64ᵀᴴ EDITION

CHAPMAN PILOTING & SEAMANSHIP

ELBERT S. MALONEY

HEARST BOOKS
A Divison of Sterling Publishing Co., Inc.
New York

Library of Congress
ISSN 1545-472X

PUBLISHER, HEARST BOOKS: JACQUELINE DEVAL
MANAGING EDITOR, HEARST BOOKS: MARYANNE BANNON
DESIGN DIRECTOR: JEANNINE FORD
BOOK DESIGN: RENATO STANISIC
ART ASSOCIATE: CHRIS DiSTASIO
LAYOUT: RENATO STANISIC/CHRIS DiSTASIO
ILLUSTRATOR: ROBERT STEIMLE
BOATING CONSULTANT: DAN FALES
CHART CONSULTANTS: JOHN WOLDRIDGE/IAN QUARRIER
PHOTO EDITOR: MATT SILVER
EDITOR: RODMAN PILGRIM NEUMANN

5 7 9 10 8 6 4

Published by Hearst Books
A Division of Sterling Publishing Co., Inc.
387 Park Avenue South, New York, NY 10016

CHAPMAN and *CHAPMAN PILOTING* and Hearst Books
are trademarks owned by Hearst Communications, Inc.

Distributed in Canada by Sterling Publishing
c/o Canadian Manda Group, 165 Dufferin Street,
Toronto, Ontario, Canada M6K 3H6

Manufactured in China

ISBN 1-58816-089-0

For information about custom editions, special sales, premium and
corporate purchases, please contact Sterling Special Sales
Department at 800-805-5489 or specialsales@sterlingpub.com.

PERSONAL ACKNOWLEDGMENTS

No book as comprehensive and authoritative as *Chapman Piloting & Seamanship* could come out of a single mind. I have indeed been fortunate in having the support and assistance of many individuals and organizations. To them, and others too numerous to list, my sincere appreciation and personal thanks.

U.S. Coast Guard:
Frank Parker; Edward LaRue;
Thomas Willis

National Weather Service:
Robert W. Jacobson
(and others who assisted him)

National Ocean Service:
Capt. Nick Perugini;
Richard Silcox; Michael Brown;
Tom Kendrick

Canadian Hydrographic Service:
Paul Holroyd

National Imagery & Mapping Agency:
Tim Doherty

United States Power Squadrons:
James Roeber

Canadian Sail & Power Squadrons:
Brian Burch

Other: Charles Husick;
Jonathan F. Swain

My very best thanks to my wife, Florine Carley Maloney, for proofreading my manuscript and saving me much embarrassment by correcting my poor typing and imprecise grammar before my text was sent to New York. She is now one of a very small group that can truly say, "I have read every word in *Chapman*." (And my love and appreciation for allowing me to neglect her and family obligations for several thousand hours over many months while this book was in preparation.)

My sincere thanks to Dan Fales for his expert technical review of the manuscript, and for his comments and suggestions that materially improved the book. He, too, now joins the "Every Word" group.

To my "strong right arm"—my Editor, Rodman Pilgrim Neumann—I can only offer my greatest thanks and appreciation. His meticulous scrutiny of my words, their context, and meaning, as well as the overall structure, has made the book more nearly "perfect" than I could have ever done. And best thanks to Matt Silver, who had the task of finding material for all the illustrations that make *Chapman Piloting & Seamanship* such a useful book—I would not have wanted that job!

And of course, this project would never have reached fruition were it not for the continued strong support of Maryann Bannon, Managing Editor, Hearst Books, and Jacqueline Deval, Publisher, Hearst Books. I shall never forget the email of 30 October 2000 in which Jacqui asked what I would do "if I were given a free hand in making broad changes in the book." Little did she know how much would be changed, and how happy I would be to make them!

Contents

Part V Electronics

Part VI Further Aspects of Boating

Part VII Appendices

Foreword

I first met Charles F. Chapman at a United States Power Squadrons meeting on marine radio communications; it was New York, in early 1959. As is all too often the situation with me, I disagreed with the speaker on some topics, and stood up to say so—a lively discussion ensued. After the meeting, Mr. Chapman introduced himself—hardly necessary, since everyone, including me, knew of "Chap," a Past Chief Commander and holder of USPS membership certificate No. A1.

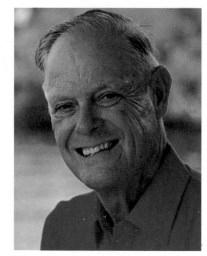

Still actively involved in keeping Chapman Piloting & Seamanship *up to date, Mack Maloney lives with his wife Florine, in Pompano Beach, Florida. They cruise in local waters much of the year, and in the Bahamas most summers.*

We had a short but pleasant conversation, and soon thereafter he asked me to write a series of feature articles on marine electronics for the magazine *Motor Boating*, of which he was the editor. For the next 40-plus years, I wrote for the magazine, which became *Motor-Boating & Sailing* for a while, but is now back to *MotorBoating*.

My relationship with Chap continued even after I retired from the U.S. Marine Corps in May of 1964, bought a boat and went cruising—no home berth, just cruising from the Florida Keys to New England or Canada, and back when it got too cold up North; and doing it again the next year! During this time, I wrote, at Chap's request, a chapter on marine electronics for *Piloting, Seamanship & Small Boat Handling*, which was then the name of the book.

In September of 1965, a message caught up to me: Chap wanted me to come to New York. He wanted me to take his job as publisher of the magazine so that he could retire; he was then 84 years of age. I couldn't help but wonder if he knew that my wife was beginning to pressure me to stop cruising and go back to work! Although the offer was attractive, I was reluctant to take an office job in New York City. To make a long story short, I eventually agreed to take over the writing, reorganizing, and updating of his book.

The book is now many years and many editions older, with a new and simplified title of *Chapman Piloting & Seamanship*. This 64th edition not only has been again updated with the help of numerous organizations and professionals in various fields, but it has also been entirely restructured, while taking advantage of the latest digital technologies with many new color photographs, sketches, and diagrams. Chapters have been revised and rearranged to provide the reader with a more organized, logical, and useful flow of information.

Whether you have been boating as long as I have, or you are experiencing your first thrill on the water, I join the *Chapman* editorial team in offering you "The Bible of Boating" for powerboaters and sailors, men and women, young and not-so-young alike. Following in the true *Chapman* tradition, it remains clear, thorough, and always comradely—a manual designed to help you and everyone aboard your boat stay safe, have fun, and become as skilled a boater as you aspire to be. Above all, I wish you as much joy from your boating years as I have had from mine.

Elbert S. Maloney

The Tradition of Chapman

Few books in today's world are used with equal enthusiasm by parents, children, and grandchildren. Few books grow with the changing technology of an age-old art and science. Few books are loved and respected—and at the same time are so authoritative that they are relied upon to set standards in a court of law. One of these rare books is *Chapman Piloting & Seamanship,* now in its tenth decade.

The story of how this book became so famous and has endured so long has many fascinating parts. The tradition began with a dynamic personality, and its evolution parallels the extraordinary growth of boating as one of North America's favorite recreational activities, and testifies to the talent and dedication of the hundreds of people who have been directly involved with developing the content and maintaining the very high editorial standards for all the 64 editions.

The Early Days

The story of the book begins during World War I, when Franklin D. Roosevelt, then Assistant Secretary of the Navy, asked Charles F. Chapman, editor of *Motor Boating* magazine, to write a manual of instruction in small boat seamanship for young men who were joining the Navy, Coast Guard, or Merchant Marine. He did so in an incredible three days, and in 1917 the first edition of *Practical Motor Boat Handling, Seamanship, and Piloting* was published. This small book contained 144 pages in a 5-inch by 7-inch format—its subtitle tells all:

"A handbook containing information which every motor boatman should know. Everything prepared for the man who takes pride in handling his own boat and getting the greatest enjoyment out of cruising. Adapted for the yachtsman interested in fitting himself to be of service to his Government in time of war."

Some of the information came from government sources. Part of the handbook was a fascinating excerpt from the Cunard Line's instructions to deck officers on its transatlantic steamships. Much of the book was a paste-up of instructional articles from what was already one of the world's leading boating magazines.

In addition to preparing the manual, Chapman offered the Navy the use of the Power Squadrons' "machinery ready to put into instant

This is how it all began! Chap assembled material that had been published in Motor Boating *magazine, and created a handbook for instruction of volunteer boatmen assisting the U.S. Navy in World War I. This slim volume, which would evolve into the "Chapman" that we know today, was listed in this April 1917 advertisement at a paperbound price of 50 cents.*

CHARLES F. CHAPMAN

The man who created and developed this nautical bestseller, Charles Frederic Chapman, was born in Norwich, Connecticut in 1881. With easy access to the nearby Thames River, Chap, as he was affectionately known throughout his life, became interested in boats, and quickly decided that his life's interests lay afloat. At Cornell University he studied naval architecture and marine engineering, graduating in 1905.

Settling in Manhattan, he bought his first motorboat; she was the *Megohm*, a trim 16-footer powered by a pint-size, one-cylinder Detroit engine that produced all of two horsepower. He joined the New York Motor Boat Club, where he was later to become its Commodore. This club was active in the new American Power Boat Association, and Chap became chairman of the APBA's racing commission, the sanctioning body for motor boat races in the U.S. He wrote the first power boat racing rules, and was secretary of APBA for 25 years.

But it wasn't all on paper. He began racing himself, and soon was declared a rising star among motorboat pilots. He finished high up in many important races in the 1920s. To dramatize

As Chief Commander of the United State Power Squadrons, Charles F. Chapman is seen reviewing the fleet at a Squadron summer activity.

operation the training of great numbers of men required for the Naval Reverse Forces." Roosevelt accepted this offer with gratitude and within a year more than 5,000 men who had attended Squadrons' classes and used the instruction manual entered the armed services.

The Story of the Book Continues

As boating grew, so, unfortunately, did boating accidents and fatalities. In an effort to increase safe practices on the water and create a more informed group of participants, Chap used the pages of *Motor Boating* to start what he called "The Correspondence Course." Each month an article on a particular subject would appear, and would end with a series of questions. Readers from all over the country sent in answers, and those who passed were given a certificate. This

was to become the first formal boating safety course in the nation, and it led to a forerunner of the book you now hold in your hands.

By 1922 Chap's book had undergone six revisions and in that year was retitled *Piloting, Seamanship & Small Boat Handling*. Now the emphasis of the book was clearly small-craft operation and safety. Still mostly a compilation of articles from the magazine, the book took on the appearance of a scrapbook of the sea and a self-instruction course in boat operation. It was constantly being revised to keep up with advances in the boating industry and ever-changing government regulations.

The book grew—in size and in usage. The United States Power Squadrons used it for free courses for the public, as well as for advanced courses for its members. The U.S. Coast Guard

the speed potential of motorboats, he organized and participated in long distance races—such as, Gar Wood's hydroplane against the famous train, the "Twentieth Century Limited". Chap served as navigator when the speedboat won the race from Albany to New York City in 1923. Another boat versus train race was from Miami to New York, and there is still a Motor Boat Trophy for the fastest time in a powerboat between these two cities.

In 1909 the boat Chap was skippering in an ocean race from New York to Marblehead, Massachusetts, caught fire and sank. While three men balanced in a tiny dinghy, three others clung to life by hanging on to its gunwales. Eventually, the entire crew was rescued by a passing schooner. No doubt the incident played a large part in Chap's lifelong dedication to instruction in boating safety.

By 1912, he was brought to the attention of a man busy building his own reputation—William Randolph Hearst. Hearst owned the magazine Motor Boating and was looking for an editor. "It's yours, Chap. Take it and run it as you wish," was the assignment. And that is exactly what Chap did—for the next 56 years.

The year Chap took over the helm of the magazine it sold for ten cents a copy and reached a few thousand readers a month. Chap set his sights high, declaring, "The boating business is a sleeping giant and I'm trying to wake it." Motor Boating soon began to grow in both stature and circulation. In 1987, then called Motor Boating & Sailing, the magazine celebrated its 80th anniversary and a circulation of some 142,000 subscribers. Now, renamed *MotorBoating*, the magazine remains a leader in its field.

Chap also used his knowledge elsewhere to further the cause of boating education. In 1913 and 1914 he was one of ten men who met first at the Boston Yacht Club and later at the New York Yacht Club to form the United States Power Squadrons. He was for many years the chairman of the flag and etiquette committee and designed the USPS ensign. At various times, he was Treasurer, Vice Commander, and for two terms, Chief Commander. He administered the first national boating tests. The organization, in recognition of his long and valuable service, gave him USPS Certificate No. 1.K°

Auxiliary adopted it for its courses given by various flotillas around the country. Boaters whose navigating skills were part of their lives took pride in having a copy of the book on board. The book also acquired nicknames: "The Blue Book," "The Bible of Boating," and just plain "Piloting" or "Chapman."

Help from Many Quarters

While Chap directed each new edition for almost 50 years, he counted on help from many assistants, and indeed, from the book's readers. With each new edition came suggestions from staff members, professional boat captains, airplane pilots, amateur sailors, cruising boaters, and others who love the sea. He also relied on the cooperation of the U.S. Power Squadrons, the U.S. Coast Guard Auxiliary, the Army Corps

of Engineers, the Coast & Geodetic Survey and the Lake Survey (both now a part of NOS, the National Ocean Service), the U.S. Navy, and most of all the U.S. Coast Guard. Scores of manufacturers of equipment, boats, instruments, and other nautical gear have always aided by providing illustrations.

Through all those years, a handful of individuals have made contributions that may be almost as responsible as Chap himself for keeping the first 50 or so editions of this book the most popular, authoritative, and current book on boating published. Their names include William H. Koelbel, who worked closely with Chap for more than 20 years and wrote a number of chapters during that time; Morris Rosenfeld, the famed marine photographer; and Morris's son Stanley, who continued the tradition; there were also Peter Barlow, Gardner Emmons, Dr. John Wilde; Robert Danforth Ogg, co-inventor of the Danforth anchor, and Gale Foster of the Cordage Institute.

Also to be mentioned as contributors are the readers, the unofficial helpers. The members and instructors of the U.S. Power Squadrons make suggestions, catch the minor typographical mistakes, sometimes argue with the editor about flag etiquette or fine points of navigational techniques and, perhaps most importantly, ask hundreds of meaningful questions.

The "Modern" Era

"Chapman's" continued to grow in the years following World War II, in which it was again used for the training of many men in the use of military small craft. But it had something of the appearance of a hodgepodge scrapbook, and in 1966 a complete reorganization of the book was planned by Chap and John Whiting (who succeeded to the title of Publisher in 1968 when Chap retired at the age of 86). The publishing plan became one for a "living book" that could adapt to the technological and governmental changes that were happening to boating.

First, Elbert S. Maloney (better known as "Mack") was assigned to the work of completely rewriting the book, several chapters a year, with updates in every chapter as a flood of governmental and technology changes swept over recreational boating.

Tom Bottomley joined the crew working on the book in 1968. It was indeed a crew. There was an exceptional degree of cooperation and dedication between Bill Koelbel and Tom, and between the various outside contributors and the staff at the office, and among the notable support people, particularly Ruth Smith (Mrs. Harold McCann), who had been Mr. Chapman's famous assistant for four decades.

Tom Bottomley (just like Bill Koelbel) had first been on the editorial staff of *MotorBoating* magazine. Bottomley's involvement with "Chapman's" began in 1968, and he served as the book's managing editor for a dozen years. His familiarity with every law and regulation passed

The New York Yacht Club, where many of the early organizational meetings of the United States Power Squadrons were held.

over the years, and his technical acumen and book-production expertise were called upon countless times. This book could not have reached its state of excellence without the benefit of Bottomley's work.

Mack Maloney, in sheer volume of work as well as its excellence, deserves special singling out. He spent his boyhood in Virginia Beach, Virginia, where his front yard was the Atlantic Ocean. Since then he has never been far from salt water, even during his 28 years in the Marine Corps. By the time Chap was preparing to retire, Mack had already written a number of chapters in the book and was recognized as an authority on many boating subjects. It was Chap's personal request that Mack step in for him and take over the principal authorship of the book.

Even in retirement, Chap kept his eyes on the book. In his home, "Bylandorsea," situated on the Connecticut River near Essex, he welcomed visitors from the staff. He deferred comments, saying "You are closer to it all today"—but the staff always had in mind keeping up the same standards with the new book that he had set for the original volume sixty years and nearly two million copies ago. He was honored in 1955 by the Ole Evinrude Boating Foundation with a silver bowl bearing engraved "No other man deserves so much from so many of us in the World of Boating." Mr. Chapman died in Essex on March 21, 1976.

He would have been proud to know that his blue book has become part of one of the largest adult education programs in the United States. More than two hundred thousand boaters take serious, well-planned courses in recreational boat operation every year. Many of them use *Chapman* as their textbook and as their "keep-aboard book" afterwards.

Ever since 1966, Mack Maloney has been the man in constant touch with the appropriate agencies in Washington, DC, and the man behind the typewriter and computer—adding chapters, rewriting specialists' contributions where necessary, making the book work as a textbook, keeping track of the necessary changes, and working with the editors in the planning and execution of each new edition. Through the 60th Edition, Mack was, indeed, the author of "Chapman." With the extensively revised 61st edition, he became the Senior Editor, the reviewing authority for all material prepared by other authors and editors, and has remained the principal writer for the each edition of the book ever since. This 64th edition has been extensively reorganized and rewritten from the first to the last page, with many new color illustrations and photographs throughout.

Maloney is deeply involved in the bridge between high technology and age-old seamanship. Mack is a member of the Institute of Navigation and served on its governing council. He is a member of the U.S. Naval Institute and author of two editions of its well-known *Dutton's Navigation & Piloting*. He was a member and Vice-Chairman of the U.S. Coast Guard Navigation Safety Advisory Council. He is Chairman Emeritus of the National Advisory

Chap was an avid and highly competent motorboat racer. Over the years, he won many trophies, including the Gold Cup shown above.

Council of BoatU.S. He has been a member of the national education staff of the U.S. Power Squadrons for many years, serving with distinction as Director of Education from 1971 to 1976.

Although *Chapman Piloting & Seamanship* has passed its three millionth copy, it is somewhat astonishing to realize that the book has had only two principal authors, four publishers, and just two publishing companies in all those years. From the days when William Randolph Hearst used to visit Chap's office regularly to look at the pictures of new boats and quiz the editor on new developments until today under the auspices of Sterling Publishing Co., Inc., the Hearst Corporation has always fully supported the continuing work that has enabled this famous book to remain in its rightful place, indispensable, as "the Bible of Boating."

Nautical Terms

The Language of Boating • The Words That Describe the Vessels, Their Construction, Equipment & Operation • The Terminology That Will Help You Have a Safer, More Enjoyable Time on the Water

Welcome to the Wonderful World of Boating. Whether sail or power, yacht or small boat, cruising, fishing, or just "getting out on the water"—whatever is your style of recreational boating—it can be safer and more enjoyable when done with knowledge. The foundation of any knowledge is built on understanding the special words and phrases of the subject—and so we begin this book.

The language of boats and boating is different from that of the land and landsmen. It has been developed over centuries of use by those who travel the waters, yet is flavored by terms invented in recent memory. When you speak of the "stern" of a boat you are using a word that goes back centuries through several languages; yet when you say that you have a "stern-drive" engine, you are using a term that has been in existence only a relatively short time.

A boater needn't be excessively "salty" in his speech, but there are strong reasons for knowing and using the right terms for objects and activities around boats. In times of emergency, many seconds of valuable time may be saved when correct, precise terms are used for needed actions or equipment. In correspondence and other written material, use of the right word often shortens long explanations and eliminates doubt or confusion.

Learning and using proper nautical terms will mark you as one who is truly interested in boating. Above all, forming the habit of *thinking directly* in nautical terms, not in "shore" terms with mental translation, will help you use the proper words consistently. Soon you will find them coming naturally.

Opposite Page: Figure 1-01 Powerboats range from the smallest outboard-powered runabout to large luxury yachts.

The terms discussed in this chapter are not all-inclusive for the field of boating. No two "experts" would agree on what constitutes a "complete" list, and any such list would far exceed the space available here. What follows is intended as a basic nautical vocabulary, to prepare you for the various topics presented in detail in succeeding chapters. Many terms will be covered more fully later in the book, and more specialized words and phrases will be introduced at that time. Terms in this chapter will be described in simple, brief remarks rather than comprehensively defined as in dictionaries. Nautical glossaries are available from marine bookstores for those who prefer exhaustive definitions; a Glossary of Selected Terms, Appendix G, is also provided at the end of this book.

BASIC TERMS

Some terms apply to all types and sizes of waterborne vessels, others apply only to smaller craft; see **Figure 1-01**. Many have found their way into everyday language on shore, such as "making headway" to indicate that progress is being made on a task or project.

What is a Boat?

The term BOAT has no precise definition. It is a waterborne vehicle smaller than a ship, which is usually thought of as being used for ocean travel. Indeed, one definition of a boat is a small craft, such as a lifeboat, carried on board a SHIP. Many consider a boat as being not over 65 feet in length. Another dividing point might be (20 meters) 65.6 feet, as used in the Navigation Rules; see Chapters 4 and 5. (Approximate metric equivalents are given in parentheses following customary units, except for Navigation Rules that are defined in meters; see also Appendix E.)

The term CRAFT or SMALL CRAFT is often used interchangeably with "boat."

VESSEL is a broad term for all water-borne vehicles and is used without reference to size, particularly in laws and regulations relating to maritime matters. A YACHT is a power or sail vessel used for recreation and pleasure, as opposed to work. The term often connotes luxurious accommodations, and it usually is not used for boats under approximately 40 feet (12.2 m) in length, but there are no established limits in this respect. This term is also applied to government craft used by officials and dignitaries, such as a "presidential yacht" or a "state governor's yacht."

Although more and more people refer to boats with the neuter pronoun "it," the traditional "she" is also correct in speaking or writing about almost any type of vessel. Both words are used throughout this book to refer to boats and other vessels.

Categories of Boats

Boats may be subdivided into POWERBOATS, SAILBOATS, and ROWBOATS as determined by their basic means of propulsion; see **Figure 1-02**. MOTORBOAT is a term used interchangeably with powerboat; these may have either gasoline or diesel engines. Sailboats with AUXILIARY ENGINES are

Figure 1-03 A motorsailer is a sailboat that has a larger engine than the typical auxiliary; it can take advantage of both sail and powered propulsion, but with some sacrifice of efficiency in both modes.

Figure 1-02 Sailboats get their propulsion from the force of the wind on their sails. They may also have auxiliary motor power for use in calms or for close-quarters maneuvering.

often called AUXILIARIES; are legally considered to be motorboats when propelled either by engine alone or by both engine and sails simultaneously. Small sailboats without engines are frequently called DAYSAILERS. A MOTORSAILER is a boat in which sails are used, but their area is reduced and the engine power is increased; see **Figure 1-03**. Like most compromises, motorsailers are somewhat less efficient under sail than sailboats and slower under power than motorboats. Some pure motorboats, such as the popular TRAWLER type, have one or more STEADYING SAILS; this is not for propulsion but rather for an easier ride in rough seas. Within the broad rowboat category are such craft as CANOES and KAYAKS.

The term CRUISER indicates a type of boat with at least minimum accommodations and facilities for overnight trips. The type of propulsion may be added to form such terms as OUTBOARD CRUISER or INBOARD CRUISER. The term is also applied to many sailboats to distinguish them from others designed primarily for racing. HOUSEBOATS include both cruising craft whose superstructure is larger and designed more for living aboard, and

Figure 1-04 Sailboarding is a popular water sport, especially among the young and fit.

many smaller vessels that appear to have evolved from land trailers and mobile homes. Houseboats offer more living space than cruisers do, but generally at some sacrifice of seaworthiness and rough-water cruising ability.

A DINGHY (often contracted to "dink") is a small open boat carried on or towed by a larger craft; it may be propelled by oars, sails, or an outboard motor. A TENDER is a dinghy or a larger LAUNCH used to carry persons and supplies to and from large vessels. A PRAM is a small, square-bow vessel often used as a dinghy.

HYDROFOIL BOATS move on below-hull structures called FOILS that are scientifically designed to give lift, much like the wings of an airplane, when moving through the water at high speeds. The submerged foils permit the boat itself to "fly" just above the water surface with little drag and at increased speeds.

A SAILBOARD is basically a large surfboard with a mast and small sail. The sail is partially supported by the person standing on board who steers by shifting both the positions of the sail and his or her weight on the board; see **Figure 1-04.**

Most boats have only a single main body or HULL, but others may have two or three, and are known collectively as MULTI-HULLS. Among these latter types are CATAMARANS with two hulls, which may be identical or mirror images of each other; see **Figure 1-05.** TRIMARANS have

three hulls; a larger center one and two smaller outer hulls. Originally, multi-hulls were almost all sailing craft, but recent years have seen an increasing interest in power catamarans in a wide range of sizes.

INFLATABLE BOATS are usually associated with tenders of less than 10 feet (3 m), but they can be much larger. Inflatables of 25 feet (7.6 m) or longer are occasionally seen. A major advantage of inflatables as tenders is that they can be deflated and stowed in a small space. In this mode they often double as life rafts though they lack many of the protective features that are associated with a proper life raft (Chapter 3).

Inflatables provide greater capacity and more stability for the same length as compared to conventional tenders. The soft contours of their inflated tubes spare the finish of the main hull when the tender is alongside. Unfortunately,

Figure 1-05 Boats, power or sail, with two hulls are called catamarans. They have additional stability and a good measure of speed. Craft with three hulls—the center one is usually much larger than the outer ones—are termed trimarans.

Wave-Piercing Catamarans

The native people of the South and Southwest Pacific have built and used multi-hull craft for many generations. Thus it is not unexpected that the newest concept in catamarans has developed in Australia and New Zealand. This is the WAVE-PIERCING CATAMARAN, a design that offers a number of advantages, the principal one of which is described by its name—the vessel quite literally pierces oncoming waves rather than riding up and over them.

The basic design typically has the appearance of a normal deep-V hull held just clear of the water surface by a pair of DEMI-HULLS; these are long, narrow shapes with quite sharply pointed bows, their tops just above the water. They penetrate the waves, and the vessel as a whole rides much more steadily with less pitching motion. Large waves may come up as high as the bow of the main hull, but its deep-V design cuts through their tops

with no problems (some variations in design appear more like a conventional catamaran with a broad structure tying the two demi-hulls together high above the water). A wave-piercing catamaran can maintain a much higher speed than a conventional catamaran when the going gets rough.

they can be difficult (if not impossible) to row under windy or choppy conditions, so are usually powered with a small outboard motor.

Primary considerations with inflatables are the quality of the fabric and gluing process used in their construction. High-quality fabrics that resist abrasion and sunlight and high-strength seams are expensive; consequently, quality boats are more costly than ordinary inflatables of similar size. For safety, any inflatable should have two or more separate air chambers. If damage causes one to deflate, the other, undamaged, chamber will keep the boat afloat.

Inflatable and conventional boat construction are combined in what is called a RIGID-HULL INFLATABLE BOAT or RIB. Some people refer to RIBs as rigid bottom inflatables. RIBs are built with a two-part hull: the lower closely resembling the lower part of a high-speed fiberglass powerboat; the upper consisting of inflated

Figure 1-06 Inflatable boats with rigid hulls, often called RIBs, are used both as dinghies and as larger sportboats. They combine the benefits of a conventional hull with the flotation and stability characteristics of an inflatable.

Figure 1-07 A personal watercraft, usually called just a PWC, is much like a motorcycle on the water—the operator "rides" the PWC by standing or sitting behind a set of handlebars with a throttle grip. PWCs are, however, a "vessel" and must comply with all navigation rules and other regulations relating to boats.

tubes. This gives RIBs both the efficient, high-speed performance of a conventional powerboat and the great stability of an inflatable; see **Figure 1-06.** These can be rowed with much greater success than "soft" inflatables. Many RIBs are purchased not as tenders but as primary boats.

PERSONAL WATERCRAFT, usually referred to as PWCs, have become widely popular both for owners and as rental boats. There are numerous definitions of the term, all of which vary slightly but do not seriously conflict. The PWC Industry Association coined the term and defined it as "An inboard vessel; less than 4 meters (13 ft) in length that uses an internal combustion engine powering a jet pump as its primary source of propulsion, and is designed with no open load-carrying area that would retain water"; see **Figure 1-07.** "The vessel is designed to be operated by a person or persons positioned on, rather

than within, the confines of the hull." (Organizations of manufacturers and users of canoes and kayaks are disputing this definition, claiming that their boats are also "personal water craft.") A PWC might be considered a motorcycle on the water—the operator sits astride or stands and controls the craft using a handlebar with a throttle on one of the grips. Many models can carry one or two additional persons seated behind the operator. They are often referred to by the brand names of the principal manufacturers—Jet Ski, Wave Runner, or Sea-Doo. *It is important to note that PWCs are "vessels," and must be registered similarly to other boats and are subject to all the same equipment requirements, navigation rules, etc., as other boats.* They are intended for use only during daylight hours; they can be operated legally only between sunrise and sunset as they are not equipped with navigation lights.

JET BOATS are a development from PWCs. Similarly propelled by a water jet, they are larger, usually with seating for about four persons; those on board sit inside the hull and remain dry. They are usually fitted with navigation lights that allow their use after dark.

JET DRIVE is a form of water-power propulsion found more and more often in larger powerboats.

Boaters & Yachtsmen

The owner-operators of recreational small craft, whether they are men or women, can be referred to as BOATERS. He or she also may be called, informally, the SKIPPER or CAPTAIN; the usual legal term is "Operator." The designation of YACHTSMAN is typically reserved for the owners of larger craft. Others on board are the CREW if they participate in the operation of the craft, or GUESTS if they are not so involved.

All persons on a boat are referred to as being ON BOARD; the term ABOARD is less correct.

Directions On Board a Boat

The front end of a boat is the BOW; the other end is its STERN. These terms can also be used to indicate larger areas of the boat without specific limits; in the middle, the area is termed MID-

Orienting Yourself on Board

Life afloat is always oriented to the boat, and not to the individual members of the crew. The PORT side, for instance, is always the left side of the boat no matter which way the observer is facing. Likewise, STARBOARD always refers to the boat's right side.

Anything toward the bow is FORWARD, while anything to the stern is AFT. A position aft of an object is ABAFT of it. (A landmark may be said to be "abaft the beam.") Something is ABEAM when it lies off either side of the boat at right angles to the keel.

Parts of the vessel, such as seats of a swim platform, which run across the boat are ATHWARTSHIPS. Along the vessel's centerline is FORE-AND-AFT.

Anything in the middle of the boat is AMIDSHIPS, whether fore-and-aft or athwartships. INBOARD is toward the center, OUTBOARD away from it. Going BELOW refers to a person moving from the deck to a lower cabin inside the hull. The reverse is going ABOVE (decks). The term ALOFT is used for climbing the rigging and masts.

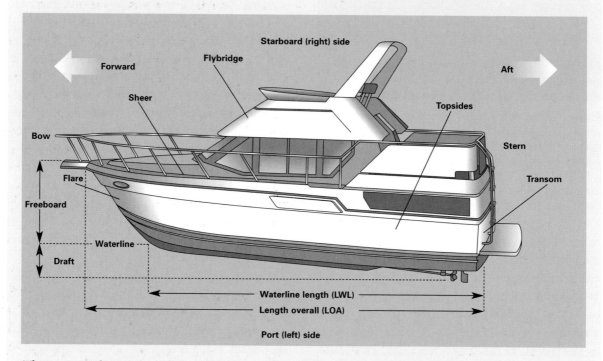

These terms relate to the hull and directions on board a boat. Note that port and starboard remain the same no matter which way a person is facing, and that length overall (LOA) is figured similarly for sailboats. Refer to Chapter 8 for terms specific to sailboats.

SHIPS. PORT and STARBOARD (pronounced "star-b'd") are lateral terms. Port designates the left side and starboard the right when on the vessel and facing the bow or, to express it differently, when facing FORWARD. By turning around and facing the stern, one is looking AFT; the port and starboard sides of the vessel do not change.

The bow is the forward part of the boat; the stern is the AFTER part. When one point is aft of another, it is said to be ABAFT it; when nearer the bow, it is FORWARD of the other. When an object lies on a line—or in a plane—parallel to the centerline of the vessel, it is referred to as lying FORE-AND-AFT, as distinguished from

ATHWARTSHIPS, which means at right angles to the centerline.

The term AMIDSHIPS has a double meaning. In one sense, it refers to an object or area midway between the boat's sides. In another sense, it relates to something midway between the bow and the stern. INBOARD and OUTBOARD, as directional terms, draw a distinction between objects near or toward amidships (inboard) and those away from the centerline or beyond the sides of the craft (outboard).

To express the idea of "overhead in the rigging," one says ALOFT. Note that ABOVEDECK means on deck rather than within the boat, and not actually above it as does "aloft." BELOW means the opposite location or direction than above.

Terms Relating to the Boat

The basic part of a boat is its HULL. There is normally a major central structural member called the KEEL; beyond this, however, the components will vary with the construction materials and techniques. Boats may be of the OPEN type, or may be covered with a DECK. As boats get above the smallest sizes, they may have a SUPERSTRUCTURE above the main deck level, variously referred to as a DECKHOUSE or CABIN (the term "cabin" is also used for spaces below the level of the deck). Small, relatively open boats may have only a SHELTER CABIN, or CUDDY, forward.

A vessel floats because water exerts a buoyant force on it. This force exactly equals the weight of the water that is displaced by the hull. To benefit from the force, the vessel must weigh not more than the water it displaces. If the boat should weigh more, the buoyant force would be inadequate, and it would sink.

Floating in salt water is different than in fresh water. Since salt water is heavier, and thus more dense than fresh water, a hull will displace a smaller volume of salt water, and its draft—the distance vertically from the water surface to the lowest point on the boat—is less. For sailboats and displacement powerboats (see page 22), the lowest point is normally the bottom of the keel;

on planing motorboats (see page 23), however, it is usually the propeller tips.

As a boat settles into the water—imagine it being lowered in slings from a crane—it reaches a level of equilibrium where the weight of displaced water matches that of the boat. This level on the hull is the waterline. Just above the waterline, a stripe of contrasting color is often painted on the hull; this is the boot-top. Below the waterline, anti-fouling paint is usually applied to the hull to reduce the accumulation of marine growth, such as barnacles.

Terms Relating to the Hull

SHEER is a term used to designate the curve or sweep of the deck of a vessel as viewed from the side. Sheer is normally gracefully upward, but in some designs it can be downward, resulting in REVERSE SHEER. The side skin of a boat between the waterline and deck is called the TOPSIDES; the structural element at the upper edge is the GUNWALE (pronounced "gun'l"). (Note that "gun-*whale*" is *not* the correct spelling.) If the sides are drawn in toward the centerline away from a perpendicular as they go upward, as they often do near the stern of a boat, they are said to have TUMBLEHOME. Forward, they are more likely to incline outward to make the bow more buoyant and to keep the deck drier by throwing spray

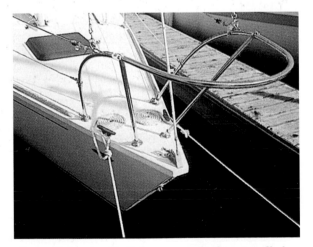

Figure 1-08 A rail all the way at the bow is called a bow rail or pulpit. It is an important safety feature on sailboats, and often appears on powerboats as well. It should have adequate strength and be solidly mounted.

aside; this is FLARE. When the topsides are carried substantially above the level of the deck, they are called BULWARKS, and at the top of the bulwarks is the RAIL. More common than bulwarks are TOE RAILS, narrow strips placed on top of the gunwale to finish it off and provide some safety for persons on deck. LIFELINES are used on larger craft at the edges of the side decks to prevent people from falling overboard. These lines usually consist of wire rope, often plastic-covered, supported above the deck on STANCHIONS. If made of solid material—wood or metal—they are called LIFERAILS. Boats may also have waist-high BOW RAILS of rigid tubing for the same safety purpose. A PULPIT is a forward extension, usually a heavy structure with rails extending up from it; see **Figure 1-08**. Bow rail installations on sailboats are also often called pulpits, whether they extend forward of the hull or not. Many sailboats also have stern pulpits, and these are sometimes called PUSHPITS.

Along the sides of the hull there will be protrusions, either molded in or added externally, to protect the topsides from the roughness of piles and pier faces. These RUB RAILS or GUARDS are usually faced with metal strips for their own better protection.

Many hulls are fitted with a SPRAY RAIL external to the topsides just above the waterline. Such a rail usually extends about halfway aft from the leading edge of the hull, or STEM, and deflects downward any spray from the bow wave.

Bows & Sterns

The STEM is the extreme leading edge of a hull; on wooden craft it is the major structural mem-

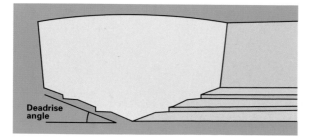

Figure 1-10 Hulls with deadrise angles of 16° to 19° are considered to be modified-V types. Steeper angles, some as high as 23°, are designated as deep-V hulls.

Figure 1-09 A chine—the sharp angle at which the sides of a boat's hull meet the bottom—provides this deep-V powerboat with better control and a dry ride at planing speeds. One of a pair of trim tabs is also seen in this photo (arrow).

ber at the bow. The stem of a boat is PLUMB if it is perpendicular to the waterline, or RAKED if inclined at an angle. The term OVERHANG describes the projection of the upper part of the bow, or stern, beyond a perpendicular up from the point where the stem or stern intersects the WATERLINE. EYEBOLTS or RINGBOLTS—to which all kinds of lines, ropes, and blocks may be attached—are frequently fitted through the stems of boats.

The flat area across a stern is called the TRANSOM. If, however, the stern is pointed, resembling a conventional bow, there is no transom and the boat is called a DOUBLE-ENDER; it can also be said to have a CANOE STERN. The QUARTER of a boat is the after portion of its sides, particularly the furthermost aft portion where the topsides meet the transom.

Additional Hull Shape Terms

The lower outer part of the hull where the sides meet the bottom is called the TURN OF THE BILGE. If the boat is flat or V-bottomed, the bottom and the sides of the boat meet at a well-defined angle rather than a gradual curve—this is the CHINE of the boat; see **Figure 1-09**. The more abrupt the angle of intersection of these planes, the HARDER the chine. SOFT CHINE craft have a lesser angle; this term is sometimes applied to round-bottom boats, but this is not correct. Some modern boats are designed with MULTIPLE CHINES (LONGITUDINAL STEPS) for a

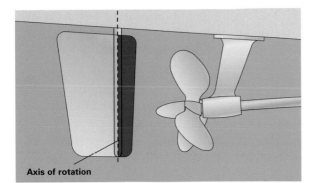

Figure 1-11 A balanced rudder has a portion of the rudder blade (red area) that is forward of the axis of rudder shaft. This offsets much of the force required to turn the rudder to steer the boat.

softer ride at high speeds in rough water; this is often referred to as DEEP-V design.

Larger round-bottom vessels may be built with BILGE KEELS—secondary external keels at the turn of the bilge, actually fins—which reduce the vessel's tendency to roll in beam seas.

The significance of the term DEADRISE can be appreciated by visualizing a cross-section of a hull; see **Figure 1-10**. If the bottom were flat, extending horizontally from the keel, there would be no deadrise. In a V-bottom boat, where the bottom rises at an angle to a horizontal line outward from the keel, the amount of such rise is the deadrise, usually expressed as an angle, but sometimes as inches per foot.

With normal sheer, the deck of a boat, as viewed from the side, slopes up toward the bow, and the stern is at least level with amidships. FLAM is that part of the concave flare of the topside just below the deck. If it curves outward sharply, it will both increase deck width and reduce the amount of bow spray that blows

aboard. The CUTWATER is the forward edge of the stem, particularly near the waterline. STEM BANDS of metal are frequently fitted over the stem for protection from debris in the water, ice, pier edges, etc. The FOREFOOT of a boat is the point where the stem joins the keel.

If the boat has an overhanging stern, this part of the hull is the COUNTER. Her lines aft to the stern are her RUN; lines forward to the stem are her ENTRANCE (or ENTRY). The descriptions FINE and CLEAN are often applied to the entrance and run. The term BLUFF is applied to bows that are broader and blunter than normal.

Terms Relating to the Keel & Rudder

The keel is the major longitudinal member of the hull. The RUDDER of a boat is the flat surface at or near the stern that is pivoted about a vertical or near-vertical axis so as to turn either side and thus change the direction of movement of the vessel through the water. A boat's rudder is said to be BALANCED when a portion of its blade area extends forward of the axis of rotation: see Figure 1-11. Such a rudder is easier to turn. A metal fitting extending back from the underside of the keel for protection of the rudder and propeller is called a SKEG.

The upward extension of the rudder through which force is applied to turn the rudder is the RUDDERPOST (or RUDDERSTOCK). A STUFFING BOX keeps the hull watertight where the rudderpost enters. (A stuffing box is also used where a PROPELLER SHAFT goes through the hull.) The rudder is linked to and turned by the vessel's WHEEL; the connection may be by mechanical linkages, cables, or hydraulic lines. Some vessels

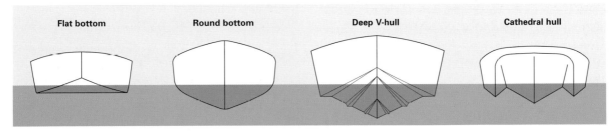

Figure 1-12 A flat-bottomed boat is inexpensive to build, but pounds. A round bottom provides a soft ride at displacement speeds, but is unsuitable for planing. The deep-V hull is used on high-speed craft; cathedral hulls have good stability.

Figure 1-13 The force exerted by the wind on the sails creates a heeling effect as well as forward motion. This causes a sailboat to lean away from the wind.

may be steered by a TILLER—a lever attached directly to the top of the rudderpost.

Hull Shapes

The lowest portion of the hull below the waterline is termed its BOTTOM. This may be one of three basic shapes—FLAT, ROUND, OR V—or it may be a combination of two shapes, one forward gradually changing to the other toward the stern. There are also more complex shapes such as CATHEDRAL-HULL, DEEP-V, MULTI-STEP, and others; see **Figure 1-12**.

Displacement Hulls

A displacement hull is one that achieves all of its buoyancy (flotation capability) by displacing a volume of water equal in weight to the boat and its load, whether underway or at rest. All cruising sailboats and large, low-speed powerboats (such as trawlers, see page 28) take advantage of the low power demands of this type of hull; see **Figure 1-13**. Little driving force is needed to move one of these boats until hull speed is reached. After this, no reasonable amount of increased power results in any efficient increase in speed. A close approximation of any vessel's hull speed (in knots, see page 50 for a definition of knots) can be found by multiplying the square root of its length at the waterline (LWL) in feet by the constant 1.3. For example: a boat with a LWL of 36 feet has a theoretical hull speed of 7.8 knots $-\sqrt{36} \times 1.3 = 6 \times 1.3 = 7.8$.

The need for an easily driven hull is obvious in a sailboat. In a powerboat, a displacement hull allows long-range cruising with a minimal expenditure of fuel. Cruising ranges in hundreds of nautical miles (see page 50 for an explanation of nautical miles) are not exceptional, especially for a trawler-type boat with a single diesel engine. Another advantage of a displacement hull is the ability to carry heavy loads with little penalty in overall performance.

Displacement hulls are normally round-bottomed. If one is flat-bottomed, it is usually for ease of construction rather than any reason of efficiency.

Figure 1-14 Hydrodynamic force lifts a planing hull partially out of the water, reducing drag and wave-making resistance. This makes high speed possible.

Planing Hulls

A PLANING HULL is one that achieves a major part of its underway-load-carrying ability by the dynamic action of its underside with the surface of the water over which it is rapidly traveling; at rest, a planing hull reverts to displacement buoyancy; see **Figure 1-14**. Planing action greatly reduces drag and wave-making resistance, allowing relatively higher speeds. Nearly all modern motorboats have planing hulls. Small, light sailboats with large sail plans can reach planing speeds in ideal conditions.

A planing hull is characterized by a flat run aft that meets the transom at a sharp angle. This

SAILBOAT HULLS

Unlike other types of boat, a sailboat needs a hull with a large amount of lateral resistance. Without this resistance it would blow sideways with the wind instead of sailing forward. Small, unballasted sailboats use movable appendages called CENTERBOARDS or DAGGERBOARDS to provide lateral resistance. A centerboard is hinged and swings down out of a centerboard trunk, whereas a daggerboard goes down vertically and can be completely removed from the boat. Another method of obtaining lateral resistance, now seldom used, is through two LEEBOARDS, which look like centerboards, attached to the gunwales on either side.

Larger sailboats have permanently attached, fixed external keels designed to provide lateral resistance. Older designs have a full keel that starts near the bow and continues aft until it joins the rudder. In recent years, FIN KEELS have become popular because they allow greater maneuverability and improved upwind performance. The rudder of a fin-keel boat may be attached to a small SKEG for protection, or it may be a separate appendage known as a SPADE RUDDER.

Both full and fin keels also serve as the craft's fixed ballast. Modern practice is to form these keels out of lead or cast iron so the ballast is outside and below the hull where it will have the maximum countering effect on heeling. Ballast has no effect until the boat begins to heel. As the angle of heel increases, the ballast exerts an increasing force to right

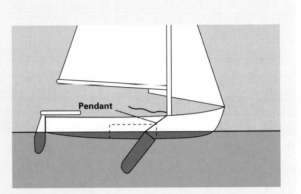

A centerboard is raised or lowered in its trunk by a pendant (also called "pennant") to permit adjustment according to the point of sail or for shallow water.

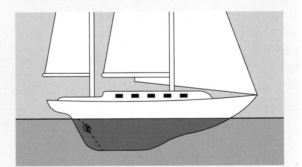

A full keel is usually found on larger boats. It may have internal ballast or exterior ballast bolted onto the hull—which also acts as a grounding shoe.

the boat. A ballasted sailboat will typically HEEL—tip sideways—rather easily at first, and then become "stiffer" as the ballast takes effect. Each sailboat has an angle of heel where the hull achieves maximum performance.

angle allows the water flowing under the hull to "break away" cleanly from the transom. Hydrodynamic forces on the flat aft run lift the boat until only a small portion of its bottom is in the water. Distinct chines aid in speed and directional control as speed increases.

It takes considerable horsepower (hp) to achieve planing speeds and that means greater fuel consumption. As a result, the cruising range of a planing hull is generally much less than that of a displacement boat carrying the same amount of fuel. Of course, the planing hull gets to its destination a lot sooner!

V-hulls

POUNDING—coming down hard on successive waves—inevitably occurs when any boat is driven through rough water at high speeds. It is accentuated by the broad, flat sections required of an efficient planing hull. Slowing down eliminates the problem, but many planing hulls become much more difficult to maneuver at slow speeds. The need to compromise between planing speeds and sea-keeping qualities has led to the almost universal acceptance of the V-hull, a design developed in the 1960s. A steep deadrise provides acceptable wave riding along with sufficient planing ability to achieve high speed. Many variations in hull design have been tried, but almost all of them fall within the modified-V type, typically considered to include boats with deadrise of approximately 16° to 19°.

TRIM TABS are rectangular control flaps that project parallel to the water's surface at the lower edge of the transom; refer to **Figure 1-09**. Deep-V and modified-V hulls are very sensitive to trim tab adjustment. Adjusting the tabs down changes the boat's trim by pushing the stern up and the bow down. These hulls are also sensitive to small changes in the angle of propeller thrust. This angle is fixed on a conventional inboard boat, but is adjustable with an outboard motor or inboard/outboard drive.

Semi-Planing Hulls

A SEMI-PLANING (or SEMI-DISPLACEMENT) hull is one that gets a significant portion of its weight-carrying capability from dynamic action, but which does not travel at a fast enough speed for full planing status. It is often a hull that is round-bottomed forward, gradually flattening out toward the stern to provide a planing surface.

Ballasted Hulls Whereas heeling is the sideways tipping of a boat caused by wind in the sails, LISTING is tipping caused by improper weight distribution. A sailboat must be able to resist this force, which acts high above the deck where it has maximum impact on stability. The boat can fight the heeling force with hull shape and BALLAST (weight put on board specifically for this function). Considering STABILITY, a flat-bottom hull presents immediate and strong resistance to heeling, but will ultimately give up with a sudden capsize, turning bottom up. At the other extreme, a round hull required for efficient sailing offers little initial resistance to heeling. Likewise, a fine hull offers less resistance to heeling than a beamy one.

On smaller sailboats, the crew can act as "live ballast," shifting to the windward side to counteract the heeling. Some larger sailing craft have BALLAST TANKS on each side of the hull so that water ballast can be pumped from one to the other to be more effective.

Deck Terms

A deck is an important horizontal structural part of a boat, its design dictated as much for strength as by aesthetics. If a deck is arched to aid in draining off water, it is said to be CAMBERED. Similarly, camber occurs on the tops of cabins, deckhouses, etc. The deck over the forward part of a vessel, or the forward part of the total deck area, is termed a FOREDECK. Similarly, the AFTERDECK is located in the after part of the vessel. SIDE DECKS are exterior walkways from the foredeck aft. Safety demands that all walking areas of exterior decks be treated with nonskid material.

HATCHES (sometimes called HATCHWAYS) are openings in the deck of a vessel to provide access below. COMPANION LADDERS or steps lead downward from the deck; these also are termed COMPANIONWAYS.

Figure 1-15 On board sailboats (above) and power-boats, the galley is frequently part of the main cabin. There is often an adjacent dinette, the table of which can be lowered to make an additional sleeping berth.

COCKPITS are open wells in the deck of a boat outside of deckhouses and cabins. The deck of a cockpit, or of an interior cabin, is often called the

SOLE. COAMINGS are vertical pieces around the edges of cockpit, hatches, etc., to prevent water on deck from running below.

Interior Terms

Vertical partitions, corresponding to walls in a house, are called BULKHEADS. WATERTIGHT BULK-HEADS are solid or are equipped with doors that can be secured so tightly as to be leakproof. The interior areas divided off by bulkheads are termed COMPARTMENTS—such as an engine compartment—or cabins—such as the main cabin or after cabin. Some areas are named by their use; the kitchen aboard a boat is its GALLEY; see **Figures 1-15 and 1-16**. The toilet area is the HEAD; the same name is also given to the toilet itself, which will be attached to some sort of MARINE SANITATION DEVICE (MSD). OVERHEAD is the nautical term for what would be the ceiling of a room in a house; if made of soft material, it can be called the HEADLINER. CEILING, on a boat, is light planking or plywood sheeting on the inside of the frames, along the sides of the boat. FLOORS, nautically speaking, are not laid to be walked upon, as in a house, but are structural parts adjacent to the keel.

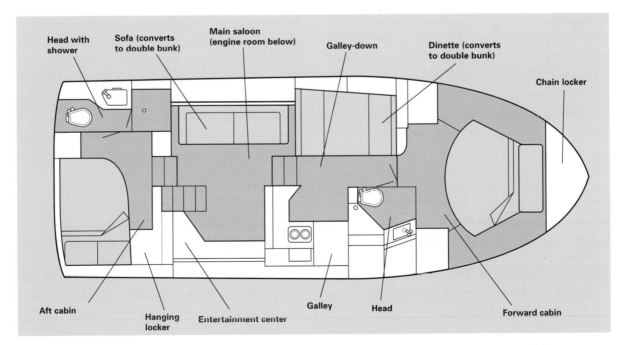

Figure 1-16 This view shows the interior arrangements of a mid-size power cruiser with comfortable accommodations for four persons, expandable when needed for two to four more. On this boat, the main saloon is raised above the engines, and the galley is "down."

The term BILGE is also applied to the lower interior areas of the hull of a vessel. Here water that leaks or washes in, or is blown on board as spray, collects as BILGE WATER, to be later pumped overboard by a BILGE PUMP.

BERTHS and BUNKS are seagoing names for beds aboard a boat. Closets are termed LOCKERS; a HANGING LOCKER is one tall enough for full-length garments; a WET LOCKER is one specifically designated for soggy FOUL-WEATHER GEAR (rain jackets and pants). Chests and boxes may also be called lockers. A ROPE or CHAIN LOCKER is often found in the bow of a boat for stowing the anchor line or chain; this area is called the FOREPEAK. LAZARETTES are compartments in the stern of a vessel used for general storage.

When something is put away in its proper place on a vessel, it is STOWED. The opposite of stowing, to BREAK OUT, is to take a needed article from its locker or other secure place.

HELM is a term relating to the steering mechanism of a craft. An individual is AT THE HELM when he or she is at the controls of the boat; he is then the HELMSMAN (male or female). The BRIDGE of a vessel is the location from which it is steered and its speed controlled. On small craft, the term CONTROL STATION is perhaps more appropriate. Many motorboats have a FLYING BRIDGE, an added set of controls above the level of the normal control station for better visibility and more fresh air. These, also called FLYBRIDGES, are sometimes open, but often have a fixed or a collapsible ("Bimini") top for shade, and perhaps

Figure 1-17 A power cruiser's flying bridge, usually called a flybridge, is an upper steering position originally intended as a platform to spot game fish.

clear plastic CURTAINS forward, aft, and around the sides for protection from the weather; see **Figure 1-17.** Medium-size and larger boats, particularly sailboats, may have a specially designated area in a cabin below for a NAV STATION equipped with a CHART TABLE.

Portholes & Portlights
On a boat, a PORT (or PORTHOLE) is an opening in the hull to admit light and air. The glass used in it to keep the hull weather tight is termed a PORTLIGHT if it can be opened, and a DEADLIGHT if it cannot. Openings in cabins above the deck are generally WINDOWS that open by sliding to one side.

The Dimensions of a Vessel
The length of a boat is often given in two forms: LENGTH OVERALL (LOA) and LENGTH AT THE WATERLINE (LWL) also known as the LOAD WATERLINE; see page 18. LOA is measured from the fore part of the stem to the after part of the stern along the centerline, excluding any projections that are not part of the hull, such as the bowsprit. Thus a boat with a LOA of 35 feet (10.7 m) might have a total length of 42 feet (12.8 m) when these appendages are taken into consideration. In many of today's powerboat designs, the swim platform is part of the hull and thus included in any LOA measurements. The waterline of a boat is the plane where the surface of the water touches the hull when it is loaded normally; LWL is measured from stem to stern in a straight line along this plane. The greatest width of a vessel is its BEAM; boats of greater than normal beam are described as BEAMY. A vessel's DRAFT is the depth of water required to float it; it is said to "draw" that depth. Draft should not be confused with the term DEPTH, which is used in connection with large vessels and documented boats and is measured inside the hull from the underside of the deck to the top of the keel. The height of a boat's topsides from the waterline to the deck is called its FREEBOARD; this is normally greater at the bow than at the stern. HEADROOM is the vertical distance between the deck and the cabin or canopy top, or any overhead structure.

Figure 1-18 The walk-around style of this outboard-powered boat includes elements of the center-console and cuddy types. A narrow sidedeck allows access to a low foredeck with rails. The cabin provides basic accommodations and storage space. This configuration is well suited for fishing.

Powerboat Types

Powerboat builders use numerous terms to distinguish boat types, and they are not always consistent. However, a few basic terms seem to be universal, surviving changes in style. A RUN-ABOUT usually seats four to six persons. BOWRIDER runabouts have additional seating in the bow accessed via a walk-through windshield. A runabout has no formal sleeping accommodations, but its seats may fold down for sunning or napping.

On runabouts with a length of about 20 feet (6.0 m) or more, the space at the bow becomes large enough for a small enclosure or cabin, termed a CUDDY (the oft-heard "cuddy cabin" is redundant). While not luxurious, the cuddy does offer shelter in wet weather and may also enclose a portable head.

Center-consoles & Daycruisers

A CENTER-CONSOLE boat has its helm and engine controls located on the centerline approximately midway between the bow and stern; see **Figure 1-18**. These craft are popular with anglers as they have the maximum deck space for a boat's overall length (LOA). Seating is usually limited to a pair of swivel or bench seats, sometimes with additional seating in the stern. Fishing enthusiasts can handle rods or swing nets around the boat's entire perimeter. The lack of enclosed space makes this type undesirable for cruising.

Center-consoles range in size from less than 15 feet (4.6 m) to about 35 feet (10.7 m).

In the range of 20 feet to 25 feet (6.1 to 7.6 m), DAYCRUISERS are large enough to have a small cabin forward with seated headroom. This will probably have a V-BERTH, a portable head, and a small galley consisting of a tabletop stove and a basin, with a folding table.

Express & Sedan Cruisers

Longer than about 25 feet (7.6 m), powerboat styles begin to diverge. Differences in accommodation layout are reflected in differences in their hull and superstructure shapes. EXPRESS CRUISERS form one branch of powerboat design, whereas another is composed of SEDAN CRUISERS, sometimes called CONVERTIBLES; see **Figure 1-19**.

An express cruiser takes the basic sportboat or runabout configuration and enlarges it to a length of 40 feet (12.2 m) or more. The craft's FOREDECK is long and unobstructed, interrupted only by hatches that provide ventilation to the enclosed space below. The control station, or bridge, is set well aft and often slightly higher than the level of the open cockpit near the stern. A radar arch is sometimes included to provide high and clear mounting space for radar and other antennas. An express cruiser is typically quite stylish and high-powered.

A sedan or convertible cruiser puts the main interior space on the same level as the cockpit.

Figure 1-19 The express cruiser is a modern, sporty design that enlarges the sportboat configuration to include accommodations in the forward cabin and an open raised bridge. It has a planing hull.

The interior is divided into two parts: a main cabin or SALOON at the level of the cockpit and a forward cabin lower and under the foredeck. ("Saloon" is the proper nautical word, although "salon" will be seen in some advertising literature.) Smaller sedans usually will have their galleys within the main cabin; this is known as a GALLEY UP layout. The GALLEY DOWN layout has the galley between the saloon and the forward cabin, at the level of the latter.

Aft-cabin Cruisers

As length increases, it becomes possible to have sleeping quarters below the level of the deck at the stern in an AFT CABIN. The engines are moved forward to the middle area of the hull beneath the main cabin, and the resulting design is called a DOUBLE-CABIN cruiser. (If the boat is large enough, there may be a second sleeping cabin aft, and the design becomes a TRI-CABIN or TRIPLE-CABIN cruiser.)

Sport Fishermen

A sport-fishing boat can be a convertible or sedan that is rigged for fishing, or it can be a true SPORT FISHERMAN (sometimes colloquially called a "SPORTFISH") with a longer foredeck, shortened main cabin, and much larger cockpit aft. Purpose-designed game-fishing craft usually have a TUNA TOWER with a set of controls at a maximum height for better spotting fish; some

have a control station in the cockpit for boat handling during the final fighting and boarding of game fish. The boat will have OUTRIGGERS for additional trolling lines and the cockpit will be outfitted with special fighting chairs.

Recreational Trawlers

Within the commercial fishing community, the word "trawler" has a specific meaning relating to a style of fishing, but in recreational boating the term is used much more loosely. In general, a cruiser that does not have sufficient horsepower to get into a planing mode is known as a TRAWLER

The trawler's hull is a displacement design to ride through and not over the water; see **Figure 1-20**. It can vary from one with soft bilges to one with hard chines. Nearly all trawlers have a significant external keel. Speed is normally limited to hull speed; the engine can be either single or twins. These craft have very modest fuel consumption characteristics and are popular for traveling at speeds of 7 to 10 knots over long distances. There are available so-called "fast trawlers" with speeds of 12 to 16 or more knots, but the term is really an oxymoron and incorrect.

Powerboat Cockpits & Bridges

The central element of a small powerboat is the CONTROL CONSOLE. Controls such as the STEERING

Figure 1-20 A trawler was originally designed as a low-speed, seaworthy commercial fishing vessel. As a recreational boat, trawlers are fuel-efficient and offer many on-board living advantages.

Figure 1-21 *A swim platform of a boat makes easier entry into and exit from the water or a dinghy; they can also be very helpful in a man-overboard situation. Be sure the engine is shut off when people are in the water near the boat.*

WHEEL and SHIFT LEVERS must be placed within easy reach. There must be good sight lines so that engine instruments and electronic displays are readily viewable. As the length of a powerboat increases, it is possible to raise the control position above the level of the cockpit sole—where it can be given the traditional name, "bridge."

Limited space makes it a challenge to install all of the radio communication and navigational electronic equipment on the console in a practical fashion. One common and sometimes overlooked problem is that of placing the COMPASS in a position from which it can be easily read, but which leaves it as free as possible from undesired magnetic influences.

At about 30 feet (9.1 m) of overall length, it becomes possible to provide a flybridge. This location for the controls has become popular as it provides better visibility all around the horizon. Sun and weather protection is usually provided by a Bimini top, frequently with all-around curtains.

Many motorboats have dual steering stations, one in the cabin below, and one on the flybridge.

Steering and engine controls are duplicated, as are some of the electronics. This design allows for a comfortable operating position in any weather.

Powerboats often have SWIM PLATFORMS just aft of the transom that serve additionally as boarding platforms for dinghies; see **Figure 1-21**. Some sport-fishing craft will have gates in the transom for easier access to this platform when boarding large game fish.

Sailboat Types

Sailboats are seldom identified as to their cabin layouts as are powerboats, probably because less variety is possible. Instead, sailing craft are usually known by their SAIL PLANS: the number of masts and the position of their sails (described on pages 32 and 33). Smaller sailboats almost always have a cockpit at or near the stern. Interior accommodations are forward in one or more cabins. While interior space receives the most attention from new boat buyers, it is actually the cockpit where most sailors' time is spent; see **Figure 1-22**.

SAIL PLANS FOR VARIOUS RIGS

The Sloop

The most popular plan is the sloop, which has one mast forward of amidships and two sails. The forward sail is the HEADSAIL or JIB, and the aft one is the MAINSAIL, also called the MAIN. A sail's leading edge is its LUFF; its after edge is the LEECH and its bottom edge is the FOOT. The jib is attached to the HEADSTAY with HANKS, strong hooks with spring-loaded closures. An alternative design uses a semi-flexible track, or FOIL, on the stay that accepts a BOLTROPE sewn along the sail's luff. Such tracks offer better airflow over the luff, making the sail more efficient; this also allows ROLLER FURLING to reduce sail area in heavy weather. Other sails may be roller furled into a slot in the mast or around the boom, or more often are partially lowered and fastened to the boom with short pieces of line attached to the sail called REEF POINTS; refer also to **Figure 1-23**.

Headsails can have many names, depending on their size, weight, and shape. The smallest is a storm jib, followed by a heavy-weather jib, and a working jib. A genoa, an oversize jib reaching well past the mast, comes in a number of sizes and may have a surface area greater than the mainsail.

When a sloop's jib is hoisted from a stay running to the top of the mast, it is a masthead sloop. If the jib is hoisted to a lower point, the sloop has a fractional rig. The headsail of this type of rig only reaches to a fraction of the height of the mast—typically three-quarters or seven-eighths.

The foot of a working jib may be attached to a small spar called a club. This arrangement allows the sail to be self-tending because it can be controlled by one sheet rather than two. A club-footed jib can be tacked (turning the boat so the wind blows on the other side) without releasing one sheet and hauling in on the other. A self-tending jib is much easier for one person to handle.

The Cutter

A single-masted sailboat similar to the sloop, the CUTTER has its mast more nearly amidships, leaving room for a larger FORETRIANGLE filled by two headsails. The outer headsail is the jib, while the inner is a STAYSAIL. A cutter rig has two advantages. First, it divides sail area among the smaller sails that are more easily handled. Second, it provides more sail reduction options in rough going than does a sloop. And when sail is reduced, the remaining area is closer to the mast, giving added safety in a seaway. This rig has been a longtime favorite among cruising sailors who prefer a one-mast rig.

The Ketch & Yawl

The KETCH and YAWL look somewhat alike. Both have a tall MAINMAST and a shorter MIZZENMAST (a smaller mast aft of the mainmast) that flies a MIZZEN sail. The distinction between a ketch and a yawl is a common topic of debate among sailors. Traditionally, the governing rule is the location of the mizzenmast: If it is ahead of the rudderpost, the boat is a ketch; however, if it is behind the rudderpost, the boat is a yawl.

Ketches and yawls are DIVIDED RIGS, meaning the sail area is divided between two masts. Either craft may have a masthead or a fractional rig forward of the mainmast with one or more headsails. Individual sails are more manageable in size and more easily handled by a small crew. Both may fly a large jib-like sail between the masts called a MIZZEN STAYSAIL. Because of the extra rigging and mast surface area exposed to the wind, these rigs have more WINDAGE. This rig is less effective on smaller boats where windage is relatively more important. The ketch and yawl rigs are popular among cruising sailors for long-distance voyages. Mizzenmasts are a practical location for mounting electronic antennas.

The Schooner

A SCHOONER is a vessel with at least two masts (in the last century, some carried up to seven). On two-masted schooners, the mainmast is aft, and is at least as tall or taller than the forward mast, or FOREMAST. Most schooners used multiple headsail combinations including—from top down—the flying jib, the jib, and the FORESTAYSAIL. The number of headsails and their names varies with the location and the time period.

Schooners were originally workboats, mainly fishing vessels. Equipped with tall, powerful rigs, they raced back home from the Grand Banks (southeast of New Foundland) to get top dollar for their catches. These became some of the first sailing competitions in the United States.

Schooners were originally GAFF RIGGED with four-sided sails on the mainmast and foremast supported by a spar—the GAFF—at their top edges. Often, a triangular topsail was flown above both the main and foresails. For extra power, a sail called a FISHERMAN was set between the masts. These complex rigs required more deck hands than are standard today. The modern schooner rig may carry a MARCONI or JIB-HEADED main and foresails (triangular as in the mainsail on a sloop). The foresail may be LOOSE-FOOTED, not fitted with a boom, and there may be only one headsail.

Schooners are most comfortable in steady trade winds on long ocean passages. Although they do not go to windward as well as other rigs, they make up for it when the wind is on or aft of the beam.

The Catboat

A boat that caries only one mast set well forward and no headsails is known as a CATBOAT. Traditionally, these were small, inshore boats. The catboat was a very useful and practical design for coastal fishermen because there was less rigging to get in the way when handling nets in the water or unloading the catch ashore. Also, the boat's single sail was easier for one person to handle.

Recent cat-rigged designs make use of UNSTAYED masts (masts that have no standing rigging, being supported only by the deck). With less windage, and high, narrow sail plans, modern catboats can often perform nearly as well as sloop rigs. The catboat concept of unstayed masts has extended into the ketch category, and occasionally a cat-schooner may be seen.

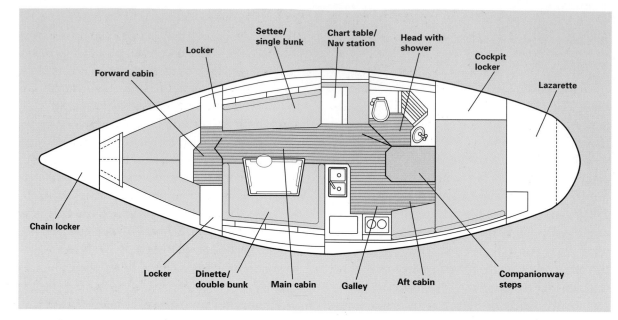

Figure 1-22 *Interior layouts for sailboats vary widely depending on the length and beam of the craft. This mid-size cruising sailboat offers generous accommodations for several crew and guests.*

Many larger sailboats are of the CENTER-COCKPIT style, roughly corresponding to the double-cabin type of powerboats. With sufficient beam at the stern, it becomes possible to have an adequate aft cabin behind or partially under the cockpit. As this cabin grows in size with increasing hull length, the cockpit itself can be moved forward to a more central location. However, to have useful space below, it is necessary to raise the cockpit sole to the level of the deck. The result is ungainly in center-cockpit boats of less than about 40 feet (12.2 m) in length.

As sailcloth, rigging wire, and metal masts have improved in strength, taller masts have become possible without increasing weight. Greater height allows more sail area, or the same area in a more efficient shape. Reduction in rigging weight, more stable hulls, and better deck equipment have made possible simpler sail plans.

Sailing Rigs

RIG is the general term applied to the arrangement of a vessel's masts and sails. Most recreational sailing craft are now fitted with triangular-shaped sails and are said to be MARCONI-RIGGED (or JIB-HEADED). If a four-sided sail with a gaff is used, the boat is described as GAFF-RIGGED.

The principal sail of a boat is its MAINSAIL. A sail forward of the mast—or ahead of the most forward mast if there is more than one—is a HEADSAIL; a single headsail is usually termed a JIB.

If a boat has no headsails, it is a CATBOAT; she may be either Marconi-rigged or gaff-rigged. A boat having a single mast, with a mainsail and a jib, is a SLOOP. On some boats additional headsails are set from a BOWSPRIT, a spar projecting forward over the bow (see page 289, in Chapter 8, for more on masts and spars).

A modern CUTTER is a variation of the sloop rig in which the mast is stepped further aft, resulting in a larger area for headsails. A cutter normally sets two headsails—a FORESTAYSAIL with a jib ahead of it.

YAWLS have two masts, the after one of which is much smaller and is stepped abaft the rudderpost. A KETCH likewise has two masts with the after one smaller, but here the difference in height is not so marked and the after mast is stepped forward of the rudderpost. The taller mast is the MAINMAST; the shorter mast of

Figure 1-23 When the wind blows too strongly for safety or comfort, it is time to take in a reef in the mainsail, usually by tying the reef points under the foot of the sail, as described in Chapter 8.

either rig is the MIZZENMAST, and the after sail is the MIZZEN.

SCHOONERS have two or more masts, but unlike yawls and ketches the after mast of a two-masted schooner is taller than the forward one (in some designs, the two masts may be the same height). Thus the after mast becomes the mainmast and the other the FOREMAST. Additional names are used if there are more than two masts.

Square-Rigged Vessels

Vessels on which the principal sails are set generally athwartships are referred to as SQUARE-RIGGED. These four-sided sails are hung from horizontal spars known as YARDS. Headsails are carried, as on other rigs, forward of the foremost mast. STAYSAILS may also be set between the masts, and the aftermost mast of a square-rigged vessel normally carries a fore-and-aft sail. Very limited use is made of this rig for recreational sailing vessels.

Sailboat Cockpits

Because the cockpit of a cruising sailboat serves as both an entertainment and a control center, compromises must be made between access to HALYARDS and SHEETS (lines to hoist and trim sails) or to WINCHES (devices to increase the pull on such lines) and the comfort of those on board; see **Figure 1-24.** Typical cockpits have facing bench seats on each side that are close enough together that individuals can brace themselves as the boat heels. Cockpit seats often lift open to reveal SEAT LOCKERS—stowage for SAIL BAGS, an uninflated life raft, dock lines, sheets, winch handles, and the accumulated etceteras of life afloat.

A PEDESTAL with steering wheel may stand near the aft end of the cockpit. On top of this may be a BINNACLE, a case that houses a compass (refer to Chapter 13). The pedestal may also support shift and throttle levers for an auxiliary engine. On smaller sailboats, there may be no pedestal, with steering being accomplished using a tiller.

Connecting the sailboat cockpit to the main cabin below is a companionway consisting of a steep set of ladder-like steps, GRAB RAIL, and a SLIDING HATCH. The part of the cockpit that must be stepped over at the top of the companionway is called a COAMING, an important safety feature. If the cockpit were to fill with water from a large wave, this barrier would prevent it from going down into the interior and collecting in the bilge.

Figure 1-24 A winch revolves in one direction only, resisting the strain of sheets and providing extra power for trimming sails. Self-tailing winches, as shown above, allow one person to do the work of two.

Water in the cockpit drains through at least two SCUPPERS (drain holes) leading from the lowest points on the cockpit sole through the hull. Of course, the cockpit sole must be at a height above the waterline at any angle of heel for these drains to work.

Aft of the cockpit there is often a lazarette, accessed through a hatch. In some more recent designs, there will be a set of steps leading down to a swim platform just above the water. This platform, in addition to being used for getting into and out of the water for swimming, is useful for boarding or disembarking from a dinghy; it can also be useful in retrieving a person from the water in a man overboard (MOB) situation.

Construction Terms

The term FASTENING is applied to various screws, bolts, or specially designed nails that hold equipment and other gear to the hull or superstructure. THROUGH FASTENINGS are bolts that go all the way through the hull or other base timbers, secured with a washer and nut on the inside; a BACKING BLOCK is generally advisable for spreading the stress and to gain additional strength. BEDDING COMPOUND, a sealer and adhesive, should be used between any fitting and the surface on which it is mounted.

SEA COCKS are valves installed just inside THROUGH-HULL FITTINGS where water is taken in or discharged for engine cooling, operation of heads, etc. Sea cocks are important safety devices as they can shut off the flow of water if a hose breaks or a piece of equipment must be worked on.

Areas that are varnished to a high gloss are termed BRIGHTWORK. (In naval usage, this term may be applied to polished brass.) A TACK RAG is a slightly sticky cloth that is wiped over surfaces that are to be varnished or painted just before the brush is applied, to remove all dust and grit.

When the rudder of a boat is exactly centered, one spoke of the steering wheel should be vertical; this is the KING SPOKE and is usually marked with special carving or wrapping so that it can be recognized by feel alone. (The wheel of a hydraulic steering system may not have an unvarying center position.) Some craft will have on the instrument panel an electrical RUDDER ANGLE INDICATOR.

Many motorboats are constructed with a small SIGNAL MAST from which flags can be flown (refer to Chapter 25). These flags are hoisted on SIGNAL HALYARDS. When partially hoisted on any mast, flags are said to be AT THE DIP; when fully hoisted, they are termed TWO-BLOCKED.

Vessels, including boats, are normally designed by a NAVAL ARCHITECT. In doing so, he or she prepares detailed PLANS and SPECIFICATIONS, including the LINES (shape) of her hull. CLEAN is a term applied not to a boat's condition, but rather to her lines. If the lines are FINE, so that she slips easily through the water, the lines are said to be clean.

A MARINE SURVEYOR is a highly experienced person whose job it is to make detailed inspections (SURVEYS) of boats and ships to determine the condition of hull, equipment, machinery, etc.; see **Figure 1-25.**

Fiberglass Construction

There are some recreational boats still in use that are of wood construction, and a few are still built each year. While there are dedicated

Figure 1-25 Generally, a survey is conducted when the boat is out of the water. A marine surveyor gives the person who has commissioned the survey an extensive report on all structural elements of the boat, including suggestions regarding needed repairs.

wooden-boat enthusiasts and popular publications targeted for them, the vast majority of recreational boats are made of FIBERGLASS. The full name of this material is "fiber-reinforced plastic," which properly describes the material as glass fibers embedded in a thermosetting plastic, usually polyester but sometimes epoxy (stronger, but more expensive). In recent years glass has sometimes been replaced with other fibers made of carbon or synthetics such as Kevlar for greater strength. Large yachts are often made of aluminum or with steel hulls and aluminum superstructures.

There are many advantages to fiberglass construction; see **Figure 1-26**. Surfaces can be of any desired compound curvature; multiple identical hulls, superstructures, and lesser components can be made economically from reusable molds; and plastic hulls completely resist attack by marine organisms, although they do require antifouling paint.

Fiberglass construction uses a female mold into which multiple layers are placed. Each layer is LAID UP in turn following a MOLD SCHEDULE, or list of layers. Typically, this might consist of a GEL COAT (which will be the outer skin of the hull), alternating layers of MAT (cloth made of irregular short fibers), regular fiberglass CLOTH, and possibly chopped strand sprayed onto the surface by means of a pneumatic gun. This series of layers might be followed by core material and further interior layers. Each layer might be hand-rolled against the previous layer, but more modern methods involve VACUUM BAGGING. A special layer, called an OSMOSIS BARRIER, is usually placed just under the gel coat to prevent the movement of water through the gel coat that could eventually cause BLISTERS.

Molded construction is also used for one-off, high performance racing boats—both power and sail. While the methods used are similar to production boats, these often make use of better (more expensive) materials, such as UNIDIRECTIONAL, BIAXIAL, or even more specialized glass cloths. EPOXY resins frequently replace the polyesters used in more conventional boats. The strength and adhesive properties of epoxy

Figure 1-26 *Fiberglass construction allows multiple hulls, superstructures, and other components to be made economically from reusable molds. Surfaces can be of any desired compound curvature. In addition, plastic hulls resist attack by marine organisms—but they do require antifouling paint.*

are superior to polyester, but it is more expensive. Reinforcing materials other than glass fiber, such as Kevlar and CARBON FIBER, are sometimes used.

Secondary parts of the boat are laid-up in their own molds, usually with a simpler schedule than is used for the hull. These parts are then removed from their molds, fitted with various hardware and other components (cleats, hatches, rails tanks, electrical wiring harnesses, etc.), then assembled to complete the craft.

Fiberglass is strong, but heavy and not very stiff. Sufficient stiffness can be achieved, without undesired weight, by using CORED CONSTRUCTION, also called COMPOSITE CONSTRUCTION. Two layers of fiberglass are separated by a light but compression-resistant core, typically a rigid FOAM CORE of balsawood. Stiffening can also be achieved by the use of box-like sections called HIGH-HAT SECTIONS forming a grid or running longitudinally inside the hull or under a deck.

The principal engineering problem, once the molding is complete, is how best to attach the deck to the hull. Theories abound, but in general

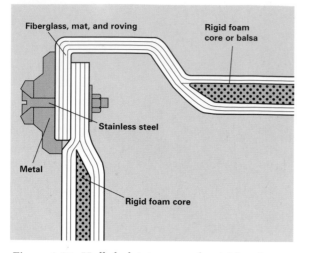

Figure 1-27 Hull-deck joints must be rigid and watertight. Most are molded box-sections that are liberally caulked with adhesive sealants. Stainless steel through-bolts provide additional security. The hull-deck joint shown above is typical of a small powerboat.

the best HULL-DECK JOINTS offer large surfaces for bedding compound or other sealers and adhesives; see **Figure 1-27**. Thick wood or metal bearing plates for through-bolt attachments are also requirements. Finally, there must be provisions for RUB RAILS and STANTION BASES.

Fiberglass is useful also in covering wood, either in new construction or in the repair of older boats, where its properties of ADHESION are important.

Sailboat Masts & Spars

While carbon fiber is also used in the construction of sophisticated racing sailboat masts, the majority of modern sailing craft have spars that are made of extruded aluminum alloy. Most masts and booms are simple tubes. Where more efficient shapes are required, they can be fabricated by cutting and rewelding basic extrusions.

Aluminum is strong, so mast failures are rare except on hard-pressed racing boats. Its main advantage is the material's light weight, which keeps the boat's center of gravity low and improves sailing performance.

Terms Relating to Equipment

CHOCKS are deck fittings, usually of metal, with inward curving arms through which mooring,

anchor, or other lines are passed to lead them in the proper direction both on and off the boat; they should be very smooth to prevent excess wearing of the line. CLEATS are fittings of metal or wood with outward curving arms, called HORNS, on which lines can be made fast; see **Figure 1-28**.

While cleats are generally satisfactory for most purposes on a boat, wooden or metal BITTS are recommended if heavy strains are to be made. These are stout vertical posts, either single or double. They may take the form of a fitting securely bolted (never screwed) to the deck, but even better—as in the case of a SAMSON POST—passing through the deck and STEPPED at the keel or otherwise strongly fastened. Sometimes a round metal pin, called a NORMAN PIN, is fitted horizontally through the head of a post or bitt to aid in BELAYING the line; see **Figure 1-29**.

Where lines pass through a chock, or rub against a surface, they should be protected from wear by a CHAFE GUARD; see **Figure 1-30**.

FENDERS are relatively soft objects of rubber or plastic used between boats and piles, pier sides, seawalls, etc., to protect the topsides from scarring and to cushion any shock of the boat striking a fixed object. Fenders, sometimes referred to in a landlubberly fashion as "bumpers," are also used between boats when they are tied, or RAFTED, together; see **Figure 1-31**. FENDER BOARDS are short lengths of stout

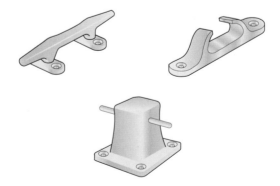

Figure 1-28 Cleats, chocks, and bitts (seen above clockwise from upper left) are used on both powerboats and sailboats. Their shape and size may vary with the size of the craft that they are on, but all are basic deck hardware.

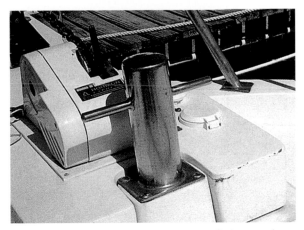

Figure 1-29 A sampson post, a strong fitting on the foredeck, secures the anchor rode or dock lines. The norman pin, which passes through it, keeps the line from slipping up and off the post, and provides a means of securing the line with half-hitches.

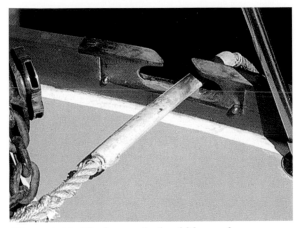

Figure 1-30 Chafe guards should be used on any lines that pass over an abrasive surface. They may he a purchased item, as shown above, but can be homemade by using a split garden hose or special tape applied to the lining.

planking, often with cushion material or metal rubbing strips on one side. They are normally used horizontally with two fenders hung vertically behind them to provide a wider bearing surface against a single pile.

A LIFE PRESERVER—also called a PERSONAL FLOTATION DEVICE, abbreviated PFD—provides additional buoyancy to keep a person afloat when he is in the water. They take the form of cushions, belts, vests, jackets, and ring buoys. PFDs must be of a Coast Guard-approved type to meet the legal requirements as set forth in Chapter 3.

A BOAT HOOK is a short shaft of wood or metal with a hook fitting at one end shaped to aid in extending one's effective reach from the side of the boat, such as when putting a line over a pile or picking up an object dropped overboard. It can also be used for pushing or FENDING OFF.

A BOARDING LADDER is a set of steps temporarily or permanently fitted over the side or stern of a boat to assist persons coming aboard from a low pier or float. A SWIMMING LADDER is much the same except that it extends down into the water.

GRAB RAILS are hand-holding fittings mounted on cabin tops or sides, or in the interiors of boats, for personal safety when moving around the boat both on deck and below.

Magnetic compasses are mounted near the control station, often in binnacles. Compasses are swung in GIMBALS, pivoted rings that permit the compass BOWL and CARD to remain relatively level regardless of the boat's motion. To enable the helmsman to steer a COMPASS COURSE, a LUBBER'S LINE is marked on the inside of the compass bowl to indicate direction of the vessel's bow (see Chapter 13 for more on compasses).

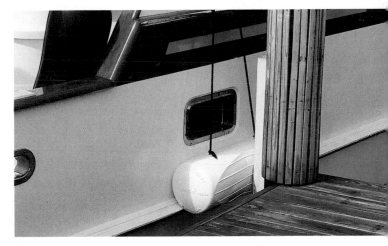

Figure 1-31 A fender is used to protect the side of a boat from damage by a rough pile or pier face. It also cushions any shocks to the boat from waves or the wake of passing vessels. Fenders can be hung horizontally or vertically as required by the surface that they bear upon.

A LEAD (pronounced led) LINE is a length of light rope with a weight (the lead) at one end and markers at accurately measured intervals from that end. It is used for determining the depth of water alongside a vessel. A DEPTH SOUNDER is an electronic device for determining the depths; often such devices are referred to as "fathometers"—a term that was actually the trademark of one manufacturer of electronic depth sounders. Boats frequently used in shallow waters may be equipped with a long, slender SOUNDING POLE with depth in feet and fractions marked off from the lower end; there may be a special mark indicating the craft's draft.

A BAROMETER is often carried aboard a boat; it measures and *indicates* atmospheric pressure. A BAROGRAPH *records* changing atmospheric pressure. Knowledge of the amount and direction of change in atmospheric pressure is useful in predicting changes in the weather (see Chapter 24).

A BINOCULAR is a hand-held device for detecting and observing distant objects. Separate sets of lenses and prisms enable the user to see with both eyes at the same time. (The term is properly singular, as in "bicycle," but the plural form, "pair of binoculars," for a single unit is often mistakenly used.)

A WINCH is a mechanical device, either hand or power operated, for exerting an increased pull on a line or chain, such as an anchor line or a sailboat's halyards or sheets.

Ropes & Lines

Generally speaking, the term ROPE is used but little aboard a boat; the correct term is LINE. "Rope" may be bought ashore at the store, but when it comes aboard a vessel and is put to use it becomes "line." MARLINESPIKE SEAMANSHIP is the term applied to the art of using line and the making of KNOTS, BENDS, HITCHES, and SPLICES (see Chapter 23, which is devoted to this important subject).

Lines used to make a boat fast to a shore structure are called MOORING LINES or DOCK LINES. BOW LINES and STERN LINES lead forward and aft from those respective parts of the boat. SPRING LINES lead aft from the bow or forward from the stern to prevent the boat from moving ahead or astern; refer to **Figure 6-23**.

A PAINTER is a line at the bow of a small boat, such as a dinghy, for towing or making fast. The line by which a boat is made fast to a mooring buoy is called a PENNANT (sometimes PENDANT). The pennant is SLIPPED when it is cast off so the boat can get underway.

Lines have STANDING PARTS and HAULING PARTS. The standing part is the fixed part, the one which is made fast; the hauling part is the one that is taken in or let out as the tackle is used. Lines are FOUL when tangled, CLEAR when ready to run freely. Ends of lines are WHIPPED or SEIZED when twine or thread is wrapped around them to prevent strands from untwisting or UNLAYING. Ragged ends of lines are said to be FAGGED.

HEAVING LINES are light lines usually with a knot or weight at one end, which makes it easier to throw them farther and more accurately. The knot that encloses a weight at the end of a heaving line is called a MONKEY'S FIST.

HAWSERS are very heavy lines in common use on tugboats and larger vessels.

Flags

Strictly speaking, a vessel's COLORS are the flag or flags that it flies to indicate its nationality, but the term is often expanded to include all flags flown. An ENSIGN is a flag that denotes the nationality of a vessel or its owner, or the membership of its owner in an organization (other than a yacht club).

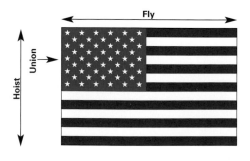

Figure 1-32 The principal parts and dimensions of a flag are shown here. For most flags the ratio between the fly and the hoist is 3:2, but this will vary with pennants. Flags should always be flown correctly.

Figure 1-33 A pier, as shown here, is a structure that projects out from the shore. A wharf is a structure that is parallel to the shore for making fast all types of vessels.

A BURGEE is a triangular, rectangular, or swallow-tailed flag usually denoting yacht club or similar unit membership. A PENNANT is a flag, most often triangular in shape, used for general designating or decorative purposes.

The HOIST of a flag is its inner vertical side; also its vertical dimension. The FLY is its horizontal length from the hoist out to the free end; see **Figure 1-32**. The UNION is the upper portion near the hoist—in the U.S. national flag, the blue area with the white stars. The UNION JACK is a flag consisting solely of the union of the national flag (see Chapter 25 for more on flags and how they should be flown).

Terms Used in Boating Activities

In addition to the numerous terms for the boat itself, there are many others to be learned in connection with boating in general. The list of these is virtually endless, and those that follow are only the more basic and often-used ones.

Docks, Piers & Harbors

There is a difference between strict definition and popular usage by many in boating for the term "dock." Properly speaking, a DOCK is the water area in which a boat lies when it is MADE FAST to shore installations—and "made fast" is the proper term rather than "tied up." In boating, however, the term "dock" is usually applied, albeit incorrectly, to structures bordering the water area in which boats lie. TO DOCK a vessel is to bring it to a shore installation and make it fast.

A DRYDOCK is one that can be shut off from the surrounding water and pumped out in order to make repairs on a vessel's bottom. A WHARF (or QUAY, pronounced "key") is a structure parallel to the shore, whereas a PIER projects outward from the shoreline; see **Figure 1-33**. PILES (or PILINGS) are substantial elongated objects driven into the bottom to which craft may be made fast or which support a structure. A group of piles driven close together and bolted or bound with wire cables into a single structure is called a DOLPHIN. (The name "dolphin," of course, is also given to a species of marine mammal as well as separately to a species of ocean game fish.) Piles are often used to form SLIPS out from a pier or wharf in which boats can be DOCKED or BERTHED; short CATWALKS (or FINGER PIERS) may extend out between the slips for easier access to the boats. A boat is made fast to a pile, in a slip, or alongside a pier or wharf.

An ANCHORAGE may be a carefully chosen, protected body of water suitable for anchoring, or an area specifically designated by governmental authorities in which vessels may anchor; special regulations may prevail in these areas. A HARBOR is an anchorage that affords reasonably good protection for a vessel, with shelter from

Figure 1-34 Marinas provide sheltered dockage and various services for small craft and yachts. Piers extend out from the shore, and finger piers project from them to provide better access to each boat. A self-propelled sling lift can take boats out of the water for work. Smaller powerboats are often lifted out and stacked in dry storage ashore with a large forklift truck; they are taken off the rack and launched for each use on the water.

wind and sea; strictly speaking, it applies to the water area only. PORT is a term that includes not only the harbor but all the facilities for freight, passengers, and services, such as wharves, piers, or warehouses. A MARINA or YACHT BASIN is a protected facility primarily for recreational craft; see **Figure 1-34.**

JETTIES are embankments connected to the shore; when these are used to protect an inlet or harbor, and have no connection to the land, they are BREAKWATERS. GROINS are jetty-like dikes built out at roughly a 90° angle from the shore to lessen erosion of the shoreline.

Boats are HAULED OUT of the water on inclined planes at the water's edge called WAYS (also MARINE WAYS or RAILWAYS). The framework that supports a boat as she is hauled out is a CRADLE. Boats are also lifted bodily out of the water and set on shore for storage or work in SLINGS, which are lowered, passed under the hull, and raised by a CRANE or a STRADDLE CRANE (often called a "Travel Lift," the name of one brand).

HEAVE is a nautical term for throwing or pulling on a line. One HEAVES IN on a line when he pulls in the slack and TAKES A STRAIN on it.

When a line is let out, one PAYS IT OUT; to lessen the strain on a line or let it out slightly or slowly, one EASES it. A line is SNUBBED when its outward run is checked; CAST OFF when let go. (A boat is cast off when all lines have been taken off the pier or other object to which it has been made fast.)

The BITTER END of a line is the extreme end, the end made fast when all line has been paid out. The middle part of a line not including either end is the BIGHT, particularly when formed into a loop. If a strain is put on a line heavy enough to break it, it PARTS.

BELAY has two meanings. A line is belayed when it is made fast without knotting to a CLEAT or BELAYING PIN; "belay," as a command, signifies "stop" or "cease" an action.

TACKLE is a broad, general term applied to equipment and gear used aboard a boat. It has a specific use, however, to mean a combination of line and BLOCKS (pulleys) used to increase a pulling or hoisting force. The wheels or rollers of the blocks are the SHEAVES (pronounced "shivs"). When a line is passed through a block or hole it is REEVED; to RENDER is to ensure that the line will pass freely through a block or hole.

Anchors & Moorings

An ANCHOR is a specially shaped metal device designed to dig efficiently into the bottom under a body of water and hold a vessel in place despite winds and currents (see Chapter 9, which is devoted to anchors and their use). GROUND TACKLE is a general term embracing anchors, lines, and other gear used in anchoring. On small craft, the anchor line or chain may be referred to as the RODE. The anchor carried on a boat for most normal uses is its WORKING ANCHOR. A heavier model carried for emergencies is termed a STORM ANCHOR, and a smaller, lighter anchor for brief daytime stops when the boat will not be left unattended is popularly called a LUNCH HOOK. Anchors come in many designs and many sizes for each design; refer to Chapter 9, **Figures 9-02 to 9-11.**

The term KEDGE is applied to an anchor of any type that is used for getting a boat off when it has run AGROUND in water shallower than its draft. The kedge is carried out by a dinghy or other means and set so that a pull on the line will help get the boat off, or at least keep it from being driven harder aground; this process is called KEDGING.

When a boat is anchored, the ratio of the length of line in use to the distance to the bottom of the water measured vertically from the deck is termed the SCOPE.

A MOORING is a semi-permanent anchorage installation, consisting of a heavy anchor (usually of the mushroom type) or block of concrete, chain, a mooring buoy, and a pennant of nylon or other synthetic line.

Motions of a Boat

A vessel GROUNDS when it touches bottom; if stuck there, it is aground. When a boat moves through the water, it is said to be UNDERWAY. According to government regulations, a vessel is underway at any time that it is not aground, at anchor, or made fast to the shore. The direction in which it is moving is made more specific by stating that it makes HEADWAY (moving forward), STERNWAY (moving backwards), or LEEWAY (to one side or the other, as when pushed by a beam wind). A boat is said to be UNDERWAY WITH NO WAY ON when it is free of the bottom or shore, but is making no motion through the water (ADRIFT); it may be moving with respect to the bottom as a result of wind or current. A vessel has STEERAGEWAY if it is moving fast enough through the water for its rudder to be effective. A vessel's anchor is said to be AWEIGH when it has broken out of the bottom and has been lifted clear.

The disturbed water that a boat leaves astern as a result of its motion is its WAKE. The flow of water that results from the action of its propeller or propellers is termed WASH. Both of these effects are commonly lumped together as "wake"; see **Figure 1-35.**

Sidewise rotational motion of a boat in rough water is called ROLL; vertical motion as the bow rises and falls is termed PITCHING. A boat YAWS when it runs off its course to either side, as it might if struck on the quarter by a following sea; see **Figure 1-36.** If it yaws too widely and is thrown broadside into the TROUGH of the waves (between the CRESTS and parallel to them), it may

Figure 1-35 Take care that your wake—the area of disturbed water behind you—does not disturb or damage other craft.

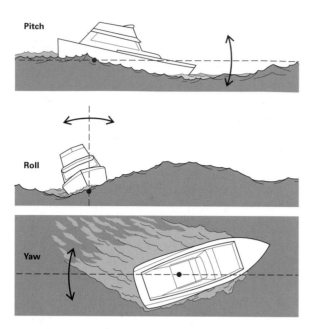

Figure 1-36 Pitching, rolling, and yawing are normal motions of a boat in moderate seas, although they may combine to create uncomfortable results. In rough seas, they can be dangerous.

BROACH (or BROACH TO), a dangerous situation that should be carefully avoided. In very rough seas a small boat can be thrown end-over-end; this is PITCHPOLING.

A boat may CAPSIZE without FOUNDERING. A boat knocked down so it lies on its side in the water or turns over has capsized; when it fills with water—from any cause—and sinks, it has foundered. If a boat fills with water from over the side, it SWAMPS. Before his vessel is reduced to such straits, the wise skipper HEAVES TO, reducing headway and generally lying with the bow slightly off from meeting the waves head on. He may put out a SEA ANCHOR that will hold the bow at the most favorable angle; this is usually in the form of a canvas cone or nylon "parachute" that does not go to the bottom, it merely serves as a drag. A DROGUE is a similar device set from the stern.

Trim

TRIM relates to the way a boat floats in the water. When it floats properly as designed, it is on an EVEN KEEL, but if it inclines to port or starboard, it lists. Heel conveys the same idea as list, a sideward inclination from the vertical, usually temporary, particularly when under sail. If a vessel is too heavily loaded forward, it TRIMS BY THE HEAD (or is DOWN BY THE BOW). If its draft is excessive aft, it TRIMS BY THE STERN (or is DOWN BY THE STERN).

Directions From the Boat

DEAD AHEAD refers to any point or object that the vessel is approaching directly on a straight course. DEAD ASTERN is, of course, the opposite direction. An object that is at right angles (90°) to the centerline (keel) of a boat is ABEAM, or BROAD ON THE BEAM. If the boat passes near to it, it is said to be CLOSE ABOARD. Vessels are ABREAST of one another when they are underway side-by-side.

The direction midway between abeam and dead ahead is BROAD ON THE BOW, port or starboard as the case may be. Similarly, an object seen midway between abeam and dead astern is BROAD ON THE (PORT or STARBOARD) QUARTER.

To express the direction of another vessel or object relative to our boat, we say that it BEARS so-and-so, using the phraseology above. For intermediate directions through a circle centered on the observer's boat, the traditional POINT SYSTEM can be used, with 32 points making a complete circle; see **Figure 1-37**. Each direction in the point system is named. A ship or other object seen from your craft might be said to bear TWO POINTS ABAFT THE PORT BEAM, ONE POINT ON THE STARBOARD BOW, etc. Half-points and quarter-points do exist but are rarely used. Many skippers now use the "clock" system to indicate direction from the boat, with the bow at 12 o'clock, and the stern at 6 o'clock. The direction of a remote object is its BEARING.

WINDWARD means toward the direction from which the wind is blowing. A boat goes to windward, but in speaking of the side of a vessel, and the objects on that side, on which the wind is blowing, it is better to refer to this as the WEATHER SIDE.

Opposite to windward is LEEWARD (pronounced loo'ard), the direction away from the wind, toward which it is blowing. The LEE SIDE OF

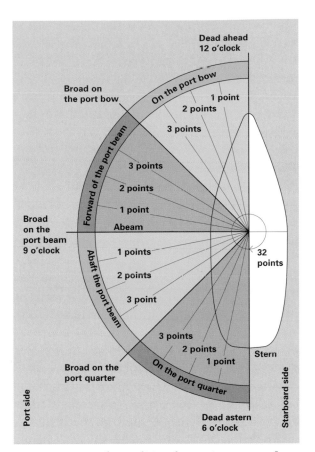

Figure 1-37 *In the traditional 32-point system of relative bearings, the circle in which the boat is centered is divided into eighths. These eighths start at dead ahead and continue on each side through the bow, forward to the beam, on the beam, on the quarter, and on to dead astern. Each of the pie-shaped sections is further divided into points, each of which is 11¼ degrees of arc.*

a boat is the side away from the wind—a boat makes leeway when blown sideways off its course. However, the vessel finds shelter in the LEE OF THE LAND when it is under a WEATHER SHORE.

Powerboat Terms

Certain basic boating terms apply specifically to craft equipped with some form of engine, whether INBOARD (mounted within the hull) or OUTBOARD (mounted on the transom and detachable).

Propulsion

THRUST for the movement of the boat through the water is achieved by the rotation of a PROPELLER, which draws in water from ahead and pushes it out astern; see **Figure 1-38**. Often-used boating slang for a propeller are "WHEEL" or "SCREW." Boats with two engines and propellers are referred to as TWIN-SCREW craft. A more recent development is the STERN-DRIVE or OUTDRIVE (or I-O, for INBOARD-OUTBOARD); see **Figure 1-39.** Here the engine is of the inboard type mounted within the hull at the stern; its external driving unit is roughly similar to the LOWER UNIT of an outboard motor, and similarly can be tilted up. Power is applied to the propeller through two right-angle sets of gears. More and more boats are JET PROPELLED, achieving their thrust from the reaction of a water jet connected to an engine.

Engine Mountings

An inboard engine is placed on ENGINE MOUNTS that are fastened above ENGINE BEDS—stout structural members running fore-and-aft. A SHAFT LOG is the device on a boat through which the PROPELLER SHAFT passes to reach the outside water; a STUFFING BOX prevents water from entering at this point. On many boats, a propeller shaft is supported externally under the hull by one or more STRUTS; see **Figure 1-40.**

Some boats have a V-DRIVE, in which the engine is mounted so that the drive shaft extends forward

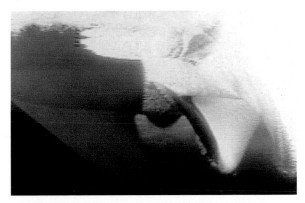

Figure 1-38 *A propeller basically moves a boat through the water on the same principle that a wood screw advances into a timber when turned. To increase efficiency, the blades are made in the shape of foils to create a pressure difference—low on the forward side and high on the after side. This foil shape is designed for forward rotation, one reason that propellers are less effective in reverse.*

Figure 1-39 A stern-drive's lower unit permits the coupling of a powerful inboard engine with a steerable and trimmable propeller shaft. This configuration is popular for powerboats from 18 to 28 feet (5.5 to 8.5 m), and some larger craft.

to a gearbox, which reverses its direction to come out under the hull in a normal manner; this permits a compact engine-in-the-stern arrangement.

Reverse & Reduction Gears

REVERSE GEARS change the direction of rotation of the propeller so as to give thrust in the oppo-

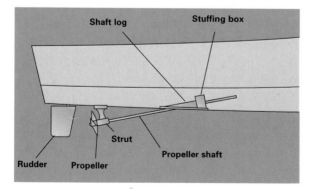

Figure 1-40 On a boat with an inboard engine (or engines), a propeller shaft for each engine extends from inside the craft through the shaft log to the propeller. A strut supports the outer end and a stuffing box keeps water from entering the hull.

site direction for stopping the craft or giving it sternway. REDUCTION GEARS are often combined with the reversing function so that the propeller, turning at a slower rate than the engine, will have increased efficiency. The gears of outdrive and V-drive units include the reversing capability and a reduction ratio if required.

Engine Accessories

A complete engine assembly normally includes a FUEL PUMP to feed fuel under pressure, an OIL PUMP to supply lubricating oil where needed within the engine, and one or more WATER PUMPS for circulating cooling water. An engine is RAW WATER-COOLED if water for cooling is drawn from the water in which the craft is floating, through a hull fitting, circulated in the engine, and then discharged overboard. A CLOSED COOLING SYSTEM uses a separate quantity of fresh water or coolant to circulate solely within the engine; heat picked up by this water is transferred to raw cooling water in a HEAT EXCHANGER, or is dissipated in the water in which the boat is floating by means of an external KEEL COOLER.

Engine instruments usually include gauges for indicating oil pressure, cooling water temperature, and battery charging or discharging

Figure 1-41 View of a typical marine inboard engine.

(AMMETER). A TACHOMETER indicates the speed of the engine in revolutions per minute (rpm), and may indicate the total revolutions or operating hours as a guide for routine maintenance. Gasoline engines are fitted with FLAME ARRESTERS—screen-like metal fittings over the air intakes of carburetors so that any flame from a backfire will not come out dangerously into the ENGINE COMPARTMENT.

On some quite small outboard motors, a SHEAR PIN is part of the propeller assembly. This small pin of relatively soft metal breaks apart—shears—when the propeller strikes a hard underwater object, thus saving the motor from more serious damage; the pin is easily replaced. Larger motors use a SLIP CLUTCH for the same protective purpose.

Sailboat Terms

Although some powerboat terms will also be applicable to many sailboats (especially those with an auxiliary engine), sailors have a language of their own.

All boaters, even powerboat skippers, should have a working knowledge of the basic terminology of sailboats and sailing.

Basic Sailboat Components

The principal components of a sailboat are its HULL, SPARS, and SAILS. The hull has been described earlier in this chapter.

Spars

The term spars is used broadly to cover MASTS, BOOMS, GAFFS, etc.; see **Figure 1-42**. Masts are the principal vertical spars from which sails are SET. Masts are STEPPED when put in position, and are RAKED if inclined aft at an angle. The horizontal spar along the lower edge of a fore-and-aft sail is a BOOM. When a four-sided sail has its upper edge laced to a fore-and-aft spar, that spar is a GAFF.

Rigging

All the various lines about a vessel that secure and control the sails, masts, and other spars are its RIGGING. Lines or wires bracing the mast and

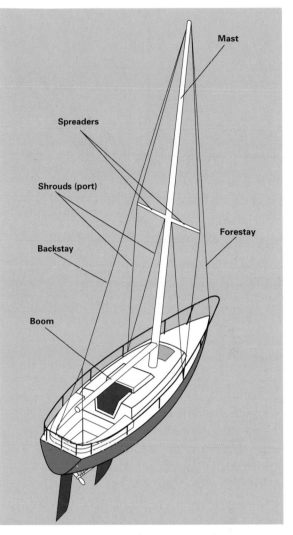

Figure 1-42 Standing rigging supports the mast against the great strains imposed by wind on the sail. The sailboat shown here has upper and lower shrouds, a single forestay, and a split backstay.

certain other fixed spars comprise the STANDING RIGGING; those used for hoisting and adjusting the sails make up the RUNNING RIGGING.

Standing rigging—usually wire rope—includes SHROUDS, from the top or upper part of masts to the sides of the boat; FORESTAYS, which run from the mast to the bow; and BACKSTAYS, which, if used, generally run from the mast to the boat's stern.

The slack is usually taken out of a stay or shroud by the use of a TURNBUCKLE, a metal sleeve threaded right-handed in one end and left-handed in the other so that when turned in one direction, eyebolts in both ends are drawn in and

Figure 1-43 *A turnbuckle is used to vary the tension on a shroud. Turned one way, it lengthens and so reduces the tension; turned the opposite way, it shortens, increasing the tension on the shroud.*

so shorten the fitting, thus tightening the standing rigging. When turned in the opposite direction, the fitting increases its overall length and provides slack; see **Figure 1-43.**

Sails

CANVAS is a general term for a boat's sails, although modern sails are made of lighter synthetic materials. Sails DRAW when they fill with wind and provide power to drive the boat through the water. One MAKES SAIL when the sails are hoisted; one SHORTENS SAIL when the area of sails in use is reduced. A sail is REEFED by partly lowering it and securing it so that it continues to draw, but with reduced area and power. The sail is DOWSED (or DOUSED) when it is lowered quickly, FURLED when it is folded or rolled and then secured to the boom or yard. One LOOSES SAIL when UNFURLING it. A SUIT OF SAILS is a complete set for a particular boat.

Sailing Terms

As sailboats cannot sail directly into the wind, the wind is almost always coming over one side or the other. When the wind is coming over the starboard side, the boat is said to be on a STARBOARD TACK; A PORT TACK is, of course, just the opposite, with the wind coming over the port side. A boat TACKS when she comes up (HEADS) into the wind and changes the side over which it blows. In tacking, a boat COMES ABOUT. Changing tacks with the wind passing astern

rather than ahead of the boat is called JIBING (pronounced with a long first *i* as in ice): JIBES (also spelled GIBES or GYBES) sometimes occur accidentally when sailing downwind (the wind nearly dead astern) and can be dangerous.

After the sails have been hoisted by their HALYARDS, they are trimmed with their SHEETS (JIBSHEET, MAINSHEET, etc.)—lines used to control their lateral position and movement. To TRIM is to haul in and tighten up on the sheet attached to a sail or its boom. As mentioned, sheets are eased when they are let out. Headsails normally have two sheets so that they can be trimmed on either tack; other sails have only one sheet.

A sailboat is CLOSE HAULED (FULL AND BY) when she is sailing with the wind as far ahead as possible, about 45° off the bow in most boats (this is also termed SAILING ON THE WIND, to WINDWARD, or BEATING). As the boat is steered further away from the wind, it BEARS OFF and is REACHING, with CLOSE REACHING, BEAM REACHING, and BROAD REACHING occurring successively as the wind moves further aft. With the wind astern, the sailboat is RUNNING (or sailing DOWNWIND, OFF THE WIND, FREE, or SCUDDING).

See Chapter 8 for a discussion of sailboat seamanship, with additional specialized terms.

Rowboats & Canoes

Although this book is primarily for the skippers of motorboats and sailing craft, it is good to know the essential facts about boats propelled by muscle-power. Dinghies are often rowed, and light motorboats are at times rowed or paddled to safety when the engine fails. The technique of paddling and rowing is an art in itself, best learned by practice under proper instruction, but the various terms involved can be made familiar here.

Rowboats & Oars

ROWBOAT is the term generally applied to light craft intended to be propelled by one or more persons using OARS. These, of course, are long, slender, round, usually wooden shafts shaped into a HANDLE (GRIP) at one end and a flat BLADE at the other; between these ends the shaft of the oar is the LOOM.

The transverse seats in rowing craft are called THWARTS. To support the thwart, a vertical piece is often fitted amidships, called a THWART STANCHION. STRETCHERS (also called FOOT BOARDS, although this creates confusion with an alternate term for bottom boards) are sometimes fitted athwartships against which the OARSMAN can brace his feet.

The terms ROWLOCK and OARLOCK are synonymous. These are the fittings in the gunwale that hold the oars when rowing. There are many styles of rowlocks; some are open, others closed; some mounted permanently, others removable; some attached to the oars. Wooden THOLE PINS (the ancient forerunner of rowlocks), driven into holes or sockets along the gunwale, are still sometimes used.

Where the loom of the oar bears against the rowlock, it is often protected from excess wear by a LEATHER (which may be of leather or rubber). On the side of the leather toward the handle, there may be a BUTTON, a ring around the oar to keep it from slipping outward through the oarlock. Where the loom becomes a blade is the NECK (or THROAT) of the oar. The TIP of the blade, its outer end, may be metal-sheathed for protection from wear.

A person who is SCULLING stands in the stern and propels the craft by working a single oar back and forth, using either one hand or two hands.

Canoes & Paddles

CANOE is the term applied to very lightly built, open craft of narrow beam and shallow draft that are paddled rather than rowed; they are normally double-ended.

A PADDLE is much like an oar except that it is shorter. The various parts of a paddle are named the same as for an oar. The grip is shaped differently since the paddle is used vertically rather than almost horizontally; the blade normally will be somewhat wider for its length in comparison with an oar.

Some paddles are double-ended (double-bladed) so that they may be more conveniently dipped alternately on either side of the canoe, an advantage when one person is propelling the boat rather than two. Double-bladed paddles are commonly used with KAYAKS, covered canoes with a small opening in the center, originally modeled on Eskimo canoes.

Water Movements & Conditions

The water in which we go boating is rarely still and motionless. It flows in various directions, and often moves up and down. Knowledge of these motions, and the proper terminology relating to them, is essential.

Tides & Currents

The word TIDE is one of the most misused of nautical terms. Properly speaking, it means only the rise and fall, the vertical movement, of bodies of water as a result of the gravitational pulls of the moon and sun. Commonly, but incorrectly, "tide" is also used to refer to the inflow and outflow of water as a result of changes in tidal level. CURRENT is the proper term for a horizontal flow of water—TIDAL CURRENT for flows resulting from tidal influences; see **Figure 1-44.** It is proper to say a "two-knot current," but not a "two-knot tide." (A knot is defined on page 50.)

HIGH WATER (HIGH TIDE) is the highest level reached by a RISING tide; LOW WATER (LOW TIDE) is the lowest level reached by a FALLING tide. The RANGE of the tide is the difference between successive highs and lows; it is not always the

Figure 1-44 Current is the horizontal flow of water. A buoy's leaning is often an indication of the speed at which the water is moving. In coastal areas, currents result from changes in tidal levels. Where normal river flows exist, the combined current effect may be in either direction.

same as the days go by. SPRING TIDES occur when the moon is new or full and have a greater range than those at other times. (The word "spring" in this instance has nothing to do with the season of the year.) NEAP TIDES are those occurring at quarter moons; these have a less than average range.

The incoming tidal current running toward the shore, or upstream in a river, is the FLOOD. The retreating, or downstream, current is the EBB. The direction in which a current flows is its SET and its velocity is its DRIFT. (The amount of leeway that a vessel makes is also its drift.) SLACK is the short period of time between flood and ebb currents when there is no observable flow in either direction. STAND is the period when there is no appreciable rise or fall in the tidal level. Slack and stand usually do *not* occur simultaneously at any given place.

For more on tides and currents, refer to Chapter 17.

Waves, Swells & Seas

Various terms are used to describe specific water movements or conditions of the surface; see **Figure 1-45.** A broad term, WAVES, is frequently used for disturbed conditions on a body of water; these actually represent vertical movement of water particles regardless of their apparent forward motion. SEA is a general term often used to describe waves and water action on the surface. RIPS are short, steep waves caused by the meeting of currents—not to be confused with RIPPLES, slight disturbances of the water's surface resulting from gentle breezes. The confused water action found at places where tidal currents meet is also called a CHOP, a term also applied to small, closely spaced waves resulting from wind action on small bodies of water.

SWELLS (GROUND SWELLS) are long, heavy undulations of the surface resulting from disturbances some distance away on oceans and seas. SURF is produced when waves coming toward the shore leave deep water, forming BREAKERS on the shore or beach as they CREST and curl over. A FOLLOWING SEA is one that comes up from astern, running in the same direction as the boat is going. A HEAD SEA is just the opposite. BEAM SEAS come from either side. CROSS or CONFUSED SEAS are irregular ones with components from two or more directions.

Navigation & Piloting

NAVIGATION is the art and science of safely and efficiently directing the movements of a vessel from one point to another. Most boaters are primarily interested in two of its subdivisions. PILOTING is navigation using visible references and the depth of the water. DEAD RECKONING is the plotting of a vessel's position using courses and distances from the last known position. Chapters 13 through 18 cover these subjects and related topics.

Another branch of navigation is ELECTRONIC NAVIGATION, used in varying degrees by inshore and offshore boatmen. With the many advances in technology, LORAN (LOng RAnge Navigation) and now GPS (Global Positioning System) have become very popular, but skippers must take care to retain their basic piloting skills; see

Figure 1-45 *Waves result from local wind action on the water surface, but may travel great distances as swells. They crest over and become breakers as they move into shallower waters. Dangerous waves form over bars, such as this one off a Pacific Coast inlet.*

Figure 1-46. Chapter 21 provides details on electronic navigation.

Then there is CELESTIAL NAVIGATION, taking SIGHTS by SEXTANT (a precision navigation instrument for measuring angles) on the sun, moon, planets, and stars, and using these data with a NAUTICAL ALMANAC and SIGHT REDUCTION TABLES (or a computer) to determine positions; a highly accurate source of time information is also needed. Celestial navigation is used for long offshore passages, primarily to backup electronic navigation systems. Celestial navigation is not covered in this book, but many texts are available, including *Dutton's Navigation and Piloting* published by the U.S. Naval Institute.

Responsibilities

Whether fishing in a small lake, cruising down a river, or crossing large bodies of water out of sight of land, the skipper of a boat has the moral and legal responsibility of knowing how to navigate and having the proper tools.

While this responsibility should weigh heavily on every boat owner, the ability to navigate also brings real rewards. Great satisfaction and pleasure can be derived from successfully navigating a vessel. Piloting and

Figure 1-46 *The use of electronic navigation systems is now widespread on boats of all sizes. The Global Positioning System (GPS) has largely overtaken Loran-C, but that older system remains in use both as a primary source of position information on some craft and as a backup to GPS on others.*

dead reckoning offer an intellectual challenge that can be matched with a sense of accomplishment.

Basic Tools

The basic tools of piloting and dead reckoning are a CHART (with appropriate plotting instruments), a MAGNETIC COMPASS, and a LOG or MARINE SPEEDOMETER. Other tools are also very useful, such as an ELECTRONIC DEPTH SOUNDER and a BINOCULAR.

Charts

A nautical chart (not "map"!) provides a wealth of information for interpretation by a knowledgeable boater. Every chart is a scaled-down representation of a water area (and some adjacent land) overlaid with a grid system. The lines of the grid system are, of course, LATITUDES and LONGITUDES. Lines of latitude are termed PARALLELS because they run parallel to the EQUATOR. Latitude is measured from 0° at the equator to 90° either North or South at the respective POLES. Longitude is measured from 0° at the PRIME MERIDIAN (Greenwich, England) to 180° East or West, which is the same longitude, and with minor variations, the INTERNATIONAL DATELINE.

Distances, Speeds & Depths

On salt water, distances are measured in NAUTICAL MILES, a unit about 1/7 longer than the land or STATUTE mile. The international nautical mile is slightly more than 6,076 feet (1852 m exactly); the statute mile used in the U.S. on shore and freshwater bodies and along the Intracoastal Waterways is 5,280 feet.

Where nautical miles are used for distance, the unit of speed is the KNOT, one nautical mile per hour. Note that the "per hour" is included in the definition—to say "knots per hour" is incorrect. MILES PER HOUR meaning statute miles is the correct term for most inland freshwater bodies, as it is on shore.

In boating, depths are usually measured in feet, but for offshore navigation, the unit FATHOM may be used—it is six feet.

Increasingly, metric units are coming into use. For distance on the oceans and seas, the nautical mile is still used, but METERS (m) are used for shorter distances. Meters and DECIMETERS (¹/₁₀ of a meter) are used for depths and heights. Useful approximate equivalencies are: 1 nautical mile = 1.852 km; 1 statute mile = 1.609 km; 1 fathom = 1.83 m.

Courses

A COURSE is the direction in which a vessel is to be steered—the desired direction of travel through the water. A TRUE COURSE is one referred to as TRUE (geographic) NORTH—it is the angle between the vessel's centerline and the geographic meridian when it is on course. MAGNETIC NORTH is the direction in which a compass would point if it were not subjected to any local disturbing effects. A MAGNETIC COURSE is one with reference to magnetic north; it is almost always different from the true course. COMPASS NORTH is the direction of north indicated by a compass on a vessel; it may or may not be the same as magnetic north. A COMPASS COURSE is one steered by reading the compass; it may or may not be the same as the magnetic course. The HEADING is the direction in which a vessel's bow points at any given moment.

Variation & Deviation

VARIATION is the angular difference between true north and the direction of magnetic north at a given point on earth. Variation is EASTERLY if the north mark of a compass card points to the east of true north, WESTERLY if the opposite. DEVIATION is the error in a magnetic compass caused by local magnetic influences on the boat. It is easterly or westerly as the compass points east or west of magnetic north. COMPASS ERROR is the resulting combination of variation and deviation. See Chapter 13 for more on the mariner's compass.

Bearings

A BEARING is the direction of an object *from* the observer and may be stated in terms of true, magnetic, or compass values. A RELATIVE BEARING is

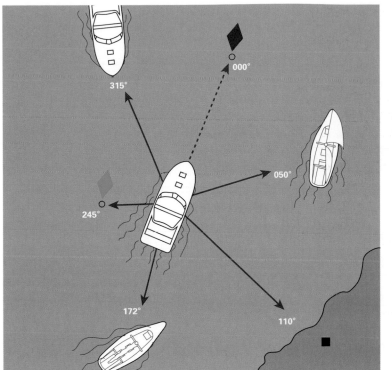

Figure 1-47 Relative bearings are measured as angles from dead ahead clockwise around the boat. Directions are always given as three-digit numbers, using leading zeros as necessary (e.g., 050, not 50).

the direction of an object from the observer measured from the vessel's heading clockwise from 000° to 360°; see **Figure 1-47.**

Plotting

In navigation, one PLOTS various data on a chart, takes bearings to determine his position (FIX),

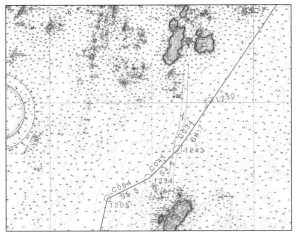

Figure 1-48 A careful skipper plots courses on a chart, and notes the time of significant events, especially changes of course or speed. Chapter 18 covers important procedures for determining position.

and TAKES DEPARTURE from a known position to commence his dead reckoning. TO CHART information is to record it on an existing chart of the area; see **Figure 1-48.**

Aids to Navigation

Various governmental authorities, and a few private organizations and individuals, establish and maintain AIDS TO NAVIGATION—artificial objects to supplement natural landmarks. These may be used to indicate both safe and unsafe waters; the boatman must know the meanings and use of each.

BUOYS are floating aids to navigation with various characteristic shapes and colors. They may be lighted or unlighted; they may or may not have audible signals, such as bells, gongs, whistles, etc.; see **Figure 1-49.**

DAYBEACONS (not "markers") are fixed aids normally consisting of distinctive signs, DAYBOARDS (also called DAYMARKS), mounted on a pile or group of piles driven into the bottom. Dayboards will have a characteristic shape and color or colors.

Figure 1-49 Aids to navigation include unlighted marks, such as the nun buoy.

LIGHTS (not 'flashers") are aids consisting of a light source mounted on a fixed object (as distinguished from lighted buoys). Each light will have a characteristic color and on-off pattern; most light structures will also have dayboards for daytime identification. The term "light" covers all such aids from the relatively weak minor light on a single pile to the largest seacoast lighthouse.

RANGES are special combinations of dayboards and lights used to guide vessels in narrow channels.

Detailed information on aids to navigation are found in Chapter 14.

MISCELLANEOUS TERMS

There are many words and phrases used in boating that do not fit neatly into one of the categories discussed thus far. When any part of a vessel's gear or equipment breaks or gives way, it CARRIES AWAY; an object GOES BY THE BOARD when it goes over the side (OVERBOARD). If a boat is STOVE (hull broken in from outside), it

SPRINGS A LEAK or MAKES WATER. When water is dipped out of a boat by hand the process is called BAILING.

The term CLEAR has many meanings. Upon leaving or entering a port when traveling between countries, a ship must clear through customs authorities. She clears the land when she leaves it, clears a SHOAL (mud or sandbank that makes shallow water) when she passes it by safely. The bilges are cleared of water when they are pumped out. Fouled lines are cleared by straightening them out and getting them ready for use.

A boat STANDS BY when she remains with another craft to give her assistance if necessary. When used as an order, "stand by" means to be prepared to carry out an instruction. AYE, or AYE AYE, is a properly nautical (if somewhat naval) way of acknowledging an order of instruction, indicating that it has been heard and understood, and will be obeyed.

ENTRIES are made in a LOG (book) to record all events occurring aboard. A PATENT LOG is a device to record distance traveled.

One RAISES a light or landmark when it first becomes visible; one MAKES A LANDFALL when the shore is first sighted on coming in from sea.

PASSAGE is generally construed to mean a run from one port to another; VOYAGE includes both the outward and homeward passages. WATCHES are periods of duty, usually four hours long, aboard a vessel; DOG WATCHES are shorter, two-hour periods between 4:00 and 8:00 P.M. (1600 and 2000 in the 24-hour system; see Chapter 16) used to ROTATE the watches so that a particular person does not have the watch for the same hours each day.

LUBBERLY is used to describe the doing of any task on board in a sloppy manner.

In nautical terminology, HARD means fully or completely—as in turning a steering wheel HARD APORT (fully to the left) or HARD OVER (in either direction).

A BAR is a build-up, usually of sand, that reduces the depth of water; it may or may not be partially exposed above the surface of the water and it usually has an elongated shape. Bars frequently form across the openings (MOUTHS) of rivers, creeks, harbors, etc. Larger, broader areas of shallow water are often termed FLATS.

A REEF is a solid underwater obstruction, generally of rock or coral formation, although artificial reefs have been constructed of various debris to attract fish. A CHANNEL is a natural or dredged path through otherwise shoal waters.

The meaning of the word LAY depends on its usage. One LAYS AFT when he goes to the stern of the vessel. The lines of a boat are LAID DOWN before it is built. A boat is LAID UP when it is decommissioned for the winter in northern climates, or is otherwise taken out of regular use. A sailboat LAYS ITS COURSE when it can make the objective without tacking. When an oarsman stops rowing, he LAYS ON HIS OARS. Referring to rope or line, lay is the direction of the twist (right- or left-hand) and its tightness (hard or soft).

When a vessel is hauled out of the water it is SHORED UP with supports to hold it upright. If it is not supported properly, so that it is held amidships while the bow and stern settle, the boat will assume a shape that is described as HOGGED. In contrast, if the amidships portion of the keel is not adequately supported and droops, the boat is said to be SAGGED.

A vessel is said to HAIL FROM its home port. A person HAILS another vessel at sea to get its attention, and SPEAKS to it when communicating with it.

CHAFING occurs when a line or sail rubs against a rough surface and wears excessively. To prevent this, line is usually encased in CHAFING GEAR made of plastic or rubber tubing. To protect sails from chafing and wearing, BAGGYWRINKLE, consisting of short lengths of old line matted together, is placed on shrouds, spreaders, and other parts of the rigging.

A SHACKLE, or CLEVIS, is a roughly U-shaped metal fitting with a pin that can be inserted through a hole in one arm of the U and screwed or pinned in the other arm to close the link; see **Figure 1-50**. Some special-purpose shackles close with a hinged SNAP or have a SWIVEL built in. A THIMBLE is a round or heart-shaped metal fitting with a deep outer groove around which line or wire can be EYE-SPLICED. It protects the line from wearing on a

shackle where it is joined to a chain, fastened to a deck fitting, etc.

A FID is a smooth, tapered pin, usually of wood, used to open up the strands of a rope for splicing.

A WATERLIGHT is an electric light, often automatically operated, that is attached to a life ring with a short length of line. It is intended for use in man-overboard (MOB) accidents at night.

The term CHARTER has usage as both a verb and a noun. TO CHARTER a craft is to lease it from the owner for a temporary period of time. It may be chartered on a BARE BOAT basis (without crew) or as a TIME CHARTER (with crew). The contract covering the use of the boat is termed the charter.

Ships and large vessels may have compartments below deck used solely for carrying cargo; these are HOLDS. The hatch giving access through the deck to such a hold is typically covered over with canvas and BATTENED DOWN with wooden or metal strips around the edges (BATTENS) to secure it against storms and water across the deck. The same term is used for the general securing of a boat against adverse weather conditions. The term "batten" is also used for small semi-flexible strips of wood or plastic inserted into pockets on a sail to help control its shape

Another vessel is said to be seen HULL DOWN when she is at such a distance that her superstructure and/or masts are visible but

Figure 1-50 A shackle, or clevis, is a horseshoe-shaped fitting that is useful in connecting chain to either an anchor or to a length of line ending in a thimble.

Figure 1-51 A bollard is a massive metal fitting placed along wharves and piers to which the lines of large vessels are made fast.

the hull is not seen due to the curvature of the earth.

FLOTSAM is material floating on the surface of the water after a vessel has broken up and sunk. Larger pieces may be dangerous to the hull or shaft and propeller of small craft. JETSAM consists of items of equipment or cargo that have been deliberately JETTISONED (thrown overboard) to lighten a vessel endangered by heavy seas.

A BOLLARD is a heavy single or double post set into the edge of a wharf or pier to which the lines of a ship may be made fast; see **Figure 1-51.**

CAVITATION occurs when a high-speed propeller develops a partial vacuum around the blades and loses its "bite" on the water, creating a loss of thrust and excessive shaft speed; continued cavitation can result in blade wear. On outboard motors where the propeller is relatively near the surface of the water and aft of the transom, a CAVITATION PLATE (more properly, an ANTI-CAVITATION PLATE) is mounted above the propeller to deflect downward the water discharge from the blades.

If the galley stove is of the type that requires its own vent above the deck, the pipe for this is called a CHARLIE NOBLE.

A boat is SHIP-SHAPE when everything is in good order; WELL-FOUND when it is well equipped. BRISTOL-FASHION is a term used to describe an especially well-cared-for vessel. To UNSHIP an item of equipment is to unfasten or remove it from its normal working location or position. One SWABS (or SWABS DOWN) the deck when he washes it down with a mop, called a SWAB in nautical language.

The term GANGWAY is applied both to the area of a ship's side where people COME ON BOARD (BOARD or EMBARK) and DISEMBARK (or DEBARK) and to the temporary ramp or platform used between the vessel and the wharf or pier; see **Figure 1-52.** In the latter usage, the terms GANGPLANK and BROW are also correct.

Figure 1-52 A gangway, or gangplank, is a ramp from a pier or wharf to a vessel. The one shown here can be converted to a series of steps.

A WINDLASS is a particular form of winch, usually used with an anchor rode, with its DRUM on which the line or chain is wrapped turning on a horizontal axis. If the drum's axis is vertical, the device may be called a CAPSTAN.

When an anchor line or chain is brought through the topsides rather than over the rail, it enters through a HAWSE HOLE and may run upward through a HAWSE PIPE. An ANCHOR CHOCK is a fitting for holding an anchor securely on a deck.

Small boats, such as dinghies and runabouts, are hoisted aboard larger craft by DAVITS—mechanical arms extending over the side or stern, or which can be swung around over the deck or swung out over the side, plus the necessary lines and blocks.

When subjected to heavy strains in working her way through high seas, a vessel is said to LABOR. If she takes the large waves easily, she is said to be SEA KINDLY. A boat that takes head seas heavily and comes down hard on successive waves is said to POUND; this is more likely to occur with a hard-chined hull. If a boat takes little spray aboard when running into a choppy sea, she is termed DRY.

To FLEMISH DOWN a line is to secure it on deck in a tight flat coil roughly resembling a mat. When a line is laid down in loose, looping figure eights it is said to be FAKED (or FLAKED) down; each loop is a FAKE (refer to Chapter 23 for more on the proper handling of lines and all aspects of marlinespike seamanship).

A boat is said to be OFF-SOUNDINGS when she is so far out from the shore (OFFSHORE) that depths (SOUNDINGS) cannot be conveniently measured for navigation; this is commonly taken as the 100-fathom line (on metric charts, the 200 meter curve is usually taken as the delineation). In contrast, a boat is ON-SOUNDINGS when she is within this line.

ADMIRALTY LAW is the body of law pertaining to ships and to navigation and commerce on the seas.

A CORINTHIAN is any nonprofessional in the field of boating.

Some boats are damaged by DRY ROT, a fungus attack on wooden areas. The term, in common use since the eighteenth century, is not strictly accurate as moisture is essential for the growth and spread of the fungus. The wood is greatly weakened by the action of the fungus. Prevention of standing water in corners and pockets, and adequate ventilation, are the best defenses against dry rot; chemical treatments can be used to prevent rot, and to attack existing rot infestations and restore strength.

BUT DON'T OVERDO IT!

There is literally no end to the list of boating terms that could be included here, but practical limitations of space must prevail. What has been covered in this chapter will serve as a framework for the remainder of the book. As the boatman gains experience in this form of recreation, his vocabulary will broaden proportionately and naturally. It is hoped, however, that his enthusiasm for boating will not cause him to toss indiscriminate AVASTS, AHOYS, and BELAYS into every conceivable nook and corner of his conversation. Strained efforts to affect a salty lingo are conspicuously inappropriate.

For additional definitions, see page 894, Appendix G, Glossary of Selected Terms.

Boating Laws & Regulations

*Federal Jurisdiction • Requirements for Boat Registration or Documentation
• Legal Responsibilities Involved in Chartering, Commercial Operations
& International Voyaging*

Boating laws and regulations can be divided into three main categories. The first deals with boat ownership: registration, numbering, and documentation, all covered in this chapter. The second category is legislation relating to equipment requirements and standards, as discussed in Chapter 3. The third category is the legal requirements for safe operation, known as the "Rules of the Road," as detailed in Chapters 4 and 5. Regulations relating to radio operation are found in Chapter 20.

A quick comparison can be made between recreational boating and the operation of motor vehicles, an activity that is so much a part of our everyday lives. Where motor vehicle laws first concentrated on operation, with legal requirements for safety features a more recent development, much of the early boating legislation, other than Rules of the Road, was already aimed at equipment requirements.

For many decades states have required the operator of highway vehicles to have drivers licenses, but the licensing of boat operators is a recent, and growing situation. Starting with juvenile skippers, licensing programs have been steadily expanding, usually phased in by age groups. It is your responsibility to become aware of any requirements in your boating waters.

FEDERAL JURISDICTION

This book will concentrate on federal boating laws and regulations rather than state and local ordinances, rules, etc., due to the wider application of the federal laws. State and municipal regulations will be touched on later in this chapter, but only in broad terms because of the variations between different jurisdictions. *You must familiarize yourself with the local requirements and restrictions for the waters that you use at home or when out cruising.*

An understanding of federal jurisdiction over navigable waters is essential for all boatmen; see **Figure 2-01.** Federal jurisdiction covers the applicability of federal laws and regulations with establishment of aids to navigation by the U.S. Coast Guard, and charting by the National Ocean Service or Army Corps of Engineers. That jurisdiction does not deprive state and local authorities of their rights to regulate aspects of waterways use that *do not conflict* with federal law or regulation—local rules might relate to speed limits, restrictions on water skiing, etc. Many state boating laws also require safety equipment beyond that called for by Acts of Congress and Coast Guard regulations.

Limits of Federal Jurisdiction

There are several terms that are used in Federal laws and regulations covering their geographic applicability. Unfortunately, specific terms are not always logical or clear to the average reader, and some have different limits for the same term. The discussion below is basic and general in nature and should not be considered to be "the final word" in all cases. Full details, in highly legalistic language, will be found in Title 33, Part 2 of the United States Code.

The starting point is the TERRITORIAL SEA BASELINE. This is the line that defines the shoreward extent of the territorial sea of the United

Opposite Page: Figure 2-01 The construction of dams, and locks for passage around them, has extended the navigable waters subject to federal jurisdiction far inland. State and local laws, such as those governing speed, may apply in the waters together with federal rules and regulations.

States. Normally, this baseline is the mean low-water line along the coast of the U.S. As will be seen below, this baseline is fundamental to the description of several offshore zones.

The TERRITORIAL SEA of the United Sates consists of the waters, 12 nautical miles wide, adjacent to the coast of the U.S., and seaward of the territorial sea baseline. This basic definition, however, has some exceptions for regulations that define the territorial sea as extending only 3 miles seaward from the baseline. (It should be noted that other nations may define their territorial sea differently.)

The term INTERNAL WATERS of the United States means the waters shoreward of the territorial sea baseline. The term INLAND WATERS, used in some laws and regulations, has the same definition.

For the purposes of the Federal Water Pollution Control Act, the CONTIGUOUS ZONE means a zone 9 nautical miles wide extending from 3 miles out from the territorial seas baseline to 12 miles out. For all other purposes, the contiguous zone is defined as all the waters within the area adjacent to and seaward of the territorial sea (as defined above) extending out to 24 nautical miles from the territorial sea baseline. Note however, that the U.S. contiguous zone does not extend into the territorial sea of another nation.

The U.S. EXCLUSIVE ECONOMIC ZONE (EEZ) includes the waters seaward of and contiguous to the territorial sea, including the contiguous zone, extending 200 nautical miles from the territorial sea baseline, except where otherwise limited by treaty or other international agreement recognized by the United States.

For some purposes, the term HIGH SEAS is used. This has several definitions, but generally can be considered as the Great Lakes and all waters seaward of the territorial sea baseline.

The phraseology WATERS SUBJECT TO TIDAL INFLUENCE and WATERS SUBJECT TO THE EBB AND FLOW OF THE TIDE appear in some laws and regulations. These are waters below mean high water as determined over a long-term tidal cycle; it does not mean high water resulting from storms, floods, etc.

The terms NAVIGABLE WATERS OF THE UNITED STATES, NAVIGABLE WATERS, and TERRITORIAL WATERS are also used in laws and regulations. In general, these terms apply to: (1) the territorial sea of the United States; (2) internal waters of the U.S. that are subject to tidal influence; and (3) internal waters that are not subject to tidal influence that are or have been used for substantial interstate or international commerce. Examples of the last category include major river systems, such as the Mississippi, Missouri, Ohio, and Tennessee Rivers; and major lakes

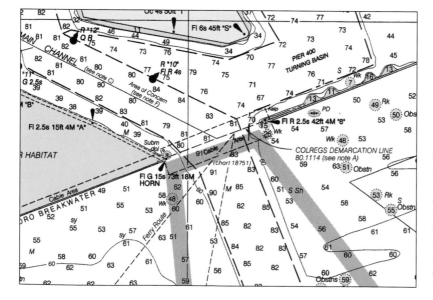

Figure 2-02 At entrances from the sea to rivers, bays and similar water bodies, as well as along some stretches of shoreline, boundary lines have been established to mark the transition from International Navigation Rules to the Inland Rules. These are shown in magenta on charts as COLREGS demarcation lines.

that border more than one state, such as Lake Mead between Nevada and Arizona, and Lake Champlain between New York and Vermont.

WATERS SUBJECT TO THE JURISDICTION OF THE UNITED STATES and WATERS OVER WHICH THE UNITED STATES HAS JURISDICTION are terms which will be found in laws and regulations. These include the navigable waters of the United States (as defined above) and other waters specifically spelled out, such as waters on lands for which the United States has acquired title, and waters made subject to U.S. jurisdiction by international agreement.

Demarcation Lines for Navigation Rules
Of special interest to boaters are the lines that separate waters governed by the International Navigation Rules from those subject to the U.S. Inland Rules (see Chapters 4 and 5). When the 1972 International Rules—termed "72 COLREGS" by the Coast Guard as a contraction of their formal name, International Regulations for Preventing Collisions at Sea, 1972—came into effect, "Demarcation Lines" separating International and Inland waters were established. In establishing these, it was found neither desirable nor practical to have an overall general line. Individual lines are defined instead, where practicable, by physical objects like fixed aids to navigation or prominent points on land, because such are readily discernable by eye rather than by instrument. The demarcation lines are set to be as short and direct as feasible, and as perpendicular as possible to vessel traffic flow. The general trend is from headland to headland, with highly visible objects used to define the line clearly. But sometimes the line is further inland than would be expected, and whole bays, harbors, and inlets are subject to the International Rules. *A boater must at all times know which set of Navigation Rules govern the waters he is in.* The demarcation lines are defined in detail in the U.S. Coast Guard publication *Navigation Rules, International— Inland* (COMDTINST M166 72.2D, or later edition) and are shown on large-scale charts; see **Figure 2-02.**

Figure 2-03 Among the various laws and regulations that relate to boating are the Navigation Rules. *The U.S. Coast Guard publication seen above contains the official text of both the International and the Inland Rules, plus other regulations. The U.S. Inland Rules require that a copy of the* Navigation Rules *be on board all vessels 12 meters (39.4 ft.) in length.*

FEDERAL LAWS & REGULATIONS

All boating and shipping is subject to "laws" and "regulations." The former consists of Acts of Congress that provide basic policies and rules upon which more specific and detailed regulations may be based. Regulations have the advantage of flexibility because they can be created, modified, or revoked more easily than laws, whose changes are subject to the full legislative process; see **Figure 2-03.**

U.S. Coast Guard Regulations

Most federal boating regulations are issued by the United States Coast Guard under authority given by Congress to the "Secretary of the Department in which the Coast Guard is operating." This rather cumbersome wording is necessary because federal law permits the transfer of this armed service from its normal peacetime Department (Homeland Security) to its wartime Department (Navy). The authority given by the U.S. Congress to the Department Secretary is, in most instances, routinely delegated to the Commandant of the Coast Guard.

Coast Guard regulations cover a wide variety of matters including boat equipment and operation, lights for vessels, aids to navigation, Inland Waters demarcation lines mentioned above, and other topics.

For technical questions regarding regulations, and information not usually available from local Coast Guard district offices, the U.S. Coast Guard has installed a toll-free telephone number in the Office of Boating Safety. The number is (800) 368-5647. This "hotline" may also be used for complaints relating to boardings by U.S. Coast Guard personnel as well as questions. By email, the address to be used is uscginfoline@gcrm.com. On the Internet, go to www.uscgboating.org.

Other Regulatory Agencies

Boaters on some waters will also be affected by regulations issued by other federal agencies such as the U.S. Army Corps of Engineers and the National Park Service (see Chapter 22, which covers Inland Boating). The operation of radio and radar transmitters on boats on all waters is subject to the rules and regulations of the Federal Communications Commission (FCC) as explained in Chapter 20.

Federal Boat Safety Act of 1971

The Federal Boat Safety Act of 1971 (FBSA/71) authorizes the "Secretary" to establish minimum safety standards for boats and "associated equipment," provides for numbering of all undocumented vessels equipped with propulsion machinery, directs that a "Boating Safety Advisory Council" be established, and authorizes financial assistance to the states for boating safety programs; see **Figure 2-04.**

Figure 2-04 Federal requirements for recreational boats are covered in the free U.S. Coast Guard pamphlet shown above. It also contains many suggestions for safer boating, plus addresses where additional information may be obtained.

Definition of Terms

The FBSA/71 contains definitions that must be clearly understood, as they directly affect its applicability.

Figure 2-05 All personal watercraft, PWCs, are considered to be "boats" or "vessels" and subject to all laws and regulations covering such craft.

In this Act, the word "vessel" includes every description of watercraft, other than a seaplane, that can be used as a means of transportation on the water; see **Figure 2-05.** The term "boat" is limited to the following categories of vessels:

Those manufactured or used primarily for noncommercial use.

Those leased, rented, or chartered to another for the latter's noncommercial use.

Those engaged in the carrying of six or fewer passengers for hire.

The distinction between "vessels" and "boats" is necessary because certain sections of the FBSA/71 (notably those dealing with safety standards and equipment) pertain *only* to the category called "boats." Other sections (those dealing with numbering) pertain to a broader category—all undocumented vessels equipped with propulsion machinery. Still other provisions (the prohibition of negligent operation) pertain to *all* vessels. Note that there is *no upper size limit* in the definition of "boat" as used in the FBSA/71.

Despite its general aim toward regulating noncommercial boats and boating, craft carrying six or fewer passengers for hire (see the "passengers for hire" definition on pages 77–78 are included, because these are not covered by the laws for vessels carrying more than six passengers for hire. Livery and charter boats are included in the FBSA/71 because their operation is closely akin to noncommercial recreational use even though they are a part of a commercial enterprise.

The term "associated equipment" means:

• Any system, part, or component of a boat as originally manufactured, or as sold for replacement, repair, or improvement of a boat.

• Any accessory or equipment for, or appurtenance to, a boat.

• Any marine safety article, accessory, or equipment intended for use by a person on a boat.

The word "State" means a State of the United States, the Commonwealth of Puerto Rico, the Virgin Islands, Guam, American Samoa, and the District of Columbia.

Applicability

The FBSA/71 applies to vessels and associated equipment used, or to be used, or carried on vessels on waters subject to the jurisdiction of the United States. This Act *also* applies to every vessel owned in a "State" and *used on the high seas*—used on the waters beyond the territorial jurisdiction of the United States.

Certain limited categories of vessels are excluded from coverage by the FBSA/71; these include foreign vessels, military or public vessels of the United States (except for recreational-type craft, which are included), vessels owned by a state or political subdivision thereof and used primarily for governmental purposes, and ships' lifeboats.

Regulations

Although the Motorboat Act of 1940 (MBA/40) is no longer generally applicable to the "boats" of the 1971 Act, the Coast Guard regulations that implemented the MBA/40 are retained and will remain in effect until replaced. The MBA/40 also remains in effect for commercial craft, such as fishing boats, less than 65 feet (19.8 m) in length.

Classes of Boats

For the purpose of applying graduated requirements for equipment as the size of the craft increases, the MBA/40 divides all motorboats into four "classes" based on length. This is "length overall" (LOA) as measured in a straight line parallel to the keel from the foremost part of the vessel to the aftermost part, excluding sheer and excluding bowsprits, boomkins, rudders abaft the transom, outboard motor brackets, etc. (refer to Chapter 1, **Figure 1-08**).

Class A	less than 16 feet (4.9 m) in length
Class 1	16 feet and over, but less than 26 feet (7.9 m) in length
Class 2	26 feet and over, but less than 40 feet (12.2 m) in length
Class 3	40 feet and over, but not more than 65 feet (19.8 m)

Note: As mentioned, regulations derived from the authority of the FBSA/71 have no upper limit of length. A number of FBSA/71 requirements use a 20 foot (6.1 m) length as a cut-off limit.

Required Equipment

The regulations of the MBA/40, applicable until superseded by new rules, contain provisions for

Figure 2-06 *Although it is not a U.S. federal requirement, in some states sailboats without mechanical power must be registered. All boats, including this sailboat, are subject to U.S. Coast Guard requirements for equipment such as personal flotation devices.*

Figure 2-07 A boat must be registered and numbered in its "state of principal use" even though this is not the state of the owner's residence, nor even that of where the boat may be stored on its trailer when out of the water (dry-docked).

required equipment, including personal floatation devices, fire extinguishers, and other items (see Chapter 3). It is specifically stated in the FBSA/71 that regulations will be issued covering items not now required on board, such as ground tackle and navigation equipment, but this has not yet been done. Any such new requirements will not become effective without considerably study and wide publicity.

Numbering of Boats

The FBSA/71 provides a system of boat numbering that is uniform throughout the United States, although the Act permits the actual process of issuing certificates and number assignments to be done individually by the states; see **Figure 2-06.**

The FBSA/71 establishes broad standards for the numbering of vessels and provides for the issuance of more detailed regulations by the "Secretary." The individual states prepare their boat-numbering laws and regulations in accor-

dance with federal standards and then submit them to the Secretary for approval. The Secretary can later withdraw approval if the state does not administer its system in accordance with the federal requirements.

Vessels Subject to Numbering The FBSA/71 requires the numbering of *all* vessels used on waters subject to federal jurisdiction, or on the high seas if owned in the U.S., that are equipped with propulsion machinery *regardless of horsepower.* Exempted are foreign boats temporarily in U.S. waters, documented vessels, ships' lifeboats, and governmental vessels other than recreational-type craft. (States may require the registration of documented boats, and the payment of fees, even though they are not numbered.)

A state numbering system may require the numbering of other craft (sailboats, rowboats, etc.) unless prohibited by federal legislation. States *may* exempt craft used solely for racing.

Special provisions are made for tenders (dinghies) carried aboard for other than lifesaving purposes.

"State of Principal Use" It is important to note that the FBSA/71 requires that a boat have a number obtained from "the State in which the vessel is principally used." This has been interpreted literally—where the boat is most often *used on the water;* i.e., not necessarily the state where the owner lives, nor the state in which the boat might customarily set on its trailer. The term "used" is taken as meaning the time that the vessel is "on" the navigable waters of the United States whether in motion, at anchor, at a mooring, or in a slip; see **Figure 2-07.**

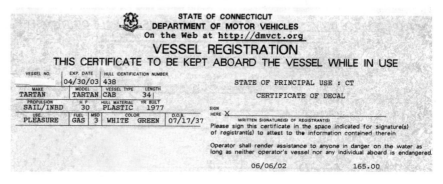

Figure 2-08 The state-issued Certificate of Number must be on board whenever a boat is in use (except for small rental craft).

Correct	Incorrect
ME 456 R	ME456R
ME-456-R	*ME 456 R*
	ME 456 R

Figure 2-09 The correct style and spacing of registration numbers is shown at left above. Letters and numbers without spacing, and use of italics or script characters (above) is incorrect and unacceptable.

Certificate of Number The identification number issued for a vessel is shown on a CERTIFICATE OF NUMBER. This Certificate must be on board whenever the vessel is in use (with exceptions for small rental boats). The FBSA/71 specifies that a Certificate of Number must be of "pocket size"; see **Figure 2-08**. Any person using a boat must present its Certificate for inspection at the request of any law enforcement officer.

Federal law states that a Certificate may not be valid for more than three years; many states issue registrations for shorter periods. All Certificates may, of course, be renewed at or prior to expiration date.

Numbering Systems The specific details of boat-numbering are covered in Coast Guard regulations. The number pattern has two parts: a two-letter symbol identifying the state of principal use, and a combination of numerals and letters for individual identification. For some states, the two-letter abbreviation is the same as that used by the U.S. Postal Service; in other states, it is different.

The individual identification consists of not more than four Arabic numerals and two capital letters, *or* not more than three such numerals and three such letters; fewer numbers or letters may be used. The letters "I," "O," and "Q" are not used because they can be mistaken for the numerals "1" and "0."

Numbers for Dinghies A state has the option of exempting dinghies from the numbering regulation. In such states, if used with a numbered vessel, a dinghy equipped with a motor of less than 10 horsepower need not be individually reg-

istered and numbered *if* it is "used as a tender for direct transportation between that vessel and the shore *and has no other purpose.*" The dinghy must display the number of the parent boat followed by the suffix "1" separated from the last letter by a space or hyphen as used in the basic number; for example, DC-4567-ED-1 or DC 4567 ED 1.

A dinghy used with a vessel *not* having a number, such as a documented boat, must be registered and have its own number as for any other boat if it is propelled by a motor of any horsepower.

Size & Style of Numbers The regulations require that boat numbers be clearly legible, and also contain specifications for style and size. The letters and numerals must be plain (no border or trim) vertical block characters not less than three inches in height. They must *not* be slanting or script style; see **Figure 2-09**. The numbers and letters should all be of one color.

Contrast Numbers must provide good contrast with their background—black on white or white on black best meets this requirement. A backing or mounting plate may be used but must be of sufficient size to provide good contrast for the numbers, and thus good legibility, without regard to the hull color.

Figure 2-10 A common misconception is that registration numbers must be at or close to the bow of a boat. The legal requirement is only that they be on the forward half of the boat. Subject to this limitation, they should be placed far enough aft to ensure easy readability.

Display of Numbers The identification number must be painted on, or attached to, each side of the *forward half* of the vessel, and no other number may be displayed there. (This does not apply to serial numbers on small validation stickers that some states and the U.S. Coast Guard issue to note payment of current fees.) In most cases the numbers are quite near the bow, but since they need be displayed only on the boat's "forward half" it is sensible, on boats with considerable bow flare, to place the numbers far enough aft to be on a more vertical surface and thus more visible; see **Figure 2-10.** Letters and numerals made of flexible rubber are available for use on inflatable boats.

Numbers are placed on a boat so as to read from left to right on both sides of the bow. They may be on the hull or on a permanent superstructure. The digits between the two sets of letters in the total number *must be separated* from those letters by hyphens or spaces. The hyphen or blank space must be equal to the width of any letter other than "I" or any numeral other than "1"; refer to **Figure 2-09.**

Identification numbers must be maintained properly to ensure legibility at all times.

Names or insignia may be displayed on the bow of a boat, but they must not detract from the legibility of the registration numbers. Only one set of numbers may be displayed at any time. If a boat is transferred to a new state, the old numbers must be removed.

Applications & Renewals The addresses of state and other authorities to whom application for a Certificate of Number must be made are listed in Appendix C.

The same numbers are reassigned for each registration period by a regular renewal Certificate. Upon transfer of ownership, if the boat continues in the same state of principal use, the old numbers stay on the craft and are assigned to the new owner.

Numbers may not be transferred from one boat to another, except for special dealers' and manufacturers' numbers issued for demonstrating, transporting, or testing boats.

Fees Under the FBSA/71, states may set their own fees for registering and numbering boats. Fees vary widely from state to state—in some jurisdictions they merely cover the cost of administering the numbering program; in others they are sources of revenue for the state.

The 1971 law specifically provides that a state may require proof of payment of state and local sales, use, and excise taxes before issuing a Certificate of Number. Withholding certification on any other grounds is *not* authorized, except that a title or proof of ownership may be required.

Reciprocity When a vessel is numbered in its state of principal use, it is considered as in compliance with the numbering system of any state in which it is *temporarily* used. There is no specific time limit stated in the federal law if such use is truly "temporary"; states often set their own time limits. This is of considerable advantage to boatmen who may cruise or trailer their craft to other state waters for vacation.

When a vessel is taken to a *new* "state of principal use," that state must recognize the validity of its number for at least 60 days before requiring new registration.

Notification of Changes If a boat is destroyed, or abandoned, or sold, or used for more than 60 days in a state other than the one that issued its Certificate, or if it is documented, a report must be made to the issuing office within 15 days. The boat's Certificate becomes invalid and must be surrendered, and its numbers (and any validation stickers) must be removed. A report must also be made if the boat is stolen and when recovered after having been stolen.

An owner's change of address must be reported to the issuing office within 15 days. A change of motor need not be reported.

Operators' "Safety Certificates"

The FBSA/71 gives states the *optional* authority to require the operator of a vessel covered by the numbering provisions to "hold a valid safety certificate issued under terms and conditions set by the issuing authority." Connecticut is one such state.

No Coast Guard regulations have been issued for this purpose, though use of the authority has been made by the states—especially in the case of young persons.

Termination of Unsafe Use

The Act also includes a provision that is unique to the general concept of boating laws and regulations: Termination of Unsafe Use. If a U.S. Coast Guard boarding officer observes a boat being used without sufficient lifesaving or fire-fighting devices, or in an overloaded or otherwise unsafe condition as defined in regulations, he may direct the operator to take immediate and reasonable steps necessary for the safety of those on board the vessel. This order may include directing the operator to return to shore or his mooring and remain there until the hazardous situation is corrected. Failure to comply with an order to terminate unsafe use of a vessel can result in arrest.

Federal regulations also designate certain portions of the Washington-Oregon coast as "regulated boating areas." When wave heights or surface currents exceed set limits, conditions are considered "unsafe" and under the Unsafe Use provision the Coast Guard may terminate boating in that area.

The Coast Guard may also forbid use of a boat that is "manifestly unsafe for a specific voyage on a specific body of water." This covers unsuitable design, improper construction or condition, or improper or inadequate operational or safety equipment.

Negligent Operation

The FBSA/71 states "no person may use any vessel in a negligent manner so as to endanger the life, limb, or property of any person." Foreign vessels, governmental vessels, and other craft normally excluded from coverage under this Act are not exempted from the prohibition against negligent operations.

The endangerment of "any person" *includes* the operator of the vessel; no other person need be involved.

Figure 2-11 Boating accidents must be reported if they involve death or personal injuries or physical damage that exceed specified limits. Accidents must be reported even if only one craft is involved. In most states, reports are made to state authorities, rather than to the Coast Guard.

Boating Accidents

Sometimes of course, despite the best of care, boating accidents do occur. They may involve only a single boat, or two or more vessels. In all cases skippers incur obligations at the scene and afterward.

Duties in Case of Accident In case of collision, accident, or other casualty involving a vessel subject to the FBSA/71 (as well as such otherwise exempted vessels as foreign or governmental craft), the operator must, to the extent that he can without serious danger to his vessel or those on board, render necessary and practical assistance to other persons endangered by the incident. The operator must also give his name and address, and the identification of his vessel, to any person injured and to the owner of any property damaged.

The duties described here apply whether or not the incident resulted from apparent negligence. They also do not preclude any other duties required by law or regulation.

"Good Samaritan" Provision Any person who complies with the accident duties described above, or any other person who gratuitously and in good faith renders assistance at the scene of an accident or other boating casualty without the objection of any person being assisted, is protected by a provision of the FBSA/71. He cannot be held liable for any civil damages as a result of rendering assistance or for any act or omission in providing or arranging salvage, towage, medical treatment, or other assistance when he acts as an

ordinary, reasonably prudent person would have under the same or similar circumstances.

Accident Reporting In case of collision, accident, or other casualty involving a vessel subject

---

OMB Control No. 2115-0003

DEPARTMENT OF TRANSPORTATION U.S. COAST GUARD CG-2692 (Rev. 4-97)	**REPORT OF MARINE ACCIDENT, INJURY OR DEATH**	RCS No. G-MOA / UNIT CASE NUMBER

SECTION I. GENERAL INFORMATION

1. Name of Vessel or Facility | 2. Official No. | 3. Nationality | 4. Call Sign | 5. USCG Certificate of Inspection issued at:

6. Type *(Towing, Freight, Fish, Drill, etc.)* | 7. Length | 8. Gross Tons | 9. Year Built | 10. Propulsion *(Steam, diesel, gas, turbine...)*

11. Hull Material *(Steel, Wood...)* | 12. Draft *(Ft. - in.)* **FWD AFT.** | 13. If Vessel Classed, By Whom: *(ABS, LLOYDS, DNV, BV, etc.)* | 14. Date *(of occurrence)* | 15. TIME *(Local)*

16. Location *(See Instruction No. 10A)* | 17. Estimated Loss of Damage TO:

18. Name, Address & Telephone No. of Operating Co. | VESSEL _____ CARGO _____ OTHER _____

19. Name of Master or Person in Charge | USCG License ☐ YES ☐ NO | 20. Name of Pilot | USCG License ☐ YES ☐ NO | State License ☐ YES ☐ NO

19a. Street Address *(City, State, Zip Code)* | 19b. Telephone Number | 20a. Street Address *(City, State, Zip Code)* | 20b. Telephone Number

21. Casualty Elements *(Check as many as needed and explain in Block 44.)*

NO. OF PERSONS ON BOARD _____
☐ DEATH - HOW MANY? _____
☐ MISSING - HOW MANY? _____
☐ INJURED - HOW MANY? _____
☐ HAZARDOUS MATERIAL RELEASED OR INVOLVED
(Identify Substance and amount in Block 44.)
☐ OIL SPILL - ESTIMATE AMOUNT: _____
☐ CARGO CONTAINER LOST/DAMAGED
☐ COLLISION *(Identify other vessel or object in Block 44.)*
☐ GROUNDING   ☐ WAKE DAMAGE

☐ FLOODING; SWAMPING WITHOUT SINKING
☐ CAPSIZING *(with or without sinking)*
☐ FOUNDERING OR SINKING
☐ HEAVY WEATHER DAMAGE
☐ FIRE
☐ EXPLOSION
☐ COMMERCIAL DIVING CASUALTY
☐ ICE DAMAGE
☐ DAMAGE TO AIDS TO NAVIGATION
☐ STEERING FAILURE
☐ MACHINERY OR EQUIPMENT FAILURE
☐ ELECTRICAL FAILURE
☐ STRUCTURAL FAILURE

☐ FIREFIGHTING OR EMERGENCY EQUIPMENT FAILED OR INADEQUATE *(Describe in Block 44.)*
☐ LIFESAVING EQUIPMENT FAILED OR INADEQUATE *(Describe in Block 44.)*
☐ BLOW OUT *(Petroleum)*
☐ ALCOHOL INVOLVEMENT *(Describe in Block 44.)*
☐ DRUG INVOLVEMENT *(Describe in Block 44.)*
☐ OTHER *(Specify)* _____

22. Conditions

A. Sea or River Conditions *(wave height, river stage, etc.)*

B. WEATHER
☐ CLEAR
☐ RAIN
☐ SNOW
☐ FOG
☐ OTHER

C. TIME
☐ DAYLIGHT
☐ TWILIGHT
☐ NIGHT

D. VISIBILITY
☐ GOOD
☐ FAIR
☐ POOR

E. DISTANCE *(miles of visibility)* _____
F. AIR TEMPERATURE _____ (F)
G. WIND SPEED & DIRECTION _____
H. CURRENT SPEED & DIRECTION _____

23. Navigation Information
☐ MOORED, DOCKED OR FIXED
☐ ANCHORED ☐ UNDERWAY OR DRIFTING
SPEED AND COURSE _____

24. Last Port Where Bound _____ | 24a. Time and Date of

25. FOR TOWING ONLY | 25a. NUMBER OF VESSELS TOWED | Empty | Loaded | Total | 25b. TOTAL H.P. OF TOWING UNITS | 25c. MAXIMUM SIZE OF TOW WITH TOW-BOAT(S) | Length | Width | 25d. *(Describe in Block 44.)* ☐ PUSHING AHEAD ☐ TOWING ASTERN ☐ TOWING ALONGSIDE ☐ MORE THAN ONE TOW-BOAT ON TOW

SECTION II. BARGE INFORMATION

26. Name | 26a. Official | 26b. Type | 26c. Length | 26d. Gross Tons | 26e. USCG Certificate of Inspection Issued at:

26f. Year Built | 26g. ☐ SINGLE SKIN ☐ DOUBLE | 26h. Draft FWD _____ AFT _____ | 26i. Operating Company

26j. Damage Amount
BARGE _____
CARGO _____
OTHER _____
| 26k. Describe Damage to Barge

PREVIOUS EDITION IS OBSOLETE

Figure 2-12 *Use of a standard official form ensures that an accident report contains all the required information.*

to the FBSA/71, the operator must make a report under certain circumstances. A report is required if the incident results in death, an injury requiring medical treatment beyond first aid, the disappearance of a person from a vessel under circumstances that indicate death or injury, complete loss of the boat, or if there is damage to vessels and other property that totals $2,000 or more, or there is a complete loss of any vessel; see **Figure 2-11.**

If death occurs within 24 hours of the accident, or a person has a reportable injury or disappears from the boat, a formal report must be made within 48 hours; otherwise, within 10 days.

Most state boating laws require that reports of boating accidents be made to a designated state office or official. If, however, there is no state provision for reporting such incidents, a report must be made to the U.S. Coast Guard Officer in Charge, Marine Inspection, nearest the site of the accident.

U.S. Coast Guard regulations on accident reporting list the information that must be furnished. The Boating Accident Report—CG-3865—may be used in reports to the Coast Guard. States normally use this form or one of their own patterned after it; see **Figure 2-12**.

Reporting requirements and forms are different for boats in commercial operation.

Accident Statistics The FBSA/71 also provides that as a part of an approved state registering and numbering system there shall be a casualty reporting plan in accordance with regulations issued by the Secretary. Detailed procedures for recording, compiling, and forwarding statistics are set forth in Coast Guard regulations.

National Statistics The Coast Guard is in turn charged with the responsibility of combining state reports with its own, to form annual national statistics on the number of registered boats by classes; accidents by type, cause, surrounding circumstances, etc; and other related data.

Privacy of Information Information about the identity and ownership of vessels numbered under the Act is made available to federal and local officials as needed in any enforcement or assistance program.

In general, files relating to boat numbering are considered "public records," and information from them may be released to anyone, subject only to reasonable restrictions necessary to carry on the work of the records office.

On the other hand, individual "Boating Accident Reports" or extracts therefrom are *not* releasable. These are intended only to assist the Coast Guard in determining the cause of accidents and making recommendations for their prevention, and compiling appropriate statistics. The privacy of accident reports permits the filing of full and accurate reports without the contents being used against an individual in civil suits.

Safety Standards The FBSA/71 authorizes minimum safety standards for "boats" and "associated equipment." Each standard must be reasonable, must meet the need for boating safety, and must be stated, insofar as practicable, in terms of performance. Under the Act's provisions, it is the responsibility of the manufacturer that all equipment on the boat when delivered meets any and all applicable safety standards of that date.

Penalties

The FBSA/71 provides for both civil and criminal penalties for violations of its provisions. It allows for variable penalties to meet situations of different degrees of seriousness, and provides for a flexible system of assessment and collection.

Civil Penalties A basic civil penalty of not more than $500 may be assessed for any violation of the FBSA/71 or any regulation issued thereunder. If the violation involves a vessel, that vessel may be liable and may be proceeded against in the U.S. federal courts. A civil penalty of not more than $200 may be assessed by administrative action; no trial is required, but procedures are established for appeals.

Criminal Penalties Any person who willfully uses a vessel in violation of the FBSA/71 or any regulation issued thereunder may be tried in court and fined up to $1,000 or imprisoned for not more than one year, or both. A person who uses a boat in a "grossly" negligent manner is subject to the criminal penalties in addition to

HOMELAND SECURITY

For many decades, boaters have been using waters that included prohibited or restricted areas. These have included waters such as CABLE AREAS and PIPELINE AREAS where navigation was not restricted, but certain actions, such as anchoring, were prohibited. There were also DANGER AREAS, including waters where bombing or naval gunfire targets were located, and RESTRICTED or PROHIBITED AREAS, generally established for the security of naval or other government facilities and property. Areas such as these might have full-time designation, or be in effect only when announced specific activities are taking place. These are described in the various volumes of the *Coast Pilot* (refer to Chapter 15, page 548), and are shown on the appropriate nautical charts, although without the details that are included in the *Coast Pilot* descriptions. Enforcement in many areas tended to be less than strict.

As an aftermath of the terrorist attacks of 11 September 2001, a considerable number of new security areas and restrictions came into existence, and the number increases almost daily. *To avoid getting into trouble with security authorities, it is imperative for every boater to know and comply with all restrictions on the waters on which he operates—enforcement is likely to be very active and strict.*

Security & Protection Zones
SECURITY ZONES are established around various onshore activities that might be a target for terrorist attack, typically all or a portion of a harbor or port, a major military or governmental facility, or a nuclear power plant. TEMPORARY MOVING SECURITY ZONES may be established around cruise ships, vessels carrying "cargoes of particular interest," typically those carrying hazardous liquids or gases, and other special vessels, usually when such vessels are entering port. TEMPORARY FIXED SECURITY ZONES are activated around these ships while they are berthed in port. NAVAL PROTECTION ZONES are always in effect around U.S. naval ships whether underway or in port—no entry within 100 yards, slow speed within 500 yards. Contact patrolling enforcement craft on VHF Channel 16 if you feel that you have to travel closer to the protected vessel, but do so *before* entering the restricted area.

Other Restricted Areas
Restricted areas with other names may be established where warranted. Restricted areas are established by the U.S. Coast Guard Captain of the Port for that vicinity in terms of specific geographic boundaries. In all cases, they are announced in the daily *Federal Register* (refer to Chapter 15, page 546) and *Local Notices to Mariners*; sometimes there will be a preliminary notice of intent to establish such a zone with a final rule and an effective date later, at other times, the restrictions will be immediate. Changes may be made after initial establishment, and, in some few cases, restricted zones may be canceled.

Safety Zones
Temporary SAFETY ZONES established for regattas, boat races, fireworks displays, etc., are distinct from the security actions described above, but boaters must be aware of these also and obey all restrictions.

Marine Sanctuaries
NATIONAL MARINE SANCTUARIES are another type of water area having special operating rules and exclusion zones.

any civil penalties. ("Simple" negligence is subject to civil penalties only.)

Penalty for Failure to Give Aid The person in charge of a vessel in collision has duties to the other vessel and those aboard her. A skipper who fails to meet these responsibilities, without reasonable cause, may be found guilty of a misdemeanor and subjected to a fine of $1,000 or imprisonment for not more than two years, or both. The vessel may be proceeded against in federal court with the penalty assessed being divided equally between any informer and the United States.

Penalty for Operation While Intoxicated Federal law now prescribes both civil and criminal penalties for operating a vessel while intoxicated. The civil penalty can be as much as $1,000. If one is tried in court and convicted, the penalty can be a fine of up to $5,000 or one year in prison, or both. Intoxication includes both alcohol and drug abuse. The Coast Guard is developing the necessary implementing regulations.

Many states have also adopted specific laws and penalties for operating a boat while "under the influence."

Written Warnings Coast Guard boarding officers may issue a *written warning,* intended to

be educational rather than punitive, for certain minor violations of boating regulations; these are awarded in lieu of a citation that would lead to a monetary penalty. Citations, not written warnings, are issued for any violation involving danger to the occupants of a craft, or when three or more violations of any type are found in a single boarding.

Written warnings are issued only for the first offense of any year; subsequent offenses are subject to more severe penalties. Appeal procedures are provided if it is felt that the warning was not warranted.

Boating Safety Advisory Council

The FBSA/71 established the BOATING SAFETY ADVISORY COUNCIL of 21 members, each of whom is expected to have special knowledge and experience in boating safety. The Council consists equally of representatives from state and local governments, boat and associated equipment manufacturers, and boating organizations and the general public. All boating safety standards and other major safety matters are referred to the Boating Safety Advisory Council before being issued.

Regattas & Marine Parades

The Coast Guard has established a set of regulations for regattas and marine parades. In some areas the authority to regulate such events has been passed on to state authorities, but with the same general requirements and procedures.

The term "regattas and marine parades" includes all organized water events of limited duration conducted on a prearranged schedule; this covers races of all types.

An application must be submitted to the Commander of the Coast Guard District in which the event will be held at least 30 days in advance; late applications are normally rejected. The application must contain information as specified in Coast Guard regulations.

Approval is often followed, in turn, by "special local regulations" governing the conduct of the event, spectator craft restrictions, patrolling

Figure 2-13 Boating laws and regulations are enforced afloat and ashore by many agencies—state and local police as well as the Coast Guard.

plans, etc. These are usually issued with Local Notices to Mariners (see Chapter 15, page 576) and carry specific penalties for violation.

Enforcement Authority

Federal boating regulations in general are enforced by the U.S. Coast Guard. USCG boarding vessels are identified by the U.S. COAST GUARD ENSIGN (see Chapter 25, page 857) and uniformed personnel. Upon being hailed by a Coast Guard vessel or patrol boat, a vessel underway must stop immediately and lay to, or maneuver in such a way as to permit the boarding officer to come on board; a search warrant is not required; see **Figure 2-13.**

Because of the many other missions assigned to the Coast Guard—drug and alien immigration interdiction, national security at ports, and others—recreational boaters are more likely to encounter enforcement by patrol boats from state and local governmental units. Skippers should be alert for posted signs or regulatory buoys indicating speed limits, "no wake," etc., and should stop immediately upon being hailed by an official craft.

Boaters in coastal waters may also be stopped and boarded by units of the U.S. Bureau of Customs & Border Protection operating in the drug and illegal immigrant interdiction efforts.

Nearly all law-enforcement vessels—U.S. Coast Guard and state or local—are equipped with a blue revolving light like those seen on police vehicles on land.

Park Regulations

The use of boats on many natural lakes and man-made reservoirs is subject to regulations issued by the National Park Service of the Department of the Interior. Other such bodies of water are controlled by state or local authorities. National Parks, Marine Sanctuaries, and similar areas in coastal waters are also policed by the National Park Service. The rules and restrictions vary from one body of water to another, and each area must be individually checked by the boater to ensure that laws are not inadvertently violated.

STATE BOATING LAWS & REGULATIONS

Federal laws and regulations now preempt state controls for boat and equipment safety standards, but FBSA/71 does allow states to impose requirements for safety equipment beyond federal rules, to meet uniquely hazardous local circumstances. The Act does *not* preempt state or local laws and regulations directed at safe boat operation. Typically, many states now have laws requiring the wearing of life preservers by children under a specified age. In addition, there are usually laws and regulations relating to boat trailers and their use.

The old saying that "Ignorance of the law is no excuse" applies to skippers of recreational boats. Each skipper should know the requirements and restrictions of his state, and should take appropriate steps to expand his knowledge before cruising in other states. He should particularly be alert to varying state laws about boat trailering on highways.

Information on applicable state laws and regulations may be obtained from each state, usually from the same office that handles registration and numbering.

DOCUMENTATION

Not all boats are numbered—many are "documented." This is a process whereby official papers on the craft are issued by the U.S. Coast Guard in much the same manner as for large ships. The "numbering" requirements of FBSA/71 do not apply to documented vessels; however, states may (and most do) require such craft to be registered, pay a fee, and display a sticker indicating that such fee has been paid. The other provisions of this Act do apply to documented boats as defined therein.

Federal documentation is a form of national registration that serves to establish a vessel's nationality, eligibility to engage in a particular employment (commercial vessels only), and eligibility to become the object of a preferred ship's mortgage. It is one of the oldest functions of Government, dating back to the 11th Act of the First Congress.

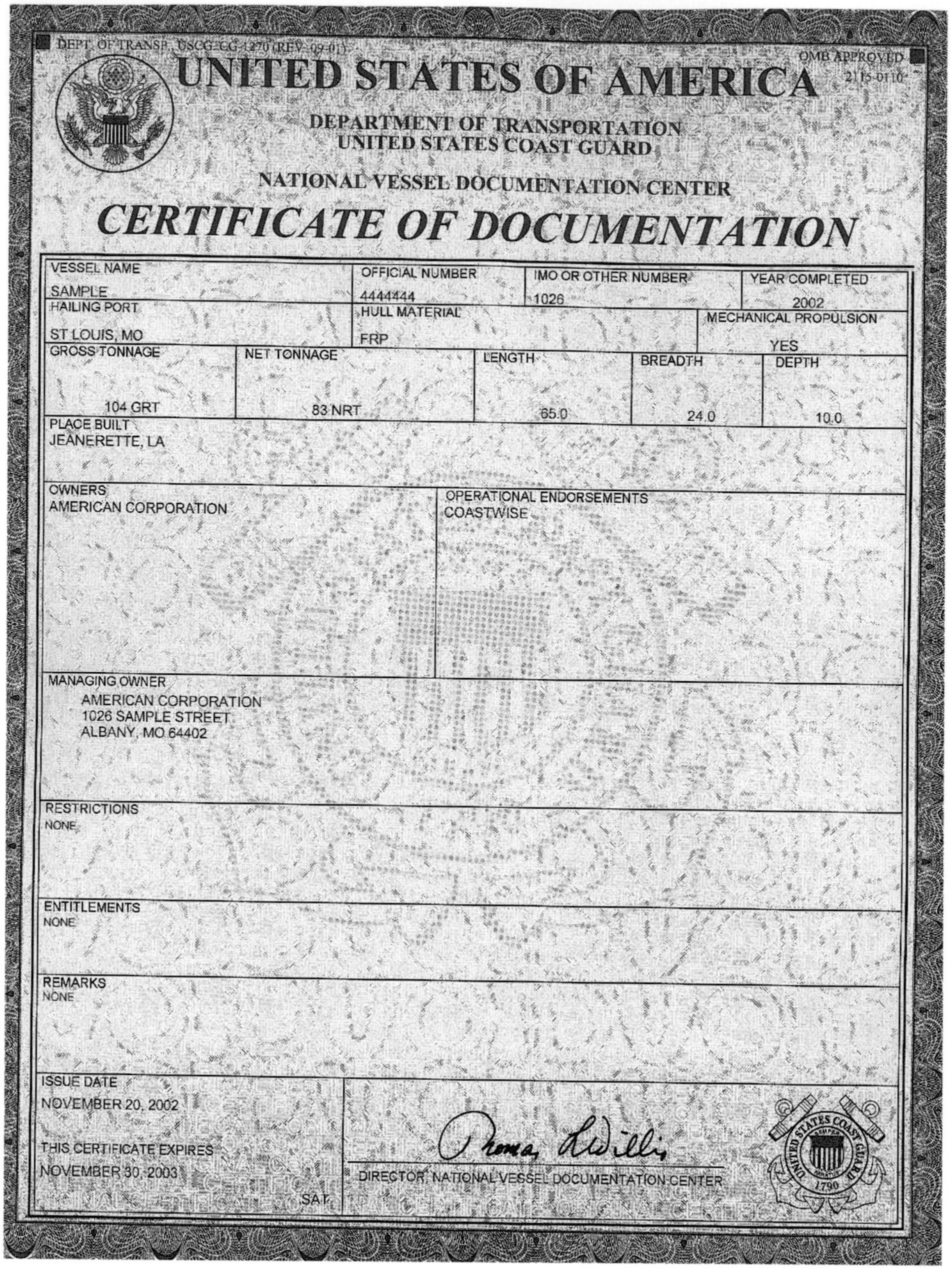

DEPT. OF TRANSP., USCG-CG-1270 (REV. 09-01)

OMB APPROVED 2115-0110

UNITED STATES OF AMERICA

DEPARTMENT OF TRANSPORTATION
UNITED STATES COAST GUARD

NATIONAL VESSEL DOCUMENTATION CENTER

CERTIFICATE OF DOCUMENTATION

VESSEL NAME	OFFICIAL NUMBER	IMO OR OTHER NUMBER	YEAR COMPLETED
SAMPLE	4444444	1026	2002

HAILING PORT	HULL MATERIAL	MECHANICAL PROPULSION
ST LOUIS, MO	FRP	YES

GROSS TONNAGE	NET TONNAGE	LENGTH	BREADTH	DEPTH
104 GRT	83 NRT	65.0	24.0	10.0

PLACE BUILT
JEANERETTE, LA

OWNERS
AMERICAN CORPORATION

OPERATIONAL ENDORSEMENTS
COASTWISE

MANAGING OWNER
AMERICAN CORPORATION
1026 SAMPLE STREET
ALBANY, MO 64402

RESTRICTIONS
NONE

ENTITLEMENTS
NONE

REMARKS
NONE

ISSUE DATE
NOVEMBER 20, 2002

THIS CERTIFICATE EXPIRES
NOVEMBER 30, 2003

SAT

DIRECTOR, NATIONAL VESSEL DOCUMENTATION CENTER

Figure 2-14 The Coast Guard issues Certificates of Documentation (Form CG-1270) for various types of vessel use, including recreation—the so-called "Yacht" document.

Basic Requirements

For any vessel, commercial or yacht, to be documented it must measure at least five net tons (see below, pages 73–74, for definition of net tonnage). Very roughly, this corresponds to a boat of 25 feet (7.6 m) or more in length, but this will vary with the type of boat.

The vessel must be owned by a U.S. citizen; a partnership association, or joint venture, all of whose members are U.S. citizens; or a corporation meeting certain requirements of control by U.S. citizens. (Vessels owned by the federal or state governments may also be documented.) The captain and other officers, but not crewmen, of a commercially documented vessel must be U.S. citizens. Vessels documented exclusively for recreational purposes do not need to be under the command of a U.S. citizen.

Documentation of a craft used *solely* for recreation is *optional,* but vessels engaged in fisheries or coastwise trade *must* be documented. Vessels engaged in foreign trade are not required to be documented, but owners usually elect to be documented to gain the protection of the U.S. flag.

Types of Documents

A CERTIFICATE OF DOCUMENTATION, Form CG-1270, is issued for all types of vessels; see **Figure 2-14.** This common basic form is ENDORSED for the authorized use or uses of the vessel—registry (for foreign trade), fisheries endorsement, coastwise license, or recreation. There may be more than one endorsement. Any commercially documented vessel may be used for recreation, but a vessel with only a recreational endorsement may not be used for any other purpose.

Advantages of Yacht Documentation

Privileges extended by documentation of vessels as yachts include (1) legal authority to fly the YACHT ENSIGN, which authority is not formally granted to other boats; and (2) the privilege of recording bills of sale, mortgages, and other instruments of title for the vessel with federal officials at the National Vessel Documentation Center (NVDC), giving constructive legal notice to all persons of the effect of such instruments and permitting preferred status for mortgages so recorded. This gives additional security to the purchaser or mortgagee, and facilitates financing and transfer of title.

Documentation is not required for recreational craft but it is advantageous for boats that cruise widely or spend major portions of the year in different states—it eliminates any concern over "state of principal use." Documentation will also be advantageous when entering foreign waters; it may even be a requirement for visiting some countries.

Obtaining Documentation

Before a vessel can be documented, it must be MEASURED for its tonnage. ("ADMEASURED" is the more formal term, but it means the same and is gradually being dropped in favor of the simpler language.) Both gross and net tonnage must be determined.

Simplified Measurement

Any vessel under 79 feet (24.1 m) in length may be measured for tonnage under procedures that are far simpler than those required for larger vessels. In brief, this method uses the numerical product of three dimensions measured in feet: the length overall (LOA, or for these purposes, simply L), overall BREADTH (B), and DEPTH (D). Measurements are in feet and inches (to the nearest inch).

As defined earlier, length overall is the horizontal distance between the outer side of the foremost part (bow) of the hull and the outer side of the aftermost part (stern) of the hull. It does *not* include bowsprits, rudders, outboard motor brackets, swim platforms that do not contain buoyant volume, and other similar fittings and attachments that are not a part of the buoyant hull.

Breadth is the horizontal distance taken at the widest part of the hull, excluding rub rails, from the outside of the "skin" on one side of the hull to the outside of the skin on the other side of the hull.

Depth is *not* the same as "draft." It is the vertical distance taken at or near amidships from a line drawn horizontally through the uppermost edges of the skin at the sides of the hull (excluding any cap rail trunks, cabins and deckhouses, and deck caps) to the outer face of the bottom of the hull, excluding the keel. For sailboats where there is not a clearly defined interface between the "bottom of the hull" and the "keel" (as is the case with an "integral" or "faired" keel), include the keel in the depth measurement.

The gross tonnage of a catamaran or trimaran (defined as having no buoyant volume in the structure that connects the hulls together) is determined by adding the gross tonnages for each hull as calculated above. Cathedral hull forms and other similar configurations with no distinct separation of the hulls are not considered multi-hulls in this context. Where the volume of the deckhouse is disproportionate to the volume of the hull—as in some designs of houseboats— the volume of the deckhouse is calculated by appropriate geometric formulas.

The dimensions discussed above are entered on the front of Form CG-5397 and submitted to the NVDC together with the Application for Documentation as described below. The NVDC will calculate the GROSS TONNAGE and NET TONNAGE from this data.

The gross tonnage of a vessel designed for sailing is assumed to be 0.5(LBD/100); for vessels not designed for sailing it is calculated to be 0.67(LBD/100).

The net tonnage of a sailing vessel is recorded as $9/10$ of the gross tonnage; for a nonsailing vessel, the multiplying factor is $8/10$. If there is no propelling machinery in the hull, the net tonnage will be the same as the gross tonnage.

An Application for Simplified Measurement, Form CG-5397 can be obtained from the Tonnage Division, Marine Safety Center, 400 Seventh St. S.W., Washington, DC 20590-0002; telephone 202-366-6480. Downloadable forms for either interactive completion or printing can be found online at www.uscg.mil/hq/msc/t3.htm; the form contains complete instructions—much other useful information can also be found at this site. The owner can take his own measurements. Certain novel or unique craft cannot be identified or categorized in the types described on Form CG-5397. In such cases, follow the instructions at the Internet site or on the reverse side of the form.

Formal Measurement

The owner of a boat may elect to have formal measurement rather than use the simplified method. This is *required* if the vessel measures 79 feet (24.1 m) or more in length, except for certain inland barges and recreational vessels operating only on the Great Lakes.

If an owner is contemplating formal measurement, it is suggested that he first estimate the tonnage by using the simplified method. If the resulting net tonnage is less than 5 tons the vessel will probably be under 5 net tons when formally measured, and thus not eligible for documentation.

The U.S. Coast Guard has delegated the function of formal measurement of vessels to several Classification Societies. Names, addressees, and contact information on each of these can be obtained from the USCG Tonnage Division as listed above.

Fees will be charged for the measurement of each vessel, and for the issuance of a measurement certificate. Owners can typically expect to pay on the order of several hundred to several thousand dollars to have a vessel formally measured, depending on vessel size, location, first-of-a-kind, etc. Appeals of decisions relating to measurement may be submitted directly to the Commandant (G-MS) at U.S. Coast Guard Headquarters, Washington, DC 20593-0001.

Application for Document

The vessel owner must submit an APPLICATION FOR DOCUMENTATION, Form CG-1258. This two-sided form is also used for changes in an existing document; an instruction sheet is available. (Some of the "instructions" are references to sections of the Code of Federal Regulations, but in general the form is simple to complete.) This form, and CG-5397 if applicable, should be sent to the National Vessel Documentation Center, 792 T J Jackson Drive, Falling Waters, WV 25419-4527; telephone 800-799-8362. Forms and general information can be obtained online at www.uscg.mil/g-m/vdoc/nvdc.htm. Forms are also available by fax 24 hours a day. Simply telephone the 800 number and follow the prompts. If you don't have a fax machine available, you may leave a voice-mail message specifying the address to which you want the forms sent.

The application for documentation must include a name for the vessel composed of letters of the Latin alphabet or Arabic or Roman numerals and may not exceed 33 characters. The name, which must be approved by the Coast Guard, may not be identical, actually or phonetically, to any word or words used to solicit assistance at sea; may not contain or be phonetically identical to obscene, indecent, or profane language, or to racial or ethnic epithets. Once established, a vessel's name may not be changed without application, fees, and the consent of the Director, National Vessel Documentation Center. There is no rule

Figure 2-15 A documented craft must have its official number permanently marked in Arabic numerals on a clearly visible interior member of the vessel.

against duplication of names for documented vessels, so hailing ports are helpful in identifying vessels.

When the Application Form is received by the Documentation Center, an "official number" will be assigned to the vessel. Although a vessel's name may be changed with appropriate permission, the official number will remain unchanged for the life of the vessel. The owner must have the vessel properly marked as described below.

If the vessel is new, evidence of the facts of construction must be submitted on a Builder's Certification, Form CG-1261.

If documentation for recreational use is sought for a used vessel for the first time, the owner has the option of presenting evidence of the complete chain of ownership, or merely a copy of the last prior registration (foreign, federal, or state) plus evidence that establishes title from that registration to the present owner.

Fees

There are several fees to be paid for the documentation process—initial issuance, commercial endorsement (but not for a recreational endorsement), duplicate for a lost certificate, recording bills of sale and mortgages, etc. These fees vary and generally slowly increase. The fees for a recreational vessel will typically be between U.S. 92 and U.S. 175.

Markings of a Documented Vessel

U.S. Coast Guard regulations prescribe precisely how a documented vessel *must* be marked. Documented vessels do not display their official numbers on the outside of the hull, but are identified by the name and hailing port. A General Information Sheet is sent with each new Certificate of Documentation; it includes clear and exact instructions for the application of the required markings.

Official Number

The OFFICIAL NUMBER assigned to a documented vessel, preceded by abbreviation "No.", must be marked by a permanent method in block-type Arabic numerals at least three inches high on some clearly visible *interior* structural part of the hull. The number must be permanently affixed so that alteration, removal, or replacement would be obvious and cause some scarring or damage to the surrounding hull area; see **Figure 2-15.**

Name & Hailing Port

The VESSEL NAME and HAILING PORT of a recreational vessel must be marked together on some clearly visible *exterior* part of the hull; see **Figure 2-16**. The vessel name of a commercial vessel must also be marked on the port and

Figure 2-16 A documented boat used for recreation purposes only must have her name and hailing port marked on some conspicuous part of its hull; this is normally done on the transom. The state must be shown as well as the city.

starboard bow and the vessel name and the hailing port must also be marked on the stern. All markings may be made by any means and materials that result in durable markings and must be at least four inches in height, made in clearly legible letters of the Latin alphabet or Arabic or Roman numerals. The "hailing port" must include *both* a place and a State, Territory, or possession of the United States. The state may be abbreviated, but *not* any part of the name of the city.

The name and port must be on the vessel itself by use of any means and materials that will result in durable markings. Having the name and port on the bottom of a dinghy carried awarthship on its side across a boat's transom, as is sometimes done, is *not* a legally acceptable substitute for markings on the documented craft itself, but can be additionally done if the dinghy obscures the name on the transom.

The vessel name and/or hailing port may be changed by filing an application for change on form CG-1258 with the appropriate fees. If your vessel is subject to a mortgage of record, you must obtain permission from the mortgagee (the lender) on form CG-4593.

A Certificate of Documentation is not valid until the vessel is properly marked. The penalty for operation of a vessel with an invalid document is $10,000 per violation, and each day of such operation is a separate violation.

Renewal of Document

A Certificate of Documentation is valid for one year from the date of issue, providing there are *no changes* other than a change of owner's address, which must be reported to the NVDC as soon as possible. The Certificate must be renewed on an annual basis. Even though it is up to the owner to ensure that the document does not expire, the Coast Guard will send a Notice of Renewal to the managing owner approximately 45 days prior to expiration. There is no fee for the yearly renewal.

It is not necessary to send back the Certificate of Documentation; simply sign, date, and return the Renewal Notice, even if your address has changed. Please note any address change. You will receive a new Certificate of Documentation each year.

You may renew your document early. The Renewal form is available at the NVDC website noted above. It may be downloaded from the Forms Menu. It may be mailed or, better yet, faxed to 304-271-2405. Be sure to cite the vessel's official number.

If you do not receive a renewal form, you should contact the NVDC not less than two weeks prior to the expiration date. The responsibility for renewal is placed on the vessel owner, whether or not a notice is received from the Documentation Center.

Sale of a Documented Vessel

If your boat is documented and you sell it, return the original Certificate of Documentation to the NVDC along with a brief note that you sold the vessel. Your Certificate is non-transferable and should not be given to the new owner unless you have sold the boat by completing the reverse side. Alternatively, when the sale is finalized you can complete a U.S. Coast Guard Bill of Sale (CG-1340) that can be used by the new owner should he wish to document the vessel. Documentation requires that the new owner send in the Certificate of Documentation completed on the reverse side, or a signed original Bill of Sale with an Application for Documentation (CG-1258) and fees. The buyer should also be able to use the Bill of Sale form as evidence of the transfer of ownership to obtain state registration and/or title if he chooses not to document the vessel with the U.S. Coast Guard.

If you have an outstanding mortgage of record against your vessel, make sure the mortgagee (the lender) completes a Satisfaction of Mortgage form and mails an original and one copy to the NVDC. Your vessel cannot be removed from documentation with an outstanding mortgage.

Other reasons requiring the surrender of a Certificate of Documentation include: (1) a change in the name of the vessel; (2) a change in ownership, such as the death of a listed owner; (3) a change in the tonnage of the vessel.

Use of Documented Boats

If a vessel is given a document for recreational use, that paper will authorize its use for noncommercial use only. A yacht document does *not* permit the transporting of merchandise or the carrying of passengers for hire (see below), such as taking out fishing parties for a fee charged directly or indirectly. Any violation of this limitation may result in severe penalties against the craft and its owner, including forfeiture of the vessel. See also the section immediately below on "Commercial Operation."

The documentation of a vessel as a yacht *does not exempt* it from any applicable state or federal taxes. Further, the fact that a boat is federally documented will not excuse the owner from complying with safety and equipment regulations of the state or states in which it is operated. State and local officials have the right to board a documented vessel for law enforcement purposes.

Vessels that are documented are neither required nor permitted to have a number issued under FBSA/71. However, in many states, these craft must be registered and the same tax or fee paid as if they were to be numbered; contact the appropriate State office in your area for further information.

COMMERCIAL OPERATION

The dividing line between noncommercial (recreational) and commercial operation of a boat may seem obvious, but a boat owner who is unfamiliar with federal regulations can get into difficulties. The amateur skipper may conclude that his activities are in no sense commercial and that guests on board are not passengers. However, there are circumstances in which authorities would disagree. A recreational boat operator who crosses the legal line may be subject to fines and may not be covered by his insurance.

The federal government requires a licensed operator on board a *motorboat* or motor yacht under 300 gross tons engaged in trade or carrying passengers for hire. Also, licensed officers are required on *motor vessels documented as yachts* of 200 gross tons and over when navigating the high seas.

Carrying Passengers for Hire

Persons wishing to operate a motorboat carrying passengers for hire must have a license. There are two categories of licensing as determined by the number of persons carried—six passengers and fewer, or more than six. Neither of these should be confused with the licenses required for pilots and engineers on vessels of more than 15 gross tons or 65 feet in length engaged in trade. Motorboats under 65 feet in length carrying *freight* for hire are not required to have licensed operators.

Definition of "Passenger" Of particular interest to boatmen who use their craft exclusively for recreation is the definition of a "passenger" in FBSA/71. A person on board a vessel is *not* considered by law to be a passenger if he is in any of the following categories: (1) the owner or his representative; (2) the operator; (3) bona fide members of the crew who have contributed no consideration for their carriage and who are paid for their services; or (4) any guest on board a vessel which is being used exclusively for pleasure purposes who has *not* contributed any consideration, directly or indirectly, for his carriage.

It is emphasized that to avoid being in a "passenger" status—which would subject the boat and its skipper to special requirements—the guest must not contribute any consideration, directly or indirectly, for his passage.

When Is a Boat Carrying Passengers for Hire? The last category above is the most troublesome. It is of considerable importance that a skipper have some understanding of circumstances that might be considered by the authorities as "carrying passengers for hire." Some situations are obvious—such as taking persons on a fishing trip for a specified amount of money for each individual or for the group as a whole—but other cases are more borderline and must be examined carefully. Typically, confusion arose when guests on board contributed toward the expenses of a purely recreational and social outing. The old regulations never defined "consideration" and local Coast Guard offices interpreted each instance on a case-by-case basis, often differently in various areas. A

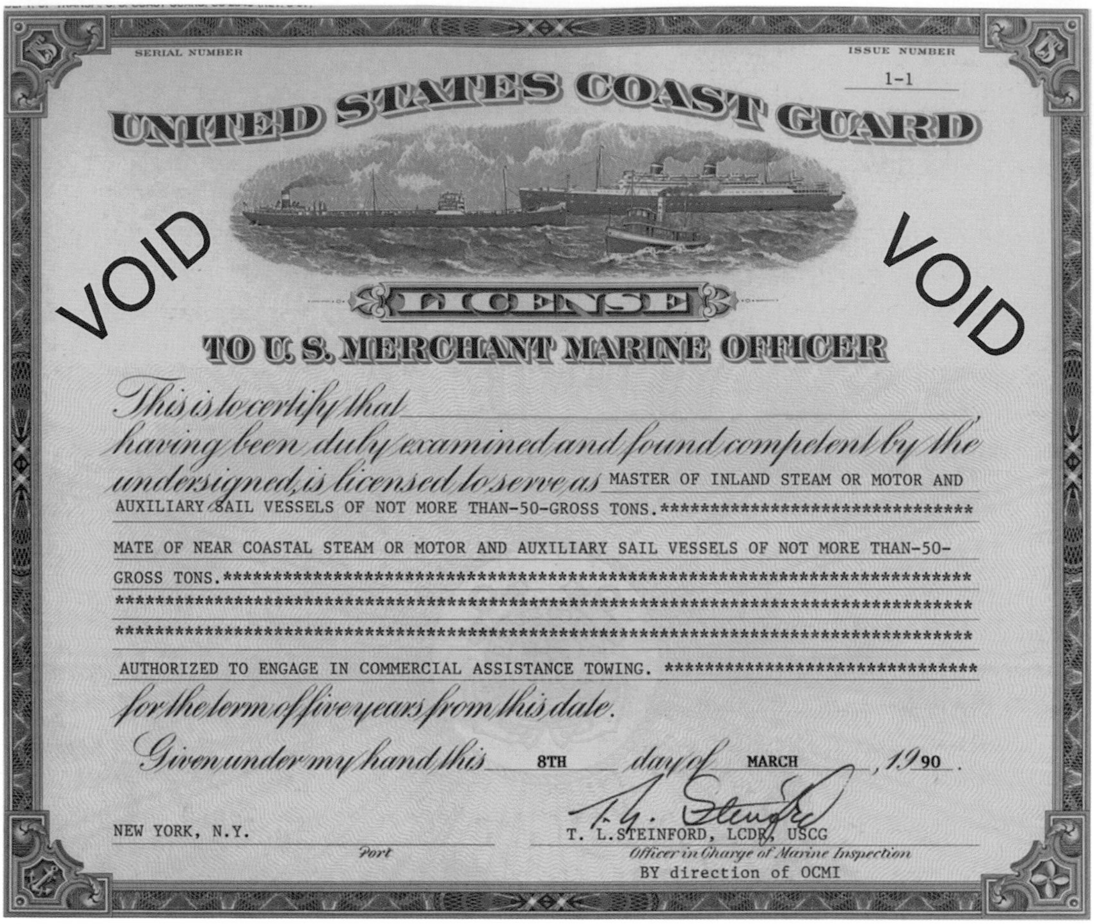

SERIAL NUMBER

ISSUE NUMBER 1-1

UNITED STATES COAST GUARD

VOID

VOID

LICENSE

TO U. S. MERCHANT MARINE OFFICER

This is to certify that

having been duly examined and found competent by the undersigned, is licensed to serve as MASTER OF INLAND STEAM OR MOTOR AND AUXILIARY SAIL VESSELS OF NOT MORE THAN-50-GROSS TONS.********************************

MATE OF NEAR COASTAL STEAM OR MOTOR AND AUXILIARY SAIL VESSELS OF NOT MORE THAN-50-GROSS TONS.**

****

****

AUTHORIZED TO ENGAGE IN COMMERCIAL ASSISTANCE TOWING. ********************************

for the term of five years from this date.

Given under my hand this 8TH day of MARCH, 1990.

NEW YORK, N.Y.

Port

T. L. STEINFORD, LCDR, USCG

Officer in Charge of Marine Inspection

BY direction of OCMI

***Figure 2-17** Licenses for the operator of a vessel carrying passengers for hire are issued in terms of the maximum tonnage of the vessel concerned, its type, and the waters for which the license is valid. If the license covers only six or fewer passengers, it is often referred to as a "Six-Pack License."*

definition has now been adopted that eliminates this confusion.

Consideration means an economic benefit, inducement, or profit (including a payment of money) accruing to the owner of the vessel. However, specifically excluded is the voluntary sharing of actual expenses of the voyage by monetary contribution or by making a donation in kind of fuel, food, beverages, or other supplies. Under these newer rules, several couples or friends may chip in to pay for the fuel, food, beverages, and other expenses for a day's outing or cruise without becoming "passengers for hire." In all other situations, where there is consideration for passage, the craft is considered as operating commercially and must be operated by someone holding an appropriate U.S. Coast Guard license.

License for Six or Fewer Passengers

Vessels of any size while carrying *not more than six passengers for hire* must be "in charge of" a properly licensed person. This license is officially titled "Operator of Uninspected Passenger Vessels" (OUPV); see **Figure 2-17**. More commonly, it is called a "six-pack" license. OUPV licenses are issued for inland, Great Lakes, or near-coastal waters (not more than 100 miles offshore).

Application for an OUPV License Licenses are issued by Officers in Charge (OIC), Marine Inspection, U.S. Coast Guard at Regional Examination Centers. Traveling Examination Teams *may* visit other ports or make specific trips to give examinations to *groups* of applicants. Much processing of applications for original license and renewals can be done by mail or on the Internet; contact the nearest OIC, Marine Inspection for details. A packet of instructions to guide prospective applicants normally accompanies the actual application form. These instructions must be followed exactly, or the application may be denied.

An applicant for an OUPV license must be 18 years of age; he or she must be able to speak and understand English as used in boating (except for licenses limited to Puerto Rico and vicinity where Spanish may be substituted). Use of dangerous drugs or conviction of drug-law violations may be a bar to issuance of a license. Fingerprints will be taken and checked. Individuals must be citizens of the United States, except that a noncitizen may receive an OUPV license limited to nondocumented vessels.

Except for special limited licenses (see below), an applicant for an OUPV license must submit proof of 12 months' experience in the operation of vessels, at least 3 months of which must have been in the last 3 years. (A "month" is interpreted as 30 days; a "day" requires at least 4 hours of operation.) If the license is for near-coastal waters, 3 months of the service must have been on ocean or near-coast waters. An applicant must submit written recommendations from three persons who have knowledge of his or her ability to carry out the duties of this type of license.

Applicants for an original license must present evidence of successful completion of one of several first-aid courses within the past 12 months, *plus* a currently valid certificate of completion of a cardiopulmonary resuscitation (CPR) course. CPR certification is not required for renewals.

Physical Fitness Required Applicants must submit a U.S. Coast Guard physical examination form, or equivalent, signed by a licensed physician or physician's assistant within the past 12 months. Visual acuity and color vision requirements are very specific, but waivers can be requested for special circumstances.

Mandatory Drug Testing The Coast Guard has established a comprehensive, mandatory drug-testing program for crews of marine vessels. All licensed crewmembers are subject to the program if they are required to be on board because of the nature of the vessel's operation, such as boats carrying passengers for hire. Unlicensed personnel are also subject to testing if they are involved in the craft's operation—such as deck hands, but not bartenders or waiters who have no duties relating to the vessel's safety.

The actual drug test (urine or blood) must be taken under five conditions: (1) Pre-employment; (2) Reasonable cause; (3) After a serious marine accident; (4) *Whenever a physical examination is required, such as original applications and renewal,* and some upgrades; or (5) Random testing. Detailed procedures have been set up for the collection of samples, analysis, review of results, reporting, and maintenance of records.

The program primarily focuses on commercially employed mariners and large ships, *but it does include self-employed individuals and recreational boaters who hold a U.S. Coast Guard license without using it for employment.* Skippers in these categories should get full details from a Coast Guard Marine Inspection office or Regional Examination Center.

Examination An applicant for a license as an Operator of Uninspected Passenger Vessels must pass a written examination. Subjects covered will be applicable to the waters concerned and may include navigation rules, chart reading and piloting; magnetic compass principles and use; tide and tidal current calculations; vessel handling, such as docking and undocking, anchoring, and in heavy weather; fire fighting and other emergency actions; first aid; rules and regulations for uninspected vessels; pollution rules and vessel sanitation laws; radiotelephone communications; and "any other subject considered necessary to establish the applicant's proficiency."

Re-examination All examinations are administered at periodic intervals. If an applicant fails three or more sections of the exam (which has four sections), a complete re-examination must be taken, but this may be done at any scheduled exam session. On the re-exam, if three or more sections are failed, at least 3 months must pass before any further retesting.

If one or two sections are failed, the applicant can be re-examined twice on these sections during the next 3 months. If these are not passed in that time period, at least 3 months must pass from the date of the last retest, and a complete re-examination must be taken.

License Issuance and Renewal Licenses are issued by an OIC, Marine Inspection. Every license must also be signed by the person to whom it is issued. It is valid for 5 years, after which it can be renewed. There are fees for the application for a license and for the examination. There are also expenses involved in the physical examination and the drug testing; there may be fees connected with the first aid course and the CPR training.

A license can be renewed in person at any Regional Examination Center, or by mail to the center that issued it. The original license (or photocopy) must be presented together with a completed application form. Evidence must be presented of at least one year of service (360 days) under the license during the past 5 years, or a comprehensive open-book exercise must be passed. Except under extraordinary circumstances, a license cannot be renewed more than 12 months in advance of its expiration date.

A license can be renewed up to 12 months after its expiration date, but it is not valid for use within this grace period. After 12 months it cannot be renewed and must be reissued; the individual will be examined to establish continued professional knowledge.

No license will be renewed if it has been suspended without probation or has been revoked, or if facts have come to the attention of the Coast Guard indicating that renewal would be improper.

Special Limited OUPV Licenses Limited OUPV licenses may be issued to employees of organizations such as formal camps, yacht clubs, marinas, and educational institutions. The experience requirement is reduced to 3 months in the type of vessel to be used, and the applicant must have a completion certificate from an approved course such as those given by the U.S. Power Squadrons or U.S. Coast Guard Auxiliary. A limited examination appropriate to the activity to be engaged in and the area concerned is required.

Lost License If a license is lost, this fact must be reported to an OIC, Marine Inspection. A duplicate license may be issued after an application and affidavit concerning the loss are submitted, and issuance of the lost license has been confirmed. This is for the unexpired term of the lost license.

Suspension or Revocation If any license holder is found guilty of incompetence, misbehavior, negligence, endangering life, or willfully violating any safety law or regulation, his or her license may be suspended or revoked. The license must then be surrendered, but a certificate will be issued covering the period during which any appeal is pending.

Licenses for More Than Six Passengers

Operation of small craft carrying *more than six passengers for hire*—"small passenger vessels"—requires a license as Master of Steam or Motor Vessels of Not More Than 100 Gross Tons. A license will be issued for not more than 50 Gross Tons if the individual's experience is on vessels of that size. The license will be further designated as Near-Coastal, Inland, or Great Lakes; near-coastal for these licenses is defined as not more than 200 miles offshore.

The required experience is 2 years of service in the deck department of ocean or near-coastal vessels. In order to get an endorsement for sail or auxiliary sail vessels, the individual must submit evidence of 12 months' service on such craft; this service may have been prior to the issuance of the license.

The physical and vision requirements are the same as discussed above for OUPV licenses. Examination subjects are expanded to cover the larger size of vessels involved.

For larger craft, there is a license level of "Not More Than 200 Gross Tons" with both "Master" and "Mate" categories, and "Ocean" as well as the other geographic limitations.

Any license issued for Inland Waters is valid for all inland waters of the United States, excluding the Great Lakes. A license issued for the Great Lakes is also valid for inland waters. A license for Near-Coastal Waters is also valid for the Great Lakes and all inland waters. A license as Master or Mate is valid for the operation of uninspected passenger vessels (six or fewer passengers).

The term of the licenses, and the requirements and procedures for renewal, are the same as for OUPV licenses.

Licenses for Towing
The Coast Guard issues licenses for Operator and Second Class Operator of uninspected towing vessels. A special endorsement is required for "Assistance Towing."

Vessel Inspection
Vessels carrying more than six passengers for hire must be inspected by an OIC, Marine Inspection. These are among the vessels generally referred to in U.S. Coast Guard regulations as "inspected vessels" and "small passenger vessels"; ordinary motorboats are categorized as "uninspected vessels."

Certificates of Inspection describe the area in which the vessel may operate, the maximum number of passengers that may be carried, the minimum crew required, and the minimum lifesaving and fire-fighting equipment to be on board, etc. Certificates are valid for 3 years.

CHARTERING
The act of renting a boat is termed CHARTERING, except for runabouts and waterskiing boats hired on an hourly or daily basis.

As a boater, you may decide that you want to charter another person's vessel, or you may want your boat to "earn her own keep" when you won't be using her. We will consider these two situations separately.

Chartering Another Person's Boat
If you have time for no boating activities at all except for a few vacation weeks each year, it may not make good economic sense to own and maintain your own boat for such limited use. Or you may have thoroughly explored the areas accessible to you with your own boat, and want to try areas further away. In either case, chartering is the way to go. Charters of both power and sailing vessels are available in almost all boating areas. Most charters begin and end at the same port, but some can be set up to cruise from "here" to "there" one-way.

Crewed or Bareboat Your charter can be either CREWED or BAREBOAT. Crewed means that the vessel's owner furnishes a captain—and often a mate/cook—who retains all responsibilities for the operation of the boat. You and your family or friends are "guests" aboard and have few responsibilities. You and your party may participate in the sailing and navigation activities if you like, but always under the supervision of the captain, who is often the vessel's owner.

On the other hand, a bareboat charter appeals to those who want to handle the boat themselves, without paid crew.

Crewed charters normally include all provisions and supplies. Bareboat charters may or may not include food and beverages, or these may be available at an additional fee (this is recommended as it permits you to get underway without delay). The CHARTER AGREEMENT states exactly what is supplied by the owner, plus his responsibilities as charterer as well as yours.

Chartering Your Boat
If you want to charter your own boat, you can do this directly, but most owners will work through an agent or broker. Any chartering must be under a written agreement. If you charter directly, the charter agreement form should be examined by a lawyer qualified and experienced in such matters. With an agent or broker, you can get customers more easily and be free from much paperwork, and you'll also know that the charter is being handled legally and efficiently. You will probably also need guidance about charges for the basic charter and for the optional services. You can get help from a professional agent or broker, but you do not need to give him an exclusive hold on your boat.

Check Your Insurance Before making even the first move toward chartering your boat, *check your insurance policy.* It most likely prohibits chartering, but the restriction can be removed with an endorsement, which requires the payment of an additional premium. You may also want to increase your liability coverage under these new circumstances.

Licenses & Regulations If you are going to captain your boat while chartering, you will be "carrying passengers for hire." In U.S. waters this will require a U.S. Coast Guard license of the proper type for the waters used, the type and size of vessel, and the number of passengers carried. If you plan to carry more than six guests your boat must be inspected by the Coast Guard and meet much more stringent requirements than for your own use or when carrying six or fewer passengers; see page 78. In the waters of other nations, the requirements may vary, and there may be restrictions as to citizenship; check carefully.

Tax Aspects of Chartering The income and expenses of operating a boat for charter will materially affect your income tax status. Check appropriate government publications and seek professional advice.

INTERNATIONAL VOYAGES

When an American boat crosses the national boundaries of the United States to visit a foreign port, or a foreign yacht visits an American port, certain customs, immigration, and other regulations must be obeyed. As a result of various provisions and exemptions applying to recreational boats, the procedure has been simplified and will not interfere with the pleasures of a foreign cruise. There are severe penalties, however, for any failure to observe the regulations that do apply.

Clearing & Entering

The terms CLEARING and ENTERING are commonly used in connection with a vessel's voyage between ports of two nations. Clearing involves obtaining permission to sail by presenting the ship's papers to a customs official. Entering relates to arrival, when the owner or master "enters" his vessel by having his ship's papers

accepted by customs authorities. Thus a U.S. vessel might be required to *clear* from an American port and *enter* on arrival at a foreign port.

If desired, BILLS OF HEALTH may be secured free of charge before leaving for a foreign port. This is not compulsory, but may make entry into the foreign port quicker and easier. Cruisers who plan to travel outside U.S. waters should check with their local health department or a travel agency for information on any inoculations or vaccinations required by specific countries.

Exemptions for Noncommercial Craft Neither a licensed yacht nor an undocumented American recreational vessel (not engaged in trade nor in any way violating the customs or navigation laws of the U.S.) is required to clear customs upon departure from the United States for a foreign port or place (with some specific exceptions, such as going to Cuba). Similarly a licensed yacht of any size or an undocumented American recreational vessel (not engaged in trade nor in any way violating the customs or navigation laws of the U.S., and not having visited any other vessel "hovering" off the coast) is exempted from *formal* entry. These craft, however, *must* make a report to the proper authorities to cover such matters as the importation of items purchased while outside the United States.

Report on Arrival

There are four separate legal aspects to entering this country from a foreign nation, each involving its own government agency and officials. These are (1) CUSTOMS, relating to bringing in dutiable merchandise; (2) IMMIGRATION, related to persons' eligibility for entry; (3) PUBLIC HEALTH SERVICE, for preventing importation of human diseases; and (4) ANIMAL AND PLANT QUARANTINE, for preventing entry of contaminated plants, fruits, and vegetables, or infected animals.

On arrival at a foreign port, the owner or captain of a recreational boat should report to the authorities mentioned above, or to such of them as exist for that port. The "Q" flag (plain yellow) should be flown where it can be easily seen—starboard spreader, radio antenna, fishing

Figure 2-18 Any boat arriving in a United States port from a foreign country must hoist a plain yellow flag—the letter "Q" of the International Code Flag set—when entering U.S. territorial waters and keep it flying until U.S. Customs and Immigration clearance has been completed.

outrigger, etc.—to indicate that the vessel desires to be boarded by customs and other governmental authorities; see **Figure 2-18.** When reporting, the captain may go ashore, if required, to report to the applicable authorities; crew and guests must remain aboard until permission has been granted to land. Any additional or local regulations to be complied with, including details in connection with clearing from that port, will be supplied by the authorities.

Every vessel, whether documented or not, arriving in the United States from a foreign port or place must come into a port where the formality of entry can be accomplished; the Q flag should be hoisted upon entering U.S. waters, 12 miles offshore. Only one person may get off the boat for the sole purpose of telephoning or otherwise notifying the authorities of the vessel's arrival; and no baggage or merchandise should be removed until the customs, immigration, and other officials have given their approval.

All boats, regardless of size, must report to the immigration authorities on return to a United States port. Any alien passengers aboard must be reported and a heavy penalty may be imposed for failure to detain passengers and crew if ordered to do so by the authorities. A report giving names, nationalities, and other information concerning any paid crew aboard must be made on a crew manifest.

In many U.S. ports a "one-stop" service has been established whereby for the simple situations of noncommercial craft from nearby foreign waters, a single government official from one of the agencies will represent all authorities and bring all necessary forms to be filled in by the skipper. In other areas, all that is needed is a telephone call to a local or toll-free number, but whatever the requirements are where you return to the United States, *they must be complied with* to avoid possible penalties.

The U.S. Customs Service now levies an annual "Processing Fee," $25 as of 2003, on boats 30 feet (9.1 m) or more in length. Most boaters who cruise out of the country send in their money in advance and get a numbered sticker to be placed on their boat in a specified location.

At the Canadian Border U.S. boats going into Canada may secure CRUISING PERMITS with the right of free entry and clearance from 1 May to 1 October. These are issued without charge by the Canadian customs authorities at the Canadian port where the craft first reports and must be surrendered when leaving the country. Provided the boat does not leave Canadian waters, she is then free to visit other Canadian ports until the permit is surrendered, though reports must be made at any port called where a customs officer is located.

A Canadian boater with a craft of less than 5 tons can enter the border waters of the United States for a day's outing without applying for admission at a U.S. port of entry. He can obtain a Canadian Border Landing Card which doesn't require advance application and is good for repeated 24-hour visits throughout the navigation season. It is good only for border waters; if the Canadian boatman wants to go farther into the U.S., he must apply at a U.S. port of entry and submit to inspection.

Additional Information In general, customs duties are assessed on articles of foreign manufacture when they are brought into the United States if the total value of items purchased exceeds a specified amount, which varies with the length of time that the individual has been out of the U.S. If you have purchased a foreign-made camera, radio, etc., in the United States and then took it with you when cruising outside U.S. waters, you would *not* be liable for any duty payment on return. It's a good idea to register such items with U.S. customs before leaving the country.

FEDERAL WATER POLLUTION LAWS

There are a number of basic laws covering water pollution, including the Federal Water Pollution Control Act of 1972 as amended and extended by the Federal Water Pollution Control Act Amendments of 1972 and the Clean Water Act of 1977. There have been additional minor revisions over the years. The Oil Pollution Act of 1990 covers spills of petroleum products of all types. These laws cover far more than discharges from boats and other vessels, but they form the basis for all implementing standards and regulations by the U.S. Coast Guard, the Environmental Protection Agency (EPA), and other federal agencies.

Discharge of Sewage

The term SEWAGE is defined as human body wastes and the wastes from toilets and other receptacles intended to receive or retain body waste. The term MARINE SANITATION DEVICE (MSD) includes any equipment for installation on board a vessel which is designed to receive, retain, treat, or discharge sewage, and any process to treat such sewage. No untreated sewage may be discharged overboard in any waters subject to the Federal laws and regulations. Treated sewage may be pumped overboard except as noted below.

Basic Provisions

The current laws and regulations relate to all watercraft. The law does, however, permit enforcing authorities to distinguish among classes, types, and sizes of vessels, as well as between new and existing vessels. There are provisions for waivers, but it has been officially stated that very few waivers may be expected and only on the strongest justification for each situation. Initially phased in over several years, the federal requirements are now applicable to all boats regardless of date of construction.

Performance Standards The general approach of the federal pollution legislation is the establishment of "standards of performance" for marine sanitation devices. The law states that performance standards must be consistent with maritime safety standards and marine laws and regulations. It specifically notes that in the development of standards consideration must be given to "the economic costs involved" and "the available limits of technology."

Operational Requirements

Present regulations divide waters into two categories: (1) freshwater lakes and reservoirs that have no navigable inlet or outlet, and (2) other waters, including coastal waters and tributary rivers, the Great Lakes, and freshwater bodies accessible through locks. Freshwater bodies in the first category above are subject to "no discharge'" rules. In the second category, the regulations also contain a provision that a state can apply for the establishment of a "no discharge zone." This is usually related to shellfish harvesting areas and public beaches, and the state must certify that there are adequate pump-out facilities to meet the needs of local and cruising boats. This provision is being implemented with increasing frequency. It should be noted, however, that craft equipped with a discharge-type MSD may be used on "no discharge" waters provided the device "has been secured so as to prevent discharge."

Marine sanitation devices are grouped into several "Types"—such as I, II, or III—based on how sewage is treated or retained on board. These devices are discussed in Chapter 3.

Vessel Requirements All vessels, including boats, with installed toilet facilities must have an operable marine sanitation device. Craft smaller than 65 feet (19.8 m) in length may have a Type I, II, or III MSD labeled as certified; larger vessels must have a Type II or III MSD.

Enforcement The law specifically authorizes U.S. Coast Guard and other enforcement personnel to board and inspect any vessel upon the navigable waters of the United States to check compliance with these provisions.

The Coast Guard has stated as a general policy that its units will not board vessels solely to check for the absence of a legal MSD. They will, however, make such an inspection whenever a boat is boarded for any other reason. Thus if your craft is boarded for a minor safety violation—such as improper navigation lights or suspected overloading—or as a routine procedure after receiving Coast Guard assistance, you can expect to be cited if you are not in compliance with the MSD requirements.

Disposal of Trash & Garbage

The U.S. Coast Guard has issued regulations to implement Annex V of the International Convention for the Prevention of Pollution from Ships, 1973, commonly known as Annex V of MARPOL 73/78. They apply to all U.S. vessels (including boats) wherever they operate (except waters under the exclusive jurisdiction of a state) and to foreign vessels operating in U.S. waters out to and including the Exclusive Economic Zone (200 nautical miles).

The regulations impose stringent requirements on the overboard disposal of trash and garbage, especially plastic items. Various restrictions apply at different distances from the shore; see **Figure 2-19** for waters other than the Great Lakes. The discharge of *all* garbage is totally prohibited in the Great Lakes and their connecting or tributary waters.

The Terminology of Garbage

PLASTIC includes, but is not limited to, plastic bags, Styrofoam cups and lids, six-pack holders, bottles, caps, buckets, shoes, milk jugs, egg cartons, stirrers, straws, synthetic ropes, and bio- or photo-degradable plastics.

GARBAGE means paper, rags, glass, metal, crockery (generated in the living spaces on board the vessel—what we normally call "trash") and all kinds of food, cargo, and maintenance waste. Garbage does *not* include fresh fish or fish parts, dishwater, or graywater (see below).

DISHWATER means the liquid residue from the manual or automatic washing of dishes and cooking utensils which have been precleaned to the extent that any food particles adhering

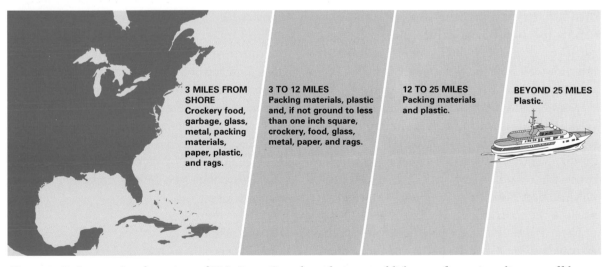

3 MILES FROM SHORE
Crockery food, garbage, glass, metal, packing materials, paper, plastic, and rags.

3 TO 12 MILES
Packing materials, plastic and, if not ground to less than one inch square, crockery, food, glass, metal, paper, and rags.

12 TO 25 MILES
Packing materials and plastic.

BEYOND 25 MILES
Plastic.

Figure 2-19 International treaties and U.S. Coast Guard regulations establish zones for various distances offshore in which the dumping overboard of specific kinds of material is prohibited.

to them would not normally interfere with the operation of automatic dishwashers.

GRAYWATER means drainage from a dishwasher, shower, laundry, bath or washbasin, but does not include drainage from toilets, urinals, hospitals, and cargo spaces.

DUNNAGE is material used to block and brace cargo—and is considered a cargo-associated waste.

Prohibited Actions

Boaters must learn and observe the various disposal prohibitions, especially the total ban on overboard disposal of plastic items in all waters, inland and offshore at *any* distance. They must learn and conform to the regulations regarding the disposal of other garbage; the restrictions gradually lessen with distance from shore; see **Figure 2-20**. For example, the rules, in effect, make it illegal within 3 nautical miles of the shore to operate a garbage disposal in a galley if it discharges overboard—even ground-up garbage. To make it easier to comply with the regulations, skippers may want to separate garbage according to the disposal limitations.

Skippers must inform crewmembers and passengers of these rules and the penalties for their violation.

Placards On craft 26 feet (7.9 m) or more in length, informational placards must be posted; depending upon the size of the vessel more than one may be required. These placards must define the limitations placed on discharging garbage in the marine environment, and specify the fines and other penalties that could be assessed for violation. Such placards must measure at least 9 inches wide and 4 inches high; they must be of durable material with letters at least ⅛ inch high. Placards that meet these specifications are available at marine stores for a small cost.

Vessels used exclusively on the Great Lakes may use the standard placard described above, or a placard that states "The discharge of ALL garbage into the Great Lakes or their connecting waters is prohibited." (In the Great Lakes, it is illegal to dump anything except fresh fish, fish

ILLEGAL DUMPING

INSIDE 3 MILES
(and in U.S. lakes, rivers, bays, and sounds)
Plastic, dunnage, lining, and packing materials that float. Any garbage except dishwater/graywater/fresh fish parts

3 to 12 MILES
Plastic, dunnage, lining, and packing materials that float. Any garbage not ground to less than one square inch

12 to 25 MILES
Plastic, dunnage, lining, and packing materials that float

OUTSIDE 25 MILES
Plastic

Figure 2-20 All boats 26 feet (7.9 m) or more in length must have one or more placards posted that specify what cannot be dumped overboard at various distances from the coast. These placards of a standard minimum size may be purchased at marine supply stores.

parts, dishwater, or graywater anywhere, regardless of distance from shore.)

Waste Management Plan In addition to the placard requirement, the regulations require a written WASTE MANAGEMENT PLAN for U.S. craft over 40 feet (12.2 m) in length that operate in coastal waters beyond three nautical miles of the shore, engage in commerce, or have a galley and berthing quarters. The plan must describe the procedures of collecting, processing, storing, and properly disposing of garbage in a way that will not violate the regulations. It must also designate the person responsible for carrying out the plan.

Vessel owners who have specific questions regarding the form or content of a Waste Management Plan should contact the nearest U.S. Coast Guard Captain of the Port: see Appendix D.

Disposal Ashore

Ports and terminals that conduct business with commercial vessels must be capable of receiving garbage from such vessels when they dock.

Recreational boating facilities (such as marinas and yacht clubs), capable of providing dockage or other services for 10 or more boats, must provide adequate garbage reception facilities for any vessel that routinely calls. (Boats must be conducting business with the marina or other facility in order to qualify for the service; facilities would not be expected to provide such service to a vessel whose sole reason for docking was to offload its garbage.) Reasonable fees can be charged for providing services for the reception of garbage. Special requirements exist for facilities that receive garbage from craft returning from international waters.

Enforcement & Penalties

The U.S. Coast Guard is responsible for the enforcement of these antipollution regulations. Civil penalties can be as great as $25,000. Additionally, criminal penalties include imprisonment for up to five years and fines up to $50,000, or both.

Notice of Violation In instances of small oil discharges (under 100 gallons) and minor violations of pollution regulations, after investigation and evaluation of an alleged violation has been completed, an issuing officer may issue a NOTICE OF VIOLATION. This will include information on the alleged violation and the applicable law or regulation; the amount of maximum penalty that may be assessed and the amount of the proposed penalty that appears to be appropriate. The Notice will also state how the penalty may be paid, and that payment will settle the case.

A Notice of Violation will advise the recipient of his right to decline the Notice and request a hearing. *Action must be taken within 45 days.* Failure to either pay the proposed penalty or request a hearing will result in a finding of default, and the Coast Guard will proceed with collection action. If the proposed penalty is paid, a finding of "proved" will be entered on the record and the case closed.

Vessels denied the ability to offload their garbage at a marina or terminal should report this to the nearest Coast Guard Captain of the Port or Marine Safety Office. Observations of vessels violating the regulations can be reported to these same offices.

Discharge of Oil

Federal regulations provide that "no person may operate a vessel, except a foreign vessel or a vessel less than 26 feet (7.9 m) in length, unless it has a placard at least 5 inches by 8 inches made of durable material, fixed in a conspicuous place in the machinery spaces, or at the bilge and ballast pump control station, stating the following":

DISCHARGE OF OIL PROHIBITED

The Federal Water Pollution Control Act prohibits the discharge of oil or oily waste into or upon the navigable waters of the United States, or the waters of the contiguous zone, or which may affect natural resources belonging to, appertaining to, or under the exclusive management authority of the United States, if such discharge causes a film or discoloration of the surface of the water or causes a sludge or emulsion beneath the surface of the water. Violators are subject to substantial civil penalties and/or criminal sanctions including fines and imprisonment.

Persons who see an oil or chemical spill can report it by calling toll-free: 800-424-8802.

Equipment for Boats

Legally Required Gear That Your Boat Must Carry • The Additional Items That Add to Your Safety • Optional Gear That Provides Comfort & Convenience

Although most manufacturers supply the basic equipment required by law, and often many other useful items, few new or used boats come with everything needed—or desired—for safe, enjoyable boating. You should select the additional gear that is best suited for your boating needs.

Categories of Equipment

Equipment for a boat can be divided into three categories for separate consideration. These groupings are:

Equipment Required by Federal, State, or Local Law. This list is surprisingly limited. It has little flexibility; items are strictly specified and usually must be of an "approved" type.

Additional Equipment for Safety & Basic Operations. This is gear not legally required, but includes items that could be considered necessary for normal boat use.

Equipment for Comfort & Convenience. This is the gear that is not necessary, but adds to the scope and enjoyment of your boating.

Factors Affecting Selection

In all three categories, the items and quantities will vary with the size of the craft and the use made of it, with the legally required items determined in most cases by the "class" of boat (see Chapter 2, page 62), as set by the Motorboat Act of 1940 (MBA/40). Other factors, such as the amount of electrical power available on board, cost, etc., will also affect equipment selection.

Opposite Page: Figure 3-01 A water-skier towed behind a boat is included in the count of number of persons on the boat in determining the number of personal flotation devices that must be on board. If the skier is wearing an approved PFD, such as a Type III, that counts toward the required number. A ski belt is not an approved PFD and does not count.

LEGALLY REQUIRED EQUIPMENT

The Federal Boat Safety Act of 1971 (FBSA/71—See Chapter 2, page 60) requires various items of equipment aboard boats. The specific details are spelled out in regulations stemming from MBA/40 and are published in a Coast Guard pamphlet, "Federal Requirements and Safety Tips for Recreational Boats" COMDTINST M16760.1, summarizes these requirements for boats in each class. The individual items are described in detail on the following pages.

Note that the FBSA/71 regulates the equipment of *all* boats *including sailboats without mechanical propulsion,* even though the regulations temporarily retained from the MBA/40 are in terms of "motorboats." The 1940 Act and its regulations remain effective for commercial vessels, such as diesel tugboats, which are not subject to the 1971 law.

State Equipment Regulations

Although the FBSA/71 provides for federal preemption over state equipment requirements, a blanket exemption has been granted which allows all state and local regulations in effect when the FBSA/71 became law to retain in force for the time being. When federal requirements have been expanded beyond the regulations of the MBA/40, this exemption may be lifted and federal rules will then prevail.

The FBSA/71 allows states and their political subdivisions, such as counties or cities, to have requirements for additional equipment beyond federal requirements, if needed to meet "uniquely hazardous conditions or circumstances" in a state or local area. The federal government retains a veto over such additional state or local requirements.

Required Equipment as a Minimum
Regard the legal requirements as a minimum. If a particular boat is required to have two fire extinguishers, for example, two may satisfy the authorities, but a third might be desirable, even necessary, to ensure that one is available at each location on board where it might be needed in a hurry. Two bilge vents may meet the regulations, but four would certainly give greater safety. Think "safety," not just the minimum in order to be "legal."

Nonapproved Items as Excess
Some boaters carry items of equipment no longer approved—older, superseded types, or items never approved—as "excess" equipment in addition to the legal minimum of approved items. This is not prohibited by regulations, but it may give a false sense of protection. The danger of reaching for one of these substandard items in an emergency must be recognized and positively guarded against. Some obsolete items of safety equipment, such as carbon tetrachloride fire extinguishers, are actually hazardous on a boat, and should never be on board.

Lifesaving Equipment
Boating is not inherently unsafe, but any time anyone goes boating there's a chance of falling overboard or the craft sinking—a small chance to be sure, but it does exist. A PERSONAL FLOTATION DEVICE—commonly called a PFD or "life jacket"—is designed to keep your head above water and assist you in maintaining a position that permits proper breathing.

PFDs are among the most essential safety items that can be on any boat. More importantly, *they must be used.* Accident data shows that 74 percent of deaths in boating accidents result from drowning, and 86 percent of those drowning were not wearing a life jacket. Many of these deaths were avoidable. An average adult needs additional buoyancy (the force, in pounds, that keeps you from sinking in the water) of 10 to 12 pounds (4.5 to 5.4 kg) in order to remain afloat. All PFDs approved by the U.S. Coast Guard and the Canadian Department of Transportation provide more than this amount of buoyancy. PFDs also provide some protection against another cause of boating accident casualties—hypothermia.

Legal Requirements
USCG regulations require that *all* recreational boats subject to their jurisdiction, regardless of means of propulsion—motor, sails, or otherwise—must have on board a Coast Guard-approved PFD for each person on board. There are a few quite minor exceptions such as sailboards, racing shells, rowing sculls, and racing kayaks. Under Federal law, sailboards are not classified as "boats" and therefore are exempt, but state laws may require PFD use. Foreign boats temporarily in U.S. waters are also exempted. "Persons on board" include those in tow, such as water-skiers; see **Figure 3-01.** The PFDs must be in serviceable condition.

An additional requirement, effective 23 December 2002, provides that all children under the age of 13 years must wear an appropriate USCG-approved PFD unless the child is below decks or in an enclosed cabin, or the craft is not underway. If a State has an established age under which children must wear PFDs, that age will be effective for the USCG requirement in that state, rather than the "under 13 years" age stated above. Note also that there is no size or type specified for the boat—the USCG regulation applies to all recreational vessels.

More stringent requirements are placed on vessels carrying passengers for hire (any number) than are applied to recreational boats.

Coast Guard approval means that the design and manufacture of the PFD has met certain standards of buoyancy and construction. Many available PFDs will provide more than the minimum buoyancy.

Types of Personal Flotation Devices
Coast Guard-approved personal flotation devices are marked with a PFD "Type" designation and descriptive name to indicate to the user the performance level that the device is intended to provide.

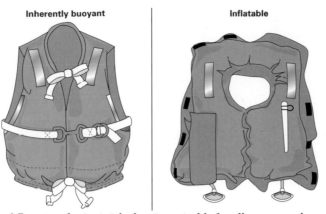

Figure 3-02 A Type I personal flotation device is "the best"—suitable for all waters and needed for rough seas. It is designed to turn most unconscious wearers to a face-up position.

Type I PFD (Off-Shore Life Preserver or Life Jacket) is designed to turn most unconscious persons from a face-downward position in the water to a vertical, face-up or slightly backward position, and to maintain that person in that position, increasing the chances of survival. A Type I PFD is highly desirable for all open, rough, and remote waters, especially for cruising in areas where there is a probability of delayed rescue. This type of PFD is the most effective of all types in rough water. A Type I PFD is, however, somewhat less "wearable" than the other types, except for the Type I INFLATABLE PFDs recently approved by the Coast Guard; see **Figure 3-02.**

A Type I PFD is available in two sizes—adult (individual weighing 90 pounds—40.8 kg—or more) and child (less than 90 pounds). Each Type I will be clearly marked as to its size; a child size is *not* suitable for an infant. A Type I PFD must have at least 22 pounds (10 kg) buoyancy for adult size and 11 pounds (5 kg) for child's size.

Type II PFD (Near-Shore Buoyancy Aid) is designed to turn the wearer to a vertical, face-up and slightly backward position in the water. The turning action is not as great as with a Type I, and will not turn as many persons as a Type I under the same conditions; note the lack of the qualification "unconscious" although some Type IIs may have a flotation collar that will assist in such turning. Tests have shown that a Type II does not provide adequate safety in rough water, and is intended for use in calm inland waters where there is a good chance of quick rescue; see **Figure 3-03.**

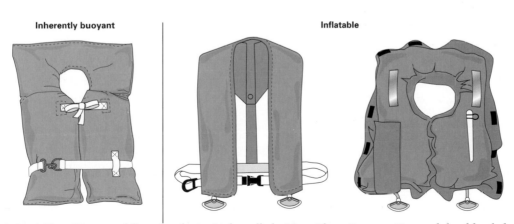

Figure 3-03 A Type II personal flotation device is also called a Near-Shore Buoyant Vest and should only be depended upon where there is a good chance of quick rescue. This will turn some unconscious wearers face up, but its turning action is less than a Type I; it is, however, somewhat more comfortable to wear.

Inherently buoyant   **Inflatable**

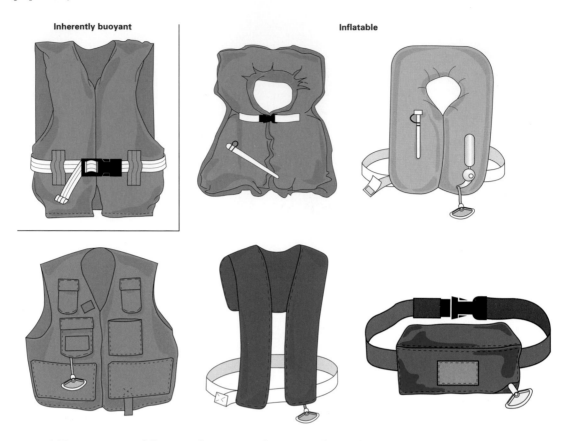

Figure 3-04 A Type III personal flotation device is a "Flotation Aid"—it should be used only in calm protected waters or where there is assurance of a quick rescue. A wearer must place himself in a face-up position; there is no inherent turning action as in Types I and II. It is generally the most comfortable to wear.

Type II PFDs are available in four sizes: Adult weighing more than 90 pounds (40.8 kg); Youth weighing 50 to 90 pounds (22.6 to 40.8 kg); Child weighing 30 (13.6 kg) to 50 pounds, and Infant (less than 30 pounds). In addition, some models are sized by chest measurement. A Type II PFD must have buoyancy of at least 15.5 pounds for Adult size, 11 pounds for Youth size, or 7 pounds (3.2 kg) for Child and Infant sizes. Here too inflatables are available in this class approved by the Coast Guard (inflatables have higher buoyancy requirements).

Type III PFD (Flotation Aid) is designed so that the wearer can assume a vertical or slightly backward position, and maintain the wearer in that position with no tendency to turn the wearer face down. The Type III can be the most comfortable to wear and is available in a variety of styles, allowing them to be matched with the individual's activities, such as skiing, fishing, canoeing, and kayaking. It is a suitable device for activities where it is especially desirable to wear a PFD because the wearer is likely to enter the water. In-water trials have shown, however, that while a Type III jacket will provide adequate support in calm waters, *it may not keep the wearer's face clear in rough waters;* this limitation should be kept in mind in the selection and use of this device; see **Figure 3-04.**

Type III PFDs must have at least 15.5 pounds of buoyancy. This is the same buoyancy as the Type II, but note that there is no turning requirement or protection for a person who becomes unconscious while in the water. Like Type II PFDs, Type IIIs are for use in inland waters with quick rescue likely. Many Type III inflatables now have Coast Guard approval. They need not be worn to be counted toward the legal minimum requirement, as do some Type V PFDs.

Figure 3-05 A Type IV personal flotation device is a throwable PFD; it can take many shapes and forms. Shown above are a life ring buoy, a horseshoe buoy, and a cushion. Type IV PFDs are intended to be grasped rather than worn, and hence are of no value to an unconscious person.

Type IV PFD (Throwable) A Type IV device is designed to be grasped by the user, rather than worn, until rescued; it is typically thrown to a person who has fallen overboard. It is designed for use in calm inland waters with heavy traffic where help is always present. Type IVs are available in a variety of forms; see **Figure 3-05** for some of these.

Buoyant cushions are made of thick foam material in plastic cases measuring approximately 15 inches square by 2 inches thick. There are two grab straps on opposite sides for holding the PFD to your chest.

Ring buoys have rope around the circumference for holding onto the device. Standard sizes are 20 inches (51 cm), 24 inches (61 cm), and 30 inches (76 cm) in outside diameter. Life rings of 18.5 inches (47 cm) diameter have been approved under the "special purpose water safety buoyant device" category and are authorized for use on boats of any size that are not carrying passengers for hire.

Horseshoe buoys are throwable devices commonly found on sailboats. Their open side makes it easier to get "inside" the PFD.

A Type IV PFD cushion must have at least 20 pounds (9.1 kg) of buoyancy; ring buoys must have from 16.5 pounds (7.5 kg) to 32 pounds (14.5 kg) depending upon diameter size.

Type V PFD (Special Use Device) is any device designed for a specific and restricted use. It may be carried instead of another type only if used according to the approval condition stated on the device's label, which often requires they be worn if used to satisfy the PFD regulation. A Type V

PFD may provide the performance of a Type I, II, or III device as marked on the label. Varieties include exposure suits, work vests, and sailboard vests. Some Type V devices provide significant hypothermia protection.

Styles of Flotation Devices

Coast Guard regulations recognize a number of different styles of PFDs and contain specifications that must be met or exceeded for each. Each device must be marked with its approval number and all other information required by the specifications.

Offshore Life Preservers Type I PFDs are available in jacket, bib, or inflatable style; refer to **Figure 3-02**. The flotation material of the jacket type is pads of kapok or fibrous glass material inserted in a cloth cover fitted with the necessary straps and ties. Kapok or fibrous glass *must* be encased in sealed plastic film covers. Type I PFDs of the "bib" type may be of cloth containing unicellular plastic foam sections of specified shape, or they may be uncovered plastic foam material with a vinyl dip coating. The bib type must have a slit all the way down the front and have adjustable body straps. This is the type commonly used on passenger ships and craft because of easier stowage than the jacket type.

Type I inflatable PFDs approved for use on recreational craft must have at least two inflation chambers, each of which must independently meet all of the in-water performance requirements for that PFD. One of the inflatable compartments must have an automatic or an automatic/manual CO_2 inflator system, and the other must have at least a manual CO_2 inflation system.

All three designs of Type I PFDs have patches of reflecting material to aid in the location of a person in the water at night.

Type I PFDs are individually inspected after manufacture. They are marked with the type, manufacturer's name and address, and USCG approval number, plus a date and place of inspection together with the inspector's initials. All Type I PFDs are now required to be INTERNATIONAL ORANGE in color.

Near Shore Buoyancy Aids Type II PFDs include BUOYANT VESTS that come in many styles and colors. They use the same flotation materials as life preservers, but vests are smaller and *provide less buoyancy,* hence somewhat less safety for a person in the water. Recent tests suggest that they are not entirely dependable for prolonged periods in rough water. The Type II is usually more comfortable to wear than a Type I, and remember, a PFD that is not worn is less likely to help you in an emergency! Boaters may prefer to use the Type II where there is a probability of quick rescue, such as areas where it is common for other craft and persons engaged in boating, fishing, and other water activities.

Buoyant vests are marked with the model number, manufacturer's name and address, approval number, and other information. These water safety items are approved by lot and are *not* individually inspected and marked.

Inflatable PFDs are a solution to the common problem of boaters who do not wear PFDs as they should because many PFDs are uncomfortable and restrict activities—keep in mind that 86 percent of the people who drown in boating accidents might have been saved if they had been wearing a life jacket. The inflatable PFD is much less bulky than conventional PFDs, many boaters find them more comfortable to wear—and hence are more likely to be worn. And when inflated, they provide even more buoyancy and life-saving capability. Besides Type III inflatables there are also Type V PFDs that may be classed as either Type II or

Figure 3-06 *Inflatable PFDs can be either manual inflation (Type III) or manual/automatic (Type V, with Type II performance). Though expensive, these are the most comfortable for routine wearing, but must be worn to count toward the legal requirement. Models are not available for children.*

Type III as determined by their buoyancy—22 pounds (10 kg) to 34 pounds (15.4 kg); see **Figure 3-06.**

Inflatable PFDs are available in either manual or automatic styles, depending on the inflation action. Manual models require action by the wearer to activate the small compressed-gas (CO_2) cylinder. Automatic models inflate when a sensing device becomes wet; they can also be activated manually. Both models can be inflated by blowing into tubes.

Inflatable PFDs are not for everyone. They should be used only by persons who can swim; they are not authorized for persons under 16 years of age. They are considerably more expensive than traditional PFDs. They require maintenance (the Coast Guard withheld approval for many years because of concern that boaters would not provide adequate maintenance). After use, inflatable PFDs must be rearmed *immediately* with a new cartridge; if automatic style, the activating unit must be replaced. Some automatic models will have a spare cartridge in a pocket so that in the case of an accidental activation it can be rearmed as a manual model.

Caution: Automatic inflatable PFDs should not be worn in cabins or other enclosed compartments. An unexpected capsize or flooding could actuate them and cause difficulties in exiting, possibly even making egress impossible.

Special Purpose Devices are a category of PFDs that may be either Type II or Type III if they are designed to be worn; they are Type IV if designed to be thrown.

The design of SPECIAL PURPOSE WATER SAFETY BUOYANT DEVICES is examined and approved by recognized laboratories, such as Underwriters Laboratories, see Chapter 11, page 380; this approval is accepted by the Coast Guard. These devices are labeled with information about intended use, the size or weight category of the user, instructions as necessary for use and maintenance, and an approval number. Devices to be grasped rather than worn will also be marked "Warning: Do Not Wear on Back."

Buoyant Cushions are the most widely used style of Type IV PFD. Although adequate buoyancy is provided—actually more than by a buoyant vest—the design of cushions does *not* provide safety for an exhausted or unconscious person; see **Figure 3-07**.

Buoyant cushions are approved in various shapes and sizes, and may be of any color. Approval is by lot and number as indicated on a label on one side, along with the same general information as for buoyant vests. All cushions carry the warning not to be worn on the back.

Life Rings are another style of Type IV PFD, more properly called LIFE RING BUOYS, which may be of cork, balsa wood, or unicellular plastic foam. The ring is surrounded by a light grab line fastened at four points; refer to **Figure 3-05**.

Balsa wood or cork life ring buoys are marked as Type IV PFDs and with other data generally similar to life preservers. They may be either international orange or white in color.

Rings of plastic foam with special surface treatment will carry a small metal plate with approval information including the inspector's initials. Ring buoys of this style may be either international orange or white in color.

Some skippers letter the name of the boat on their ring buoys; this is not prohibited by the regulations.

Horseshoe Ring Buoys are another type of "marine buoyant device, Type IV" often found on cruising sailboats and almost always on larger racing sailboats for man-overboard emergencies. These are made of unicellular foam encased in a vinyl-coated nylon cover. The shape is aptly described by the device's name—it is much easier to get into in the water than a ring buoy. These are normally carried vertically in special holders near the stern of the boat; some holders are designed to release the horseshoe ring quickly by merely pulling a pin on a cord. To facilitate the recovery of the victim, these rings are often equipped with special accessories at the end of a short length of line—a small float with a slender pole topped with a flag (and, in some cases, with a radar reflector), an

Figure 3-07 By far the most common Type IV personal flotation device is the buoyant cushion. It must always be remembered that it is primarily a life-saving device, not just another cushion on board. The straps should be grasped, but a person's arms may be placed through the straps to hold the device in front of him, never on the back.

electric flasher light that automatically comes on when floating upright in the water, a small drogue to slow the rate of drift to more nearly that of a man in the water—all or a combination of these items.

Hybrid PFDs combine inherent internal foam buoyancy with the capability of being inflated to a greater buoyancy. These are available in Adult, Youth, and Child sizes. The inherent buoyancy ranges from 10 pounds (4.6 kg) to 7.5 pounds (3.4 kg) depending upon size, with inflated buoyancies of 22 pounds (10 kg) to 12 pounds (5.4 kg). The hybrid PFD is less bulky and more comfortable to wear than other PFDs, yet the device has at least some initial support in case of accidental falls overboard with the victim possibly unconscious—and much greater buoyancy if the person is conscious and capable of inflating the hybrid PFD.

Unless the person concerned is within an enclosed space, hybrid PFDs are acceptable toward the legal requirements *only if they are being worn*. These devices should be assigned to a specific person and fitted to that individual; they should be tried on *in the water*. Hybrid PFDs are not desirable for use by guests; guests should have Types I, II or III.

Buoyant Work Vests are classed as Type V PFDs. These are items of safety equipment for crewmembers and workmen when employed over or near water under favorable conditions and properly supervised. Such PFDs are not normally approved for use on recreational boats.

PFD Requirements by Boat Size

All recreational boats must have on board at least one approved wearable personal flotation device

MAINTENANCE FOR YOUR PFDs

It is not only a requirement of Coast Guard regulations to maintain your PFDs in good condition; it is common sense—your life may depend on them some day! Don't only, take care of them, but also remember that a PFD, like any other item of equipment on your boat, eventually wears out and must be replaced.

• You and each person in your regular crew should have a specifically assigned PFD marked with their name. It should be tried regularly in shallow water. It should hold its wearer comfortably so that he or she can breathe easily.

• After each use, each PFD should be air-dried thoroughly away from any direct heat source. Then store it in a dry, well-ventilated, easily accessible place on board the boat.

• Check at least once a year for mildew, loose straps, or broken zippers (if applicable). Clean with mild soap and running water; avoid using strong detergents or chemical cleaners, and do not dry clean. Check PFD covers for tears—a cover that has torn due to

weakened fabric is unserviceable; a weak cover could split open and allow the flotation material to be lost. Badly faded colors that should be bright can be a clue that deterioration has occurred. Compare fabric color where it is protected—under a strap, for example—to where it is exposed. A PFD with a UV-damaged fabric cover should be replaced without delay. Another test is to pinch the fabric between the thumb and forefinger and try to tear it. If the cover can be torn, the PFD should be replaced.

• Check PFDs that use kapok-filled bags for buoyancy. Make sure that the kapok has not hardened and that there are no holes in the bags. Squeeze the bags and listen for an air leak. If water has entered a bag, the kapok will eventually rot. Destroy and replace any PFD that fails these tests.

• Avoid contact with oil or grease, which sometimes causes kapok materials to deteriorate and lose buoyancy

• Avoid kneeling on PFDs; do not use them for fenders.

of Type I, II, III, or V for each person on board. Though they need not be worn, except with some Type Vs, they must be near at hand. A Type V must provide the performance of a Type II or III (as marked on its label) and must be used in accordance with that label.

Boats *16 feet or more in length* must *additionally* have on board at least one Type IV "throwable" PFD.

All PFDs must be Coast Guard approved, in good condition, and of the appropriate size for the intended user. Where the type of PFD that is carried comes in sizes, such as adult and children's life preservers, and the four sizes of buoyant vests, the PFD used to meet the requirements of the regulations must be of an "appropriate" size for the person for whom it is intended.

Stowage of PFDs

The best "storage" of your PFD is on your person while your boat is underway—the need for it may arise suddenly with no time to find it and put it on. A wearable PFD may save your life, but only if you wear it.

When not being worn, it is best that PFDs be stored out of direct sunlight. Coast Guard regulations are very specific about stowage of personal flotation devices. Any required Type I, II, or III (or acceptable Type V) PFD must be "readily accessible." Any Type IV PFD required to be on board must be "immediately available." These rules are strictly enforced.

The PFDs must also be in "serviceable condition." Inspect your PFDs at least annually, and replace any that show signs of deterioration, usually found in the covering or straps.

State Requirements

With the exception of inflatable and hybrid PFDs, the federal requirements are stated in terms of flotation devices being on board, not necessarily being worn. In contrast, state regulations generally cover additional situations where PFDs must be worn. A majority of states now require that children wear flotation devices while boating; the upper age limits vary from 5 to 12 years, and the circumstances vary widely, from *at all times* to *only when underway,* or *on deck,* etc. The new Federal rule provides only two exceptions—while below decks or in an enclosed cabin, and while the boat is not underway. Previous state exceptions, which varied widely, remain applicable for state enforcement.

It is critical that a child's PFD be of the proper size and fit, and that it be tried out in a safe place in the water, such as a swimming pool. The child must not be able to slip out of the device; crotch straps are an important feature for children's flotation devices.

Fire Extinguishers

All hand-portable and semi-portable fire extinguishers and fixed fire extinguishing systems must be of a type that has been *approved by the Coast Guard.* Such extinguishers and extinguishing systems will be clearly labeled with information as to the manufacturer, type, and capacity. (See below for information on "type" and "size.")

Coast Guard approval of hand-portable extinguishers requires that they be in approved marine-type mounting brackets.

Types of Fire Extinguishers

Fire extinguishers, including those for boats, are described in terms of their contents—the actual extinguishing agent.

Figure 3-08 Most fire extinguishers on boats will be portable dry-chemical units. These must have a pressure gauge, and this should be checked regularly. Extinguishers must be USCG approved and mounted on an approved bracket.

Dry Chemical This type of extinguisher is widely used because of its convenience and relative low cost. The cylinder contains a dry chemical in powdered form together with a propellant gas under pressure. Coast Guard regulations require that such extinguishers be equipped with a gauge or indicator to show that normal gas pressure exists within the extinguisher; do not carry one that does not meet this requirement, it is not USCG approved; see **Figure 3-08.**

The dry chemical in these extinguishers has a tendency to "pack" or "cake." Mount them where there is a minimum of engine vibrations; shake them every month or two.

Carbon Dioxide Some boats have carbon dioxide (CO_2) extinguishing systems; such units are advantageous as they leave no messy residue to clean up after use, and they cannot cause harm to the interior of engines as some other types may. This type of extinguishing agent may be used as a fixed system installed in an engine compartment, operated either manually or automatically by heat-sensitive detectors; see **Figure 3-09.** There are also hand-portable units, but these are infrequently found on boats. Semi-portable extinguishers (wheeled carts) will be seen on some marina piers and in boat yards.

Carbon dioxide extinguishers consist of a cylinder containing this gas under high pressure, a valve, and a discharge nozzle, sometimes at the end of a short hose. The state of charge of a CO_2 extinguisher can only be checked by weighing the cylinder and comparing this figure with the one stamped on or near the valve. See Chapter 11, page 401, for further details on the maintenance of CO_2 extinguishers.

Vapor Systems Other chemical vapors with a fire extinguishing action are available. Halon 1301 is a colorless, odorless gas that stops fire instantly by chemical action. It is heavier than air and sinks to lower parts of the bilge. Humans can tolerate a 7 percent concentration; this is more than enough to fight a fire for several minutes. However, Halon discharged in closed spaces consumes the oxygen available for breathing and persons should evacuate as quickly as possible; the *smoke* from a Halon-extinguished fire is very toxic. Halon is used in built-in systems actuated manually or automatically; manual controls must be located outside

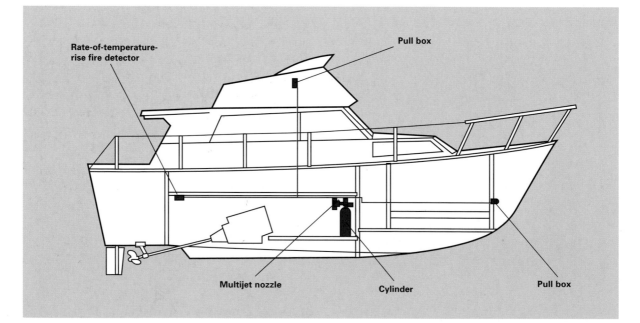

Figure 3-09 Boats powered with inboard engines, particularly those fueled by gasoline, often are fitted with a built-in CO_2 or Halon-type fire extinguishing system. It may be activated automatically by temperature-rise sensors in the engine compartment or manually at one or more remote locations on the boat.

the space to be protected. Halon 1301 has now been banned from new liquefied gas system installations because of environmental considerations, but some craft may still have this type of extinguisher installed.

An alternative chemical for vapor systems is FE-241; however, this gas is toxic and must not be used in occupied spaces. It is used in engine compartments, with the size of extinguisher matched to the volume of the space to be protected. To avoid damage to engines, especially diesels, it should be used with an automatic shutdown device. FM-200 is another chemical for fire extinguishers that is considered safe for use in occupied spaces, but is significantly more expensive.

The state of charge of a vaporizing liquid extinguisher can only be checked by weighing the cylinder and comparing this figure with the one stamped on or near the valve; see Chapter 11, page 401 for further details on the maintenance of Halon and FE-241 extinguishers.

Foam Aqueous film foam forming (AFFF) extinguishers are legally acceptable on boats, but this type is rarely used, as it leaves a residue that is difficult to clean up after use and may require a partial engine disassembly if discharged in an engine compartment.

Foam extinguishers are not pressurized before use and do not require tests for leakage. Such units contain water and must be protected from freezing. Foam extinguishers should be discharged and recharged annually.

Nonacceptable Types Vaporizing-liquid extinguishers, such as those containing carbon tetrachloride and chlorobromomethane, are effective in fighting fires but produce highly toxic gases. They are *not* approved for use on motorboats and should *not* be carried even as excess equipment because of their danger to the health—or even life—of a user in a confined space.

Classification of Extinguishers

Fires are classified—according to the general type of material being burned—into four categories, three of which are of concern to boaters: A (combustible materials), B (flammable liquids), C

FIRE EXTINGUISHER CONTENTS

Class	Foam (gals.)	CO_2 (lbs.)	Dry Chemical (lbs.)	FE-241 (lbs.)
B-I	1.25	4	2	5
B-II	2.5	15	10	10

Figure 3-10 Fire extinguishers that are approved by the Coast Guard for use on boats are hand-portable, B-I or B-II classification, and have the characteristics shown above.

(electrical components); see Chapter 12, page 420. The fourth category—D (flammable metals, such as magnesium, as stated, does not concern boaters.

Fire extinguishers are similarly classified as to "type" and in addition are placed in size groups, I (the smallest) through V; see **Figure 3-10.** (These USCG classifications—B-I, B-II, etc.—should not be confused with Underwriters Laboratories rating, such as 2-B, 5-B, 10-B, etc., which may also appear on extinguishers. The UL rating provides a better guide to extinguisher capacity, but it has not been written into USCG regulations as yet.)

The primary fire hazard on boats results from flammable liquids—so type "B" extinguishers are specified. (Some "B" extinguishers have adequate or limited effectiveness on other classes of fire; some should *not* be used on other types of fires, such as foam extinguishers on class "C" electrical fires.) Only the two smallest sizes, I and II, are hand portable, size III is a semi-portable fire extinguishing system, and sizes IV and V are too large for consideration here.

(Refer to **Figure 3-18,** which shows the type and size of extinguishers for various classes of boats.)

Requirements on Boats

Fire extinguishers on boats must be specifically marked "Marine Type U.S. Coast Guard Approved."

Class A and 1 boats (under 26 feet—9.9 m—in length) must have at least one type B-I (5-BC or higher rating) hand-portable fire extinguisher, except that boats of these classes with outboard motors and portable fuel tanks, not carrying

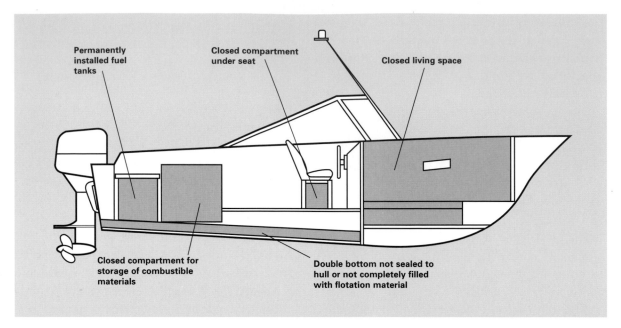

Figure 3-11 *If a craft has any one, or more, of the enclosed spaces identified above, Coast Guard regulations require that it must carry at least one fire extinguisher.*

passengers for hire *and* of such open construction that there can be no entrapment of explosive or flammable gases or vapors, need not carry an extinguisher.

A fire extinguisher *is required* on boats under 26 feet (7.9 m) in length powered with outboard motors *if one or more* of the following conditions exist; see **Figure 3-11**:

• Closed compartment under thwarts or seats in which portable fuel tanks may be stored.

• Double bottoms *not* sealed to the hull, or which are not *completely* filled with flotation material.

• Closed living spaces.

• Closed storage compartments in which combustible or flammable materials are stowed.

• Permanently installed fuel tanks. (To avoid being considered as "permanently installed," tanks must not be physically attached in such a manner that they cannot be moved in case of fire or other emergency. The size of the tank in gallons is *not* a specific criterion for determining whether it is a "portable" or a "permanently installed" tank. If the weight of a fuel tank is such that persons on board cannot move

it, the Coast Guard considers it to be permanently installed.)

The following conditions do *not*, of themselves, require that fire extinguishers be carried; see **Figure 3-12**:

• Bait wells.

• Glove compartments.

• Buoyant flotation material.

• Open slatted flooring.

• Ice chests.

Class 2 boats must carry at least *two B-I* approved hand-portable fire extinguishers, or at least *one B-II* unit.

Class 3 Boats must carry at least *three B-I* approved hand extinguishers, or at least *one B-II* unit *plus one B-I unit.*

Boats with fixed extinguisher systems in the engine compartment may have the above minimum requirement for their size reduced by one B-I unit. The fixed system must meet Coast Guard specifications.

Exemptions Motorboats propelled by outboard motors, while engaged in a previously arranged and announced race (and such boats designed solely for racing, while engaged in operations incidental to preparing for racing) are

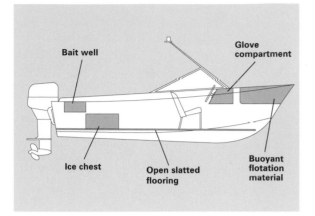

Figure 3-12 A boat of open construction, with no enclosed spaces as defined by regulations, need not have a fire extinguisher on board, but one is desirable for safety.

exempted by Coast Guard regulations from any requirements to carry fire extinguishers.

Keeping Safe

Don't merely purchase and mount fire extinguishers and then forget all about them. All types require some maintenance and checking; see pages 400 and 401 for guidance in keeping up the level of fire protection you gain when first installing new extinguishers.

All members of your regular "crew," and also any guests who may be aboard, should know both the location and operation of all fire extinguishers.

Never partially discharge a dry-chemical extinguisher with the idea of "saving" the balance of its contents for later use. There is almost always some powder left in the valve, and this will result in a slow leak of pressure, rendering the unit useless. Always recharge or replace fire extinguishers immediately after use. As the cost of recharging small extinguishers is almost the cost of a new one, replacement is the usual action.

Backfire Flame Control

Every inboard *gasoline* engine must be equipped with an acceptable means of BACKFIRE FLAME CONTROL. Such a device is commonly called a "flame arrester" and must meet Coast Guard specifications to be approved. Accepted models

will be listed by manufacturer's number in equipment lists or will have an approval number marked on the grid housing.

In use, flame arresters must be secured to the air intake of the carburetor with an air-tight connection, have clean elements, and have no separation of the grids that would permit flames to pass through; see **Figure 3-13.** Fuel-injected engines without carburetors require a backfire flame arrester over the air intake to prevent exhaust valves from backfiring into the air chamber, which might cause a fire or explosion.

An exception is made for boats constructed so that the fuel/air induction system is above the sides of the hull—typically craft used in connection with waterskiing—provided that specified conditions are met.

Ventilation Requirements

All motorboats, except open boats, that use fuel having a flashpoint of 110°F (43.3°C) or less—gasoline, but not diesel—must have ventilation for every engine and fuel tank compartment. Gasoline in its liquid and vapor states is potentially dangerous, but to enjoy safe boating, one need only follow Coast Guard regulations and good common sense.

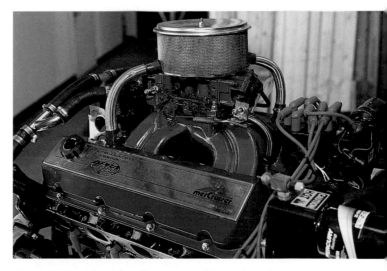

Figure 3-13 A backfire flame control is more widely known as a "flame arrester." Coast Guard regulations require an approved model on every inboard gasoline engine. Elements must be kept clean and grids must not have any separations that would let flames pass through.

The Coast Guard requires mechanical ventilation blowers on all boats built after 31 July 1980 under regulations derived from the Motorboat Act of 1940; see **Figure 3-14.** Manufacturers must provide such equipment and no person may operate such a boat that has a gasoline engine for propulsion, electrical generation, or mechanical power unless it has an *operable* ventilation system that meets the requirements. Thus the initial requirement is placed on the builder, but the owner has a continuing responsibility. Boats of "open construction" are exempted.

Open Construction Defined

The Coast Guard has prepared a set of specifications to guide the boat owner in determining whether his boat meets the definition of "open construction." To qualify for exemption from the bilge ventilation regulations, the boat must meet *all* of the following conditions:

• As a minimum, the engine and fuel tank compartments must have 15 square inches of open area directly exposed to the atmosphere for each cubic foot of *net* compartment volume. (Net volume is found by determining total volume and then subtracting the volume occupied by the engine, tanks, and other accessories, etc.)

• There must be no long or narrow unventilated spaces accessible from the engine or fuel

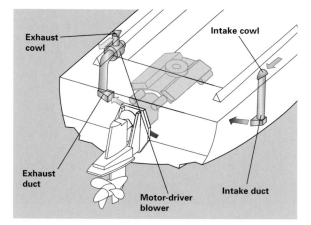

Figure 3-14 A powered ventilation system consists of one or more intake ducts plus one or more exhaust ducts with an exhaust blower. Each blower intake must draw from the lower one-third of the engine compartment, but above the normal level of bilge water.

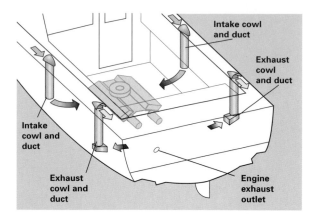

Figure 3-15 A natural ventilation system is an arrangement of intake openings or ducts from the atmosphere (located on the outside of the hull), or from a ventilated compartment, or from a compartment that is open to the atmosphere. There are also one or more exhaust ducts.

tank compartments into which fire could spread.

• Long, narrow compartments, such as side panels, if joining engine or fuel tank compartments and not serving as ducts, must have at least 15 square inches of open area per cubic foot through frequent openings along the compartment's full length.

Sailboats are subject to the same ventilation requirements as powerboats if combustible fuel is carried on board.

Be Safe—Be Sure

If your boat is home-built or does not meet one or more of the specifications above, or if there is *any* doubt, *play it safe and provide an adequate ventilation system.* To err on the safe side will not be costly; it may save a great deal, perhaps even a life.

Natural Ventilation

Except for those of open construction, a gasoline-engine-powered boat is required to have at least two ventilation ducts, fitted with cowls at their opening to the atmosphere, for each engine and fuel tank compartment. An exception is made for fuel tank compartments if each electrical compartment therein is "ignition protected" in accordance with Coast Guard standards, and fuel tanks are vented to the outside of the boat; see **Figure 3-15.**

The VENTILATORS, DUCTS, and COWLS must be installed so that they provide for efficient removal of explosive or flammable gases from bilges of *each* engine and fuel tank compartment. To create a flow through the ducting system—at least when underway or when there is a wind—cowls (scoops) or other fittings of equal effectiveness are needed on all ducts. A wind-actuated rotary exhaust fan or mechanical blower is equivalent to a cowl or an exhaust duct.

Lack of adequate bilge ventilation can result in an order from a Coast Guard Boarding Officer for "termination of unsafe use" of the boat; see Chapter 2, page 66.

Ducts Required

Ducts are a necessary part of a ventilation system. A mere hole in the hull won't do; that's a vent, not a ventilator. "Vents," the Coast Guard explains, "are openings that permit venting, or escape of gases due to pressure differential. *Ventilators* are openings that are fitted with *cowls* to direct the flow of air and vapors in or out of *ducts* that channel movement of air for the actual displacement of fumes from the space being ventilated." Each supply and exhaust duct must extend to the lower third of the compartment and must be above the normal accumulation of bilge water.

Size of Ducts

Ventilation must be adequate for the size and design of the boat. There should be no constriction in the ducting system that is smaller than the minimum cross-sectional area required for efficiency. Where a stated size of duct is not available, the next larger size should be used.

Small Motorboats To determine the minimum cross-sectional area of the cowls and ducts of motorboats having small engine and/or fuel tank compartments, see **Table 3-1,** which is based on *net* compartment volume (as previously defined).

Cruisers and Large Boats For most cruisers and other large motorboats, see **Table 3-2,** which is based on the craft's beam; this is a practical guide for determination of the minimum size of ducts and cowls.

Ducting Materials

For safety and long life, ducts should be made of nonferrous, galvanized ferrous, or sturdy high-temperature resistant nonmetallic materials. Ducts should be routed clear of, and protected from, contact with hot engine surfaces.

VENTILATION REQUIREMENTS FOR SMALL BOATS

Net Volume (cu. ft.)	Total Cowl Area (sq. in.)	Minimum Inside Diameter for Each Duct (inches)	
		One-Intake and One-Exhaust System	Two-Intake and Two-Exhaust System
Up to 8	3	2	—
10	4	2¼	—
12	5	2½	—
14	6	2¾	—
17	7	3	—
20	8	3¼	2½
23	10	3½	2½
27	11	3¾	3
30	13	4	3
35	14	4¼	3
39	16	4½	3
43	19	4¾	3
48	20	5	3

Note: 1 cu. ft. = 0.028 cu. m; 1 inch = 2.54 cm; 1 cu in. = 6.45 cu. cm

Table 3-1 Ventilation requirements for small boats.

VENTILATION REQUIREMENTS FOR LARGE POWERBOATS

Two-Intake and Two-Exhaust System

Vessel Beam (feet)	Minimum Inside Diameter for Each Duct (inches)	Cowl Area (sq. in.)
7	3	7.0
8	3¼	8.0
9	3½	9.6
10	3½	9.6
11	3¾	11.0
12	4	12.5
13	4¼	14.2
14	4¼	14.2
15	4½	15.9
16	4½	15.9
17	4½	17.7
18	5	19.6
19	5	19.6

Note: 1 cu. ft. = 0.028 cu. m; 1 inch = 2.54 cm; 1 cu in. = 6.45 cu. cm

Table 3-2 Ventilation requirements for large powerboats.

Positioning of Cowls

Intake cowls will normally face forward in an area of free airflow underway, and the exhaust cowl will face aft so that a suction effect can be expected.

The two cowls, or sets of cowls, should be located with respect to each other, horizontally and/or vertically, so as to prevent return of fumes removed from any space back into the same or any other space. Intake cowls should be positioned to avoid picking up vapors from fueling operations.

Air for Carburetors

Openings into the engine compartments for entry of air for the carburetor are in addition to requirements of the ventilation system.

Requirements for Boats

On boats built after 31 July 1980, each compartment having a permanently installed gasoline engine with a cranking motor for remote starting must be ventilated by a powered exhaust blower system unless it is "open construction" as defined above. Each exhaust blower, or combination of blowers, must be rated at an airflow capacity not less than a value computed by formulas based on the net volume of the engine compartment plus other compartments open thereto.

The engine compartment—and other compartments open to it where the aggregate area of openings exceeds two percent of the area between the compartments—must *also* have a natural ventilation system.

There must be a *warning label* as close as practicable to the ignition switch that advises of the danger of gasoline vapors and the need to run the exhaust blower for at least *four minutes* and then check the engine compartment for fuel vapors *before* starting the engine.

Natural ventilation systems are also required for any compartment containing both a permanently installed fuel tank and any electrical component that is not "ignition protected" in accordance with existing Coast Guard electrical standards for boats; or a compartment that contains a fuel tank that vents into that compartment (highly unlikely); or one having a nonmetallic fuel tank that exceeds a specified permeability rate. The USCG regulations specify the required cross-sectional area of ducts for natural ventilation based on compartment net volume, and how ducts shall be installed.

The regulations above concern the manufacturer of the boat, but there is also a requirement placed on the operator that these ventilation systems be operable any time the boat is in use. Because such systems are so desirable, it is recommended that they be installed on *any* gasoline-powered motorboat or auxiliary; see also fuel vapor detectors in Chapter 11, page 386.

Requirements for Older Boats
On boats built before 1 August 1980, only natural ventilation is required—one intake cowl and duct extending from the atmosphere to a point at least midway to the bilge or below the carburetor; there must also be at least one exhaust cowl and duct extending from the atmosphere to the lower portion of the bilge (but not so low as to become blocked by normal bilge water levels). For such boats, there is no federal requirement as to the minimum duct size, but Coast Guard policy is that the smallest acceptable size is two inches for all boats.

If the boat is equipped with a bilge blower, its duct could serve as the exhaust duct for natural ventilation as well, this is provided the size of the duct is large enough and the flow of air is not obstructed by the fan blades. A separate duct is also acceptable.

Diesel-Powered Boats
Diesel fuel does not come within the Coast Guard's definition of a "volatile" fuel, and thus bilge ventilation legal requirements are not applicable. It is, however, a sensible step to provide essentially the same ventilation system for your boat even if it is diesel-powered, particularly because diesel engines require a high volume of air for efficient combustion. Diesel fuel does not explode, but it does burn; a broken fuel line can cause a fire that could result in the total loss of your boat.

Visual Distress Signals
All boats of any type 16 feet or more in length, and all craft of any size carrying six or fewer passen-gers for hire, must be equipped with approved VISUAL DISRESS SIGNALS (VDS) at all times when operating on coastal waters. Exempted from this requirement are boats engaged in regattas or racing, manually propelled boats, and sailboats less then 26 feet (7.9 m) in length of completely open construction and not equipped with propulsion machinery.

There are two types, nonpyrotechnic such, as a special orange flag or an approved signaling light, and pyrotechnic, such as a red flare or smoke signal. If pyrotechnics are selected there must be three such signals available to satisfy the requirement. If nonpyrotechnics are chosen, one day and one night signal will suffice. Thus the VDS requirement may be met by carrying three daytime and three night pyrotechnic signals, or by carrying a special daytime flag and a nighttime special flashing light. Boats less than 16 feet in length—with the exceptions noted above—must carry distress signals when operating at night. Day signals are not required on any of these boats, though it would be prudent to do so.

Coastal waters are defined as the U.S. waters of the Great Lakes and the territorial seas (now out to 24 miles from shore) plus connected waters where any entrance exceeds two nautical miles between opposite shorelines to the first point inward where the distance between shorelines narrows to less than two miles (see Chapter 2, page 58, for more on these definitions). Shorelines of islands or points of land within a waterway are considered in determining the distance between opposite shorelines.

Types of Visual Distress Signals
Visual distress signals are classified for day (D) or night (N) use, or for both (D/N). To meet the requirements, a boat must have an orange flag with special square-and-disc markings in black (D) and an S-O-S electric light (N): *or* three hand-held or floating orange smoke signals, (D) plus three flares (N); *or* three red flares of hand-held, meteor, or parachute type (D/N). Each signal must be legibly marked with a Coast Guard approval number or certification statement. It must be serviceable and not past any expiration

Figure 3-16 Approved visual distress signals include hand-held flares, meteors and parachute flares, smoke signals, and others suitable for day or night use, or both.

date; see **Figure 3-16.** (Pyrotechnic signals will have an expiration date 42 months after manufacture.) Combinations of various flare types and smoke signals are acceptable. (The flares must carry an approval; older launchers may be used if still available.) In some states, a pistol launcher for flares may be considered a firearm and subject to licensing and other restrictions; check your local authorities before purchasing such a device. Flares marked "Not Approved for Use on Recreational Boats" are for use only on commercial craft.

All visual distress signals must be stowed so as to be "readily available."

The legal requirements are a *minimum;* prudent skippers will carry additional and more robust signals to meet their particular needs.

Visual distress signals must not be displayed on the water except where assistance is needed because of *immediate or potential danger to the persons on board.* This allows tests and demonstrations to be made from the shore, but good judgment should be used to avoid false alarms—if there is any likelihood of reports being made to the local Coast Guard unit notify them by telephone or radio of your intended actions.

The use of pyrotechnic signals is not without hazard from the flame and hot dripping ash and slag. Hand-held flares must be held over the side and in such a way that hot slag will not drip on your hand or the deck or side of your boat. Pistol-

launch flares should be fired downwind and at an angle of roughly 60° above the horizon, higher in stronger winds but never directly upward. In a distress situation do not waste signals by setting them off when no other vessel is within sight.

If you are using a pistol-type launcher, check to make sure that flares that you have now or purchase later will fit—there have been small changes in the length of some flares, and not all will fit in all launchers.

Marine Sanitation Devices

The regulatory requirements for boat to have a marine sanitation device (MSD) were discussed in Chapter 2, see page 84. This section will cover the various types of MSDs that must be installed to meet those requirements, and the level of treatment that they provide.

Type I & Type II MSDs

Type I and Type II marine sanitation devices are described in Coast Guard regulations as "flow-through" devices; the difference between the types is the level of treatment; see **Figure 3-17.**

The most common form is a MACERATOR-CHLORINATOR that takes the discharge of a marine toilet, grinds up the solids to fine particles, treats the resultant waste with a disinfectant, and pumps the treated sewage overboard. Many MSDs dispense disinfectant from prefilled reservoirs.

Figure 3-17 Type I Marine Sanitation Devices are available that more than meet the EPA and Coast Guard requirements for overboard discharge of human wastes. This device first disinfects sewage and then uses a macerator to grind it so that there are no visible floating solids.

Others make their own disinfectant by using electricity to break down seawater, using the dissolved salt (NaCl, sodium chloride) to produce chlorine, the active disinfectant. In fresh or brackish waters, ordinary table salt may be placed in a dispenser to provide the necessary chemical.

A Type I MSD must be certified as being capable of discharging an overboard waste liquid that has a coliform bacterial count of not more than 1,000 per 100 milliliters of effluent. Most devices commonly installed on boats have a bacterial count much less than required, normally producing effluent with less than 10 coliform bacterial per 100 milliliter. This type MSD must also not discharge any "visible floating solids."

A Type II MSD must be certified to a level of a bacterial coliform count of not more than 200 per 100 milliliters, and total suspended solids of not more than 150 milligrams per liter. Few boats under 65 feet in length are equipped with this type.

A reminder: sewage, whether treated or not, cannot be discharged overboard in any designated "No Discharge Zone."

Type III MSDs

Type III marine sanitation devices are described in the regulations as "non-flow-through" devices; there are two subcategories of this type.

Type III-A MSDs are designed to treat the sewage and hold it for later disposal. Typically, this is a RECIRCULATING TOILET that is "charged" with a few gallons of water and special chemicals. An example of a fixed model of this is the toilet used on passenger aircraft; boats usually use a portable model, such as a "Porta-Potti," with this device being limited to smaller craft. The treated water, plus the waste, is recirculated each time the toilet is used. The toilet can normally be used for several days before pump-out is necessary. This type also includes reduced-flush devices that ultimately evaporate and incinerate the waste to a sterile sludge or ash.

Type III-B MSDs are collection, holding, and transfer systems consisting of drain piping, HOLDING TANKS, pumps, valves, connectors, and other equipment used to collect and hold shipboard sewage waste for subsequent transfer to a shore sewage system, sewage barge, or for discharge overboard in *unrestricted* waters. Holding tanks are the common form of MSD found on boats that are not fitted with a Type I device. Tanks may be rigid in various shapes or flexible; they should be sized to fit the size and use of the boat. An indicator and/or warning system can be used with a holding tank to alert the skipper to an impending need for pump-out. Chemicals can be added to reduce any offensive odors, but these do not qualify as disinfecting the waste. Obviously, holding tanks cannot be pumped overboard in any "No Discharge Zone."

Combination Systems

An excellent solution to the boat sewage disposal problem is a combination of a Type I MSD followed by a holding tank. This allows you to treat the waste before it goes to the holding tank, reducing the possibility of unpleasant odors, and still allowing you to pump overboard where such action is legal.

Other Required Equipment

Additional items of equipment required by law or Coast Guard regulations to be on board some or all boats include a whistle, a bell, navigation lights, and, in some instances, one or more day shapes. As with other equipment, these devices are graduated with the size of the vessel, and may vary with the waters on which they are used.

These requirements are covered in the Inland and International Navigation Rules; see Chapters 4 and 5.

Federal requirements for recreational boats are summarized in **Table 3-3.**

State & Local Requirements

Boaters may expect to have to comply with additional requirements in many states, and possibly additional ones in some local jurisdictions. These are too diverse to be covered in this book, but each skipper should be aware of the possible need for additional legally required equipment in both home waters and other cruising areas.

U.S. COAST GUARD MINIMUM REQUIRED SAFETY EQUIPMENT

Equipment	Class A Less than 16 feet (4.9 m)	Class 1 16 feet to less than 26 feet (4.9-7.9 m)	Class 2 26 feet to less than 40 feet (7.9-12.2 m)	Class 3 40 feet to not more than 65 feet (12.2-19.8 m)
Personal flotation devices*	One Type I, II, III or V** device for each person (also applies to canoes and kayaks of any length).	One Type I, II, III or V** PFD for each person on board or being towed on water skis, etc., plus one Type IV*** PFD available to be thrown.	One Type I, II, III or V** PFD for each person on board or being towed on water skis, etc., plus one Type IV available to be thrown.	
Fire extinguishers* When no fixed fire extinguishing system is installed in machinery space(s)	At least one B-I class approved hand-portable fire extinguisher. Not required on outboard motorboats less than 26 feet (7.9 m) in length and not carrying passengers for hire if the construction of such motorboats will not permit the entrapment of flammable gases or vapors.		At least two B-I class approved hand-portable fire extinguishers, or at least one B-II class approved hand-portable fire extinguisher.	At least three B-I class approved hand-portable fire extinguishers, or at least one B-I class plus one B-II class approved hand portable extinguisher.
When fixed fire extinguishing system is installed in machinery space(s)	None		At least one B-I class approved hand-portable fire extinguisher.	At least two B-I class approved hand-portable fire extinguishers, or at least one B-II approved unit.
Ventilation	Boat operator is responsible for keeping the ventilation systems in operating condition, making sure openings are free of obstructions, ducts are not blocked or torn, blowers are operating properly and worn out components are replaced with equivalent equipment.			
Whistle or other sound signaling device	Boats up to 12 meters (39.4 ft.), any device capable of making an efficient sound signal.*			Boats 12 to 20 meters (39.4-65.6 ft.) device meeting technical specifications of Navigation Rules, audible 1/2 mile.
Bell	None required if boat equipped with device capable of making an"efficient sound signal."			Boats 12 to 20 meters (39.4-65.6 ft.): bell with a mouth diameter of not less than 200 millimeters (7.9 in.).
Backfire flame arrester**** (also called flame arrester)	Every gasoline engine installed in a motorboat after April 25, 1940, except outboard motors, must be equipped with an acceptable means of backfire flame control. Sailboats equipped with a motor are considered "motorboats."			
Visual distress signals*	All vessels used on coastal waters, the Great Lakes, territorial seas and those waters connected directly to them, up to a point where a body of water is less than two miles wide, must be equipped with visual distress signals. Vessels owned in the U.S. operating on the high seas must be equipped with visual distress signals. The following vessels are not required to carry day signals, but must carry night signals when operating from sunset to sunrise: • Recreational boats less than 16 feet (4.9 m) in length. • Boats participating in organized events such as races, regattas or marine parades. • Open sailboats less than 26 feet (7.9 m) in length not equipped with propulsion machinery. • Manually propelled boats.			
Navigation lights	Must comply with International or Inland Navigation Rules			

* Must be USCG-approved.
**Type V must be worn (except within enclosed space) to qualify as required safety equipment.
***Type IV not required for canoes or kayaks greater than 16 feet (4.9 m) in length.
**** Must be USCG-approved or comply with SAE-J 1928 or UL-1111 standards and be so marked.

Table 3-3 *In addition to the federal equipment carriage requirements for recreational craft summarized above, the owner/operator may be required to comply with additional regulations specific to the state or area in which the boat is being operated.*

Equipment for Commercial Craft

Boats (including sailing and nonself-propelled vessels) used for carrying six or fewer passengers for hire (paying passengers), or for commercial fishing, are "commercial uninspected vessels" subject to the Motorboat Act of 1940 and Coast Guard regulations issued under the authority of that Act.

All nonrecreational craft less than 40 feet (12.2 m) in length, *not* carrying passengers for hire, such as commercial fishing boats, must have on board at least one life preserver, buoyant vest, or special purpose water safety buoyant device of a suitable size for each person on board. "Suitable size" means that sufficient children's lifesaving devices (medium or small, as appropriate) must be carried in addition to adult sizes.

All vessels carrying passengers for hire (six or fewer), and all other vessels subject to the MBA/40 which are over 40 feet (12.2 m) in length, must have at least one life preserver of a suitable size for each person on board.

Each vessel 26 or more feet (7.9 m) in length must also carry at least one life ring buoy in addition to the life preservers or other wearable lifesaving devices required.

All lifesaving equipment must be in serviceable condition; wearable devices must be readily accessible and devices to be thrown must be immediately available.

More than Six Passengers

Vessels carrying more than six passengers for hire are subject to a separate Act and set of Coast Guard regulations (see Chapter 2, page 81). These vessels must be "inspected" and certified as being equipped with the specified minimum equipment such as lifesaving gear and fire extinguishers.

ADDITIONAL EQUIPMENT FOR SAFETY

Any newcomer to boating might think that he would be fully set to go if he ordered his new craft with "all equipment required by federal and state regulations." Actually, such is far from the real situation. Federal requirements stop too soon; state requirements—lacking uniformity—are not much help.

The list of items beyond federal requirements that you should have for safe boating is amazingly long. It is based on common sense and on the experience of many skippers over many years. Not every item will be required on every boat— the list must be tailored to your particular craft and boating activities—but you should at least consider each item discussed below.

Possible Liability

Another factor necessitating the carrying of equipment beyond the legal minimums is the possibility of LIABILITY in case of an accident. It is a mistake to think that the boating equipment specified by the government is the only equipment that you are *legally* bound to have aboard. Consider as well the far-reaching rules of NEGLIGENCE, as developed over the years in court cases. Technically, negligence is the unintentional breach of a legal duty to exercise a reasonable standard of care, thereby causing damage to someone. More simply stated, it is the failure to conduct oneself as a *reasonable* person would have under the circumstances. If, for example, a reasonable person would have carried charts, you may be liable to an injured party for an accident arising out of not having them available on board. If a reasonable person would have had an anchor, compass, lines, tools, and spare parts, etc., you may be held liable for not having them when needed. It is no defense to argue that no regulations require you to carry them.

Personal Flotation Devices

Regulations set the *minimum* number and type of PFD for your boat, but sound judgment often requires something better. Tests have shown that a Type II PFD may not keep your head sufficiently clear of the water in heavy seas—it's better to have a Type I! If you ever expect to have multiple guests on board, make sure that you have enough for each person; if children might be involved, have several of the various sizes on your boat; see **Figure 3-18.**

Figure 3-18 Children do not float well in a face-up position and tend to panic easily. Type II PFDs are best for small children; an infant vest should have built-in rollover and head-support features.

The legal requirement is for *one* throwable device. You should consider whether one is enough, and maybe there should be one each of two or more different types, such as a buoyant cushion and a small life ring with a length of light line attached. This latter device can be used to either rescue a person in the water or to float a line over to a disabled boat that cannot be approached too closely because of shoal water, fire, or other emergency condition.

PFD Lights & Reflective Material

In order to better locate persons in the water at night, boats in *commercial* operation on certain waters must now carry personal flotation devices that are equipped with a light and reflective material—on both front and back sides—that will show up in the beam of a searchlight. Although such PFDs are not required for recreational boats, it's a good idea for increased safety! Kits are available for adding reflective material to existing PFDs. A "water light" is a device that automatically comes on when it comes into contact with water; this makes a ring or horseshoe buoy much easier to locate at night; see **Figure 3-19.**

A simple whistle on a cord is a valuable aid in nighttime rescues.

Life Rafts

Boaters who use colder northern waters, or cruise more than a few miles offshore in any waters,

should consider the purchase of a life raft to supplement other lifesaving gear; they are not required by the Coast Guard. Essential features include: redundancy in buoyancy tubes, stowage on deck, gas cylinder inflation, water ballast or pockets, insulated floor, a canopy, boarding ladder and lifelines, a painter (to secure the raft to your boat so that it will not drift away), locator lights, adequate survival equipment and first-aid kit, a rainwater collector, a sea anchor or drogue, and an Emergency Position Indicating Radiobeacon (EPIRB). The raft should be able to accommodate the largest number of persons expected to be carried while offshore; more than one raft may be needed; see **Figure 3-20.**

It is important to note that life rafts are categorized by the waters on which they are intended to be used. Inshore rafts are little more than buoyant platforms that will permit survivors of a sinking vessel to get out of the water. Coastal rafts should

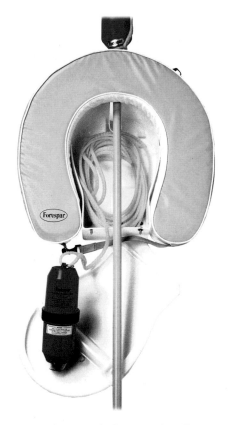

Figure 3-19 A "water light" is not legally required, but one, such as shown here to the left of a horseshoe buoy, will greatly increase the possibility of locating a man-overboard at night.

Figure 3-20 Any skipper cruising offshore, especially in northern waters, should consider equipping his boat with a life raft. These are available in models for coastal cruising and distant voyaging. Life rafts must be maintained and periodically inspected in accordance with the manufacturer's specifications.

only be used in waters where rescue can be reasonably expected in one day, typically within 20 miles (VHF radio range) from shore—they lack features for extended use. Offshore rafts extend this period to four to five days—they have canopies and multiple buoyancy tubes. Rafts that meet the international requirements for ships (SOLAS—Safety of Life at Sea Convention) are the highest category—these rafts are designed for survival of up to 30 days and have the most support features. Some rafts are not Coast Guard-approved, but may be suitable for limited boating activities; some are approved, but only for certain categories of vessels, others have full approval.

A four-person life raft is one rated to support four adults while it is half-inflated. It does not mean comfortable space for four persons; SOLAS/USCG standards require only four square feet per person, and unapproved rafts may provide even less. On the other hand, a raft loaded to capacity may be more stable and will be warmer in cold weather.

Even with today's advanced search and location techniques, your predicament and location may not be known to rescue authorities. The latest models of EPIRBs are excellent, but not

perfect. Weather may delay search and rescue for many hours. If you get into a life raft in an emergency, you should be prepared to spend an indeterminate length of time there.

Life rafts are cumbersome, expensive, and require costly annual inspections. But if you boat in any circumstances where a collision, fire, or sudden uncontrollable leak might place you and your crew in the water—away from other boats that might provide assistance, and drifting farther from shore—then you must have one. A life raft is not intended for use until an emergency occurs—but then it *must* work! It is of the utmost importance that life rafts are properly stowed, and that they are serviced periodically at an authorized facility.

Lifelines, Safety Nets & Harnesses

Make sure that everyone on board follows the traditional mariner's advice: "One hand for yourself and one for the boat." No matter how seasoned your sea legs, when the weather is rough, keep your center of gravity low whenever you move about the boat. (Further ensure stability by grasping handholds, for example.)

On sailboats, lifelines serve as boundaries for the deck, particularly when children or pets are aboard. Many people reinforce those boundaries by rigging nylon netting along the lifelines (see **Figure 3-21**), or between the hulls of catamarans

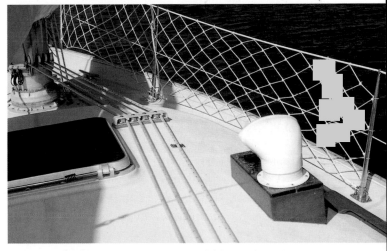

Figure 3-21 Netting rigged along the lifelines of a sailboat is an excellent safeguard against children or pets falling overboard.

Figure 3-22 A safety harness is further insurance against falls overboard, and enables you to know where your child is at all times on board a boat.

or trimarans. When small children are adventurous, however, or when the boat is pitching, rolling or heeling, safety harnesses provide additional safety insurance; see **Figure 3-22.**

In addition to ensuring that you know a child's whereabouts at all times, a safety harness is essential in other conditions for boaters of all ages. It will keep you aboard even if you fall, and should be worn anytime you are sailing alone, whenever any crew member is on deck in heavy weather, when going on deck alone at night while underway, when going aloft, or whenever you feel there is a danger that you might lose your footing.

Put on the safety harness before going on deck, and remember that a safety harness is only as strong as its attachment point. The best attachment point is a JACKLINE, or jackwire—a bow-to-stern trolley-like wire on a sailboat deck, onto which safety harness tethers are securely clipped. In the absence of a jackline, a harness should be hooked to the windward side of the boat—only onto a sturdy through-bolted fitting (a cleat, winch, or stay, for example); the mast; or stainless steel eyes of a toe rail or a grab rail. Keep in mind

that lifelines and stanchions cannot be relied upon to withstand a great deal of force; therefore, they are unsuitable attachment points.

When shopping for safety harnesses, choose only models designed for use on board a boat, with reinforced nylon webbing, stainless steel hardware, and a tested strength of at least 3,000 pounds. The harness should fasten at the chest, with a catch that responds only to firm, positive action for release; the USCG recommends quick-release-under-load catches and buckles. A harness should have a stainless steel snap hook at the end of a tether no longer than 6 feet. If you attach a sailing knife to the harness, in a sheath and with a lanyard, you will always have a tool handy.

Each safety harness aboard your boat should be adjusted to fit the person who will wear it, then labeled to ensure quick identification when needed in an emergency. Stow your harnesses in

DON'T FORGET A PFD FOR YOUR PET

Although probably the best action is to leave pet dogs and cats ashore, some skippers just can't bring themselves to do that. If you have a pet on board, he should have his own life vest. This device will provide both additional flotation and a means of retrieval by hooking with a boat hook. The flotation device should be worn at all times when on board, including when your boat is docked. Even if your pet is a good swimmer, animals that jump or fall overboard often become confused and swim away from your boat rather than toward it; strong currents can carry a pet away from a boat that is anchored or on a mooring. In either of these situations, the life vest will keep your pet afloat until you can get to him. The "PFD" must be properly sized, and the animal must be gradually introduced to wearing it; a cat will probably be more resistant to wearing a life vest than a dog.

dry places and inspect them regularly for wear and tear, along with your other safety equipment.

Fire Extinguishers

As with other required equipment, the regulations call for a *very minimum* of fire extinguishers; it would increase your safety if you carried additional units. If your boat is of the type or use category that does not require carriage of a fire extinguisher, you should consider carrying at least one unit, and two are not too many.

Extinguishers should be located around the boat where they will be close at hand if needed. One should be close to the helm and another in the galley. On many craft, it is desirable to have one in the engine compartment. It would add to the safety of your boat if an extinguisher were located close to the skipper's bunk, where it could be grabbed quickly in the event of a nighttime emergency.

A fire extinguisher rated B-I by the Coast Guard can be as small as one that is rated 5-B, C by Underwriters Laboratories. The additional cost is minimal to upgrade to an extinguisher rated 10-B, C. Note that the Coast Guard requirement is for a "BC" extinguisher, designed for fighting fires involving flammable liquids and usable on fires related to electrical circuits. As discussed earlier, there are also Class A fires; those that might occur in a trash basket, upholstery, or bedding. An even better extinguisher, one rated 1-A; 10-B, C, at only a slight increase in cost, would add a capability to fight such fires of ordinary combustible materials.

Navigation Lights

The builder of your boat was required by the Coast Guard to install navigation lights that meet the minimum requirements of the Navigation Rules; see **Figure 3-23.** But perhaps you would want your craft seen at a greater distance when out boating at night. Have you ever tried to find out from how far away your boat could be seen and recognized for the type of vessel that it is? You might be surprised, and not pleasantly, at the results of such a test.

Figure 3-23 Make sure that your navigation lights fully meet the legal requirements, and then a bit more. Check that each can be seen through the required arc, and not beyond those limits. Check the lights on your boat from a distance, from shore or by going out on another boat.

On smaller boats, especially open craft of the runabout type, there is often a problem with the white forward or all-round light. It is often not high enough that it can be seen from ahead, being blocked by a top or even by the bodies of people on board. Make sure that such a light on your boat is mounted high enough, or if on a collapsible post, it can be raised high enough to be seen from any direction.

Visual Distress Signals

If you meet the VDS requirement by carrying three hand-held flares, you are "legal," but hardly safe. Even if you are careful to wait until you feel sure that there is someone within visible range, it is highly likely that you may use all your flares and still not be seen. Be safe, carry more than the legal minimum of hand-held flares, and consider having on board several red aerial flares that can be seen from a greater distance—or even better, red aerial parachute flares that will burn longer and be more likely to be seen than a meteor flare.

Lines & Anchors

Even the smallest rowboat or dinghy needs at least one length of line for making fast to a pier, or to a mooring or anchor; and a 40-footer (12.2 m) will need some six or eight dock lines—yet none are required by Coast Guard regulations. No sensible skipper would venture far from shore without an anchor—but again none are required items of equipment.

The number and length of dock lines will naturally vary with the size of the craft that they are carried on; see Chapter 6, page 194. A heaving line of light construction is desirable if your boat is large enough to need heavy mooring lines. The use of polypropylene line, or other material that is brightly colored and will float, is recommended for this purpose.

An anchor is a valuable safety item should the engine or steering fail and your boat be in danger of drifting or being blown into dangerous waters. Much more on anchors can be found in Chapter 9; see pages 317–323 and 328, for information on the types of anchors and the size that should be on your boat. All but the smallest craft should consider carrying more than one anchor.

Bilge Pumps

The list of required equipment does not include a bilge pump to move overboard water that comes in from rain, spray, or a leak in the hull. It has been said that there is no more effective "dewatering device" (to use a Coast Guard term) than a frightened boater with a bucket. Still, there is much safety achieved by having one or more electric bilge pumps, preferably backed up with an installed manual pump; see **Figure 3-24**. Bilge pump intakes should be fitted with a screen or filter to preclude any chance of becoming blocked by debris or loose objects in the bilge.

An electric bilge pump can be a hazard as well as a "boatsaver"—the trouble is SIPHONING if the bilgewater outlet ever becomes below the surface of the outside water. Bilge pumps are often installed so that the hose runs upward from the bilge pump, then makes a U-turn downward. To avoid an unsightly stain on the topsides, the outlet is usually just barely above the normal waterline. Should the craft ever sink further into the water, this outlet then is below the surface—a constant list or heeling could produce the same result. Siphoning is simply a backflow of water from outside the boat into the bilge—most undesirable. If there is an automatic switch for the bilge pump, water is first pumped out, and then siphoned back in—and the cycle repeats until the battery is dead. A check valve in the bilge pump output hose should prevent siphoning, but a better solution is a vented loop installed at the high point of the output hose.

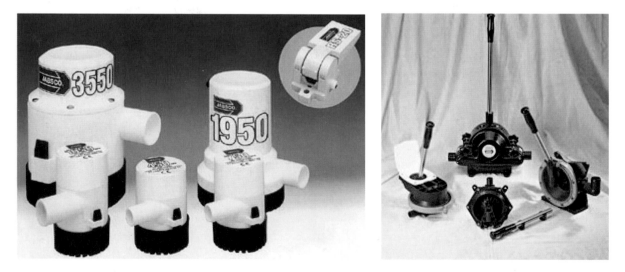

Figure 3-24 Small electric bilge pumps are suitable for most boats, but be aware of their limited pumping capacity. Every craft with such pumps should have a manual pump of adequate size to provide additional pumping capability and to back up the electric pump in case of electrical failure.

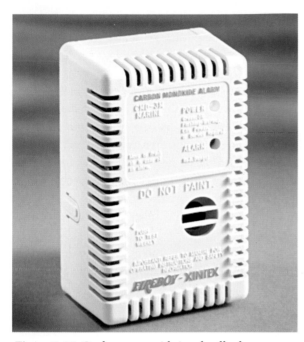

Figure 3-25 Carbon monoxide is a deadly threat on board any boat with gasoline engines for propulsion or generation of electricity, or open flame cooking and heating stoves. Passive chemical detectors indicate a dangerous condition by a change in color. Only active electronic detectors that can give an audible alarm should be used in sleeping areas.

A very useful device is an indicator at the helm position that will show when a bilge pump is operating; if the inflow from a leak is greater than the pump can handle, and you are not aware that the pump is running, you might have a major emergency situation develop without warning. There are also bilge water alarms independent of pumps than can provide a similar alert. Both of these devices should have a very bright light or an audible alarm (they can be connected to sound the boat's horn).

Smaller boats and dinghies should have a scoop-type bailer that can be bought ready-made or easily self-made by cutting down a gallon-size bleach bottle.

Carbon Monoxide Detectors

Every boat that has enclosed spaces and uses gasoline for propulsion or generation of electrical power should be—*must be*—equipped with detectors for carbon monoxide, (CO), gas. CO also results from the use of stoves, heaters and charcoal grills. This completely colorless, odorless gas is a killer, one that cannot be detected by a human no matter how alert he or she may be. It requires a chemical or electronic detector to provide a safe environment; see **Figure 3-25.** This should be a unit that is designed specifically for marine use; it is calibrated differently than those for home use.

Carbon monoxide poisoning can be accumulative—over time, even low levels of CO can have harmful effects. Electronic sensors can be designed to recognize such a condition and sound both a visual and an audible alarm. Because chemical detectors indicate the presence of CO only by a change in color—having no sound alarm—they should not be used for the protection of sleeping compartments. These are relatively inexpensive, but should be used only as supplemental detectors; they have an in-use life of one month, but a shelf life in a sealed container of several years. ABYC (American Boat & Yacht Council) standards prescribe CO detectors on all new boats with gasoline engines; if yours is an older craft at risk, buy and install units for the safety of your self and crew.

Additional information of carbon monoxide hazards will be found in Chapter 11.

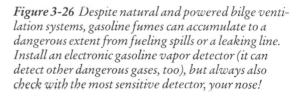

Figure 3-26 Despite natural and powered bilge ventilation systems, gasoline fumes can accumulate to a dangerous extent from fueling spills or a leaking line. Install an electronic gasoline vapor detector (it can detect other dangerous gases, too), but always also check with the most sensitive detector, your nose!

Gasoline Fume Detectors

The required natural and powered ventilation systems, and the use of ignition-protected electrical equipment, will provide a measure of protection from gasoline explosions and fires. An added measure of safety will come from the installation of a gasoline fume detector; see **Figure 3-26.** This will have one or more sensors in the engine and fuel tank compartments, with a display and alarm unit at the helm. Some models will additionally start the bilge blower(s); these do not interfere with normal manual control of blowers. Gasoline fume detectors will also give the alarm in case of leaks of cooking fuels and some other gasses such as hydrogen from batteries overcharging.

Compass

Although not required by the Coast Guard, a compass of adequate size is a definite safety addition to a boat of almost any size. Information on the selection, installation, and use of compasses can be found in Chapter 13.

Charts & Navigational Tools

Large ships are required by law to have official nautical charts on board, but for recreational boats this is left to the discretion of the operator. The conscientious skipper, however, will always have at hand the proper charts for the waters he is traveling on. These, together with the appropriate navigation tools, will do much to ensure the safety of his craft and those on board. Quite obviously, a boat should have a magnetic compass of a size appropriate to the size of the craft; see Chapter 13.

Electronic Equipment

There are a number of items of electronic equipment that are not required by regulations, but which can be placed in the "essential for safety" category. These include a depth sounder and radio for almost all boats, and radar for larger craft. These are covered in detail in Chapters 20 and 21.

Additional Operational Equipment

There are other items of equipment that are not required—and not directly related to the safety

of your boat—but which are necessary for its proper normal operation.

Fenders

An adequate number of fenders of a size appropriate to the size of the boat will prove useful in many different situations, such as normal docking or rafting up with another boat or boats; refer to **Figure 1-32.** One or two fender boards will often find use where a fender might not provide adequate protection to the boat's hull.

Boathook

A boathook will be found very useful in fending off when docking or coming alongside another craft, for placing lines over piles, picking up pennants of mooring buoys, and many other

Figure 3-27 A searchlight can be useful as an emergency signaling device and for nighttime operation. Do not aim it toward the helm of another vessel as it could temporarily blind the helmsman.

activities. Some models are designed to have at its outer end either a normal hook or a mesh net, useful for retrieval of items from the water.

Searchlights

A searchlight—mounted on larger boats, hand-held on smaller craft—can be useful, even necessary, for nighttime operation of your boat; it can also be used as an emergency signaling device; see **Figure 3-27.** A large multi-cell flashlight can serve these functions, but not so well as a searchlight.

Windshield Wiper

Although windshield wipers may seem like minor equipment, they are highly valuable in rainy or misty conditions. Wipers may be operated by hand or electric motors. The best choice of wiper is a sturdy commercial model used by tugboats and commercial fishermen.

A "clear view" screen is an effective, but expensive, alternative. This consists of a circular piece of glass spun at high speed by an electric motor; water is thrown off by centrifugal action.

There are also chemical products that when rubbed onto a windshield cause water to bead up and quickly run down the glass.

Lead Line

A simple hand-held lead line is valuable as a backup to an electronic depth sounder; see **Figure 3-28.** It is also useful when you have to probe around a stranded boat, either from on deck or by going out in a dinghy, to locate deeper water. A pole or boathook marked with depth indications at one-foot intervals can serve a similar function in shallower waters; you can add a specially colored mark for the boat's draft. Many lead weights used for this purpose have a hollowed-out space at the bottom in which can be placed wax or thick grease to bring up a sample of the bottom material, such as sand, mud, shale, etc.

First Aid Kit

A first aid kit should be on board every craft except the very smallest. The extent of its contents will be governed by the distance—actually measured in time—that your boating activities will

take you from shoreside medical assistance. Additional information on first aid kits can be found in Chapter 11.

Emergency Drinking Water

Every cruising boat, especially those that travel to relatively remote areas, should carry an emergency supply of potable water. This will be very valuable should the water pressure pumping system fail, or if a leak should drain the supply tank. (If your supply is contained in two or more tanks, never have more than one tank on line at any given time so that an undetected leak will not cause the loss of the total supply.)

A life raft should, of course, have cans of drinking water in its emergency kit, but there should also be a small supply on board your dinghy in case you should ever get stranded with a failed motor.

Supplies of emergency drinking water should be dated when put on board and periodically

Figure 3-28 Considered "old-fashioned" by some, a lead line is handy as a backup to an electronic depth sounder and for determining the nature of the bottom. It can also be used for checking depths all around a boat that has gone aground.

Figure 3-29 Spare parts should include belts, filters, and cables and hoses, as well as items such as spark plugs. You should also carry at least one spare bulb for each navigation light, and several spare fuses of each size used on board.

replaced to ensure acceptable freshness when needed. There should also be a supply of distilled water on board for servicing storage batteries—this can also be used as drinking water if necessary.

Tools, Spare Parts & Consumable Supplies

The list of tools, spare parts and consumable supplies is highly individualized by the size and type of the boat, the area and nature of its use, and the capabilities of its skipper and crew; see **Figure 3-29.** All that can be pointed out here is the vital need for careful study and list making.

EQUIPMENT FOR CONVENIENCE & COMFORT

Many, but certainly not all, of the items of EQUIPMENT FOR CONVENIENCE & COMFORT fall into the electronic or electrical categories. These items are covered more fully in Chapters 19, 20, and 21; these include navigational aids such as radio transceivers, depth sounders, radar, and sophisticated positioning equipment, such as GPS and Loran C receivers, and course plotters. Speedometers and logs will provide speed and distance information that will assist in piloting. An automatic steering mechanism—usually called an "autopilot"—adds greatly to the convenience and comfort of cruising. Loudhailers and intercom systems

increase the convenience of operating or living on board larger boats. Twin-engine vessels will benefit from engine synchronization indicators, and benefit even more from equipment that will match the engine speeds automatically.

Electrical equipment items include pressure freshwater systems, water heaters, electric stoves and microwave ovens, electrical refrigeration, showers with drain pumps, plus heating and/or air-conditioning equipment.

An anchor windlass on the foredeck will remove a major part of the physical labor involved in "getting the hook up." An electric anchor windlass is seen in **Figure 1-30,** just forward of the sampson post.

Although not required on diesel-powered craft, powered exhaust blowers can serve a very useful function after a day's run. All engines, especially diesels, become hot when operating and radiate heat into the boat's interior. This heat is reduced somewhat while the engine is running by the flow of cooling water, but when it has been shut down for the day, and no water is circulating, engine compartments and the boat in general can become very hot. Running an exhaust system for 10 to 15 minutes will remove this unwanted heat from the interior of the boat, increasing comfort and lightening the load on an air-conditioning system if one is on board.

All of the above equipment requires increased electrical power from the boat's system, either AC or DC. Auxiliary generating plants will permit the use of "shore-type" heavy-drain equipment underway or at anchor; see **Figure 3-30**. Inverters—converting DC battery power to AC—are very useful items that permit the operation of moderate-drain AC equipment, such as TVs, without the noise of running a gasoline or diesel engine-driven generator. Battery chargers will supply the needed DC power without operation of the main engine if AC power is available; these will keep the boat's storage batteries at full charge when in port.

Outside the electrical-electronic field, equipment items for convenience and comfort are numerous and varied. Many skippers will want to have a boarding/swimming ladder for ease in going over the side and returning. A swim platform across the stern of medium-size and larger boats is a great convenience for swimming or using a dinghy. The dinghy itself, perhaps with sails or a small outboard motor, may well be classed as an item of convenience equipment.

Freshwater-making equipment will often add immeasurably to a boat's cruising endurance. Stabilizers are now available for medium and larger motor yachts to eliminate much of the rolling from offshore cruising. Bow (and stern) thrusters will greatly assist in the docking of larger craft.

Weather instruments—barometer, thermometer, anemometer, and perhaps a hygrometer for measuring the relative humidity—will add to the interest of boating. With study and practice, they can add to the safety, too, of a boat and its crew. A recording barograph will provide interesting permanent records of atmospheric pressure, and thus weather, changes.

The spare parts inventory of a boat can be expanded beyond the limits of necessity into the area of convenience. Carrying spare propellers,

Figure 3-30 An auxiliary generating plant can provide a boat with "shore-type" electrical power underway or at anchor. This will allow the operation of many electrical appliances that otherwise could not be used on board.

and even shafts, can often greatly reduce delays at a strange port away from home if these major components should become damaged. These may be beyond the capability of the crew to install, but their ready availability can often reduce repair times from days to hours.

Diving gear—either of the simple mask-and-snorkel style or the more complex scuba type—can make boating in many areas more interesting, and can at times be of real value in making underwater inspections and repairs. "Wet suits" may be required for colder water areas.

Boating Insurance

Marine insurance can be bought to cover loss or damage to the boat or its equipment, protect against liability for personal injury or property damage, provide medical payments in case of injury, and cover transportation of the boat while on land. Consult a good agent. Better yet, talk to two or three agents for quotations.

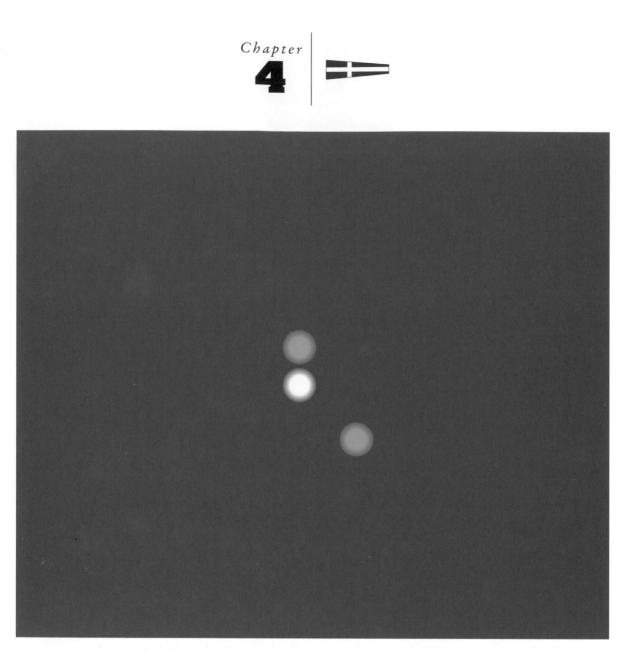

Navigation Rules
Lights & Day Shapes

*Navigation Lights & Day Shapes Required by the U.S. Inland Navigation
Rules for Vessels of All Types • The International Navigation Rules &
How They Differ From Those for U.S. Inland Waters*

The NAVIGATION RULES, often referred to unofficially as the RULES OF THE ROAD, are sets of statutory requirements enacted by Congress to promote the safety of navigation. The Rules consist of requirements for navigation lights and day shapes that are discussed in this chapter. They also include steering and sailing rules, sound signals for both good and restricted visibility, and distress signals, all covered in Chapter 5.

There are different sets of Rules for international and inland waters, with some local variations in the latter. The first International Rules of the Road were established in 1889; the most recent ones, titled the International Regulations for Preventing Collisions at Sea, were adopted in 1972. These are called the "72 COLREGS" by the U.S. Coast Guard. There are also different requirements for small and large vessels. References generally apply to all boats of any size, unless specific sizes of vessels are stated to have differing requirements.

The 1980 U.S. Inland Rules
The 1972 International Rules were unique for the U.S., because for the first time they had the status of an international *treaty*; previous sets of International Rules had the status of an international *agreement*. A treaty is more binding on a country, offering less flexibility and requiring stricter compliance with its terms. A key provision of the 1972 International Rules was the requirement in Rule 1(b) that any national rules for internal waters "shall conform as closely as possible" to the International Rules. The first

result of this requirement was that the U.S. Inland Rules no longer applied out to the offshore "boundary lines" but were effective only shoreward of new "demarcation lines" (see Chapter 2, pages 56–59.) The longer-term effect was the passage by Congress of the INLAND NAVIGATION RULES ACT OF 1980, which unified the previously separate Inland, Great Lakes, and Western Rivers Navigation Rules and their respective supplemental Pilot Rules.

State and local authorities may also issue regulations relating to boating, but these seldom relate to navigation lights and shapes.

Foreign Waters
Some foreign nations have their own set of navigation rules for their internal waters. In Canada, these are the *Collision Regulations: International Regulations for Preventing Collisions at Sea, 1972, with Canadian Modifications*. Many other countries have no national rules, and in these the COLREGS govern on their internal as well as on external waters.

Sequence of Consideration
Most recreational boaters in the United States use their craft on waters of rivers, lakes, bays, and sounds that are governed by the U.S. Inland Navigational Rules, and for this reason primary consideration will be given to these Rules, with the International Rules being presented only in terms of their *differences* from the Inland Rules. The International Rules apply, however, to all vessels once they clear the jetties or headlands at a harbor entrance. Indeed these International Rules even intrude into harbors, bays, inlets, rivers, etc., in some areas along the New England coast and in the lower Florida Keys. Check your coastal chart for the location of the demarcation lines.

Opposite Page: Figure 4-01 What do you make of this pattern of navigation lights? What action do you take? It's an underway fishing vessel engaged in trawling as viewed from its starboard side. You have to alter course and speed to avoid both the vessel and its nets.

The consideration of the Rules of the Road in this chapter and in Chapter 5 is not complete; it focuses on the points of greatest concern to boaters.

Numbered Rules

Both the U.S. Inland Rules and the International Rules consist of major subdivisions; Part A—General; Part B—Steering and Sailing Rules; Part C—Lights & Shapes; Part D—Sound & Light Signals; and Part E—Exemptions. (Part E provides specific temporary and permanent exemptions for existing vessels, to permit a smooth transition from the previous requirements for lights and sound signals. Most of these exemptions have now expired.)

Within both sets, the Rules are numbered from 1 to 38, with subparagraphs such as (a), (b), (c),

KNOW THE CURRENT NAVIGATION RULES

Each operator of a self-propelled vessel, power or sail, state registered or documented, 12 meters (39.4 ft) or more in length must carry on board and have available for ready reference a copy of the Inland Navigation Rules. [V, 88.05] Although the Pilot Rules do not explicitly say so, it is reasonable to interpret this requirement to mean an up-to-date copy of the Rules.

The official text of the U.S. Navigation Rules, as well as the International Rules, is contained in the Coast Guard publication entitled *Navigation Rules, International—Inland*. This small book carries the numerical designation of Commandant Instruction (abbreviated COMDTINST) M16672.2x, where "x" is a letter denoting the specific revised edition. This book also contains sections on the demarcation lines, penalty provisions, vessel bridge-to-bridge radiotelephone regulations, and a metric conversion table.

Changes in the Navigation Rules do not occur often, and when they do, they are usually minor in nature. Such changes are published in *Notices to Mariners* as they occur, and subsequently in a revised edition of the book. The suffix letter of the latest edition is "D" and with an edition date of March 25, 1999. Commercially published versions of this book may be available with changes promulgated subsequent to the date of the official version.

Copies of *Navigation Rules, International Inland—Inland* can be purchased from some local Sales Agents for nautical charts or by mail, phone, or via the Internet from the Government Printing Office (Stock Number 050-012-00407-2); phone 202-512-1800, fax 202-512-2250; http://bookstore.gpo.gov. Price varies from time to time; credit cards are accepted.

U.S. Department of Transportation
United States Coast Guard

NAVIGATION RULES
INTERNATIONAL—INLAND

and still lower levels indicated by (i), (ii), (iii), etc. Rules that are identical or nearly identical in both sets carry the same numbers. In order that parallel numbering can be continued in the Rules that follow, Rule 28 is omitted as it is from the U.S. Inland Rules.

Indication of References

Numbers and letters shown in brackets are references to the applicable Rule. References to Annexes are indicated by a Roman numeral, since the annexes to both sets are so designated; specific paragraphs and subparagraphs are noted by numbers and letters as appropriate. These references are shown to facilitate looking up the exact language of the Rules and Annexes in the Coast Guard publication *Navigation Rules, International—Inland* (for purchasing, see opposite page sidebar).

Why Navigation Lights & Day Shapes

On a vessel, NAVIGATION LIGHTS are lights shown that are of specified color (white, red, green, yellow, blue), arc, range of visibility, and location, as required by law and regulations. Their basic purpose is to prevent collision by alerting each vessel to the other's presence; see **Figure 4-01.** Lights also indicate the relative heading of one vessel as seen from the other, and give clues to its size, special characteristics, and/or current operations. Most important is its orientation with respect to your boat—a fact you must know to determine who has the right-of-way.

Navigation lights are sometimes referred to as RUNNING LIGHTS (those shown underway) and RIDING LIGHTS (those shown while at anchor or moored), but this terminology is unofficial and does not appear in the Navigation Rules.

In the language of the Navigation Rules, SHAPES are objects of specified shape, size, and placement on a vessel, as required by rules and regulations; all are black in color. These are often called "day shapes" as they serve some of the same purposes by day that navigation lights do by night; see **Figure 4-02.** There are no day shapes corresponding to the basic running lights as the relative aspect and motions of two vessels can be

Figure 4-02 During the day, when lights would be ineffective, shapes are used to indicate special vessel status. Other information that is provided at night by lights—type, size, relative bearing—can be determined by direct observation in daylight.

determined by observation. However, day shapes are used to indicate special situations, such as being anchored or engaged in fishing, and some conditions not detectable by eye, such as a sailboat with its sails up but with its engine also in use (such a craft is regarded as a power-driven vessel and is not entitled to any of a sailboat's right-of-way privileges merely because its sails are up).

Importance of Knowledge

Knowledge of navigation lights is important to a small boat skipper for two separate, but equally-important, reasons. First, he is legally responsible for his boat displaying lights of the proper color, intensity, locations, and visibility. Although as of November 2003 manufacturers must install only certified navigation lights on new boats, craft built before that date may or may not have lights that fully comply with the legal requirements. Thus a boat owner must know the requirements of the applicable Navigation Rules and check that his boat fully complies. If it doesn't comply, it is he—not the boatbuilder—who will be cited by the Coast Guard, and possibly fined. He must also know which lights to turn on (and which not to turn on) for various situations, and when.

Second, and perhaps even more important, he must depend on his knowledge of navigation lights for the safety of his boat when operating at night. Quite often, all the information available about another vessel is derived from interpreting its navigation lights. There are many lights and possible combinations; often a quick decision is needed, with no time to go "look it up in the book." *Know the lights* shown on both boats and ships. Even in the daytime and with good visibility, the day shapes carried by another vessel will give you information about its activities or limitations that you could not determine from simple observation. *Know day shapes* as well as lights.

THE U.S. INLAND NAVIGATION RULES

The U.S. Inland Navigational Rules are applicable shoreward of the demarcation lines separating inland and international waters that have been established at entrances to bays, sounds, rivers, inlets, etc.; see Chapter 2. They are *not applicable* to waters of harbors that are specifically designated as not covered, as along coasts with many small harbors (New England Coast especially), in the harbors of offshore landmasses, such as Block Island and Catalina Island, or in the lower Florida Keys.

The Inland Rules apply on the Western Rivers and the United States portions of the Great Lakes (see below, for definitions of "Geographic Limits"). They also apply to U.S. vessels on the Canadian portion of the Great Lakes, as long as there is no conflict with Canadian laws or regulations. [1(a)]

Basic Definitions
Rule 3 contains general definitions that are used throughout the U.S. Inland Navigation Rules.

Vessel This term applies to every size and description of water craft, including nondisplacement craft (air-cushion vehicles) and seaplanes, used or capable of being used as a means of transportation on water. The term "vessel" includes all

sizes without limit, from a dinghy or personal watercraft to a supertanker.

Power-Driven Vessel Any vessel propelled by machinery.

Sailing Vessel Any vessel propelled by sail, provided that propelling machinery, if fitted, is *not* being used. A sailboat or motorsailer using both sail and engine simultaneously is a *power-driven* vessel for purposes of the Rules of the Road.

Underway A vessel *not* at anchor, made fast to the shore, or aground. This term applies whether or not the vessel is moving ("making way") through the water.

Vessel Engaged in Fishing Any vessel fishing with nets, lines, trawls, or other fishing apparatus that restricts maneuverability. It does *not* include vessels with trolling lines, or drift fishing with hand rods and lines.

Vessel Not Under Command A vessel which through some exceptional circumstances is unable to maneuver as required by the Rules, and therefore is unable to keep out of the way of another vessel. Typically, this category would apply to a boat drifting with an inoperative engine or steering system.

Vessel Restricted in Its Ability to Maneuver A vessel which from the nature of its work is restricted in its ability to maneuver as required by the Rules, and therefore is unable to keep out of the way of another vessel. Typically, this term applies to dredges, vessels engaged in laying or repairing submarine cables or pipelines, and vessels engaged in a towing operation that severely restricts the towing vessel and its tow in their ability to deviate from their course.

Visibility Vessels are deemed to be "in sight of one another" only when one can be observed from the other. A vessel is not considered to be "in sight" if it is observed on radar, but cannot be seen visually.

Restricted Visibility Any condition in which visibility is reduced by fog, mist, falling snow, heavy rain, sandstorms, or any other similar cause.

Rule 3 also contains other definitions of interest to boaters. The term "SECRETARY" means the Secretary of the Department of the Federal Government in which the Coast Guard is operating. This is normally the Department of Homeland Security, but in time of war or national emergency, it could become the Department of the Navy by Presidential Executive Order.

Geographic Limits

Although separate sets of Rules of the Road for the Great Lakes and the Western Rivers no longer exist, these terms are still defined in the 1980 Inland Rules, because of certain exceptions and special provisions for specified waters.

The "GREAT LAKES" are defined as the lakes themselves, plus their connecting and tributary waters, including the Calumet River as far as the Thomas J. O'Brien Lock and Controlling Works (between mile 326 and 327), the Chicago River as far as the east side of the Ashland Avenue Bridge (between mile 321 and 322), and the St. Lawrence River as far east as the lower exit of the St. Lambert Lock.

"WESTERN RIVERS" means the Mississippi River, its tributaries, South Pass, and Southwest Pass to the demarcation lines for COLREGS waters; the Port Allen–Morgan City Alternate Route; that part of the Atchafalaya River above its junction with the Port Allen-Morgan City Alternate Route, including the Old River and the Red River; and the Tennessee-Tombigbee Waterway. Note that the term "Western Rivers" does *not* apply to rivers on the West Coast of the United States—such rivers as the Sacramento or the Columbia; the Inland Rules *are* in effect for all rivers emptying into the Pacific Ocean.

There are also portions of certain rivers and waterways that are "waters specified by the Secretary" as subject to different provisions of the Inland Rules. These are delineated in the Code of Federal Regulations, Title 33, and are listed in the Navigation Rules, International—Inland.

Units of Measurement

Except for distances in nautical miles, linear units of measurement in the 1980 U.S. Inland Rules are given in the metric system. Specifications such as the lengths of vessels or the spacing and height of lights will thus be in meters. The Coast Guard book on the Navigation Rules referred to above contains a conversion table for all metric values used in the Rules. In this chapter and Chapter 5, the metric values of the Rules are to be followed by customary (English) units in parentheses.

Navigation Lights

Navigation lights are discussed for various categories and sizes of vessels in the subsections below; they are also presented graphically on pages 124 to 128.

When Lights & Shapes Are Shown

Vessels are required to show the proper navigation lights from *sunset* to *sunrise* in all weather conditions, good and bad. During these times, no other lights that could be mistaken for lights specified in the Rules can be displayed, nor any lights that impair the visibility or distinctive character of navigation lights, or interfere with the keeping of a proper lookout. [20(a) and (b)]

The Inland Rules also state that navigation lights *must* be shown between sunrise and sunset in conditions of reduced visibility, and *may* be shown at any other time considered necessary. [20(c)]

Day shapes specified in the Rules must be displayed by day; although not specifically so stated, this has been taken to mean from sunrise to sunset. [20(d)]

Light Definitions

Masthead Light A white light placed over the fore-and-aft centerline of the vessel, showing an

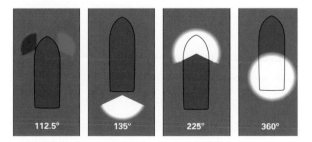

Figure 4-03 Each type of navigation light covers a specific arc of visibility. When these types and their arcs are understood, the orientation of the vessel becomes clear.

INTERPRETING RUNNING LIGHTS

The following pages are designed to help you sort out lights in the dark and guide you in identifying the boats associated with them. Refer to the legend at right: the colored text gives information on the International Rules where they differ from the Inland Rules (otherwise, they agree).

SAILING VESSEL LESS THAN 50 M IN LENGTH

None. (Masthead lights not used under sail alone.)

Separate red and green (or combination), 112.5°, vis. 2 mi.; if less than 12 m in length, vs. 1 mi.

White, 135°, vis. 2 mi.

R   Optional addition—two all-round lights at or near top of mast, red-over green separated by at least 1 m, vis. 2 mi.

POWER-DRIVEN VESSEL AT LEAST 12 M BUT LESS THAN 20 M IN LENGTH (AND VESSEL ENGAGED IN SPORTFISHING, TROLLING, OR DRIFT FISHING)

White, 225°, vis. 3 mi, at least 2.5 m above gunwale.

Separate red and green, 112.5°, vis. 2 mi, at least 1 m below masthead light.

White, 135°, vis. 2 mi.

R   After masthead light not required.

POWER-DRIVEN VESSEL LESS THAN 12 M IN LENGTH (AND VESSEL ENGAGED IN SPORTFISHING, TROLLING OR DRIFT FISHING)

White, 225°, vis 2 mi, may be less than 2.5 m above gunwale, but at lea m above sidelights.

Separate red and green (or combination), 112.5°, vis. 1 mi, at least 1 m below masthead light.

White, 135°, vis. 2 mi.

R   May be off center if necessary; may show only all-round white light, vis 2 mi, and sidelights.
Same. Less than 7 m and less than 7 kt max. speed, need have only all-round white light, and may have sidelights, if practicable.

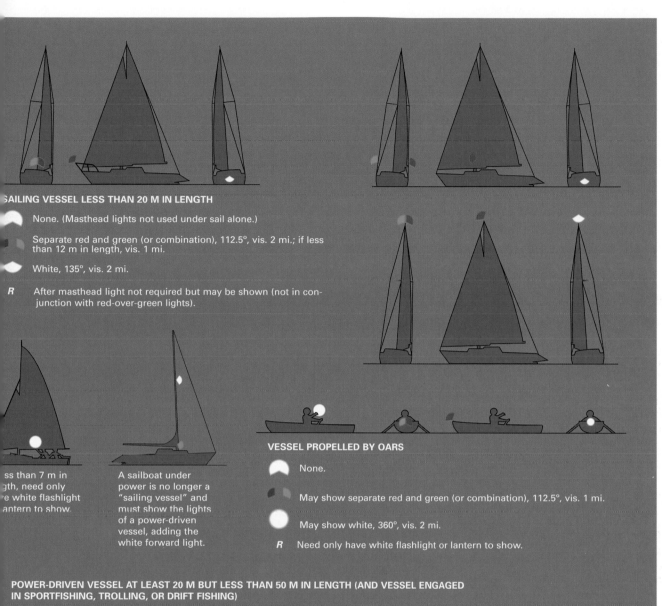

SAILING VESSEL LESS THAN 20 M IN LENGTH

None. (Masthead lights not used under sail alone.)

Separate red and green (or combination), 112.5°, vis. 2 mi.; if less than 12 m in length, vis. 1 mi.

White, 135°, vis. 2 mi.

R After masthead light not required but may be shown (not in conjunction with red-over-green lights).

ss than 7 m in
gth, need only
e white flashlight
antern to show.

A sailboat under power is no longer a "sailing vessel" and must show the lights of a power-driven vessel, adding the white forward light.

VESSEL PROPELLED BY OARS

None.

May show separate red and green (or combination), 112.5°, vis. 1 mi.

May show white, 360°, vis. 2 mi.

R Need only have white flashlight or lantern to show.

POWER-DRIVEN VESSEL AT LEAST 20 M BUT LESS THAN 50 M IN LENGTH (AND VESSEL ENGAGED IN SPORTFISHING, TROLLING, OR DRIFT FISHING)

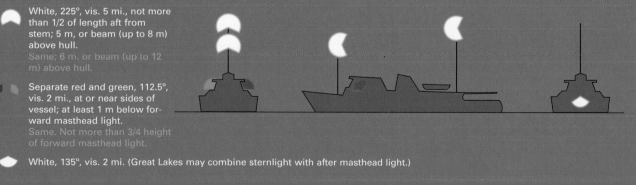

White, 225°, vis. 5 mi., not more than 1/2 of length aft from stem; 5 m, or beam (up to 8 m) above hull.
Same; 6 m, or beam (up to 12 m) above hull.

Separate red and green, 112.5°, vis. 2 mi., at or near sides of vessel; at least 1 m below forward masthead light.
Same. Not more than 3/4 height of forward masthead light.

White, 135°, vis. 2 mi. (Great Lakes may combine sternlight with after masthead light.)

R After masthead light may be shown; at least 2 m higher than forward masthead light.
Same. At least 4.5 m higher than forward masthead light.

INTERPRETING RUNNING LIGHTS (CONTINUED)

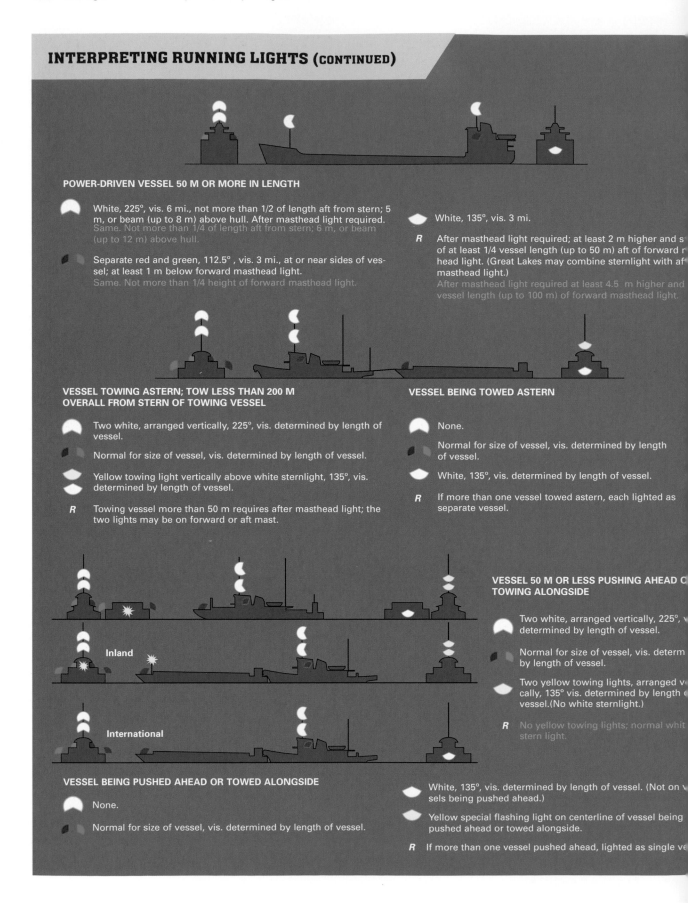

POWER-DRIVEN VESSEL 50 M OR MORE IN LENGTH

White, 225°, vis. 6 mi., not more than 1/2 of length aft from stern; 5 m, or beam (up to 8 m) above hull. After masthead light required.
Same. Not more than 1/4 of length aft from stern; 6 m, or beam (up to 12 m) above hull.

Separate red and green, 112.5°, vis. 3 mi., at or near sides of vessel; at least 1 m below forward masthead light.
Same. Not more than 1/4 height of forward masthead light.

White, 135°, vis. 3 mi.

R After masthead light required; at least 2 m higher and s of at least 1/4 vessel length (up to 50 m) aft of forward head light. (Great Lakes may combine sternlight with af masthead light.)
After masthead light required at least 4.5 m higher and vessel length (up to 100 m) of forward masthead light.

VESSEL TOWING ASTERN; TOW LESS THAN 200 M OVERALL FROM STERN OF TOWING VESSEL

Two white, arranged vertically, 225°, vis. determined by length of vessel.

Normal for size of vessel, vis. determined by length of vessel.

Yellow towing light vertically above white sternlight, 135°, vis. determined by length of vessel.

R Towing vessel more than 50 m requires after masthead light; the two lights may be on forward or aft mast.

VESSEL BEING TOWED ASTERN

None.

Normal for size of vessel, vis. determined by length of vessel.

White, 135°, vis. determined by length of vessel.

R If more than one vessel towed astern, each lighted as separate vessel.

Inland

International

VESSEL 50 M OR LESS PUSHING AHEAD O TOWING ALONGSIDE

Two white, arranged vertically, 225°, v determined by length of vessel.

Normal for size of vessel, vis. determ by length of vessel.

Two yellow towing lights, arranged v cally, 135° vis. determined by length vessel.(No white sternlight.)

R No yellow towing lights; normal whit stern light.

VESSEL BEING PUSHED AHEAD OR TOWED ALONGSIDE

None.

Normal for size of vessel, vis. determined by length of vessel.

White, 135°, vis. determined by length of vessel. (Not on v sels being pushed ahead.)

Yellow special flashing light on centerline of vessel being pushed ahead or towed alongside.

R If more than one vessel pushed ahead, lighted as single ve

SSEL TOWING ASTERN; TOW 200 M OR MORE ERALL FROM STERN OF TOWING VESSEL

Three white arranged vertically, 225°, vis. determined by length of vessel.

Normal for size of vessel, vis. determined by length of vessel.

Yellow towing light, 135°, over white sternlight, 135°, vis. determined by length of vessel.

Towing vessel more than 50 m requires after masthead light; the three lights may be on forward or aft mast.

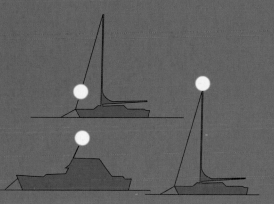

VESSEL ENGAGED IN TRAWLING

None. Replaced by all-round green-over-white lights, arranged vertically, vis. determined by length of vessel. If more than 50 m, after masthead light required; 225°, vis. determined by length of vessel.

Only when making way. Normal for size of vessel.

Only when making way. Normal for size of vessel.

R When not actually trawling, normal masthead, sidelights and sternlight for size of vessel. If less than 50 m, may exhibit after masthead light abaft of and higher than all-ground green light.

SSEL ENGAGED IN FISHING, OTHER THAN TRAWLING

None. Replaced by all-round red-over-white lights, arranged vertically, vis. determined by length of vessel.

Only when making way. Normal for size of vessel.

Only when making way. Normal for size of vessel.

When not actually fishing, normal masthead, sidelights and sternlight for size of vessel.

SSEL AT ANCHOR 50 M OR MORE IN LENGTH

None.

None.

None.

White all-round light in forepart, not less than 6 m above hull. Second white all-round light in after part, not less than 4.5 m lower than forward anchor light, vis 3 mi. If   100 m or more, deck lights illuminated

VESSEL AT ANCHOR LESS THAN 50 M IN LENGTH

None.

None.

None.

R White all-round light where can best be seen, vis. 2 mi. (Not required if less than 7 m and not anchored in narrow channel or where vessels normally navigate.)

INTERPRETING RUNNING LIGHTS (CONTINUED)

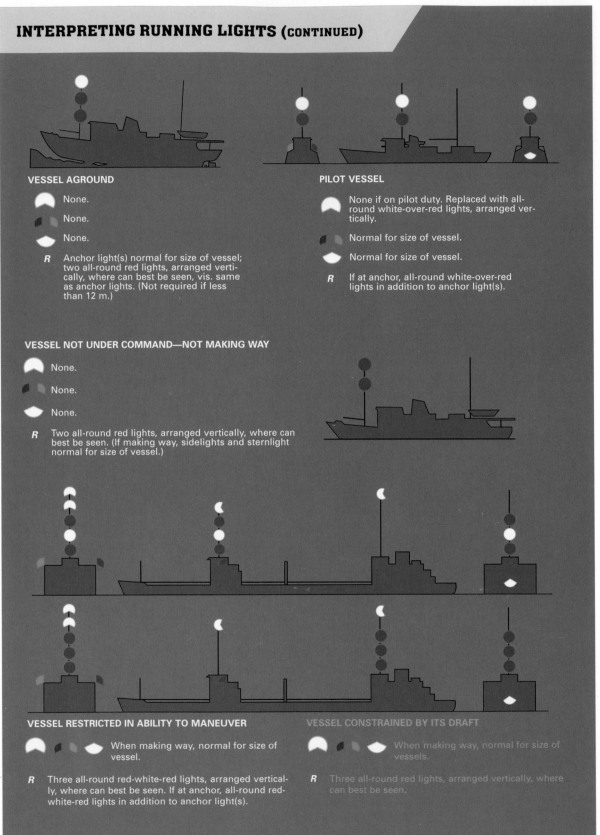

VESSEL AGROUND

None.

None.

None.

R   Anchor light(s) normal for size of vessel; two all-round red lights, arranged vertically, where can best be seen, vis. same as anchor lights. (Not required if less than 12 m.)

PILOT VESSEL

None if on pilot duty. Replaced with all-round white-over-red lights, arranged vertically.

Normal for size of vessel.

Normal for size of vessel.

R   If at anchor, all-round white-over-red lights in addition to anchor light(s).

VESSEL NOT UNDER COMMAND—NOT MAKING WAY

None.

None.

None.

R   Two all-round red lights, arranged vertically, where can best be seen. (If making way, sidelights and sternlight normal for size of vessel.)

VESSEL RESTRICTED IN ABILITY TO MANEUVER

When making way, normal for size of vessel.

R   Three all-round red-white-red lights, arranged vertically, where can best be seen. If at anchor, all-round red-white-red lights in addition to anchor light(s).

VESSEL CONSTRAINED BY ITS DRAFT

When making way, normal for size of vessels.

R   Three all-round red lights, arranged vertically, where can best be seen.

Figure 4-04 A masthead light, shown at right in this photo, is white and covers an arc of 225°. It should be mounted high, but not necessarily at the top of a mast. Directly behind are an anchor light and a GPS antenna.

unbroken light over an arc of 225°, and so fixed as to show it from dead ahead to 22.5° abaft the beam on both sides of the vessel; see **Figure 4-04.** On boats less than 12 meters (39.4 ft) in length, the masthead light may be off the fore-and-aft centerline, but must be as close to it as possible. [21(a)]

As will be seen later, the term "masthead light" is something of a misnomer. More often than not, this light is *not at the top* of a mast. On motorboats it is often on a short staff on top of the cabin. On sailboats it is usually part way up the mast and

another light, the anchor light, is actually at the masthead.

Sidelights Colored lights—red on port and green on starboard—showing over an unbroken arc of the horizon of 112.5°, from dead ahead to 22.5° abaft the beam on each side; see **Figure 4-05.**

Combination Light On a vessel of less than 20 meters (65.6 ft) length, the sidelights may be combined in a single fixture carried on the centerline of the vessel, except that on boats less than 12 meters (39.4 ft) in length, this combination light need be carried only as close to the centerline as possible. [21(b)] Note that the sum of the arcs of the two sidelights is exactly the same as that for the white masthead light; see **Figure 4-06.**

Sternlight A white light showing over an unbroken arc of the horizon of 135°, centered on dead astern; see **Figure 4-07.** [21(c)]

Towing Light A yellow light having the same arc as a sternlight, showing 67.5° to either side of dead astern. [21(d)]

All-Round Light A light, color determined by its use, showing over an unbroken arc of the horizon of 360°. [21(e)] A large vessel may require two lights on opposite sides of a structure.

Flashing Light A flashing light at regular intervals, at a rate of 120 or more flashes per minute. [21(g)] This high flashing rate is used to lessen any possibility of confusion with "quick flashing lights" on aids to navigation.

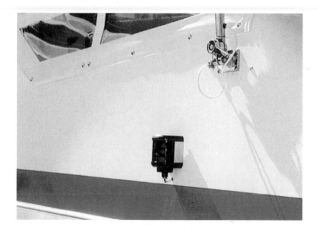

Figure 4-05 Sidelights (the red and green lights) on a vessel must each cover an arc of 112.5°, but not more. On the boat shown here, the side of the flybridge prevents the sidelight from being seen across the bow, a common failing of sidelights on many small craft. Sidelights must not be placed on the hull below the deck line.

Figure 4-06 Vessels less than 20 meters (65.6 ft) in length may carry a combined bow light in place of separate sidelights. Each half covers the same arc as one sidelight; and the total is the same 225° as that for separate sidelights.

Figure 4-07 A white sternlight with a 135° arc centered on dead astern covers the directions not covered by the sidelights and masthead light. In boats less than 12 meters (39.4 ft) in length, the sternlight may be combined with the masthead light as a single all-round white light.

Special Flashing Light A yellow light flashing at a rate of 50 to 70 flashes per minute, placed as far forward and as nearly as practicable on the centerline of a tow, and showing an unbroken light over a horizontal arc of not less than 180° nor more than 225° centered on dead ahead. [21(g)]

Lights for Various Sizes of Power-Driven Vessels Underway

The basic navigation lights for a power-driven vessel of less than 12 meters (39.4 ft) in length, when underway, are a white masthead light and a stern-light, each visible 2 miles, plus sidelights visible 1 mile. [22(c), 23(a)] The two white lights may be combined into a single all-round light [23(c)]; the sidelights may be separate or combined.

Masthead Lights

The masthead light of a vessel *12 meters (39.4 ft) or more but less than 20 meters (65.6 ft)* in length must be at least 2.5 meters (8.2 ft) above the gunwale. [I-84.03(c)] On boats *less than 12 meters (39.4 ft)* long, the masthead light need only be at least 1 meter (3.3 ft) higher than the sidelights; it must be screened if necessary to prevent interference with the helmsman's vision. [I-84.09(b)]

Vessels *more than 12 meters (39.4 ft)* in length must carry a separate forward masthead light and a sternlight. The forward light need not actually be at the masthead, but must meet placement requirements given in Annex I.

On a vessel *20 meters (65.6 ft) or more* in length, the masthead light must be not less than 5 meters (16.4 ft) above the hull, *except* that if the beam of the vessel is greater than 5 meters, then the height must be not less than the beam, but need not in any case be greater than 8 meters (26.2 ft) above the hull. [I-84.03(a)] The term "height above the hull" is defined in Annex I.

The forward masthead light must be in the forward half of the vessel, except that in boats *of less than 20 meters (65.6 ft)* length, it need only be as far forward as possible. [I-84.05(d)]

A second masthead light is required on vessels of 50 meters (164.0 ft) *or more*, and may be carried on vessels of lesser length [23(a)(ii)]. This light must be at least 2 meters (6.5 ft) higher than the forward light. [I-84.03(a)(2)] A smaller vessel may optionally show the second light.

When two masthead lights are carried, the horizontal distance between them must be at least one-fourth of the length of the vessel, except that this distance need not in any case exceed 50 meters (164.0 ft). [I-84.05(a)] *Exception*: Special provisions are made on the Western Rivers and other designated waters for vessels between 50 and 60 meters (164.0-196.8 ft) in length. [I-84.05(e)]

Value of Lights as a Range When two masthead lights are carried they form a RANGE, a valuable aid in determining the relative heading of another vessel when it is first sighted at night. Since these white lights are both brighter and higher than the sidelights, they normally will be seen well before the colored light or lights can be detected and read for their meaning.

The relative location of the two range lights will be the key. Should they be seen one directly over the other, the other vessel is heading *directly toward you* and danger of collision may exist. Should the lower (forward) range light be seen to the right or left of the higher (after) white light, the other vessel is on an oblique course and the angle can be roughly gauged by the horizontal separation between the lights; see **Figure 4-08.**

Visibility Requirements Masthead lights must have a range of visibility as follows: Boats *less than 12 meters (39.2 ft.) long*—2 miles; vessels of *12 to not more than 50 meters (39.4-164.0 ft)* in length—5 miles; except that it may be 3 miles for boats *less than 20 meters (65.6 ft)* in length; vessels *over 50 meters (164.0 ft) in length*—6 miles. [22]

In all cases, masthead lights must be placed so as to be clear of all other lights or obstructions. [I-84.03(f)]

Sidelights

Sidelights on a vessel *of any length* must be at least 1 meter (3.3 ft) lower than the (forward) masthead light; they should not be so low as to be interfered with by deck lights. [I-84.03(g)] On vessels of *20 meters (65.6 ft) or more* in length, sidelights must not be forward of the forward masthead light. [84.05(b)] On vessels of such size, sidelights must be provided with mat black inboard screens to make the necessary cut-off of light at the "ahead" limit of each arc of visibility. [I-84.09(a)] *Smaller vessels* also must have these screens, if needed to meet the cut-off requirements, and to prevent excessive

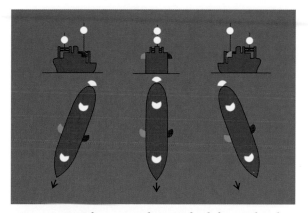

Figure 4-08 When a vessel carries both forward and after masthead lights, these form a central range that is an excellent indicator of its heading as seen from your boat. If the lower (forward) light is to the left of the after light, the vessel is heading to your port. If the lower light is to the right of the other light, the vessel is heading to your starboard. When the two lights are directly in line, one above the other, the vessel is heading toward you. These lights will normally be seen well before the colored sidelights.

spillover from sidelights. A combination light using a single *vertical filament* bulb and a very narrow division between sectors need not have a screen.

Sidelights must have a range of visibility as follows: boats *less than 12 meters (39.4 ft)* in length—1 mile; vessels of *12 to 50 meters (39.4-164.0 ft)* length—2 miles; and *vessels more than 50 meters (164.0 ft)* length—3 miles. [22]

Sternlights

The Rules and Annex I do not specify a vertical or horizontal placement for a sternlight, except that it be as nearly as possible "at the stern."

The required visibility for a sternlight is as follows: vessels *less than 50 meters (164.0 ft)* in length—2 miles; vessels *50 meters (164.0 ft) or more* in length—3 miles. [22]

A power-driven vessel operating on the Great Lakes *may* show an all-round white light in place of the normal after masthead light and sternlight. This must be carried in the same position and have the same visibility range as would have a second masthead light. [23(d)]

Lights for Various Sizes of Sailing Vessels Underway

A sailing vessel of any size underway—remember that, if any propelling machinery is in use, it is *not* a sailing vessel—will carry the same sidelights and sternlight as a power-driven vessel of the same length, but will *not* carry a forward white masthead light. [25(a)]

A sailing vessel *may* additionally carry at or near the masthead two all-round lights in a vertical line, with the same visibility range as a sternlight, the upper being red and the lower green. [25(c)]

Sailboats Under 20 Meters

If a sailboat is *less than 20 meters (65.6 ft)* in length, the sidelights and sternlight may be combined into a single fixture at or near the top of the mast where it can best be seen. (The Rules do not so state, but "the mast" can be presumed to be the mainmast if there are more than two masts.) [25(b)] The use of a combination mast-

Figure 4-09 A sailboat less than 20 meters (65.6 ft) in length, while underway under sails alone, may show a tri-color light at or near the top of its mast. This combines the sidelights and the sternlight; no other navigation lights are shown. This light must not be used when under power whether sails are hoisted or not.

head light, however, is *not* permitted when any mechanical power is being used, since there is no way to carry a white forward light higher than the colored sidelights; see **Figure 4-9.** Carrying a three-color combination light also eliminates the use of the red-over-green optional light for sailboats, and a set of conventional lights would be needed for use when the boat was under mechanical power.

A sailboat *less than 7 meters (23.0 ft)* long *should* carry normal sidelights and sternlight; but if this is not possible, it is sufficient to have an electric flashlight or lighted lantern ready at hand to be shown in time to prevent collision. [25(d)(i)] Again, if such a boat is operating under mechanical power, it must show the appropriate lights for a powerboat of its size.

Rowboats

A small boat propelled by oars may show the lights of a sailboat, or have handy an electric flashlight or lighted lantern to show to prevent a collision. [25(d)(ii)]

Lights for Vessels at Anchor

A boat *less than 7 meters (23.0 ft)* in length, when at anchor *not* in or near a narrow channel, fairway, or anchorage, or where other vessels normally navigate, need not show an anchor light.

Also, there are locations on U.S. inland waters designated as "special anchorage areas," where anchor lights are not required for vessels *less than 20 meters (65.6 ft)* long. [30(g)] These special anchorage areas are found frequently off yacht clubs and similar facilities. For a boater, they offer the possibility of legally leaving his boat unattended at a mooring, without having an anchor light burning continuously or turning one on each sunset.

In anchoring situations other than those above, vessels *less than 50 meters (164.0 ft)* in length may show only a single all-round white light wherever it can best be seen, [30(b)], or the two anchor lights that are mandatory for larger vessels; see **Figure 4-10.**

When two lights are used, the Inland Rules require a white all-round light in the fore part of a vessel at anchor, plus a second all-round white light at or near the stern, and lower than the forward light. [30(a)] The forward anchor light must be at least 4.5 meters (14.8 ft) above the other

Figure 4-10 A vessel at anchor less than 50 meters (164 ft) in length must show a white all-round light where it can best be seen. Larger vessels must show one such light forward and another aft and lower. There are exceptions for very small boats and vessels in waters officially designated as a special anchorage. The dayshape is a single black ball.

one. If the vessel is 50 *meters (164.0 ft) or more* in length, the forward light must be at least 6 meters (19.7 ft) above the hull. [I-84.03(k)]

Any vessel at anchor may, and a vessel of *100 meters (328.1 ft) and more* in length *must*, also use the available working or equivalent lights to illuminate its decks. [30(c)]

Vertical Spacing & Positioning

When the Rules require that two or three lights be carried in a vertical line, the lights must be spaced and positioned as follows: for vessels *less than 20 meters (65.6 ft)* in length, the vertical spacing must be not less than 1 meter (3.3 ft), for larger vessels, the spacing must be not less than 2 meters (6.6 ft). Where three lights are carried vertically, the spacing must be equal.

The lowest light on vessels *less than 20 meters* (65.6 ft) in length must be not less than 2 meters (6.6 ft) above the gunwale; on larger vessels, this height requirement is not less than 4 meters (13.1 ft). [I-84.03(i)] This standard of spacing and positioning applies to all lights arranged vertically (except towing lights), including lights on fishing vessels, vessels aground, pilot vessels, vessels restricted in their ability to maneuver or not under command, and the forward lights of towing vessels. The lower of the two all-round lights required on a vessel engaged in fishing must be at a height above its sidelights not less than twice the distance between the two vertically arranged lights. [I-84.03(j)]

Lights for Vessels Aground

A vessel that is aground must show the normal anchor light(s) plus two all-round red lights arranged vertically. [30(d)]; see **Figure 4-11.** A vessel *less than 12 meters (39.4 ft)* in length is exempted from this requirement.

Lights for Towing

Vessels of any size that are either towing another vessel or being towed obviously have, because of this condition, much less maneuverability than vessels proceeding singly. To indicate this situation at night, special navigation lights are prescribed for vessels towing or being towed.

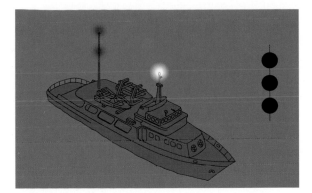

Figure 4-11 A vessel 12 to 50 meters (39.4 to 164 ft) in length, when it is aground, must show a normal anchor light plus two all-round red lights. Smaller craft are not required to show these additional lights; larger vessels, over 50 meters (164 ft), show the usual two anchor lights as well as the red ones. The day signal is three black balls hoisted vertically.

Towing Alongside or Pushing Ahead

A power-driven vessel when pushing ahead or towing another alongside must carry, in addition to its normal sidelights, two masthead white lights in a vertical line with standard spacing and positioning. [24(c)] These lights must be shown, but may be carried *either* at the position of the normal forward masthead light *or* that of the after masthead if used. However they are carried, the lowest after masthead light must be at least 2 meters (6.6 ft) above the highest forward light, to form an adequate range. [I-84.03(c)] In lieu of the normal white sternlight, it must carry two yellow "towing lights" in a vertical line, positioned so as to be showing astern.

When a pushing vessel and a vessel being pushed ahead are "rigidly connected" as a *composite unit,* they are considered a single power-driven vessel and must position their masthead lights accordingly. This is *not* the same as a tug lashed to a barge ahead, no matter how tight the fastening cables are pulled in. [24(b)]

In inland waters, vessels towed alongside or being pushed ahead must show their own lights. On a vessel being pushed ahead or towed alongside, sidelights must be shown at the forward end plus a "special flashing light" (yellow) as defined in Rule 21 (g). When towed alongside, a sternlight is added. [24(f)]

Exception On the Western Rivers (except below the Huey P. Long Bridge on the Mississippi River) and on waters specified by the Coast Guard, the prescribed lights for a vessel pushing ahead or towing alongside are only sidelights and two towing lights carried one above the other. [24(i)] It is said that masthead lights are not required on Western Rivers because of the number of low bridges that towboats must pass under.

Towing Astern

If the length of a tow astern, measured from the stern of the towing vessel to the after end of the tow, is *200 meters (656.2 ft) or less*, the towing vessel must carry *two* masthead lights in the same manner as for pushing ahead or towing alongside, plus sidelights, a sternlight, and one towing light above the sternlight. If the length of the tow is *greater than 200 meters (656.2 ft)*, *three* masthead lights are carried in a vertical line, rather than two. [24(a)]

A vessel towed astern carries sidelights and a sternlight, but no white forward lights. [24(e)]

An inconspicuous, partially submerged vessel or object must carry special lights, rather than those just described. If it is less than *25 meters (82.0 ft) in beam*, it must carry one all-round white light at or near each end; if it is *25 meters (82.0 ft) or more in beam*, four all-round white lights at or near corners. If it exceeds *100 meters*

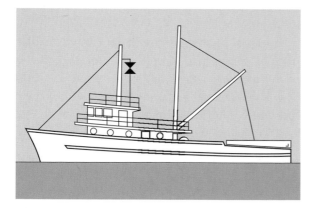

Figure 4-12 By day, a fishing vessel, whether trawling or fishing by other means, must show a shape consisting of two cones point-to-point without vertical spacing. At night, the special fishing lights are green over white for trawling; red over white for other fishing methods.

(328.1 ft) in length, it must have additional all-round white lights, placed so that the distance between such lights is not more than 100 meters (328.1 ft). These white lights must be visible for 3 miles. This rule exists to provide for the proper lighting of large liquid-filled bags (called "dracones"), log rafts, and other nearly awash objects.

Multiple vessels or objects towed alongside are lighted as a single vessel or object. [24(g)]

When it is impractical for a towed vessel to carry the prescribed lights, Rule 24(h) directs that all possible measures be taken to light the vessel or object being towed, or at least to indicate the presence of that vessel or object.

Small Boat Towing

Although the 1980 Inland Rules make no special provisions for small boats when towing, Rule 24(j) covers situations where towing is not the normal function of a vessel engaged in such work, and the towed vessel is in distress or otherwise in need of assistance. In this instance, all possible measures must be taken to indicate the relationship between the two boats, including the use of a searchlight to illuminate the towed vessel.

Lights for Special-Purpose Vessels

Specific lights or combinations of lights are prescribed for various categories of vessels, so they may be more easily identified at night.

Fishing Vessels

A vessel engaged in fishing, whether underway or at anchor, must show *only* the lights specified in Rule 26; see **Figure 4-12**. Remember, however, that the definition of "fishing" does *not* include trolling lines.

A vessel engaged in *trawling*—dragging a dredge net or "other apparatus used as a fishing appliance"—must show two all-round lights vertically, green over white, plus sidelights and a sternlight when making way through the water. It must also carry a white masthead light abaft of and higher than the green light if it is *50 meters (164.0 ft) or more in length*; shorter vessels may, but do not have to, carry this light. [26(b)]

A vessel engaged in fishing *other than trawling* shows red-over-white all-round lights, again with sidelights and sternlight, if making way. If there is outlying gear more than 150 meters (492.1 ft) horizontally from the vessel, an all-round white light must be shown in that direction. This light must be not less than 2 meters (6.6 ft) nor more than 6 meters (19.7 ft) horizontally away from the all-round red and white lights. [26(c)]

In both cases just mentioned, the lower of the two vertical lights must be at a height above the sidelights not less than twice the spacing between the two vertical lights. The required visibility range is the same as for sternlights.

A vessel that is fishing close by other vessels also fishing *may* exhibit the additional signals described in Annex II. These signals would aid trawlers and purse seiners working in groups to coordinate their movements. [26(d)]

A fishing vessel *not* engaged in fishing will show the normal navigation lights for a vessel of its length. [26(e)]

Pilot Vessels

A pilot vessel, when on pilotage duty, does not show normal lights for a vessel of its size, but rather two all-round lights in a vertical line, white over red, at or near the masthead. These lights have the same visibility distance requirement as a sternlight, which together with sidelights, must be shown when underway. At anchor the pilot vessels show normal anchor lights as well as the white-over-red lights. [29(a)]

A pilot vessel *not* on duty carries only the normal lights for a vessel of its length. [29(b)]

Lights for Vessels with Limited Maneuverability

The U.S. Inland Navigational Rules prescribe special lights for various types of vessels that have limited maneuverability because of their condition or their operations. [27] A vessel less than 12 meters (39.4 ft) is not required to show these lights and shapes, but may do so. [27(g)]

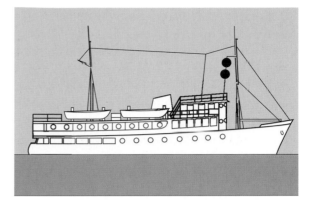

Figure 4-13 A vessel 12 meters (39.4 ft) or more in length and not under command (see text) shows two ball shapes vertically. At night, she shows two red all-round lights, plus sidelights and a sternlight if making way through the water.

Vessels Not Under Command

A vessel "not under command"—such as one with disabled engines, or one that for some reason cannot direct its movement in a specific direction—will show two red all-round lights vertically spaced where they can best be seen; see **Figure 4-13.** When making way through the water, such a vessel must also show sidelights and a sternlight, but no masthead lights. [27(a)]

Vessels Restricted in Maneuverability

A vessel of any size restricted in its ability to maneuver, except one engaged in mineclearance operations, will show three all-round lights with standard vertical separations, red-white-red. Underway or at anchor the vessel will also show the usual lights for that status. [27(b)]

A vessel engaged in a towing operation that severely restricts the tow's ability to deviate from its course will show normal towing lights, plus red-white-red vertical lights. [27(c)] It is *not* intended, however, that vessels engaged in routine towing operations can declare that they are restricted in their ability to deviate from their course.

In addition to the red-white-red lights, a vessel engaged in dredging or underwater operations involving an obstruction to navigation will also show two vertically spaced red all-round lights on the side on which the obstruction exists and two green all-round lights, one above the other, on the side on which it is safe to pass; these lights shall be at the maximum practical horizontal distance, but never less than 2 meters (6.6 ft) from the red-white-red lights, and the upper light of these pairs must not be higher than the lower red light. A vessel of this category will not show anchor light(s) but will show underway lights, if applicable. [27(d)]

Diving Operations

Whenever the size of a vessel engaged in diving operations makes it impractical to exhibit all the lights prescribed in Rule 27(d) above, it must instead show three all-round lights, placed vertically, red-white-red; see **Figure 4-14.** [27(e)]

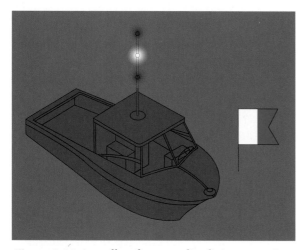

Figure 4-14 A small craft engaged in diving operations at night that restrict its ability to maneuver must show three lights vertically, red over white over red. During the day, it must show a rigid replica of the code flag for the letter "A"; flying an actual flag is not adequate to meet the requirements of the Rules. Though official only in some states, a flag of red field with white diagonal stripes is sometimes used by recreational divers.

Mineclearance Vessels

A vessel engaged in mineclearance operations (often called "minesweeping") will show, in addition to all normal underway lights for a power-driven vessel, three green all-round lights. One of these will be at the foremast head and one at each end of the foreyard. These lights indicate that it is dangerous to approach within 1,000 meters (1094 yds) of the mineclearance vessel. [27(f)]

Smaller Boats

Boats *less than 12 meters (39.4 ft)* in length, except when engaged in diving operations, are not required to show the lights of Rule 27, but larger craft must comply. [27(g)]

Not Distress Signals

The various lights of Rule 27, especially those for vessels not under command, should be understood by other vessels as signals of limited maneuverability, not as signals of vessels in distress and requiring assistance. [27(h)]

Miscellaneous Provisions of the Rules

Rule 1(b) of the Inland Rules allows vessels equipped with lights meeting the requirements of the International Navigation Rules to use such lights on inland waters *in lieu* of the lights specified by the 1980 Inland Rules. Lights must be complete for one set of Rules or the other—no mixtures. (Consult the Coast Guard publication *Navigation Rules, International—Inland* for the applicable provisions of the International Rules.) This option is of value to the owners of boats that may be operated outside the Inland Rules demarcation lines at night, since it eliminates any need for making a change in lights when going from one body of water to the other.

The navigation lights of the International Rules are permitted on inland waters, *but not vice versa;* a boat lighted for the Inland Rules may be in violation when proceeding seaward of the demarcation lines.

Exemptions for Government Vessels

Any requirements for lights and shapes—their number, placement, range of arc of visibility—do not apply to a Navy or Coast Guard vessel whose department Secretary certifies that its special construction—such as for submarines and aircraft carriers—makes this impossible. In such cases, however, their lights must comply as closely as feasible. [1(e)]

Rule 1(c) allows the use of special station or signal lights by naval ships and vessels proceeding in convoy. These additional lights, so far as possible, shall be such as cannot be mistaken for any lights of the Rules of the Road.

Special Submarine Lights

Because of their low height and close spacing, a submarine's normal navigation lights are sometimes mistaken for those of small boats, although submarines are large, deep-draft vessels with limited maneuverability on the surface. The Rules do not provide for any special lights for submarines at the surface, but under the authority of Rule 1(e), the United States has established a special distinctive light for its submarines; this light is in addition to all other required lights.

The distinctive light characteristic is an amber (yellow) beacon with a sequence of one flash per second for three seconds, followed by three seconds of darkness; see **Figure 4-15.** The light is located where it can best be seen, as nearly as possible all around the horizon; it will be not less than 2 feet (0.6 m) above or below the masthead light.

Signals to Attract Attention

The Inland Rules authorize a vessel to make light or sound signals to attract the attention of another vessel, provided that such actions cannot be mistaken for one of the normal lights or signals. A vessel may also direct the beam of its searchlight toward a danger, but not in such a way as to impede the navigation of any other vessel. [36] See Distress Signals in Chapter 5, page 171.

Air-Cushion Vessels

An air-cushion vessel, when operating in the nondisplacement mode ("flying"), must show the normal navigation lights for a vessel of its length, plus an all-round flashing yellow light where it can best be seen. [23(b)]. There are no special lights for hydrofoil vessels.

Lights for Seaplanes

A seaplane is defined as including any aircraft designed to maneuver on the water. [3(a) and (e)] Seaplanes, while on the water, are thus in theory required to show the same lights as a ship of the same size. Because this will probably be imprac-

Figure 4-15 *Because it is a large vessel, but with little above the water surface, a special identifying light is established for U.S. submarines—an all-round flashing amber (yellow) light that flashes once a second for three flashes, off for the next three seconds, then repeating.*

tical, the Rules offer an exception allowing them to show lights "as closely similar in characteristics and position as is possible." [31]

Technical Details for Lights

Annex I to the U.S. Inland Rules also contains highly technical specifications for the "chromaticity" (color specifications) of navigation lights, and for the necessary luminous intensity to achieve the various ranges of visibility specified in the Rules. Specifications are also included for horizontal and vertical sectors, so that adequate light brightness is maintained fully over the specified arc, yet rapidly decreases outside the set limits. The requirements for horizontal sectors are the same for all vessels, but the vertical sector specifications for sailing vessels differ from the requirements for power-driven vessels. When buying lights, specify the type and size of the vessel they are intended for.

Day Shapes

In the interest of collision prevention and greater overall safety on the water, the Navigation Rules prescribe a number of shapes for certain situations and categories of vessels. Objects of specified shape and minimum size are used in the daytime, when lights are ineffective. The general requirements for the display of shapes are given in the numbered Rules, with details of configuration, size, and placement set forth in Annex I.

Ball Diameter of not less than 0.6 meter (2.0 ft).
Cone Base diameter not less than 0.6 meter (2.0 ft) and height equal to base diameter.
Diamond Two cones, each as above, base to base.

If more than one shape is hoisted, they shall be spaced at least 1.5 meters (4.9 ft).

Small Boats Vessels *less than 20 meters (65.6 ft)* in length may display smaller shapes scaled down to be commensurate with the vessel's size; the vertical separation may be correspondingly reduced.

Vessels Under Sail & Power

A vessel proceeding under sail in the daytime, when also being propelled by machinery, must

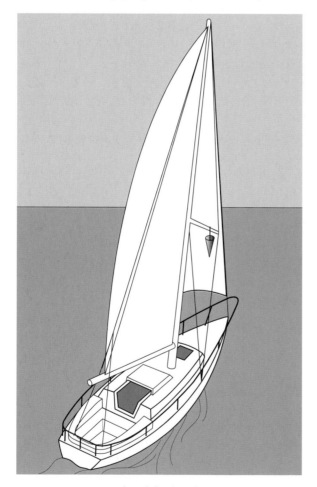

Figure 4-16 A vessel with both sail and mechanical propulsion must show a cone shape, point down. Inland Rules exempt sailboats less than 12 meters (39.4 ft) in length, but on waters subject to the International Rules, all sailboats must comply regardless of length.

carry forward, where it can best be seen, a black conical shape with its point downward. Under Inland Rules only, a vessel of *less than 12 meters (39.4 ft)* length is not required to exhibit this shape, but may do so. [25(e)] This day shape signals that such a vessel is *not* entitled to a sailboat's Rule 18 right-of-way privileges even though its sails are set; see **Figure 4-16**.

Vessels at Anchor or Aground

Although larger vessels must display certain shapes by day whenever they are at anchor or aground, this does not apply to *small boats* in most situations. Vessels *under 7 meters (23.0 ft)* in length need show no shape if they are *not* at anchor in or near a narrow channel or fairway, anchorage, or where vessels normally navigate.

Vessels *under 20 meters (65.6 ft)* in length need not display shapes when at anchor in a special anchorage area. Vessels *less than 12 meters (39.4 ft)* in length are not required to show shapes when aground or operating with limited maneuverability, except for diving operations; refer to **Figure 4-13**. [27(g) and 30(f)]

In all other situations, vessels at anchor must hoist a ball shape forward where it can best be seen; see **Figure 4-17**. [30(a)] This is the signal displayed by the large vessels whenever at anchor. Similarly, a vessel *12 meters (39.4 ft) or longer* aground must display three ball shapes in a vertical line; refer to **Figure 4-11**. [30(d)]

Vessels Towing & Being Towed

Between sunrise and sunset, a power-driven vessel having a tow astern that is longer than 200 meters (656.2 ft) must carry a diamond shape where it can best be seen. [24(a)]

In such cases, the vessel being towed must also show a diamond shape where it can best be seen. [24(e)]

Vessels Engaged in Fishing

Vessels engaged in fishing by day must indicate their occupation by displaying, where it can best be seen, a shape consisting of two cones in a vertical line with their points together (in this case only, no vertical separation between the two

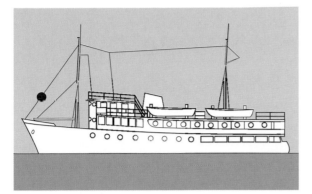

Figure 4-17 Vessels at anchor by day must hoist a ball shape. Boats less than 7 meters (23.0 ft) anchored clear of traffic need not show this shape. Craft less than 20 meters (65.6 ft) in length are also exempted if in a designated "special anchorage area" (U.S. inland waters only).

shapes). [26(b) and (c)] These shapes are used on vessels engaged in either trawling or in fishing other than trawling (but not on vessels trolling or drift fishing); refer to **Figure 4-12.**

If its outlying gear extends more than 150 meters (492.1 ft) horizontally from the vessel, a vessel engaged in fishing, other than trawling, will show a day shape of a single cone, point up, in the direction of the outlying gear. [26(c)]

Vessels 12 Meters or More with Limited Maneuverability

A vessel not under command will show as a day signal two black balls one above the other; refer to **Figure 4-13.** [27(a)]

A vessel "restricted in its ability to maneuver" will hoist three shapes in a vertical line, ball-diamond-ball; refer to **Figure 4-02.** [27(b)]

A vessel engaged in a towing operation that severely restricts the tow's ability to deviate from its course, will show the ball-diamond-ball shapes, in addition to any other required day shapes.

Vessels engaged in routine towing operations, however, cannot declare that they are restricted in their ability to deviate from their course.

A vessel engaged in dredging or underwater operations when an obstruction to navigation exists will hoist two balls vertically on the side on which the obstruction exists, with two diamond

shapes on the side on which another vessel may pass. [27(d)] If the size of a vessel engaged in diving operations makes it impracticable to exhibit these shapes, it shall show instead a *rigid replica* of the International Code flag "A" (white and blue, swallow-tailed) not less than 1 meter (3.3 ft) in height, arranged to ensure all-round visibility; refer to **Figure 4-14.** [27(e)] This requirement for visibility in any direction will normally require multiple rigid "flags" in a criss-cross or square arrangement. An "A" *flag*—made of cloth—is *not* an acceptable substitute for the "rigid replica" required by the Rules.

While there is no official recognition in the International or U.S. Navigation Rules for the familiar "diver's flag"—rectangular red with one white diagonal slash—it is still advisable to fly it in the close vicinity of any persons engaged in diving as a warning to other craft to stay clear; this can be done by mounting the flag on a small float that moves along with the divers. Some state laws require that the red-and-white flag be flown when there are divers in the water; it should *not* be flown routinely when this condition does not exist. The "A" flag replica relates only to the status of a vessel and is not required, nor should it be displayed, if maneuverability is not limited, such as by having divers connected by hoses and lines.

A vessel engaged in minesweeping will show three balls, one at the foremast head and one at each end of the foreyard; these have the same significance as the green lights shown at these positions at night. [27(f)]

Pilot Rules for Inland Waters

The PILOT RULES for inland waters under the 1980 Inland Rules are found in Annex V. The Pilot Rules require that a copy of the Inland Navigation Rules be carried on board every "self-propelled vessel" *12 meters (39.4 ft) or more* in length. [V-88.05] These are found in Coast Guard publication *Navigation Rules, International—Inland,* available for purchase from the Superintendent of Documents, Government Printing Office, Washington, D.C. 20401, or from regional GPO Bookstores; Internet http://bookstore.gpo.gov; it may also be available from some local sales agents for charts and nautical publications.

The Pilot Rules contain certain additional provisions for navigation lights:

Law Enforcement Vessels

Law enforcement vessels of the United States, and of the States and their political subdivisions, may display a flashing *blue* light when engaged in direct law enforcement activities. This must be located so as to not interfere with the visibility of the vessel's navigation lights. [V-88.11]

Public Safety Vessels

Vessels engaged in government-sanctioned public safety activities, and commercial vessels performing similar functions, may display an alternately flashing red and yellow light; this must be a single light, not two separate red and yellow flashing lights. Typically, these are small craft patrolling an authorized regatta, race, or similar marine event, and small towing assistance vessels; other examples are fire and rescue boats, search and rescue craft, and medical assistance vessels [V-88.12]

This special light does not replace—nor should it be located as to interfere with—normal navigation lights. It is only a means of identification and does not convey any special privileges. Vessels showing this light must abide by all applicable Navigation Rules and not presume that they have any precedence or right-of-way.

Lights on Dredge Pipelines

Dredge pipelines that are floating or supported on trestles must display lights at night and in periods of restricted visibility. There must be yellow lights along the pipeline, approximately equally spaced and no more than 10 meters (32.8 ft) apart when a pipeline crosses a navigable channel; when the pipeline does not cross a navigable channel, the lights must be sufficient to clearly show the pipeline's length and course. Each light must be visible all around the horizon, flash 50 to 70 times per minute, and be located not less than 1 meter (3.3 ft) nor more than 3.5 meters (11.5 ft) above the water. There

PENALTIES

The Navigation Rules do not include provisions for penalties, but the U.S. federal law that makes them effective does provide stiff penalties for violations. An important aspect of these penalties that is not widely understood is the concept that the vessel can also be penalized *in rem,* or "under the law" (see below). Under several penalty provisions, it is possible for the operator, the owner, and the vessel itself to each be penalized.

Theoretically, this could result in an owner paying several penalties for the same violation. Additionally, many boating actions could be violations of state or local laws and subject to nonfederal penalties.

Operation in Violation of the Rules

Any person "who operates a vessel" in violation of either the Inland or International Rules, or any regulation issued thereunder—and this includes the various Annexes—is liable for a civil penalty of not more than $5,000 for each violation. The vessel may also be subject separately to a similar penalty.

It should be noted that this penalty is not a "fine" requiring conviction in a federal court, but it is a civil forfeiture imposed by the Secretary or his delegate. The penalty may not be assessed until the person charged has received notice of the violation and had an opportunity for a hearing. The Secretary or his delegate may remove or mitigate any penalty assessed. If a penalty, as finally determined, is not paid, the matter can be taken to a Federal District Court for collection and/or appropriate action.

Negligent Operation

Anyone operating a vessel in a negligent manner (which can include a careless action that endangers a person or property) is liable to a civil penalty of as much as $1,000.

Gross Negligent Operation

Anyone operating a vessel in a grossly negligent manner is subject to a fine of up to $5,000 or imprisonment for up to 1 year, or both.

Duties in an Accident

A vessel that is involved in a collision ("marine casualty") must render assistance to anyone else involved in the accident, as long as such assistance can be done without endangering the passengers, crew, or the vessel rendering aid.

The operator ("master") must give his or her name and address and the identification of the vessel to anyone else involved in the accident.

Anyone who fails to provide assistance and/or who does not provide proper identification is subject to a fine of up to $1,000, imprisonment for up to 2 years, or both. The vessel is also liable to be fined *in rem*.

Obligation to Render Assistance

Anyone who encounters another person or vessel at sea who is in need of assistance must render that assistance as long as it can be done without endangering the passengers, crew, or the vessel rendering aid. Anyone who fails to provide such assistance is subject to a fine of up to $1,000, imprisonment of up to 2 years, or both.

The "Good Samaritan" Provision

Anyone who complies with the required duties listed above, or who gratuitously and in good faith renders assistance at the scene of an accident or other boating casualty without the objection of any person being assisted cannot be held liable for any civil damages as a result of rendering assistance, or of any act or omission in providing or arranging salvage, towing, medical treatment, or other assistance where the individual acts as an ordinary, reasonable, and prudent person would have done under the circumstances.

Penalties Against Vessels

In maritime law, a vessel itself can be held to be in violation and be subject to penalties if operated contrary to any provision of the Inland Navigational Rules Act of 1980 or regulations issued thereunder, including the Annexes. The same maximum penalty, $5,000 for each violation, can be assessed, and in this case the vessel may be seized and proceeded against in any Federal District Court. The same procedures for due notice and hearings are available to the owner of a vessel charged with a violation as are available to individuals as described above.

The law also allows the withholding or revocation of U.S. Customs clearance for any vessel whose owner or operator is subject to a penalty for violation of the Inland rules. This is an important consideration for foreign vessels operating in U.S. waters. If penalty proceedings are not complete before the vessel's sailing date, clearance may be granted upon the filing of a bond or other surety satisfactory to the Secretary.

must also be two all-round red lights (not flashing) at each end of the pipeline, 1 meter (3.3 ft) apart vertically, with the lower red light at the same height above the water as the flashing yellow lights. [V-88.15]

Lights on Barges at Bank or Dock

Section 88.13 of Annex V describes the circumstances requiring lights on barges moored at banks, docks, or on moorings, and the characteristics of such lights. Basically, the Rules require white lights visible for 1 mile on a clear, dark night.

Modifications while Passing Under Bridges

Any vessel, when passing under a bridge, may lower any light or day shape if it needs to. When clear of the bridge, the lights or day shapes must be repositioned immediately. [V-88.09]

INTERNATIONAL NAVIGATION RULES

Careful study of the 1980 U.S. Inland Rules of the Road provides an excellent basis for understanding the "INTERNATIONAL REGULATIONS FOR PREVENTING COLLISIONS AT SEA, 1972"— the formal name for what are generally called the INTERNATIONAL RULES OF THE ROAD or "72 COLREGS." The International Rules were made applicable to U.S. waters and U.S. vessels by Presidential Proclamation and subsequent Act of Congress. The 1972 International Rules consist of 38 numbered "Rules," grouped together into the same "Parts" as for the U.S. Inland Rules, plus four "Annexes" (the International Rules do not have Pilot Rules, the fifth Annex of the U.S. Inland Rules). Some of these Rules and Annexes relate to lights and day shapes, and are discussed here. Other Rules and Annexes are concerned with right-of-way, whistle signals, and distress signals; these are considered in Chapter 5.

Figure 4-18 A power-driven vessel less than 12 meters (39.4 ft) in length may have an all-round white light in lieu of the masthead and stern lights under both Inland and International Rules.

Applicability

The International Rules, as established under the U.S. authority, apply to vessels in two situations:

• To all vessels in waters within the United States sovereignty, outside the prescribed demarcation lines at entrances to bays, rivers, harbors, etc.; see page 59. In the absence of demarcation lines, they are also applicable *within* bays, harbors, and inlets, along specified stretches of coasts, and up the connecting rivers to their limits of continuous navigation.

• To all U.S. vessels on the high seas, not subject to another nation's geographic jurisdiction.

Although the International Rules state that they are applicable "Upon the high seas and in all waters connected therewith navigable by seagoing vessels" [1(a)], there is a provision for a nation to prescribe its own rules for harbors, rivers, and inland waterways [1(b)]; this is the basis for the U.S. Inland Rules.

Manner of Presentation

The 1980 U.S. Inland Navigation Rules were derived from the 1972 International Rules, and nearly match them rule for rule, and annex for annex, in format. Considerable effort was taken to make the language identical wherever possible. Where there are differences, they exist because different operating conditions on the inland waters of the United States require rules for safety of navigation different from those applicable on the high seas. On inland waters, vessels are generally smaller in size and the distances are less. The International Rules, of course, do not contain the several special provisions for the Great Lakes or Western Rivers.

Thus, the consideration of the International Rules for lights and day shapes can be limited to the relatively few points of difference. *Where a difference is not noted, the International and 1980 U.S. Inland Rules are identical,* except for minor editorial modifications of no significance to vessel operation.

Navigation Lights

The requirement for showing navigation lights and day shapes is the same for waters governed by the International Rules as for those where the U.S. Inland Rules apply.

Definitions

The International Rules definitions *do not include a* "special flashing light"—the yellow light used at the bow of barges pushed ahead on inland waters.

The International Rules *do include* a definition not used in the Inland Rules. A "vessel constrained by her draft" is considered a power-driven vessel which, because of her draft in relation to depth and width of navigable water, is severely restricted in her ability to maneuver.

Lights for Power-Driven Vessels Underway

Small craft with sidelights flush-mounted in the hull below the rub rail *do not comply* with the International Rules requirement that such lights be above the "uppermost continuous deck."

Lights for Vessels Anchored or Aground

The International Rules contain *no provision* for special anchorage areas as established in inland waters. The *only exception* to the requirement for an anchor light is for vessels *under 7 meters (23.0 ft)* in length anchored in areas free of water-borne traffic. Vessels *under 12 meters (39.4 ft)* in length are exempt from the requirements to show special lights and day shapes when aground.

Lights for Vessels Towing

A vessel pushing a tow ahead or towing alongside must show a normal white stern light (rather than two yellow towing lights in a vertical line, as required by Inland Rules). [24(c)] A vessel pushed ahead or towing alongside will *not carry* the special flashing yellow light used at the bow of such barges on inland waters.

Lights for Vessels Constrained by Draft

International Rule 28 *permits* a vessel that is "constrained by her draft" to show three red all-round lights in a vertical line wherever they can best be seen; see **Figure 4-19.** (This is the Rule that is omitted from the U.S. Inland Rules.)

Day Shapes of the International Rules

International Rule 25(e) requires the use of a cone, with point downward, as a day shape on *all* sailing

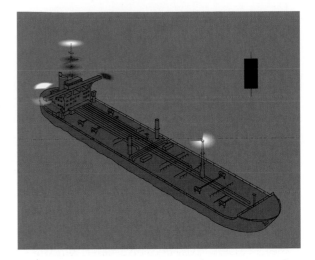

Figure 4-19 Only the International Navigation Rules recognize a vessel "constrained by her draft"; this category does not appear in the Inland Rules. At night, such a vessel shows three all-round red lights arranged in a vertical line; by day, it exhibits a cylindrical shape.

vessels using machinery for propulsion while its sails are up. There are *no exceptions* in this rule for smaller sailboats.

The exception for showing an "anchor ball" is *limited* to vessels *under 7 meters (23.0 ft)* in length, when anchored in waters not subject to water-borne traffic. A similar exception for vessels under 12 meters (39.4 feet) applies to the requirements for showing three balls in a vertical line if aground. [30(e) and (f)]

International Rule 28 *permits* a vessel "constrained by her draft" to show a day shape consisting of a cylinder. The cylinder must be not less than 0.6 meter (2.0 ft) in diameter with height twice the diameter.

General Cautions

Although they are not strictly a part of the Inland or International Rules or their Annexes, several other navigation light matters should be considered by every skipper.

Interpreting What You See

All that has gone before in this chapter has related to what lights are placed where on various vessels. If you have learned this, great—but that is only the beginning! You must also learn how to interpret the navigation lights that you see when you are underway at night—and for your safety, learn it well.

If you see a red navigation light on the other vessel, you immediately know that it has the right-of-way and you must yield—that's why it is red.

If you see two or three white vertical lights, that could be a tug with a tow astern. Look for the lights on the towed vessel, and don't try to pass between the tug and its tow.

And there are other lights and combinations of lights that you must be able to instantly recognize—the lights for a sailboat that is privileged over a motorboat, the special lights of various fishing vessels, a dredge, or a vessel not under command. Study the requirements for navigation lights from the viewpoint of a "looker" as well as a boat owner.

Certification of Navigation Lights

As of November 2003, the U.S. Coast Guard is requiring boat manufacturers to install on the boats that they build only navigation lights that have been certified as meeting the requirements of the Navigation Rules with respect to color, arc of coverage, and intensity. The manufacturer must not only use certified lights, but must install them so that the requirements of the Navigation Rules are met.

Craft constructed prior to November 2003 may or may not (all too often "not") meet the specifications contained in the Rules and their Annexes. Even lights that do meet the design requirements are often installed improperly. The most frequent discrepancy is a sidelight that can be seen across the bow, sometimes by as much as 30 or more degrees. Such improper lights, usually on smaller boats, make it difficult or impossible at night to determine the heading of that craft. Another frequent problem is an all-round white light at the stern that is too low, so its light is blocked by persons on board, a canvas top, or other structural part of the boat, and it can not be seen by another craft traveling in the opposite direction.

Misuse of Navigation Lights

Boats are often seen underway at night showing both running lights and the anchor light. This presents a confusing picture to another boat approaching from astern of the first vessel—two white lights such as would be seen from ahead of a larger vessel under the Inland Rules. This illegal situation is usually caused by carelessness on the part of the skipper—he turned on one too many switches! Check your lights each time you turn them on.

Another problem is the small Class A or 1 boat at anchor that shows its combination red-and-green light as well as its all-round white light aft. Here the illegal situation is caused by the manufacturer who installed only one switch for all navigation lights—making it impossible for the boat to show only the white light as an anchor light, without also showing the red and green sidelights. The solution is for the skipper to install a second switch, or a single switch with two separate "on" settings, so that the colored and white lights may be controlled independently.

Maintenance of Navigation Lights

Lights should always be checked before leaving dock if night operation is scheduled. Many boats are used only in the daytime, but the wise skipper checks all navigation lights once a month—whether they have been used or not. One or more spare bulbs and fuses, each of the proper type and size, should always be on board.

It is common for the color of plastic sidelight lenses to begin to fade after a few years of service. Red lenses tend be affected most noticeably, often to the point where the light through a faded lens appears almost white. It is the owner/operator's responsibility to replace faded lenses to ensure that the sidelights show their proper colors.

Navigation Rules
Right-of-Way & Sound Signals

*Actions to Take & Signals to Sound to Avoid Collision • Sound Signals Required in
"Thick" Weather When Underway or at Anchor • Distress Signals*

Most of us have had the experience of walking down a street and meeting another pedestrian headed toward us. We turn to one side to avoid hitting him, only to have him dodge simultaneously to the same side. Then perhaps there's a quick turn by both in the opposite direction, followed by a collision, or we manage to pass without hitting. To pedestrians on a sidewalk such actions are merely comical, and fairly simple to avoid. Between vessels on the water, they are serious indeed, and boaters need to understand and follow the applicable Navigation Rules to avoid collisions.

Except for marked channels, there are no clearly defined paths for boats to follow. They have an open expanse of water on which to navigate, and their courses often cross the tracks of other vessels in the same waters. The caution needed on the water, even though traffic is much less than on land, is thus just as important as on sidewalks, streets, and highways, or even more so.

"Ignorance of the law is no excuse" applies to boating as well as activities on land. Skippers of boats of all sizes have been found liable for criminal and civil penalties of substantial sums when they ignored or violated right-of-way rules. Before paying claims, insurance companies may ask skippers to prove that they operated their craft in accordance with the Navigation Rules.

More important, knowing and obeying the Rules can save your life and the lives of your family and guests on board. Whether you operate a boat 60 feet (18.3 m) in length or a personal watercraft, knowledge of the Navigation Rules is a *must*.

Previous Page: Figure 5-01 Many boating areas are relatively open areas without specific channels. Boats may approach from more than one direction, often several at a time. Every skipper must know who has the right-of-way, and what signal to give, in each situation.

Rules & Regulations

To prevent collision, carefully considered rules clearly state the duty of the skipper of any vessel encountering another vessel. These rules are of three general classes: the *International Regulations for Preventing Collisions at Sea, 1972* (known as the 72COLREGS); the *1980 U.S. Inland Navigational Rules*; and regulations issued by departments and agencies of the federal government. Most of the latter category are promulgated by "the Secretary of the Department in which the Coast Guard is operating," or by the Commandant of the Coast Guard, under authority delegated to him by the Secretary. The principal Federal Regulations are the five annexes to the Inland Rules, including Annex V, Pilot Rules.

State & Local Regulations Both the International and Inland Rules are focused on the prevention of collisions between vessels. They do not cover matters such as "no wake" zones or the operation of watercraft near swimming beaches. These types of regulations are the responsibility of state and local authorities. In general, such special regulations conform to the Inland Rules and Coast Guard regulations, but elaborate on certain minor details. The wide variety of such regulations makes it impossible to consider them here, except to remind all skippers to be alert for them.

Many states have regulations prohibiting boat operation in restricted areas above and below dams. The towing of water-skiers may be restricted in some waters. Boats are often prohibited from operating within a specified distance, usually 100 yards of craft displaying a state-recognized "diver down" flag. State laws may give public safety vessels displaying the appropriate flashing blue light the right-of-way over other vessels.

Foreign Waters

Some foreign nations have their own set of navigation rules for their internal waters. In Canada, these are the *Collision Regulations: International Regulations for Preventing Collisions at Sea, 1972 with Canadian Modifications.* Many other countries have no national rules, and in these the COLREGS govern on their internal as well as external waters.

Sequence of Consideration

The U.S. Inland Navigational Rules will be considered in detail here. They apply on waters *shoreward* of demarcation lines at the entrances to most, but not all, harbors, bays, rivers, and inlets (see Chapter 2, pages 56–59). They probably thus apply to most recreational boatmen in the U.S.

The International Navigation Rules will be discussed in detail only where their provisions differ significantly from the U.S. Inland Rules. As discussed in Chapter 4, the Inland Rules are derived from the International Rules and closely parallel them; the various provisions are matched rule for rule and annex for annex. Many Rules are identical, but in a number of instances the content and language has been changed to reflect the generally smaller size of vessels and shorter distances involved in inland waters; in a few places an editorial change has been made for greater clarity.

Annexes II and IV are identical; Annexes I and III have minor differences, and Annex V of the Inland Rules has no counterpart in the International Rules since there are no Pilot Rules for those waters.

The consideration of the Navigation Rules in this chapter and Chapter 4 is not complete; it focuses primarily on points of greatest interest to boaters.

Numbered Rules

Both the U.S. Inland Rules and the International Rules consist of major subdivisions; Part A—General, Part B—Steering and Sailing Rules, Part C—Lights and Shapes, Part D—Sound and Light Signals, and Part E—Exemptions. (Part E provides specific temporary and permanent

Figure 5-02 *In crowded waterways, it is essential to understand the Navigation Rules. If every skipper knew the "Rules of the Road" as he should, it would do much to bring calm to what could be a chaotic situation.*

exemptions for existing vessels, to permit a smooth transition from the previous requirements for lights and sound signals. Most of these exemptions have now expired.)

Within both sets, the Rules are numbered from 1 to 38, with subparagraphs such as (a), (b), (c), and still lower levels indicated by (i), (ii), (iii). Rules that are identical or nearly identical on both sets carry the same numbers, so that parallel numbering can be continued in the Rules that follow. (Rule 28 is omitted from the U.S. Inland Rules.)

Indication of References

Numbers and letters shown in brackets are references to the applicable Rule. References to Annexes are indicated by a Roman numeral as the annexes to both sets of Rules are so designated; specific paragraphs and subparagraphs are noted by numbers and letters as appropriate. These references are shown to facilitate looking up the exact language of the Rules and Annexes in the U.S. Coast Guard publication *Navigation Rules, International—Inland.*

THE U.S. INLAND RULES

The Rules covered in this chapter are in addition to those in Chapter 4. Taken together, they make up the sum of the two sets of Navigation Rules. The term "Right-of-Way" is not used in the text of the Rules, but it is commonly understood language and will be used in the following discussion.

Definition of Terms

The definitions of the Inland and International rules that were discussed in Chapter 4 on page 124 are also equally applicable in this chapter. Additional definitions follow:

Whistle Any sound-signaling equipment capable of producing the prescribed blasts, and which complies with the specifications in the Annex III. [32(a)]

Short Blast A blast of about one second's duration.

Prolonged Blast A blast of from four to six seconds' duration. (The term "long blast" is no longer used in the Navigation Rules.)

The geographic limits of Rule applicability to the Great Lakes, the Western Rivers, and specified waters described in Chapter 4 are similarly applicable to this chapter.

"Privileged" & "Burdened" Vessels

For generations, skippers have used the terms BURDENED and PRIVILEGED to define the status of two vessels encountering each other. The privileged vessel is the one that has the right-of-way—the right to proceed unhindered by the other. The burdened vessel is the one that does not have the right-of-way, the one that must take any necessary action to keep out of the way of the privileged vessel.

These terms do not appear in the 1972 International Rules and the 1980 Inland Rules—but the concept remains. Officially, the privileged vessel is now the STAND-ON vessel; the burdened vessel is the GIVE-WAY vessel. (Although these terms are used in the titles of Rules 16 and 17, they are not included in the definitions of either set of Rules.) The new terms were adopted as they were considered to be more descriptive of the required actions. The terms "burdened" and "privileged"

continue in use by maritime personnel on an informal basis.

Steering & Sailing Rules

The basic purpose of any set of rules of the nautical road is to prevent collisions (indeed, this is the title of the International Rules). A major subdivision, Part B, termed "Steering and Sailing Rules," is particularly aimed at that goal with three subparts covering conduct of vessels in any condition of visibility [Rules 4-10]; when within sight of each other [Rules 11-18]; and when in restricted visibility [Rule 19]. Part D, Sound and Light Signals also largely focuses on collision prevention [Rules 32-37].

Technically, the right-of-way rules do not come into effect between two vessels until the possibility of a collision exists; see **Figure 5-03**. Privilege and burden are not necessarily established when vessels first sight each other, but rather at the moment when a "risk of collision" develops. Although not an actual rule, a basic principle of collision prevention is that, where the depth of the water permits, two vessels should never get so close to each other that the risk of a collision can materialize. A collision between two vessels is almost impossible if each skipper fully and properly obeys the Navigation Rules.

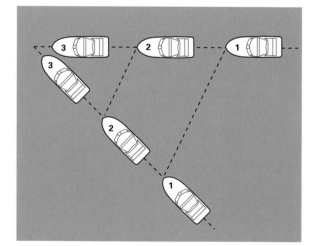

Figure 5-03 The Navigation Rules come into force whenever there is risk of collision. In a crossing situation, keep a check on the relative bearing of the other craft. To be safe, there should be a distinct change in this angle, forward or aft; a constant or slow change in bearing indicates a risk of collision.

Determining Risk of Collision

Every vessel shall use all available means appropriate to the prevailing conditions to determine if risk of collision exists. If there is any doubt, such risk shall be deemed to exist. [7(a)]

Every vessel must at all times maintain a proper watch by sight and hearing, as well as all available means appropriate in the prevailing conditions so as to make a full appraisal of the situation and of the risk of collision. [5]

An excellent method (and prescribed by the Rules) of determining whether your boat is on a collision course with another is to watch the compass bearing of the other vessel; see **Figure 5-04.** If this bearing does not change appreciably, either forward or astern, a risk of collision

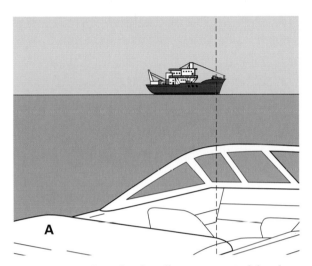

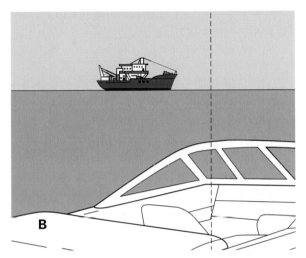

Figure 5-04 These sketches illustrate a typical developing situation. Even without the use of a compass, another vessel can be "eyeballed." On first sighting (A), this freighter gives no clue as to its speed. The small-boat skipper lines it up with the windshield and the corner of the companionway.

In B, the ship seems to be falling behind the bearing line. If the small boat has kept a constant speed and heading since the first sighting, it will pass ahead of the freighter.

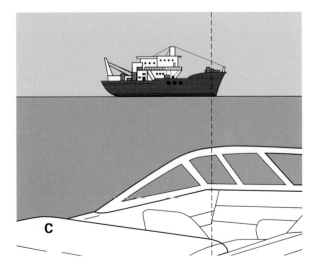

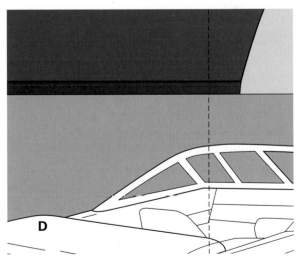

Now however, in C the ship has pulled ahead of the bearing line and collision is possible. The small boat is actually the privileged vessel, but it would be extremely risky and foolish to try and claim that right.

In D, a collision appears probable. The small craft should have altered course or speed, or both, in order to prevent this situation from occurring. Survivors of collisions between ships and boats are nearly always those persons who are on the ship.

exists. [7(d)] The Navigation Rules then apply, and appropriate action must be taken.

Boaters are cautioned, however, against presuming there is no risk when there is an appreciable change in bearing. Each situation must be considered in light of its own conditions. [7(d)]

In reduced visibility, you must make proper use of any operational radar equipment on board, including long-range scanning, and of radar plotting or equivalent systematic observation of detected objects. [7(b)]

Do not make assumptions on the basis of scanty information, especially scanty radar information. [7(c)]

Safe Speed

Clearly, the safe speed for a motorboat operating on a little-traveled waterway in the middle of a week may be completely different than the safe speed for the same boat in a crowded harbor on the Fourth of July weekend. The prevailing circumstances and conditions are quite different, and that's just what the Rules want to be taken into account. Every vessel must proceed at a safe speed at all times. [6]

Rule 6(a) lists specific factors to be considered in determining a "safe speed," including but not limited to:

- The state of visibility;
- Traffic density, including concentration of fishing or other vessels;
- Your vessel's maneuverability, with special reference to stopping distance and turning ability;
- At night, the presence of background lights such as those from shore, or from the backscatter of your vessel's own lights;
- The state of wind, sea, current, and the proximity of navigational hazards;
- The vessel's draft in relation to the available depth of water.

Rule 6(b) provides additional guidance for determining a safe speed for a ship or boat fitted with an operational radar.

Actions to Avoid Collision

The rules specifically require that any action taken to avoid collision, if the circumstances

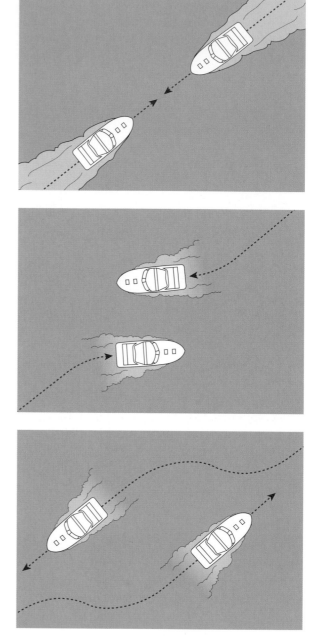

Figure 5-05 All changes of course in the presence of another vessel should be so pronounced and definite that they will be noticed and properly evaluated by the other skipper. Slight changes may fail to make your intentions clear. Changes in speed are often less noticeable than changes in course.

allow, will be positive, made in ample time, and in keeping with good seamanship. Any change of course or speed should be large enough to be readily apparent to the other vessel visually or by radar; avoid a series of small changes. Your judgment—your "seamen's eye"—may tell you that only a slight change will be sufficient, but that change might well go undetected and leave the other skipper in doubt; see **Figure 5-05.** With some boats, particularly those with displacement hulls, a change of course is preferable to a change in speed as the latter is less likely to be noticed.

The action taken must be sufficient to result in passing at a safe distance; continue to check its effectiveness until the other vessel is clear. If you have to, you must slow down *or take all way off* by stopping or reversing. [8]

Basic Responsibilities

Two Navigation Rules are of such primary importance that every skipper should know them by heart. These are "the rule of good seamanship," and "the general prudential rule."

The Rule of Good Seamanship

Rule 2(a) is the broad, summing-up RULE OF GOOD SEAMANSHIP. It provides that nothing in the rules shall exonerate any vessel, or its owner, master, or crew, from the consequences of failing to comply with the rules, or of neglecting any precaution that may be required either by the ordinary practice of seamen or by the special circumstances of the case. Whatever you can do to avoid a collision, you must do!

The General Prudential Rule

Rule 2(b) is often termed the GENERAL PRUDENTIAL RULE and is of great importance due to its wide applicability. In obeying and construing the Rules of the Road, due regard must be given to all dangers of navigation and collision, and to any special circumstances, including the limitation of the vessels, which may render a departure from the rules necessary to avoid immediate danger. The Rules must not be literally, blindly followed into a collision.

Interpretation of "Dangers" Courts have placed considerable emphasis on the word "dangers" of Rule 2(b) in rendering their decisions. The basic principle is that the rules must not be abandoned whenever *perceptible* risk of collision exists, but only when *imperatively required*

by special circumstances, as when the actions of one vessel alone will not avoid a collision.

Lookouts

Every vessel must at *all* times maintain a proper lookout by sight and hearing as well as by all other available and appropriate means, to keep fully appraised of the situation and any risk of collision. [5]

The need for a proper lookout is often taken too lightly on small boats. Under normal circumstances, the helmsman will satisfy this need, but he must be qualified, alert, and have no other responsibilities. The use of an automatic steering mechanism (an "autopilot"; see Chapter 21) is not justification for the absence of a human helmsman at the controls, observing all around the horizon and ready to take over immediately if needed. The use of radar at night or in fog does not justify the absence of an additional person as a lookout, stationed outside the bridge, usually forward, where he can hear as well as see; see **Figure 5-06.**

Figure 5-06 It is the responsibility of the skipper of a boat of any size that a proper lookout is maintained at all times. Failure to do this raises serious questions of liability in case of an accident.

The noise level of most motorboats renders the helmsman totally ineffective as a listening watch.

The Rules do not prohibit single-handed boating or operating with a short-handed crew. It is not the intent of Rule 5 to require additional personnel forward if none is needed for safety. The burden of proof, however, will continue to be on each vessel involved in a collision to establish that a proper lookout could not have prevented the accident.

General Right-of-Way Provisions

Except for vessels specifically designated otherwise—such as vessels in narrow channels and Traffic Separation Schemes and those overtaking—vessels may be "ranked" for right-of-way as follows:

- Vessels not under command
- Vessels restricted in ability to maneuver
- Vessels engaged in fishing
- Sailing vessels
- Power-driven vessels

Each type of vessel in this list must yield right-of-way to vessels listed higher, and will be privileged with respect to those lower on the list. [18] Rules 9, 10, and 13 cover the exceptions.

Caution Required

Be aware that not all skippers know the Rules! Be prepared to take whatever steps are necessary to avoid collision, even if technically your boat has the right-of-way.

Actions by the Give-Way Vessel

Actions by a vessel that is required by the Rules to keep out of the way of another vessel (a burdened vessel) are simple and straightforward: "So far as is possible, take early and substantial action to keep well clear." [16]

Actions by the Stand-On Vessel

The vessel that has the right-of-way must maintain its course and speed, at least initially. [17] But the privileged vessel is never allowed to proceed blindly into a collision. The best way to think of the stand-on vessel's responsibility is as a three-stage action.

Stage One The approaching vessel on a collision course is still some distance away. The stand-on vessel must at this time keep its course and speed to allow the other vessel full opportunity to maneuver. [17(a)(i)]

Stage Two The other vessel, which is required to give way, continues approaching and is getting uncomfortably close. It appears that it does not realize the situation and is not intending to maneuver. At this point, the privileged vessel may maneuver to avoid a collision. [17(a)(ii)] If the stand-on vessel chooses to maneuver, however, it must not alter course to port for a vessel on its own port side. [17(c)]

Stage Three The separation between the vessels continues to decrease and the situation becomes one in which no action by the give-way vessel can avoid a collision. At this point, the stand-on vessel is *required* to take any action that is necessary to avoid a collision. [17(b)]

It should be noted that Rule 17 does not relieve the give-way vessel of its obligation to keep out of the way of the privileged vessel.

Sound Signals

One- and two-blast whistle signals used between power-driven vessels encountering each other are discussed in this section, along with the determination of right-of-way and the necessary actions to be taken by the vessels.

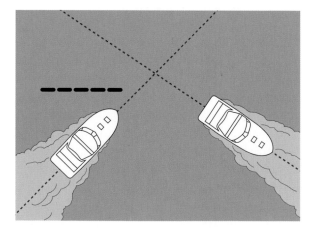

Figure 5-07 The danger signal is five (or more) short blasts sounded rapidly. It is used when danger is evident, or there is doubt about another vessel's actions or intentions. Here, the boat on the right is backing into danger.

"THE RULE OF TONNAGE"

The Inland and International Navigation Rules must be interpreted with common sense. A collision between a large steel ship and a fiberglass boat of almost any size will not result in equal damage and casualties on both vessels. This harsh reality leads to the *very unofficial* "Rule of Tonnage" that says that small, lightweight craft should always avoid close-quarters situations with big ships of heavy tonnage. In the language of the Rules in many cases, all vessels are equal, but in actuality "some are more equal than others."

The speed of a large ship first seen at a distance can be difficult to judge, particularly when viewed head-on. Large tankers and containerships often travel at four or more times the speed of a sailboat or trawler-type powerboat. A dot on the horizon can become a close-quarters situation in less than 15 minutes. The time between first sighting and collision can shrink to a minute or less in reduced visibility. Small craft must look out all around the horizon, not just ahead.

Installing larger, brighter navigation lights greatly improves the possibility of a small boat being seen. Flags, sails, and other equipment on board must never be allowed to obscure navigation lights, especially a sternlight.

Large vessels use radar for collision avoidance, but this is no guarantee that a nonmetallic boat will be visible on the screen. Sea clutter and other natural phenomena can prevent the echo from a small boat being detected. A radar reflector, mounted high and in the "catch-rain" orientation, increases the size of the radar echo returned to the ship, making the craft more visible on the display on the ship's bridge.

A boat can make itself more visible at night by shining a light on its deck or cabin, or onto its sails. If the approach of a large ship becomes uncomfortable, an attempt to communicate should be made on VHF Channel 13 or 16 (or 70 using DSC, see Chapter 20, page 694). Finally, small craft should always consider the advisability of making major course changes to avoid a close-quarters situation with a large ship. Sailboats should start their auxiliary engine in preparation for motoring out of harm's way.

These signals are to be used *only* when the vessels are in sight of each other and are meeting or crossing at a distance within half a mile of each other. [34] These signals must never be used in fog or other conditions of reduced visibility; where the vessels are not visible to each other by eye, only the fog signals of Rule 35 may be sounded at such a time.

Danger Signal

In any situation where two vessels are approaching each other, if one fails to understand the actions or intentions of the other, or if not sure that sufficient action is being taken by the other to avoid collision, the vessel in doubt must give the DANGER SIGNAL—*five or more* short and rapid blasts on its whistle; see **Figure 5-07.** [34(d)]

A skipper also uses this signal to indicate that he considers the actions of the other vessel dangerous to either vessel—such as a negative reply to a proposal to pass in a certain manner.

Giving a danger signal does not relieve a vessel of its obligations or responsibilities under any Rule.

Although not specifically covered in the Rules, a careful skipper who either hears or sounds a danger signal will *at once* slow or stop his vessel until the situation is clarified for all concerned.

Equipment for Sound Signals

The term "whistle" dates back to the beginning of steam propulsion for ships. Today, the Navigation Rules accept not only a steam whistle, but also an air horn or electric horn to make the required signals.

Annex III of the Rules specifies the tone of the whistle for various sizes of vessels—the smaller the vessel, the higher the pitch of the whistle or horn. A vessel pushing another vessel or vessels may sound a whistle whose characteristics are determined by the combined length of the tug and tow.

A vessel *12 meters* (39.4 ft) *or more* in length must have a WHISTLE and a BELL; a vessel of 100 meters (328.1 ft) or more in length must also have a GONG, the tone and sound of which cannot be confused with those of the bell. [33(a)]

A vessel *less than 12 meters* (39.4 ft) in length need not carry the sound-signaling equipment required on larger vessels, but if it does not, it must have "some other means of making an efficient sound signal." [33(b)] There are no requirements for small boats in terms of range (0.5 mile would be a reasonable minimum) or source of power—only in terms of efficiency—and sailboats have the same requirements as motorboats. (Some states do have requirements for sound equipment on smaller vessels.)

For vessels *over 12 meters* (39.4 ft) in length, however, Annex III contains detailed specifications for sound-signaling equipment, including whistle tones, and ranges of audibility. Higher-pitched tones are used for smaller vessels; for those of *less than 75 meters* (246.1 ft) length, the band of frequencies is 250 to 525 Hz. Required ranges of audibility gradually increase, from 0.5 mile for vessels *12 but less than 20 meters* (39.4 to 65.6 ft) in length, to 2 miles for vessels *longer than 200 meters* (656.2 ft); all distances are coordinated with specific sound pressure levels (loudness). [III-86.05] A vessel normally used for pushing ahead or towing alongside may carry a whistle with characteristics matched to the length of the longest towed-and-towing combination customarily operated, and may use it even when operating singly. [III-86.15] The Annex specifies directional properties and positioning for whistles, and a limitation on sound pressure level at the vessel's own "listening posts" (lookout or helm position). [III-86.07 and 86.09]

All bells and gongs must be made of corrosion-resistant material and be designed to give a clear tone. Specifications for bells and gongs include different sizes for smaller and larger vessels, and a minimum sound-pressure level. A bell on boats *under 20 meters* (65.6 ft) in length must be not less than 200 mm (7.9 inches) in diameter at the mouth. Bells on larger vessels must be at least 300 mm (11.8 inches) in diameter. The mass of the striker for any size of bell must not be less than 3 percent of the mass of that bell. [III-86.21 and 86.23]

The bell or gong, or both, on a vessel may be replaced by "other equipment" (usually electronic) having the same sound characteristics, provided that the prescribed signals can always be sounded manually as well. [33(a)]

Maneuvering Lights

Whistle signals may be supplemented by a light signal synchronized with the whistle; the flashes have the same significance as the whistle blasts. This is a single all-round light, white or yellow, visible for at least two miles regardless of the size of the vessel. [34(b)(iii)] This MANEUVERING LIGHT must be placed in the same vertical plane as the "masthead" light(s), at least one-half meter (19.7 in) above the forward masthead light, and at least one-half meter (19.7 in) above or below the after masthead light. If a vessel carries only one masthead light, as will be the case for nearly all small craft, the maneuvering light can be carried where it can best be seen, but not less than one-half meter (19.7 in) vertically apart from the masthead light. Remember that a maneuvering light is an all-round light and should not be significantly obscured in any direction. [I-84.23]

Rules for Power-Driven Vessels Underway

The Navigation Rules recognize three types of encounters between two approaching vessels—meeting, crossing, and overtaking; see **Figure 5-08**. The rules governing right-of-way, whistle signals to be given, and actions to be taken with regard to course and speed changes, are given below for power-driven vessels underway. Remember that a boat being propelled by both sails and machinery is considered in the Navigation Rules as a power-driven vessel.

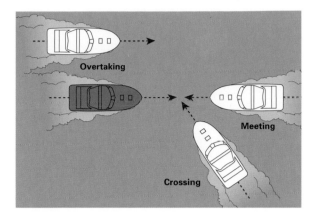

Figure 5-08 The Navigation Rules recognize three types of encounters in reference here to the dark blue boat and one of the other boats—meeting, crossing, and overtaking. Specific provisions of the Rules govern the actions taken and signals given by both vessels in each of these situations.

Meeting Situation

When two power-driven vessels are approaching one another head-on, or nearly head-on, this is a MEETING SITUATION. In this situation, unless otherwise agreed each should pass on the port side of the other. [14(a)] Neither vessel has the right-of-way over the other, and both must alter course to starboard, if necessary, to provide sufficient clearance for safe passage; see **Figure 5-09.** This is exactly the same, it will be noted, as for two cars meeting on a narrow road. This is colloquially referred to as a "port-to-port" or a "one-whistle" passing.

For the Rule of the meeting situation to apply, two requirements must be met: the vessels must be meeting in such a manner as to involve risk of collision, and they must be on reciprocal or nearly reciprocal courses. Such a situation is deemed to exist by day when a vessel sees the other ahead or nearly ahead, and by night when it can see the masthead lights of the other in a line or nearly in a line, or sees both sidelights. [14(b)] Although the rules do not set mathematical limits for the meeting situation, court interpretations and decisions over the years have established an arc of one point (11.25°), with half on either side, as the practical boundaries of the zone within which vessels will be considered as meeting each other.

This Rule does not apply to two vessels that will, if both keep on their respective courses

without change of heading or speed, pass clear of each other.

When a vessel has any doubt that a meeting situation exists, it must assume the situation does exist and act accordingly; that is, change course to starboard. [14(c)]

In a winding channel, a vessel may first sight the other at an oblique angle rather than "head on, or nearly head on." Nevertheless, the situation is to be regarded as a meeting situation since they will be "head on or nearly head on" when the actual passing occurs. Each should keep to its own right side of the channel and neither has the right-of-way over the other.

Exception A power-driven vessel operating on the Great Lakes, the Western Rivers, or other waters designated by the Secretary, and proceeding downbound with the current, has the right-of-way over an upbound vessel. The downbound vessel proposes the manner of passing and initiates the whistle signals. [14(d)]

Signals When power-driven vessels are within sight of each other and meeting at a distance of a half-mile or less, each vessel *must* sound whistle as follows:

One short blast, meaning "I intend to leave you on my port side."

Two short blasts, meaning "I intend to leave you on my starboard side."

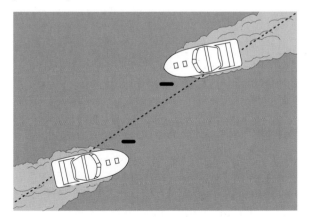

Figure 5-09 In a meeting situation, both vessels must sound one short blast, alter course to starboard, and pass port-to-port. Either vessel can signal first; neither vessel has the "right-of-way." If there is any doubt as to whether the courses of the boats are reciprocal, a meeting situation must be assumed to exist and appropriate actions taken.

Three short blasts, meaning "I am operating astern propulsion" (engines in reverse gear).

Upon hearing the one- or two-short-blast signal from the other, a vessel will, if in agreement, sound the same signal and take any steps necessary to effect a safe passage. If it doubts the safety of the proposed maneuver for any reason, it must sound the danger signal of five or more short, rapid blasts *and* take appropriate precautionary action until a safe passage agreement is made. [34(a)] The rule does not state which vessel should signal first—both boats are on an equal basis and either can make the first signal to the other.

Note that a vessel should *never* answer a one-blast signal with two blasts, nor a two-blast signal with one blast. This is known as CROSS SIGNALS and can only lead to confusion and a hazardous situation.

When one vessel sounds the danger signal in a meeting situation, both vessels should immediately stop or reduce their forward speed to bare steerageway. [8(e)] Neither vessel should attempt to proceed or pass until agreement is reached through the exchange of the same whistle signal, either one short blast or two.

Crossing Situation

When two power-driven vessels are not meeting head-on, or nearly so, and each has the other forward of a direction 22.5° abaft the beam, a CROSSING SITUATION exists.

When two power-driven vessels are crossing so as to involve risk of collision, the vessel that has the other on its own starboard side must avoid crossing ahead of and must keep out of the way of the other. [15] See **Figure 5-10.**

This leads to the unofficial definition of a boat's DANGER ZONE—a concept not explicitly stated in the Navigation Rules, but one very valuable for safety. This is the arc from dead ahead to 22.5° abaft the starboard beam; see illustration in sidebar "The Danger Zone." If you see another vessel within this danger zone, it most likely is the stand-on (privileged) vessel; yours is the give-way (burdened) vessel and must change course or speed to avoid collision.

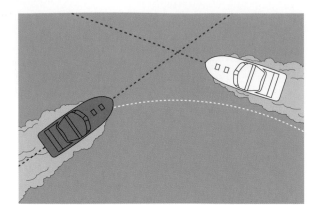

Figure 5-10 When two power-driven vessels encounter each other not in a meeting situation but with each having the other forward of a direction 22.5° abaft the beam, this is a crossing situation. The vessel that has the other on its starboard side is the give-way (burdened, colored dark blue) vessel and must take action to avoid collision. It can slow down, stop, or turn to starboard (but never to port!).

The stand-on (privileged) vessel has the right-of-way and maintains course and speed unless the other vessel fails to take suitable action.

Exceptions On all waters, a vessel must not cross a narrow channel or fairway in such a way as to impede the progress of a vessel which can only navigate safely within that channel or fairway. The vessel in the channel shall use the danger signal if it is in doubt as to the intention of the crossing vessel. [9(d)]

Further, on the Great Lakes, the Western Rivers, and any other waters specified by the Secretary, a vessel crossing a river must keep clear of a power-driven vessel proceeding up or down that river. [15(b)] This situation is analogous to a road intersection on land, where the side street has a "Stop" sign to prevent interference with traffic on the main street.

Signals The Inland Rules *require* whistle signals in both meeting and crossing situations. If the vessels are in sight of each other and will pass within a distance of a half-mile [34(a)], one, two, and three short blasts are used with the same meanings as described above for meeting situations. Again, the Rules do not state which vessel should signal first, but by custom it is most often the vessel that is privileged, or believes itself to be privileged. A one- or two-short-blast signal is

THE DANGER ZONE

A power-driven vessel of any size has a so-called "danger zone" from dead ahead to 22.5° abaft its starboard beam (see below). It must give way to any crossing vessel that approaches within this zone. The danger zone is a concept that is implicit—although not specifically mentioned—in the Navigation Rules.

Note that the danger zone of the give-way vessel has the same arc of visibility as its green sidelight. Thus the stand-on vessel sees a "go" light from the other vessel. Conversely, the give-way vessel sees the red ("stop") light of the stand-on vessel—a very logical situation!

Most often, altering course to starboard is the best action for the give-way vessel to keep clear; this allows that vessel to pass safely astern of the other. Slowing down or stopping are other options. The give-way vessel should not turn to port for a vessel forward of its beam.

The danger zone is not, however, applicable in all crossing situations. On the Great Lakes, the Western Rivers, and other specified waters, a power-driven vessel going upriver or down does not have to yield to a vessel in its danger zone if that other vessel is crossing the river. [15(b)]

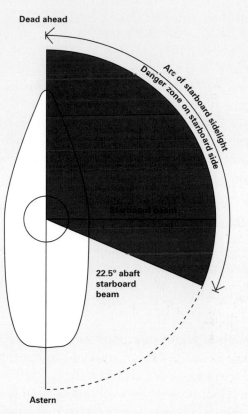

The "danger zone" is a concept implicit in the rules of the road, and should be firmly understood by every boater.

A somewhat similar exception applies in all waters to small vessels crossing a narrow channel or fairway. [9(b)]

answered with the same number of blasts if the other vessel is in agreement and will take the steps necessary to effect a safe passage. The danger signal of five or more short, rapid blasts is used in the same way to indicate doubt in the safety of the actions taken or in the signaled intentions of the other vessel.

A maneuvering light may show one, two, three, or five or more flashes synchronized with the whistle blasts.

Note that this rule applies only if there is risk of collision. If two vessels will cross free and clear of each other, neither is the stand-on or give-way vessel, and thus whistle signals are inappropriate.

In case of doubt, however, the safe procedure is to assume that the intentions of each are not known to the other.

Overtaking Situation

A power-driven or sail vessel is considered to be OVERTAKING when it is coming up on another, from a direction of more than 22.5° abaft either beam of the other vessel, and making greater speed so as to close the distance between them; see **Figure 5-11**. At night, this situation exists when the vessel astern cannot see either of the sidelights of the vessel ahead. By day, the overtaking vessel cannot always know with certainty whether it is

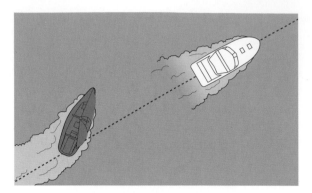

Figure 5-11 Any vessel approaching another from more than 22.5° abaft the other's beam, either side, is overtaking. As such it must keep out of the way of the vessel being overtaken. This rule applies even to a sailboat overtaking a motorboat. The overtaking boat remains in the give-way status for the remainder of the encounter and must keep clear until fully past even though this takes it through the other vessel's danger zone.

forward or abaft a direction 22.5° abaft the other vessel's beam; if in doubt, it should assume that it is an overtaking vessel. [13(b) and (c)]

Notwithstanding any other provision in the Navigation Rules, every vessel overtaking another must keep out of the way of the overtaken vessel. The overtaking vessel is burdened; the overtaken vessel is privileged. [13(a)]

The Rules state specifically that once a vessel is in an overtaking status, it remains so for the remainder of the encounter; no subsequent alteration of the bearing between the two vessels will serve to make the overtaking vessel a crossing vessel within the meaning of the rules, or relieve it of its duty to keep clear of the overtaken vessel until it is finally past and clear. In other words, should the overtaking vessel come up on the starboard side of the overtaken vessel, and move into its danger zone, the overtaking vessel does not by this movement become the privileged vessel with the right-of-way. [13(d)]

Signals If the overtaking vessel desires to pass on the port side of the vessel ahead—as would be normal if the slower vessel were keeping to the right of a channel (see **Figure 5-12**, left)—it must sound a two-short-blast signal. If the privileged vessel agrees with such a passing, it should immediately sound the same signal. The faster vessel then directs its course to port and passes as proposed and agreed.

Should the vessel astern desire to pass on the other's starboard side—not normal, but legally permissible (see **Figure 5-12**, center)—it must sound a one-short-blast signal, which is returned in kind by the privileged vessel if it consents. [34(c) and 9(e)]

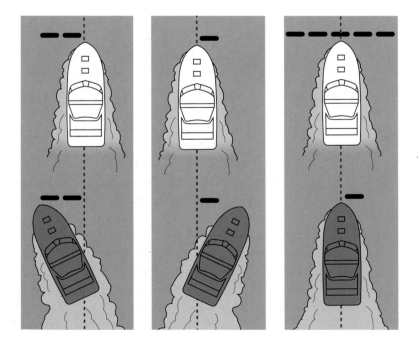

Figure 5-12 The overtaking boat (burdened, colored dark blue) signals first: two blasts for "I intend to overtake you on your port side" (the normal method); one blast for "I intend to overtake you on your starboard side" (legal, but less desirable). Note that the wording differs from that used with the meeting and crossing signals, found on pages 157 and 158. If the signaled action is safe, the overtaken boat replies with the same signal. If it is not safe, that boat sounds the danger signal, five or more short blasts.

If in either of the above situations the vessel ahead does not consider that the proposed passing can take place safely, it must immediately sound the danger signal of five or more short, rapid blasts. (The danger signal should also be sounded if the overtaking boat attempts an unsafe passing without first giving a whistle signal of its intentions.)

An overtaking vessel receiving a danger signal in reply to its stated intention to pass should immediately cease all actions related to passing, and reduce speed so as to close no further on the overtaken vessel; see **Figure 5-12,** right. No attempt should be made to pass until the proper signals have been given and answered. Although not provided for in the Rules, it is reasonable for a privileged vessel to give the danger signal, pause, and then give the other passing signal to the burdened vessel—saying in effect, "The side that you proposed is unsafe, but the other is OK." This action by the privileged vessel is not normal, but it is often logical because the leading vessel has a better view of the conditions ahead.

As in the meeting situation, cross signals—answering one blast with two, or two blasts with one—makes for an unsafe situation. Answer a signal only with the same signal received, or with the danger signal.

Even though the slower vessel ahead is privileged, it must never attempt to cross the bow or crowd the course of the passing vessel.

Although the overtaken (stand-on) vessel is required by Rule 17(a)(i) to keep its course and speed, it is often a desirable action in narrow channels or confined waterways for a boat to slow down so that the passing craft can likewise slow and thus pass with less wake. This action is a departure from the basic Rules, but it is covered by the language in Rule 9(e)(i) that the overtaken vessel may "take steps to permit safe passing." It is also covered by Rule 2(b).

Use of Radio Communications

Vessels 20 meters (65.6 ft) or more in length, or greater than 100 tons carrying passengers, or 26 feet (7.9 m) or more in length engaged in towing must have a Bridge-to-Bridge VHF-FM radio.

The Inland Rules state that vessels that have reached agreement in a meeting, crossing, or overtaking situation by using radio (Channel 13 in most areas, but 67 on the lower Mississippi River) need not sound whistle signals, but may do so. If agreement is not reached, then whistle signals must be exchanged "in a timely manner," and these will govern the actions taken. [34(h)] The use of radio is highly desirable as it permits the exchange of so much more information than can be communicated by simple whistle blasts; it should be the preferred means of signaling in all passing situations.

Narrow Channels

A vessel in a narrow channel must keep to the right and as close to the outer limit of the channel as is safe and practicable. [9(a)(i)] This places a burden on a vessel on the *left* side to (1) be there only if it must, and (2) establish agreement for a starboard-to-starboard passage.

Exception On the Great Lakes, the Western Rivers, and any other waters specified by the Secretary, a power-driven vessel operating in a narrow channel or fairway and proceeding *downbound with a following current* has the right-of-way over an upbound vessel and shall initiate maneuvering signals as appropriate. The vessel proceeding upbound against the current must hold as necessary to permit safe passing. [9(a)(ii)] This does not apply in tidal waters where there might be doubt as to the direction of the current, but by common courtesy a vessel proceeding against the current yields to the other.

Rounding Bends in a Channel

A special sound signal is provided for a situation in which a vessel approaches a bend or channel area where other vessels may be unseen because of an obstruction such as the banks, vegetation, or structures. In this situation the vessel sounds the "blind bend" signal of one prolonged blast. This signal must be answered with one prolonged blast by any approaching vessel within hearing. [34(e)] If such an answer is received, normal whistle signals must be exchanged when the vessels come within sight of

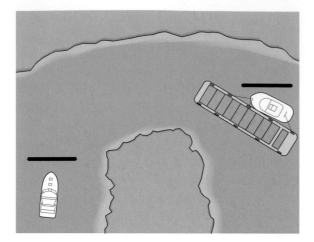

Figure 5-13 When a vessel is approaching a bend in a river where vessels coming from the other direction cannot be seen, it should sound a special "blind bend signal" of one prolonged (4 to 6 seconds) blast. A second vessel approaching from the other direction answers with the same signal, and both vessels proceed with due caution exchanging normal signals when within sight of each other.

one another; see **Figure 5-13.** If no reply to its signal is heard, the vessel may consider the channel ahead to be clear. All vessels in such situations must be navigated "with particular alertness and caution." [9(f)]

In each such situation, a vessel with limited maneuverability or one requiring most of the channel width will often make a "security call" on VHF Channel 13 or 16, or both, to announce its position and direction of travel. Such calls should be answered by any vessels approaching the area.

Leaving a Berth

A power-driven vessel leaving a dock or berth must sound a warning signal of one prolonged blast. [34(g)] The same signal should be given by a boat exiting a side canal into a river or waterway.

Note that, although it is not explicitly so stated in the Navigation Rules, it may be inferred that a boat just emerging from a slip or berth does not have the right-of-way over another vessel passing in the channel or nearby open water, even though it is in the other's danger zone—its privileged status in a crossing situation is not established until it is "fully in sight."

Don't Impede Other Vessels

A vessel less than 20 meters (65.6 ft) in length, or a sailing vessel, must not impede the passage of a vessel that can navigate safely only within a narrow channel or fairway. [9(b)]

A vessel engaged in fishing must not impede the passage of any other vessel navigating within a narrow channel or fairway. [9(c)]

A vessel must not cross a narrow channel or fairway in such a manner as to impede the progress of a vessel that must stay within that channel or fairway. The latter vessel must use the danger signal if there is doubt about the intentions of the crossing vessel. [9(d)]

If the circumstances allow, a vessel must not anchor in a narrow channel. [9(g)]

Ferry Boats

Although there are no express provisions in the Inland Rules that give special privileges to ferry boats, the courts have repeatedly ruled that ferries are entitled to a reasonable degree of freedom of entrance to and exit from their slips.

Boats should avoid passing unnecessarily close to piers, wharves, etc., where they may be caught unawares by movements of other vessels.

Rules for Sailing Vessels Underway

The provisions of Inland Rule 12, which are stated below, apply only to situations involving two sailing vessels; neither may be under power, or a combination of sail and power.

When two sailing vessels are approaching one another so as to involve risk of collision, one of them must keep out of the way of the other in accordance with the following conditions:

• When each has the wind on a different side, the vessel with the wind on its port side must keep out of the way of the other; see **Figure 5-14.** [12(a)(i)]

• When both have the wind on the same side, the vessel to windward must keep out of the way of the vessel that is to leeward; see **Figure 5-15.** [12(a)(ii)]

• If a vessel with the wind on its port side sees a vessel to windward and cannot determine with certainty whether the other vessel has the wind on its port or starboard side, it must keep out of the way of that vessel. [12(a)(iii)]

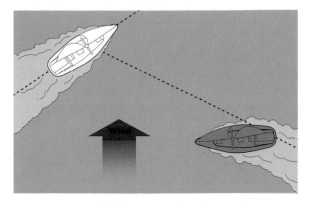

Figure 5-14 Sailboats meeting may be on opposite tacks—one with the wind to starboard, the other with the wind to port. The boat with the wind to starboard is on a starboard tack and is the stand-on vessel, having Right-of-Way. The boat (colored dark blue) with the wind to port is burdened and must give way. If in doubt, a skipper should assume that his boat does not have the Right-of-Way.

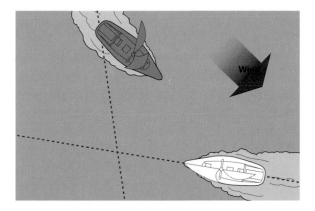

Figure 5-15 When two sailboats meet on the same tack (both with the wind on the same side), one will be to windward of the other—farther in the direction from which the wind is blowing. This is the windward boat (burdened, colored dark blue), which must keep clear of the leeward boat (privileged). A leeward boat might have its wind blocked and be hampered in its ability to maneuver.

For the purpose of Rule 12, the windward side is the side opposite that on which the mainsail is carried (or in the case of a square-rigged vessel, the side opposite that on which the largest fore-and-aft sail is carried). [12(b)]

Signals Sound signals are not required to be used in passing situations between two sailing vessels. Note, however, that sailing vessels are required to sound all reduced visibility ("fog") signals, whether on a whistle, horn, or bell.

Encounters Between Sailing & Power Vessels

In general, a sailing vessel has the right-of-way over a vessel propelled by machinery or by both sail and machinery. The power-driven vessel must keep out of the way of the sailing vessel. [18(a)(iv)] Passing signals are not required to be given, but are not prohibited; if a powerboat signals a sailboat, it should not expect a reply; see **Figure 5-16.**

There are, however, some exceptions and they should be thoroughly understood. Should a sailing vessel overtake a power-driven vessel, the overtaking situation rule prevails and the sailing vessel is the burdened one, regardless of the means of propulsion. [13]

Likewise, a sailing vessel is not the privileged vessel in an encounter with certain vessels engaged in fishing (but this does not include trolling), a vessel not under command, or a vessel restricted in its ability to maneuver; see **Figure 5-17.** [18(b)]

Vessel Traffic Service

A VESSEL TRAFFIC SERVICE (VTS) is established by U.S. Coast Guard regulations to provide mariners with information relating to the safe navigation of a congested waterway or area of special hazards. Normally advisory only, under certain circumstances a VTS may issue directions to control the movement of vessels in order to

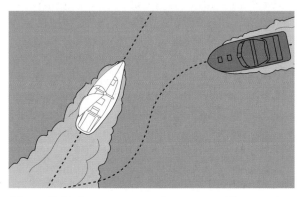

Figure 5-16 In an encounter between a sailboat and one driven by power, the powerboat (burdened, colored dark blue above) must keep out of the way of the sailing craft. However, if the sailboat is overtaking a powerboat—an unlikely, but possible situation—the sailboat is the burdened vessel.

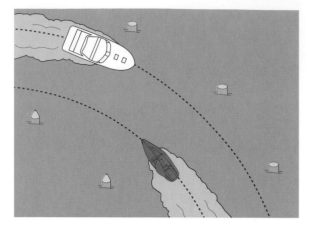

Figure 5-17 *A sailboat must keep clear of a vessel that cannot navigate outside of the channel it is using, most fishing vessels, and vessels not under command. The sailboat (colored dark blue) above is the burdened vessel.*

minimize the risk of collisions between vessels, or damage to property or the environment. The master or person directing the movement of the vessel remains at all times responsible for compliance with the applicable Navigation Rules.

A VTS consists of a system of regulations, communications, and monitoring facilities established at selected ports and confined waterways to provide active position monitoring, collision avoidance services and navigational advice. For each VTS area, a set of reporting-in points and precautionary areas are established. In most locations, vessels report their position, speed and other information to a VESSEL TRAFFIC CENTER (VTC) on a designated VHF radio channel. The VTC monitors conditions in the area with one or more remote radar sites, and in some cases, remote TV cameras. Some VTS are voluntary, but most are compulsory for specified classes of vessels when navigating—all power-driven vessels over 40 meters (131 ft), all towing vessels over 8 meters (26 ft), and all vessels certificated for 50 or more passengers when engaged in trade. In some ports, vessels at anchor are required to monitor a separate designated channel.

Recreational boats are not normally subject to VTS regulations, but should be aware of the restrictions placed on the movement of larger vessels. They may monitor the VTS radio channel, but should not transmit.

Automatic Vessel Identification An AUTOMATIC IDENTIFICATION SYSTEM (AIS), where established and for ships so equipped, provides for the continuous transmission of a vessel's movement to a VTC, and to other ships with equipment to receive and display such information. A GLOBAL POSITIONING SYSTEM (GPS) receiver (see Chapter 21, page 727) supplies position, course, and speed data to a radio that then transmits it, plus other vital information such as type of vessel, call sign, etc., digitally on a designated VHF channel. The system is capable of handling more than 2,000 messages per minute, with updates as frequently as every two seconds. AIS will eventually be operational on all waters, including the high seas.

Conduct in Restricted Visibility

Fog is the usual reason for restricted visibility, but not the only one. Other causes include heavy rain or snow, sandstorms, or even dense smoke from on shore. Rule 19 applies to vessels that are not in sight of each other in *or near* areas of restricted visibility. They must proceed at a "safe speed adapted to the prevailing circumstances and conditions." [19(b)] The Rules make no reference to a specific speed that would be considered "safe." This is left for the skipper of each vessel to decide, but the obvious intent of the rule is that vessels should *slow down*. There is no mention of the old adage of "being able to stop in half the distance of visibility," but that does make good sense. If both vessels followed this procedure, they would not collide. The use of radar is not a justification for failing to operate at a safe speed; nor is it an excuse for not posting appropriate lookouts. Each skipper must consider Rule 6 carefully to determine the application of all factors to the particular situation at hand.

Vessels must also have due regard for the steering and sailing rules that prevail under all conditions of visibility. [19(c)]

Close-Quarters Situations

When a fog signal of another vessel is heard apparently forward of the beam, the boat hearing it is required to reduce speed to bare steerageway. If

TAKING ALL WAY OFF

The following excerpt is taken from Cockroft & Lameijer's *A Guide to the Collision Avoidance Rules:*

The courts have held that a vessel operating without radar in restricted visibility should reverse engines to take all way off in the following instances:

- A fog signal is heard for the first time in close proximity.
- A fog signal is heard dead ahead.
- A fog signal appears to be a narrowing beam that is moving toward the bow.
- Another vessel is seen looming out of the fog, but its course cannot be determined.
- A sailboat's fog signal is heard forward of the beam.
- A fog signal is heard of a vessel at anchor and the tide is setting toward it.

There are many other situations in which taking all way off is indicated. When this is done, however, it should be kept in mind that the sound of the engines reversing may block out further fog signals from other vessels.

necessary, the boat hearing the signal must take all way off (stop dead) and "in any event, navigate with extreme caution until danger of collision is over." The same requirement to slow down or stop applies to any boat that knows it is in close quarters with another vessel, even if it has not heard a fog signal. [19(e)]

How "close" is close-quarters? The Rules make no statement on this question. On the high seas, this distance is generally regarded as about 2 nautical miles, or the audible range of the typical ship's fog signal.

It is important to remember that the apparent direction of sound signals can be very misleading in fog. Additional lookouts should be posted and instructed to both look and listen. Never alter course until the position of the other vessel is

known with reasonable certainty. If radar is available, it must be used.

Engine Availability

Whenever visibility is restricted, a power-driven vessel must have its engines ready for immediate maneuver. [19(b)] The same advice also makes good sense for sailboats with auxiliary power, but is not required by the Rules.

Using Radar Information

Vessels that have radar on board must use it properly, including plotting or equivalent systematic observation of detected objects to obtain early warning of a risk of collision, but most especially in restricted visibility. [7(b)] If a close-quarters situation with another vessel is detected by radar alone, the vessel using radar must take action to avoid the risk of collision in ample time—but certain types of actions must be avoided.

- An alteration of course to port for a vessel forward of the beam, other than a vessel being overtaken. [19(d)]
- An alteration of course toward a vessel abeam or abaft the beam. [19(d)(ii)]

Any action to avoid risk of collision in restricted visibility should be monitored to ensure that a new risk does not develop. Lookouts must be posted and the radar observed continuously with plotting or equivalent systematic observation of detected objects. [7(b)]

IF COLLISION IS UNAVOIDABLE

It's not a happy thought, but the rule of thumb is this:

- Stop as quickly as possible and face the danger. If there's any doubt on which side a vessel approaching directly and at a relatively high speed may attempt to pass, present as small a target as possible. The effects of a collision will be much less if the impact is taken end-on rather than broadside.

Sound Signals in Restricted Visibility

Rule 35 prescribes sound signals to be given by different types of vessels in various conditions when in *or near* an area of restricted visibility. These are often termed "fog signals," but they apply equally in any of the conditions included in the definition of restricted visibility (see above, page 164). They also apply equally day or night. The same equipment is used for these whistle signals as for maneuvering and warning signals.

Courts have held that fog signals should be sounded when visibility is reduced to the distance at which sidelights are required. These sound signals serve two purposes: they alert nearby vessels to the presence and approximate position of the signaling vessel; and they may indicate its status (underway or not) or limitations of maneuverability (towing, being towed, sailing, fishing, etc.).

Power-Driven Vessels Underway

A power-driven vessel making way through the water must sound one prolonged blast at intervals of *not more than two minutes.* [35(a)]

Such a vessel underway but stopped and making no way through the water (also described as "underway with no way on") must sound, at the same intervals, a signal of two prolonged blasts in succession separated by an interval of about two seconds. {35(b)]

A vessel towing or pushing another ahead, a vessel not under command, a vessel restricted in its ability to maneuver (underway or at anchor), and a fishing vessel (underway or anchored) all sound the same signal—one prolonged blast followed by two short blasts. [35(c)]

Sailing Vessels Underway

A sailing vessel underway makes the same sound signal in restricted visibility conditions as does a towing vessel, fishing vessel, etc., just as described above—one prolonged blast followed by two short blasts. [35(c)] Note that a sailing vessel, while not required to have a whistle for passing signals, must have some means of signaling in reduced visibility.

NOT TOO OFTEN!

The Rules prescribe an interval of "not more than two minutes" between the soundings of most fog signals from a vessel, and two minutes is the interval normally used. This is long enough for lookouts to recover their hearing after their own vessel sounds its fog signal, yet not so long as to allow other vessels to approach too closely without warning. Timing is best done automatically, and many electronic hailers have the capability to generate a fog signal regularly through their external sound system. If no automatic device is available, the sweep-second hand of a watch or clock may be used. The silent periods between blasts are intended for listening for signals from other vessels. (Note that the interval is one minute for bell and gong signals.)

Two minutes is a relatively brief interval and normally should not be further reduced by skippers concerned about collision. Use the interval between your blasts to listen for other vessels' signals; this is as valuable for safety as blowing your own whistle or horn. If your signals are sounded automatically, interrupt them from time to time to make sure you are not signaling in synchronization with another vessel.

Vessels at Anchor

A vessel at anchor *must*, at intervals of not more than *one minute*, ring its bell rapidly for about five seconds. If it is 100 meters (328.1 ft) or more in length, the bell must be sounded in the forepart of the vessel and immediately thereafter a gong must be sounded rapidly in the after part of the vessel. [35(f)]

A vessel at anchor *may* additionally sound a three-blast whistle signal—one short, one prolonged, one short—to give warning of its position, and the possibility of collision with an approaching vessel. [35(f)]

Special Anchorage Areas Inland Rule 35(j) permits the omission of fog signals for vessels in a "special anchorage area" (see Chapter 4, page 134), if they are less than 20 meters (65.6 ft) in length, or if they are a barge, canal boat, scow, or "other nondescript craft."

Vessels Aground

A vessel aground must sound the bell signal of a vessel at anchor (and the gong signal, if applicable) and additionally give three separate and distinct strokes on the bell immediately *before and after* the rapid ringing of the bell. [35(g)] It does not sound the whistle signal of an anchored vessel.

A vessel aground may also sound an appropriate whistle signal on detecting the approach of another vessel, if there is the possibility of collision. [35(g)] This rule is not specific as to the number and length of the blasts, but it could be the letter "U" of the International Code (short-short-long) for "You are standing into danger."

Vessels Being Towed

If manned, a vessel being towed (or the last vessel if several are being towed in a string) must sound a fog signal of four blasts—one prolonged and three short blasts—at intervals of not more than two minutes. When possible, this signal should be sounded immediately after the signal of the towing vessel; see **Figure 5-18.** [35(e)] Unmanned towed vessels are not required to sound a fog signal.

Pilot Vessels

A pilot vessel, when engaged on pilot duties in restricted visibility conditions, *may* sound an "iden-

tity signal" of four short blasts. This would be in addition to the normal signals of a vessel underway, underway with no way on, or at anchor. [35(i)]

Exception for Small Craft

Craft *less than 12 meters* (39.4 ft) in length may, but need not, sound the above fog signals; but if they do not, they must make "some other efficient sound signal" at intervals not exceeding two minutes. [35(h)]

Other Rules & Procedures

There are a number of other, somewhat unrelated, rules and procedures with which a skipper should be familiar.

Signals to Attract Attention

To attract the attention of another vessel, any vessel may make light and/or sound signals that cannot be mistaken for any signal authorized in the rules, or may direct the beam of his searchlight in the direction of the danger in such a way as to not embarrass any vessel. [36] The practical meaning of this prohibition is that you should not shine your searchlight directly into the pilot house or flybridge of another boat.

Use of high-intensity flashing ("strobe") lights for the purpose of attracting attention is illegal. They are an official distress signal.

Signals for Drawbridges & Locks

U.S. Coast Guard regulations—not a part of the Inland Rules or Pilot Rules—prescribe uniform

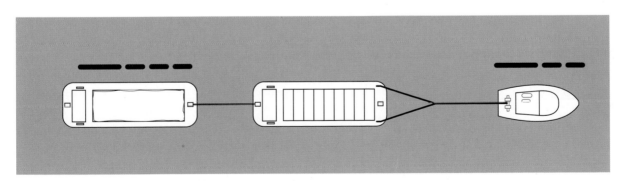

Figure 5-18 *A vessel towed astern (or the last vessel if more than one is being towed), if manned should sound a fog signal of one prolonged blast followed by three short blasts at intervals of not more than two minutes. If practicable, this signal should be sounded immediately after the fog signal—one prolonged followed by two short blasts—of the towing vessel.*

and unmistakable whistle signals for drawbridge operation. A vessel wishing to open a drawbridge for its passage will sound one prolonged whistle blast followed within three seconds by one short blast; this signal has no other meaning in any set of Rules of the Road. The regulations also provide for making the opening signal by horn, bell, or shout, or by any similar device whose sound can be clearly heard. The vessel's signal should be repeated until acknowledged by the drawtender (also called a bridge tender) before proceeding close to the bridge.

Intent to Open the Draw If the drawtender will open the draw immediately, he responds with a similar one-prolonged-one-short-blast signal. If the draw cannot be opened immediately, the drawtender will sound five short blasts. When this signal has been sounded from the bridge, a vessel is specifically prohibited from attempting to pass through the closed draw.

Immediate Closing When an open drawbridge must be closed immediately, the drawtender must first sound the five-short-blast signal. This signal must be acknowledged by the vessel by sounding the same five-short-blast signal; if the vessel does not acknowledge the drawtender's signal, the drawtender must repeat it until that is done. The same five-short-blast signal is sounded before a routine closing of a bridge; it is not replied to by a vessel unless it is still in the draw and would be endangered by the bridge being closed, in which case, the boat sounds five blasts. Other vessels must not enter the draw after the bridge tender has sounded the five-blast signal.

Approaching an Open Draw A vessel approaching a bridge that is already open still must give the opening signal. If no acknowledgement is received within 30 seconds, the vessel may proceed, with caution, through the draw.

Use of Visual Signals Visual signals may also be used, if weather conditions may prevent signals from being heard, or if sound-producing devices are not functioning properly. (Sound signals may also be used with visual signals.) A vessel signals with a white flag of sufficient size as to be readily visible for a half-mile by day, or a white light bright enough to be seen at the same distance at night. This signal is raised and lowered vertically, in full sight of the bridge tender, until acknowledged. The tender signals that the bridge will open immediately by repeating the same signal. The signal from the bridge that it cannot be opened immediately, or if open must be closed immediately, is a red flag waved horizontally by day, or a red light swung back and forth horizontally at night, in full sight of the vessel. (Some bridges may have mechanical devices and/or flashing electrical lights to signify the same meanings.)

Use of Radio Communications Radio communications may be used to request a bridge opening and to receive information about the bridge's status and the actions to be taken. (Bridges equipped with radios will have signs to that effect with a plain language statement or a symbol consisting of a shape of a telephone handset horizontally with a lightning flash superimposed. The preferred calling channel will be stated in the lower-left corner of the sign, and the preferred working channel in the lower-right corner.) If agreement is reached by radio, sound or visual signals are not required; both the vessel and the bridge must continue to monitor the selected channel—often 13, occasionally 16 or 9—until the vessel has cleared the draw. If radio contact cannot be established and maintained, sound or visual signs must be used.

Two or More Drawbridges Coast Guard regulations require that a vessel wishing to pass through two or more bridges close together must give the opening signal for the first bridge, and after acknowledgement it must give the opening signal for the second bridge, and so on, until all bridges have acknowledged that they will be opening promptly.

Two or More Vessels If two or more vessels approach the same drawbridge at nearly the same time, from the same or opposite directions, the regulations require that each vessel must signal independently for the opening of the draw. The drawtender need not reply to signals by vessels accumulated at the bridge for passage during a scheduled open period.

Restricted Operations Some bridges have restricted hours of operations because of the volume of land traffic. The Coast Guard may authorize periods of no openings or openings only on specific schedules, such as hourly, or every 30, 20, or 15 minutes. The restrictions may be for all day, or only for morning and evening rush hours. The restrictions will be posted on signs on each side of the bridge. During such periods, certain privileged vessels—government craft, tugs with tows, etc.—can request an opening by sounding five short blasts in lieu of the normal signal.

Do Not Cause Unnecessary Openings Clearance gauges are maintained on most drawbridges; skippers should know the vertical clearance required for their craft. Coast Guard regulations provide penalties for vessel owners and operators who cause unnecessary bridge openings because of "any nonstructural vessel appurtenance which is not essential to navigation or which is easily lowered." On the other hand, the same regulations provide penalties for any bridge tender who "unnecessarily delays the openings of a draw after the required signal has been given."

Canal locks Signals for the operation of canal locks are often the same as those for bridges nearby, but not always; radios can be very effective in obtaining information on the status of a lock. Major ship canals have elaborate sets of lights and/or horn signals to control water-borne traffic. Consult the appropriate volume of the *Coast Pilot* or Navigation Regulations for the proper signals and VHF radio channel to use before approaching any lock.

Pilot Rules for Inland Waters

As noted in Chapter 4, the Pilot Rules are in Annex V to the Inland Navigation Rules. Among other provisions, these require that a copy of the Inland Rules be kept on board every self-propelled vessel 12 meters (39.4 ft) or more in length.

Penalties

The penalties for violation of the Navigation Rules are described in Chapter 4; see pages 142 and 143.

INTERNATIONAL NAVIGATION RULES

Certain of the International Rules relate to navigational lights and shapes; these were discussed in Chapter 4. This chapter considers only those rules and annexes relating to right-of-way, conduct of vessels in restricted visibility, and sound signals.

Manner of Consideration

Study of the U.S. Inland Rules provides an excellent base for learning the International Navigation Rules. Hence, the International Rules are considered in detail here only where they differ from the U.S. Inland Rules. Topics are discussed in the same sequence.

Definitions

The International Rules contain one definition that is not used in the U.S. Inland Rules. A VESSEL CONSTRAINED BY ITS DRAFT is a power-driven vessel which, because of its draft in relation to the available depth and width of navigable water, is severely restricted in its ability to deviate from the course that it is following. [3(h)]

Steering & Sailing Rules

The rules for signals are very nearly identical in the two sets, but where they do differ, the difference can be considerable and significant.

Sound Signals

The one- and two-short-blast whistle signals in the Inland Rules under conditions of good visibility are *signals of intent and agreement*, whereas those of the International Rules are indications of *taking action to alter course*. The International Rules signals are often termed RUDDER SIGNALS; they *do not* require a reply; see **Figure 5-19**. In some instances the other vessel will take similar action and so sound the same signal. The three- and five-or-more short blast signals have the same meaning in both sets of Rules. The 1980 Inland Rules retained the former U.S. signals (rather then adopting those of the 1972 International Rules) because of their long established use, plus the belief that they were simpler, clearer, and more suitable for confined inland waters.

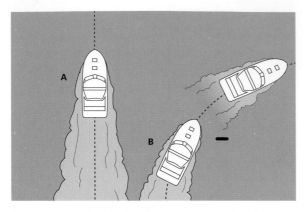

Figure 5-19 *Whistle signals of the International Navigation Rules indicate course changes rather than intent to pass. Such signals are not returned by the other vessel.*

Equipment for Sound Signals

Annex III of the International Rules differs from the corresponding U.S. Inland Rules annex, but the differences are essentially technical and of little concern to small craft skippers. Several changes were made to this International Rules annex in November 2003 relating to frequencies, intensities, and ranges of audibility for vessels of various sizes.

The International Rules now no longer require that vessels less than 20 meters (65.6 ft) in length carry a bell and use that device for sound signals while at anchor or aground.

The International Rules *do not* contain the provision allowing a vessel normally used for towing alongside or pushing ahead to use a whistle matched to the length of the customary combination of towed and towing vessels (see page 156).

Sound-signaling equipment that is acceptable to the International Rules can also be used on inland waters, as provided for in the Inland Rule 1(b) (ii).

Maneuvering Lights

A maneuvering light used in conjunction with whistle signals must be white; yellow is not acceptable as it is under the Inland Rules. The light must have minimum range of 5 miles, and it need not be synchronized with the vessel's whistle although the same number of flashes are made as blasts are sounded. Each flash shall be of about one second duration, and the interval between successive signals must be at least 10 seconds. [34(b)]

Rules for Power-Driven Vessels

The rules for meeting and crossing situations are the same in both sets, except for whistle signals. The International Rules *do not have* the one-half-mile closest-point-of-approach requirement for signaling intent to pass, nor the reply signals of agreement. They *do* require a whistle signal for each change of course, without reply signals from the other vessel. On winding rivers where the vessel's course follows the waterway, however, no whistle signals are used for the many necessary changes of course.

Overtaking Vessels

International Rule 9(e) for vessels in an overtaking situation applies only in a narrow channel or fairway and only if the overtaken vessel has to take some action to permit safe passing [9(e)(i)] (not in all waters and in all overtaking situations, as in the Inland Rules). The whistle signals are very different, and quite complex. [34(c)]

A vessel overtaking another will signal its intention by two prolonged blasts, followed by one short blast ("I intend to overtake you on your starboard side") or by two prolonged blasts followed by two short blasts ("I intend to overtake you on your port side"). The vessel about to be overtaken signals its agreement not with the identical signal, as Inland Rules specify, but with one prolonged, one short, one prolonged, and one short blast—this is the letter "C" in Morse Code and the international signal for "yes." In case of doubt, the vessel about to be overtaken will sound the five-or-more short and rapid blasts.

Use of Radio Communication

The International Rules *do not* contain provisions for the use of radiotelephone communications in place of whistle signals. This does not mean, however, that such additional procedures are not an excellent means of ensuring a safe passage, and they are normally used.

THE DUTY TO KEEP A LOOKOUT

Both the Inland and the International Navigation Rules are quite specific about requiring a "proper lookout." This requirement has been further amplified by U.S. court decisions arising out of collisions. One of the earliest rulings dates from 1833 when a sailing vessel was held liable for a collision with another sailing vessel. The first vessel had no watch on deck other than the man at the helm. Later court decisions extended the ruling to power-driven vessels.

The courts have repeatedly defined a "lookout" as a person who is specially charged with the duty of observing lights, sounds, echoes, and any obstruction to navigation with all of the thoroughness that the circumstances permit. "Specially charged" in this context means that the lookout has no other duties at that time that might in any way detract from the keeping of a proper watch. Except in limited circumstances mostly involving smaller vessels, the operator of a vessel is *not* legally complying with the Rules by keeping a lookout from the pilothouse.

A lookout should be someone who has had the training and experience to do the job. Normally the lookout should be stationed outside any cabin in order to hear sound signals. In fog, the traditional wisdom is to place the lookout as far forward and as low down as possible.

Radar-Equipped Vessels

The Rules require the proper use of radar on vessels that are so equipped. The person using the radar must know the characteristics, efficiency, and limitations of the equipment. Targets detected by radar must be systematically observed and plotted to determine their actual course and speed. Rule 7 is absolutely clear—assumptions should never be made from scanty radar information.

The sea state, weather (such as rain), and even transmissions from other nearby radars can cause targets to disappear from radar screens for periods of time. Small boats, particularly fiberglass-constructed recreational craft, may not always be detected in time to avoid collision. Use of a single range scale can be misleading. On long-range settings, small targets at short range may not be detected. Or at short-range setting, the approach of a large vessel at some distance may not be detected.

Narrow Channels

International Rule 9(d) *differs* from its Inland Rules counterpart in that the sounding of a danger signal by a vessel that observes another crossing a narrow channel or fairway is optional, rather than mandatory.

Leaving a Berth

The International Rules *do not* include a signal for a power-driven vessel leaving a berth, as does Inland Rule 34(g). Such a signal, however, is not prohibited and would be a good idea, even on those U.S. coastal waters subject to the International Rules.

Sound Signals in Restricted Visibility

The International Rules *do* prescribe a sound signal in restricted visibility (such as fog) for a vessel constrained by its draft; this is the same signal, "one prolonged blast followed by two short blasts," as has been prescribed for a sailing vessel, a towing vessel, a vessel engaged in fishing, and a vessel that is restricted in its ability to maneuver. [35(c)]

The International Rules *do not* provide for "special anchorage areas," where fog signals need not be sounded by small boats, and by barges, scows, and the like.

TRAFFIC SEPARATION SCHEMES

A Traffic Separation Scheme (TSS) is one of several routing measures adopted by the International Maritime Organization (IMO) to improve the safety of navigation in areas of converging traffic, congested areas, or where the freedom of navigation is constrained in some way. These are usually found at the entrances to major ports and "choke points" where heavy volumes of shipping are forced to pass through narrow straits. TSSs are usually in waters outside demarcation lines, but their use is covered by Rule 10 in both the International and Inland Rules.

A TSS separates opposing traffic streams by appropriate means—such as the establishment of traffic lanes. Each traffic lane is reserved for one-way traffic of large ships with the direction indicated by an arrow on the chart. For small craft skippers, the regulation of particular interest is the one stating that vessels less than 20 meters (65.6 ft) and sailing vessels must not impede the safe passage of a power-driven vessel following a traffic lane. [10(j)]

A separation zone or line keeps apart the traffic lanes of vessels that are traveling in opposite directions. It also may divide traffic lanes from adjacent open waters, or it may separate the traffic lanes designated for particular classes of vessels that are heading in the same direction. There can be inshore traffic zones that comprise a defined area between the landward boundary of a TSS and the adjacent coast. Where lanes converge, there will be a precautionary zone.

Ships that are using a TSS proceed in the appropriate traffic lane. So far as practicable, they are obliged to keep clear of a traffic separation zone or line. Vessels not using a traffic separation scheme must avoid it by as wide a margin as possible.

Normally, ships enter or leave a traffic separation lane at the termination of that lane. If they must join or leave a lane from either side, they should do so at as small an angle to the general flow of traffic as possible.

Vessels are advised to avoid crossing traffic lanes. If this cannot be avoided, crossing should be done as nearly as practicable at right angles to the general direction of traffic flow. Other than when crossing, vessels should refrain from entering a separation zone, except in emergencies or to fish within the separation zone.

Vessels less than 20 meters (65.6 ft.) in length, sailing vessels and fishing vessels are free to use an inshore traffic zone if one exists. Otherwise, inshore traffic zones are not normally used by through-traffic.

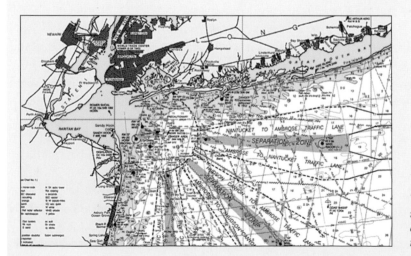

Traffic separation schemes are indicated on NOS charts. The example shows the approaches to New York harbor.

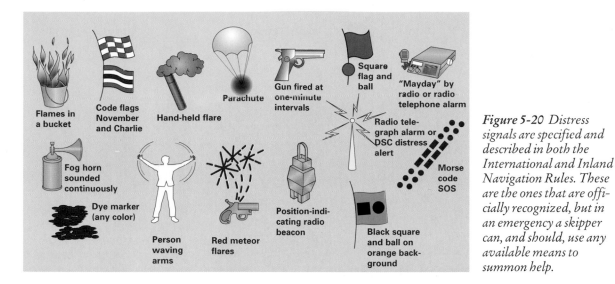

Figure 5-20 Distress signals are specified and described in both the International and Inland Navigation Rules. These are the ones that are officially recognized, but in an emergency a skipper can, and should, use any available means to summon help.

General Right-of-Way Provisions

The International Rules contain the *same* general right-of-way "ranking" of vessel types as the Inland Rules do (see page 154), *plus* a provision that any vessel except one not under command or restricted in its ability to maneuver must avoid impeding the safe passage of a vessel constrained by its draft, a category not included in the Inland Rules. [18(d)]

DISTRESS SIGNALS

Because of their great importance, the accepted forms of DISTRESS SIGNALS have been written into both the International and U.S. Inland Rules of the Road. These are contained in Annex IV, which is identical in both sets of rules, except that the Inland Rules additionally list a white high-intensity "strobe" light flashing 50 to 70 times per minute.

Figure 5-20 lists the *officially* recognized signals, but in an emergency a skipper can, and should, use any means he can to summon help.

Supplemental Signals

In the category of "supplemental signals," Annex IV lists a piece of orange-colored canvas, with both a black square and a circle, or other appropriate symbol, for identification from the air. (Actually, the circle should be solid, more properly termed a "disk"; and although "other appropriate symbol" is not defined, the word "HELP" in large black, block letters is often used.)

Unofficial Distress Symbols

An unofficial but well-recognized signal, especially in inland and coastal waters, is a red-orange flag of any size, waved from side-to-side.

Most American boatmen would recognize the flying of an inverted U.S. national or yacht ensign as a signal of distress. Remember that such a signal has no official sanction, however, because many national flags have no "top" or "bottom" and appear the same if turned upside down.

Use of radiotelephones for distress communications and the new Digital Selective Calling (DSC) distress alert are covered in Chapter 20.

KNOW THE RULES—BUT USE GOOD JUDGMENT

When your boat encounters another in a situation involving a possible collision, you must know the Navigation Rules, take the proper actions, and if appropriate, sound the prescribed sound signal. But that is not enough; you must be alert and use good judgment. The other skipper may or may not know the Rules, and he may not take the actions prescribed by the Rules. If the situation progresses to the point where an accident is likely, you must take any action necessary to avoid collision—this deviation from the normal procedures of the Rules is allowed, even required, by Rule 2.

Seamanship Under Power

*Helmsmanship • Propeller & Rudder Actions • Single-Screw Inboard Maneuvering •
Maneuvering in Tight Quarters • Dock Lines & Their Uses • Twin-Screw Maneuvering •
Maneuvering with Directed Thrust*

Boat-handling ability is at the very heart of good seamanship. Some of the finest exhibitions of boat handling are given by boaters who have never read a printed page on the subject of seamanship. Their proficiency, developed over long years of meeting every conceivable situation, manifests itself almost as an instinct, prompting the skipper to react correctly whether he can think the problem out beforehand or not.

A recreational boater, particularly a novice, will not have these years of experience. He can gain much from a study of the basic factors involved, and then build up his experience. In approaching a study of the principles of boat handling, keep in mind that the goal is to understand *why* your boat reacts the way it does when you are out there handling it. If your craft stubbornly refuses to make a turn under certain conditions, or persists in backing one way when you want it to go the other, you are less likely to make the same mistake repeatedly once you understand the reasons behind its behavior.

HELMSMANSHIP

The ability to steer well—called HELMSMANSHIP, whether involving men or women—is a quality that cannot be learned from a book or in a classroom. However, understanding the basic principles of boat handling will make it easier for you to perform in a variety of situations.

It is important to realize that boats are nearly as individualistic as people, particularly in their steering characteristics. Deep-draft and shallow-draft vessels handle differently. Boats that steer by changing their thrust direction—outboards, stern-drives, and jet drives—respond differently than boats steered by rudders. The response of heavy displacement hulls to helm changes is quite unlike that of light planing hulls.

The secret of good helmsmanship is to know your boat. If you skipper your own craft, this comes quickly as you gain experience with it. If you take the wheel or tiller of a friend's boat, however, take it easy at first with helm changes, until you get the "feel" of the craft's response.

Steering by Compass

Boats are often piloted by running compass courses; see **Figure 6-01.** You must keep the compass lubber's line on the mark of the card that indicates the course to be steered. If the course to be steered is 100°, and the lubber's line is momentarily at 95°, you must "swing the boat's head" with right rudder, 5° to the right, to bring the lubber's line around to 100. *Remember, the card stands still while the lubber's line swings around it.* Any attempt to bring the desired course on the card up to the lubber's line will produce exactly the *opposite* result.

As a vessel swings with a change in course, an inexperienced helmsman tends to allow it to swing too far, due to the momentum of the turn and the lag between the turn of the wheel and the response of the craft. The experienced helmsman knows how to steady on the new course without over-swinging. In almost all power cruisers, this requires that the helmsman return the rudder to the neutral, midships, position *before* the craft reaches the intended new heading. You will often need to use a slight amount of opposite rudder to check the boat's swing.

Opposite Page: Figure 6-01 On open water, away from marked channels, the only way a person at the helm can maintain the proper course is by keeping an eye on the compass. When possible, sight on a distant object that is ahead in the direction that you want to go—but do not use clouds.

A zigzag course brands the helmsman as inexperienced. The goal is a straight course; this can be achieved, after the boat has steadied, by only slight movements of the wheel. An experienced boater at the helm anticipates the vessel's swing and, turning the wheel slowly and deliberately, makes corrections with *little* rudder instead of going well off course before correcting.

A good helmsman will also turn the wheel slowly and deliberately. The actual manner of steering is a characteristic of each craft, and is learned only by experience.

When holding a course, it helps to pick out a distant landmark or other fixed object, if there is one, to steer by. At night, a star can be used, but remember that the apparent positions of stars change over a period of hours. This helps to keep a straight course, as a boat compass is smaller and less steady than one aboard a large vessel. Avoid steering on cloud formations; these move with the wind and change shape. Drop your eyes periodically to the compass to check your course, and always remember to look *back* frequently at the aids or landmarks you have passed, making sure that you remain on your proper track. Even though you may be steering quite precisely toward your objective, the wind of a crosscurrent may be setting you to one side. If in a narrow channel, you could soon be out of it and aground. Look back at the aids to navigation that you have passed, or any prominent feature, and be sure that you are on your proper track, not off to one side.

If steering by an electronic device, such as an autopilot or electronic chart plotter, always monitor the off-course error, called crosstrack error; see Chapter 21, page 747.

BASIC PRINCIPLES OF BOAT HANDLING

The proper approach to boat handling is a balance of study and practice. Learn all you can about the principles by which *average* boats respond under *normal* conditions; supplement this with experience in *your own boat* and others. In this way you will learn to act so that the controlling elements aid you rather than oppose you.

In boat handling, there are three primary types of powered craft to consider—inboard single-screw, inboard twin-screw, and outboard (as well as stern-drive and jet drives) whether single or multiple. The first two use a rudder or rudders in combination with a constant thrust from the propeller or propellers; the last uses directed water thrust, usually without a rudder. The handling characteristics of each type are different from the others, but as the single-screw, single-rudder inboard is the basic type, we will cover it in considerable detail. Note that the principles apply equally for a sailboat being moved through the water by inboard auxiliary power.

No two boats will behave in an identical manner in every situation. Just how a boat performs depends on many things—among them the form and shape of the hull's underbody; the construction; the shape, position, and area of the rudder; the trim; speed; weight; load; the strength and direction of wind and current; and the nature of the sea.

Basic Boat-Handling Terms

Certain basic boating terms apply specifically to boats equipped with one or more engines—whether inboard (mounted within the hull), outboard (mounted on the transom and detachable), or the combination inboard-outboard (I/O) type, also called stern-drives. Thrust for the movement of the boat through the water is achieved by the rotation of a propeller (or "screw"), which draws in water from ahead and pushes it out astern. A boat with one propeller is termed a single-screw type. Boats with two propellers are referred to as twin-screw craft. Sailboats fitted with an engine are called auxiliaries; their handling characteristics are similar to those of a single-screw powerboat, although engines are usually of lesser horsepower.

Steering is accomplished in one of two ways. An inboard engine operates according to a "fixed-screw": Turning a rudder or rudders diverts the thrust developed by the propeller(s), which in turn turns the boat; see **Figure 6-02**. An outboard or I/O powered boat operates without a rudder. Moving the motor and propeller, or outdrive unit,

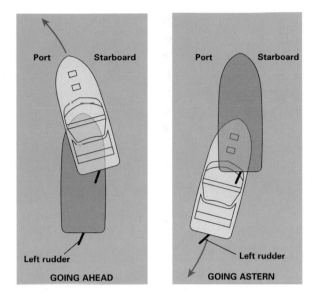

Figure 6-02 With left rudder on a boat going ahead (above, left), the stern is moved to starboard, and the bow turns to port. With left rudder when going astern (above, right), the stern moves to port. The movement of the bow is initially unchanged in this case.

directly turns the propeller thrust, changing the boat's direction.

Just as a person has a left and right side, a boat has a left—or port—side and a right—or starboard—side as you stand and look forward on it. The left and right sides of a person stay the same no matter from which direction you look; similarly turning around while on board and looking aft will not change the boat's port and starboard sides.

A boat is said to be making headway when it is going forward in the water and sternway when it is backing up. A boat is turning to port when its bow is moving to the left when making headway. A boat is said to be going to port when making sternway if its stern is moving to the left.

The terms RIGHT RUDDER and LEFT RUDDER refer to how the *bow* would turn if the boat were making headway. The same is used for the same position of the rudder when making sternway. A boat with left rudder applied will turn its bow to port while making headway and swing its stern to port when making sternway. In **Figure 6-02,** the boat has left rudder in both cases. Right rudder is not illustrated, but would be just the opposite.

A BALANCED RUDDER is one whose blade surface lies partly ahead of its rudderstock; refer to **Figure 1-12.** (An UNBALANCED RUDDER, seldom seen, is one whose blade surface is fully behind the rudderstock.) While the portion of this forward balance area may be only 20 percent of the total rudder area, it exerts considerable effect in taking strain off the steering gear and making the steering easier.

Right- & Left-Hand Propellers

Propellers are said to be RIGHT-HAND or LEFT-HAND depending on the direction they turn (looking forward from aft of the propeller). The difference is important because propeller rotation has a considerable bearing on how a boat maneuvers, especially when reversing. A propeller that turns clockwise when driving the boat ahead is right-handed, one that turns counterclockwise is considered left-handed. To determine the "hand," with the boat out of the water, stand astern of the propeller and look forward at the driving face of the blades; the forward edge of each blade cuts through the water. If the propeller will turn clockwise when driving the boat forward, it is right-handed; if it would turn counterclockwise, it is left-handed. In **Figure 6-03,** the propeller at left is left-handed; the one at right is right-handed. It is not always easy to determine the hand of a propeller by looking at the rotation of the engine alone. The engine is connected to a transmission

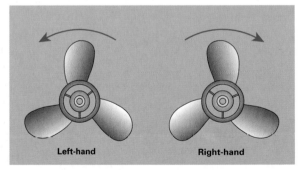

Figure 6-03 If you stand at the stern of a boat that is out of the water, and look at its propeller, you will be looking at the driving face of the propeller blades. If the propeller must turn to the right (clockwise) to push water toward you, the propeller is right-handed. If it would have to turn in the opposite direction for the same effect, it is left-handed.

that may change engine rotation depending on its reduction gearing. The rotation of the coupling connecting the transmission to the propeller shaft is, however, a true indication of the propeller rotation. If, looking forward toward the transmission from aft of it, the shaft and coupling rotate clockwise when the transmission is in forward, then the shaft has a right-hand propeller.

Most, but not all, single-screw boats have right-hand propellers. In the maneuvering situations below, the propeller on a single-screw craft is *right-handed* unless otherwise noted.

Twin-screw craft almost always have the tops of the blades turning outward when going ahead for best maneuverability. **Figure 6-03** can be viewed as the two propellers of a twin-screw craft; the port engine will turn a left-hand propeller, also called a "wheel," and the starboard engine a right-hand propeller. Whereas skippers sometimes refer to propellers as "wheels," especially when describing right- or left-handedness, since most of the discussion in this chapter is about steering, we will use "propeller" exclusively.

Hull Shape

In addition to propeller and rudder configuration, the hull shape of a boat has a strong influence on how it handles. Given the same wind and sea conditions, a trawler with its heavy displacement hull and deeper draft will behave differently than a lighter sport-fishing boat with its shallower draft, planing hull, flying

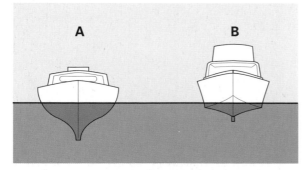

Figure 6-04 A deep-draft displacement hull, A, will tend to be set off course by adverse water currents, but its low freeboard and superstructure offer lesser resistance to the wind. Conversely, a typical planing hull, B, floats high in the water and a wind on the beam will result in considerable leeway.

Figure 6-05 This sport-fishing boat with its planing-type hull has only part of its hull in contact with the water when it is on a plane.

bridge and, possibly, tuna tower; see **Figures 6-04** and **6-05**.

Displacement-type hulls are heavily built and have a large load-carrying capacity, but are limited in the speed at which they can be driven through the water. Sailboats, trawlers, and most large yachts fall into this category. Planing-type hulls are generally lighter in weight. They have less draft, and can be driven through the water fast enough to cause the hull to rise up out of the water and plane on top of it, keeping only a part of the hull in contact with the water. As a planing hull eventually slows down, it reaches a point where it reverts to the displacement mode.

Wind & Current

A boat's handling characteristics are affected by wind and current, no matter what type of hull and power combination it has. Keeping a course or maneuvering in close quarters may be straightforward on a calm day during a slack tidal current, but the boat may become quite ill-mannered when coping with a stiff crosswind or crosscurrent. Since bows on many powerboats are higher than the sterns, they tend to fall off the wind when backing, despite anything that is done with the helm.

Hull type has the most effect on how a boat reacts to the current. Displacement-type hulls with considerable draft are affected by current to a greater extent than shallower-draft, lighter, planing-type hulls. Water is much denser than air, so a half-knot crosscurrent may have more effect on a displacement cruiser than a stiff 15- to 20-knot wind (a moderate to fresh breeze). On the other hand, given the same conditions, a planing type hull with a high tuna tower could be more affected by wind than by current. Neither a displacement nor planing boat can ignore either the wind or the current. Skippers of both will find one of them a major factor affecting the boat's maneuverability. This becomes most apparent while running at low speed in close quarter.

Two boats of roughly the same size, one with a considerable hull draft forward but little aft, and another with relatively greater draft aft but more superstructure forward, have radical differences in their handling qualities. The governing factor is the relative area presented above the water to the wind, compared with the areas in the water, both fore and aft.

Helmsman Must Develop Judgment

From the above and other variations in behavior, it is obvious that a boater must develop judgment based on understanding his boat and the forces acting on it. Combinations of conditions can be infinite, so he or she must be able to appraise the situation and act promptly.

Try to foresee possibilities, and have solutions in mind before problems arise. For instance, if you are running down a channel with a strong wind on your beam, and you have the choice of which side of the channel to use, the windward side is the better bet. Should your engine stop, or your steering fail, you will have more of a chance to get an anchor down before going aground on the leeward side.

By the same reasoning, you shouldn't skirt the windward side of a shoal too closely. Or suppose that you are approaching a bridge (see **Figure 6-06**), with a narrow draw opening and a strong wind or current pushing you along. If you approach the opening at an angle and power fails, you will be in a jam. But if you think to straighten out your course while still some distance away, so that you will be shooting down the center of the opening in alignment with it, you will be safer because your straight course will carry you through in the clear.

In developing your "boat sense," draw from as many sources as possible. Watch how experienced boaters handle their craft, but allow for differences in your own boat when you try similar maneuvers. And it almost goes without saying, if you are at the helm of a strange boat, go more slowly than normal, taking additional precautions.

UNDERSTANDING PROPELLERS & RUDDERS

When under power, boats are driven through the water by the action of their propellers, which act like pumps—drawing in a stream of water from forward (when going ahead), and throwing it out astern. Moving these streams of water aft creates an opposite forward thrust at the propellers, which is transmitted to the boat through the propeller shaft and its supporting structure. This drives the boat forward.

How Propellers Create Thrust

The curved blades of the propeller are similar to other curved foils found on boats, for example a sailboat's sail or a fin keel. When such a foil passes through a fluid, the flow is divided into two streams, one on either side of the foil. When a rudder is in a straight position, the water flows evenly on both sides. Turning the rudder causes an uneven flow, building pressure on one side and

Figure 6-06 When approaching a bridge with a narrow draw, aim for the opening, so that if power should fail, your course will tend to carry your boat through in the clear.

reducing it on the other. With this pressure difference, the rudder will then tend to move toward the low pressure, creating what is called lift, and turning the boat in that direction.

A propeller blade creates force in a very similar way to the rudder. If the propeller were designed with blades that were flat rather than curved, and if the blades were simply spun around without any angle to their direction of travel, the propeller would turn through the water like a disk with equal flow on each side. However, this is not the case. The blades of the propeller are both curved and angled; as they pass through the water, they create lift. There is a low-pressure area on the side of the blade facing forward and a high-pressure area on the side facing aft.

Although the water drawn into the propeller does not actually flow from directly ahead like a thin column of water, for our purposes here it can be considered as coming in generally parallel to the keel. As the propeller ejects the water, it imparts a twist or spiral motion to that water. (The direction of rotation is dependent on the way the propeller turns.) This flow of water is called the SCREW CURRENT.

Suction & Discharge Screw Currents

Regardless of whether the propeller is rotating to move the boat ahead or astern, the part of the current that flows into the propeller is called the

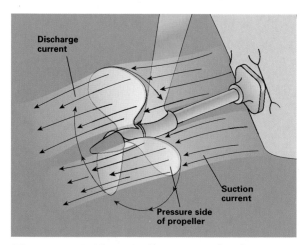

Figure 6-07 With a propeller turning ahead, suction screw current is developed by the water flowing toward the propeller and discharge current is driven out astern.

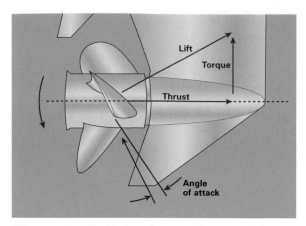

Figure 6-08 The blades of a propeller act as foils, providing lift, thrust, and torque.

"suction screw current." The part of the current ejected from the propeller is called the "discharge current"; see **Figure 6-07**. Discharge current, spiral in motion, is a compact stream of water that exerts greater pressure than the broader suction current.

Placing the rudder behind the propeller in the discharge current increases the steering effect because the rudder is acting in an accelerated flow. (Of course, there is a small rudder action from any flow of water past it even if the propeller is not turning.) A twin-screw cruiser has twin rudders, one behind each propeller, keeping the rudder blades directly in the propellers' discharge currents.

The pressure difference created by the propeller blade creates lift, and its force is roughly perpendicular to the blade itself. Lift can be divided into two components—a thrust component in the direction of travel and a torque component in the opposite direction of propeller rotation; see **Figure 6-08**. You can easily see the effect of propeller torque when a runabout with a large engine accelerates; as the propeller begins to accelerate, the boat tends to dip on one side (generally on the port side with a right-hand propeller).

There is also WAKE CURRENT—a body of water that is carried along by a vessel due to the friction on its hull as it moves through the water. This has its maximum effect at the surface, and little effect at keel depth.

Unequal Blade Thrust

Turning propellers not only create forward or reverse thrust with their discharge current, they also produce forces that tend to push the propeller to one side or the other, depending on the direction of rotation.

This effect is most noticeable on inboard boats that have a propeller shaft set through the hull at an angle to the horizontal. Since the propeller is attached to the end of this shaft, it is positioned at the same angle and the water that flows into it meets the blades at different angles depending on whether they are on the downward or upward part of their circle. The actual pitch of the blades as manufactured is the same, of course, but the effective pitch of one blade is increased, the other reduced. For example, a forward-turning right-hand propeller would have the pitch of its starboard (descending) blade increased, while the pitch of the port (ascending) blade would be decreased. The relatively greater blade pitch on the starboard side creates a stronger thrust on that side; see **Figure 6-09**. The importance of this factor is reduced as the shaft angle is decreased, and naval architects sometimes take pains to have the engine installed as low in the hull as possible so as to keep the propeller shaft nearly parallel to the flow of the water past the blades. This contributes to propeller efficiency and is a factor worth considering if it is consistent with other design

Figure 6-10 A high-performance system, such as the Arneson Drive, is designed to reduce drag while enhancing positive-thrust steering. It uses surface-piercing propellers.

requirements. In practical terms, the effect of unequal blade thrust varies with each design.

Effect of Unequal Blade Thrust

The relatively greater blade pitch on the starboard side creates a stronger thrust on that side. As far as this single factor is concerned, the stern of a single-screw boat with a right-hand propeller thus has a natural tendency to go to starboard when the propeller is going ahead. The opposite effect occurs when the propeller is reversing.

When such a craft has headway, its bow tends to turn to port, and a certain amount of right rudder may be needed to maintain a straight course. To correct this tendency, a small trim tab may be attached to the after edge of the rudder and bent to an angle that provides the proper compensation; refer to **Figure 1-10**.

The effect of unequal blade thrust is so small for some boats as to be negligible, and quite pronounced on other craft. With left-hand propellers, the effect is, of course, just the opposite of that described above.

However, when the shaft angle is parallel to the flow of water into the propeller, another effect, the paddle wheel, or propwalk, may come into play. As an outboard motor is progressively raised, the propeller will eventually break the surface of the water. As this occurrence

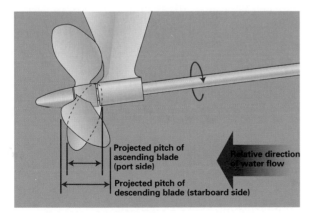

Figure 6-09 A propeller shaft at an angle to the horizontal has the effect of increasing the pitch of the descending blade relative to that of the ascending blade. This produces greater thrust to starboard in a right-hand propeller. A left-hand propeller would produce a greater thrust to port.

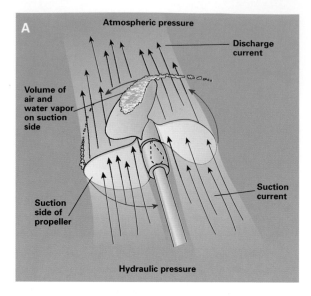

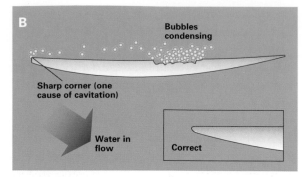

Figure 6-11 Cavitation results from a partial vacuum formed, A, by the blades of a propeller, with a consequent lost of thrust. There is also the danger of damage to the propeller when the cavitation bubbles collapse, as shown in B.

increases, a blade sweeping across the top, fanning through aerated water, will not pull as hard in a sideways or propeller torque direction as the fully submerged blade sweeping across the bottom of the propeller arc. This will cause a right-hand rotation propeller to "walk" to the right, much as a paddle wheel would do. This action in turn tries to pull the aft end of an outboard or stern-drive to the right, causing the boat to go into a left-hand turn, if not resisted at the steering wheel.

Unequal blade thrust becomes more of a concern to lighter single-engine craft at higher speeds when the propeller is elevated closer to the water surface; the paddle wheel (propeller) effect, also called propwalk, will eventually dominate any steering torque situation.

Ventilation & Cavitation

Since all but a few high-speed, surface-piercing propellers (see **Figure 6-10**) rely on the smooth flow of water over their blades to create lift, a slight disturbance to this flow limits the overall efficiency of the propeller.

Ventilation occurs when air from the water's surface or exhaust gases from the exhaust are sucked into the discharge current. The propeller then loses its grip on the water and over-revs, losing much of its thrust. Trying to turn an outboard-powered boat too tightly at too high a speed often results in propeller ventilation.

Cavitation usually occurs at the tip of a propeller that is turning too fast. A spot on the tip of a propeller blade travels farther and faster during each revolution than does one near the hub. As the propeller rpms increase, the tip reaches a point where water simply can't flow past the tip without creating a partial vacuum, breaking down and forming small bubbles, much like boiling water; see **Figure 6-11, A**. As these water vapor bubbles move along the surface of the metal, they eventually find an area of higher pressure where they collapse and cause damage. When collapsing, the bubbles release their stored energy onto the metal, acting like tiny jackhammers; the result is known as "cavitation burn"; see **Figure 6-11, B**.

Cavitation may result from a number of causes, including nicks in the leading edge, sharp leading-edge corners (as shown), improper polishing, poor propeller design, severely bent blades or broken blade tips, or ventilation.

How a Rudder Acts

Most inboard boats have a vertical rudder blade located at the stern, attached to a rudderpost that extends through a watertight stuffing box into the boat. Movement of the steering wheel turns the rudder to port or starboard. As described earlier, the position of the rudder creates a higher pressure on one side of the rudder and a lower pressure on the other, creating lift. As the rudder is pushed and pulled into its own lower pressure area, it takes the stern of the boat with it.

Steering wheels on boats are rigged in such a way that they turn with the rudder—turning the helm to port accordingly turns the rudder to port. Turning the helm to port therefore gives left rudder; this then moves the stern to starboard, so that the bow in effect moves to port, starting a turn to the left. Conversely, turning the helm to starboard gives right rudder, throwing the stern to port so that the boat then turns to starboard (to the right). On sailboats with tillers, the opposite is true.

Propeller Current's Action on Rudder

If a boat is motionless in the water (regardless of motion with respect to the bottom caused by wind or current), turning the rudder will have no effect—there must be a flow of water past the rudder for it to exert a force on the stern of the craft. However, if the propeller is turning, the situation is quite different. Now the rudder blade is directly in the discharge current of the propeller, which is pumping a strong stream of water astern. Turning the rudder to one side deflects the stream to that side. Small rudders are effective when there is considerable propeller current; but they develop little turning force at slow speeds or when the propeller is not turning. Sailboats and most single-prop, heavy displacement powerboats have larger rudders and respond to the helm adequately at slow speeds.

At very slow propeller speeds, the boat's headway may not be sufficient to given control over the boat if wind or current is acting upon it. Take, for example, a strong wind on the port beam. Even with the rudder hard over to port, it may not be possible to make a turn into the wind until the propeller is speeded up—enough to exert a more powerful thrust against the rudder blade. As a vessel travels through the water, the minimum speed at which it can be controlled is what is meant by steerageway.

Turning Circles

When any boat has headway and the rudder is put over to make a turn (to starboard, for example),

the stern is first pushed to the opposite side (in this example, to port). The boat then tends to slide off obliquely, in a crablike fashion. Its momentum will carry it some distance along the original course before settling into a turn, in which the bow describes a smaller circle than the stern; see **Figure 6-12**. The pivoting point is usually aft from the stem between one-fourth and one-third of the boat's length, see **Figure 6-13**, varying with different boats and changing for any given boat with its trim. While there is always a loss of speed in making a turn, the size of a boat's turning circle varies little with changes in speed, assuming a given rudder angle.

However, the size of the turning circle is much larger for single-screw inboard boats as compared with outboards (or stern-drive boats) because the shaft and propeller of the inboard are fixed on the centerline and cannot be rotated. The twin-screw inboard, on the other hand, provides excellent maneuverability, as will be seen later.

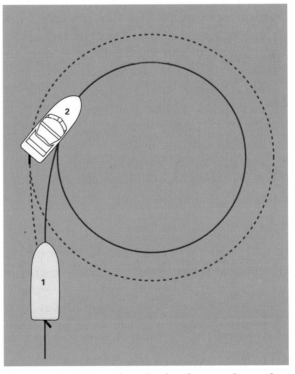

Figure 6-12 When a boat has headway and its rudder is turned to one side to make a turn, the stern moves in the opposite direction. Then, after sliding obliquely along the course from 1 to 2, it settles into a turn in which the bow follows a smaller circle (solid red line) than the stern (dotted red line).

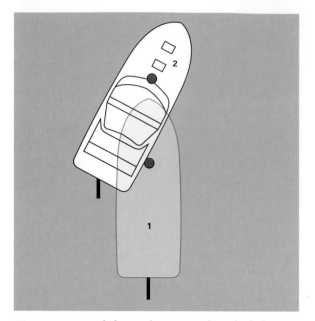

Figure 6-13 With forward motion, when the helm is put over to one side, a boat pivots around a point about one-third its length from the stem. Note that this causes the stern to swing in a wider arc than the bow.

It is important to consider the position of the rudder with respect to the pivot point of the hull when the boat is reversing. In this case, the pivot may be about one-fourth of the hull length from the transom; see **Figure 6-14.** Therefore, the rudder is acting on a much shorter lever arm as it tries, sometimes in vain, to swing the hull off course.

When the boat has sternway (reversing), there is no powerful discharge current past the rudder, only the weaker, more diffuse suction screw current. The rudder normally would be turned to port (left rudder) to turn the stern of the boat to port; right rudder should normally turn the stern to starboard in backing. Under certain circumstances, the effect of the reversing propeller "walking" itself the other way may more than offset the steering effect of the rudder. The boat may actually continue to turn to the right, for example, despite left rudder angle.

Water depth also has an effect on a boat's steering. Even though the keel may be a foot or so above bottom, a boat's response to rudder action in shallow water is almost always very sluggish.

Keep Stern Free to Maneuver

If a boater understands the underlying difference between the steering of a boat and of a car, he will be aware of the need to keep the stern free to maneuver in close quarters. The stern must have room to swing in the opposite direction from that in which the bow is being turned. This is especially important when the craft lies close to a pile or solid vertical surface; see **Figure 6-15.**

This is also very important when towing either a skier or another boat. To ensure the maneuverability of the towing craft, a towline must be attached forward of the stern; see **Figure 6-16.**

The Tendency to Stray Off Course

Different boats require varying rudder angles to compensate for the tendency to fall off from a straight course. Depending on differences in construction, arrangement of rudder blade, and the hand of the propeller, the bow may fall off to port or to starboard.

For example, a certain group of boats of almost identical design had a strong tendency to pull off course to port. In some of them, the condition was corrected simply by lowering the rudder blade, without changing its size or shape but merely by lengthening the stock an inch or two.

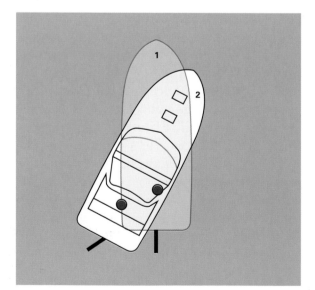

Figure 6-14 When backing down with the rudder to port, the pivot point is about one-quarter of the boat length forward of the stern. The bow, therefore, describes a wider arc than the stern.

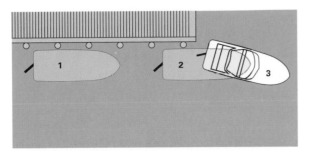

Figure 6-15 With right rudder, as the boat moves from 1 to 2, the stern is driven against the piles, with risk of damage. The rudder should be centered until the boat is clear (or the boat should be backed away from the face of the pier).

Before that correction, the boats would make a quick and easy turn to port but would be obstinate in turning to starboard. As a matter of fact, unless steering controls were rigged with worm and gear to hold the wheels against pressure on the rudders, the boats would swing into a short circle to port the instant the wheels were left unattended. This exaggerated condition is far from normal, but it does illustrate the handling characteristics the helmsman must pay attention to, especially in an unfamiliar boat.

Figure 6-16 A towline should be attached to a fitting well forward of the transom. This will allow the stern to swing more freely to either side for turning and provide greater overall maneuverability.

PROPULSION "PODS"

The latest design feature of cruise ships—large passenger vessels—are propulsion "pods." These are large streamline bodies beneath the after part of the hull where propellers would normally be. Each pod contains a large electric motor that drives a forward-facing propeller. The pods can be rotated horizontally through 360° for steering; there are no rudders. Power is supplied by electrical cables from several generators driven by multiple, large diesel engines or gas turbines. The advantages are vastly increased maneuverability and the flexibility to locate the power-generating machinery anywhere in the ship. Increased fuel efficiency is achieved—only the number of engines/turbines and generators need be run to meet the power needs of the moment.

Propulsion pods have been installed on all cruise ships built or planned since 1998. Most ships have two pods, but some will have three or four, with the additional pods being fixed rather than rotating. Vessels range in size from 40,000 to 142,000 gross tons, or more. Individual pods are rated at 9,000 to 21,500 horsepower (21.5 to 6.65 MW). Who knows when the first recreational craft will appear with propulsion pods?

Steering with Propeller Thrust

Here is a procedure that can often be helpful. In close quarters, a boat can often be turned in a couple of lengths by applying brief bursts of engine power. If, for example, the rudder is set hard to starboard (right rudder) while the craft has no headway, and the throttle is suddenly advanced significantly, then quickly closed, the stern can be kicked around to port before the boat has a chance to gather significant headway; see **Figure 6-17.** The exact technique of turning in limited space is described in detail later in this chapter.

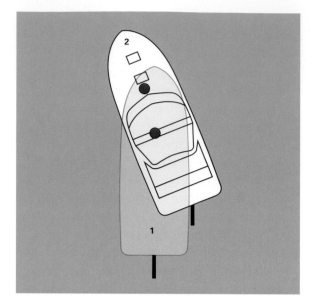

Figure 6-17 *With the boat dead in the water (1), when forward gear is engaged, the stern is moved to starboard. The amount of movement depends upon the boat form and the amount of throttle applied. If the rudder is put over to port, the movement is greater.*

BOAT HANDLING WITH A SINGLE-SCREW

While this section focuses on the handling of single-screw boats, twin-screw boats as well as craft using directed thrust—outboard motors, stern-drives, and jet-drives—are all considered in this chapter. Although single-screw inboard-engine boats may be in the minority of modern small craft, the basic principles of boat handling are best explained by first considering the actions and reactions of a craft with one inboard engine, one shaft, one propeller, and one rudder.

A single-screw inboard boat relies on water flowing past the rudder for maneuvering power. This is provided by the movement of the boat through the water and by the discharge current from the propeller (or suction current if backing down). How well your boat responds to the helm in any given situation will depend largely on constant factors such as unequal blade thrust, propwalk, and hull type. The variable factors are wind, current, and the amount of rudder angle being used.

Every time you leave your berth, certain basic maneuvers are necessary—getting underway, turning, stopping, and backing down. Next is a description of how to perform these maneuvers in a single-engine inboard boat with a right-hand propeller. In addition, you will learn about why your boat sometimes seems to have a mind of its own.

Gathering Headway

Getting underway should be straightforward, but when you put the boat into forward gear with the rudder centered, it may not behave as you would expect. When you shift into forward gear and the propeller starts to turn ahead, the unequal blade thrust tends to move the stern to starboard. This can be frustrating when pulling away from a starboard-side berth. If you don't get your boat far enough away from the pier or wharf, the stern may swing in and hit it.

Compensating by using right rudder may help, but it could also hamper the maneuver of getting away from the structure. The truly proper way to depart a wharf or pier is to back out—here the natural tendency of a boat will pull the stern out, and when the boat is clear of the structure, it can go forward, parallel to the wharf or pier face, at an adequate distance from it. If there is any tendency for wind or current to pin the boat against the wharf or pier face, go ahead on an after bow spring to get the stern out (see page 207).

As the boat gathers headway, wake current (from the movement of the boat through the water) enters the picture, increasing pressure against the rudder. This tends to offset the effect of unequal blade thrust, and the average boat tends to hold course in a straight line fairly well.

From a purely theoretical standpoint, the unequal blade thrust, with a right-hand propeller, should tend to move the stern to starboard, and the bow to port. Once underway, the effect of unequal blade thrust is quite slight. Only in comparatively few cases will unequal blade thrust have a pronounced effect on steering, and in these it can be corrected by a small rudder tab.

Turning

Now that your boat has headway, assume the rudder is turned to starboard. The water flowing past the hull strikes the rudder on its starboard side, forcing the stern to port. The propeller's discharge current intensifies this effect by acting on the same side, and the boat's bow turns to starboard, the same side on which the rudder is set.

How fast a boat will react to the helm is dependent on the size of the rudder and hull shape, but the most influential factor is how fast the boat is moving through the water. At slow speeds, with the engine idling or turning slowly, a heavy boat will have a considerable lag between the time its helm is put over and the time the boat actually begins to turn. At idle speeds, there is less water flowing past the rudder, and the propeller discharge current is weak; so it may take a boat several seconds to begin a turn. You may also have to give the boat considerably more rudder to get the same response you achieve at higher speeds.

Of course, the opposite is also true. A boat traveling fast has a very powerful flow of water past the rudder; with a very strong propeller discharge current, it responds much more quickly to helm movement. At speed, a light, fast, planing-type inboard has a very positive feel to the helm, with no noticeable lag between helm movement and turning.

The boat's turning radius is determined by how much the helm is turned at both high and slow speeds. How quickly the boat responds to helm movement is basically a factor of how fast it is moving.

Stopping

A boat has no brakes—stopping is achieved by reversing the propeller. Assume that your boat has headway, with the rudder centered, propeller turning in reverse. The rudder has decreasing steering effect as the boat slows, and unequal blade thrust of the reversed propeller tends to throw the stern to port. At the same time, on some boats the propeller blades on the starboard side are throwing their discharge current in a powerful column forward against the starboard side of the keel and bottom of the boat, with little on the port side to offset this pressure. This also adds to the forces moving the stern to port.

If wind and current permit, an experienced boater will make a portside approach to a pier with a single-engine boat that has a right-hand propeller. By reversing the propeller, the stern then is moved in toward the pier, instead of away from it.

Backing Down

If the boat is lying dead in the water with no headway, rudder centered, and the propeller turning in reverse, we again have the strong tendency of the stern to go to port as the discharge current strikes the starboard side of the hull. In each case where the discharge current of the reversing propeller is a factor, the strong current on the starboard side is directed generally toward the boat's bow but upward and inward in a spiral movement. The descending blade on the port side, on the other hand, tends to throw its stream downward at such an angle that its lesser force is largely spent below the keel. Therefore, the two forces are never of equal effect.

Until the boat gathers sternway from its backing propeller (right-hand), it would not matter if the rudder were over to port or starboard. The discharge current against the starboard side is still the strong controlling factor, and thus the stern will be moved to port.

Now visualize the boat gathering sternway as the propeller continues to turn in reverse. Here arises one of the seemingly mystifying conditions that baffle many a new helmsman. The novice assumes that in order to back in a straight line the rudder must be centered, just as it must be when going ahead on a straight course. But under certain conditions the boat may even respond to *right* rudder as the boater reverses by going to *port*, which is totally unexpected.

If the boater is learning by trial-and-error, it is easy to come to the conclusion that it depends on the boat's fancy, while rudder position has nothing to do with control. Fortunately, something can be done about it.

Backing with Left Rudder

Consider a boat in reverse with left rudder. Here there are four factors all working together to throw the stern to port. Unequal blade thrust is pushing the stern to port; the discharge current of the propeller is adding its powerful effect; and now we add the steering effect of the wake current acting on the after side of the rudder blade, against which the suction current of the propeller is also working.

Remember this condition well, for it is the answer to why *practically every single-screw vessel with right-hand propeller easily backs to port,* although it may be obstinate about going to starboard when reversing.

Backing with Rudder Centered

If, while backing to port, you bring the rudder amidships, you eliminate the effects of suction current and steering from the rudder. This leaves unequal blade thrust and the discharge current to continue forcing the stern to port.

Backing with Right Rudder

Assuming further that you have not yet gathered much sternway, you might expect that putting the rudder to starboard should make the boat back to starboard. The forces of unequal blade thrust and discharge current still tend to drive the stern to port, but the suction current of the propeller wants to offset this.

The effect of the discharge current is stronger than the suction so the overall tendency is still to port. With sternway, the steering effect of the right rudder is to starboard, but as yet you haven't way enough to make this offset the stronger factors.

Steering while Backing

Opening the throttle to gain more sternway finally has the desired effect; with full right rudder you will find that the steering effect at considerable backing speed is enough (probably) to turn the stern to starboard against all the opposing factors. How well the boat will back to starboard—in fact, whether it will or not—depends upon the design of the craft.

All of this means that if the boat will back to starboard with full right rudder, it may also be made to go in a straight line—but *not* with the rudder centered. There's no use trying. The boat will need a certain amount of right rudder

depending both on its design and on speed. While most boats always back to port much better than to starboard, a boater can learn to control a particular boat with a reasonable degree of precision.

In some cases, boats may even be steered backwards out of crooked slips or channels—not, however, without a lot of backing and filling when there is much wind to complicate the situation. Generally, the trick is to keep the boat under control, making the turns no greater than necessary to keep the boat from swinging too much.

In backing situations, set the rudder first and *then* add maneuvering power by speeding up the propeller.

Killing Sternway

There is one other situation to be considered, where you want to kill sternway by engaging the propeller to turn ahead. Regardless of the rudder position, unequal blade thrust with the propeller going ahead now tends to throw the stern to starboard, while the suction current is of little or no consequence. In this situation, unequal blade thrust may or may not be offset by the steering effect and the discharge current.

With rudder amidships, there is no steering effect and the discharge current does not enter into calculations. Therefore the stern will go to starboard. Now if you turn the rudder to port, the discharge current of the propeller strikes the rudder and pushes the stern to starboard—even though the normal steering effect of left rudder would be to send the stern to port, with sternway. The powerful discharge current from the propeller going ahead is the determining factor.

If the rudder is turned to starboard, the steering effect works with the unequal blade thrust, tending to move the stern to starboard, but the discharge current strikes the starboard side of the rudder and acts to kick the stern to port. Be sure to apply enough power so that the force of discharge current outweighs the other factors, and the stern will indeed go to port.

Propeller Action Governs

From the above analysis it is clear that in a single-screw inboard boat you must be

STEP-BY-STEP DOCKING WITH A SINGLE-SCREW BOAT

With a right-hand propeller, back to port in order to line up with your slip. How fast you can turn your boat determines where to stop and when you should begin backing. A high freeboard and flybridge may react to a crosswind, so choose your moment so as to avoid sudden gusts.

Propeller action will help most single-screw boats turn to port when backing. With the helm hard to port, the boat should begin a turn to line up with the slip.

Usually a boat will need some help kicking its stern farther to port to align itself with the slip. Going ahead with a short burst of power, with helm over to starboard, will accomplish this. Some right rudder will probably be needed to make the boat back in a straight line into the slip, but remember that the torque of the propeller to port (in reverse) often has more influence than the position of the rudder. If a short burst of power is needed, position the rudder first, then apply power.

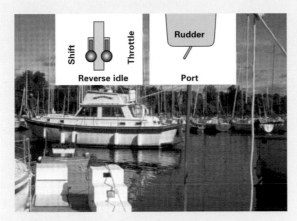

1 Shift into reverse to stop the boat, then put the helm over hard to port to start the turn into the slip. A slight increase in power will cause the boat to turn a bit quicker.

2 Shift into forward as you enter, put the helm over to starboard and open the throttle for a short burst of power. This kicks the stern to port, aligning the boat with the slip.

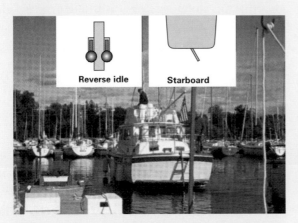

3 Shift into reverse and keep the helm to starboard in order to overcome the propeller walk to port and back straight into the slip.

4 When fully in the slip, put the gear in forward briefly to stop sternway. Keep the helm to starboard in order to kick the stern closer to the dock—or to port if it is too close.

constantly aware of what the propeller is doing, in order to know how best to use the rudder. What the propeller is doing is even more important than whether the boat has headway or sternway.

It's Different with Left-Hand Propellers

A minority, but a significant number, of single-screw powerboats, typically displacement types, and auxiliary-powered sailboats have left-hand propellers. Many commercial boats also have left-hand propellers as this makes it easier for them to execute a starboard-side approach and departure from a pier or wharf.

If your boat is equipped with a left-hand propeller, you can generally reverse "port" and "starboard" in the foregoing discussions. But to be absolutely sure, make tests for all possible situations.

MANEUVERING IN TIGHT QUARTERS

Since most marinas and anchorages are congested places, handling a boat in these confined spaces can be a real test of your skills. In fact, in some harbors, leaving and returning to your berth can be the most harrowing part of a cruise. Most of the basic maneuvers that you will need to get underway from, and return to, your slip safely are covered below.

Getting Underway

As skipper, you are responsible for the safe operation of your boat. Before you leave the berth, be sure that all your getting-underway procedures are completed. Make sure that all electrical cords and hoses are disconnected before taking off last-minute dock lines. Avoid spending too much time at the pier warming up the engine; long periods of idling are not good for the motor or transmission. The engine will warm up faster under a light load.

Getting Clear of Your Berth

When the boat lies alongside a pier or another craft, and the skipper wants to pull away, the wheel should never be put hard over until the stern is clear.

To set the rudder to starboard while lying portside to a pier or wharf, for example, and then attempt to pull away by going ahead (refer to **Figure 6-15**) only tends to throw the port quarter against the piles and pin it there, to slam into one pile after another, possibly damaging the boat.

Checking Headway

Stopping a boat's headway will require reversing the propeller. Experiment with stopping the boat from different speeds. This will give you an idea about the propeller's ability to check the boat's headway. Consider the following:

• Generally, a larger diameter propeller, acting on a large volume of water, will exert a greater effect. Small propellers, especially those on outboards, may do a lot of churning before they can overcome the boat's momentum.

• You can stop a fast boat in a short distance by cutting the throttles. Then, as the boat comes off of plane, shift into reverse and apply power.

• When practicing these maneuvers, take the following precaution: When you need to go from forward to reverse or vice versa, *slow the engine down* before going through neutral. Also warn crewmembers and passengers of your intentions so that they will not be unexpectedly thrown off balance, possibly being injured. Never make a practice of shifting from full ahead into full astern—you will tear up the gears.

• Always remember to approach piers as well as other craft at a very slow speed. Failure of the transmission, or an unexpected stopping of the engine, can result in embarrassment or damage, or both.

Turning in Close Quarters

Although turning a boat in a narrow channel or other confined waterway not much wider than the boat itself may seem impossible to the novice, it is really no more difficult than turning a car around on a narrow road.

Suppose, for example, that you have reached the head of a dead-end canal and must turn around. (See the sequential illustrations in **Figure 6-18.**) Assuming you have a single-screw boat

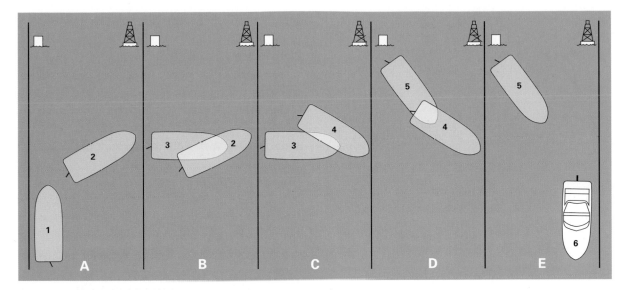

*Figure 6-18 Turning in close quarters: In **Step A**, at 1, the boat starts to turn at the left side of the channel; make allowance for the stern to swing to port. Headway is checked at 2 by reversing the propeller, with the rudder kept to starboard throughout this series of maneuvers. Unequal blade thrust and discharge current forces the stern to port as the boat backs from 2 to 3 in **Step B**. Going ahead again with a short burst of engine power, **Step C**, the stern is kicked around more at 4 before the boat has a chance to gain headway. Reversing once more in **Step D**, headway is checked at 4, and the boat backs to 5. (This forward and backing maneuver can be repeated as necessary.) Finally, in **Step E**, the boat goes ahead from 5 to 6 completing the change of direction by 180°.*

with a right-hand propeller, steer to the left side of the channel and make all forward maneuvers to starboard and backing maneuvers to port, to take advantage of the boat's natural tendencies. Now, running at slow speed, put the rudder hard over to starboard and, as the boat begins to turn, check headway by reversing. Leave the wheel hard over to starboard (right rudder). Very little is gained by applying right rudder while going ahead and left rudder while going astern, since the boat will make little way through the water. As the reversing propeller stops the boat, open the throttle for an instant; the stern will be kicked farther to port. Then put the gear in forward and open the throttle for a short burst of power, to check any sternway and keep the stern swinging to port. As soon as the boat gathers headway, shift into reverse and back down to kick the stern to port; then shift into forward again.

Most single-screw inboard boats can be maneuvered in very tight quarters by using this technique. Unequal propeller thrust in combination with rudder action turns the boat. Remember, however, that his applies only for a

right-hand propeller; reverse the technique for a left-hand propeller.

Backing to Port from a Slip

When leaving a slip, an experienced skipper will back a single-screw boat with a right-hand propeller to port. Suppose the boat is lying in a slip and you intend to back out into the channel. With left rudder, it will likely turn fast enough as it gathers sternway, aligning with the channel in one maneuver.

Before putting the boat in reverse, pull the boat to the port side of the slip, ensuring as much clearance as possible on the starboard side. Although some room is necessary on the port side because the stern immediately starts to move to port, more room is required on the starboard side because the bow will swing this way as the boat backs.

The starboard bow and port stern are the places to watch in executing this maneuver. If the boat turns sharper than expected, the starboard bow is in danger of touching the adjacent pier (see **Figure 6-19**) or a boat in the adjacent slip. This could be corrected by going ahead with the propeller a few

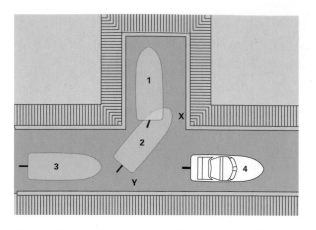

Figure 6-19 To back out of a slip, a boat should be able to make a short turn to port from 1 to 3 when reversing with left rudder. However, if the bow swings too wide, it may hit at X or Y.

revolutions while backing out of the slip. Once the bow is clear of the slip, right rudder followed by a short burst of power in forward will help kick the stern over to port if it is not turning fast enough while making sternway.

Backing Around to Starboard

In a different scenario, suppose you want to back out of the same situation outlined above or from a slip into a narrow canal that would require a sharp turn to starboard; see **Figure 6-20.**

Reversing with full right rudder, you will not be able to turn short enough to steer around the 90° angle before you would come up on the opposite canal bank. Most likely, you will back to a position somewhere in the middle of the canal

with the stern slightly to starboard. Now, by going ahead with left rudder, the stern is kicked farther over to starboard.

Reversing once more, with full right rudder, the boat backs to starboard and, just as it begins to make sternway, you go ahead once more with left rudder. This checks the sternway and kicks the stern to starboard in alignment with the channel.

Backing into a Berth Between Piles

Many marinas and yacht clubs provide slips in which boats are berthed at right angles to a pier or wharf and made fast to piles. Normally, a short secondary pier, often called a finger pier or catwalk, extends out between each pair of slips. In this situation, it is much easier to board the boat if it is moored with the stern toward the main pier or wharf. This arrangement makes for an easy departure, but requires backing into the slip upon return.

There are many variables that come into play as you back into a slip. Wind, current, and the location of other boats are just a few. At times, some of these factors may be so disconcerting that you may decide not to back into the slip, but instead to dock bow first until conditions improve. A wise man who said "Discretion is the better part of valor" must have been thinking of this situation.

Now let's consider a typical situation: You have spent a nice day on the water and are returning to your slip—one of hundreds located on a pier in a large marina; you want to back in. As you turn into the channel, the slip is to port and you are moving with a light wind and current astern. The

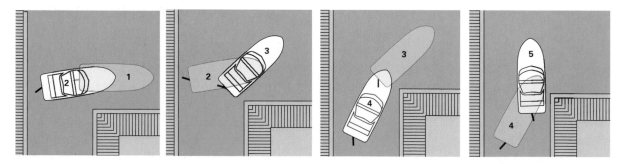

Figure 6-20 To back around to starboard where space is limited, the boat starts at 1 with right rudder and backs to 2 as it cannot turn sharply to starboard. At 2, the rudder is turned to port, and the stern is kicked to starboard at position 3 with a brief burst of engine power. From 3, the boat is backed to 4 with full right rudder. Here the rudder is put over to port again, and the boat moves forward to 5. Backing down from 5, it will need a certain amount of right rudder to maintain a straight course.

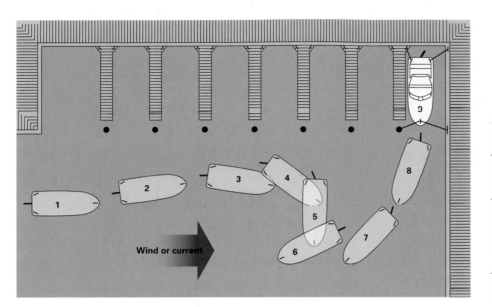

Wind or current

Figure 6-21 Backing into a slip between piles in a basin, if space allows, make a turn ahead under power to maneuver the bow partly into the wind before backing down. Note that the right rudder from positions 6 through 8 keeps the stern from swinging to port.

channel is only a couple of boat lengths wide, so there is not much room for maneuvering. In this situation, the port side of the channel should be favored to allow for wind and current. Begin your turn before the slip, in order to position the boat upwind and/or up-current of it.

Depending on how quickly the boat can be turned, put the helm over to starboard well before you reach the slip. Because the channel is narrow, the boat will not be able to turn more than 90°, almost into the wind, in a single maneuver; see **Figure 6-21.** As the bow approaches the other side of the channel, shift into reverse and open the throttle to stop headway and kick the stern to port. As soon as the boat gathers sternway, reduce throttle, then shift to forward and open the throttle again to kick the stern farther to port; position the boat at about a 45° angle to the slip.

The turn should be timed so that the final position of the boat is slightly upwind from the slip, with the wind and current off the starboard bow. If you are not upwind of the slip, complete the turn and run upwind until you are. If you are too far upwind, wait for the current to push you down closer to the slip.

Begin backing with right rudder. As soon as you start backing, the current and wind will push the bow to port so that, by the time the stern is entering the slip, the boat will be nearly in line with the slip. Remember, when backing a boat

with a right-hand propeller, use left rudder in combination with a short burst of forward power to move the stern to starboard. Left rudder with propeller reversing should move the stern to port.

Getting Clear of a Pile

In maneuvering around slips and piles, you may be caught in a position where the wind and/or current hold the boat against the pile, preventing any maneuver. The solution is to rig a forward spring line from the pile to an aft cleat, preferably on the side of the boat away from the pile; see **Figure 6-22.** Then, by reversing with left rudder, pivot the boat around the pile and bring the bow into the wind or against the current. You can then clear the pile by going ahead with power as the spring is cast off.

In getting clear from this point, you may need a little left rudder to keep the stern clear of the pile, but don't use enough to throw the stern so far over that the starboard quarter is in danger of hitting an adjacent pile.

Plan Maneuvers in Advance

Obviously the number of possible situations—considering the differences in boats and the strength, direction, and effect of wind and current—is almost infinite. Usually, however, applying one of the principles above, modified as needed, will permit a seamanlike handling of the problem.

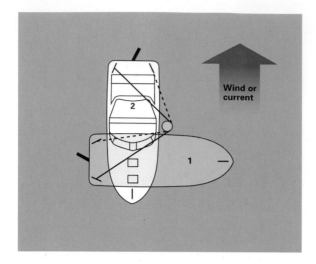

Figure 6-22 *If pinned against a piling, use a forward spring line from a stern cleat to swing the boat into the wind or current.*

Even though you know the principles, however, it pays to think ahead about the steps you will take. With a clear plan of action, you can take each step slowly and easily, and have time to keep the boat under perfect control. To avoid confusion, tell your crew the steps you plan to follow, the actions that each crewmember will have to take, and the orders you will give when these actions are required. Even on occasions that call for swift and decisive action, you'll need calm, ordered judgment.

If your plan of action requires total abandonment because of unforeseen conditions, don't hesitate to act accordingly. For example, if you plan for a clean approach to a pier or wharf has been upset by a freak current you couldn't calcu-

late, or by a passing boat's wake, back off and square away for another attempt. That in itself is good seamanship, regardless of how some may judge your apparent "miss" on the first try. Common sense, if you act with deliberation, will enable you to work out a solution for any combination of conditions.

When you are at the helm and you have people on deck handling lines, give orders to each so that all action is under your control, instead of having two or three acting independently at cross-purposes. This is especially imperative when your crew is not familiar with boats or with your method of boat handling.

DOCK LINES & THEIR USES

Dock lines (also called mooring lines) play an important part in the handling of vessels at a pier. Obviously, as boat size increases, more and heavier lines are needed. A small, light outboard craft requires fewer lines for secure docking than does a heavy 50-foot trawler. But both skippers should know and understand how lines are used, so that they can decide which lines are appropriate.

In addition to securing a boat in its berth, the proper use of lines can aid maneuvering close to piers and wharves.

Dock Line Terminology

Although most skippers speak quite loosely of bow and stern lines, it generally matters little as long as the line is made fast forward or aft. However, there are several lines that can be

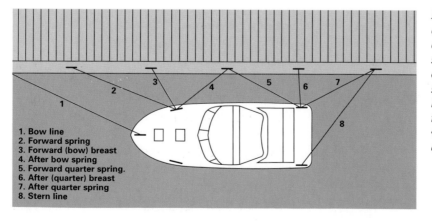

1. Bow line
2. Forward spring
3. Forward (bow) breast
4. After bow spring
5. Forward quarter spring.
6. After (quarter) breast
7. After quarter spring
8. Stern line

Figure 6-23 *The various possible dock lines for a vessel include the eight shown here. A small craft skipper will never need to use all of them at the same time. The stern line, 8 in the diagram, is best run to the offshore side of the boat to gain better control while still holding the stern in closer to the wharf or pier.*

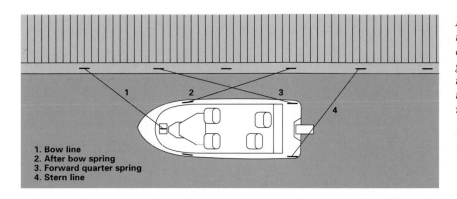

1. Bow line
2. After bow spring
3. Forward quarter spring
4. Stern line

Figure 6-24 *As shown in this typical small craft docking, crossing spring lines provides greater length for each. This is particularly desirable where there is a significant tidal range.*

secured to the bow or stern and, depending on their direction and use, these are given other names. (Note that "forward" and "after" relate to the direction in which a line runs from the vessel, and not to where it is made fast on board.) **Figure 6-23** illustrates eight possible lines; **Figure 6-24** shows just those lines that might be used in a typical small-craft docking situation.

Bow & Stern Lines

According to correct nautical terminology, there is only one BOW LINE. This is made fast to a forward cleat and run forward along the pier to prevent the boat from moving astern. The STERN LINE leads from an after cleat to a pile or cleat on the pier astern of the boat; this line checks the boat from going ahead. For securing a small craft, these lines are often the only ones that are required. If they are given the proper slack, they can allow for considerable rise and fall of the tide.

Breast Lines

BREAST LINES are lines, secured to the bow and stern, that lead athwartships nearly at right angles to the vessel and to the pier or wharf. They are used on larger vessels to keep the craft from moving away from the pier or to pull it in for boarding. Large craft may use bow or quarter breasts, depending on where they are secured. Naturally, breast lines on large vessels are more important than on small ones.

Additional Cleats

Smaller recreational boats frequently will have only one bitt or cleat forward, and one or two aft,

for securing dock lines. Additional cleats along the sides, properly through-bolted, give better flexibility in the use of dock lines.

Spring Lines

Although only two SPRING LINES generally are used at any one time, there may be as many as four: the forward bow spring, the after bow spring, the forward quarter spring, and the after quarter spring. Bow springs are made fast to the vessel near or at the bow; quarter springs are near or at the stern. Forward springs lead forward from the vessel to the pier or wharf, and control movement sternward. After springs lead aft from the vessel, and check movement ahead.

Spring lines are used to prevent movement in a berth, ahead or astern. They work with the bow and stern lines to keep a boat in position when there is a significant rise and fall of tide. This is particularly desirable where boat movement forward and aft must be minimized so that fenders are kept in place against piles, or where the gap between adjacent vessels is quite small.

Sizing the Line to the Boat

On most recreational boats, dock lines are usually made from nylon, either of twisted rope or braided core and cover. Nylon is the preferred material because it stretches absorbing shock loads, is chafe-resistant for long life, and is easy on the hands.

A line's size varies with the boat. Typically, a 20- to 40-foot craft will use ½-inch-diameter nylon lines, with larger yachts using ⅝- or ¾-inch lines. Smaller boats can use ⅜-inch nylon. Dock

BOW THRUSTERS

Many medium-size and larger craft are now equipped with a BOW THRUSTER. This is a small propeller (or two of them) mounted in a tunnel that crosses from one side of the hull to the other just below the waterline and very near the bow. Bow thrusters on boats are simply smaller versions of devices found on most large ships. They are powered by either an electric or a hydraulic motor; electrically powered thruster installations are simpler and less expensive unless the vessel already has a hydraulic power system for other machinery. Smaller units have a single propeller; larger units have two counter-rotating propellers or two propellers with opposite blade angles turning in the same direction; there does not seem to be any significant advantages or disadvantages in these variations in design. Thrusters are generally rated in pounds of thrust developed.

Bow thrusters are reversible, sending a jet of water from either side to the other. Controls usually consist of a small joystick at each helm position, together with an ON-OFF switch. Motors are operated in either direction at a fixed speed. To keep size and weight at a minimum (highly desirable at the bow), electrical motors are small and must be operated intermittently to prevent heat buildup and damage. On very sophisticated installations, a thruster may be retractable rather than in a tunnel, being lowered for use and retracted within the hull when not needed so as to reduce drag.

Bow thrusters are of the greatest assistance to single-screw vessels, but will also be quite useful on twin-screw craft. They are primarily used in docking and undocking, situations where they can be of significant help. They may also assist in making sharp turns in rivers and channels. The fact that they are used only infrequently does not detract from their overall value—when you need one, it's good to have it!

Seldom seen, but quite practical, are STERN THRUSTERS. These have the motor and small propeller of a bow thruster, but not the tunnel. They are usually mounted beneath a swim platform on single-screw craft such as trawlers. The purpose is the same as for bow thrusters: assistance in docking or other close-quarters maneuvers.

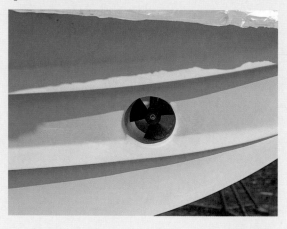

lines should be strong enough to hold the boat and have enough bulk to resist chafe, while not being so heavy as to lose their shock-absorbing characteristics. A light boat pulling against a ⅝-inch line will come up hard against the line because the weight of the boat is not enough to cause the line to begin to stretch. On the other hand, a light ⅜-inch line holding a heavy boat will be very springy and probably only strong enough for favorable conditions. Moreover, ⅜-inch lines provide no margin for wear and chafe when under heavy strain.

Making a Boat Fast to a Pier

Although many people will speak of "tying up" a boat in a slip or to a pier, this is *not* correct nautical terminology. A vessel of any size is "made fast" to the shore.

As described above (and illustrated in **Figure 6-23**) there are at least eight dock lines that might be used to secure a boat; they are not all used at the same time. Most average-sized boats can be made fast to a pier or wharf using four lines. The after bow spring is crossed with the forward quarter spring and secured to separate pier cleats or piles; refer to **Figure 6-24.** This arrangement provides longer springs, which can be drawn up rather snugly and still allow for a rise and fall of tide. If only one pile or cleat is available on shore, position your boat so that this point is opposite amidships; then run both springs to it. The lines will be shorter, but still effective.

The bow and stern lines should make roughly a 45° angle with the pier. The stern line can be secured to the near-shore quarter cleat, but will work better if run to the offshore quarter cleat. The longer line will allow the boat to rise and fall with the tide and better keep the boat in close to the pier.

If there is an offshore wind blowing, you may want to rig a slack breast line to the near-shore quarter cleat in order to pull the boat into the pier against the wind for easy boarding. However, you must always remember to loosen the line as the tide rises or falls, and to allow plenty of slack during the night, or when the boat is not tended.

Dock lines frequently have an eye splice in one end, but not the other. You must decide whether to use the end with a loop on shore or on the boat. If you are going to be on board, it is better to retain the plain end on board. This means that you can make adjustments without getting off the boat. If there will be no one on the boat, use the end with the eye on board; the plain end ashore will allow adjustment without the necessity of boarding. **Figure 6-25** illustrates the most secure method of making the eye end of a line fast to a cleat. For securing the plain end to a cleat, see Chapter 23, page 783.

Heaving Lines & Monkey's Fists

A part of good seamanship is knowing when a certain procedure is applicable to the size of vessel that you are on, as when getting dock lines from your boat to the shore or another craft. The lines of a big ship are heavy hawsers, hard to handle and impossible to heave. The

Figure 6-25 Most cleats on boats consist of a crossbar elevated from the deck by two legs (see Figure 1-29). The most secure method of attaching a line to such a cleat is by passing the eye through the gap between the legs and then back over each end of the crossbar.

deck crew of such a vessel makes use of HEAVING LINES, light lines weighted at one end with a MONKEY'S FIST (an intricate woven knot enclosing a weight) for greater accuracy in heaving. This light line is attached to the hawser near the eye splice–but not in the loop where it might get jammed when a strain is placed on the hawser–and the line is heaved over from the ship to the pier or wharf as soon as possible as a MESSENGER. The heavier line or hawser is then pulled over and made fast.

Small Craft Practices On recreational boats, heaving lines is more of a technique to be learned and then filed away for possible later emergency use. Normally, your crew can hand a line to someone ashore, or throw it a short distance.

To throw a line to someone on shore or another boat, coil the line in your left hand (if you are right-handed), making clockwise loops. Coil the line smoothly, avoiding figure-eights, then transfer about half the loops to your throwing (right) hand and hurl them with a strong swinging motion while letting the loops play out freely from your other hand. Hold tightly to the bitter end or, better yet, secure it to a cleat. **Figure 6-26** shows a line being thrown by a right-handed person. If necessary a weight can be added to carry a line farther, but this is seldom needed. If you need to pass over a heavy

MAKING FAST

When mooring your boat, fasten the lines securely at both ends. Often you will loop the eye splice of the dock line around a pile. If your boat has much freeboard, or the tide is high, the mooring line will lead down sharply from deck to pier. To prevent it from being pulled up off the pile, loop the eye splice around the pile twice. If the eye in your mooring line is too small to go around the pile twice, or even fit over the pile once, pull the line through the spliced eye to make a new loop.

If yours is to be the second line on a pile or cleat, it is both prudent and courteous to dip your line through the first loop. The other skipper may not know the trick of getting his line clear without removing yours. To drop a line over a pile that already holds another boat's line, run the eye of your line up through the first eye from below, then loop it over the pile; see the illustration below. This will allow either line to be removed without disturbing the other.

If you find that another skipper has dropped the eye in his line over yours on a pile or cleat, simply reverse the process. Get a little slack in the other line, and then slip your eye up through its loop and over the top of the pile. Your line then can be dropped through the eye of the other and pulled clear.

When leaving a pier or maneuvering against spring or other dock lines, it is convenient to be able to release the line from the pile or cleat—from on board the boat—as soon as you get away from the pier. By looping a long line around the pile or cleat, and having both ends on board, you can

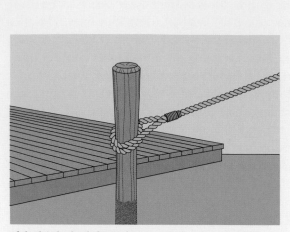

If the lead is high from the pier or wharf to the deck, take an extra turn around the pile with the eye splice to prevent the line from slipping up off the top of the pile.

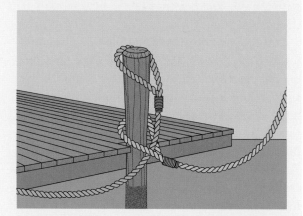

If you need to place your line on a pile that already has one on it, pass the loop of your line up through the loop of the first line and then over the top on the pile.

easily release it. Slip one end around the pile or cleat, then pull it back on board. Be sure to release the end of the line without the eye splice, so it will run freely around the pile or cleat without hanging up at the splice.

towline, however, break out your heaving line and use it to good advantage.

If Lines Are Doubled
If two lines are used with the idea of getting double the strength of one, they must be of equal length. Otherwise, the short one

carries the full load until it breaks, leaving the single longer line to then carry the same full load.

Allowing for Tidal Range
Boaters on fresh-water streams and lakes have no tides to worry about when they make fast to a

Figure 6-26 A properly coiled dock line can be thrown a significant distance if you start with half the coil in each hand.

pier. But in tidal waters, failure to consider the tides can part lines, and may even sink the boat.

Long spring lines provide the most effective method for leaving a boat free to rise and fall. They also keep the boat from going ahead or astern, moving off fenders, or twisting in such a way as to get caught on pier projections. The longer a spring, bow, or stern line can be, the greater the tidal range it can accommodate with a minimum of slack. Long lines allow each line to be adjusted, so that all do not come taut together at either extreme stage of the tide; see **Figure 6-27.**

Adjust the dock lines to come up almost taut at either of the extreme tidal ranges; this adjustment may take some experimentation. Observe the boat at both high and low tide, and adjust the lines so they are snug, but not tight, at these stages.

If you keep your boat in a slip, it is important to check the lines at times of extreme high and low tides. Make sure the lines are not so slack that the boat can move against a pile or finger pier.

When berthing in a narrow slip with a large tidal range, it may be impossible to keep the boat from coming up against a pile or pier at mid-tide; careful placement of fenders, either on the boat or secured to the pier or piling, may be the only way to protect your boat.

Maneuvering Against Dock Lines

Depending on current and weather conditions, getting in and out of your slip or away from a pier can at times be challenging. Spring lines are the most useful dock lines since they can be used to assist maneuvering.

Going Ahead on an After Bow Spring

If it is possible to secure an after spring amidships or close to the boat's pivot point (about one-third the way aft from the bow), the boat can then be worked into a pier by running ahead slowly with the rudder turned away from the pier; see **Figure 6-28.** Since the stern is free to swing as the discharge current acts on the rudder, the boat will move toward—and come in closer to—the pier. This technique is especially useful when maneuvering short-handed, bringing the boat against the pier by simply passing a single line ashore. It is also helpful when maneuvering a large boat against a stiff offshore wind, where hauling in on bow and stern lines would require great effort. This is typically more theoretical than practical on many small boats, which have only the bow and stern (or quarter) cleats for securing spring

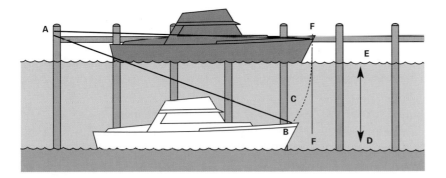

Figure 6-27 This illustration shows how long spring lines are used with considerable changes in tidal levels. If the water drops 11 feet from E to D, a 32-foot after bow spring line (A to B) would cause the boat to move astern only the distance from B to F, roughly 2 feet. F represents the position of cleat C at high water.

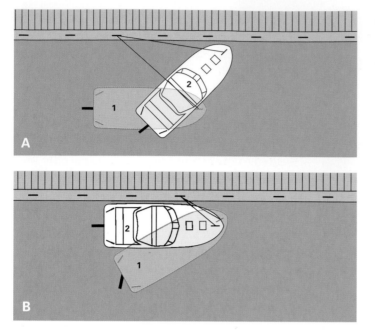

*Figure 6-28 By going ahead on an after bow spring line, as shown at **A**, a boat's bow is pulled into the pier, but the stern swings away from shore. If the rudder is turned away from the pier, as at **B**, the stern will swing in as power is applied. This maneuver works best if there is a cleat back from the bow, nearer the pivot point of the boat.*

lines to, while the pivot point is well aft of the bow. If it is at all possible, install a cleat on each side of your boat slightly forward of amidships.

Reversing on a Spring Line

The stern is swung sharply toward the pier by the action of the forward quarter spring when reversing; see **Figure 6-29.** Since stern movement is restricted, there is much less control. The bow is free to swing away from the pier with the wind or current. If you back on a forward bow spring, or on a bow line, the stern is not as restricted, and the line has less effect on turning the boat; see **Figure 6-30.** Unless there is a strong offshore wind or current, the boat will probably back parallel to the pier.

LANDING WITH CONTROL

Whenever you approach a pier or wharf, your close-quarters boat-handling skills will be tested. Although this maneuver is not difficult, a challenging situation can arise from a combination of wind, current, and adjacent congestion. Your knowledge of turning a boat in limited space will stand you in good stead when you tackle the problem of bringing your boat in neatly to a pier, wharf, or float.

As a matter of proper terminology, here is a reminder that you should not refer to a "dock" when you actually mean a "pier" or "wharf." A pier projects out from the shoreline, usually but not always at a right angle. A wharf (sometimes called a quay, pronounced "key") is a structure generally parallel to and not far from the shore. Technically, a dock is the adjacent *water* area that can be occupied by a vessel. In boating, however, the term is often used loosely to mean the structure itself. The space occupied by a vessel, or available for its use, is its berth.

The action of coming alongside the structure, whatever it is, is referred to as docking (sometimes mooring, although it is less confusing if this term is limited to picking up the pennant of a floating mooring buoy). Departing is undocking, a term more often used with ships than boats.

This section covers the basic guidelines to consider when approaching a pier or docking a boat in the type of conditions you will likely encounter.

Approach with Caution

Since boats do not have brakes, and must rely on reversing the propeller thrust to stop, it is prudent to maneuver at slow speeds while in congested areas. Monitor your boat's wake as you make your way to your berth; it can affect your boat, as well as other craft nearby.

Don't come in at a high speed with a grand flourish. Depending on conditions, throttle down gradually to keep the boat under control. The goal is to proceed through the harbor or marina slowly, but with enough way on to maintain control. When you consider that you have enough way on to reach the dock, shift into neutral; use reverse power as and when necessary to check headway as you reach your desired location.

If your speed has been properly estimated, you will be several boat lengths from the pier when you shift into neutral. Approaching a pier too fast will require you to shift into neutral far from your berth. Even though the boat is moving through the water, the propeller is not turning and, consequently, there is no propeller discharge current acting on the rudder. Keep in mind that most boats have better slow-speed maneuverability if the propeller is turning: A slow approach allows you to keep the boat in forward until you are almost alongside the pier.

This is a good time to exercise judgment—keeping on the way needed for maneuverability, yet using no more speed than required. If you have been running at any speed, hold off briefly and let your own wake pass by your boat.

Have the dock lines ready to use fore and aft. Also have fenders ready so that they can be put in place as soon as the boat is secured, keeping it from chafing against piles or pier edges. Lead all docking lines outboard of stanchions and shrouds, so that they will be clear when taken ashore.

The biggest mistake novice deckhands make is to secure a dock line before the boat has lost all headway. If you have a couple of hands on board, assign one to the bow and one to the stern, with instructions not to make fast until headway is checked. Use reverse to stop the boat, cautioning your crew that securing the bow or stern lines while the boat is still moving can cause the bow or stern to come crashing into the pier. An after bow spring line is the only dock line that should be used to stop the boat. If you are maneuvering into a tight berth, or against strong current or wind, this line will likely be the first one secured.

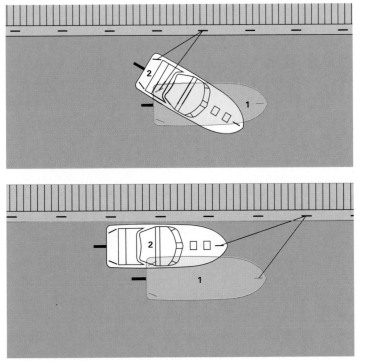

Figure 6-29 When backing on a forward quarter spring, the stern swings in but the bow swings out away from the pier.

Figure 6-30 By reversing on a bow line, a boat can be sprung in nearly parallel to a pier or wharf face.

MAKING USE OF FENDERS

Fenders (they are *not* to be called "bumpers") are relatively soft objects of rubberlike plastic and filled with air under low pressure. They are used between boats and piles, pier sides, and seawalls to protect topsides from scarring and to cushion any shock of the boat striking the fixed object. Some fenders can be inflated to different pressures with a hand pump. Most fenders are circular or square in cross section and of varying length.

Most fenders have eyes molded in each end for attaching a short length of line that is used to suspend them along the side of a boat. Some models have a hole through their center through which a piece of line is run and knotted at each end.

Good quality fenders are not inexpensive, but they are well worth the investment. Half a dozen substantial fenders are not too many for the average cruiser to carry.

Fenderboards

When fenders hang vertically from the boat's side, they give protection against the face of a solid pier or wharf as the boat moves fore and aft. If the boat lies against vertical piles, vertical fenders will not stay in place during the boat's forward and afterward movement.

The solution to protecting the hull in many situations is with fenderboards—short lengths (approximately 4 to 6 feet) of heavy boards (2 inches by 6 inches is common),

sometimes faced on one side with metal rub-strips on rubber cushions. Holes are drilled, and lines attached, allowing the board to be hung horizontally, backed by two fenders hung vertically.

The horizontal fenderboard rests against the pile bridging the two fenders. The boat can then move back and forth the length of the fenderboard and still be protected from chafing against the pile.

Fenderboards also give excellent cushioning between two or more craft rafted together. One boat should put out the usual two fenders behind a fenderboard; the other puts over only its own two fenders. A second fenderboard should not be used, since one board could tangle with the other.

Calm Conditions

Without wind or current to complicate landing, a skipper operating a boat with a single right-hand propeller will want to make a port-side approach to the pier. Time your approach speed so you will be several boat lengths from the pier when you shift into neutral. Since a reversing right-hand propeller will move the stern to port, approach the pier at a 10° to 20° angle; see **Figure 6-31**. When alongside, shift into reverse to stop

headway. Depending on your speed, a short burst of throttle may be necessary to stop the boat and to kick the stern to port, with the boat alongside and parallel to the pier.

Though a port-side approach is preferable, you can, with care, make a good landing with the pier on the starboard side (remember, we are on board a single-screw boat with a right-hand propeller). Approach the pier slowly at a much shallower angle, as nearly parallel as possible to the pier; see

Figure 6-32. Just before you have to reverse to check headway, turn the rudder to full left, swinging the stern in toward the pier. If it does not respond, give the propeller a brief spurt of ahead engine power while the rudder is full left, in order to kick the stern to starboard. Then reverse to check your headway.

You can also bring the boat in parallel to the pier with an after bow spring line. Secure this line to a pile or cleat ashore, then put the gear in forward with the rudder still full left. The spring line prevents forward movement while the stern moves toward the pier.

Wind or Current Parallel to Berth

Because water is many times denser than air, in most cases current should be given primary consideration when planning an approach to a pier or wharf. If the wharf happens to be on the shore of a river, or the bank of a tidal stream, the current will flow generally parallel to it. In this case, the direction of the current should determine how you approach. Heading into the current will enable you to keep the propeller turning over slowly and water

moving past the rudder—right up to the moment of reaching the wharf—if the current is strong enough.

If you were to approach the pier from the opposite direction, moving with a half-knot current, you would not only have to stop the boat dead in water. You would also have to begin making half-knot sternway before your relative movement past the pier would stop.

The wind also must be reckoned with. Since propellers are not as efficient when reversing as when going forward, attempting to stop your boat in a strong following wind takes extra time. During this time, the rudder will be in the propeller's suction current, so it will be of little use in steering the boat. Stopping a boat going upwind is much easier, and, if the wind is strong enough, the propeller can be kept turning ahead even as the boat comes dead in the water.

When approaching a pier with a current running or strong wind blowing parallel to it, stop your boat in the channel. Assess the directions and relative strengths of the wind or current (at times they may be opposing) before deciding on which approach is best:

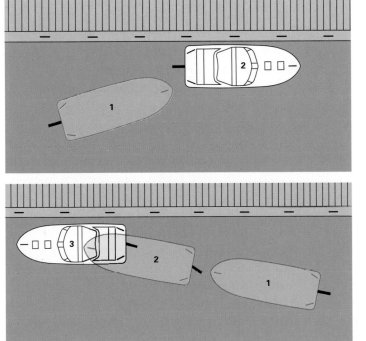

Figure 6-31 With a right-hand propeller, approach a pier or wharf for a landing, as at 1, at an angle of 10° to 20°. Discharge current of the reversing propeller will set the stern to port as at position 2, even though the rudder is centered.

Figure 6-32 When it is necessary to make a landing starboard side to the pier in a craft with a right-hand propeller, approach slowly as at 1, as nearly parallel as possible to the pier or wharf face. The rudder is turned to full left at 2, and the stern is swung to starboard with a short burst of engine power. Check the forward motion at position 3.

• If the wind or current is at your back, then pass downwind or downstream of the pier, turn around and proceed toward the dock upstream. In starting a turn such as this, even at some distance from the berth, throttle down well before the wharf comes abeam. Otherwise your wake may carry along and have you wallowing in it just when you are coming alongside.

• In coming up against wind or current, you can use that force to check your headway, instead of reverse. In the case of a strong current, your boat should respond to the helm when its relative movement to the pier has stopped, because there will still be a flow of water past the boat and its rudder.

Landings Downwind or with Current

If you can, avoid any landing in which wind or current is setting you down toward your berth. In this case, you are totally dependent on your reverse gear for stopping the boat. An error in judgment or an engine failure would put you in an embarrassing, if not dangerous, situation.

Sometimes, however, space will not permit you to turn before docking. Suppose, for example, you are coming into a canal lock with a strong wind astern. Proceed in, as slowly as possible while retaining control. With a single-screw, right-hand-propeller boat, if possible, choose the port side of the lock, so that your stern will swing in against the lock face when you reverse. Once the boat's headway has been checked, get a line out from the stern or port quarter; the boat can lie temporarily on this line alone. If you get a bow line secured ashore first, and miss making the stern line fast, you risk being turned end-for-end by the wind or current.

Handling the Lines

If you have a couple of hands aboard, assign one to the bow and one to the stern to handle lines, with instructions not to make fast until headway is checked. The seriousness of checking the boat's way by means of a snubbed bow line instead of reversing the propeller is only too obvious. If single-handed you will have to work smartly, with a stern line fast to the after cleat coiled ready to carry ashore, and a bow line run in advance along the deck back to the cockpit. All docking lines, of course, would have to be led outboard of stanchions and shrouds, to be clear when taken ashore.

The problem is similar if you are making your landing with a following current. In either case, be ready with reverse gear on the approach, using it as strongly as necessary to hold the boat against its momentum and the push of wind or current. The propeller ordinarily should be turning over slowly in reverse for the last boat length or two of headway, the throttle being opened gradually and as needed to kill all headway at the right instant.

Landing on the Leeward Side of a Pier

Since the wind can blow from any direction, it's not uncommon to find yourself approaching a pier with the wind blowing at right angles to the pier. If you have a choice as to which side of the pier you land, choose the leeward side. If the wind is strong, the windward side can be uncomfortable and your boat may pound against the piles. The rougher it is, the more important it becomes to dock on the leeward side. The wind will then hold the boat clear of the pier instead of pushing the craft against it.

Unless there is current to consider, make the leeward approach so the port side will rest against the pier. Depending on wind strength, you may have to point the bow into the wind a bit more than usual to keep it from falling away during your approach. Your biggest problem will be getting the stern to come into the pier against the wind.

Since you are going upwind, you can approach the pier a bit faster then normal, and then reverse a bit harder, kicking the stern toward the dock. You may need to put the rudder hard right and go forward for short burst to help get the stern in.

Have the crew take or pass the bow line—or after bow spring line—ashore first. Then secure the stern line. If the stern begins to drift away from the pier before you can secure the stern line, run ahead on the bow line slowly with the rudder hard right. It will act as an after spring to help bring the stern into the pier.

Be careful that neither the bow nor topside is damaged by the pier during this operation; have your fenders ready.

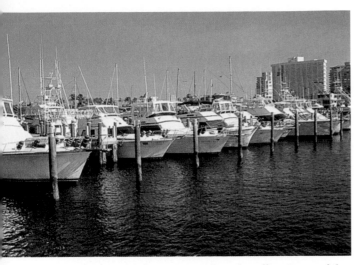

Figure 6-33 Close-quarters boat handling is one of the most important skills that a boater can acquire. The key to success is understanding the fundamentals, plus much practice—an opportunity that is ever-present (often with other skippers watching) in most marinas and yacht clubs.

If you have a large, heavy boat, secure the after spring on a beam cleat first; then secure the stern line.

Close Quarters

Often you will find that the only empty berth in a crowded marina or yacht club lies between two docked boats. There may be little more than a boat length to squeeze into; see **Figure 6-33.** Here again, the spring line comes into play.

A port-side approach is preferable. Since boats are on both sides of the docking area, you will have to approach at a greater angle than if the pier were clear of other vessels; see **Figure 6-34.** The aim is to place the bow as close to the pier as possible, without running up on the forward boat. Be sure you leave ample clearance on your port side so that, when you back down to check headway, the stern does not hit the bow of the boat astern of you.

Have your crew stand by, ready to go ashore with the after bow spring line, or ready to throw the line ashore to someone on the pier who will make it fast. After the spring line is secured ashore, put the rudder over full right and go ahead slowly. While the propeller discharge current acting on the right rudder pushes the stern into the pier, make certain that the spring line is adjusted so that the boat cannot possibly move forward into the boat ahead. Then, as the boat swings in, the spring line may be slacked off a little bit. Quite often you may find that a fender or two might be necessary at the point of contact.

A Mediterranean Moor

In some areas, especially along the Mediterranean coast in Europe where docking space is very limited, boats of all types and sizes are docked with the stern to the shore without the use of piles and finger piers. An anchor is dropped off shore and the vessel is slowly backed down, paying out the anchor rode, until it is close enough for persons to get on and off using a short gangplank. Have fenders in place along both sides if there are adjacent craft.

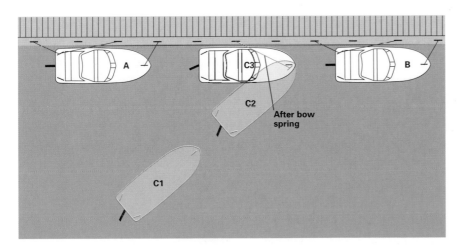

Figure 6-34 Landing between boats A and B, boat C approaches at a greater than normal angle. At position C2, a spring line is run aft from at or near the bow to the pier or wharf. Going ahead with engine power and right rudder, the boat swings into its berth at position C3.

Holding with One Spring Line

The use of a spring line works well for temporary holding on the lee side of a pier or wharf. Assume that you have run up along the leeward side of a wharf, to remain there for a short time while you pick up guests or perhaps put someone ashore. Instead of getting lines out to make fast fore and aft as you would for a longer stay, or expecting the crew to hold the boat against the wind's pressure, try using one line as an after bow spring. First come alongside, then rig this line and go ahead easily till it takes a strain; now with rudder turned away from shore, go ahead with just power enough to hold the stern up against the pier. This is a maneuver that you can accomplish single-handed without too much difficulty by having your spring line fast to the forward cleat as you come in, with the end ready to pass ashore for someone on the pier to drop over a pile or cleat.

Doubling a Spring Line

Single-handed, you might prefer to use the spring doubled, with the bight of line around the pile or cleat on shore and both ends of the line made fast to your boat. Then when you are ready to leave, you can slip the engine into neutral, cast off the one line, and haul the spring back aboard without leaving your boat. This would be helpful when the wind is of some force, the shoreside cleat well back from the pier's edge, and there is no one on shore to assist. This way there would be no risk of the boat's being blown off as you step ashore to cast off the line.

In any case, when the line has been cast off, the wind will cause the boat to drift clear of the dock, the bow ordinarily paying off faster than the stern. Whether you go ahead or reverse to get under way will depend on whether there are other structures and boats nearby, and whether your course is to be up- or down-wind.

This same maneuver is appropriate if it is current rather than wind that is tending to move your boat away from the pier.

CLEARING A BERTH

Getting safely away from alongside a pier or wharf can be either simple and easy, or complex and difficult, depending on wind direction, the set of any current, and the proximity of other craft. Take advantage of any help you can get from the wind and current, and make good use of spring lines.

With Wind or Current Ahead

When facing wind and current ahead, leaving a berth is not difficult. The biggest problem that skippers often create for themselves is to start forward without providing sufficient clearance between the pier and their boat. Remember that, for a boat to turn, the stern must be free to move. To pull away from a port-side pier, the stern must swing to port before the boat will begin to turn to

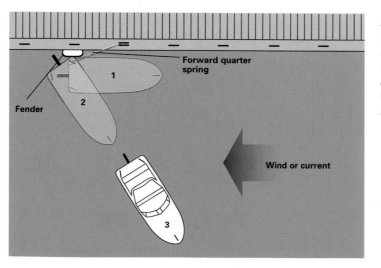

Figure 6-35 One technique that can be used when the wind or current is ahead is to back on a forward quarter spring line to turn the stern in and the bow out, angling to get clear to go ahead with the rudder centered. Use a fender as shown here.

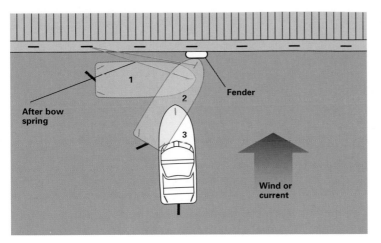

Figure 6-36 *An after bow spring line is often needed to depart from the windward side of a pier or wharf face. The boat goes ahead on the spring from 1 to 2, with the rudder turned toward the shore. Use of a fender may be needed as shown here. At 3, the line is cast off, and the boat backs into the wind or current.*

starboard away from the pier. It is not uncommon to see a boat rub its stern against the whole length of the face of a wharf as the skipper turns the wheel more and more to starboard in an effort to pull away; refer to **Figure 6-15.**

With smaller, lighter craft, all that may be needed to gain the necessary clearance from the pier is for someone to give the bow a push off. Backing on a forward quarter spring line will allow the current to turn the bow out and away from the pier or wharf; use a fender to cushion the port quarter of the hull; see **Figure 6-35.** On the other hand, a larger boat will find it better to go ahead on the after bow spring, with the rudder turned in toward the pier. The natural action of the propeller plus rudder will swing the stern clear of the pier. You can then back down a short distance, and be clear of the pier to go ahead; remember that as you turn to starboard your stern will swing to port, bringing it back toward the pier. With either procedure, don't try to cut away too sharply; your stern could come back in enough that your port quarter would strike the pier.

From a Windward Berth

Clearing a berth where the wind or current is pushing the boat against the pier does not necessarily have to be difficult, except in extreme conditions when it may be impossible to get the boat off the pier without working with the after bow spring.

Since the wind or current is holding the boat against the pier, cast off all dock lines—except the aft bow spring line. If the boat has only bow and stern lines, cast off the stern line, then transfer the bow line to an amidships position on the pier to convert it into an after spring.

Go ahead easy on the spring with the rudder turned toward the wharf; see **Figure 6-36.** The bow of the boat will come into the pier, and the stern will move away from the pier. If it does not respond with the rudder hard over, open the throttle to provide the kick necessary to work the stern around.

Depending on the nature of the pier and the type of boat, you may need a fender or two at the critical spots between pier and boat.

Continue until the boat has turned enough. The stern should be angled far enough from the pier so it will not be blown back against the pier when backing away. Get the spring line and fenders on board, and back the boat away with rudder centered. The stronger the wind or current, the more power is necessary to move the boat against it. If there are other boats moored to the pier near you, back away with considerable power to gain sternway and some steerage as soon as possible.

Continue backing away until well clear; a boat that is dead in the water will make much more leeway than one that is moving.

With Wind or Current Astern

Instead of merely casting off all lines and going ahead, get the maneuverable stern out away from the pier and go astern before going ahead on the course.

Run ahead on the after bow spring. This allows the stern to go out into the current, or be kicked out if necessary by power, going ahead with the rudder turned toward the wharf. If the current or wind is noticeable, often the stern swings out without aid of the engine. When the boat has swung out, anywhere from 45° to 60° degrees depending on the situation, the spring is cast off. The boat backs off far enough to clear the structure before you go ahead with opposite rudder.

Backing Around

We have already discussed backing out of a slip. But at times, it may be necessary to back out of the slip and make an almost-immediate sharp turn because of congestion, or to come up to the adjacent pier. In either case, the forward quarter spring line can be used in much the same way as described for using the after spring; see **Figure 6-37.**

For example, let's say your boat is lying in its slip, starboard side to the land. The first step is to make the spring ready from a point near the corner of the slip to the after cleat—either amidships, if there is only one, or the cleat on the starboard quarter, if there are two.

With the spring ready, but left slack and tended, ease off on the bow line, tended by someone on shore. Back the boat slowly with full right rudder. When the boat is about halfway out of the slip, take a strain on the spring to prevent backing farther. This will cause the boat to pivot as the stern is pulled around to starboard by the

spring line. Be sure to protect the boat from the pier with a fender.

As you continue to back, the spring will pull the boat up to the pier. At this point, you should slack the spring as the boat comes parallel to the pier so you can back farther. If you plan to secure the boat to the pier, you can use the spring as one of your dock lines, adding others as needed.

This method is especially useful when there is a breeze off the structure that would tend to blow the boat away if maneuvering without lines. No human power is required, and it can be accomplished in a leisurely and seamanlike manner. But, as in any case where the stern is made fast to the shore with the bow free, take special care to keep the boat under control.

If the boat is to get underway after being backed around, no bow line is needed. When the boat has pivoted far enough, with starboard quarter near the corner of the pier, idle the engine while casting off the shoreward end of the spring and bringing it on board. To get underway from such a position, keep the rudder amidships until the stern of the boat is clear of the pier.

Turning in a Berth

At times you may find it easier to turn your boat around at the pier than to attempt to leave the berth with adverse current conditions—particularly if the area surrounding the pier is congested.

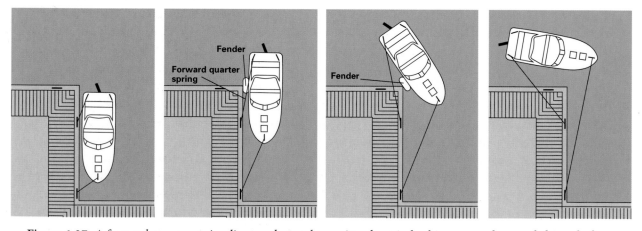

Figure 6-37 A forward quarter spring line can be used to assist a boat in backing out and around the end of a pier. When the spring line becomes taut, the boat reverses with full right rudder. Use a fender as necessary to protect the hull.

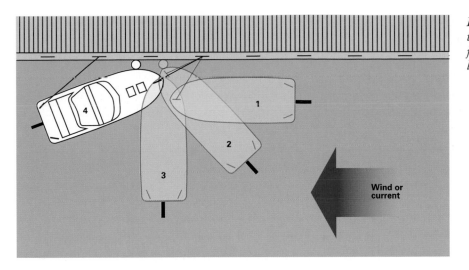

Figure 6-38 A boat can be turned end for end using just the current and spring lines.

To turn a boat with the starboard side against a pier, current coming from astern, first let all lines go except the after bow spring. Often the effect of the current will then be sufficient to throw the bow in toward the pier and the stern out into the current; see **Figure 6-38.** If any factor, such as a beam wind, tends to keep the stern pinned against the pier, kick the stern out by going ahead easy with right rudder. Keep a fender handy as a protection for the starboard bow.

Take steps to prevent the bow from catching on the pier as it swings. A small boat will usually require a fender, but a large craft may have to reverse the engine just enough to keep the bow clear.

As it swings in with the current, the fender should be made ready near the port bow. Also transfer the after bow spring from the starboard side to the port side. As the boat moves with the current, this line becomes the port forward bow spring. If the boat does not come alongside readily, even when helped by going ahead a little with right rudder, rig a forward quarter spring. Take a strain on the quarter spring and ease the bow spring. The current will push the boat back against this line and pull it parallel to the pier.

On a larger vessel, you will need to go ahead on an after bow spring rigged on the port side. Going ahead easily with right rudder on this spring alone, the boat stays under control and eases in

nicely. In turning a boat this way, make the turn with the bow to the pier, rather than the stern.

Turning with Power

Consider a situation as described above with the starboard side against a pier, except there is neither wind nor current to assist in turning. Here the power of the engine can be used to swing the boat. Go ahead on an after bow spring with right rudder. This throws the stern out away from the pier; use a fender to protect the bow. Allow the bow to nose up against the pier, using another fender, if necessary, to cushion it.

As the boat swings toward a position at right angles to the pier, ease the spring. With the bow against the pier, the engine going ahead slowly, and the rudder amidships, hold the boat in this position. Meanwhile, cast off the bow spring from on shore; re-rig it as an after bow spring on the port side (or use a second line for the port side). With right rudder again, the stern will swing all the way around; shift the fenders once more to protect the port bow.

In any maneuver involving the use of engine power against the spring, the strain on the line must be taken up slowly and easily. A surge of power puts a shock load on deck fittings that they were never designed to carry, and may even tear out the cleats. And with such a surge, if the fastenings hold, the line may part.

Once the strain has been taken up easily, proper deck fittings and good line of adequate

TRIM TABS

The performance of a boat with a planing or semi-planing hull is considerably affected by its trim. A high bow-up angle of pitch results in less efficient operation and greater wake. The proper use of TRIM TABS will bring the bow down for a better running angle. These are metal plates attached by a hinge to a portion of the lower edge of the transom; refer to **Figure 6-39.** In appearance, they are much the same as the flaps seen on the trailing edge of the wings of an aircraft. In the retracted, or "up," position they are in line with the bottom of the craft. Moved to a "down" angle of 10° to 20° degrees, they provide added lift at the stern with an accompanying lowering of the pitch angle as the bow comes down. A slight increase in drag occurs, but this is insignificant as compared with the more desirable effects of a better running angle. Trim tabs are normally installed in pairs, and are raised or lowered by one or more actuators for each tab. Actuators are usually small hydraulic cylinders and pistons operated by their own hydraulic pump.

Trim tabs must be used intelligently. When a boat is at rest in its berth, the tabs should be in the fully up position—this provides the maximum protection for the "piston rods" from marine fouling. Starting from a standstill, operating in the displacement mode, the tabs will have no effect and should be left in the up position. As additional throttle is applied to get "on plane," the tabs should be lowered—how much will have to be learned from experience with each individual boat. Properly used, the tabs will significantly help the boat to get on plane, and will reduce the engine power required to stay on plane. Speed for a given engine rpm should be increased by several knots, and fuel efficiency should increase slightly. Once on plane, the best adjustment of the tabs will have to be found experimentally. Trim tabs are not always used with their maximum down angle; it is possible in some cases to get the bow angle down too low, with the result that the boat could tend to yaw from side to side. Most installations will have some sort of indicator for the angle of the tabs; they may be labeled "Tab Up" or "Bow Up"—the effects are exactly the opposite. Make small adjustments up or down, and after each, wait a half-minute or so for the boat to settle into the new running angle.

Trim tabs should not be used in all conditions. They probably should not be used in a following sea, as it is then desirable for the craft to have a greater bow-up attitude for more positive steering control. In significant head seas, the bow should be up more than in calmer waters, and thus less tab action is called for. Tabs should always be in the up position when backing down—if the tabs are down there will be water pressure on their upper surfaces that may damage the actuator.

A pair of trim tabs is normally operated together, the same angle on each tab. Controls for each tab are separate, however, and they can be adjusted individually. They can be so used to correct for a lateral imbalance, such as a list to port or starboard—an increased angle of tab is used on the low side.

size will stand the application of plenty of power. Always bear this principle in mind when you are preparing to tow, or when you are passing a line to a stranded boat. Also remember that most docking lines are nylon, and can store considerable energy as they stretch. When the boat is put in neutral, or the throttle is closed, the boat can be pulled back toward the pier. If a nylon line is stretched to the breaking point, it can snap back with dangerous, or even lethal, effects.

Figure 6-39 Maximum maneuverability of twin-screw craft is gained by placing twin rudders behind the propellers, where the discharge current can act upon them most effectively. Note also the trim tabs located at the lower edge of the transom.

BOAT HANDLING WITH TWIN-SCREWS

This chapter has thus far related almost exclusively to a single-screw inboard boat. Although this permits a better study of the basic factors of boat handling, attention must also be given to twin-screw craft.

In twin-screw craft, there are twin rudders as well, one directly behind each propeller; see **Figure 6-39.** The propellers are counter-rotating, which balances any steering pull, and will generally rotate "outward"—the right-hand rotation on the right side and the left-hand rotation on the left side. The effect of this is to provide a maximum of maneuverability.

Going ahead with the starboard engine for a turn to port, the offset of the propeller from the centerline adds greatly to its effect of throwing the stern to starboard. Similarly, offset of the port propeller going ahead helps the steering effect when the port propeller is going ahead for a turn to starboard.

When reversing, the starboard propeller throws its discharge current against the starboard side of the hull to help the turn of the stern to port. Likewise, the port propeller reversing throws its stream against the port side of the hull to help the swing of the stern to starboard.

The important factors in turning and steering are thus combined by the outward-turning

propellers. The steering effect is exerted in the same direction as the turning movement caused by the off-center location of the propellers.

Gathering Headway

Unlike a boat with a single propeller, if the transmission gears of a twin-screw boat are put in forward together, the boat will begin to make headway without any tendency to pull to starboard or to port.

Turning

Clearly, having two propellers gives you the means of shifting one propeller or the other ahead or astern, independent of rudder control. In fact, much of a twin-screw boat's slow-speed maneuvering is done without touching the steering wheel; working the clutches and throttles is the key to controlling the boat's movements.

One Propeller Going Ahead or Reversing

A boat's stern may be put to one side or the other by going ahead or backing down one propeller, without turning the other. Some headway or sternway in these cases accompanies the turn.

Referring to **Figure 6-40,** powering ahead on the port engine (*A*) moves the stern to port and the bow to starboard; right rudder would assist this turn, but is not necessary. The opposite action,

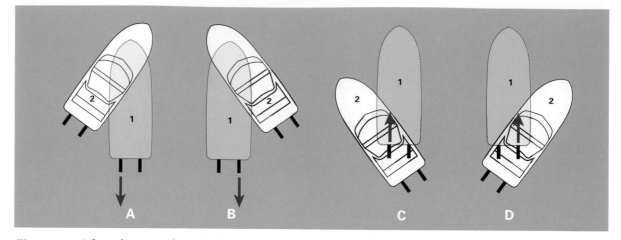

Figure 6-40 These diagrams show the actions of a twin-screw craft when power is applied to only one propeller, with the rudder centered. (Arrows show discharge current). One propeller turning ahead turns the stern of the boat to its side. When one propeller is in reverse, the boat backs to the opposite side.

using power ahead on the starboard engine (*B*) has the opposite result, stern to starboard and bow to port.

Reversing on one engine results in the same turning action as going ahead on the other. At (*C*), the port engine has been put in reverse, and at (*D*), the starboard engine has been reversed.

The maximum turning effect is, of course, obtained when one propeller is turning ahead and the other is in reverse—the two effects are additive; see **Figure 6-41.**

Maintaining Control while Backing

A twin-screw boat starting from a position dead in the water, with both engines at the same speed in reverse, has a great advantage over a single-screw craft as it can be made to take any desired course by steering with the rudders. In such a boat, the counter-rotation of the propellers means that the force that normally would throw a single-engine boat off-course is balanced out. Rudder action, however, will be less than when going ahead as the propellers' discharge currents are directed away from the rudders rather than onto them.

In addition to the ability to use the rudders, a twin-screw boat offers the possibility of using the throttles to speed up one engine or the other as an aid to steering while maintaining its sternway. There is also the possibility of stopping one engine

completely, or going ahead on it, for maximum control in backing up.

While a twin-screw craft backs as readily to starboard as to port, it is still subject to the effect of wind, waves, and current. The helmsman, however, has a greater ability to exercise control over these external forces.

Steering with the Throttles

In maintaining a straight course with a twin-screw boat, the speed of each engine can be adjusted so that the leeward engine compensates for the effect of leeway. This is done by running the leeward engine at a slightly faster speed to hold the bow up into the wind. The disadvantage of using this technique is that an undesirable "beat note" or throb sound may be heard when the speeds of the two engines are not the same—when the engines are not "in sync."

Turning in a Boat's Length

With practice, you can easily turn a twin-screw boat in a circle only a little larger than the boat's length, as shown in **Figure 6-41.** For example, to turn to starboard, the rudders can be set amidships while the port engine goes ahead and the starboard engine reverses; on most boats, turning the rudder is not necessary, but will tighten the turn.

STEP-BY-STEP DOCKING WITH A TWIN-SCREW BOAT

Most twin-screw boats are maneuvered in close quarters by using the direction of rotation of the propellers. Depending on wind or current conditions, stop the boat in front of the slip, or slightly to windward or up-current. (The rudder may be used if needed.)

The sequence below is intended as an example. Depending on the circumstances, this will sometimes be done in the opposite manner, swapping "starboard" for "port" and vice versa. In this example, both throttles are in idle

and you begin backing. As the boat gathers way, it will begin to back to port. By going forward with the port engine, the boat can be made to pivot and to align with the slip. When alignment is satisfactory, the port engine is also put in reverse to continue backing into the slip. Slight adjustment in direction can be made by putting either gear momentarily in neutral or forward. (On some craft, the placement and grouping of the shift lever and throttles will vary from that shown below.)

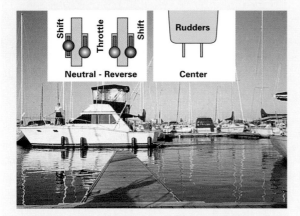

1 *Stop headway with the starboard engine in reverse; the stern will begin to move to port. Then continue backing, with the starboard and port engines at idle.*

2 *As sternway builds and you enter the slip, go ahead with the port engine to align the boat with the slip.*

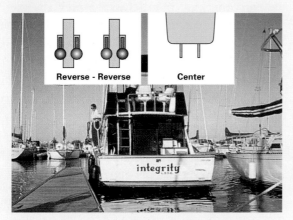

3 *With the boat aligned with the slip, put both engines in reverse; continue backing into the slip. If either engine is put in forward, the stern will move in the same direction.*

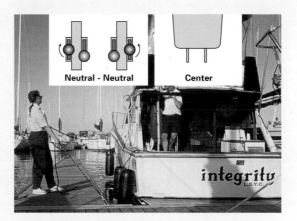

4 *When fully in the slip, put both engines in forward momentarily to kill all sternway. Secure the boat.*

Start this type of turn with the engines at idle or turning slowly at the same speed. To turn to the right, put the port gear in forward and the starboard gear in reverse. As the boat begins to turn, it may start to make some headway. (This is not surprising, since a boat drives forward more easily than it goes astern, and the propeller develops more thrust at a given rpm while turning ahead than astern because the propeller blades are curved so as to produce lift on the forward side.) To compensate, you probably will have to open the starboard throttle slightly to increase the rpm of the reversing starboard propeller. For both engines, a rate of rpm can be found so that the balance will turn the boat in its own length.

When the port engine is speeded up a little, the circle is larger and the boat makes some headway. If the port engine is slowed down, the circle is also larger, but the boat makes some sternway as the reversing starboard propeller pulls it around, stern to port.

Handling a Partially Disabled Boat

If your boat happens to sustain damage to the steering gear, it can still make port by steering

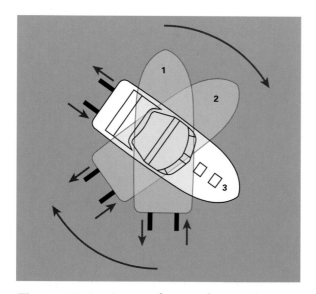

Figure 6-41 A twin-screw boat can be turned in its own length. With rudders centered, go ahead on one engine with the other in reverse (small arrows show screw discharge current). Changing engine speed on one propeller can give the craft headway or sternway if this is desired.

with the throttles (provided that the rudders are not jammed hard over to one side). One engine can be allowed to turn at a constant speed—the starboard one, for example. Then open the throttle of the port engine to speed up the port propeller and cause a turn to starboard. Closing the throttle of the port engine slows down the port propeller and allows the starboard propeller to push ahead, causing a turn to port—keep your speed moderate when doing this, as steering is not as positive as with rudders. Since most slow-speed maneuvering is done with the propellers, when you get back to port you will be able to maneuver into your berth.

Stopping

A twin-screw boat is stopped by reversing its propellers, but unlike a single-screw vessel, this will usually not throw the stern to one side.

Docking a Twin-Screw Boat

When docking, the experienced helmsman of a single-screw boat usually tries to make a port-side approach so that, when the vessel is stopped, the reversing propeller will swing the stern toward the pier (or wharf). The skipper of a twin-screw boat can use this technique on both port and starboard approaches. By reversing the offshore engine to check headway when coming up parallel to the pier, the stern will move in. On a port-side approach the reversing starboard right-hand propeller will move the stern to port. When approaching to put the craft's starboard side to the pier, the reversing port propeller will conveniently move the stern to starboard.

Landing at a pier or wharf, a twin-screw boat should approach at an angle of 10° to 20°, as is the case with a single-screw craft. When it has just enough way to carry it in nicely, the rudders are turned to the side away from the pier to bring the stern in as it comes up parallel to the structure, and the engines are shifted into neutral. To check headway as it comes parallel to the structure, the offshore engine is briefly put into reverse.

Using Spring Lines with a Twin-Screw Boat

When a twin-screw boat is lying in a berth and a spring line is used to throw the bow or stern out as an aid to getting clear, one engine may be used. For example, with an after bow spring, going ahead on the outside engine only throws the stern out away from the pier; in addition, the inside engine could be put in reverse.

Sometimes a twin-screw vessel is gotten clear of a wharf by rigging a forward bow spring and reversing the propeller on the wharf side to throw the propeller discharge current on that side forward between the boat and structure as a "cushion". Naturally this is most effective if the wharf under water is solidly bulkheaded rather than built on open piling. The discharge current from the inside wheel forces the boat away from the wharf and the line is then cast off. Further reversing on the propeller nearest the wharf while the other propeller turns ahead, as necessary, shapes the boat up to get the stern clear. The speed of the two engines will vary with conditions of wind and current, and the rudder is left amidships till the boat is clear and ready to pull away.

Other Twin-Screw Maneuvers

If one propeller is stopped while the boat has headway, the bow necessarily turns in the direction of the propeller that is dead. Consequently, if one engine of a twin-screw power-plant fails, and the boat must proceed on the other alone, a certain amount of rudder angle on the side of the operating engine is necessary to maintain a straight course, or, less efficiently, some kind of a drag must be towed on the side of the working propeller.

When a twin-screw boat has headway, both propellers turning ahead, and a quick turn to starboard is desired, the starboard engine can be reversed and right rudder applied. The fact that the craft has headway means that the right rudder adds to the steering effect to shorten the turn. A turn to port is accomplished by similar, but opposite, action.

With sternway, both propellers reversing, if a quick turn to port is wanted, the port engine is shifted to ahead and left rudder is applied. Again, due to the craft's sternway, the rudders' effect is added to that of the propellers to cause a quick turn to port. Return the port engine to reverse as the stern moves onto the desired heading.

If a twin-screw boat has considerable headway and its engines are reversed with rudders hard over, the stern will normally swing away from the rudders (to port with right rudder, and vice versa) until the headway is overcome by the reversing engines. After it has gathered sternway, the stern tends to work toward the side on which the rudders are set.

MANEUVERING WITH DIRECTED THRUST

Outboard and inboard/outboard (I/O) boats do not have rudders. The boat is steered by directing the propeller thrust—by turning the outboard motor or stern-drive unit on which the propeller is mounted. Maneuvering an outboard or stern-drive boat is usually easier than a single-propeller inboard boat of the same type.

Directed propeller thrust makes slow speed maneuvering easier, and turns at normal speeds much sharper; see **Figure 6-42**. The propeller discharge current is turned from side to side to create turning forces, unlike a boat with a rudder that must have water flowing by it to be effective. Outboard and stern-drive units have very little or no shaft angle, so the propeller does not produce as much unequal blade thrust as does the propeller on an inboard boat. Larger, more powerful outboard motors and high-power stern-drives do, however, produce considerable propeller torque—twin drives of either type normally have counter-rotating propellers to balance out this undesirable effect.

How a particular outboard or stern-drive boat reacts to the helm is difficult to predict exactly, but there are some general principles that apply in most typical situations. Some of these situations—basic maneuvers that any boater will likely have to complete during regular daily operation—are described below. This discussion assumes a typical boat with single outboard or stern-drive power.

Figure 6-42 The pivoting drive unit of a stern-drive boat (above, left) permits a tight turn, while an inboard craft, even a twin-screw boat (right), with its fixed propellers, responds only to the rudders. Jet-drive craft can likewise make very sharp turns at high speeds, even to the point of their being dangerous.

Gathering Headway

When an outboard or stern-drive boat is "dead in the water," that is, not moving forward or sternward, and the propeller is not turning, the boat will not respond to the helm. Since the propeller is not turning, it is not creating any discharge current, so no turning forces are created. Even though the boat may be moving over the bottom with a current, no water is passing by the lower unit of the outboard or stern-drive; therefore, it cannot act as a rudder.

As soon as the outboard or stern-drive is shifted into forward gear, the propeller's action creates a discharge current and generates thrust. If the engine or stern-drive is centered, the discharge current is directed straight back causing the boat to begin to move forward in a straight line.

If you open the throttle quickly on a boat with a single large outboard or stern-drive, as you would when pulling a water-skier, for instance, torque will pull the stern of the boat to one side, usually starboard, similar to a single-screw inboard. Large outboards and some stern-drives have small trim tabs located behind the propeller that help compensate for these forces, but a firm grip on the helm, before the throttle is opened, is also necessary.

As the boat gathers headway and the propeller begins to operate in the faster water flow for which it was designed, this imbalance usually lessens. If your boat wants to turn to port or starboard as soon as you let go of the helm at typical operating speeds, the steering trim tab needs adjustment.

Turning

After a boat has gathered headway, with the helm amidships and the lower unit tilted so that the boat is planing at a slight bow-up angle, the average boat tends to hold its course in a straight line fairly well. Once underway, the outboard or stern-drive boat is not affected to any significant degree by propwalk unless the lower unit is trimmed too far out or in.

If the helm is turned to starboard, the outboard motor or stern-drive is also turned in the same direction. The propeller's discharge current is directed to starboard, forcing the stern to port. Water flowing past the hull hits the lower unit on its starboard side, creating additional turning forces. The stern begins to move to port, causing the bow to turn to starboard.

If the helm is turned to the left, the motor or stern-drive turns to port; the stern of the boat moves starboard as the bow begins to turn to port.

At low speeds, there can be a time lag between when the helm is put over and when the boat actually begins to turn. At high speeds, there is little lag in helm

STEP-BY-STEP DOCKING WITH A STERN-DRIVE BOAT

Outboard- or inboard/outboard-powered boats are relatively easy to back up, but that may be scant comfort to the novice in a busy marina. The reversing propeller is turned in the direction you want to go by using the wheel or motor handle or tiller. On some light displacement boats with shallow draft, the bow tends to be influenced by the wind (coming from left in photos below).

When backing down in a crosswind, allow maneuvering room (to port in this example)

and watch the bow carefully. If it begins to swing downward you may have to stop backing, leave the helm over to port (toward the wind) and go in forward to straighten the boat. A quick burst of power is all that is usually needed, but be careful that you don't throw your crew or guests off balance with a sudden maneuver.

Set your speed to just enough to overcome the effect of a crosswind. If doesn't work, abort the maneuver early, reposition, and wait for a lull in the wind.

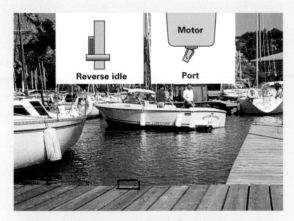

1 Bring the boat to a stop by shifting into reverse. Put the helm over to port and begin backing in. Slow your speed by momentarily shifting into neutral.

2 Continue backing, with the helm over hard to port. Watch the bow, and begin to straighten the helm as the boat enters the slip.

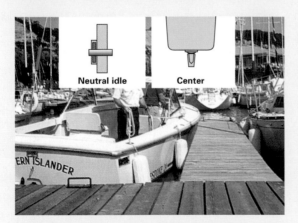

3 Center the helm to align the boat parallel to the pier. If the stern is too far from the pier, shift to neutral, then put the helm over to port and go forward for a second or two.

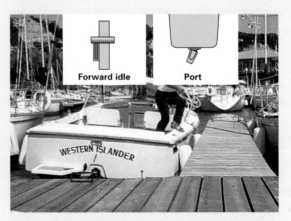

4 When fully in the slip, stop sternway by shifting into forward. Put the helm to port to kick the stern over close to the pier if necessary. Shift into neutral and secure the boat.

response. Small movements of the helm result in immediate action by the boat. The faster the boat moves through the water, the greater the forces generated by the water hitting the lower unit of the outboard or stern-drive, which provides a small amount of "rudder action." Also, the discharge current increases in strength as the throttle is advanced and propeller rpm increases.

It is important to remember that the response of each boat depends on the maneuver and the speed at which it is undertaken. Actual experience at the helm at different speeds is the only way to become familiar with the handling characteristics of any boat.

In order for the boat to begin its turn, the stern must be free to move. For example, the force of a water-skier towline secured to the stern can make steering difficult, since it may prevent the stern from swinging to port. That is why competition ski boats secure the line to a towing post located well up into the boat, forward of the transom; refer to **Figure 6-16.**

Stopping

Unlike a car with brakes, your boat depends on reverse thrust in order to stop. Assume that the boat has headway, with the helm centered and the propeller turning in reverse. Now the propeller discharge current is directed forward, past the lower unit of the stern-drive or outboard.

Depending on the throttle setting, the screw current may not be strong enough to reverse the water flowing past the lower unit. As power is increased, the propeller discharge current becomes strong enough to stop the flow of water past the lower unit and, as the throttle is opened, more completely reverses its flow.

While water is flowing past the lower unit, there is some steering force generated, but when the discharge current stops that water flow, the boat will temporarily not respond to the helm. When the strong propeller discharge current starts to flow past the lower unit, steering is again restored. In addition to the force of the water hitting the lower unit, the propeller discharge current is directed by turning the outboard or stern-drive, adding to the steering forces.

The propwalk of the reversing propeller tends to throw the stern to port, but to a lesser extent than a comparable inboard engine craft.

Backing Down

If your boat is dead in the water with the outboard motor or stern-drive centered, and you put it into reverse gear, the stern will be pushed slightly to port by the reversing propeller. The tendency to back to port can easily be overcome by turning the engine or stern-drive slightly to starboard.

Since outboards and stern-drive boats have the advantage of directing the propeller discharge current, and not relying on a rudder for steerage, you can also maneuver your boat by the judicious use of the throttle. The technique is to position the drive unit with the steering wheel while out of gear or while at very low speed, then to give a short, sharp burst of throttle. The overall effect will be to push the stern in the desired direction while not adding an appreciable forward or sternward motion to the boat.

As the boat begins to gather sternway, the water passing by the lower unit will begin to contribute to the steering force. Unlike most single-screw inboard boats, outboard and stern-drive boats back predictably. If the helm is put over to starboard, the motor or stern-dive will turn to starboard, and will direct the propeller discharge current to port, moving the stern to starboard.

However, wind and current will affect how a boat of this type backs. Outboard and stern-drive powered boats tend to be light-displacement, shallow-draft craft, and when backing down in a strong crosswind, the bow will tend to fall off downwind. This can cause steering difficulties.

Remember that, in addition to the force of the wind on the forward topsides, the hull's pivot point has also moved aft, much closer to the drive unit. The steering forces are now acting on a much shorter lever as a result.

Usually, once sufficient sternway is gained, the force of the keel moving through the water is enough to keep the boat on track. Also remember that, when backing, the stern will lead as it moves to port or starboard, before the boat begins to turn.

Jet Drives

Jet drive boats essentially have a propeller within the hull of the craft—in effect this is a pump, drawing in water from ahead and ejecting it out the stern. There is no rudder–steering is accomplished by pivoting the jet nozzle from side to side of the centerline. Reversing is done by lowering a deflection plate into the discharged water so as to create rearward thrust.

The vast majority of jet drives will be found on personal watercraft (PWCs), but this type of propulsion is by no means so limited. Jet drives have been used on vessels of all sizes, including yachts of 100 feet (30.5 m) or more in length.

The use of jet drives on small, fast personal watercraft provides a very high degree of maneuverability and fast acceleration. Steering response

OTHER SEAMANSHIP TOPICS

Although boat handling is one of the major aspects of seamanship, there are many others.

These include Anchoring (*Chapter 9*), Special Techniques (*Chapter 10*), Safety & Emergencies (*Chapters 11* and *12*), River Seamanship (*Chapter 22*), and Marlinespike Seamanship (*Chapter 23*).

Seamanship for sailing craft is covered in Chapter 8.

is immediate and turns can be very sharp. Persons taking their first ride on a PWC should start out slowly and get the feel of the craft's response to throttle and steering before operating at high speed and making sharp maneuvers.

Small Boat Seamanship

The Boat • The Motor & Its Accessories • Equipment • Outboard Motor Basics • The Trailer • Trailer Operations • Launching & Retrieving • Small Boat Seamanship • Inflatable Boats • Jet-Drive Boats • Waterskiing

The pleasures of recreational boating are not in any way related to the size of one's craft, although it is true that size has a real bearing on the type of boating activities that can be accomplished. Whereas there are some elements of seamanship that apply to every type of boat, there are significant differences between the requirements for small, open outboard or stern-drive craft and larger inboard-powered cruisers and sport fishermen.

This chapter focuses on smaller craft, up to 26 feet (7.9 m) long—boats that are generally suited for trailering if the owner so desires. These are the U.S. Coast Guard categories of Classes A and 1—about 96 percent of all the boats in the United States.

THE BOAT

Outboard boats, those craft suitable for a detachable motor, come in a wide range of size, design, construction material, and cost. At the lower end are the 8-foot (2.4-m) or smaller prams that can be car-topped or used as a dinghy. At the upper end of the scale are the center-console and cruiser hulls that can take two, three, or even four motors of as much as 300 or more horsepower (hp). And there are many sizes and styles between these extremes; see **Figure 7-01**.

Also at the upper end of this size range are boats with stern-drives that combine the desirable qualities of an inboard engine with the flexibility of a drive unit generally similar to the lower-unit of an outboard motor.

Opposite Page: Figure 7-01 An outboard motor clamps onto the transom; large, heavy motors are usually bolted in place. Smaller motors are portable and can be removed when not in use. To lessen the chance of water entering the craft, a self-bailing motor well, not present here, would make a good safety feature.

The Use of the Boat

The key to selecting the "right" boat for a particular skipper is the use, or uses, for which the craft is intended. Obviously, the boat for waterskiing is not the boat for trolling, and the boat for an after noon outing may not be the perfect one for a week's cruise. Not all boating families will agree on just one or even two uses, and few families can afford a separate craft for each type of activity desired.

Compromise is inevitable, but if all possible factors are considered in advance, the likelihood of disappointment is reduced. Be sure to take into consideration the type of waters on which the boat will be used—protected lakes and rivers, coastal bays, or offshore.

Hull Designs

There are two basic hull types—displacement and planing—and many variations of the latter. Although, in general, displacement boats cruise through the water, and planing hulls lift and skim over the surface, often it is difficult to make a sharp distinction between these types.

Planing hulls receive a large part of their support at normal speeds from dynamic reaction of water against the bottom, and a lesser part of their support from buoyancy that diminishes with increased speed but never quite disappears at any speed. Generally, planing begins when the water breaks cleanly away at the chines and transom. With today's availability of motors with high horsepower, most cruisers have some planing action, and practically all runabouts are of the planing type.

Small boats designed to take outboard or stern-drive power can be classified into the following hull forms:

• **Flat bottom** (displacement type) Usually rowboats or skiffs 14 to 18 feet (4.3 to 5.5 m); used for fishing or utility purposes on shallow streams and small protected lakes. Generally these are heavy and roomy for their length, and slow. Many of these are made of aluminum.

• **Round bottom** (displacement type) Dinghies, tenders, car-top boats, occasionally runabouts 12 to 18 feet (3.7 to 5.5 m). At slow speeds these hulls are often more easily driven and maneuvered than the flat-bottom craft. (Some light, round-bottom boats will also plane.)

• **V bottom** The most popular type of hull design, the V bottom is used for runabouts, utility craft, and cruisers when speed is a factor. It is available in the following varieties:

The flat bottom, popular on the U.S. west coast, has a bottom that is either flat or a shallow V. The trihull (or cathedral) is a V bottom with two smaller V shapes on each side of the hull. The deep V uses a degree of deadrise at the transom running from 22° to 26° (see Chapter 1, page 21). The modified V has a deep V in the front and tapers off to a shallow V in the stern, and has a hard or soft chine. This is the most popular competition-ski-boat construction type. Twin-hull catamarans are increasing in popularity because of the stable platform that they offer.

• **Hydroplanes** Generally used for racing. The bottom, which is flat, may be "stepped"—that is, divided into two levels, about amidships. The resultant notch reduces wetted surface, increasing speed.

Size & Loading

Because overloading a small boat can be exceedingly dangerous, *the safe limits for a particular boat must be known.* Coast Guard rules require that U.S. boats under 20 feet (6.1 m) (except sailboats and some special types) manufactured after October 31, 1972, carry a "capacity plate" showing maximum allowable loads. Since August 1980, plates for outboard boats have shown a maximum horsepower for motor(s), maximum number of persons, and maximum weights, both for persons only and for motor, gear, and persons; see **Figure 7-02**. Plates for inboard, stern-drive, and nonpowered vessels omit the maximum power rating. Boats manufactured before this

Figure 7-02 For an outboard craft, a U.S. Coast Guard capacity plate shows the maximum horse-power as well as the limits for number and weight of persons, and total maximum weight for persons, motor, and gear.

regulation may carry no capacity plate, or one based on a formula that is no longer used; such craft are now seldom seen.

Added Buoyancy

Boats less than 20 feet (6.1 m) in length, manufactured since July 31, 1973, carry built-in flotation installed in accordance with U.S. Coast Guard regulations (the exceptions again being sailboats and some special types). It is possible to add positive flotation to older boats to ensure the safety of yourself and your passengers. This can be in the form of sealed air chambers, or masses of plastic foam.

The buoyancy units should be located as high as possible in the hull so that the boat, if swamped, will remain in an upright position and not capsize. This provides greater safety than a capsized hull; persons in the water will be able to hold on easily, and they may be able to recover some form of emergency signaling, bailing, or other needed equipment.

Special Design Features

A highly desirable safety feature is a self-bailing MOTOR WELL. Most boats powered with an outboard motor have a transom that is "cut down" or lowered where the motor is to be attached. This is necessary so that the motor will be low enough that its propeller will be well below the bottom of the hull. Such a transom will provide efficiency for the motor, but will seriously jeopardize the safety of the craft by providing an easier point of entry in the hull for water. Safety can be maintained by having an inner bulkhead forward of the motor that is *not* cut down, one that is fully as high as the sides of the boat; see **Figure 7-03.** The space aft of this bulkhead to the cut-down transom is the motor well; it should have self-bailing drains at each after corner.

Many boats will have special features for particular applications, such as sport fishing. These invariably add to the cost of the boat and are worth it only if the craft is to be used for such special purpose.

THE MOTOR & ITS ACCESSORIES

Trailerable boats are typically powered by outboard motors or inboard-outboard power packages (I/O, also called stern-drives or outdrives). For some styles of fishing on

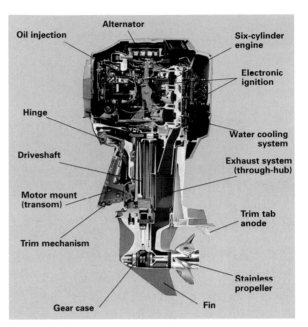

Figure 7-04 A two-stroke outboard motor provides a higher horsepower-to-weight ratio than an inboard motor but has the disadvantages of poorer fuel economy, greater pollution, and a higher noise level. These drawbacks are greatly reduced in the newer four-stroke outboards.

Figure 7-03 On the craft shown here, the motor is mounted on a cut-down portion of the transom, but there is a full-height bulkhead forward of the motor. This design allows the motor to be at an optimum height with respect to the hull without increasing the danger of water entering the boat from astern.

protected waters, the main propulsion may be supplemented by a small and quiet electric motor powered by an automotive-type storage battery.

Outboard Motors

An outboard motor is a detachable power plant, complete with driveshaft and propeller, that operates on one to six cylinders; see **Figure 7-04.** The fuel tank and operating controls are usually separate; on the smallest motors, they may be mounted on the powerhead itself. Although usually a gasoline-fueled motor (two-stroke or four-stroke operation, many now with fuel-injection to reduce pollution), it may be diesel-powered—or electric for trolling or other low-power applications.

The outboard is clamped or bolted to a cutout in the transom, or mounted on a bracket bolted to the transom. Smaller motors are clamped on for easy removal; medium and larger motors are bolted on, and removal is possible but infrequent. The motor can be tilted into or out of the water, either by hand for smaller units or, on larger units,

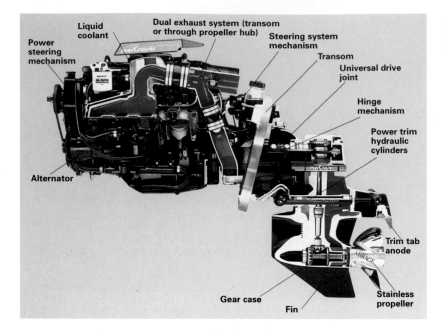

Power steering mechanism

Liquid coolant

Dual exhaust system (transom or through propeller hub)

Steering system mechanism

Transom

Universal drive joint

Hinge mechanism

Power trim hydraulic cylinders

Alternator

Trim tab anode

Gear case

Fin

Stainless propeller

Figure 7-05 A stern-drive propulsion package, also called an outdrive or an inboard/outboard, combines a typical medium-size inboard gasoline or diesel engine with an external drive unit that is very similar to the lower unit of an outboard motor.

with the help of hydraulics. The smallest outboards are generally steered by a hand-held tiller. The medium range has wheel-controlled steering with push-pull cables; larger units will be assisted hydraulically (power steering).

Stern-Drives

At and above about the 100 hp mark, the stern-drive power package is often used. This combines the inboard, four-stroke gasoline or diesel engine mounted inside the hull with an externally mounted drive unit that resembles the lower section of an outboard motor; see **Figure 7-05.** This is intended to combine the greater power and efficiency of an inboard engine with the directed-thrust steering, tilt-up capability, and other advantages of outboard propulsion.

Boats of stern-drive design can be considered with outboards, except for matters directly relating to the engine itself. They are usually in the size category of medium and larger outboard boats, handle similarly, are used for the same general purposes, and can be trailered.

Outboard vs. Stern-Drive

Two-stroke outboards offer trailerboaters a great advantage by providing a much higher horsepower-to-weight ratio than four-stroke stern-drives. Two-stroke outboard motors are

built of lightweight cast aluminum, and also pull more horsepower out of smaller-displacement blocks. For example, a 115-hp stern-drive (with an engine built of cast iron) which has 181-cubic-inch (3.0 liter) displacement weighs in at 625 pounds (283 kg) while a 115-hp outboard with 105-cu. in. (1.7 liter) displacement, built by the same manufacturer, weighs in at 315 pounds (143 kg), about half the weight for the same power. (Motors of all types are now also rated in metric terms; 1 hp = 0.746 kW.) Increasingly, however, manufacturers are changing to four-stroke outboard motors, which have cleaner exhaust emissions but which are about 10 percent heavier than two-stroke engines, and more costly.

Outboard motor wells use up valuable cockpit space. However, if the boat is designed for them, outboard "brackets" can be attached to the boat's full transom, placing the motors outside the boat. Putting the motor a couple of feet aft of the transom places the propeller in "cleaner" water, away from any turbulence created by the hull, allowing the propeller a better "grip" on the water. Brackets are generally used with large outboards and boats in the 20- to 30-foot (6.1 to 9.1 m) range. Brackets can prove particularly useful for twin-motor installations and are most popular in 24- to 28-foot (7.3 to 8.5 m) offshore-style fishing boats, where increased cockpit space is appreciated, but twin engines are needed.

Stern-drive engines offer the greater fuel efficiency of four-stroke engines and the convenience of inboard-engine maintenance, but they do use up interior space. Stern-drives are suitable for boat designs where the owner wants the convenience of an outboard (a drive leg that tilts out for servicing or prop maintenance and helps the boat reach optimum trim) and the appearance of an inboard, where the engine is hidden inside the boat.

Outboard Motor Selection

While horsepower always seems to be the first thought in most people's motor selection, other factors, such as weight, starting method, and price, may in fact be even more important. With the wide range of motors available, however, it is not difficult to select a model suitable for almost any application.

The horsepower required for a boat will depend upon size and weight of the boat (loaded), and the desired speed. A displacement hull of 14 feet (4.3 m) or so will serve adequately for lake and river fishing with a 10-horsepower motor; any greater horsepower would be wasted in an attempt to drive the boat faster than hull speed.

For waterskiing behind a planing hull of 16 to 18 feet (4.9 to 5.5 m), motors of 40 to 75 horsepower are suitable. A larger outboard will make the boat go faster, provided the hull has the capacity for greater power, but speed does not increase in direct proportion to motor power. Very roughly, horsepower must be tripled, or even quadrupled, to double speed.

Two-Stroke or Four-Stroke?

Until recent years, all outboard motors were of the two-stroke carbureted type, notorious for their "dirty" exhaust emissions. The Environmental Protection Agency (EPA) has steadily pushed for cleaner engines of all types, but especially outboard motors. Manufacturers have responded with two different types of motors, both much cleaner in operation—fuel-injected two-stroke motors and four-stroke motors (also fuel-injected).

Existing old-style motors can be used in most areas until they wear out, and until 2006, when very stringent EPA emission standards come into effect, a carbureted two-stroke motor can still be purchased, but most boaters are looking ahead and opt for one of the newer designs.

Two-Stroke Carbureted Motors Traditional two-stroke outboard motors do have advantages (but of course, clean operation is not one of them). These engines are simpler in design, resulting in less weight and less initial cost. They have a power output advantage in that a two-stroke cycle has a power stoke for each revolution of the crankshaft, rather than one for every other revolution as in four-stroke cycle engines, providing better acceleration. They are easier and less expensive to maintain and repair.

There are a number of disadvantages, however, in addition to the emissions problem. Special oil must be mixed with the gasoline fuel—this is an additional chore for each refueling, and an added expense. Problems may be encountered in cold starts, and raw fuel may be initially discharged in the exhaust. Although maintenance problems are not greater, in general the life span of a traditional two-stroke outboard motor is less than can be expected of the newer designs. And traditional outboard motors are known for the noise that they make.

Fuel-Injected Two-Stroke Motors Fuel-injection eliminates the carburetor, where many of the problems of a two-stroke engine begin. Exactly the correct amount of a fuel-air mixture is injected into each cylinder at exactly the correct moment of crankcase revolution. (There are some fuel-injected models that take in air normally and inject only fuel under high pressure.) The fuel is better atomized, resulting in a more-complete, cleaner burn (remember, fuel in an internal combustion engine does not explode, it burns). This in turn results in more fuel efficiency and lesser harmful components of the exhaust.

Fuel-injected two-stroke outboard motors have an oil injection system that eliminates the need for mixing oil and gasoline by hand. By feeding oil into the fuel stream only as needed by the engine speed and load, less oil is used and less

ENGINE CYCLES

Internal-combustion engines—gasoline or diesel, land or marine, inboard or outboard—operate on CYCLES of several STROKES. A stroke is *one* travel of the piston in the cylinder, up *or* down. (Customary usage is to call inboard power plants on boats "engines," but for outboard craft, call them "motors"—there is no real difference in the two terms.)

The majority of engines operates on a cycle of four strokes and are usually referred to as FOUR-STROKE ENGINES, although the term "four-cycle" is occasionally used. The cycle is normally considered to start with the INTAKE STROKE—this is a downward movement of the piston resulting in a partial vacuum in the COMBUSTION CHAMBER and an inflow of air or a mixture of air and fuel through one or more INTAKE VALVES. Next is the COMPRESSION STROKE—an upward movement of the piston, reducing the volume of the combustion chamber and increasing the pressure and temperature of the air or mixture, called the CHARGE. In a gasoline-fueled engine, near the end of this stroke an electrical SPARK is caused to occur which results in the rapid burning (not explosion) of the fuel-plus-air mixture. In a diesel engine, the COMPRESSION RATIO (the ratio of the volume in the cylinder when the piston is all the way down to the volume when it is all the way up) is greater than in a gasoline engine. Only air is compressed; fuel is injected at or near the top of the piston's travel. There is no spark, the initiation of burning being caused by the very high temperature resulting from the greater compression. The rapid burning of the air and fuel results in the generation of large amount of COMBUSTION GASES (sometimes called "products of combustion") which force the piston down in the POWER STROKE. After completing this stroke, the piston again moves upward in the EXHAUST STROKE,

forcing out the expanded gasses through the EXHAUST VALVE, which has been opened for this purpose; the cycle is then complete. (In some engines, there may be more than one of each type of valve. In FUEL-INJECTION gasoline engines, fuel may be injected into the cylinder much the same as for a diesel engine, but a spark is used to ignite the charge as the compression ratio is less.)

As will be seen from the above description, power is generated by the engine on only one of the four strokes, on only one of each two revolutions of the CRANKSHAFT. For each cylinder, the other three strokes are carried through by power strokes in other cylinders and/or the momentum of a FLYWHEEL

Another type of engine has only two strokes in each cycle; this type of operation is termed TWO-STROKE CYCLE, commonly called TWO-STROKE (or sometimes "two-cycle" as in the designation of outboard motor oil as TC-3W, where "TC" stands for two-cycle and "W" for water-cooled). The inflow of air and fuel and the outflow of exhaust gases are through openings in the cylinder walls; there are no valves as in four-stroke engines. These PORTS are closed off by the sides of the piston for most of each stroke, opening at different times in the upward and downward movement of the piston. Near the bottom of the downward stroke, the exhaust port is uncovered and the remaining pressure in the COMBUSTION CHAMBER forces out the burnt gases. The intake port opens slightly before the exhaust port (on the opposite side of the cylinder wall) is covered; the incoming charge, under slight pressure, helps in pushing the burned gases out, but in so doing, some of the unburned fuel of the new charge goes out also, increasing the pollution. Each downward power stroke of the piston serves to slightly increase the pressure in the CRANKCASE so that, when an intake port is uncovered shortly after exhaust port is uncovered, a fresh charge of fuel and air will flow into the COMBUSTION CHAMBER to be compressed on the subsequent upward stroke. When the piston nears the top of its travel, a spark ignites the charge and the cycle repeats.

The advantages of a two-stroke outboard engine are simplicity and less weight—no valves and a less-complicated lubrication system, and more power for a given weight—one power stroke for every engine revolution of the crankshaft rather than one for each two revolutions. The principal disadvantage is its "dirtier" exhaust—oil for lubrication is mixed into the gasoline fuel and as a result combustion is less complete; the use of ports rather than valves further contributes to pollution. (Some larger two-stroke motors now use oil injection rather than mixing it into the fuel; this somewhat lessens pollution.) Two-stroke engines are also noisier and have more vibration than four-stroke models.

gets into the exhaust stream as a pollutant. These engines are more economical in the use of both oil and gasoline.

But there are disadvantages. A fuel-injected two-stroke outboard motor is heavier and more complex. It is more costly than a carbureted model and requires more expertise in maintenance. And it is just as noisy as motors of the older design

Four-Stroke Motors Four-stroke outboard motors have many design features in common with automobile engines. There are intake and exhaust valves for each cylinder and fuel is injected. Oil is not mixed into the fuel flow but is stored separately and applied by a pump for lubricating the crankshaft, connecting rods, cylinder walls, and other parts of the engine.

Four-stroke motors are easier to start, are smoother running, and have better fuel economy. They are much quieter in operation. The elimination of oil from the combustion chamber, plus the fact that the exhaust and intake valves of any cylinder are never open at the same time, results in a cleaner exhaust, one that is freer of undesirable hydrocarbon products.

The disadvantages of four-stroke outboard motors include their greater weight and initial cost. Maintenance and repairs are more complicated and may also be more costly than for two-stroke motors. With a power stroke for each cylinder only once every two revolutions of the crankshaft, acceleration may be less than with a two-stroke engine.

Small (Trolling) Motors & Electrics

Very small single-cylinder gasoline outboards, ranging from 2-hp models that weigh under 25 pounds (11.3 kg) to 4- and 5-hp motors of 45 pounds (20.4 kg) or less, offer inexpensive, reliable power for dinghies, small inflatables, and small sailboats. Most of these outboards are simple, with integral gas tanks, 360° steering (allowing you to reverse by spinning the entire engine), and no transmission.

Even smaller 12-volt electric motors, in various sizes rated in pounds of thrust, are bow-mounted on small fishing boats as auxiliary motors to pull them along at trolling speeds.

Figure 7-06 For fishing in protected waters, a boat will often have a high-horsepower motor for a speedy run to the fishing area, plus a bow-mounted electric motor for quietly moving around to the various spots where the fish might be.

These motors are quiet and usually rigged for remote control, with the operator controlling the motor with his feet, while using his hands to do his fishing; see **Figure 7-06**.

Several electric outboard motors are available for the main propulsion power of smaller and slower boats. These are of limited horsepower and are used in special applications, such as where no engine emissions are permitted. The motors are quite light, but require several hundred pounds of batteries. (There are also small craft with inboard electric motor/battery propulsion.)

Electric Starting

All small outboard motors, and some medium-power models, are started by pulling a rope that is wound around the top of the flywheel. This is not practical for the larger motors, so electric starting systems are provided. The electrical system, with its battery and alternator, has the added bonus of making possible the use of navigation lights and electronic gear on the boat.

Electric starting means added weight and cost, but this is offset by the greater convenience that this type of starting provides. In general, motors less than about 9 hp will be manually started; those of more than 40 hp will have electric

Figure 7-08 This multi-purpose open-deck, 25-foot catamaran-type boat has twin high-horsepower outboard motors. The greater beam of this type of hull provides greater stability for fishing and cruising and a wider spacing for the motors, increasing maneuverability.

starting; motors between these sizes may have either method of starting.

Single or Twin Installation

Many outboard hulls are designed to allow the fitting of either one or two motors on the transom. There are definite advantages and disadvantages to each arrangement, given the same total horsepower.

The most common reason for twin motors rather than a single one is the added safety that such an installation provides; see **Figure 7-07**. Properly maintained outboard motors are extremely reliable, but if one should fail, the other will bring the boat home. Disadvantages of the twin rig include the greater initial cost—about 1 1/3 times the price of a single larger motor of the total horsepower—an additional battery (or larger single one), more complex control systems, greater weight in the boat (about 50 percent more), greater underwater drag, and greater fuel consumption (not doubled, but greater by 1/3 to 1/2). Twin motors, and their batteries and fuel tanks, take up more space than that needed for a single-motor installation. Pairs of larger engines are available with counter-rotating propellers; this is highly desirable to balance out strong torque effects; see **Figure 7-08**.

Figure 7-07 Twin outboard motors give a greater degree of security from loss of power. The disadvantage is higher initial investment, compared with the cost of a single motor of the total horsepower, plus more weight and greater fuel consumption.

Figure 7-09 Because large motors are not designed to run at slow speeds for long periods of time, some skippers choose to mount a second, small motor that will push the boat at a trolling speed. Such a motor can also bring the craft home should the large motor fail.

A special case is the large outboard cruiser where use of two motors is required to meet horsepower needs, and the weight and space requirements are less important. In such an installation, twin motors will also allow the use of more efficient propellers with larger blade area.

If a boat is performing to certain standards with a single motor, what will result if a second motor of the same power is added (assuming that boat is rated to handle the double horsepower)? The added weight and drag, combined with hydrodynamic factors, will hold the speed increase to about 25 percent, although this will vary widely with specific installations. Fuel consumption, with both engines running at the same rpm (revolutions

per minute), will be about 1½ times that of the single motor installation.

A combination to be considered is a single large motor adequate for all normal operation, plus a smaller motor of 4 to 10 hp. The smaller motor is used for trolling while fishing—large motors should not be run at slow speeds for extended periods—and for emergency backup; see **Figure 7-09**. A 6-hp motor will move a medium-size outboard hull at 3 to 4 knots and get it home or to assistance.

Propellers

Although most outboard motors are sold complete with a "stock" propeller, suitable for an average boat under average conditions, some motors, especially the larger ones, are offered with a choice of several propellers. Keep in mind that a stock propeller may not have the optimum diameter or pitch, or both, for a particular application. Your first step should be to become familiar with the basic parts of a propeller; see **Figure 7-10**.

Manufacturers publish tables of recommended propeller sizes for various applications, but these should be used only as initial guides. If you know another owner who has an identical boat and motor combination, whose style of boating matches yours, and who is getting the desired performance from his craft, your decision may be easy.

Otherwise, the answer lies in experimentation. In any case, the "right" propeller for any boat in a specific application is the one that allows the

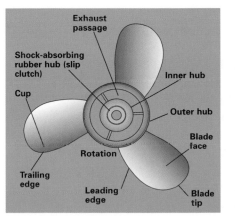

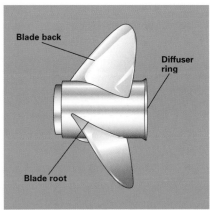

Figure 7-10 An understanding of propellers should start with knowledge of the basic parts. The propeller shown here is typical, but there are some design differences in other models.

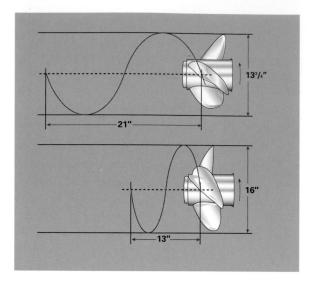

Figure 7-11 Diameter is the distance across the circle that the blade tips trace as they revolve; note that for a three-bladed propeller it is not a tip-to-tip measurement. Pitch is the distance that a propeller would advance in one revolution in a solid substance, as a screw would advance in wood. Shown here are two propellers of different diameter and pitch.

motor to turn up to its full rated rpm, but no more. It is necessary for the motor to turn to full rated rpm in order to develop full rated power. However, if it will turn faster than that, the propeller is too small and full power is not being developed at the rated maximum rpm (which must never be exceeded, except for very brief bursts).

If the boat is used for more than one type of activity—cruising and fishing or waterskiing, for example—the same motor will require different propellers for the most efficient operation in each type of use. As a spare propeller is an excellent safety item, the purchase of a more efficient one is not all "added expense"—the stock propeller becomes the spare.

Diameter & Pitch
Diameter is defined as the distance across the circle made by the blade tips as the propeller rotates; see **Figure 7-11.** Its size is determined by the rpm at which the propeller will be turning, as well as the amount of power delivered through it. Note that diameter will need to be greater as horsepower increases and conversely as rpm

decreases. Diameter will tend also to be larger as propeller blade surface increases.

The pitch of a propeller determines its "bite" on the water, and thus the rpm that the motor can turn up (this is also affected by propeller diameter). Motor rpm is, of course, related to boat speed and weight—a lighter, faster boat, for example, will use a propeller of greater pitch than a vessel that is heavy and designed for slower operation. Once again, experimentation is really the only way of selecting the best match of propeller to suit the craft.

A propeller is described by stating its diameter and pitch, usually in inches—for instance, the lower propeller in **Figure 7-11** with a 16-inch diameter and a pitch of 13 inches would be described as "16 by 13," typically written as "16 x 13"; it would also be designated as "right-hand" or "left-hand" (see Chapter 6, page 177).

If a single motor is "doubled up" with another similar to it, this will require a change of propeller on the original motor. The faster speed obtained with the additional horsepower will call for a greater pitch, probably one, but possibly two, inches more—but only actual trials will tell for sure.

Materials
Most stock propellers on outboards and sterndrives are made of aluminum. These are well suited for a conventional purpose and are also relatively easy to repair. Propellers of stainless steel and other high-strength alloys are advantageous for special applications such as waterskiing and racing. They are more expensive both to purchase and repair. Plastic is used mainly for propellers of the smaller motors, such as those for electric trolling and on dinghies.

Shear Pins & Slip Clutches
Because outboard boats often operate in fairly shallow water, the driveshaft, gears, and other internal parts of the motor are subject to damage should the propeller hit an underwater object. To prevent such damage, the motors are equipped with either a shear pin (older smaller motors only) or a slip clutch (all current models) on the propeller shaft.

A shear pin is made of a relatively soft metal. It transmits the drive from the propeller shaft to the propeller, and is just strong enough for this. Upon impact with a rock or other hard object by a propeller blade, this pin is broken, sheared off near the end, and the impact is not transferred to the inner parts of the motor. To restore operation it is necessary to remove the propeller and install a new pin, so be sure to always carry spares.

To overcome the nuisance of having to replace sheared pins, manufacturers developed slip clutches in which a rubber inner hub is used to transmit the drive power. Under normal loads there is no slippage, but upon impact with a hard object (or even with the sudden load of a too-quick shift of gear or advance of the throttle), the rubber hub slips somewhat to absorb the strain from the propeller blade. Obviously there is no internal component to be replaced after impact,

PROPELLER TYPES

Propellers are classified according to their construction, materials, and design. Six types are generally available, four of which are shown below.

• The aluminum propeller can be run fully submerged or slightly surfaced with light loads. Some have special blades to avoid becoming fouled with weeds in shallow-water operation.

• High reverse thrust is useful for workboats, large slower boats, and auxiliary sail-power applications. The blades provide the same thrust in forward or reverse.

• The cleaver-style surfacing propeller has the trailing edge of its blades cut on a straight line. This is a true high-rev racing performer designed for surface-piercing stern-drives and outboard applications. It provides less bow lift than the chopper.

• The chopper-style, another surfacing propeller, is for sport boaters for speeds higher than 50 mph. It has considerable bow-lifting capabilities and is known for the tenacious way in which it refuses to break loose on a plane, a much-desired characteristic. It comes with weed-chopping fingers.

• A basic stainless-steel propeller is similar in design to the conventional propeller of aluminum, but it has slightly thinner blades and higher strength and durability for a wide variety of medium- to high-horsepower applications. It is also resistant to corrosion in salt water.

• Stainless-steel high-performance or racing propellers are of the cleaver type with higher-pitch range because of the combination of high horsepower and lightweight boats. Speeds are in the 90 mph range.

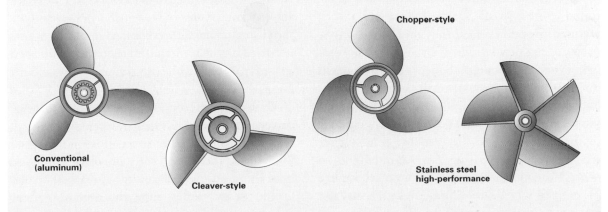

Conventional (aluminum)

Cleaver-style

Chopper-style

Stainless steel high-performance

and it provides adequate protection for the motors. Time and overuse may cause a slip clutch to weaken and slip more often than desired; replacement is not difficult. Some propellers are constructed with removable blades so that one or two damaged blades can be replaced; carrying extra blades rather than an extra propeller can save space, weight, and money.

EQUIPMENT

From the moment it is launched, each boat—even the smallest, including personal watercraft (PWCs)—must meet all federal requirements for a craft of its size and type of use (refer to Chapter 3), plus any additional equipment required by state or local regulations. Boaters venturing into new waters subject to other regulations than "at home" should check with a marina operator, park ranger, or other local authority to avoid inadvertent violations. The prudent traveler will be aware of, or will find out about, any further local requirements, such as anchoring limitations, special cruising permits, speed limitations, etc.

Navigation Lights

Even if you intend to never use your boat at night, it should be equipped with navigation lights (refer to Chapter 4). Engine trouble, fuel problems, unexpectedly good fishing, or other situations may keep you out longer than expected. (PWCs are not operated at night, and thus are not expected to have navigation lights.)

Nearly all outboard boats are delivered with a red-green combination light at the bow and an all-round white light aft. Such lights are legal if they are used properly *and if they meet the requirements of the regulations*. All too often the after light is not high enough to meet the requirement for *all-round* visibility, especially when the boat is underway and the bow rises, or when the canvas top is used. Some lights are on a telescoping pole so that they may be lowered for convenience when not in use during the daytime, and to protect the mounting from damage; see **Figure 7-12**. Even when raised, these lights are usually too low to be seen from ahead. Be sure that your

Figure 7-12 A stern light may be mounted on a telescoping pole so that it can be kept low and out of the way during the day. When operating at night, be sure to extend the staff to full height so that the light will be visible from all directions. See Chapter 4 for all details regarding navigation lights.

boat can be seen from all directions at night; the white light is more important than the colored lights as it will be seen at a greater distance. Have someone on shore, or on another boat, check as you run past at various angles, and then let your boat go dead in the water to check the stern light as an anchor light.

Power-driven vessels less than 39.4 feet (12 m) in length have the *option* under both the Inland and International Navigation Rules of carrying a single all-round white light, visible two miles, in lieu of separate forward and stern lights. This light *may* be placed off the fore-and-aft centerline if centerline mounting is not practicable. Under the International Rules only, if such a light is shown, the sidelights must be combined in one light that is carried on the fore-and-aft centerline or located as nearly as practicable on the same fore-and-aft line as the all-round light

Under the International Rules only, a power-driven vessel that is less than 23 feet (7 m) in length and whose maximum speed does not exceed 7 knots—typically a lightly powered dinghy—may show only an all-round white light that is visible for two miles. Sidelights are not mandatory, but should be shown if practicable.

Under both International and Inland Rules a vessel less than 23 feet (7 m) propelled solely by sail or oars need have only a flashlight handy to show a white light in sufficient time to avoid a collision. Dinghy owners take note.

Equipment for Safety

Equipment for safety and convenience was covered in Chapter 3; some items will be covered again here with special emphasis on their applicability to smaller craft.

Lifesaving Devices

Smaller boats, especially those with outboard motors, are more likely to capsize or sink than are larger inboard boats; consequently, there is a greater possibility that the occupants will find themselves in the water. Do not skimp on personal flotation devices; carry at least the number legally required (see Chapter 3, page 90). Wearable PFDs of the proper size are required for each person on board. (Additionally, a throwable PFD, such as an approved cushion, is required on each craft over 16 feet, (4.9 m), in length.) Adult nonswimmers, handicapped persons, any one wearing a cast, and children should wear life preservers at all times when underway. (There are legal requirements regarding children in most jurisdictions.) Special purpose flotation devices *approved by the U.S. Coast Guard*, such as some hunter's jackets and some waterskiing vests are legally acceptable; many water-skiers wear a belt

Figure 7-14 An anchor and line is required by some states, but not by federal regulations. In any case, however, it is a good safety practice to have a means of anchoring in an emergency, such as an engine failure. It is desirable that a short length of chain be connected between the anchor and line.

rather than a jacket, this does not count toward the required number of PFDs.

Paddle or Oars

Required by regulations in some state and local jurisdictions (and by plain "common sense" everywhere), a paddle or pair of oars should be on all smaller boats. They could be the only way of reaching safety in the event of motor failure. Most outboard boats row or paddle quite clumsily and with considerable effort, but the means to do so should be on board; see **Figure 7-13.**

Anchor & Line

Another item of common sense, and in some areas, boating regulations, is a suitable anchor and line long enough to anchor in all areas where the boat is used; see **Figure 7-14.** (Obviously, this concept must be applied with reason when the boat is used off very deep coasts, but when purchasing line it is better to get too much than too little.) See Chapter 9 for details on anchoring.

Bailer

All small boats should be equipped with a manual bailer. This can be a scoop purchased for this purpose, or one homemade from a household

Figure 7-13 No matter how dependable a motor may seem, a paddle or pair of oars should be carried on all small boats for emergencies.

plastic jug. Transom drains are effective underway for many fast boats, but these must have a means of positive closure when not in use. Electric bilge pumps will be found on many larger outboard or stern-drive boats. A large sponge is frequently convenient for getting that last little bit of water out of a small boat.

Flashlight or Lantern

Every small boat should be equipped with a flashlight or electric lantern, whether or not plans include using the boat after dark. The light should be waterproof, and it should float if accidentally dropped overboard. Extra batteries, stored in a waterproof container, will often prove valuable in an emergency. Batteries in the flashlight or lantern, and the spares, should be renewed at the start of each boating season, regardless of their apparent condition. The flashlight is also important while traveling on the roads in case of trailer or car trouble.

Visual Distress Signals

All boats 16 feet (4.9 m) or more in length operating in coastal waters of wide connecting bodies *must* carry a specified minimum of visual distress signals; smaller boats need carry them only when operating at night. The signals must be U.S. Coast Guard approved; signals are classified as for day or night use, or a combination of both. Common sense suggests carrying more than the legal minimum. See Chapter 3, pages 105 to 107, for additional details.

Radio

A radio—VHF/FM—is often installed when the outboard has a battery for electric starting and an alternator to keep the battery charged. VHF equipment, with its smaller antennas, is especially suitable for smaller boats. Small handheld VHF sets (refer to Chapter 21) are useful in outboard boats, especially if used with an installed antenna.

Operational Equipment

In addition to equipment carried on board for safety reasons, there are many items that will be needed or useful in the normal operation of smaller boats. The specific items will, of course, vary with the size of the craft and the uses to which it is put.

Compass

Except when used on the smallest of lakes, no outboard or similar boat should be without a magnetic compass. Select one of adequate size and quality, and install it properly. Refer to Chapter 13 for more information.

As most smaller boats are relatively open, it is particularly important that the compass is shielded from the sun's direct rays. When not in use, remove it and store it out of the light, or place a light-tight cover over it.

Charts

Carry charts for the waters that you use; on inland lakes and rivers, these may be called "maps"; refer to Chapter 15. Learn to use a chart with your compass, and do use it often under favorable conditions even when not strictly necessary. This practice is excellent training and will prepare you for using the chart with confidence and efficiency should an emergency arise. Make a point of keeping track of where you are at all times.

Tools

Every boat, no matter how small, should carry at least a few simple hand tools. The minimum should be a screwdriver, pliers, and an adjustable open-end wrench. Consideration might be given to having two or more screwdrivers as well as wrenches of different sizes. A spark-plug wrench suitable for your motor is recommended.

Safety Chain

Most outboard motors are clamped to the craft's transom (some of the larger ones may be through-bolted). To protect against accidental loss overboard should the clamps loosen with vibration, a short safety chain (or cable) is often used between a connecting point on the motor and a ring securely fastened to the hull. Chains or lengths of steel cable, frequently plastic-coated to reduce rusting, may be inexpensively purchased for this purpose already equipped with snap fittings at each end. This is "cheap insurance" against the total loss of an expensive motor in deep water. With locking fittings, they also provide some security against theft.

Extra Fuel Tanks

The very smallest outboard motors have an integral fuel tank, but those of four or more horsepower typically operate from remote tanks that are more convenient with their larger capacity. Boats of 18 feet (5.5 m) or so in length, with high-horsepower motors, usually have built-in tanks.

It is often necessary to carry additional fuel to make long runs without stopping. Select a spare tank or container carefully; it must be made for that specific use. The material of the tank and its design must be intended specifically for containing gasoline in a marine (often salt water) environment. Homemade or converted tanks are hazardous. Tanks from the manufacturer of your motor, or a reputable manufacturer specializing in marine tanks, are best.

Fuel tanks should be stored in a well-ventilated area, and secured against unnecessary movement. They should be protected from spray or rain, and inspected at least once each season. Dents and scratches can damage the plating that protects underlying steel from rust; a tank that shows any signs of rust should be replaced.

Steering & Other Controls

The simplest outboard motors have controls right on the motor itself; see **Figure 7-15**. A steering handle, or tiller, is used to turn the motor from side to side. A throttle may be built into the steering arm, or it may be a separate lever on the motor. A gearshift lever for forward, neutral, and reverse is usually located on the side of the powerhead. Controls for choking and carburetor-jet adjustment are usually on the front of the motor.

Remote steering and engine controls may be an option on motors of about 10 to 25 hp and are standard on larger engines. This allows the operator to sit forward in the boat for greater visibility, with a wheel for steering, and levers for shift control. A control also may be provided to

Figure 7-15 On smaller motors, all controls are mounted on the powerhead. On the motor shown here, the shift lever is on the side and the throttle is part of the steering arm.

change the angle of the engine against the transom to adjust the riding trim of the boat (see page 238).

Steering controls may consist of a continuous loop of metal cable (usually plastic-covered) running from one side of the engine forward, around a drum on the shaft of the steering wheel, and then aft to the other side of the motor. Pulleys are used to guide the cable, which may run forward on one side of the boat and aft on the other, or may run fore and aft on the same side.

Rod steering uses a rack-and-pinion gear at the steering wheel to push and pull a stiff cable through a protective housing. The other end of the cable is attached to the motor, moving it from side to side around its central pivot as the steering wheel is turned back and forth. Rod steering gives smooth control and is free of the hazards of the exposed cables of the other type.

In hydraulic systems, steering wheel motion is transmitted through fluid-filled lines to the stern, activating a push-pull rod attached to the motor(s).

Throttle and gearshift controls consist of a stiff cable within a sheath to transmit the back-and-forth motion required. In some models, the two controls are combined at the helm in a single lever that is pushed forward to go ahead and pulled backward, through a neutral center position, to go astern. This mechanism is somewhat more complex than separate throttle and gearshift controls.

Tachometer

This instrument, when properly calibrated, indicates engine revolutions per minute (rpm). A tachometer is important when running trials to select the optimum propeller, and it often is used as a reference for operating at cruising or trolling speeds. In the absence of a speedometer, a series of timed runs at regular increments of engine speed can be used to establish a speed curve for the boat. This curve then gives you a boat speed through the water at any engine setting. See Chapter 16, page 577, for details on establishing a speed curve.

An electronic tachometer can be fitted to almost any outboard motor; it is a simple job requiring little technical know-how and very little time.

Speedometer

As an alternative to developing a speed curve with a series of timed runs, a speedometer can be

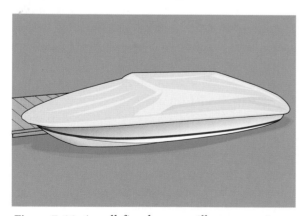

Figure 7-16 A well-fitted cover will prevent rain and falling debris from entering the boat in its berth afloat or ashore, or while traveling. Covers may cover the entire boat, or only the open portion; the motor may or may not be covered.

installed, and speed taken directly from it. This instrument also is quick and simple to install, and the more expensive models offer a reasonable degree of accuracy. Many models can be calibrated by doing a series of timed runs, but even if a speedometer is not accurate in absolute terms, it can be used to determine the relative speeds obtained with various motor and propeller combinations. Calibration is necessary, however, when it is to be used in navigation. Remember, on board speedometers measure only speed through the water not over the bottom like a GPS or Loran receiver (refer to Chapter 21).

Electronic Depth Sounder

Many smaller craft can carry an electronic depth sounder and put it to good use. Special transom mounts for the transducer are available for smaller craft where through-hull mounting may not be practicable. More on this very useful device will also be found in Chapter 21.

Boat Covers

A cover keeps dirt out of the boat and helps to protect the interior during off-season storage; see **Figure 7-16.** Usually of Dacron or similar synthetic fabric, covers may be available in a style that covers your entire boat, from stem to stern, including the outboard motor; others may cover only the open parts of the boat. Covers are excellent for keeping out rain as well as the dirt and leaves that accumulate when the boat is on its trailer. Be sure that the cover provides adequate ventilation for the interior to prevent rot of interior woodwork and other forms of fungus growth.

The cover must fit the boat and must be capable of being adequately secured by means of snaps or drawstring. (Snaps or other mechanical fasteners should be protected from corrosion by a nonstaining lubricant; a silicone grease stick is excellent for this purpose.) A cover is of the greatest value when a boat is being trailered, but it must be fastened down adequately to prevent wind damage. In outdoor storage, a cover must also be adequately supported internally to prevent the formation of pools of rainwater that

Figure 7-17 The addition of a top, often with side and rear panels including clear plastic, can make a boat more comfortable in rainy or cool weather. Often such a craft can be used for weekend cruises or other short trips.

will stretch—and eventually tear—it, dumping the water into the boat.

For some outboards, tops are available to provide protection against rain and shade from the hot sun while the boat is in operation. Side and rear panels, with clear plastic inserts, also may be available, offering considerable protection against rain and spray, as well as allowing comfortable boating in cool weather; see **Figure 7-17.** Such tops and panels should be removed before trailering a boat at highway speeds.

Registration & Numbering

Although requirements vary in details for various states, nearly all boats, including personal watercraft, will require registration and the affixing of numbers on each bow; refer to Chapter 2 and Appendix C.

OUTBOARD MOTOR BASICS

A boat equipped with an outboard motor or inboard/outboard drive can be used for widely varied recreational purposes, some of which include fishing, waterskiing, cruising, and diving. In any application, greater safety and enjoyment will result when you understand and employ the following boating practices.

Adjusting the Motor

Begin your outboarding by installing the motor properly on the boat, according to the manufac-

turer's diagrams. Seat a single motor squarely on the center of the boat's transom and securely tighten the bracket screws. Some motors come equipped with a special mounting plate; with others, you may want to make use of a rubber pad to help cushion vibrations and to prevent the transom from being marred. Be sure to connect a safety chain or cable from the motor to the boat's hull; a lock may be desirable for security against theft.

Twin motors are usually installed by a dealer, as are large single motors of the high-horsepower

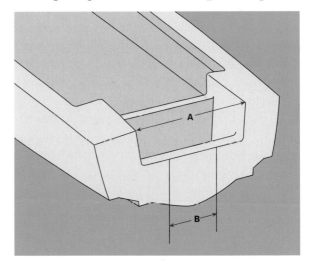

Figure 7-18 Standards are set by the American Boat and Yacht Council for the width of transom cutouts ("A" above) and for the center-to-center spacing of twin outboard motors ("B"). The ABYC standard also includes other critical dimensions.

range. Twin motors should have the proper spacing—22 inches (56 cm) is recommended by the American Boat and Yacht Council (ABYC) for motors up to 75 hp, and 32 inches (81 cm) for higher-horsepower motors on single-hull craft. Standard motor position dimensions are furnished to the boat manufacturers; see **Figure 7-18.** Motors on catamarans are normally placed at the stern of each hull; this wider spacing is an advantage in maneuvering.

If a combination of a large and small motor is used, the large one is mounted on the boat's centerline, with the small "kicker" off to one side, usually on a bracket specifically designed for such use. (Such a bracket allows the motor to be raised entirely clear of the water when it is not in use, thereby reducing drag.) The low horsepower of the small motor will not present any significant steering problems from its off-center position.

Motor Height

Although there is a high degree of standardization in the design of transom cutouts for motor mounting, it is wise to check that the lower unit of the motor is correctly located with respect to the bottom of the hull. Standard shaft lengths are 15 and 20 inches (38 and 51 cm), and 25 inches (64 cm) for the high-horsepower engines. There are some variations, however, and a transom can be modified, if necessary, to ensure proper motor positioning. The "anti-cavitation plate" on the lower unit should line up with the transom chine, except for some installations on deep-V hulls.

If the motor is located too high, a smooth flow of water will not reach the propeller; it will not be able to get a proper "grip" on the water. This may cause "ventilation," in which the propeller spins in aerated water with possible damage to the engine from excessive rpm. If the motor is located too low, drag will be increased due to both the greater area of the lower unit in the water and a distorted flow over and under the anti-cavitation plate. Attention to this detail of motor installation will help provide both increased speed and decreased fuel consumption.

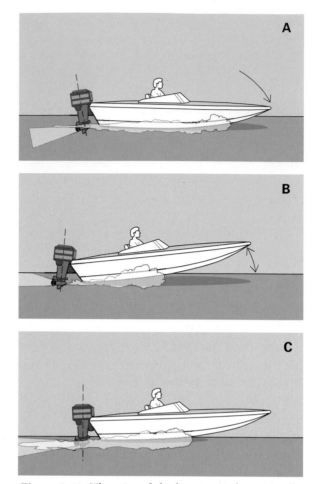

*Figure 7-19 The trim of the lower unit has a significant effect on the planing angle of the boat, which alters top speed and handling. At **A**, the drive is trimmed too far "in," while at **B** it is too far "out." The drive at **C** is properly trimmed.*

Thrust-Line Adjustment

Most outboard motors are equipped with a tilt adjustment, allowing a boater to vary the angle of thrust of the propeller. For best performance, the drive of the propeller should be in a line parallel to the flat surface of the water at the boat's most efficient operating angle, whether as a planing hull or in the displacement mode.

If the motor is in too close to the transom, the thrust line is downward from the horizontal, pushing the stern up and the bow down, making the boat "plow" through the water unnecessarily. On the other hand, if the motor is tilted too far out from the transom, the thrust line is upward, and the bow is forced up too high while the stern "squats"; see **Figure 7-19.**

Boats differ in design, and loading conditions vary widely with any specific boat, so manufacturers make tilt-angle adjustment as easy as possible. On stern-drive engines and some larger outboard motors, an electro-hydraulic control is provided; just push the button for "up" or "down."

Be aware of the inefficiency of an improper thrust angle, and do not neglect to change the adjustment to your current operating conditions. The best angle may vary with water conditions. On some boats, an adjustment with the motor tilted out (bow up) for smooth water may give more speed, and a better ride in rough water may be obtained with the motor trimmed in a bit. Remember that only with actual trials on your boat will you be able to tell for sure.

Special Applications of Tilt

While underway, the tilt feature of outboard motor and stern-drive lower units can be used to advantage for several special situations. If the propeller becomes fouled with weeds, it is, for example, often a simple matter to stop the motor, tilt it up, clear off the vegetation, lower the motor, restart it, and then continue on your way. If a smaller motor shears its pin, it is often possible to replace it with the motor tilted up, making it unnecessary to unmount the motor completely in order to work on it in the boat.

It is also possible to tilt the outboard motor or lower unit up far enough so the boat can clear shoal areas. Take care not to tilt it so much that the cooling water intake comes above the surface, and watch out that the propeller does not strike rocks or other hard objects that might damage it. Proceed slowly when using this technique.

With I/Os, many manufacturers recommend not to operate with the drive unit partially or all the way up. Otherwise, you risk excessive wear on the flexible couplings.

Mixture Controls

Many smaller outboard motors have controls for adjusting the fuel-air ratio; see **Figure 7-20.** This

Figure 7-20 Smaller outboard motors have one or more carburetor controls brought out to the front of the motor case to make possible the adjustment of fuel-air mixtures for various operating conditions. Be sure to follow the instructions in your operator's manual.

adjustment allows you to obtain optimum performance while cruising at low speeds and, in the case of some smaller motors, for high speeds as well. Adjustment controls are located outside the motor cover so that they can be used easily while underway.

You can minimize the possibility of engine damage due to improper settings and help achieve the best results by strictly following the instructions in your owner's manual.

Changes in fuel, air temperature, and altitude (such as going from mountain lakes to a lower elevation, or vice versa) may require changes in mixtures. Any adjustment should be made with the motor thoroughly warmed up and the boat loaded to normal trim. Many motors also have a manual choke or control for added fuel injection for starting.

Fuels & Oils

The drive for a cleaner environment has resulted in the mandated use of "no-lead" gasoline with other chemicals added to maintain octane ratings. In many cases these fuels have given the older motors a few problems. Recent models are designed for current gasolines.

The typical smaller outboard motor has its lubricating oil mixed into the gasoline fuel supply; there is no separate crankcase. Consequently, special oil properties such as "low ash" are required, and many normal features such as detergents must be limited or avoided.

The best oil to use in a two-stroke motor is one specifically made and sold for that purpose by oil companies or outboard manufacturers. The oil will be certified as TC-W (two-cycle, water-cooled) and it will contain no harmful compounds. Take note that although the motor manufacturers do not *make* the oils that bear their names, presumably they set the specifications for them. Using oil from the motor's manufacturer will ensure greater compatibility between the oil and motor (and possibly lessen any difficulties with future warranty claims).

The current TC-W specification is now TC-W3; this addresses the higher horsepower engines. It meets even more demanding specifications in order to cope with the now-common use of low-grade "pipeline" gasolines. It can be used in any size motor. (TC-W and TC-W2 oils are no longer produced and sold.)

Outboard motors are generally of low compression ratio and can use fuels of modest octane rating. Actually these engines now are designed for these fuels (many boaters find it desirable to use mid-grade 89 octane gasoline). Keep in mind that marine engines normally operate under a constant load, unlike autos and trucks that go uphill and downhill, with frequent changes of load. It is always best to follow the fuel recommendations in your owner's manual. Remember, with the newer four-stroke, no fuel/oil mixture is required. But with two-stroke outboard motors using a mixture of gasoline and lubricating oil it is essential that both of these be of the correct type and that the mixture ratio be that specified by the manufacturer.

Oil-Fuel Mixture Ratios

Motor manufacturers specify the correct ratio of gasoline to oil for their models. Although for older motors the ratio was 24 to 1, for most of today's motors it is 50 to 1. Motors made outside of the U.S. may have different requirements. The amount of oil to be used is sometimes given as ounces or fractions of a pint that should be added for each gallon of gasoline; see **Table 7-1**.

Some marinas now have a special pump installed that dispenses premixed gas and oil. In some instances this mixture is fixed at an established blend, usually at a 50 to 1 ratio; however, at other pumps, controls can be set to any one of several standard gas/oil ratios.

Many outboard motors are now oil injected, providing an optimum ratio for any speed. This is especially valuable for the higher horsepower sizes, enabling them to be used at the lower end of their speed range without fouling the motor; see **Figure 7-21**.

Fueling Procedures

There are two aspects of fueling an outboard boat that must be given careful attention—safety and the proper mixing of the oil and gasoline. Fueling a boat safely is an essential element of good seamanship. Whether you are planning a day's outing or an extended cruise, before starting out make sure you have enough fuel on board, and if any is needed, fill your tanks safely. Refer to

Ratios of Oil to Gasoline

Pints of oil added to gallon of gas

Actual Ratio Gals.	1 Gal.	2 Gals.	3 Gals.	4 Gals.	5 Gals.	6
96:1	1/12	1/6	1/4	1/3	5/12	1/2
48:1	1/6	1/3	1/2	2/3	5/6	1
24:1	1/3	2/3	1	1 1/3	1 2/3	2
16:1	1/2	1	1 1/2	2	2 1/2	3

Table 7-1 The row for 48:1 is commonly used for a "50 to 1" mix, and the row for 96:1 when a 100 to 1 mix is specified.

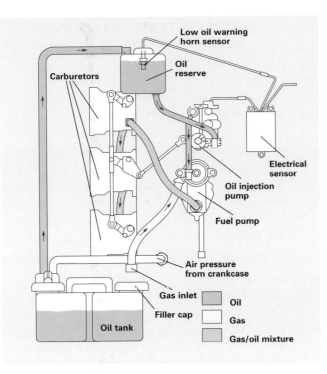

Low oil warning
horn sensor

Carburetors

Oil
reserve

Electrical
sensor

Oil injection
pump

Fuel pump

Air pressure
from crankcase

Gas inlet

Filler cap

Oil tank

Oil

Gas

Gas/oil mixture

Figure 7-21 An oil-injection system will automatically mix oil and fuel to the precise operating ratio between 50 to 1 and 100 to 1. It reduces oil consumption at idle speeds to reduce smoke and pollution. The oil reservoir is about the size of a battery box and can hold enough oil to treat at least 150 gallons (568 liters) of gasoline.

Chapter 11 for information about the safety aspects of fueling.

Tanks of smaller than 6 gallons should be removed from the boat when refueling; see **Figure 7-22.** Newer outboard motor oils make filling portable tanks easy because they mix readily with gasoline. Use the engine manufacturer's recommendations to determine the amount of oil for the required amount of fuel. Pour the oil into the tank, and then fill it with gasoline. The inward flow of the fuel will cause the oil to mix thoroughly and additional mixing is not needed. (If the tank is empty—dry—it is best to fill it about one-quarter full of gasoline before pouring in the oil.) Shaking the tank is not necessary. Wipe off the outside of the tank and return it to the boat after any odor of fumes has disappeared.

For safety, portable tanks should be secured in the boat. A simple way is to provide wooden blocks on the hull or floorboards to prevent sideways or endways movement of the tank, with straps over the top of the tank to hold it down in rough going.

If your fuel tanks are larger than 6 gallons, they are best left in the boat for filling. These, and

permanently installed tanks, are not filled before all doors, hatches, windows, etc. are closed to keep any gasoline vapors from getting below. After fueling and cleaning up, open all hatches and ports, and allow time for ventilation to clear bilges and any enclosed spaces before starting the engine.

Pour oil into the fill pipe of a fixed tank before it is filled with gasoline. Fuel flow will carry the

Figure 7-22 As a safety measure, portable fuel tanks should be removed from a boat and filled on the gas pier or wharf. Wipe the tank clean and dry before it is put back on board.

oil into the tank where the newer outboard motor oils mix rapidly. Most higher horsepower engines now have separate gasoline and lubricant tanks that eliminate mixing oil into the fuel. Lubricant is automatically mixed with the fuel in metered amounts. This results in lower oil consumption and cleaner-burning engines.

Extra Fuel Tanks

If is often necessary to carry additional fuel to make long runs without stops. Select a spare tank or container carefully; *it must be made for that specific use.* The material of the tank and its design must be intended specifically for containing gasoline in a marine (often salt water) environment. Homemade or converted tanks are hazardous. Tanks from the manufacturer of your motor, or a reputable manufacturer specializing in marine tanks, are best.

Any additional fuel tanks should be carried on board in a well-ventilated area and secured against unnecessary movement. They should be protected from spray or rain. Inspect at least once each season. Dents and scratches can damage the plating that protects underlying steel from rust. *A tank that shows any signs of rust should be replaced.*

THE TRAILER

The addition of a trailer to your boating outfit provides considerable operational flexibility to the skipper. It allows traveling to distant boating areas that would be otherwise inaccessible, and storage of the boat at the owner's home—saving marina fees and facilitating routine maintenance. Also, there is less of a chance for marine organisms to attach themselves to the hull. This reduces the need for periodic and costly applications of antifouling paint.

Selecting the Right Rig

The owner of a trailered boat faces the unique challenge of not only having to determine what type of boat and propulsion will meet their needs, but also to match up that boat with a trailer and a vehicle that can safely haul, launch, and retrieve his craft; see **Figure 7-23.** (The combination of a boat,

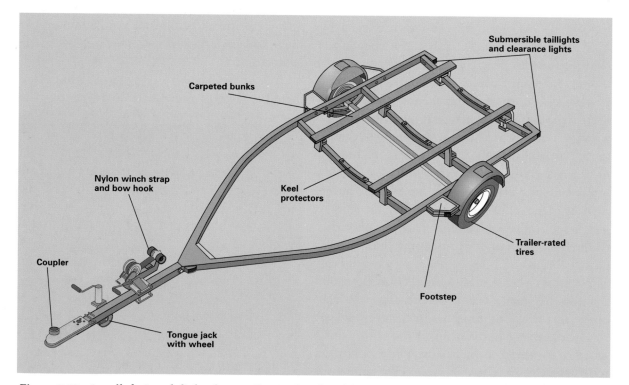

Figure 7-23 A well-designed, light-duty trailer is often fitted for one size and weight of boat only, but can still offer reliable and affordable use over many years if properly maintained.

motor, and trailer is often referred to as a "rig.") This imposes definite limits on the size and style of boat. Most trailerboats will fall into the 14- to 25-foot (4.3 m to 7.6 m) category and weigh 1,000 to 4,000 pounds (454 to 1,814 kg). Although boats up to 40 feet (12 m) or longer can be trailered legally without special permits, 8.5-foot (2.6 m) width limitations in most states and provinces mean that only high-performance or specialty boats much over 25 feet (7.6 m) fall into the trailerable category.

Trailerboaters are also limited in a practical sense by the expense of specialized tow vehicles that are needed to haul large and heavy loads. The choice of tow vehicle, boat, and trailer must be made carefully so the combination works well, while fitting the boater's needs. If you already own a boat, shop carefully for a suitable trailer and vehicle. If you already own a vehicle suited and equipped for towing, you will be limited in your purchase of a boat and trailer by the vehicle's rated towing capacity.

Considering Vehicles

Since the more a tow vehicle weighs, the more sway it can absorb, a tow vehicle should weigh at least as much as the rig it is pulling. In other words, weight determines whether the tow vehicle will be in firm control of the trailer or the trailer will be pushing the vehicle around. A heavier trailer can throw both vehicles into a violent swaying motion that could cause the driver to lose control.

Wheelbase length is another important factor to consider when gauging the ideal fit between trailer and tow vehicle. Cars and small trucks with short wheelbases make poor tow vehicles. Alternatively, long-bed pickups, with their equally long wheelbases, perform excellently. Just like a tow vehicle that is too light, one that is too short may be controlled by a trailer. But note that vehicles with long wheelbases can be hard to maneuver in tight quarters.

Horsepower is another consideration when choosing the ideal tow vehicle. How much is enough? One rule of thumb suggests adding the weight of the boat and trailer and then knocking off one of the zeros. The remainder gives an idea of how many cubic inches of engine displacement you need to adequately haul the load. For example, a 3,000-pound rig would require a 302-cu. in. (5.0-liter) engine, while a 3,500-pound rig requires a 351-cu. in. (5.8-liter) engine. Similarly a large 4,600-pound rig needs a 460-cu. in. (7.5-liter) big-block vehicle engine.

When looking at vehicles, there are other factors that should be added to the equation. Remember that four-wheel-drive vehicles work as well on slippery launch ramps as they do on ice and rain-soaked pavement. Also note that a manual transmission's clutch will wear out sooner than an automatic transmission when it is used for extensive towing. In addition, the automatic is much easier to use, giving you freedom from the constant up- and down-shifting necessary to keep the engine on the proper portion of the torque curve.

Depending on the engine's horsepower rating and its rear axle ratio, a tow vehicle is assigned what is called a Gross Vehicle Weight (GVW) rating. This figure specifies the maximum loaded weight in pounds of the tow vehicle, its boat, and the trailer. In other words, the number tells you how large a trailered boat your car or truck can safely pull.

Vehicle Modifications

A car used with a trailer may need some modifications to give fully satisfactory performance. Rear springs and/or shock absorbers may require replacement by heavier duty units because of the added weight transferred from the trailer tongue. The turn-signal flasher unit may need replacement with one that can handle the added load of the trailer's signals.

If a heavy trailer is to be pulled, it may be desirable, or even necessary, to add a cooler for crankcase oil and transmission fluid. Vehicle manufacturers are becoming increasingly specific in the maximum loads that can be towed without modifications, and just what modifications are available. When in doubt, be sure to check your owner's manual, and be careful *not to void your warranty.*

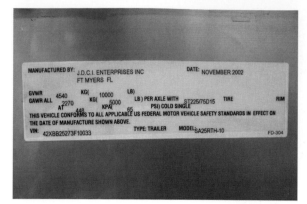

Figure 7-24 The capacity plate on this trailer tongue shows its load capacity, tire size and required pressure, and other data.

Because trailering a big boat imposes heavy loads on the engine, the drivetrain, suspension, electrical system, brakes, and tires, any vehicle destined to pull a boat really needs the special factory towing package that is usually available. This will greatly extend the life of your vehicle.

Driving with a boat trailer behind the car is not as easy as ordinary driving, especially when the craft is high and wide. An external rear-view mirror on the car's right side will make passing both safer and easier. If the boat is quite wide, it is best to install external mirrors (refer to **Figure 7-38**) that project out far enough to give a clear view behind the boat; these are the mirrors often used on cars that pull house trailers.

Selecting a Trailer

Like boats and motors, trailers also come in many varieties; they range in price from economy to premium. A light-duty trailer, such as **Figure 7-23,** may be adequate if all your boating is done locally; a heavy-duty one may be needed if you plan long hauls.

In general, premium models use better construction techniques and materials, and they are often better designed. Economy-priced trailers tend to have fewer cross-members along their frames, which means they have fewer support rollers, with wider spaces between them. Many inexpensive models also use a lighter-gauge steel stock in their frames and are usually bolted together rather than welded—a good weld is a far stronger bond.

Adequacy

The trailer for your boat must be adequate in both weight-carrying capacity and length. Under-buy in either of these aspects and your craft will ultimately suffer. Each trailer will have a "capacity plate" with various data on it; see **Figure 7-24.**

The trailer must be able to carry the weight of your boat, motor(s), *and the gear stowed in the boat.* As a general rule, it is important to remember that the capacity of the trailer should exceed the combined gross weight of boat and motor by about 20 percent. This surplus capacity

Figure 7-25 As the full weight of an outboard motor or stern drive is carried on the boat's transom, adequate support under this part of the hull is essential.

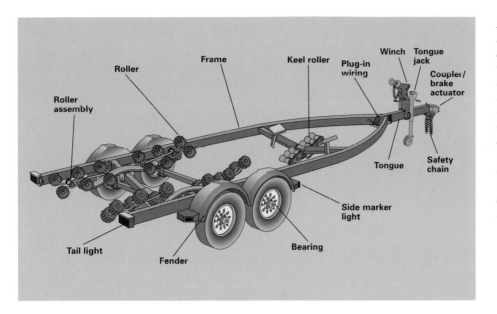

Figure 7-26 A system of pivoted arms with pairs of rollers lets this load-leveler type of tandem-axle trailer conform to the shape of a boat's bottom automatically, after being adjusted for length and beam. Three-axle trailers are used for heavier craft.

is intended to handle the extra weight of any gear you will be carrying on board. If there is any doubt, buy the next larger model. Don't underestimate weights; boat weights given by manufacturers may be for basic models, so try to account for all equipment. Make a detailed list of each item that you plan to install or carry in the boat and its weight, and be sure to include a generous allowance for "miscellaneous." If possible, use a truck scale to weigh the trailer alone, then the trailer with empty boat and motor, and finally the complete rig with all gear and fuel—you may be surprised at the final gross weight!

Length

Trailer length is critical because the boat's stern area, particularly the transom, must have adequate support. The boat must be able to fit onto the trailer bed so that the aftermost supports extend at least an inch or two beyond the transom; see **Figure 7-25**. If there is any overhang, the hull will be distorted. This is also true for stern-drive craft, but it is particularly important for outboards, where the full weight of the motor(s) is on the transom. A "hook" (a downward bend) in the hull at the stern, caused by a too-short trailer, can affect both the boat's speed and its general handling characteristics.

Supports

In a boat's natural environment—the water—the hull is uniformly supported; there are no concentrations of pressure on the hull. However, a trailer can provide support only in limited areas or even points, so the trailer bed must fit the contours of the hull as closely as possible. Plenty of padding and bracing also may be needed.

Supports may take the form of rollers or of padded bars or STRINGERS (BUNKS), or a combination of some of each. Some trailers, with multiple pairs of rollers on pivoted bars, are designed to conform to the hull shape automatically; these are the SELF-LEVELING models. Each type of support system has its advantages and disadvantages; the way the boat will normally be launched and loaded must be considered.

Rollers of hard rubber are widely used on trailers that tilt and allow the boat to move backward into the water by gravity; see **Figure 7-26.** Their disadvantage is that each roller has very little area of contact with the hull with consequence of high pressure in those areas. The more rollers there are, the better, *provided* that the height of each is adjusted properly; the depth of the indentation into the roller by the keel is a rough guide as to the weight being carried at that point.

Padded bar supports provide the maximum area in contact with the hull, and thus the

TRAILER TERMINOLOGY

Ball Mount That part of the hitch that connects the hitch ball to the coupler on the trailer.

Bearing Buddy A commercial product that replaces the dust cover on the axle hub; as well, this item allows the wheel bearings to be greased without disassembly.

Bumper hitch Trailer hitch bolted to the rear bumper. Usually rated for Class I towing applications.

Class I, II, III, and IV hitches Weight-carrying hitches whose various capacities are rated at gross trailer weight and tongue weight. See text for more details.

Coupler That part of the trailer that connects the tongue to the hitch ball.

Electric brakes independent braking system for a trailer, actuated electrically from the tow vehicle.

Frame-mounted hitch A hitch that is mounted or welded to the frame of the tow vehicle.

Gross axle weight rating (GAW) Specifies the maximum weight an axle is designed to carry. This figure includes the weight of the vehicle plus any load supported by the axle. Caution: Never exceed the GAW.

Gross trailer weight rating (GTW) Weight of the trailer with all of its cargo.

Gross vehicle weight rating (GVW) The maximum weight the vehicle is designed to carry—includes the weight of the vehicle itself plus any load normally added.

Hitch ball That part of the hitch that couples to the trailer—in essence, a ball joint. The ball allows the trailer to swivel freely when cornering.

Hitch receiver The component part of a hitch that receives the shank. Also called a hitch box.

Receiver hitch A hitch with a receiver, from which the hitch shank can be removed.

Safety chains Required by law in most states, these connect the trailer to the hitch, providing an extra measure of safety.

Spring bars Spring steel bars in a weight-distributing hitch that distribute weight throughout the tow vehicle and trailer.

Step bumper hitch A hitch found on many utility vehicles.

Surge brakes A hydraulic braking system that is activated by the momentum of the trailer pushing against the tow vehicle during deceleration.

Tongue weight The amount of trailer weight that is measured at the tongue.

Weight-carrying hitch A trailer hitch that accepts all of the tongue weight of a trailer.

Weight-distributing hitch A frame-mounted hitch that consists of a shank, a ball mount and spring bars, as well as hookup brackets.

Wiring harness Wiring connecting a trailer's lights to the tow vehicle's electrical system.

---

minimum of point contact pressure. These are excellent for boats that normally are lifted from the trailer, as by a crane's slings. They have considerable surface friction, however, and are generally less suitable for sliding the boat off the trailer into the water—unless special features are provided.

There are trailers that use a combination of rollers and padded bars, with a lever system that lowers the bars for launching and retrieval, and raises them for additional support when the boat is fully onto the trailer.

There also should be side supports to hold the boat firmly in position on the trailer bed, and a bow chock to keep the boat from moving farther forward. All of these supports must be adjustable and positioned so that they can carry out their functions. Location of the bow chock, for example, should be adjusted so that the transom

Figure 7-27 When the weight of a boat becomes too great for a single axle, it is time to consider a multi-axle trailer. Models are available with two, three, or more axles for larger craft.

will be directly over its supports. The boat's position on the trailer also affects the weight at the trailer tongue and coupling. Any unbalanced condition, once the hull is properly mated to the trailer bed, is properly corrected by shifting the location of the axle and wheels, *not* the bow chock.

Wheels & Tires

Many trailer tires are smaller in diameter than automotive tires. Small wheels position the axle closer to the ground so that the trailer rides as low as possible. A low center of gravity optimizes stability during turns and in crosswinds.

But the downside is that smaller tires sink deeper into potholes and turn at a higher rpm than the tires on the car. These two factors translate into a shorter tire life. As a rule, small tires are best for light boats over short hauls, while larger and/or tandem tires are better for heavier rigs and long hauls. The larger tires provide a smoother ride.

Larger trailers, over 3,000 lb (1,360 kg) capacity, often come with tandem wheels—four tires on two axles; see **Figure 7-27**. Still larger trailers, over 9,000 lb (4,080 kg) capacity, have three axles and six tires. There are benefits and drawbacks to multi axle arrangements. On the one hand, they cost more to purchase and maintain. And because they resist sharp turns, maneuvering in close quarters is more difficult. On the

other hand, four or six wheels track very straight—an immense help when backing a big rig down a launch ramp.

All trailers should have a spare tire already mounted on a wheel. The spare can be locked to the trailer tongue. Trailer tires are often odd sizes and not always readily available when on the road. As a general rule, buy the best tires you can afford for both tow vehicle and trailer; they will last longer. Tires made specifically for trailer use will generally give better service than those designed for automotive use.

Suspension

Although more expensive, torsion-bar suspension is superior to the leaf-spring type. Wheels are suspended independently, making for a softer ride for the boat over bumps and potholes. The trailer will track better and torsion-bar suspension will allow the frame and boat to ride lower for better stability. This type will have a longer life than the leaf-spring type, which eventually may rust together and lose effectiveness.

Hitches & Couplers

The hitch is a very important component of a towing vehicle and trailer combination; it is the main link between it and the trailer. HITCHBALLS are mounted on fixed platforms or on draw-bars that insert into receiver-type hitches. COUPLERS are mounted on the front of the trailer tongue are designed to fit nearly over the various balls, with a lever or screw on top that engages a latch that encloses the ball. Once the screw or lever is engaged, the coupler prevents the trailer tongue from bouncing off the ball, while still allowing the trailer to pivot from side to side and, to a certain extent, up and down.

Hitches are divided into four classes:

• **Class I hitches** (standard fixed-ball bumper hitches) are designed for light-duty loads of up to 2,000 pounds gross trailer weight (GTW) with no more than 200 pounds of tongue weight (amount of trailer weight measured at the tongue). The utility bumper of a light truck or van fits in this category. Some may have frame attachment points.

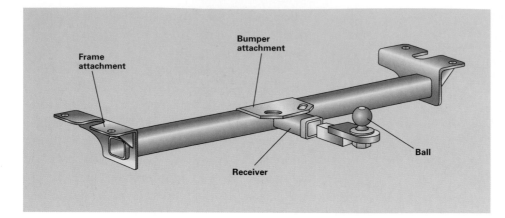

Figure 7-28 This Class II frame-mounting hitch features a removable ball mount for better appearance and convenience.

• **Class II hitches** are weight-carrying hitches, fixed ball or receiver type, designed to tow up to 3,500 pounds GTW loads with no more than 300 pounds tongue weight. These are basically bumper hitches for the heavier-duty trucks and vans, or brackets installed on the car's frame and the bumper, since few car bumpers can now handle alone this kind of weight. **Figure 7-28** shows a hitch of this class.

• **Class III hitches** are weight-carrying or weight-distributing receiving hitches designed to tow in the range of 5,000-7,500 pounds (GTW), depending on the size and structure of the tow vehicle. These frame hitches distribute weight using spring bars, mounted between the trailer and the hitch, that transfer a portion of the tongue weight to the front wheels of the tow vehicle.

• **Class IV hitches** are weight-carrying or weight-distributing hitches designed to tow in the range of 7,500-10,000 pounds (GTW), depending on the size and structure of the tow vehicle.

A trailer hitch should be secured to the towing vehicle's frame either with bolts (using lock washers) or by welding.

Hitch Balls & Chains

Hitch balls on the towing vehicle must match the coupler on the trailer tongue and its GTW rating. Balls vary in diameter from $1\frac{7}{8}$ inches to $2\frac{5}{16}$ inches; shanks vary from $\frac{3}{4}$ inch to $1\frac{3}{8}$ inches. For the same size balls, shanks may vary and have different GTW ratings. The diameter and GTW rating are normally stamped on each ball. *Never use a mismatched coupler and ball.*

At least one SAFETY CHAIN between the trailer and the towing vehicle is a *must*, and two are desirable; see **Figure 7-29.** When hooking them to the hitch, cross them so that the trailer will remain attached to the towing vehicle and under control. It is highly desirable that they cradle the tongue of the trailer and prevent it from dropping to the roadway, but this may not be possible if the chains are long enough to permit the required turns.

Keep in mind that the chains need to be long enough so that they don't bind in the middle of a tight turn or when backing down a launching ramp, yet not so long that they drag on the pavement—never hook the chains to the bumper. Chains must have adequate strength; chains

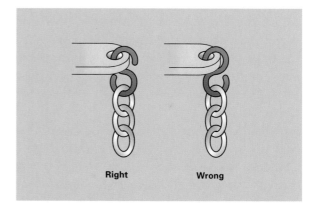

Figure 7-29 There is a right way and a wrong way to hook up trailer safety chains. The open end of the hook should go up through the hole, not down through it, so that the hook cannot bounce out. Use of a shackle would provide greater safety. Cross the chains under the trailer tongue so that they will support the tongue if the trailer coupling should fail.

furnished with a new trailer will normally more than meet this requirement but may be too long and require shortening. If cables are furnished rather than chains, it is desirable that they be replaced with chains.

On trailers equipped with surge brakes (see below), there may also be a third chain. Attach it to the auxiliary brake handle mounted on the tongue. Should the trailer break free, the crisscrossed chains will keep the trailer from pole-vaulting, while the third chain activates the surge brake.

There are also available now coupler and hitch combinations, such as the Saf-T-Tow, that provide positive action to prevent the trailer tongue from dropping to the road surface or crashing into the rear of the towing vehicle should the coupler come off the ball of the hitch.

Brakes

Generally, a lightly loaded trailer can be easily handled by the towing vehicle's brakes. Larger loads need an independent trailer braking system. Minimum trailer weights for brake requirement regulations vary from one state to another. It is wise to have even better brakes than the minimum legal requirement. Some trailer manufacturers suggest trailer brakes for any load over 1,000 pounds.

Trailers can be equipped with electric brakes that are activated in tandem with the towing vehicle's hydraulic system, or manually via a dashboard or steering-column control. This system can be adjusted according to the trailer load and works well on the road, permitting independent braking of the trailer to either slow down or even stop the whole rig. On the other hand, when backing up, the system tends to be less efficient. It's also prone to corrosion and component failures after being immersed in water.

A very popular choice is surge brakes; see **Figure 7-30.** Hydraulically operated and independent from the tow vehicle, these are activated by a pressure-sensitive master cylinder in a special coupler mounted on the trailer tongue. These brakes are activated when the tow vehicle slows down: As the trailer surges forward, the trailer brakes come on, and the harder the load pushes,

Figure 7-30 The surge type of coupler shown above senses the trailer's momentum when the towing vehicle slows and automatically applies the trailers hydraulic brakes.

the harder the brakes are applied. The brakes come off as the trailer slows and the load on the coupler is relieved. In this way, the surge brakes control themselves, according to the trailer's braking needs.

Trailer manufacturers warn trailerboaters with surge brake couplers not to shift into a lower gear, rather to use the tow vehicle's engine as a brake constantly instead of intermittently. This could result in overheating the trailer's brakes and putting them out of commission. It is better to approach a hill slowly, then brake repeatedly while heading down the hill, giving the brakes time to cool between applications.

Surge brake couplers are now designed to tolerate backing up without the need to deactivate them unless you are backing up a gradient or steep hill. Most states require that the brakes be equipped with a "breakaway" connection that activates the surge brakes if the trailer parts company with the tow vehicle.

Boaters are also warned to avoid getting the brakes wet whenever possible and, if they do get wet, to allow them to dry while the trailer is running. Test the brakes before each trip and after greasing the trailer wheels; inspect the brake linings regularly and replace them when worn.

Winches

A winch is needed to help ensure the orderly launching of the boat and easier effective retrieval;

Figure 7-31 Winches are used to gain added pull when loading a boat back onto its trailer. Both single- and two-speed models are available; the latter is preferable for all but the lightest of boats.

see **Figure 7-31.** While a single-speed manual winch will work fine for small boats up to about 1,000 pounds, most trailers should be equipped with a two-speed manual winch. This allows you to pull the boat out of the water quickly during the initial stages of retrieval, while the boat still has some buoyancy. The increased pulling power of the lower speed is then available when the boat has cleared the water and the winch is pulling its entire weight.

Electric winches are also available, making recovery of the boat a matter of hooking up and flipping a switch; see **Figure 7-32.** Powerful elec-

Figure 7-32 An electric trailer winch is especially desirable for loading heavier boats, often in less-than-perfect conditions.

tric models (expensive) are especially desirable for heavy boats that are often launched under less-than-ideal conditions, for example, on very steep ramps.

Whether manual or electric, the winch must be mounted so that the winch-line runs level with the boat's bow-eye. It should have an unimpeded run aft and, during recovery, should bring the bow snug against the bow-stop roller. A manual winch needs to be cleaned and greased regularly, while an electric winch should be maintained according to the manufacturer's specifications.

Tie-Downs

Do not depend on the bow-winch cable to hold the boat onto the trailer, and/or hold the bow down into its chock. There should be an additional TIE-DOWN of a lashing and turnbuckle. Moving aft, there should be straps of webbing across the hull to hold it firmly in place against the supports of the trailer, and to prevent any bouncing up and down on the trailer when on rough roads. There should be additional lashings at each side of the transom; see **Figure 7-33.** If a trailer as purchased does not have these fittings, they should be added before any extensive trip is made.

Electrical System

A trailer's electrical system powers its lights—tail, stop, turn signal, marker, and license plate—and in many cases, a braking system. Good-quality components and careful installation are essential for safety and long trouble-free operation. Wires should be protected from mechanical abrasion, road splash, and other physical damage. It is important that there is a ground wire as part of the electrical system between the trailer and the towing vehicle; the coupler and hitch ball do not provide an adequate "return path" for electrical current. Connectors should be heavy-duty and waterproof.

All states require trailers to be equipped with signal, safety, and stop lights operated by the driver. State regulations vary, but generally trailers less than 6 feet 8 inches (2 m) wide need red reflector lights at the back combining stop,

Figure 7-33 *When being transported, a boat must be held firmly on the trailer so that it cannot shift or bounce on the bed. In storage at rest, tie-downs should be slacked off a bit to reduce any distorting strains on the hull.*

tail and, signal lights, along with a white license-plate light. Also required are yellow marker lights on each side of the frame, just ahead of the wheels. Trailers wider than 6 feet 8 inches must add a group of three red identification lights in the middle of the back cross frame, as well as an amber clearance light mounted on the front of each fender. It is often recommended that rear lights be mounted high—usually on a bar across the boat's transom—but in some jurisdictions this may not be acceptable.

While many trailers being built today are equipped with fully waterproof lights, many still have lights that are simply "submersible." That means the lights can be submerged in water and will drain on their own. Such lights, however, must be disconnected from the automobile—their power source—before boat launching time. Even with waterproof lights, disconnecting is always a good idea in order to rule out the possibility of any leaks or shorts in the wiring that could blow bulbs or fuses.

The standard trailer wiring harness, best installed by professionals but easy to repair in a pinch, is a four-prong connector with the green wire going to the right turn signal, yellow to the left, brown to tail lights, rear markers and rear side lights, and white to ground. That means left gets a combination of yellow and brown wires, while right gets a green and brown combination. Seven-wire harnesses are also available with a blue wire for trailer brakes or other extra equipment, red for charging batteries in the trailer or boat, and light green for backup lights.

Trailer builders suggest that you check your wiring for corrosion, bare wires, cracked insulation or other potential shorts at least twice a year; replace and repair any worn or damaged parts and apply waterproof grease to plug contacts and bulb bases to prevent corrosion. Check that all your lights are working before you head out onto the road, day or night.

Trailers are normally sold equipped with several light reflectors. Additional reflectors or reflecting tape may be added as deemed necessary by the owner.

Mast & Other Supports

Sailboat spars can be carried lashed to the boat's deck, on special brackets built onto sailboat trailers, or in custom-made crossbar brackets mounted on the deck or cabin-top. However, if the spars protrude aft beyond the boat's transom or outboard motor, the end of the spar must be marked with a red signal flag (and a light at night) for safety.

Trailer Accessories

The items and features discussed above can be considered "essentials"; there are many others that will add to the ease and convenience of using a boat trailer. There are nonskid walkways that can be attached to the frame (see **Figure 7-34**), allowing you to stay higher and drier during launching and recovery; guide posts, guide rollers, and padded bunk guides that help keep the boat properly aligned on a still-submerged trailer; and even waterproof lights that will light up the frame of a submerged trailer, making it an easier target in the dark.

There are a number of accessories available to help line up your hitch ball and trailer couple single-handed, including "aerials"—with balls

Figure 7-34 A walkway may be a part of a trailer, or it can be added. Extending along one or both sides of the trailer bed, it can make it easier to guide the boat when it is being launched or retrieved, and it can keep your feet dry, too.

and "guides" that lead the coupler toward the ball. With practice you should be able to park your hitch very close to the trailer coupler with great regularity.

One accessory, the dolly-style tongue jack, should be standard equipment for trailers. The jack, equipped with a wheel to allow the tongue and entire trailer to be moved by hand, is usually raised and lowered by a handle-operated worm gear; see **Figure 7-35**. It should have a pivot and pin that allow it to be flipped up out of the way once the trailer is hitched to the tow vehicle. The dolly wheel and the jack allow you to raise the trailer tongue above the level of the hitch ball, back the vehicle into place, then easily maneuver the coupler right into place, and drop it effortlessly onto the ball. A great advantage of this method is that it prevents bruised knuckles and fingers.

Regulations & Licensing

All trailers must be registered with state or provincial transport departments and must bear an affixed license plate. As long as the boat and trailer combined do not exceed 8 feet 6 inches (2.6 m) in width, about 75 feet (22.9 m) in length and 13 feet 6 inches (4 m) in height, no additional permits are needed. If you're hauling a double- or triple-axle trailer, though, you will have to pay more to use toll roads. However, keep in mind

that these are general guidelines,; for specifics, check your local authorities.

If you're planning to haul a rig larger than maximum dimensions, arrange for special permits: Contact state highway authorities in areas you wish to transit. These permits might differ from one state to the other.

Insurance

Know fully the status of your insurance coverage in regard to pulling a trailer with your car. Some automobile policies allow this, others do not, and some provide limitations on hauling a trailer. Check your policy carefully and, if necessary, consult your insurance agent. If an endorsement is needed, don't delay or neglect to get it, even at the cost of a small additional premium. *Be protected, especially in your liability coverage.*

TRAILER OPERATION

Safe, trouble-free trailering depends as much on proper preparations as on correct procedures when "on the road." Preparations are not complicated or difficult, but even a single item overlooked can make problems.

Loading the Boat for Travel

Store heavy items as low as you can, keeping the center of gravity as low as possible. All sharp

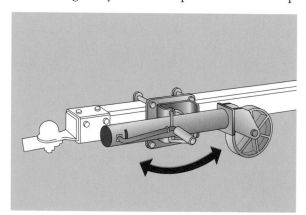

Figure 7-35 Using a dolly-style tongue jack is like having an extra person helping to move the trailer manually. It swings down to support the tongue, or up for traveling on the road. Some models remain vertical and are cranked up or down.

objects should be padded and propped in such a way that they will not shift should you have to jam on the brakes in an emergency, or inadvertently ride onto a curb. Whether or not the boat is covered by a tarp, any gear left inside (especially if it is light enough to be blown away) should be either stored in a locker or below decks or removed. Carefully secure any loose gear.

Also avoid the unnecessary weight of a full fuel tank, and carry empty water containers; you can easily fill up once you near or reach the launch area.

Balance the Boat Properly

Check the weight at the trailer tongue *after loading the boat with everything to be carried in it;* if necessary, shift gear and/or axle(s) as needed to achieve proper weight distribution. Tongue weight should be between 5 and 10 percent of GTW. With a small rig, the tongue weight can be determined using a bathroom scale; on heavier rigs, use a shipper's scale.

Too much weight applied on the tongue pushes down the back of the tow vehicle, forcing it to "squat." As well as putting undue strain on the vehicle's suspension, this can take needed weight off the tow vehicle's front wheels, making the vehicle hard to steer.

Too little weight on the tongue makes the trailer "tippy" and gives it the tendency to pull up on the tow vehicle. That makes the trailer unstable and more likely to swing from side to side or "fishtail."

The only proper way to balance a trailer is to move the axle(s) until the desired ratio is obtained. In balancing the whole rig, another very important guideline to consider is the gross axle weight rating (GAW), which is the maximum weight an axle is designed to carry, and is closely related to the tires; see **Table 7-2.** This figure includes the weight of the vehicle plus any load supported by the axle.

It is important never to exceed the GAW. This can be achieved by reading the appropriate figures on each of your tires; they will have a maximum for

Load Capacity of Trailer Tires

Tire Size	Ply Rating	Pounds of Tire Pressure (Measured Cold)											
		30	35	40	45	50	55	60	65	70	75	80	85
4.80/4.00 x 8	2	**380**											
4.80/4.00 x 8	4	380	420	450	485	515	545	575	**600**				
5.70/5.00 x 8	4		575	625	665	**710**							
6.90/6.00 x 9	6		785	850	915	970	1030	**1080**					
6.90/6.00 x 9	8		785	850	915	970	1030	1080	1125	1175	1225	**1270**	
20 x 8.00-10	4	825	**900**										
20 x 8.00-10	6	825	900	965	1030	**1100**							
20 x 8.00-10	8	825	900	965	1030	1100	1155	1210	1270	**1325**			
20 x 8.00-10	10	825	900	965	1030	1100	1155	1210	1270	1325	1370	1420	**1475**
480/4.00 x 12	4	545	550	595	635	680	715	755	**790**				
5.30/4.50 x 12	4	640	700	760	810	865	**915**						
5.30/4.50 x 12	6	640	700	760	810	865	915	960	1005	1045	1090	**1135**	
6.00 x 12	4	855	935	**1010**									
6.00 x 12	6	855	935	1010	1090	1160	1230	**1290**					
6.50 x 13	6	895	980	1060	1130	1200	**1275**						

Table 7-2 Figures in boldface are the maximum recommended inflation-load values for tires of each size at highway speeds. Axle loads are the sum of two tire loads.

single wheel and one for dual wheel. It cannot be stressed enough that these loads must never be exceeded per axle. To ensure safety, take your rig either to a transport company scale or the local highway trucker scale and ask them to give you a reading per axle.

Weight-distributing hitches spread the tongue weight among all trailer and vehicle wheels. Such hitches are generally used to handle heavy loads that would otherwise put too much weight in back of the vehicle, but must be approached with some caution. Trailer manufacturers warn that such hitches, if overloaded or improperly installed, can cause malfunctions or impairment in operation of hydraulic surge brakes.

Covering & Securing the Boat

A canvas or synthetic cover, fitted to cover the top of the boat neatly and fitted with a drawstring to pull it tight under the gunwales, will help keep highway grime off the boat. Such a cover, however, must be well secured to stay tied down on the road, and may require a web of extra covering ropes. Once your boat is loaded onto a trailer, with the bunks or rollers all making close contact with the hull, you must ensure that it is well secured before heading out onto the highway. (If a cover is to be used, put it on before fastening the tie-downs.) Most trailers are designed so that the boat can be secured with

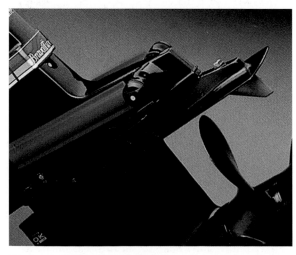

Figure 7-36 Trailering clips (seen in red above) are often available to protect stern-drive components while on short or long hauls.

a safety chain or U-bolt at the bow and two nylon-web tie-downs on the transom. The winch line attached to the boat's bow-eye should be tight, but you cannot count on it alone to hold the boat.

For a long highway trip, you may wish to secure the boat with additional tie-downs on each side of the boat, near the stern, where the engine—and most of the boat's weight—is located. These tie-downs must be padded when in contact with the boat. They act like sandpaper and actually can work their way through the gel coat and fiberglass; they also wear out the anodizing of the aluminum.

Powerboat lower units, outboard or inboard-outboard, are often best trailered and stored in the full-down position; check your owner's manual for your motor. If this doesn't allow enough clearance off the road, the engine or drive can be tilted up, and a wooden block wedged into the gap to take some of the strain. Also check your motor manual to determine optimum block placement. Also remember to remove the blocking before attempting to tilt the motor or stern-drive back down. Special accessories may be available to ensure safe travel of a stern-drive; see **Figure 7-36**.

A fixed-keel sailboat, with a high center of gravity, will obviously need to be well secured by a network of tie-downs to the sides, front and back of the trailer. The mast and boom can be set on pads and secured to the boat's deck, if it is flat enough, or in specially built cross-member frames that hold the mast level, allowing it to be secured above the boat's superstructure. Such a rig must be lower than the 13 feet 6 inches (4 m) height limit set by most states and provinces.

Use a Predeparture Checklist

It is an excellent idea to make a checklist, *and use it*. Such a list can be typed and then sealed in plastic; thus waterproofed it can be attached to the trailer tongue where it won't be overlooked; see **Figure 7-37**. Make it a habit to run through the checklist in the same sequence each time and you will never overlook any potential problem. See the sidebar "Using a Checklist," on pages 256-257.

Figure 7-37 Begin a trip only after all preparations have been made. Use a checklist to make sure that nothing is left undone. If traveling a long distance, plan on stopping at intervals to check tie-downs, wheel bearings, and all lights on the trailer.

A Final Check

Just before starting out on the road, make a final rundown of the checklist. Check all lights with someone in the car operating the switches for all the lights, depressing the brake pedal, and operating the turn signals. And don't forget to ask each member of the crew, "Have you forgotten anything?"

Driving with a Trailer

Driving and steering a vehicle with a 20- to 30-foot articulated extension is neither easy nor intuitive. There will be slower acceleration, passing will be more difficult, and more time and distance will be required for stopping. Although some drivers readily adjust, most need practical advice and practice. Practice in light traffic before taking to the crowded weekend highways. Perhaps the best and simplest advice is to *slow everything down.* Consider and plan your moves carefully, and remember that you cannot move as quickly in, for example, your van and boat-trailer combination as you would in your two-door coupe.

Safety First

The first rule in driving with a trailer behind is "No passengers in the boat." This practice is unsafe, and it is illegal in many jurisdictions. Do not even allow pets to ride in the trailer.

Drive as smoothly as possible—no sudden jerks in starting, and well-anticipated, easy stops. Jerks and sudden stops put added loads on the car-trailer connection, the boat itself, and the gear stowed in it. Avoid quick turns and sudden swerves; these can make the rig harder to handle.

Just as soon as you start out—before you leave your own property if possible—test your car's brakes and those of the trailer, if it is so equipped.

Attach big frame-mounted mirrors, if those are needed to see back past the boat and trailer; see **Figure 7-38.** Watch the trailer in the rearview mirrors as much as possible, and keep an ear out for the development of any unusual noises. If a car passes you with its driver or passengers making hand signals to you, pull off the road as soon as possible and check to see what might be wrong.

Observe all speed limits; these are sometimes less for cars with trailers, and for good reasons. Don't tailgate; your stopping distance is increased

Figure 7-38 Many boats are of such size or shape that they obstruct normal rearward vision. A large mirror on right side of the vehicle, as well as one on the left, overcomes this limitation.

Using a Checklist

Check the Boat

• Make sure that the outboard or stern-drive has adequate clearance from the road. As discussed above, check with the manufacturer for proper transport position: You may have to tilt the motor up as far as possible, and lock or tie it in order to relieve tilt mechanism strain.

• Check that all container lids and caps are secure—from fuel, water, and holding tank deck plates to two-stroke oil can caps. Protect loose containers from possible puncture. Should a spill occur, it should be restricted to the immediate area.

• Ensure that the battery is secure in its box and that the box is lashed down firmly.

• Check that the towing eye is secure and free of play.

• Remove all loose gear (antennas, flags, lines, cushions, etc.) from the deck and cockpit; store these items below.

• Take down any fabric top and side curtains; secure them against the winds of highway speeds.

• For safety during transport, remove a fire extinguisher from the boat and put it in the towing vehicle. This is especially recommended if the boat is covered, as a stray cigarette butt from a passing car could land on the cover and start a fire. (Don't forget to return the extinguisher to the boat before launching!)

Check the Trailer

• Ensure proper coupler function; a dab of oil or grease goes a long way in preventing rusting. Check the locking mechanism and have a security pin in place. A padlock can replace that pin to prevent theft.

• Check for proper tire pressure, including the spare tire. Grease wheels, using a grease gun if the trailer is equipped with bearing fittings. Check the sidewalls for cracks—if any are present, change the tires. Check the tightness of wheel lugs.

• Check rollers and bunks, and adjust for proper support of the boat.

• If the winch handle is removable, place it in the back of the car. If it is permanently mounted, check to see that the mounting nut is secure. Check the cable or strap in the winch drum—if frayed, it is unsafe. Make sure that the locking lever has a positive engagement; lubricate the mechanism.

• Check the wiring harness for either bare wires or nicks, and repair as necessary.

Check the Towing Vehicle

• Adjust tire pressure to manufacturer's recommendations. Check the spare tire at the same time.

• Check that your rearview mirrors on both sides are set properly for the best view of the boat.

• Check hitch installation and tightness of the ball mount.

• Check engine and transmission oil, and as well as radiator coolant. (Remember, these fluids will need to be working harder to accommodate the extra load).

• Check that all necessary tools and spare parts are stowed in the vehicle's trunk compartment.

Tie Everything Down

• Check your tie-downs; one nick in a strap or cable will greatly reduce its load rating.

• You need to take precautions against the boat shifting forward if you need to jam on the brakes. The boat should be secure against the bow chock on the trailer. Should there be a possibility that the bow of the boat may ride up the bow chock, add one or two other tie-downs from the eye to a strong point on the trailer.

• If you decide on extra side tie-downs, it is important that you prepare in three ways: First, use a piece of carpeting or custom sleeve fitted over the tie-downs to protect the boat against gel coat damage.

Second, avoid routing the straps over anything, such as a cleat, windshield, cushions, the plastic hatch cover, or a railing. Use a ratchet mechanism on the tie-down to tighten it, but don't overtighten. Remember that the tension that can be generated by a ratchet often equals the weight of the boat and can permanently damage any part of it.

Third, do your best to position the ratchet mechanism on the driver's side of the road for ease of checking through his mirror. This way, if a tie-down goes slack, the driver will be able to spot it.

• Avoid positioning a tie-down ratchet against or close to any part of the boat. The vibration generated by the wind pressure will cause knocking on the hull or part of the boat. This can result in a pitted patch of gel coat or aluminum. If you must, use padding under the ratchet device.

• Always tie loose end of a tie-down securely to any object; if the tie-down is left hanging, it will fly in the wind and fray to shreds.

• Make sure that all tie-downs are tight enough to prevent the boat from bouncing on the trailer, but no not too tight so as to distort the hull. The boat should travel with the trailer as one, with the trailer's suspension absorbing the shocks of the road.

Cover the Boat
Consider the following points when you are covering your boat for on-the-ground travel:

• Be sure the cover is snug and well tied. If it has a chance to flap in the wind, it will destroy itself. Dust, dirt, and rain must not be able to get under it.

• If you travel on dirt roads, cover the winch in order to reduce the possibility of grit and debris getting into the mechanism and damaging it.

Hooking Up
When hooking up your trailer to the tow vehicle, use the following checklist:

• Coat the hitch ball with a light coat of grease in order to reduce friction.

• After joining the coupler to the hitch ball, always make sure the coupler is tightened properly and locked according to its design; when in doubt, refer to the manufacturer's instructions.

• Connect the safety chains immediately, so they won't be forgotten. If they have an "S" hook, make sure that the open end of the hook goes up through and not down through; it will prevent it from bouncing off. A shackle is probably better. Cross your chains.

• Raise the tongue jack to its "on the road" position.

• If you have a weight-distributing hitch, be sure to set up the spring bars and adjust them so that the bars will level both the trailer and the tow vehicle. The tow vehicle should never squat.

• Systematically check that all lights on the trailer and tow vehicle, including the parking lights, turn signals, emergency flasher, brake lights, and license plate lights are in good working order.

• Finally, before leaving, make sure that you are carrying all necessary documentation, including your car, trailer, and boat registrations and proof of insurance, as well as any necessary road permits.

Figure 7-39 Keep in mind that boat tops are designed for cruising speeds on the water, not the rigors of high-speed roadway trailering. Take down any fabric top and side curtains and secure them so that they won't be damaged.

because of the trailer. When driving at highway speeds, allow more room between yourself and the vehicle in front than you normally would; this gives you plenty of time to slow down if the vehicle in front hits the brakes.

Use added caution in passing; remember that your overall length is twice as much as normal, or more, and your car will have to be well ahead of the passed vehicle before there is room for you to get back into your previous lane. Remember, too, that it will take longer for you to accelerate to passing speed. Keep in the proper lane; on multi-lane highways, this will normally be the right-hand lane. If there is only one lane in each direction, and traffic begins to pile up behind you, it is courteous and a contribution to safety to pull off the road (where you can safely do so), and let the faster traffic get past you. On multilane roads, signal well before you need to turn, and be sure that drivers in the other lane—who may be moving faster—have slowed down and are expecting your move. Even through you are already keeping a sharp lookout on the rearview mirrors, you will want to watch even more closely when changing lanes.

When turning left at an intersection, the boat will tend to follow the path of the tow vehicle as you'll have lots of room to make a smooth arcing turn. When turning right, into a right-hand lane, you may need to swing a bit wide into the left-hand lane in order to keep the trailer clear of the

right-side curb or the roadside margin—it can be embarrassing to bump the trailer tires up over the curb when turning a street intersection. With a turn in any direction, do not cut too closely; at worst, you could jack-knife the tow vehicle into the boat and trailer.

Be wary of parking lots or driveways that don't give you enough space to maneuver.

Stop & Check

On long highway trips at relatively high speeds, it is important to stop occasionally and see how the rig is traveling; see **Figure 7-39**.

You might stop after the first 1 or 2 miles (2–3 km), then again after about 50 miles (80 km), and then every 100 miles (160 km). The initial check is made soon after departure so that any small problem can be detected and corrected before it becomes a major one. Make each inspection a thorough one. Stopping intervals must, of course, be adjusted to the availability of suitable locations.

Inspection Procedure Follow a regular procedure on each check to make sure that nothing is overlooked. Check the hitch for tightness, and the safety chains for the right amount of slackness. Check tires visually; there is a normal amount of pressure build-up; don't bleed off air in the belief that it is excess. Feel all wheel bearings; warmth is acceptable, but if they are too hot to touch, you have a problem. Let them cool off and then drive as slowly as possible to a service station for disassembly and inspection. Be sure to check the cover and all tie-downs; take a look inside the boat at the stowed gear. Check all lights, especially stop and turn signals.

Check the car's tires and lights as part of your inspection. Car cooling systems are pressurized; do not remove the fill cap unless you know that there is trouble, and then do so very carefully (check the vehicle's operator manual).

When Conditions are Bad

Driving in rain, fog, or other conditions of reduced visibility is always a bit more hazardous; it is more so if you are pulling a trailer. Consider the added length of the trailer, and your less favorable acceleration and stopping characteristics. High winds, especially cross winds, present added hazards, and trailer rigs may be banned from some roads and bridges at these times.

Pulling Tandem-Axle Trailers

It has been found that the "following" characteristics of trailers with two axles can be improved in some cases by *not* inflating all four tires equally. If you are experiencing any weaving back and forth at highway speeds, try varying the tire pressures by 5 or 10 psi with the front wheels softer than the rear, or vice versa. No specific guidance can be given, except to try various combinations and check for either improved or worsened conditions.

At Your Destination

Upon arrival at your destination, take time to make an inspection similar to those you did en route. Even if tie-downs are to be removed soon, it is useful to know whether or not they have loosened. Likewise, check the hitch and chains. Hot wheel bearings, or even warm ones, should be allowed to cool before launching (see below). If bearings are really hot, it indicates a possible seizure problem that you should have corrected before starting home.

Maneuvering a Trailer while Backing

The guidelines below are intended to help hone your skills in negotiating a trailer. Along with practice, these will help you anticipate how both trailer and vehicle will behave, and to take the necessary actions required for safety.

Driving a trailer backward is trickier than going forward, and takes even more practice. If you're just starting out, try to find a large deserted parking lot—an office or mall parking lot on Sunday, for example—where you can practice backing in peace, without hazardous obstacles or curious onlookers. That way, you'll have plenty of confidence when you first pull up to a launching ramp. Remember that in backing up, the vehicle is pushing rather than pulling the trailer. That means, if you want the trailer to back straight, you have to keep the tow vehicle running exactly straight and aligned with it; see **Figure 7-40.**

• Turning the steering wheel right will turn the back of the tow vehicle right and the back of the trailer left. Moreover, if you keep going, the rig will jack-knife.

• When you want the boat to keep backing up to the left, you have to follow the trailer and swing the car around in an arc behind it, which means steering back in the opposite direction.

• Turning the steering wheel left swings the back of the tow vehicle left and moves the trailer sharply to the right.

• When you want to keep moving the trailer to the right without jack-knifing, you have to swing the steering wheel back to the right, bringing the tow vehicle roughly in a line with the arc of the trailer.

• The trick with backing up is to maneuver the trailer into the direction in which you want to move it, then follow it, driving either in a wide arc or straight back.

• When moving straight back, use a series of *shallow* S-shaped turns for "correction," to keep the rig moving straight.

Land Storage

Because most trailerable boats are stored on land between uses and during the off-season, such boats usually spend more time on a trailer bed than in the water. In addition to keeping both the trailer and boat in good repair, there are other guidelines for safe and careful storage of both, which are covered below.

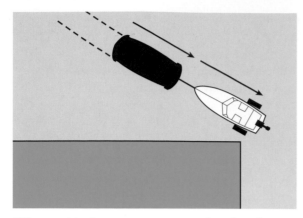

When positioning at a ramp, remember that the trailer always backs in the direction opposite to that of the car. As you approach in reverse, swing close to the ramp.

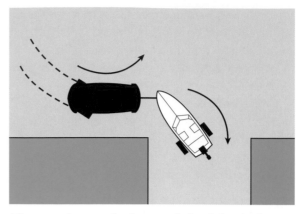

Then cut the car wheels toward the right. As the car swings slightly to the left, the trailer angles toward the ramp.

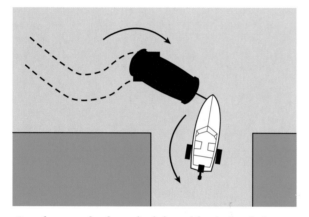

Cut the car wheels to the left and back slowly into the ramp as the trailer moves to the right.

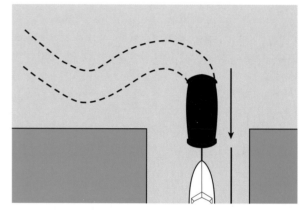

Finally, straighten the car wheels to follow the trailer as it backs straight down the ramp.

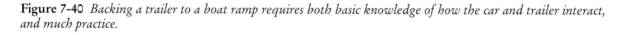

Figure 7-40 *Backing a trailer to a boat ramp requires both basic knowledge of how the car and trailer interact, and much practice.*

• **Protect Against Theft and Damage** You can create at least partial protection against the theft of your boat and its trailer by installing a special fitting that is secured to the trailer coupling with a keyed lock; see **Figure 7-41**. Remember, if they can't "hitch up," they can't haul it away.

When the car is not pulling the trailer, cover the hitch ball with an old, split-open tennis ball or a ball cover. This will prevent any grease on the ball from rubbing off on clothing and will provide some protection against rust. Some owners unbolt the ball from the hitch and store it in the trunk or in another protected spot (additional theft protection).

With a receiver-type of hitch, the shank can be removed and stored.

If your boat will be stored outside for an extended period of time, it is wise to remove the battery, electrical components, and even the motor—if possible—and store these items indoors for greater protection against both theft and corrosion.

• **Keep Water Out** Rainwater in the boat is undesirable for many reasons—mainly because water collection can rapidly increase weight on the trailer, often beyond its capacity. A cover is desirable, and should be supported so that pockets of rainwater cannot form, stretching the

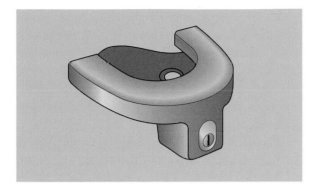

Figure 7-41 Locks for trailers parked without their towing vehicle can either be of the specialized type shown here, or of the padlock style.

fabric and breaking through it. Cross-supports under the cover and frequent fastening points around the edge will keep the cover sag-free; allow some "give" in the cover if the fabric is subject to shrinking when wet.

• **Drain Accumulating Water** Whether your boat is protected with a cover or not, the best way to get rid of accumulated water is to raise the tongue of the trailer, allowing water to run aft and out the drain hole. Crank down the parking wheel to raise the tongue, or, alternatively, block it up securely. Make sure the drain is *open*.

• **Ease Strains on the Hull** If tie-downs remain taut after over-the-road travel, slack them off or remove them. This will eliminate any strains and possible distortions to the hull that might occur during long storage periods.

• **Block Up the Trailer** If you do not expect to use your rig for several weeks or months, the trailer frame should be jacked up and placed on blocks in order to reduce the strain on springs and tires. Be sure to use enough blocking to prevent distortion of the trailer frame—which in turn could distort the hull of your boat.

The blocks need be just high enough to take the greater part of the load, but if the trailer wheels are clear of the ground, reduce air pressure in the tires by 10 to 15 psi. Remember that you must have means at hand to restore pressure when the blocks are later taken out for the next trip—do not deflate tires unless you can pump them up again right on the spot before starting off.

MAINTENANCE, TOOLS & SPARES

Boat trailers are often neglected, and of all their components their wheel bearings are the most critical. Trailers are frequently driven for long times on the highway, often loaded close to their limit. Then after a short, if any, rest period, they are immersed in water during launching and retrieval.

The water seeps into their wheel hubs because of the partial vacuum resulting from the cooling effect of the water on the hot metal. The water emulsifies the grease on the bearings, destroying its lubricating capabilities. If left unattended for any length of time, the water will corrode the bearings' rollers, resulting in grit in the mixture. Of all stranded trailers, wheel bearing failure is one of the principal causes.

Keep Tools Handy

When traveling, keep some tools handy for any of the most common incidents. Include the usual screwdrivers, pliers, and wrenches; wire cutters and strippers; hammer and small sledge hammer; tire pressure gauge; a small hydraulic jack; a lug wrench and a large wrench for the spindle nut; a grease gun loaded with axle grease; a good flashlight or electric lantern; a few rags, and last, but not least, some waterless hand cleaner.

Always keep a few spares on hand. Include a complete hub assembly (hub, pre-packed wheel bearings, seals, lug nuts, and cotter pins); a spare wheel with a mounted tire; a few feet of wire and some terminals; and a spare of each type of light bulb used on the trailer, plus a few fuses for the electrical system. Roadside flares or reflective warning triangles might come in handy and perhaps a 12-volt tire pump that connects to a battery.

Figure 7-42 Make prelaunch preparations well away from the ramp so as to help avoid delays and lengthy lines for ramp use.

• **Check the Rig Frequently** When your boat is stored and out of regular use, try to set up a schedule of weekly visits by yourself or someone else acting on your behalf. (Checking at the same time each week will help you remember to do so.) On each visit, thoroughly inspect the vessel for peeling paint and any other visible signs of physical deterioration. It is recommended that you take the necessary corrective action immediately, before any minor problems escalate into major ones.

LAUNCHING & RETRIEVING

Both launching a boat from its trailer and its retrieval (loading) are important skills. In each instance, the steps to be taken must be carefully planned and executed to avoid damage to the boat or motor, as well as injuries to people; see **Figure 7-42.**

Using a Ramp

Although a ramp is not the best way to get a boat into the water, it is the method used most often. Ramps vary widely in their characteristics—many are surfaced with concrete, while others are hard-packed dirt or sand, sometimes reinforced with wood or steel planking. Some ramps are wide enough for only one launching operation at a time; others can accommodate many rigs simultaneously.

The quality of a ramp depends on its slope, how far it extends into the water, and the condition of its surface. The angle of slope is not critical, but it should be deep enough so the trailer need not be backed down so far into the water that the wheel bearings of the tow vehicle become submerged.

If the slope is too steep, however, you may need an excessive pull to get a loaded trailer up and off the ramp. It is very important that the ramp extends far enough into the water that trailers can be backed down without running off the lower end, even in low water conditions. (Many surfaced ramps develop a sharp drop-off at their lower end; if the trailer has rolled past this point, getting trailer wheels back up over this lip can be a major problem.) A dirt or sand ramp must be firm enough to support the trailer and car or truck wheels. A surfaced ramp must not have a coating of slime that could make footing dangerous, and provide inadequate traction for the car.

Preparing for Launching

While the trailer's wheel bearings are cooling down (highly desirable), remove the boat cover,

Figure 7-43 Raising the mast of a sailboat can be trouble free if proper preparations are made. This trailer has rear guide posts and a built-in ladder at the bow hitch.

fold it, and store it in the car or boat. Tie-downs can be removed and stored in a safe place, but leave the winch line taut. If the outboard motor or stern-drive lower unit has been in the down position during trailering, tilt it up. If the trailer's lights will be submerged, disconnect the plug to the vehicle's electrical system.

If you are launching a sailboat, now is the time to untie the mast and rigging and proceed to hoist the mast. On most trailerable sailboats, hoisting the mast is more easily done on land than when afloat; see **Figure 7-43.**

Remove or relocate equipment stowed in the boat so that the boat will trim properly when launched. If the fuel or water tanks are empty, or only partially filled, it may be most convenient to top them up now, unless there is a fuel pier nearby.

Use Two Lines
Ensure adequate control of the boat by using two lines. Attach both a bow and a stern line; a boat cannot be adequately controlled by a single line. If you are planning to move the boat to a pier or seawall once it is in the water, put in place any fenders that might be needed.

"Preview" the Launching
Study the ramp and surrounding water area for any hazards, such as a slippery or too-short surface; estimate the wind and current effects; see **Figure 7-44.** If in doubt, as mentioned above, don't hesitate to ask another skipper who has just launched or retrieved a boat. If you have time, it is useful to watch the launching operation of others, noting any peculiarities of a ramp that is new to you.

Now check the drain plug, if one is used. (Occasionally even an experienced skipper launching a boat suffers the embarrassment of water pouring in the drain.) Look about to make sure that no item of preparation has been forgotten, then *check the drain plug again.*

Launching the Boat
Line up the car and trailer so that the backing process will be as straight and as short as possible; see **Figure 7-45.** (If you have a rear-wheel-drive car, it might be advantageous to use a secondary

hitch on the front of the vehicle for maneuvers on the ramp.) On a wide ramp, give due regard to others and don't take up more than your share of space.

Back the rig down, preferably to the point where the trailer tires—but not the axle bearings—are in the water. Next, set the parking brake on the towing vehicle; for added safety, block a wheel on each side of the vehicle. Then have one person man the winch controls, while one or two other helpers take the bow and stern lines; see **Figure 7-46.**

Release the trailer tilt latch, if it is of this type. Tighten the winch brake and release the anti-reverse lock. *Do not,* under any circumstances, disconnect the winch cable from the boat. At this stage, a craft should slide easily off the trailer, its

Figure 7-44 Make sure that you have inspected the ramp before you line up to use it; make any last minute checks. If you are not familiar with the ramp, take time to talk to someone who has just used it and learn of any peculiarities or problem aspects.

Figure 7-45 Line up the car and trailer, then back the rig down the ramp as described in the text.

Figure 7-46 While a crewmember disconnects the bow hitch cable, one or two others control the boat with lines attached at the bow and stern.

Figure 7-47 Make sure that one or two crewmembers have hold of the bow and stern lines before giving the boat a light push to float it off the trailer.

Figure 7-48 Make the boat fast temporarily while parking the vehicle and trailer. In this illustration, the trailer is still in the water showing how far it needs to enter the water in order to launch the boat.

speed controlled by the winch brake; in some instances, a push or two may be needed to get it started; see **Figure 7-47.** Be sure that the motor is tilted up so the propeller and skeg will not dig into the bottom as the boat slides down.

When the boat is floating free of the trailer, unhook the winch line. Move the boat aside and make it fast to a pier, beach it, or otherwise secure it temporarily; see **Figure 7-48.** Return a tilted trailer bed to a horizontal position, and latch it in place. The winch line may be rewound on the drum if desired, or secured by catching the hook on a rear member of the trailer frame and taking up the slack.

Remove the blocks from the towing vehicle's wheels, and drive the vehicle to an authorized parking area—be sure to give consideration to others by clearing the ramp promptly, and selecting a parking spot that will neither take up unnecessary space nor block others from using the ramp. If it is possible, hose down with fresh water any parts of the trailer that got wet during a launch into salt water.

Use a padlock on the coupling or safety chain to prevent theft of the trailer. Place the chocks at the wheels of the trailer if it is detached from the car and if the parking area has any slope.

At the boat, lower the outboard motor or stern-drive unit to its operating position, and connect the fuel line if necessary. Complete any preparations needed for getting underway—transferring equipment to the boat from the car for example. Then load up your crew, and clear away from the launching area as rapidly as can be done with safety.

Reloading on the Trailer
Beach the boat or make it fast to a pier, and get the car and trailer from the parking area. If the boat will not be used in the next day or so, it is a good idea to disconnect the fuel line of an outboard motor while it is running at a fast idle. Let it run until all the fuel in the motor is used up; this will help prevent the formation of gum and deposits in the carburetor and fuel lines.

Back the trailer to the water's edge; make sure that the electrical plug at the vehicle is discon-

Figure 7-49 Except for dealing with the mast, launching and retrieving a sailboat are identical to the processes for a powerboat. Always be sure to check carefully for any overhead power lines, and use great care if there are any nearby.

nected. Set the towing vehicle's brakes and block the wheels. If the trailer bed tilts, release the latch and push the frame into the "up" position. Then tilt up the boat's motor or stern-drive unit, and work the boat into position to move onto the first rollers, with the keel of the boat in line with the trailer.

As with launching, both a stern and bow line help in boat maneuvering during reloading. It may be possible for one of the crew to wade into the water to guide the boat into position. (You can keep your feet dry by using a walkway installed on the trailer frame; refer to **Figure 7-34.**) Run out enough winch cable to engage the hook in the boat's stem eye; be careful to watch out for kinks in the cable and remember never to handle a steel wire line except with gloves.

Crank in the winch line and the boat should come onto the trailer bed; a tilted frame will come down to the horizontal position by itself when the boat moves up it; see **Figure 7-49.** Often a winch has a higher-speed mode that is useful to get the boat started onto the trailer, and a more-powerful mode when the pull gets more difficult.

Do not allow anyone to be in line with the winch cable. A cable under load may snap like a rubber band when it breaks, and can throw a hook or fitting great distances; so *keep clear.*

When the boat is fully onto the trailer, latch down the tilt mechanism (if it is of this type), remove the wheel blocks, and move the rig clear from ramp so others can use it. Do not overlook the other preparation required for road travel, but move away from the launch area to do them. It is always desirable to hose off the boat with fresh water, but this is especially necessary if it was used in saltwater; *this should be done as soon as possible after reloading—do not wait until you get home.*

Launching & Retrieving by Crane

The use of a crane or traveling lift with padded slings is the launching method that is probably the easiest on the boat. When it is exercised with care, this method of launching minimizes strains on the hull; see **Figure 7-50.**

Although the slings are usually provided by the crane operator, check to make sure that these are of adequate strength before entrusting your boat to them. You also should be familiar with the

Figure 7-50 Where a ramp is not available, a crane or traveling lift can be used to lift a boat from its trailer and lower it into the water.

proper placement of slings so as to ensure a safe balance for your boat—your dealer should be able to provide you with this information.

While the boat is in the slings, use both bow and stern lines to control any swinging motion during transit from the trailer to the water, or vice versa.

Clean Your Boat & Trailer

Whether you use a ramp or a crane, fresh water or salt, it is essential that you clean your boat and trailer before you leave the area where the craft was removed from the water. The waters of the United States and Canada are seriously infested with "invasive nuisance" species of aquatic weeds and animals. The most widely publicized of these is probably the zebra mussels (*Dreissena polymorpha*) now spreading from the Great Lakes into the waters of many states and provinces, but there are many others—a recent appearance of giant salvina (*Salvinia molesta*), an invasive aquatic fern, is causing major environmental damage in many areas. These infestations are of major concern as they crowd out desirable native plants and fishes, and cause damage to vessels and shore installations.

Boaters who do not thoroughly wash down their craft and trailers are guilty of spreading undesired and harmful plants, shellfish, and even fish. All mud and plants must be removed before starting out on the road.

SMALL BOAT HANDLING

Although boat handling of outboard and stern-drive craft is covered in Chapter 6, there are some details that specifically relate to lighter, trailerable craft. We will deal with those concerns in this section.

Although the vast majority of trailerable boats have wheel steering, some are equipped with outboard motors with tiller handles. The operator sits in the stern of the boat and pushes the tiller handle away from the direction of the intended turn. On the smallest outboards, reverse is achieved by rotating the engine 180°.

The smaller the boat in relation to the size of the engine, the more you will feel the effect of the engine's torque. In proportion to the engine's force, the boat will tend to heel to one side as a reaction to the powerful spin of the propeller. A propeller with more pitch will tend to "walk" sideways as it achieves higher speeds in the water.

Trim

Remember that the number of seats in a boat is not an indication of the number of persons that it can carry safely. Overloading is a major cause of boating accidents, so stay within the true limits of your craft (check the official capacity plate). The factors affecting trim become increasingly critical as the load approaches the boat's capacity, and also as boat size decreases.

Before getting underway, trim your boat as well as possible, as shown in **Figure 7-51.** In smaller craft it is dangerous for passengers to change places or to move about while the boat is moving along briskly. If such movement becomes essential, slow or stop the boat first. (In rough water remember to maintain sufficient momentum to retain steerage control, and to keep the boat headed into wind and waves.) Anyone moving must keep low and near the boat's centerline.

Stability

Since outboard-powered craft are often operated at relatively high speeds, their stability becomes an important safety issue. Some hulls will run straight ahead quite steadily, but have a tendency to heel excessively, or even flip over, when turned sharply.

The underwater shape of the hull is a key factor in stability. Today, most outboard and stern-drive boats are of deep-V or modified-V form, or of the multiple-hull cathedral type; refer to Chapter 1, **Figure 1-12.** These designs provide a higher degree of stability in normal operation; however, they resist turning—attempts to make a sharp turn at high speed may cause broaching (uncontrolled turning broadside to the seas or to the wind). This is also the case with some older, flat-bottom hull forms that have keels to provide directional stability.

Conversely, a flat-bottom boat without a keel has little directional stability, and may skid out sideways when a turn is attempted at excessive

Proper lateral trim is important for safety.

If the load is concentrated to port, the boat might capsize in a tight left turn or if hit by a wave or wake.

Overload forward causes boat to "plow." Running with the bow down may allow the boat to dig into an oncoming wave.

Overload aft causes boat to "squat," placing the transom dangerously low to the water.

Distribute passengers and gear so the boat is level; fore-and-aft trim is important for best performance and comfort.

Figure 7-51 *The proper trim of a small boat make for both safer and more efficient operation.*

speed. Initially the boat will point off in the new direction, but actually will continue to travel along what is essentially its old track.

In any case, the faster a boat goes, the more important it is to reduce speed to a safe level before starting a turn; never turn more sharply than necessary Normal operation seldom requires a sudden, sharp, high-speed turn.

Reversing

Most outboard motors have a reverse gear that enables them to be backed down. Unless restrained, an outboard motor has the tendency to tilt itself up and out of the water when thrust is reversed. On many models, there is a manually operated reverse lock that must be latched into place to keep the motor down while engaged in

Figure 7-52 An inflatable boat combines lightness of construction with a safe, wide platform and soft contours. Many have a rigid hull beneath the side tubes for better speed and control.

backing maneuvers. For normal running, however, it is important that this latch be released so that the lower unit will be free to tilt up if it strikes an underwater obstruction.

INFLATABLE BOATS

Inflatable boats are constructed of air-filled tubes, with flexible or rigid floors. The transoms and seats are built of wood, metal, or fiberglass.

These highly stable platforms have found widespread acceptance as dinghies for larger craft, dive boats, workboats, and all-around recreational boating. The material used to build most inflatables is high-strength woven polyester or nylon fabric that is impregnated with flexible but durable "plastomer" coatings. The inside layers of some inflatables are made of neoprene—a stretchy but airtight rubberlike material expanded with air; see **Figure 7-52.**

Inflatables are stable, unsinkable when inflated, and capable of carrying great weights; many of them also have the advantage of collapsing into small, portable packages. Although most models are difficult to row, inflatables are easily driven by outboard motors. Because they are made of fabric that is subject to abrasion and wear, care should be taken during use and while being inflated and deflated.

Types

The traditional inflatable dinghy or tender was built with plywood floors and inflatable tube seats and controlled by a tiller-mounted outboard. Inflatables are now available with more sophisticated accommodations such as remote-control consoles with rigid seats and even "radar-arch" bars for mounting radio antennas and lights. The flat-bottom inflatable hull has given way to a wide variety of hull shapes, including inflated V-hulls and V-hulls with inflated "sponsons." Some very rigid inflatable floors are also available.

Rigid-hull inflatable boats (RHIBs or RIBs) combine the stability and sea-keeping ability of regular inflatables with the speed and handling capability of regular V-hulls. Because of the hulls' added strength and stiffness they can carry more powerful motors; rigid seats, consoles or storage areas can also be added. Most RIBs are, in fact, small fiberglass V-hulls surrounded by inflatable tubes. Strength can be built into the boat and the stability for which inflatables are known is available when needed—while the boat is operating at slow speeds or at rest—but the V-hull comes into play when the boat is on plane and running at speed. While traditional inflatables are usually deflated and disassembled for travel, rigid inflatables are normally left inflated and carried on a bunk-style trailer.

Inflatables need lower horsepower to perform the same work as heavier types of boats; overpowering an inflatable adversely affects maneuverability and balance. Be sure to check the height of the motor to reduce excessive spray around the engine while underway.

Towing

Inflatables being towed behind larger boats should have all loose equipment removed. The tow should be from "tow" rings—usually installed by the manufacturer—mounted on the forward underside of the inflatable's bow area. From these tow rings, a bridle should be created, centered forward of the inflatable's bow.

A popular position for towing inflatables with sailboats and slower powerboats is snugged up against the transom of the tow vessel. With faster powerboats, a dinghy is normally towed astern on a longer line; to reduce strain on the line, it should ride on the forward side of a stern wave. Note that using three-strand nylon lines for towlines (or trailer tie-downs) is not recommended. This type of line, with exposure to sun and salt, can be quite abrasive, and constant rubbing against the inflatable can cause damage. Braided lines of polyester or polypropylene are the best choice because they float; a few floats of the type often used in swimming pool can be strung along the towline at intervals to aid in preventing the line from becoming fouled in propellers and rudders.

Maintenance

Most manufacturers of inflatable boats recommend mild detergent cleaners. Mild abrasive scrubbers will help remove serious grime. Minor cuts and abrasions can be repaired using sandpaper, cleaner, glue, and a patch. Extensive repairs should be done by a professional.

Like other boats, inflatables will grow barnacles or become coated with scum if left in the water unprotected. A special anti-fouling paint is available for them. A properly inflated RIB will be rigid in the water and will not sag or flex with the waves; the operating pressure of a properly inflated boat varies among manufacturers.

Since wet wood will eventually warp and rot, wood components of any model need regular painting and varnishing. Also, metal components should be kept clean and free from corrosion. Valves should be cleaned once or twice a year, or monthly if the boat is regularly inflated and deflated. Valve cleaning should be done with mild soapy water and an old toothbrush. Check the O-rings; if cracked or pitted, they permit air leakage and should be replaced. Do not use petroleum jelly, silicones, or petroleum distillates on the valves. Clean the boat fabric with mild soapy water at least twice a year with the floor system removed and the bilge well cleaned. As for fiberglass components, treat them as any other fiberglass item, with regular compounding and waxing.

JET-DRIVE BOATS

Various boats, ranging from planing to displacement-type hulls, and from small "personal watercraft" (PWCs) to very large yachts, use water jet propulsion; see **Figure 7-53.** Although handling characteristics can differ significantly depending on the boat, the major features of a jet boat include the following:

• Instant response in accelerating, stopping, or making any sort of turn.
• Low drag because of the lack of appendages.
• Shallow draft.
• Safety around people in the water.
• Absence of hull vibration or torque effects, which eliminates high-speed cavitation.

The principle of operation is borrowed from aircraft jet propulsion. Rather than having a traditional propeller immersed below the hull, the water jet system draws water through an intake duct and debris screen fitted flush to the bottom of the hull. A high-performance axial flow impeller pumps high volumes of water, discharging it via a nozzle projecting through a sealed transom opening. This results in a powerful forward thrust. Steering is normally accomplished by swiveling the jet stream from side to side; occasionally, there will be a pivoting deflector blade in the jet stream. There are some models of outboard motors that have a jet-drive lower unit rather than a conventional propeller drive.

Figure 7-53 Jet-drives are most often seen on personal watercraft (PWCs), but they are also used on small "jet boats" where the operator and passengers are inside a hull, and occasionally on large fast yachts.

Jet-drive craft have no steering capability if there is no jet discharging. Reverse is achieved by lowering a deflector or "clam shell" to divert the flow of water forward. If done suddenly on a small boat, it stops the boat in its own length—a maneuver that should not be done at high speed because of possible injuries to the operator and any passengers, and/or somersault of the light craft. Because there is no gearbox, shifting from forward to reverse at any speed does not overload the engine—only the direction of the external water stream is altered in stopping or reversing. The pivot point of a light displacement jet boat can be as little as two feet forward of the jet nozzle. Without rudder or lower unit drag, sharp turns can be made; it is possible to reverse course in little more than the boat's length. Getting into a tight space at a pier can be accomplished by using short bursts of power alternatively in forward and reverse.

Jet-drive boats with the best handling characteristics are those designed specifically for this means of propulsion. Their hulls are designed to ensure that the aerated water from the bow wave does not enter the jet, thus avoiding the creation of slip and minimizing power loss.

Personal Watercraft

A personal watercraft (PWC) is a common introduction to boating for young people. Because such craft sometimes use the same waters as other powerboats, it is important that boaters be informed about their use and about how to avoid collision.

A personal watercraft is classified by the U.S. Coast Guard as a "Class A Inboard Boat" and is subject to the same laws and requirements as conventional boats. According to the Navigation Rules, there is no difference between operating a personal watercraft and any other craft. As skipper of a PWC, you are operating a highly maneuverable type of boat, but you have the same privileges and obligations as the operator of any other vessel. With no navigation lights installed, a personal watercraft *may not be used after dark*.

Remember that both the owner and the skipper are responsible for the safety of

Personal Watercraft Operation: Do's & Don'ts

• Do know how to swim, but always wear a PFD. Always attach the throttle safety lanyard to your vest before starting the engine.

• Do go slowly until you are in a clear area.

• Do make sure you can be seen at all times.

• Do have available an up-to-date chart of the waters where you are intending to go boating.

• Do check for, and obey, "no wake" signs.

• Do look behind you for traffic as you prepare for each turn.

• Do keep a substantial distance between your watercraft and every other person or craft in or on the water.

• Do avoid ship channels whenever possible; if absolutely necessary, cross them vigilantly and quickly.

• Do operate courteously. Showing respect to others will help maintain a high public regard for your sport. Keep in mind that only a few irresponsible operators can lead to restrictive local regulations that may reduce your chances to fully enjoy your craft.

• Do slow down and be extra cautious on your way home. Numerous studies have shown that fatigue caused by the glare, motion, noise, and vibration during a day on the water will reduce your reactions to nearly the same level as if you were legally intoxicated.

• Do *not* speed in congested areas.

• Do *not* speed in fog or stormy conditions.

• Do *not* come too close to another vessel.

• Do *not* engage in wake-jumping— crossing close astern of larger boats underway.

everyone on board, as well as any damage that may occur from the PWC's wake—an important consideration when lending or borrowing such a craft. Manufacturers recommend that no privately owned PWC be operated by anyone below the age of 14 or rented to anyone below the age of 16. There may be state or local age restrictions; these will vary from one jurisdiction to another.

WATERSKIING

Since every boater is likely to encounter water-skiers at one time or another while underway—or to participate in the sport—a mention of water-skiing is relevant in terms of safety. This brief coverage of the subject is intended to help the boater anticipate dangerous situations and to respond quickly and effectively.

The Boat

Waterskiing doesn't require a large boat with a high-powered engine. Although tournament and show skiers use very sophisticated equipment, the average skier can use the family boat, whether outboard, inboard or stern-drive. Although it is possible to ski behind a boat as small as a personal watercraft—and even behind an inflatable with a 20-hp (14.7 kW) engine—the normal length is 14 to 20 feet (4.3 to 6.1 m). It is generally accepted, though, that 75 hp (55 kW) is approximately the minimum size for a tow motor. The most important factor is the size of the engine: It must be more powerful than the required minimum for the activity. Otherwise, the waterskiing can overload the motor, reducing its useful lifespan.

When pulling skiers, it is important to maintain constant speed—ideally using a speedometer and/or a tachometer to ensure that the engine won't exceed its maximum rpm. To achieve maximum efficiency when towing skiers, using a smaller pitch propeller will help to keep the power to its maximum in the ranges of speed used. Top-end speed may be lower but acceleration will be better. The towline for the skier must be mounted either on a high point inside the transom on a post called the "pylon" or on a bridle attached at two points through-bolted on the stern that are designed for this purpose. Never tie to one corner only; this could cause a small boat to upset and greatly hinder maneuverability on larger boats.

Since verbal communication between the skier and the boat's crew is difficult if not impossible, it is essential that a universally accepted group of signals be used. Using the observer as a intermediate to the driver, the skier is able to communicate his wishes by these gestures, shown below; see **Figure 7-54.**

Safe Waterskiing: Do's & Don'ts

• Do learn good swimming skills. This is important for the skier and for the boat's crew.

• Do wear a PFD that is secure, durable, and is not too bulky or awkward.

• Do familiarize yourself with safe boating procedures (refer to Chapter 3). Although most boating fatalities result from collision, capsizing, or falls overboard, with personal watercraft and waterskiing, falling overboard is often considered part of the fun.

The Skier

• Do learn about waterskiing from a qualified instructor.

• Do make yourself visible if you fall in waters where traffic exists. Hold a ski halfway up to alert boats nearby.

• Do *not* put any part of your body through the bridle or place the handle behind the neck or knees. A fall in this position has the potential for serious injury.

• Do insist on having a competent observer in addition to the driver—someone who is appointed to watch the skier at all times and report to the driver of the boat. That observer should be able to physically assist the skier in case of need. Above all, the lookout should remember that objects and other boats present the greatest danger. Be aware that an observer is a legal requirement in most states.

• Do *not* dry land at a dock or beach. Any error in judgment could result in an injury.

Safe Operation of Small Craft

A carefully matched boat, motor, and propeller, operated in accordance with the law and with courtesy, will go a long way toward eliminating many accidents and worries. But some possibility for trouble always exists; the wise boater should be prepared to act in an emergency. Much of the information listed below is of particular interest to small boat and personal watercraft operators as well as waterskiers. Refer also to Chapters 11 and 12 for more extensive safety-on-the-water and emergency information.

Common Causes of Accidents Involving Small Craft

- Overloading, overpowering, and improper trim.
- High speed turns, especially in rough water.
- Failure to keep a lookout for obstructions and other boats.
- Going out in bad weather (or not starting for shelter soon enough when weather starts turning bad).
- Standing up in a moving boat.
- Having too much weight too high in the boat, such as when someone sits on the deck of a small outboard.
- Leaks in the fuel system.
- Going too far offshore.

Safe Operating Procedures

- **Allow no one off the bow.** A crewmember who slips off the boat may be run over by the boat before the skipper can take action.
- **Stand clear of hazards.** Strong river or tidal currents around large objects, such as moored barges and vessels, can create a hazard for small boats, which can be pulled beneath the surface. Give such situations a wide berth.
- **Slowing and stopping.** Watch your own stern wave; it could overtake you and swamp your boat.

- **Fuel consumption.** There is no excuse for running out of fuel. Keep tanks near full and know the fuel consumption on a per-hour or per-mile basis. Always plan for a reserve of at least one-third of your total capacity.
- **Leave word behind.** If you are going offshore or for a long run on inland waters, or even just fishing some distance away from home, tell someone ashore what your plans are, giving as much detail as possible (Chapter 11).
- **Watch the weather.** The smaller the boat, the more vulnerable it is to approaching bad weather. Take early evasive action; head for safe waters while there is ample time. Always keep an eye on the weather.
- **Carry distress signals.** Even though the size of your craft might not warrant the need to carry emergency equipment and flares during the day, it is nevertheless good practice to carry some in case you are delayed or stranded. Learn the proper emergency procedures.
- **Watch for squalls and storms.** If you get caught in bad weather, the information included in Chapter 10 is good even for small craft. The basic safety rules apply: Everyone should wear a PFD. Go slowly. Check your weight distribution. If the motor quits, keep the bow to the waves. Don't let water accumulate in the boat.
- **Know what to do if you capsize.** Unless your life is threatened, stay with the boat, which is easier to spot than a swimmer alone. All small boats built after July 1973 must carry flotation to keep them upright.
- **Know what to do in case of accident.** If you are involved in a boating accident, you are required to stop and help if you can without endangering your boat or passengers. You must identify yourself and your boat to any person injured or to the owner of the property damaged. See Chapter 12 for information on reporting accidents and recovery procedured.

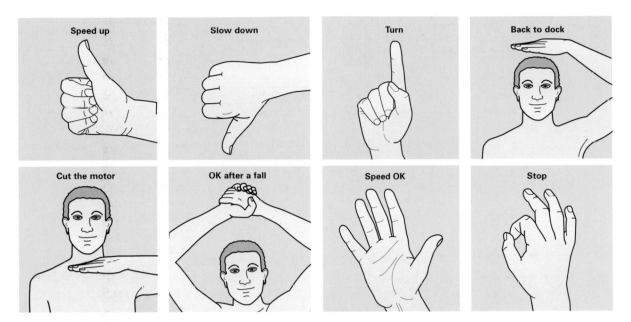

Figure 7-54 Since verbal communication between the skier and the towing boat crew is difficult, if not impossible, it is essential that hand signals be used. It is helpful if a standardized, universally accepted system of signals is employed. Using an observer as an intermediary to the boat driver, the skier is able to communicate his status or wishes by these gestures

The Boat Operator

• Do always look ahead. Plan your speed and turns according to the skier's ability.

• Do return quickly to a fallen skier.

• Do *not* drive on any course that could jeopardize the skier's safety—for example, when circling closely to follow a skier, a boat could inadvertently strike the skier if he or she should fall.

Both Skier & Boat Operator

• Do check equipment regularly, especially before skiing; skis with nicks could cut or scrape skin. Make sure ski lines are free of tangles, loops and knots.

• Do *not* ski in shallow water—water less than about 6.5 feet (2 m) deep.

• Do *not* ski at night (established as being from one hour after sunset until sunrise).

• Do *not* ski near boats, docks or swimming, scuba diving, sailing and fishing areas. Also avoid close proximity to the shore, stationary objects, narrow channels and harbors, and busy areas.

• Do *not* prevent people on shore, or other boaters, from enjoying the peacefulness of open waters and beaches. Noise carries farther over the water than on land, particularly when it is otherwise quiet. Remember that early morning and late afternoon are times when many boaters value quiet most. When waterskiing or operating PWC at high speeds, stay away from anchorages, shoreline areas with homes, campgrounds, and other places where people go for peace and quiet.

Seamanship Under Sail

*How a Boat Sails • The Parts of a Sailing Rig • Basic Sail Trim • The Points of Sailing
Tacking • Jibing • Docking Under Sail • Anchoring & Mooring Under Sail
Sail Handling & Storage • New Sailboat Types*

Sailing is an old and complex art—sailors can spend a lifetime at it and still find that there is more to learn. It is also a simple and enjoyable activity. A beginning sailor can have a fine time in a sailboat on his or her first day out, provided a few precautions are observed regarding the weather and safety on the water.

Experienced powerboat people, as well as those new to watersports, are taking up sailing in increasing numbers. While most of the seamanship and piloting chapters in this book apply equally to sailboats and powerboats, there are terms used specifically on sailboats and special equipment used to accomplish many sailing seamanship maneuvers.

HOW A BOAT SAILS

The art of sailing, one of the oldest studies in the world, has been joined by the science of sailing with its complex laws of physics and the lofty mathematics that describe them. Fortunately, along with the wind tunnels, sensing devices, and computers that confront us with all of sailing's complexity has come technology that has broadened the methods and materials we use to build and sail boats. The improvement in construction and safety of sailboats is obvious—and no less so the ability of modern sailors to take advantage of it—but both the art of sailing and the science of sailing are very much works in progress.

While sailors can take heart that the underlying physical phenomena can be used without being completely understood, it should be noted that sailing has been studied assiduously for centuries. The interaction of the wind, water, hull, sails, and keels—to say nothing of the involvement of sailors—is complex, often simultaneous, and indeed, at times invisible and even intuitive. But each progression in its under standing has led to easier and faster ways to sail.

Keep in mind that while the following discussion of how and why a boat sails is broken into sections so as to be intelligible, the elements that are discussed in isolation are in fact seldom isolated. On a sailboat, little happens that doesn't have an effect on everything else.

Bending the Flow

Sails extract energy from the flow of air (the wind) by bending as it goes by. This is true of every kind of sail, ancient or new, and it is true whether the sail is moving across the wind, or being blown along with it. As they create a driving force, or lift, from the wind, sails also create a small amount of drag—the smaller the better.

The underwater surfaces of a boat, whether they are the carefully shaped hulls and highly efficient fins of racing yachts, or old-fashioned cargo hulls, also act as foils bending the flow of water that passes around them. The interesting thing about sails ("airfoils") and keels ("hydrofoils") is that, while they are in one sense opposite, the principles that govern them are the same.

Push Equals Shove

A sailboat hull, driven by aerodynamic forces, accelerates until resistance from various forms of drag, both aero- and hydrodynamic, equals the driving forces. At that moment, the sailboat stops accelerating and travels at a constant speed—constant, that is, until something changes. This equalization of driving and dragging forces may be short-lived as the boat sails into a changing wind, is buffeted by waves, or when the delicate flow patterns are disturbed by its crew. Of course, if sailing carefully, the crew is trying to upset the equalization in favor of the driving forces—trying

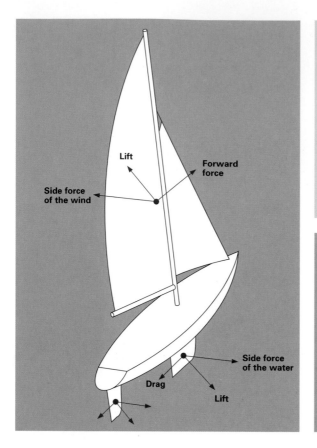

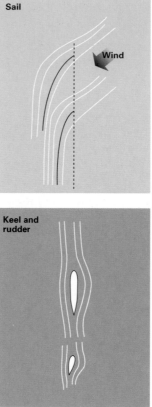

Figure 8-01 The sails and underwater surfaces of a boat both act as foils. The sails bend the flow of air over their surfaces, converting some of its energy into forward and lateral motion ("lift"), and some into drag. At the same time, water flowing past the hull and its appendages produces lift to windward, as well as drag.

to make the boat accelerate. When the crew is successful, a larger drive is soon countered by a larger drag and, once again, the boat settles into a "steady state"—but at a higher speed.

Airfoils vs. Hydrofoils

Sailboats and airplanes bear some kinship because both depend on a careful use of fluid motion over curved surfaces. But a sailboat operates within two fluid media—air and water, whereas an aircraft operates in only one. The airplane's airfoils (wings) pull in one direction—upward.

The sailboat's foils pull in nearly opposite directions—the sails to leeward and the keel to windward; see **Figure 8-01,** left. Each depends on the other to make the sailboat work—to make it move. Sails could not extract energy in any useful way without the work of the keel, and the keel could not do its work if the boat were not being pushed; see **Figure 8-01,** right.

Historically, the airfoils on a sailboat (its sails) have received a lot more attention than the hydro-

foils. Designers have developed complicated ways to make them more efficient over a range of wind speeds by changing their shape and their angle to the hull. On the other hand, hydrofoils have been left pretty much on their own while the boat is underway. But this is changing. Designers are now finding ways to modify the shape and orientation of fin keels too, as any America's Cup spectator knows.

Bernoulli's Discovery

In the early 1700s, the Swiss scientist Daniel Bernoulli established that changing the velocity of flow of a fluid, such as air or water, at a specific point brings about a consequent inverse change in pressure at the same point. Bernoulli's law led to its application in the venturi effect—such as when the flow of a fluid in a tube is constricted resulting in increased velocity and decreased pressure—and the development of the curved foil. The most convincing demonstration of the venturi effect is easy to perform in the kitchen. First, run a stream of water from the faucet. Then, dangle a soup-spoon by the tip of its handle and move its convex surface slowly toward the stream. Rather than being pushed away, as your intuition might suggest, it is pulled into the stream.

Action of Flow Over Foils

The most familiar practical application of the venturi effect is seen in the behavior of an airfoil, such as an airplane wing. As the aircraft moves along a runway, the induced airflow (from the plane's motion) separates as it strikes the leading edge of the wing. The velocity of the airflow forced to travel over the airfoil's convex upper surface increases because it spans a greater distance than the air that travels beneath the wing.

Following Bernoulli's law, the increased velocity on the upper surface of the wing is accompanied by a decrease in pressure, relative to that on the under surface; see **Figure 8-02**, lower. Since a region of high pressure will try to push into one of low pressure, a force is produced. Aviators began calling this force LIFT, and we use the same term when talking about boats. (The term "lift" also has another meaning, discussed later in this chapter.) Depending on the shape of the surface, the speed of the flow, the angle at which the foil meets the airflow, and other factors, more or less lift is produced. The faster an aircraft's forward motion induces airflow across its wings, the greater the pressure differential and the greater the lift. Ultimately, the high-pressure area beneath the wing, in attempting to displace the increasingly lower pressure area above it, lifts the wing—and the aircraft to which it is attached—upward and off the ground.

An asymmetrical airplane wing, curved on the upper surface and almost straight on the lower surface, can produce some of its lift even when it is pushed in a line parallel with the oncoming airflow—that is, with no ANGLE OF ATTACK. The sails on a sailboat, acting as a vertical wing or airfoil, ordinarily don't have thickness the way an airplane wing does. Without thickness and being asymmetrical (because they have to produce lift alternately on both sides), sails must be presented to the flow of air at an angle; see **Figure 8-02**, upper. This is

why sailboats lose their drive, or end up IN IRONS, when they are steered too close to the wind.

When sails are set at an efficient angle, air flows across their convex leeward surface and a low-pressure area is created. The sail tries to move into it, impelled by the relatively higher pressure on its windward side. This driving force created by the sails is transmitted to the hull through the mast, sheets, and sail attachments. The boat begins to move, but not necessarily in the right direction—not yet.

Drag

At the same time that lift is being created, there is another force at work on the sails. This is the DRAG that results from friction and turbulence along the sail's surface and at its edges. Boats rely on the flow of the wind—relatively slow compared to the much faster airflow generated by an engine-powered aircraft. They are severely limited in the amount of energy they can exploit. When resources are scarce, skills are challenged even more. Being able to change the sail's shape and the

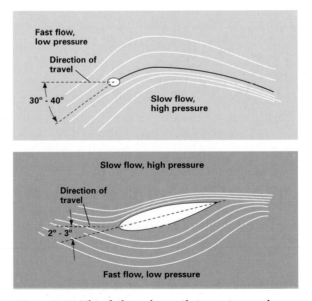

Figure 8-02 Thin foils, such as sails (upper), must be presented to the wind at an angle in order to create a low-pressure area across their leeward surface. The sails try to move into that low-pressure area, producing forward and lateral movement of the boat. Thick foils, such as fin keels (lower), also must be presented to the water flow at an angle in order to create high- and low-pressure areas and "lift." This angle is exaggerated in the lower diagram.

angle at which air flows over it to suit varying wind strengths and directions is critical to extracting the required lift from the available wind energy and to minimizing the inevitable drag.

If there is no corresponding hydrofoil already at work, the result of this careful sail trimming is just unresisted sideways motion, resulting in slower airflow, resulting in less speed—in other words the boat slides aimlessly. You have probably seen this happen when a sailing dinghy leaves the pier with its centerboard up.

Underwater Foils

The addition of underwater fins—a keel or centerboard, and a rudder—vastly increases lateral resistance. Again, unlike most airplane wings, a sailboat's foils are symmetrical (because they have to work the same way on both sides). Hydrofoils, like sails, also have to meet the oncoming flow at an angle, called their angle of attack, before they develop any lift. Since most keels are rigidly attached to their hulls, the whole boat has to be aimed a couple of degrees to windward of the course it actually travels; see **Figure 8-02,** lower.

As the dinghy sailor lowers the centerboard, he or she might also allow the sail to aim its effort in a more forward direction by letting it out just a little. Now the airfoil and hydrofoil get down to work—against each other. As each begins to encounter faster flow (we are dealing in less than walking speed here, so "fast" is a relative term) each foil begins to produce lift. The centerboard produces lift to windward, as well as drag, while the sail produces lift to leeward, and slightly forward. It's the "slightly forward" that makes things happen.

Creating more lift (and causing less drag) is the ultimate objective of high-performance sail and keel design. (This also explains why there are now designers who specialize in "appendages," keels and rudders, and othesr who design hulls—both separate from the people who design sails.) Of course, they have contrived a whole set of labels and rules to talk about it. Two important labels in this discussion are CENTER OF EFFORT (CE) and CENTER OF LATERAL RESISTANCE (CLR). These

are really just two sides of the same coin because both centers involve foils—"effort" for the sails, and "lateral resistance" for the keel and rudder; see **Figure 8-03.**

Now that computers are able to analyze the contribution of every carefully shaped square inch of foil surface, the center of effort and its twin, the center of resistance, are much easier to find. Both centers are simply the sum of all of the lift and drag forces at work anywhere on the foil. If you had to attach a string somewhere on the sail and another on the underwater surface, and pull the boat along by these two strings—creating the same force and balance as a particular strength and direction of wind—the center of effort is the place where you would attach the sail's string, and the center of lateral resistance is the place you would have to attach the underwater string.

Yacht designers used to estimate the position of the center of effort by finding the geometric center

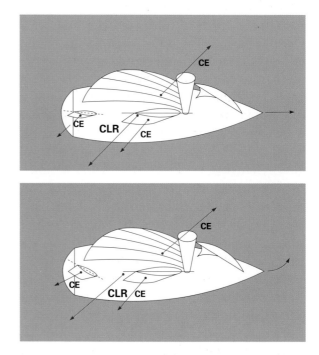

Figure 8-03 The center of effort (CE) is the position of the sum of all the lift and drag forces produced by the sails. The center of lateral resistance (CLR) is the equivalent position of all forces produced by the hull and its appendages. When the two centers are balanced against each other, the boat travels in a straight line (upper). When they are out of balance, the boat turns. Changing the rudder angle (lower) shifts the position of the CLR aft so that the boat turns to leeward.

of the triangles in a sail plan, connecting them, segmenting the connecting line in ratio to the areas of the triangle, then using their experience to estimate how far forward or aft the real balance point might be. The center of lateral resistance was found in a similar fashion. Today, designers still use experience, but it is supplemented by wind tunnel and tank testing of various shapes.

The Balancing Act

Both centers (CE and CLR) are constantly changing with boat motion and sail adjustment. Unfortunately, the net effect of lift and drag that the CE represents does not pull the boat straight ahead. (Remember that we said the boat would start to move, but not in the desired direction.) The force acting at the CE on the sails actually pulls mostly sideways, and the forces acting on the CLR on the hull, keel, and rudder, act to windward and slightly aft. These forces are in balance when the boat is traveling in a straight line. When they are out of balance, the boat turns; refer to **Figure 8-03**.

Keeping in mind that boats sail fastest when their keel and rudder are presented to the water flow at a slight angle, designers place the sails on the hull in such a way that, if no steering force were applied with the rudder, the boat would turn itself gently toward the direction of the wind (WEATHER HELM). When the boat is sailed, a straight-line course is achieved by the gentle application of 2° or 3° degrees of rudder angle in the opposite direction; see **Figure 8-04**. Balance between CE and CLR is achieved (the boat does not turn), and both underwater foils, keel and rudder, are presented to the oncoming flow of water at a slight angle of attack—so that both foils develop a force that pulls the boat to windward. However, you can also have too much of a good thing. An excessive imbalance between CE and CLR, one that requires more than a slight rudder correction, causes the rudder to develop drag commensurate with the greater lift it is being forced to create. The boat decelerates—slower speed means less drive from the sails—and things settle back into the drive-drag equilibrium at a slower constant speed.

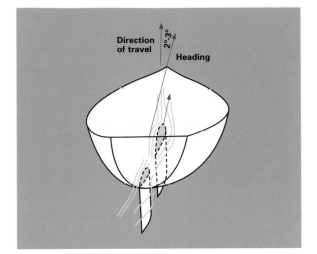

Figure 8-04 Since the keel and rudder must be presented to the water at a slight angle of attack (ideally 2° to 3°) in order to create maximum lift, the boat must be steered in one direction—its heading—to travel ("make good") in a slightly different direction.

In moderate wind (up to 10–14 knots), a sailboat that is properly balanced exhibits a weather helm—a tendency to turn into the wind. This is counteracted by pulling the tiller slightly to weather (the direction of the wind) or turning the wheel away from the wind. A sailboat that acts in this way is considered safer because in the event of gear failure or lack of attention to the helm, it will round up (head into the wind) rather than fall off into a possibly dangerous jibe (pronounced with a long "i" as in "ice"). Weather helm should decrease as wind strength abates.

A LEE HELM is the opposite of weather helm, a tendency for the boat to wander off to leeward; many sailboats develop a slight tendency for lee helm in light air. Acceptable in very light winds, it is not desirable in heavier wind. A straight-line course can only be achieved when the rudder is turned to create a force pulling to leeward (so the bow is pushed to windward). This means that no windward lift is being created by the rudder, so all of it has to be created by the keel. The keel then ends up at a more extreme angle of attack to produce this lift, and in the process creates more drag. As a result, everything slows down.

It should be noted that all of these differences in balance are important to the cruising sailor as well as the racer. Though they are difficult to perceive—3° is hard to see and often difficult to feel in the helm—they produce substantial differences on almost all points of sail. The racing sailor may lose a race, but the cruising sailor may make serious errors in navigation by failing to account for large leeway angles that result from excessive imbalance.

Incidentally, keels and rudders can be a lot smaller in area than sails because they operate in a denser medium. In addition, when they are pushed through the water at greater speeds, they can produce sufficient side forces with less area—that's why the crews of fast, planing catamarans often reduce drag by pulling up their foils (usually daggerboards) a few inches at high speeds, even though they are sailing upwind.

Conversely, if there is no speed at all, there is no flow and neither the keel nor the rudder can do its job. A boat that has no way on cannot be steered, which is why STEERAGEWAY is so important. Skippers will often do whatever they can to get a boat settled down and underway so as to create some flow past the keel and rudder before they worry about what precise direction they're going.

Outsailing the Wind

For most novice sailors, the idea that a boat can sail faster than the wind is questionable at best. Even the less ambitious claim—that a boat can receive more power from the wind as the boat picks up speed—seems contrary to common sense. After all, there is no source of power other than the wind.

The Effect of Apparent Wind

But it's true, and an understanding of APPARENT WIND, the stronger wind partly created by the boat's own speed, is crucial to sailing. Let's look at two extreme examples—a very slow boat and a very fast boat.

The slow boat is a Spanish galleon. It has no separate keel and, by modern standards, inefficient sails. It sails most effectively with the wind behind it, and even then, it doesn't sail very fast. If the galleon were just getting underway, and if

the wind were exactly on its stern and blowing at 10 knots, the wind felt by someone standing on deck would be 10 knots. As the galleon picked up speed, the wind felt on deck (the apparent wind) would decrease, because the ship would be moving along with it. The effect of the wind on the moving sails would also decrease. At somewhere around 2 knots of vessel speed through the water, the decreasing force created by the sails would exactly balance the increasing resistance of the hull (discussed later) and the galleon would stop accelerating and settle down for a long trip to its destination. Vessel speed would be 2 knots, wind speed 10 knots, apparent wind speed 8 knots.

Now take the fast boat—an iceboat—in a similar situation. With almost no hull resistance to overcome, the iceboat picks up the same 10 knots of wind from directly astern and, within seconds, the skipper is aware of a rapidly decreasing apparent wind. His boat reaches a balance between the decreasing force of the wind and the increasing resistance of the iceboat at, for example, 9 knots (boat speed 9 knots, wind speed 10 knots, apparent wind speed 1 knot).

Now, 9 knots would be pretty exciting in a Spanish galleon, but in an iceboat, it's not worth chilly feet. So the iceboat skipper turns his boat so that it begins to travel on a line perpendicular to the wind. He does this without losing any speed, so his initial speed, after the turn, is still 9 knots. At that instant, the iceboat skipper feels the full force of the 10-knot wind, because he's no longer traveling away from it. He also feels the force of a 9-knot wind, just as if he were on a bicycle pedaling at 9 knots. These two vectors, at right angles to each other, can be added (vector addition is discussed in Chapter 17) with an apparent wind of about 13.5 knots flowing into the iceboat at an angle of about 47°.

The Spanish galleon, still traveling at 2 knots, also turns so that it is sailing on a line perpendicular to the wind. The new wind across its decks is also a vector sum of the 10-knot wind and the 2-knot boat speed. The result is a less-then-impressive 10.3 knots at an angle of about 79°.

The galleon responds to this slightly stronger apparent wind (which is still hitting at an angel wide enough for its square sails to make use of) by accelerating. Again, the force on the sails is balanced by the increasing resistance of the hull, and things settle down again—at 2.5 knots.

However, aboard the iceboat, things start to happen. Its highly efficient sail and almost-zero hull resistance respond to the new, stronger wind. It begins to accelerate again. The first one-knot increase in boat speed, to 10 knots, brings a new apparent wind; 14.1 knots, at a new angle of 45 degrees. This angle is still no problem for an iceboat sail so it responds to the new apparent wind strength by gaining another knot. Now the apparent wind is very close to 15 knots and the angle is still comfortable—producing more acceleration.

Where does it all end? Well, this is not perpetual motion (though, in an iceboat, it can often feel that way!). Things start to level of when the apparent wind goes so far forward that the sail begins to point too directly into the wind. It can no longer achieve a useful angle of attack and it luffs. At this point the iceboat is probably experiencing an apparent wind of almost 45 knots and is doing almost 40 knots of boat speed—pretty good for wind strength of 10 knots. In fact, with strong winter winds and cold,

dense air, iceboats routinely travel at speeds of more than 50 knots. At that speed, their sails are strapped in tight regardless of what direction the "real" wind is blowing—their apparent wind is far more important, and it's blowing from almost straight ahead; see **Figure 8-05.**

The effects of apparent wind on most sailboats are far more dramatic than aboard the galleon and far less than aboard the iceboat. Even a heavy racing sloop might increase its speed by 25 percent as a result of a stronger apparent wind. Sailboats that are less limited by their weight can easily double their speed with careful use of apparent wind.

There are some fundamental rules about apparent wind:

• Except when sailing directly downwind, apparent wind will always come from "farther ahead" than the true wind does.

• Sailing on any angle ranging from perpendicular to the wind to an angle quite close to the wind, apparent wind will always be greater than the wind.

• As wind strength increases, the angle of the apparent wind moves farther aft; conversely, as wind strength decreases, the apparent wind moves farther forward. A strong gust of wind is usually welcome because it provides more power applied from farther aft.

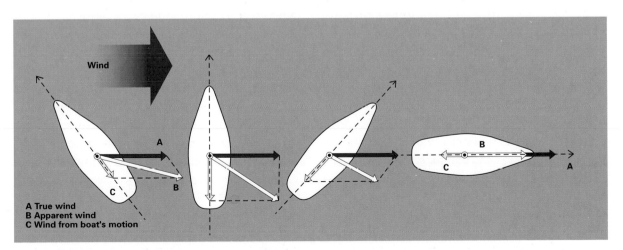

A True wind
B Apparent wind
C Wind from boat's motion

Figure 8-05 *Apparent wind is the direction of the wind as it appears to a person on board. Both boat speed and the boat's angle to the true wind affect the direction and strength of the apparent wind. In the vector diagram shown here, the yellow arrow is the wind from the boat's motion, and the white arrow is apparent wind. Apparent wind is greatest when the boat is sailing perpendicular to, or at an angle close to, the actual wind.*

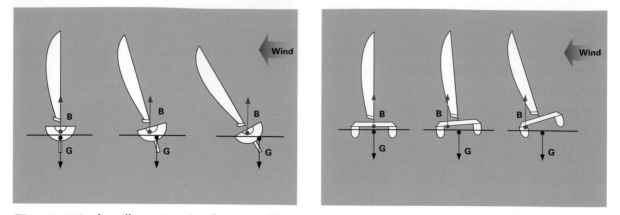

Figure 8-06 *In these illustrations, B is the center of buoyancy and G is the center of gravity. Sailboats can use either weight (left) or width (right) to remain upright against the force of the wind. A hull stabilized primarily with weight has a very small righting moment as it begins to heel, but that increases steadily as the craft heels farther over. Such boats are initially "tender" and ultimately "stiff." As the wind increases, a ballasted hull will lean over, increasing the righting moment, but the wide, unballasted hull has already achieved its maximum righting moment and is becoming increasingly unstable as the angle of heel increases.*

Heeling

For the most part, boats sail most efficiently in an upright position so that aerodynamic and hydrodynamic lifts are converted into forward motion. But the same dynamic forces that pull the boat forward also try to push it over.

The sails, which have their CE at about 40 percent of the height of the mast, and the keel with its corresponding CLR well below the water, both act as levers with the hull in the middle as their fulcrum.

In general, there are two ways to counter these forces and prevent them from pushing the boat over and capsizing it. These are weight and width. Both have disadvantages. Energy extracted from the wind is partly absorbed in the work of moving weight, especially if that weight begins to move up and down through waves, so any extra weight robs speed. Width makes a hull harder to push through the water (unless the boat is separated into two hulls, or three, that are spread apart).

Most sailboats use both weight and width to stay upright. The width of the hull is the first line of defense because buoyancy begins to provide substantial righting moment (it pushes back) as soon as the hull begins to heel. Fixed ballast gains in importance as the hull heels farther over.

Different sailboat designs rely more heavily on one or the other method. The classic heavy, narrow "meter boats," such as the 12-meter class formerly used in American's Cup competition, were intended to balance at a substantial angle of heel sailing close to the direction of the wind. Designers took advantage of this fact by shaping their hulls in such a way that they would have greater potential speed in their heeled underwater shape than in their upright underwater shape. The basic method is explained below in discussion of form resistance.

Most recent racing designs, such as the J-24, rely more on a wide, shallow hull. With this hull type, crew weight becomes even more important, especially because crew weight can begin to provide righting moment even before the hull begins to heel. That's why the best-sailed dinghies sail through gusts of wind without heeling—their crews move into position in perfect synchronization with the changing aerodynamic forces, converting every increase in power into forward acceleration, rather than heeling.

As the boat begins to heel, several factors combine to rob it of forward speed. The force created by the sails is now aimed partly downward (instead of parallel to the water), thereby helping to immerse the hull into the water rather than pulling it forward. Less sail area is exposed to the horizontal movement of the wind. A corresponding deterioration takes place underwater where the flow of water across the keel and rudder are compromised. The part of the hull that is underwater becomes asymmetrical, creating turning forces that have to be counteracted; see **Figure 8-06,** left.

A more subtle change also takes place. The forces created by sails and keel are no longer acting directly above and directly below the hull—they're both displaced sideways. The effect is similar to what would happen if you were pulling the hull with a towline. When the boat is upright, the towline pulls along the hull's centerline. As the boat heels, the effect is as if the towline were uncleated and made fast again at the gunwale near the widest point of the beam. In this case, you would expect to fight the boat with its rudder to keep it on a straight course. When the boat heels, its propulsion forces operate away from the hull's centerline. That's why boats that are allowed to heel too far under the pull of a spinnaker are so vulnerable to broaching. It also explains why, when a sailboarder leans back into the wind at high speed, he must also move to the tail of his board, holding the sail well aft of the point on which the board pivots when it changes direction.

Achieving Stability

It's no wonder the Polynesian solution—dividing the hull into two (or three) units and placing them far apart—is attractive. With no penalty in weight, a catamaran or trimaran achieves huge righting moment at the slightest angle of heel.

However, that's not the whole story. When stability is achieved entirely by righting moment from hull width (or by spreading the hulls farther apart), righting moment is typically very high at small angles of heel—but decreases steadily to nothing as the boat heels farther over. In one sense, when you need it most, it's all gone; see **Figure 8-06,** right.

The righting moment provided by fixed ballast is typically very small as the hull begins to heel, but steadily increases as the hull heels farther; in other words, the boat is initially TENDER and ultimately STIFF. In the extreme case, the mast is almost parallel with the surface of the water and the fixed ballast is held at a similar angle, almost

sideways. At this radical stage, righting moment is at a maximum and heeling force at a minimum.

Keep in mind that these examples are highly simplified. Many other factors, such as the wave conditions present when such extreme heeling forces are at work, have to be considered by yacht designers. For example, even though the fixed-ballasted boat may not heel beyond this extreme angle, it may be filling itself with water. Even though the powerfully rigged, unballasted multihull may potentially capsize, it is less likely actually to founder (since it is generally lighter than water).

Boat Speed

Few activities so inspire participants to seek the smallest improvement in speed that sailing does. Indeed, it is the potential for almost infinitesimal improvement that is one of the joys—and at times the frustration—of sailing.

Most sailors are not particularly concerned with going faster than any other sailboat—they're more concerned with getting the most speed out of a sailboat that has been designed with speed-limiting rules. They want to maximize the potential of a boat that has been designed to sail within a class of boats that are all very much the same, if not actually identical in performance characteristics.

This historical limitation of sailboat design has led to a paradox: While sailors have developed the art of boat preparation, sail trim, and steering to a high degree of refinement, and yacht designers have squeezed every last fraction of a knot from conventional hulls, keels, and sails, the vast majority of sailboats have remained within a narrowly defined set of basic configurations. The imaginative application of pure science and engineering has not had much impact on the activities and experience of most sailors. Nevertheless, the principles that determine how fast a sailboat can go are eagerly studied and applied with an increasing degree of subtlety.

One of the chief enemies of speed for a sailboat, as for any vehicle traveling through a fluid—whether water or the atmosphere—is drag. But sailboats encounter two kinds of drag whose relative importance varies with speed. The first and most obvious is the drag caused by

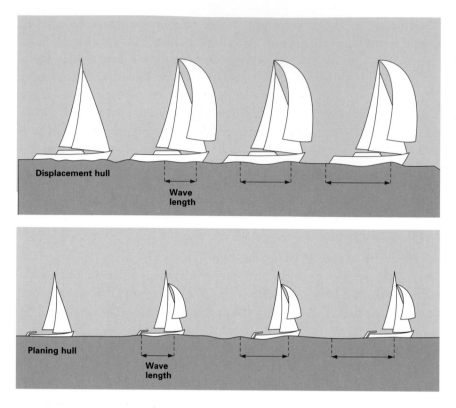

Figure 8-07 When a hull moves through the water, It produces waves that result in energy loss. The maximum speed of a conventional displacement hull (upper) is a function of the longest wave that it can make, which in turn is determined by hull length. No amount of sail can create enough power for it to go faster. On the other hand, the planing hull (lower) like a racing dinghy and some multihulls, can carry enough sail to push it over its own bow wave and onto a plane.

the friction of air and water flowing over large surfaces that can never be perfectly smooth. For that reason, yacht designers take great pains to reduce the wetted surface of the hull. For any given volume, the shape with the least wetted surface is a sphere (that's why soap bubbles are spherical), but a sphere is not very useful for a hull. The next best compromise might be a round tube. Many hulls are developed from that principle and have almost a circular cross section.

Drag is also caused by turbulent flow around the awkward shapes of deck fittings, rigging attachments, through-hull fittings, and even the crew themselves. While attempts are made to streamline these, there are practical and rule-oriented limitations that most sailors happily accept.

Drag from friction and turbulence is most important at low speeds—not because it diminishes at higher speed (it doesn't) but because on the conventional sailboat another form of drag becomes even more difficult to control. This is FORM DRAG, the process of energy loss through the formation of waves.

Hull Speed

Imagine a sailboat moving through the water at less than a knot. Tiny wavelets stream from the hull at several points along its waterline. They don't seem to be connected. As speed increases, the wavelets grow into waves and seem to join, the trough of one running up into the crest of the next; see **Figure 8-07,** upper. At this point, you could measure the boat's speed by measuring the distance between one wave crest and the next: The speed of a surface wave is strictly related to its length. To measure the relationship, in knots, of waves in water, yacht designers use the square root of the wave length, in feet, multiplied by 1.34.

Three crests along the side of the boat indicate that it is traveling at about half of its maximum speed. As speed increases, the bow wave grows in height and length, pushing the midships wave aft. As the last fraction of a knot is reached, the stern wave is almost falling behind the hull—but it can't. As the stern wave pulls aft, the stern settles down into it. Drag increases because the hull is actually inclined upward against the slope of the bow wave. The hull is trapped.

The implication is that you should always have enough propulsion power to climb over the bow wave and convert from a floating or displacement mode of support to a planing mode. That option is available to very light boats that can carry lots of sail (racing dinghies, multihulls, sailboards, and even foil-supported boats), but it's not available within the realm of ballasted monohulls.

Therefore the implication for conventional boats is that, as long as a hull is trapped in its own wave, the vessel will never go faster than the longest wave it can make. That is the reason why longer boats are faster—and why, almost from the beginning of sailboat racing, length has been heavily factored into rating rules.

The challenge, within the limitations of rules and economics, is to make a longer wave, so that the hull has a higher potential speed when the propulsion power (wind) is available, but to do so without seriously compromising the hull's performance when windpower is scarce; see **Figure 8-07,** lower.

Designing for Speed

One common strategy is to design a hull that has two "personalities"—a shape that is relatively narrow and fine at the ends of the waterline when upright (at low speed when form resistance is less important), and a heeled, or high-speed, shape that is full at the ends. An overhang at the stern is very useful in this regard; as the stern wave builds, the waterline becomes longer and fuller, delaying the point at which the stern begins to settle down into the wave.

Obviously, this dual personality has limitations. In fact, if the designer has made the bow and stern of the boat especially fine so that they will be easier to push through the water, the waterline will actually seem short to the wave and the top speed will be lower. This leads to the paradox that hulls meant to travel at or near hull speed most of the time tend to be rather full in the bow and the stern, while hulls expected to travel more slowly, while making more efficient use of lighter winds, might be finer fore and aft.

If heavy winds were always available on demand, and if sailboats always traveled with large apparent winds, yacht design would, of course, be much simpler. However, maximum driving power from a sailboat rig is rarely available and conventional hulls therefore have to be designed in order to strike the best compromises.

Some very light sailboats, such as racing dinghies, are able to provide lots of propulsion power by having their crews hike out against the power of very large sails; see **Figure 8-08.** Since they are short, these boats reach their wave-resistance limit at a very low speed (just over 5 knots). But they have lots of propulsion power still to absorb. Without much fuss, they rise over their bow waves and plane, just like powerboats, often reaching a respectable 17 to 20 knots. Of course, it takes two heavy sailors and perhaps three straining sails to do it, but that's all part of the attraction.

Multihulls

Catamarans and trimarans, with their unique stability, also have physics on their side when it comes to making waves. Because their hulls can be so much narrower than a monohull, the waves they produce are consequently much smaller. While the relationship between wave length and speed still holds, the "hole in the water" that is created by the passage of a narrow hull is much

Figure 8-08 This racing dinghy is moving at high speed on a plane, literally leaping out of the water. Its crew must "hike out" on a trapeze to keep the boat reasonably level.

smaller. The stern of a narrow hull doesn't have so far to settle, and drag does not increase as much or as suddenly. In one sense, the narrow hull of a catamaran or a trimaran doesn't have to plane because it has broken the hull-speed rule.

THE PARTS OF A SAILING RIG

Technology has contributed many innovations to the art of sailmaking, mainly in the area of sail material. The woven polyester fiber, usually referred to by the trade name Dacron, that replaced canvas and cotton, remains the most common of the new fibers. Nonetheless, in the constant quest for greater strength and less weight and stretch, Dacron has itself been surpassed by such wonder materials as Mylar, a nonwoven polyester, as well as Kevlar and Spectra.

With few exceptions (such as the spinnaker, discussed separately later), a conventional triangular shape has emerged as the most popular sail configuration. The luff of a mainsail is attached to the mast while the foresail's luff is attached to a forestay. While some mainsails are "loose footed" and attached only at the fore and aft corners (the tack and clew), more often they are attached along the length of the boom either by a boltrope sewn into the sail or by slides. Most foresails are loose footed. See **Figure 8-09,** for

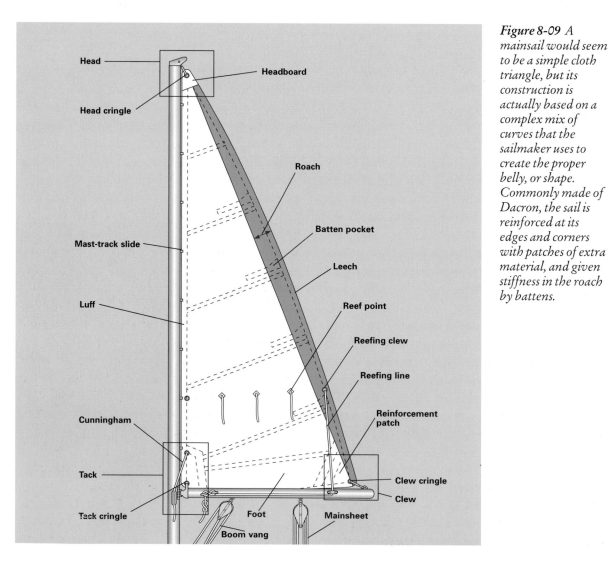

Figure 8-09 A mainsail would seem to be a simple cloth triangle, but its construction is actually based on a complex mix of curves that the sailmaker uses to create the proper belly, or shape. Commonly made of Dacron, the sail is reinforced at its edges and corners with patches of extra material, and given stiffness in the roach by battens.

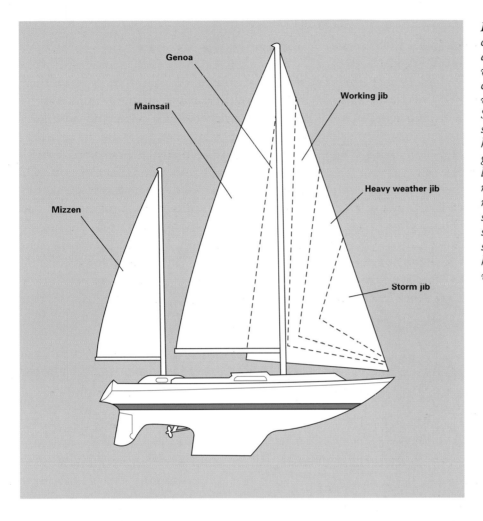

Mizzen

Mainsail

Genoa

Working jib

Heavy weather jib

Storm jib

Figure 8-10 A boat may carry many sails of different sizes and weights to suit different conditions of wind velocity or points of sail. Shown here are the basic sails that a ketch might have on board. The genoa, for example, is the largest headsail, but is made of the lightest material to catch the slightest breezes. The storm jib is the smallest sail, and is made of the heaviest material to withstand strong winds.

the various parts of a sail; see **Figure 8-10**, for typical sails of various sizes.

Sails are not flat like paper. They are very carefully cut and assembled so as to present a subtle shape, curving both along their horizontal lines and along their vertical lines. The quality of these curves and their ability to be slightly altered underway are what makes sailmaking such a competitive science. Not only must sailmakers design the right curves for each boat and for a variety of wind and wave conditions, they must also design a structure that will maintain its shape despite heavy stress and the effects of violent shaking and sunlight.

The largest stress on most sails, especially mainsails, is along the leech from the clew to the head. This unsupported edge has to accept the pull of the mainsheet and must also take the pressure of the wind flowing off its windward side.

On almost all recent designs, the leech also carries a deep outward curve, a ROACH. To counter these loads, most sailmakers lay out the sail material so that the low-stretch fibers of the weave run parallel to the leech. That design dictates panels of material that slope down from leech to luff.

But many other patterns are in use as well. Some place different materials at high-stress areas of the sail, even going so far as to stitch and weld strong fibers in elaborate elliptical curves that radiate out from the foot and luff. At the other extreme are cruising sails that can easily be rolled onto furlers and have very straight, soft leeches.

Battens provide additional support at the leech of a mainsail. Traditionally, they are flexible slats of wood or plastic that slide into long pockets. But that tradition is changing too. Catamaran sailors discovered that by extending battens from the leech all the way to the luff they could have a sail that would maintain a curve at very narrow angles to the oncoming airflow. Such sails have become popular even among cruising sailors who feel that, although they add extra weight, they are easier to manage and will last longer. Full-batten mains have led to a number of additional items of sail hardware to allow the forward end of the batten to be flexibly attached to the aft face of the mast, and so slide up and down freely despite the pressure.

Most sailors attach ribbon or pieces of wool to both sides of the sail; these TELLTALES, or TICK-LERS, indicate the efficiency of airflow over the sail. Often sailmakers sew windows of plastic near the telltales to make the action of a leeward one more visible. Large windows are sometimes sewn into dinghy mainsails and "deck-sweeping"

foresails for better leeward visibility when racing or sailing in confined conditions.

Spinnakers, in all their variations, are usually made of nylon. Since spinnakers generate their drive from the push of the wind, they can be allowed to stretch, thereby taking full advantage of the ultimate strength and lightness nylon provides. However, the architecture of spinnakers is just as complicated as it is for other sails. The goal is to produce a very full CAMBER, but one that still stands up the flow of air from one edge to the other—spinnakers do not simply fill with air like a balloon. Lightness is a requirement to allow the sail to set high and away from the interference of the mainsail, and to present the largest possible area to the wind. The fact that spinnakers are usually colorful is a matter of tradition more than function, but it does mean they are easier to examine against a bright sky for fine-tuning the trim.

Standing Rigging

Standing rigging is the structure designed to support the sails and to help transmit the power they develop to the hull. In most discussions, the mast itself is considered to be the main component of the standing rigging. The idea that the standing rigging is set up permanently and should not move (hence "standing") has given way to high-performance engineering and tinkering. It is now fairly com-mon to find standing rigging that is substantially altered while underway, and masts that are not only allowed, but forced, to bend.

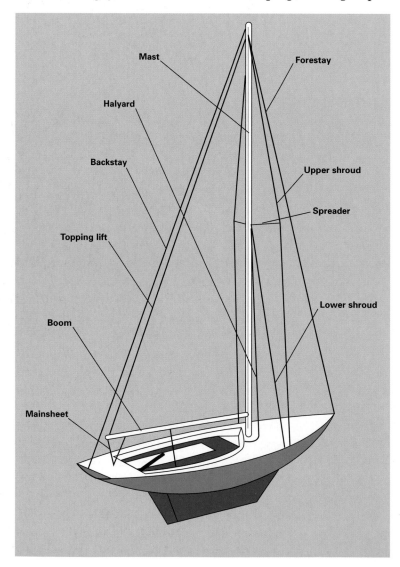

Figure 8-11 *Standing rigging supports the sails and transmits to the hull the power that they develop. The most common arrangement is a mast supported by stays and shrouds. Running rigging includes halyards for hoisting the sails and sheets for trimming them.*

The distinction between standing and running rigging has begun to blur. **Figure 8-11** illustrates the major components of standing rigging.

Masts

The evolution of mast making has focused on attempts to increase strength while reducing weight aloft. The challenge to make the structure lighter and stronger is complicated by the fact that for any given sail area, more power can be extracted with a tall narrow shape than with a short wide one. The ASPECT RATIO of sails (the relation between height and width) is limited by the fact that they become harder to trim as they get taller; but in general, masts can never be too tall or too thin—and are often extremely expensive.

Traditional wooden masts and booms have given way to extruded aluminum tubes and, more recently, to tubes made of composites of such materials as carbon fiber and epoxy. The simplest mast for a small, single-sail dinghy (such as the Laser) is a round aluminum tube held in a simple socket in the deck. The sail is attached to the mast by means of a sleeve extending the full height of the luff.

Although free-standing masts are sometimes used on larger sailboats (some even have more than one free-standing mast and sail-sleeve attachment), a much more common arrangement uses traditional stays and shrouds as guy wires from the mast to the deck. The mast may pass through the deck to rest on a step at the keel (KEEL-STEPPED) or fit into a step or tabernacle on deck (DECK-STEPPED).

Stays & Shrouds

There are almost infinite configurations for stays and shrouds, but at the forward side, there is always a forestay running from the bow (or near it) to the top of the mast (or near it). When the forestay is attached to a point below the top of the mast (called a fractional rig), the top of the mast can be pulled backward to create a slight bow shape. (The reasons for doing this are described in the section on sail trim.) There might also be a secondary inner stay at the bow, either for more

Figure 8-12 Many small cruising sailboats adjust their backstay by pulling a choker downward over a Y-shaped bridle. Larger vessels usually use a hydraulic tensioning system.

precise control of the mast bend or, as on a cutter rig, for carrying a second inner staysail.

On high-performance rigs there might also be a JUMPER STAY running from the mast, over a strut (JUMPER STRUT or DIAMOND STRUT) and back to the mast at the top. Tension on this stay holds the mast tip against the pull of the mainsail leech, especially in a fractional rig.

A backstay, running from the mast tip (TRUCK) to the stern, may be a single wire or be split into a bridle and attached to the aft deck at two points. Splitting the backstay makes it easy to adjust its tension because the bridle can be pulled together with a simple block and tackle; see **Figure 8-12.** The configuration also allows easier access to the cockpit over the transom.

Additional backstays are sometimes used on high-performance rigs, and are considered part of the running rigging because they can be loosened completely when underway. In fact, one has to be loosened and the other tightened on each tack or jibe, the windward running backstay is tensioned to add to mast stability, while the leeward one is slackened to allow the mainsail to be trimmed out.

Needless to say, the cockpit of such a boat is a noisy, crowed place on each tack.

Smaller boats may run shrouds directly from TANGS (attachment fittings) on the mast to CHAINPLATES on the hull at or near the deck. Taller masts cannot use this simple arrangement because, to get the required angle between the shrouds and the mast, the attachment at the deck would have to be outboard of the hull. Instead, struts called spreaders provide needed support by giving a wider angle between the upper shrouds and the mast. They push the shrouds outward to maintain supporting pressure on the upper mast.

Single spreaders extend athwartships from the mast a little more than halfway to the top. They are either horizontal or have a shallow upward angle. Some are swept back slightly. Smaller rigs get extra control over mast bend by swinging their spreader tips in a fore-and-aft arc. Larger boats often have multiple spreaders with several shrouds, each to a different level of the mast.

No matter what their arrangement, shrouds and stays are meant to keep the mast standing against the forces of wind and sails, or when the mast is deliberately bent, to change the shape of the mainsail.

Stays and shrouds on most modern boats are made of 1x19 stainless-steel wire of appropriate diameter for the size of the rig being supported. Stainless steel rod, though more expensive, has been growing in popularity because it has less stretch and more resistance to corrosion than wire. Rod diameter required to provide the same tensile strength is smaller than that of stranded wire and so has less windage (surface exposed to the wind).

Integral to the strength of the standing rigging itself is the attachment point at the deck. Usually, shrouds and stays terminate in turnbuckles that are attached to the eyes of chainplates, which in turn are bolted directly to the hull.

Tuning the standing rigging involves careful tightening of the turnbuckles until the shrouds on both sides of the mast have the same tension and the mast remains in column vertically with no sideways bends.

Once the shrouds are tuned, the forestay and backstay(s) are tensioned by means of tackle or hydraulic pumps to induce mast bend or mast rake to accommodate different sailing conditions underway.

Running Rigging

Running rigging includes all the gear used to raise and trim sails—and sometimes there is a bewildering amount of it. Many crews resort to color-coded lines to distinguish one piece of running rigging from another. Perhaps the easiest way to understand running rigging is to go through the sequence that most crews would follow to get underway. We will assume that the boat is a 25-foot cruising and racing sloop with a centerboard—a fairly common type.

If it's not already attached to the boom, the first step is to pull the boltrope on the foot of the mainsail into the groove of the boom. The clew is pulled out to the end of the boom by hand and attached to a short wire called an OUTHAUL that will later be adjusted. (Alternatively, there may be slides attached to the sail; these are slid onto and along a track on the upper side of the boom.) The tack is attached to the GOOSENECK (the articulated fitting that couples boom to mast) by a short pin. Above the tack is another hole (a CRINGLE) where another short adjusting line—the CUNNINGHAM—may be attached. Many items of running rigging are illustrated in **Figure 8-11.**

Now, presuming the boat is ready to be cast off, or is already underway with engine running, the mainsail can be pulled to the top of the mast. This requires that the main halyard be shackled to the headboard of the main and that the luff boltrope be slid into the groove of the mast (there might be sail slides on a track instead). The halyard runs loosely up the truck of the mast, over a sheave (a wheel) and back down the mast to the deck. It may simply be cleated to the mast, or it may run through a block (pulley) to a cleat or LINESTOPPER near the cockpit. Part of the halyard's up-and-down journey may be inside the mast. Before the main is raised, a check is made to ensure that all of the lines attached to it will not restrict the main on its way up the mast.

When the skipper has headed the boat into the wind and gives the word, the halyard is hauled, the head of the main rises to the top of the mast, and the end of the halyard is cleated in place. Later, small adjustments may be made. With the main exposed to the wind, the sail flaps until the mainsheet is trimmed in. The mainsheet attaches near the end of the boom and controls the in-and-out position of the boom the way your arm controls the swing of a door. Now is also the time to make initial adjustments of the outhaul (and cunningham, if used); by tensioning the cloth along the edges, the position of the deepest part of the sail's curve is controlled. After the tail of the main halyard is coiled and stowed, it might be necessary to ease the TOPPING LIFT—a line or wire that supports the boom in a level position when the boat is at rest. Now the BOOM VANG should be checked. This line, or telescoping pole, runs from the butt of the mast to the underside of the boom and resists the mainsail's tendency to lift up the aft end of the boom. Of course, the mainsheet has a role to play here, too.

Selecting & Raising the Jib

Now it's time to raise the headsail. First, the skipper chooses which one to raise. It's common to have two or three, ranging from a small storm jib to a large genoa—collectively, "all jibs." Bigger jibs are used in lighter winds.

The tack of the headsail is attached by a short pin or a shackle to a point close to the bottom of the forestay. Some boats are equipped with a foil on the forestay, which contains a groove to hold the boltrope sewn into the forestay's leech. Otherwise, the foresail is attached to the stay with a series of HANKS—spring-piston hooks. The headsail itself is loosely bundled on the foredeck; it may be necessary to tie it to the lifelines temporarily. The halyard is attached to the head and made ready to haul, then sheets must be attached to the clew. Unlike the mainsheet, these are normally stowed when not in use. The headsail sheets are best tied through the clew cringle and led back, one on each side of the boat, through their sheet blocks (or fairleads) and draped over the coaming of the cockpit. It's important not to have them catch while the sail is being raised. (Sometimes, one long line is used for both sheets, attached to the clew at its midway point.)

When the word is given, the crew hauls the halyard and the headsail raises up the forestay. It luffs noisily for a few seconds while the halyard is cleated or stopped, then one of the sheets (depending on which tack the boat takes) is hauled in. Now, minor adjustments can be made to halyard tension and position of the jibsheet leads (which are often moveable fore and aft on a track).

Now the boat is fully under sail. The engine is turned off. The centerboard, very likely, is lowered completely, perhaps using a light winch with a crank for a boat this size. Smaller boats employ a block and tackle called a centerboard tackle, and very small boats have a simple pendant. Obviously, sailboats with a keel skip the final steps above.

Adjusting the Sails

From this point, most sail adjustments take place from the cockpit, using the mainsail and headsail sheets. The position of the TRAVELER—a car that moves on a rail set athwartships on the boat to adjust the angle of pull on the mainsheet—also has to be set. Depending on many variables (refer to "Basic Sail Trim," page 296), the traveler car is either pulled up to the windward side or let down to leeward; see **Figure 8-13**. Once it is fixed in place, frequent small adjustments are made to the mainsheet to account for changes in apparent

Figure 8-13 Shown here on a small sailboat, a traveler is a car that slides on an athwartship track to aid in the proper adjustment of the mainsheet; see text for its use.

wind speed and angle. These adjustments both position the boom laterally and release or apply tension to the leech, depending on the traveler car's position. In some racing boats, the traveler tackle becomes the principal control for the main while sailing close to the wind.

Likewise, the headsails are frequently adjusted—some crews would say too frequently. Sail trim of the main and headsail are often coordinated in an effort to shape the layer of air that flows between them. Jib sheet adjustments are made with a winch; see **Figure 8-14.** On boats larger than about 20 feet (6.1 m), even if the extra mechanical advantage of a winch crank is not necessary, the winch helps by snubbing the sheet until another handgrip is taken. When the wind increases, the headsail can hardly be moved without the mechanical advantage provided by the winch's gear ratio. (Set aside winch handles carefully; they're expensive and they sink.) Now, many headsail winches are fitted with a self-tailer, a circular jaw that holds enough tension on the sheet to prevent it from slipping against the surface of the winch drum. As the sheet is cranked in, the tail is peeled out of the jaw automatically. This means sail trim can be accomplished by one person, instead of two. For cruising, this is progress; for racing, it means less work for the crew.

The sails on a 25-foot boat are fairly easy to raise without the help of winches, but a larger boat might have a halyard winch, either mounted at the foot of the mast, or, more commonly, on the aft end of the roof of the cabin. Since winches are expensive, they are often shared among halyards and other adjusting lines. To hold one line in place while another is being winched, boats may now have linestoppers—simple levered clutches that clamp onto the line without damaging it. These are arranged, one per line, in front of the shared winch.

In place of linestoppers, lines may be held by camcleats with spring-loaded jaws that permit line in, but not out. Mainsheets, with their load-reducing block and tackle to provide mechanical advantage, are almost always held by large camcleats. Otherwise, camcleats are more common on small boats or for smaller, lightly loaded adjusting lines on large boats. Line is released by lifting up and out of the jaws.

Ordinary horned cleats are also useful for sheets, although they are less and less common for running rigging. Used properly, cleats can provide prefect holding power and quick release. (Refer to Chapter 23 for more information on cleating.)

So far we have explored all the line and hardware needed to get the sails up, adjust their shape, change their angle in relation to the apparent wind, and pull the centerboard up and down. We've pulled on the backstay, moved the traveler car, and positioned the headsail leads. The next step—flying the spinnaker—perplexes and intimidates novices.

Flying the Spinnaker

For this discussion, we will assume a conventional spinnaker because the other styles are simplifications of it. The spinnaker is attached at three points—the head and the clews. (Note that spinnakers have two clews although some sailors may logically refer to the windward clew as the tack.) The head is attached to the mast by a halyard just like other headsails. The clews are attached to the deck with sheets, just like all headsail—except that there are always two separate sheets. The uniqueness of a conventional spinnaker is that it is symmetrical, so that one sheet and one luff are on the windward side of the spinnaker on one tack, but the leeward side on the other tack. As they change sides, they change names.

The leeward side of the spinnaker is the simplest. A sheet is attached to the clew; it runs aft to a block on the deck and is trimmed with a winch. When the spinnaker luffs, you pull the sheet in. The windward side is more complicated. Here, the clew also attaches to a sheet that runs aft to the deck at the stern. In this position, on the windward side, the sheet is now called the guy—though it's still the same piece of line. However, it is held away from the mast by a pole—a SPINNAKER POLE—jutting out at right angles and attached to the mast with an articulated coupling. The outboard end of the pole has a piston hook (or a similar device) that the guy runs through. The spinnaker itself is not actually attached to the pole.

That sounds simple, except that the pole has to be held both up and down. This is done with a pole uphaul and downhaul running from the pole (or a bridle on the pole) to the mast. Both up- and downhaul need their own blocks and, sometimes, winches. The loads created by the spinnaker can be heavy and variable.

For the cruising sailor, the chief advantage of the ASYMMETRICAL SPINNAKER is that so much of this spinnaker gear is eliminated. Asymmetry does away with the two clews and the sheets that change names. The cruising spinnaker is really a larger, lighter headsail that is tacked and jibed much the same way as a normal headsail, but is not attached along the forestay. Instead, it flies freely away from the forestay.

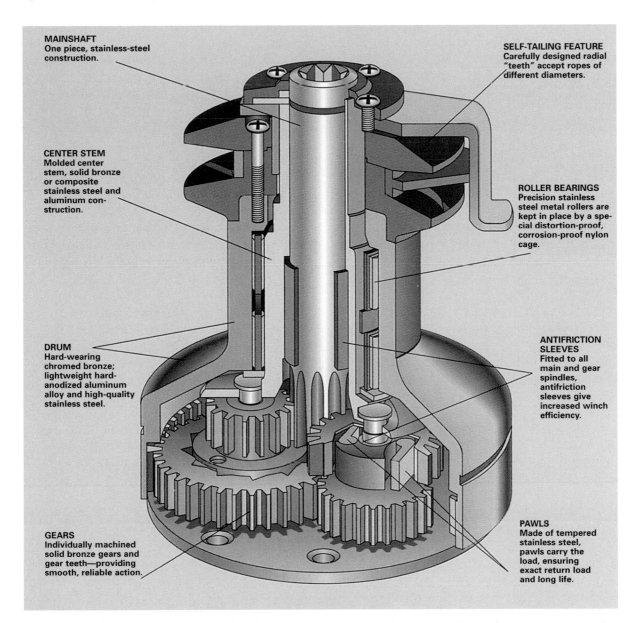

MAINSHAFT
One piece, stainless-steel construction.

SELF-TAILING FEATURE
Carefully designed radial "teeth" accept ropes of different diameters.

CENTER STEM
Molded center stem, solid bronze or composite stainless steel and aluminum construction.

ROLLER BEARINGS
Precision stainless steel metal rollers are kept in place by a special distortion-proof, corrosion-proof nylon cage.

DRUM
Hard-wearing chromed bronze; lightweight hard-anodized aluminum alloy and high-quality stainless steel.

ANTIFRICTION SLEEVES
Fitted to all main and gear spindles, antifriction sleeves give increased winch efficiency.

GEARS
Individually machined solid bronze gears and gear teeth—providing smooth, reliable action.

PAWLS
Made of tempered stainless steel, pawls carry the load, ensuring exact return load and long life.

Figure 8-14 On all but the smallest sailboats, winches are used to provide mechanical advantage for trimming the headsail sheets. Most modern winches are now equipped with self-tailing devices so that a single crewmember can handle the winch.

The racing approach to asymmetrical spinnakers is a little different. A pole is still used, but it has become a telescoping bowsprit. The spinnaker is typically not flown directly downwind (because these new, light boats sail fastest by tacking downwind), but is flown like a headsail, even though it is as big and almost as round as a conventional reaching spinnaker.

BASIC SAIL TRIM

With practice, and by noting the results during trial and error experimentation, helmsman and crew will develop a feel for a boat's characteristics in different conditions and take appropriate measures to keep it "in the groove." Sail trim is a major component of achieving that goal, whether or not you are racing. The following are some elementary aspects of sail trim on each point of sail.

Sail Shape

To some degree, the shape of a sail is restricted to the amount of camber designed into it by the sailmaker. But the depth of the camber (DRAFT) can be controlled, and the position of the deepest part of the draft, with respect to the luff of the sail, can

also be controlled; see **Figure 8-15.** A more familiar, and eminently changeable, element of sail trim is the angle of incidence—the angle at which the leading edge meets the apparent wind.

As discussed in the preceding section on sailboat parts, a host of controls is available for trimming and shaping the sails for the conditions encountered. Be forewarned, however: There are no hard and fast rules for the order or degree with which each is used. Observation of the telltales on the sails and instruments in the cockpit, ability to hold a desired course, and the "feel" of the helm all measure the success of each action or combination of actions. Moreover, actions that produce a positive response on one boat may not produce the same response on another. But if experimentation is the rule of sail trim, there are some fundamentals worth learning.

Mainsail Trim

Changing the shape of the mainsail involves changing the depth of the draft to produce a flatter or fuller sail. Moving the mainsail's draft fore and aft is also a factor in improving the balance of the boat. Most of the time, the ideal position for maximum draft is one-third to one-half the way

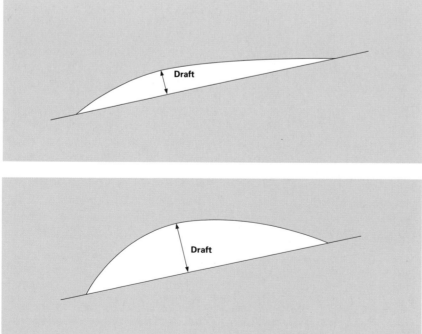

Figure 8-15 Changing the shape of a sail is accomplished by changing the depth of the draft to produce a flatter or fuller sail. The amount of draft required in different conditions varies with the point of sailing. In general, flatter sails (upper) are more efficient upwind than fuller ones (lower).

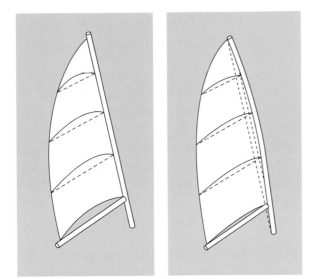

Figure 8-16 Using the backstay to tension the top of the mast aft will bow the middle of the mast forward, and so flatten a mainsail. The effect is to reduce draft and move it forward.

back from the mast. When sailing upwind, the object is to make the sail fuller at the leading edge, to direct total lift force forward and reduce side forces. When reaching, draft position is usually farther aft. Tensioning the clew outhaul to pull the clew aft reduces draft and moves it forward. The same effect is achieved by tensioning the backstay and boom vang to bend the top of the mast aft and bow the middle of the mast forward. As the mast bows forward, it pulls the middle of the mainsail and flattens it out; see **Figure 8-16.** Increasing halyard tension and taking up on the cunningham are also effective measures to move draft forward.

The mainsheet, combined with the boom vang and traveler, controls the tension on the leech of the mainsail. Leech tension is important for several reasons but the two principal considerations are twist and trailing-edge shape.

In general, wind flows faster the higher it is from the water. That means that the top of a sail has to be trimmed to a different angle than the bottom, with the greater angle at the top—hence sail twist; see **Figure 8-17.** To achieve a high degree of twist, you would usually ease the mainsheet, allowing the boom to rise. You might have to pull the traveler car to windward to prevent the boom from swinging too far from the boat's centerline. The boom vang would be slack.

The opposite effect, removing twist, is achieved by trimming harder on the mainsheet, placing more

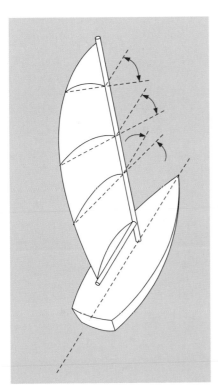

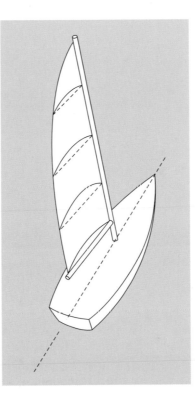

Figure 8-17 Because wind speed is faster higher above the water, sails need to be trimmed to a different angle at the top than at the bottom, with the greater angle at the top. Sail twist is achieved by easing the mainsheet, allowing the boom to rise (far left). To remove twist (near left), trim the mainsheet in, and use the traveler to position the boom slightly farther off the boat's centerline.

THE POINTS OF SAILING

The relationship between the boat's head and the direction of the wind has a traditional set of names. When there is the smallest practical angle between wind direction and heading, the boat is said to be "close-hauled," meaning that it sails (or "yards" on square-rigged vessels) are hauled in close to the hull. Another name for this is "beating."

When the angle between heading and wind direction is increased, the boat begins to "close reach," and when the angle is about 90°, the wind is on the beam, so the boat is "beam reaching."

Further increases in angle bring the boat to a "broad reach"; with the wind almost directly aft, the boat is "running."

The term "running" sounds fast, and in square-riggers, it may well have been. But the fastest point of sail for most modern boats is close reach, and running today is actually very slow.

Remember that this diagram shows the relation between the boat and the wind, while the more important factor, especially for today's faster boats, is the relationship between the boat and its apparent wind—the wind that the sails feel. Very fast boats, like catamarans and racing dinghies, might seem to be swinging from a close reach right through to a broad reach in terms of the true wind, when they are in fact close reaching the apparent wind.

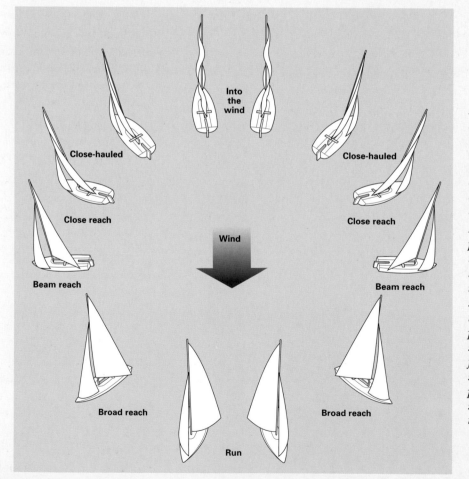

A Sailboat cannot sail directly into the eye of the wind, but modern sailboats usually can sail to within 45° of the wind, or closer, when close-hauled. A reach is the fastest point of sail, with the sails eased about halfway out. A run is aerodynamically simpler, but can be the most dangerous point of sail. The sails are extended as far out over the sides of the boat as possible, and can swing across with tremendous force.

tension up the leech, letting the traveler car down to position the boom somewhat away from the boat's centerline, and using a tight boom vang. More pressure is carried high and aft by the mainsail and the leech "closes up"—begins to push airflow away to windward instead of just letting it flow easily aft.

While the basic decision to twist or close up the leech might be made according to the general wind strength and the point of sail, at the same time, gusts and lulls require adjustments to the mainsheet; see sidebar, "The Points of Sailing." Typically, the mainsheet is tensioned in lulls and eased (or even released) to open the leech and depower the sail in gusts. Upwind, the mainsheet usually provides most of the leech control. Off the wind or on a reach when the main is eased, the vang controls the leech. Many sails also have a LEECHLINE and a small cleat built into them to provide fine control as an adjunct to the coarse control of the mainsheet and vang. Care must be taken that the leechline is not so tight as to actually hook the leech to windward.

The traveler, of course, provides a means of balancing the mainsheet's vertical and horizontal pull on the boom. As the mainsheet is eased, and the boom moves to leeward, the angle of pull on the boom becomes more horizontal, removing tension from the leech. When the traveler car is eased to leeward, the pull of the mainsheet becomes more vertical, increasing leech tension.

The traveler car can also be pulled to windward in light air so that the mainsheet tension is more horizontal but the angle of the boom is still very close to, or right over, the centerline of the boat. This allows sufficient twist, but a smaller angle of incidence to the flow of air at the luff. However, care must be taken not to overtrim the main. A rule of thumb is to keep the batten second from the top parallel to the boom; no battens—in fact, no part of the sail—should ever point to windward.

Headsail Trim

The headsail, or jib, of many boats supplies as much drive as the main, or more. Not only are headsails often as large as the main, especially in masthead rigs with genoas, but the sail is presented to the airflow without disturbing windage of the mast.

The tension on the forestay is the second most important control of the headsail shape, after the position and tension on the sheet itself.

A loose forestay (created by loosening the backstay) creates sag, which in turn creates a full (deep draft) headsail. Sailmakers build a degree of allowance for forestay sag into the sail shape, but manipulating tension in the forestay has the same effect as straightening the mast: The sail is pulled tighter across the middle and becomes flatter.

Upwind, particularly in brisk winds, the jib halyard should be tensioned in order to keep the position of the deepest part of the draft as far forward as possible.

Key to trimming the jib, however, is the position of the clew. As the leeward sheet is eased, the clew will tend to move outboard and upward. The effect is a fuller sail. Tensioning the sheet pulls the clew aft, down and inboard, flattening the sail and decreasing the angle of incidence with the airflow.

Twist in the headsail is controlled by the position of the sheet lead (also known as the fairlead). As the lead is moved forward, the sheet pulls more on the leech—more downward. But as the lead is moved aft, the sheet pulls more on the foot—more backward.

In practice, it is often difficult to see the angle of the jib sheet accurately. But if the leech is fluttering, it indicates that the fairlead is too far aft, creating too much twist at the top of the sail; if the foot of the sail is fluttering or bellied out too far, the fairlead is too far forward, flattening the top of the sail too much.

Telltales

The most effective sail trim is often elusive, even for experienced sailors. Yet while no one can actually see the wind, there remains a relatively simple solution: Place pieces of ribbon or yarn about eight or nine inches long—TELLTALES—at or near the luff on both sides of the headsail, and sometimes also on the mainsail. Their movement will reveal the action of the wind; see **Figure 8-18.** Jib telltales can serve to fine-tune sheet lead position and sheet tension. Although telltale positions will

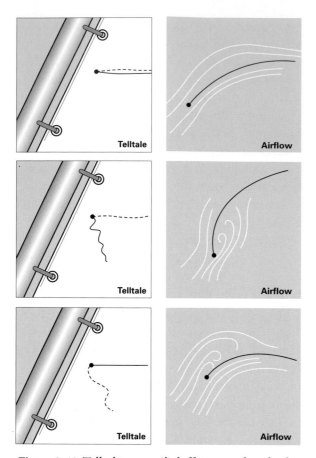

Figure 8-18 Telltales on a sail's luff stream aft on both sides of the sail (dashed line is to leeward) when airflow is even and smooth (upper). A drooping telltale (middle) indicates a dead pocket of air, with no force being extracted. Lifting and fluttering telltales on the leeward side (lower) indicate that air is curling around the sail's edge.

vary with preference, in general three telltales are placed on the jib about a foot behind the luff so that they divide the luff into four roughly equal sections. (It's a good idea to avoid placing telltales too close to seams. It can be frustrating when they become caught on stitching in light air.)

Some sailors also favor telltales at the point of maximum draft on their mainsail, and one at each batten pocket along the leech, in addition to three telltales at the luff positioned as for the jib.

In general, the object when trimming a sail is to have all the telltales streaming aft at the same time, indicating that the airflow across the two sides of the sail is even and smooth. When telltales lift and flutter, air is curling around the edge of the sail

nearest the telltale instead of flowing strongly past it. When telltales droop, it's an indication that an "empty pocket" of air has been created and no energy is being extracted at that point.

If the leeward telltales are lifting or fluttering, they indicate that the boat can be steered on an angle closer to the apparent wind because the airflow is hitting the edge of the sail and tipping over it, resulting in a curl. If it is not necessary, or even desirable, to steer closer to the wind—if the boat is not sailing upwind, but reaching—the same corrective effect can be achieved by letting the sail out. The leading edge of the sail thus meets the airflow more smoothly, and as a consequence the telltales stream aft.

Conversely, if a windward telltale lifts and flutters, the boat is too close to the apparent wind and must be LAID OFF, or steered at a wider angle to the apparent wind. If a course change is not desirable, the airflow can be corrected by pulling the sheet tighter and the sail closer to the boat's centerline.

If the telltales nearer the foot of the sail (usually the headsail) are acting differently from the telltales nearer the head, then there is something wrong with the amount of twist. The sheet lead position should be changed until the telltales all react in a similar manner to changes in steering angle or sheet tension. For example, if the upper windward telltales are lifting while the lower ones are streaming, this is an indication that the sail has too much twist and the leads should be moved forward.

Fluttering or drooping telltales on the leech of the mainsail indicate that the air leaving the after edge is curling, creating drag; this is created by loosening of the leech tension, known as OPENING UP THE LEECH. This drag can be reduced or eliminated by tightening the leech.

The Slot

The mainsail and the headsail work very closely together to shape the air that flows between them. This area between the sails is called the SLOT. The headsail accelerates the air across the leeward surface of the main, helping it produce lift and substantially enhancing the low-pressure venturi effect.

If the jib sheet is eased, it permits the clew to rise and go too far outboard. The slot may become too open, so that there is no accelerated flow. If the jib is sheeted too tightly, the slot closes and the jib forces airflow to curl into the back of the main—BACKWINDING the main and destroying the low pressure that is the whole object of the trimming. (Sometimes this backwinding is acceptable if there is too much airflow and sufficient power is being taken from the headsail while the main acts to balance the pressures fore and aft to control steering.)

The jib should generally be trimmed for course and conditions first, then the main trimmed so that the twist of the leech matches that of the jib, making the slot effective. On an upwind course, jib and main are usually trimmed as close to the centerline as wind force will permit. On some boats, a second fairlead track or BARBER-HAUL system permits the headsail sheet lead to be positioned closer to or farther from the centerline, as well as fore and aft, with much the same effect as adjusting the mainsheet traveler.

Other Rigs

When measured against the relatively complex rigging of conventional sailboats, the popularity of wishbone cat-rigs is easy to understand; see **Figure 8-19,** far right. One sail does all the work and is controlled, for the most part, by one line— the mainsheet. The wishbone boom is suspended at its forward end by a choker line that attaches to a block on the mast and leads down to the foot of the mast and back to the cockpit. At its aft end, it is suspended, like a conventional boom, by the sail. The tightness or looseness of the choker line determines the depth or shallowness of the curve of the main in somewhat the same way that a conventional outhaul does.

Very small sailboats may have a variety of rigs, as shown in **Figure 8-19.**

Upwind Techniques

The closer to the wind a boat sails, the less distance it must travel to reach an upwind destination. But it also sails slower. Conversely, the farther off the wind it sails, the faster the boat moves. But it must sail a greater distance; see **Figure 8-20.**

The objective of sailing upwind (variously called POINTING, BEATING, or SAILING CLOSE-HAULED or TO WEATHER) is to reach a specific point as quickly as possible by sailing a course that strikes the best compromise between higher speed and longer distance on the one hand, and lower speed but shorter distance on the other. The exact best compromise changes with wind speed and wave conditions.

In general, flatter sails are more efficient upwind than are full ones; refer to **Figure 8-15.** They also should be sheeted as close to the center-line as the wind strength will allow. The crew

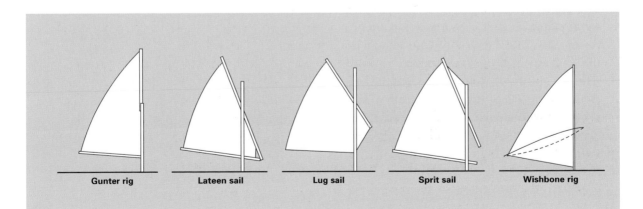

Gunter rig **Lateen sail** **Lug sail** **Sprit sail** **Wishbone rig**

Figure 8-19 Very small sailboats may have a variety of rigs as shown here. Most commonly seen is the lateen rig, used on board boats such as the Sunfish, and the wishbone rig used on board sailers. The rigs shown above are in addition to the common marconi and gaff rig.

TACKING

Since a boat cannot set a direct course to a destination to windward, it must tack upwind. Each tack has a predeterminable compass heading, a factor of leeway and estimated speed; its length must be calculated to achieve the most efficient progress in tacking to windward.

A well-crewed boat should be able to tack smoothly, a fundamental maneuver of sailing. In preparation, the helmsman announces "Ready about," and bears off the wind a few degrees to add speed. The windward foresail sheet is prepared with a turn or two around the windward winch, while the leeward foresail is uncleated but kept on the winch ready to free. The winch handle should be at hand. If the traveler car is to windward, the crew member assigned to the mainsheet readies the car to be moved.

The helmsman should check the compass heading on the original tack. Once the boat and crew are readied, the helmsman announces, "Helms a'lee" or "Coming about," and smoothly luffs up into the wind, ensuring that the rudder is not cranked over so hard as to stall the boat.

As the headsail passes through the eye of the wind, the helmsman pushes the tiller or wheel over until the course is about 95° or 100° from the original course. The original leeward sheet is cast off, and the new leeward sheet hauled in by hand until taut, then wrapped two more times around the winch. The winch handle is inserted for final foresail trimming. Simultaneously, the helmsman gradually lets the boat gather speed as the mainsheet trimmer moves the traveler and trims the main to complement the trim of the foresail. The objective bearing on the new tack will be about 90° from the previous one, and 45° to the true wind on the new windward bow. But the helmsman should allow the boat to accelerate slightly off the wind before sails are trimmed perfectly and the boat is steered up to the desired heading.

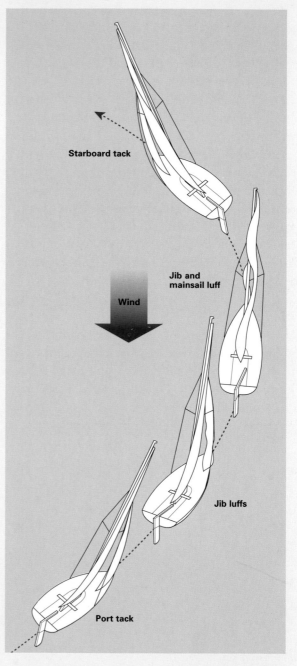

In the tacking diagram shown at right, the boat begins to turn at the bottom figure. Sails begin to luff as the bow heads into the wind. Momentum carries the boat onto the new tack (in this case, the starboard tack), and the sails are then trimmed.

should be prepared to depower sails during gusts—either by easing the traveler car to leeward or by easing the mainsheet—so that excessive heeling doesn't contribute to leeway. Positioning crew to windward and even asking them to hike over the side will also help to counter heeling, thus allowing the keel to produce more lift and less leeway.

Constant adjustment of sails is called for in alternating gust and lulls when close-hauled. Alternatively, the helmsman can PINCH UP in puffs and gusts, temporarily depowering the sails and keeping the boat ON ITS FEET (albeit at a temporary loss of speed), and bear off in lulls to accelerate.

Sailing close-hauled, the helmsman must determine how well the boat is balanced. If too much weather helm is required to keep the boat sailing a straight course, the center of effort has moved too far aft or the boat has heeled too much. To balance the boat, the sails can be depowered (flattened), the leech can be opened up, the boom can be eased out away from the centerline, or all three.

To sail a windward course well, a crew must deal with several trade-offs in order to develop a strategy for reaching a windward mark. Factors such as wind strength, the possibility of a wind shift, sea conditions, strain on the boat, crew comfort (and if in a race, how the competition is doing) must be weighed in order to set a course that efficiently and economically moves the boat toward the target.

Reaching Technique

Bearing away from a close-hauled course onto a reach is a technique that puts most boats onto their fastest point of sailing. But caution must be taken whenever this maneuver is put into practice—continued care is required in order to maintain the boat's balance. Weather helm, as the boat tries to round up into the wind, is usually strongest on a close reach because an overtrimmed main will tend to keep the center of effort back and to twist the boat into the wind.

Moving the main traveler to leeward will change the angle of incidence of the leading edge of the sail to the apparent wind and ease heeling.

But while main and jib should be trimmed for the course and wind strength, care must be taken that the main isn't eased so far that wind strikes its lee side too directly and stalls the boat. In centerboard boats, it helps to raise the board slightly to move the center of lateral resistance aft and more in line with the center of effort. A skilled crew might wish to cope with gusts by alternately easing and sheeting sails. But the helmsman should bear in mind that the rule that applied when close-hauled is now the opposite: When reaching, bear off in gusts and head up in lulls. It is essential to bear off because, as boat speed increases, the apparent wind moves forward. In a light boat, a quick jab to leeward will also help to "put the hull under the sails" and stabilize it momentarily.

In order to keep the rudder "biting" when reaching in heavy weather, crew weight should be aft and to windward. This is especially important in a following or quartering sea, because waves moving under the hull from behind can lift the stern and rudder out of the water, causing the boat to yaw with a momentary loss of steerage. But a helmsman who learns to STEER THE WAVES can often surf down them and exceed theoretical hull speed, one of the most exhilarating experiences in sailing. The boom vang should be used to adjust the curve of the leech and control the boom.

Reaching in very light conditions calls for different tactics. Moving crew weight forward and to leeward induces heel, making the sails "fall" to leeward and giving them a better airfoil shape to utilize what little airflow exists.

Offwind Technique

Sailing off the wind can be a pleasant respite after a long beat or reach. More sail may be carried because the apparent wind is not as strong. On the other hand, downwind sailing is not usually as fast as other points of sail, and unless caution is taken it can be the most dangerous point of sail; see **Figure 8-20**.

Bearing off a reach onto a straight downwind course, ease the main as far out as possible. If possible, ease tension on the backstay (leeward running backstay, if so equipped)

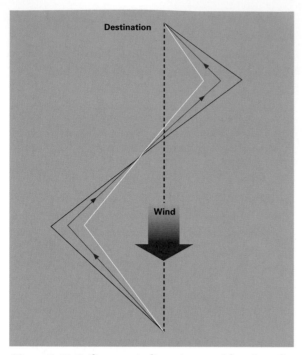

Figure 8-20 Sailing upwind requires consideration of several factors, including wind speed, wave conditions, and desired level of comfort. In the example above, any of the three routes shown will lead to the same destination.

for fuller sail shape of the headsail. Sufficient tension on the upwind running backstay may be applied to give extra support to the mast. Most sailors prefer to broad reach downwind, jibing toward the target rather than sailing dead downwind. This is usually preferable for a light, fast boat. But even broad reaching, the narrowest angle toward the target may be best. And unless the wind comes slightly over one quarter, a jib will become blanketed by the main's wind shadow. To put the foresail in clear air, it can be jibed across to the other tack so the boat is sailed GOOSEWINGED (WING-AND-WING), with the lee side of both sails 90 degrees to the wind.

Maintaining steady wind on a boomless foresail when goosewinged is often a problem. The remedy is a whisker pole extended from a fitting on the mast to the clew of the foresail—the precursor of the spinnaker pole. Some long-distance sailors, if sure that the wind won't shift, and reluctant to deal with the extra care a spin-

naker requires, go so far as to fly two boomed foresails at once, one out each side, often with the main reefed or furled altogether.

Whenever the boom is outboard of the boat (sometimes when reaching and always when running), the mainsheet has less downward pull. In heavier weather downwind, waves may cause the boom to rise and fall as the boat rolls. Tightening the boom vang will help steady the boat. The mainsail may be at right angles to the centerline of the boat, but if the boom is allowed to move too far forward, the boat will be SAILING BY THE LEE.

The Dangers of Jibing

If there is a danger that the wind might catch the front of the main and cause a FLYING JIBE (uncontrolled), a PREVENTER can be rigged. The mast attachment of a tackle type of boom vang can be moved farther outboard, toward the toerail. In heavy seas, however, care must be taken that the boom, which is held down by the vang, doesn't dip into the water as the boat rolls. Furthermore, too much tension on the vang may result in over-flattening the main sail. To maintain sail shape, the topping lift and vang can always be adjusted in concert.

While a vang attached to the toerail will partially prevent the main from filling on its leeward side and jibing accidentally, it may also cause damage to the rigging if you do jibe uncontrollably. A better, perhaps safer, preventer can be rigged from the clew of the main to a block on the foredeck, and led to the cockpit where it can be eased if necessary.

In general, crew weight when sailing off the wind should be amidships fore and aft, and as far outboard as possible on both sides. In fresh conditions (17-21 knots) when a following sea is lifting the stern of the boat, moving weight aft is a measure that will help maintain steerage.

When sailing downwind, it is important to remember that wind strength is greater than it seems. Before HARDENING UP to a reach, sails should be tended accordingly, perhaps even changed or reefed if the boat will be over-canvassed for the new point of sail.

JIBING

Uncontrolled jibes are to be avoided as they are hard on gear and a fast-moving boom is potentially dangerous. A controlled jibe, however, should be a normal part of sailing and is not something to be feared. When ready to jibe, the helmsman announces, "Prepare to jibe," and steers slightly off the wind. The mainsheet trimmer hauls the sheet in and cleats it as other crew releases the leeward headsail sheet and hauls in the windward sheet.

The helmsman then steers back toward the wind until the boom swings across the boat and is held by the cleated mainsheet. The mainsheet is then eased to the new windward side as the headsail is trimmed for the new course.

In the diagram at right, the boat is already sailing goosewinged (also called wing-and-wing), with the mainsail on the port side and the jib to starboard. The helmsman prepares to jibe the mainsail turning the stern into the wind (bottom). The wind then catches the mainsail and whips it across the boat (middle), under control of the main sheet.

Port tack

Wind

Mainsail jibes

Starboard tack

Spinnakers

Sailors who wish to achieve maximum speed when sailing off the wind invariably turn to a spinnaker. Perhaps no sail has as many variations as the spinnaker (often called "chute" or "kite"). Sails that fall into the category are often called FLYING SAILS as they are attached to the boat only at their three corners, and do not have the stabilizing support at the luff that other headsails do; refer to **Figure 8-21.**

The chute itself is constructed of lightweight material that fills easily, packs in a small launching bag or box, and is cut to billow with a full shape and curved luff and leech. Contrary to popular view, a spinnaker does not merely catch wind from behind to "push" the boat. Rather, air passing over its leeward side from luff to leech creates a mini low-pressure area into which the sail moves.

For the most part, spinnakers fall into one of two categories: conventional and asymmetrical. A conventional symmetrical spinnaker (luff and leech are of equal lengths and interchangeable) is more efficient directly downwind than asymmetrical models.

Before it is launched, care must be taken that the spinnaker has been properly packed with no twists, and that the head and two corners of the foot of the sail are accessible, preferably color-coded for port (red) and starboard (green).

Assuming that the spinnaker is being launched on the port side, clip the inboard end of the spinnaker pole to the mast eye, with the pole sticking out the starboard (windward) side. Adjust the mast end to the height at which it is anticipated that the pole will be held when the sail is set.

The guy is run through the pole end (still on deck or lower than the pole end attached to the mast) and around the forestay, then clipped to the green-patched (starboard) spinnaker clew and led aft outside the shrouds. The sheet is attached to the red-patched port clew, then led outside the shrouds and aft to a turning block on the aft quarter. The halyard is attached to the head of the sail by means of a swiveling shackle. The spinnaker should be flown from a mast block that is above and ahead of the forestay.

Raise the spinnaker pole using the pole uphaul lift until it is at right angles to the mast. Take up the pole downhaul and cleat it, leaving just a little slack.

Before raising the sail, ensure that the pole is a few feet from the forestay and pay out some of the sail so that the tack is allowed to reach the end of the pole as the guy is tensioned and cleated.

Finally, hoist the spinnaker and cleat the halyard. If the foresail is still flying, it is now lowered and secured on deck or roller-furled. As the spinnaker fills, trim the sheet and guy, first positioning the guy (and the pole with it) according to the apparent wind angle. The pole should be (very roughly) at a right angle (90°) to the apparent wind.

Sailing the Chute

The primary rule of spinnaker sailing is to keep the luff from curling and the pole as square as possible to the wind. The closer the course is to dead downwind, the farther aft the pole is pulled and the more the sheet eased to add to sail fullness. In some cases, the halyard may be eased slightly as well to permit the spinnaker to move forward out of the disturbance from the main.

To reach, allow the pole to move forward, and trim the sheet. Care must be taken that the pole doesn't rest on the forestay; the power of a spinnaker is such that forestay damage is possible. A spinnaker is also capable of heeling the boat dramatically. The helmsman must bear off in gusts and "sail under the chute."

To jibe the chute, begin by swinging the main boom across the centerline. Next, unclip the pole at the mast and, using the remote line to open the pole-end fitting, clip the former mast end over the sheet, which is to become the new guy. The final maneuver consists in attaching the former outboard pole end to the mast eye and trimming the former guy, which at this point becomes the sheet.

An alternative "dip-pole" jibe requires either a pole that fits inside the forestay, or one that can be retracted in such a way that allows it to do so. Throughout, the mast end remains attached to the mast. During the jibe, the guy is released by the remote trip line, the pole is retracted if necessary, and the pole topping lift is released in order to permit the pole to be dipped below and behind the forestay. Finally, the pole end is then clipped onto the former sheet, which now becomes the new guy, and the new sheet (which formerly was the guy) is hauled in and trimmed.

Dousing the Chute

The surest way of bringing down (DOUSING) the spinnaker is first to depower by steering so that the spinnaker is blanketed by the main when the guy is eased forward. The foredeck crew unclips the guy from the pole using the remote trip line and the guy is eased. The sail, now held in the wind by the head and sheet, essentially becomes a large flag. Taking care not to let the sheet or guy fall into the water, one crewmember eases the halyard while another gathers the sail by the leech, under the main boom. With practice, it is possible to gather it directly into the storage "turtle," leaving the two lower corners and head exposed and ready for rehoisting.

Cruising Spinnakers

From the foregoing, it isn't hard to see why conventional spinnakers are often eschewed by cruising sailors who sail short-handed. But all sailors seek to improve downwind performance, and the asymmetrical spinnaker, often called a CRUISING CHUTE, is viewed by many as the cruiser's answer. For reaching in particular, asymmetrical spinnakers, distinguished by a luff that is shorter than the leech, are also gaining favor with racers.

In the cruising form, a line at the tack is led through a block at the stemhead and run back to the cockpit cleat or stopper. The sheets are usually run outside the forestay. Sailing under cruising chute is much like reaching, though easing the sheets by easing the tack line, and perhaps the halyard, brings the sail forward and free of the main's shadow.

Jibing a cruising chute inside the forestay as one would a conventional foresail risks wrapping the halyard around the forestay, as well as damaging the large sail on foredeck fittings. Consequently, a cruising chute is usually jibed by letting the sheet go as the stern comes through the wind. The clew of the sail is allowed to fly free around the front of the headstay and the new sheet on the opposite side is taken up so that (unlike a conventional spinnaker) the reverse side of the chute is now the leeward side.

The asymmetrical chute's effectiveness decreases as the boat sails more downwind. Only in very light conditions should it be poled out like a genoa. However, it is often better than a symmetrical spinnaker for close reaching. A recent trend among larger racing yachts, including those in the America's Cup competition, has been adapted from racing dinghies such as the International 14 class. This system features a permanently mounted pole that can be extended forward through the hull at the bow to become a long sprit (like a bowsprit). Attaching the asym-

Figure 8-21 *"Flying" a spinnaker off the wind can be a breathtaking experience. This powerful sail demands skill and constant attention.*

metrical chute to the pole end means effective exposure to the wind when reaching.

Yet another variation on the spinnaker theme is the so-called gun-mount spinnaker system, which features a pole mounted at its middle on the fitting of a reinforced pulpit. The sail is tacked at both ends of the pole and the pole acts as a boom. Sheets to each end of the pole are used to trim the sail according to the course; refer to **Figure 8-21**.

BOAT HANDLING UNDER SAIL

In most, but not all, situations a sailboat will be under auxiliary engine power when maneuvering in close quarters, such as leaving a berth and coming back in, anchoring, or picking up a mooring. But if for any reason mechanical power is not available, a skipper must be able to

Figure 8-22 Leaving a pier under sail power alone must be done with due caution. Here the crew is about to sheet in the jib, and the boat should gather way and begin to sail. Care should be taken that the boat does not drift back into the pier.

carry out the required maneuver under sail power alone.

The wind that propels a sailboat can also be used to put on the brakes. That's why a skipper who wants to slow down, or stop, will begin by spilling the wind from the boat's sails (letting them out), then will point the bow of the craft into the direction from which the wind is coming. The whole rig, acting as windage, will slow the boat down, stop it, and eventually force it backward.

Docking & Undocking Under Sail

In most instances a day's sail will begin and end at a pier or wharf, or perhaps from a berth in a slip. The first situations are not too great a problem; departing from a slip can be more difficult.

Departing a Pier Under Sail

Frequently, the wind and current will permit a straightforward departure from a pier even under sail. When everyone is on board and all gear is stowed, sails should be readied for hoisting, with the halyards attached.

If the wind will help move the boat from the pier, it is a simple matter to take in the dock lines and raise the first sail. This is usually the mainsail. The boat will be maneuverable as soon as the sail is hoisted and sheeted properly, provided there is sufficient wind; steerageway may be gained by a shove off or along the pier. Other sails may be raised later when clear of the pier; see **Figure 8-22**.

If the wind or current is pushing the boat onto the pier, departure may be more difficult. In extreme conditions, when it is rough or windy and therefore impossible to position the boat for a safe departure from the end of a pier, then either another boat, or an anchor set to windward, will be needed to pull the boat away from the pier.

Coming into a Pier Under Sail

Using the wind to slow down, and eventually stop, a sailboat is a technique that is useful for landing at a pier or wharf; see **Figure 8-23**. Providing that you can choose an "approach path" that heads the boat into the wind, you can sail across the wind, round up, and, as the boat slows, guide it gently into position for docking.

In stronger winds, everything is noisier and more exciting, but the braking action is also greater. It can be further strengthened if the crew pushes the boom outward against the wind as the boat is headed up. This is called BACKING THE MAIN.

Figure 8-23 Arriving at a pier under sail requires practice to prevent crash landings. In the light breeze shown here, sails can be left up and allowed to luff completely. Usually, however, it is wiser to douse the sails just before reaching the dock, in case an unexpected puff of wind comes up to fill the sails.

Careful crew work and a little practice will allow a skipper to judge just how far the boat will carry on as the braking force of the wind is applied. Some skippers claim that they can even back down into a slip, but in a marina, this maneuver should be reserved for emergencies.

When approaching a pier or wharf for a landing under sail, the jib may be dropped some distance away, according to the skipper's judgment. This will slow the boat's speed but keep maneuverability. Lines and fenders should be prepared and ready to use, just as they would be for a landing under power.

The skipper must have an idea of how far the boat will coast after the last sail is lowered or allowed to luff, and before the boat loses maneuverability. This can be learned in open water by heading the boat up into the wind and allowing the sails to luff, observing how far she carries her way. A lightweight centerboard boat will stop in the water almost immediately, while a heavy keelboat may travel for several boat lengths before stopping, depending on wind and sea conditions; see **Figure 8-24.**

When the boat is judged to be the right distance from the dock, she is brought into the wind with the sheets freed, sails luffing. The boat coasts in, still with maneuverability. The right distance will vary with each boat, and in each set of wind and sea conditions.

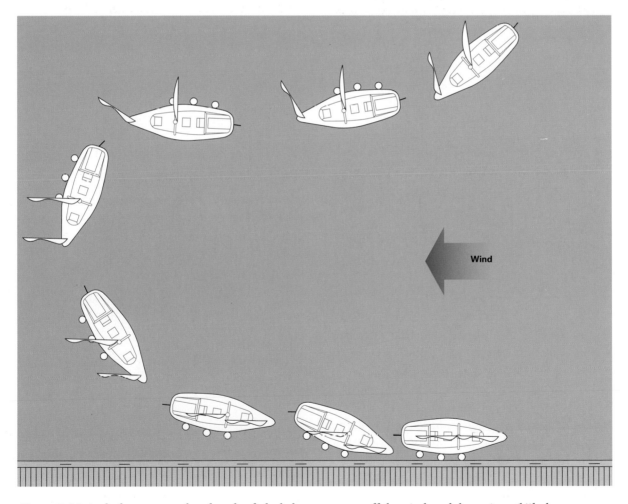

Figure 8-24 As the boat approaches the wharf, the helmsman steers off the wind, and the main and jib sheets are loosened to spill the wind. Once the craft has depowered, the helmsman uses the remaining momentum to steer the boat across the wind, then round up into it at the desired berth. The distance that the boat will coast under such conditions must be gauged by experience; additional braking force, if needed, can be supplied by backing the main against the wind.

Ideally, the boat should lose way and come to a stop of her own accord within arm's reach of the pier, then lines can be neatly placed ashore and the boat secured.

Don't Be Embarrassed to Try Again If the landing looks bad, the skipper should not hesitate to use the last of his maneuverability to turn away from the pier. This allows the skipper to get away and make a fresh approach.

Anchoring Under Sail

When anchoring a sailboat, the skipper must, of course, remember that most sailboats require more water than most powerboats, and he must be mindful of his draft when selecting an anchorage. Furthermore, it is important to remember that because of their keels, and because of their lofty rigging, sailboats are affected differently by wind and current than are powerboats. When anchored too close together, a sailboat and a powerboat will swing differently, and may collide. For this reason, and because of their greater draft, sailboats tend to anchor together in deeper water (see Chapter 9, pages 345-346).

The procedures for setting and retrieving an anchor from a boat with only sail power are generally similar to those for setting and retrieving an anchor under power. However, it can be difficult to set the anchor properly without using an engine in reverse to back down on it and dig it into the bottom.

Setting an Anchor Under Sail

Approach the chosen anchorage under reduced sail, perhaps under mainsail alone. Experiment with your boat and find out what is best.

Follow the recommendations given in Chapter 9, Anchoring. Instead of backing down in reverse gear while paying out scope, however, it is necessary to back down under sail. (See Chapter 9, page 333, for discussion of scope.)

Backing down is best done by backwinding the mainsail firmly and allowing the wind to catch it and back the boat down. If the boat spins and will not back down in a straight line, straighten it up by pushing the boom out to the other side. This can be a tricky maneuver because the boat will

start to sail away, and may not back down properly. It may be necessary to drop all sail, settle back to full scope, and then raise sail again, briefly, to apply pressure on the anchor to set it.

Raising an Anchor Under Sail

To raise the anchor without the use of power in a small boat is as simple as pulling up the anchor line, then pulling up the anchor hand over hand. The sail should be already up and luffing, or ready to raise as soon as the anchor is up; see **Figure 8-25.**

In larger craft, that might be too heavy to pull upwind while bringing in the anchor line, other measures will be necessary. The anchor line can be brought in on a windlass, or the boat can be sailed in short tacks up to the anchor, with the crew bringing in the rode by hand as the boat travels over it until the anchor is at short scope. Then the

Figure 8-25 This anchor is being raised by hand while the mainsail is already raised and allowed to luff. When the anchor has been secured in place, the boat will drift backwards in irons, and must be skillfully handled to get off on the proper tack. Take care not to drift back onto other boats while getting underway.

crew must cleat the anchor line promptly, and the momentum of the boat will beak out the anchor, and it can then be raised by hand.

Using a Mooring Under Sail

The use of a mooring by a sailboat without mechanical power is much like the process of anchoring. The primary difference is that when picking up a mooring the point of action is more precisely defined; boat handling in the final moments must be much more carefully done.

Departing a Mooring

Leaving a mooring under sail is just as simple as leaving under power, perhaps simpler because there is less worry of fouling the mooring in the propeller. The mainsail may be hoisted before casting off the mooring pennant, but the jib is often hoisted later, to keep the foredeck clear for the person throwing off the pennant.

Getting Off on the Right Tack By waiting for the natural swing of the boat, by backwinding a sail as discussed below, or by holding the pennant far out to one side (and perhaps moving aft a bit while holding the pennant out), the person releasing the mooring can send the bow of the boat off in a chosen direction, to port or to starboard, allowing the mainsail to fill on one side, and the boat to pick up speed.

Caution must be taken that the pennant is not released when the boat is exactly head to wind, because it is then "in irons" and may drift backwards "in irons" without steerageway. It may continue to drift without any wind in the mainsail until she fetches up on a boat moored astern, or in the shallows near shore.

Picking Up a Mooring Under Sail

When picking up a mooring under sail, the skipper's knowledge of the particular boat is called upon. Again, wind, current, and sea conditions must be considered, and practice will pay off.

As the boat nears the mooring, station a crewman forward to pick up the pennant, or be prepared to go forward quickly yourself if you are alone. Turn the boat directly into the wind, and let the sails luff while the boat is still a few boat

Figure 8-26 *To pick up a mooring under sail, a slow approach is made with a crewmember stationed forward. The boat must not approach too fast, but must have enough speed to maintain steerage. When the mooring pennant has been picked up and secured, the sails should be dropped promptly. Practice is required and a good sailor makes it look much easier than it actually is.*

lengths away from the mooring buoy. It should have the momentum to keep going ahead and stop with her bow just at the pennant, but this takes practice; see **Figure 8-26.** Just how many boat lengths to allow is part of the skill involved, and the distance will change from day to day depending on the wind and current, and from boat to boat.

As with coming into a pier for a landing, if the maneuver isn't working right—just head the boat around, trim the sails, and try again.

SAIL HANDLING & STOWAGE

Sails are expensive—ask any sailboat skipper/owner! The proper handling and stowage of sails will do much to extend their life and reduce overall costs. Some variations may be necessary on different craft, but the general procedures given below will cover most situations.

Headsails

Roller furling for headsails is one of many innovations that promote simplified, convenient handling of sails; not surprisingly the system has been growing steadily in popularity. The furling mechanism typically consists of a headfoil that is fitted over the forestay. The foresail halyard is then attached to a swivel that can both slide up and down the foil as well as swivel around on it. A reel-like drum at the base of, and fixed to, the foil has a furling line that is wound around it. The furling line finally leads back to the cockpit. Some models feature a continuous line around the reel that is led aft on blocks; see **Figure 8-27**.

To raise the sail initially, the head is attached to the swivel and the boltrope fed into the groove of the foil. The tack is attached to the drum. The halyard on the swivel pulls up both the swivel and sail. When the furling line is hauled aft, the drum and foil turn around the forestay, rolling the sail

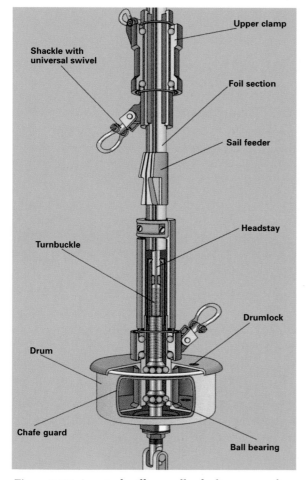

Figure 8-27 A typical sailboat roller furling system for a headsail uses a reel-like drum to contain the furling line. The furling line can be controlled from the helm position.

around it as well. The furling line is cleated to store the sail furled on the forestay. To protect the sail from ultraviolet deterioration, a sacrificial protective strip is often sewn along the leech and foot. To set the sail, the furling line is released. Tension on a sheet unrolls the foresail, assisted by the wind once the aft part of the sail beings to fill.

In addition to saving storage space, foresail furling systems also permit the sail to be partially furled or reefed. To maintain proper angle of the sheets when the sail is reefed, jib fairleads must be moved forward on their tracks.

Mainsails

Roller furling systems exist in a number of variations for mainsails as well. Some feature an in-mast or behind-the-mast furler that begins by winding the luff of the sail, pulling the clew forward. The disadvantage of such systems is that they preclude the use of battens, often require a loose-footed main, and add weight aloft.

In-boom furling systems that furl the foot of the sail on an internal roller are actually a refinement of older roller reefing systems that worked by wrapping the sail around the boom itself. In practice, the boom is supported by the topping lift while the halyard is released and a handle winds the roller in the boom. The customary difficulty of getting a proper sail set, which used to affect older systems, has been eliminated on many modern versions.

A more commonly employed (and distinctly less expensive) means of reefing is a SLAB or JIFFY system that makes use of cringles at two or three reef points on each of the luff and leech. Reefing lines are fastened to the boom, led up through the cringles on the leech and down to a sheave at the boom end, and then forward to the gooseneck. To reef, the boat is taken head to wind, and the topping lift is tensioned in order to take the weight of the boom. The halyard and outhaul are then eased off and the reef cringle at the luff is hooked onto a tack hook. As the halyard is tensioned, the appropriate reefline is taken up to pull the new clew down and aft, and the topping lift is eased. The new foot of the sail is then secured, either by means of permanent lines on the sail or with sail ties led through cringles spaced between the leech and luff reefing points.

As unwieldy as all this sounds, with a certain amount of planning, a reef using a jiffy reefing system can usually be taken in or let out in less than a minute, and the resulting shortened sail can be set well.

Spinnakers

The lack of luff support makes spinnakers more unstable and more difficult to launch, jibe, and douse (take down). Some new designs are equipped with a reinforced patch and a cringle in the center to which a "take down" or "retriever" line is attached to assist in dousing the sail, and sometimes for pulling the sail through a tubular launcher incorporated into the hull with a funnel-like outlet on deck. The retriever is then led through the tube to the cockpit. Now the doused sail, which is now stored in the tube, is ready to be redeployed whenever it is needed.

Another technique for hoisting the spinnaker entails careful packing beforehand. The sail is pulled through a funnel-like device equipped with elastic bands stored on its narrow end. As the head of the sail is pulled out the narrow end, bands are placed around it at intervals. The spinnaker is rigged and hoisted with the bands in place. When the sheet and guy are trimmed, the bands break and let the sail fills.

A tubular sleeve with rings at each end (variously called a SOCK, or SALLY, or CHUTE SCOOP, etc.) may also be used. The spinnaker is stored inside the sleeve and attached to it. The sleeve is hoisted on the spinnaker halyard.

A line running the length of the sleeve is threaded through a block at the halyard end, and from there is attached to the ring at the bottom. The sock is hoisted fully with the sail inside, and then the line is pulled in such a way that it will slip the sleeve upward. Wind filling the bottom of the sail usually helps to move the bottom ring and sock toward the halyard until the spinnaker billows and fills. The sleeve, meanwhile, remains at the head of the spinnaker while it is flying, and the line from the sleeve is cleated on deck. To douse the spinnaker, the sheet and guy are eased

Figure 8-28 *To store a lowered mainsail, pull the sail aft from the leech, flaking it on opposite sides of the boom as you go.*

and the line attached to the sock's bottom ring is hauled in so as to pull the sock down over the sail. In addition to being useful in dousing, a sock also can be used to control the sail while jibing whenever the boater is sailing shorthanded. The sock is merely pulled down over the sail, set up on the opposite tack, and pulled again to set the sail.

Storing Sails

Foresails not stored on a roller system should be dry and FLAKED—folded accordion-style—before being bagged; see **Figure 8-28**. Though not always the easiest thing to do in rough weather, the crew can control a hanked-on sail as it comes down on the side-deck by moving forward and pulling aft on the leech, securing the sail to the rail as they go. Ideally, another crewmember, sitting back-to-bow in the bow pulpit, can control the luff to assist with flaking. If the flaked sail is to be bagged, the sheets are untied, and it is rolled neatly from the clew forward, ready to fit in the bag opening.

Hanks can be left on until the sail is stored. Sails that fit into a headfoil present a difficulty since they are controlled only by the halyard and tack when dropped. Care must always be taken to ensure that the sail does not fill on deck and then blow overboard.

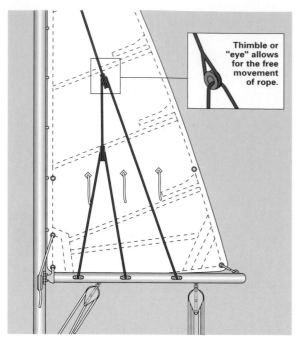

Thimble or "eye" allows for the free movement of rope.

Figure 8-29 *Lazy jacks, shown here, are designed to help control the mainsail as it is dropped by cradling it on the boom.*

An elongated bag—aptly referred to as a SAUSAGE BAG—is often used in place of a conventional sail bag whenever using headsails constructed from new sail materials, such as Mylar or Kevlar, that can be damaged if they are folded too tightly. The zipper on the bag is opened lengthwise and clipped to the lifelines before the sail is dropped to the deck. Then, once the sail is dropped and flaked in the open bag, the full-length zipper is closed to enclose the sail.

A number of systems exist to help control the mainsail. LAZY JACKS—ropes or wires running from mid-mast to the boom—keep the sail on the boom when it is dropped; see **Figure 8-29**. Another system, called a DUTCHMAN, features vertical lines running from the topping lift (or a similar line), through cringles on the sail and down to the boom. When the halyard is released, the vertical lines hold the sail in line with the boom.

To store the lowered mainsail on the boom, begin at the leech and pull the sail aft, flaking it on alternative sides of the boom. Sail ties can be used at intervals to lash the sail to the boom. As soon as possible, the sail should be covered to prevent ultraviolet degradation. Lazy jacks and the Dutchman may necessitate a special sail cover.

NEW SAILBOAT TYPES

Sailing is undergoing another major step in its evolution. Techniques explored by sailboarders, multihull sailors, and racing dinghy sailors for the last 20 years are now finding their way into the mainstream of sailing. In addition, techniques rooted in pure science and aircraft speed engineering—such as rigid wings and hydrofoils—are finding practical, if not widespread, application.

Several factors are making sailing a faster and more exciting sport. One is the simple fact that most North Americans enjoy speed. Yet the cost of moving across the water at speed is very high. Many recreational boaters just can't afford to run a fast powerboat. For them, the thrill of a catamaran at high speed, not to mention the challenge of handling it, is an affordable choice.

Another factor is the availability of strong and light materials. In fact, many of the designs we consider recent and new had been around in slightly different forms for most of the twentieth century. For example, extremely light, flat-hulled racers with lots of sail area and asymmetrical spinnakers are very like the "sandbaggers" that were raced in New York Harbor late in the nineteenth century.

What's different now is that light, highly stressed designs can be built of strong materials, making ownership by mainstream sailors possible. Sandbagger sailing, on the other hand, was semi-professional and certainly not for the family man—just as America's Cup sailing today is very distant from family-oriented racing.

Multihulls

The most obvious "new" sailboat type is the catamaran or trimaran. In fact, the idea is ancient and was tried out as a racing design also in the nineteeth century.

Multihulls first gained acceptance in the 1960s as light and fast recreational boats, but began to be seen as a practical (and even potentially safer) solution to long-distance cruising. Their high construction cost (at least in a production setting) and the general conservatism of the North American market kept them in the background through the `60s and `70s. However, in the `80s, European and some exceptional North American sailors successfully sailed multihulls in the open trans-ocean competition offered by such races as the Single-Handed Trans-Atlantic Race; see **Figure 8-30.**

There are now several successful builders of production multihulls in Europe and North America and their general superiority, at least for racing, has been well demonstrated in various professional-level ocean races as well as Dennis Conner's famous defense of the America's Cup in 1988.

Along with the huge stability provided by two or three separate hulls, multihull designers have introduced such innovations as the rotating mast and the full-batten sail. By allowing the mast to rotate on a vertical peg at the foot, catamaran sailors are able to point the mast into the airflow and to induce the least amount of drag. By "over-rotating" they can more precisely control the shape of the full-batten sail. A rotating mast can also be built with a lighter and stronger section, because its wider surface can be regarded as sail area rather than parasitic drag.

Rigid-Wing Sails

The wide rotating mast and very stiff, full-batten sails of catamaran competition eventually led to the rigid-wing sail. First regarded as belonging exclusively to the radical realm of catamaran competition, and with no practical relevance to ordinary recreational sailing (or conventional "yacht club" racing), the rigid wing is now proven as a feasible cruising rig. John Walker, the British

Figure 8-30 North American sailors resisted multihulls for years, but designs such as this Jeanneau trimaran are winning them over.

former aircraft designer, has created a cruising multihull, called the Planesail, powered by a three-part, rigid-wing sail. The trim on the sail is automatically controlled and electronically adjusted so that sailing the Planesail is more like driving a vehicle (or flying an aircraft). The skipper sits in a chair and manipulates switches and levers. There is no winch grinding, halyard hauling, or, in fact, any of the procedures described in the previous sections for sailing a conventional sailboat. Yet the Planesail has crossed the Atlantic under the power of wind, sometimes in rough weather. This remarkable achievement owes almost nothing to the conservative traditions of racing-oriented yacht design.

Rigid wings have also been used in catamaran competition, where their somewhat higher weight can be compensated for with very widely spaced hulls that are able to yield much greater stability.

Planing Hulls

Sailboats have been planing since the early 1900s, but it is only in the last 30 years that light, high-powered sailboats have become extremely popular. Boats with wide, light hulls are common, and many of these are equipped with trapezes that allow their crew (sometimes both skipper and forward hand) to suspend themselves horizontally over the surface of the water on the windward side.

The enormous increase in stability that trapezing allows is exploited by very large sail areas in relation to the weight of the boat and crew. Planing a boat of this type is possible even in gentle winds of only 12 or 13 knots.

Trapezing is only practical on boats no longer than about 20 feet (6.1 m). At this size, the complexity of crew work and the number of trapeze artists required takes such boats out of the realm of recreation and into the realm of pure sport.

However, even without trapezes, there are many light, but ballasted, keelboats that are capable of planing in heavy winds. While such planing episodes can be brief (and are often assisted by a following sea that induces surfing),

these light, flat-keel boats nevertheless achieve speeds well beyond the normal limit of the speed of a wave length equal to their displacement waterline.

Keels & Ballast

One of the refinements that has made it possible for a ballasted boat to sail beyond displacement hull speed is the use of very deep, and consequently narrower, fin keels.

A given volume of lead ballast, if stretched downward, acts on the hull with a longer lever and can, therefore, provide more righting moment for the same weight. There are practical limits to the extent of draft, however, that have to do with the mechanical stresses placed on a lifting surface like a fin keel, especially when it is swung violently by wave action at the surface (not to mention shallow water).

Recent design trends among America's Cup boats have suggested that the development of bulb keels will continue as a way to concentrate more ballast farther away from the hull.

Ironically, the wing keel, made famous by the first successful challenge of the America's Cup (by Australia, in 1983), was a successful design innovation that was very tightly tied to the design rules of the 12-meter class—which insisted on very high ratios of ballast to overall weight. Wing keels have found popular application outside of competition, in cruising boats that need both good windward performance and shallow draft; see **Figure 8-31.** The volume of lead needed to provide righting moment can be formed into a shallower shape, which, with winglets, needs not be hydrodynamically inefficient.

The quest for greater righting moment without the penalty of weight has found yet another expression in the use of movable and expendable water ballast. There are two common approaches. In the most obvious method, water is taken on board, and held in tanks at the extreme beam of the hull. If the boat is working to windward on starboard tack, for example, its water ballast is pumped into the starboard tank where its weight provides the best righting moment. As or before the boat tacks, water is transferred, by pump or

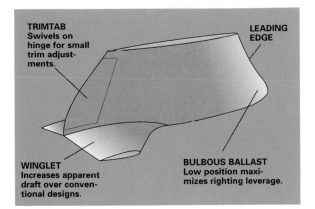

TRIMTAB
Swivels on hinge for small trim adjustments.

LEADING EDGE

WINGLET
Increases apparent draft over conventional designs.

BULBOUS BALLAST
Low position maximizes righting leverage.

Figure 8-31 Wing keels are designed to position more ballast weight lower, without adding significantly to the craft's draft. Originally created for competition racing, they are now being used on cruising boats.

gravity, to the port tank, ready for the new tack. Of course, great care must be taken that the boat is not completely disabled should the ballast end up on the wrong side in heavy winds. The amount of water ballast carried, in relation to the boat's other stability, has to be carefully calculated by the designer. Obviously, racing boats, especially single-handed ocean racers with the most to gain, take greater calculated risks.

Another type of water ballast has nothing to do with racing or risk-taking. Several small, trailerable cruising sailboats have a different kind of water ballast, which allows them to be light enough to tow behind a car but heavy enough to achieve good stability. A long, low internal water tank is built into the hull at the lowest part of the bilge. A hole allows water to flow freely into and out of the tank. When the dry boat is launched, the tank fills up, adding, perhaps, a couple of hundred pounds at the lowest, and therefore, most advantageous, part of the hull. While this seems counter-intuitive to many sailors, it's easy to understand if you imagine, for a moment, that, instead of adding 100 pounds of water, you add 100 pounds of soft drink cans to the bilge. The effect is the same.

When it's time to go home, the (heavy) boat is pulled onto the trailer and, as it begins to rise above its load waterline, the ballast tanks begin to empty. By the time the boat is at the top of the ramp, it's losing weight rapidly.

Sailboards

Currently, the second-fastest sailboat in the world is hardly a boat at all—it is a sailboard, or wind surfer. Surprisingly, it doesn't look much different from the high-tech sailboards you see at any beach. As an exercise in motive efficiency, the sailboard is a very sophisticated device.

First, of course, its hull can hardly help but plane. But more important, it carried a huge amount of sail area in relation to its (and its crew's) overall weight. Since the mast is not stayed, the responsibility for holding it up does not fall on the hull. Rather, the weight of the crew is partly suspended against the very efficient lifting surface of the sail. Here, the aircraft notion of "lifting" has real merit; in fact, many sailboards are capable of short flights, given the right wave.

However, in setting a world speed record, the sailboard in question stayed very firmly on the water, finally reaching just over 44.66 knots.

Unfortunately, the sailboard may already have reached its maximum size. If it were any larger, it could not be controlled by one person.

Anchoring

*Types of Anchors • Anchor Lines • Anchoring Techniques • Special Anchoring
Situations • Permanent Moorings*

Of all the skills involved in seamanship, the art of anchoring is one the boater must master if he is to cruise with an easy mind. Perhaps you have been getting by with inadequate gear and bad practices acquired in home waters. Sooner or later, carelessness and lack of technical know-how will lead to difficulty—probably inconvenience, possible danger.

The essence of successful anchoring is to "stay put," without dragging, whenever the anchor is set. And don't forget the need to respect the rights of nearby boats that could be fouled or damaged if your anchor drags.

Though anchoring skill may not be learned from printed pages alone, this chapter should help the beginning skipper to get off to a good start and the seasoned boater to verify or update his technique.

In quiet anchorage, in familiar surroundings, ground tackle (the gear used) and the methods employed are seldom put to test. Cruising into strange waters, being obliged to use inadequate shelter in an exposed anchorage during a hard blow, and unexpected variations in wind and current will surely take the measure of both tackle and technique.

The problem, then, breaks down into two principal parts—(1) the equipment that every boat should carry, and (2) knowledge of how to use it.

GROUND TACKLE

Anchors have evolved over centuries from the simple stone fastened to a crude rope to modern designs that have been carefully engineered to achieve the greatest holding power for the least weight. It did not take long for mariners to realize that what was needed was an anchor that would *dig in* and *hook* the bottom, rather than merely a weight that might drag across it. Simple wooden hooks were first added, later changing to iron. Still later a STOCK was installed perpendicular to the plane of the hooks so as to put them in a better position to get a bite of the bottom. Holding power in softer bottoms was improved by adding broad FLUKES to the hooks. Now, anchors have highly engineered designs that enable them to quickly and deeply bury themselves in the bottom, thus achieving the maximum holding power for the least weight.

Some Terms & Definitions

To prevent confusion in the use of terms, refer to the labeled illustration of the parts of an anchor, **Figure 9-01,** and the definitions in the sidebar on page 319 (also refer to Appendix G for further information). A popular version of the classic anchor was chosen to illustrate the parts. Subsequently we shall see how the proportioning and placement of parts have varied with the introduction of later designs.

The ANCHORING SYSTEM is all the gear used in conjunction with the anchor, including the line, chain, shackles, and swivels. The anchor line, including any chain, is often called the RODE.

Types of Anchors

Scan a marine hardware catalog and, without experience, you may be confused by the diversity of designs. What you should be buying, essentially, is holding power; sheer weight is no index of that. On the contrary, scientific design is the key to efficiency, and a modern patented anchor, if properly manufactured, stands at the top of the list on a holding-power-to-weight basis.

Lightweight-type Anchors

The LIGHTWEIGHT TYPE of burying anchor introduced just prior to World War II was developed by R.S. Danforth. Its efficiency in service was so

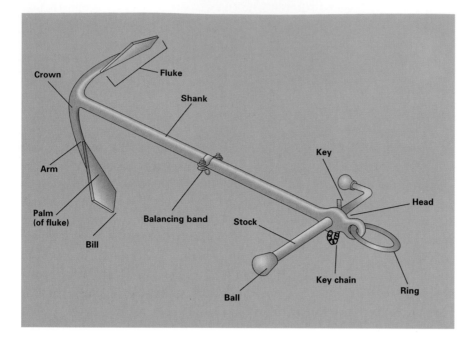

Figure 9-01 Anchor parts are identified here on a traditional kedge anchor, but many of the terms are the same for most modern types.

high that it permitted the retraction of grounded amphibious vessels during assaults on enemy-held beachheads. After that war, models were developed specifically for recreational and small commercial craft, and these are widely used. The term "Danforth," although the trade name belonging to one manufacturer, is often used generically for all anchors of this general design.

Although refinements by a number of subsequent manufacturers have led to minor changes, the Danforth design remains generally the same as the original. The lightweight anchor's high holding-power-to-weight ratio (the ultimate measure of an anchor's desirability) makes it a standard piece of equipment on many recreational vessels.

In this type of anchor, pivoting flukes are long and sharp so that heavy strains bury the anchor completely; see **Figure 9-02.** It tends to work down through soft bottoms to firmer holding ground below, often burying part of the line as well; see **Figure 9-03.** On some designs, the angle between the flukes and stock can be varied for improved performance on soft or hard bottoms. In place of a stock through the head, the lightweight type has a round rod at the crown end to prevent the anchor from rolling. This placement of the stock does not interfere with the shank being

drawn into the hawsepipes of larger craft for stowage. (Many skippers place protective rubber tips over the stock ends to prevent scarring the boat's topsides and the bringing up of mud and sand from the bottom if the stock is a hollow rod.)

In use, a lightweight-type anchor at first rests flat on the bottom. A forward pull with a slight

Figure 9-02 Lightweight-type anchors made of steel were originated by Danforth, but are now also made, with minor variations, by several other companies. Note the angled plates on the crown.

upward angle on the shank turns its broad, pivoted flukes downward so that their sharp points dig into the bottom. The stock at the crown prevents the anchor from rolling and disengaging one or both flukes. A key element in the high performance of lightweight-type anchors is the design of the crown. The two flat, inward-sloping surfaces force the thin, sharp flukes to dig into the bottom and penetrate deeply. The surfaces of the crown are placed away from the plane of the flukes in order to help reduce clogging with mud, grass, or bottom debris that might possibly interfere with the penetration of the anchor and its holding power.

After the initial strain placed on the line, and thus on the shank, has buried the flukes into the bottom, subsequent pull on the line continues to bury the anchor until the force of the pull and the resistance of the anchor's broad flukes are balanced against each other; refer to **Figure 9-03.**

Compared to other anchors, this popular type is easy to handle and stow. Its holding power is most effective in favorable bottoms such as sand, mud, or clay; on a rocky bottom, the flukes may or may not catch. Where there are weeds or grass, this type of anchor will often skip across the bottom without digging in; if it does set, it may be in the grass or weeds that will then pull out with a complete loss of holding power.

A number of manufacturers produce anchors of the lightweight, burying type. In selecting an anchor, remember that all manufacturers have their own concepts of design, and "look-alikes" do not necessarily hold similarly. Be sure to check both design and construction integrity. Variation between the angles of the flukes to the shank on similar sized anchors from the manufacturer may

ANCHORING TERMINOLOGY

• **Anchor** Device designed to engage the bottom of a waterway, and through its resistance to movement, to maintain a vessel within a given radius.

• **Anchor chocks** Fittings on the deck of a vessel used to stow an anchor when it is not in use.

• **Anchor rode** Line or chain, or a combination of both, connecting an anchor to a vessel.

• **Bow chocks** Fittings on a vessel's rail at or near the bow having jaws that serve as fairleads for an anchor rode or other lines.

• **Breaking out the anchor** Unsetting it by pulling up on the rode when above it.

• **Changing the nip on an anchor rode** Preventing wear from occurring at the same place over an extended period of time by pulling in or letting out a short length of the anchor rode.

• **Ground tackle** An overall term for anchors, anchor rode, fittings, etc., used for securing a vessel at anchor.

• **Hawsepipe** A cylindrical or elliptical pipe or casing in a vessel's hull through which an anchor rode runs.

• **Horizontal load** The horizontal force that is placed on an anchoring device by the vessel to which it is attached.

• **Mooring bitt** A post through or attached to the deck of a vessel that is used to secure an anchor rode or other line to the vessel. A Samson post is one form of a mooring bitt.

• **Scope** The ratio of the length of the anchor rode currently in use to the vertical distance from the bow chocks to the bottom of the water (depth of water plus the height of the chocks above the water).

• **Tripping an anchor** Using a line attached to the crown or head of an anchor fouled in the bottom to pull it out backwards (to "trip" it).

• **Vertical load** The downward force placed on the bow of the vessel by its anchor rode.

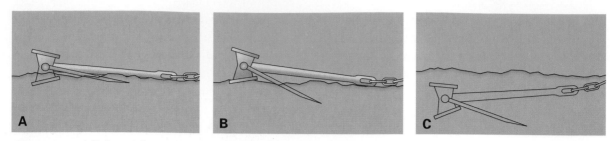

Figure 9-03 *A lightweight-type anchor lands with its flukes flat against the bottom (**A**). A strain on the anchor line causes the flukes to penetrate the bottom (**B**). Further strain on the rode causes the flukes, and sometimes the entire anchor and part of the rode, to be buried (**C**).*

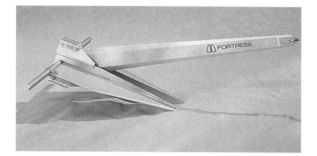

Figure 9-04 *The Fortress anchor, made of aluminum alloy, has high holding power per pound of weight. It does better in softer bottoms and performs poorly in grass and weeds. The shank angle can be adjusted to the type of bottom.*

indicate inadequate quality control. Carefully inspect all welds—if the anchor breaks in use, its most attractive feature, holding power to weight ratio, becomes meaningless

Lightweight-type anchors are also made of aluminum, with the trade names of Fortress and Guardian As a result of careful engineering, these anchors have shown even greater holding power than steel anchors of comparable size, plus increased ease in handling from their significantly lighter weight. These anchors can be disassembled and stowed as a flat package. Another desirable feature of Fortress anchors is their ability to be assembled in either of two ways for different fluke angles in order to maximize holding power in normal or soft mud bottoms; see **Figure 9-04.** One drawback is that these anchors have a tendency to plane or fly off in the water as they are lowered.

Plow Anchors

The PLOW anchor resembles none of the other anchor types. It was invented in England by Professor G.I. Taylor of Cambridge University; he called it the CQR (which stands for "secure"). Its most distinctive feature is a shank that pivots longitudinally on a hinge; this reduces its tendency to break out from the bottom when the boat swings and the direction of pull changes; see **Figure 9-05.** Similar models have since been developed and manufactured in the United States and other countries. It has found wide acceptance because of its demonstrated efficiency in a variety of bottoms. Opinions vary as to its effectiveness in heavy grass or weed, which

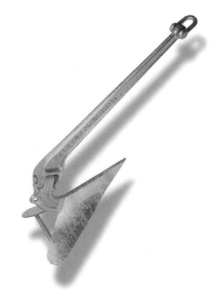

Figure 9-05 *The plow anchor gets its name from the shape of its single deep-burying fluke pivoted at the end of the shank.*

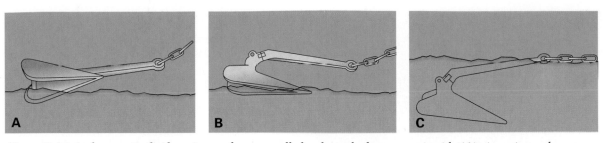

Figure 9-06 A plow or similar burying anchor normally lands on the bottom on its side (A). A strain on the anchor rode causes it to turn more upright and quickly bite into the bottom (B). Further stain on the line results in the anchor burying itself in the bottom (C).

is not surprising in that many weed growths resist penetration by any anchor.

When a plow anchor is lowered, it first lies on its side on the bottom; see **Figure 9-06.** Then when a pull is put on the line, it rights itself after moving a short distance, driving the point of the plow into the bottom and finally burying the anchor completely if the bottom is soft. Suggested weights for CQR anchors may vary from 15 pounds (6.8 kg) for a 25-foot (7.6 m) boat to 60 pounds (27.2 kg) for a 60-foot (18.3 m) craft, with heavier sizes available for larger vessels. For best performance, the manufacturer recommends a minimum of 18 feet (5.5 m) of chain between the anchor and a fiber line.

Because of the pivoting feature of its shank, the plow anchor tends to remain buried over moderate changes in direction of pull on the line caused by wind or current shifts. There is no projecting fluke to foul the anchor line and the plow breaks out easily when the pull is vertical for raising the anchor. Plow anchors do not stow well on deck and are usually hoisted to a bow roller fitting where they are secured.

As with lightweight types, plow anchors are produced by a number of manufacturers and effectiveness may vary between different units; forged models are stronger than cast versions. A variation of the plow, the Delta anchor, has a solid, nonpivoting shank, but otherwise the same basic design; see **Figure 9-07.** It is weighted so that the pointed fluke is ready to dig in as soon as it reaches the bottom. This anchor design is also somewhat easier to stow on a bow roller, as it does not have the bulky hinge.

The Bruce Anchor

Another anchor from the United Kingdom is the BRUCE. Originally developed for use with offshore oil and gas well drilling rigs, it has been scaled down for use with small craft in sizes from 5 to 50 kg (11 to 110 pounds)

A burying type, the very strong Bruce anchor is designed to right itself no matter how it lands on the bottom while digging in within two shank lengths; it breaks out easily with a vertical pull; see **Figure 9-08.** The design is particularly focused on quick resetting should the anchor disengage from the bottom after a change in direction of pull.

Variations on this basic design are used by different manufacturers, such as the Horizon Claw anchor, which is very similar, and the SuperMax that has larger fluke area; see **Figure 9-09.** Recommended sizes are roughly the same as for plow anchors.

Figure 9-07 The Delta anchor is similar to the CQR plow, except that it is one piece, eliminating the swivel joint between the shank and fluke. Its holding power is said to be slightly superior to other plow types.

Figure 9-08 The Bruce anchor is shaped so that once it has been set, should it pull out from a wide change in direction of pull, it will reset almost immediately. Intentional breakout, however, is easy on a vertical pull. The anchor is said to work well in sand and mud, and is strong enough to be used in rocks.

Kedge Anchors

In discussing KEDGE anchors it is important to distinguish between the more massive ancient types and the later versions designed for small boats. In glossaries, "kedge anchors" are often defined as light anchors (of any design) carried out from a vessel aground to free her by winching in on the rode. Here, however, we refer to the kedge as an anchor with the more traditional type of arms, flukes, and stock as distinguished from newer lightweight types.

Kedge anchors are not widely used on modern recreational boats, but they do have their place in special applications. Some models have relatively sharp bills and small flukes to bite better into hard sand bottoms; see **Figure 9-10.** Others will have broader flukes on heavier arms for greater holding power in softer bottoms and greater strength when hooking into rocks or coral heads. A kedge anchor is normally an excellent choice for bottoms with heavy growth of grass or weeds— one arm will penetrate the vegetation and dig into the bottom beneath. Typical designs are the Herreschoff, Fisherman, and Yachtsman, all varying in small details.

Kedge anchors are not of the "burying" type, as the shank lies on the bottom and one arm remains exposed. On the other hand, a kedge's "hook" design recommends it, probably above all other types, on rocky bottoms where one fluke can find a crevice. Retrieval, with proper precautions, is not too difficult. (More about this later; see page 338.) Modern kedge designs have a diamond-shaped fluke to lessen the risk of anchor line fouling on the exposed arm, but this possibility must be considered if a change in direction of pull of a half-circle or more occurs.

Stock & Stockless Types The plow and Bruce anchors are of the STOCKLESS type. Others are classified as being of the stock type, although the stock, as we have seen, may be at either the ring or crown end. Those with the stock at the crown end, such as the lightweight type, have a fixed stock. On nearly all designs where the stock is at the ring end, such as the various kedge anchors, the stock is loose and can be folded for better stowage. Frequently, a key is required to pin the stock of a kedge in its open position when set up ready for use; the key is lashed in its slot to hold it in place.

Anchors of Special Design

The NORTHILL is an anchor with a design its own. At its crown end, two arms with sharpened flukes extend at right angles to the shank and two arms

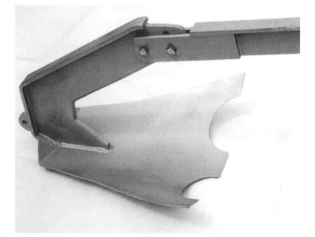

Figure 9-09 The SuperMax anchor's greater holding power seems to come from the extra size fluke. The adjustability of the shank allows the angle to be set for use in varying types of bottoms.

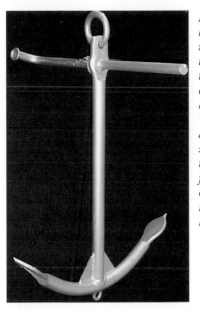

Figure 9-10 The kedge anchor must be heavier than a burying type anchor for equivalent holding power. The thin arms and sharp flukes shown here make this model better for use in weeds or grass; it is also useful on hard bottoms.

without flukes act as a stock. In some versions, all four arms can be folded flat against the shank for stowage.

Several manufacturers sell anchors of distinct proprietary designs, and with what can only be called unique names. Among these are the Barnacle, Bullwagga, Hans C-Anchor, Spade, Vetus, and others. Some of these may disappear from the market, and others will surely be developed. Several have performed very well in impartial tests. The best advice on the selection of one of these more specialized designs is to consider what types are being used in your boating area, and how satisfied are the skippers who use them.

Other Anchor Types

Another design of anchor is frequently referred to as NAVY TYPE. Inexperienced boaters when seeing them on large ships sometimes conclude that they are best for all vessels, including small boats—this is simply not so. Ships use them because such stockless anchors can be hauled up into hawsepipes. The ratio of weight to holding power for these anchors is so small that, if weight is held within reason for a small boat, holding power is far below safe limits.

GRAPNELS, though used by some commercial fisherman, are not recommended for general anchoring service aboard recreational boats. These are also stockless models with, as a rule, five curved, sharp-billed, claw-like prongs symmetrically arranged around the crown end of the shank. Eyes may be cast in both ends of the shank—at the head in lieu of a ring for attachment of a rode (if used as an anchor) and at the crown end for a buoyed trip line (see page 339). By dragging a small grapnel back and forth, a boater may GRAPPLE for a piece of equipment lost on the bottom; see **Figure 9-11.**

FOLDING anchors are those which allow all parts to fold against the shank into the smallest possible space for the most convenient stowage—at some sacrifice of holding power and strength. In one stockless type, there are two pairs of flukes at right angles to each other, almost in the manner of a grapnel. In rocky bottoms they hook readily and may be rigged to pull out easily, crown first. Such anchors are often excellent in bottoms with heavy growths of grass or weeds as one or two arms penetrate the vegetation to get a bite into the bottom. They typically have less than desirable holding power in loose sand or soft mud due to small fluke area.

MUSHROOM anchors are principally used in conjunction with permanent moorings, and are discussed in more detail under that heading; see page 344. Modified versions of the mushroom are manufactured for small craft such as canoes and rowboats, but their efficiency as anchors is so slight as to be almost nonexistent.

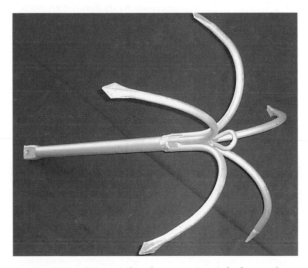

Figure 9-11 A grapnel is shown as it might be used to recover a mooring chain. With a trip line rigged to its crown end, it can be used to anchor a boat on a rocky bottom.

Sea Anchors

All the anchors under discussion in this chapter are designed to keep a boat from drifting by engagement with the bottom; SEA ANCHORS do not fall in this category. These are intended to float at or just below the surface, serving merely as a drag to hold a boat's bow (or stern) up toward the oncoming seas so as to prevent her from lying in the trough. Sea anchors are seldom used aboard recreational boats, and then only in the heaviest weather offshore, where there is room to drift to leeward. See Chapter 10 (pages 356–357) for a discussion of sea anchors and their use in rough weather.

The Anchor Line

All of the gear, taken collectively, that lies between a boat and her anchor is called the RODE—whether it is synthetic fiber (like nylon), chain, or a combination of the two.

Twisted Nylon

Nylon, in three-strand twist or double-braid form, is by far the most widely used material for anchor lines; other synthetics, such as Dacron, polypropylene, and polyethylene, have less desirable characteristics. Chain makes a good anchor rode, but its weight, while desirable for anchoring, may necessitate your having a winch or other mechanical assistance on board to hoist it. On a small boat, the weight of an adequate length of chain, stowed in the bow, may be too great for proper trim.

For anchoring, nylon's greatest asset is its characteristic of stretching under load; it has a working elasticity of 15 to 25 percent. When a boat surges at anchor in steep seas, there is a heavy shock load on fittings and ground tackle—unless provision is made to absorb it gradually. Nylon's elasticity does exactly that.

Some boaters unwittingly lose part or most of the advantage inherent in nylon by using too large a line. Within the limits of safe working loads, the smaller the diameter the better the elasticity for given conditions. A practical limit is reached when small diameters (though rated high enough for breaking strength) are not convenient to handle. Some experienced boaters use nylon as light as ³⁄₈-inch (10 mm) diameter on the working anchors of their 30- to 40-foot (9-12 m) craft. Nylon line—as also discussed in Chapter 23 on marlinespike seamanship—is highly resistant to rot, decay, and mildew, but can be damaged by rust from iron fittings or a rusty chain. Nylon line should be stored out of direct sunlight to prevent a gradual deterioration from ultraviolet rays.

Braided Synthetic Line

Most nylon used for anchor lines is laid up by twisting three strands. Synthetics can, however, be laid up by BRAIDING. For anchoring (as well as mooring or towing) a braided outer cover of nylon surrounds a braided inner synthetic core—this is commonly called "double-braided" or "braid-on-braid" line. The result is a line of exceptional stability with no inherent tendency to twist because of the nature of its lay. Consequently, it can be fed down into rope lockers without fear of kinking.

When braided nylon is handled on deck, it is advisable to fake (of flake) it down in figure-eight pattern, rather than the conventional clockwise coil used with twisted fibers. Because of the relatively smoother surface of braid, with more fibers to take the wear, chafing is less of a problem than it is with the twisted three-strand lay. Braided nylon retains an adequate degree of elasticity (14 percent at working leads, as against 25 percent for twisted nylon).

Chain

As the size of the vessel increases, so does the required diameter of nylon anchor line. For yachts 65 feet (20 m) or more, nylon would run to diameters of up to fl inch or larger. This is getting to a size that is difficult to handle; the alternative is CHAIN.

From this it should not be inferred that chain is not also suitable for use on smaller craft. Boats that cruise extensively and have occasion to anchor on sharp rock or coral often have chain; in some cases it is regarded as indispensable—it stands chafing where fiber won't.

In larger diameters, the weight of chain makes a sag in the rode that cushions shock loads due to surging. Once the slack has been taken up, however, the shock on both boat and anchor is very much greater than with nylon. You must thus be sure to use adequate scope with chain, as is discussed below. Shock loads can be further mitigated by using a SNUBBER—a short length of nylon line. After the anchor is set, one end of several feet of nylon line is hooked into a link in the chain between the boat's deck and the water surface; the other end is made fast on deck. Then the tension on the chain is slacked off so that the load is carried by this short length of stretchable nylon line.

The three kinds of chain most used as anchor rode are "BBB," "Proof Coil," and "High Test." Chain is designated by the diameter of material in the link, but the various types have links differing slightly in length. It is necessary to match the chain to the pockets of the WILDCAT (a pulley designed for use with chain, also called a GYPSY) of the anchor windlass. The differences in link length are slight, but they are enough to cause trouble if there is a mismatch. (Most windlasses have a capstan for line and a gypsy for chain, but special models are available where the gypsy can handle both.)

Any type of chain may be used for anchoring—BBB is slightly stronger than Proof Coil; High Test is significantly stronger than either. The selection of specific chain type and size for your boat involves several factors, the first of which is adequate strength. A safe standard to use is a WORKING LOAD—figured from the size of the boat and the conditions to be encountered—at 20 percent of the chain's breaking strength when new. But you must also consider weight. The chain must be heavy enough to provide a proper sag to cushion shock loads, but the length required for normal anchoring depths must not be so heavy, when stored on board, that it affects the boat's handling characteristics or even its safety. The weight factor may dictate a combination of chain and line.

Nylon & Chain

In current practice the consensus appears to be that for most craft in average conditions, the ideal rode is a combination of nylon line with a short length of chain between the line and the anchor. The chain length should be 6 to 8 or more feet (2 to 3 m); even longer is desirable.

One effect of chain in this combination rode is to lower the angle of pull, because chain tends to lie on the bottom. Of equal, perhaps greater, significance is the fact that modern lightweight anchors often bury completely, taking part of the rode with them. Chain tolerates the chafe, and sand has less chance to penetrate strands of the fiber line higher up. Sand doesn't stick to chain, and mud is easily washed off. Without chain, nylon gets very dirty in mud.

Chain used in this manner may vary from /inch (6 mm) diameter for 20-foot (6 m) boats up to $7/_{16}$-inch (11 mm) for 50-foot (16 m) craft. It should be galvanized to protect against rust. Neoprene-coated chain is an added refinement, as it will not mar the boat, but such coating has a limited life in active use.

Securing the Rode

The complete ANCHOR SYSTEM consists of the anchor and the rode, usually made up of a length of line plus a length of chain. Each element of the system must be connected to its neighbor in a strong and dependable manner.

Eye Splice, Thimble & Shackle

There are various methods for securing the rode to the anchor ring. With fiber line, the preferred practice is to work an EYE SPLICE around a THIMBLE and use a SHACKLE to join the thimble and ring; see **Figure 9-12**. With nylon line you can use a plastic thimble, one of galvanized metal, or one of stainless steel; be sure to keep the thimble in the eye of the line. A right, snug splice will help, and seizings around the line and the legs of the thimble, near the V, will keep the thimble in the eye splice when the line comes under loads that stretch the eye (see Chapter 23, page 790). A better thimble is available in bronze alloy; this is designed to hold and protect the line; see **Figure 9-13**.

Where a shackle is used, it is a good idea to put a bit of silicone spray or waterproof grease on the threads of the shackle pin to keep it from

Figure 9-12 A shackle and eye splice, with thimble, are commonly used to secure anchor and anchor line to the anchor ring, or better, to a short length of chain between the line and the chain.

seizing up over a period of time; a good practice is to turn the pin all the way in tight, and then back it out a quarter- or half-turn. *Be sure to safety the pin to prevent its working out accidentally;* stainless steel wire can be used, but a nylon "cable tie" is easier to work with (use a black one, they better withstand prolonged sunlight exposure); see **Figure 9-14.** Watch for corrosion if different metals are used in thimbles, shackles, and rings. Also beware of rust stains on nylon; cut out and resplice in a new thimble if the line becomes rust-stained.

A thimble and shackle provide a ready means for including, if desired, a length of chain in your rode, shackling the chain in turn to the anchor ring. Shackles should be large enough so as not to bind against the ring, and at least as strong as the chain itself.

Anchor Bends & Bowlines

Some skippers would rather fasten their line directly to the ring using an anchor bend, seizing the free end to the rode. Others use a bowline with an extra turn around the ring, see **Figure 9-16.** In either case, these procedures make it easy to turn the line end-for-end occasionally, or to remove the line from the anchor for easy handling when stowing.

Turning a line end-for-end greatly extends its useful life, as the lower portion of the line that has carried the load for each anchoring, and the lower end that has chafed on the bottom, become the inboard portion seldom used with normal scope. Eye splices may be used at both ends of the rode, or added as necessary when the rode is turned.

Even where the regular working anchor is kept made-up with a combination of line and chain, you should know how to bend a line directly to an anchor. This is often the handiest way to drop a light anchor for a brief stop, or to make up a second anchor when a bridle or stern anchor is needed.

Use shackles to secure chain rode to the anchor; stout swivels are a desirable refinement. As swivels are a weak point, they must be large. On an all-chain rode they are essential. Swivels, however, should not be used with twisted soft-laid synthetic lines; a hockle (kink) may be the result. Double-braided synthetic lines will not hockle, even though subjected to very heavy strains.

Figure 9-13 A special type of thimble of bronze alloy or plastic should be used with synthetic line to prevent the line from jumping out of the thimble when the eye splice stretches under load.

Figure 9-14 This shackle, used to attach a short length of chain to another shackle on the anchor is secured by running a nylon cable tie through the eye of the pin and around the side of the shackle. Stainless-steel wire can also be used for this.

At the Bitter End

To guard against accidental loss of the anchor system, the bitter (inboard) end of the anchor rode should be made fast to some part of the boat. You may do this by leading the line below, perhaps through a deck pipe, and securing it to a built-in eye or an eyebolt through a strong structural part. On sailboats you can secure it to the foot of a mast. On small boats where the entire length of rode is carried on deck, you can have an eye splice in the bitter end to fit a securely fastened ring or eyebolt. In any case, make sure that the bitter end is fastened, but always have handy some means of quickly cutting the anchor line in an emergency—even if you think that you could unfasten it in a hurry.

How Many—& How Heavy?

The number of anchors you should carry depends upon several things—the size of your

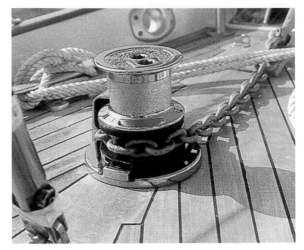

Figure 9-15 This vertical windlass has a smooth drum on top for line with a gypsy for chain beneath it; they can be operated independently. The anchor chain passes around the gypsy and through a deck opening to the chain locker below. The smooth drum can be used with a dock line to warp the boat into a berth.

boat, whether it is used only in sheltered waters or cruises extensively to many harbors, and, to some extent, the type of anchor.

Some small boats like runabouts and utilities have only a single anchor, but this cannot be considered adequate. Even discounting the possibility of fouling one anchor so badly that it cannot be retrieved, there are occasions when it is desirable to use two. Further, one anchor heavy enough for extreme conditions could be a nuisance in ordinary weather.

Figure 9-16 An anchor bowline, above, with its extra turn around the ring, is a secure way to bend the rode to the anchor; for greater security, the loose end can be seized—wrapped with twine or thread—to the adjacent line (here only the end has been whipped).

SUGGESTED SIZES FOR WORKING

Boat length ft(m)	Rode length ft(m)	Rode size in(mm)	Chain size* in(mm)	Danforth standard model	Fortress model no.	Plow lbs. (kg)	Bruce lbs. (kg)	Delta lbs.(kg)
Up to 15 (4.0)	100 (01)	¼ (6)	³⁄₁₆ (5)	4-S	FX-7	20 (9.1)	11 (5)	14 (6.4)
15 to 35 (4.6 to 7.6)	150 (46)	³⁄₈ (10)	³⁄₁₆ (5)	8-S	FX-7	20 (9.1)	11 (5)	14 (6.4)
26 to 30 (7.9 to 9.1)	180 (55)	³⁄₈ (10)	¼ (6)	13-S	FX-11	20 (9.1)	16.5 (7.5)	22 (10)
31 to 35 (9.4 to 10.7)	200 (61)	³⁄₈ (10)	¼ (6)	22-S	FX-11	25 (11.4)	22 (10)	22 (10)
36 to 40 (11.0 to 12.2)	250 (76)	⁷⁄₁₆ (11)	⁵⁄₁₆ (8)	22-S	FX-16	35 (16)	33 (15)	35 (16)
41 to 50 (12.5 to 15.2)	300 (91)	½ (12)	³⁄₈ (10)	40-S	FX-23	45 (20.4)	44 (20)	35 (16)
51 to 60 (15.5 to 18.3)	300 (91)	½ (12)	³⁄₈ (10)	65-S	FX-37	60 (27.2)	66 (30)	55 (25)

*Recommended chain length, ½ foot of chain for each foot of boat length. Larger vessels should use an all-chain rode.

Table 9-1 The sizes above are suggested for use under moderate conditions of wind and waves, with good holding ground and a scope of 5:1. For less favorable conditions, increase anchor size by one bracket and increase scope. For a "lunch hook" under good conditions with a person remaining on board, one bracket smaller can be used.

Many boats carry two anchors, with the weight of the heavier one about 1.5 times the weight of the lighter one. For cruising boats, three are undoubtedly better. This allows for two to be carried on deck—a light LUNCH HOOK for brief stops while someone is aboard, and a WORKING ANCHOR for ordinary service, including anchorages at night in harbor. The third might well be a big spare STORM ANCHOR, possibly stowed below, selected with an eye to its holding no matter what else lets go, even under extreme conditions of wind and weather.

Anchor Size & Holding Power

Down through the years there have been repeated attempts to reduce anchor weights to a simple formula or table based on boat length or tonnage. Recommendations have varied widely, gradually becoming lighter as more modern designs replaced old-fashioned kedge anchors. With the development of patented designs, however, came the problem of minor variations between manufacturers of anchors of the same general type. Thus any table of anchor size vs. boat size, such as **Table 9-1** can only be a broad recommendation, to be modified for individual craft and local situations.

Stowage

A boater's seamanship skills can be evaluated by the attention he gives to stowing his craft's ground tackle. Exactly how he goes about it depends to some extent on the kind of boating he does, the size of his boat, and the way it is equipped. In any case, unless his deck is uncluttered—with gear ready for immediate use, yet secured so that it cannot shift—he will never rate high as a seaman.

Ordinarily a cruising boat will carry one, sometimes two, anchors on deck, made up and ready for use. On some small boats, where it is not feasible to leave anchors on deck at all times, or in cases where lines are stowed below at the home berth, at least one anchor and line should be prepared and made ready before getting underway from your slip or mooring. If your boat lowers its anchor from a windlass,

Figure 9-17 Anchors are normally stowed in fitted chocks on the foredeck, but working space can be gained if they are hung from the rail as shown above.

Figure 9-17. Many boats with bowsprits or pulpits have a roller at the outboard end, to carry an anchor in this outboard position as a regular working anchor; see **Figure 9-18.** Some larger yachts have provision for hauling the anchor into a hawsepipe fitted into the topsides forward.

The load can be taken off the anchor windlass by using a chain TENSIONER or STOPPER. This small device is suitable for an all-chain rode or the chain portion of a combination rode. It mounts on the deck and either hooks into a link of the chain or clamps around it.

Stowing the Storm Anchor

As the big spare storm anchor is used only on rare occasions, you can carry it in some convenient location below, or in a lazarette or stowage space below a cockpit deck, accessible through a hatch. Chocks here should be arranged to ensure that the anchor is held in place securely. If the big anchor

power to that device should be on. Engines and steering systems do fail, and when they do it's likely to be at an embarrassing moment, with wind or current setting you down on a shoal or reef. It's too late then to think about breaking out gear that should have been ready at hand.

An anchor lying loose on deck is a potential hazard. If the boat happens to roll or pitch, it may slide across the deck, leaving scars in it wake and damage to equipment. Conceivably it could go over the side, taking line with it that might foul a propeller. Every anchor on deck should be stowed in chocks which are available at marine supply stores to fit standard anchors. Lashings hold the anchors in the chocks. Hardwood blocks, properly notched, have often been used in lieu of metal chock fittings.

As an alternate of chocking to deck, anchors carried aboard sailboats may be lashed to bow rails or shrouds, off the deck, where there is not risk of their getting underfoot, and less risk of their fouling running rigging; see

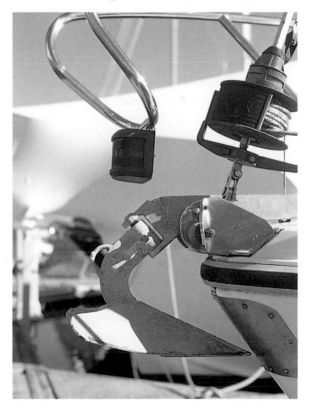

Figure 9-18 Many boats, both power and sail, have short bowsprits that have a roller at the outer end. The anchor line passes over this roller and the anchor can be drawn up tight against it.

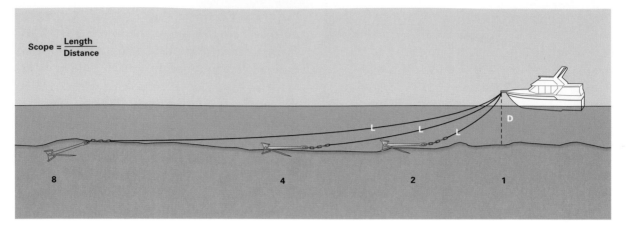

Figure 9-19 *Scope, the ratio of rode length L to the distance D, from the bow to the bottom (1), is critically important to safe anchoring. At (2) the rode length is twice the distance D, but the angle of pull tends to pull the anchor free. At (4), with L four times D, the anchor can dig in, but there is still too much upward pull on the rode. At (8), scope 8:1, the short length of chain at the anchor lies flat on the bottom, and any pull acts to pull the anchor in deeper.*

gets adrift, it could easily break through the hull. Some anchors, such as the Fortress can be broken down into parts and stowed in a box or fitted bag; they can be assembled in only a few minutes with two ordinary wrenches.

The big risk in stowing a spare anchor away in some out-of-the-way corner is the possibility that other gear may be allowed to accumulate over and around it. You must guard against that happening. The sole value of a storm anchor may some day depend upon your being able to get that big hook over quickly, bent to a long and strong spare rode that must be equally accessible.

Lunch hooks are small and seldom needed without warning, so there's justification for stowing them in some convenient locker. Keep them away from the compass, however, as they can be a potent cause of deviation (except, of course, for aluminum anchors).

Rope & Chain Lockers
Although small craft often carry their lines coiled on a forward deck or in an open cockpit, many cruising boats have a rope locker in the forepeak that can be used. Nylon dries quickly and can be fed down into lockers almost as soon as it comes aboard. Lockers must be well ventilated and arranged to assure good air circulation at all times. Dark, damp lockers are an invitation to rot and mildew. A vented hatch over the rope locker will permit exposure to a good flow of air.

The rode should always be ready to run without fouling. Line is often passed below through a deck pipe, slotted so that it can be capped even when the line is in use. Slots must face aft to prevent water on deck from finding its way below. Some cast mooring bitts are made with an opening on the after face, through which line can be passed below.

Chain won't soak up moisture and is easy to stow in lockers. Where weight of chain in the bow of a small offshore cruising boat is objectionable, it can be overcome by splitting a long rode into two or three shorter lengths, stowed where convenient and shackled together as necessary. The chain portion of a combination nylon-and-chain rode is ordinarily shackled in place for regular use, but nylon, if left on deck, should be shaded as much as possible from the sun to protect surface fibers from damage by ultraviolet rays.

Scope
Once you have chosen an anchor of suitable design and size to provide adequate holding power, you must consider SCOPE. It is a major factor that determines whether your vessel will, in fact, hold or drag. Too short a scope can destroy the efficiency of the best anchor.

Although some books use the term "scope" to refer to the length of anchor rode in use, most often it is recognized as the *ratio* of the length of the anchor rode to the height of the bow above the bottom of the body of water, as shown in **Figure 9-19.** Note two important factors: the height of the bow chocks above the surface, and the range of the tide.

Let's assume you anchor in 10 feet of water with 60 feet of rode paid out. At first glance, this is a reasonable scope of 6:1. But if your bow chock is 5 feet above the surface, the ratio is immediately cut to 4:1 (60:15). Six hours later the tide has risen another 5 feet and now you have an actual scope of 3:1 (60:20), exactly half the original theoretical ratio, and much too slight for safety.

What Is a Proper Scope?

Under favorable conditions using nylon line, 5:1 might be considered a *minimum;* under average conditions, 7 or 8:1 is regarded as satisfactory. Tests show that proper scope ratios range between 5:1 and 10:1, the latter for heavy weather. Even in a very hard blow, in an exposed anchorage, you will probably never need a scope of more than 15:1 with an anchor of suitable holding power. Effective scope for given conditions varies with the type of anchor. In our hypothetical example above, allowing for the range of tide, the length of rode paid out should have been 140 (7:1) to 160 (8:1) feet; 100 feet (5:1) might be regarded as a minimum.

With all-chain rodes, a scope from 3:1 to 5:1 is adequate for all normal condition.

For maximum efficiency, all anchors require a low angle of pull—preferably less than 8∞ from the horizontal. With short scope, holding power is reduced because the angle of pull is too high, tending to break the anchor out. As the pull is brought down more nearly parallel with the bottom, flukes dig in deeper with heavier strains on the line. Surging, as a boat pitches in a sea, throws a great load on the anchor, particularly on a short scope. With long scope, the angle of pull is not only more horizontal at the anchor, but the elasticity of a long nylon line cushions the shock loads significantly.

Marking a Line for Scope

Granting that we know how much scope is required, how do we know when we have paid out enough? Estimates are risky. Plastic cable markers, see **Figure 9-20**, come in sets to mark various lengths, such as 25, 50, 75, 100, 125, 150, and 200 feet (or corresponding metric lengths), and are attached by inserting them under a strand or two of the line. In daylight such markers are fine, but in the dark, the traditional markers of strips of leather, bits of cotton or flannel cloth, and pieces of marline with knots have the advantage of being able to be "read" by feel. Plastic markers have the further disadvantage of being rapidly chewed up by anchor windlasses.

For all practical purposes, five or six marks at intervals of 20 feet (6 m) (say from 60-140 feet; 18-30 m) should be adequate. One practical method is to paint wide and narrow bands of a red vinyl liquid called Whip-End Dip at significant points, calling wide bands 50 feet (15.3 m), narrow ones 10 (3 m). On chain rodes, as a measure of scope, some boaters have painted links white at intervals.

If you anchor frequently in the same harbor areas, you may want to put a whipping—wrapping the line with twine or thread—to prevent chafe at two or three predetermined places on the rode; see Chapter 23, page 799.

Figure 9-20 Numbered plastic markers can be inserted in laid line to indicate the amount of rode let out. Alternatively, colored rings can be painted on the rode.

ANCHORING TECHNIQUES

Thus far we have discussed only equipment, or ground tackle. Let's now consider the technique—the art of anchoring. Before you can think about *how* to anchor, however, you must decide *where* you will anchor, and here, as in all phases of seamanship, a little foresight pays off handsomely.

Selecting an Anchorage

There will be times, of course, when you will stop briefly in open water, coming to anchor for lunch, for a swim, to fish, or perhaps to watch a race—but more often, the real problem of finding an anchorage comes down to the choice of some spot where there's good holding bottom, protection from the wind and waves, and water of suitable depth. Such an anchorage is the kind you'd want for spending the night, free from anxiety about the weather.

Types of bottoms vary widely, and there are good (though perhaps not "best") types of anchors for each bottom. Since it is impractical to carry the optimum anchor for every type of bottom, it is necessary to select an area that best fits one of the anchors that you do have on board.

Using a Chart

A chart is the best guide in selecting a suitable location. Alternatively, "cruising guides" for many boating areas often name anchorages that have been used and found suitable. Sometimes you will be able to find a harbor protected on all sides, regardless of wind shifts. If not, the next best choice would be a cove, offering protection at least from the existing direction of the wind, or the quarter from which it is expected to come. As a last resort, anchorage may be found under a windward bank or shore—that is, where the wind blows from the bank toward the boat. In these latter two cases, watch for wind shifts, which could leave you in a dangerous berth on a lee shore.

Anchorages are sometimes designated on charts with an anchor symbol. Areas delineated on the chart by solid magenta lines, perhaps with the water area marked with yellow buoys, may be designated (U.S. inland waters only) as special anchorage areas, where anchor lights are not required on vessels less than 20 meters (65.6 ft) in length; see **Figure 9-21.** Never anchor in cable or pipeline areas or in channels, both indicated on charts by broken parallel lines in magenta.

Adequate but shallow depths are preferred for an anchorage, because a given amount of rode will then provide a greater scope for better holding. You must consider the range of tide, however, so that a falling level does not leave you aground or bottled up behind a shoal with not enough depth to get out at low water. You also must be alert to the special problems of reversing tidal currents, if such exist where you are anchoring.

Characteristics of the Bottom

The character of the bottom is of prime importance. While the type and design of anchor flukes have a direct bearing on its ability to penetrate, it may be stated broadly that mixtures of mud and clay, or sandy mud, make an excellent holding bottom for most anchors. Firm sand is good *if* your anchor will bite deeply into it; loose sand is undesirable. Soft mud should be avoided if possible. Rocks prevent an anchor from getting a bite except when a fluke is lodged in a crevice. Grassy bottoms, while they provide good holding for the anchor that can get through to firm bottom, often prevent a fluke from taking a hold on anything but the grass, which then pulls out by its roots.

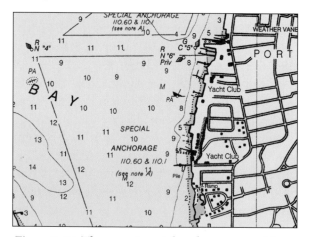

Figure 9-21 There are "special anchorage areas" in U.S. inland waters where anchor lights and shapes are not required on vessels less than 65 feet (19.8m) in length. These are shown on charts; the boundaries may or may not be marked by buoys.

Sometimes bottoms, which would otherwise provide reasonably good holding, are covered with a thick growth of vegetation that positively destroy the holding power of any anchor. Even if you happen to carry one of the fisherman's sand-anchor types, with its thin spidery arm and small flukes, expect it to pick up half a bushel of this growth. All you can do is clean it off and try elsewhere.

Characteristics of the bottom are normally shown on charts; see **Figure 9-22.** By making a few casts with a hand lead armed with a bit of hard grease you can bring up samples of bottom as a further check. Chart abbreviations for some bottom characteristics are shown in **Table 9-2.**

How to Anchor

Having selected a suitable place, and having the proper ground tackle on board, the next step taken is the actual process of anchoring—the approach, getting the anchor down, setting it, and making the anchor line fast. Each step must be done properly if a boat is to be secure. *Never anchor a small boat by the stern*—the freeboard is less and swamping is much more likely to happen.

Approaching the Anchorage

Having selected a suitable spot, run in *slowly*, preferably on some range ashore selected from marks identified on the chart, or referring your position to visible buoys and landmarks to aid you in locating the chosen spot. Use of *two* ranges will give you the most precise positioning; refer to **Figure 9-22.** Later these aids will also be helpful in determining whether you are holding or dragging, especially if the marks are visible at night and it begins to blow after dark.

If there are rocks, shoals, reefs, or other boats to consider, give them all as wide a berth as possible, keeping in mind a possible swing of 360° about the anchor with wind shifts or current changes.

Remember, too, that large yachts nearby may swing to a much longer scope than you allow—and, conversely, that you may swing much farther than a smaller craft nearby lying on shorter rode. A vessel anchored by chain will normally have a

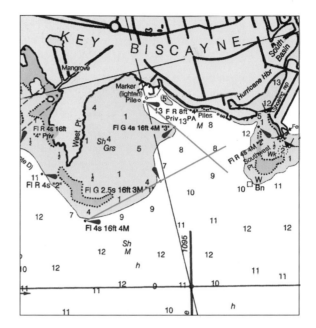

Figure 9-22 Fixed aids to navigation, not buoys, or any pair of charted objects that form a range are useful in selecting an anchorage spot, and as a means of checking to make sure that the anchor is not dragging. An ideal anchoring spot is at the intersection of the two ranges shown above.

lesser scope and thus a smaller swinging circle. A boat on a permanent mooring will have the smallest movement of all. Observe how the boats that will be your neighbors are anchored or moored, visualize how you will swing with your intended scope, and don't get into a situation of overlapping swinging circles.

The risk of fouling a neighboring boat is aggravated when, in a current, a deep-draft vessel holds

Basic Characteristics

Cl. clay	M. mud	Oys. oyster	stk. sticky	gn. green
Co. coral	Rk. rock	hrd. hard	bk. black	gy. gray
G. gravel	S. sand	rky. rocky	br. brown	wh. white
Grs. grass	Sh. shale	sft. soft	bu. blue	yl. yellow

Table 9-2 Knowledge of the character of the bottom is very important in anchoring. Charts provide this information by the use of abbreviations, some of which are shown above.

her position while a light-draft boat swings to a shift of wind not strong enough to influence the other. Keel sailboats may lie one way in a light current, powerboats in another way.

The boat that has already established her location in an anchorage has a prior claim to the spot and can't be expected to move if you later find yourself in an embarrassing position. Consequently, allow room enough so that you can pay out more scope if necessary in case of a blow, without being forced to change your anchor spot, perhaps at night.

The way other boats lie, together with the set of nearby buoys, will help to determine how you should round up to the chosen spot. Estimate the relative effects of wind and current on your own boat and come up *slowly,* against the stronger of these forces—in other words, heading as you expect to lie after dropping back on the anchor. Running through the anchorage, take care that your speed is reduced to a point where your wake will not disturb other boats.

Letting the Anchor Go

These preliminaries disposed of, you are ready to let the anchor go. Unless you must work single-handed, station one person on the forward deck. Enough line should be hauled out of the locker and coiled down so as to run freely without kinking or fouling. If previously detached, the line must be shackled to the ring, and the stock set up (if of the stock type) and keyed. Many an anchor has been lost for failure to attach the rode properly. Rodes, too, have gone with the anchor when not secured at the bitter end. Lightweight anchors are always ready for use and do not have to be set up, but always check to see that the shackle is properly fastened.

Despite what may be seen all too often, an anchor *should not* be lowered when your boat has *any headway at all.* In a motorboat, or a sailboat under power, the bow should be brought slowly up to the spot where the anchor is to lie, and headway checked with reverse power. Then, just as the boat begins to gather sternway slowly in reverse, the anchor is lowered easily over the side until it hits bottom,

crown first. (Anchoring under sail only is covered on page 308.)

Never stand in the coils of line on deck and don't attempt to "heave" the anchor by casting it as far as possible from the side of the boat. Occasionally, with judgment, a light anchor in a small boat can be carefully thrown a short distance if such action is required—taking care that it lands in its holding position—but the best all-round rule is to *lower* it as described. That way the possibility of fouling is minimized.

Setting the Anchor

An anchor must be "set" properly if it is to yield its full holding power. The best techniques for setting an anchor will vary from type to type; only general guidelines can be given here, and you should experiment to determine the best procedures for your boat, your anchors, and your cruising waters.

With the anchor on the bottom and the boat backing down slowly, pay out line (sometimes spoken of as VEERING) as the boat takes it, preferably with a turn of line around the bitt. When the predetermined length has been paid out, snub the line promptly and the anchor will probably get a quick bite into the bottom. A lightweight, burial type like a Danforth or Fortress is frequently set with a scope as short as 3:1 or 4:1, especially in a soft bottom. Anchors such as a kedge or plow or Bruce seem to set better with a scope of 5:1 to 8:1.

Sometimes the anchor may become shod with a clump of mud or bottom grass adhering to the flukes; in these cases, it is best to lift it, wash it off by dunking at the surface, and try again.

After the anchor is set, you can pay out or take in rode to the proper length for the anchorage, and for the prevailing and expected weather conditions. Scope must be adequate for holding, but in a crowded anchorage you must also consider the other boats.

When you must work single-handed, get your ground tackle ready to let go long before you arrive at the anchorage. Bring the boat up to the chosen spot and then lower the anchor as the boat settles back with wind and current, paying out line as she takes it.

Regardless of the type of anchor, after you have paid out full scope, reverse your engine to apply a back-down load in excess of any anticipated strains. This is particularly important if your boat is to be left unattended.

You must make a positive check that the anchor is holding, and not dragging. There are several ways to do this. If the water is clear enough that you can see bottom, you can detect any movement easily. If you cannot see bottom (which is generally the case) select two objects on the beam that form a natural range and watch for any change in their relationship—if none occurs, your anchor is holding. An even simpler method is possible if you are using a buoyed trip line from the crown of your anchor (see page 339). When you are applying reverse power to test the anchor's holding, the float on this line should continue to bob up and down in one spot unaffected by the pull on the anchor rode. If you see the float making a path through the water, however, you can be sure that your anchor is dragging. In warm, clear tropical waters, it is an excellent practice to put on a mask and fins and "swim to the anchor," checking visually how well it is buried.

Making Fast

After the anchor has gotten a good bite, with proper scope paid out, make the line fast and shut off the motor.

On boats with a forward bitt (or samson post), an excellent way to secure the anchor line is to make two to four full turns around the bitt, and then finish off with a half-hitch around each end of the pin through the bitt. The bitt takes the load and the pin secures the line; this way, the line is more easily taken off the bitt than with a clove hitch or any other hitch. Do not depend on the brake of a windlass to carry the load of an anchor rode.

Where a stout cleat is used to make fast, take a full turn around the base, one turn over each horn crossing diagonally over the center of the cleat, and finish with a half-hitch around one horn; see Chapter 23, page 788.

The fundamental idea in making fast is to secure in such a manner that the line can neither slip nor jam. If the strain comes on top of a series of turns on a cleat, then you will find it nearly impossible to free the line if you want to change the scope; you must first taking the strain off it.

If you must shorten the anchor line, first clear the bitt or cleat of old turns and hitches. Do *not* place new turns over old ones.

A trick worth using when the sea is so rough that it is difficult to go forward on deck—especially if you are single-handed—is to set up the anchor in the aft cockpit, lead the line forward on deck through a closed chock and then back aft to the cockpit. (If there are stanchions for lifelines, the lead off the rode from chock to anchor must obviously be outside them.) When you're ready to let go the anchor can be dropped on the weather side from the cockpit, with the line running through the bow chock and secured on a bitt or cleat aft.

Hand Signals

Anchoring, like docking, is one of the situations where it's a great help to have another hand on board. A problem is communication between the person on the foredeck and the skipper at the helm. With engine and exhaust noise, or a howling wind, it's usually difficult for the skipper to hear, even though the man on deck can. A helmsman handling the boat from a flying bridge can usually hear better and, from his higher position, can see the trend of the anchor line.

In any case, it helps to have a prearranged set of hand signals. There is no need for standardization on this, as long as the helmsman clearly understands the crew's instructions. Keep the signals as simple as possible. Motion of the hands, calling for the helmsman to come ahead a little, or back down, can take the most obvious form; pointing ahead or aft will do it. Simply holding up a hand palm out—a "traffic policeman's signal"—may be used to indicate a "stop" to whatever action is then taking place.

When the Anchor Drags

Let's assume now that you have anchored with a scope of 7:1, have inspected the rode, and taken bearings, if possible, as a check on your position.

Though the wind has picked up, you turn in, only to be awakened near midnight by the boat rolling. Before you reach the deck you know what has happened: the anchor is dragging and the bow no longer heads up into the wind.

This calls for instant action, not panic. A quick check on bearings confirms what the roll indicated: You're dragging, with the wind abeam. Sizing the situation up swiftly, you note that danger is not imminent; there is still plenty of room to leeward and no boats downwind to be fouled. Otherwise you would have to get underway immediately, or be prepared to fend off.

The first step in trying to get the anchor to hold is to let out more scope. Don't just throw over several more fathoms of line; pay it out smoothly, with an occasional sharp pull to try to give it a new bite. If you're dragging badly and can't handle the rode with your hands, take a turn around the bitt and snub the line from time to time. If this doesn't work, start the engine and hold the bow up into the wind with just enough power to take the strain off the rode. This gives the anchor a chance to lie on the bottom and perhaps get a new bite as you ease the throttle and let the boat drift back slowly.

If you haven't held when the scope is 10:1, get the anchor back aboard and try again with your larger storm anchor, or in another spot.

Sentinel—or Buoy?

Suppose, now, that you have no spare storm anchor to fall back on. Can anything be done to increase your holding power? Here we enter an area of controversy with something to be said for two quite different techniques. One has the objective of lowering the angle of pull on the anchor line, and the other the lessening of the shock loads on the anchor or on the boat itself. We'll consider both procedures in turn.

For generations, cruising boaters have used a device known as a SENTINEL (sometimes called a KELLET); see **Figure 9-23.** In principle, the sentinel is nothing more than a weight sent more than halfway down the rode to lower the angle of pull on the anchor and put a greater sag in the line that must be straightened out before a load is thrown on the anchor. Working only with what came readily to hand in such a case, boaters have shackled or snapped their light anchor to the main anchor line, and sent it down the main rode with a

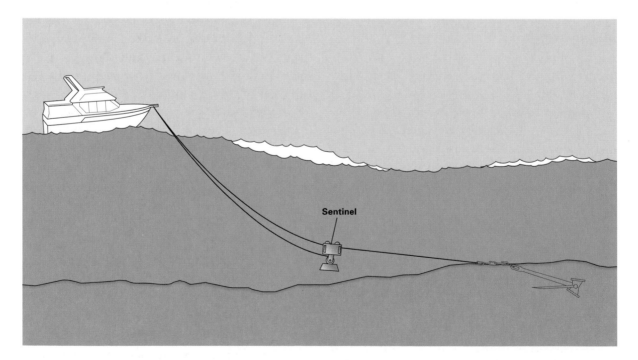

Figure 9-23 A sentinel (kellet) is a weight, typically about 25 pounds (11.6 kg), suspended from the rode to help keep the pull on the anchor as horizontally as possible to prevent dragging in rough weather.

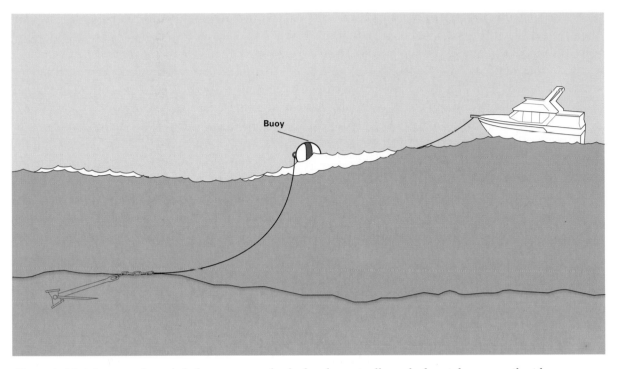

Figure 9-24 A buoy on the rode helps to act as a shock absorber as it allows the boat's bow to easily ride up wave crests without excessive strain being transmitted to the anchor itself.

line attached to its ring, to be stopped at a suitable distance. A pig of ballast or other weight would do as well, provided it could be readily attached. Commercially made devices are available that do this easily and neatly. On the other side of the picture, if the sentinel is to be used, it should be done *with ample scope,* and every precaution taken to avoid chafing the main rode.

The other school of thought would use a buoy, see **Figure 9-24,** rather than a weight, claiming that, properly used, the buoy can carry most of the vertical load in an anchoring or mooring system, limiting the basic load on the boat to the horizontal force required to maintain the boat's position. The argument is advanced that the buoy permits the boat's bow to ride up easily over wave crests, rather than being pulled down into them, with excessive loads on both rode and anchor.

If a buoy is used, it should be of the type found in a permanent mooring system; see **Figure 9-25.** Its connection into the anchoring system should be as for a permanent mooring (as discussed below, page 346) with all strain carried by the rode—this ensures that there is no "weak link." A proper buoy should be carried on board rather than trusting to a makeshift device improvised under the stress of severe weather.

An Alternate System

The chain and sentinel techniques can be combined. Carry a boat-length of substantial chain and a 25-pound (11.3-kg) pig of lead with a ring bolt cast in it. Stow them away somewhere in lieu of ballast. When the chips are down, with breakers to leeward, shackle the chain to your biggest and best anchor, and the chain in turn to

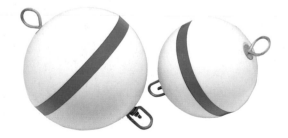

Figure 9-25 A plastic foam buoy usually transmits the strain through the buoys by a solid rod. Some models have the two connecting rings at the same end of the buoy.

your best and longest nylon rode, with the ring of the pig lead shackled in where chain and nylon join. It cannot be anything but an improvement over the same long scope of nylon without benefit of the extra length of chain and added weight. This would seem to eliminate the twin problems of chafe (at the sentinel) and any tendency to hold the boat's bow down in the surge of pitching seas.

Getting Underway

When you are ready to WEIGH ANCHOR and get underway, run up to the anchor slowly under power, so that the line can be taken in easily without hauling the boat up to it. Ordinarily the anchor will break out readily when the line stands vertically. If your craft is equipped with an anchor windlass, do *not* use it to pull the boat forward, use it only to take in anchor rode as it becomes slack.

As the line comes in, you can whip it up and down to free it of any grass or weeds, before it comes on deck. If the anchor is not too heavy, wash off mud by swinging it back and forth, and dunking it up and down, near the surface as it leaves the water. With care, the line can be snubbed around a bitt and the anchor allowed to wash off as the boat gathers way, preferably sternway. Two things must be watched: don't allow the flukes to hit the topsides, and be careful that water flowing past the anchor doesn't get too good a hold and take it out of your hands.

Although nylon anchor line will not be harmed by stowing without drying, it is undesirable to carry this additional moisture below decks. Coil the line loosely on deck and allow it to dry, but expose it to sunlight no longer than necessary.

In all anchor handling, try to avoid letting the anchor hit the hull at any time. Whether your boat is made of fiberglass, metal, or wood, some gouges, dents, or nicks may result. Guests are often eager to "help" by getting the anchor up, but unless they have had some experience, it's better to handle this part of the job yourself. Handle and stow lines carefully. If a bight or end of line slips over the side it is certain to run back under the bottom and get fouled in the propeller.

In a boat under sail alone, have your mainsail up before you break the anchor loose. The same procedure is used as stated above but there is no motor to help. However, it is possible to use your sails to assist. See pages 308–309 for details.

If you have been anchored for a day or two in a brisk wind, the anchor may be dug in deep. Don't wait till you're ready to get underway; 20 minutes before departure shorten the scope— *but keep a sharp watch.* The boat's motion will tend to loosen the anchor's hold and save a lot of work when you finally go to break it out and raise it.

Clearing a Fouled Anchor

If an anchor refuses to break out when you haul vertically on the line, snub it around the bitt and go ahead with the engine a few feet. If the anchor

Figure 9-26 If your anchor fouls on a rocky bottom, your first attempt to free it should be by reversing the original direction of pull (left) with moderate scope, to draw it out (right).

doesn't respond to this treatment, it may have fouled under some obstruction. First try pulling on the line in the opposite direction with moderate scope, about 2:1 or 3:1; see **Figure 9-26.** If this doesn't free it, try making fast to the bitt and running slowly in a wide circle on a taut line. Changing the angle of pull may free it, or a turn of line may foul an exposed end of the stock or a fluke (if it's a kedge) and draw it out.

Probably the best way to break out of a fouled anchor is with a BUOYED TRIP LINE—if you have been wise enough to rig one beforehand. Use a light line, but one that is strong enough to stand the pull of a snagged anchor—⅜-inch (10 mm) polypropylene (which floats) is a typical choice. Attach this line to the crown of the anchor (in some models an eye is provided for this; a hole can be drilled in one of the crown plates of a Danforth or similar anchor). The trip line should be just long enough to reach the surface in waters in which you normally anchor, with allowance for tidal changes. Pass the line through a wooden or foam float (you can even use a plastic disposable bottle if it has a handle) and end the line in a small eye-splice that can be caught with a boathook. If the anchor doesn't TRIP in a normal manner, pick up the trip line and haul the anchor up crown first.

If you haven't rigged a trip line, sometimes you can run a length of chain down the anchor line, rigged so that another boat can use her power to haul in a direction opposite to that in which the anchor line tends, thus changing the angle of pull 180°. With kedges, if one fluke is exposed, a chain handled between dinghies can usually be worked down the rode to catch the upper arm and draw the anchor out, crown first.

If the anchor is not fouled in something immovable but merely set deeply in heavy clay, you can generally break it out by securing the line at low water and allowing a rising tide to exert a steady strain. Or, if there is a considerable ground swell, snub the line when the bow pitches low in a trough. There's some risk of parting the line this way, in case the fluke is fouled worse than you think.

Figure 9-27 On the Hooker Quik-Set anchor, the rode is attached to a ring that slides in a slot in the shank allowing the anchor to be drawn out backwards if necessary. For use when snagging is unlikely, the rode can be shackled directly to the eye at the end of the shank.

There is a type of anchor in which the ring is free to slide the full length of shank. Properly rigged, it is claimed to be virtually snag-proof; see **Figure 9-27.** If the anchor should snag, the theory is that when the boat is brought back over the anchor, the sliding ring can slip down the shank so the anchor will be drawn backwards. There is, however, some risk; if there should be a near-180° shift of wind or current, the anchor might pull out when you wanted it to hold. Some models have an eye at the end of the shank separate from the slot; if the anchor line is attached there, the anchor functions in the normal manner.

Using Two Anchors

For increased holding power in a blow, two anchors are sometimes laid. If your working anchor drags, you can run out your spare storm anchor without picking up the working anchor. The important thing to remember is to lay them out at an angle, not in line, to reduce the risk of having one that drags cut a trough in the bottom for the other to follow; see **Figure 9-28.**

Special care is necessary for a boat with two anchors out if she is subject to extreme wind shifts, as might occur with the passage of a squall line. A change of pull on the anchor lines of 180°, more or less, can bring the two rodes into contact with each other in such a way *neither* anchor will hold or reset if pulled out. In some situations, one anchor is actually safer than two!

When setting two anchors, make the rodes fast separately to two bitts or cleats. Do *not* put one rode on top of the other in case you have to make adjustments later.

To Reduce Yawing

Deep-draft sailboats usually lie well head to the wind, but motorboats often "tack" back and forth at anchor, which is called YAWING. Skiffs, with high freeboard and little draft forward, are among the worst offenders in this respect.

You can lessen yawing by laying two anchors, lines leading out from either bow, making an angle of about 45° between them. To do this, let one anchor down first and have a crewman tend the line carefully as you maneuver the bow off to one side before letting the other go. Then you can settle back on both lines, adjusting scope as necessary.

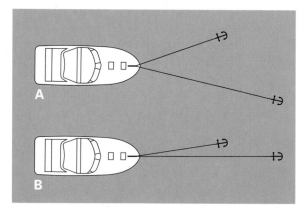

Figure 9-28 If two anchors are set out ahead of a boat, it is best to have the rodes at a wider angle, as at A, rather than nearly in a line, as at B, to reduce the possibility of their fouling each other as the boat swings to wind or current.

With skillful handling, you can get two anchors down single-handed. The easiest way is to settle back on one anchor, making fast when the proper scope has been paid out. Then go ahead easily with the propeller, rudder over enough to hold the line out taut so you can keep an eye on it at all times. When the line stands out abeam, stop your headway, go to the foredeck and let the other anchor go, then drop back, snub the line to set the anchor, and finally, adjust the lines to equal scope.

If a dinghy is available, the second anchor can be carried out in it; the coiled anchor line should be in the stern of the dinghy so that it pays out freely as you move away from your boat. If an attempt were made to pay the line out from the deck of the boat, the dinghy might well become unmanageable when conditions include a wind or strong current. Both rodes should be adjusted as required after the two anchors are set.

Guard Against Wind or Current Shifts

Sometimes you will need to anchor where the tidal current reverses, or wide wind shifts are likely. Here it is wise to set two anchors as security against an anchor breaking out and failing to set itself again.

The anchors are set 180° apart with the bow of the boat at the midpoint between them; see **Figure 9-29.** With both lines drawn up tight, the bow remains over essentially the same spot and swinging is limited to the boat's length. This "Bahamian moor" works best for a reversing tidal current with the wind blowing across the current so as to keep the boat always on one side of the line between the two anchors. When setting a second anchor for such a mooring, set the up-current anchor in the conventional way and then back down until double the normal scope is out. After the down-current anchor is set, adjust the scope at the bow chocks until both are equal. When going ahead with a rode tending aft, take care not to foul the propeller.

If the two-anchor technique is used in a crowded anchorage to limit your swinging radius, remember that other nearby boats may lie to one anchor only. Thus, since your swing will not be in sync with theirs, the risk of having their swinging circles overlap your limited swing is increased.

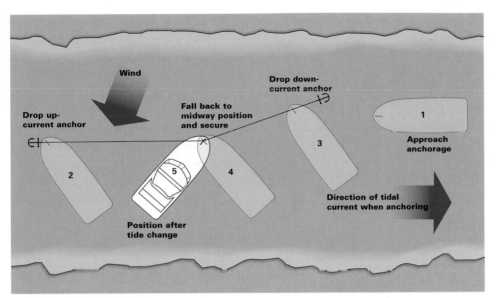

Figure 9-29 When anchoring in a narrow waterway with reversing tidal current, two anchors should be set from the bow in a "Bahamian moor," as shown. Adequate scope should be used on each anchor, with the rodes adjusted so that there is no slack in one when the other is taut.

Stern Anchors

In some anchorages, boats lie to anchors bow and stern. The easiest way to get these down is to let the bow anchor go first, and then drop back with wind or current on an extra long scope, drop the stern anchor, and then adjust the scope on both as necessary, taking in line forward. In tidal waters, just as with a single anchor, make allowance for increasing depth as the tide rises. The value of this arrangement is generally restricted to areas where permanent moorings are set explicitly for this purpose, as in narrow streams, or on occasions where there is no risk of getting a strong wind or current abeam. Under such conditions, the strain on a vessel's ground tackle could be tremendous.

Sometimes a stern anchor will be useful if you seek shelter under a windward bank. Let the stern anchor go from aft, carefully estimating scope as it is dropped, and pay out more scope as you run up toward the bank or beach. Bed a second anchor securely in the bank, or take a line to a structure or tree ashore. The stern anchor will keep the stern off and prevent the boat from ranging ahead. But, again, *watch that stern line while the propeller is turning!*

At Piers & Wharves

Docking on the windward side of a pier or wharf is undesirable, as considerable damage can be done to a boat pounding heavily against piles, even with fenders in place. Anchors can help to ease the situation in a case where such a berth is unavoidable. Keeping well up to windward, angling into the wind as much as is practicable, have someone go drop an anchor on a long scope off the quarter (the port quarter if you'll lie starboard side to the pier). As this line is paid out, run ahead and get another anchor off the port bow, judging positions of both so you can drop down to leeward toward the pier on equal scope, with lines tending off at a 45° angle. Properly executed, this maneuver will prevent your vessel from hitting the pier, and the lines you then carry ashore will be needed only to prevent the boat from moving ahead or astern. See also Chapter 6, pages 202-208.

Rafting

At a rendezvous several boats frequently lie to a single anchor. Sometimes as many as ten or more boats raft together (rather too many for safety even in a quiet cove). After one boat is anchored, the second pulls alongside with plenty of fenders out on both. Stay six to ten feet away from the anchored boat and heave bow and stern lines. If this can't be done, run up to the anchored boat's bow at an angle of about 45° and pass a bow line first, then your stern line. Make sure you have no headway when lines are passed. As soon as the bow line is aboard the anchored boat, stop your

Figure 9-30 In rafting, only one boat should be anchored. The other boat(s) is made fast to it so that all will move as a unit. Raft only in light breezes and in calm water.

engine so that there will be no chance of going ahead, breaking the anchor out.

For a powerboat—but not a sailboat—you would allow your boat to drift astern until transoms align. Because of the dangers of spreaders tangling in a rocking situation, it's best to line up rafting sailboats so that the rigging is clear at all points aloft. Then let the bow swing off and pull the sterns in close so it will be easier to step from one boat to another. To keep the boats in line and fenders in position, run a spring line from the stern of the arriving boat to a point well forward on the anchored boat. A second spring line in the opposite direction is useful.

If a third boat makes fast, the anchored boat should be in the middle; if more tie up always alternate them, port and starboard of the anchored boat. Each succeeding boat should use the same technique, always with a spring from the stern of the outboard boat forward to the one next inboard. Keels of all boats in the group should be nearly parallel. For safety, boats should raft only when there is little wind and a relatively smooth surface. When four or more are tied together, it is a good precaution for the outboard boats to carry additional anchors out at a 45° angle.

When it's time to turn in for the night, every boat should have its own separate anchor.

Special Situations

Although the foregoing sections have covered nearly all the problems in anchoring, there are still a few that might be termed "special situations."

Anchoring at Night

When anchoring overnight, if you have no ranges to check your position (or if those you have are unlighted) you can rig a drift lead (the lead line will do). Lower it to the bottom, leave some slack for swinging, and make fast. If it comes taut, you've dragged. Don't forget to pick it up before getting underway. Many electronic navigation systems include an "anchor alarm" that will sound if your boat moves from the designated location by more than an amount that you have preset.

In general, vessels anchored at night must show an anchor light, two lights if over 50 meters (164.0 ft) in length. Anchor lights are not required, however, for vessels under 20 meters (65.6 ft) in a "special anchorage area," or for craft less than 7 meters 23.0 ft) when *not* in a channel, fairway or where other vessels normally navigate. See details in Chapter 4, pages 134–136.

Requirements for "Anchor Ball"

With the same exceptions as noted above for anchor lights, a vessel anchored during daylight hours must hoist a black ball shape where it can best be seen. This shape must be not less than 0.6 meter (23.6 in) in diameter for ships, but may be of lesser size for small craft. See Chapter 4, page 140.

Rocky Bottoms

Earlier certain steps that could be taken to clear a fouled anchor were discussed. Avoid rocky bottoms or those with coral heads; they are hazardous at best, regardless of the type of anchor

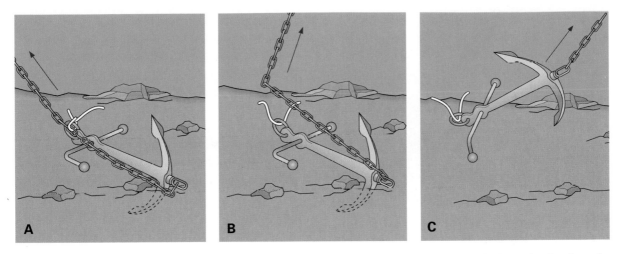

Figure 9-31 *When "scowing" an anchor, the rode is attached to the anchor crown, led back along the shank, and lashed at the ring. If the anchor becomes snagged (A), an upward pull (B) breaks the lashing and the anchor can be drawn out crown first (C).*

used. Before leaving a boat unattended, apply a test load to the anchor well in excess of any expected load.

If you normally anchor in rocky bottoms or suspect that the bottom is foul in the area where you must anchor, it is better to forestall trouble. One time-tested device is the buoyed trip line described on page 339.

An alternate scheme is to SCOW the anchor by attaching the rode to the crown, leading it back along the shank, and stopping it to the ring with a light lashing of marline; see **Figure 9-31.** With sufficient scope, the strain is on the ring and not on the lashing. When hove up short, the strain is on the lashing. When this parts, the anchor comes up crown first.

Kedging off a Shoal

The term KEDGING is applied to the use of a light anchor (not necessarily kedge-type) carried out to deep water in a dinghy to haul a stranded boat off a shoal. If you ever have to resort to this, make sure that the line is in the dinghy rather than on deck. See also Chapter 10, page 362.

Anchoring for a Sailboat

The procedures used for selecting and approaching an anchorage are the same for a sailboat skipper as for the operator of a powerboat.

There are some differences in lowering and setting the anchor; these are covered in Chapter 8, page 308.

Some Cautions

Take great care to avoid chafe on fiber lines. Wherever the line comes in contact with chocks or rails and rubs back and forth under continuous strain, outer fibers may be worn to such an extent as to seriously weaken the line. Mooring pennants are particularly susceptible to this, as are dock lines.

When lying at anchor, you can "freshen the nip" by paying out a little more scope from time to time, or protect the line at the point of chafe with strips of canvas wrapped around it.

Modern chafing gear is available in the form of plastic or rubber sleeves that can be snapped over the line, centered in a chock, and seized with thongs on either side to prevent shifting; see **Figure 9-32.** Chafing gear also comes in the form of lacing line or a white waterproof tape, to be applied around the line at bitts, chocks, and other points of contact.

The increasing use of relatively light anchor rodes of small diameter (as small as ⅜-inch) points up the necessity of preventing chafe. The chafe that a ¾-inch line could tolerate might render a ⅜-inch line unsafe.

Figure 9-32 Split plastic tubing can be used to cover a line where it passes through chocks to protect it against abrasion.

Chocks, Bitts, Cleats & Other Fittings

Chafe is aggravated wherever a fitting has a rough surface to accelerate abrasion of the fibers. Even small nicks and scratches in a chock can damage a line by cutting fibers progressively, one at a time. Serious weakening of a line develops when it is forced to pass around any fitting with relatively sharp corners, such as a square bitt with only a minimum rounding of the edges, especially when the bitts are too small for their job. Theoretically, the ideal bitt or samson post is round and of generous diameter. The best chocks are those of special design with the largest possible radius at the arc where the line passes over it.

Mooring bitts especially must be fastened securely. The best bitt is the old-fashioned wooden bitt, long enough to have its heel fastened solidly to the boat's keel; see **Figure 9-33.** If a cast fitting is used on deck, it must be through-bolted and the deck below reinforced with a husky backing plate.

Protection from Ultraviolet Ray Damage

The outer layers of all types of rope are subject to some degree of damage from ultraviolet rays that are part of the normal spectrum of sunlight. With nylon line of relatively large diameter (upward of ¾-inch) such damage is probably negligible. As the diameter decreases the problem becomes proportionately more serious; in ⅜-inch nylon it is an important factor because so much of the line is in

the outer fibers. Take care to shield such lines from unnecessary exposure to direct sunlight. Often the rode can be fed down into a locker. If it must be carried on deck, shade it or assign it to less critical uses and get new anchor line.

PERMANENT MOORINGS

PERMANENT MOORINGS, as distinguished from ordinary ground tackle in daily use, consist of the gear used when boats are to be left unattended for long periods, such as at yacht club or municipal anchorages. The traditional system often consists of a mushroom anchor, chain from the anchor to a buoy, and a pennant of stainless steel or nylon from the buoy to a light pick-up float at the pennant's end; see **Figure 9-34.**

Mushroom anchors, especially the type with a heavy bulb cast in the shank can, through suction, develop great holding power under ideal conditions if they have enough time to

Figure 9-33 A substantial, well-rounded samson post is shown behind the drum of an electric windlass. Note the horizontal norman pin that keeps the line from slipping up and off.

bury deeply into bottoms that permit such burying ; see **Figure 9-35**. Unfortunately, ideal bottom conditions are not always present. Often large cast concrete blocks, similar to those used by the Coast Guard to moor buoys, are put down in lieu of mushroom anchors.

Complicating the problem is the fact that anchorages are becoming increasingly crowded so that boats cannot have adequate scope because of overlapping swinging circles. Add to this the threat of abnormally high hurricane tides, which reduce scope to a ratio allowing no safety factor, and you have contributing factors to the devastation wrought by several hurricanes along the Atlantic Coast.

Typical Mooring Systems

The problem faced by the Manhasset Bay Yacht Club at Port Washington, NY, is typical. Here about 200 boats are moored in a limited space. If each boat could use a length of chain equal to 5 to 7 times the depth of water (maximum 30 feet), safety would be assured, but this would require a swinging radius of several hundred feet for each boat, which was not feasible. After exhaustive study, the Manhasset boaters prepared a set of recommended standards, given in **Table 9-3**. A generally similar system was adopted by the Lake Michigan Yachting Association; refer to **Figure 9-34**.

Guest Moorings

Often a cruising skipper will find guest moorings available at yacht clubs and municipal anchorages, and at some marinas. The launch operators will know which of those not in use for the night are heavy enough to hold your boat. As a rule, it's easier and safer to pick up such a mooring rather

Manhasset Bay Yacht Club Mooring System

	Overall Boat Length (Feet)	Mush-room Anchor Minimum Weight (Pounds)	Heavy Chain		Light Chain		Permanent			Total Minimum Length of System, Chocks to Mush-room Anchor (Feet)
			Length (Feet)	Diameter (Inches)	Length (Feet)	Diameter (Inches)	Minimum length (feet)	Diameter Nylon	Stainless Steel (inches)	
Motorboats	25	225	30	7/8	20	3/8	20	7/8	9/32	70
	35	300	35	1	20	7/16	20	1	11/32	75
	45	400	40	1	20	1/2	20	1 1/4	3/8	80
	55	500	50	1	20	9/16	20	1 1/2	7/16	90
Racing Sailboats	25	125	30	5/8	20	5/16	20	7/8	9/32	70
	35	200	30	3/4	20	3/8	20	1	11/32	70
	45	325	35	1	20	7/16	20	1 1/4	3/8	75
	55	450	45	1	20	9/16	20	1 1/2	7/16	85
Crusing Sailboats	25	175	30	3/4	20	5/16	20	7/8	9/32	70
	35	250	30	1	20	3/8	20	1 1/2	11/32	70
	45	400	40	1	20	7/16	20	1 1/2	3/8	80
	55	550	55	1	20	9/16	20	2	1 1/2	95

System is based on maximum water depth of 20 feet; for greater depths, length of light chain should at least equal the expected maximum.

Table 9-3 Specifications for mooring system used at the Manhasset Bay Yacht Club.

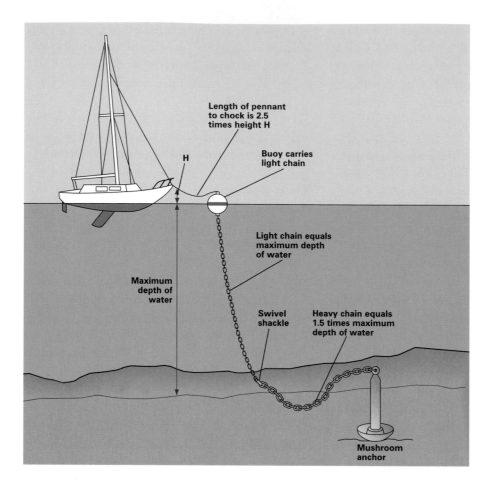

Length of pennant
to chock is 2.5
times height H

H

Buoy carries
light chain

Maximum
depth of
water

Light chain equals
maximum depth
of water

Swivel
shackle

Heavy chain equals
1.5 times maximum
depth of water

Mushroom
anchor

Figure 9-34 In this diagram of mooring practice recommended by the Lake Michigan Yachting Association, total scope is the combined length of heavy chain, light chain, and pennant. Minimum space between adjacent moorings should be 1.25 times the total scope plus the length of any boat likely to use the mooring. Be sure the chain or rod running through the buoy is of sufficient strength. Otherwise connect the pennant directly to the light chain below the buoy.

than anchoring. In most places, a charge will be made for the use of the mooring, and for launch service, if desired.

Mooring Buoys

To comply with U.S. Coast Guard regulations, mooring buoys should be white with a horizontal blue band. Buoys used in any mooring system should be of a type that transmits strain *directly through* the buoy, using chain or rod of acceptable strength; refer to **Figure 9-25.** Buoys perform a useful function in removing much of the vertical load; the pennant is under a more nearly horizontal load, and the boat's bow is freer to lift to heavy seas.

Stainless-steel pennants are often preferred because of failures traceable to the chafing of fiber pennants. When fiber is used for the pennant, protect it with chafing gear especially if there is a bobstay against which it can saw; refer to **Figure 9-32.**

Annual Inspection Necessary

Because ordinary moorings often need a period of time for silting-in before achieving their full holding power, annual inspection of chain, links, shackles, and pins should be made early in the season—never picked up for checking just about the time storm warnings are issued. On the other hand, it is also wise to give the pennant from buoy to boat a double-check in mid-season, just before the August-September months when hurricanes most often strike in the East.

Screw-In Moorings

A new technology has been developed for permanent moorings, promising greater security for craft exposed to the forces of hurricanes and other major storms. In lieu of a heavy anchor or sinker on the bottom, a HELICAL ANCHOR is literally screwed into the bottom much as a cork-puller is screwed into the cork of a wine bottle. Tests have shown that a helical anchor provides three to fives times the holding power of a typical mushroom anchor or concrete block. They are particularly useful in situations where the bottom is rocky or too hard to let a mushroom anchor bury itself, or where the bottom is too soft for a mushroom anchor to develop enough holding power.

Typical helical anchors are made of 1¾-inch galvanized steel rod fashioned into helices of 8-, 10-, 12-, or 14-inch diameter. These anchors are installed using special machinery mounted on a barge, and both skill and experience is required for proper installation. Measurements of the force required to screw the anchor into the bottom can be used to predict the holding power; additional sections can be added is it is necessary to force the anchor down deeper. Smaller helical anchors for small boats can be installed by a diver.

Picking up & Leaving a Mooring

Approach a mooring buoy in the same manner as you would an anchorage spot, as previously described in this chapter—slowly and into the prevailing wind or current, whichever has the stronger effect on your craft. A person on the bow will need a boathook with which to pick up the pennant streaming from the buoy. Typically, this line will have an eye that can be placed over the forward bitt or samson post. Often, however, the pennant is a polypropylene line (so that it will float on the surface) that has accumulated considerable marine growth—this can be quite messy on the crew's hands and on the foredeck. A solution is to use a short length of braided nylon line with an eye in one end. Place the eye of this line on the bitt, and, when the pennant is hauled up to deck level on the boat hook, pass the other end of the braided line through the eye of the pennant and then back to the bitt or a forward cleat—this allows the fouled pennant to stay clear of your boat.

Departing a mooring should be no problem, just keep clear of the mooring buoy that you are leaving and other nearby craft. The person on the bow can lift the eye of the pennant off the bitt and drop it overboard; if an additional line has been used as suggested above, the free end can be uncleated and pulled back, dropping the pennant. It is best to just let the wind or current carry you

away from the buoy, but a touch of reverse engine power may be used if necessary; the person on the bow can signal the helmsman as to the location of the mooring buoy until it can be seen from the helm.

Picking up a mooring, or getting away from one, with a sailboat is covered in Chapter 8, page 309.

A Multiple-Anchor System

One hurricane that ravaged the North Atlantic Coast swept through an anchorage in the New York area and tore almost every boat from her moorings. Only two survived. What these two had in common was an "unconventional" mooring system—multiple (3) anchors bridled to a common center, with chain and pennant leading from that point to the boat.

The obvious advantages of the system are shown in **Figure 9-36.** Regardless of how the wind shifts, the boat swings through a small circle, despite the advantage of a relatively long total

Figure 9-35 Mushroom anchors can develop great holding power under ideal conditions if they have enough time to bury deeply.

GROUND TACKLE MAINTENANCE

A boat's ground tackle includes all the anchors, anchor rodes (nylon line or chain), and shackles that are used to connect components together into an anchor system. Adequate ground tackle is *essential* to the safety of a vessel of *any* size. Unfortunately, time and use take their toll. Proper inspection and care are required to get the greatest possible life out of any component of an anchoring system.

At least once a year, every set of ground tackle should be hosed clean, and the chain and rode should be checked for any deterioration. All shackles (and swivels, if used) should be closely examined. All pins should be safetied with stainless wire or nylon cable ties to keep them from working loose; replace each safety tie once a year.

The rope/chain locker should be cleaned out. Ensure that the bitter end of each working anchor rode is securely fastened to prevent the accidental loss of the anchor.

Fiber Lines

Keep fiber lines free from sand and grit. Use a low-pressure hose to wash off grit, or slosh the line overboard, tied in a loose coil. Don't use a high-pressure nozzle—it may force grit deeper into the line.

Make sure that lines are straight before any load is applied. Placing a strain on a kinked line can damage or break the fibers. To a lesser degree, sharp bends are harmful; blocks should always have sheaves of adequate diameter; see Chapter 23, page 787.

Inspect all lines regularly. Check the effect of abrasion, cuts, rust on nylon, broken or frayed yarns, variations in strand size or shape, burns, rot and/or acid stains, and fiber "life." Nylon line may fuzz on the surface although the yarns are not broken. This seems to act as a cushion, reducing further outside abrasion.

Compare the line to new rope. Untwist and examine the inside of strands; they should be clean and bright as in new rope. If powder or broken fibers appear, the line has been overloaded or subject to excessive bending. Nylon may be fused or melted, either inside or out, from overloads.

Check any splices. All splices should have absolute integrity. (For complete safety, the only splice in an anchor rode should be the eye splice that has a thimble connecting the rode to the chain near the anchor.)

Keep in mind that most chafe and wear comes on the anchor end. Periodically, lines in regular use should be turned end-for-end. If you use one size for all anchor and mooring lines, you can put a new spare anchor line aboard each spring, put the former spare into regular use, and make the oldest anchor line into dock lines after cutting out any chafed sections.

Become familiar with the special techniques that are required in working with nylon line, as when making up eye splices, or even unreeling it from a coil. These techniques are covered in detail in Chapter 23.

Anchors & Chain

Consider the appearance of your anchors. Galvanized anchors are usually coated by the hot-dip process that leaves a tough protective finish, and normally require no care except washing off mud. They can be occasionally freshened up in appearance by a coat of aluminum paint. You can also buy a spray coating that is heavy in zinc, a "cold galvanize." This coating will temporarily improve the appearance of anchor and chain that are starting to rust, but it has poor wearing qualities when compared to hot-dip galvanizing.

Don't store a dirty anchor chain. If it comes up fouled with mud, give it a thorough cleaning. Some larger yachts have a faucet and

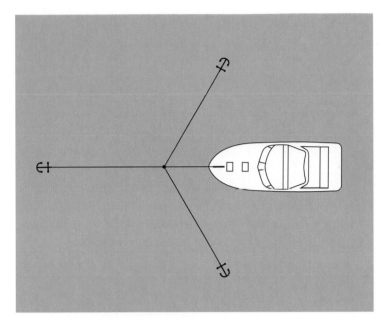

Figure 9-36 *A modern permanent mooring system designed to be an improvement over the single mushroom anchor uses three lightweight-type anchors bridled 120° apart. A relatively short rode limits swinging.*

hose near the bow connected to a fresh- or salt-water pressure system for this purpose.

Periodic Inspection

At least once a year, the complete anchoring system should be inspected. Check the line or chain, shackles and any swivels that are used, and the anchor itself. All shackles should be safetied with either stainless wire or nylon cable ties to keep them from working loose; replace any doubtful ones. Clean out the rope/chain locker. Verify that the bitter end of each rode is securely fastened to prevent accidental loss of the anchor and rode.

scope from the boat to the anchor. The short rode up from the three-way bridle minimizes any "tacking" tendency. Always there will be one or two anchors to windward, the strain tending in the same direction. Using modern lightweight anchors instead of mushrooms, the greater the load, the deeper they bury. Mushrooms often need a relatively long period to bed-in securely, but lightweight anchors will dig in almost immediately. Next to each anchor, use a heavy chain with a length one and a half times the maximum depth of the water—the objective is to have a three-anchor system with a holding power equal to the design holding power of a permanent mooring for the same size craft.

Special Seamanship Techniques

Boat Handling Under Adverse Conditions • Running Aground
• Assisting & Towing Other Vessels

While boaters would all prefer to be out on the water in pleasant conditions, experienced skippers recognize that sometimes there will be bad weather, they may run aground, or they may need to assist another vessel in trouble. They may well encounter emergencies such as a man overboard, fire, or the need to abandon a sinking boat. Every skipper should be thoroughly familiar with the special seamanship techniques, presented in this chapter, that are required to safely cope with these conditions. The particulars of specific serious situations aboard, such as man overboard, fire, and abandoning ship, are covered in Chapter 12, "Emergencies Underway."

BOAT HANDLING UNDER ADVERSE CONDITIONS

Perhaps the most important test of a skipper's abilities comes in how he handles his boat in adverse weather conditions. Boat size has little bearing on seaworthiness, which is fixed more by design and construction. The average power cruiser or sailboat is fully seaworthy for normal conditions in the use for which it is intended. Which means: "Don't venture into waters or weather conditions clearly beyond what your boat was designed for." Remember also that what a boat will do is governed to a great extent by the skill of its skipper; a good seaman might bring a poor boat through a blow that a novice could not weather in a far more seaworthy one.

Rough Weather

"Rough weather" is a relative term, and what might seem a terrible storm to the fair-weather

Opposite page: Figure 10-01 Reefed, with lee rail awash, this yawl is being driven hard in moderate seas.

boater may be nothing more than a good breeze to an experienced weather-wise skipper.

On large, shallow bodies of water like Long Island's Great South Bay, Delaware Bay and River, or Lake Erie, even a moderate wind will cause an uncomfortable steep sea with crumbling crests. Offshore or in deeper inland water the same wind force might cause moderate seas, but the slow, rolling swells would be no menace to small craft; see **Figure 10-1**.

Know Your Boat

Boat handling under adverse conditions is an individual matter, since no two boats are exactly alike in the same sea conditions. When the going gets heavy, each hull design reacts differently—and even individual boats of the same class may behave differently because of factors like load and trim.

Each skipper must learn the particulars of his boat, to determine how best to apply the general principles covered in the following sections. Reading this book and taking courses are important first steps. You can learn basic good seamanship by absorbing facts and principles, but you'll have to pick up the rest by using your book and classroom learning on the water when the wind blows.

Even when conditions do not force you to undertake special seamanship techniques, involve yourself with theoretical situations. Ask yourself and your crewmembers how to handle various difficulties. While cruising along on a calm day, for example, ask what each person should do if the boat suddenly ran aground. This not only makes for interesting conversation, but also provides a good basis for practicing procedures.

Head Seas

The average well-designed power cruiser or larger sailboat should have little difficulty when running generally into head seas. If the seas get

PREPARATIONS FOR ROUGH WEATHER

In anticipation of high winds and rough seas, a prudent skipper takes certain precautions. No single list fits all boats or all weather conditions, but among the appropriate actions are those listed below. Storms can be a tremendous test of the knowledge, endurance, courage, and good judgment of the skipper and crew. A well-prepared craft and its crew are more likely to survive a storm.

• Break out life preservers and have everyone on board, including the skipper, wear one before the situation worsens; don't wait too long.

• Secure all hatches; close all ports and windows. Close off all ventilator openings.

• Pump bilges dry and repeat as required. ("Free" water in bilges adversely affects a boat's stability.)

• Secure all loose gear; put away small items and lash down the larger ones, including all anchors, spinnaker pole, and life raft.

• Break out emergency gear that you might need—hand pumps or bailers, sea anchor or drogue, etc.

• Make sure that navigation lights are working. Hoist the radar reflector, if it is not up. Check batteries in all flashlights and electric lanterns.

• Get a good check of your position, if possible, and update the plot on your chart.

• Make plans for altering course to sheltered waters, if necessary.

• If towing a dinghy, bring it on board and lash it down securely.

• If sailing, prepare all reefing lines; set up the storm jib and trysail (see page 355) if this can be done independently from the mainsail and foresails. Be ready to change to storm sails quickly. If running before the wind, rig a strong preventer that can be released from the helm. Wear your safety harness at all times; it should fit snugly over your clothing. Charge your batteries and avoid unnecessary drains on them until the weather improves.

• Remember that being cold can affect a person's judgment. Have everyone put on appropriate clothing. Choose clothing that will keep you warm even when wet—wool or polypropylene.

• Give all hands a good meal while you have the opportunity; it might be a while until the next one. Prepare some food in advance; put coffee or soup in a thermos, and store something that can be eaten easily and quickly—perhaps sandwiches—in a watertight container.

• Get out the motion sickness pills; it is much better to take them before you get queasy.

• Reassure your crew and guests; instruct them in what to do and not to do, and then give them something to do to take their minds off the situation.

too steep-sided or if you start to pound, slow down by easing the throttle or shortening the sail. This gives the bow a chance to rise in meeting each wave instead of being driven hard into it. (A direct consequence of driving hard into a wave could be that the force of the water hitting the superstructure would break ports and windows.)

Match Speed to Sea Conditions

If conditions get really bad, slow down until you're barely making headway, holding your bow at an angle of about 45° to the swells. The more you reduce headway in meeting heavy seas, the less the strain on the hull and superstructure, and the less the stress on the persons onboard.

Avoid Propeller "Racing"

You must reduce speed to avoid damaging the hull or power plant if the seas lift the propeller clear of the water and it "races." This sounds dangerous—and it may be. First, there's a rapidly increasing crescendo of sound as the engine winds up, then excessive vibration as the propeller bites the water again. Don't panic—slow down and change your course until these effects are minimized.

Keep headway so you can maneuver your boat readily. Experiment to find the speed best suited to the conditions.

Adjust Trim

You can swamp your boat if you drive it ahead too fast or if it is poorly trimmed. In a head sea, a vessel with too much weight forward will plunge rather than rise. Under the same conditions too much weight aft will cause it to fall off. The ideal speed will vary with different boats—experiment with your craft and find out its best riding speed.

Change the weight aboard, if necessary. On outboards, shift your tanks and other heavy gear. In any boat, direct your passengers and crew to remain where you place them.

Meet Each Wave as It Comes

You can make reasonable progress by nursing the wheel—spotting the steep-sided combers coming in and varying your course, slowing or even stopping momentarily for the really big ones. Just as you adjust your speed when driving a car on a winding road, you must vary your boat's speed to get through waves. If the person at the helm can see clearly and act before dangerous conditions develop, the craft should weather moderate gales with little discomfort. Make sure the most experienced person aboard acts as helmsman, with occasional breaks in order to stay sharp.

In the Trough

If your course requires you to run broadside to the swells, bouncing from crest to trough and back up again, your boat may roll heavily, perhaps dangerously. In these conditions in a powerboat it is best to run a series of "tacks" much like a sailboat.

Tacking Across the Troughs

Change course and take the wind and waves at a 45° angle, first broad on your bow and then broad on your quarter; see **Figure 10-02.** You will make a zigzag course in the right direction, with your

Figure 10-02 This U.S. Coast Guard utility boat is taking waves at a 45° angle to its stern. With judicious use of power and helm, it will remain under control despite the breaking seas.

boat in the trough only briefly while turning. With the wind broad on the bow, the boat's behavior should be satisfactory; on the quarter, the motion may be less comfortable but at least it will be better than running in the trough. Make each tack as long as possible to minimize how often you must pass through the trough.

To turn sharply, allow your powerboat to lose headway for a few seconds, turn the helm hard over, then suddenly apply power. The boat will turn quickly as a powerful stream of water strikes the rudder, kicking you to port or starboard, without making any considerable headway. You won't be broadside for more than a minimum length of time. This is particularly effective with single-screw boats. With twin-screw powerboats, the engine on the side in the direction of the turn may be throttled back or even briefly reversed.

Running Before the Sea

If the swells are coming from directly behind you, running directly before them is safe if your boat's stern can be kept reasonably up to the seas without being thrown around off course. But in heavy seas, a boat tends to rush down a slope from crest to trough, and, stern high, the propeller comes out of the water and races. The rudder also loses its grip, and the sea may take charge of the stern as the bow "digs in." At this stage, the boat may yaw so badly as to BROACH—to be thrown broadside, out of control—into the trough. Avoid broaching by taking every possible action. Unfortunately, modern power-boat design emphasizes beam at the stern so as to provide a large, comfortable cockpit or after-deck—this width at the transom increases the tendency to yaw and possibly broach.

Reducing Yawing

Slowing down to let the swells pass under your boat usually reduces the tendency to yaw, or at least reduces the extent of yawing; see **Figure 10-03.** While it is seldom necessary, you can consider towing a heavy line or drogue (see page 357) astern to help check your boat's speed and keep it running straight. Obviously the line must be carefully handled and not allowed to foul the propeller. Do not tow soft-laid nylon lines that may unlay and cause hockles (strand kinks).

Cutting down engine speed reduces strain on the motor caused by alternate stern-down laboring and stern-high racing.

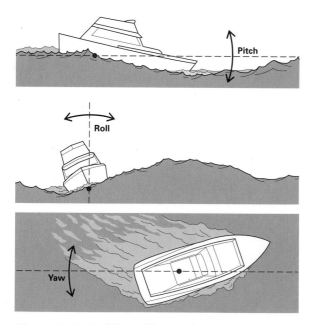

Figure 10-03 Pitching, rolling, and yawing are normal motions of a boat. If they become excessive, or combine, they may be uncomfortable, even dangerous.

Pitchpoling

The ordinary offshore swell is seldom trouble-some when you are running before the seas, but the steep wind sea of some lakes and shallow bays make steering difficult and reduced speed impera-tive. Excessive speed down a steep slope may cause a boat to PITCHPOLE, that is, drive its head under in the trough, tripping the bow, while the succeeding crest catches the stern and throws her end over end. When the going is bad enough that there is risk of pitchpoling, keep the stern down and the bow light and buoyant, by shifting weight aft as necessary.

Shifting any considerable amount of weight aft will reduce a boat's tendency to yaw, but too much might cause it to be POOPED by a following sea breaking into the cockpit. Do everything in moderation, not in excess. Adjust your boat's trim bit by bit rather than all at once, and see what makes it more stable.

Tacking Before the Seas

Use the tacking technique also when you want to avoid large swells directly astern. Try a zigzag track that puts the swells alternately off each quarter, minimizing their effects—experiment with slightly different headings to find the most stable angle for your boat—but keep it under control to prevent a broach.

Running an Inlet

One of the worst places to be in violent weather is an inlet or narrow harbor entrance, where shoal water builds up treacherous surf that often cannot be seen from seaward. Inexperienced boaters, nevertheless, often run for shelter rather than remain safe, if uncomfortable, at sea, because they lack confidence in themselves and their boats.

When offshore swells run into shallower water along the beach, they build up steep waves because of resistance from the bottom. Natural inlets on sandy beaches, unprotected by breakwaters, usually build up a bar across the mouth. When the swells reach the bar, their form changes rapidly, they become short, steep-sided waves that tend to break where the water is shallowest.

Consider this when approaching from offshore. A few miles off, the sea may be relatively smooth while the inlet from seaward may not look as bad as it actually is. Breakers may run clear across the mouth, even in a buoyed channel.

Shoals shift so fast with moving sand that buoys do not always indicate the best water. Local boaters often leave the buoyed channel and are guided by appearance of the sea, picking the best depth by the smoothest surface and absence of breakers. A stranger is handicapped here because he may not have knowledge of uncharted obstructions and so may not care to risk leaving the buoyed channel. He should thus have a local pilot, if possible, or he might lay off or anchor until he can follow a local boat in.

If you must get through without local help, these suggestions may make things more comfortable.

• Contact the local U.S. Coast Guard station, if there is one, for recommendations. In the absence of a Coast Guard unit, try to contact a local marina or local fishing boats that frequently use the inlet.

• Make sure that your boat is ready—close all hatches and ports, secure all loose gear, and get all persons into lifejackets, briefing them on what to do and what not to do.

• Don't be in a hurry to run the inlet; wait outside the bar until you have had a change to watch the action of waves as they pile up at the most critical spot in the channel, which will be the shallowest. Typically, waves will come along in groups of three, sometimes more. The last sea will be bigger than the rest and by watching closely you can pick it out of the successive groups.

• When you are ready to enter, stand off until a big one has broken or spent its force on the bar, and then run through behind it. Watch the water both ahead and behind your boat; control your speed and match it to that of the waves.

An ebbing tidal current builds up a worse sea on the bars than the flood does because the rush of water out works against and under the incoming swells. If the sea looks too bad on the ebb, it is better to keep off a few hours until the flood has had a chance to begin. As deeper water helps, the

very best time is the slack just before the tidal current turns to ebb. Do not use the times of high and low water to plan for the time of slack—these times are rarely, if ever, the same; see Chapter 17 for more on tides and currents.

Departing through inlets is less hazardous than entering, as the boat is on the safe side of the dangerous area and usually has the option of staying there. If you do decide to go out, you can spot dangerous areas more easily, and a boat heading into surf is more easily controlled than one running with the swells. On the other hand, the skipper of a boat outside an inlet may conclude he has no other choice but to enter, but should only attempt it in the safest possible manner.

Heaving-To

When considerations get so bad offshore that a boat cannot make headway and begins to take too much punishment, it is time to HEAVE-TO, a maneuver whose execution varies for different vessels. Powerboats, both single- and twin-screw, will usually be most comfortable if brought around and kept bow to the seas, or a few points off, using just enough power to make bare steerageway while conserving fuel; it may be necessary to occasionally use brief spurts of greater power to keep the craft headed in the best direction.

Sailboats traditionally heave-to with the helm lashed downwind, to keep the boat headed up. A small, very strong STORM JIB is sheeted to windward to hold the bow just off the wind, while a STORM TRYSAIL is sheeted flat. This is a small, strong triangular sail with a low clew and a single sheet, it should have a separate track on the mast so that it can be set up before the mainsail is dropped. A loose-footed sail, it is not bent to the boom, which is secured in its crutch. The jib-trysail combination balances the tendency of trysail and rudder to head the vessel into the wind against the effect of the jib to head it off, and the result is, ideally, that the boat lies 45° from the wind while making very slow headway.

Lying Ahull

For a sailboat, the next step down as the wind increases is LYING AHULL. The crew takes these steps: all sail is dropped and secured, the helm

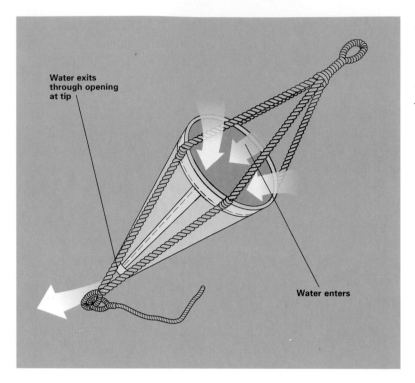

Water exits through opening at tip

Water enters

Figure 10-04 The towline of a traditional sea anchor is made fast to the thimble at right. A trip line is fastened to the apex of the cone; this end has a small opening to let some of the water flow through.

lashed to prevent damage to the rudder, and the vessel left to find its own way.

Sea Anchors

In extreme weather you may use a SEA ANCHOR, traditionally a heavy fabric cone with a hoop to keep it open at the mouth; it appears much like a megaphone. Its leading edge has a bridle of light lines leading to a fitting attached to a heavier towing line. The apex of the cone has a small, reinforced opening to allow a metered amount of water to pass through from the wide end; see **Figure 10-04**. Sea anchors may also be a series of plastic floats that fold compactly for storage and are said to be more effective than the traditional kind. Newer designs borrow their general shape from aircraft parachutes. Some have lightweight canopies much like a parachute, while others use a lattice of webbing.

Sea anchors range in size from a few feet to 40 feet (1 to 12 m) or more in diameter depending upon the style of the sea anchor and the size and weight of the craft; they are more common on sailing craft than on powerboats. The bigger the diameter, the more effective a sea anchor will be.

Whatever style of sea anchor you carry, test it in moderate weather a few times to make sure it is big enough to be effective. A small one may be easier to stow, but there's no point to having it if it won't do the job.

The line that attaches a sea anchor to the boat should be the same diameter as the rode for the craft's conventional working anchor. A lightweight trip line attached to the smaller end allows the sea anchor to be pulled back to the boat, always an easier task than pulling the boat up to the sea anchor.

Improvised Sea Anchors In the absence of a regular sea anchor, try any form of drag rigged from spars, planks, canvas, or other material at hand that will float just below the surface and keep your boat from lying in the trough.

Using a Sea Anchor

The classic use of a sea anchor is to hold the bow of a boat to within a few points of the wind and waves as it drifts off to leeward when it is not making way through the water on its own power. A sea anchor is not meant to go to the bottom and hold, but merely to present a drag that keeps the boat's head up; see **Figure 10-05**. A sea anchor will usually float just beneath the water's surface. It should be streamed at lease one wavelength away from the vessel, although the proper length may change with the circumstances. Chafing must be carefully guarded against; a short length of chain used where the rode comes on board is one solution. Such a sea anchor can reduce drift up to 90 percent, but that much reduction can cause the boat to take considerable punishment from wave action. Holding position, however, can save a vessel that has lost powcr off a lee shore (a shore to leeward of her). If engine repairs are possible, they are much more easily and quickly accomplished if the vessel is head to the seas rather than rolling in the trough. Another use is to allow a crew to rest after hours of battling a major storm at sea.

When retrieving a sea anchor, motor very slowly up to the recovery float (refer to **Figure 10-05**), taking in the rode so as to not foul the craft's propeller. Pick up the float and trip line with a boathook.

Drogues

A close relative of the sea anchor is the DROGUE, which is towed astern to keep a craft from yawing extremely or broaching. A drogue has a larger vent opening to provide a lesser drag, because it is for use on a boat making way through the water. A drogue must be secured *ahead of the rudderpost* in order to keep the boat maneuverable.

Cautions

Setting a sea anchor that is too small off the bow will allow the boat to drift backwards. This backward movement may result in damage to the rudder, espccially on sailboats, or allow the boat to yaw and possibly fall off into a broaching position. One rule of thumb for sizing a cone-shaped sea anchor is to have the larger end one inch in diameter for each foot of the craft's length at waterline (LWL). With parachute-type sea anchors, it is best to follow the manufacturer's recommendations.

Whether streamed off the bow or stern, all types of sea anchors and drogues put a tremendous strain on a boat, which must be strongly built to withstand any waves that may pound on deck Sailboats towing a drogue astern must have a watertight, self-draining cockpit with fast-draining scuppers. This prevents seawater from getting into the interior of the boat should it be pooped by a wave breaking over the stern and into the cockpit. Sport-fishing models of powerboats are not designed to survive being pooped, so

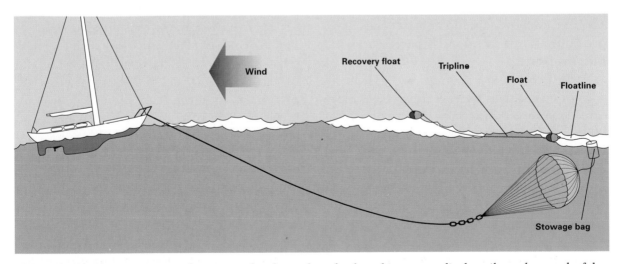

Figure 10-05 When using a parachute sea anchor, let out lots of rode as this system relies heavily on the stretch of the nylon line for yielding to the seas (and not standing up against them). Even in moderate conditions, you should pay out at least 200 feet (60 m) of rode; use 10 to 15 times the length of the boat in heavy weather conditions.

towing a drogue astern of such craft cannot be recommended.

There is controversy over the safety and efficacy of sea anchors, especially in survival conditions offshore. Modern fin-keel sailboats may not lie quietly to a sea anchor off the bow without a small steadying sail. Such a sail may also keep a powerboat from "dancing" on its rode.

Sea anchors work only if there is sufficient sea room, because they do permit a steady drift to leeward. When a vessel is driven down onto a lee shore, it must use its regular ground tackle to ride out a gale. It is imperative that constant watch to guard against dragging toward a lee shore. Use your engine to ease the strain during the worst of the blow, and give the anchor a long scope for its best chance to hold. Don't confuse "lee shore"—a shore onto which the wind is blowing, a dangerous shore—with being "in the lee" of an island or point of land, being on the sheltered, safer side.

Other Uses

Sea anchors can also prove useful in less stormy weather. A vessel that loses power in water too deep to anchor conventionally can drift many miles while waiting for assistance. Staying as closely as possible to the location of the original distress call greatly assists rescuers; boats that drift from their reported position can be difficult to locate. By limiting drift, a sea anchor can keep a disabled boat in reasonable proximity to the location where rescuers will start their search.

Sport fishermen sometimes use a small sea anchor to slow their boat's drift over schools of fish. Controlled drift is typically desired by fishermen, so a fishing sea anchor is smaller than one intended for use in an emergency. Commercial fishermen also use them as a means of "anchoring" at sea where depths do not permit normal anchoring; this is useful for resting between periods of fishing activity.

Use of Oil with Sea Anchors

Sea anchors sometimes have an OIL CAN that permits oil to ooze out slowly and form a slick on the surface, thus preventing seas from breaking. The oil might also be distributed from a bag punctured with a few holes and stuffed with cotton waste saturated with oil. (See also the following section on the use of oil.)

Make sure this equipment—sea anchors, trip lines, oil bag lines—is in good condition and not rotten from long disuse and stowage in the bottom of some locker.

Using Oil on Rough Water

Experienced seamen have long known the value of oil for modifying the effect of breaking seas. Oil is easily dispensed and quickly dispersed; the effect of even small amounts is significant.

Note: Discharging oil onto the water is a violation of U.S. Coast Guard antipollution regulations even though only a small quantity is used. Information given here does not advocate its use. Use of oil should be avoided, restricted only to an emergency situation involving immediate danger.

Here is a summary of information on its emergency use and behavior:

• On free waves, i.e., waves in deep water, its effect is greatest.

• In a surf or in waves breaking on a bar, its effect is uncertain, as nothing can prevent the larger waves from breaking under such circumstances. Even here, however, it has some value.

• The heaviest and thickest oils are most effective. Kerosene is of little use; but animal and vegetable oils and waste oil from the engines will all have a useful effect.

• A small quantity of oil suffices, if applied so that it spreads to windward.

• In cold water, the oil is thickened by the lower temperature and spreads more slowly, so will be less effective. The loss of effectiveness will vary with the type of oil used.

• For a boat at sea, the best way to apply oil is to hang one or two small canvas bags over the side that can hold 1 to 2 gallons (3.8-7.6 liters) of oil; prick the bags with a sail needle to facilitate leakage of oil.

The position of these bags is determined by the circumstances. Running before the wind, hang them on either bow and allow them to tow in the water.

With the wind on the quarter, the effect seems to be less than in any other position, as the oil goes astern while the waves come up on the quarter.

Lying-to, hang them from the weather bow and another position farther aft, using sufficient line for them to draw to windward while your boat drifts.

• To cross a bar with a flooding tidal current, pour oil overboard and allow it to float in ahead of your boat, which then follows with another bag towing astern. The oil is less dependable in this situation, however.

Entering across a bar with the tidal current ebbing, it is probably useless to try oil.

• To approach a stranded boat, pour oil overboard to windward of her before going alongside. The effect in this case will depend upon the set of current and depth of water.

• For a boat riding from a sea anchor in rough water fasten the oil bag to a line rove through a block on the sea anchor. The oil is thus diffused well ahead of the boat and the bag can be hauled on board for refilling.

• Remember that the purpose of using oil is to spread a calming slick to windward and around your boat, so that she stays in the slick. If the oil goes off to leeward or astern, it is of no use.

Seamanship in "Thick" Weather

Another "adverse condition" that requires special skills is "thick" weather—conditions of reduced visibility, caused by fog, heavy rain or snow, or haze. Fog is probably the most often encountered and most severe condition.

Seamanship in thick weather is primarily a matter of avoiding collisions. Piloting and position determination, the legal requirements for sounding fog signals, and the meteorological aspects of fog are all covered elsewhere in this book (see Contents and Index). Here we will consider only the aspects of boat handling and safety.

Avoiding Collision

The primary needs of safety in conditions of reduced visibility are to see and be seen—to hear and be heard. The wise skipper takes every possible action to see or otherwise detect other boats and hazards, and simultaneously takes all steps to make his presence known to others.

Reduce Speed

You need, of course, to detect other vessels by sight, sound, or radar early enough to take proper action to avoid collision. Both the Inland and the International Rules require reduced speed for vessels in low visibility—a "safe speed appropriate to the prevailing circumstances and conditions" see Chapter 5, page 164.

It is best to be able to stop short in time, rather than to have to resort to violent evasive maneuvers, to avoid a collision. The Navigation Rules require that, except where it has been determined that a risk of collision does not exist (by radar plot, perhaps), any vessel which hears another's fog signal apparently forward of her beam must "reduce her speed to the minimum at which she can be kept on course. She shall if necessary take all way off, and, in any event, navigate with extreme caution until danger of collision is over"; see Chapter 5, page 165.

Lookouts

Equally important with a reduction in speed is posting LOOKOUTS. This is a requirement of the Navigation Rules, but it is also common sense. Most modern motor and sail boat designs place the helmsman aft, or fairly far aft, where he is not an effective lookout, so you will probably need one or two additional people on board as lookouts in thick weather.

Look . . . & Listen

Despite the "look" in "lookout," such a person is as much for listening as for seeing; see **Figure 10-06.** A person assigned as a lookout should have this duty as his sole responsibility while on watch. A skipper should certainly post a lookout as far forward as possible when in fog, and, if the helmsman is at inside controls, another lookout

Figure 10-06 How you respond to the challenge of navigating in fog is one of the greatest measures of seamanship.

for the aft sector is desirable. Lookouts should be relieved as often as necessary to ensure their alertness; if the crew is small, an exchange of bow and stern duties will provide some change in position and relief from monotony. If there are enough people on board, a double lookout forward is not wasted manpower; but the two should take care not to distract each other.

A bow lookout should keep alert for other vessels, listen for sound signals from aids to navigation, and watch for hazards like rocks and piles, breakers, and buoys. Note that in thick weather, aids to navigation without audible signals can indeed become hazards. A lookout aft should watch primarily for overtaking vessels, but he may also hear fog signals missed by his counterpart on the bow.

The transmission of sound in fog is uncertain and tricky. The sound may seem to come from directions other than the true source, and it may not be heard at all at otherwise normal ranges. See the discussion of fog signals in Chapter 5.

Stop Your Engine
When underway in fog in a boat under power, slow your engines to idle or shut them off entirely,

at intervals, to listen for fog signals of other vessels and of aids to navigation. This is not a legal requirement of the Navigation Rules, but it is an excellent, practical action.

In these intervals, keep silence on the boat so you can hear even the faintest signal. The listening periods should be at least two minutes to conform with the legally required maximum intervals between the sounding of fog signals. Don't forget to keep sounding your own signal during the listening period—you may get an answer from close by! Vary your timing to avoid being in sync with the signals of another vessel.

When proceeding in fog at a moderate speed, slow or stop your engines immediately any time your lookout indicates he has heard something. The lookout can then have the most favorable conditions for verifying and identifying what he believes he has heard.

Radar & Radar Reflectors
Radar has its greatest value in conditions of reduced visibility. If your craft has a radar, the Navigation Rules—both International and Inland—require that it be used. It must be on a long enough range scale as to give early warning of the possibility of collision and all targets must be followed systematically. Use of radar, however, is not a substitute for adequate lookouts.

Whether or not you have radar, you should carry a passive radar reflector (see Chapter 21); this is the time to open it and hoist it as high as possible. This increases the chances of your boat being detected sooner, and at a greater distance, by a radar-equipped vessel (your own radar may not make your craft easier to detect).

Cruising with Other Boats
If you are cruising with other boats and fog closes in, you may be able to take advantage of a procedure used by wartime convoys. Tie onto the end of a long, light line, some object that will float and make a wake as it moves through the water. A life ring or a glass or plastic bottle with a built-in handle will do quite well. The object is towed astern with the boats traveling in single file, one object behind each craft except the last; each bow lookout except

the first can keep it in sight even though he cannot see the vessel ahead, or even hear its fog signal.

Anchoring & Laying-to

If the weather, depth of water, and other conditions are favorable, consider anchoring rather than proceeding through conditions of poor visibility. Do not anchor in a heavily traveled channel or traffic lane, of course.

If you cannot anchor, then perhaps laying-to—being underway with little or no way on—may be safer than proceeding at even a much reduced speed.

Remember that different fog signals are required when you are underway, with or without way on, and when you are at anchor (see pages 166–167). By all means, sound the proper fog signal and keep your lookouts posted to look and listen for other craft and hazards.

Use Your Radio

In areas of heavy traffic, especially large vessels, some skippers of small fiberglass boats, not easily detected on radar even with a reflector aloft, make "Securite" calls on VHF channels 16 and 13 to advise others of their presence.

RUNNING AGROUND, ASSISTING & TOWING

It is an unwritten law of the sea that a boater should always try to render assistance to a vessel in need of aid. This is one of the primary functions of the Coast Guard, of course, but there are plenty of occasions when timely help by a fellow boater can save hours of effort later after the tide has fallen, or wind and sea have had a chance to pick up.

Often, giving assistance means getting a towline to another skipper to get him out of a position of temporary embarrassment, or perhaps to get him to a Coast Guard station or back to port. The situation can also be the other way around—you may go aground, or a balky motor or gear failure force you to ask a tow from a passing boat.

In either case, you should know what to do and why. Thus the problems of running aground, and

their solutions, will be considered from both the viewpoint of being in need of assistance, and of being the one who renders aid to another vessel.

Running Aground

Simple running aground is more often an inconvenience than a danger, and with a little know-how and some fast work, the period of stranding may be but a matter of minutes.

If grounding happens in a strange harbor, chances are you have been feeling your way along and so have just touched bottom lightly. You should be off again with little difficulty if your immediate actions do not put you aground more firmly.

If it becomes apparent that you are not going to get free quickly, of if the situation becomes serious because of weather, call the U.S. Coast Guard and report the incident. Unless your vessel or your crew is endangered, do not make this a "Mayday" call; simply call them and report the problem and your location—they will probably refer you to commercial assistance. If you accept commercial assistance, be sure to negotiate the price before any work takes place; this agreement should be in writing, if practicable.

Right & Wrong Actions

The first instinctive act on going aground is to gun the engine into reverse in an effort to pull off; this may be the one thing that you should not do. You could damage the rudder or propeller; you might also pile up more of the bottom under the boat, making you harder aground. You may have already, or, if not, might suck mud or sand into the engine cooling system. All of these events are highly undesirable!

First, check for any water coming in; if there is any, stopping the leak takes precedence over getting off. If no water is coming in, or when it has been stopped, and you are in tidal waters, immediately check the state of the tide. If the tide is rising, and the sea quiet enough so that the hull is not pounding, time is working for you, and whatever you do to assist yourself will be much more effective later rather than now. If you grounded on a falling tide, you must work quickly and do exactly the right things—or you will be fast for several hours or more.

About the only thing you know offhand about the grounding is the shape of you boat's hull, its point of greatest draft, and thus the part most apt to be touching. If the hull tends to swing to the action of wind or waves, the point about which it pivots is the part grounded.

Check the water depth around the boat. Deeper water may be to one side rather than astern. You can use a lead line, or a boathook or similar item. Check from your deck all around. If you have a dinghy, use it to check over a wider area. Examine also the point where the water level meets your hull—if your normal waterline is well above the surface, you are more severely grounded than if there is no apparent change. Also check the raw water intake strainers to your engine or engines. Clean out if clogged with sand, gravel or mud before using engine power.

Cautions in Getting Off

Consider the type of bottom immediately. If it is sandy and you reverse hard, you may wash a quantity of sand from astern and throw it directly under the keel, bedding the boat down more firmly. Take care also not to suck up sand or mud into the engine through the engine's raw water intake.

It the bottom is rocky and you insist on trying to reverse off, you may drag the hull and do more damage than with the original grounding.

Also, if grounded forward, remember that reversing a single-screw boat with a right-hand propeller may swing the stern to port, and thus push the hull broadside onto adjacent rocks or into greater contact with a soft bottom.

Kedging after Grounding

The one right thing to do immediately after grounding is to take out an anchor in a dinghy, if available, and set it firmly, initiating the process of kedging your boat off a shoal; see **Figure 10-07**.

Unless your boat has really been driven on, the everyday anchor should be heavy enough. Put the anchor and the line in the dinghy, make the bitter end fast to the grounded boat's stern cleats and power or row the dinghy out as far as possible, letting the line run from the stern of the dinghy as it uncoils. Taking the line out this way makes the task much easier to row the dinghy or control it if an outboard motor is being used than if the line is dragged with the dinghy through the water.

If you do not carry a dinghy, you can often swim out with an anchor, providing sea and weather conditions do not make it hazardous to go overboard. Use life preservers or buoyant cushions—one or two of either—to support the anchor out to where you wish to set it. Be sure to wear a life jacket or buoyant vest yourself, to save your energy for the work. And have a light line attached from you to the boat so that you can be pulled back if you become exhausted.

If there is no other way to get a kedge anchor out, you may consider throwing it out as far as possible. Although this is contrary to basic good anchoring practice, getting an anchor set is so important that it warrants the technique. You may need to throw several times before you get it set firmly.

When setting out the anchor, consider the sideways turning effects of a reversing single screw and, unless the boat has twin screws, set the anchor at a compensating angle from the stern. If the propeller is right-hand, set the anchor slightly to starboard of the stern. This will give two desirable effects. When pulling the anchor line while in reverse, the boat will tend to back in a straight line. When used alternately, first pulling on the line and

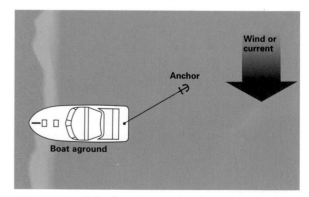

Figure 10-07 The first thing to do after going aground is to check hull integrity; next, to get a kedge anchor out to keep from being driven farther aground. It may also provide a means of pulling free as waves or the wake from another craft lift your boat.

then giving a short surge with the reverse, the resulting wiggling action of stern and keel can be a definite help in starting the boat moving.

With sailboats, it is often helpful to put out an anchor with a line running to or near the top of the mast. This can be used to heel the boat over, reducing its draft.

Getting Added Pulling Power

If you have a couple of double-sheave blocks and a length of suitable line on board, make up a HANDY-BILLY or FALL and fasten it to the anchor line. Then you can really pull! A handy-billy should be part of a boat's regular equipment (refer to Chapter 23, pages 796–798).

During the entire period of kedging the boat after grounding, keep the anchor line taut. The boat may yield suddenly to that continued pull, especially if a passing craft throws a wake that helps to lift the keel off the bottom.

Two kedges set out at an acute angle from either side of the stern and pulled upon alternately may give the stern a wiggle that will help you work clear.

If the bottom is sandy, that same pull with the propeller going ahead may wash some sand away from under the keel, with the desired result. If the anchor line is kept taut, try this maneuver with caution.

Move your crew and passengers quickly from side to side to roll the boat and make the keel work in the bottom. If you have spars, swing the booms outboard and put people on them to heave the boat down, thus raising the keel line. Shift ballast or heavy objects from over the portion grounded to lighten that section and if you can, remove internal weight by loading it into the dinghy or by taking it ashore; pump overboard excess water in your tanks. Unloading a boat is especially practical when running aground at or near high tide—while the tide is going down and coming back up, you have time to unload the heaviest items in order to create more buoyancy.

When to Stay Aground

All of the above is based on the assumption that the boat is not holed. If it is holed you may be far

Figure 10-08 If you go aground on a falling tide, your boat may be left completely "high and dry." If so, try to brace the boat so that it will stay as upright as possible; it will be easier to refloat.

better off where it lies than you would be if it were in deep water again. If it is badly stove, you may want to take an anchor ashore to hold it on or pull it farther up until temporary repairs can be made.

As the tide falls the damaged hull may be exposed far enough to allow some outside patching, if you have something aboard to patch with. A piece of canvas, cushions, and bedding can all be used for temporary hull patches.

What to Do While Waiting

While waiting for the tide to rise, or for assistance to come, do not sit idle. Take soundings all around you. If circumstances permit, put on a mask and snorkel and take a look. A swing of the stern to starboard or port may do more for you than any amount of straight backward pulling; soundings will locate any additional depth—or, conversely, shallow areas or rocks.

If another boat is present, it may be able to help you even if it cannot pull. Have the other skipper run his boat back and forth to make as much wake as is safely possible. His wake may lift your boat just enough to permit you to back clear.

If your boat is going to be left high and dry with a falling tide; keep an eye on its layover condition. If there is anything to get a line to, even another anchor, you can make it lie over on whichever side you choose as it loses buoyancy. If the boat is deep and narrow, it may need some assistance in standing up again, particularly if it lies over in soft mud. Both the suction of the mud and the boat's own deadweight will work against it; see **Figure 10-08**.

If the hull is undamaged, and you are left with a falling tide to sit out for a few hours, you might as well be philosophical about it—get over the side and make good use of the time. Undoubtedly you would prefer to do it under happier circumstances, but this may be an opportunity to make a good check of the bottom of your boat, or do any one of a number of little jobs that you could not do otherwise, short of a haul-out.

Assisting a Stranded Boat

If you are not stranded but able to help another boat that is, you must know what to do and what not to do.

The first rule of good seamanship in this case is to make sure that your boat *does not join the other craft in its trouble*! Consider the draft of the stranded vessel relative to yours. Consider the size and weight of the grounded boat relative to the power of your engines—don't tackle an impossible job; there are other ways of rendering assistance. Passing close by, making as large a wake as possible, may be all that is needed. Consider also your level of skill—it is often better not to try to be a "hero." If you decide that you can safely and effectively assist, follow these guidelines. Otherwise, just stand by until the proper help arrives.

Getting a Line Over

It may seem easiest to bring a line in to a stranded boat by coming in under engine power, bow on, passing the line and then backing out again, but do not try it until you are sure that there is enough water for you. Make sure also that your boat backs well, without too much stern crabbing due to the action of the reversed propeller. Wind and current direction will greatly affect the success of this maneuver. If conditions tend to swing your boat broadside to the shallows as it backs, pass the line in some other manner.

Try backing in with wind or current compensating for the reversing propeller, keeping your boat straight and leaving its bow headed out. In any case, after the line is passed and made fast, do the actual pulling with your engines going ahead, to get full power into the pull. For greater maneuverability of your boat, make the line as far forward of the stern as practical.

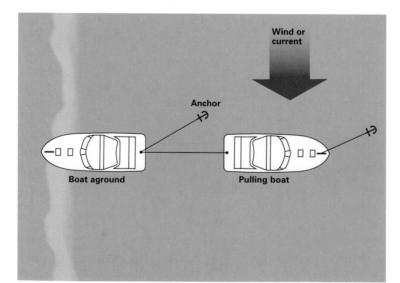

Figure 10-09 Most recreational boats pull with the towline cleated astern, which restricts maneuverability. For safe control, put out a bow anchor and take up on its line as the stranded boat becomes free. This arrangement prevents the pulling boat from being carried into shoal water.

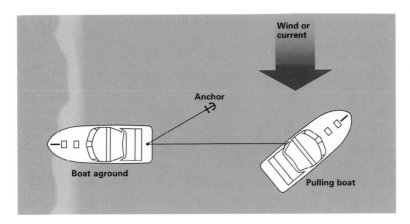

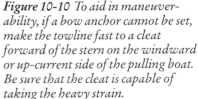

Figure 10-10 To aid in maneuverability, if a bow anchor cannot be set, make the towline fast to a cleat forward of the stern on the windward or up-current side of the pulling boat. Be sure that the cleat is capable of taking the heavy strain.

For safe control, you might drop your own bow anchor or anchors, and then send a line over from your boat to the stranded boat; see **Figure 10-09.** If a close approach seems unwise, anchor your own craft, and then send the line in a dinghy, or buoy it and float it over.

Making the Pull

If wind or current, or both, are broadside to the direction of the pull, keep your boat anchored even while pulling and keep a strain on your anchor line. Otherwise, as soon as your boat takes the pulling strain (particularly if the line is fast to its stern), you will have lost maneuverability, which could eventually put your boat aground broadside.

If you are pulling with your boat underway, secure the towline well forward of your stern so that while hauling, your boat can angle into the wind and current and still hold its position; see **Figure 10-10.**

Tremendous strains can be set up, particularly on the stranded boat, by this sort of action, even to the point of carrying away whatever fitting that the towline is made fast to. Ordinary recreational craft are not designed as tugboats.; the cleats or bitts available for making the line fast may well be not strong enough for such a strain, and they are probably not located advantageously for such work. It is far better to run a bridle around the whole hull and pull against this bridle rather than to risk damaging some part of the stern by such straining. Use a bridle on your boat, too, if there is any doubt of its ability to withstand such concentrated loads; see **Figure 10-11.**

When operating in limited areas, the stranded craft should have an anchor out for control when it comes off. It should also have another anchor ready to be put over the side, if necessary, to keep it from going back aground if it is without power. Through all of this maneuvering, keep all lines clear of the propeller and make sure no sudden surge is put on a slack line.

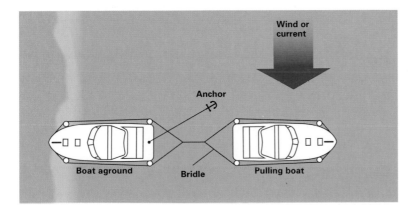

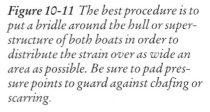

Figure 10-11 The best procedure is to put a bridle around the hull or superstructure of both boats in order to distribute the strain over as wide an area as possible. Be sure to pad pressure points to guard against chafing or scarring.

Towing

At some time you will probably need to take another vessel in tow. In good weather with no sea running, the problem is fairly easy. It involves little more than maneuvering your boat into position forward of the other boat, and passing it a towline. (Note that the "old saying" about whose towline is used in determining liability in case of an accident has no validity.)

Generally speaking, the towing boat should pass her towline to the other craft. You may want to send over a light line first (such as a plastic water ski towline that floats is excellent), and use that to haul over the actual towing line.

When approaching a boat that is dead in the water to pass it a line, do not be dramatic and move in too close if there is any kind of sea running. Just buoy a long line with several life preservers, tow it astern, and take a turn about the stern of the disabled vessel, but don't foul its propeller in doing so. The crew of the vessel being assisted can pick the line up with a

TOWING PRINCIPLES

Start off easy! Don't try to dig up the whole ocean, and merely end up with a lot of cavitation and vibration. A steady pull at a reasonable speed will get you to your destination with far less strain on boats, lines, and crewmembers.

• When towing, keep the two boats "in step" by adjusting the towline length to keep both on the crest or in the trough of seas at the same time. Sometimes, as with a confused sea, this may not be possible, but the idea is to prevent a situation where the boat being towed is shouldering up against the back of one sea, presenting maximum resistance, while the towing boat is trying to run down the forward slope of another sea. Then when this condition is reversed, the tow alternately runs ahead briefly and then surges back on the towline with a heavy strain. If there is any degree of uniformity to the waves, the strain on the towline will be minimized by adjusting it to the proper length.

• As the tow gets into protected, quiet waters, shorten up on the line to allow better handling in close quarters. Swing as wide as possible around buoys and channel turns so that the tow has room to follow.

• A small boat in tow should be trimmed a little by the stern; trimming by the head causes her to yaw. In a seaway this condition is aggravated and it is increasingly important to keep the bow relatively light.

• It is easy for a larger boat to tow a smaller vessel too fast, causing it to yaw and capsize. Always tow at a moderate speed, something less than hull speed (1.34 times the square-root of the waterline length in feet), and make full allowance for adverse conditions of wind and waves.

• In smooth water, motorboats may borrow an idea from tugs, which often take their tow alongside in harbor or sheltered waters, for better maneuverability. The towing boat should make fast on the other craft's quarter; refer to **Figure 10-12**.

• In relatively calm water, even a dinghy with a small outboard motor can tow a medium-size boat at slow speed, enough to get it into harbor or to a pier; tow astern or alongside as required for maneuverability.

Towing Alongside

• Towing alongside may be necessary when the towed craft has lost its steering capability, or when only one person is on board the disabled boat and is using its dinghy to tow. Towing alongside is better than towing astern in congested areas where maneuvering is more critical.

boathook from the cockpit with far less fuss than by any heave-and-catch method, as long as you are to windward.

The most logical place to attach the line on the boat to be towed is that boat's forward bitt or cleats, but be sure that such fitting can take the load. The bitt or cleat should be fastened with through bolts of adequate diameter, washers, and nuts—never with wood or self-tapping screws. If the fastening is to the deck, this must be reinforced on the underside with a backing plate of sufficient area. Even better is a bitt fastened to a major structural member. Be cautious; if an item of deck hardware pulls out under heavy load, the stretched towline can act as a slingshot, hurling the bitt or cleat with great force, enough to cause serious injury or death.

A trailerable boat will have a bow eye that makes an excellent place of attaching a towline; if it is a cast-type bow eye, it could snap off from an improper alignment of the pull. On a small sailboat with the mast going through the deck, wrap the towline around the mast; if the mast is stepped on deck, do not fasten to it—you will only pull it off.

Towing Lines

Three-strand twisted nylon has excessive stretch and dangerous snap-back action if parted under load; it should not be used if its use can be avoided.

Polypropylene line floats and is a highly visible bright yellow, but it has little elasticity and shock loads are heavily transferred to fittings on both the towed and towing craft. Further, it has less strength (requiring larger sizes), and is stiff, making it difficult to stow and handle; it is also particularly subject to chafing damage. With all these disadvantages, this line, in sizes up to ⅝-inch, is suitable only for light towing loads in protected waters.

The preferred line for towing is double-braided (braid-on-braid) nylon. It has sufficient elasticity to cushion shock loads, but not so much as to create a snap-back hazard. This line is stronger than three-strand twisted nylon of the same size and will not kink. Its disadvantage is that it does not float and must be watched to avoid entanglement in the towing vessel's propeller. It is the most expensive type of line, but for moderate- and heavy-duty towing it is well worth the difference.

Handling the Towing Boat

The worst possible place to make the tow line fast is to the stern of the towing boat, because the pull of the tow prevents the stern from swinging properly in response to rudder action, limiting the boat's maneuverability. The towline should be made fast as far forward as practicable, as in tug and towboat practice. The deck hardware of the towing boat must be capable of carrying the load—the same as described above for the towed craft. If there is no suitable place forward, make a bridle from the forward bitts, running around the superstructure to a point in the forward part of the cockpit. Such a bridle will have to be wrapped with chafing gear wherever it bears on the superstructure or any corners, and even then it may cause some chafing of the finish.

Cautions in Towing

Secure the towline so that it can be cast loose, if necessary, or, failing that, have a knife or hatchet ready to cut it. This line is a potential danger to anyone near if it should break and come whipping forward. Three-strand nylon acts like a huge rubber band when it breaks, and there have been some bad accidents. Never stand rear or in line with a highly stressed towline, and keep a wary eye out at all times.

On board the towed boat, have an anchor ready to drop in case the towline breaks or must be cast off.

If for any reason you must come near a burning vessel to tow it (for instance, to prevent it from endangering other boats or property), approach from windward so the flames are blowing away from you. Your lightest anchor with its length of chain thrown into the cockpit or through a window of the burning boat could act as a good grappling hook.

When the towing boat is smaller than the towed craft, it will often encounter heavy resistance from waves hitting the larger vessel; these waves can slow or even stop the progress of the

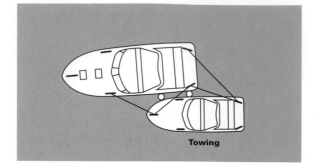

Towing

Figure 10-12 Spring lines are used as shown above when a boat takes a larger craft in tow alongside. Fenders are used at points of contact, and springs are made up with no slack. Both boats respond as a unit to the towing boat's rudder action.

tow. Crosswinds may make you drift off course faster than you are prepared for. One way to avoid these problems is for the towing boat to make fast alongside the towed craft near its quarter; see **Figure 10-12.** This will make the towing more efficient—even a dinghy with an average outboard motor can usually tow a much larger craft in this manner.

In any towing situation, never have people fend off the other vessel with hands or feet; even the smallest boats coming together under these conditions can cause broken bones or severed fingers. With large vessels, the risk is the loss of a whole limb, or worse.

Never allow anyone to hold a towing line while towing another vessel, regardless of its size. They could receive badly torn tendons and muscles, they might lose the towline over the side, or they could be dragged overboard.

When Not to Tow

Towing can be a dangerous undertaking, as well as an expensive one, if not properly done. If you are not equipped for the job, stand by the disabled vessel. If your craft's engine would be barely adequate for the task, as in the case of a small sailboat with a small inboard or outboard auxiliary engine, towing another boat in less than perfect conditions might be awkward. You may be able to put a line across and assist by keeping the other craft's bow at a proper angle to the sea until help comes.

Call the U.S. Coast Guard or other towing agency, and turn the job over to them when they arrive. Don't try to be a hero, as you are more than likely neither trained nor experienced in this type of work. Remember that the most important concern of a skipper is the safety of persons on board, not the safety of the craft itself. No boat is worth a life!

Chapter
11

Safety Afloat

Duties & Responsibilities of the Skipper • Basic Operating Procedures
Safety Organizations • Construction for Safety • Engines & Fuel Systems
Electrical Systems • Lightning Protection • Equipment for Safety
Maintenance for Safety • Safety in the Water • First Aid Afloat

Although boating is not an inherently unsafe activity, there are many actions that can make it safe and carefree without spoiling its enjoyment. Good seamanship begins with knowledge and use of safe practices in all aspects of boating. For the skipper, this includes knowing his duties and responsibilities, as well as having an understanding of the construction of boats, their equipment, operation, and maintenance. While not allowing it to detract from his enjoyment of boating, the wise operator practices safety at all times while afloat and studies it frequently ashore. He recognizes the importance of safety, and it is always in the back of his mind. He views safety not as an arbitrary set of rules, but as the practical application of special knowledge and common sense.

Most boating accidents and difficulties arise from ignorance and could have been avoided. A person does not knowingly put his life, and the lives of others, and the safety of valuable property in jeopardy, but he may do so through lack of knowledge.

DUTIES & RESPONSIBILITIES OF THE SKIPPER

As the skipper you are responsible for the safety of your boat and the people on board. You are also responsible for the safety of nearby craft and the people on them, for swimmers and water-skiers in your vicinity, and anyone else who might be affected by your boat's course or wake. This

Previous Page: Figure 11-01 At least one person on board other than the skipper should be fully capable of sending a distress message, recovering a person who falls overboard, or returning the boat to port should the skipper become incapacitated.

applies to all sizes of boats, on all waters, and at all times. One of the challenges of boating is accepting this responsibility without letting it detract from your enjoyment of boating.

Leadership

Leadership and discipline are subjects rarely considered by recreational boaters but they are valuable assets, particularly should an emergency occur.

Discipline means prompt and cheerful obedience to laws and regulations designed primarily for safety. It also means a square deal to shipmates; the skipper who expects discipline of his crew must likewise discipline himself.

Discipline does not mean a long string of commands with a crew constantly scurrying about the deck. There can be discipline on board the smallest craft without there being any apparent show of it. Real discipline is a function of leadership and leadership can be exercised in casual clothing on any boat. If you establish your authority as the leader and delegate with tact, each outing on your boat can be both fun and safe.

Leadership is based on three things: (1) each skipper must know himself, his abilities, and his limitations; (2) he must know his job, know it so well that he doesn't have to think about the details of doing it; (3) he must know his crew and his boat and what he can reasonably expect of them in an emergency.

Foresight

Next to leadership comes forehandedness or foresightedness. A first-class skipper doesn't wait for an emergency to arise; he has already formulated solutions to any emergency he may face. "Plan ahead" is one of the best pieces of advice you can be given in boating.

Even the most experienced skipper will admit that he has at times been fooled by unexpected effects of wind or current. Dangerous situations can develop with great suddenness—so even when all looks well, watch out! You should have an answer to every threat, and a plan to take you out of every danger.

Vigilance

Next in importance is vigilance. As skipper, you must see intelligently all that comes within your vision, outside and inside the boat. And your vigilance must extend beyond this to foreseeing situations as well. An aircraft pilot's rule that he must be able to get into alternate fields as well as the airport of his destination holds equal meaning for the boat skipper, too.

You must be able to concentrate—distractions such as loud music or rowdy passengers must not be allowed to divert your attention from your important tasks. Maintain a safety consciousness at all times.

Common Sense

One more checkpoint: common sense. The successful skipper has a sense of proportion and of the fitness of things. We can all recall cases where through lack of common sense, we did things that later looked rather ridiculous. Use your head!

Check of Equipment

Before you get any boat underway, check to see if it is really ready to go. Not only should all equipment required by law (Chapters 2 and 3) be on board and in proper condition for use, but all navigational and other equipment should be at hand. Check water and fuel tanks, inspect ground tackle, check stores, and complete all those other small jobs that can be done easily at the mooring or safe in a slip, but not at sea in an emergency.

Prepare a "predeparture checklist" (see page 376) and keep it updated. Don't trust to memory or routine to ensure that *everything* necessary is on board—have a list and use it.

Physical Condition of the Skipper

Also relevant to a boat's safe operation is the physical condition of its skipper. The constant vigil that is necessary requires his complete possession of his faculties and a sense of physical well-being. Except in cases of extreme emergency, no skipper should expose his boat or his people to danger unless he is in good physical and mental condition.

Although the partaking of alcoholic beverages is commonly a part of many boating activities, the prudent skipper abstains while underway or when getting underway is anticipated in the next few hours. Alcohol adversely affects memory, balance, night vision, and muscular coordination; tests have shown that effects of sun and wind encountered in boating tend to aggravate these effects. Think before you drink—especially when boating.

Avoiding Risk

Do not permit any of your crew or guests to take needless risks. If someone must do a dangerous job that could result in his being swept overboard insist that he wear a life jacket—an approved PFD.

Carefully observe the current weather and check the forecast before getting underway. If the weather doesn't look good, stay in port until conditions improve. A day on the water is not worth the risk of your boat or a life.

Acting Moderately

A major part of common sense is acting moderately. Make all changes of course and speed with moderation. Don't accelerate from a stop or slow speed so abruptly as to possibly cause other persons on board discomfort or injury. Full-throttle starts are not necessary, except perhaps for getting a water-skier up and going. Likewise, don't make sudden and abrupt changes in heading unless necessary.

If appropriate, as it will be in many cases, make an announcement or warning of what you are about to do. A simple "Here we go" or "Hold tight" will do much to avoid a preventable accident.

Maintaining a Lookout

A small craft cannot readily use the lookout routine of the large vessel, but the vigilance and caution of that routine should be acknowledged. Having a lookout is not only a requirement of the Navigation Rules, it is good common sense. Make it a matter of pride that you as skipper will observe any danger before anyone else does; this is definitely your responsibility. On the water, a dangerous situation can develop with amazing speed; you should try to be "one step ahead" of any developing hazard.

Specific Responsibilities

The responsibilities of the skipper or of the individual on watch are as follows:

- Safe navigation of the boat.
- Safe and efficient handling of the boat in the presence of other boats.
- Safety of personnel and material on board.
- Rendering assistance to all in danger or distress.
- Smart handling and smart appearance of the boat.
- Comfort and contentment on board.
- A good log.

The Crew

Recreational boating is usually a family affair—indeed, one of its most pleasing aspects is that essentially the whole family can share in activities.

One aspect of boating that should not be overlooked is the *training* of the crew. No boat of any appreciable size should depart its slip or mooring for an afternoon's run or a cruise measured in days without an adequately trained crew, *especially an alternate for the skipper*; see **Figure 11-01.** One other person should be fully competent to take the helm at least under all normal conditions of wind and waves, and really should be able to do so under adverse weather conditions. The mate should be capable of bringing the boat alongside a pier or of anchoring it. A sudden incapacitating illness or accident may thrust heavy responsibilities upon the mate without warning. If that person has been trained ahead of time, the emergency will be significantly less drastic and much more easily handled.

Training the Crew

A training program need be neither onerous nor unpleasant; in fact, it need not be even apparent to the "students"! It should, however, be planned and carried out on a formal basis so that the skipper can be sure that everyone knows what he has to know. The secret to a successful family crew-training program is to make it fun and not let it take the pleasure out of boating.

With just a little imagination a man-overboard drill can be made into a game without losing one bit of its effectiveness. With patience and adequate opportunities for practice, the mate and older children can be developed into skillful helmsmen. Every member of the crew should know where the fire extinguishers are *and should have had actual experience in using them*; see **Figure 11-02.** It is well worth the small price of recharging one or two extinguishers to gain the experience of putting out a fire with one. (By the way, have *you* ever actually put out a fire with an extinguisher of the type now on your boat?) This practice should

Figure 11-02 It is not enough that approved-type fire extinguishers be on board at appropriate locations; every member of the crew should be trained in how they are used before getting underway.

not, of course, be carried out on the boat, but it is easily done ashore.

The mate, at least, and preferably several others of the crew, should know how to place the radio in operation, how to change channels, which channel is to be used for emergencies, and what to say.

Instruction plus Practice

A proper training program consists of instruction plus practice. First, learn for yourself what should be done and how, and then pass this information on to your crew. For routine matters such as boat handling, give each crewmember the chance to become proficient—it may be quicker and easier on your nerves always to bring the boat alongside a pier yourself, but you should have the patience to let others learn how by doing. For emergency procedures, have both planned and unannounced drills.

All aboard, *including you*, should be trained to do the right thing instinctively and quickly in a real emergency.

Guests on Board

When you have guests on board, they may or may not become part of the crew. If qualified, give them some clearly defined job(s) to do—and be sure to tell the regular crewmember who normally performed those duties to supervise or stand aside as appropriate.

If your guests have had little or no boating experience, take them on a tour of the boat. Without overdoing it and frightening them, point out possible dangers such as cleats on the deck that might be a cause of tripping, the hazards of riding on the bow, the boom of a sailboat—you know the possibilities on your boat, point them out to your guests. Show them the location of PFDs, *and how to put them on*; show them the location of the fire extinguishers, and how to operate them. Tell them what they can do to help with the operation of the boat, and even more importantly, what they should not attempt to do.

Important Actions Underway

Here is a short checklist of things to do and not do:

• Check and plot the boat's position frequently when in sight of land or aids to navigation; be certain of the identification of the objects used to fix position.

• Keep a close eye on the depth sounder. If your boat has one, set the minimum depth alarm to a suitable depth. Don't be caught by surprise by shallower water.

• Note the effect of wind and current on the boat, especially in close waters or when maneuvering near other boats.

• Do not follow other boats blindly; steer a safe course, and do not assume that another craft is on a safe course.

• When in doubt about your position, slow down; do not wait until the last minute.

• Remember that the other skipper may not see you, and always be alert to take immediate steps to prevent a collision.

BASIC OPERATING PROCEDURES

There are a number of basic operating procedures that are done repeatedly in everyday boating. After doing them routinely time after time, there is a tendency to do them semiautomatically, perhaps cutting corners and slighting some steps—that is simply human nature. Periodically, take time to stop and think; refresh your mind and perform each step properly one by one. Being fully safe requires constant attention to detail.

Fueling

Fueling a boat properly is an essential element of good seamanship. Before starting out make sure that you have enough fuel on board, and if any is needed, put it in safely. Certain precautions must be carefully and completely observed every time that a boat is fueled with gasoline. (Diesel fuel is nonexplosive, but it will burn; the step-by-step procedures given below should be followed with both fuels.)

Before Fueling

1. Make sure that your boat is properly secured to the fueling pier. Fuel before dark, if possible.

Figure 11-03 Overloading is a major cause of boating accidents and can worsen the outcome of any mishap while underway. Be sure to check your craft's capacity plate before loading.

2. Stop engines, motors, fans, and other devices that could produce a spark. Turn off the master switch for the batteries if the electrical system has one. Put out all galley fires and open flames.

3. Close all ports, windows, doors, and hatches so that fumes cannot blow aboard and below.

4. Disembark all passengers and any crewmembers not needed for the fueling operation.

5. Prohibit all smoking on board and nearby.

6. Have an approved, well-maintained fire extinguisher close at hand.

7. Measure the fuel in the tanks and do not plan to put in more than the tank will hold; allow for expansion.

While Fueling

8. Keep nozzle or can spout in contact with the opening to guard against static sparks.

9. Do not spill any fuel, especially gasoline.

10. Do not overfill. Filling a tank until fuel flows from the vents is *dangerous.*

11. For boats with outboard motors, remove any portable tanks from the boat and fill on shore.

After Fueling

12. Close fill openings.

13. Wipe up any spilled fuel; dispose of wipe-up rags on shore.

14. Open all ports, windows, doors, and hatches; turn on bilge blower. Ventilate boat at *least* four minutes.

15. Sniff low down in tank and engine compart-

ments. *If odor of gasoline is present, do not start engine;* continue ventilation actions until odor can no longer be detected. Check for any drips and liquid fuel.

16. Be prepared to cast off lines as soon as engine starts; get clear of pier promptly.

Loading

Overloading is a major cause—perhaps the greatest single cause—of accidents in smaller boats and dinghies, and also has significance for medium-size boats; see **Figure 11-03**. Overloading is particularly hazardous because people do not fear it as they do fires and explosions. Many a skipper, cautious in his handling of gasoline, will unknowingly load his craft far beyond safe limits. The number of seats in a boat is *not* an indication of the number of persons it can carry safely.

Determining Capacity

"Loading" and "capacity" are terms primarily related to the weight of persons, fuel, and gear that can be safely carried. The safe load of a boat in persons depends on many of its characteristics, among them hull volume and dimensions; what it is made of; for outboards whether there is an effective engine well inboard of the transom notch where the engine is mounted; and how heavy the engine is.

  USCG Capacity Plates Boats under 20 feet in length (6.1 m)—inboard, outboard, and stern-drive, other than sailboats and certain special

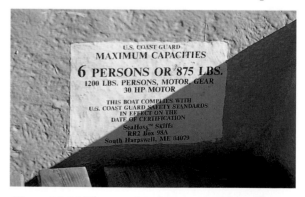

Figure 11-04 The capacity plate on an outboard boat shows the limits of loading in terms of number of persons and the maximum weight of persons, and the total weight of motor, fuel gear, and persons. A maximum horsepower rating is also shown.

```
          U.S. COAST GUARD
     MAXIMUM CAPACITIES

  7  PERSONS OR   900 LBS

  970   LBS. PERSONS, GEAR

     THIS BOAT COMPLIES WITH U.S. COAST GUARD SAFETY
     STANDARDS IN EFFECT ON THE DATE OF CERTIFICATION
```

Figure 11-05 A capacity plate for a boat with an inboard engine or a stern-drive shows only the maximum allowable number and weight of persons, and the maximum weight for persons and gear. Exceeding these numbers or weights is not a violation of federal law but may be considered in case of accidents.

types—must carry a capacity plate specified by U.S. Coast Guard regulations issued under the Federal Boat Safety Act of 1971. These capacities are computed from rather complex formulas. Plates on craft powered by one or more outboard motors show both the maximum weight for persons, the maximum number of persons, and the total maximum weight for motor, fuel, gear, *and persons*; these plates also show the maximum horsepower capacity, total horsepower if more than one engine is mounted; see **Figure 11-04.** Plates for inboard and stern-drive craft show only the maximum number of persons capacity in terms of weight and number of persons, and the maximum weight for fuel, gear, and persons; see **Figure 11-05.** Your boat's capacity plate must be mounted where you can see it when you are preparing to get underway.

Limits on capacity plates apply for boating in good to moderate weather conditions. In rough waters keep the weight well below the limit. The presence of a capacity plate does *not* relieve you of responsibility for sound judgment. You should know probable future weather conditions as well as those prevailing when starting out.

Safe Loading

Remember that people represent a "live" load; they move about and affect a boat quite differently than static loads like the engine or fuel tank.

If your boat's capacity is fully utilized, or the weather gets rough, distribute the load evenly, keep it low, and don't make abrupt changes in its distribution. Make any shift in human or other weights only after stopping or slowing.

Horsepower Capacity

A second aspect of capacity for smaller craft is the maximum horsepower motor that it can *safely* carry; this capacity is exceeded perhaps as often as the weight-carrying one.

You need not use the maximum safe horsepower; most boats give satisfactory and more economical service with motors of lesser horsepower. A larger engine does not always mean more speed; it does mean that the increased weight of the engine, and of its fuel and accessories, will significantly reduce the number of people that can be safely carried.

Boarding a Boat

There is a safe way to step aboard a small boat—outboard or dinghy—and an unsafe way; see **Figure 11-06.** In boarding from a pier, step into the boat as near to the center as possible, keeping body weight low. If you're boarding from a beach, come in over the bow. Keep lines tight or have someone steady the boat.

Figure 11-06 Do not attempt to step aboard a dinghy carrying heavy or bulky items. One person should board and another hand the items over from on shore or a larger craft. If alone, line up the items on the pier, step aboard, and then reach over for the gear or packages.

Never jump into a boat or step on the gunwale (edge of the hull). If you must take a motor or other gear aboard, place it on the edge of the pier where you can easily reach it from the center of the boat. Better yet, after you are in the boat, have someone on the pier hand it to you.

If stepping into a canoe or light dinghy on a beach, remember that the unsupported parts of a hull out of the water are quite vulnerable. A rock could be driven through the hull by your weight all on one foot.

The boarding cautions above are primarily focused on a "hard" dinghy—an inflatable, with its buoyancy tubes at each side is more stable, but care should still be taken.

Predeparture Actions

Another measure of good seamanship is the procedure you follow before actual departure. If you will be gone for overnight or longer, you should repeat many of these steps each day before getting underway.

Final Weather Check

Few boats are so large that their skipper can ignore weather conditions. You should make a final weather check close to departure time. Know the time of best weather broadcasts, radio and TV (including cable), in your home area (these broadcasts vary widely in their scope and suitability for boating); know the telephone numbers of agencies to call for last-minute information. When away from your home waters, find on arrival at each overnight stop how you can get early morning forecasts before departure.

The Marine Weather Services Charts published each year by the National Weather Service (see Chapter 24, pages 832 and 833) give information on major radio and TV weather broadcasts as well as the location of regional Weather Service broadcast antennas. NWS is also steadily expanding the number of VHF-FM radio transmitters that broadcast continuous weather information; also available on the web at www.nws.noaa.gov; see also Chapter 24.

Predeparture Checklist

Prepare your own predeparture checklist *and use it*. Review and revise the list if you change boats or boating areas.

The following items apply generally; you may not need them all and you may add some of your own. Check that:

• All safety equipment is aboard, accessible, and in good working condition, including one Coast-Guard-approved PFD for each person.

• The bilge has no fuel fumes and little or no water. Ventilate or pump out as necessary. (On a gasoline-powered inboard-engine craft, operate the blower for at least four minutes, then "sniff" the bilge for any fumes.)

• All navigation lights operate satisfactorily (even if you do not intend to be out after sunset); horn works properly.

• All loose gear is stowed securely. Dock lines and fenders should be stowed immediately after getting underway.

• Engine oil levels are adequate; both crankcase and reverse-reduction gears; water level is sufficient in closed cooling systems. After starting engines, check overboard flow of cooling water.

• Fuel tanks are as full as you need and compartments have been properly ventilated; see **Figure 11-07**. Know your tank capacity and fuel consumption at various rpms, and the cruising radius this gives. Make sure there is enough fuel aboard for your anticipated cruising, plus an adequate reserve if you must change your plans for weather or other reasons. For a day's outing and return home, follow the

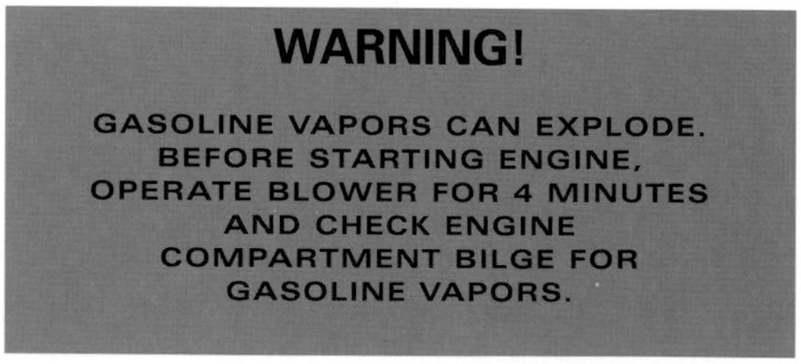

WARNING!

GASOLINE VAPORS CAN EXPLODE. BEFORE STARTING ENGINE, OPERATE BLOWER FOR 4 MINUTES AND CHECK ENGINE COMPARTMENT BILGE FOR GASOLINE VAPORS.

Figure 11-07 A warning label is required near an ignition switch on a boat in order to comply with the powered ventilation requirements of the Coast Guard. Help prevent disaster by posting a warning label in any unventilated compartment into which a crewmember might place gasoline or a cleaning solvent container.

PREDEPARTURE FLOAT PLAN

1. NAME & PHONE NUMBER OF PERSON FILING THE FLOAT PLAN

2. DESCRIPTION OF BOAT

Name of boat; length; make; type; color of hull, deck, and trim, including any canvas top; any other distinguishing features; registration number.

3. ENGINE TYPE

Number of engines, horsepower, fuel capacity.

4. PLANNED OPERATIONS

Departure point; destination; route; planned date and time of arrival at destination; expected date and time of return.

5. PERSONS ON BOARD

Name of skipper and his boating experience. For all persons: name, age, address, and phone number. Any person with a medical condition or problem.

6. MARINE RADIO

Type and frequencies/channels; EPIRB (type).

7. SAFETY & SURVIVAL EQUIPMENT

Personal flotation devices, visual distress signals; flashlight; anchor and line; food and water; paddles; dinghy or life raft; other safety or emergency equipment.

8. OTHER PERTINENT INFORMATION

If applicable: vehicle information—color, make, type, license tag number, where parked. If applicable: trailer—type, where parked. Any other useful information.

9. SUGGESTED DATE & TIME FOR HOLDER OF FLOAT PLAN TO CALL COAST GUARD OR LOCAL AUTHORITY

List all appropriate telephone numbers.

"rule of thirds"—one third for the trip outbound, one third for the return run, and one third for reserve.

• All guests have been properly instructed in safety and operational matters—both dos and don'ts.

• There is a second person on board capable of taking over for you if you are disabled.

Float Plan

Before departing, tell a responsible relative or friend where you intend to cruise and when you expect to make port again; make sure he or she has a good description of the boat. (Do not attempt to file this "Float Plan" with the U.S. Coast Guard; they do not have the manpower to keep track of boats as the FAA monitors aircraft flights.) After departure, tell that person of any changes in your cruise plans, so he can tell the Coast Guard where to search and

what type of boat to look for if you are overdue. And be sure to check in with him or her when you return to prevent false alarms about your safety.

Forms are not required for float plans, but they do make it easier to record the necessary information and ensure against omissions; see sidebar above. A typical Float Plan form is printed in the Coast Guard pamphlet "Federal Requirements and Safety Tips for Recreational Boats"; similar formats are in many books and periodicals. Forms are available also from many marine insurance offices.

Safety Organizations

There are many public and private organizations devoted to the promotion of boating safety. Several teach boating safety; others are concerned with the material and operational aspects of boats and boating.

Figure 11-08 The United States Power Squadrons is an organization of volunteers dedicated to making boating safer through education. Boats skippered by a USPS member are usually identified by the distinctive flag with blue-and-white vertical stripes, shown here.

Educational Organizations

United States Power Squadrons The USPS is a volunteer organization of more than 60,000 members organized into over 450 local Squadrons. These units, located throughout the United States and in some overseas areas, offer educational programs of basic safety and piloting to the public, and more advanced courses to members; see **Figure 11-08.**

It is a nonprofit, self-sustaining private membership organization dedicated to teaching better and safer boating. Despite the word "Power" in its name, the USPS today includes many sailboat skippers in its ranks, and has added the phrase "Sail and Power Boating" to its literature, and many local squadrons have added "Sail" to their name. USPS also has several public service programs, including the reporting of chart corrections and the Vessel Safety Check (VSC) program (see pages 396-399). The boats of members can be identified by the USPS Ensign with its blue and white vertical stripes; see Chapter 25.

Many thousands of boaters and families receive free instruction in the USPS Boating Course every year. For information on local classes, write USPS Headquarters, P.O. Box 30423, Raleigh, NC 27622-0423; www.usps.org. You can also call 800-336-BOAT, a central listing service maintained by BoatU.S.

The Canadian Power and Sail Squadrons are organized similarly to the USPS, with modifications to fit Canada's laws and customs.

Additional information on the USPS and CPS appears in Chapter 26.

United States Coast Guard Auxiliary The USCGAux is a voluntary civilian organization of owners of boats, private airplanes, and shore radio stations; it is a nonmilitary group, although administered by the U.S. Coast Guard. It promotes safety in operation of small boats through education, boat safety checks, and operational activities.

Although organized along military lines and closely affiliated with the regular Coast Guard, the Auxiliary is strictly civilian in nature; it has no law enforcement powers. See Chapter 26 for more information and illustrations of USCGAux flags and uniform insignia.

The Auxiliary carries on a program of public boating courses free of charge except for the cost of materials.

Members take specialty courses to increase their knowledge and abilities.

Vessel Safety Check (formerly known as Courtesy Marine Examination) is a well-known program of both the Coast Guard Auxiliary and the United States Power Squadrons. Specially trained USCGAux and USPS members conduct

Figure 11-09 Boat owners can request the free Vessel Safety Check given by members of the Coast Guard Auxiliary, shown here, or by USPS members. Craft that meet all the requirements are awarded a decal for the current year.

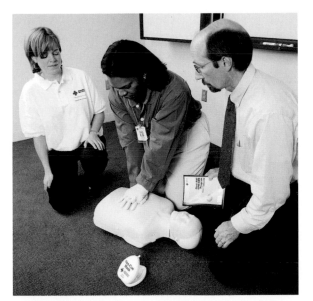

Figure 11-10 Local chapters of the American Red Cross teach swimming, life saving, and other water safety subjects, including First Aid and CPR (cardiopulmonary resuscitation), to persons of all ages. Every person who goes boating should try to become an adequate swimmer.

annual checks on boats, but only with the consent of the owner; see **Figure 11-09** and pages 396–399. Boats that meet a strict set of requirements are awarded a distinguishing decal. If a boat fails to qualify, the owner is urged to remedy any defects and request a reexamination. No report of failure is made to any authority.

The Auxiliary promotes safety afloat by assisting the Coast Guard in patrolling regattas and racing events. In many areas, the Auxiliary also participates in search and rescue for vessels that are disabled, in distress, or have been reported overdue.

Information on public classes of the Auxiliary or membership in the organization may be obtained from a local Flotilla or by writing to the appropriate Coast Guard District Headquarters, or you can call 800-336-BOAT. More information on the USCGAux appears in Chapter 26.

American National Red Cross The Red Cross offers programs of water safety education through its more than 3,000 local chapters in all areas of the United States; see **Figure 11-10.** The swimming and water safety skills taught by the Red Cross range from beginning through

advanced swimmer, survival swimming, and life-saving. The small craft safety courses include canoeing, rowing, outboard boating, and sailing.

Red Cross first-aid training is also available to the public through local chapters. A wise skipper would do well to learn the proper action to be taken in common emergencies. Training in cardiopulmonary resuscitation (CPR) is desirable for all skippers, but it is essential for those cruising offshore; it is now a requirement for USCG licenses.

Textbooks used in Red Cross training programs may be purchased from larger bookstores or through local chapters; all are valuable reference publications. Available texts from the Red Cross include *Swimming and Water Safety, Lifesaving and Water Safety, First Aid, Basic Canoeing, Canoeing, Basic Rowing, Basic Outboarding,* and *Basic Sailing;* all are reasonably priced.

The Red Cross publishes a variety of safety pamphlets and posters and produces informational and instructional films. These are available

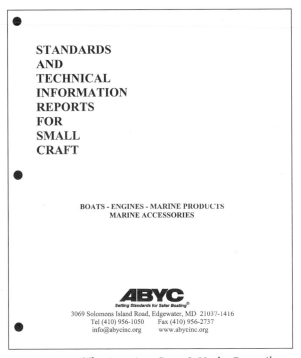

Figure 11-11 The American Boat & Yacht Council, Inc., is a nonprofit, public-service organization founded to increase safety in the design, construction, equipping, and maintenance of small craft. The volumes of its "Safety Standards" are worthwhile reading for skippers of all boats.

free to interested groups. Information on classes, publications, films, and other safety activities can be obtained from local chapters.

Boat & Equipment Organizations

In addition to the national volunteer groups working toward greater safety afloat through education, there are several organizations related to the boating industry that promote safety through standards for boats and equipment, including installation and use.

American Boat & Yacht Council, Inc. The ABYC is a nonprofit public-service organization founded in 1954 to "improve and promote the design, construction, equipage, and maintenance of small craft with reference to safety." Membership is open to companies and individuals.

The American Boat & Yacht Council develops and publishes "Safety Standards" which are recommended specifications and practices for making small boats as free from dangerous defect or deficiency as possible; see **Figure 11-11.** They also offer the most extensive technical education and technician certification program in the marine industry. Standards are stated in terms of desired performance. They are prepared by Project Technical Committees formed as broadly based groups of recognized authorities. All safety standards and technical reports are advisory; ABYC has no powers of enforcement.

The ABYC does not "approve" boats, equipment, materials, or services. Some standards refer to standards of other organizations or to testing laboratories. Standards are reviewed at least every five years. New and revised standards are sent out as supplements to the complete compilation published in loose-leaf form. Included are standards for such diverse matters as "good visibility from the helm position," "lifesaving equipment," "gasoline fuel systems," "AC electrical systems on boats," "lightning protection," "hydraulic systems," and "propulsion control systems." The full set of 64 recommended standards is published as *Standards and Technical Information Reports for Small Craft,* available from the Council at 3069 Solomons Island Road, Edgewater, MD 21037-1442; 410-956-1050; www.abycinc.org.

Although expensive, this is a good book to have on hand for reference.

Design, safety, and construction standards for boats as well as motors are also prepared by Underwriters Laboratory (UL), the American Bureau of Shipping (ABS), Society of Automotive Engineers (SAE), Lloyds of London, North German Lloyds, International Organization of Standards (ISO), and Det Norske Veritas. Boats manufactured in any country may be built to conform to the standards set by any of these organizations.

The Marine Department of Underwriters Laboratories, Inc. Underwriters Laboratories is a not-for-profit corporation that dates from 1894; it has marine testing facilities in North Carolina, as well as other locations—UL Laboratory and Testing Facility, 12 Laboratory Drive, P.O. Box 13995, Research Triangle Park, NC 27709-3995; 919-549-1534; www.ul.com. It serves industry and the boating public by conducting safety investigations and tests of marine products, by developing Marine Safety Standards, and by preparing special Marine Supplements to UL Electrical Safety Standards.

The principal activity of the Marine Department is testing boating equipment for safety, a process that begins with manufacturers voluntarily submitting product samples. These are often tested for compliance with appropriate safety requirements, and evaluated for overall design and construction in relation to their use. After a product has successfully completed the evaluation and complied with all of the UL requirements, the Marine Department conducts a follow-up investigation at the factory to confirm that the manufacturer's production controls comply with UL requirements.

A device that passes all its tests is "listed" by Underwriters Labs and may carry both on the product and in its advertising the UL "Listing Mark," consisting of the Laboratory's name or symbol, the product name, a control number, and the word "listed"; see **Figure 11-12.** The name of the device is included, with the name of the manufacturer, in the annual UL Marine Product Directory and in the online certification database

Figure 11-12 Boating products that have passed a safety evaluation buy the Marine Department of Underwriters Laboratories are "listed." The UL label, shown above, can be used in advertising the items and may be found on them in the form of stickers or tags.

on the UL website. UL does not approve or disapprove anything. Listing is an expression of UL's good-faith opinion, based on tests, that the item meets minimum applicable safety standards. It is not a warranty of quality or performance, nor are all listed products of the same category necessarily equivalent in quality, performance, or merit.

Only products commercially available are eligible for listing. New products may be submitted in their model stage for evaluation, but no final listing action is taken until production units are submitted.

The presence of a UL or UL-Marine label on any device means that a production sample has been successfully evaluated relative to safety requirements, and nothing more. The label may, however, be the basis on which "authorities having jurisdiction" grant approval for use. Such authorities include individuals making judgments for their own purposes, industry people making judgments for components of original equipment installations, marine surveyors for insurance purposes, and administrators of regulations making judgments required by law.

National Fire Protection Association This organization's activities extend far beyond boating and marine interests to include all aspects of the science and methods of fire protection. NFPA issues codes, standards, and recommended practices for minimizing losses of life and property by fire.

NFPA does not approve, inspect, or certify any installations, procedures, equipment, or materials, and it does not approve or evaluate testing laboratories. It does prepare, by coordinated action of committees of experts, codes and standards for the guidance of all persons in the matter of fire protection. Frequently, NFPA codes and standards are written into law or regulations by various government units.

Of interest to boaters is NFPA's booklet *Fire Protection Standard No. 302 for Pleasure and Commercial Motor Craft;* see **Figure 11-13.** It is available from the National Fire Protection Association, 1 Batterymarch Park, P.O. Box 9101, Quincy, MA 02269-9101; 617-770-3000; www.nfpa.org.

United States Sailing Association (US SAILING) This organization is the national governing body for the sport of sailing, whose mission is to encourage participation and excellence in sailing and racing in the United States. There is a strong emphasis on all safety aspects.

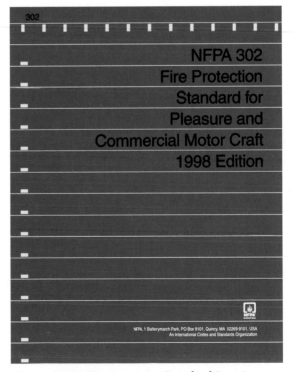

Figure 11-13 Fire Protection Standard Requirements for Pleasure and Commercial Motor Craft, NFPA No. 302, is a safety bulletin issued by the National Fire Prevention Association. It will provide useful information for any boat owner.

Contact US SAILING at P.O. Box 1260, 15 Marine Drive, Portsmouth, RI 02871-0907. www.ussailing.org.

CONSTRUCTION FOR SAFETY

Safety afloat starts with the design and construction of the boat itself. The typical skipper most likely did not build his own boat, but he should be able to recognize proper design features and sound construction characteristics. A boater should be reasonably familiar with safe and unsafe aspects of boat construction—the points that should be checked in determining whether or not a particular boat, new or used, should be bought—and thus avoid those that fail to measure up to desirable standards.

A boater thinking of buying a used boat should seriously consider the services of a qualified MARINE SURVEYOR, who is an expert in determining the condition of the hull, engine, and equipment. The surveyor may well discover defects that the would-be buyer overlooked and his impartial survey is sound protection for a purchaser; the modest cost is well justified. Surveys are often required before a boat-buyer can get a loan or insurance, particularly on older boats.

Hull Construction

Modern boats, built by reputable manufacturers, are basically seaworthy if they are honestly constructed to proven designs. This points out the proper course in selection of a good, sound boat. If you have no experience in selecting a boat, get the guidance of someone who is better qualified; be sure to talk to several people to avoid personal biases.

Where possible, two means of exit should be provided from compartments where people may congregate or sleep. Thus in a small boat with only one cabin and cockpit, a forward hatch is a desirable feature.

Construction Materials

For seaworthiness, materials suitable for boat building and high-quality construction are both essential. Fire-retardant materials should be used wherever possible. Boats may be built equally well of wood, fiberglass, steel, or aluminum. Combinations of materials may also be used, such as an aluminum superstructure on a steel hull. Note too that boats can also be built poorly in any of these materials.

Safety on Deck

A medium-size or large craft may have side decks on which individuals move forward to the bow. It is essential that four safety features be present.

First, these decks must be wide enough for secure footing, even though the space may be measured in inches.

Second, if the deck is made of a material that is slippery when wet (and most are), antislip protection must be provided at critical points. This may consist of a built-in roughness in fiberglass decks, grit added to deck paint, or special nonskid strips attached to the deck with their own adhesive backing. Any place where someone has slipped—or could slip—needs nonskid protection; see **Figure 11-14.**

Third, there must be enough hand-holds—places to grab and hold on—that no one is ever beyond a secure grasp when moving forward and aft, or when coming aboard or leaving the boat. The old saying "one hand for the boat and one for

Figure 11-14 Antislip protection on deck walkways and at boarding areas is a must. Adhesive strips offer another means of preventing falls on decks that otherwise would be slippery, particularly when wet.

yourself" is an excellent one—even in calm waters; at all times, hold on to something strong enough to bear your weight.

Fourth, no boat large enough for them should be without lifelines or life rails. They are often carried forward to join low metal rails (pulpits) at the bow and stern to enclose the deck completely.

Owners of offshore cruising sailboats would be wise to meet the requirements established by the Offshore Racing Council: There should be lifelines supported on stanchions effectively continuous around the working deck. Horizontal rails may be substituted in pulpits. Lifelines should be permanently supported at intervals of not more than 7 feet (2.1 m) and should not pass outboard of supporting stanchions. Pulpits should be permanently installed and their upper rails should be at no less height above the working deck than the upper lifelines, which should be 24 inches (61 cm) above the working deck. Lifelines should be stranded stainless-steel wire of not less than 5/32 inch (4 mm) for boats under 43 feet (13.1m) LOA, or 3/16 inch (5 mm) for larger boats. These requirements are compatible with those of the American Boat & Yacht Council for lifelines and rails on both power and sail boats.

Just because a boat has lifelines doesn't mean you can rely on them. The stanchions should be well-made and through-bolted. On fiberglass boats, you must rely on the quality of the deck construction, but check to be sure that each stanchion base bolts through a generous backing block under the deck.

Even if your lines and stanchions pass muster, don't conclude they are the best point of attachment for the snap of a safety harness in bad weather. A dock line stretched between the mooring cleat on the foredeck and the cleat on the stern has a number of advantages as a point of attachment, as it allows you to move about the deck without having to stop, unsnap, and snap on again as you must do at each stanchion if you rely on the lifelines.

Superstructure & Stability

The belief that a boat can carry weight anywhere as long as it appears to trim right can be

Figure 11-15 Every through-hull fitting should have a seacock to shut off water entry should a hose fail, or to work on equipment served by that fitting. A solid pipe extending to above the water line, not shown here, is a desirable added safety feature.

dangerous. Addition of more superstructures, such as a flying bridge, is often particularly bad, as is shifting heavy weights such as motors, ballast, tanks, and machinery. Where stability is concerned, no shifts of major weights or changes in design should be considered without advice of a qualified naval architect. Boat owners sometimes ruin boats and reduce their safety factors by deviating from architect's specifications for weight distribution.

Through-Hull Fittings

Through-hull fittings which pass through near or below the waterline should have SEACOCKS installed to permit positive closing. It is desirable to have solid, noncorroding metal pipe extend from the seacock to a level above the waterline, from which point flexible hoses may be run to the pump or other accessory; see **Figure 11-15.** Where hose is placed over pipe nipples for connections, use double hose clamps. There are now available through-hull fittings and seacocks that have been safety evaluated and "listed" by the Underwriters

Laboratories. ABYC *Safety Standard H-27* furnishes additional information on these.

ENGINES & FUEL SYSTEMS

Fires and explosions on boats are usually traceable to the engine room or galley, where improper equipment, faulty installation, or careless operation and maintenance are the direct cause. All these causes are under the owner's control.

Engine Installation

Engines should be suited to the hulls they power. Extremes of either underpowering or overpowering can be dangerous. Original installations and subsequent changes require the advice of a naval architect or someone thoroughly familiar with that phase of boat design.

Amateur conversions of automobile engines for marine use may be a source of trouble because of basic differences between the two types. Lubrication and cooling are the chief problems. Select an accepted type of marine engine or a commercially produced conversion instead.

Pans should be installed under the engine to catch any oil and grease drippings and prevent these from getting into the bilge. Remove accumulations promptly for fire safety.

Fuel Systems

The primary aspect of fuel system safety is the prevention of fires and explosions. Not to be overlooked, however, are the reliability aspects of the system that will ensure a continuous flow of clean fuel to the engine. The discussion that follows is principally concerned with boats using gasoline engines; exceptions and requirements relating to diesel fuel systems are covered separately.

The Coast Guard has a set of complex technical requirements for fuel systems of all boats under 20 feet (6.1 m) in length having gasoline engines for mechanical or electrical power on board, or for propulsion. These are requirements placed on manufacturers of new boats, but they can serve as an excellent guide for all boat owners. These standards can be found in the *Code of Federal Regulation,* available in the reference department

Figure 11-16 A carburetor on a marine gasoline engine (other than outboard motors) must be equipped with a flame arrester. A downdraft carburetor as shown here does not require a drip pan, but an updraft model (now rare) requires one.

of larger local libraries, as Chapter 33, Part 183, Subpart J; the *CFR* can also be accessed on the Internet at www.gpo.gov/nara/cfr/index.html.

Fire Prevention

A boat's entire fuel system must be liquid- and vapor-tight with respect to the hull interior. Gasoline fumes mixed with air are an explosive combination. These fumes, several times heavier than air, settle to the bottom of the bilge. A concentration of gasoline in the air as low as 1.25 percent—a half-teacup, a few ounces of gasoline—can create enough explosive vapor to totally destroy a large boat.

The obvious answer is *prevention*—make it impossible for gasoline, either in liquid or gaseous form, to get into the bilge in the first place. Then keep the bilge clean and ventilate the engine compartment thoroughly, and there will be nothing that can be ignited.

Leakage of liquid gasoline into the bilge can be prevented by a properly installed fuel system that uses strongly built gasoline tanks, approved tubing for fuel lines, leakproof connections, tight fittings, and lengths of flexible metallic fuel hose to take care of vibration. As discussed earlier, keep gasoline vapors created when the tanks are filled from finding their way down through open hatches and companionways. Finally, do not permit sparks and flames in the engine room.

Carburetors

Carburetors must be equipped with flame arresters for protection against backfire; see **Figure 11-16.** If not of the downdraft type, they should also have a pan covered with a fine mesh screen attached under the carburetor to collect any drip. Leakage will be sucked back into the engine if a copper tube is run from the bottom of the pan to the intake manifold. Keep flame arresters clean both for safety and best engine operation.

Fuel Tanks & Gauges

Permanent fuel tanks must be installed securely to prevent any motion in a seaway. Using portable tanks below decks is not good practice.

Fuel tanks must be constructed of a metal that is compatible with both the fuel and a normal marine environment. Copper, copper alloys of certain specific composition, hot-dipped galvanized sheet steel, and aluminum are all used for gasoline tanks. In each case, construction, installation, and inspections should be in accordance with standards of the American Boat & Yacht Council. Terneplate steel should be used only on outboard boats and then only for tanks that will be above cockpit decks; annual inspections are a must.

Gasoline tanks must not be integral with the hull. The shape of the tank should be such that there are no exterior pockets that would trap moisture after the tank is in its installed position. Tank bottoms must not have sumps or pockets in which water could accumulate.

Internal stiffeners and baffle plates are used to provide necessary rigidity and resistance to surging of liquid in the tanks. Baffles must meet certain specified design criteria to prevent formation of liquid pockets in the bottom of tanks and vapor pockets in the tops.

There should be no drains or outlets for drawing off fuel from the tank, nor outlets or fittings of any type in the bottom, sides, or ends of tanks. Fuel lines to the engine should enter the tank at its top and internally extend nearly to the bottom.

A fuel-level indicator, if used, should be of an approved type.

Fuel Filler Pipes & Vents

One of the most essential requirements in the proper installation of a fuel system is that there be a completely tight connection between the gasoline tank and the filling plate on deck. The fuel fill must be located so any spillage will go overboard, *not inside the hull,* and tight pipe connections between deck plate and tank will prevent leakage or spillage below. Fill pipes, at least 1½-inch (3.8 cm) inside diameter, should run down inside the tank nearly to the bottom to lessen the production of vapors.

A suitable vent pipe for each tank should lead *outside the hull;* vents should *never* terminate in closed places such as the engine compartment or under the deck. Minimum inside diameter of vent pipes should be $\frac{7}{16}$ inch (11 mm). Where a vent ends on the hull, the outlet should be fitted with a removable flame screen to protect against flashbacks from outside sources of ignition. In boats that normally heel, such as auxiliary sailboats, it may be necessary to have dual vents with the port tank vent led to the starboard side and vice versa.

Nonmetallic hose may be used as a coupling between sections of metallic fill piping. The hose must be reinforced or of sufficient thickness to prevent collapse. A grounding jumper wire must be installed across the nonconducting section to provide a complete electrical path from the deck fitting to the fuel tank, which in turn is grounded.

If the fuel supply for an auxiliary electric plant is not drawn from the main tank, the separate tank should be installed with its own filler and vent.

Fuel Lines

Fuel lines should be of seamless copper tubing, run in sight as much as possible for ease of inspection, protected from possible damage, and secured against vibration by soft nonferrous metal clips with rounded edges. A short length of flexible tubing with suitable fittings should be used between that part of the fuel line that is secured to the hull and that part which is secured to the engine itself—this will prevent leakage or breakage as a result of vibration.

Reinforced nonmetallic hose may be used for the full distance from the tank shutoff valve to the engine only if the line is fully visible and accessible for its entire length. Wherever used, nonmetallic hose must be dated by the manufacturer and not used for a period longer than that recommended by the maker. With the increasing use of alcohol additives to gasoline, increased caution and more frequent inspections are necessary.

Tube fittings should be of nonferrous drawn or forged metal of the flared type, and tubing should be properly flared by tools designed for the purpose.

A shutoff valve should be installed in the fuel line directly at the tank connection. Arrangements should be provided for ready access and operation of this valve from outside the compartment in which tanks are located, preferably from abovedeck. Where engine and fuel tank are separated by a distance exceeding 12 feet (3.7 m), an approved-type manual stop-valve should be installed at the engine end of the fuel line to stop fuel flow when servicing accessories.

Valves should be of nonferrous metal with ground seats installed to close against the flow. Types which depend on packing to prevent leakage at the stem should not be used. For fuel and oil lines a type of diaphragm packless valve is available which is pressure-tight in any position. A UL-listed electric fuel valve shuts off the flow of gasoline whenever the ignition switch is turned off; it can also be independently turned off in an emergency.

Fuel Pumps & Filters

Electric fuel pumps, where used, should be located at the engine end of fuel lines. They must be connected so that they operate only when the ignition switch is on.

A filter should be installed in the fuel line inside the engine compartment, properly supported so that its weight is not carried by the tubing. Closure of the filter must be designed so that opening it for cleaning will not cause fuel to spill. It should also be designed so that the unit can be disassembled and reassembled in dim light without undue opportunity for crossing threads, displacing gaskets or seals, or assembling parts in an improper order that might result in fuel

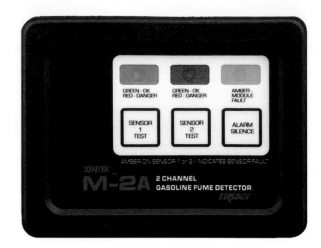

Figure 11-17 Fuel-vapor detectors are considered essential safety items onboard a vessel using gasoline as a fuel, but the human nose is the best and most reliable detector.

seepage after assembly. Fuel filter bowls should be highly resistant to shattering from impact and resistant to failure from thermal shock.

Fuel-Vapor Detectors

A FUEL-VAPOR DETECTOR is considered by many boaters to be an essential item of safety equipment on board any craft using gasoline as a fuel. These devices provide a visual, and in many units an audible, warning of the buildup of any dangerous concentration of fuel vapor in the engine space and bilges; see **Figure 11-17.** It is important to remember, however, that they are *not an absolutely positive means of alerting you to a hazardous condition*; they are not as infallible as the human nose. If in doubt, open the spaces and use your nose—it is the best "bilge sniffer."

Fuel-vapor detectors come in several designs, each with good points and disadvantages. These include hot-wire, cold-sensor, and semiconductor types of detector units. Price does not vary much between these types, and a choice should be made on the features of the designs and their suitability for your particular installation. Some sensors will detect hazardous levels of other gases such as propane (LPG), alcohol, or hydrogen (from storage-battery charging).

Installing a fuel-vapor detector is not difficult electrically or mechanically, but it *must* be done correctly. The location of the detector unit is most important; the alarm must be where it will be seen and heard. When completed, have your installation inspected by a surveyor or a safety inspector from your insurance company.

Fuel Systems for Outboards

Fuel tanks and systems permanently installed in the hull of outboard-powered boats should be designed, constructed, and installed in accordance with the above principles. No pressurized tanks should be built into or permanently attached to the hulls. A quick-disconnect coupling may be used between motor and fuel line but, when disconnected, it must automatically shut off fuel flow from the tank; see **Figure 11-18.** Arrangements should be provided so that making and breaking the connection can be accomplished with a minimum of spillage.

Be extremely cautious in using plastic containers for storing gasoline; they can accumulate a static electricity charge that is not drained off by grounding connections. A static electricity-generated spark could ignite vapors in the container.

Plastic containers should meet fire retardance and fuel-compatibility requirements of ABYC. The containers should carry the approval of a national listing agency or a major city fire department. *Do not use any other type of plastic*

Figure 11-18 Portable fuel tanks used with outboard motors are equipped with quick-disconnect fittings designed to minimize fuel linkage when connecting and disconnecting.

container for gasoline or other flammable liquid. Stow any portable fuel container in a well-ventilated place, protected from both physical damage and exposure to direct sunlight. Any leakage or vapors must drain overboard.

Be extremely careful that not even a single drop of gasoline finds its way into the bilge. Proper bilge ventilation is a strict legal requirement and it is a vital safety measure; see Chapter 3.

Fuel Systems of Diesel-Powered Boats

Fuel systems of diesel-powered boats generally conform to safety standards for gasoline-fueled vessels, with a few exceptions as required or permitted by the nature of the fuel and characteristics of diesel engines.

Tanks for diesel fuel may be iron or steel as well as nickel-copper. They may be painted if not galvanized externally; iron tanks must not be galvanized internally. Diesel tanks may have a sump or pocket in the bottom for collection of water. Tanks for diesel fuel may be integral with the hull.

Fuel lines for diesel fuel may be of iron or steel pipe or tubing in addition to the metals approved for gasoline. A return line to carry excess fuel from the engine back to the tank is needed.

Additional Information

Many additional technical details on gasoline and diesel fuel systems for boats will be found in ABYC *Safety Standards H-24, H-25,* and *H-33.*

Underwriters Laboratories Marine Division has evaluated and accepted for listing a number of tanks, filters, valves, and related equipment by various manufacturers.

Exhaust Systems

Exhaust lines and pipes should be installed so that they cannot scorch or ignite woodwork. Where necessary, gratings can be used to prevent gear from touching the line. Exhaust systems must be gas-tight, and constructed and installed so that they can be inspected and repaired readily along their entire length. Any leaks must be rectified *at once* to prevent escape of exhaust gases into various compartments. *Carbon monoxide is a deadly odorless gas.*

SAFEGUARDING AGAINST CARBON MONOXIDE

Although most recreational boaters are conscious of the potential dangers on the water, the risk of carbon monoxide poisoning is often overlooked. It is important to know the facts about this invisible killer, and to take the necessary steps to ensure safety on board. Carbon monoxide (CO) gas is clear and odorless, and may be present even when exhaust smoke is not.

Its initial toxic symptoms are deceptively similar to those of seasickness: headaches, dizziness, and lack of coordination, as well as other symptoms, such as drowsiness. Moreover, the individual who experiences symptoms of carbon-monoxide poisoning tends to lose any healthy fear that danger is imminent.

When carbon monoxide is inhaled, CO molecules attach themselves to red blood cells—as oxygen molecules do in a person who is breathing clean air. The result is a lack of oxygen for the tissues with subsequent death of the tissue and, if prolonged, death of that person.

Precautions

A boater whose craft is equipped with a permanently installed gasoline engine, gasoline-powered genset (auxiliary generating plant for 120-volt AC power, see Chapter 19), stoves, heaters, or charcoal grills should be alert to the dangers of CO poisoning. He should ensure sufficient ventilation, be aware of the situations when danger is heightened, and inspect his exhaust systems frequently.

Cabin cruisers are particularly susceptible to problems involving carbon-monoxide poisoning. The best way to prevent CO from getting into passenger areas and sleeping spaces is to provide alternate sources of air. For example, leave a part of the windshield open and open a deck hatch. If you can feel a flow of air coming aft through the cabin and cockpit areas, you can reduce the chances that carbon monoxide will be pulled forward and into the boat due to backdrafting.

Backdrafting is caused by air movement over or around a boat, creating a low-pressure area at the stern that can increase CO levels on board. Dangerous concentrations of CO can also accumulate when a boat's engine or generator is operated while the boat is alongside other boats, next to a seawall, or in a confined area such as a boathouse. Be aware of the effect that your craft's exhaust may have on other vessels; likewise, be aware that another vessel's equipment may affect the CO levels on your boat.

The way to prevent CO leaks from exhaust systems is with regular inspections and proper maintenance. Look and listen for leaks in exhaust systems of generators and propulsion engines. Look for discoloration around joints in the system. Make sure that all hose clamps in the exhaust system are secured properly. Double-clamping rubber hose connections at each end will help prevent the exhaust hose from vibrating loose. Make sure that engine room bulkheads are completely sealed against leaks into sleeping areas. All holes or gaps in the engine room bulkheads for plumbing, wiring, and controls should be sealed.

Carbon monoxide gas detectors should be considered by all safety-conscious skippers.

What to Do

In the event that a person on board displays symptoms of CO poisoning, immediately evacuate all enclosed spaces; give the affected individual oxygen if it is available; contact medical help, and if the person is not breathing, perform cardiopulmonary resuscitation (CPR).

A "wet" exhaust system requires a continuous flow of cooling water (from the heat exchanger or the engine block) discharged through the exhaust line, entering as close to the manifold as possible. Exhaust systems of the "dry stack" type (no cooling water) operate at considerably higher temperatures and their use is relatively rare except on larger vessels.

An exhaust system should be run with a minimum number of bends. Where turns are necessary, long-sweep elbows should be combined to achieve a 45° ells are recommended to avoid tight bends. The exhaust system must not cause back pressure at the exhaust manifold greater than that specified by the engine manufacturer. A small pipe tap, located not more than 6 inches (15.2 cm) from the exhaust manifold outlet, should be provided for measuring back pressure.

The exhaust system should be designed to prevent undue stress on the exhaust manifold, particularly where an engine is shock-mounted. All supports, hangers, brackets, and other fittings in contact with the exhaust should be noncombustible and so constructed that high temperatures will not be transmitted to wood or other combustible materials to which fittings are secured.

The exhaust piping or tubing should have a continuous downward pitch of at least ½ inch per foot (1 cm per 24 cm) when measured with the vessel at rest. It must be designed and installed to eliminate any possibility of cooling water or seawater returning to the engine manifold through the exhaust system.

Exhaust Systems for Sailboat Engines

Exhaust systems for auxiliary-powered sailboats should be designed to prevent sea or cooling water from running back into the engine when these are installed close to or below the waterline. A riser should reach above the waterline sufficiently to allow a steep drop-off; see the manufacturer's installation instructions for the specific height. The high point should be a gooseneck, with cooling water injected aft of this point; see **Figure 11-19.** Any dry section of an exhaust

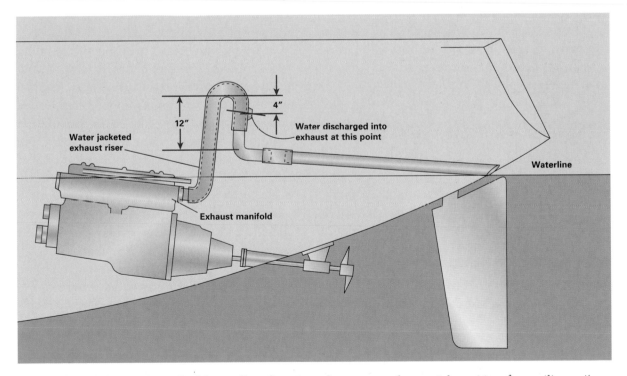

Figure 11-19 The ABYC standard for small-craft engine exhaust systems has special provisions for auxiliary sailboats. When an engine is located below the waterline, a high-rising loop must be installed in the exhaust line to bring it above the waterline. Dimensions may vary; see the instruction manual for your engine.

system must be adequately insulated with materials that can withstand the high temperatures involved. As an alternate arrangement, installation of a water-trap silencer is recommended.

Flexible Exhaust Lines

Steam hose or other nonmetallic material may be used for exhaust lines where greater flexibility is desired. Every flexible line of this type must be secured with adequate clamps of corrosion-resistant metal at each end. Hose used for this purpose must have a wall thickness and rigidity sufficient to prevent internal separation of plies, or collapse. Full-length nonmetallic exhaust tubing may be used in wet exhaust systems providing it is water-cooled throughout its length and is not subjected to temperature above 280°F (138°C). Tubing used for exhaust service should be specifically constructed for that purpose and so labeled by the manufacturer. Tubing should be installed in a manner that will not stress or crimp the inner or outer plies.

Additional Information

ABYC *Safety Standard P-1* provides much additional information on "wet" and "dry" exhaust installations. It should be studied by anyone building or rebuilding a boat equipped with an inboard engine.

ELECTRICAL SYSTEMS

A boat's entire electrical installation should comply with the best safety practices. Requirements of marine installations are more exacting than other applications where salt- and moisture-laden atmospheres are not prevalent. Wiring and other electrical equipment should be installed correctly in the beginning and kept safe by frequent inspection. Detailed information on boat electrical systems can be found in Chapter 19.

Lightning Protection

You only infrequently hear of a boat, power or sail, being struck by lightning, but this can, and does, happen. And when it does happen, serious, even fatal, consequences may ensue. You can add to both your physical safety and your peace of mind by getting adequate basic information and taking certain precautions.

The voltages involved in lightning are tremendous—materials normally considered to be nonconductive become conductors, and that includes the human body. The voltages are so high that if they start to travel through a boat's structure—say, through its mast—then meet high resistance—for instance, the hull's skin—the current discharge, in its drive to reach ground potential, may simply blow a hole in the nonconductive barrier.

Protection Principles

The theory in any shipboard lightning protection system is to create what is known as a "Faraday's cage," after the nineteenth-century scientist Michael Faraday. The principle of a Faraday's cage is to provide a surrounding, well-grounded metal structure, all of whose parts are bonded together and at the same electrical potential. Such a "cage" may possibly increase the likelihood of a lightning strike, but if one does occur, it carries the charge directly to ground, thereby protecting life and limb within its boundaries.

On a boat, the "cage" is formed by bonding together, with heavy conductors, a sailboat's mast and all other major metal masses—for example, engines, stoves, air-conditioning compressors, railings, arches and the like—and providing a direct, low-resistance conductive path to ground (the water) usually via the engine and propeller shaft, or keel bolts, or, even better, a separate external ground plate, at least 1 ft² (0.093 m²) in area. (Although actual data are not available, it is believed that a long narrow strip, for example, 1 inch by 12 feet, is more effective that a one-foot square plate.) Of course, it's necessary to ensure that crew fall within the protection of the confines of the "cage," something that is not always feasible when the vessel is not built of steel or aluminum. And in this respect, on a fiberglass or wooden craft, it's advantageous to have a mast or other conductive metal protrusion extending well above the vessel, creating what is known as a "cone" or zone of protection.

It's generally accepted that this zone of protection extends 45 degrees from the vertical from all around the tip of such a metal protrusion; see **Figure 11-20.** Thus, if the aluminum mast of the average sailing vessel is properly bonded to the vessel's other major metal masses and given a direct, low-resistance conductive path to ground, essentially the entire boat should fall within the protected zone, that is, inside the "cage." If a sailing vessel has a wooden or plastic composite mast, the same effect can be achieved by installing a 6- to 12-inch metal spike at the masthead and running a sufficiently heavy conductor from it down the mast and as directly as possible to ground. To provide an adequately grounded conductor or protective mast, the *entire* circuit from the masthead to the ground (water) connection should have conductivity equivalent to a No. 4-gauge wire, recently increased from the previous recommended size of No. 8. (Any copper strip used should not be thinner than No. 20 gauge, 0.032 inch, 0.8 mm.) An aluminum or steel hull, of course, constitutes an excellent ground connection to the water. The path followed by the grounding conductor should be essentially straight with no sharp bends.

In the case of powerboats, ensuring sufficient mast height is quite often difficult; and it may not be possible, given the limitations, to ensure that a person standing on deck always falls within the zone of protection. Keep in mind that you cannot rely on fiberglass radio antennas for this purpose, as they do not afford a sufficiently low-resistance path, and possibly because of their construction, no path at all. (The most common antennas, those used for VHF, CB, or SSB radios, offer no conductive path.) The best advice in such cases is to work with an expert in the field, if you're considering the possibility of using an antenna as a lightning mast.

It is possible in a powerboat to install a separate lightning mast. But, if the mast is hinged for getting under bridges or for general nonthreatening conditions, a jumper of adequately heavy wire should be installed to provide a bypass around the hinge. In all cases on powerboats, it will generally be necessary to pay close attention to keeping crew within the zone of protection and isolated from contact with any metal objects during a lightning storm.

If there are metal objects of considerable size within a few feet of the grounding conductor, there will be a strong tendency for sparks or side flashes to jump to them from the grounding conductor. To prevent such possibly damaging flashes, an interconnecting conductor of the same size should be provided at all likely places.

Metal objects situated wholly on a boat's exterior should be connected to the grounding conductor at their upper or nearest end. Metal objects within the boat may be connected to the lightning protective system directly or through the bonding system for underwater metal parts.

Metal objects that project through cabin tops, decks, etc., should be bonded to the nearest lightning conductor at the point where the object emerges from the boat and again at its extreme lowest end within the boat. Spotlights and other objects projecting through cabin tops should be solidly grounded regardless of the cone of protection.

Remember: *A lightning protection system offers no protection when the boat is out of the water.*

Additional information on lightning protection will be found in *ABYC Standard E-4.*

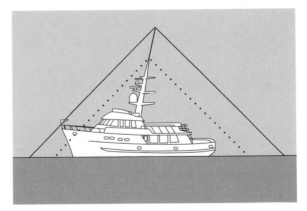

Figure 11-20 A measure of lightning protection can be obtained by using the principle of a "Faraday's cage." A high, pointed conductor, heavily wired to all of the conductive parts of the boat, seems to cast a cone-shaped umbrella in which lightning does not strike. Instead, the electricity is conducted safely to "ground" in the water via submerged metal parts such as the rudder and propeller, sailboat keel, or special ground plate.

LIGHTNING PROTECTION FOR PERSONNEL

The basic purpose of lightning protection is safety for people; everyone on board should take the following precautions.
• Stay inside a closed boat as much as possible during an electrical storm.
• Avoid making contact with any item connected to a lightning protective conductor, and especially in a way that bridges two parts of the grounding system. For example, do not touch both the reverse lever and spotlight control at the same time.
• Stay out of the water; keep hands and feet out of the water.

Danger from Overhead Power Lines

Although it is not related to lightning hazards, a skipper should be aware of the fact that sailboats face a serious danger from contact with overhead power lines—both underway and, more often, as they are being launched or hauled out. Sailors must always be aware of power lines and be sure of their clearances. Remember: *A lightning protection system is not designed to provide protection if any part of the boat comes in contact with power lines while afloat or ashore.*

EQUIPMENT FOR SAFETY

Some safety equipment is required by laws and Coast Guard regulations. These requirements are generally written in such broad language, however, that boaters need additional knowledge and guidance. Boats need to have numerous additional items of equipment beyond the legal minimum to achieve a full measure of safety. Still further pieces of equipment are desirable for operational efficiency and convenience. Many of these are discussed in Chapter 3 and other chapters. This chapter supplements equipment considerations covered elsewhere in the book.

Lifesaving Equipment

As noted in Chapter 3, each boat must, by law, have a personal flotation device (PFD) for each person on board, and water-skiers towed behind are counted as being "on board." A wise skipper does not skimp on quality or quantity of his PFDs, making sure that he has enough even if a few unexpected guests show up.

Where the type of PFD used comes in different sizes, such as adult and children's life preservers, or the three sizes of buoyant vests, the PFD must be of an appropriate size for the person who is to wear it.

Although the regulations allow a choice from three or four categories of PFDs, the safety-conscious skipper will choose Type I. This type provides the maximum buoyancy and will hold a person's face clear of the water so he can breathe even though unconscious. The only exception to this maxim is the use of inflatable PFDs—there greater degree of comfort while being worn increases the likelihood that they will be worn a greater percentage of the time on board.

Fire Extinguishers

Beyond the legal minimum requirements, ABYC *Safety Standards A-4* makes a number of recommendations that should be considered. On inboard or inboard/outboard boats with an engine compartment, there should be provision for discharging a CO_2 or Halon-type extinguisher directly into the engine space *without opening the primary access.* This will prevent the addition of oxygen that would further fuel the fire; remaining outside the compartment containing the fire will also increase the personal safety of the individual using the extinguisher. A caution sign should be posted to not open the engine compartment.

The ABYC *Standards* includes recommendations for the appropriate size of Halon or CO_2 extinguishers for various volumes or engine compartments. Regardless of the type or size of installed system, it is recommended that there be a sign at each helm position to shut down the engine immediately when the extinguisher activates—if the engine is not shut down, a portion of the extinguishing agent will be sucked into the engine and thus its extinguishing capability will be lost.

Pumps & Bailers

There are no federal requirements that a boat (if used exclusively for recreation) be equipped with a bailing device, but all boats should be equipped with some form of pump or bailer. Too many skippers place their *full* dependence on electrical bilge pumps, and perhaps on only one of those. Once water rises in the bilge high enough to short out the battery, the pump is out of action. (On most boats the batteries are placed low in the bilge—excellent for stability, but not for safety if the boat starts taking on water.)

Only the smallest boats should depend on a hand bailer or bucket. Other boats should be equipped with a manually operated pump of generous capacity. Such an item can be either a fixed installation or a portable pump stowed where it can be quickly and easily reached when needed.

Bilge Water Alarms

Electric bilge pumps are normally actuated by float switches. These are generally reliable and provide a great convenience, but are not to be solely depended upon. Safety is much enhanced by the installation of a BILGE WATER ALARM. This quite simple system consists of an additional regular float switch mounted at a level that is a few inches above that of the switch that operates the bilge pump. This is wired to a source of 12-volt DC power and one or more alarms, both visible and audible. One such alarm should be at the normal helm position and another near the skipper's sleeping location. The audible alarms should be loud enough to be heard over the normal noise level of the engines, and loud enough to awaken a sleeping person. Additional alarms around the boat are probably not needed as conditions are quiet enough at anchor or when docked that one or both of the alarms will be heard. For boats stored in a slip, an external alarm may be rigged to alert marina personnel of a flooding condition.

Distress Signaling Equipment

A boat's radiotelephone is probably the most often used means of summoning assistance in an emergency. Use of the radio for this purpose is covered in Chapter 20. The legal requirements for varying visual distress signals are covered in Chapter 3, on pages 105–108.

Without special equipment, a distress signal can be made to other vessels in sight by standing where one is clearly visible and slowly raising and lowering one's outstretched arms.

Signal flares may be projected several hundred feet into the air by a special type of pistol. The laws of several states regulate possession of these and similar explosive projectile devices; check carefully before putting one aboard, but if permissible, these are effective and desirable items of safety equipment.

There are also hand-held flares of the single- and double-ended types, the latter producing a bright flame at one end for night use and a dense smoke at the other end for day distress situations. Before using any flare, read all instructions carefully so as to avoid personal injury or aggravation of the emergency. Read carefully *before* any emergency arises. Your preparation for emergencies and the training of your crew should include familiarization with all distress signaling equipment.

Distress signaling equipment of any type should be stored in protective, waterproof containers and stowed where it is readily available for use in an emergency or to be taken off the boat if it must be abandoned. Containers should be opened and contents inspected at least annually; flares have an expiration date and must be replaced periodically.

Miscellaneous Items of Safety Equipment

There are many small items of equipment that increase safety and convenience.

All but the smallest boats should be equipped with several FLASHLIGHTS and at least one battery-powered ELECTRIC LANTERN. Flashlights should be distributed where they will be quickly available in an emergency. One should be within reach of the skipper's bunk.

There should also be a flashlight in the guest cabin, if any, and another on the bridge. Batteries in all units should be checked monthly to be sure of sufficient power. All should be completely waterproof, and lanterns should be the kind that will float if dropped overboard.

An installed searchlight of adequate intensity is desirable on medium-size and large boats. It is useful both in routine navigation and docking, and in emergencies such as man-overboard situations or assisting another boat in distress. On smaller boats, the electric lantern can serve as a hand-held searchlight.

Boats of medium or large size should have on board some means, such as a hatchet, of cutting lines in an emergency.

TOOLS and REPAIR PARTS for the engine and major accessories can be considered parts of a boat's essential safety equipment. Personal experience and conversation with seasoned skippers will offer the best guidance to just what tools and parts should be carried aboard any particular boat. Insofar as possible, tools should be of rust-proof metal; tools susceptible to rust or corrosion, and all spare parts, should be given a protective coating, and stowed to protect them from adverse effects of a marine environment.

All but the smallest boats should carry EMERGENCY DRINKING WATER and FOOD supplies—a life raft must, and a dinghy should, have such items; see **Figure 11-21.** The amount will vary with the number of persons normally on board. The type of food is not important—anything will do when you get hungry enough! Nonperishability over a long period is important, but it might be wise once each year to consume your emergency supplies (a shipwreck party?) *after* they have been replaced with a fresh stock. Such items can usually be purchased from marine supply stores or from Army-Navy surplus stores; food should be simple and compact, but sustaining and energy-producing.

FIRST-AID KITS are essential safety items; refer to the sidebar, "Basic First-Aid Kit."

NAVIGATION EQUIPMENT, CHARTS, and GROUND TACKLE are all items of safety equipment, but each is considered in detail elsewhere in this book; see index.

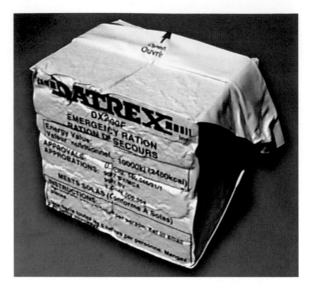

Figure 11-21 Every boat, even a dinghy, should carry a supply of emergency water and food, with the type and amount based on the size of the boat, its crew, and its normal cruising area. Prepared kits of long shelf life products can be purchased, or a boater can assemble his own package of emergency supplies.

Safety Aspects of Other Equipment

Several items generally found on boats are not safety equipment per se, but have definite aspects of safety about their design, installation, or operation that must be considered by boat owners.

Galley Stoves

Galley stoves should be designed, manufactured, and approved for marine use. Types of fuel that are ordinarily used include alcohol, kerosene, electricity, and liquefied petroleum gas (LPG) also known as propane. Some boats are now using compressed natural gas (CNG) as stove fuel. Stoves fueled with coal, wood, diesel oil, or canned heat (solidified alcohol) are only rarely seen. Gasoline is *not* a safe stove fuel and should never be used on a boat.

Electricity is probably the safest source of heat for cooking, but shore power or an auxiliary generating plant is required to produce the large amounts of AC power required. Because of the inexpensive and simple nature of the equipment, alcohol stoves are widely used on boats despite their rather high fuel costs; with moderate and reasonable precautions, such

BASIC FIRST-AID KIT

In addition to at least one comprehensive first-aid manual, your boat should be equipped with a first-aid kit designed specifically for your needs, according to the length of your voyages and the areas in which you cruise. Day and weekend boaters, for example, need at least a kit stocked with basics, such as a thermometer, tweezers, alcohol, sunscreen, bandages of various sizes, scissors, an eye-washing cup, and a hot-water bottle/ice bag. Use of more advanced items requires proper training. Depending on the cruising waters and the crewmembers aboard, it may also be wise to stock items such as remedies for seasickness and jellyfish stings. Long-range offshore cruisers require more extensive first-aid supplies and lifesaving equipment, as well as a wide range of prescription medications. In order to reduce the caregiver's risk of infection, every first-aid kit should also include a waterless antiseptic hand cleaner and disposable gloves.

When assembling your first-aid kit, consult more than one source to assess your needs. There are a number of books available on the subject of first aid for boaters and medical emergencies at sea. Also discuss your needs with the instructors of any first-aid or safe-boating courses in which you enroll. Finally, get your doctor's advice. If you stock prescrip-

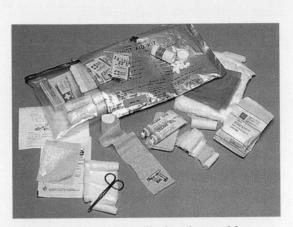

A number of companies offer kits designed for various boating needs—ranging from basic kits for day outings (above) to more extensive offshore cruising kits. Be sure to add any necessary supplies not included in the kit.

tion medications, make sure the expiration dates are clearly marked, and that each prescription is replaced when necessary. An off-the-shelf kit may be the starting point, but you may need to add further items to meet your specific needs. Once your supplies are assembled, store them in a watertight container (plastic to avoid rusting problems) in a dry, secure compartment. Review your kit periodically, making sure that it continues to suit your needs, that each item is in good working order, and that medicines have not become outdated.

installations can be quite safe. Plain water will extinguish alcohol fires.

LPG stoves are excellent for cooking but can present a serious safety hazard unless installed and operated in accordance with strict rules. An excellent guide to a safe LPG installation will be found in *ABYC Safety Standard A-1*. As of 1 April 2002, propane tanks for marine use must have an overfill protection device (LOPS) when they are bought or taken in for a refill; the only exception is for certain horizontal tanks. Existing tanks can be retrofitted with an OPD valve at a cost of about one-third that of replacing the tank.

Stoves should be permanently and securely fastened in place when in operation. Portable stoves are not recommended; if one must be used, it should be secured while in use. Adequate ventilation should be provided to prevent too much heat when a stove is operated for extended periods of time. All woodwork and other combustible material around a stove, including smoke stacks, must be effectively protected with noncombustible sheathing; see **Figure 11-22**; 1/8-inch (3.1 mm) heat-resistant board covered by sheet metal is recommended.

VESSEL SAFETY CHECK REQUIREMENTS

The long-time "Courtesy Marine Examination" program of the U.S. Coast Guard Auxiliary has now been expanded, revised, and renamed. The new "Vessel Safety Check" (VSC) program now includes checks by members of the United States Power Squadrons as well as members of the USCG Auxiliary.

A Vessel Safety Check is a courtesy examination of your boat to verify the presence and condition of safety equipment required by federal regulations, plus certain additional requirements. A boat must also meet any requirements of the state in which it is being examined.

Following the examination, the specially trained examiner will also make recommendations and discuss safety issues that may make you a safer boater. This is not a law enforcement action; no citations will be issued as a result of the examination. You will receive a copy of the evaluation of your boat so that you may follow the suggestions given. The examination is free, and boats that pass the examination will be able to display the distinctive VSC decal (actually, a sticker). This does not exempt your boat from law enforcement boarding.

The requirements for the decal, listed below, make a good checklist for any well-equipped boat.

Numbering & Paperwork

The boat must be properly registered by a state or documented by the Coast Guard; the paperwork must be on board; refer to Chapter 2.

For state registered boats, the registration numbers must be permanently displayed on each side of the forward half of the boat; they read from right to left, and there must be no other such numbers. The letters and numerals must be plain, vertical, block characters not less than three inches high, and in a color contrasting with the background. A dash or a space equal in width to a letter must separate the numerals from the letters that precede and follow them; for example, **FL-1235-AB** or **FL 1234 AB**. Any state validation sticker should be placed in accordance with that state's requirements.

For a documented boat, the documentation number must be permanently marked on a visible part of the *interior* structure. A recreational craft's name and hailing port must be displayed on the *exterior* hull in letters not less than four inches in height; on some clearly visible exterior part of the hull; no specific location is required. The hailing port must consist of *both* a city and a state; *only* the state may be abbreviated.

Personal Flotation Devices (PFDs)

An approved personal flotation device in good serviceable condition, and of a suitable size, is required for each person on the boat, with a minimum of two (one wearable and one throwable) for boats 16 feet and over. Children must have properly fitted PFDs designed for children and suitable for their size (child PFDs come in various sizes marked for the weight of the user).

Wearable PFDs including inflatable PFDs must be *readily accessible*; throwable devices must be *immediately available*. PFDs must not be stored in unopened plastic packaging. All PFDs on board will be examined if there are more than the legally required minimum.

For an inflatable PFD to count toward the legal requirements, the person (16 or more years of age) for whom it is intended must be wearing it at the time of the examination.

Visual Distress Signals

To receive VSC approval, recreational boats 16 feet and over used on coastal waters or the Great Lakes must have Coast Guard-approved day and night visual distress signals (VDS) that have not reached their expiration dates. Manufacture and/or expirations dates must be legible to meet decal requirements. Signals with expired dates are allowed on board as excess equipment. VDSs must be properly protected from moisture damage and readily accessible for use. Some signals, such as red flares, can serve for both day and night requirements.

Fire Extinguishers

All boats must have at least the minimum number of USCG-approved Type B fire extinguishers of the number and size required by regulations; see Chapter 3, pages 99–100.

Seals and tamper indicators must not be broken or damaged. Pressure gauges or indicators must be in the operable range. There must be no obvious physical damage or deterioration, no clogged nozzles.

CO_2 and Halon or Halon-type extinguishers must have been weighed and tagged by a recognized authority within one year of the examination. Manual controls for fixed systems must be located outside the space being protected.

All hand-portable extinguishers should be mounted, but this is not a requirement for award of the VSC decal.

Ventilation

The VSC examiner will check that the boat meets the Coast Guard requirements for manual and powered ventilation of spaces where explosive vapors might collect; see Chapter 3. All such spaces must be opened for examination; there must be no evidence of any fuel leaks.

Ducts and openings must not be blocked; blowers must be operational.

On boats built after July 31, 1980, the manufacturer's Certificate of Compliance will be accepted as proof that the ventilation system is properly designed and installed *provided* that it does not appear to have been altered and has been adequately maintained.

Backfire Flame Control

Every boat with a gasoline engine installed, except outboard motors, must be equipped with an acceptable means of backfire flame control. Fuel-injected engines must have such a flame arrester over the air intake. In both cases, the device must be attached with a flame-tight connector. The approval number must be clearly visible.

Sound-Producing Device

To receive the VSC decal, a boat must meet the legal requirements for a "sound producing device."

A craft 12 meters (39.4 ft) or more in length must have on board a horn or whistle ("athletic whistles" are not acceptable). There must also be a bell measuring not less than 200 millimeters (7.9 in) in diameter at the mouth.

A boat less than 12 meters (39.4 ft) in length need not have the above devices, but must have "an efficient sound signaling device." This may be a whistle, horn, or other means to signal their intentions and/or position in periods of reduced visibility—"athletic whistles" are acceptable.

Navigation Lights

The law does not require that a boat operated only in the daylight have navigation lights, but in order to meet the VSC standards for all craft 16 feet or more in length such a boat that does have lights they must be properly mounted and functioning. Proper lights for use both under way and at anchor must be shown. A sailboat with an auxiliary engine must be capable of showing the lights of both a sailboat and a powerboat; the lights must be wired so that they can be changed from one display to the other.

Cracked or discolored lenses are not acceptable. The decal will not be awarded if lights are grossly misplaced, even if they are operable. Navigation lights must show unbroken light through the prescribed arcs of visibility. All-around lights may not be obstructed for more than six degerees by items such as collapsible canopies, Bimini tops, masts, and similar items.

Pollution Placards

A boat 26 feet or more in length with a machinery compartment must have an "oily waste pollution" placard, not smaller than 5 by 8 inches and made of a durable material, posted in the machinery space or where the bilge pump switch is located. Boats of this length must also display a 4 by 9 inch "MARPOL" trash placard (garbage dumping restrictions) "in a prominent location." Craft 40 feet and over must have a written Trash Management Plan describing the procedures for collecting, processing, storing, and disposal of garbage; this plan must designate the person in charge of carrying out the plan.

Marine Sanitation Device

Any installed MSD must be a Coast Guard-approved device. Overboard discharge outlets must be capable of being sealed. Special local or state restrictions may apply.

Overall Boat Condition

The boat must be free from fire hazards and in good overall condition, with bilges reasonably clean and visible hull structure generally sound. The use of automobile parts on boat engines is not acceptable. The engine horse-power must not exceed that shown on any capacity plate.

The electrical system must be protected by fuses or trip-free circuit breakers. Wiring must be in good condition, properly installed, with no exposed areas or deteriorated insulation. Batteries must be firmly secured with terminals covered.

Any self-circling or kill-switch mechanisms must be in proper working order. All Personal Watercraft (PWCs) must have a self-circling or kill-switch mechanism.

Portable fuel tanks (normally 7 gallons or less) must be of nonbreakable material and must be free of corrosion and leaks. All vents must be capable of being closed. The tank must be secured and have a vapor-tight, leak-proof cap. Each permanent fuel tank must be properly vented.

Galley stoves and heating systems must have fuel tanks that are properly secured with no flammable material nearby.

VSC RECOMMENDATIONS

The VSC program also recommends a number of items for the safety and proper operation of a boat—items beyond those required for award of the decal. The actual selection of items from this list will depend on the size and use of the boat involved; the VSC examiner will make recommendations and suggestions. The VSC list includes the following items:

Marine radio

Dewatering device and backup (scoop or bilge pump)

Mounted fire extinguishers in appropriate locations

Anchor and line, suitable for area

First-aid kit

Person-in-the-water kit (one extra wearable PFD and a throwable device with line attached)

Visual distress signals for inland boating

VSC examiners may also discuss operational and educational matters in the interest of increased safety. These topics might include:

Accident reporting

Operator responsibilities

Offshore operations

Charts and aids to navigation

First aid and survival tips

Fueling and fuel management

Float plans

Insurance consideration

Boating checklists

Safe-boating classes

Additional information on the VSC program is available on the Internet at www.safetyseal.net.

A Final Word on Fire Extinguishers

When it comes to equipping your boat with fire extinguishers, it is prudent to go beyond even the VSC requirements. Consider installing extinguishers in the following locations, or wherever else you deem necessary to meet the needs of your own boat:

The helm, where there is always someone when underway

The engine compartment

The galley

Adjacent to the skipper's bunk, for quick reach at night.

Fuel for alcohol and kerosene stoves may be supplied to the burners either by gravity or pressure systems, provided fuel tanks cannot be filled while the burners are in operation except where the supply tank is remote from burners and the filling operation will not introduce a fire hazard. A removable or accessible liquid-tight metal drip pan at least ¾-inch (1.9 cm) deep should be provided under all burners. Pressure tanks should have suitable gauges and/or relief valves.

Refrigeration

Ice is used on some boats as a means of keeping food fresh and for cooling beverages. It offers no safety hazards, but water from melting ice should be piped overboard rather than into the bilge; a fresh-water drip tends to promote rot and/or odor. A collection sump, with pump, may be used, but is less desirable.

Mechanical refrigeration is normally of the electric-motor-driven compressor type similar to units found in the home. On some boats a compressor is belt-driven from a main engine.

Safety aspects of mechanical refrigeration include use of a nontoxic and nonflammable refrigerant, nonsparking motors, safety valves on high-pressure portions of the system, and general construction adequate to survive the rigors of marine service.

Some kerosene and bottled-gas refrigerators have a constant small open flame; this can produce an explosion hazard. Models are now available that work without a pilot light and are said to be safe for marine use.

Heaters

Cabin heaters are sometimes used on boats in northern waters; gasoline should never be used as a fuel in these, and portable kerosene or alcohol heaters are not recommended. Diesel heaters, however, are gaining in popularity. Built-in electrical heaters are safe; portable electrical heaters should be used only if secured in place while in operation.

Any heater discharging combustion products must be vented through a stovepipe and a "charley noble" set in a water-cooled deck plate or other

Figure 11-22 *Galley stoves should be permanently and securely fastened in place. They should have guardrails that will keep pots and pans from sliding off the front. On sailboats, stoves are often gimbaled so that the cooking surface remains nearly level when the boat heels.*

fire-preventive fitting. Many sailors favor coal- or charcoal-burning heaters, despite the mess they create and the problems of storing fuel, because of the even, dry heat that they deliver.

LPG (propane) heaters should have an automatic device to shut off the fuel supply if the flame is extinguished; pilot lights should not be used.

Many models of air-conditioning equipment used on boats are of the "reverse cycle" or "heat pump" type and can supply warmth rather than cooling when needed, provided that the surrounding water is not too cold. This is a thoroughly safe heating method.

MAINTENANCE FOR SAFETY

No matter what item of equipment is placed on board to enhance safety, *it must be properly maintained to ensure continuous safety.* Continual attention is needed for some safety gear; for others, periodic checks at weekly, monthly, or annual intervals is sufficient. The important thing is that these checks of safety equipment be made *regularly* when needed; use of a checklist is strongly recommended; see **Figure 11-23.**

Keep Your Boat Clean
Cleanliness is an important aspect of safety. Accumulations of dirt and trash in the bilge will soak up oil and fuel drippings and become a fire hazard. Such accumulations may also stop up limber holes and clog bilge pumps. Keep your bilge *absolutely* free of dirt and trash; check frequently and clean out as often as needed.

Lifesaving Equipment
The maintenance of PFDs is covered in Chapter 3—make sure that these actions are listed on your safety maintenance checklist. *Do not delay in replacing below-par lifesaving devices;* attempt repairs *only* where *full* effectiveness can be restored. In case of doubt, ask the Coast Guard.

If you have a life raft on board, ensure that it receives the required periodic inspections at an authorized facility—not more than 24 months after manufacture, and at 12-month intervals thereafter.

Fire Extinguishers
Installed fire-extinguishing systems should be checked at least annually, more often if recommended by the manufacturer whose maintenance procedures should be followed. An excellent procedure is to inspect at the beginning of the year's boating activities, and again at mid-season. ABYC *Standard A-4* recommends that portable extinguishers be checked at least monthly.

Dry-Chemical Extinguishers
Pressurized dry-chemical extinguishers have a gauge that should be checked for an indication of adequate pressure—needle in center or green area of scale. Do not, however, merely read the gauge; tap it lightly to make sure that it is not stuck at a safe indication. If it drops to a lower reading take the extinguisher to a service shop for recharging. Even if the gauge reads OK, take the unit out of its bracket and shake it a bit to loosen the dry chemical inside to keep it from settling and hardening; the natural tendency to pack is increased by the motions and vibrations on a boat. If the contents of the extinguisher become tightly packed, some of it may not be discharged when the unit is used, and the fire-fighting effectiveness would be reduced.

Any areas on the exterior of the cylinder showing rust should be cleaned and repainted. *Do not* test by triggering a short burst of powder. The

Figure 11-23 When inspecting any system on a boat, use a checklist so that nothing is overlooked. When you are finished, be sure to follow up and correct any deficiencies that are found.

valve probably will not reseat fully, and the pressure will slowly leak off.

Dry-chemical stored-pressure extinguishers should be discharged every 6 years and have the shell hydrostatically tested at intervals of from 5 to 12 years depending upon the material from which the shell is made; see *NFPA 10, Standard for Portable Fire Extinguishers*.

CO_2 Extinguishers

Carbon dioxide extinguishers must be checked annually by weight. Any seals on the valve trigger must be unbroken. Portable units and built-in systems have a weight stamped at the valve. If the *total* weight is down by 10 percent or more of the *net* weight of the contents, the cylinder must be recharged. The gauge of these units may indicate almost the full amount of pressure even if the cylinder is nearly empty of the extinguishing agent. Weighing is normally the only check for CO_2 fire extinguishers, but it must be done accurately. Portable units can be checked by the skipper if he has suitably precise and accurate scales. Built-in systems are best checked by a professional serviceperson who has special knowledge and equipment.

CO_2 cylinders also should have the date on which the cylinder was last hydrostatically pressure-tested. (This is done by emptying the cylinder of its extinguishing agent, then filling it with water and increasing the pressure to a value significantly greater than the working pressure; this testing will require a commercial facility) Testing should be done every 5 years if the cylinder is not discharged. If the extinguisher is used, it must be pressure-tested before it is recharged if this has not been done within the preceding five years. If a used CO_2 extinguisher is purchased, it should be discharged, hydrostatically tested, and recharged before it is installed aboard. The pressure in these cylinders is tremendous, and if the cylinder has been damaged through rust or corrosion, it is just like a time bomb, and you do not know when it may go off!

Carbon-dioxide extinguishers should not be installed where bilge or rainwater will collect and cause rust. Any exposed metal should be painted at each annual inspection. If a cylinder becomes pitted from rust, have it hydrostatically tested for safety. Replace any damaged hoses or horns on this type of extinguisher.

Halon-Type Extinguishers

Automatic systems using Halon-1301, or similar halonagenated agents, must be checked by weighing the cylinder and comparing actual weight with that stamped on it. Check every six months, or more often if recommended by the manufacturer; a loss of only several ounces is significant. Use accurate scales; bathroom scales are not precise enough. Cylinders will require hydrostatic testing similar to CO_2 extinguishers.

Periodic Discharges

It is a good policy to discharge a fire extinguisher periodically even though it is not needed for fighting a fire. An effective way of doing this would be to discharge one of the portable units each year on a regular rotation basis. This should be done in the presence of the whole crew and, as discussed earlier, preferably in the form of a drill, putting out an actual small fire—off the boat, of course—in a metal pan or tub. Probably 99 percent or more of all persons who go boating have never discharged a fire extinguisher, let alone used one to put out an actual fire. There is not time to read the instructions carefully and practice after a fire has started on your boat. A word of warning with respect to CO_2 extinguishers: *never* unscrew the hose from the cylinder and then discharge it openly; always hold the nozzle by its wooded handle.

Make sure that when fire extinguishers are removed for testing or practice discharge they are serviced by a competent shop and reinstalled *as soon as possible*. It is also wise not to denude your boat of fire protection by removing all extinguishers at the same time for servicing; do a half or a third at a time.

Log Entries

Make an entry in the boat's log of all inspections, tests, and servicing of fire extinguishers. This will help keep these essential checks from being overlooked and may prove valuable in the event of insurance surveys or claims.

Engine & Fuel System

Check the engine and fuel system frequently for cleanliness and leaks. Wipe up any oil or grease drippings and stop leaks as soon as possible. *Take immediate action in the case of any gasoline leaks.* Do not use the boat, and disconnect the leads from the battery (with all loads turned off so that no spark will jump) so that the engine cannot be started.

Check the entire fuel system annually inch by inch, including fuel lines in areas not normally visible. Look for any evidence of seepage of fuel or external corrosion of the lines. If any suspicious joints or lengths of tubing or hose are found, call in a qualified mechanic without delay.

Bilge Ventilation System

Although it is the manufacturer's responsibility to install a powered ventilation system on certain types of boats, it is the operator's responsibility to ensure that the system continues to perform properly (and to use it!). Even if yours is an older boat, built before these requirements came into effect, maintain your bilge ventilation system in top operating condition.

Carbon-Monoxide Detectors

If your boat is equipped with a carbon-monoxide (CO) detector—and it should be—its proper operation must be checked periodically at the intervals and in the manner prescribed in its owner's manual. You probably never will have a situation that activates this safety device, but you must be sure that it will function if needed—it could mean saving your life and that of others on board. Should it ever sound, take immediate action for the safety of personnel, and when that has been accomplished, then look for the CO source that set it off.

Electrical Systems

A boat's electrical system should be inspected thoroughly every year, including all wiring in areas not normally visible. This should be done by a person qualified to evaluate what he finds—by you if you have the necessary knowledge and experience, or by an outside expert if needed.

Search for any cut or chafed insulation, corrosion at connections, excessive sag or strain on conductors, and other visible signs of deterioration. A leakage test should be made by opening each circuit at the main distribution panel and measuring current flow when all loads are turned off. Ideally there should be no current flow; current of more than a few milliamperes indicates electrical "leakage" that should be tracked down and corrected without delay.

Maintenance of storage batteries is covered in Chapter 19.

Bonding Systems

If all through-hull fittings, struts, shafts, etc., are electrically connected by an internal bonding system, this wiring should be checked annually. Especially careful checks should be made where connections are made to the protected fitting or other metal part. Connections in the bilge are subject to corrosion and development of poor contacts with high electrical resistance.

The skipper can make a visual check of the bonding system, but an electrical expert with specialized equipment is needed for a thorough evaluation. Should any signs of corrosion at points of connection between bonding wires and through-hull fittings be noted, a complete electrical test is recommended.

With respect to possible electrolysis (stray current corrosion) damage, a bonding system with one or more poor connections may be worse than no system at all. Electrolysis can and does cause weakening of through-hull fittings, bolts on struts and rudderposts, etc., that could result in serious safety hazards.

Hull Safety Maintenance

Boats normally kept in the water should be hauled out periodically for bottom cleaning and repainting. This occasion provides an opportunity for a *safety* inspection of hull and fittings below the waterline. On wood boats, check hull planking for physical damage and for any general deterioration from age. Check fiberglass hulls for any cracks, especially at points of high stress. Call in an expert if you find any suspicious areas.

Through-Hull Fittings
Each time your boat is hauled, check inside and outside to see that through-hull fittings and their seacocks are in good condition. All seacocks should be checked quarterly, if not monthly—they should operate freely; disassemble and lubricate if necessary. Include in your inspection all fastenings susceptible to damage from electrolytic action.

Underwater Components
Check underwater fittings annually. This includes shafts, propellers, rudders, struts, bearings, stuffing boxes, and metal skegs. Stuffing boxes should be repacked as often as necessary to keep them from leaking excessively. Shafts should be checked for alignment and excessive wear at strut bearings, and propellers examined to see if they need truing up.

Each "zinc"—galvanic corrosion protectors—should be checked and replaced if more than half has eroded away.

Follow-Up of Inspections
Nothing is gained if prompt and thorough follow-up actions are not taken on findings of periodic safety inspections. *Maintenance related to safety must not be delayed. Do not operate a boat that has a known safety defect.*

SAFETY IN THE WATER
Anyone who goes boating regularly should know how to care for himself in the water. Fortunately, most boaters and their families do know how to swim, but this may be limited to taking a few strokes in a calm, relatively warm pool, with safety and rest only a few feet away. Give special attention to staying afloat under adverse conditions of water temperature and waves. Seldom is it necessary, or even desirable, to swim any distance; the problem is staying afloat until help arrives. The skipper and crew should all have instructions in "drown-proofing."

Safety *in* the water can well start with a swimming and/or lifesaving class at the local "Y" or community recreational center. Local American Red Cross chapters also give instruction in these subjects.

Lifesaving Devices
A person in the water following a boating accident should, of course, have a PFD of some sort—life jacket or buoyant cushion. It is important that these devices be worn or used properly. Buoyant cushions are far from the best flotation device, but are widely used because of their convenience and low cost. Buoyant cushions are *not* intended to be worn. The straps on a buoyant cushion are put there for holding-on purposes and also to aid in throwing the device. Because they must be grasped, cushions are not suitable for small children or injured persons, and are not desirable for nonswimmers. Cushions should never be worn on a person's back since this tends to force his face down in the water.

The PFD providing the greatest safety is the canvas jacket with flotation material in sealed plastic pouches. Stow these PFDs in several locations about your boat, so fire or other disaster cannot cut you off from all of them; they must also be easily accessible. Inflatable PFDs fall into this category as well, but really should be worn for the greatest safety. As mentioned, everyone on board, including guests, *must* know where the PFDs are stowed. You and your regular crew should have tried them on and should be able to get into them quickly even in the dark (practice while wearing a blindfold). Most importantly, order everyone into PFDs *in advance* of their need, if you can. At night, anyone on deck should routinely wear a PFD; nonswimmers, young children, and persons physically handicapped should wear one at all times when not below decks—a person with a cast on an arm or leg goes down like a rock without added buoyancy.

Never carry on your boat any nonapproved, damaged, or condemned lifesaving devices as "extras"—someone might grab one of them in an emergency.

Monitoring Vital Life Signs

You, as skipper, should have had basic first-aid instruction and CPR training, such as given by the American Red Cross, the American Heart Association, and local health and emergency agencies, and have adequate references on board. *But only someone educated and properly qualified to practice medicine should attempt to act as doctor.*

A primary survey can help you check for life-threatening conditions and give urgent first-aid care; see **Steps 1-6.** While another crewmember is calling for help, check quickly for the following danger signs: unconsciousness, loss of breathing, loss of heartbeat (pulse), and severe bleeding. If you are the only other person on the boat and you find the victim is unconscious, call for help immediately, then return and complete your check of the victim's vital signs. If the victim is a child, don't delay: Immediately give any necessary rescue breathing or CPR—for one minute—then go and call for emergency medical help.

If the respiratory or the circulatory system fails to function properly, the supply of oxygen to the body is decreased. In such cases the victim needs rescue breathing or CPR to stay alive until emergency help arrives. Otherwise, keep the victim comfortable and wait for emergency assistance; continue to monitor the victim's breathing and pulse rate.

If the victim vomits, or you must leave an unconscious person, roll him or her onto his or her side and clear the mouth and throat. Stabilize the person by bending his or her upper leg at the hip and knee. Raise the victim's head slightly, extend the lower arm straight out under it, and gently lower the head until the extended arm supports it.

Rescue breathing or artificial respiration is a way of breathing air into someone's lungs when natural breathing has stopped or when a person cannot breathe properly on his or her own. The air that you breathe into the victim contains more than enough oxygen to keep that person alive.

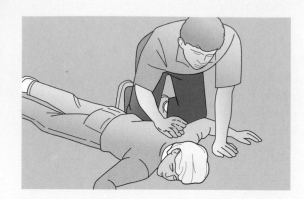

1 Check for reponsiveness. Determine whether or not the victim is conscious. Tap or gently shake the victim, and ask, "Are you all right?" If the person responds, he is conscious and breathing, and has a pulse. If the victim could be injured, do not move him; most injured people will find the most comfortable position for themselves. Caution: If you suspect that the victim has suffered a spinal injury, move him only if absolutely necessary, keeping the head and back in a straight line. If there is no response, and if no one has yet called for emergency help, send or have someone send an urgent radio call, as described in Chapter 12.

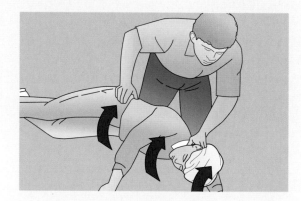

2 Roll the victim onto his back if necessary to check for breathing. Remember that unconsciousness can indicate a life-threatening condition. The tongue may have relaxed and fallen to the back of the throat, blocking the airway. This can cause breathing to stop, then the heart to stop. Therefore the next step is to open the victim's airway.

If it is necessary to move the victim into a face-up position, kneel facing the person. Place one hand on his shoulder and the other on his hip. Then roll him toward you as a single unit, moving your hand from the person's shoulder to support the back of his head or neck.

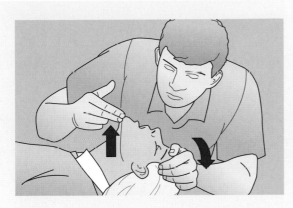

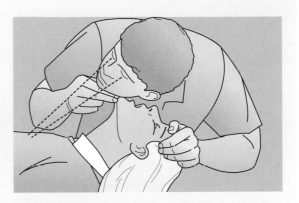

3 *Open the airway. Opening the passage that allows the victim to breathe is the most important action for successful resuscitation. If the victim is unconscious, open the airway with a gentle head-tilt/chin-lift action, as shown by the arrows.*

4 *Check for breathing. For 3 to 5 seconds, watch the chest to see if it rises and falls, listen for breathing and feel for air coming out of the victim's nose and mouth. (Chest movement alone does not mean that the victim is breathing.)*

If the victim is not breathing, act immediately, giving two full, slow breaths (Step 5) to get air into the lungs. If the person is breathing, keep the airway open and monitor breathing. Check for severe bleeding and contol it, if necessary.

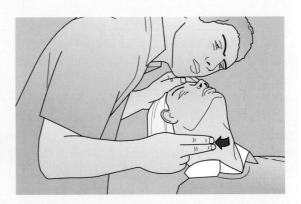

5 *Rescue breathing: Give two full, slow breaths. Keeping the vicitm's head tilted back and chin lifted, pinch the nose shut. Seal your lips tightly around the person's mouth. Give two full, slow breaths each lasting 1½ to 2 seconds. Watch for the chest to rise, indicating that your breath is going in.*

If the chest rises, check for pulse (Step 6). If you do not see the victim's chest rise and fall as you give breaths, you may not have the head tilted far enough back to open the airway adequately. Retilt the vicitm's head and try again to give breaths. If your breaths still do not go in, the airway could be obstructed: While a crewmember calls for emergency medical service, give first aid for an airway obstruction.

6 *Check for pulse. Locate the victim's Adam's apple, then slide your fingers into the groove on the side of the neck. Applying moderate pressure, feel for the pulse, as shown, for 5 to 10 seconds.*

If the person does not have a pulse, check for and control severe bleeding. Then begin CPR as trained. If there is a pulse, check for, and control, any severe bleeding, then continue to monitor breathing: Give one breath every 5 seconds (as in Step 5); recheck pulse and breathing approximately every minute or after 10 to 12 slow breaths. Continue rescue breathing until emergency medical help arrives.

Swimming Tips

Even with the best lifesaving equipment aboard, you may find yourself in the water without the aid of a buoyant device or approved PFD. If your boat stays afloat or awash, *stay with it.* Search vessels and aircraft can spot a boat or its wreckage far more easily than an individual whose head only is above water.

While swimming you may find temporary relief from fatigue by floating or by varying your style of swimming. Cold or tired muscles are susceptible to cramps. A leg cramp can often be overcome by moving your knees up toward your chest so that you can massage the affected area. Save your breath as much as possible; call for help only when there is definitely someone close enough to hear you.

FIRST AID AFLOAT

At the beginning of this chapter we considered certain responsibilities of the skipper. Another of these is caring for minor injuries and illnesses of his crew and guests. Your boat should have at least simple first-aid supplies and equipment, plus a manual of instructions for their use; you should have had basic first-aid instruction and CPR training.

But no one who is not educated and properly qualified to practice medicine should attempt to act as a doctor. There are, however, many instances where the availability of a first-aid kit (see page 395), some knowledge on the part of the boater, and a ready reference book have materially eased pain or even saved the life of a sick or injured person on a boat. All skippers should be prepared to render emergency first aid, doing no more than is absolutely necessary while getting the victim to a doctor or hospital as rapidly as possible.

Responding Quickly To Medical Emergencies

On land, emergency medical assistance is usually just moments away. But on the water, you are on your own—at least for a longer period of time. As skipper of a boat, you are responsible for dealing with medical emergencies aboard, an obligation

WATER SAFETY TIPS

• Know your personal limits; avoid overextending yourself.

• Always swim with at least two other persons, never alone.

• Before diving, make sure that the water is deep enough and hazard-free; check for any change in tide level since last swimming. For the first "dive," enter the water feet-first.

• When tired or overheated, stay out of the water.

• Rely on your swimming ability for support, not on inflatable or inherently buoyant objects, such as plastic toys or air mattress rafts.

• If you are a nonswimmer, do not go into the water without a personal flotation device (PFD).

• Do not engage in, or allow, dunking and pushing, which can be dangerous.

that relies on formal first-aid training and stocking the necessary supplies. It also means knowing the physical condition, and any medical problems, of everyone aboard your boat.

Your confidence and competence in handling medical emergencies should be on a par with your seamanship skills. That level of confidence comes from knowledge and practice; both can be acquired and honed by basic and advanced first-aid courses. Perhaps most important, you learn to stay calm in emergencies because you know what to do; see **Figure 11-24.** You can then make decisions and take the appropriate steps to keep a victim alive or to keep injuries stabilized until you can obtain emergency medical service.

Your Legal Responsibility

Legally, a victim must give consent before a person trained in first aid begins to help him or her. The law assumes that an unconscious person would give consent. If a victim is conscious, make sure you ask permission before administering first aid. If you are helping a victim previously unknown to you, ask a simple question: "My name is . . . I know first aid and I can help you until emergency assistance arrives; is that all right?"

You must be aware that emergencies in which the victim is an infant or child younger than eight years old may require special training and similar but varied techniques than for an adult or a child eight years or older. If you are likely to have infants or children under eight aboard your boat frequently, you should enroll in a first-aid course that specializes in first-aid techniques for that age group.

Calling for Emergency Help

In any medical emergency, it is essential to make sure that help is on the way—soon rather than too late. Even when in doubt about the severity of the victim's condition, save precious seconds by immediately sending an urgent call using "Pan-Pan" (see Chapter 12). Remember the old adage that it's better to be safe than sorry; you can always cancel the call if you get the situation under control.

There is the possibility that help will come from boats in the immediate vicinity. Until help arrives, take whatever first-aid measures you are qualified to perform. You usually can make contact with a doctor through the Coast Guard on VHF Channel 16 or SSB frequency 2182 kHz; or equivalent DSC channels. The USCG has access to military and U.S. Public Health physicians and,

Figure 11-24 As you first take immediate action in a medical emergency, check the victim for a medical information bracelet or pendant. This may provide vital information about a diagnosed medical condition, allergy, sensitivity, or prescribed medication.

through its AMVER (Automated Mutual-Assistance Vessel Rescue) system, keeps track of ships at sea that have medical staff aboard. If you cannot reach the USCG, try to contact Medical Advisory Systems, Inc. on SSB frequency 2182 kHz or 16,590 kHz. This private company operates the Medical Telecommunications Response Center in Owings, Maryland (301-855-8070; fax 410-257-2704; www.mas1.com), staffed around the clock by its own physicians. It serves primarily commercial marine vessels and remote industrial locations that subscribe to its services, but will provide assistance to nonsubscribers in a life-threatening emergency. There are also other similar agencies, such as MedLink (877-633-2473; www.medaire.com).

Chapter
12

Emergencies
Underway

Preparing for Emergencies • Flooding • Fires & Explosions • Man Overboard
Other Emergencies • Helicopter Rescue • Abandoning Ship

Whether caused by rough weather, overconfidence or just plain carelessness, emergencies on board a boat are the greatest test of a skipper's abilities. How quickly he or she can react to—and minimize the effects of—an accident, a fire, or other crisis on board can often make the difference between mishap and disaster, or even life and death.

This chapter deals with preparing for potentially serious situations—flooding, fires, and explosions, man overboard, and others—and dealing with them should they occur. Less serious "everyday" emergencies—heavy weather, fog and reduced visibility from other causes, running aground, assisting other vessels in trouble, and towing and being towed—are considered special seamanship situations and are covered in Chapter 10. The medical aspects of emergency situations are covered in Chapter 11, pages 404-407.

This chapter also explains how to call for help when you need it, and how to cope with helicopter rescue and abandon-ship emergencies.

PREPARING FOR EMERGENCIES

Experienced skippers prepare themselves for dealing with emergencies as a matter of routine. They also prepare their crew. Whether their crewmembers are part of a proficient, competitive team, or family and friends, or guests out for a casual afternoon cruise, the seasoned skipper is already aware of, and prepared for, dangers that may present a threat to the safety of the craft and

Opposite Page: Figure 12-01 As a basic action toward preventing an emergency from arising, every boat should be well maintained and have proper safety equipment, such as personal flotation devices (PFDs). Collisions and capsizing are among the accidents that are responsible for the principal number of fatalities.

BOATING ACCIDENTS

According to USCG statistics on 40,084 reported boating accidents during a recent five-year period, the following thirteen causes are cited, in order of frequency of occurrence. The consequences were serious; 3,909 fatalities, 22,065 injuries, and more than $142 million in property damage. Although each type of accident resulted in some fatalities, those indicated with an asterisk were responsible for approximately 90 percent of total fatalities.

- Collision with other vessels.*
- Collision with a fixed object.*
- Capsizing.*
- Other casualty; unknown.*
- Falls overboard.*
- Grounding.*
- Fire or explosion of fuel.
- Collision with floating object.
- Swamping/flooding.
- Sinking.
- Struck by boat or propeller.
- Falls within boat.
- Non-fuel-related fire or explosion.

The U.S. Coast Guard statistics do not include every accident to a recreational boat. Some are not included as no report is required; others go unreported because of ignorance of the requirement and a lack of enforcement of the law. It has been officially stated that the Coast Guard believes that "only a small portion of all boating accidents are reported." The more serious the accident, the greater the likelihood of it's being reported; it is probable that nearly all fatal accidents are officially reported.

TRANSMITTING A MAYDAY DISTRESS CALL & MESSAGE BY VOICE

Only when grave and imminent danger threatens life or property and immediate help is required should you use the distress procedure Mayday. Transmitted on VHF Channel 16 or 2182 kHz (SSB), your message should be heard by boats, USCG stations, and other shore stations that are within communications range. Speaking slowly, clearly, and calmly, use your marine radio (see Chapter 20) to communicate the following information:

1 "MAYDAY... MAYDAY... MAYDAY"

2 "THIS IS (boat name)... (boat name)... (boat name)."

3 "MAYDAY (boat name) POSITION IS (vessel position in degrees and minutes of latitude NORTH or SOUTH and longitude EAST or WEST, or as a distance and magnetic or true bearing from a well-known navigation landmark)."

4 "WE (nature of your emergency)."

5 "WE REQUIRE (type of assistance required)."

6 "ON BOARD ARE (number of adults and children on board) AND (safety equipment aboard). (State conditions of any injured.)"

7 "(Boat name) IS A (boat length in feet)-FOOT (type: sloop, sportfisherman, etc.) WITH A (hull color) HULL AND (trim color) TRIM."

8 "I WILL BE LISTENING ON CHANNEL (16 or 2182)."

9 "THIS IS (boat name). OVER."

all on board. The location of emergency equipment—fire extinguishers, personal flotation devices, radio, visual distress signals, etc.—should be shown to everyone on board.

The first thought to be given to any preparation for a specific emergency should be how to prevent that situation from ever arising. A well-maintained boat is an important precaution; see **Figure 12-01**. The emergencies that are most often reported as accidents, listed in the sidebar "Boating Accidents," can usually be prevented by the actions described in Chapter 11, Safety Afloat. The practice of good seamanship is an essential element in the elimination of emergencies; safe operating procedures for various types of boats are covered in Chapters 6, 7, and 8.

The Importance of Emergency Drills

The general importance of practice and drills was pointed out in Chapter 11; this is even more important in relation to the preparation for emergencies. Even the best plans are valuable only if tried out and evaluated, revised as necessary, and then practiced periodically. Rehearse the procedures discussed in this chapter until they are second nature. Practice each operation with the entire crew at the beginning of each boating season, then once again on a staggered schedule later in the season. Make every effort to keep the drills enjoyable without reducing their serious nature. Have some drills without your participation, as if you had become incapacitated.

Think of invited guests as "temporary crew." You may not be able to train them in drills, but they should be shown where the PFDs are and how to use them. Inform them in a relaxed manner, not with an air of alarm. If guests are aboard for an extended cruise, expand their knowledge to such items as the location and use of fire extinguishers and bilge pumps.

SUMMONING ASSISTANCE

The marine environment can be unforgiving, and what may initially be a minor problem can rapidly develop into a situation beyond your control. For this reason, let someone know when you are experiencing even relatively minor difficulties—before your situation turns into an emergency.

TRANSMITTING A PAN-PAN URGENCY CALL & MESSAGE

Send the Pan-Pan urgency signal to indicate that you have a "very urgent" message regarding the safety of your vessel or the safety of a person.

1 "PAN-PAN . . . PAN-PAN . . . PAN-PAN" [properly pronounced "pahn-pahn"].

2 "ALL STATIONS (or the name of a particular vessel)."

3 "THIS IS (boat name) . . . (boat name) . . . (boat name)."

4 "WE (nature of your emergency)."

5 "WE REQUIRE (type of assistance required or other useful information such as your position, a description of your vessel, and/or the number of people on board)."

6 "THIS IS (boat name). OVER."

CANCELING A PAN-PAN

If you transmit a Pan-Pan call, then find that you no longer require assistance, you must cancel the message.

1 "PAN-PAN, PAN-PAN."

2 "HELLO ALL STATIONS, HELLO ALL STATIONS."

3 "THIS IS (boat name)."

4 "TIME IS (transmission by 24-hour clock)."

5 "CANCEL PAN-PAN."

6 "THIS IS (boat name). OUT."

Note: When distress traffic ends or radio silence is no longer needed, the controlling station must transmit: "MAYDAY . . . HELLO ALL STATIONS (said three times) . . . THIS IS (station identification) . . . (time) . . . (name and call sign of distressed vessel) . . . SEELONCE FEENEE or PRU-DONCE."

The USCG serves as Search and Rescue (SAR) coordinator for all maritime emergencies in U.S. waters and is the appropriate contact on safety issues. If you are in "distress"—if you and/or your boat are threatened by grave or imminent danger requiring immediate assistance—the USCG will take immediate action. Increasingly, though, help for situations less than an emergency will be provided by commercial assistance operators for a fee. There will, however, be instances where speed of response or lack of commercial towing craft will result in the use of USCG or USCG Auxiliary assistance.

There are four ways to broadcast a signal informing the rest of the world that you need assistance. First there's the voice Mayday call on VHF-FM or single sideband SSB-MF/HF, or both. You can send such a Mayday in an open broadcast, or, if your radio is so equipped, you can push the red distress button and send out an automatic signal. This new system is called Digital Selective Calling (DSC), and it is required on all new transceivers. When you push the button, a distress message (Mayday) is transmitted, naming your vessel, the type of emergency (fire, sinking, etc.) and, if a GPS is connected to the radio, your position; see Chapter 21.

Another Mayday signal can be sent automatically from an Emergency Position Indicating Radio Beacon (EPIRB); see Chapter 20. Here, too, vessel data and position can be sent, this time via satellite connections to rescue forces.

And finally there's the newest technology called a Search and Rescue Transponder (SART); see Chapter 20. When this unit is activated by pulses from a radar on another vessel, it responds with a series of "dashes" that will appear on that vessel's radar screen and lead it to your location.

In situations other than Mayday, more traditional voice communication techniques are used. These are listed in the sidebars.

How to Signal Distress & Urgency

Aboard most boats, the radio is the primary means for getting assistance. (For information on radio operation, see Chapter 20.) Channel

16 VHF/FM and frequency 2182 kHz MF/SSB are dedicated distress and calling frequencies monitored by the USCG at all times. USCG stations no longer monitor Citizen's Band (CB) channels.

Offshore farther than about 20 nautical miles (37 km), you should call the USCG on one of their 4 to 6 MHz, or higher, working frequencies. The Global Maritime Distress and Safety System (GMDSS) is now in operation. GMDSS consists of several subsystems, including satellite detection of 406 MHz EPIRBs (see Chapter 20, page 705), NAVTEX receivers (see page 707), MF, HF and VHF transceivers using DSC (see page 709) and search-and-rescue radar transponders, mentioned earlier. The USCG will not have VHF DSC radios on Channel 70 at shore stations and on cutters until perhaps 2005; distress calls should continue on Channel 16. DSC calls on 2187.5 kHz can be received at some USCG stations, but coverage is not complete. Even so, as DSC radios proliferate, distress messages will be heard by other vessels that may be able to help or at least pass the alert on to the Coast Guard.

The USCG's primary SAR role is to assist mariners in distress. If you are in distress, first use, if possible, the DSC button. Next, immediately transmit a Mayday voice call on the radio. Speaking slowly, clearly, and calmly, use the format suggested in the sidebar on page 410.

If you require the assistance of other vessels, but the danger is not life-threatening—in the case of a person overboard, for example—the situation is one of URGENCY. Broadcast the Pan-Pan urgency signal. The Pan-Pan signal has priority over all transmissions except the Mayday distress call and message. Once the Pan-Pan emergency is over, a signal "to all stations" must be transmitted. The end of a distress situation must be announced by a "Seelonce Feenee" or "Pru-donce" message.

Every skipper must understand what does *not* constitute a distress or urgent situation. Mere running out of fuel or having a dead battery, for example, does not constitute using Mayday or Pan-Pan unless truly bad weather threatens.

Radio Silence

"Seelonce (French pronunciation of 'silence') Mayday" has been adopted internationally to control transmissions on the distress frequency, telling all other stations to leave the air and maintain radio silence. This signal is to be used only by the unit in distress or the station controlling the distress traffic. Any other station that considers it necessary to advise one or more stations of the need to keep off the air should use the signal "Seelonce Distress" followed by its identification.

The signal to indicate the end of radio silence and permission to resume normal operation is "Seelonce Feenee" (French for "silence ended") or "Pru-donce" (French for "prudence"). This signal may be transmitted only by the station that has controlled the distress traffic.

If You Hear a Mayday Call

If you are not in distress but you hear a Mayday call, listen carefully—*do not transmit*. As you listen, try to determine if your boat is in the best position to take the necessary action, or if some other vessel is better located or better equipped to deal with the situation.

If yours is the logical boat to render assistance, reply with a call to the distressed vessel as follows: "(Name of boat in distress) . . . (name of boat in distress) . . . (name of boat in distress). This is (your boat name) . . . (your boat name) . . . (your boat name and call sign). Received Mayday."

When the other vessel has acknowledged your call, continue with your offer of assistance by giving your position, your speed toward the scene of distress, and the estimated time to get there. But be sure before you transmit that you will not be interfering with the signal of another vessel better situated to render immediate assistance. Keep in mind that the "Good Samaritan" provision (see Chapter 2) protects you from liability.

If yours is not the logical boat to take action, maintain radio silence but monitor the frequency closely for any further development. Start making notes so that you can record the events in your boat's log. When another station retransmits a distress message, the words

"Mayday Relay" must be spoken three times before station identification.

Making a Non-Distress Emergency Call

If your situation is not a distress, simply call "Coast Guard." If alternative sources of assistance are available, the Coast Guard will normally coordinate the efforts to assist you. If you have a friend, marina, or commercial firm that you want contacted, for example, the Coast Guard will attempt to do so. You may also contact them directly on Channel 16 VHF/FM or through the marine operator. If this is unsuccessful, the Coast Guard will make a Marine Assistance Request Broadcast (MARB) on your behalf. This announces that you need help, gives your location, and invites others to come to your aid.

Thereafter, if you do not accept services offered in response to the first MARB, you have two options. The USCG will supply information about commercial firms, if available, so you may contact them directly. Or, if you request, the USCG will make a second MARB to see if other help is available.

Keep in contact with the Coast Guard at regular intervals and tell them when help arrives. If someone offers help but cannot get to you within a reasonable time, usually not to exceed one hour, contact the Coast Guard to arrange other assistance. In addition, inform the Coast Guard if conditions change sufficiently to cause alarm—for example, if a medical emergency develops, a storm approaches, your boat begins taking on water, or your last reported position changes.

If the Coast Guard or Coast Guard Auxiliary arrives to assist you and you require a tow, they normally will tow you to the nearest location where you can either arrange for repairs or a tow back to your homeport. However, if a commercial firm is available to help you safely in a reasonable time, the Coast Guard will not provide direct on-scene assistance. Since you will have to pay for the commercial firm's services, inquire about fees and salvage commitments before accepting that service.

Remember that, if you agree to the assistance of a commercial firm and then refuse this service when it arrives, you still may be legally obligated to pay a fee.

In addition to Coast Guard, Coast Guard Auxiliary, and commercial firms, others that may be available to assist you include a fellow boater, a local fire or police department, or another public agency. Keep in mind that a Good Samaritan, although well-meaning, may not have the equipment or skills needed to help you safely and effectively.

If You Do Not Have a Radio

If you do not have a marine radio, or yours is not working, attempt to signal a fellow boater who can either assist or call the Coast Guard for you. In a distress situation, use flares or any other distress signaling device to catch the attention of people aboard other boats in the vicinity. Refer to the officially recognized signals shown in Chapter 5; refer to **Figure 5-20**.

COLLISIONS

Accident statistics for a recent year make very interesting reading. For all reported accidents involving recreational boats, 38 percent involved the collision of one craft with another, an additional 13 percent involved the collision of a boat with a fixed or floating object. Thus, collisions

USING A CELL PHONE TO GET HELP

A cellular telephone can often be used to summon assistance if you are in a coverage area—it has advantages and disadvantages. A good feature is that transmissions will be clear and free of interference. You should have the telephone number of the local Coast Guard station available on your boat; in some areas, a call may be made directly to "*CG." The disadvantage in the use of a cell phone to request assistance is that your call will not be heard by other boats, and often help is more readily available from a nearby craft; as well the range may be limited and the battery may run low.

Figure 12-02 Many boating areas are relatively open expanses of water without specific channels. Craft may approach from one or more directions, often several at a time. To avoid collisions, every skipper must know who has the right-of-way and what signal to give in each situation.

totaled 51 percent of all reported boating accidents. Clearly, collisions are a primary category of underway emergencies. With more boats using our waters every year, and faster speeds becoming common, every skipper must learn to use special caution to avoid a collision; see **Figure 12-02**.

Avoiding Collisions

In recent years, among the most frequent "causes" of boating accidents were "operator inattention," "no proper lookout," and "operator carelessness." If your course appears to be converging with another vessel's, take careful compass or relative bearings every few minutes; increase their frequency as the gap narrows. If the bearings move forward, the other vessel will cross ahead of you; if the bearings move aft, the boat will cross behind you. But if the bearings remain constant, you are on a collision course and must take immediate action. Do not wait until the last moment. If the other vessel is a boat, take action in accordance with Navigation Rules, giving way or maintaining course and speed if you are the stand-on vessel.

Although a converging course is difficult to judge with any boat, large commercial vessels offer a particular challenge. As soon as you spot a freighter, tanker, or ferry, assign a crewmember to lookout

duty. Nothing should distract this person from looking at and taking bearings on the vessel until the chance of collision has clearly passed. Unless you are certain that you will cross its bow at least one mile ahead of it, alter your course so that you will pass astern of the larger vessel. If your boat is on a bow-to-bow reciprocal course with another vessel, alter course to starboard by at least 20 degrees.

Even if you have the right away, the Navigation Rules (see Chapter 5) require you to do everything you can to avoid collision—even if it means reversing. If a collision seems imminent, and the other vessel's crew obviously doesn't see you, do everything you can to make your boat visible.

Attract attention to your vessel by shining a bright hand-held light on your sails, or fire flares from your vessel to attract the other crew's attention.

In summary, to be safe when encountering another vessel, you should:

• Know the Navigation Rules for the waters that you are using.

• Obey the Navigation Rules.

• Assume that the operator of the other vessel does not know the Navigation Rules and will not be obeying them.

If You Do Have a Collision

If despite your best effort a collision does occur, your first actions should be for the safety and welfare of persons on your boat and the other craft. If people are in the water, throw them PFDs or any other item that would help them remain afloat until they can be helped on board your or another craft. If there are injuries, apply such first-aid measures as you can; see Chapter 11.

As the statistics show, despite knowing the Rules of the Road and taking proper precautions, collisions do occur. If you are involved in one— your fault or the other skipper's—you are in most instances required to file an accident report. In some instances, this report will be made to the Coast Guard on Form CG-3865. In most cases, however, the report will be made to a state agency using a form required by that agency; this form will usually be very similar to the Coast Guard form. The circumstances that require the submis-

REPORTING BOATING ACCIDENTS

Boating Accident Reports are intended to assist the Coast Guard in determining the cause of accidents and making recommendations for their prevention, and in compiling appropriate statistics. In case of collision, accident, or other casualty involving a vessel subject to the Federal Boat Safety Act of 1971 (FBSA/71), the operator must make a formal report within 48 hours if the incident results in any of the following circumstances:

• Death, although local authorities must be notified immediately.

• An injury requiring medical treatment beyond first aid.

• The disappearance of a person from a vessel under circumstances that indicate death or injury. The report must be filed within 10 days if the accident results in either property damage totaling more than $2,000 or in complete loss of a vessel. Most state boating laws require that reports of boating accidents be made to a designated state office or official. If, however, there is no state provision for reporting such incidents, a report must be made to the Coast Guard Officer in Charge, Marine Inspection, nearest the site of the accident.

Coast Guard regulations on accident reporting list the information that must be furnished. The Boating Accident Report Form—CG-3865—may be used in recreational boat reports to the Coast Guard; states normally use this form or one of their own patterned after it. (Note that reporting requirements and the form are different for craft in commercial operation.)

sion of an accident report, and the time requirements for its submission are shown in the sidebar above, see also Chapter 2, pages 66–68.

FLOODING

Be prepared mentally and in terms of equipment to take immediate action at the first sign of water entering your boat. Try to identify where the water is coming in. If your boat is damaged by collision with another boat, or if you hit a submerged object, especially at high speed, the location of the leak will probably be obvious. In other situations, the source of the inflow may not be easy to determine.

A likely cause of leaks is failure of through-hull fittings and related parts such as hoses, keel bolts, underwater exhausts, stuffing boxes, and rudderposts; check these locations first. This is where a thorough knowledge of your boat is essential. If you have taken the time to diagram the location of every through-hull fitting in your boat, you will be well prepared to find the problem quickly and to deal with the situation in a calm, logical manner.

Preparing in Advance for Leak Control

Even if you can't prevent a leak, you can be well prepared to repair it with speed and confidence. The following precautions may help when your boat begins taking on water:

• Install the largest possible manually operated diaphragm pump; such units are available with a capacity of one gallon per stroke. Mount the pump so that you can operate it continuously without excessive fatigue.

• Have on board softwood plugs—one of appropriate diameter for each size of through-hull fitting in your boat, tapered so they can be driven into place from the inside; see **Figure 12-03**.

• To prepare for the possibility of hull damage, stock a small, strong tarpaulin with corner grommets. When dock lines are attached, the tarpaulin can be maneuvered to cover a damaged hull area from the outside, then secured. Alternatively, there is a commercially available product that operates as a "leak umbrella," which is inserted from the inside of the boat through a large opening in the hull, then opened up in umbrella-like fashion to cover the

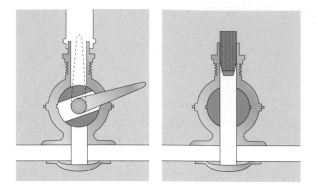

Figure 12-03 If the cause of the leak is a damaged hose, closing the seacock (above left) should solve the problem. If, however, a through-hull fitting fails and the seacock or gate valve cannot be closed, hammer in a plug to stop the inflow of water (above right). Such a plug must be watched closely lest it come out undetected.

hole and secured with the handle. Although these actions may not stop all leaking, they can significantly reduce the water inflow.

• Be prepared to take advantage of the engine to gain full pumping capacity, as shown in the sidebar "Increasing Pumping Capacity," on page 417. The alternative system can also be used to admit a small, controlled amount of water into the bilge for testing the operation of automatic bilge pump controls, and for cleaning.

Taking Immediate Action

As soon as you suspect damage that might cause a threatening leak, switch on all electric bilge pumps. (Even if you discover no leak, the pumps will not be damaged by a brief run without water to pump.)

Assign someone the task of calling for emergency assistance (see above, page 410)—even before you are sure that you will need help. Activate a manual pump if you have an extra person on board. Then investigate for possible damage.

Caution for boats connected to shore power, or when an onboard 120-volt AC genset is running: If your boat has suffered hull damage as the result of a collision with another boat or an object, consider the possibility that the collision might also have damaged the vessel's electrical system. If a live electrical wire has been knocked

loose and is discharging current into bilge water, anyone stepping into that bilge water could suffer a serious, possibly fatal, shock. If electrical wires have been pulled loose and come into contact with bilge water, or you notice any electrical sparking, shut down the main breakers in your AC and DC electrical panels before exposing yourself to the water in the bilge.

Remember that a boat floats as long as water is pumped out at least as fast as it comes in. Assign someone to investigate the extent of the damage by checking the bilge. If conditions permit, make this investigation yourself. If leaking is rapid, plug the leak and do everything possible to remove the water. Do whatever works fastest with the materials at hand, from the emergency pumping procedure shown in the sidebar, "Increasing Pumping Capacity," to forming a bucket brigade. If your leak occurs offshore, keep in mind that USCG aircraft carry pumps that can be dropped in floating containers to boats that need them. Emergency operating instructions are on and in the containers.

Stopping the Inflow of Water

The action that you take to stem the flow of water into your boat will depend on the nature of the leak itself. Almost anything soft can be stuffed into a hole in the hull—from cushions and pillows to bedding and spare sails (never use PFDs; you might need them). As quickly as possible, reinforce soft plug materials with something flat and solid, such as a hatch cover, battens, or bed slats. Assign a crewmember to hold the plug in place. The plug should be monitored at all times by a crewmember, while others continue pumping overboard the water that has entered the boat. In the meantime, head the boat to a nearby destination where necessary repairs can be made. If it gets really bad, you might consider beaching the boat at the nearest landfall.

If the material is applied from the outside—the most effective method, since water pressure will help to hold it in place—the boat must be stopped while the temporary patch or plug is positioned and secured. If you are going to try to

INCREASING PUMPING CAPACITY

In an emergency underway, when the bilge is flooding and uncontrolled by the boat's pump(s), the engine's cooling system can be valuable to stem the inflow of water in one of the following ways:

• You can improvise by simply shutting the seacock to the engine and removing the intake hose, keeping it below water level in the bilge; make sure the new intake point is ahead of the engine's raw water strainer.

Important: Make sure your boat is equipped with a replacement hose. When removing the intake hose, you may discover that it has bonded to the seacock and will rip or have to be cut away. Unless you have a replacement hose in good condition, you will lose the use of your engine.

• Alternatively, you can modify your intake system as shown here—by installing a "T" connection and hose, fitted with a strainer, to the lowest point in the bilge; this should be ahead of the engine's raw water strainer. This hose must have an in-line shut-off valve—keep it closed in normal

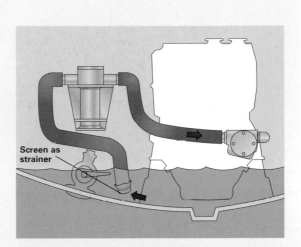

In most systems, the end of the intake hose can be removed and placed in the bilge.

operation. To activate the emergency pumping system, close the seacock and open the valve in the bypass line. The engine will then use the bilge water as coolant.

Important: When activated, this system must be constantly monitored to prevent damage to engine(s) if water drops below the pickup level; the two valves can each be partially opened and adjusted to match the pumping action in the inflow volume. In addition, when engines are shut down, the bypass must be turned back to seacock mode once the leak is under control. This system is only for emergency pumping—never use it to flush out dirty bilges.

If a "T" connection and in-line valve are installed, as shown, protect the engine by tying the valve handle. (An accidental switch of the handle could ruin the engine.)

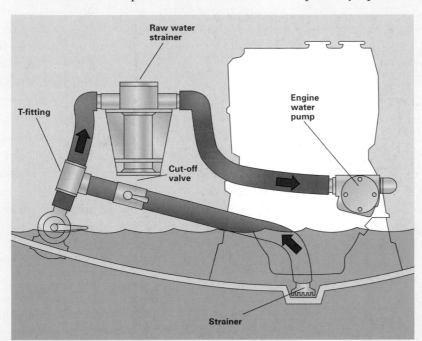

reach shore with such a rig in place, make certain its top edge is well above your vessel's waterline and proceed slowly.

FIRES & EXPLOSIONS

Fire on a boat is a very serious matter. Your surroundings are burning and you have nowhere to go except overboard into the water. Fire safety is something that everyone who owns or operates a boat should practice. Each year, boating fires and explosions injure hundreds of boaters and cause millions of dollars in property damage. While there is a greater chance of a fire or explosion on a boat than on land, most of these accidents can be prevented.

Preventing Fires on Board

Keep in mind that most fires are preventable. A boat kept in shipshape condition, with clean bilges and proper stowage of fuel and gear, is not likely to have a fire. Prevention requires constant attention; whenever you see a condition on your boat that might contribute to a fire, correct it at once.

Fires do occur despite a skipper's best efforts, so always keep the firefighting gear accessible and in good working condition. Stow some PFDs well forward in case of fire aft, or in case you must abandon ship over the bow.

Fuel and fuel vapors are two of the leading ingredients in all boating accidents involving fires and explosions. Follow the guidelines for safe fueling (see Chapter 11, pages 373-374), as well as the following reminders provided by the United States Coast Guard and the National Fire Protection Association.

General & Seasonal Checks

• Be alert for damage to your boat's fuel system. Over a period of time, fuel fittings and fuel hoses wear out. Inspect all fittings and hoses regularly, especially near the engine where engine heat and vibration can accelerate deterioration.

• Inspect fuel tanks annually. Pay particular attention to bottom surfaces, which may have been in contact with bilge water, and also any part of the tank that touches the boat structure. The tank could have rusted or been damaged due to rubbing and abrasion. A suitable vent pipe for each tank should lead outside the hull; vents should never terminate in closed spaces such as the engine compartment or under the deck.

• Be sure the fuel fill pipe is tightly fitted to the fill plate and located outside closed compartments. Also, the fill pipe should be located where any spilled fuel will be directed overboard. Look for fuel fill hoses that are dry and cracked or soft and mushy. Such hoses should be replaced with marine fuel hoses immediately.

• If a hose or fuel tank leaks, replace it before using your boat again, even for a short time.

• On a boat with portable fuel tanks, make sure the vents can be closed and that the tanks have vapor-tight, leak-proof caps. The vent on a portable tank should be open when the motor is running, but when the tank is not in use, the vent and the cap should be tightly closed.

• Never leave motor fuel or other flammable liquids in open buckets. Choose nonvolatile fluids.

• If the boat has powered ventilation (a bilge blower), make sure the blower operates.

• If your engine is equipped with a backfire flame arrester, keep the flame arrester screen on the carburetor clean.

• Be sure heating and cooking appliances on board are secured and operate properly. Refer to the owner's manual for the appliance for guidance on inspecting for leaks in valves and connections; never use a match.

• In the galley, fit splash-proof covers to appliances and controls. Keep the galley clean, especially the sides of pans and any grease filters. Never leave the galley unattended when power or fuel is switched on.

• Make sure that flammable items are stowed safely and cannot come into contact with cooking or heating appliances or hot engine parts.

• Install a sniffer-type alarm if your galley stove uses a heavier-than-air fuel, such as propane, or if the boat has a gasoline engine. Otherwise, fumes from these fuels may settle in the bilge, undetected by crewmembers; an open flame or spark could ignite the fumes.

• Make sure that Coast Guard-approved fire extinguishers (refer to Chapter 3, page 97) on board are in working order—that gauges register and that nozzles are clear. Take a boating safety course that teaches the correct use of a fire extinguisher aboard a boat. The time to learn is *before* a fire occurs.

• Look for bare wires or loose electrical connections; these might cause a short in your boat's electrical system, which could start a fire.

• Do not store small disposable propane cylinders or charcoal lighting fluid on board.

• Discourage or minimize drinking of alcohol while the boat is underway.

• Do not permit anyone to smoke when they are in bed, refueling, or changing gas bottles. Advise all on board to never leave a lighted cigarette unattended; to put it out when finished, and to use an ashtray that will not slide off a table and overturn should the boat rock or heel over.

• Dispose of paper and packing material as soon as stores are broken out.

• Keep light bulbs clean; make sure that wattage is proper for each fitting.

• Never store oily cloths or combustible material in lockers.

• If working with wood chips, sawdust, and shavings, sweep up and dispose of the scraps as soon as possible.

• When hauled out, if your boat does not have a metal hull, install an earth lightning conductor.

• Conduct a bow-to-stern inspection, checking for loose fuel, gas fumes, and any malfunctioning instruments.

Before Casting Off

• "Sniff" your bilges. Usually your nose is the best fuel/vapor detector. This will mean getting down on your hands and knees; however, it is the best way to check.

• Operate the bilge blower for at least four minutes before starting an inboard gasoline engine. If you still smell fumes after four minutes, find what is causing them and make repairs before starting the engine.

• Make sure the locations of your fire extinguishers are known to all persons on board.

• When refueling, close all hatches, ports, and other openings; shut off all engines and motors; and ensure that all persons refrain from smoking. Fill all portable tanks on shore.

• After refueling, wipe up or wash off any excess or spilled fuel; open all hatches and ports, and let the boat air out. "Sniff" your bilges. Operate the bilge blower for at least four minutes before starting an inboard engine.

Fighting a Fire on Board

Unfortunately, sometimes fires do occur despite a skipper's best efforts. Chances are, however, that this will result in a less severe emergency than it might if the required firefighting gear (pages 97-101) is on board, in good working condition and readily accessible, and if those aboard respond with speed. See **Table 12-1** for information on the various types of extinguishing agents and the type of fires on which each should be used.

Explosions & Fires

A fire may start with a dramatic explosion or on a much smaller scale. The skipper of every boat should have in mind the action to be taken if fire strikes; see **Figure 12-04.** The first consideration must be for the passengers, and the skipper should have a plan for abandoning ship if need be; see page 430. If you have a gasoline explosion, there usually is little you can do except reach for a PFD if you can

Figure 12-04 Fire on board a boat is a very serious matter. If the fire starts with an explosion, there is usually little that you can do except grab a life preserver and go over the side without delay.

ASSESSING FIRE EXTINGUISHER CONTENTS

Contents	Use (type of fire)*	Advantages	Disadvantages	Precautions
CO_2	A, B, C	Smothers a fire and does not conduct electricity, so can be used on any fire.	Less effective in open areas where winds or drafts exist. If ignition source has not been removed, fire can re-flash. Will stop a running engine. Can asphyxiate user in a close space.	Do not touch discharge horn when in operation. Use caution in unventilated areas.
Dry Chemicals	A, B, C or B, C	Inhibit chemical process of combustion.	Can stop an engine. Can leave a residue that can damage electronic equipment or machinery.	Should never be partially discharged. If discharged even briefly, the nozzle may later leak. Discharge completely and recharge.
Foam	A, B	Most effective with Type B fires; will work on Type A fires.	Leaves a messy residue. Should not be used on Type C fires.	
Halon-type	Halon 1211 and 1301 can no longer be used in new fire extinguishers; other chemicals such as FE241 are available that are less damaging to the environment. Existing Halon units can remain in use and can be refilled if recycled Halon is used. Fixed FE241 systems are used to fight all classes of fire.			Gauges may be unreliable; have weight tagged annually.
Pyrene and Carbon Tetrachloride	Commonly used in past; still found in older extinguishers. GENERATE TOXIC GAS THAT CAN BE FATAL. DO NOT USE.			DO NOT USE.

*A=Ordinary combustibles: wood, cloth, rubber, paper, many plastics
B=Flammable liquids: gasoline, solvents, grease, oil, some paints
C=Electrical equipment: wiring, fuse boxes, energized electrical equipment

Table 12-1 *Familiarize yourself with the various types of extinguishing agents and the kinds of fires for which they are suitable.*

and go over the side. When clear of the danger, account for all crewmembers. Give whatever assistance you can to anyone injured or in the water without a buoyant device. Keep everyone together in a group—for morale and to aid rescue operations.

If abandoning ship is not immediately indicated, take the following steps as quickly as possible:

• Head the boat, if possible, so the flames blow outboard, not inboard.

• Make a radio distress call (page 410), if time permits, giving the boat's location.

• Make sure the passengers move to the safest areas of the boat, such as forward with the bow into the wind, with their life preservers on.

• Reach for the appropriate fire extinguisher (pages 97-101), and fight the fire as described below.

Fighting Fires of Various Types

Fires require four elements for their existence— fuel, oxygen (air), heat, and uninhibited chemical chain reactions—remove or interrupt any of these and the fire will go out. Many fires are fought by smothering (shutting off the flow of air) or by cooling them below the temperature that will support combustion. Others are extinguished by interrupting the chain reactions of the combustion process—this is the action of dry-chemical extinguishers so widely used on small boats.

In fighting a fire, specific procedures and precautions must be followed. Hold the extinguisher upright and pull the pin. Stand back from the fire roughly 10 to 15 feet (3-5 m), and squeeze the handle. *Always remember that a typical small marine fire extinguisher has a discharge time of only 8 to 20 seconds.* From the start of the discharge, aim at the base of the fire, not the smoke. As the flames begin to die down, slowly approach the fire more closely. *Never prematurely consider the fire to be extinguished until the material has substantially cooled down—be alert for a flashback.* Wait until you believe that the burned material has sufficiently cooled down— and then wait a while longer. Opening an access hatch prematurely can let in enough fresh air (oxygen) to turn a smoldering fire into an inferno. *Never get into a position where the fire, burning or "extinguished," is between you and a safe exit.*

• **Galley Fires** Fires in the galley are most likely to be fueled by flammable liquids such as grease, propane, or alcohol, or by combustible solid materials such as paper, wood, or fabric. A U.S. Coast Guard-approved Class ABC extinguisher will be effective against both kinds of fires; see **Figure 12-05**. If no extinguisher is available, use materials at hand such as baking soda or a water-soaked towel. If using baking soda, pour

some in your hand, then throw it at the base of the flames. Do not use water on grease fires; the grease will float on top of the water and can carry flames to other parts of the vessel. The same can happen with a fire involving alcohol stove fuel.

• If your stove uses propane for cooking, turn off the fuel supply from the tank. (The shut-off valve should be near the stove, but neither behind it nor in a location that will require reaching through flames.) Once the fuel supply is cut off, let the fire burn itself out. If necessary, soak nearby wooden or fabric surfaces with water to keep the fire from spreading.

• **Gasoline, Diesel Oil, or Grease Fires** Use a Class B dry-chemical, CO_2, or foam extinguisher. Do not use water, which will only spread the flames. A common source of deck fires aboard boats is the gasoline used to fuel the dinghy's outboard motor. Although Coast Guard regulations do not require that a fire extinguisher be carried in most dinghies, you should keep a Class B extinguisher on board and make certain it is nearby whenever you are handling gasoline.

• **Fires Belowdecks** Fires in a vessel's cabins or lockers will most often be fueled by combustible material such as wood, paper, or fabric. You should have a Class A extinguisher mounted below where you and your crew can get to it

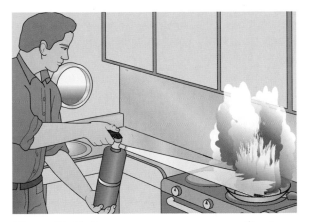

Figure 12-05 Do not use water on a grease fire; it may spread the flames. In using a hand-portable extinguisher, pull out the lock pin and squeeze the two handle levers together. Aim at the base of the flames with a sweeping action if the burning area is large. Keep the stream steadily on the base of the flames until the fire is out—or until the extinguisher is empty, a matter of only 8 to 20 seconds.

easily, even in the dark. If no Class A extinguisher is available, flood the fire's base with water and/or rob the fire of oxygen by closing a door or hatch to snuff it out. Throw burning materials over the side if you can.

If you must open a door or hatch behind which fire may be burning, feel its exterior first. If it is too hot for you to touch, the fire is probably still burning. If you must open the door or hatch, have a portable Class A extinguisher ready, open the door slowly, stay as low as possible, and keep the door or hatch between yourself and the possible fire.

• **Engine Fires** If the engine-room fire extinguisher system has not discharged automatically, activate it manually. Stop all engines and generators in the engine space involved with the fire—if any engine continues to run, it will draw in some of the fire suppressant gasses, reducing the amount available to fight the fire, and at the same time draw in outside air that will further fuel the fire; automatic shut-down devices are available. Close all engine-room doors and hatches.

Order a trained crewmember to stand by the life raft and prepare to launch it; order the crew into life jackets. Transmit a Mayday distress call and message or Pan-Pan urgency call and message (see page 411). If the engine-room fire extinguisher has discharged, keep all engine-room doors and hatches closed for 15 minutes before opening.

If you must use a portable fire extinguisher, aim it at the base of the flames, through the smallest access hole to the engine compartment; this minimizes the flow of air into the area of the fire and avoids spreading the flames into the rest of the boat. It is highly desirable that engine compartments have one or more small "fire ports" just large enough for the nozzle of an extinguisher

• **Electrical Fires** Use an approved Class C fire extinguisher designed specifically for this purpose; never use water, which conducts electricity. Fires in electrical-wiring insulation cannot sustain themselves without a great deal of oxygen; if your circuit panels are encased in a heavy metal box, in many cases closing the box will be sufficient to extinguish a fire.

MAN OVERBOARD

One of the most frightening emergencies that can occur aboard a vessel is a crewmember or other person falling overboard. Although man-overboard (MOB) drills have been a routine element of boating courses for many decades, they have been largely overlooked by many otherwise responsible powerboat and sailboat operators.

In recent years, on-the-water research on sailboats and powerboats alike has resulted in some dramatic changes to recommended man-overboard techniques. Testing by the Naval Academy Sailing Squadron in Annapolis and the Sailing Foundation of Seattle, Washington, has shown that the priority is getting the boat near the man-overboard victim as soon as possible so that he or she stays in sight of those on deck. Once the person in the water disappears from sight, the odds of a successful rescue are low.

Man-overboard victims face a number of dangers, including panic, injury during the fall, and hypothermia. For those on board the boat, quick thinking and coordinated action are essential to an effective rescue. Control of the situation is most likely to be maintained by those who have prepared themselves with regular drills. For such boaters, the retrieval of the person overboard will be automatic and effective without many shouted orders, and the passage or outing will continue without undue stress.

Immediate Actions

The simplest and most efficient procedure is to follow the four steps below:

1. Shout "MAN OVERBOARD" and keep eyes on the victim. When someone has fallen overboard, immediate action is vital. Any crewmember who sees a person go overboard should immediately and loudly shout, "MAN OVERBOARD STARBOARD" or "MAN OVERBOARD PORT," while at the same time keeping his or her eyes on the victim, pointing emphatically to the person in the water; see

Figure 12-06. This crewmember should not be assigned or accept any other duties.

Every second counts; this is an all-hands-on-deck procedure. The other crewmembers on board should put on approved PFDs and harnesses. (The last thing you want is another person overboard to recover.) All crewmembers should come on deck to assist in the maneuvers. Some crew will be assigned exact duties while others will automatically add eyes on the victim.

2. Simultaneously, throw over a man-overboard rig. One crewmember will jettison the rig—depending on the particular equipment aboard. This might range from a PFD to a sophisticated man-overboard module containing a single-person life raft with a drogue to slow down its drift, a life vest, and 8-foot pole, a strobe light, a radio beacon, survival food, etc.

For most boats, however, a practical and effective system is a buoyant pole at least 8 feet long, with its top marked by a large international orange flag and a water-activated strobe light and a weight at the other end. Such a rig usually includes a horseshoe life ring, a whistle, and a small drogue. It is highly visible, and serves a double purpose: It focuses the action so that both the skipper of the boat and the victim will try to aim for the lighted pole

Figure 12-06 Constant vigilance is essential in a man-overboard rescue. Anyone who sees the person fall should shout immediately and loudly, "Man overboard, starboard (or port)." Make sure that one or more crewmembers keep the victim in sight at all times.

The rig must be launched quickly—in a matter of seconds. If you do not have such a man-overboard rig, throw the buoyant device that can be deployed the fastest—for example, a United States Coast Guard-approved cockpit cushion (ideally, high-visibility red or orange) or a quick-release life ring. Throw the device upwind of the victim so that it can blow toward him or her. (Other boats use a Lifesling or other patented recovery device, which should be used according to the manufacturer's specific instructions.)

In addition, three other tasks should be assigned: One crewmember should note compass heading, wind speed, wind direction, and time. Another crewmember should be issuing a Pan-Pan radio call (see page 411) to alert both the Coast Guard and other boats in the vicinity of the emergency. Finally, throwing a constant line of floating debris will aid in tracking the victim.

Most electronic navigation devices, such as a GPS or Loran receiver, will have a "MOB" button on the front panel. Press this immediately to record the latitude and longitude (or Loran readings) of the position where the person went overboard. Many of these devices will automatically display a course back to the scene of the incident.

3. Also, simultaneously the helmsman should stop the boat's forward progress as soon as possible and then quickly reverse course.

• On a powerboat, go briefly into reverse to slow down and at the same time turn toward the victim in a simple circle.

In a study conducted by the Seattle Sailing Foundation's Safety at Sea Committee, 300 actual live-victim recoveries were made. After testing four different maneuvers for boats under power, the Committee found that this simple turn—involving an immediate reduced-speed return—meets all of the criteria for small craft man-overboard rescue. It keeps the boat close to the victim, and is the safest, most reliable, and quickest of all the methods tried—regardless of the experience of the operator.

At night or in reduced visibility, and when you are not sure when the person fell overboard, the Williamson Turn, see **Figure 12-07**, might be your best way of reversing course: Put the helm hard

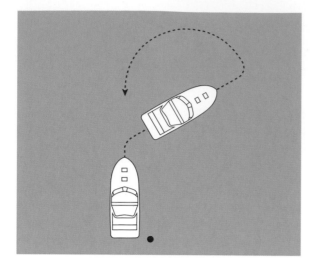

Figure 12-07 The Williamson Turn, a traditional rescue technique, is usually the method of choice for a motorboat when the location of the person in the water is uncertain. This method is also used in compass compensation, as described in Chapter 13.

over, turning toward the side (if known) over which the person fell overboard, until your heading has changed 60 degrees. Then quickly reverse the rudder and come around 240 degrees.

You should then be heading back on the exact reciprocal course.

• On a sailboat, it is always best to head into the wind immediately, using the Quick-Stop method shown in **Figure 12-08.** (Even if you opt to start your engine, continue, at least initially, under sail. Dropping the sails costs precious time and sacrifices some control of the boat.)

If the spinnaker is set, lead the guy forward to the forestay, round up into the wind and haul the sheet tight. Drop the halyard (or cut it, if need be) and collect the spinnaker under the boom and into the hatch. Do not worry about neatness; only the speed of the recovery is important.

In a case where the MOB marker has clearly been launched some time after the person has fallen overboard, it may be best to jibe, as this maneuver has a greater likelihood of reversing course with the fastest speed, moving the boat nearer the person in the water. (Remember that the victim may drift downwind, especially in large waves.)

After Reaching the Victim

1. Getting closer to the victim. Under power, you can motor slowly alongside the victim, aiming just to windward or leeward according to your judgment. The direction is controversial: If coming from windward in high winds and wave action, you may drift over the victim. Otherwise, in general, recovery is easier if you come from windward; see **Table 12-2.**

Plan to get no closer than 10 feet, and to reach a dead slow speed as you draw alongside. Remember that a boat traveling at more than one knot is impossible to either hang onto or stay with, even if a line is thrown from the deck.

If you are sailing to the victim, you may choose one of the two options described below; both methods also help to steady the deck for the actual recovery. (If you are unfamiliar with any of the sailing terms used here, refer to Chapter 8 and/or the Glossary, Appendix G).

• The Rod-Stop Method. If you are on a close reach, use the "Rod-Stop Method," named for the well-known sailor and yacht designer Rod Stephens. As you approach the person in the water, dowse, roll up or luff the jib. Cast off the main sheet and tie a preventer to the boom, bringing the boom all the way out to leeward. Hold the boom down and flatten the sail, using

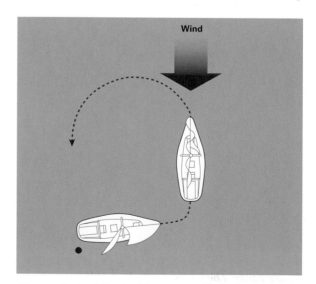

Figure 12-08 The Quick-Stop method of rescue stops a sailboat's forward progress by immediately heading into the wind and tacking back to the person overboard.

the boom vang, cunningham, and outhaul. The sail will fill at one moment on one side, at another moment on the other side, moving the boat ever so lightly forward. To get underway again just let go of the preventer and trim the sails.

• Heaving-to. Another option—if the boat is either close-hauled or on a close reach—is to "heave-to" until you reach the person overboard. (Heaving-to, described in Chapter 10, involves setting the sails so that a boat makes little headway.) Then you can either tack, leaving the jib backed, or stay on the same tack and haul the jib sheet to back it. The boat will then stop and keep going forward slightly.

2. Recovering the person overboard. One way to quickly recover your victim is to use the increasingly popular MOB retrieval system called the Lifesling. This patented product features a padded sling at the end of a long line that you tow behind your boat, moving around in a circle until the victim can grab it in order to place under his or her arms for hoisting and retrieval, as shown in **Figure 12-09.**

Figure 12-09 *The Lifesling is a system that greatly increases the chance of rescuing a conscious victim. In order to recover an unconscious person, another crewmember must enter the water to position the sling on the victim for hoisting aboard.*

WINDWARD VERSUS LEEWARD APPROACH

	Advantages	Disadvantages
Windward	• Creates a lee for the victim. • Ease of throwing a line or horseshoe ring. • Best position from which a swimmer can assist victim.	• Wave action can suddenly throw a smaller boat on victim with disastrous results. • A fast-drifting boat can push a victim under water.
Leeward	• Victim is protected from the boat going over or pounding on top of him. • Close enough to pick up victim.	• Wave action can throw victim against the boat. • Difficulty of staying to leeward. • Boat may drift away faster than victim. • Difficulty of throwing line or horseshoe ring against wind to victim. • If victim is unconscious or injured, a swimmer might have to fight heavy waves to reach him or her.

Table 12-2 *The direction of approach to a person in the water is controversial. Determine what is best for your craft and practice man-overboard drills often. Make sure that you consider various wind and wave conditions, and vary the approach accordingly.*

Whether you use a Lifesling or another method of retrieval, getting an exhausted, heavy victim on deck can be quite a challenge. In most cases, the person in the water will not be able to climb aboard due to extreme fatigue and waterlogged clothing. This stage can have tragic consequences if not acted upon efficiently and immediately. You must make a quick decision as to whether the recovery will be active or passive, as described below.

• **In an active recovery,** the victim is able to assist in getting on deck. You can use a sturdy ladder amidships. (Beware of using the transom; the victim could be pulled under the stern.) You can also rig two or three different lengths of line between a stanchion and another stanchion or a cleat, forming a makeshift ladder. Another alternative is to rig a line from a fixed point amidships, so that it reaches below water level, then lead it back around a stanchion to the windlass. Use this line as a lift to help the victim aboard. (Watch toes and limbs so as not to be caught against the hull.)

• **In a passive recovery,** however, the victim may be hypothermic, exhausted, or injured. (When falling overboard, a person often hits the lifelines and grabs on, dislocating a shoulder.) Or, even worse, the person overboard may be unconscious. If the victim is a child or slight person, two or more strong adults may be able to lift him or her on board. But if the victim is a full-size adult with waterlogged clothes, you will need a mechanical advantage.

On a powerboat, a safety line may help; otherwise, try a block and tackle. Unless you are certain of being able to come back on board, do not go over the side, even wearing a PFD. If you must enter the water, it is absolutely essential that you wear a PFD—for added buoyancy and to keep both hands free and ready to use. In a small boat, there is also a danger of capsizing while recovering, so take special care.

On a sailboat, recovery can be easier because of the opportunities of using the boom with a block and tackle (the boom vang); be careful to prevent the boom from flogging back and forth while winching up. Another way is to lift the victim in the belly of the jib. (Although some people recovered this way have experienced claustrophobia, they were brought aboard nonetheless.) A third alternative is to use the main halyard, if the mainsail is down, or any other halyard that can be a lead to a sturdy winch.

OTHER EMERGENCIES

The most-likely major emergencies have been listed and discussed here—but there are others. Study your craft in detail and try to visualize what could go wrong—and then prepare plans for dealing with such occurrences. Some of the more typical emergencies are covered below.

Deadheads & Shipping Containers

A deadhead is a log or large piece of timber that has become so waterlogged that little buoyancy remains. It usually floats with one end down, showing only a few inches of the other end; it barely rises and falls and is extremely difficult to spot, particularly from a fast boat or any boat at night. Deadheads are more dangerous than rocks or reefs because they are uncharted and may appear almost anywhere. The only action a boater can take is precautionary; maintain a sharp lookout while underway.

A generally similar hazard is a freight container that has fallen overboard. Every year literally

Figure 12-10 Many thousands of freight containers are transported on all oceans all the time. Some are lost overboard in violent storms. Most of these will sink, but some will continue to float for lengthy periods; while floating, they constitute a serious hazard to small craft.

WHAT TO DO IF YOU FALL OVERBOARD: SURVIVAL FLOATING

Just as important as acquiring the skills necessary for rescuing a person overboard is a knowledge of how to help yourself if you are the person overboard. The following tips can help you stay afloat until you are recovered.

• Keep your clothes on. If your shoes are light enough for you to swim comfortably, leave them on. If they weigh you down, however, remove them. Remove any heavy objects from any pockets in your clothing.

• If you can float on your back fairly easily, save energy by doing so. Kick only when necessary.

• While signaling for help or waiting for rescue, tread water to stay in an upright position, moving your hands back and forth and using a kick that requires little energy.

Remember, the more you move around in cold water, the quicker your body temperature will drop, and the faster hypothermia can set in.

• In warm water, conserve your energy by using the facedown floating technique shown below, called survival floating. Each move you make should be slow and easy.

• Every second counts. As soon as a heaved line reaches you, quickly tie a bowline (refer to Chapter 23) around your chest. If a Lifesling reaches you, slip into it immediately; refer to **Figure 12-09**.

• As the rescue boat approaches, stay away from both the stern and the bow of the boat.

• When trying to board the boat, don't rush; it is important to make effective use of your remaining energy.

With your mouth above the water's surface, hold your breath, put your face in the water, let your arms and legs dangle for several seconds. Then tilt your head back to raise your face above the surface, only high enough for your mouth to clear the water. As you raise your face, exhale. As your mouth clears the water, gently press down with your arms and bring your legs together. This will help keep your mouth above water. Take another breath and repeat the cycle.

thousands of them fall from the decks of container ships in rough seas; see **Figure 12-10**. These large objects, roughly 8 feet (2.4 m) square and 20 to 40 feet (6 to 12 m) in length, are designed to flood and sink if this happens—but that doesn't always happen! Those that remain floating are a real hazard to small craft, especially at night. If your boating takes you into or across shipping lanes, add "floating containers" to your list of dangers that you must guard against.

Dismasting

A broken sailboat mast can result from improper tension on the standing rigging or—as in the case of ocean racing—pushing the boat past its designed performance limits. In any case, this emergency demands immediate attention. Make sure that all crewmembers are wearing PFDs, then direct them to take quick action to clear and secure all stray lines, rigging, sails, and other loose gear—anything that could foul the propeller, or create such a drag as to affect the controllability of the boat. That done, now it is safe to turn on the auxiliary engine.

One great danger of dismasting is severe damage to your hull; see **Figure 12-11.** In this case you must decide immediately to cut the mast loose and get free of it, or to try to save it. In the latter case, it is essential to secure the mast tightly against the hull and cushion it with a mattress or pillows.

Some resourceful sailors can jury-rig a new spar—from the mast stump or a whisker pole, for example—in order to catch at least some wind.

Swamping, Foundering & Capsizing

A boat is "swamped" when it fills with water from over the side. The causes can vary, from large waves coming over the gunwales or the transom to reduced freeboard because the boat is over-loaded. Or swamping may result from a sudden squall or a heavy wake from a larger vessel. Small wooden boats have enough buoyancy to remain afloat, and will not founder—sink—when swamped; most small fiberglass boats have buoyancy built into them in the form of plastic foam

Figure 12-12 Small fiberglass craft have built-in added buoyancy so that when swamped they will not sink, but will remain floating in a level attitude. As long as possible, stay with your boat—you will be more likely to be located and rescued sooner.

flotation material; see **Figure 12-12.** Use anything at hand to bail out the water; otherwise, hand-paddle to the nearest shore.

A boat is "capsized" when it is knocked down so it lies on its side in the water or turns over—a frequent occurrence among small sailboats that are especially sensitive to sudden changes in the wind. Most small boats will remain in that position, unless righted, and will float enough to support any crew that had been on board.

Having capsized or swamped, it is important to remain calm and conserve energy. The general rule is to ensure that all crewmembers are wearing PFDs and that they stay with the boat; there may be possibilities of righting it, and rescuers will be able to find you more easily. Leave the boat only if it is headed toward a hazard. If the capsized boat is a small centerboard sailboat, improve your chances of recovery by trying to keep it from turning over. Get into the water immediately and stand on the centerboard, providing lever action; this is a technique taught in most basic sailing

Figure 12-11 While just being dismasted is bad enough, the spars and sails in the water alongside the craft can be a hazard to the hull and must be cut away or secured without delay.

courses. If possible, have a crewmember attach a life jacket or other flotation device to the end of the mast. If you can, remove all sails before attempting to right the boat.

Take precautions against swamping and capsizing: Watch that loaded items do not shift from side to side; guard against too much power or speed on turns, and the wash of large boats. Take waves head on, or fine on the bow, at low speeds, giving the hull a chance to ride over rather than dive into them. Do not broach.

HELICOPTER RESCUE

The U.S. Coast Guard uses helicopters as well as surface craft for search and rescue work. The USCG has equipped fixed-wing aircraft with droppable VHF radios. This equipment may be delivered to the distressed vessel if the Coast Guard is unable to establish communication.

When Coast Guard assistance is provided by helicopter rather than surface craft, the distressed boat's skipper must know how to participate in the action. Such a rescue is most effective with the advance preparations described below.

Prior to helicopter arrival

• If possible, listen continuously to VHF Channel 16 (156.8 MHz) or other specified frequency.

• Select and clear the most suitable hoist area. For sailboats and powerboats, this often means clearing a dinghy or raft from the deck, and towing it astern.

• If the hoist is to be performed in the dark, light the pickup areas as well as possible. Avoid shining any lights on the helicopter, however; this could blind the pilot. If there are obstructions in the vicinity, focus a light on them, making the pilot aware of their positions.

• To facilitate the helicopter pilot's approach, make sure that he or she knows the pickup area location before the helicopter arrives.

• Remember that there will be a high noise level and significant downwash under the helicopter, so conversation between the deck crew will be almost impossible. Arrange a set of hand signals between those who will be assisting.

Assisting the Hoist

• Change the boat's course, permitting the craft to ride as easily as possible with the wind on the bow, preferably on the port bow. The helicopter pilot rides on the starboard side of the helicopter, which helps to give him or her the best view of the boat; see **Figure 12-13.**

• Reduce speed, if necessary, to ease the boat's motion, but continue to maintain steerageway.

• On a small craft, there is not enough deck space to permit hoisting directly from the boat. In that case, you must assist the victim into the dinghy for hoisting from there.

• If you do not have radio contact with the helicopter, give a "thumbs up" signal when you are in all respects ready for the hoist; use a flashlight at night.

Figure 12-13 Helicopter rescues are often made by the U.S. Coast Guard. Boaters being so aided must assist in the operation. Know what to do, and what not to do. Even though a helicopter may not be a part of your drill, practice what actions you would take if it were an actual rescue.

MOB RADIOBEACON

Microelectronics has come to the rescue of the man-overboard situation. A radio transmitter operating on 121.5 MHz can transmit a signal to a receiver on board the boat that will both alert the crew that someone has fallen overboard—especially desirable for craft with small crews where there may be only one person on deck—and also provide signals for a direction finder on the boat to find the MOB when it turns around and goes back. The transmitter may be actuated either manually or automatically upon immersion in water (it is not affected by rain or spray). The device may be a small clip-on unit or even a fully functionally wristwatch that be only slightly larger than normal. The range is said to be about a mile to a surface vessel and more than 10 miles to an aircraft, such as a searching helicopter. The internal battery will operate the device for approximately six hours under normal circumstances.

The watch type of this device is waterproof to 150 feet (46 m) and can be useful to a diver who might surface out of sight of his dive boat.

There is also a new device known as a personal locator beacon; see Chapter 20, page 706.

• Avoid static shock by allowing the basket or litter to touch down on the deck prior to handling.

• If a trail line is dropped by the helicopter, use it to guide the basket or litter to the deck; *do not fasten it to the boat.*

• Place the person to be lifted in the basket, sitting with hands and arms completely inside, or strap him or her in the litter. If possible, the person should be wearing a life jacket. Signal the helicopter hoist operator when ready for hoist; ask the person in the basket or on the litter to nod his head if he is able, and deck personnel to give a "thumbs-up" signal.

• When the individual is ready to be hoisted, hook up the cable and signal the hoist operator that you are ready to hoist. Steady the litter to keep it from swinging or turning.

• If necessary to take a litter away from the hoist point, unhook the hoist cable, keeping it free for the helicopter to haul in. *Do not secure the cable to the vessel or attempt to move a litter without unhooking it.*

• If a trail line is attached to the litter, use it to steady the litter, while maintaining moderate tension. Make sure that crewmembers' feet are clear of the line.

ABANDONING SHIP

The act of abandoning ship is filled with potential hazards and should be undertaken only if your vessel is fully on fire or is in imminent danger of sinking. Abandon ship only as a last resort: In many cases, even vessels that have been seriously damaged will remain afloat for hours, even days, due to their natural buoyancy or to air trapped inside their hulls or superstructures.

Preparations for Abandoning

At the first indication that a fire or a breach of your hull's integrity may become grave enough to require abandoning ship, mentally run through the procedure, as discussed here, and alert your crew that you are considering that extreme course of action. Give the abandon-ship order only when you are sure that no other option is viable.

• As soon as you even wonder if you might have to abandon ship, make certain that all crewmembers are warmly dressed and wearing personal flotation devices. In waters below 60°F (15°C), crewmembers should also put on immersion suits if they are available. Remember that exposure to hypothermia (extreme loss of body heat) is one of the greatest dangers. Long pants, long-sleeved shirts, sweaters and jackets—even if they are soaked—can help preserve valuable body heat. If you have to order your crew into the raft, they could very well wind up in the water, and warm clothing and a PFD could prove to be the difference between life and death.

In offshore situations, all the PFDs aboard should be Type 1 and, at a minimum, should be fitted with reflective patches and a whistle. Even better, they should also be equipped with strobe-type personal rescue lights and mini-B EPIRBs (see Chapter 20).

• Instruct a trained crewmember to stand by the life raft and prepare to launch it. If you carry your life raft belowdecks and/or it must be manually inflated, the crewmember should know where it is located as well as how to inflate it quickly, and that it must be inflated on deck rather than belowdecks or in the cockpit.

Actions When Abandoning

• The moment you decide to abandon ship, transmit a Mayday distress call and message (see page 410). After transmitting the distress message, wait 30 seconds for any vessel receiving it to respond. Then, if there is no response, transmit the distress call and message a second time over that same channel. If there is still no answer, retransmit the distress call and message on any channel frequently used in the area. A good second choice of VHF would be Channel 22A (157.1 MHz), which is the primary USCG liaison channel. Good choices of SSB frequencies would be 2.182, 4.125, and 6.215 MHz (all simplex, transmit and receive on the same frequency); these are monitored by all U.S. Coast Guard long-range communications facilities.

• Gather emergency supplies. If you are boating offshore, you should have an abandon-ship bag accessible at all times, stowed where you can grab it quickly on your way to the life raft. Such a bag should include signaling equipment; medical supplies; provisions, including at least a half-gallon of fresh water per person or a hand-operated reverse-osmosis watermaker or solar still; clothing and fishing supplies. Also make sure that your vessel's EPIRB (see Chapter 20) gets into your life raft.

• Make certain that your life raft is tethered to the boat, and launch it. In heavy seas, launch to leeward amidships—the boat's most stable point. Once you have launched the raft, one crewmember should steady it while a second crewmember boards.

• Load the rest of your crew into the life raft and have them fend it off from your vessel while you load your emergency gear, to avoid snagging the life raft on anything that might puncture it. If at all possible, the crew should step or jump directly from your vessel into the life raft rather than jumping into the water and then trying to crawl up into it. This not only lessens the danger of crewmembers being swept away from the raft, but in cold waters, it also reduces the danger of hypothermia.

• Make sure your EPIRB is securely attached to your life raft. Activate it as soon as you enter the raft, and leave it activated. If you have reason to believe that someone is within visual range, fire a red meteor or parachute flare as soon as you depart your vessel.

• If your boat is afire or about to sink, cut the lines tethering the life raft to it. But if it is merely awash, remember that an awash vessel is a larger target to spot than a lone life raft. Keep the life raft tethered to the boat as long as possible. (In heavy seas, free the heaving line and pay out the full length of the raft's tether—keeping the raft away from the boat to avoid a puncture or being trapped beneath the boat.)

The Mariner's Compass

How a Compass Works • How They Should Be Selected & Installed
How They Should Be Used • Variation & Deviation • Compass Compensation

The marine compass is a remarkable instrument, and the single most important navigational tool on any boat. It requires no power source; it guides you on all oceans and waterways, in fair weather and foul.

Your boat's safety may well depend on her compass, and on your ability to use it properly. On long runs out of sight of land or aids to navigation, your compass enables you to steer accurately to your destination. In poor visibility you may have no other means of keeping on your course. Knowing the limitations of your magnetic compass is essential, but within these, you should trust it to guide you safely.

HOW A COMPASS WORKS

Magnetism is a phenomenon that can only be known from its effects. It is a basic natural force and one that is essential to a vast number of devices, from incredibly complex electronic equipment to your boat's simple magnetic compass.

Magnetism appears as a physical force between two objects of metal, usually iron or an alloy of iron and other metals, at least one of which has been previously magnetized and has become a MAGNET. The area around a magnet in which its effect can be detected is called a MAGNETIC FIELD. This is commonly pictured as innumerable LINES OF FORCE, but these are purely a convention for illustration and actual lines, as such, do not exist; see **Figure 13-01,** left, which is a typical illustration of a BAR MAGNET with some of the lines of force shown. (An electric current flowing in a wire also creates a magnetic field; more on this later.)

Basic Law of Magnetism

Each magnet, regardless of size, has two POLES where the magnetic action appears to be concentrated. These poles have opposite characteristics and are termed NORTH and SOUTH; refer to **Figure 13-01,** left. The basic law of magnetism is very simple: Opposites attract; likes repel. Thus an N pole is attracted to an S pole, but repels another N.

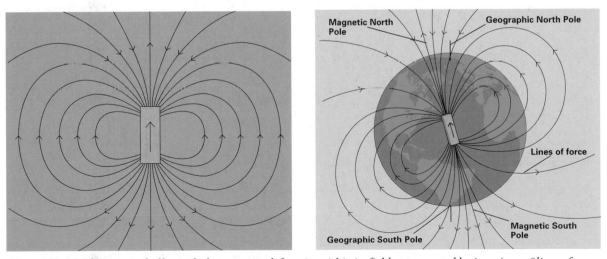

Figure 13-01 *The external effects of a bar magnet, left, exist within its field, represented by imaginary "lines of force." The magnetic properties of the earth can be visualized as a powerful bar magnet, right, at its center, but not aligned with the earth's axis of rotation, the geographic poles.*

The Earth

The earth as a whole has magnetic properties and can be thought of as having a powerful bar magnet near its center, refer to **Figure 13-01**, right. The magnetic properties of the earth are not uniformly distributed, and as a consequence its magnetic poles are *not* at the locations of geographic poles. The magnetic pole in the northern hemisphere is named the NORTH MAGNETIC POLE because of its general location; actually, it is more than 600 miles from the North geographic pole, the pole of the earth's rotation. The SOUTH MAGNETIC POLE is the one located nearly 1500 miles from the South geographic pole.

The Basic Compass Principle

The basic principle of a magnetic compass is simple—a small bar magnet freely suspended in the earth's magnetic field will align itself parallel to the lines of force of that field, and thus establish a DIRECTION. The end of a magnet that points generally north is termed its NORTH POLE although it is actually the "north-seeking" pole; the other end is its SOUTH POLE. Normally, the compass will not point to geographic north, nor even provide the correct direction to the North magnetic pole. It gives, however, a reliable and consistent direction, and for the purposes of navigation this can be considered as being relatively constant over a period of several years.

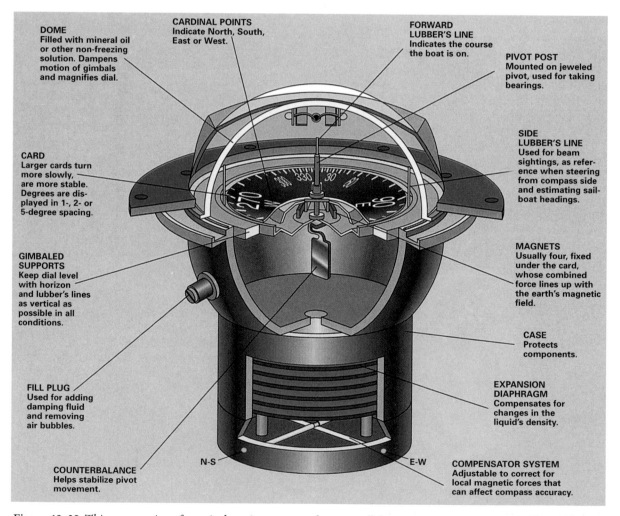

DOME
Filled with mineral oil or other non-freezing solution. Dampens motion of gimbals and magnifies dial.

CARDINAL POINTS
Indicate North, South, East or West.

FORWARD LUBBER'S LINE
Indicates the course the boat is on.

PIVOT POST
Mounted on jeweled pivot, used for taking bearings.

CARD
Larger cards turn more slowly, are more stable. Degrees are displayed in 1-, 2- or 5-degree spacing.

SIDE LUBBER'S LINE
Used for beam sightings, as reference when steering from compass side and estimating sailboat headings.

GIMBALED SUPPORTS
Keep dial level with horizon and lubber's lines as vertical as possible in all conditions.

MAGNETS
Usually four, fixed under the card, whose combined force lines up with the earth's magnetic field.

CASE
Protects components.

FILL PLUG
Used for adding damping fluid and removing air bubbles.

EXPANSION DIAPHRAGM
Compensates for changes in the liquid's density.

COUNTERBALANCE
Helps stabilize pivot movement.

N-S

E-W

COMPENSATOR SYSTEM
Adjustable to correct for local magnetic forces that can affect compass accuracy.

Figure 13-02 This cross-section of a typical marine compass shows parallel permanent magnets mounted beneath the card. The magnets and card are attached to a light frame, which is supported on a pivot. The space inside the compass is filled with a liquid to dampen oscillation, and a diaphragm to allow for expansion and contraction with temperature changes. Other features, not labeled here, include a protective hood over the compass dome and a night light, usually red.

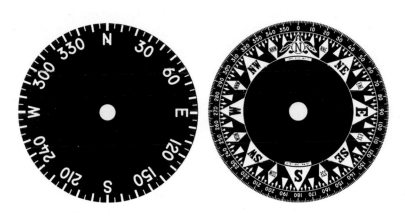

Figure 13-03 Compass cards are graduated in various styles; those used on boats at 5-degree intervals, left, with the 10-degree marks heavier for easier reading. Numbers are usually at 30-degree intervals, and cardinal headings—North, East, South, West—may be shown as letters rather than numbers. Compasses for larger vessels may have finer graduations, two degrees or even one. Intercardinal and combination headings are often shown, right; on the largest cards, "by-points" and even individual points, half-points, and quarter-points maybe shown. See page 436 for explanation of the "point" system.

The navigator usually has at hand information and rapid means for converting the reading of his compass to true geographic directions. He knows that if any local influences from magnetic geologic formations, iron or steel objects, and electrical wires can be neutralized (or measured and recorded), his compass will be a dependable magnetic direction finder, needing neither mechanical nor electrical power.

COMPASS CONSTRUCTION

The construction of a typical compass is shown in **Figure 13-02;** it has more than one bar magnet from which to derive its force to align with the earth's magnetic field. A circular disk of light, nonmagnetic material is mounted on a wire frame, also of nonmagnetic material. This is the CARD of the compass; it is marked around its circumference with graduations from which the direction can be read. Two or more magnets are attached to the frame, aligned with the N-S markings on the card.

Centrally placed under the frame is a BEARING that rides on a hard sharp point called the PIVOT; this in turn is supported from the outer case, which is the BOWL of the compass. A cover of transparent material, the DOME, is rigidly fastened to the top of the bowl with a leakproof seal; this may be either flat or hemispherical. Through a pluggable opening, the bowl is filled with a special

nonfreezing liquid. An EXPANSION DIAPHRAGM in the lower part of the bowl allows the fluid to expand and contract with temperature changes without bubbles being formed.

A FLOAT may be attached under the frame to partially suspend the card and magnets, and thus reduce friction and wear on the bearing and pivot. The compass liquid also helps to dampen out any rapid oscillations or overswings of the card when direction is changed or rough weather is encountered. GIMBALS, when provided, either internally or externally, are intended to help the compass card remain essentially level despite any rolling or pitching of the vessel. The best arrangement is two sets of rings, one pivoted on a fore-and-aft axis and the other on an athwartship axis.

Compass Cards

The card of a modern compass is divided into DEGREES, 360° to a full circle; the degrees increase *clockwise* around the card. North is 0° and the scale continues on around through 90° (East), 180° (South), and 270° (West) back to North, which is 360° or 0°. The spacing between graduations on the card will vary with the size of the compass, but 5-degree spacings are typical for most small-craft compasses, see **Figure 13-03,** left, with some larger compasses having 2-degree cards. Ships will normally have compasses with cards having one-degree divisions; see **Figure 13-03,** right; note that this card is also marked

Figure 13-04 When a compass is designed for front viewing, the lubber's line is on the side nearest the helmsman. The readings increase to the left, and a person accustomed to a conventional card must take care to avoid confusion when reading values between marks. These compasses are sometimes found on smaller craft. The bulkhead-mounted compass can be read from the top or front; the scale below the bowl indicates the angle of heel.

with the "points" of the compass (see , page 436). Numbers may be shown every ten degrees from 10°to 350°; every 20 degrees from 20° to 340°; or every 30 degrees from 30° to 330°.

Over or just outside the card is the index mark against which the graduations are read. This is the main or forward LUBBER'S LINE; it may be a mark on the inside of the bowl or it may be a part of the internal gimbal system; see **Figure 13-04,** and refer to **Figure 13-02.** There may also be additional marks at 45° and/or 90° from the main mark.

The lubber's line should be close enough to the card so that there is minimal PARALLAX ERROR, the change in the *apparent* value of a reading when viewing from one side of the compass as compared to reading the card from directly to the rear.

On some compass cards, the *width* of the major degree marks and the lubber's line have significance. If the lubber's line is one degree in width, for example, that fact can be used to estimate values that are intermediate between markings on the compass card; refer to **Figure 13-05.**

Front-Reading Compasses

Some smaller and medium-size compasses are designed for mounting with direct reading from the front rather than from above or nearly so. Here the lubber's line is nearer the helmsman rather than on the far side of the card. This results in the larger numbers being to the left of the lubber's line rather than to the right; refer to **Figure 13-04.** This fact can be confusing to a skipper accustomed to a more conventional "top-reading" compass, and must always be kept in mind when determining an exact value between the numbered marks on the card. Some compasses can be read from above using the lubber's line at the front of the card, or directly viewed, using the lubber's line nearer the user—great care must be taken to understand the use of this style of compass; **see Figure 13-06.**

The Point System

In olden days, compass cards were subdivided into POINTS—32 points to a complete circle, one point equal to 11¼ degrees (or 11°15'); refer also to **Figure 1-37.** These were named, not numbered, and a seaman early learned to "box the compass" by naming all the points. There were also half and quarter-points when a smaller subdivision was needed.

The CARDINAL points, North, East, South, and West—and the INTERCARDINAL points, Northeast, Southeast, Southwest, and Northwest—are still in common use as rough directions and as descriptions of wind directions.

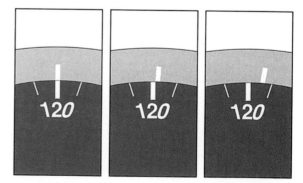

Figure 13-05 On some compasses, the width of the lubber's line equals 1° on the card. The center drawing above shows how this feature can be used to read one degree either side of a main graduation. As shown at right, a reading slightly more or less than halfway between marks would indicate two or three degrees more or less than the nearest graduation.

Figure 13-06 *Compasses offer a variety of mounting possibilities. The light-shielding hood, center, cuts off excessive sunlight to aid in reading the compass. Most modern compasses have two sets of internal compensating magnets, usually at the bottom of the binnacle.*

The COMBINATION points, such as NNE, ENE, and so on, are sometimes used for general directions, but the BY-POINTS, N by E (North by East), NNE by N, NNE by E, and their like, are rarely used.

The combination point system is now otherwise effectively obsolete. For those who do not wish to forget the past, or want to learn points for ease in steering sailboats, a table of conversions between the point and degree systems is provided as **Table 13-1.**

Some modern compass cards label the intercardinal points as well as the cardinal headings, and a few mark all points and even quarter-points; refer to **Figure 13-03,** right. The examples and problems that follow, however, will all be in terms of degrees. Note, however, that some statements of direction will be in degrees and minutes, there being 60 minutes in one degree. Minutes will have to be converted to decimal fractions for calculations.

Spherical Compasses

When the top over a compass is hemispherical, the dome serves to magnify and make the card appear much larger than it actually is. This aids in reading it closely, making it possible to steer a better

CONVERSION OF POINTS & DEGREES

Direction	Points	Degrees
North to East	N	0°00′
	N by E	11°15′
	NNE	22°30′
	NE by N	33°45′
	NE	45°00′
	NE by E	56°15′
	ENE	67°30′
	E by N	78°45′
East to South	E	90°00′
	E by S	101°15′
	ESE	112°30′
	SE by E	123°45′
	SE	135°00′
	SE by S	146°15′
	SSE	157°30′
	S by E	168°45′
South to West	S	180°00′
	S by W	191°15′
	SSW	202°30′
	SW by S	213°45′
	SW	225°00′
	SW by W	236°15′
	WSW	247°30′
	W by S	258°45′
West to North	W	270°00′
	W by N	281°15′
	WNW	292°30′
	NW by W	303°45′
	NW	315°00′
	NW by N	326°15′
	NNW	337°30′
	N by W	348°45′
	N	360°00′

Table 13-1 *The point system was in common use before World War II. Few boaters now will learn to "box the compass" through all its 32 points, but the major directions are still familiar and very useful. In descending order, the points are known as cardinal (N, E, S, and W), intercardinal (such as NE and SE), combination points (such as NNE and ENE), and by-points (such as N by E, NE by N, etc.).*

course or take a better bearing. On some compasses with a hemispherical cover, the card itself is concave or dish-shaped, rather than flat. This feature, combined with the shape of the dome, makes it possible to read the compass from a lower angle and at considerably greater distances; it is not necessary to stand more or less directly over the compass to read it. A compass with such a card of 5-inch (12.7 cm) "apparent diameter" (actually somewhat smaller in diameter) can be read from as far as 10 feet (3m) or more away.

If the compass as a whole is spherical, bowl as well as dome, there is a considerable gain in stability of the card. The effect of a whole sphere is to permit the fluid inside to remain relatively undisturbed by roll, pitch, or yaw; the result is superior performance in rough seas.

Some compasses have special features for use on sailboats. These include more extensive gimbaling so as to permit free movement of the card at considerable angles of heel, and additional lubber's lines at 45 degrees and 90 degrees to either side of the one aligned with the craft's keel as an aid in determining when to tack. These additional lubber's lines are also useful when the helmsman sits to one side, as when sailing with a tiller. They can also be used to sight distant objects to determine distance off.

Binnacles

Compasses are sometimes mounted directly on or through a horizontal surface. More often, however, the compass is mounted in an outer supporting case called a BINNACLE. This can be a simple case, sometimes with a light-shielding hood, which is then fastened down; refer to **Figure 13-06**. Or it can be a complete pedestal stand as might be used on larger sailboats. On smaller sailboats, a compass is sometimes mounted on a vertical, or near-vertical bulkhead forward of the helm position.

The outside of the binnacle or compass case, or any mounting bracket, should be black, preferably with a dull finish. There should be no shiny chromed parts that could reflect sunlight into the eyes of the helmsman.

Lighting

When compasses are lighted for night use, the lighting system is often a part of the compass case, cover, or binnacle. The light should be red in color and its intensity at a suitable level. If the light is not red, or is too bright, there is a risk of loss of the helmsman's night vision—this will make it more difficult, or even impossible, for him to see other vessels, aids to navigation, or other objects. On the other hand, a too-dimly lit compass can be a source of eyestrain and a detriment to good steering. In some installations, a means is provided for varying the intensity of the light; this is a desirable feature.

Internal Compensators

As will be detailed later in this chapter, it usually is *not* possible to have a situation where there are no magnetic effects from iron and steel objects on the boat. The compass must then be COMPENSATED (ADJUSTED) with small additional bar magnets located and polarized so they counteract these unwanted magnetic influences. Such COMPENSATORS may be external to the compass and binnacle, but are more likely to be internal, usually a part of the binnacle unit; refer to **Figures 13-02** and **13-05**, right. Refer to pages 443–444 for more on local magnetic influences and compensation.

SELECTION

Although a compass is a relatively simple mechanism in terms of its construction and operation, it is probably the most important navigational tool on board any boat. Considerable thought should be given to its selection. This is not the place for a hasty decision, or for saving money by buying a small, cheap unit. In fog or night, or any other form of reduced visibility, your compass is the basic instrument that shows direction—*your safety will depend upon it, it has to be right!*

Quality

Almost any new compass will look fine in a store or on board a boat in the quiet motion of a marina slip or at a mooring. But its behavior underway, when the sea makes up and the craft pitches, rolls, and yaws, is of supreme importance. Will the card stick at some angle of heel? Will its motion be jerky, or smooth and easy? Are the card graduations legible and are different headings easily distinguished? Is the compass protected against large temperature changes? What if a bubble appears under its glass that might distract the helmsman? The answers to these questions will depend upon the quality of the compass. Select a compass fully adequate for your expected needs, and if a choice must be made, choose the better quality.

Examine a number of compasses before buying one. Pick them up; tilt and turn them, simulating motions to which they would be subjected in actual use afloat. The card should have a smooth stable reaction, coming to rest without oscillating about the lubber's line. Reasonable tilting, comparable to the rolling and pitching of your boat, should not appreciably affect the reading. In fairness to the compass, however, if it has internal correctors, they must have been zeroed-in before you make these motion tests; see pages 442–443, on zeroing-in.

Size

All too often, a small compass will be selected and installed on a small boat for the simple reason that the boat is just that, small. This is *not* the correct approach. Because the boat is small, it will be subject to greater movement, both in normal operation and in rough waters. A small, cheap compass will have less stability and may even be completely unusable in severe conditions, perhaps just when it is most needed.

A compass for a boat should be as large as the physical limitations of mounting space sensibly allow—and the quality should be just as high as the owner's budget can possibly allow.

Card Selection

In selecting a compass for your boat, pay particular attention to the design of the card. Its graduations should be suited to the intended use. That a large craft may be held on course more easily and precisely than a small one is readily understandable. Thus the larger the vessel, the greater the number of divisions normally found around the outer edge of the card. Skippers of large ocean-going craft seem to prefer cards that can be read directly to two degrees, or even to single degrees.

Studies have shown, however, that subdivisions smaller than five degrees may not be desirable. Cards with finer subdivisions may produce more eyestrain, require a higher intensity of illumination, and may result in greater steering action although no better course is made good. The experiences and preferences of the individual must govern here.

Choosing a Sailboat Compass Card

The helmsman of a sailboat is usually in an unprotected cockpit exposed to the weather. Spray and rain on the glass cover of the binnacle may obscure or distort the markings on the compass card. The smaller and more uniform the markings on the card, the easier it is for the helmsman to confuse one marking for another, lose his place on the card, and wander off course. This is especially true at night or offshore when he has no landmarks to warn him that he has been steering, for example, 055° instead of his intended course of 065°. And when he discovers his error, he may not know for how long he has been off course.

If the pattern on the card shows a large and prominent patch of contrasting color at the cardinal points and an even larger one at "North," even an inexperienced helmsman can steer with surprising accuracy by relying on the general position of this distinctive pattern as his guide, vague and blurry though it may be.

Testing

Although not always reliable, price is generally a fair indicator of quality. There are, however, simple tests that you can make yourself to aid in judging between different units. When making any of these tests, make sure that any other compasses are at least four feet (1.2m) distant.

Test for minimum pivot friction (it should be zero) by turning the compass as a whole until a card graduation mark is exactly aligned with the lubber's line, then bring a small magnet or an iron/steel object just close enough to the compass to cause the card to deflect 2 to 5 degrees to either side. Next, take it well away from the compass quickly, watching the card as you do so. The card should return to its former position *exactly*. This test is completed by drawing the card off to the other side—by moving the magnet or iron/steel object to the other side of the compass. Again the card should return to its initial position when the influence of the external magnet or steel object is removed. (Make sure that the object is moved far enough away each time for a fair test; turn a small magnet end-for-end—the card should not be affected.) Sticky pivots are rare, but they do occur, and the test is too simple and easy to make to omit doing it. Do not purchase a compass that does not pass this test.

Repeat the above procedure, but this time draw the card off to each side about 20 to 30 degrees. Release the external influence abruptly and observe the amount of overswing as the card returns back to, and past, its original setting. A compass with proper dampening will have a minimum overswing and will return to its proper position with a minimum of oscillation about that position.

These tests are relative; there are no absolute values to use as a standard. Thus these tests should be made on comparative basis between several different compasses of the same model and between different models. Be fair, be careful—try to see that comparable tests are made on each compass.

INSTALLATION

The installation of a compass, from initial site selection through to the actual mounting, is of critical importance to its performance. If any step is omitted or is not done carefully, it may never be possible to get the compass properly adjusted for precise navigation. Follow each step in detail and don't rush the work.

Locating the Compass

The first step is selecting the location in which to mount the compass. There are a number of factors to be considered, and some limitations that must be faced. Actually, you should consider where to place the unit *before* you buy the compass.

On Larger Craft

Ideally, the compass should be directly in front of the helmsman, placed so that he can read it

without physical stress whether he sits or stands. Give some thought to comfort in rough weather, and in conditions of poor visibility, day or night. His or her position is fairly well determined by the wheel or tiller. The compass has to be brought into what might be called his "zone of comfort." Too far away, he bends forward to watch it; too close, he bends backward for better vision. Much of the time he may not be only the helmsman but the forward and after lookout as well. So put the compass where he can bring his eyes to it for reading with a minimum of body movement. For the average person, a distance of 22 to 30 inches (56-76 cm) from his eyes with the head tilted forward not more than 20 degrees is about right. Additional details will be found in *ABYC Standard S-17*.

On Smaller Boats

Locating a compass on a small boat may be more of a problem. It must, of course, be located where it can be easily seen by the helmsman, preferably directly before him; see **Figure 13-07**. Such a location may not be physically possible, or it may be subject to undesirable magnetic influences that will cause DEVIATION in the compass readings (see pages 449–450). It may be necessary to locate the compass to one side of the helm position. If so, check carefully for PARALLAX ERROR—the change in *apparent reading* when the compass is viewed from one side as compared with from directly behind. A slight difference in reading, perhaps up

Figure 13-07 Boats smaller than this one nearly always present a major problem in locating a compass due to limited space and a poor magnetic environment. Finding the best location takes ingenuity and patience.

SUMMARY OF SELECTION CRITERIA

When shopping for a compass, choose a quality instrument. Consider the points below, and remember that your compass is the most important navigation tool on board your boat.

• The compass (and binnacle if applicable) should be of a design that can be mounted on board your boat in a location that allows accurate comfortable viewing.

• The card should be easily read and graduated to your preference.

• The card should remain level and not stick through reasonable angles of pitch or roll.

• The card should move, but slightly and uniformly, during any course change (simulated by slowly and smoothly rotating the compass through 90 degrees or more). Some small lag due to the inertia of the card is permissible, but the card should be dead-beat, swinging but once to a steady position, not oscillating about the lubber's line.

• There should not be any significant parallax error when viewed from the side as compared from the rear.

• The compass or its binnacle should have built-in compensating magnets.

• The compass or binnacle should include provision for night lighting. (A means of adjusting the intensity of the light is desirable.)

• The dome should be hemispherically shaped, rather than flat.

• The compass should have a fully internally gimbaled card and lubber's line.

• The compass should be of a design that can be mounted on your boat in the most suitable position for it with easy access to the adjusting screws for the internal compensators.

• The compass should have a metal or rubber expansion bellows or diaphragm in the assembly to prevent bubbles forming in the liquid due to temperature changes.

• The compass or binnacle should be waterproof and have some form of light-shielding hood.

• If the compass is second-hand, it should be very carefully checked.

• Buy a quality instrument and pay the price. This is no place to cut corners; you get what you pay for.

---

to 3 degrees, may be accepted, but more than that, which can easily occur, will result in defective and perhaps dangerous navigation. If you have this mounting problem, check several models of compasses, as some designs will have less parallax error than others.

On All Craft

A compass is often located off the centerline of the boat, and special care *must* be taken to ensure that it is properly aligned. A line running through the center of the card and the lubber's line *must* be parallel with the centerline of the hull; see **Figure 13-08**.

On some boats that are either wide or are steered from one side or the other—such as catamarans, racing sailboats, or even workboats—

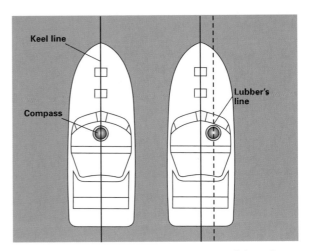

Figure 13-08 If the compass is not mounted directly over the keel line, take care to make sure that a line through the center of the card and the lubber's line is exactly parallel to the centerline of the boat.

additional compasses can be mounted at either side to make viewing more direct and accurate.

Zeroing-In

A modern compass with internal compensators should be ZEROED-IN before being mounted on a boat. Zeroing-in is nothing more than adjusting the internal compensating magnets so that they have no effect on the compass. A compass that is subject only to the earth's field has no need for compensation; there is no deviation to be removed. Thus before being installed, any deviation caused by the improper position of the compensators themselves must be removed so that the unit can go on board ready for whatever magnetic influences the boat may have. With these magnets properly set, any deviation will come from external sources. A quality compass will have been shipped with its internal compensating magnets set to "zero," but check before installation to be sure that the settings have not been changed. The slots of the screws for the N-S and E-W compensators should be horizontal, but aligning the screw slots by eye, or with marks on the case, may not be sufficient for accurate navigation. Zeroing-in by trial-and-error is simple and effective. It does not require any knowledge of the direction of magnetic north.

How to Zero-in a Compass

Zeroing-in must be done off the boat and in an area well away from any magnetic influence such as iron or steel pipes and girders, radios, electric motors, etc. Don't work wearing a steel belt buckle or wristwatch strap; keep all tools well away from the work area.

Select a board with two exactly parallel edges. Temporarily mount the compass on this board using nonmagnetic screws or tacks. Line up the lubber's line with the parallel edges as closely as possible, but precise alignment is not necessary. On a level, flat surface—a plank will do fine, but not a table that may have screws or braces of magnetic material—place a reference edge, such as a book or straightedge, and the compass on its small board. Move the board with the compass into close contact with the reference edge; see

Figure 13-09. Rotate the board and reference edge as a unit until the compass reads exactly North. Hold the reference edge steady in this position; it provides a fixed direction reference. Remove the board and compass, turn it end for end, then bring the other parallel side of the board snugly against the reference edge. The lubber's line has now been exactly reversed. If the compass now reads South exactly, the N-S internal compensator is already zeroed-in and requires no adjustment.

If, however, the reading is not exactly South, an adjustment is needed; read the difference from 180° and make a note of it. Adjustments must be made with a nonmagnetic tool—a "screwdriver" made from a piece of brass rod with one end ground or filed down to a flat blade is often used; bend the other end over by 90° to form a handle that will facilitate small turns. A thin coin, such as a dime, can be used with some compasses. Slowly turn the N-S screw until *half* this difference is removed. (If the difference increases when you first turn the screw, turn it in the opposite direction until the desired result is obtained.) Now slightly realign the reference edge until the compass reads South exactly. Hold the reference edge firmly and again reverse the board.

The compass should now read N exactly. If it does not, the difference should be much smaller than the initial difference at South. If there is a difference, halve it by turning the N-S adjusting screw. Next, slightly realign the straightedge and board until the compass reads exactly North, always keeping the board snug against the reference edge. Once again, reverse the board, and check to see if the compass reads South. If it does not read South exactly, again halve the difference. Continue this procedure until the reversal yields zero difference, or as nearly zero as possible. When this process has been completed, the North-South axis of the compass coincides with the magnetic meridian.

Next adjust the East-West compensators in the same way. Line up on either an East or West heading, reverse the board and compass, and if the reading is not the exact opposite, halve the difference by turning the E-W screw in the correct direction as determined by trial-and-error. Continue working on the East and West headings just as on North and South until the desired results are obtained.

If exact reversals are not attainable, some unseen magnetic influence may be present. Move the zeroing-in project to a different location, and try again as above. It is also possible, although unlikely, that the compass is defective.

If the compass manufacturer provided instructions for zeroing-in, they should be followed.

Do not discard the temporary mounting board. It may be useful in testing for a possible site on the boat.

Check for Magnetic Influences

With the compass properly zeroed-in, and the best location selected from the viewpoint of visibility and use, now check for undesirable magnetic influences. The site should be at least 2 feet (0.6 m) from engine instruments, radios, bilge vapor indicators, electric gauges and instruments, and any iron or steel. (Stainless steel is nearly always nonmagnetic, but there are many different alloys and each item of such metal should be checked.) When one or more of these magnetic influences is too close, either it or the compass must be relocated. Fortunately, magnetic influence is subject to the "inverse square law"— double the distance from a disturbing force to the compass and you have reduced the effect to one-fourth; triple the distance and the effect is down to a relatively insignificant one-ninth.

Test for magnetic materials or influences that may be concealed from ready view. Make your test with the compass itself. Move the compass slowly and smoothly all around the proposed location without changing its orientation with the boat's centerline. Watch the card; one thing only will make it turn: a magnetic influence—find this with the compass. If the influence cannot be moved away or replaced with nonmagnetic material, test to determine whether it is merely magnetic metal, a random piece of iron or steel, or a magnetized object. There is a difference between the effect of an object that is magnetized and one that is merely made of magnetic material.

Successively bring the North and South poles of the compass near it. Both poles will be attracted if it is unmagnetized. If it attracts one pole and repels the other, the object is magnetized. Demagnetization may be attempted; see page 465.

Metal objects that move in normal operation should be moved. Turn the steering wheel fully in both directions; work the throttle, move the gearshift lever; open and close the windshield if it is near the compass. Try to duplicate all the changes that can occur in normal operation of the boat.

Check for Electrical Influences

Electrical currents flowing in wires near the proposed location can also exert undesired influences on the compass. Hold or tape down the compass at the proposed location, then test every circuit that might affect the compass. Switch on and off, one at a time, *all* the electrical loads, radio, bilge pump, depth sounder, lights, windshield

Figure 13-09 A board with parallel edges and a large book are all that is needed to accomplish the zeroing-in process. A nonmagnetic screwdriver or a thin coin must be used to turn the adjusting screws for the compensating magnets.

wipers, etc.; don't overlook anything controlled by a switch on the panel or located near the proposed compass site. Start the engine so that its electrical instruments will be operating. If there is an auxiliary generating plant, start it. Make full sets of checks with the boat on two cardinal headings 90 degrees apart.

The two wires of a circuit can be twisted together to avoid the creation of a magnetic field. Make sure that the wiring for the compass light is twisted. Wiring beneath the compass and instrument panel should be in twisted pairs, one pair for the two wires to each instrument of switch. The grouping of pairs is not important.

Make a Complete Check

In summary, check everything, *one item at a time*, that might influence the compass at the intended location, carefully watching the card as items are switched on and off, moved back and forth, started and stopped. When the card moves during any of these tests, the compass has been affected. Ideally, the compass should be relocated or the cause of the influence removed or demagnetized. In actual practice, however, you may have to settle for two separate states of magnetic environment; for example, with and without windshield wipers working.

Vibration

Vibration can make a compass completely unusable at an otherwise desirable location. It can actually make a card slowly but continuously spin. Even if vibration does not cause the card to spin, it could result in excessive pivot wear. Mount the compass temporarily but firmly in the planned location and watch for vibration at all ranges of engine rpm and boat speed; vibration is unpredictable and may occur only at certain engine speeds.

To avoid compass vibration, mount it on as solid a part of the boat as possible; a beam or deck is better than a wood or fiberglass panel. If vibration remains a problem, it may be eliminated or reduced by forcing a block of foam rubber between the bottom of the compass and the boat's

structure. Craft with slow-turning diesel engines may require a special vibration-dampened binnacle.

Mounting

Once the zero setting of the compass has been verified, and the prospective location checked for undesirable magnetic influences, you can proceed to the actual compass mounting. Certain basic requirements must be met.

• The compass must be securely fastened to the boat.

• A line from the center of the card through the lubber's line must be exactly parallel to the keel, the centerline of the boat; refer to **Figure 13-08.** (Ideally, the compass would be directly *over* the centerline. This often is not practical, but *it must be kept at least parallel to* the centerline.)

Establishing this line parallel to your boat's centerline is quite simple, but it almost always takes a little more patience and time than you anticipate. Find the center of the transom using a measuring tape, and accurately mark that center on a piece of masking tape (so as not to permanently mark the boat). This is usually easy. Next you need a second center point at some convenient location forward of the compass position—this might be the mainsail track of a sailboat. Alternatively, you can use the bow and a second location aft of the intended position of the compass.

With help from some additional pairs of hands, stretch a string tightly between the two center points. Accurately measure out (athwartship) to the location you selected for your compass, and after marking off this distance at your transom and forward location, move the string to this new pair of points. If the string is higher than the area where the compass base will be, use a plumb bob to transfer the line. Of course the boat must be on an even keel if a plumb bob is used.

Once you have checked to make sure you have accurately established your compass mounting line parallel to the boat's centerline, you might just want to carefully scratch or mark a short permanent line for future reference. You must install your compass so the lubber's line is exactly lined up with it. Many compasses have small alignment marks (forward and aft) where the housing touches the mounting surface, to aid in positioning on the scratch marks.

This alignment is extremely important, because an improperly aligned compass can never be properly adjusted for deviation, and will have a constant error (in addition to deviation) no matter what your boat's direction.

• The compass *should be* level; this is often at least partially accomplished by mounting brackets; if the compass has a cylindrical case, the bottom may need to be shimmed so that the unit is level. Bulkhead-mount compasses must be of the type intended for such installation; the mounting should be no more than a few degrees from true vertical.

• Magnetic material in the vicinity of the compass should be minimal. Wires near it, carrying direct current, must be twisted.

Fastening the Compass Down

Drill one mounting hole only. If during compensation later the compass must be slightly turned to correct any misalignment of the lubber's line, more than one hole could present problems. When compensation has been accomplished, the remaining hole(s) can be drilled and the fastening job completed; a check of the compensation should be repeated after this is done. *Use only nonmagnetic screws,* and if possible, nonmagnetic tools.

A compass bracket that has only two holes for mounting requires precise alignment and leaves very little room for further adjustment. Often circular compass mounts have slots built in for fastening, and fasteners are tightened when alignment is completed. If such slots are not present, try using either masking tape or duct tape to hold the compass temporarily in place.

If Your Boat Already Has a Compass

If you have a boat and it already has a compass installed, or if you are buying a boat that comes equipped with a compass, you can still benefit from the above information as all too many factory- and owner-installed compasses have lubber's lines not truly parallel to the centerline.

Electronic Compasses

A simple magnetic compass is a basic navigation tool that should be on every boat. However, more and more small craft are additionally fitted with electronic compasses; nearly always this is a FLUXGATE COMPASS; see **Figure 13-10.** These are more expensive than the previously described ordinary magnetic compasses, but not greatly so. A fluxgate compass has an electronic output that can be used in several ways. Applications can include digital displays, with as many remote readouts as you wish, or signals to an autopilot, or input data to electronic navigation systems. Various designs are used, but the basic principle is the sensing of the earth's magnetic field by coils of wire and the amplification of these very weak signals by solid-state electronics. There are no moving parts, thus avoiding such problems of an ordinary magnetic compass as friction, lag, etc.

Electricity is required for the operation of a fluxgate compass, but not a significant amount; in the event of a loss of electrical power, an electronic compass, of course, becomes inoperative, and you are back to your regular old-fashioned mariner's compass. Fluxgate compasses are subject to the same disturbing influences as are more ordinary compasses, but the sensing unit can be remotely located in a position where the "bad" effects are absent or at a minimum. (A common location is under a forward berth.) If needed, compensation can be applied, either with magnets or electroni-

Figure 13-10 Electronic fluxgate compasses react to the same magnetic field of the earth as do traditional compasses, but there are no moving parts. The output is a digital signal that can be displayed for steering, used as the input to an autopilot, or as an input to electronic navigation systems.

USING AN UNCOMPENSATED COMPASS

A compass that has not been compensated—had deviation removed or else had a deviation table prepared—cannot be used to navigate with a chart, but there are simple and practical uses for it.

An uncompensated compass may not measure directions correctly relative to magnetic north, but it does indicate directions in a stable, repeatable way if local conditions on the boat are unchanged. You can proceed from one point to another— for example, from one channel marker to the next, read the compass when you are right on course, and record that value. If you make the same run on another day, the reading will be the same, provided that you haven't changed any magnetic influences near the compass. Thus if the day comes when it is foggy, or night catches you still out on the water, you can follow with confidence the compass heading that you recorded in good visibility.

It's a good idea to record compass headings on all the runs you regularly make, particularly a route you might follow during period of reduced visibility. Run the route in clear weather and record the compass headings. One word of caution, however: run the course in both directions for each heading. You cannot add or subtract 180 degrees from the forward run to get a reading for the return; residual deviation may give an erroneous reading.

cally. Variation can be electronically inserted so that the instrument gives true headings and directions. Careful alignment of the sensor unit with the vessel's centerline is just as essential as for an oridnary mariner's compass, but the remote readout units can be positioned anywhere that is convenient and these have no need for precise alignment.

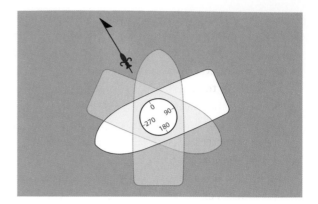

Figure 13-11 When a boat changes heading, it is the boat itself and the lubber's line of the compass that turns—the compass card maintains the same orientation as before the turn.

A more sophisticated, high-tech (and more expensive) version of a fluxgate compass includes three-axis gyro stabilization for improved accuracy and precision. Its electronic output can be used with a variety of navigation devices, such as autopilots, chart plotters, and radar displays, as well as a direct display of heading. The normal output is a magnetic heading, but if a GPS receiver (see Chapter 21, page 729) is connected, or variation is entered manually, a true heading is available.

USING A COMPASS

A compass is read by observing the graduation of the card that is opposite the lubber's line. The card of a typical boat compass has major graduations every ten degrees with lighter marks at intermediate five-degree intervals; refer to **Figure 13-03,** left. On some models the width of the lubber's line is just about one degree. Thus it is possible to use this width to estimate fairly accurately a reading of one degree more or less than each card marking. A reading of slightly less or more than midway between the card markings gives the individual degree values; refer to **Figure 13-06.**

Always remember when a boat turns, it is the boat, and the lubber's line, that turns—the compass card maintains the same orientation; see **Figure 13-11.**

Like all other piloting instruments and techniques, your compass should be used frequently.

Use it in good weather and sea conditions, even though it might not be actually needed. This will make you more familiar with how it is used and increase your confidence in it when it becomes a vital piloting tool at night or reduced visibility. Line up with a channel whose magnetic heading you know. Does your compass read that value (with any correction for deviation that is necessary)? Make note of your readings on frequently run tracks. Keep your compass course records handy and check the various headings frequently. If there is a change, look for the reason and eliminate it.

Using a compass for steering a boat and taking bearings is covered in later chapters.

Protection When Not in Use

The worst enemy of a compass is direct sunlight. When a boat sits day in and day out in a marina slip, or on a mooring, something can and should be done about excess sunlight.

When a compass is not in use, it should be thoroughly shielded from the sun to prevent discoloration of the liquid, and perhaps of the card. Sometimes a binnacle will have a light-shielding hood; if so, keep it closed whenever the compass is not in use. If such a shield is not a part of your compass, improvise one of lightproof material; if you use cloth, make sure that it is a tight weave that will not "leak" direct sunlight.

COMPASS ERRORS

Before a compass can be used for accurate navigation, you must understand COMPASS ERRORS—the differences between compass readings and true directions measured from geographic North. Normally, when working with your charts, you will record and plot courses and bearings with respect to true North. Some experienced boatmen, however, work in terms of magnetic directions.

Variation

The first and most basic compass error is VARIATION (V or VAR). For any given location on land or sea, this is the angle between the magnetic meridian and the geographic meridian; see **Figure 13-12.** It is the angle between true North and magnetic North as indicated by a compass that is free from any nearby influences. Variation is designated as EAST or WEST in accordance with the way the compass needle is deflected. Any statement of variation, except zero, must have one of these labels: E or W.

Variation is a compass error about which a navigator can do nothing but recognize its exis-

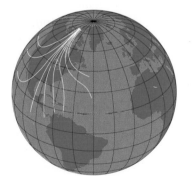

Figure 13-12 Variation is the angle between the magnetic and the true meridians. Variation depends on geographic location but is the same for all vessels in any vicinity. In North America, right, variation is generally easterly on the Pacific Coast and westerly on the Atlantic Coast and on the Great Lakes. There is a line of zero variation between these areas.

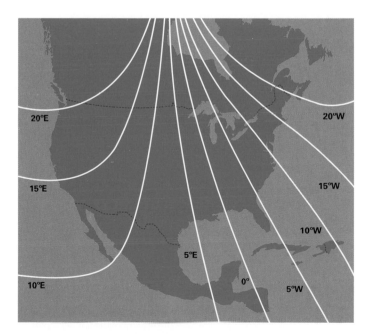

tence and make allowances for. Variation is the compass error that would exist on a boat entirely free from any on-board magnetic materials or other internal magnetic influences.

General Variation

The earth's magnetic field is not uniform, and, because the magnetic poles are not at the geographic poles (refer to **Figure 13-01,** right), *variation changes with location;* refer to **Figure 13-12.** The result of failure to apply different variation as a vessel moves from one location to another can be seen in **Figure 13-13.**

At any given place, the amount of variation is essentially constant. There is usually a small annual change, but if you are using a chart not more than two or three years old, this quite small amount of change can be ignored. The amount of

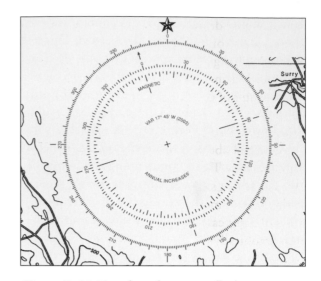

Figure 13-14 Most charts have several compass roses that show the variation both graphically and descriptively. They are located so as to be convenient for plotting. On any chart, especially small-scale charts covering large areas, always use the compass rose nearest the vicinity concerned.

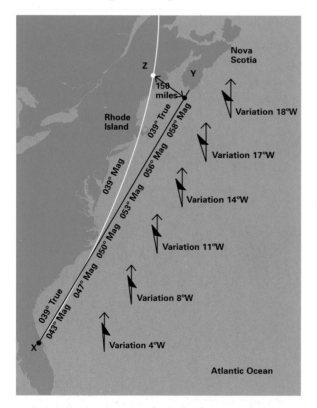

Figure 13-13 Do not overlook the change in variation with change of location. In this example, the true and magnetic courses from X to Y are initially very nearly the same, but the magnetic course soon changes, while the true remains constant. By staying on the same magnetic heading, an aviator would soon be at Z, 150 miles west of his destination—but the skipper of a boat would have run aground on the Rhode Island coast!

variation, and its annual rate of change, is found within each COMPASS ROSE on the chart; see **Figure 13-14.** On nearly all types of charts published by the National Ocean Service part of NOAA (National Oceanic and Atomospheric Admisnistration) there will be found several compass roses suitably placed for convenient plotting. These are circular figures several inches (perhaps 5 to 10 cm) in diameter with three concentric circular scales. The outer scale is graduated in degrees and it is oriented so that its zero point, indicated by a star symbol, points to true (geographic) North. The inner pair of scales is graduated in degrees and in the point system down to quarter-points. The zero point of these scales, identified by an arrow symbol, shows the direction of magnetic North at that point. On some charts, the innermost scale in points is omitted.

The angle at the center of a compass rose between the star and arrow symbols is the variation *in that vicinity* for the year stated. This information is printed at the center of the rose to the nearest 15′; for example, in **Figure 13-14,** "Var 17° 45′ W (2003)." The annual rate of change is noted to the nearest 1′, and whether the variation is increasing or decreasing; for example, "Annual Increase 2′ " or "Annual Decrease 6′ " or "No Annual Change." On older charts, apply the accumulated annual change to the variation value at the center of the rose. In all cases, use variation to the nearest whole degree—fractions are not practical for small craft.

As noted above, magnetic variation changes with location. Thus, except for charts of a limited area, such as a single harbor and its approaches, variation will most likely be different in various areas of a typical chart. For this reason, the variation graphically indicated by the several compass roses on any particular chart will be different. It is important *always* to refer to the compass rose that is *nearest your position* on the chart to read variation or to plot from its scales. If you have to fold your chart, try to do so that it will have a compass rose on each panel.

Local Attraction

In addition to the general overall magnetic variation, the navigator may also encounter LOCAL ATTRACTION. (Here "local" means a limited geographic vicinity, as opposed to magnetic influences on board the boat.) In a few localities, the compass is subject to irregular magnetic disturbances in the earth's field over relatively small areas. A striking example is found at Kingston, Ontario, Canada, where variation may change as much as 45 degrees in a distance of a mile and a half (2.4 km).

Charts of areas subject to such local attraction will bear warnings to this effect. Other means of navigation are needed when within range of such disturbances.

Deviation

A boat's compass rarely exists in an environment that is completely free of nearby magnetic materials or influences. Normally it is subject to magnetic forces in addition to those of the earth's field. Material already magnetized, or even capable of being magnetized by the magnets of the compass, will cause the compass needle to deviate from its proper alignment with the magnetic meridian. Currents flowing in improperly installed electrical wiring can have the same effect.

The deflection of the compass from its proper orientation is called DEVIATION (D or DEV). It is the angle between the magnetic meridian and a line from the pivot through the North point of the compass card; it is the angle between the direction the compass would point if there were no deviating influences and the direction in which it actually does point. Theoretically, it can range from 0° to 180°, but in practice large values cannot be tolerated. Just as for variation, deviation can be EAST or WEST depending on whether compass North lies to the east or west of magnetic North. Deviation *must* carry one of these labels, E or W, unless it is zero; see **Figure 13-15.**

While variation changes with geographic location, *deviation changes with the craft's heading* and does not change noticeably in any given geographic area. (Causes for this effect will be explained later, see page 466.) To cope with these changes a vessel needs a DEVIATION TABLE—a compilation of deviations, usually for each 15 degrees of heading by the compass; see **Table 13-2.** For added convenience, a deviation table can also be prepared in terms of magnetic headings; see **Table 13-3.** (Note: In these examples, the values of deviation are large for purposes of illustration. They are typical of an uncompensated compass in a poor magnetic environment.)

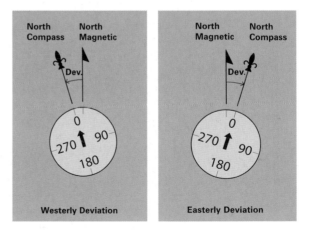

Figure 13-15 Deviation is the difference between North as indicated by the compass and magnetic North. It can be easterly or westerly, and depends on the magnetic conditions on the vessel. It changes with the boat's heading, but is not noticeably affected by changes in position within a geographic area.

Deviation Determination by Compass Headings

Boat's Compass Heading	Range Bearing by Compass	Magnetic Range Bearing	Deviation
000°	082°	087°	5°E
015°	086°	087°	1°E
030°	091°	087°	4°W
045°	096°	087°	9°W
060°	100°	087°	13°W
075°	104°	087°	17°W
090°	106°	087°	19°W
105°	106°	087°	19°W
120°	104°	087°	17°W
135°	101°	087°	14°W
150°	097°	087°	10°W
165°	093°	087°	6°W
180°	089°	087°	2°W
195°	085°	087°	2°E
210°	082°	087°	5°E
225°	079°	087°	8°E
240°	076°	087°	11°E
255°	073°	087°	14°E
270°	070°	087°	17°E
285°	069°	087°	18°E
300°	070°	087°	17°E
315°	072°	087°	15°E
330°	075°	087°	12°E
345°	078°	087°	9°E

Table 13-2 The first deviation table prepared will be in terms of compass heading; see page 456 for the procedure. This table is useful for correcting compass bearings so that they can be plotted. (Note that the table's figures are much larger than would be tolerated in actual piloting. If deviations are this large, the compass needs compensating to reduce deviation to zero or nearly so.)

Using Deviation Tables

For ordinary navigation, it is normally sufficient to use the value of deviation from the line of the table that is nearest to the craft's actual heading, either compass or magnetic. This is particularly true for compensated compasses where the deviations will rarely exceed a few degrees.

For more precise navigation, such as in contests and perhaps some races, it will be necessary to *interpolate* between tabular entries to get a more precise value of deviation; see page 468 for interpolation procedures.

Changes in Deviation

Note that any deviation table is valid *only* on the boat for which it was prepared, and *only* for the magnetic conditions prevailing at the time the table was prepared. If magnetic materials within the radius of effect—some 3 to 5 feet (0.9-1.5 m)—are added, taken away, or relocated, a new deviation table must be prepared, or at a minimum, sufficient checks must be made of the old table to ensure that its values are still correct. If any electronic equipment is installed, removed, or relocated, check to see if a new table is needed.

COMPASS CALCULATIONS

A boat's course is the direction in which it is intended to be steered, or of a line on a chart, with respect to some other line of reference. (Its heading is that angle at any given moment.) Three lines of reference have been established: the direction of true North or the true meridian; the direction of the magnetic meridian; and the direction of

Deviation Determination by Magnetic Headings

Boat's Magnetic Heading	Deviation
000°	7°E
015°	1°E
030°	6°W
045°	12°W
060°	17°W
075°	19°W
090°	18°W
105°	17°W
120°	14°W
135°	11°W
150°	8°W
165°	5°W
180°	2°W
195°	2°E
210°	4°E
225°	6°E
240°	9°E
255°	11°E
270°	14°E
285°	16°E
300°	17°E
315°	17°E
330°	15°E
345°	11°E

Table 13-3 Deviation in terms of magnetic headings, rather than compass headings, is needed to determine the compass course to be steered for a plotted magnetic direction. Here the values have been calculated and tabulated for each 15° magnetic heading.

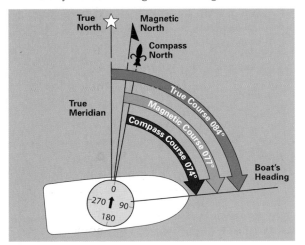

Figure 13-16 A course, heading, or bearing can be named in any one of three systems based on the reference direction used.

the North point of the compass. Thus *there are three ways to name a course or heading:* TRUE, MAGNETIC, or COMPASS. The three reference lines and the three measurements of direction for one heading are illustrated in **Figure 13-16.** The above remarks also apply to the measurement of directions for bearings.

Applying Variation & Deviation

To be able to use your compass fully, you must develop an ability to CONVERT directions of one type to the other two quickly and accurately. These directions include headings, courses, and bearings. You use compass courses in steering your boat; you get compass bearings when you take a reading across your compass to a distant aid to navigation or landmark. You normally plot true directions on your chart and record them in your log. There are also magnetic directions—the intermediate steps in going from compass to true—which are also some-

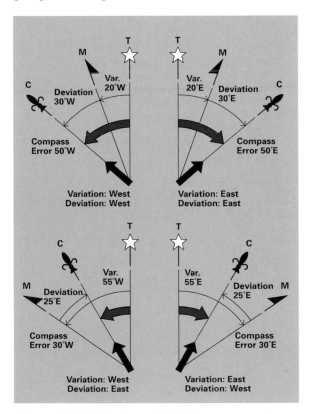

Figure 13-17 Variation and deviation are sometimes combined algebraically into a single value, "compass error (CE)." These intentionally exaggerated drawings show the four possible combinations of easterly and westerly variation and deviation.

times directly useful in themselves. Hence, there is need for continual interconversion between the three systems of naming direction.

Variation and deviation can be in the same direction (have the same label), or they may be opposite, and thus partially canceling; see **Figure 13-17**. (The amount of variation and deviation in this figure is exaggerated for greater clarity.)

Single-Step Calculations

Although most compass calculations involve the double conversion from true to magnetic to compass, and vice versa, it is best to consider single-step computations first.

The terms "correct" and "correcting" are used in easily remembered phrases to help determine whether to add or subtract deviation and variation. This is done by considering true directions as being more "correct" than magnetic, and magnetic as being more "correct" than compass directions. This can be rationalized and easily

EXAMPLE 1
Given: The magnetic course is 061°; from the chart, the variation for the area in which we are navigating is 11°E; there is no deviation.
Required: The true course, TC.
Calculation: The conversion is one of correcting because we are going from magnetic to true. The variation is east, so the basic rule is used, Correcting add east.
061° + 11° = 072°
Answer: TC 072°

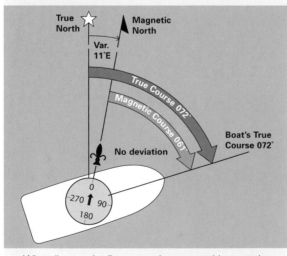

When "correcting" a magnetic course with easterly variation to a true course, add the variation.

EXAMPLE 2
Given: The magnetic course is 068°; the variation is 14° W; there is no deviation.
Required: The true course, TC.
Calculation: The conversion is correcting and the variation is westerly. In the basic rule, EAST has been changed to WEST; one word has been changed, another must be. Since this calculation is correcting, "add" must become "subtract." The rule to be applied here is thus: Correcting subtract west.
068° - 14° = 054°
Answer: TC 054°

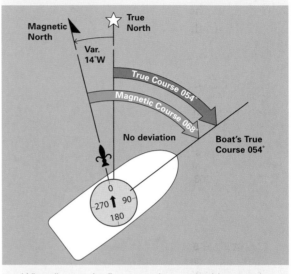

When "correcting" a magnetic course with westerly variation to a true course, subtract the variation.

EXAMPLE 3
Given: The course of the boat by its compass is 212°; the deviation for that heading is 5°E.
Required: The magnetic course, MC.
Calculation: The conversion is correcting and the deviation is easterly; the application rule is Correcting add east.
212° + 5° = 217°
Answer: MC 217°

remembered by observing that true has no errors, magnetic has one error (variation), and compass includes two errors (variation and deviation). Going from magnetic to true—or compass to magnetic—can thus be termed "correcting." Conversely, the term "uncorrecting" is used when going from true to magnetic, or from magnetic to compass.

The basic rule is: *When correcting, add easterly errors,* which can be shortened to *"Correcting add east"* and memorized as "C-A-E"; see **Example 1.**

The basic rule is easily altered for application to the three other operations of conversion. Remember to *always change two, but only two, words* in the phrase for any application—never only one, never all three; see **Examples 2 and 3.**

Now consider the reverse process, uncorrecting. We again change two, but only two, words to the basic rule and we get: *Uncorrecting add west* and *Uncorrecting subtract east.* (Don't worry about remembering all four rules. It's easier to remember the basic rule of C-A-E and how to change it to fit the other situations); see **Examples 4 and 5.**

EXAMPLE 4

Given: The true course is 351° and the variation is 12°W; there is no deviation.
Required: The magnetic course, MC.
Calculation: The conversion is uncorrecting and the variation is westerly. The applicable rule is Uncorrecting add west.
351° + 12° = 363° = 003°
Answer: MC 003°

EXAMPLE 5

Given: The magnetic course is 172° and the deviation for that heading is 7°E.
Required: The compass course, CC.
Calculation: The conversion is uncorrecting and the deviation is easterly. The application rule is Uncorrecting subtract east.
172° - 7° = 165°
Answer: CC 165°

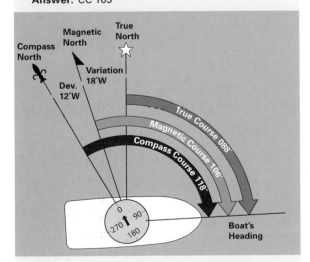

In this example, a true course is "uncorrected" to a compass course, with the error of variation and deviation both westerly.

Two-Step Conversions

The same rules apply when two-step conversions are made from true to compass, or from compass to true. It is important to remember that the proper rule must be used for *each step separately*. It will always be correcting or uncorrecting for both steps, *but* the addition or subtraction may not be the same as this is determined individually be the east or west nature of the variation and deviation; see **Examples 6 and 7.**

EXAMPLE 6

Given: The true course is 088°, the variation is 18°W, and the deviation is 12°W.
Required: The compass course, CC.
Calculation: Both conversions are uncorrecting and both errors are westerly. The rule for both calculations is Uncorrecting add west.
088° + 18° + 12° = 118°
Answer: CC 118°

EXAMPLE 7

Given: The compass bearing is 107°; the variation is 6°E, and the deviation for the heading that the boat is on is 2°W.
Required: The true bearing, TB.
Calculation: Both conversions are correcting; the variation is easterly but the deviation is westerly, so two rules are required: Correcting add east, subtract west.
107° + 6° - 2° = 111°
Answer: TB 111°

Other Memory Aids

The basic rule of *Correcting add east* and its variations is only one set of memory-aids for compass calculations; there are many more. You need to know only one; study several and pick the one that is easiest for you to remember and apply.

Another that is easily memorized and used is *Compass least, error east; Compass best, error west.* This can be used for conversions such as those shown in the examples above, but it is of particular value when the difference between compass and magnetic is known numerically and it must be decided whether the deviation is east or west. For example: if the magnetic course is known to be 192° but the compass reads only 190°, what is the deviation? The numerical difference is 2° and the compass is "least"—190° is less than 192°—so the error is east; deviation is 2°E. If on the same heading, the compass had read 195°, the compass would then have been "best"—195° being more (better) than 192°—and the deviation would be 3°W.

When considering the variation as the difference between true and magnetic, apply the same phrase but with magnetic substituted for compass—the rhyme is not as good, but the principle is the same. For example: if a true bearing is 310°, and the variation is 4°W, then the magnetic bearing would be "best" (more than the value of the true bearing), 314°. If the variation had been easterly, then the magnetic bearing would have been "least" (or less than the true bearing), 306°.

Visual Aids

Many boatmen find a pictorial device a better memory-aid than a phrase or sentence. Letters are arranged vertically, representing the three ways of naming a direction—true, magnetic, and compass—with the respective differences—variation and deviation—properly placed between them. The arrangement can be memorized in several ways, such as *True Virtue Makes Dull Company* or in the reverse direction as *Can Dead Men Vote Twice.*

On each side of the letters, an arrow is drawn to indicate the direction of conversion; on the left, down for true to compass, and on the right, up for compass to true. Also on each side, the appropriate arithmetic process is indicated for use with easterly or westerly errors; see **Figure 13-18.** The right side indicates correcting; the left side illustrates uncorrecting. If one memorizes D-A-W for *Down add west,* then the correct signs can always be added to the letters and arrows. (The three other actions follow the same pattern as above—always change two, but only two, words. Thus it would be Down subtract east, Up add east, or Up subtract west; see **Examples 8A, 8B, and 9.**)

Always Trust Your Compass

If you must depend on your compass for navigation, make a quick check for any objects near it that could cause additional, unmeasured deviations—typical objects that get placed too close to a compass include knives, beer and soft drink cans (if not

---

EXAMPLE 8A

Given: From the chart, the true course is 107° and the variation in the locality is 5°E.
Required: The magnetic course, MC.
Calculation: The conversion is uncorrecting, so use the left side and read down the diagram. The variation is easterly so it is to be subtracted.
107° - 5° = 102°
Answer: MC 102°.

Down	T	107°
Subtract	V	(-) 5°E
East	M	102°

EXAMPLE 8B

Given: For this magnetic heading, the deviation aboard this boat is 4°W.
Required: The compass course, CC.
Calculation: The conversion is still uncorrecting, so read downward on the diagram; continue to use the left side. The deviation is westerly so it must be added.
102° + 4° = 106°
Answer: CC 106°.

Down	M	102°
Add	D	(+) 4°W
West	C	106°

EXAMPLE 9

Conversions such as Examples 8A and 8B could be done in a single operation.
Given: A boat is on compass course (CC) 193°. Its deviation on this heading is 6°E; the variation for the vicinity is 9°W.
Required: The true course, TC.
Calculation: The conversion is correcting, upward on the diagram; use the right side. Easterly deviation is to be added; westerly variation is to be subtracted.

T	190°	Read up
V	(-) 9°W	Add
M	199°	EAST
D	(+) 6°E	Subtract
C	193°	WEST

Answer: TC 190°

---

aluminum), small radios, some cameras, your flashlight, and tools of all sorts. If you have nonboater guests on board, be especially careful that one of them doesn't unknowingly bring a "forbidden" object into the vicinity of the compass.

If your magnetic situation has been checked and is all clear, then trust your compass to direct you to your destination—it is better than your instincts!

The Importance of Accurate Helmsmanship

Keep in mind the results of not running an accurate course. If your compass or compass calculations should be in error by only 5 degrees, you will be a full mile off course for every 11ft miles run (1 km for every 11.4 km). This could be hazardous when making a landfall or a coastal run at night or in poor visibility. Also, running a narrow channel in poor visibility with an inaccurate compass would be dangerous. Note the increasing seriousness of even small errors as shown in **Table 13-4.**

DETERMINING DEVIATION

Deviation is a property of each individual boat, and its effect must be determined for your own craft. It is the angle between the compass-card axis and the magnetic meridian; refer to **Figure 13-15.** On board any boat, the direction of compass North is easily learned by a quick glance at the compass card. Not so the direction of the magnetic meridian—magnetic North. Thus it is not possible to compare visually the angle between these two reference directions, to determine the deviation on that heading. But the difference between an observed compass bearing and the known correct magnetic direction for that

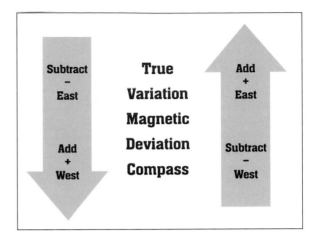

Figure 13-18 A pictorial "TVMDC" diagram can be an aid in remembering the rules for converting between true, magnetic, and compass directions. The basic rule is "Down Add West" but the other rules can be derived by changing two, but only two, of these three words.

bearing yields that value.

Deviation should always be checked after purchase of a boat, new or used, and before it is taken on its first cruise. It is also desirable that deviation be checked annually, usually at the beginning of a boating season, and after the installation of any new electronic or electrical equipment near the compass. If a compass is replaced a new deviation check is required even if the new unit appears identical to the old one.

Deviation by Bow Bearings

The bearing is sighted over the compass with the boat headed directly toward the object or range. The magnetic direction is taken from the chart. The distant target can be a range of two objects, or it can be a single object if the location of the boat can be fixed precisely, such as close aboard an aid to navigation with the object far enough away that any slight offset of the boat is immaterial.

The range technique is the more accurate and is done as follows: Select two accurately charted, visible objects that are on shore or fixed to the bottom. From the chart, measure and record the magnetic direction from the nearer to the farther mark. (The best ranges are those in the *Light List*; their true direction is given precisely, just apply variation to get magnetic.) See **Figure 13-19;** A and

Error in Course	Number of feet off course after sailing one nautical mile	Miles sailed to be one mile off course
1°	106	57.3
2°	212	28.6
3°	318	19.1
4°	425	14.3
5°	532	11.4
6°	639	9.5
7°	746	8.2
8°	854	7.1
9°	962	6.3
10°	1071	5.7

Table 13-4 This table shows the effect of getting off course, for various steering errors—the distance off course after traveling one mile, and the distance traveled before being one mile off course.

Compass Heading (boat)	Cross Bearing (range)	Mean Magnetic (range)	Deviation
000°			
015°			
030°			
045°			
060°			
075°			
090°			
105°			
120°			
135°			
150°			
165°			
180°			
195°			
210°			
225°			
240°			
255°			
270°			
285°			
300°			
315°			
330°			
345°			

Compass Heading (boat)	Cross Bearing (range)	Mean Magnetic (range)	Deviation
000°	095°		
015°	095°		
030°	096°		
045°	097°		
060°	098°		
075°	098°		
090°	099°		
105°	098°		
120°	097°		
135°	096°		
150°	091°		
165°	090°		
180°	090°		
195°	092°		
210°	093°		
225°	094°		
240°	095°		
255°	095°		
270°	096°		
285°	095°		
300°	094°		
315°	094°		
330°	095°		
345°	095°		

$$\frac{2,278}{24} = 94.91 \ (95°)$$

Table 13-5A *When determining deviation values, the first step is to construct a table as shown above. You already know that you will be reading range bearings at every 15° of compass heading, so list the compass headings in the first column of the table.*

B are two visible objects, with B visible behind A. The magnetic direction of this range is 075°. The boat is run straight toward A on the range, keeping A and B visibly in line. While steady on this heading, the compass is read and recorded. In this example it reads 060°; the amount of the difference is the deviation, 15 degrees. Reference to any of the conversion rules makes it clear that the deviation is east. You can set up other ranges and find the deviation on such headings by repeating the bow bearing procedure as above. Use the side of a long object (pier or large building) as a range, if the direction can be determined from the chart. Use a buoy and a fixed object, or even two buoys, only if a range of fixed objects is unavailable. Remember that the charted position of a buoy is that of its anchor, and wind or current, or both, may swing it around its

Table 13-5B *For the second step, use a pelorus to obtain range bearings for every compass course heading, and record them in column two. Then find the average of your range bearings by adding all the values and dividing by the number of values; round off to the nearest whole degree. This is what the range bearing would have been if the compass had no deviation. (These are illustrative values; they will be different for your boat.)*

charted position. Large ships and tugs sometimes move buoys off-station inadvertently by collision in thick weather. Buoys thus give less accurate deviation table results; replace the data as soon as you can with a table made under better conditions.

Deviation by Courses

Steering a visual course from one aid to navigation to another and noting the compass heading will, if the observation is made *at the start of each leg*, give reasonably good values of deviation when compared with the magnetic direction from the

Compass Heading (boat)	Cross Bearing (range)	Mean Magnetic (range)	Deviation
000°	095°	095°	0°
015°	095°	095°	0°
030°	096°	095°	1°W
045°	097°	095°	2°W
060°	098°	095°	3°W
075°	098°	095°	3°W
090°	099°	095°	4°W
105°	098°	095°	3°W
120°	097°	095°	2°W
135°	096°	095°	1°W
150°	091°	095°	4°E
165°	090°	095°	5°E
180°	090°	095°	5°E
195°	092°	095°	3°E
210°	093°	095°	2°E
225°	094°	095°	1°E
240°	095°	095°	0°
255°	095°	095°	0°
270°	096°	095°	1°W
285°	095°	095°	0°
300°	094°	095°	1°E
315°	094°	095°	1°E
330°	095°	095°	0°
345°	095°	095°	0°

$$\frac{2,278}{24} = 94.91 \ (95°)$$

Table 13-5C The third step is to determine the difference between each range bearing (column 2) and the calculated magnetic bearing (column 3). This difference, entered in column 4, is the deviation. If the compass bearing is larger than the magnetic bearing, the deviation is west; if it is smaller, the deviation is east. From this table, another table in terms of magnetic headings can be calculated; refer to Table 13-3.

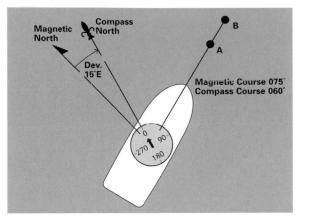

Figure 13-19 The simplest way to determine deviation on any heading is to locate two objects to use as a range whose magnetic direction can be established from the chart. Head your boat toward this range and read the compass. The difference is the deviation on that heading; if there is no difference, the deviation on this heading is zero.

On a calm day, the boat *Water Witch* sails across this range on compass headings successively 15 degrees apart. Using sight vanes and an azimuth circle mounted on the compass her skipper takes bearing of the range for each crossing, and records and tabulates the results; see **Table 13-5A.**

The skipper averages the various compass bearings and gets 94.91°; see **Table 13-5B.** He notes that this is very close to the magnetic bearing of the range from the chart and decides he has a good set of data.

The first and last columns of this table now constitute a deviation table for *Water Witch* provided *no changes are made in the magnetic environment of the compass;* see **Table 13-5C.** Note also that the table's deviations are in terms of *compass* headings. These are not, of course, the same as magnetic headings; when on a heading of 090° *magnetic* the boat's bow points in a direction quite different from when she heads 090° by *compass.* This leads to a problem. The skipper determines from the chart his magnetic course; he then wants to know what deviation to apply to get the compass course he should steer. Use of **Table 13-5C** for that purpose requires time-consuming trial-and-error steps. To avoid this, he makes a second table listing the deviations in terms of *magnetic* headings; refer to **Table 13-3.** This can

chart; see **Figure 13-20.** Sighting down the center of a long straight channel defined by aids to navigation or banks close by on either side is another excellent means of getting a compass heading to compare with the chart.

Deviation Table by Swinging Ship

A precise technique for developing a deviation table is to SWING SHIP about a compass by running different headings across a range, recording the compass bearing of the range of each crossing. For example, two prominent charted objects are on a range with a magnetic bearing measuring 087°.

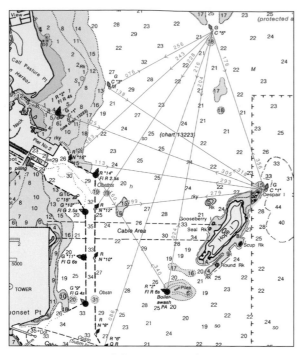

Figure 13-20 Carefully run courses between two charted positions can be used to determine deviation on a number of headings. Deviation will not be the same for reciprocal courses, and each direction must be run individually.

be done by trial-and-error method (but needs doing only once to make the table, rather than each time such deviation is needed.)

COMPENSATION

It can be assumed that at boat's compass will have deviation errors. The area available for a control station on most craft, especially motorboats, is so limited that it is impossible to have magnetically undesirable objects at a safe distance from the compass. It is possible to live with known values of deviation provided they are not too large—deviations much over about 6 degrees can cause trouble in rough waters. It is, however, much better if the compass is COMPENSATED (also referred to as ADJUSTED) so that the deviation is reduced to zero, or nearly so, on as many headings as possible. This procedure is within the capabilities of the average skipper.

The procedures described below are applicable to boats made of fiberglass, wood, or aluminum; see page 470 if your craft is made of steel.

Two Methods

Two basic techniques are used to adjust compasses; both use one or two pairs of small COMPENSATING MAGNETS. In one instance the magnets are internal to the compass case or binnacle, in the other they are external and are mounted near the compass location. The objective of both methods is the same—to provide weak magnetic fields that cancel out the disturbing influences.

Compensation consists of adjusting the effect of each of these magnets to achieve the counterbalances of their fields with the fields of the disturbing influences.

Using Internal Compensators

Most modern boat compasses now have internal compensating magnets. The two magnets, or pairs of magnets, are installed at right angles to each other. Usually there are two slotted screw heads at the edge of the compass; one marked E-W, and the other N-S; refer to **Figure 13-05.** (If external magnets must be used, see page 469.)

Preliminary Steps

As discussed on page 438, the internal compensators should be at zero effect before the compensation procedures are begun. Check also that the line from the center of the compass through the lubber's line is *exactly* parallel to your boat's centerline (see page 441). Select an object at least one-half mile (0.9 km) distant. With your boat held absolutely motionless, sight on that object both down the centerline and then over the compass; the sight lines should be the same.

Have a *nonmagnetic screwdriver* available to adjust the screws of the compensating magnets. (You could use a dime or a piece of heavy sheet copper or brass, or a brass machine screw filed down to a flat point.)

Store each magnetic article of the boat's gear in its regular place, put the windshield wiper blades in their normal "off" position, and keep no magnetic material near the compass. Steel eyeglass frames, steel partial dentures, or even the steel grommet in a yachting cap, if brought within a few inches of the compass, might cause deviation;

someone may be working that close to the compass during adjustment.

Disposable Buoys Several disposable buoys will be needed. Excellent ones can be made of cardboard milk cartons or plastic bleach bottles ballasted with some sand or dirt. Newspapers wadded into a ball about the size of a basketball and tied with string will work if they are weighted with a small heavy object such as a large bolt or old spark plug at the end of three or four feet (0.9-1.2 m) of string; wire or rope should not be used for such a buoy; see **Figure 13-21.**

Running Reciprocal Courses

The essential element of compensating a compass by running reciprocal courses is achieving accurate reversal, putting and holding the boat on a course over the bottom which is exactly the reciprocal of the original unknown magnetic heading. This is not as difficult as might be expected.

Establishing the Courses Between any two visible marks, or on a range, reversing the magnetic heading is obviously easy. In the procedures of compensation, however, there is need to run at least the four cardinal *magnetic* directions; East and West, North and South. Seldom will you find in your local waters natural marks or aids to navigation on these exact magnetic headings. If you are fortunate, you may find special ranges on these headings that have been established for compass adjustment purposes. More likely, though, you must make your own temporary basic courses.

The basic technique is quite simple—departing from a fixed mark (a buoy will do, but a daybeacon or light is better), run on a steady compass heading until ready to reverse your course. Drop a disposable buoy creating the desired range. (With many high-speed craft, the path through the water may be distinctive enough that a marker will not be required.) Next, execute a "buttonhook" turn (known technically as a Williamson turn)—line up the disposable buoy with the object marking the original departure point, steady on this range visually, and *ignoring the compass*, head for the initial point. Run down

the disposable buoy, and continue back toward the departure point; see **Figure 13-22.** Make the turn as tightly as possible, keeping the buoy in sight, so as to complete the turn before the buoy has had time to drift from the spot at which it was dropped. Choose a right or left turn, whichever can be made tighter if there is any difference; swing enough to the *opposite* side before making the main turn so that when the main turn is completed, you can pick up the desired reciprocal course smoothly without overshooting and having to apply opposite rudder. This maneuver is not difficult to learn; all that is required is a few trials and then some practice. It has other uses, too; for example, it is the quickest and most accurate procedure for returning to the spot where a person or object has been lost overboard.

This maneuver will put the boat accurately on a reciprocal course, providing that the buoy remained where it was dropped and that no wind or current set the boat to either side of her heading on the *outward* run from the starting point.

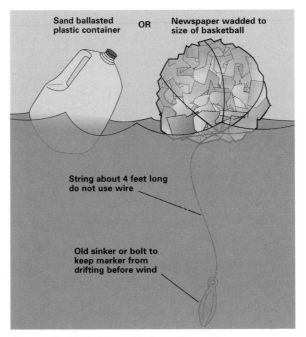

Figure 13-21 A disposable buoy for use in maneuvering to determine compass deviation can be made from either a ballasted plastic container or a ball of wadded newspapers attached to a small weight. All such buoys should be picked up and properly discarded after the operation is completed.

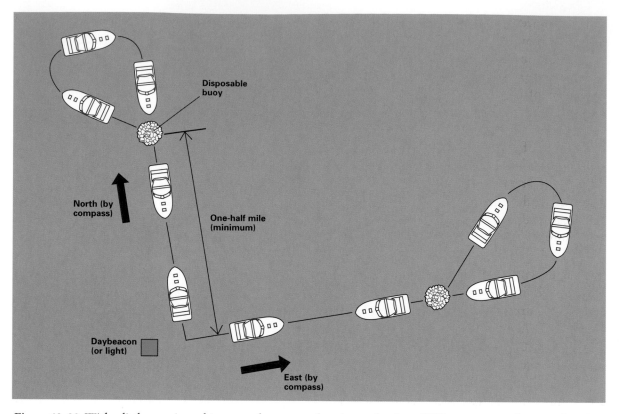

Figure 13-22 With a little practice a skipper can learn to make a buttonhook, or Williamson, turn of 180° and come back directly over the spot where the turn was started. Swing out far enough initially on the opposite side of the turn so that the reciprocal course can be picked up without overshooting it.

Compensation will be inaccurate if the boat has moved crabwise, headed one way but actually going another. The various courses of compass compensation procedures must therefore be run when wind and water conditions will produce no leeway.

The skipper who hesitates to run directly over the disposable buoy should take it very close alongside, touching it if possible. On a range of ½ nautical mile, when the buoy is 10 feet (3m) to one side of the boat's centerline, the course error will be only 11′, less than ⅕ of a degree.

Compensation on Cardinal Headings

As noted above, compensation must be accomplished when wind and current will not set the boat to either side of the intended course; the winds and seas must also be such that accurate steering is possible. Adjustments are made on two cardinal headings, East-West first.

East-West Adjustments

First steer 090° (or 270°) by compass from the chosen departure mark, holding rigorously to this course by the compass for at least a half-mile; a mile would be better, but you must be able to see the starting mark. It makes no difference whether the initial run is toward the east or west; this can be determined by the available water area and object used for a departure mark. Have someone drop a disposable buoy over the stern, execute the turn described above, and run the reciprocal course; refer to **Figure 13-22.** Run this course *not* by the compass, but by heading for the original departure point. Read the compass and record the figures.

If the compass reading is now 270° (or 090°), there is no deviation on east or west headings and compensation is not needed; the E-W internal compensator should not be touched.

If the compass reading for a return to the starting point is not 270° (or 090°), compensation is required. Use your nonmagnetic screwdriver to remove *half* the difference between 270° (090°) and the observed reading. Halving the difference is based on the assumption that the deviation of reciprocal courses is equal and opposite. This may not be exactly so, but it serves as a good initial approach.

Assume, for example, that the compass reading was 290°; then one-half of the 20-degree difference, or 10 degrees, is to be removed while the reciprocal course is carefully run. Turn the E-W adjusting screw, and watch the compass closely. If the compass reading increases rather than decreases, the screw has been turned in the wrong direction (there is no way to tell in advance which is the correct direction); turn the screw in the opposite direction. Move the screw slowly until the compass reading is 280° while the boat is exactly on the reciprocal course.

Return to the starting mark and make another E-W run. Head out again on a compass course of 090° (or 270°), the track through the water will *not* be the same as for the first run; drop a new disposable buoy, turn, and line up for the reciprocal course back to the point of departure. If the compass reading is not now 270° (or 090°)—it should be close—again remove half the difference by turning the screw of the compensating magnets.

Repeat these east-west runs until the deviation is eliminated or reduced to the smallest possible amount on these headings. Do not touch the E-W adjusting screw again after it is finally set.

North-South Adjustments

Follow a similar procedure on north-south headings. Run from a starting point—it can be the same as for E-W runs, or it can be a different one as required by the available water area—on a compass heading of 000° (or 180°) by compass, drop a disposable buoy, make the turn, and head back visually toward the departure point. Remove half of the error by adjusting the screw marked N-S.

Repeat such runs as necessary just as was done for the east-west compensation.

When the north-south compensation has been completed, make a quick check for any east-west deviation; it should not have changed, but it doesn't hurt to be sure. The deviation on all cardinal headings should now be zero, or as near zero as is attainable in this boat.

Residuals on Intercardinal Headings

You can determine any deviations remaining on the intercardinal headings—NE, SE, SW, and NW—by any of the methods discussed earlier in this chapter; or you can estimate them by making reciprocal runs on these headings. In this method, the deviation will be half the difference between the outward course steered by compass and the reading of the compass when the turn has been made and the craft pointed back to the starting point. Be sure to note the direction of the deviation, east or west. *Do not touch the N-S or E-W adjustment screws.*

Intercardinal heading errors can be especially troublesome on craft with a steel hull, or if there is a larger mass of iron near the compass. In such situations, the services of a professional compass adjuster should be obtained.

Failure to Achieve Compensation

When compensation cannot be achieved satisfactorily, you undoubtedly have an undetected magnetic field on your boat. Prime suspects are the tachometer cable(s) and the steering mechanism. Test them with a thin piece of steel; a machinist's thickness gauge for a few thousands of an inch (0.05 to 0.10 mm) is ideal. Make sure that this thin piece of steel is not itself magnetized.

Touch one end of this thin piece of steel to the part being tested for magnetism and gently pull it away. If it tends to stick to the part, the latter is magnetized. Test all around thoroughly. Open the wheel housing or look under the instrument panel; test all metal parts found.

If a magnet is located, demagnetization will be required. You may need professional advice and assistance, but try your own hand at the job first, using the procedures on page 465.

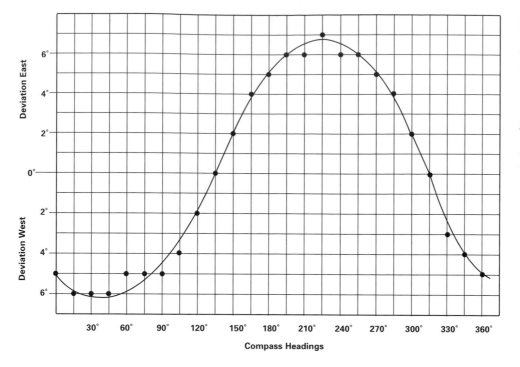

Figure 13-23
When you have all your data, and before making a final deviation table, make a simple plot of the values to spot any that are not consistent with the others.

The Final Deviation Table

When the compass has been adjusted to the greatest possible extent, make a complete deviation check and prepare a table for any deviations found; use any of the methods described earlier.

Make this check under all conditions in which the compass might be used; check with the navigation lights on and off (they may be distant from the compass but wires running to their switch will be nearby), with the windshield wipers operating and not operating, and with the electronic depth sounder, radio direction finder, and radio each on and off. Look also for other electrical equipment whose operation could affect the compass. Remember to check on two cardinal headings 90 degrees apart. Most of this equipment will not disturb the compass, *but some could,* and you must be aware of it. If any checked items have to be on when the compass is in use, you may need to have more than one deviation table. You may also sometimes have to turn on certain equipment, whether needed or not, to re-create the magnetic environment that existed when the deviation table was prepared. A sailboat may need different deviation tables for port and starboard tacks because of different heeling errors. If two or more deviation tables are necessary, it is a good idea to use different color paper for each.

Before preparing the final deviation table, plot a simple graph of the values to be used. Lay out a horizontal base line for compass headings from 0° to 360°; plot easterly deviation vertically above the base line and westerly deviations below that line at a suitable scale; see **Figure 13-23.** When all values of deviation have been plotted, draw a *smooth* curve through the points, but don't expect all values to be exactly on that line since the deviations have been measured only to the nearest whole degree. You should be able to get a smooth curve through or near all of the points; if any value lies significantly off the curve, it is probably in error and should be rechecked. If you can draw a smooth curve, but its center axis does not coincide with the horizontal base line for 0° deviation, the lubber's line may be out of alignment; recheck carefully.

The final deviation table can be alternatively prepared as a direct-reading table of critical values; see page 468 and **Table 13-6.** Whichever style of deviation table you choose to prepare, it can be used with confidence if care is taken to see that the magnetic environment is not altered.

Check it each year, even though you think that no changes have been made that would upset the deviation table.

COMPASS MAINTENANCE

In addition to protecting the instrument from direct sunlight when not in use, compass maintenance has two aspects. The first is the preservation of the magnetic environment that surrounds it. Except for occasional testing, no piece of iron or steel should be brought or installed near it, lest it cause unknown deviations. The second aspect of maintenance consists mainly of getting to know your compass. Watch how it swings. Check that its readings are consistent on frequently run courses. Note if it appears to become sluggish and above all if it becomes erratic—these conditions warn you of undetected disturbances or a damaged pivot bearing.

CONVENTIONAL DEVIATION TABLE

Magnetic Heading (in degrees)	Deviation (in degrees)	Compass Heading (in degrees)	Deviation (in degrees)	Magnetic Heading (in degrees)	Deviation (in degrees)	Compass Heading (in degrees)	Deviation (in degrees)
000	7°E	000	5°E	105	17°W	105	19°W
015	1°E	015	1°E	120	14°W	120	17°W
030	6°W	030	4°W	135	11°W	135	14°W
045	12°W	045	9°W	150	8°W	150	10°W
060	17°W	060	13°W	165	5°W	165	6°W
075	19°W	075	17°W	180	2°W	180	2°W
090	18°W	090	19°W	195	2°E	195	2°E

CRITICAL VALUES TABLE

Magnetic Heading (in degrees)	Deviation (in degrees)	Compass Heading (in degrees)	Magnetic Heading (in degrees)	Deviation (in degrees)	Compass Heading (in degrees)
000-003 223-229	7°E	351-355 217-222	019-020 179-182	1°W	019-021 181-182
004-005 216-222	6°E	356-359 211-216	021-022 174-178	2°W	022-024 177-180
006-007 211-215	5°E	000-002 206-210	023-024 167-173	3°W	025-026 172-176
008-009 205-210	4°E	003-005 202-205	025-026 163-166	4°W	027-028 168-171
010-011 198-204	3°E	006-008 196-201	027-028 160-162	5°W	029-030 166-167
012-013 193-197	2°E	009-010 192-195	029-030 154-159	6°W	031-032 161-165
014-015 188-192	1°E	011-115 188-191	031-033 148-153	7°W	033-036 157-160
016-018 183-187	0°	016-018 183-187	034-035 143-147	8°W	037-040 153-156

Table 13-6 A deviation table—shown here in two formats—permits the conversion of directions from magnetic to compass, or from compass to magnetic. A conventional table, upper, requires interpolation to get values between the lines of data. For example: for a magnetic heading of 10°, the deviation lies between 7°E for 000° and 1°E for 015°; interpolation gives 3°E. With the critical values table, lower, you can go directly to the value needed, no interpolation is required. (Deviation values have been exaggerated for clarity; on an actual vessel, they would have been reduced by compensation.)

Test for a damaged bearing or undue pivot friction by deflecting the card two or three degrees with a small magnet or piece of iron. If the card does not return to its former position, the compass should be removed from the boat and taken to a reputable shop for tests and, probably, repair.

As mentioned, a bubble can be removed by adding some liquid, but the liquid must be the same as that with which the compass is filled. This is best left to a compass repair shop.

Lightning strikes on board or near by may change the craft's magnetic field; electric welding can have the same effect. After exposure to either of these, check deviations.

In northern waters, care should be taken that metal objects on the boat have not acquired a magnetic field over the winter storage period; a newly magnetized piece of metal could, of course, confuse the compass and require readjustment of the compensators, or the making of a new deviation table.

Do read and follow the manufacturer's instructions for winter storage if the boat is taken out of regular service. Doing so may add years to the compass's useful life.

ADVANCED COMPASS TOPICS

The following sections on various topics on magnetism and compasses are generally beyond the "need-to-know" of the average skipper. Some, however, will be of value to those with special problems, and many others will be of interest to those skippers who want to have a bit more than the minimum knowledge.

Magnetism

Contrary to some popular ideas, the location of the earth's MAGNETIC POLES is of little interest to the navigator. (Should he ever get to their vicinity, he would then have to rely for directional information on some instrument other than his magnetic compass.)

Variation is *not* the angle between the direction to the true and magnetic poles. This concept, a fictitious visualization useful in helping students to realize that true and magnetic north are usually different directions, has been accepted by many as truth. This must be recognized as merely a learning aid, not a factual representation. The magnetic pole does not control the compass. The controlling force is the earth's magnetic field. The compass magnet does not necessarily point in the precise direction of the magnetic pole.

Actually, two specific points on the earth's surface that are the magnetic poles do not exist. There are north and south MAGNETIC POLAR AREAS containing many apparent magnetic poles, places where a dip needle would stand vertically. If this seems strange, consider the problem of pinpointing the precise point in the end of a bar magnet that is the pole.

For scientific purposes, approximate positions of the theoretical North and South Magnetic Poles have been computed from a large number of continuing observations made over the world for many years. They are not diametrically opposite each other as are the geographic poles. The magnetic poles do not stay in the same place; they wander about with both short-term and long-term cycles. They are relatively distant from the geographic poles. Very roughly, the North Magnetic Pole is at 76° N, 100° W with the South Magnetic Pole at 66° S, 139° E. A magnetic compass at 80° N, 100° W would show north in a direction truly southward of the compass.

A magnetic meridian is generally not a segment of a great circle passing though the magnetic poles, since only one great circle can pass though any two surface points not at the ends of a diameter. Not so obvious, but just as true, the magnetic meridian is generally not part of a great circle from a given point to the adjacent magnetic pole.

Isogonic Lines

On smaller scale charts covering larger areas, variation may be shown by ISOGONIC LINES; every point on such a line has the same variation. Each line is labeled with the amount and direction of variation, the date, and the annual rate of change. The line joining all points having zero variation is called the AGONIC LINE; see **Figure 13-24**.

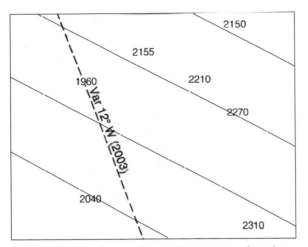

Figure 13-24 Offshore charts of large areas often show magnetic variation by a series of broken lines for each degree of variation. Each such isogonic line is labeled with its variation.

Induced & Permanent Magnetism

Masses of iron or related metals that do not show any magnetic properties under usual conditions will acquire INDUCED MAGNETISM when brought near a magnet and into its field. The polarity of an induced pole is *opposite* to that of the nearest pole of the magnet that caused it. When the inducing field is removed, any magnetism that remains is termed RESIDUAL. If the object retains magnetism for a long period of time without appreciable reduction in strength, this is PERMANENT MAGNETISM.

Magnetism from Electrical Circuits

Although the copper of electrical wires is nonmagnetic material, currents flowing in them produce magnetic fields. It is this effect that makes possible electrical motors, generators, relays, electromagnets, etc. A direct current in a wire results in a field that can affect a vessel's compass. (Alternating-current electricity also produces magnetic fields, but not of the type to disturb a compass.) The polarity of a field around a wire carrying DC is related to the direction of the current, a fact that can be used to advantage. The two wires carrying power to any load have currents in the opposite directions, thus producing opposing fields. If these wires are

twisted together, the field around one wire cancels out the field produced by the other, and the net effect on the compass will be *zero*, or nearly so.

Always use two wires, don't use a common ground for return current, and always twist pairs of wires that pass near a compass. Don't fail, however, also to make an actual check by observing the compass closely as the electrical circuit is switched on and off; make this test on two cardinal headings 90 degrees apart.

Demagnetization

If tests with a thin strip of steel (see page 461) have shown that some metal object at the control station is magnetized, it *may* be possible to DEMAGNETIZE it with a device used by electronic repair shops, such as a degaussing coil for TV sets or a magnetic-tape bulk eraser. If the magnetized object cannot be removed from the boat for undertaking this effort, it is *mandatory* that the compass be taken off lest the effectiveness of its magnets be destroyed.

The demagnetizing device is operated from 120-volt shore power; it uses alternating currents to produce magnetic fields that reverse at the 60 Hz frequency. Hold the device about a foot (0.3 m) from the target object and turn on the power; do not turn off the device until the full process has been carried out. Advance the demagnetizer slowly toward the object until it touches; move it around slowly over all the accessible surfaces of the object. Remove the device slowly away until it is at least the starting distance away and then turn it off. (If power to the demagnetizing device was interrupted at any time during the process, start over again and repeat all steps.) Take care not to demagnetize anything that is properly magnetic, such as electrical instruments or radio speakers.

Now test the disturbing object again with the thin strip of steel. If it has been possible to reach all of the object, it should be demagnetized. Often, however, complete access is not possible, and the object may have to be disassembled and/or removed from the boat for complete demagnetization.

After the demagnetization process is completed, remount the compass, and, in *all* cases, make an entirely new deviation table.

Why Deviation Depends on the Boat's Heading

Aboard a boat, the compass is subject to two magnetic forces, that of the earth and that of objects on the craft. If the boat were absolutely free of magnetism—no permanent magnets, no material subject to acquiring induced magnetism, and no fields from electrical currents—there would be no deviation on any heading; see **Figure 13-25.** The earth's force depends upon geographic locations; the compasses of all vessels in the same harbor are subject to the same variation. The deviations aboard these ships and boats will be dissimilar because of the differences in the magnetic characteristics of each vessel. Thus if all of them put in identical magnetic headings, their compasses would differ, except in the remote circumstance that each compass was completely compensated.

DEVIATION, it will be remembered, *varies with the craft's heading* because of magnetic material on board. A few examples may make this clearer. Refer again to **Figure 13-25,** the nonmagnetic boat. No heading of this craft affects its compass card; its North point always lies on the magnetic meridian; the compass has no deviation. As the boat changes heading, the lubber's line, turning with the bow, indicates the magnetic heading on the card.

Now put aboard the craft, in the vicinity of the compass, items such as radios, electronic depth sounders, electrical gauges, and other instruments. Also on the boat, but usually farther from the compass, are metallic masses such as anchors, chain, fuel and water tanks, and other magnetic items, including the engine (the engine is by far the largest mass of magnetizable material, but it is relatively distant from the compass). The boat has now acquired a magnetic character of its own; in addition to any permanent magnetism of some objects, there are now masses of unmagnetized material that can affect the compass by acquiring induced magnetism.

The effects on the compass of permanent magnetism and induced magnetism are different and must be considered separately.

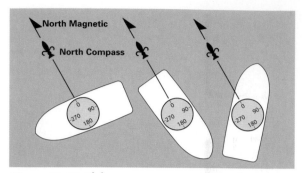

Figure 13-25 If there are no magnetic disturbances on the boat to disturb its compass—which is rarely the case—there is no deviation on any heading.

Effect of Permanent Magnetism

On typical boats of wood or fiberglass, the effect of permanent magnetism is by far the greater. To visualize this, let us assume that the same net effect would be exerted by a single permanent magnet located aft of the compass and slightly askew of the boat's centerline; see **Figure 13-26.** This representation by an imaginary magnet is quite applicable; it simulates conditions found on most boats other than those with a steel hull. (The exact position of the imaginary magnet, its polarity, strength, and angle of skew are not important in this illustration of principles.)

Two forces, that of the field of the earth and that of the field of the imaginary magnet, now affect the compass; its poles are attracted or repelled in accordance with the basic law of magnetism. Without the influence of the imaginary magnet, the compass magnets and card will line up with the magnet meridian. The 0° mark of the card is an N (north-seeking) pole, and the 180° mark is at an S pole. Now, in addition to the effect of the earth's magnet poles on them, the N and S poles of the compass magnets will be attracted or repelled by the S pole of the imaginary magnet (the pole nearer the compass in these examples). The result is easterly deviation on some headings, westerly on others, and zero on those where the sign of the deviation changes from east to west, or from west to east.

Consider a typical boat, *Morning Star,* headed north (000°) magnetic; see **Figure 13-26A.** The S pole of the compass, 180° on the card, is repelled by the S pole of the imaginary magnet. The result

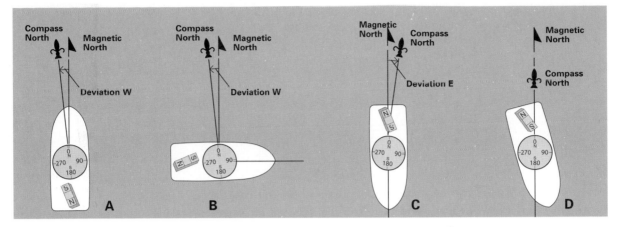

Figure 13-26 On a north magnetic heading, A, the S pole of the compass is repelled by the S pole of the imaginary magnet representing the net effect of all magnetic influences on the boat. The card is deflected counter-clockwise; there is westerly deviation. On an east heading, B, the N pole of the compass is nearer the S pole of the imaginary magnet, and is attracted toward it. The deflection is still counter-clockwise; the deviation is still westerly. On a south magnetic heading, C, the N pole of the compass is nearest the S pole of the imaginary magnet and is attracted to it. The card is deflected clockwise; the deviation is easterly. On an intermediate heading, D, the N pole of the compass is attracted to the S pole of the imaginary magnet, but is already as close to it as it can get. There is no deflection, and thus no deviation on this heading.

is that the card is rotated counterclockwise; the compass reading is increased, 006° in this instance, and there is westerly deviation.

On a south magnetic heading, as in **Figure 13-26C,** the N pole of the compass magnet, 000° on the card, is nearer the S pole of the imaginary magnet and is attracted by it. The card is deflected clockwise and the compass reading decreases, to 174° and deviation is easterly.

If the magnetic heading of *Morning Star* is to the east, as in **Figure 13-26B,** the N pole of the compass magnet is the nearer pole to the S pole of the imaginary magnet and it is attracted. This results in a counterclockwise rotation of the compass card giving westerly deviation. On a west magnetic heading, the deflection of the card is clockwise for easterly deviation. (It is a good exercise to diagram this situation for yourself.)

In the above examples, the deviation is westerly on an east magnetic heading, but easterly on a south magnetic heading. Thus there must be some intermediate heading where the deviation passes through zero as the sign changes from west to east. This situation is approximated in **Figure 13-26D.** There is still attraction of the N pole of the compass by the S pole of the imaginary magnet, but on this heading the compass card has

its N pole as close to the S pole of the magnet as it can get. Thus there is no deflection of the card in either direction, no deviation.

As has been illustrated above, deviation resulting from permanent magnetism will normally swing through one cycle of west to east and back to west in 360°, with two headings having zero deviation.

Do not assume that the location, polarity, and angle of skew of the imaginary magnet would be the same on any other boat as in the above examples, which are for the sole purpose of illustrating principles. A change of one or more of these factors would result in an entirely different set of deviations.

Effect of Induced Magnetism

The effect of induced magnetism on a compass can be visualized in a series of examples much like the above with an imaginary mass of magnetizable material. In this case, the disturbing pole would be the one induced in that mass and its sign would change as determined by the changing sign of the nearer pole of the inducing magnet. The sign of the deviation would change *four* times in 360 degrees, with *four* headings having zero deviation.

If the effects of permanent and induced magnetism are combined, a complex situation results; fortunately, this is unlikely for most small craft.

Effect of Geographic Position

Deviation can change with changes in MAGNETIC LATTITUDE of a vessel. The strengths of most magnetic influences on a boat are unchanged at different geographic positions, but the horizontal component of the earth's field lessens in higher latitudes. Hence the interaction of these two forces, the cause of deviation, changes with varying magnetic latitudes.

Compass Calculations

COMPASS ERROR (CE) is sometimes used in compass calculations as a specific term. It is the algebraic sum of the variation and deviation. Because variation depends on geographic location, and the deviation upon the craft's heading, there are various possible combinations of these two quantities; refer to **Figure 3-17.** Similarly to variation and deviation, it is expressed in degrees and direction, for example 5°E or 7°W; in boating, it is given to the nearest whole degree.

This is a term used for convenience. The compass is not actually in error; it is operating according to the forces that control its behavior. Compass error is merely the angle between true north and compass north.

Interpolation

The process of determining intermediate values between tabular entries is called INTERPOLATION. It is most easily explained by several examples. Consider the following extract from a deviation table:

Compass Heading	Deviation
090°	7°E
105°	4°E

Assume that we need the deviation for a compass heading of 100°. The interval between tabular entries is 15 degrees; the difference between deviation values is 3 degrees. Since 100° is

$^{10}/_{15}$ of the way between 090° and 105°, we multiply the value difference by that fraction: $3° \times {}^{10}/_{15} = 2°$. Since the deviation is decreasing, this is subtracted: 7°E - 2° = 5°E, the deviation for 100°.

If the values are not so even as above, an answer with a fraction will result. If we had desired the deviation for 098°, the fraction would have been $^{8}/_{15}$, and the result $3° \times {}^{8}/_{15} = 1.6°$; then 7° - 1.6 = 5.4°E; but for boat use deviation is not used more precisely than the nearest whole degree and thus the deviation for 098° would be recorded and used as 5°E. If the fractional value is 0.5°, use the nearest even, not odd, degree.

Caution must be used when the two values of deviation are of *opposite* name. The value difference between 3°W and 1°E is *four* degrees, not two.

Critical Values Tables

A skipper will need deviation values in terms of both compass headings (for correcting calculations) and magnetic headings (for uncorrecting). A simple way to combine both of these, and have a more easily used table as well, is to prepare a direct-reading table of CRITICAL VALUES. Such a table is prepared in basic terms of deviations rather than headings. There is a line in the table for each whole degree of deviation; opposite this is listed on one side the range of compass headings for which that value of deviation is applicable; on the other side is the range of magnetic headings which have that value of deviation. See the below partial example and **Table 13-6,** where different numbers are used.

Magnetic	Deviation	Compass
133°-144°	0°	133°-145°
145°-153°	1°E	146°-153°
154°-163°	2°E	154°-162°
164°-176°	3°E	163°-174°
177°-187°	4°E	175°-185°

Special Compensation Situations

The procedures of compensation described earlier in this chapter will fit most, but not all, recreational boats and their compasses. Special situations are discussed below.

Using External Magnets

If the boat's compass (or binnacle) does not have internal compensating magnets, it still can be adjusted to near zero deviation if there is space to place external magnets where they are needed.

Two compensating magnets will be needed. Each is an encased permanent magnet having two holes in the case for screw fastening. The ends of the magnets will either be marked N and S, or be colored red on the north end and blue on the south. Masking tape is good for temporary fastening; be sure that the screws used for final fastening are nonmagnetic. Carefully mark the longitudinal center of each magnet. In the areas where the external magnets will be placed, carefully mark out in chalk two lines through the compass center, for fore-and-aft and one athwartships; see **Figure 13-27**.

General Procedures The compensation process consists of making outward runs on cardinal headings by compass, dropping a disposable buoy, turning, and heading back toward the point of departure. All this is done in the same manner as was done for internal compensators. Keep all external magnets far from the compass until each one is to be used.

Adjustment on E-W Headings If compensation is shown to be needed—for example, the compass reads 290° on the reciprocal of a 090° outward run—the correction is made by placing an external compensating magnet in a fore-and-aft position centered on an athwartship chalked line. This can be placed on either side of the compass in position Λ or Λ' of **Figure 13-27**, right. Should the compass reading now become more than 290, the compensation is increasing the deviation; move the magnet to the other side of the compass or turn it end-for-end (but don't do both). The card will then move in the desired direction, toward 270°.

Should the card stop moving before 280° (the reading for removal of half of the error), the compensator, in a position such as at D, is too far from the compass. On the other hand, if the card moves past 280°, the compensator is too close to the compass, as at C, and must be moved farther away. Move the external magnet closer to or farther from the compass until the desired reading is attained. Now tape the compensator down; no screws yet. *Do not let it get off the centerline as at* E. As with internal compensators, a second E-W run is then made, or perhaps more, until zero deviation is achieved.

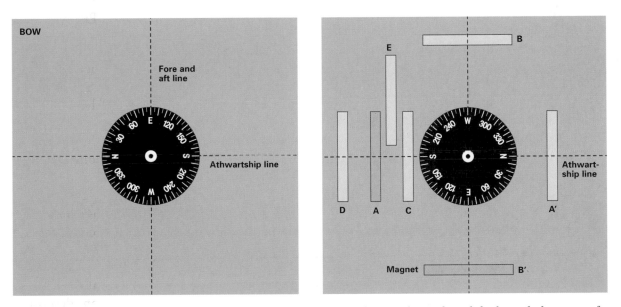

Figure 13-27 Before installing external compensating magnets, chalk in two lines, above left, through the center of the compass mounting location. The magnets must always be placed so that their centers are on one of these lines. Magnets are placed forward or aft of the compass and on one side, above right. When final placement has been determined, they are fastened down with nonmagnetic tacks or screws.

Adjustments on N-S Headings After the turn back on a north or south run, one-half of any deviation is adjusted out by placing a compensator in an athwartship position *centered* on the fore-and-aft line, such as at B′ in **Figure 13-27, right**. If there is no room for the magnet in front of the compass, place it aft of the instrument in the vicinity of B′. Move it closer to the compass or farther away—and reverse ends if needed—in the same manner as on east-west runs.

When, after sufficient runs, the deviation is zero, or reduced to a minimum, screw down the magnets (remember, nonmagnetic screws) with care that their position is not shifted. It is wise to make one more E-W and then N-S run after the magnets have been secured in place as a final test of your work.

Compensation by Shadow Pin

A method of sailing reciprocal courses without setting up temporary ranges with disposable buoys uses a vertical shadow pin in the center of a horizontal disc graduated similar to a compass card; the disc should be gimbal-mounted.

As the craft heads east (or west) by the compass, the disc is rotated by hand so that the shadow of the pin caused by the sun falls on the 090° (270°) mark. The turn is made and the boat is steadied on such a heading that the shadow falls on the opposite side of the disc, exactly on the 270° (090°) mark. If the compass now reads 270° (090°), there is no deviation on E-W headings. If not 270° (090°), the previously described procedures are followed for adjustment. A similar technique is used for north-south headings.

This procedure has advantages. The boat need not run far on any heading. No departure mark or disposable buoy is required. Neither the wind nor current will affect the result. But there is one complicating factor—the sun and its shadow do not stand still. Regardless of how steady the boat is being held on a heading, the shadow is moving. Time becomes a factor in execution of the procedure; compensators must be adjusted before the shadow moves enough to upset the process, taking the boat off a true reciprocal heading.

Compensation on Sailboats

Sailing craft, heeling out of a horizontal trim, frequently require HEELING MAGNETS below the compass to reduce their deviation. Small-craft skippers can make a rough compensation, but an exact adjustment is a job for a professional compass adjuster.

Place your sailboat on a N-S heading and heel her slightly, maintaining a constant heading. Place a correction magnet vertically under the compass so as to eliminate *only* the deviation induced by heeling; reverse the ends of the magnet if necessary. Even if you are unable to make this adjustment, try heeling your sailboat to see the effect on your compass.

Compensation on Steel Boats

Steel hulls may present problems whose solution may require installation of soft iron QUADRANTIAL SPHERES; **see Figure 13-28**. Another solution might be the use of FLINDERS BARS, or possibly heeling magnets. All this is for the professional adjuster, or for the skipper who has achieved professional competence.

Iron and steel vessels are subject to changes in deviation upon large changes in latitude. This must be considered when cruising in such craft.

OTHER INSTRUMENTS

Several other direction instruments will be of general interest to boatmen although few skippers will have more than one or two of them.

Hand-bearing Compass

A small compass (some equipped with a handle) designed to be easily held in front of one's face is termed a HAND-BEARING COMPASS; see Chapter 16, page 562. This instrument is normally used for taking bearings, especially those that cannot be conveniently sighted across the steering compass.

A more sophisticated (and more expensive) hand-bearing compass combines a 5 x 30 monocular, a digital compass, an electronic rangefinder, and a chronometer in a single lightweight, handheld instrument. It can show the distance to an object as well as its compass bearing and the time

Figure 13-28 Vessels, including boats, with steel hulls present special cases for compass compensation. It will normally be necessary to mount two quadrantal spheres of soft iron on the binnacle and then adjust them very carefully—this is work for a professional compass adjuster.

of the observation; up to nine bearings can be recorded with the push of a button.

In an emergency, a hand-bearing compass can be used for steering the boat.

Tell-Tale Compass

A TELL-TALE COMPASS is one located belowdecks, usually overhead above the skipper's bunk. These go back to the days when the captain used one to keep an eye on the course steered when he was not on deck. Today, they can serve the same purpose on long passages, but the more likely use is to watch out for wind and current shifts when riding at anchor for the night.

A tell-tale compass is an ordinary magnetic compass built upside-down so that the bottom of the card can be read. Some models have markings on both sides of their cards so that they can be used equally well in normal fashion or inverted as a tell-tale mounted overhead.

Pelorus

A PERLORUS is an instrument having sight vanes and a compass-like card, either of which can be clamped in a fixed position. Sometimes referred to as a DUMB COMPASS, it is used to take bearing when it is not possible to do so across the steering compass. The pelorus is placed in a location suit-able for observation; its zero point is adjusted to either compass North or the boat's current heading, depending upon whether compass or relative bearings are desired.

Gyrocompass

Ships and the largest of yachts will normally be fitted with a GYROCOMPASS, a complex device that senses changes in the direction of the vessel. One type of gyrocompass holds a preset orientation, but gradually drifts off; it is independent of the earth's magnetic field. Another, more complex type orients itself with respect to the earth's rotation. This is the ultimate device for measuring direction at sea, yielding true, rather than magnetic, directions. Such units, however, are generally too large and too expensive for typical small craft. But even gyrocompasses are not perfect, they must occasionally be reset, and adjustments are required for changes in latitude. Details on gyrocompasses are beyond the scope of this book.

Interested readers are referred to *Publication No. 9—Bowditch—*of the National Imagery and Mapping Agency, or to *Dutton's Navigation and Piloting* published by the U.S. Naval Institute.

GPS Compass

The signals that GPS receivers (refer to Chapter 21, page 726) use to determine position can also be used by a GPS COMPASS (also called a SATELITTE COMPASS) to determine the heading of a vessel. This can be done whether or not the vessel is underway; normal GPS receivers can display course-made good (also called course-over-the ground), but this is not the same as instantaneous heading and cannot be determined when the vessel is stationary.

Two GPS antennas are mounted on a fixed fore-and-aft baseline, either in a small dome or in the open (other orientations are possible by entering alignment details into the system). The GPS signals from satellites arrive at these antennas at the same time only for a specific orientation; at other times, there is a difference in the phase of the signals. Sophisticated computer technology uses the phase difference to determine the direction that the signals are coming from, and hence the heading of the vessel. As only phase information is used, these signals need not be differentially corrected. Three-axis solid-state gyro rate sensors ensure the continuity of heading information during periods of signal dropout for any reason, such as passing under a bridge. Some models use a third GPS antenna to reduce the negative effects of vessel motion in pitch, roll, and yaw. Headings are displayed to tenths of a degree; accuracy is typically better than 0.5°. The output of a GPS compass is in true headings; these can be changed to magnetic values by the introduction of variation information.

GPS compasses are not affected by the vessel's speed, acceleration, latitude, or magnetic conditions on board. The heading information can be used by many types of on navigation equipment, such as autopilots, course plotters, and radar displays. GPS compasses also provide the normal output information of a GPS receiver, and benefit from having multiple sources of data.

Sun Compass

A SUN COMPASS is not a true compass; it is an instrument for taking bearings of the sun. The observer looks not at the sun, but at a shadow cast by a small pin in the center of the card. The card is graduated clockwise through 360° starting with zero at south. The shadow thus marks the sun's bearing. If the instrument is properly oriented with the vessel's heading, the shadow will show the ship's true course. The difference between its reading and the ship's compass is the compass error, CE. Applying variation yields the deviation of the ship's compass on the heading. Accuracy depends upon knowledge of the sun's true bearing. Since latitude, date, and time affect this, and since the rate of change of the sun's true bearing is not constant, the procedure is complex and requires experience for satisfactory results. Some spherical compasses have a shadow pin mounted on the card directly above the pivot. A knowledgeable skipper can use this in checking deviation by azimuths of the sun. (This pin is also very useful when bearings are taken directly over the compass.)

Aids to Navigation

Buoys • Daybeacons • Lights of All Sizes & Types • Sound Signals
Ranges & Directional Lights—All Vitally Necessary for Safe Navigation

Unlike the roads and highways that we drive on, the waterways we go boating on do not have road signs that tell us our location, the route or distance to a destination, or of hazards along the way. Instead, the waterways have AIDS TO NAVIGATION, all those man-made objects used by mariners to determine position or a safe course. These aids also assist mariners in making landfalls, mark isolated dangers, enable pilots to follow channels, and provide a continuous chain of charted marks for precise piloting in coastal waters. An aid to navigation system is designed, and intended, to be used with a nautical chart. The exact meaning of an aid may not be clear to a navigator unless the appropriate chart is consulted, as the chart illustrates the relationship of the individual aid to channel limits, obstructions, hazards to navigation, and to the total aids to navigation system.

The term "aid to navigation" includes buoys, daybeacons, lights, lightships, radiobeacons, and sound signals (The United States no longer has any lightships or marine radiobeacons, but these may be found in some foreign waters.). Also included are the Global Positioning System (GPS), Loran, and other electronic systems that are covered in Chapter 21. The term covers all the visible, audible, and electronic signals that are established by government and private authorities for piloting purposes. The U.S. Coast Guard uses the acronym ATON.

Note that the term NAVIGATION AID is far broader, including charts, instruments, and methods that assist in marine navigation.

Aids to navigation are shown on the appropriate charts. Good piloting starts with the ability to correlate what appears on the charts with what you actually see on the water.

Previous Page: Figure 14-01 Buoys, daybeacons, and minor lights all follow a systematic pattern of shapes and colors, whereas primary lights, such as lighthouses, are more distinctive and diverse.

Aids established by the federal government are placed only where the amount of traffic justifies their cost and upkeep. Within bounds of necessity and cost, each aid is designed to be seen or heard over the greatest possible area.

Operating Agencies

The U.S. Coast Guard is the agency responsible for maintaining aids to navigation on U.S. waters that are under federal jurisdiction or that serve the needs of the U.S. armed forces. Each Coast Guard District has supply and buoy depots, and special vessels for maintaining the aids.

State-Maintained Aids

On bodies of water wholly within the boundaries of a single state, and not navigable to the sea, the state is responsible for establishing and maintaining aids to navigation.

Although each state keeps authority over its waters, a uniform system of aids and regulatory markers was established in 1966, see page 490, but this is now being phased out in favor of aids conforming to the system used in coastal waters.

"Private" Aids to Navigation

With prior approval, aids to navigation may be established in U.S. federal waters by individuals or agencies other than the U.S. Coast Guard. Commercial, naval, scientific, sporting, or other private organization may establish aids for their own specific purposes. These might consist of such diverse activities as lights on loading docks, data-gathering devices for oceanographers, or racing marks for regattas. These PRIVATE AIDS must be patterned after federal aids, and any fixed structure planned for navigable waters requires a permit from the U.S. Army Corps of Engineers. See any Coast Guard District Headquarters for details and procedures.

All such aids to navigation—whether established by an individual, a corporation, a state or local government, or even a federal agency other than the Coast Guard, such as the Navy—are private aids. They must have the same appearance as Coast Guard-maintained aids, but are specially designated in the *Light Lists;* see page 549.

Protection by Law

Whether or not established by the Coast Guard, all aids to navigation are protected by law. It is a criminal offense to cause any damage or hindrance to the proper operation of any aid. Do not deface, alter, move, or destroy any aid to navigation. Never tie your boat to a buoy, daybeacon, or light structure. Avoid anchoring so close to a buoy that you obscure the aid from sight of passing vessels. If you should unintentionally or unavoidably collide with or damage an aid to navigation, report the fact to the nearest Coast Guard unit without delay.

Suggestions for improvements to aids to navigation should be submitted in writing to the Commander of the Coast Guard District concerned; see Appendix D.

TYPES OF AIDS TO NAVIGATION

The term "aid to navigation" encompasses a wide range of floating and fixed objects ("fixed" meaning attached to the bottom or shore), ranging from a small buoy or a single pile of wood, concrete, or metal with a sign to lighthouses with an array of visible, audible, and electronic signals. Informal aids such as bush stakes marking natural channels or hazards in a creek are not a part of the organized system of aids to navigation.

Prominent buildings, cupolas, smokestacks, and other structures ashore as well as unique land features, also can be used as signposts for navigation. These are LANDMARKS, as distinguished from aids established solely for navigation.

Major Types

BUOYS are floating objects—other than lightships—that are anchored to the bottom as aids to navigation. They have distinctive shapes and colors as determined by location and purpose, and may have visual, audible, and/or electronic signals; see pages 476–481.

BEACONS are aids to navigation structures that are permanently fixed to the earth's surface, on shore or in the water; they may be of any size, from a lighthouse to a single pile. Lighted beacons are called LIGHTS; unlighted beacons are called DAYBEACONS.

Beacons are equipped with one or more DAYMARKS of a distinctive shape and color for daytime identification. Lights are classified by the U.S. Coast Guard and other authorities as PRIMARY SEACOAST LIGHTS, SECONDARY LIGHTS, or MINOR LIGHTS, as determined by their location, importance, and physical characteristics. A light's range and intensity vary with its classification. The shape and color of its supporting structure may be distinctive to identify it, but these characteristics do not convey information as they do for buoys. The term LIGHTHOUSE is often applied to primary seacoast lights and to some secondary lights; see **Figure 14-01.**

SOUND SIGNALS are audible signals sounded to assist mariners during periods of low visibility. They may occasionally be separate aids, as when located on the end of a jetty, but are generally part of a buoy, light, or larger aid to navigation.

RANGES are pairs of unlighted or lighted fixed aids that, when observed in line, show the pilot to be on the centerline of a channel. Individual structures may also serve to mark a turn in a channel.

LIGHTSHIPS are specially equipped vessels anchored at specific locations to serve as aids to navigation. They are of distinctive shape and color, and have lights, sound signals, and radiobeacons. In U.S. waters lightships have been replaced by permanent towers and large, specially equipped buoys, as explained later in this chapter.

RADIOBEACONS are transmitters broadcasting a characteristic signal specifically to aid navigation at night, in fog, or at distances exceeding normal visibility. These are usually at another aid, such as a major light, but may be located separately.

RADIONAVIGATION SYSTEMS are radio transmitters ashore and on satellites that emit special signals for use in navigation in fog or when beyond sight of land or offshore aids. The systems include Loran-C and Differential Global Positioning System (DGPS) operated by the Coast Guard, the Global Positioning System (GPS) operated by the Department of Defense, and aeronautical radiobeacons and Omni stations run by the Federal Aviation Administration. There are also some private systems, but these will seldom be available to recreational boaters.

BUOYS

Buoys are anchored to the bottom at specific locations, and are shown on charts by special symbols and lettering that indicate their shape, color, and visual and/or sound signals (if any). They vary widely in size. Buoys are secured to the bottom, using chain, to heavy concrete "sinkers" weighing up to six tons or more. The length of the chain will vary with the location, but may be as much as three times the depth of the water.

The buoyage system adopted for United States waters consists of several different types of buoys, each kind designed to serve under definite conditions. Broadly speaking, all buoys serve as daytime aids; many have lights and/or sound signals so that they may be used at night and in periods of poor visibility.

A buoy's shape, color, and light characteristics, if any, give a navigator information about his location and the safe guidance of his vessel. A buoy's size is usually determined by the importance of the waterway and size of vessels using it, and the distance at which the buoy must be seen.

Buoy Characteristics

Buoys may be unlighted or lighted, sound buoys, or combination buoys (having both an audible and a visual signal). The Coast Guard maintains about 20,000 unlighted and 4,100 lighted and combination buoys in waters under its jurisdiction. Additional buoys are maintained by state and private agencies in nonfederal waters.

Buoy Shapes

Unlighted buoys may be further classified by their shape.

CAN BUOYS have a cylindrical above-water appearance, like a can or drum floating with its axis vertical and flat end upward; see **Figure 14-02.** Two lifting lugs may project slightly above the flat top of a can buoy, but they do not significantly alter its appearance.

NUN BUOYS have an above-water appearance like that of a cylinder topped with a cone, pointed end up; see **Figure 14-03.** The cone may come to a point or be slightly rounded. Smaller nun buoys have a single lifting ring at the top; larger buoys have several lugs around the sides.

Unlighted buoys come in standardized sizes; a nun's above-water portion may vary from 30 inches (0.76 m) to 14 feet (4.27 m); can buoys range from roughly 18 inches (0.46 m) to nearly ten feet (3.05 m) above the waterline. Boaters should remember that a considerable portion of a buoy is under water, so that it is actually much larger and heavier than would appear from casual observation. Some smaller temporary buoys are now made of plastic materials.

SPHERICAL BUOYS are now used in the revised U.S. lateral system for a specific purpose as discussed later in this chapter, see page 485.

Other buoys of special shapes will sometimes be found in use as markers, but these are not

Figure 14-02 A can buoy is cylindrical in shape with its long axis vertical. On some buoys, the upper part is made of metal plates at right angles to each other, making it an excellent radar reflector. Most, but not all, can buoys are constructed in this manner.

regular aids to navigation. The Coast Guard has now eliminated the use of SPAR buoys, but they may be used in some other nations or in private systems. They are usually large vertical logs, trimmed, shaped, and appropriately painted; they are anchored at one end by a chain.

Lighted, sound, and combination buoys are described by their visual and/or audible signals rather than by their shape, as discussed below; see **Figure 14-04.**

Sound Buoys

A separate category of unlighted buoys includes those with a characteristic sound signal to aid in their location in fog or other reduced visibility. Different sound signals are used to distinguish between different buoys that are within audible range of each other.

BELL BUOYS are steel floats surmounted by short skeleton towers in which a bell is mounted; see **Figure 14-05.** They are effective day and night, and especially in fog or other conditions of reduced visibility; their use is favored because of their moderate maintenance requirements. Bell buoys are operated by motion of the sea using four tappers, loosely hung *externally* around the bell. When the buoy rolls in waves, wakes, or ground swells, a single note is heard at irregular intervals. Bell buoys, and other types that require some sea motion to operate, are not normally used in sheltered waters; a horn buoy is used there instead if a fog signal is needed.

Figure 14-03 A nun buoy is cylindrical up to just above the waterline, from there it tapers to form a conical top. This small nun buoy has a lifting ring at its top; this has no navigational significance. The upper part of some nun buoys consists of metal plates at right angles to reflect radar signals.

Figure 14-04 Buoys with lights or sound signals, or both, have no significant shape, although most will appear similar to the one shown above. Lifting lugs are at the base of the superstructure.

Figure 14-05 A bell buoy has four tappers that are outside the bell. These strike the bell making similar sounds in an irregular pattern as the buoy rocks due to the motion of the sea.

Figure 14-06 A lighted buoy has a light at its top that flashes in one of several regular patterns. The light is turned off in daylight by a photoelectric sensor. Power is obtained from a battery that is kept charged by a solar panel.

GONG BUOYS are similar in construction to bell buoys, except they have multiple gongs instead of a single bell. They normally have four gongs of different tones with one tapper for each gong. As the sea rocks the buoy, the tappers strike against their gongs, sounding four different notes in an irregular sequence.

WHISTLE BUOYS have a whistle sounded by compressed air that is produced by sea motion. Whistle buoys are thus used principally in open and exposed locations where a ground swell normally exists.

HORN BUOYS are rather infrequently used. They differ from whistle buoys in that they are electrically powered; they are placed where a sound signal is needed and sea motion cannot be depended upon.

Lighted Buoys

Buoys may be equipped with lights of various colors, intensities, and flashing characteristics (called RHYTHMS). Colors and characteristics of the light convey specific information to the mariner. Intensity depends upon the distance at which the aid must be detected, as influenced by such factors as background lighting and normal atmospheric clarity.

Lighted buoys are metal floats with a battery-powered light atop a short skeleton tower; see

Figure 14-06. Lighted buoys can operate for many months without servicing, and have "daylight controls" that automatically turn the light on and off as darkness falls and lifts. The lights are powered by storage batteries that are kept charged by panels of solar cells near the top of the buoy.

Lights on buoys may be red, green, white, or yellow according to the specific function of the buoy; the use of these colors is discussed later in this chapter; see page 486.

Combination Buoys

Buoys with both a light and sound signal are designated COMBINATION BUOYS. Typical of these are "lighted bell buoys," "lighted gong buoys," and "lighted whistle buoys." There will be only one type of sound signal on any buoy; see **Figure 14-07.**

Offshore Buoys

As a replacement for lightships, and for use at important offshore locations, the U.S. Coast Guard had developed LARGE NAVIGATIONAL BUOYS (LNBs) These aids—sometimes referred to as "super buoys"—had combined a light and sound signal, and often also had a radiobeacon.

Figure 14-07 This combination buoy has both a light and a whistle as a sound signal. The whistle is operated by air that is compressed by the motion of the buoy.

This type of buoy had been roughly 40 feet (12.2 m) in diameter with a superstructure rising to 30 feet (9.1 m) or more.

Because of their high initial cost and considerably greater maintenance costs, LNBs have been replaced with EXPOSED LOCATION BUOYS (ELBs). Although not of the size of LNBs, these are still quite large, being 9 feet (2.74 m) in diameter. ELBs are equipped with lights and sound signals, as well as weather and electronic navigation devices. Power is supplied by batteries kept charged by solar cells and a generator powered by wave motion; see **Figure 14-08.**

Color of Buoys

Buoys may be of one solid color, or have a combination of two colors in *horizontal bands* or *vertical stripes*. The colors used in the IALA system are red, green, yellow, white, and black. The specific application of colors is discussed later in this chapter in connection with the uses of various buoys.

Optical Reflectors

Almost all unlighted buoys are fitted with areas of reflective material, to help boaters find them at night by using searchlights. The material may be red, green, white, or yellow in banding or patches, and it has the same significance as lights of these colors. It can also be placed on the numbers or letter of lighted and unlighted buoys of all types.

Radar Reflectors

Many buoys have RADAR REFLECTORS—vertical metal plates set at right angles to each other so as to greatly increase the echo returned to a radar receiver on a vessel. The plates are shaped and mounted to preserve the overall characteristic shape of an unlighted buoy or the general appearance of a lighted buoy; refer to **Figure 14-04.**

Light Rhythms

The lights on lighted buoys will generally flash in one of several specific rhythms, for these reasons:

• Flashing conserves the energy source within the buoy.

• A flashing light can be more easily detected against a background of other lights.

• The light can signal specific information during hours of darkness, such as the need for special caution at a certain point in a channel.

• Different flashing patterns can be used to distinguish clearly between buoys of similar functions that are within visible range of each other.

FLASHING lights are those that come on for a single brief flash at regular intervals; the time of light is always *less* than the time of darkness. Coast Guard-maintained flashing buoys will flash their light not more than 30 times per minute; this is the more generally used characteristic. It is sometimes referred to as "slow flashing," but this is not an official designation.

QUICK FLASHING lights will flash not less than 60 times each minute. These buoys are used for special situations where they can be more quickly spotted and where particular attention to piloting is required.

Figure 14-08 Exposed location buoys (ELBs) are usually equipped with a RACON (radar transponder), light, and sound signal; some will have meteorological sensors. These typically have both solar and wave-actuated power sources.

CAUTIONS IN USING BUOYS

Do not count on floating aids always maintaining their precise charted positions, or unerringly displaying their characteristics. The Coast Guard works constantly to keep aids on station and functioning properly, but obstacles to perfect performance are so great that complete reliability is impossible.

Buoys are heavily anchored, but may shift, be carried away, or sunk by storms or ships. Heavy storms may also cause shoals to shift relative to their buoys.

Lighted buoys may malfunction and show no light, or show improper light characteristics. Audible signals on most buoys are operated by action of the sea, and may be silent in calm water; or they may fail to sound because of a broken mechanism.

A buoy does not maintain its position directly over its sinker, as it must have some scope on its anchor chain. Under the influences of current and wind, it swings in small circles around the sinker, which is the charted location. (See page 522 for the charting of buoys.) This swinging is unpredictable, and a boat attempting to pass too close risks collision with a yawing buoy. In extremely strong current, a buoy may even be pulled beneath the water surface.

Buoys may be temporarily removed for dredging operations, and/or in northern waters they may be discontinued for the winter, or changed to special types in order to prevent damage or loss from ice flows. The *Lights Lists* show dates for changes or for seasonal buoys, but these are only approximate and may be changed by weather or other conditions.

Temporary or permanent changes in buoys may be made between editions of charts. Keep informed of existing conditions through reading *Notices to Mariners* and/or *Local Notices to Mariners*—see page 553.

All buoys (especially those in exposed position) should, therefore, be regarded as warnings or guides, and *not as infallible navigation marks*. Whenever possible, navigate with bearings or angles on fixed aids or objects on shore (see Chapter 18), and by soundings, rather than by total reliance on buoys.

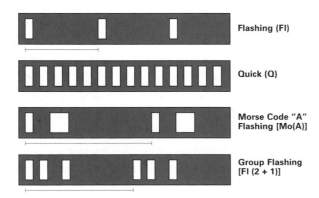

Figure 14-09 Characteristic light patterns identify buoys. They are named (as indicated in these schematic patterns) and identified on charts by abbreviations. One period is indicated by ├────┤ (quick flashing is continuous and does not have a period).

GROUP FLASHING (2+1) lights show two brief flashes, a brief interval of darkness, a single brief flash, and then an interval of darkness of several seconds duration.

MORSE CODE (A) FLASHING lights have a cycle of a short flash, and a brief dark interval, then a longer flash and a longer dark interval, repeated every eight seconds. This is the "dot-dash" of the letter "A" in Morse code.

The above light rhythms are shown diagrammatically in **Figure 14-09**. The PERIOD of a light is the time it takes to complete one full cycle of flash and dark interval, or flashes and dark intervals. A light described as "Flashing 4 seconds" has a period of four seconds. One flash and one dark interval lasts just that long before the cycle is repeated. Three standard periods are used for flashing lights—intervals of 2.5, 4, and 6 seconds.

The term CHARACTERISTICS as applied to a lighted aid to navigation includes the color as well as the rhythm, and may also cover physical features, such as nominal range.

DAYBEACONS

DAYBEACONS are unlighted aids that are fixed, rather than floating like buoys. They may be either on shore or in waters up to about 15 feet (4.6 m) deep.

Daybeacons vary greatly in design and construction, depending upon their location and the distance from which they must be seen. Daybeacons in U.S. waters, and their chart symbols, are illustrated in the ATON *Light List* plates, on pages 500-501.

Daybeacon Construction

The simplest daybeacon is a single pile with signboards, called DAYBOARDS, at or near its top, usually two, facing in opposite directions; see **Figure 14-10.** The pile may be wood, concrete, or metal.

Figure 14-10 Most daybeacons consist of a single pile with two dayboards. At some locations, such as channel junctions, where the daybeacon can be approached from more than two directions, there will be an additional dayboard. Some daybeacons consist of multiple pile structures; this has no navigational significance.

A larger, more visible, and more sturdy daybeacon is the "three-pile dolphin" type: three piles a few feet apart at their lower ends, bound tightly together with wire cable at their tops. There are also some five-pile dolphins (four piles around one central pile.) The Coast Guard maintains approximately 10,000 daybeacons.

Dayboards

To serve its purpose on an aid to navigation, a dayboard usually bears identification in the form of a number or, occasionally, a letter or a number plus a letter.

Dayboards are normally either square or triangular, corresponding to can and nun buoys. Square dayboards are green with green reflective border. Triangular dayboards are red with red reflective border. The number or letters will also be of reflective material. In special applications, a dayboard may be octagonal (eight-sided) or diamond-shaped, carrying a brief warning or notice.

The Uses of Daybeacons

For obvious reasons the use of daybeacons is restricted to relatively shallow waters. Within this limitation, however, it is often more desirable than a buoy because it is firmly fixed in position and taller, thus easier to see and identify. Daybeacons also require less maintenance than buoys.

Daybeacons are used primarily for channel marking, and they serve in the same manner as buoys in the buoyage systems to be described later in this chapter.

MINOR LIGHTS

Just as daybeacons are sometimes substituted for unlighted buoys, so may lighted buoys be replaced with MINOR LIGHTS. These are fixed structures of the same overall physical features as daybeacons, but equipped with a light generally similar in characteristics to those found on buoys; see **Figure 14-11.** Most minor lights are part of a series marking a channel, river, or harbor; also included, however, are some isolated single lights if they are of the same general size and characteristics. The term "minor light" does not include the more impor

Figure 14-11 Most minor lights are little more than a daybeacon to which has been added a light, with its battery box and solar panels. The minor light seen here has a more elaborate structure and has three dayboards.

tant lights marking harbors, peninsulas, major shoals, etc.; these have lights of greater intensity and/or special characteristics—these are designated as "secondary" or "primary seacoast" lights and are discussed in detail later in this chapter.

Features of Minor Lights

Minor lights are placed on single pile, on multiple-pile dolphins, or on other structures in the water, or on shore; see **Figure 14-12**. Minor lights carry dayboards for identification, and reflective material for nighttime safety should the light be extinguished.

Light Characteristics

A minor light normally has the same color and flashes with the same phase characteristics as a lighted buoy; refer to **Figure 14-09**. Intensity will generally approximate that of a lighted buoy, but visibility may be increased by its greater height above water and its more stable platform. A combination of storage batteries and solar cells is used in the same manner as on lighted buoys.

Sound Signals

Minor lights may, in some locations, have an audible sound signal—an electrically operated horn or siren. In some cases, the signal operates continuously for months when reduced visibility conditions can be expected.

BUOYAGE SYSTEMS

Most maritime nations use either a LATERAL SYSTEM OF BUOYAGE or a CARDINAL SYSTEM, or both. In the lateral system, the buoys indicate the direction to a danger relative to the course that should be followed. In the cardinal system, characteristics of buoys indicate location of the danger relative to the buoy itself; see **Figure 14-13**. The term "cardinal" relates to cardinal points of the compass; see page 436.

The IALA Systems of Aids to Navigation

The International Association of Marine Aids to Navigation and Lighthouse Authorities (formerly the International Association of Lighthouse Authorities, still known as the IALA) had the goal of establishing a single global system of aids to navigation, but was unable to do so and had to settle for two regional systems. These systems have many identical characteristics, but also one fundamental difference—the colors used for the lateral marks. Both systems have provisions for the use of topmarks, small shapes, such as spheres and triangles, placed above the basic buoy structure.

The IALA-B System

The full name is "System B—The Combined Cardinal and Lateral System (Red to Starboard)." System B uses five types of "marks"—those of lateral and cardinal systems, plus three different marks for isolated dangers and safe waters, and for special indications. These are all of a designated design, but may vary in size. Nations using this system must use aids conforming to the basic designs, but need not use all types. As indicated by the title, lateral marks on the starboard side of channels entering from the open sea are colored red, with the port side being marked by green aids. **Table 14-1** summarizes the IALA-B System.

The IALA-B system is used in the Western Hemisphere, Japan, Korea, and the Philippines.

The U.S. Aids to Navigation System

The United States has long used a "lateral system" of buoyage; this has now been converted to conform, as noted above, to the colors and shapes established by the International Association of Lighthouse Authorities (IALA) for "System B." Wherever you travel in the navigable waters of the United States, Canada, and other countries of the Western Hemisphere, the basic system is the same; you needn't learn a new system for new waters. (The IALA-A system is used in U.S. possessions west of the International Date Line and south of 10° North latitude; see sidebar, right.)

In the United States, the lateral system of buoyage is uniformly used in all federal-jurisdiction areas and on many other bodies of water where it can be applied. In this system, the shape,

THE IALA-A SYSTEM OF AIDS TO NAVIGATION

The IALA-A system uses the same cardinal marks, isolated danger marks, safe water marks, and special marks as the IALA-B system. The difference is that the lateral marks are directly opposite in color—marks left to starboard when entering from the sea are colored green, those on the port side are colored red. The shapes of the lateral marks are the same in both systems, only the color is different.

The IALA-A system is used in all waters worldwide that are not covered by the IALA-B system. This, of course, includes European, African, and nearly all Asian waters.

coloring, numbering, and light characteristics of buoys are determined by their position with respect to the navigable channel, natural or dredged, as such channels are entered and followed *from seaward* toward the head of naviga-

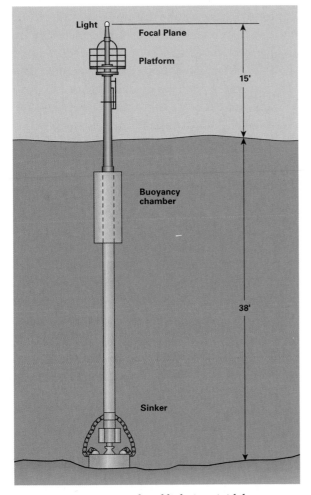

Figure 14-12 An articulated light is a rigid, buoyant structure fixed (with an articulated coupling) to the seabed. It provides more precise location than an anchored lighted buoy. Without the light, it would be an articulated daybeacon.

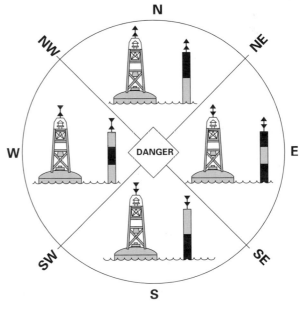

Figure 14-13 Cardinal marks, named for the four points of the compass, indicate that the navigable water lies to the named side of the mark. If lighted, the color is white.

tion. This is termed the "Conventional Direction of Buoyage."

As not all channels lead or appear to lead from seaward, certain arbitrary assumptions are used in order that the lateral system may be consistently applied. In coloring and numbering offshore buoys along the coasts, the following system has been adopted: proceeding in a southerly direction along the Atlantic Coast, in a northerly then westerly direction along the Gulf Coast, and in a northerly direction along the Pacific Coast will be considered the same as coming in from seaward. This can be remembered as proceeding around the coastline of the United States in a *clockwise* direction.

Thus there's a very important exception to red-right and green-left. As noted above it occurs in the United States when a channel that appears to come from the sea has in fact been designated by the U.S. Coast Guard as part of the "clockwise direction" rule. It happens in coastal waters including rivers and especially in the Intracoastal Waterway. Many unexpected groundings have

occurred because the navigator did not study the charts or does not understand the clockwise rule.

On the Great Lakes, offshore buoys are colored and numbered as proceeding from the outlet end of each lake toward its upper end. This will be generally westerly and northward on the Lakes, except on Lake Michigan where it will be southward. Buoys marking channels into harbors are colored and numbered just as for channels leading into coastal ports from seaward.

On the Mississippi and Ohio rivers and their tributaries, characteristics of aids to navigation are determined as proceeding from seaward toward the head of navigation, although local terminology describes "left bank" and "right bank" as proceeding *with* the flow of the river.

Not all types of marks are used in all waters, but those that are used will conform to the IALA-B system with respect to shapes, colors, top-marks, and light color and rhythm (characteristic). The U.S. system does not use cardinal buoys, but does use safe water buoys and a few isolated danger buoys. The IALA-B system makes no mention of

IALA-B LATERAL SYSTEM OF BUOYAGE

Returning from sea*	Color	Number	Unlighted Buoy Shape	Lights or Lighted Buoys		Daymark Shape
				Light Color	Light Rhythm	
To your starborad	Red	Even	Nun	Red	Flashing or quick flashing	Triangular
To your portside	Green	Odd	Can	Green	Flashing or quick flashing	Square
Preferred channel	Red-and-green horizontally banded**	Not numbered; may be lettered	Nun or can **	Red or green	Group flashing (2 + 1)	Triangular or square **
Midchannel of fairway	Red-and-white white vertically striped	Not; numbered; may be lettered	Spherical or sound buoy	White	Morse code "A" flashing	Octagonal

* or entering a harbor from a larger body of water, such as a lake.
** preferred channel is indicated by color of uppermost band, shape of unlighted buoy and color of light, if any.

Table 14-1 This table summarizes the color numbering, shape, and lights or buoys used in the IALA-B system of buoyage. Be aware of the "clockwise direction" rule in the coastal waters of the United States, see text.

sound signals such as gongs or whistles on buoys, and the previous U.S. usage has not been changed. The U.S. system also includes daybeacons and lights on fixed structures, aids that are not covered by either IALA system.

The U.S. system of lateral aids to navigation is supplemented by nonlateral aids where appropriate; see **Figure 14-14.**

Coloring

All buoys are painted distinctive colors to indicate on which side you should pass them, or to show their special purpose. In the lateral system the significance of colors is as described below; the traditional phrase "red, right, returning" helps in remembering the system.

Red buoys mark the starboard ("right") side of a channel when entering ("returning") from seaward, or a hazard that you must pass by keeping the buoy to starboard.

Green buoys mark the port (left) side of a channel when entering from seaward, or an obstruction that must be passed by keeping the buoy on the left hand.

Red-and-green horizontally banded buoys are used to mark the "preferred" channel (usually the major channel) at junctions, or hazards that you may pass on *either* side (but check your chart to be sure). If the topmost band is green, the preferred channel is the buoy to port of your boat—it is treated as if it were a can buoy. If the topmost band is red, the preferred channel is with the buoy to starboard. (Note: When proceeding *toward* the sea, it may *not* be possible to pass such buoys safely on either side. This is particularly true in situations where you are following one channel downstream and another channel joins in from the side; see **Figure 14-15.** When such a buoy is spotted, be sure to consult the chart for the area.)

Red-and-white vertically striped buoys are "safe water marks"; they are used as offshore approach points (often called "sea buoys"), and to mark a fairway or midchannel. If lighted, there will be a red spherical TOPMARK above the light that is roughly one-fifth the diameter of the buoy. If unlighted, these may be spherical or they may

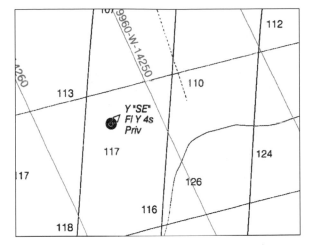

Figure 14-14 There are some circumstances in the IALA-B system where yellow buoys that have no lateral significance are used. Generally, these mark anchorages, exclusion areas, etc.

be similar in construction to sound buoys and will have a topmark.

Red-and-black horizontally banded buoys are used o mark obstructions; the top band will be black.

Note carefully that areas of color running horizontally are "bands"; if the areas are arranged vertically, they are "stripes." These terms are used in other color combinations in the case of special-purpose buoys.

Shapes of Buoys

In the lateral system of buoyage, unlighted buoys have definite shape characteristics that indicate which side of the channel they mark. The ability to distinguish shapes is particularly essential when you first sight a buoy in line with the sun and can see only its silhouette, rather than its color.

Can buoys, painted green, mark the port (left) side of the channel when returning from seaward, or a hazard that you must pass by keeping the buoy to port.

Nun buoys, painted red, mark the starboard (right) side of channels, or hazards that must be passed by keeping the buoy to starboard.

Channel junction may be of either can or nun shape as determined by which is the primary channel. If the buoy is a *can*, the uppermost band is *green*; if the buoy is a *nun*, the uppermost band is *red*; refer to **Figure 14-15**. Obstruction buoys follow the same color scheme.

Unlighted red-and-white vertically striped buoys are spherical in shape with a topmark.

No special significance is to be attached to the shape of sound, lighted, or combination buoys. The purpose of these is indicated by their coloring, number, or the rhythm of the light. Special caution must be exercised when a buoy is first sighted under conditions that its color cannot be determined, such as when proceeding in a direction toward a sun low in the sky.

Numbering

Most buoys have "numbers" that actually may be numbers, letters, or a number-letter combination to help you find and identify them on charts. In the lateral system, numbers serve as yet another indication of which side the buoy should be passed. The system is as follows:

Odd-numbered buoys mark the port (left) side of a channel leading in from seaward. In accordance with the rules stated above, these will be green buoys, cans if they are unlighted.

Even-numbered buoys mark the starboard (right) side of a channel; these will be red (nun) buoys.

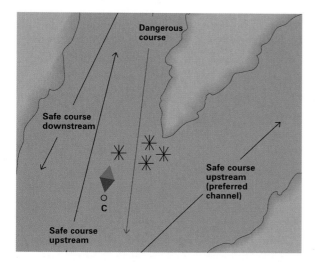

Figure 14-15 A junction buoy, painted with red and green bands, must be treated differently depending upon whether you are proceeding toward the sea or away from it. Upstream, either course is safe; downstream one course is dangerous.

Numbers increase from seaward and are kept in approximate sequence on the two sides of a channel by omitting numbers as appropriate if buoys are not uniformly placed in pairs. Occasionally, numbers will be omitted on longer stretches without buoys, to allow for possible later additions. Numbers followed by letters, such as "24A" and "24B," are buoys added to a channel after the initial numbering system was established, and with the series not yet renumbered.

A buoy marking a wreck will often carry a number derived from the number of the buoy next downstream from it, preceded by the letters "WR." Thus, a buoy marking a wreck on a channel's left-hand side between buoys 17 and 19 would be "WR17A." A wreck buoy not related to a channel may be designated by one or two letters, relating to the name of the wrecked vessel or a geographic location.

Letters without numbers are sometimes used for red-and-white vertically striped buoys marking fairways or harbor entrances, and for green-and-red horizontally banded buoys.

Numbers followed by letters may be used on aids to navigation marking offshore dangers. For the buoy marked "1JR," the number has the usual sequential significance and the letters "JR" indicate that it is off "Johnson Reef."

Color of Lights

For all lighted buoys in the IALA-B lateral system, the following system of colors is used:

Green lights on buoys mark the left-hand side of a channel returning from seaward; these are on green odd-numbered buoys, or green-and-red horizontally banded buoys with the green band uppermost.

Red lights on buoys mark the right-hand side of a channel when entering from sea (red even-numbered buoys) or red-and-green horizontally banded buoys with the red band uppermost.

White lights in the IALA-B system are used only on safe water marks with the Morse letter "A" rhythm, and on marks at isolated dangers with a group flashing (2) rhythm. (Some white lights remain in use on the Western Rivers (see Chapter 4, page 125) but will eventually be eliminated.)

Yellow lights are used only on special marks; the rhythm may vary, but usually is flashing or fixed.

Light Rhythms

Flashing lights are placed only on green or red buoys, or on special purpose buoys.

Quick flashing lights are placed only on channel-edge-marking green and red buoys; these are used to indicate that *special caution* in piloting is required, as at sharp turns or changes in the width of the waterway, or to mark hazards that must be passed only on one side.

Group flashing (2 + 1) lights are used only on buoys with red-and-green horizontal bands. These are the buoys at channel junctions and at obstructions that can be passed on either side.

Morse code "A" flashing lights are placed only on red-and-white vertically-striped buoys that mark a fairway or midchannel; these are passed close to on either side, and are always white.

Fixed lights show continuously; they are rarely used because of excessive power requirement as compared to the various types of flashing lights.

Daybeacons & Minor Lights

The lateral system of buoyage has been described in terms of unlighted and lighted buoys, but the descriptions apply fully to comparable daybeacons and minor lights.

Daybeacons with red triangular dayboards may be substituted for nun buoys, or ones with green square dayboards may replace can buoys. Minor lights may be used in place of lighted or combination buoys. Structures subject to being repeatedly struck by vessels may be set back from the channel edge, as noted in the *Light List*.

If a daybeacon is used to indicate the preferred channel at a junction, or an obstruction, the dayboard will be red-and-green horizontally banded, with the color of the uppermost band indicating the main or preferred channel. The dayboard shape will be either square or triangular as determined by the color or the top band, as with a can or nun buoy used for this purpose.

Safe-water daybeacons marking fairways or the midchannel have an octagonal-shaped dayboard, painted red and white, divided in half vertically down the middle.

A diamond-shaped dayboard has *no* significance in the lateral system. A typical application might be to increase the daytime detectability of a minor light that is not a part of a channel or waterway series. These are often used to mark a shoal, rock, submerged object, or other hazard; they are also used to mark prohibited areas where boats must not enter.

Minor lights, and the lights on buoys, are equipped with electronic DAYLIGHT CONTROLS that automatically turn the light on during periods of darkness and off during daylight. These controls are not of equal sensitivity; therefore all lights do not go on and off at the same time. Take care to identify aids correctly during twilight periods when some may be on and others are not.

Wreck Buoys

Buoys that mark dangerous wrecks are generally lighted, and placed on the seaward or channel side of the obstruction and as near to it as possible. Wreck buoys are solid red or green if they can be safely passed on only one side; horizontally banded otherwise, and numbered as previously discussed. Be careful around wreck buoys, because sea action may have shifted the wreck since the last Coast Guard visit. Wreck buoys are also used in some instances where a fixed aid to navigation has been knocked down, but the remains have not been removed.

Isolated Danger Marks

In addition to the widespread lateral system of buoyage, the U.S. Coast Guard maintains a few aids to navigation in the cardinal system of buoyage. Such an aid is erected on, or moored above or near, an "isolated danger" that has unobstructed water on all sides. These marks should not be approached closely without special caution. Colors are red and black, horizontally banded; if lighted, the light is always white and group flashing (2), 6 seconds. A topmark of two black spheres vertically arranged is used on lighted and unlighted buoys; no numbers are used, but they may be lettered.

Seasonal Buoys

In some areas subject to severe icing during winters, the normal buoys are removed to prevent damage or loss. These are temporarily replaced with ICE BUOYS, lighted or unlighted buoys of special sturdy construction. The placement and removal of such buoys are announced in *Local Notices to Mariners* and *Light List* changes. In some instances, lights on shore may be activated to guide vessels in the absence of buoys.

Racons

Some major aids to navigation are equipped with RADAR BEACONS, commonly shortened to RACONS. When a racon is triggered by pulses from a vessel's radar, it transmits a reply that results in a better defined display on that vessel's radarscope, thus increasing accuracy of range and bearing measurements.

The reply may be coded to facilitate identification, in which case it will consist of a series of dots and dashes (short and/or long intensifications of the radar blips beginning at and extending beyond the racon's position on the radar screen). The range is the measurement on the radarscope to the dash nearest its center. If the racon is not coded, the beacon's signal will appear as a radial line extending from just beyond the reflected echo of the aid, or from just beyond where the echo would be seen if detected. Details of racon coding will be found in the *Light Lists.* The coded response of a racon may not be received if the radar set is adjusted to remove interference (IF) or sea return from the scope; interference controls should be turned off when reception of a racon signal is desired.

Special-Purpose Aids

The Coast Guard also maintains several types of special purpose aids, with no lateral significance, to mark anchorages, fish net areas, dredging limits, etc.

In the IALA-B system of buoyage, these are all yellow, regardless of the usage to which they are being put. These may be of can or nun shape, and, if lighted, the light will be yellow with any rhythm, fixed or slow flashing preferred. (Some are equipped with xenon-discharge-tube lights that give a very bright, but very brief, flash.) Dayboards on a daybeacon or minor light will be diamond shape and all yellow in color.

Reporting Discrepancies

All boaters should realize that the U.S. Coast Guard cannot keep the many thousands of aids to navigation under constant observation, and for that reason, it is impossible to maintain every light, buoy, daybeacon, and fog signal operating properly and on its charted position at all times. The safety of all who use the waters will be enhanced if every person who discovers an aid missing, off station, or operating improperly will notify the nearest Coast Guard unit of the situation that has been observed. Use radio, land telephone, Internet e-mail, or postal mail, as dictated by the urgency of the report.

Variations in the Basic U.S. System

Although all U.S. waters are marked by the basic U.S. Aids to Navigation System, there are some areas in which additional or modified markings are used to meet local needs.

Buoyage on the Western Rivers

Buoyage on the "Western Rivers"—the Mississippi River and its tributaries above Baton Rouge, LA, and on some other rivers that flow toward the Gulf of Mexico (see page 124)—differs from the basic U.S. system in several ways:

- Aids to navigation are not numbered.
- Any numbers on aids to navigation are of no lateral significance, but show mileage (statute) from a fixed point—usually the river mouth.
- Diamond-shaped crossing dayboards, red-and-white or green-and-white as appropriate, are used to indicate where the river channel crosses from one bank to the other.
- Lights on green aids to navigation show a single-flash characteristic, which may be green or white.
- Lights on red aids to navigation show a group

(2) flashing characteristic, which may be red or white.

• Isolated danger and safewater marks are not used.

In an effort to eliminate white light from the lateral buoyage system, the U.S. Coast Guard is attempting to restrict its use to only crossing daymarks.

Intracoastal Waterway Aids to Navigation

The Intracoastal Waterway (ICW) runs parallel to the Atlantic and Gulf coasts from Norfolk, Virginia, to the Mexican border. The purpose of the ICW is to provide a protected route for vessels making coastwise passages. Distances along the ICW are in statute miles as the waterway is maintained by the U.S. Army Corps of Engineers.

Distinctive ICW markings Aids to navigation on the ICW are conventional buoys, daybeacons, and minor light, but with added identification of yellow triangles on "red" aids and yellow squares on "green" aids; see **Figure 14-16.**

The conventional direction of buoyage in the ICW is generally southerly along the Atlantic coast, and first northerly then westerly along the Gulf of Mexico coast. Intracoastal Waterway aids are numbered in groups, usually, but not always, not exceeding "99," beginning again with "1" or "2" at specified natural dividing points.

Buoy lights follow the standard system of red lights on red buoys and green lights on green buoys. Colors of minor lights fit the same pattern. Range lights, not being a part of the lateral system, may be of any standard color.

Dual-purpose aids The ICW was stitched together out of local rivers, channels, and fairways (with some additional land cuts created), which are marked in the conventional manner of the basic U.S. system. Some aids to navigation on these local waterways may also serve the Intracoastal Waterway. If they have this DUAL PURPOSE, some portion of them is identified with either a yellow square (indicating a can buoy) or a yellow triangle (indicating a nun buoy). In some cases, a green can buoy marking a local channel may carry a yellow triangle for the ICW.

No matter what its basic shape, any aid of any shape carrying a yellow triangle should be left to starboard when following the ICW from north to south and on the Gulf Coast. Similarly, any aid with a yellow square should be left to port. Where dual markings are employed, the ICW skipper disregards the basic shape and coloring of the aid on which the yellow square or triangle is placed and pilots his craft *solely* by the shape of the yellow markings. The numbers on the aids will be those of the local channel's lateral system, and in some instances where the southward ICW proceeds *down* a river, the numbers will be temporarily decreasing rather than increasing; see page 486.

Nonlateral aids in the ICW—such as safe water marks, isolated danger marks, and ranges—will have a horizontal band or bar in yellow.

Uniform State Waterway Marking System

Each state has authority over control of navigation on waters that lie wholly within its boundaries and are not subject to federal jurisdiction; see page 474. This includes the responsibility for establishing and maintaining aids to navigation. In 1966, the UNIFORM STATE WATERWAY MARKING SYSTEM (USWMS) was developed for these

Figure 14-16 The dayboards on daybeacons and minor lights on the Intracoastal Waterways carry the usual numbers but also a yellow triangle or square. Buoys also have such a mark.

OTHER BUOYAGE SYSTEMS

In Canadian waters, the lateral system of buoyage is essentially the same as in the United States. Minor differences in the physical appearance of buoys may be noted, but these are not great enough to cause confusion. Cardinal buoys of the IALA-B system are used in some areas; boaters there should familiarize themselves with the appearance and meaning of such aids. Chart symbols, likewise, may be slightly different from those standardized for use on the U.S. charts.

Skipper's Responsibility

Familiarize yourself with the system of buoyage that you expect to encounter before entering coastal waters of another nation. Consult the appropriate official publications or cruising guides for the necessary information.

waters to indicate safe boating channels and areas by marking the presence of either natural or artificial hazards. With trailer-borne boats traveling freely over the highways from state to state, the gain for recreational boaters from the uniform system is obvious.

A major defect in the USWMS, however, was its evident contradictions with the U.S. Aids to Navigation system that is based on IALA-B. The U.S. Coast Guard initiated a plan in 1998 to replace aids of the USWMS with aids consistent with the system used in coastal waters. The USWMS will have been completely superseded by December 31, 2003.

Inland Waters Obstruction Mark To meet the needs of boaters on inland waters after the demise of the USWMS, one new aid to navigation was created. On inland navigable waters (see Chapter 2, pages 58–59) designated by the Commandant of the Coast Guard as "State waters," and on nonnavigable waters of a state where there is no defined head of navigation, such

as lakes, the INLAND WATERS OBSTRUCTION MARK will be used to indicate that an obstruction extends from the nearest shore out to that buoy. This buoy will have black-and-white vertical stripes, and its meaning will be "Do not pass between this buoy and the shore." If lighted, it will have a quick-flashing white characteristic. It replaces the red-and-white vertically striped buoy of the USWMS, which color had a different, and contradictory, meaning in the basic coastal system.

Information & Regulatory Markers

Although not derived from the IALA-B system, the U.S. Aids to Navigation System includes INFORMATION & REGULATORY MARKS (often called "markers"). These are used to alert skippers to various warning or regulatory matters. They may be either buoys or beacons.

These marks have orange geometric shapes against a white background. The meanings associated with the orange shapes are as follows:
• An open-faced diamond signifies danger.
• A vertical diamond shape with a cross centered within it indicates that vessels are excluded from the marked area.
• A circular shape indicates that certain operating restrictions are in effect within the marked area.
• A square or rectangular shape contains directions or instructions lettered within the shape.

When a buoy is used as an information or regulatory mark, it must be white in color with two horizontal orange bands placed completely around the buoy circumference. One band must be near the top of the buoy body, with the other just above the waterline; both bands must be clearly visible.

PRIMARY SEACOAST & SECONDARY LIGHTS

PRIMARY SEACOAST and SECONDARY LIGHTS in the U.S. are so designated because of their greater importance as aids to navigation. They differ from minor lights previously considered by their greater physical size, intensity of light, and complexity of light characteristics. These lights are more diverse than minor lights and buoys; only broad, general statements can be made about them as a group.

Primary seacoast lights warn the high-seas navigator of the proximity of land. They are the first aids seen when making a landfall (except where there may be a light tower). A coastwise navigator can use these lights to keep farther offshore at night than by using other visual aids. These are the most powerful and distinctive lights in the U.S. system of aids to navigation.

Primary seacoast lights may be located on the mainland or offshore on islands and shoals. Offshore, they may mark a specific hazard or they may serve merely as a marker for ships approaching a major harbor.

Many primary seacoast lights are classified according to the importance of their location, the intensity of light, and the prominence of the structure. Other aids are classed as secondary lights because of their lesser qualities in one or more of these characteristics. The dividing line is not clear, however, and lights that seem to be more properly in one category may be classified in the other group in the *Light Lists* (see pages 549–550). The difference in classification is of no real significance to boaters and can be ignored in practical piloting situations.

Structures

The physical structure of a primary seacoast light and of many secondary lights is generally termed a LIGHTHOUSE although this is not a designation used in the *Light Lists.* The structure's principal purpose is to support a light source and lens at a considerable height above water. The same structure may also house a sound signal or other equipment, and quarters for the operating personnel. Auxiliary equipment and personnel are sometimes housed instead in a group of buildings nearby with the whole group referred to as a LIGHT STATION.

Lighthouses vary greatly in their outward appearances, depending on where they are, whether they are in the water or on shore, the light importance, the ground they stand on, and the

prevalence of violent storms; see **Figures 14-17, 14-18,** and **14-19.**

Lighthouse structures also vary with the range of visibility they need; a lengthy range requires a tall tower or a high point of land, with a light of high CANDLEPOWER—the standard measure of brightness. At points intermediate to principal lights, however, and where ship traffic is light, long range is not so necessary and a simpler structure can be used.

Coloring of Structures

Lighthouses or other light structures are marked with colors, bands, stripes, and other patterns to make them stand out against their backgrounds, and to assist in their identification; see **Figure 14-20.**

Light Characteristics

Primary seacoast and secondary lights have distinctive light characteristics—lights of different colors, and lights that show continuously while others show in patterns. Their three standard colors are white, red, and green.

Light Rhythms

Varying the intervals of lights and darkness in both simple and complex ways yields many different rhythms for major lights.

Fixed A light is termed "fixed" if it is always on with no periods of darkness.

Figure 14-17 New London Ledge Light, Connecticut.

Figure 14-18   *Split Rock Lighthouse State Park, Lake Superior, Minnesota.*

Opposite Page: Table 14-2 The light phase characteristics of primary and secondary lights permit rapid identification at night. One full cycle of changes is the light's period. Light phase characteristics can be combined—fixed and flashing, for example. Eclipses refer to periods of darkness.

Flashing   The term "flashing" has already been defined as a light that is on less than it is off in a regular sequence of single flashes occurring less than 30 times each minute. Some primary seacoast and secondary lights will "flash" in accordance with this definition although their characteristics will have no relation to the flashes of buoys and minor lights. In general, a flashing major light will have a longer period (time of one complete cycle of the characteristic) and may have a longer flash—for example, Cape Hatteras Light flashes once every 15 seconds with a 3-second flash.

Figure 14-19   *Kilauea Point Lighthouse, Kauai, Hawaii.*

Figure 14-20   *Bands of stripes of various colors are often used to aid in distinguishing lighthouses from their background, and as a aid to identification.*

CHARACTERISTICS OF LIGHTS

Flashing pattern & period (⊢─┤)	Type	Description	Abbreviation
	Fixed	A light showing continuously and steadily.	F
	Fixed and flashing	A light in which a fixed light is combined with a flashing light of higher luminous intensity.	F Fl
	Flashing	A flashing light in which a flash is regularly repeated (frequency not exceeding 30 flashes per minute).	Fl
	Group flashing	A flashing light in which a group of flashes, specified in number, is regularly repeated.	Fl (2)
	Composite group	A light similar to a group flashing light except that successive groups in the peiroid have different numbers of flashes.	Fl (2+1)
	Isophase	A light in which all durations of light and darkness are equal.	Iso
	Single occulting	An occulting light in which an eclipse, of shorter duration than the light, is regularly repeated.	Oc
	Group occulting	An occulting light in which a group of eclipses, specified in numbers, is regularly repeated.	Oc (2)
	Composite group	A light, similar to a group-occulting light, except that successive groups in a occulting have different numbers of eclipses.	Oc (2+1)
	Quick	A quick light in which a flash is regularly repeated at rate of 60 flashes per minute.	Q
	Interrupted quick	A quick light in which the sequence of flashes is interrupted by regularly repeated eclipses of constant and long duration.	IQ
	Group quick	A group of 2 or more quick flashes, specified in number, which are regularly repeated. (Not used in the waters of the United States.)	Q(3)
	Morse Code A	A light in which lights of two clearly different durations(dots and dashes) are grouped to represent a character or characters in the Morse code.	Mo (A)
	Alternating	A light showing different colors alternately.	Al RW
	Long flashing	A flashing light in which the flash is 2 seconds or longer.	LFl

In most instances, however, the actual light source is constant, and the "flashes" are produced by a rotating set of optical lenses; at close ranges, a weak steady light may be seen. Although a few major lights have a "fixed" characteristic (a continuous light without change of intensity or color), the light phase characteristics of primary seacoast or secondary lights are generally more complex, as described below (with current abbreviations); see **Table 14-2.**

Group Flashing (Fl [n]) The cycle of the light characteristic consists of two or more flashes separated by brief intervals and followed by a longer interval of darkness. (The "n" in the abbreviation indicates the number of flashes.)

Alternating Flashing (Al Fl) Flashes of alternating color, usually white and red, or white and green.

Occulting (Oc) The light is on more than it is off; the interval of time that the light is *lighted* is greater than the time that it is ECLIPSED—its period of darkness.

Isophase (Iso) Intervals of light and darkness are equal; the light is described in the *Light List* or on charts in terms of the period, the lighted and eclipsed portions each being just half of that time. This was formerly known as an "equal interval light."

Group Occulting (Oc [n]) Intervals of light regularly broken by a series of two or more eclipses. This characteristic may have all eclipses of equal length, or one greater than the others. (The "n" in the abbreviation indicates the number of eclipses.)

Complex Characteristics

The above light phase characteristics may be combined. Examples might include Gay Head Light "Alternating White/Red 15 seconds (Al W R 15s)" where there is a white flash for 0.2 seconds, an eclipse (period of darkness) for 7.3 seconds, a red flash for 0.2 seconds, and an eclipse of 7.3 seconds, for a total period of 15 seconds; or Minots Ledge Light "Group Flashing White 45 seconds (Fl W (1+4+3) 45s)" where 1.5-second white flashes occur at 1.5-second intervals in groups of one, four, and three separated by 5-second intervals and

followed by a 15.5-second longer interval to indicate the proper starting point of the 45-second period; or other characteristics of a generally similar nature.

Sectors

Many lights will have SECTORS—portions of their all-around arc of visibility in which the normally white light is seen as red or green. These sectors mark shoals or other hazards, or warn of land nearby.

Lights so equipped show one color from most directions, but a different color or colors over definite arcs of the horizon as indicated on charts and in the *Light List.* A sector changes the color of a light when viewed from certain directions, but *not* the flashing or occulting characteristic. For example, a flashing white light with a red sector, when viewed from within the sector, will appear as flashing red; see **Figure 14-21,** left.

Sectors may be a few degrees in width, as when marking a shoal or rock, or wide enough to extend from the direction of deep water to the shore. Bearings referring to sectors are expressed in degrees *as they are observed from a vessel toward the light.*

You should almost always avoid water areas covered by red sectors, but you should also check your chart to learn the extent of the hazard. Some lights are basically red (for danger) with one or more white sectors indicating the direction of safe passage, but a narrow white sector of another light may simply mark a turning point in a channel.

Lights may also have sectors in which the light is *obscured*—cannot be seen. These will be shown graphically on charts; see **Figure 14-21,** right, and described in the *Light Lists.*

The Visibility of Lights

A light's theoretical visibility in clear weather depends on two factors: its intensity and its height above water. Its intensity fixes its NOMINAL RANGE, which is defined in the *Light Lists* as "the maximum distance at which the light may be seen in clear weather (meteorological visibility of 10 nautical miles)."

Height is important because of the earth's curvature; height determines the GEOGRAPHIC RANGE at which the light can be seen. It is not affected by the intensity (provided that the light is bright enough to be seen out to the full distance of the geographic range).

The nominal range of major lights is generally greater than the geographic, and the distance from which such aids can be seen is limited only by the earth's curvature. Such lights are often termed "strong"; a light limited by its luminous range is a "weak light."

The glare, or LOOM, of strong lights is often seen far beyond the normal geographic range, and under rare atmospheric conditions the light itself may be visible at unusual distances. The range of visibility is obviously also lessened by rain, fog, snow, haze, or smoke.

U.S. Coast Guard *List Lights* show the nominal range for all lighted aids except private aids, navigation ranges, and directional lights (see page 502), and show how to convert nominal range to LUMINOUS RANGE—the maximum distance at which a light may be seen in specific *existing* visibilities. Both nominal and luminous ranges take no account of elevation, observer's height of eye, or the curvature of the earth. (Any height of eye on board the vessel increases the effective geographic range for that specific situation.) For lights of complex characteristics, nominal ranges are given for each color and/or intensity.

The geographic range of lights is not given in the *Light Lists* but can be determined from the given height of the light source. The distance to the horizon may be taken from a table in the front pages of each *Light List* volume, or calculated using the equation $D = 1.17\sqrt{H}$ (where H is the height in feet and the distance is in nautical miles) or $D = 2.12\sqrt{H}$ (where H is in meters and distance is still in nautical miles). For distances in statute miles, the factors are 1.35 and 2.44.

For any situation, the light's range, as limited by the earth's curvature, will be the distance to the horizon for the light *plus* the distance to the horizon for *your* height of eye—determine each distance separately, then add; *do not add heights and make a single calculation.* Boaters should know their height of eye when at the controls of their boat (and the height of any other position on board to which they can climb to see farther).

Lights on inland waters, where their radius of usefulness is not great, are frequently "weak" lights whose intensity need not reach the full limit of their geographic range.

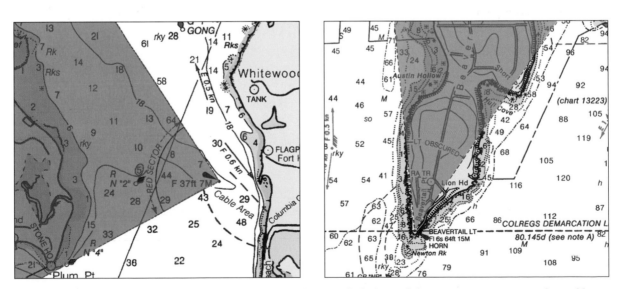

Figure 14-21 *A hazardous area is often covered by a red sector of a light, and this sector (or sectors) is indicated by words along the arc on a chart (left). Aside from being red, the sector shows the same characteristics as the normal white sector of the light. A light may also be obscured over a sector, and this, too, is indicated on the chart. Note: The colors used here are for clarity and do not actually appear on a normal chart.*

CAUTIONS IN USING LIGHTS

Complex lights with several luminous ranges may appear differently at extreme distances where, for example, a white fixed (or flashing) light could be seen but a red flash of the same light was not yet within luminous range. Examination of a *Light List* will show that usually the nominal range of a red or green light is 15 percent to 30 percent *less* than that of the white light from the same aid. Be cautious when identifying lights like these.

The effect of fog, rain, snow, and haze on the visibility of lights is obvious. Colored lights are more quickly lost to sight in poor weather than are white lights. On the other hand, refraction may also cause a light to be visible from a greater distance than normal.

Be cautious also when using light sectors in your navigation. The actual boundaries between the colors are not so distinct as the chart suggests; the lights shade gradually from one color into the other.

Note, too, that the increasing use of brilliant shore lights for advertising, illuminating bridges, and other purposes may cause marine navigational lights, particularly those in densely populated areas, to be outshone and difficult to distinguish from the background lighting.

A light can also be extinguished for some reason. Unattended lights that are broken may not be immediately detected and corrected. If you do not see a light reasonably soon after your course and speed suggest that you should, check the situation carefully. Do not rely on any *one* light, except perhaps for making a landfall. For positive identification, use several lights *together* as a system, checking each against the others.

Identification of Lights

Charts can only briefly describe the characteristics of a primary seacoast or secondary light, by means of abbreviations and a notation of the total period of the light cycle. You will often need to consult the *Light Lists* for details of the characteristics to help you identify it positively.

When you first see a light, note its color and time its full cycle of light changes. If color, period, and number of flashes per cycle match the *Light List* information, the light has been identified. As a precaution, however, check the charts and *Light Lists* to be sure that no other light in the vicinity has similar characteristics.

Emergency Lights

Emergency lights of reduced nominal range are displayed from many light stations when the main light is inoperative. These standby lights may or may not have the same characteristics as the main light. The existence of the standby light (if any) and its characteristics (if different) is noted in the *Light Lists*.

SOUND SIGNALS

Any sound-producing instrument operated in time of fog or other condition of reduced visibility from a definite point shown on a chart serves as a useful sound signal. To use it effectively as an aid to navigation, you must be able to identify it and know its location.

As mentioned, the simpler sound signals used on buoys are operated by sea action and thus you may have difficulty identifying them. Sound signals at all lighthouses and other lights are electrically or mechanically operated on definite time schedules, however, so are easier to identify positively.

Signal Characteristics

Sound signal characteristics are described in terms of the length of a total cycle of one or more BLASTS

CAUTIONS IN USING SOUND SIGNALS

Sound signals obviously depend upon the transmission of sound through the air. As aids to navigation, they thus have inherent limitations that you *must* consider. Because sound travels through air in a variable and unpredictable manner, you should note that:

• The distance at which a sound signal can be heard may vary at any given instant with the bearing of the signal, and may be different on different occasions.

• Under certain atmospheric conditions you may hear only part of a sound signal that is a siren or that has a combination of high and low tones.

• There are sometimes areas close to a signal where you will not hear it, perhaps when the signal is screened by intervening landmasses or other obstructions, or when it is on a high cliff.

• The apparent loudness of a sound signal may be greater at a distance than in its immediate vicinity.

• A patch of fog or smoke may exist at a short distance from a manned station but not be seen from it. Thus the signal may not be placed in operation.

• Some sound signals require a start-up interval.

• You may not hear a sound signal with your boat's engine on, but you may hear it suddenly when it is off or if you go forward on board away from its noise.

In summary, sound signals are valuable as warnings, but do not place implicit reliance upon them in navigating your vessel.

Based on the above established facts, you must *NOT* assume:

• That you are out of the ordinary hearing distance of a sound signal because you do not hear it.

• That because you hear a sound signal faintly, you are at a distance from it.

• That you are near to the sound signal because you hear it clearly.

• That the sound signal is not sounding because you do not hear it, even when you know that you are nearby.

• That the detection distance and sound intensity under any one set of conditions is an infallible guide for any future occasion.

of specific length and one or more SILENT INTERVALS, also of definite lengths. These times are shown in the *Light Lists* to aid in identification. (Normally, only the type of sound signal, without further details, is indicated on charts.) When you are counting the blasts and timing the cycle, refer to the *Light Lists,* for its details.

Sound Signal Equipment

Sound signals also differ from each other in tone, which helps in identification. The signal type for each station is shown in the *Light Lists* and on charts.

Diaphones produce sound by means of a slotted reciprocating piston activated by compressed air. Blasts may consist of two tones of different pitch, in which case the first

part of the blast is higher pitch and the latter is lower. These alternate-pitch signals are termed "two-tone."

Diaphragm horns produce sound by means of a disc diaphragm vibrated by compressed air or electricity. Duplex and triplex horn units of different pitch are sometimes combined to produce a more musical signal.

Sirens produce sound by means of either a disc or cup-shaped rotor actuated by compressed air, steam, or electricity. These should not be confused with "police sirens"; these aids may produce a sound of constant pitch much like a diaphragm horn or a whistle.

Whistles produce sound by compressed air, emitted through a slot into a cylindrical bell chamber.

Operation of Signals

Sound signals at stations where a continuous watch is maintained are placed in operation whenever the visibility decreases below a limit set for that location; typically, this might be five miles.

Sound signals at locations without a continuous watch may not always be sounded promptly when conditions of reduced visibility occur, or may operate erratically due to mechanical difficulties.

Where sound signals are operated continuously on a seasonal basis or throughout the year, this information will be found in the *Light Lists.*

On buoys where sound signals are operated by sea motion, the signals may be heard in any condition of visibility.

RANGES & DIRECTIONAL LIGHTS

Ranges and directional lights serve to indicate the centerline of a channel and thus aid in the safe piloting of a vessel. Although they are used in connection with channels and other restricted waterways, and shown on all the appropriate charts, they are not a part of the lateral system of buoyage.

Ranges

A RANGE consists of two fixed aids to navigation so positioned with respect to each other that when seen in line they indicate that the observer's craft *may* be in safe waters; see **Figure 14-22**. The aids may be lighted or unlighted as determined by the importance of the range.

The conditional phrase "may be in safe waters" is used because observation of the two markers in line is *not* an absolute determination of safety. *A range is "safe" only within specific limits of distance from the front marker.* A vessel too close or too far away may be in a dangerous area. The aids that comprise the range do not in themselves indicate the usable portion of the range; check your chart and other aids.

Ranges are described in the *Light Lists* by first giving the position of the front marker, usually in terms of geographic coordinates—latitude and longitude—and then stating the location of the rear marker in terms of direction and distance

from the front marker. This direction, given in degrees and minutes, true, need not be used in ordinary navigation, but is useful in making checks of compass deviation. The rear dayboard (and light, if used) is always *higher* than the one on the front aid; see **Figure 14-23**.

Because of their fixed nature, and the accuracy with which a vessel can be positioned by using them, ranges are among the best aids to navigation. Use a range whenever one is available; and use a buoy only to determine the beginning and end of the usable portion of the range.

Ranges are used outbound just as they are inbound. Make sure that you do not meet head-on with a vessel using the range in the opposite direction to your own.

Unlighted Ranges

Although any two objects may be used as a range, the term is properly applied only to those pairs of structures built specifically for that purpose. Special shapes and markings are used for the front and rear aids of a range for easier identification and more accurate alignment. Differing designs have been used in the past, but the Coast Guard has now standardized on the use of rectangular dayboards, longer dimension vertical, painted in vertical stripes of contrasting colors, see page 500. The design of specific range dayboards will normally be found in the *Light Lists.*

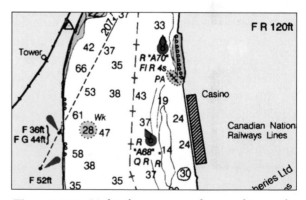

Figure 14-22 Lighted ranges are often used to mark channels in rivers, particularly where cross-currents exist. This range is on the St. Clair River on a true bearing of 207°. Range front light structures sometimes have all-round "passing lights" lower than the range light. The crossed-dashed line is the international border.

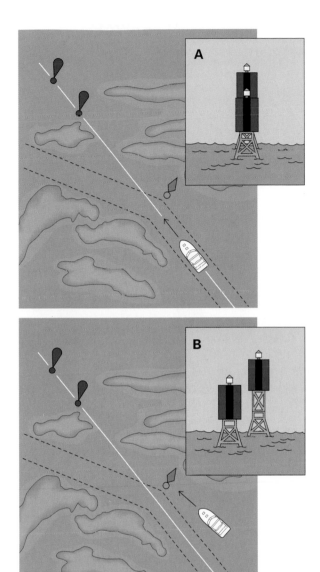

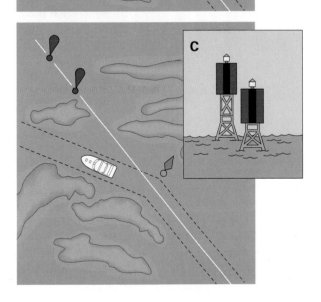

Lighted Ranges

Because of their importance and high accuracy in piloting, most range markers are equipped with lights, in addition to the usual dayboards, to extend their usefulness through the hours of darkness. Entrance channels are frequently marked with range lights; the Delaware River on the Atlantic Coast and the Columbia River on the Pacific Coast are examples of this.

Range lights may be of any color used with aids to navigation—white, red, or green—and may show any of several characteristics. The principal requirement is that they be easily distinguished from shore backgrounds and from other lights. Front and rear lights will, however, normally be of the same color (white is frequently used because of its greater visibility range), with different rhythms. Since both lights must be observed together for the proper steering of the craft, range lights often have a greater "ON" interval than other lights do. Range rear lights are normally on more than their front counterparts; many ranges now show an isophase (equal interval) rear light and a quick-flashing front light.

Many range lights are fitted with special lenses that give a much greater intensity on the range centerline than off of it; the lights rapidly decrease in brilliance when observed from only a few degrees to either side. In some cases, the light will be visible only from on or very near to the range line; in other cases, a separate, lower light of lesser intensity may be seen all around the horizon—this can be either from the main light source or from a small auxiliary "passing" light. Light is shown around the horizon when the front aid also serves to mark the side of a channel at a turn of direction.

Most lighted ranges are lit only at night or during periods of reduced visibility that will

Figure 14-23 A skipper can keep within a narrow channel by following a range. At A, front and range markers are in line with the higher rear range mark directly over the lower front mark. If he gets "off range," the markers will not be aligned, as shown in B. The channel may turn before reaching the range front marker, as in C; the turning point is normally marked by a buoy.

U.S. AIDS TO NAVIGATION SYSTEM
on navigable waters except Western Rivers

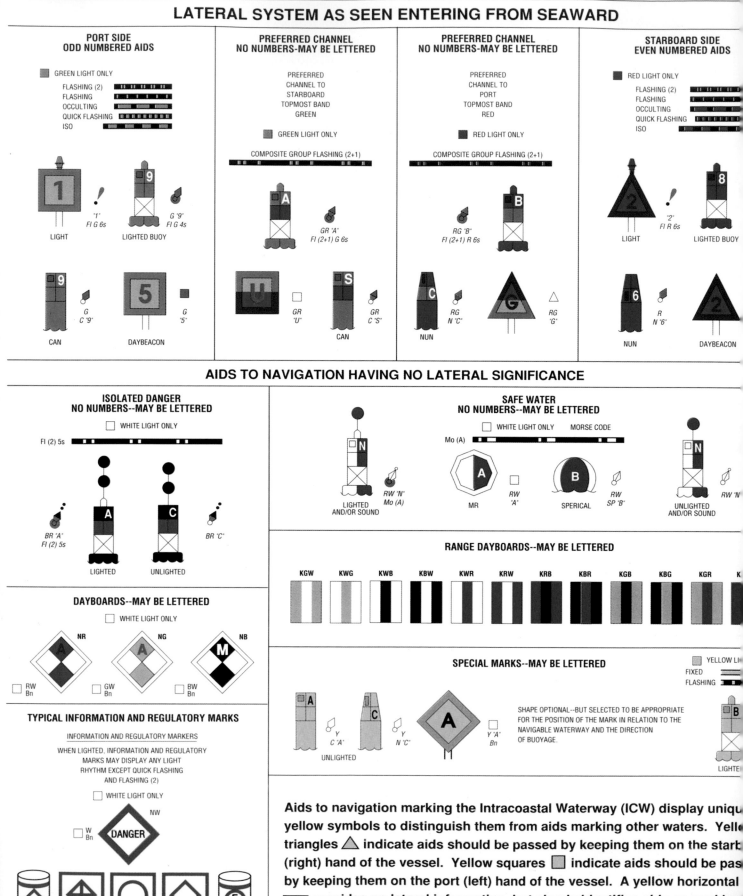

LATERAL SYSTEM AS SEEN ENTERING FROM SEAWARD

PORT SIDE ODD NUMBERED AIDS

GREEN LIGHT ONLY

FLASHING (2)
FLASHING
OCCULTING
QUICK FLASHING
ISO

"1" FL G 6s — LIGHT

G "9" FL G 4s — LIGHTED BUOY

G C "9" — CAN

G "5" — DAYBEACON

PREFERRED CHANNEL NO NUMBERS-MAY BE LETTERED

PREFERRED CHANNEL TO STARBOARD TOPMOST BAND GREEN

GREEN LIGHT ONLY

COMPOSITE GROUP FLASHING (2+1)

GR "A" FL (2+1) G 6s

GR "U"

GR C "S" — CAN

PREFERRED CHANNEL NO NUMBERS-MAY BE LETTERED

PREFERRED CHANNEL TO PORT TOPMOST BAND RED

RED LIGHT ONLY

COMPOSITE GROUP FLASHING (2+1)

RG "B" FL (2+1) R 6s

RG N "C" — NUN

RG "G"

STARBOARD SIDE EVEN NUMBERED AIDS

RED LIGHT ONLY

FLASHING (2)
FLASHING
OCCULTING
QUICK FLASHING
ISO

"2" FL R 6s — LIGHT

8 — LIGHTED BUOY

R N "6" — NUN

2 — DAYBEACON

AIDS TO NAVIGATION HAVING NO LATERAL SIGNIFICANCE

ISOLATED DANGER NO NUMBERS--MAY BE LETTERED

WHITE LIGHT ONLY

FL (2) 5s

BR "A" FL (2) 5s — LIGHTED

BR "C" — UNLIGHTED

DAYBOARDS--MAY BE LETTERED

WHITE LIGHT ONLY

NR — A — RW Bn

NG — A — GW Bn

NB — M — BW Bn

TYPICAL INFORMATION AND REGULATORY MARKS

INFORMATION AND REGULATORY MARKERS

WHEN LIGHTED, INFORMATION AND REGULATORY MARKS MAY DISPLAY ANY LIGHT RHYTHM EXCEPT QUICK FLASHING AND FLASHING (2)

WHITE LIGHT ONLY

W Bn — DANGER — NW

EXCLUSION AREA | RESTRICTED OPERATIONS | DANGER

SAFE WATER NO NUMBERS--MAY BE LETTERED

WHITE LIGHT ONLY   MORSE CODE

Mo (A)

RW "N" Mo (A) — LIGHTED AND/OR SOUND

A — RW "A" — MR

B — RW SP "B" — SPERICAL

RW "N" — UNLIGHTED AND/OR SOUND

RANGE DAYBOARDS--MAY BE LETTERED

KGW | KWG | KWB | KBW | KWR | KRW | KRB | KBR | KGB | KBG | KGR | K

SPECIAL MARKS--MAY BE LETTERED

YELLOW LI
FIXED
FLASHING

A — Y C "A" — UNLIGHTED

C — Y N "C"

A — Y "A" Bn

SHAPE OPTIONAL--BUT SELECTED TO BE APPROPRIATE FOR THE POSITION OF THE MARK IN RELATION TO THE NAVIGABLE WATERWAY AND THE DIRECTION OF BUOYAGE.

B — LIGHTE

Aids to navigation marking the Intracoastal Waterway (ICW) display uniqu yellow symbols to distinguish them from aids marking other waters. Yelle triangles △ indicate aids should be passed by keeping them on the starb (right) hand of the vessel. Yellow squares ▢ indicate aids should be pas by keeping them on the port (left) hand of the vessel. A yellow horizontal ▬ provides no lateral information, but simply identifies aids as marking the ICW.

U.S. AIDS TO NAVIGATION SYSTEM
on the Western River System

AS SEEN ENTERING FROM SEAWARD

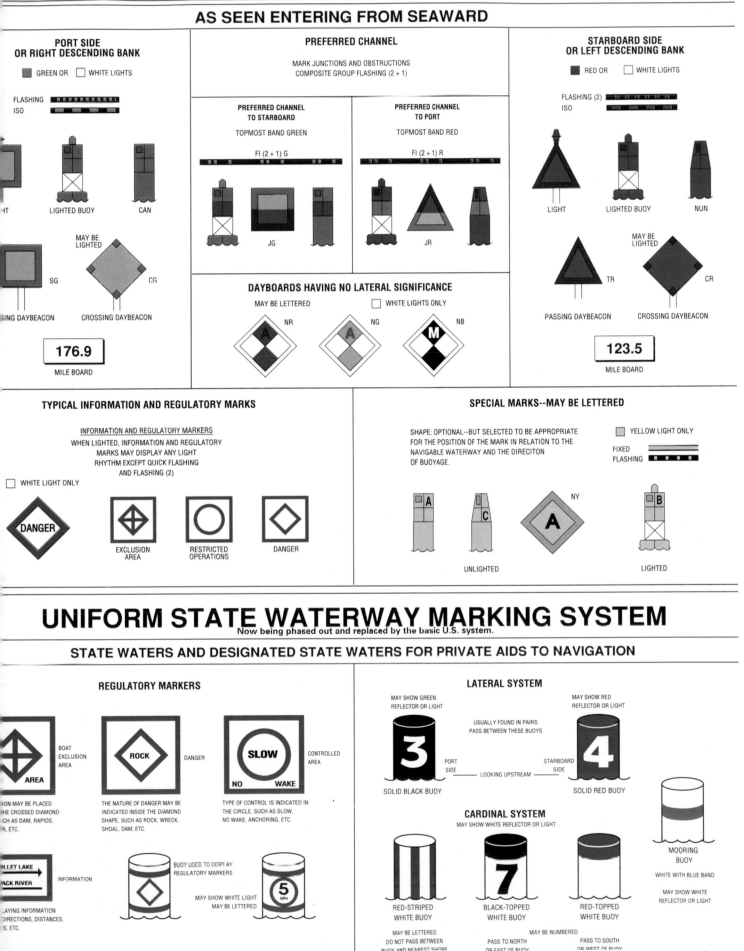

PORT SIDE OR RIGHT DESCENDING BANK

GREEN OR ☐ WHITE LIGHTS

FLASHING
ISO

LIGHTED BUOY — CAN

MAY BE LIGHTED

SG — GG

...SING DAYBEACON — CROSSING DAYBEACON

176.9 MILE BOARD

PREFERRED CHANNEL

MARK JUNCTIONS AND OBSTRUCTIONS
COMPOSITE GROUP FLASHING (2 + 1)

PREFERRED CHANNEL TO STARBOARD
TOPMOST BAND GREEN
Fl (2 + 1) G
JG

PREFERRED CHANNEL TO PORT
TOPMOST BAND RED
Fl (2 + 1) R
JR

DAYBOARDS HAVING NO LATERAL SIGNIFICANCE
MAY BE LETTERED   ☐ WHITE LIGHTS ONLY
NR — NG — NB

STARBOARD SIDE OR LEFT DESCENDING BANK

RED OR ☐ WHITE LIGHTS

FLASHING (2)
ISO

LIGHT — LIGHTED BUOY — NUN

MAY BE LIGHTED

TR — CR

PASSING DAYBEACON — CROSSING DAYBEACON

123.5 MILE BOARD

TYPICAL INFORMATION AND REGULATORY MARKS

INFORMATION AND REGULATORY MARKERS
WHEN LIGHTED, INFORMATION AND REGULATORY
MARKS MAY DISPLAY ANY LIGHT
RHYTHM EXCEPT QUICK FLASHING
AND FLASHING (2)

☐ WHITE LIGHT ONLY

DANGER — EXCLUSION AREA — RESTRICTED OPERATIONS — DANGER

SPECIAL MARKS--MAY BE LETTERED

SHAPE: OPTIONAL--BUT SELECTED TO BE APPROPRIATE
FOR THE POSITION OF THE MARK IN RELATION TO THE
NAVIGABLE WATERWAY AND THE DIRECITON
OF BUOYAGE.

☐ YELLOW LIGHT ONLY
FIXED
FLASHING

A — C — NY A — B

UNLIGHTED — LIGHTED

UNIFORM STATE WATERWAY MARKING SYSTEM
Now being phased out and replaced by the basic U.S. system.

STATE WATERS AND DESIGNATED STATE WATERS FOR PRIVATE AIDS TO NAVIGATION

REGULATORY MARKERS

BOAT EXCLUSION AREA
AREA

ROCK — DANGER

SLOW
NO   WAKE
CONTROLLED AREA

...ION MAY BE PLACED
...HE CROSSED DIAMOND
...CH AS DAM, RAPIDS,
..., ETC.

THE NATURE OF DANGER MAY BE
INDICATED INSIDE THE DIAMOND
SHAPE, SUCH AS ROCK, WRECK,
SHOAL, DAM, ETC.

TYPE OF CONTROL IS INDICATED IN
THE CIRCLE, SUCH AS SLOW,
NO WAKE, ANCHORING, ETC.

...LLET LAKE
...ACK RIVER
INFORMATION

...AYING INFORMATION
...IRECTIONS, DISTANCES,
...S, ETC.

BUOY USED TO DISPLAY
REGULATORY MARKERS

MAY SHOW WHITE LIGHT
MAY BE LETTERED

5 MPH

LATERAL SYSTEM

MAY SHOW GREEN
REFLECTOR OR LIGHT

USUALLY FOUND IN PAIRS
PASS BETWEEN THESE BUOYS

MAY SHOW RED
REFLECTOR OR LIGHT

3
PORT SIDE — LOOKING UPSTREAM — STARBOARD SIDE
4

SOLID BLACK BUOY — SOLID RED BUOY

CARDINAL SYSTEM
MAY SHOW WHITE REFLECTOR OR LIGHT

RED-STRIPED
WHITE BUOY

7
BLACK-TOPPED
WHITE BUOY

RED-TOPPED
WHITE BUOY

MAY BE LETTERED
DO NOT PASS BETWEEN
BUOY AND NEAREST SHORE

MAY BE NUMBERED
PASS TO NORTH
OR EAST OF BUOY

PASS TO SOUTH
OR WEST OF BUOY

MOORING BUOY
WHITE WITH BLUE BAND
MAY SHOW WHITE
REFLECTOR OR LIGHT

actuate their daylight sensors; during daytime; these ranges are used by aligning the dayboards. A more recent development is the "day/night range" that has two lights each on front and rear towers at slightly different heights; these lights will have the same flashing characteristic, but often different arcs of visibility and ranges. In addition to the daytime light, these ranges still have their distinctive dayboards.

Directional Lights

The establishment of a range requires suitable locations for two aids, separated adequately both horizontally and vertically. In some areas, this may not be possible and a single light of special characteristics will be employed.

A DIRECTIONAL LIGHT is a single light source fitted with a special lens so as to show a white light in a narrow beam along a desired direction, with red and green showing to either side. Width of the sectors will depend upon the local situation, but red will be seen if the pilot is to the right of the centerline as he approaches the aid from seaward, and green if he is to the left of the desired track.

A typical example is the Thames River Upper Directional Light (Connecticut) that shows an isophase 6-seconds white light, over an arc of 3 degrees, with green and red sectors 3-degrees wide on either side; it cannot be seen from any other direction. A quite different light is the Kailua Bay Entrance Directional Light (Hawaii) that shows an occulting 4-seconds white light, 3 degrees either side of the correct heading of 023 degrees True, with a green sector 34-degrees wide and a red sector 70 degrees in width.

Directional lights will normally have an occulting or isophase characteristic, so that they are easily followed.

Caution Regarding Directional Lights

A skipper should not place too great reliance on the various colors of a directional light for safe positional information. As noted for light sectors, the boundaries between colors are not sharp and clear; the light shades imperceptibly from one color to the other along the stated, and charted, dividing lines.

Nautical Charts & Publications

The Importance of Charts • Charts vs. Maps • Chart Features • Symbols &
Abbreviations • Chart Projections • Navigational Publications

To travel anywhere safely in his boat, a skipper must have knowledge of water depths, shoals, and channels. The location of aids to navigation and landmarks must be known, and where ports and harbors can be found. At any given position, depth can usually be measured and some landmarks seen; but for true safety a boater has to know the depth ahead, the actual location of the aids to navigation seen, and where more aids lie on the course that will be followed. To plan the best route to his destination, he must know the dangers to navigation along the way. This information can best be determined from up-to-date nautical charts. The skipper must not only have the required charts on board, he or she must also know how to use them.

In addition to the traditional paper charts, electronic charts are now available to many boaters. These wonders of digital electronics come in various packages and can be used either with dedicated chart plotters, other electronic devices such as some radars and fish finders, and personal computers, even pocket computers. They offer some advantages, but on small craft should not be considered as a replacement for paper charts; see pages 543–546, and Chapter 21, pages 736–738.

CHARTS VS. MAPS

A MAP is a representation in miniature—usually at some proportional scale—on a plane surface, of a portion of the earth's surface for use on land in which the emphasis is on roads, cities, and political boundaries; see **Figure 15-01.**

A NAUTICAL CHART is a similar representation in miniature—to scale—emphasizing the water areas and natural and man-made features of particular interest to a navigator; see **Figure 15-02.** A chart includes information about depth of water, obstructions and other hazards to navi-

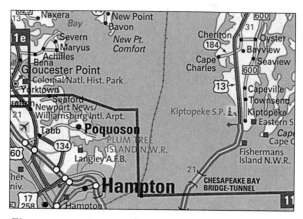

Figure 15-01 A map is designed to emphasize information about land features such as roads—as shown here on this map of the lower Chesapeake Bay area of the Atlantic Coast. Underwater and coastal features are almost ignored.

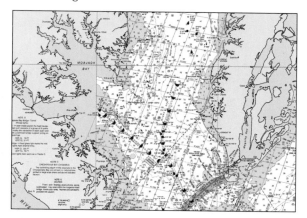

Figure 15-02 A chart of Chesapeake Bay is far more detailed than a map of the same area. It is almost exclusively concerned with navigation on the water. Note the amount of data that is conveyed by each square inch of the chart—all achieved without compromising its clarity.

gation, and the location and type of aids to navigation. Adjacent land areas are portrayed only with details that aid a navigator—the shoreline, harbor facilities, and prominent natural or man-made features. Charts are printed on heavyweight, durable paper so that they may be used as worksheets on which courses may be plotted and positions determined. For skippers of small craft, there are even special charts with details on marinas and similar facilities.

A chart's basic purpose is to give the navigator information that enables him to make the *right decision in time to avoid danger*. Charts differ from road maps both in kinds of information and in the precision of their details: for safety, charts must be extremely accurate. Even a small error in charting the position of a submerged obstruction can be a serious hazard to navigation.

Various "cruising guides" are available for many boating areas. These are useful in planning a nautical trip with chart reproductions or extracts, textual information, useful data, and even aerial photographs. What these lack, however, are provisions for revisions between printings comparable to *Notices to Mariners* changes for official charts. Take advantage of the information available in cruising guides, but do *not* try to substitute them for genuine nautical charts.

Geographic Coordinates

Charts show a grid of intersecting lines to aid in describing a specific position on the water. These lines are charted representations of a system of GEOGRAPHIC COORDINATES that are imagined to exist on the earth's surface.

The earth is nearly spherical in shape—it is slightly flattened along the polar axis, but the distortion is minimal and need concern only those who construct the charts, not boaters. A GREAT CIRCLE is the line traced out on the surface of a sphere by a plane cutting through the sphere at its center; see **Figure 15-03,** upper. It is the largest circle that can be drawn on the surface of a sphere. A SMALL CIRCLE is one marked on the surface of a sphere by a plane that does not pass through its center; see **Figure 15-03,** lower.

Meridians & Parallels

Geographic coordinates are defined by two sets of great and small circles. One is a set of great circles each of which passes through the north and south

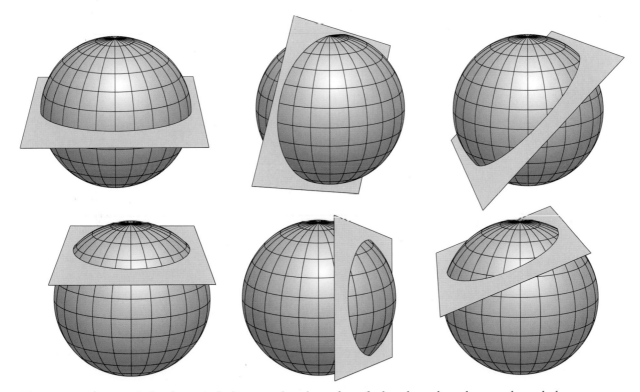

Figure 15-03 *A great circle, above, is the line traced on the surface of sphere by a plane that cuts through the center of the sphere. A small circle, below, is a line traced on the surface of a sphere that does not cut through the sphere's center.*

geographic poles—these are the MERIDIANS OF LONGITUDE; see **Figure 15-04,** left. The other set is a series of circles each established by a plane cutting through the earth perpendicular to the polar axis. The largest of these is midway between the poles and thus passes through the center of the earth, becoming a great circle; this is the EQUATOR. Other parallel planes from small circles are known as the PARALLELS OF LATITUDE; see **Figure 15-04,** right.

Geographic coordinates are measured in terms of DEGREES (one degree is 1/360th of a complete circle). The meridian that passes through Greenwich, England is the reference for all measurements of longitude and is designated as the PRIME MERIDIAN, or 0°. The longitude of any position on earth is described as so many degrees East or West of Greenwich, to a maximum in either direction of 180°. The measurement can be thought of as either the angle at the North and South Poles between the meridian of the place being described and the prime meridian, or as the arc along the equator between these meridians; see **Figure 15-05,** left. The designation of "E" or "W" is an essential part of any statement of longitude, abbreviated as "Long," or "Lo" or as "l" (the Greek letter *lambda*).

Parallels of latitude are measured in degrees north or south from the equator, from 0° at the equator to 90° at each pole. The designation of latitude (abbreviated as "Lat." or "L") must include "N" or "S" as necessary to provide a complete position; see **Figure 15-05,** right.

For greater precision in position definition, degrees are subdivided into MINUTES (60 minutes = 1 degree) and SECONDS (60 seconds = 1 minute). In some instances, minutes are divided decimally, and for very high precision, seconds can be so divided.

From **Figure 15-05,** left, you can see that the meridians of longitude get closer together as one moves away from the equator in either direction, and converge at the poles. Thus the *distance* on the earth's surface between adjacent meridians is not a fixed quantity but varies with latitude. On the other hand, except for extremely small technicalities, the parallels of latitude are equally spaced and the distance between successive parallels is the same. One degree of latitude is, for all practical purposes, 60 nautical miles; *1 minute of latitude is used as 1 nautical mile,* a relationship that we will later see is quite useful.

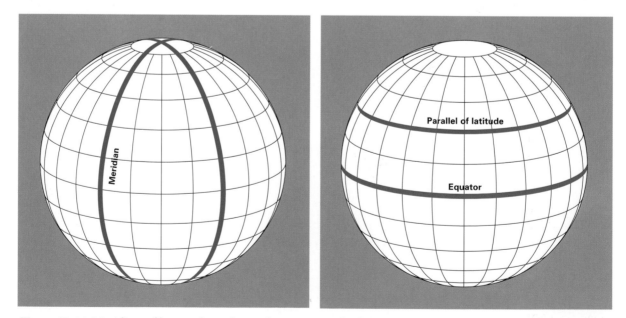

Figure 15-04 Meridians of longitude on the earth are great circles, left, that pass through both the north and south poles. Parallels of latitude, right, are small circles that are parallel to the plane of the equator. The equator is a great circle that is perpendicular to the earth's axis.

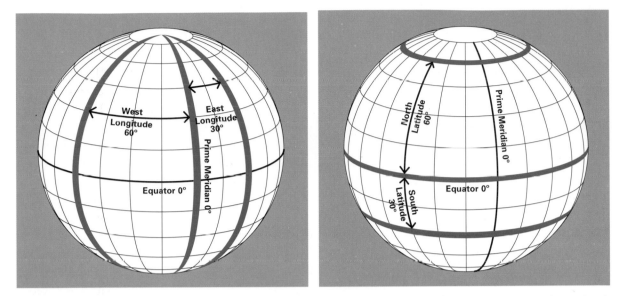

Figure 15-05 *Longitude, left, is measured from the prime meridian (0°), which passes through Greenwich, England, east or west to a maximum of 180°. Latitude, right, is measured north or south from the equator (0°) to the poles (90°). Meridians of longitude and parallels of latitude are shown at 15° intervals.*

Chart Construction

The construction of a chart presents the problem of representing a spherical, three-dimensional surface on a plane, a two-dimensional sheet of paper. It is actually impossible to accomplish this exactly, and a certain amount of distortion is inevitable, but various methods, called PROJECTIONS, can provide practical and sufficiently accurate results.

The transfer of information from the sphere to the chart's flat surface should be accomplished with as little distortion as possible in both the shape and the size of land and water areas, the angular relation of positions, the distance between points, and other more technical properties. Each projection is superior to others in one or more of these qualities; none is superior in all characteristics. In all projections, as the area covered by the chart is decreased the distortion diminishes, and the difference between types of projections lessens.

Of the many projection techniques that are used, two are of primary interest to boaters. The MERCATOR PROJECTION is an example of the most common; it is used for charts of ocean and coastal areas. The POLYCONIC PROJECTION is employed for National Ocean Service (NOS) charts of the Great Lakes and some inland rivers. The average skipper can quite safely navigate his boat using either type of chart without a deep knowledge of the techniques of projection. (For those who would like to know more about the various projection methods, see pages 538-543.)

Direction

DIRECTION is defined as the angle between a line connecting one point with another and a base, or reference, line such as the geographic or magnetic meridian passing through the original point; the angle is measured in degrees clockwise from the reference line. Thus direction on charts may be described as so many degrees TRUE (T) or so many degrees MAGNETIC (M). The difference between these directions is VARIATION and must be allowed for, as described in Chapter 13. The principal difference in the use of charts on the Mercator projection from those on the polyconic projection lies in the techniques for measuring direction; this is covered later in this chapter; see page 541.

Measurement of Direction

To facilitate the measurement of direction, as in plotting bearings and laying out courses, most charts have COMPASS ROSES printed on them. A compass rose consists of two or three concentric circles, several inches in diameter and accurately subdivided; see **Figure 15-06.** The outer circle has its zero at *true* North; this is emphasized with a star. The next circle or circles are oriented to magnetic North. The next inner circle is *magnetic* direction expressed in degrees, with an arrow printed over the zero point to indicate magnetic North. The innermost circle, if there are three, is also magnetic direction, but in terms of "points," and halves and quarters thereof; its use by modern boaters will be limited. (One point = 11¼ degrees.) The use of points with the mariner's compass is covered in Chapter 13.

The difference between the orientation of the two sets of circles is the magnetic variation at the location of the compass rose. The amount of the variation and its direction (Easterly or Westerly) is given in words and figures in the center of the rose, together with a statement of the year that such variation existed and the annual rate of change. When using a chart in a year much later

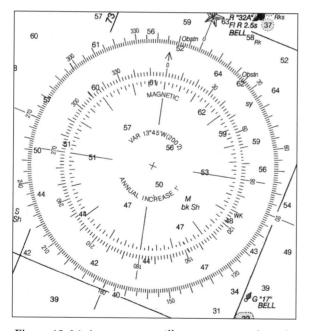

Figure 15-06 A compass rose illustrates true and north magnetic directions. The outer circle is in degrees with zero at true north. The inner circles are in degrees and "points" with their zero at magnetic north. Several compass roses are located on each chart at locations convenient for plotting course and bearings. Some charts of the Small Craft series omit the innermost circle with its point system of subdivision.

UNIT CONVERSION

On salt water, distances are measured in nautical miles, while the statute mile is used on shore, in fresh-water bodies, and along the Intracoastal Waterways. Depths are usually measured in feet on inshore and near-coastal waters; offshore, the unit of depth measurement is the fathom—which is 6 feet (1.83 m). Increasingly, metric units are coming into use for depths and short distances.

While it is easy to make conversions graphically by using the various unit scales presented, you may also need to make conversions by using numeric conversion factors given below (factors are rounded, except where shown as "exactly"), or by using quick rules of thumb, as shown at bottom.

- nautical miles x 1.15 = statute miles
- statute miles x 0.87 = nautical miles
- nautical miles x 1,852 = meters (exactly)
- meters x 0.00054 = nautical miles
- nautical miles x 2,025.4 = yards
- yards x 0.00049 = nautical miles
- statute miles x 1,609 = meters
- meters x 0.00062 = statute miles
- statute miles x 1,760 = yards (exactly)
- yards x 0.9144 = meters
- meters x 1.094 = yards
- fathoms x 6 = feet
- feet x 0.16667 = fathoms
- fathoms x 1.828 = meters
- meters x 0.5468 = fathoms

Rules of Thumb

Roughly 7 nautical miles equals 8 statute miles, so you can convert nautical to statute by multiplying nautical miles by 8 and dividing the product by 7. To reverse the conversion: statute miles times 7, then divide by 8. A nautical mile has about 2,000 yards—close enough for quick calculations.

than the compass rose date, it *may* be necessary to modify the variation shown by applying the annual rate of change. Such cases are relatively rare as rates are quite small and differences of a fraction of a degree may generally be ignored. Each chart has several compass roses printed on it in locations where they do not conflict with navigational information.

Until a skipper has thoroughly mastered the handling of compass "errors," he should use only true directions and the true (outer) compass rose. Later, the magnetic rose may be used *directly*, thus simplifying computations.

Several cautions are necessary when measuring directions on charts. For large-area charts, the magnetic variation can differ for various portions of the chart. Check each chart when you first start to use it, and, to be sure, always use the compass rose *nearest* the area for which you are plotting. Depending upon a chart's type and scale, graduations on its compass rose circles may be for intervals of 1°, 2°, or 5°. On some charts, the outer (true) is subdivided into units of 1° while the inner (magnetic) circle, being smaller, is subdivided into steps of 2°. Always check to determine the interval between adjacent marks on each compass rose scale.

Distance

DISTANCES on charts are measured in statute or in nautical miles. Use of the STATUTE (LAND) MILE of 5,280 feet (approximately 1609 m) is limited to the Great Lakes, inland rivers, and the Atlantic and Gulf Intracoastal Waterways. The NAUTICAL MILE of 6,076.1 feet (exactly 1,852 m) is used on ocean and coastal waters.

In navigation, distances up to a mile or so usually are expressed in YARDS, a unit that is the same no matter which "mile" is used on the chart. Foreign charts will commonly use METERS for shorter distances, and this unit may come into wider use on U.S. charts.

Conversion factors and rules of thumb are shown opposite; more complete conversion tables will be found in Appendix E.

Conversions can also be made graphically using graphic bar scales; see **Figure 15-07**. A distance measured on one scale by using a pair of dividers can be measured on another scale to determine the equivalent distance; refer to Chapter 16, **Figure 16-05.**

Chart Scales

The amount by which actual distances are reduced for representation on a chart is known as the SCALE of that chart; many different scales are used. Scale may be expressed as a ratio, 1:80,000 meaning that 1 unit on the chart represents 80,000 units on the actual land or water surface, or as a fraction 1/80,000 with the same meaning. This is termed the NATURAL SCALE of the chart.

The ratio of chart to actual distance can also be expressed as a NUMERICAL or EQUIVALENT SCALE, such as "1 inch = 1.1 miles,"—another way of expressing a 1:80,000 scale. Equivalent scales are not as commonly used on nautical charts as on maps, but they may be encountered in publications such as cruising guides.

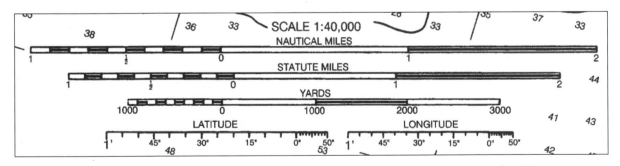

Figure 15-07 NOS charts of scales of 1:80,000 and larger will have a scale of nautical miles and one of yards; those for the Great Lakes, inland rivers, and the Intracoastal Waterways will also carry a scale of statute miles. This 1:40,000 small-craft chart additionally has latitude and longitude scales showing subdivisions of one minute.

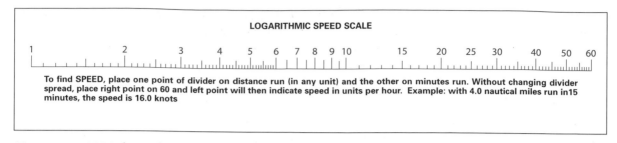

Figure 15-08 NOS charts of 1:40,000 or larger scale carry a Logarithmic Speed Scale that can be used to graphically solve problems of time, distance, and speed. Its use in explained in Chapter 16.

Charts at a scale of 1:80,000 or larger (e.g. 1:40,000) will normally carry, in addition to a statement of scale, two sets of GRAPHIC BAR SCALES each subdivided into conveniently and commonly used units; refer to **Figure 15-07**. Note that one basic unit is placed to the *left* of the scale's zero point and is subdivided more finely than is the main part of the scale. The use of these graphic scales is covered in Chapter 16.

When using Mercator charts, the navigator can take advantage of the fact that one minute on the *latitude* scale on each *side* of the chart is essentially equal to one nautical mile. (Do *not* use the longitude scale at the top or bottom of the chart.) On charts of a scale 1:80,000 and smaller (e.g. 1:1,200,000) the latitude scale will be the only means of measuring distance.

It is important to fix in your mind the scale of the chart you are using, lest you misjudge distances. Quite often in a day's cruise you may use charts of different scales, changing back and forth between small-scale coastal charts and larger-scale harbor charts. Unless you are aware of the differing scales, you may find yourself in a dangerous position.

A LOGARITHMIC SPEED SCALE is printed on all charts of 1:40,000 or larger scale; see **Figure 15-08**. It is useful for graphically solving problems of time, speed, and distance; the technique is explained in Chapter 16.

Chart Sources

Charts are prepared and issued by several agencies of the U.S. federal government. This is not duplication, however, because different agencies are responsible for different areas and types of charts.

Most boaters use charts prepared by the National Ocean Service of the National Oceanic and Atmospheric Administration, U.S. Department of Commerce. NOS charts (sometimes referred to as NOAA charts) cover the Great Lakes and the coastal waters of the United States, including harbors and rivers extending inland to the head of tidal action.

The National Imagery and Mapping Agency (NIMA) publishes charts of the high seas and foreign waters based on its own and other nations' surveys; see page 555 for a recent name change. Some of these charts may still bear the name of a former publishing agency, Defense Mapping Agency Hydrographic/Topographic Center,

LARGE-SCALE & SMALL-SCALE

When chart scales are expressed fractionally, confusion sometimes results from the use of the terms "large-scale" and "small-scale." Since the number that is varied to change the scale is in the denominator of the fraction, as it gets larger, the fraction, and hence the scale, gets smaller. For example, 1/80,000 is a smaller fraction than 1/40,000, so a chart to the former scale is termed a smaller-scale chart.

The terms "large-scale" and "small-scale" are relative and have no limiting definitions. Scales may be as large as 1:5,000 for detailed harbor charts, or as small as 1 to several million for charts of large areas of the world.

DMAHTC. Boaters will use NIMA charts, for example, when cruising in the Bahamas.

Charts of major inland rivers such as the Mississippi and Ohio are issued by the U.S. Army Corps of Engineers. Also available are charts of many inland lakes and canal systems.

Canadian waters are charted by the Canadian Hydrographic Service, an agency of the Department of Fisheries and Oceans.

Chart Catalogs

The catalogs from issuing agencies indicate the area covered by each chart, the scale used, the price, and the type of radionavigation system (LORAN) charted, if any. These catalogs are useful for planning a cruise into unfamiliar waters.

The National Ocean Service publishes four free chart catalogs; see page 548.

The NIMA chart catalog, available as nine individual catalogs, is discussed on page 551.

Where to Buy Charts

Charts may be purchased directly from the headquarters or field offices of the issuing agencies, or from retail sales agents. The addresses of NOS and NIMA distribution offices are given in Appendix A. Sales agents are widely located in boating and shipping centers. The names and addresses of local sales agents for NOS charts and publications are listed in the various chart catalogs. These lists are footnoted to indicate agents also stocking NIMA charts and USCG publications. Each volume of the NIMA chart catalogs lists sales agents, including those in foreign countries.

The price of NOS and DMAHTC charts has risen significantly in recent years and continues to rise nearly every year. The cost of a full set for many boating areas has become a major expense for a boater. These greater prices, however, still do not cover the full costs of surveys, data compilation, printing, and distribution. Even so, Government charts should be considered a bargain considering the extent, accuracy, and importance of the information that they provide.

A discount is allowed to each local sales agent for his quantity purchases. It is also possible for a boat or yacht club or other boating organization to purchase charts in quantity for a discount.

Reproductions of government charts are also available from commercial organizations in bound volumes for greater convenience and at somewhat lower cost.

You should keep a full set of charts aboard for the waters you cruise, and regularly replace worn-out or outdated charts with new ones. Failure to have a proper chart could be a factor in determining liability in the event of an accident.

WHAT CHARTS SHOW

Charts include much information that you should study thoroughly before you actually use the chart for navigation. Clear the kitchen or dining room table and spread your charts out—do it before you cruise into any unfamiliar waters. Study charts can also be displayed on computer using chart-planning programs. This can provide a measure of "boating fun" when the weather is too cold or too wet and windy to get your craft underway. There is an amazing amount of information on every nautical chart; learn how to get every bit of it.

When hydrographic surveys have been completed, cartographers are presented with vast amounts of information—so much so that if they were to include it all, charts would be a useless mass of black and colored ink. The cartographer's task is to edit the survey information, to make decisions as to what to include and what to leave out. Even so, such a large amount of data remains that every element on the printed chart must be made to carry meaning. To learn to read a chart, you must recognize that nothing has been placed there without significance.

Basic Information

Located on the chart where space is available is the GENERAL INFORMATION or TITLE BLOCK; see **Figure 15-09.** Here is the chart title describing the waters covered (the chart number does not appear here, but rather in several places around the margins); a statement of the type of projection used and the scale; the unit of depth measurement

PRINT-ON-DEMAND CHARTS

A recent development in nautical charting is the NOAA program of "Print-on-Demand" (POD). This is the use of large-format inkjet printers to produce charts at a decentralized location. Files are maintained in NOS databases and updated weekly with data that is published in *Notices to Mariners* and *Local Notices to Mariners*, as well as information from NOS field activities and cooperating organizations not yet published. Updated digital chart images are transmitted from NOS to the printing activity each hour. Here the actual printing is done only when an order is received by a retail agent and the chart is shipped for overnight delivery. The technology is not suitable for walk-in service or for implementation at all sales agencies

Print-on-Demand offers the following benefits for users:

• Nautical charts that are up-to-date when they are purchased, instead of charts that may be many months, even years, old when sold. A new edition is available five to eight weeks before the conventionally printed chart is in the distribution system. Additionally, a user can go to the Internet site www.chart maker. ncd.noaa.gov/pod and see the schedule for prospective new editions, thus avoiding buying a chart that will soon be replaced.

• POD charts are even better than before— brighter colors and higher contrast for improved readability in various light conditions. The paper used is water and abrasion resistant. Charts can be furnished in a double-sided laminated version for a small additional cost.

• Charts that are normally overprinted with Loran-C lines may now be ordered without such lines; this will result in charts with greater clarity for the many users who no longer use Loran as a navigation tool. (Some notes relating to Loran will not be removed and will remain on the face of the chart or in the margins.) A probable future development is the capability to print charts customized for a user's specialized needs, such as routes in water areas and additional features in land areas. Other products, such as reduced-scale "Pocket charts," are also being considered in this still-developing area of navigational aids.

Print-on-Demand provides the following benefits for sales agents and the government:

• Reduction of the need for space and costs of maintaining inventories.

• Elimination of the wasteful condemnation of obsolete charts when a new edition is issued.

Print-on-Demand charts are official and sufficient to meet all legal requirements where applicable. (Current editions of charts are not required on board recreational small craft, but their availability and use will be beneficial in case of accidents, lawsuits, etc.) POD charts carry the usual edition number and publication date, but also have an "Additional Corrections" box in the lower-left corner that notes the latest NIMA and *Local Notices to Mariners* for which the chart has been corrected.

There are, however, some disadvantages. Conventional POD charts are somewhat larger than the normally printed version. This added space is put to good use with additional information, but the larger size may make handling more difficult on smaller boats. NOS produces many charts as "small-craft editions" printed on both sides of lighter-weight paper and accordion-folded for ease of use in limited spaces; see page 533. When prepared as Print-on-Demand charts these are printed on one side of regular-weight paper with multiple parallel strips covering the various section of the route concerned—these are often even larger than conventional POD charts and could present quite a problem in use at the helm of smaller boats.

Nearly all NOS charts (98 percent as of early 2003) are now available in the Print-on-Demand format—information on availability can be found at the website mentioned above. These charts can be purchased from many of the larger chart sales agents—again, see the website for the current list of retail dealers. Charts that are ordered at one of these dealers (in person or by phone, fax or Internet) will normally be available the next business day; they can be picked up at the store or dropped-shipped directly to the user. (Occasionally, a retail agent may have in stock a POD chart that is up-to-date for all corrections.)

The cost of a Print-on-Demand chart is a few dollars more than a conventionally printed chart. The POD system supplements, but does not replace, the long-standing chart distribution system and charts as we have known them for many years remain available.

POD Charts in Canada

The Canadian Hydrographic Service (CHS) also provides a print-on-demand chart service. There are some differences from the NOS operations, but the result is similar for users.

The information for many CHS charts is now stored in digital databases that are updated on a continuous basis from *Notices to Mariners*; CHS prints the charts in Ottawa using large-format inkjet printers. As of early 2005, about half of the 950 CHS charts were in the POD files and conversion work is continuing. Charts not yet in the database are printed lithographically as before and commercial charts continue to be hand amended prior to being issued to dealers. A few charts of a specialized nature will continue to be press-printed. Charts that are printed in the POD system are not available in the older printing-press format. Charts are printed only when an order from a dealer has been received.

With the POD system, CHS no longer needs to print large inventories of charts and hand-correct them with cumulative *Notices to Mariners* before distribution to dealers. For customers, this means that charts are completely machine printed and up to date as of the time they are printed. Print-on-Demand allows CHS to issue charts to customers six to eight weeks faster and to have continual availability as compared to press-printed charts.

Because these charts are up-to-date at the time of printing, customers no longer receive charts that contain hand-drawn amendments and ironed-on patches. The product is a fresh, clean, completely machine-drawn chart.

POD charts from CHS are priced the same as the lithographically printed charts they replace.

Future plans being considered include expanding POD printing to the dealer level. CHS is evaluating the business case and supporting technologies.

(feet or fathoms—one fathom equals six feet—or meters), and the datum plane for such soundings. (Caution: if the chart has INSETS—"blow-ups" of areas of special interest—these will be at a larger scale than the chart as a whole.)

Elsewhere on the chart where space is available (normally in land areas), you will find other information including the meaning of certain commonly used abbreviations, units and the datum for heights above water, notes of caution regarding dangers, tidal information, references to anchorage areas, and a statement of the applicable volume of the *Coast Pilot* (see page 548). Read *all* notes on charts; they provide important information that cannot be graphically presented; see **Figure 15-10**.

Editions & Revisions
The edition number and publication date of a chart at the lower left-hand corner; immediately

Figure 15-09 The title block of a chart shows the official name of the chart, the type of projection, and scale, plus the datum and unit of measurement for depths. Printed nearby is much valuable information, so be sure to read all notes before using any chart.

Figure 15-10 Notes printed on charts may concern navigation regulations, hazardous conditions at inlets, information on controlling depths that cannot be printed conveniently alongside a channel, or other matters that relate to navigation.

following these figures is the date of the latest revised printing, if any. Under a policy adopted in late 2002, only the month and year of the chart's printing will be shown, and nearby will be separate information indicating the dates of the latest NIMA *Notice to Mariners* and USCG *Local Notice to Mariners* through which the chart has been corrected; see **Figure 15-11**. These dates may be several weeks prior to the printing date due to the time require for actual printing after the final data input; they are provided to indicate to the user the starting point for keeping the new edition corrected from *Notices*. Most NOS charts are printed to supply a normal demand of one or two years for active areas, and from four to 12 years in

areas where few changes occur. (Print-on-Demand charts will carry additional dates indicating the more recent application of information from *Notices* and other sources; see sidebar page 512.)

Charts may be printed as-is when the stock runs low, but a REVISED PRINT is more likely if a new edition is not published. Revisions include all changes that have been printed in *Notices to Mariners* since the last revision. When major changes occur, such as significant differences between charted depths and actual conditions revealed by new surveys, a NEW EDITION will be published. This will also include all other changes that have been made in aids to navigation, shore-side features, etc.

NOS is increasingly publishing nautical charts compiled using an automated information system. Every item of information on the chart—every symbol, abbreviation, sounding, line, color, *everything*—is stored on magnetic media as bits of digital data. Negatives for the printing of each color are made by laser beams controlled by a computer. Since a digital database is easily updated, the revision of charts for new editions is becoming an easier and faster process as this technique is extended to all NOS charts. Digitizing also allows downloading of data to electronic charts.

Use only the latest edition of a chart. All new editions supersede older issues, which should be discarded. New editions contain information published in *Notices to Mariners* and *Local Notices to Mariners.* They also include other corrections from extensive application of hydrographic and topographic surveys considered essential for safe navigation but not published in the *Notices.* To ensure that you know what are the latest editions, check the small NOS booklet *Dates of Latest Editions,* issued quarterly and found at local sales agents for charts and other NOS publications; this is also available online at www.chartmaker.ncd.noaa.gov and at www. NauticalChart.gov.

Between editions, correct your own charts from information published in *Notices to Mariners* and *Local Notices to Mariners* (see page 553). Charts kept in stock by the National Ocean Service or

Figure 15-11 The edition number and date, month and year, of printing of each NOS chart are printed in the margin, at the lower left corner along with the chart number. Also shown are the dates of the last Notice to Mariners and Local Notice to Mariners data that was available when the chart was prepared. Between editions, a chart may be revised; the date of revision will also be shown in the margin.

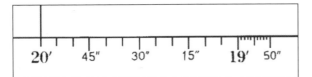

Figure 15-12 On charts at scales of 1:40,000 or larger, latitude and longitude scales are subdivided into minutes and seconds. This extract from a harbor chart shows meridians drawn at 5-minute intervals, tick marks at 1-minute intervals, and a 1-minute interval subdivided into 5-second units. Note the ten 1-second longitude units at the right of the 19′ figure.

Figure 15-13 On charts of relatively small scale, the latitude and longitude border markings are in minutes and fractions of minutes. On this 1:80,000 chart, meridians are drawn at 10-minute intervals; subdivisions are in minutes and tenths of minutes. On smaller scale charts, the smallest subdivisions might be fifths, halves, or whole minutes.

sales agents while awaiting sale are not updated or corrected before sale. When you buy a new chart, check all *Notices* subsequent to the printed edition date and enter all applicable corrections. Changes for NOS charts are also available on the Internet; searches can be made by chart number or by Coast Guard District (but not smaller geographic area). Go to http://www.ch artmaker.ncd.noaa.gov (files may be quite large; a high-speed connection is desirable). Changes for NIMA charts may be derived from *U.S. Notices to Mariners*, available on line at http://pollux. nss.nima.mil/index/. For *Local Notices to Mariners* go to www. navcen.uscg.g ov/lnm/ default.html.

Latitude & Longitude Scales

Conventional nautical charts have the geographical north direction toward the top of the sheet, unlike some small-craft charts and chart books that may be oriented to follow the general direction of a river or the coastline without respect to north. Such conventional charts have latitude scales in each side border and longitude scales in the top and bottom borders. Meridians and parallels are drawn across the chart as fine black lines, usually at 2-, 5-, or 10-minute intervals as determined by the scale of the particular chart.

On NOS charts with a scale of 1:50,000 and larger, such as on harbor charts, the subdivisions in the border scales are in terms of minutes and seconds of latitude and longitude; see **Figure 15-12.**

On small-scale charts, the subdivisions are in minutes and fractions of minutes—charts at a scale of 1:80,000, such as *Training Chart 1210Tr*, use minutes and tenths of minutes; see **Figure 15-13.** Even smaller-scale charts use minutes and fifths or halves, or even full minutes.

Where skewed projections are used, and North is not at the top of the sheet, such as on small-craft charts of the Intracoastal Waterway, divisions of latitude and longitude are indicated along parallels and meridians at several convenient places, and/or separately near the graphic distance scales.

Use of Color on Charts

Nearly all charts use color to emphasize various features and so facilitate reading and interpretation. The colors vary with the agency publishing the chart and its intended use.

The NOS color system uses five multipurpose colors in either solid color or shades—black, magenta, gold, blue, and green. Land areas are a screened tint of gold (urban or built-up areas are often shown in a darker screened tint of that color); water areas are white (the color of the paper), except for the shallower regions, which are shown in a screened blue. Areas that are submerged at some tidal stages but uncovered at others, such as sand bars, mud flats, coral reefs, and marshes, are green. On some charts, water areas that have been swept with wire drags to ensure the absence of isolated rocks or coral heads may be shown by a screened green with the depth of the sweep indicated.

Magenta ink is used for many purposes on charts; it has good visibility under red light, which is used for reading charts during the hours of darkness, because it does not destroy night vision as white light does. Red buoys are printed in magenta, as are red daybeacon symbols. Lighted buoys of any color have a magenta disc over the small circle portion of the symbol to assist in identifying it as a lighted aid. A magenta flare symbol extending from a position dot (much like an exclamation mark) is used with lights, lighted ranges, etc. Caution and danger symbols and notes are printed in magenta; also compass roses, usually, and recommended courses where shown. Black is used for most symbols, contour lines, man-made features, and printed information.

The use of colors on NIMA charts is generally the same as described above for NOS charts, except that gray (screened black) is used for land areas.

Lettering Styles

To convey as much information as possible in the clearest form, certain classes of information are printed in one style of lettering and other classes in another style. By knowing what type of lettering is used for which class of information, you can more easily and quickly grasp the data being presented.

Vertical lettering is used for features on NOS charts that are dry at high water and not affected by movement of the water (except for the height of the feature above the water, which may be changed by tidal action). See the use of vertical lettering for the landmark stacks and spires, and the horn signal in **Figure 15-14**. Depth information also uses vertical numbers.

Slant (italic) letters, such as those in **Figure 15-14,** are used for water, underwater, and floating features, except depth figures. Note also the use in

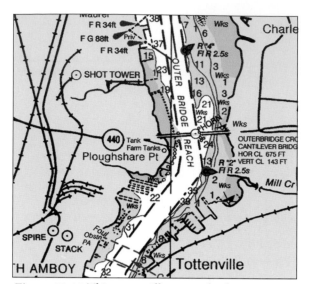

Figure 15-14 This excerpt illustrates the distinction between vertical lettering for features that are above the water—such as "STACK" and "SPIRE" in contrast to leaning (italic) letters for underwater features, such as "Wks" for wrecks and "Obstn" for an unidentified obstruction.

Figure 15-14 of slanted lettering for bottom features and buoy characteristics.

On smaller-scale charts, a small reef (covering and uncovering with tidal action) often cannot be distinguished by symbol from a small islet (always above water); the proper name for either might be "____ Rock." The feature in doubt is an islet if the name is in vertical letters, but is a reef if lettered in slanting characters. (The small reef would be indicated by a symbol that resembles an asterisk. A small islet would be exaggerated if far enough from shore and filled in with a gold tint.)

Similarly, a piling visible above water at all tidal stages is charted as "Pile," but one beneath the surface is noted as *"Subm pile."*

Periods after abbreviations are omitted in water and in land areas, but lower-case "i" and "j" are dotted. Periods are used only where needed for clarity, as, for example, in certain notes.

Water Features

The information shown on charts is a combination of the natural features of the water and land areas and various selected man-made objects and features. Each item shown is carefully chosen for its value to those who navigate vessels of all sizes.

Depths

The principal feature of concern to boaters is the DEPTH. For any system of depth information there must be a reference plane, or DATUM. This is obvious in coastal areas where depths may change hourly as a result of tidal action; it is likewise true in inland areas where lake or river levels may also change, though more slowly on a seasonal basis. Each chart has on it a statement of the datum from which all depths, also called SOUNDINGS, are measured. The choice of the reference plane is based on many factors, most of them technical, but the primary consideration is that of selecting a datum near to normal low-water levels.

Planes of Reference On NOS charts the datum for the depths is MEAN LOWER LOW WATER; this is of greatest significance in areas such as the Pacific Coast where each tidal day has two low tides of different heights; refer to **Figure 17-06**. However, this datum is now on all NOS charts.

By definition, "mean lower low water" is an average of all lowest water levels for tidal days over a period of time (usually 19 years). Thus on some days the lower low tide will be *below* the datum. This will result in *actual* depths being *shallower* than the charted figures. Many charts will have a small box with a tabulation of the extreme variations from charted depths that may be expected for various points; see **Figure 15-15**.

Prolonged winds from certain directions, or persistent extremes of barometric pressure, may cause temporary local differences from charted depths. *Remember that there are exceptional conditions at which times the water may be much shallower than indicated on the chart.*

The datum for water depths on the Great Lakes and other inland bodies of water is an arbitrarily established plane, usually at or near long-term low averages. This datum will be clearly indicated on the chart.

How Depths Are Shown

Depth information is shown on a chart by many small printed figures. These indicate the depth at that point, usually measured in feet or fathoms. Some newer U.S. charts, and many of other nations, have depth measured in meters and

TIDAL INFORMATION				
Place	Height referred to datum of soundings (MLLW)			
Name (LAT/LONG)	Mean Higher High Water	Mean High Water	Mean Low Water	Extreme Low Water
	feet	feet	feet	feet
Plum Gut Harbor (41°10'N/72°12'W)	3.1	2.8	0.2	-3.0
Sag Harbor (41°00'N/72°18'W)	3.0	2.7	0.2	-3.0
Saybrook Jetty (41°16'N/72°21'W)	4.2	3.8	0.3	-3.5
Stratford Shoal (41°04'N/73°06'W)	7.1	6.8	0.2	-3.5
(100)				

Figure 15-15 Coast and harbor charts often carry information on the normal range of tides, and the extreme variations from charted depths that may be expected. Check all newly purchased charts for this important information.

decimeters (tenths of a meter). The printed depth figures are only a very small fraction of the many soundings taken by the survey team.

Only the more significant and representative depth data are selected for use on the final chart. A skipper can form some opinion of the characteristics of the bottom by noting the density of the depth information. Where depth figures are rather widely spaced, he can be assured of a reasonably flat or uniformly sloping bottom. Wherever the depths vary irregularly or abruptly, the figures will be more frequent and more closely spaced.

Depth Curves Most charts will have contour lines, usually called DEPTH CURVES, connecting points of equal depth. Such lines will appear at certain depths as determined by the scale of the chart, the relative range of depths, and the type of vessel expected to use the chart. Typically, depth curves are shown for 6, 12, 18, 30, and 60 feet, and multiples of 60 feet (note the relationship to fathoms). Depth curves are shown as continuous solid lines with depth labels or various combinations of dots and dashes to code the depth along each line, but it is often easier to learn a line's significance by inspection of the depth figures on either side of it.

On many charts, a blue tint is shown in water areas out to the curve that is considered to be the danger curve for the majority of important marine traffic that is expected to use that particular chart. In general, the 6-foot curve is considered the danger curve for small-craft and

Intracoastal Waterway charts; see **Figure 15-16.** The 12- or 18-foot curve is considered the danger curve for harbor charts, and the 30-foot curve for coast and general charts. (These types of charts are discussed in more detail on pages 531–533.) On some of the latter charts, the area beyond the 18-foot curves may be tinted in a lighter shade of blue than the shallower areas. Thus it can be seen that, while blue tint means shallow water, this coloring does not have exactly the same meaning on all charts. Check each chart you plan to use to determine at just what depth the coloring changes.

Isolated offshore areas that have depths corresponding to the tinted areas alongshore waters will also be tinted in the appropriate shade of blue.

Charts without depth curves or dashed curves must be used with caution, as soundings may be too scarce to allow the lines to be drawn accurately.

Avoid an isolated sounding that is shallower than surrounding depths, particularly with a solid or dotted line ring (depth curve) around it, as it

may be doubtful how closely the spot has been examined and whether the least depth has been found.

Dredged Channels

Dredged channels are shown on a chart by two dashed lines to represent the side limits of the improvement. The channel's depth and the date on which such data were obtained are often shown within the lines or close alongside; refer to **Figure 15-14.** A dredged basin will be similarly outlined with printed information on depths and date. The depth shown, such as "*6 Feet Oct 2001,*" is the controlling depth through the channel on the date shown, but does not mean this depth exists over the full width of the channel; some charts may indicate that the stated depth is only "on centerline."

Channels are sometimes described in terms of specific width as well as depth; for example, "*8 Feet for a Width of 100 Feet*"; a date for this information is often included. Depths may have subsequently changed from either shoaling or further dredging, so if your boat's draft is close to the depth shown for the channel, get local information, if you can, before entering. Detailed information for many dredged channels is shown in tabular form on applicable charts, with revisions of the data published in *Notices to Mariners* or *Local Notices to Mariners* as changes occur.

Nature of the Bottom

The nature of the bottom, such as sand, rock, mud, grass, or "hard" or "soft," is indicated for many areas by abbreviations. This information is especially valuable when you are anchoring, so take advantage of it wherever it appears. The meanings of these and other abbreviations are usually given on the face of the chart near the basic identification block; many are self-evident.

The Shoreline

The shoreline shown on charts is the MEAN HIGH-WATER LINE for tidal areas; it is the HIGH-WATER LINE in lakes and nontidal areas, except in marsh or mangrove areas where the outer edge of vegetation is used. Natural shoreline is represented by a

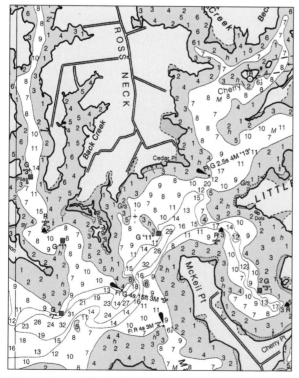

Figure 15-16 This inshore chart shows depth curves at 6, 12, and 18 feet. The blue tint emphasizes the 6-foot line and indicates dangerous shallow water.

slightly heavier line than man-made shoreline. Unsurveyed shoreline, or shoreline connecting two surveys that do not join satisfactorily, is shown by a dashed line. The low-water line is marked by a single row of dots. The outer limits of marsh are indicated by a fine solid line. The region between the high- and low-water lines is tinted green, and may be labeled "Marsh," "Grass," "Mud," "Sand," etc.

Features of Land Areas

Features and characteristics of land areas are shown on nautical charts in only such detail as will assist a navigator on the water. Details are usually confined to those near the shoreline or of such a prominent nature as to be clearly visible for some distance offshore.

How Topography Is Shown

The general topography of land areas is indicated by contours, form lines, or hachures. CONTOURS are lines connecting points of equal elevation. Their specific height, usually measured in feet, may be shown by figures placed at suitable points along the lines. The interval of height between adjacent contours is uniform over any one chart. On NOS charts of tidal areas, heights are measured from a different datum than depths; usually this is Mean High Water; in nontidal areas, the same datum is established for both depths and heights.

FORM LINES, or SKETCH CONTOURS, are shown by broken lines and are contour approximations meant to indicate terrain formations without giving exact information on height. They are used in areas where accurate data are not available to do otherwise. The interval between form lines is not necessarily uniform and no height figures are given.

HACHURES are short lines or groups of lines that indicate the approximate location of steep slopes. The lines follow the general direction of the slope, with the length of the lines indicating the height of the slope.

Cliffs, Vegetation & the Shore

Cliffs are represented by bands of irregular hachures. The symbol is not an exact "plan view," but rather somewhat of a "side elevation"; its extent is roughly proportional to the height of the cliff. For example, a perpendicular cliff of 100 feet height will be shown by a hachured band wider than one representing a cliff of 15 feet with slope.

Spot elevations are normally given on nautical charts only for summits or the tops of conspicuous landmarks; see **Figure 15-17.**

The type of vegetation on land will sometimes be indicated by symbols or wording where this information may be useful to mariners.

The nature of the shore is sometimes indicated by various symbols—rows of fine dots denote a sandy beach, small circles indicate gravel, or irregular shapes mean boulders.

Man-Made Features

Man-made features on land are shown in detail to the extent that they can be useful to water-borne traffic. Examples are piers, bridges, overhead power cables, and breakwaters. Other man-made features on land, such as built-up areas, roads, and streets, may be shown in some detail or generalized as determined by their usefulness to navigation and the scale of the chart. On large-scale charts the actual network of streets may be shown with public

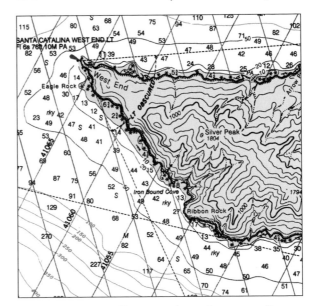

Figure 15-17 *Landforms are shown by contour lines and the tops of conspicuous landmarks are identified by height and name. Heights are usually measured from mean high water in feet. The metric system is used on some charts.*

buildings such as the post office and customhouse individually identified; see **Figure 15-18,** upper. On less detailed charts, the town or city may be represented by a cross-hatched or more heavily screened area for the approximate limits of the built-up area, with major streets and road shown by single heavy lines; see **Figure 15-18,** lower.

Locations of prominent isolated objects, tanks, stacks, spires, etc., are shown accurately so they may be used for taking bearings.

Specific descriptive names have been given to certain types of landmark objects to standardize terminology. Among the more often used are the following:

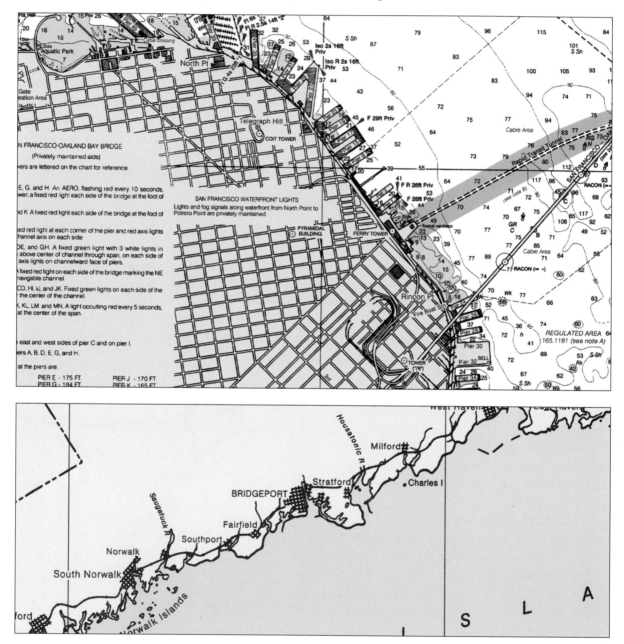

Figure 15-18 On relatively large-scale charts, upper, detailed information may be shown of the streets and buildings of a city or town, particularly near the waterfront. Some street names may be given, as well as the location of public buildings such as a customhouse or post office. On smaller-scale charts, lower, cities, town and built up areas are indicated by cross-hatching, as shown, or by heavier screening that shows up as a darker, but not black, area. Single heavy lines indicate principal roads.

• BUILDING or HOUSE—the appropriate term is used when the entire structure is a landmark, rather than any individual feature of it.

• CHIMNEY—a relatively small projection for conveying smoke from a building to the atmosphere. This term is used when the building is more prominent than the chimney, but a better bearing can be taken on the smaller feature.

• CUPOLA—a dome-shaped tower or turret rising from a building, generally small in comparison with the building.

• DOME—a large, rounded, hemispherical structure rising above a building; for example, the dome of the United States Capitol in Washington.

• FLAGPOLE—a single staff from which flags are displayed. This term is used when the pole is not attached to a building.

• FLAGSTAFF—a flagpole arising from a building.

• LOOKOUT STATION or WATCH TOWER—a tower surmounted by a small house from which a watch is regularly kept.

• RADIO MAST—a relatively short pole or slender structure for elevating ratio antennas; usually found in groups.

• RADIO TOWER—a tall pole or structure for elevating ratio antennas.

• SPIRE—a slender, pointed structure extending above a building. It is seldom less than two-thirds of the entire height of the structure, and its lines are rarely broken by intermediate structures. Spires are typically found on churches.

• STACK—a tall smokestack or chimney. This term is used when the stack is more prominent as a landmark than the accompanying buildings.

• STANDPIPE—a tall cylindrical structure whose height is several times it diameter.

• TANK—a water tank elevated high above ground by a tall skeleton framework. GAS TANK and OIL TANK are terms used for distinctive structures of specialized design, and are usually lower than a water tank and not supported by a skeleton framework.

• TOWER—any structure with its base on the ground and high in proportion to its base, or that part of a structure higher than the rest, but having essentially vertical sides for the greater part of its height.

• TREE—an isolated, conspicuous tree useful as a navigational landmark (seldom used).

Bridges over navigable waterways are shown with the type of bridge—bascule, swing, suspension, etc.—and both horizontal and vertical clearances in feet, the latter measured from mean *high* water (or other shoreline plane of reference used for heights of objects). Vertical clearance should be stated as the height available at the lowest point over the channel; this "low steel" figure for arched bridges may be supplemented by a sign indicating the amount of additional clearance available at the center. Some bridges will have a sign merely stating "Clearance at Center."

When two similar objects are so located that separate landmark symbols cannot be used, the work "TWIN" is added to the identifying name or abbreviation. When only one of a group of similar objects is charted, a descriptive legend is added in parentheses; for example "(TALLEST OF FOUR)" or "(NORTHEAST OF THREE)."

Radio broadcasting station (AM) antennas are shown on charts where they may be used for taking visual or radio bearings. The call letters and frequency are often shown adjacent to the symbol marking the location of the towers.

Stacks, radio towers, and other tall towers are required to have lights to indicate their presence to aircraft. When these lights are useful for marine navigation, they appear on charts as "FR," "Occ R," or "Fl R"; see page 493. Also there are structures with multiple very-high-intensity, very-short-flash lights that are charted as "Strobe." These are visible in daylight as well as at night and eliminate the need for the tower or stack to be painted with alternating red and white bands.

SYMBOLS & ABBREVIATIONS

The vast amount of information shown on a chart, and the closeness of many items, necessitate an extensive use of symbols and abbreviations. You should be familiar with all symbols and abbreviations on the charts you use. You must be able to read and interpret your charts quickly and accurately; the safety of your boat may depend on this ability.

International Standards

Chart SYMBOLS are conventional shapes and designs indicating the presence of a certain feature or object at the location shown. No attempt is made at an accurate or detailed representation of the object, but the correct location is shown. Symbols and abbreviations used on NOS and NIMA charts are standardized and appear in a small pamphlet as *Chart No. 1*; see **Figure 15-19**. This is also available as a CD-ROM and on the Internet at http://pollux.nss.nima.mil/pubs or at www.chartmaker.ncd.noaa.gov/. Generally similar information is printed on the reverse side of *Training Chart 1210Tr*. The symbols and abbreviations are in general conformance with worldwide usage as adopted by the International Hydrographic Organization (IHO).

The standardized symbols and abbreviations are shown in part on pages 523–529.

Basic Symbols & Abbreviations

Simple inspection of many symbols will reveal a pattern in the way that they are formed. If you know the general principles of chart symbols, you'll have an easier time learning the details.

Buoys

BUOYS, except mooring buoys, are shown by a diamond-shaped symbol and a small open circle indicating the position. (A circle is used rather than a position dot in recognition of the fact that a buoy will swing about its anchor on a length of chain.) To avoid interference with other features on the chart, it is often necessary to show the diamond shapes at various angles to the circle; the orientation of the diamond shape has no significance.

On charts using the normal number of colors, RED BUOYS are printed in magenta; the letter "R" may also be shown adjacent to the symbol. GREEN BUOYS are shown in that color with the letter "G" nearby.

A buoy symbol with a line across its *shorter* axis indicates a HORIZONTALLY BANDED BUOY. For a junction buoy both colors are used; magenta (for red) over green, or green over magenta, as the buoy itself is painted. The letters "RG" or "GR," respectively, appear near the symbol.

An open buoy symbol with a line across its *longer* axis represents a VERTICALY STRIPED BUOY. No colors are used on this symbol; the colors are indicated by the abbreviation "RW" for red-and-white.

Special purpose buoys are shown by an open, uncolored symbol and the letter "Y."

The type and shape of UNLIGHTED BUOYS is normally indicated by an abbreviation such as "C" for can or "N" for nun.

Because they are a potential hazard to navigation, "superbuoys" are charted with a special symbol, see **Figure 15-20**. This category includes exposed location buoys, offshore data collection buoys, and buoys for mooring tankers offshore while loading or unloading.

LIGHTED BUOYS are indicated by a small magenta disc over the small circle that marks the buoy's position. The color and rhythm of the light, and the "hull" colors are indicated by abbreviations near the symbol.

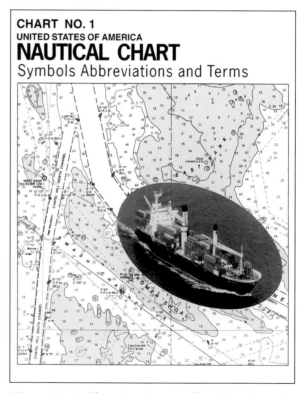

Figure 15-19 Chart No. 1 is not really a "chart" at all. It is a most useful booklet showing all chart symbols used on U.S. charts and the charts of other national jurisdictions.

ANATOMY OF A CHART

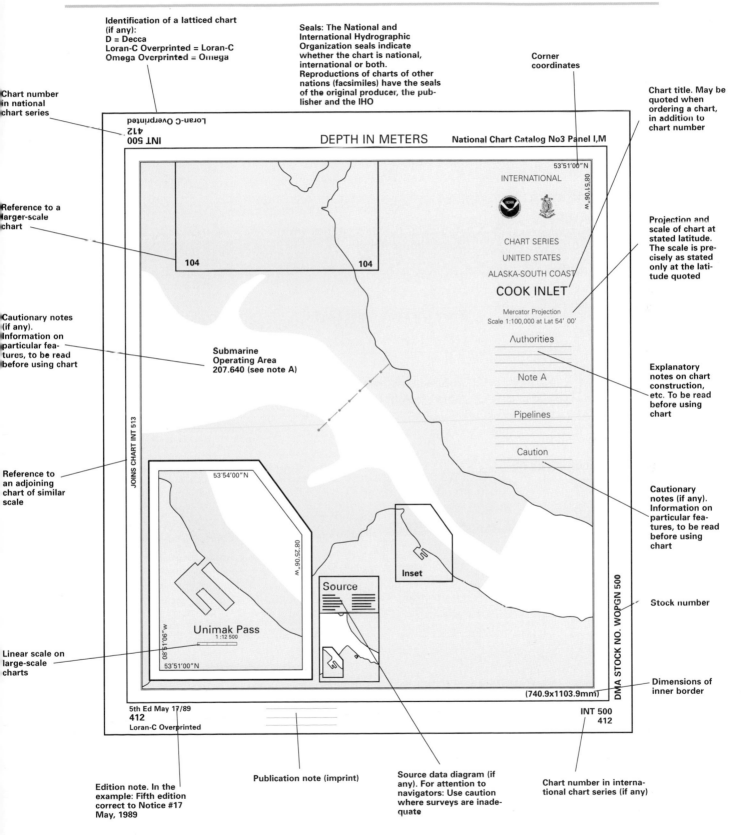

Identification of a latticed chart (if any):
D = Decca
Loran-C Overprinted = Loran-C
Omega Overprinted = Omega

Seals: The National and International Hydrographic Organization seals indicate whether the chart is national, international or both. Reproductions of charts of other nations (facsimiles) have the seals of the original producer, the publisher and the IHO

Corner coordinates

Chart title. May be quoted when ordering a chart, in addition to chart number

Chart number in national chart series

Reference to a larger-scale chart

Cautionary notes (if any). Information on particular features, to be read before using chart

Projection and scale of chart at stated latitude. The scale is precisely as stated only at the latitude quoted

Reference to an adjoining chart of similar scale

Explanatory notes on chart construction, etc. To be read before using chart

Linear scale on large-scale charts

Cautionary notes (if any). Information on particular features, to be read before using chart

Stock number

Dimensions of inner border

Edition note. In the example: Fifth edition correct to Notice #17 May, 1989

Publication note (imprint)

Source data diagram (if any). For attention to navigators: Use caution where surveys are inadequate

Chart number in international chart series (if any)

EXCERPTS FROM CHART NO. 1; NATURAL FEATURES

RELIEF

Plane of Reference for Heights → H

Supplementary national symbols: f

10		Contour lines with spot height	
11	256	Spot heights	
12		Approximate contour lines with approximate height	
13		Form lines with spot height	
14		Approximate height of top of trees (above height datum)	

WATER FEATURES, LAVA

Supplementary national symbols: g, h

20		River, Stream	
21		Intermittent – river	
22		Rapids, Waterfalls	
23		Lakes	

CULTURAL FEATURES

15		Embankment	
16		Tunnel	
17		Airport, Airfield	

OTHER CULTURAL FEATURES

Supplementary nationals symbols: e, f

20	VERT CL 6 FT ⊤6	Vertical clearance above High Water	
21	HOR CL 28 FT ⊢28⊣	Horizontal clearance	
22		Fixed bridge	
23		Opening bridge (in general)	
23.1		Swing bridge	
23.2		Lifting bridge	
23.3		Bascule bridge	
23.4		Pontoon bridge	
23.5		Draw bridge	
24		Transporter bridge	
25		Overhead trasnporter. Telepheric with vertical clearance	

PORTS

29.1	Floating oil barrier	Oil barrier
29.2	Oil retention (high pressure pipe)	Oil barrier
30	Works on land, with year date	Dock under construction (1987)
31	Under construction	Works at sea. Area under reclamation with year date	Area under reclamation (1987)
32	Under constr	Works under construction, with year date	Under construction (1987) Works in progress (1987)
33.1	Ruins	Ruins	Ru
33.2	Subm ruins	Ruined pier, partly submerged at high water. Submerged ruins	Pier (Ru)
34	*Hk*	Hulk (actual shape on large scale charts)	Hulk

CANALS, BARRAGES

Clearance ➞D   Signal Stations   T

40	Canal Ditch	Canal	°km 32	°km 46
41.1	Lock 6 10 8 6 ⊙SPIRE	Lock (on large-scale charts)		Lock
41.2	Canal ➞Lock Ditch Sluice Tidegate, Floodgate	Lock (on smaller-scale charts)		
42		Caisson		
43		Flood barrage		Flood barrage
44		Dam		Dam

TIDES, CURRENTS

TIDAL LEVELS & CHARTED DATA

Tide gauge ➤T

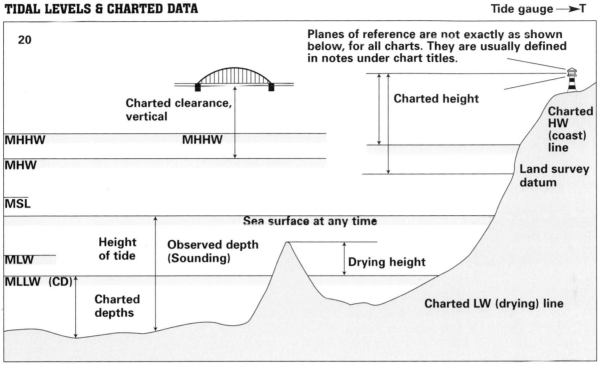

20

Planes of reference are not exactly as shown below, for all charts. They are usually defined in notes under chart titles.

Charted height

Charted clearance, vertical

Charted HW (coast) line

MHHW   MHHW

MHW

Land survey datum

MSL

Sea surface at any time

Height of tide

Observed depth (Sounding)

Drying height

MLW

MLLW (CD)

Charted depths

Charted LW (drying) line

TIDAL STREAMS & CURRENTS

Supplementary national symbols: m – t

Breakers ➤K

Tide Gauge ➤T

40	2 kn ➤	Flood stream (current) with rate	2,5 kn ➤
41	2 kn ➤	Ebb steam (current) with rate	2,5 kn ➤
42		Current in restricted waters	⫸➤
43		Ocean current with rates and seasons	2.5-4.5 kn ↝ Jan-March (see Note)
44	Tide rips 〜〜〜 Symbol used only in small areas	Overfalls, tide rips, races	〜〜 〜〜 〜〜 〜〜 〜〜
45	Eddies ℮℮℮ ℮℮℮ Symbol used only in small areas	Eddies	℮ ℮ ℮ ℮ ℮
46	⟨A⟩ ⟨B⟩	Position of tabulated tidal data with designation	⟨A⟩

DEPTHS & NATURE OF THE SEABED

DEPTH CONTOURS

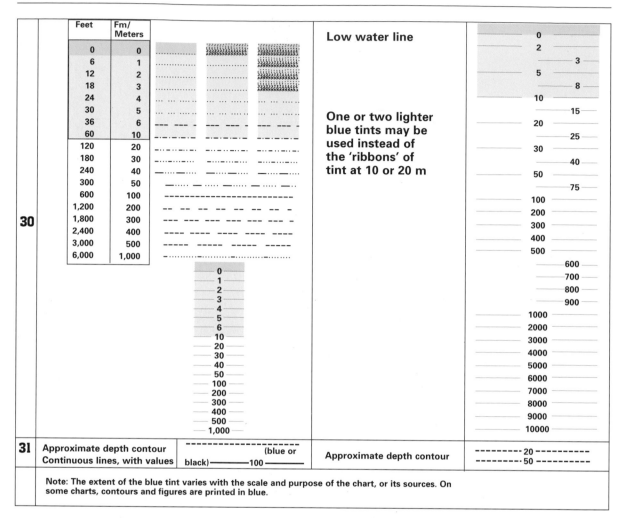

Feet	Fm/Meters
0	0
6	1
12	2
18	3
24	4
30	5
36	6
60	10
120	20
180	30
240	40
300	50
600	100
1,200	200
1,800	300
2,400	400
3,000	500
6,000	1,000

30

Low water line

One or two lighter blue tints may be used instead of the 'ribbons' of tint at 10 or 20 m

31 Approximate depth contour
Continuous lines, with values

(blue or black) ———100———

Approximate depth contour

Note: The extent of the blue tint varies with the scale and purpose of the chart, or its sources. On some charts, contours and figures are printed in blue.

TYPES OF SEABED, INTERTIDAL AREAS

20.1	Gravel	Area with stones, gravel or shingle	G St
20.2		Small area with stones or gravel	
21	Coral	Rocky area, which covers and uncovers	
22	Rock	Coral reef, which covers and uncovers	

ROCKS, WRECKS, OBSTRUCTIONS

31	*Foul* *Wks* #	*Foul* *Wks* *Wreckage*	Remains of a wreck or other foul area, a non-danger to navigation but to be avoided by vessels anchoring, trawling, etc.	# $\boxed{Foul}$	# fB

OBSTRUCTIONS

Plane of Reference for Depths ➤ H   Kelp, Sea-Weed ➤ J

40	Obstn	Obstn	Obstruction, depth unknown	Obstn	Obstn	#
41	5¼ Obstn	5¼ Obstn	Obstruction, least depth known	4₆ Obstn	16₈ Obstn	
42	21 Obstn · 5 Obstn	21 Obstn · 5 Obstn	Obstruction, least depth known, swept by wire drag or diver	4₆ Obstn	16₈ Obstn	
43.1	⊥ Subm Stakes, piles Perches	Subm piles Subm piling	Stumps of posts or piles, wholly submerged	Obstn ⋎ ⋎	⋏ Ⓣ Subm piles	
43.2	∘∘ Snags	∘∘ Stumps	Submerged piles, stake, snag, well or stump (with exact position)	⋎	⋏ ⋏ Ⓣ	
44.1	⊥⊥⊥⊥⊥ Fsh stks		Fishing stakes			
4.2			Fish trap, fish weirs, tunny nets			
45			Fish trap area, tunny nets area	Fish traps	Tunny nets	
46.1	Obstruction (fish haven) (actual shape)	Obstruction (fish haven)	Fish haven (artificial fishing reef)			
46.2	Obstn } Fish haven (Auth min 42 ft)		Fish haven with minimum depth	(2₄)	2₄	
47	*Oys*		Shellfish cultivation (stakes visible)	Shellfish		

Daybeacons

The symbol for DAYBEACONS—unlighted fixed aids to navigation—may be either a small triangle or square.

The square symbol, colored green and with the letter "G" nearby, is used for daybeacons that have a solid green dayboard of this shape.

The triangle symbol, colored magenta and with the letter "R" nearby, is used for daybeacons with solid red dayboards of this shape.

The symbol for a daybeacon with red-over-green triangular daymarks is an open triangle with the letters "RG"; for a daybeacon with green-over-red square daymarks it is an open square symbol with the letters "GR." The symbol for an articulated daybeacon is the usual square or triangle with a small circle added to the bottom as in **Figure 15-20**, plus a label "ART."

All octagonal, diamond-shaped, round, or rectangular daymarks will be represented by open square symbols and letter abbreviations as appropriate for the colors concerned.

Lights, All Types

The chart symbol for lights of all sizes—from the simple light on a single pile in inland waters to the largest of primary seacoast lights—is the same. This is a black position dot with a magenta "flare" giving much the appearance of a large exclamation mark. In addition to color and characteristics, there may be information on the height of the light and its nominal range (no allowance made for curvature of the earth or observer's height of eye).

The symbol for an articulated light combines the small circle of the buoy symbol and the magenta flare for a fixed light.

Fog Signals

The type of FOG SIGNAL on buoys and lights so equipped is indicated by a descriptive word or abbreviation adjacent to the chart symbol.

Identification by Number

Buoys and lights are usually NUMBERED (or less frequently, designated with letters or combinations of letters and numbers). This identification is placed on the chart near the symbol and is enclosed in quotation marks to distinguish the figures from depth data or other numbers. Primary and some secondary lights are named; the words, abbreviated as necessary, are printed near the symbol where space permits.

Ranges

RANGES are indicated by the two symbols of the front and rear markers (lights or daybeacons), plus a line joining them and extending beyond. This line is solid *only* over the distance for which the range is to be used for navigation; it continues on as a dashed line to the front marker and on to the rear marker; see **Figure 15-21.**

Dangers to Navigation

Symbols are also used for many types of DANGERS to navigation. Differentiation is made between rocks that are awash at times and those which remain below the surface at all tides, between visible wrecks and submerged ones, and between hazards that have been definitely located and those whose position is doubtful. There are a number of symbols and abbreviations for objects and areas dangerous to navigation. Spend adequate time studying them, with emphasis on the types commonly found in your home waters.

Accuracy & Precision Problems

The art and science of navigation has not been immune from the advances of technology. The most obvious new technology in piloting is the

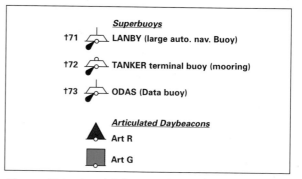

Figure 15-20 Special chart symbols are used to indicate the position of large automatic navigation buoys, tanker terminal buoys, and ocean data buoys—all types known as "superbuoys."

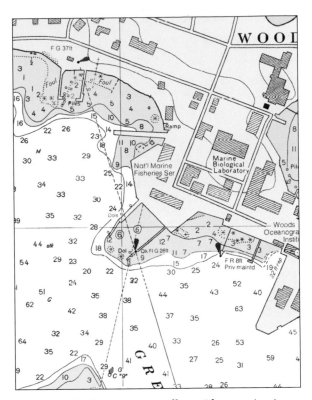

Figure 15-21 Ranges are excellent aids to navigation; they are charted by showing the front and rear marks (lighted or unlighted) with a line between them that denotes the range. The line is solid over the portion that is to be navigated, and dashed where it should not be followed.

Differential Global Positioning System (DGPS). Navigation systems using DGPS for locating a vessel's position have put mariners in a counter-intuitive predicament. In many cases, the DGPS position is more accurate than the technology that was used to put the soundings and features on the chart.

This discrepancy is even more pronounced when the chart scale is taken into consideration. The width of a line or line symbol on a paper chart is typically 0.1 to 1.5 millimeters (0.004 to 0.06 inches). A feature's actual position can fall anywhere within that line or symbol. Thus, on a typical 1:40,000 harbor chart, a feature could have a potential error of 40 to 80 meters (130 to 260 feet) due to scale alone; a line plotted on a chart would have a similar range of possible error. DGPS errors do not normally exceed a few meters (10 to 15 feet), and are often less. This is

often the cause of the "ship on pier situation" in which a vessel made fast to a pier shows on an electronic navigation system as being on the pier rather than along side.

CHART NUMBERING SYSTEM

All NOS and NIMA charts are numbered in a common system. This is based on REGIONS and SUBREGIONS. Boaters will generally be concerned only with charts having *five-digit* numbers; such charts have a scale of 1:2,000,000 or larger. The first digit refers to a region of the world, and the second, together with the first, to a subregion; the final three digits, are assigned systematically within the subregion, to denote the specific chart.

Region 1 includes the waters in and around the United States and Canada. Region 2 covers Central and South America, Mexico, the Bahamas, and the West Indies.

Region 1 has nine subregions designated counterclockwise around North American from Subregion 11 for the Gulf of Mexico and the Atlantic Coast up to Cape Hatteras. Subregion 12 extends to the eastern tip of Long Island, and 13 goes on to the Canadian border. Subregion 14 covers the Great Lakes; Subregion 18 is the U.S. Pacific Coast; Subregion 19 covers the Hawaiian Islands and adjacent waters. **Figure 15-22** shows the regions and subregions of the world.

The final three digits of a five-digit number are assigned counterclockwise around the subregion or along the coast. Many numbers are skipped over and left unassigned so that future charts can be fitted into the system.

The Five NOS Chart Series

As previously mentioned, charts are published in a wide range of scales. For general convenience of reference, the NOS has classified charts into "series" as follows:

• SAILING CHARTS—the smallest scale charts covering long stretches of coastline; for example, Cape Sable, Newfoundland to Cape Hatteras, NC; or the Gulf of Mexico; or San Francisco to Cape Flattery, Washington; see

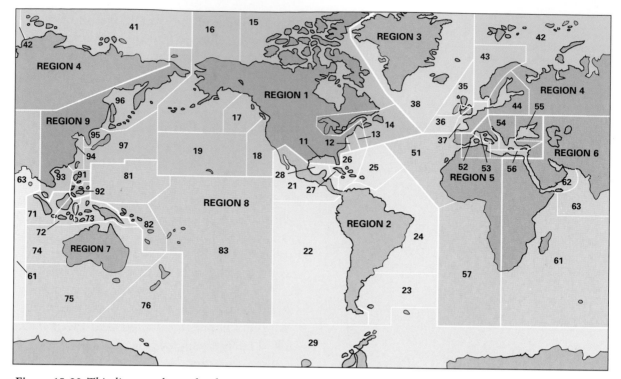

Figure 15-22 This diagram shows the chart regions and subregions of the world. Region 1 covers the United States and Canada. The number of the subregion forms the first two digits of a five-digit chart number.

Figure 15-23. The charts of this series are published at scales of 1:600,000 or smaller. Sailing charts are prepared for the use of the navigator in fixing his position as he approaches the coast from open ocean, or when sailing between distant coast ports. They show the offshore soundings, the principal lights and outer buoys, and landmarks visible at great distances. Other than for ocean cruising races, the average boater will have little use for charts in this series, except perhaps to plot the path of hurricanes and other tropical disturbances.

• GENERAL CHARTS—The second series comprises charts with scales in the range of 1:150,000 to 1:600,000. These cover more limited areas, such as Cape May, NJ to Cape Hatteras, NC; or Mississippi River to Galveston Bay; or San Francisco to Point Arena, CA. General charts are intended for coastwise navigation outside of offshore reefs and shoals when the vessel's course is mostly within sight of land and her position can be fixed by landmarks, lights, buoys, and sounding; see **Figure 15-24.**

• COAST CHARTS—This next larger scale series consists of charts for close-in coastwise navigation, for entering and leaving harbors, and for navigating large inland bodies of water. The scales used range from 1:50,000 to 1:150,000 with most at 1:80,000; see **Figure 15-25.** Typical examples of coast charts are the widely used *Training Chart No. 1210Tr,* and such navigational charts as the series of five which cover Chesapeake Bay or 18746 which takes the California skipper from Long Beach or Newport to Santa Catalina Island and back. The average boater may use several charts from this series.

• HARBOR CHARTS—This is the largest-scale and most-detailed series; see **Figure 15-26.** Scales range from 1:50,000 to 1:5,000 with an occasional inset of even larger scale. The scale used for any specific chart is determined by the need for showing detail and by the area to be covered by a single sheet.

• SMALL CRAFT CHARTS—These compact charts provide the small-craft skipper with a convenient, folded-format, small-size chart designed primarily

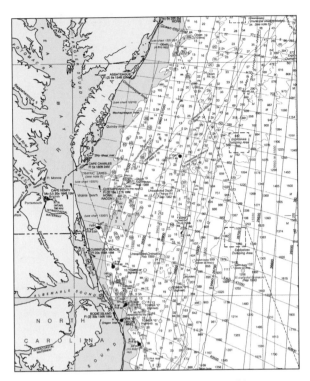

Figure 15-23 Sailing chart 13003, Cape Sable, Nova Scotia, to Cape Hatteras, North Carolina, scale 1:1,200,000. This chart would be used for far offshore passages; it shows very little detail of inshore aids to navigation. The entrance to Chesapeake Bay is just above the middle of this chart extract. On this chart, 1 inch equals 16.46 nautical miles.

for use in confined spaces; see **Figure 15-27.** One of the formats is designed to cover long, narrow waterways; another is a folded multi-page chart covering larger areas. All small-craft charts include a tabulation of public marine facilities, tide tables, weather information sources, and similar data of particular value to boaters. This small-craft series is described in greater detail below.

Stowage & Use

NOS charts in the first four series above are printed by accurate techniques on highly durable paper. Individual charts range in size from about 19 x 26 to 36 x 54 inches. (483 x 660 to 914 x 1,372 mm). Some U.S. charts are now printed in the international standard size of 841 x 1,189 mm (33.1 x 46.8 inches). They are among the navigator's most important tools, so should be given careful handling and proper stowage. If circum-

stances permit, they should be stowed flat or rolled, and in a dry place. Charts of this type should not be folded, if this can be avoided.

Make any permanent corrections in ink so they will not be inadvertently erased; make all other lines and notations lightly in pencil so they may be erased without damaging the chart.

Selecting the Proper Chart

From a consideration of the five categories of charts discussed above, you can see that most boating areas will appear on two charts of different series, and that some areas will be covered by three or four charts of different scales. Such charts will vary widely in the extent of the area covered and the amount of detail shown. Choosing the proper chart for your use is important. In general, the closer you are to shoal water and dangers to navigation, the larger you will want the scale of your chart.

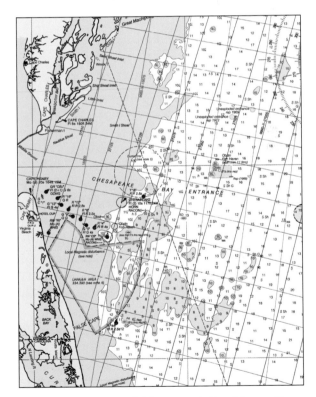

Figure 15-24 General Chart 12200, Cap May to Cape Hatteras, scale 1:419,706. This chart does not extend as far offshore, and would be used for the initial approach from sea toward Chesapeake Bay Entrance; additional details of aids to navigation are shown. On this chart, 1 inch equals 5.76 nautical miles.

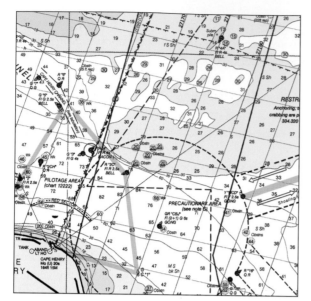

Figure 15-25 Coast Chart 12221, Chesapeake Bay Entrance, scale 1:80,000. This chart gives details of the water depths, hazards, aids to navigation, etc., within the coastline. Its scale of 1 inch equals 1.10 nautical miles would be suitable for navigating into the bay.

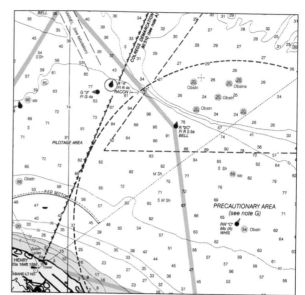

Figure 15-26 Harbor Chart 12222, Cape Charles to Norfolk Harbor, Scale 1:40,000. This chart shows all details of the water and aids to navigation. It can be used for piloting down channels and to anchorages. On this chart, 1 inch equals 0.55 nautical miles.

What Coast Charts Show

Coast charts show the major hazards and aids to navigation, and give general information on depths. Some charts in this series entirely omit any details in certain areas that are covered by larger-scale charts. For example, Narragansett Bay appears on Chart 13218, but no details at all are given, merely a small note "(Chart 13221)." Other coast charts include in their area coverage portions of the Atlantic Intracoastal Waterway, but the navigator is referred to the ICW route charts for all information on the inland route. Many coast charts include a small diagram outlining the areas covered by each larger scale chart. On Chart 13218, this amounts to all portions of 13 more-detailed charts.

What Harbor Charts Show

Harbor charts show more numerous soundings and *all* aids to navigation, and permit the most accurate fixing of position from plotted bearings. The question may be asked, why ever select any but the largest-scale chart? The answer lies in the fact that as the scale is increased the area covered is proportionately decreased. Thus for a given

cruise, many more charts from the harbor series would be required than from the coast series. Further, in some areas continuous coverage from port to port is not possible with harbor charts alone. Yet another problem is that the increased number of harbor charts would complicate the task of laying out a long run between ports.

Selecting the proper charts will usually mean that you have a mixture of coast charts for the longer runs and harbor charts for entering ports and exploring up rivers and creeks. For some areas, you will find it useful to have one or more general charts in addition to the coast and harbor charts. For example, the best overall route up Chesapeake Bay is more easily plotted on one general charts, 12280, than on a series of five coast charts, 12221 to 12273. The coast charts will be desirable for the actual trip, however, when used with some harbor charts.

In the margin of many charts, you will find helpful information regarding the next chart to use when you are going in a particular direction. This note will take the form of a statement such as "(Joins Chart 13233)" or "(Continued on Chart 13236)."

Small-Craft Charts

The charts in the first four series discussed above are referred to as "conventional charts" and are intended for flat or rolled storage. The fifth series, small-craft charts, is quite different, designed for more convenient use in the limited space available on boats, and for folded storage; refer to **Figure 15-27**. There are approximately 90 small-craft charts, each numbered in the normal five-digit style.

Types of Small-Craft Charts

Small-craft charts are printed in three general formats termed ROUTE, FOLIO, and AREA as follows:

Small-craft ROUTE CHARTS, consisting of a single sheet printed front and back and accordion folded; some are slipped into a suitable jacket. These are sometimes referred to as POCKET FOLD CHARTS.

Small-craft FOLIO CHARTS, consisting of three or four sheets printed front and back, accordion folded, and bound in a suitable cover.

Small-craft AREA CHARTS, usually consisting of a conventional chart printed on lighter-weight paper with additional data for the small boat skipper. Half the chart is printed on each side of the paper with a slight area of overlap. The chart is accordion folded and may be issued in a protective jacket.

Route and area charts are being redesigned into a 5-inch by 10-inch "pocket fold" format without a cover jacket. All information once shown on the separate jackets is now included on the margins of the chart itself. The elimination of the jacket allows a lower price.

Facilities Data

A unique feature of these small-craft charts is the variety of data printed on the chart or the protective jacket; see **Figure 15-28**. Repair yard and marina locations are clearly marked on the chart, and the available services and supplies are tabulated. A tide table for the year, marine weather information, Rules of the Road, whistle signals, and warning notes are included for ready reference.

Small-craft charts make frequent use of insets to show such features as small creeks and harbors

in greater detail at a larger scale. **Figure 15-29** shows an inset from Chart 11467 showing waters just south of Miami, Florida.

Courses Indicated

Many of the folio and route types of small-craft charts indicate a recommended track to be followed. The longer stretches of these tracks are marked as to *true* course and distance in miles and tenths. Route charts of the Intracoastal Waterway also have numbered marks every five *statute* miles indicating the accumulated distance southward from Norfolk, Virginia to Florida, and eastward and westward from Harvey Lock, Louisiana (also westward across the Okeechobee Waterway and

Figure 15-27 For use on small boats, particularly open boats, a small-craft chart has many advantages over a large sheet-like conventional chart. The SC chart can be easily opened only to the area of immediate interest. Additional information, such as facility data and tidal predictions, is also available on these charts for the use of boaters.

northward along the Florida Gulf Coast); see **Figure 15-30**. Facilities along the ICW are designated in accordance with a numbering system that starts over again with "1" on each chart of the series.

Periodic Revision

Many, but not all, small-craft charts are revised and reissued annually or biannually, sometimes to coincide with the start of the boating season in the locality concerned. These charts are *not* hand corrected by the NOS after they are printed and placed in stock. Check the publication *Dates of Latest Editions* to be sure that you are using the latest chart, keep your chart up-to-date between editions by applying all critical changes published in *Notices to Mariners* and *Local Notices to Mariners*. This is not a great chore, *if* you keep up with the changes and don't get behind.

Other Charts for Small Craft

MODIFIED ROUTE CHARTS are identical in construction and format with small-craft area charts and are used in areas that are not adaptable to the route chart style used for long, narrow waterways.

RECREATIONAL CHARTS are a series of large-scale charts, published in book format, providing sequential coverage for selected areas.

MARINE FACILITIES CHARTS are conventional charts with small-craft facility information overprinted on the chart and tabulated on the reverse side.

CANOE CHARTS covering the Minnesota—Ontario Border Lakes are designed to meet the needs of operators of small, shallow-draft craft.

Great Lake Charts

Polyconic projection (see page 541) is used for most of the NOS charts of the Great Lakes; a few smaller-scale charts are also published in Mercator projection editions, as are all those published in metric editions. Other small variations between these and coastal charts may be noted. Often courses and distances (in statue miles) will be shown for runs between important points.

On the Great Lakes and connecting waters, special editions of charts for small craft are available for a number of boating areas. These are bound into SMALL CRAFT BOOK CHARTS booklets with individual charts at various scales.

NIMA Charts

Charts from the National Imagery and Mapping Agency are used by skippers making long ocean voyages or visiting waters of other nations (except

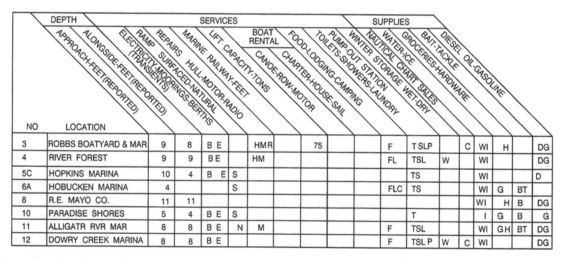

THE LOCATIONS OF THE ABOVE PUBLIC MARINE FACILITIES ARE SHOWN ON THE CHART BY LARGE MAGENTA NUMBERS.
THE TABULATED "APPROACH-FEET(REPORTED)" IS THE DEPTH AVAILABLE FROM THE NEAREST NATURAL OR DREDGED CHANNEL TO THE FACILITY.
THE TABULATED "PUMPING STATION" IS DEFINED AS FACILITIES AVAILABLE FOR PUMPING OUT BOAT HOLDING TANKS.

Figure 15-28 Table on a small-craft chart lists the tide ranges, depths, and the services and supplies available at marine facilities in the area covered. The numbers at the left are keyed to locations on the chart.

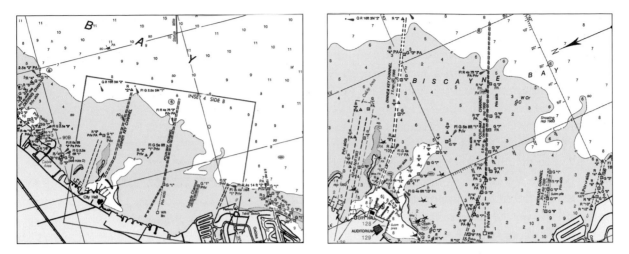

Figure 15-29 Insets are frequently used on small-craft charts to show specific areas at a larger scale with greater details. The inset, right, from Chart 11467 of the ICW in the Miami, Florida area, is typical. On these charts water areas with depths less than 6 feet are shown in blue; aids to navigation are in green and magenta.

Canada). The way of showing information does not differ much from the more familiar NOS charts; symbols and abbreviations will be familiar to the coastal boater, but land areas are shaded gray rather than gold. Symbols are different for lighted buoys and those with radar reflectors. Most charts based on non-U.S. sources will show depths and heights in meters and fractions, rather than in feet or fathoms; increasingly, NIMA-originated charts will also use metric units.

The NIMA—and it predecessor agency, DMAHTC—have published special editions for some of the major ocean sailing races. These are regular editions of the applicable charts overprinted with additional information for the yachtsman, including the direct rhumb line, typical sailing tracks for seasonal winds, additional current data and other useful items. These charts are listed in the section on Miscellaneous Charts and Publications in NIMA *Chart Catalog* (see Appendix A).

Remember that many NIMA charts are based on surveys done by other nations; see **Figure 15-31.** The authority for the charted information is always given, as is the date of the surveys.

Inland River Charts

Boaters on inland rivers use charts that differ in many respects from those used in coastal waters.

Often the inland river charts are issued in book form with several pages covering successive stretches of a river; frequently, they are called "navigational maps."

Probably the most obvious difference is the usual lack of depth figures. In lieu of these, there is generally a broken line designating the route to be

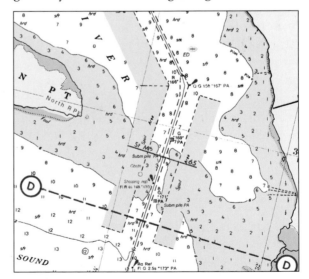

Figure 15-30 Charts of the Atlantic Intracoastal Waterway show a fine magenta line that indicates the route to be followed. Tick marks are placed at five-mile intervals along this course line and are labeled with the accumulated mileage (statute) south from Norfolk, Virginia. The "D—D" line on this excerpt is a matching line to facilitate shifting to the adjoining Intracoastal Waterway chart.

followed. To make the best use of each paper sheet, pages may be oriented differently; North is seldom toward the top and its actual direction is shown by an arrow. Some symbols may vary slightly in appearance from those on "salt water" charts, and additional ones may be used as required by local conditions. Distances are stated in terms of statute miles, and locations are described in distances *upriver* from a specified origin point.

More detailed information on river charts will be found in Chapter 22; see pages 756-758. An extensive listing of where river charts and related publications can be obtained will be found in Appendix A.

Bathymetric Charts

Charts designed to give maximum emphasis to the configuration of the bottom show depths beyond the 100-fathom curve by depth contours similar to contours shown on land areas to indicate graduations in height. These are called BATHYMETRIC CHARTS.

CHART PROJECTIONS

You can safely navigate your boat without knowledge of the various types of PROJECTION used in the preparation of charts. As in almost any field, however, greater knowledge will assist in understanding and using nautical charts. Hence the following paragraphs offer additional information on chart projections (which are actually mathematical constructions rather than true graphic projections).

The MERCATOR projection used in ocean and coastal waters, and the POLYCONIC projection used for inland lakes and rivers, have both been mentioned earlier in this chapter. These, plus the GNOMONIC PROJECTION used in polar regions, will now be presented in more detail. There are other systems of projection, but each has limited application and need not be considered here.

Mercator Projection

The Mercator projection is often illustrated as a projection onto a cylinder. Actually, the chart is

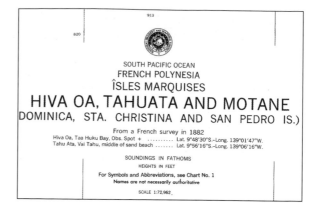

Figure 15-31 Many charts issued by NIMA are based on surveys done by other nations, frequently decades or even centuries ago. This is noted in the chart's title block. Such charts should be used with caution if the surveys are many years in the past.

developed mathematically to allow for the known shape of the earth, which is not quite a true sphere. The meridians appear as straight, vertical lines; see **Figure 15-32,** upper. Here is our first example of distortion—the meridians no longer converge, but are now shown as being parallel to each other. This changes the representation of the shape of objects by stretching out their dimensions in an east-west direction.

To minimize the distortion of shape—one of the qualities that must be preserved as much as possible—there must be a stretching-out of dimensions in a north-south direction. The parallels of latitude appear as straight lines intersecting the meridians at right angles. Their spacing increases northward from the Equator; see **Figure 15-32,** lower, in accordance with a mathematical formula that recognizes the slightly oblate shape of the earth. This increase in spacing is not obvious in the case of charts of relatively small areas, such as in the harbor and coastal series, but it is quite apparent in Mercator projections of the world.

The Mercator projection is said to be CONFORMAL, which means that directions can be determined correctly, and distances measured to the same scale in all directions. By the Mercator technique of distortion, then counter-distortion, the shape of areas in high latitudes is correctly shown, but their size appears greater than that of similar

CAUTIONS REGARDING USE OF CHARTS

Producing charts for the vast coastline and contiguous waterways of the United States is a major undertaking. The U.S. Atlantic coastline exceeds 24,500 nautical miles, the Gulf Coast 15,000 miles, the Pacific Coast 7,000 miles, and the Alaskan and Hawaiian shorelines total more than 30,000 nautical miles. NOS publishes almost 1,000 charts covering over 3.6 million square miles, and both of these figures increase each year. In meeting its global responsibilities, NIMA puts out charts numbered in the thousands, and there are, in addition, many U.S. Army Corps of Engineers charts and navigational maps.

Keeping so many charts up-to-date is obviously a staggering task. Surveys are constantly being made in new areas and must be rechecked in old areas, but this work generally is dependent on the limitations of funding by taxpayers through the U.S. Congress. NOS has an extensive program of cooperative reporting by boaters to supplement its own information-gathering capability. Formal programs are established in the United States Power Squadrons and the U.S. Coast Guard Auxiliary, but *all* individual skippers are encouraged to report any corrections, additions, or comments to the chart's issuing agency. Comments are also desired on other publications such as the *Coast Pilots.* Send comments to the Director, National Ocean Service, Silver Spring, MD 20910-3233.

Charting agencies make every effort to keep their products accurate and up-to-date with changing editions. Major disturbances of nature such as hurricanes along the Atlantic Coast and earthquakes in the Pacific Northwest cause sudden and extensive changes in hydrography, and destroy aids to navigation. The everyday forces of wind and waves cause slower and less obvious changes in channels and shoals.

Be alert to the possibility of changes. Most charts will cite the authorities for the information presented and frequently the date of the information. Use additional caution when the surveys date back many years. Half of NOS charts are based on surveys made before 1940, many using lead lines. The surveys of some NIMA charts go back more than a century.

Another possible problem lies in the HORIZONTAL DATUM used on the chart. Various datums have been used over the years; the standard now is the 1984 World Geodetic System (WGS 84). The 1983 North American Datum is essentially the same, but other datums may be found on charts from other regions or nations that will require adjustments to positions of charted features. This is primarily of concern to vessels using electronic navigation systems; see Chapter 21.

areas in lower latitudes. An island, for example, in 60° latitude (Alaska) would appear considerably larger than an island of the same size located at 25° latitude (Florida). Its shape, however, would still be true to the actual proportions.

Advantages & Disadvantages

The great value of the Mercator chart is that straight-line meridians of longitude intersect straight-line parallels of latitude at right angles to form an easily used rectangular grid. Directions can be measured with reference to any meridian or parallel, or any compass rose. The geographic coordinates of a position can easily be measured from scales along the four borders of the chart. *We can draw upon a Mercator chart a straight line between two points and actually run that course* by determining the compass direction between them; the heading is the same all along the line. Such a line is called a RHUMB LINE. However, a great circle, the shortest distance between two points on the earth's surface, is a curved line on a Mercator chart; refer to **Figure 15-35.** This is more difficult to calculate and plot. For moderate runs, the added distance of a rhumb line is insignificant, so the rhumb is the track that is used.

The scale of a Mercator chart varies with the distance away from the equator as a result of the N-S expansion. The change is unimportant on charts of small areas such as harbor charts, and the graphic scale may be used. The change in scale with latitude does become significant, however, in charts covering greater areas, as on general, coastal, and sailing charts. On such charts, when you measure distances using the latitude scale on either side margin, *take care that distance is measured at a point on the latitude scale directly opposite the region of the chart being used. Never use the longitude scale at the top and bottom of the chart for measuring distance.*

Polyconic Projection

Another form of chart construction is the *polyconic* projection. This method is based on the develop-

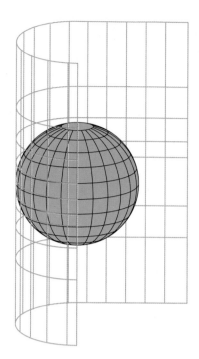

Figure 15-32 A Mercator projection, above and below, can be visualized as the placement of a cylinder around the earth, parallel to the polar axis, and touching the earth at the equator. In actuality, the projection is accomplished mathematically. A Mercator chart shows considerable distortion in the near-polar latitudes.

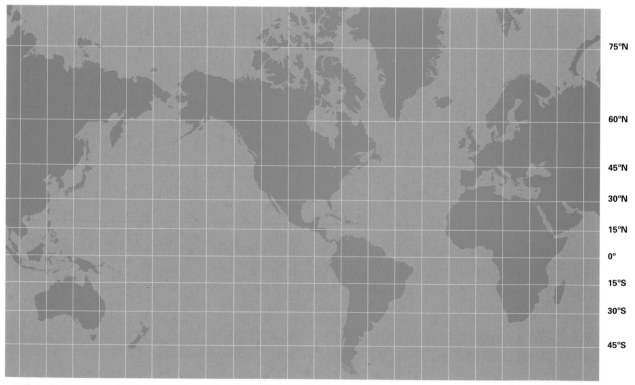

75°N

60°N

45°N

30°N

15°N

0°

15°S

30°S

45°S

105°E 120°E 135°E 150°E 165°E 180° 165°W 150°W 135°W 120°W 105°W 90°W 75°W 60°W 45°W 30°W 15°W 0° 15°E 30°E 45°E 60°E 75°E

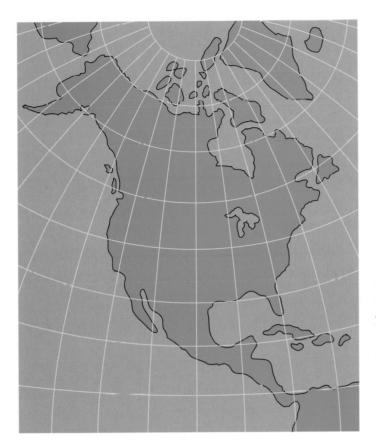

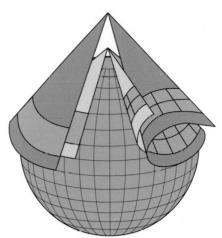

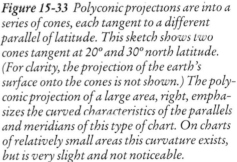

Figure 15-33 Polyconic projections are into a series of cones, each tangent to a different parallel of latitude. This sketch shows two cones tangent at 20° and 30° north latitude. (For clarity, the projection of the earth's surface onto the cones is not shown.) The polyconic projection of a large area, right, emphasizes the curved characteristics of the parallels and meridians of this type of chart. On charts of relatively small areas this curvature exists, but is very slight and not noticeable.

ment of the earth's surface upon a series of cones, a different one being used for each parallel of latitude; see **Figure 15-33.** The vertex of the cone is at the point where a tangent to the earth at the specified latitude intersects the earth's axis extended.

The polyconic projection yields little distortion in shape, and relative sizes are more correctly preserved than in the Mercator projection. The scale is correct along any parallel and along the central meridian of the projection. Along other meridians, the scale increases with increased difference in longitude from the central meridian.

Parallels appear as non-concentric arcs of circles and meridians as curved lines converging toward the pole, concave toward the central meridian; refer to **Figure 15-33,** right. These characteristics contrast with the straight-line parallels and meridians of Mercator charts, and are the reasons why this projection is not so widely used in marine navigation. Directions from any point should be measured relative to the meridian passing through that point; in actual practice, the

nearest compass rose is used. Great Lakes charts have a graphic PLOTTING INTERPOLATOR for close measurements of latitude and longitude.

A variation of this type is the LAMBERT CONFORMAL PROJECTION based on one cone that *intersects* the earth's surface at two parallels. It is used mostly by aviators because a straight line nearly approximates a great circle, and radio bearings can be plotted without the corrections needed when using a Mercator chart.

Gnomonic Projection

A gnomonic chart results when the meridians and parallels of latitude are projected onto a plane surface tangent to the earth at one point; see **Figure 15-34.** Meridians appear as straight lines converging toward the nearer pole; the parallels of latitude, except for the equator, appear as curves.

Distortion is great, but this projection is used in special cases because of its unique advantage—*great circles appear as straight lines.* Probably the easiest way to obtain a great circle track on a Mercator or

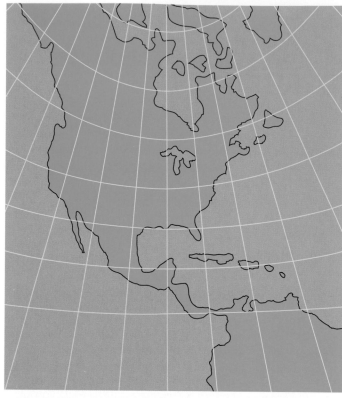

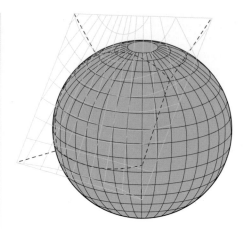

Figure 15-34 A gnomonic projection is made by placing a plane surface tangent to the earth's surface at a given location. Points on the earth's surface are then projected onto the plane. A chart made on the gnomonic projection, left, shows meridians as straight lines converging toward the nearer pole. Parallels, other than the equator, appear as curved lines.

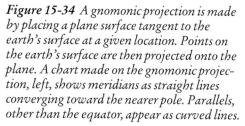

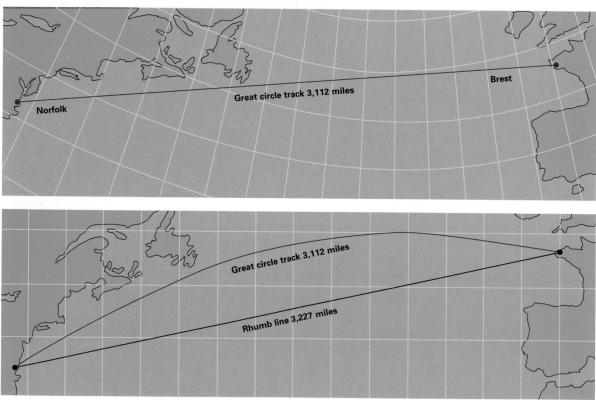

Figure 15-35 A great circle provides the shortest distance between any two points on the earth's surface, and can be plotted as a straight line on a gnomonic chart, upper. To plot it on a Mercator chart, lower, the geographic coordinates at each meridian crossing are transferred and connected by a series of straight lines that appear to form a curve.

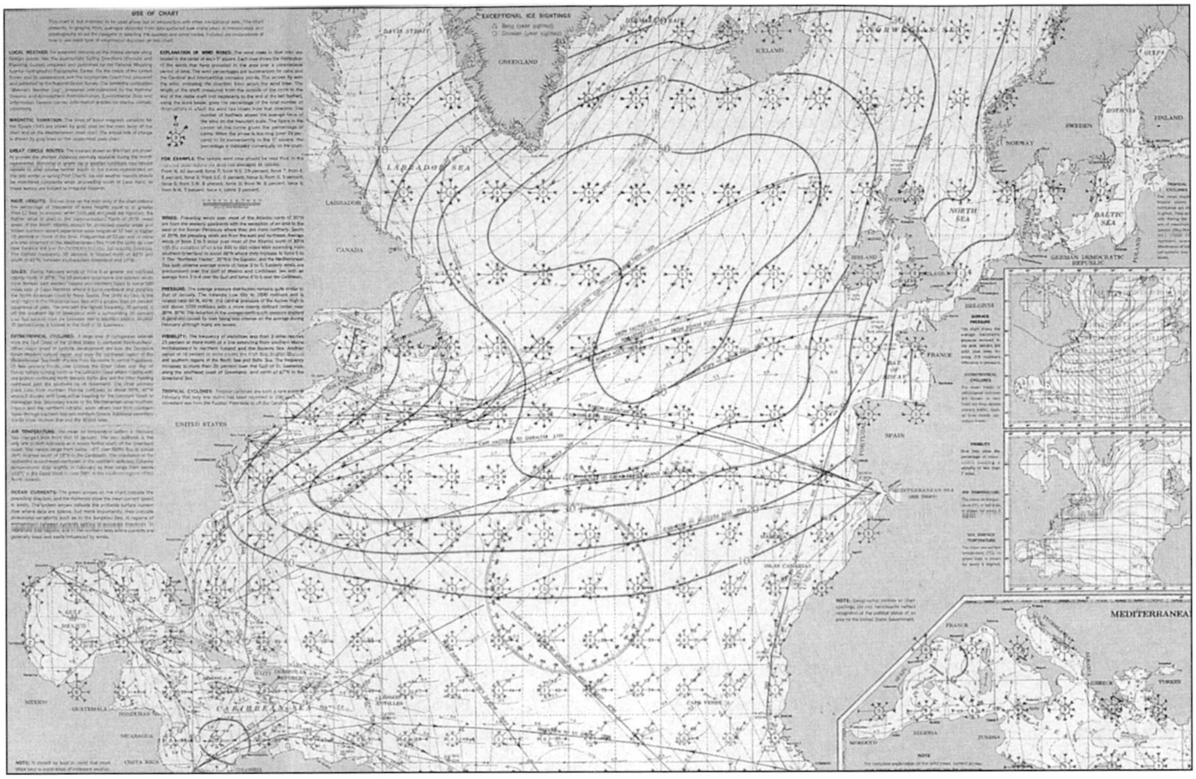

Figure 15-36 *A pilot chart, prepared for each month, is not intended to be used alone, but in conjunction with other navigational aids. Such a chart provides general information based on averages of many years on magnetic variation, great-circle routes, wave heights, gales, cyclones, temperature, ocean currents, prevailing winds, wind strengths, pressure, and visibility.*

polyconic chart is to draw it as a straight line on a gnomonic chart and then transfer points along the line to the other chart using the geographic coordinates for each point. The points so transferred are then connected with short rhumb lines and the result will approximate, closely enough, the great circle path; see **Figure 15-35.**

A special case of gnomonic chart projection occurs when a geographic pole is selected as the point of tangency. Now all meridians will appear as straight lines, and the parallels as concentric circles. The result is a chart easily used for polar regions where ordinary Mercator charts cannot be used.

Pilot Charts

No discussion of nautical charts would be complete without a mention of a unique but valuable chart issued quarterly by the NIMA. These PILOT CHARTS present in graphic form information on ocean currents and weather probabilities

for each month, plus other data of interest to a navigator; see **Figure 15-36.** Articles of great navigational interest are printed on the reverse side of each chart. They are published quarterly in two editions: *Chart No. 16, North Atlantic Ocean,* and *Chart No. 55, North Pacific Ocean.*

ELECTRONIC CHARTS

The latest "high-tech" development in charting is the ELECTRONIC CHART—a full nautical chart presented on a viewing screen. Electronic charts were first suggested in the 1970s, but their implementation and development had to await faster processors and more economical large data storage capabilities—that time is now here, and electronic charts are suitable for ships of all types and sizes and small craft of nearly any size.

With the chart created electronically, it is possible to add information on the vessel's position from GPS or Loran; objects detected by radar; heading, speed, and depth information; etc. The charts are "digitized" and stored magnetically on disks as used in personal computers or on plug-in cartridges. In this chapter, we consider the charts themselves, and in Chapter 21 their display on a CHART PLOTTER with a computer-like screen, or on a personal computer using special electronic navigation software; see **Figure 15-37**.

Electronic Charting Terminology

There are many terms, with corresponding acronyms, and these can be confusing unless used specifically and correctly. Additional terms relating to display systems will be found in Chapter 21.

"Raster" vs. "Vector" Charts

The first distinction must be between the basic ways that the data of an electronic chart is generated.

A RASTER CHART, which can also be called a "bit-mapped chart," is essentially a digital photograph of a conventional nautical chart. Raster data is composed of an array of dots arranged in rows and columns. Each dot, or pixel, has a specific position in this array. Each pixel is assigned a color which when viewed with other pixels in the array produces an image.

Raster charts are relatively easy and economical to produce. Each separate color plate that was used to print the paper chart is scanned at a high resolution that is later reduced to make the commercially distributed raster chart. When viewed, they appear just like the original paper chart with which all boaters are (or should be) familiar, although only a portion of the chart is viewable at any given time. NOS maintains a master database of raster charts to which corrections are applied weekly; this is used to print new editions of paper charts and to provide information for updating print-on-demand charts. As the technology is generally available and charts are not copyrighted, commercial activities that wish to do so can scan paper charts to produce raster charts.

A VECTOR CHART consists of lines—straight or curved—that are stored as digital data. These lines are defined by mathematical elements called VECTORS that contain the geometric qualities of each line. These lines can be as simple as a straight line connecting two points, or a long sinuous line defining a section of shoreline. They often take the form of geometrical shapes such as rectangles, circles, or triangles. Vector data can also contain point and area information; they frequently are composed of areas that are completely enclosed and can be filled with a single color. Vector data is essentially a database of chart features that can be used to intelligently process the information and draws the display. Initial versions of vector charts were intended for large-ship use and omitted coverage of some areas where such vessels do not travel. Recent NOS vector charts now contain everything that is on the paper/raster chart, with a few exception of some features on land that are not valuable to a navigator.

Advantages & Disadvantages of Each Type

The advantage of raster charts lies in their ease of production, and the fact that when viewed they can appear similar to the original chart. The disadvantage, however, is that it is difficult to link chart features to information in a database as each pixel is a separate entity. Another negative factor is that the data file of a raster chart is quite large and the files expand exponentially as the resolution of the image is increased (the higher the resolution, the better the chart will look when viewed). Raster charts are also scale-dependent. When such a chart is zoomed out (to a smaller scale, larger area), pixels must be dropped; this degrades the image. When a view is zoomed in from the original image, pixels appear to be enlarged (actually they are repeated) often to a point where the image can no longer be recognized. This can have grave consequences when a raster chart is used for navigation. Raster charts should be displayed and used at their base scale on a display that has sufficient resolution.

The advantage of vector charts is that each entity, such as each charted feature, can be linked to information about that entity in a database. They are also usually considered to be scale-

Figure 15-37 Electronic charts can be displayed on a "chart plotter," shown above, or on a personal computer using special charting software.

independent—they retain their legibility as the user zooms out. Another desirable characteristic of a vector chart is that the data files are very compact and relatively small as compared to a raster chart. Vector charts are composed of LAYERS of information. One layer might consist of only shoreline features, another of just depth figures, another of aids to navigation, etc. The person using the chart can display all layers simultaneously, or only a limited number to reduce clutter; the appearance of each layer may differ from equivalent information shown on a conventional or raster chart. A disadvantage of vector charts is that they are much more difficult to produce—the chart is essentially completely redrawn by cartographers from existing chart database information plus other original source data; special care must be exercised that errors are not made. NOS produces vector charts to the standards of the International Hydrographic Organization (IHO) as do other nations to ensure the interoperability of all such charts. Another disadvantage is that vector chart systems may use symbols, abbreviations, and other characteristics that are different from conventional charts. The user, therefore, must familiarize him- or herself with the differences before he or she can use a vector chart with the

same ease, speed, and accuracy as a conventional paper chart or a raster chart.

The initial NOAA project to digitize charts was to produce only vector charts, but the work was tedious and proved exceedingly time consuming, requiring too great a number of cartographers. Work on the preparation of vector charts, referred to by NOS as ELECTRONIC NAVIGATION CHARTS (ENC), continues to meet the demand for such charts in ELECTRONIC CHART AND DISPLAY INFORMATION SYSTEMS (ECDIS) used on large ships. NOS has, however, all of its charts digitized as RASTER NAUTICAL CHARTS (RNC); these are used in the Print-on-Demand system, described on page 51. ENCs are available for download from NOS without charge at www.chartmaker. ncd.noaa.gov, but are not on any hard media. Several ENC viewers are available free at www.openecdis.org/ freeware/index. html. ENCs and RNCs are available from commercial sources on such media as CD-ROMs and proprietary cartridges. The National Imagery and Mapping Agency (NIMA) produces vector charts for naval use, terming them DIGITAL NAVIGATION CHARTS (DNC); these are not available to the public.

NOS keeps its files updated for both raster and vector charts as changes of all types—hydrographic, aids to navigation, hazards, etc.—occur. This includes all information included in *Notices to Mariners* and *Local Notices to Mariners*, plus other information not suitable for such publication. It is relatively simple to transmit vector chart corrections to users either directly or via the Internet. Until recently, this was not possible for raster charts, giving vector charts a definite advantage in this respect. Now, however, computer techniques have advance to a point where "patches" can be similarly sent to users for updating raster charts.

As vector charts become available for more and more maritime areas, they will replace raster charts and become the standard for shipboard use.

Accuracy & Precision Problems

The problems, described on pages 530–531, concerning the relative accuracy and scale of charts and electronic positioning systems, apply to charts derived from paper charts, such as raster charts and any vector charts that were created by digitizing a paper chart.

NAVIGATIONAL PUBLICATIONS

Most persons think first of charts when we consider government publications designed to make piloting easier and boating safer. It is certainly true that charts are the predominant form of government piloting information, but we can't overlook the dozens of other publications that make piloting easier and more accurate. Generally, these are available from the same agencies that issue charts, as listed below (also refer to Appendix A, for more details, and consult the *Federal Register* for new restrictions at www.gpoaccess.gov/nara/index.html).

Publishing Agencies in the United States

In addition to various commercial organizations, agencies of the U.S. Federal Government that issue publications valuable to the boater include:

- National Imagery and Mapping Agency (NIMA).
- National Weather Service (NWS), a component of National Oceanic and Atmospheric Administration (NOAA).
- Office of Coast Survey (OCS), part of National Ocean Service (NOS), also a component of NOAA.
- U.S. Army Corps of Engineers (District Offices).
- U.S. Coast Guard, a component of the Dept. of Transportation.
- U.S. Government Printing Office.
- U.S. Naval Observatory.

The Government Printing Office, an independent agency, does, or contracts for, much of the actual printing of federal publications dealing with piloting. The Office of the Superintendent of Documents sells most of the publications, but there seems to be no clear rule about whether a publication is sold by the GPO or by the government agency that prepared it.

Publications sold by the GPO can be bought by mail from: Superintendent of Documents, Government Printing Office, Washington, DC 20402. You can also buy them at a retail bookstore in the GPO building, North Capital and H Streets in Washington, DC, and by mail or in person from GPO Regional Bookstores in many major cities. Make your checks payable to the "Superintendent of Documents," or charge to your VISA or MasterCard account. The GPO Bookstore is online at http://bookstore.gpo.gov/.

State Agencies

State agencies also produce a variety of publications of interest to boaters, but there are too many of them to list here. Some of these publications are listed in Appendix A, but you should also check with authorities in your own state, and write ahead to other states when you expect to cruise in new waters. Refer to Appendix C for the name and address in each state. Be as specific as possible in requests for information and literature. Information may be obtained that will add to safety and convenience, possibly avoiding legal embarrassment as well. Remember, "Ignorance is no excuse" applies afloat as well as on shore.

Sales Agents

Federal government agencies have designated certain boating supply stores and marinas as official sales agents for their publications. Authorized sales agents may carry publications of the National Ocean Service, the National Imagery and Mapping Agency, the Coast Guard or a combination of these. It does not hold true that because an establishment is an agent for one source of publications it will necessarily have available documents from the others.

Charts and other publications of the National Ocean Survey are now sold by the FAA Distribution Division (AVN-50), National Aeronautical Charting Office, 6501 Lafayette Ave., Riverdale, MD 20737-1199. Purchases can be made in person at the address above; by mail to that address; by telephone to 301-436-8301; or 800-638-8972; by fax to 301-436-6929; or by e-mail to 9-ANC-chartsales@faa.gov. Payment

Figure 15-38 *Tide Tables and Tidal Current Tables, similar in format for either coast, provide predicted heights of tide for one and strengths and direction of current for the other, for virtually any location along the coasts. The printing and sale of these publications is now done commercially under contract from NOS, which supplies the data.*

must be made in advance by cash, check (payable to FAA on a U.S. bank), or by credit card (Visa, MasterCard, or Discover).

Authorized Sales Agents are listed on each NOS and NIMA Chart Catalog (see below). The location of these agents may also be found on the Internet at www.chartmaker.NCD.NOAA.gov.

Tide & Tidal Current Tables

The National Ocean Service is charged with the responsibility for the survey of the coast, harbors and tidal estuaries of the United States and its insular possessions. NOS publishes charts, *Chart Catalogs* and *Coast Pilots*. NOS provides data to commercial publishers who now print *Tide Tables* and *Tidal Current Tables* in book format; these are usually available at local chart sales agents; see **Figure 15-38.**

Tide Tables are of great value in determining the predicted height of the water at almost any place at any time. The tables are calculated in advance and are published annually in four volumes, one of which covers the East Coast of North and South America (including Greenland) and another the West Coast of these continents (including the Hawaiian Islands). The other volumes are for Central and Western Pacific Ocean (including the Indian Ocean), and for Europe and West Coast of Africa (including the Mediterranean Sea).

The *Tide Tables* give the predicted times and heights of high and low waters for each day of the year at a number of important points known as "reference stations." Additional data show the difference in times and heights between these reference stations and thousands of other points, termed "subordinate stations." The tables and their use in piloting are discussed at length in Chapter 17.

The *Tidal Current Tables* have much the same format of reference and subordinate stations as the *Tide Tables.* However, instead of indicating the times of high and low waters, these tables give the times and directions of maximum currents (ebb and flood), and the times of minimum currents. These times do not correspond to times of high and low tides, and the *Tide Tables* cannot be used for current predictions. Strength of the current is given in knots and direction in degrees true.

Tidal Current Tables are published in two volumes: Atlantic Coast of North American, and Pacific Coast of North America and Asia. Each volume includes tables for calculating current velocity at any intermediate time, and the duration of slack water or weak currents. *Tidal Current Tables* and their use in piloting are covered in detail in Chapter 17.

Although no longer publishing these tables in book format, NOS does make available all six tables in PostScript format on a CD-ROM, with a PostScript reader included to allow viewing individual pages on a computer screen. The same information is also available on a set of 3.5-inch disks. Each year, new tables for the coming year are available by December 1.

Tidal (and sometimes tidal current) data are often included on chart CD-ROMs used with navigational programs to be used on chart plotters and personal computers.

Coast Pilots

Information on nautical charts is limited by space and by the system of symbols used. You will often need additional information for safe and convenient navigation. The National Ocean Service publishes such information in the *Coast Pilot,* covering the United States coastlines and the Great Lakes in nine separate volumes; see **Figure 15-39.**

Each *Coast Pilot* contains channel descriptions, anchorages, bridge and overhead cable clearances, currents, prominent features, pilotage, towage, weather and ice conditions, wharf descriptions, dangers, routes and traffic separation schemes, small-craft facilities, and Federal regulations applicable to navigation.

Atlantic Coast

No. 1 Eastport to Cape Cod
No. 2 Cape Cod to Sandy Hook
No. 3 Sandy Hook to Cape Henry
No. 4 Cape Henry to Key West
No. 5 Gulf of Mexico, Puerto Rico and Virgin Islands

Great Lakes

No. 6 Lakes Ontario, Erie, Huron, Michigan and Superior, and St. Lawrence River

Pacific Coast

No. 7 California, Oregon, Washington, and Hawaii

Alaska

No. 8 Dixon Entrance to Cape Spencer
No. 9 Cape Spencer to Beaufort Sea

Coast Pilots are published every two or three years, except No. 6, which is published annually. Each edition is corrected through the date of *Notices to Mariners* shown on the title page; do not use them without checking the *Notices*

Figure 15-39 Each Coast Pilot provides valuable information that cannot be shown on charts by symbols and abbreviations.

issued after publication. Changes that affect the safety of navigation and have been reported to NOS in the interim period between new editions are published in *Notices to Mariners* and *Local Notices to Mariners,* except those for No. 6, which are published only in *Local Notices.*

As of early-2003, online versions of the *Coast Pilot* volumes were available on a test basis; they are not certified for navigation purposes. The digital files are those of the printed version; these are not kept up to date for changes published in *Notices to Mariners.* It was expected that by the end of 2003 fully certified versions would be available. Chapters, tables and other sections of each volume are separate pdf files that can be viewed, printed, or downloaded.

Catalogs

The National Ocean Service publishes free *Chart Catalogs.* There are four catalogs:

• Atlantic and Gulf Coasts, including Puerto Rico and the Virgin Islands

• Pacific Coast, including Hawaii, Mariana, and Samoa Islands

• Alaska, including the Aleutian Islands

• Great Lakes and Adjacent Waterways.

These catalogs are actually small-scale outline charts with diagrams delineating the areas covered by each NOS chart; see **Figure 15-40.** They are also sources of information on other NOS publications and charts, as well as publications of other agencies; they also contain a listing, organized by state, of the names and addresses of local sales agents for nautical charts and other publications.

The National Imagery and Mapping Agency publishes catalogs of its maritime products.

NOS Offices

For information about National Ocean Service charts, publications and activities, write, phone, fax or e-mail to:

Director, Office of Coast Survey
SSMC-3, Room 6147
1315 East-West Highway
Silver Spring, MD 20910-3282
Phone: 1-301-713-2770
Fax: 1-301-713-4019
http://www.chartmaker.ncd.noaa.gov/
Regional Marine Centers are located at Norfolk, Virginia and Seattle, Washington.

U.S. Coast Guard Publications

The Coast Guard has publications about the safety of navigation, covering such topics as aids to navigation, applicable rules and regulations, and general safety matters. Refer to Appendix A for a more complete listing. Some of these publications are available free, others are available for a nominal charge.

Light Lists

The United States Coast Guard produces a series of publications for the coastal and inland waters known as the *Light Lists.* These books provide more complete information concerning aids to navigation than can be shown on charts but they should not be used for navigation in lieu of *Coast Pilots* and charts; see **Figure 15-41.**

The *Light Lists* describe the lights (all classes), buoys, daybeacons, RACONs, and Differential GPS sites maintained in all navigable waters of the U.S. by the Coast Guard and various private agencies. (In this usage, the Navy and all other non-USCG governmental bodies are considered "private agencies.") The data shown in the *Light Lists* include a reference number, official name of the aid, its position (for many, but not all), light characteristics (if any), height, range, structure (as applicable), and remarks.

The *Light Lists* are published in seven volumes:

Volume I Atlantic Coast from St. Croix River, Maine, to Ocean City Inlet, Maryland

Volume II Atlantic Coast, from Ocean City Inlet, Maryland, to Little River Inlet, South Carolina

Volume III Atlantic Coast, from Little River Inlet, South Carolina, to Econfina River, Florida, and the Greater Antilles

Volume IV Gulf of Mexico, from Econfina River, Florida, to Rio Grande, Texas

Volume V Mississippi River System

Volume VI Pacific Coast and Pacific Islands

Volume VII Great Lakes

Within each volume, aids to navigation are

Figure 15-40 *A catalog of nautical charts includes listings of other useful NOS publications and other agencies. It shows the area covered by each chart, the scale, and the price.*

listed by Coast Guard Districts in the following order: seacoast, major channels, minor channels, and Intracoastal Waterway (if applicable). Lighted and unlighted aids appear together in their geographic order, with amplifying data on the same page.

Seacoast aids are listed in sequence from north to south along the Atlantic Coast, from south to north and east to west along the Gulf Coast, and from south to north along the Pacific Coast. Great Lakes aids are listed in a generally westerly direction. On the Atlantic and Gulf coasts, aids along the Intracoastal Waterway are listed in the same sequence. For rivers and estuaries, the aids to navigation are shown from seaward to the head of navigation. An aid serving a channel leading in from sea and the ICW is listed in both sequences.

All volumes of the Coast Guard *Light List* are available for purchase through the Superintendent of Documents, Government Printing Office; the volume for a particular area may be sold by authorized chart and publication sales agents within that area. *Light Lists* for other areas also may be available. *Volumes I-IV and VII-VIII* are published annually; *Volume V* is published every two years.

The Coast Guard Navigation Center (www.navcen.uscg.gov) has an online data file of the current edition of each Light List volume, plus the Navigation Aid Reference Guide. Also available is a Summary of Corrections, for each volume separately, that will allow a user to keep his Light List up to date; this is updated regularly. Each volume can be downloaded and the portions of interest extracted and printed or saved to a CD-ROM or other storage media; if the media is re-writable, the information can be updated periodically. Light List data are also available from NGA (http://pollux.nss.nga.mil). The full text is not downloadable, but the database can be searched by Light List number or geographic area.

Navigation Rules

The Coast Guard has prepared an excellent booklet on the two sets of Rules of the Road. This is *Navigation Rules, International-Inland* officially designated as *Commandant Instruction*

M16672.2D (subsequent editions will change the final letter); refer also to Chapters 4 and 5. This edition contains all changes for both sets of rules as of its publication date of March 25, 1999; any subsequent changes will be published in *Notices to Mariners* and *Local Notices to Mariners*. This booklet presents the various Rules and Annexes on facing pages—International on the left, Inland on the right. Illustrations for specific rules appear near the applicable text.

There are many illustrations of lights and shapes, each adjacent to the applicable rule. The demarcation lines separating U.S. Inland Rules waters from International Rules waters are described in detail. The booklet also describes penalties for violations of rules or regulations; it outlines regulations relating to regattas and marine parades, and provides useful information on Vessel Traffic Service and Vessel Separation Schemes at many major ports and harbor entrances.

Copies of *Navigation Rules, International-Inland* may be ordered from the Superintendent of Documents, Government Printing Office or Regional or online GPO Bookstores; or purchased from local sales agents for charts and nautical publications.

Other USCG Publications

Federal Requirements for Recreational Boats and Safety Tips is a small pamphlet that will be very useful to all skippers. Topics include laws and

Figure 15-41
Light Lists,
published by the
U.S. Coast
Guard, provide
more detailed
information on
all types of aids to
navigation than
can be shown
conveniently on
charts.

U.S. Department
of Transportation
United States
Coast Guard

LIGHT LIST

Volume IV

GULF of MEXICO

Econfina River, Florida to
Rio Grande, Texas

This publication contains a list of lights, sound
signals, buoys, daybeacons, and other aids to navigation.

IMPORTANT
THIS PUBLICATION SHOULD BE CORRECTED
EACH WEEK FROM THE LOCAL NOTICES TO MARINERS
OR NOTICES TO MARINERS AS APPROPRIATE.

2001
COMDTPUB P16502.4

regulations, numbering and documentation, reporting accidents and approved equipment. This publication and others can be obtained by writing USCG Headquarters, Washington, DC 20593. Copies may also be available at Coast Guard District offices and some local USCG stations.

NIMA Publications

The National Imagery and Mapping Agency has several publications of interest to boaters. Charts, publications and other products of NIMA are identified with a prefix to the individual chart or publication number.

The nautical chart identification system uses a numeral of one to five digits, without prefix, as determined by the scale and assigned to regions and subregions.

Oceanographic products, primarily publications related to the dynamic nature of the oceans or the scientific aspects of oceanography, are printed by the Naval Oceanographic Office and carry numbers with prefixes that reflect the nature of the particular publication.

NIMA has begun the transition from producing and distributing hardcover nautical publications to digital format on CD-ROM and/or availability for electronic access on the Internet. By the year 2005, it is expected that all publications produced by NIMA will be in digital format only; some publications will be available only via the Internet, no printed copies sold. These datasets will be more robust, expansive, and user-friendly than the current printed versions. Users can expect to have access to data links between publication datasets video streams, links to other websites, timely up-to-date information, and current state-of-the-art graphics, photos, and commercial satellite imagery.

NIMA digital publications can be updated using a binary executable called "Publication Data Update (PDU)"; PDU updates will be found on the Maritime Safety Information Division homepage (http://pollux.nss.nima.mil). Users may download PDU updates for any nautical publication at their leisure; however, PDU updates will be sequential and must be applied in date order, oldest to newest. PDU files can be applied to a publication on a CD-ROM by transferring the publication text to a computer hard drive and applying the PDU to that file. Then the updated text can be used from the hard drive or written to a new CD-R or CD-RW. A PDU file cannot be printed and applied to a printed copy of the publication concerned. Complete instructions for using PDU updates will be found at the homepage listed above.

Bowditch (Publication No. 9)

The *American Practical Navigator* (known as *Bowditch*), originally written by Nathaniel Bowditch in 1799, is an extensive treatise on piloting, celestial navigation and other nautical matters. It is Publication No. 9 of NIMA.

Bowditch has long been an accepted authority on piloting and other forms of navigation. The current 2002 edition is a single volume available in hardcover format with a digital version on CD-ROM included. While it is intended as a replacement for the 1995 and prior editions, it is recommended that the 1984 Volume I and 1981 Volume II be retained as these contain some topics that have been dropped from the more recent editions.

Other NIMA Publications

The National Imagery and Mapping Agency publishes a series of *Sailing Directions* that provides supplementary information for foreign coasts and ports in a manner generally similar to the *Coast Pilots* for U.S. waters.

The *Lists of Lights* published by this agency likewise covers foreign waters and does not duplicate the Coast Guard *Light Lists*. These are NIMA Pubs. No. 110 through 116.

Other NIMA publications that may be useful to a boater include Pub. 117, *Radio Navigational Aids*, and Pub. 102, *International Code of Signals*.

NIMA charts and publications are listed in the *NIMA Catalog of Maps, Charts and Related Products, Part 2—Hydrographic Products, Volume I—Nautical Charts and Publications*. The contents are grouped into nine regions that correspond to the chart numbering system, plus a section for

Miscellaneous Charts and Publications.

NIMA publications include a number of tables for the reduction of celestial observations, and tables and charts for plotting lines of position from Loran-C measurements. These are of interest only to those yacht skippers making extensive voyages on the high seas.

Other NIMA publications are listed in Appendix A.

Obtaining NIMA Publications

NIMA charts and nautical publications can often be purchased from the same agents as for NOS products (see above); the same forms of payment may be used. The *NIMA Catalog, Part 2, Volume I—Nautical Charts and Publications* is available as nine individual catalogs, each covering a different region. Each catalog contains general, ordering, and nautical products information; lists of charts available in the region; graphics displaying chart location; and a miscellaneous charts and publications section.

The catalogs are free of charge and available from your local NOS chart sales agent or may be ordered from the NOS Distribution Branch. The stock numbers of catalogs for the nine regions are listed below:
- DMANC1 United States, Canada
- DMANC2 Central and South American, Antarctica
- DMANC3 Western Europe, Iceland, Greenland, the Arctic
- DMANC4 Scandinavia, Baltic, the Former Soviet Union
- DMANC5 Western Africa, the Mediterranean
- DMANC6 Indian Ocean
- DMANC7 Australia, Indonesia, New Zealand
- DMANC8 Oceania
- DMANC9 East Asia

Naval Observatory Publications

The Naval Observatory participates and assists in publishing the *Nautical Almanac* and the *Air Almanac* annually. There is also the annual *Almanac for Computers,* useful for programmable calculators and microcomputers; complete almanac and other data are now available on a single floppy disk. These books contain astronomical data that is helpful for celestial navigation.

The Naval Observatory also participates in and assists the publication of other navigational documents such as the *Tide Tables* and celestial sight reduction tables, but it is not the agency directly responsible for them.

U.S. Army Corps of Engineers Publications

The Corps of Engineers of the Unites States Army has the responsibility for navigational and informational publications on major inland (non-tidal) rivers such as the Tennessee, Ohio and Mississippi, and many lakes and reservoirs behind large dams.

Intracoastal Waterway Booklets

The Army Corps of Engineers has prepared two paperbound booklets on the Intracoastal Waterway, which comes under its jurisdiction. These booklets contain descriptive material, photographs, small-scale charts and tabulated data.

Unfortunately, these publications are not periodically updated and they are of far less value than the corresponding volumes of the NOS *Coast Pilots* with their annual editions and frequent changes in *Notice to Mariners.*

Bulletins on the Intracoastal Waterways are issued periodically by the Engineers District Offices. Addresses of these offices are given in the Appendix A.

Rivers & Lakes Information

Regulations relating to the use of many rivers and lakes (reservoirs), *Navigational Bulletins* and *Notices to Navigation Interests* are issued by various offices of the Corps of Engineers, as listed in Appendix A. Other government publications relating to inland river and lake boating are also listed on that page, together with information on their availability.

National Weather Service Publications

The National Weather Service, a part of NOAA, prepares weather maps that appear in many newspapers, but boaters generally make greater use of radio and television broadcasts for weather and sea conditions.

To assist mariners and boaters in knowing when and where to listen for radio and TV weather broadcasts in or near the continental United States, NWS publishes a series of *Marine Weather Services Charts.*

Boaters who cruise far off U.S. shores and in foreign waters should use the NWS publication *Worldwide Marine Weather Broadcasts,* which contains information on frequencies and schedules of stations transmitting in radiotelephone, radiotelegraph and radioteletype modes.

Keeping Publications Up to Date

You should be sure to keep charts and certain other navigational publications fully up to date. Outdated information can be more harmful than no information at all.

Coast Pilots and *Light Lists* are the primary publications that need continual correction. Fortunately, the government has provided a convenient means for executing this important function. The time and effort required are not great, provided a skipper keeps at it regularly and does not permit the work to build up a backlog.

U.S. Notice to Mariners

The National Geospatial-Intelligence Agency publishes a weekly *U.S. Notice to Mariners* that is prepared jointly with the National Ocean Service and the U.S. Coast Guard; see **Figure 15-42,** left. These pamphlets advise mariners worldwide of important matters that affect navigational safety, including new hydrographic discoveries, changes in channels and navigation aids, etc; they contain information that is primarily of interest to ocean-going vessels. Besides keeping mariners informed generally, the *Notice to Mariners* gives information specifically useful for updating latest-edition nautical charts and publications. Each issue has instructions on how it is to be used to correct charts and other publications. Supplementary information is published in *Notice* No. 1 of each year; lists of recently affected charts are included in each issue.

Printed copies of the *U.S. Notice to Mariners* are no longer distributed to the public. The full contents are available online at http://pollux.nss.nga.mil; click on "U.S. Notices to Mariners." They are in a single pdf file or in a zipped file that includes both the complete *Notice to Mariners* in pdf format and high-quality graphics as jpg files; these may be either viewed online or downloaded. Notices are available as a whole or section by section. The contents and appearance are the same as the formerly mailed *Notices.* Back copies are available as far back as No. 39 of 1999. A free subscription service is available by which you will be notified by email of the availability of each issue as it comes online. (Printed copies may be available from commercial sources.)

NIMA also publishes a semiannual *Summary of Corrections* in regional volumes. Each issue contains the full text of all accumulated corrections from *Notice to Mariners,* except for *Light Lists* and certain other navigational publications. It is easier to use than a file of *Notices* for bringing up to date a chart that has not been kept corrected. The *Summary* does, however, require a paid subscription.

Local Notices to Mariners

The Commander of each Coast Guard District issues weekly *Local Notice to Mariners.* These provide corrections for applicable charts, *Light List,* and *Coast Pilot* volume; they also include current security regulations, general information of interest on bridges, local events, proposed changes to aids to navigation, etc.; see **Figure 15-42,** right. *Local Notices to Mariners* bring information to users several weeks in advance of the *Notices to Mariners* printed in Washington by the National Geospatial-Intelligence Agency (formerly the National Image and Mapping Agency) and mailed from there. *Local Notices* are of particular interest to small-craft skippers, as the NGA *Notices* do not carry information on inland waterways and other waters not used by large ocean-going vessels.

The first *Local Notice* of each calendar month is termed the "Monthly Edition" and contains a summary of all current information; subsequently there are "Weekly Supplements" that furnish new information and may repeat important items. Effective in April 2004, the Coast Guard Districts stopped printing and mailing copies of *Local Notices* to persons and activities on their mailing lists. For all Districts, they are now available only on the Internet at the website of the USCG Navigation Center, http://www.nav-cen.uscg.gov/lnm. There is a free "one-way email service" that allows you to register and be automatically notified each time a new *Local Notice* is posted for the district or districts in which you are interested. This notification will also include information on the status of the online *Light List* and other relevant marine information updates.

Additional Navigation Information Available Online

The U.S. Coast Guard operates the USCG Navigation Information Service (NIS); this is available 24 hours a day, 7 days a week. This can be reached by the Internet (www.nav-cen.uscg.gov) or telephone (703-313-5900). In addition to *Local Notices to Mariners,* up-to-the-minute status information on GPS, DGPS, and LORAN-C is available.

The National Geospatial-Intelligence Agency operates the Maritime Safety Information website at http://pollux.nss.nga.mil. In addition to *Notices to Mariners,* this site has information on charts and publications issued by NGA, and a complete catalog of NGA nautical products.

Report All Useful Information

As emphasized earlier, all boaters are urged to help governmental agencies maintain the buoyage system by reporting damage to aids, malfunctioning of lights, shifting of shoals and channels, or new hazards. Use a radio if the matter is urgent; otherwise, reports of defects and suggestions for improvement of aids to navigation should be sent to the Commander of the applicable Coast Guard District.

Information concerning dangers to navigation, changes in shoals and channels, and similar information affecting NOS charts or publications should be sent to the Director, Coast Survey, National Ocean Service, 1315 East-West Highway Silver Spring, MD 20910-3282; telephone 301-713-2729.

Similar information relative to NIMA charts and publications should be sent to The Maritime Safety Information Division (ST D44), National Imagery and Mapping Agency, 4600 Sangamore Road, Bethesda, MD 20816-5003; telephone 301-227-2588; fax 301-227-5745.

Reports on the degradation or loss of radionavigation services can be made via the Internet to nisws@navcen.uscg.mil or by telephone to 703-313-5900.

Quasi-governmental Publications

Besides the agencies and their publications noted above, several activities best described as "quasi-governmental" produce publications of interest to boaters. Two are discussed on page 555.

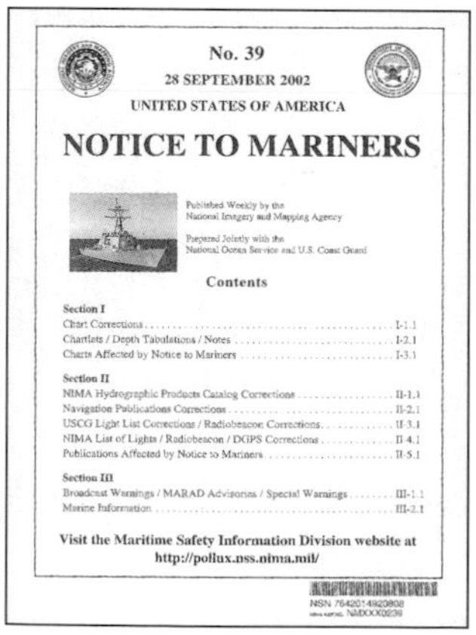

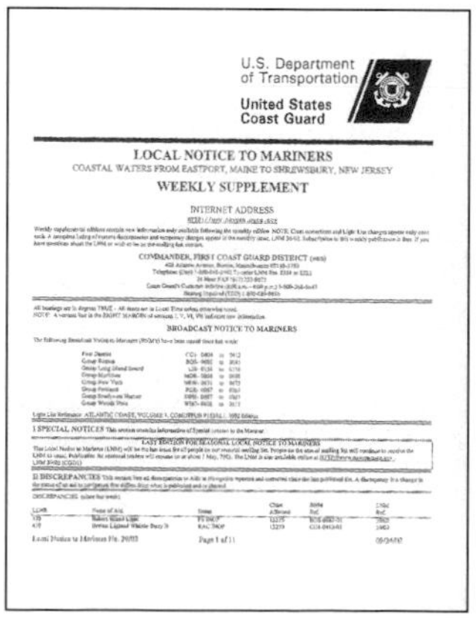

Figure 15-42 Notice to Mariners is published in two versions: (1) a weekly edition, published by NIMA, covers the entire world, except for inland waters not used by ocean shipping. (2) A local edition is published monthly, with weekly updates, by each U.S. Coast Guard District.

RTCM

The Radio Technical Commission for Maritime Services, better known as RTCM, includes individuals from governmental agencies such as FCC, the Coast Guard, NOAA, Maritime Administration and others—user organizations such as ocean steamship operating groups, Great Lakes shipping interests, and the U.S. Power Squadrons; equipment manufacturers; labor organizations; and communication companies such as the Bell System. The RTCM does not have authority to make binding decisions, but it wields considerable influence as a meeting place for and resolution of conflicting views and interests Radio Technical Commission for Maritime Services, P.O. Box 19087, Washington, DC 20036-0087.

Naval Institute Publications

The United States Naval Institute, it should be noted, is not a governmental agency; rather it is a private association dedicated to "the advancement of professional, literary and scientific knowledge in the Navy." As a means toward this goal, one of the Institute's principal activities is the publication of books dealing with naval and maritime matters.

The Naval Institute publishes a number of excellent books on the Navigation Rules, as well as the familiar text *Dutton's Navigation and Piloting*. Like the classic *Bowditch*, this volume has come to be recognized as an all-round authority on matters of piloting and navigation. The current volume is an outgrowth of years of development and expansion from an early work; the book on which it is based was initially known as *Navigation and Nautical Astronomy* by Benjamin Dutton. This useful book can be purchased in boating supply and bookstores and is also available from Naval Institute Press, 2062 Generals Highway, Annapolis, MD 21401-6769, or 800-233-8764, or www.navalinstitute.org.

Publications Available in Canada

Numerous Canadian Aids to Navigation (primarily seacoast aids) are listed in USCG *Light Lists Volumes I, VI, and VII*. These are most useful when they appear visually and/or electronically to mariners transmitting in U.S. waters adjacent to Canadian waters. The listing of some Canadian Aids to Navigation in the USCG *Light Lists* is not intended to be a substitute for the equivalent official Canadian publication, which is called *List of Lights*.

National Imagery & Mapping Agency (NIMA) Becomes National Geospatial-Intelligence Agency (NGA)

American navigators have always required accurate charts and nautical publications for the waters beyond the boundaries of the United States. Many foreign nations publish such data, but the coverage is not complete. The gap was first filled by the Navy Hydrographic Office, which later became the Navy Oceanographic Office. Following the consolidation of the U.S. military activities, the Defense Mapping Agency was created; its Hydrographic-Topographic Center (DMAHTC) combined the charting and navigational publication capabilities of the military services. Advances in technology resulted in a name change to the National Imagery & Mapping Agency (NIMA) and in November of 2003 a further redesignation as the National Geospatial-Intelligence Agency (NGA).

Civilian mariners and boaters should be aware of these governmental reorganizations and redesignations, but need not be concerned with them. Charts and publications, and their numbers, will generally not be changed, and only the title blocks will appear differently. Over time, charts and publications may be found in use bearing the imprint of NGA or any of its predecessor organizations.

Chapter
16

Basic Piloting Procedures

*The Dimensions & Tools of Piloting • Dead Reckoning • Precision & Accuracy,
Rounding Numbers • Making a Speed Curve*

PILOTING is the use of landmarks, aids to navigation, and soundings to conduct a vessel safely through channels and harbors, and along coasts where depths of water and dangers to navigation require constant attention to the boat's position and course; see **Figure 16–01.**

Piloting is one of the principal subdivisions of NAVIGATION—the science and art of directing the movements of a vessel from one position to another in a safe and efficient manner. It is a science because it uses principles and procedures based on centuries of observation, analysis, and study; it is an art because interpretations of observations and other information require individual judgment and skill.

An adjunct to piloting is DEAD RECKONING, a procedure by which a boat's approximate location is determined at any time by its movements since the last accurate determination of position. The term is said to have evolved from *deduced* reckoning, often abbreviated "de'ed" reckoning in old ships' logs.

Other types of navigation include CELESTIAL and ELECTRONIC NAVIGATION. Typical radio-based systems applicable to small craft are covered in Chapter 21; celestial navigation is covered in more advanced texts, such as *Dutton's Navigation and Piloting.*

THE IMPORTANCE OF PILOTING

Piloting is used by boaters in rivers, bays, lakes, sounds, as well as close alongshore when on the open ocean or large lakes—all areas known as PILOT WATERS. The navigator of a boat of any size in pilot waters must have adequate training and knowledge; he or she must be constantly alert, and give his task close attention. Frequent determinations of position are usually essential, and course or speed changes may be necessary at relatively short intervals.

Always keep in mind that the use of "high-tech" electronic navigation instruments does not make basic piloting and chart work obsolete as many users of Global Positioning System (GPS) and Loran-C receivers seem to believe. It is not simply a matter of providing a backup against the possible failure of your electronic navigation equipment, though this in itself is a sufficient reason to learn and practice piloting.

The reason that piloting and chartwork are still an integral part of electronic navigation is that without a graphic representation of your pilot waters you cannot know what lies ahead along your course. Without a chart, and without plotting your electronically-derived position on it, you cannot know whether or not you are headed into danger.

Electronic charts are coming into wider usage every year, but that in itself will not preclude the need for a basic understanding of piloting.

The High Seas vs. Pilot Waters

On the high seas, or well offshore in such large bodies of water as the Great Lakes, your navigation can be more relaxed. An error or uncertainty of position of a few miles presents no immediate hazard to the safety of boat and crew. But when you approach pilot waters, you need greater precision and accuracy. An error of only a few yards, for example, can result in your running aground with possibly serious consequences. The presence

Opposite Page: Figure 16–01 Piloting involves the use of specialized equipment and procedures. Learn how to use the various tools; follow standard practices in taking measurements and plotting the results.

of other vessels nearby underscores your constant need to know where the dangers lie, and where your own boat can be steered safely if you need to maneuver to avoid a collision with another craft.

The Enjoyment of Piloting

You will enjoy piloting most when you can do it without anxiety; which means that you need a background of study and practice. Try "over-navigating" in times of fair weather so you acquire the skill needed to direct your boat safely through fog, rain, or night without fear or strain. Despite the availability and use of electronic systems, a good navigator will retain his or her basic skills because piloting a boat with a chart and a pencil is a satisfying activity and a pleasure.

THE DIMENSIONS OF PILOTING

The basic dimensions of piloting are direction, distance, and time. Other quantities that must be measured, calculated, or used include speed, position, and depths and heights. You must have a ready understanding of how each of these dimensions is measured, expressed in units, used in calculations, and plotted on charts.

Direction

DIRECTION is the position of one point relative to another point without reference to the distance between them. As discussed earlier in Chapters 13 and 15 on compasses and charts, modern navigation uses the system of angular measurement in which a complete circle is divided into 360 units called "degrees." In some piloting procedures, degrees may be subdivided into minutes (there are 60 minutes in one degree), or into common or decimal fractions of a degree.

True, Magnetic, or Compass

Also as discussed, directions are normally referenced to a base line running from the origin point toward the geographic North Pole. Such directions can be measured on a chart with reference to the meridians of longitude and are called TRUE DIRECTIONS. Measurements made with respect to

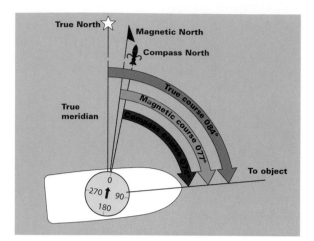

Figure 16-02 Direction, one of the basic dimensions of piloting, can be measured with respect to True, Magnetic, or Compass North. The reference used must always be designated when stating a direction.

the direction of the earth's magnetic field at that particular point are termed MAGNETIC DIRECTIONS. Those referred to local magnetic conditions as measured by the vessel's compass are designated COMPASS DIRECTIONS; see **Figure 16-02.**

To ensure accuracy, it is essential that you always designate the directorial reference used: magnetic (M) or compass (C); true is assumed when there is no letter designation.

Directions & Angles

The basic system of measurement uses the reference direction as 0° (North) and measures clockwise through 90° (East), 180° (South), and 270° (West) around to 360°, which is North again. Directions are expressed in three-digit form, such as 005°, 030°, 150°. Note that zeros are added before the direction figures to make a three-digit number, for example, 005° or 055°; see **Figure 16-03,** left. ANGLES that are *not* directions are expressed in one, two, or three digits as appropriate; 5°, 30°, 150°; see **Figure 16-03, right.** The use of three digits for directions helps distinguish them from angles.

Reciprocals For any given direction, there is its RECIPROCAL direction: its direct opposite, differing by 180°. Thus the reciprocal of 030° is 210°, and the reciprocal of 300° is 120°. To find the reciprocal of any direction, simply add 180° if the given direction is less than that amount; or subtract 180° if it is more; see **Figure 16-04.**

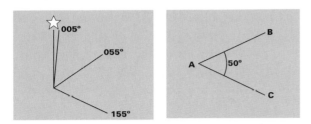

Figure 16-03 *Directions are always designated by a three-digit number. Add zeros before a single-digit or two-digit value (left). An angle between two directions (right), as distinguished from the directions themselves, is not expressed as a three-digit number.*

Distance

DISTANCE is defined as the spatial separation between two points without regard to the direction of one from the other. It is the length of the shortest line that can be drawn between the two points on the earth's surface.

The basic unit of distance in piloting in the U.S. is the MILE, but as noted in Chapter 15, a boater may encounter two types of miles. The familiar STATUTE MILE is used on many inland bodies of water, such as the Mississippi River and its tributaries, the Great Lakes, and the Atlantic and Gulf Intracoastal Waterways. It is 5,280 feet in length; the same mile as commonly used on land. On the high seas and connecting tidal waters, the unit of measurement is the NAUTICAL MILE set at 6,076.1 feet. This "salt-water" mile was conceived as equal to one minute of *latitude*, and this relationship is often used in navigation on both the sea and in the air. The conversion between nautical and statute miles is a factor of 1.15; roughly, seven nautical miles equals eight statute miles.

You may cruise from an area using one kind of mile into waters where the other kind is used. Be sure to determine which type of mile is to be used in your calculations. For shorter distances, a few miles or less, the unit of measurement may be the YARD; feet are seldom used except for depths and heights.

With the coming of the metric system, boaters must be prepared for greater use of METERS (m) and KILOMETERS (km); they must be familiar with these units and conversion to and from conventional units. Factors are: 1 foot = 0.3048 meter; 1 yard = 0.9144 meter; 1 statute mile = 1.609 kilometers, 1 nautical mile = 1.852 kilometers exactly. See Appendix E for additional conversion factors. Even though many charts will use mostly metric measurements, distances will probably continue to be stated in nautical miles because of its relationship to latitude.

Time

Although a navigator in pilot waters does not need so accurate a knowledge of the exact time of day as does a celestial navigator, ability to determine the passage of time and to perform calculations with such ELAPSED TIME is essential.

Units of Time

The units of time used in boating are the everyday ones of hours and minutes. In piloting, measurements are seldom carried to the precision of seconds of time although decimal fractions of minutes may occur occasionally in calculations. Seconds and fractions of minutes may be used in competitive events such as races and predicted log contests, but seldom otherwise.

The 24-Hour Clock System

In navigation, including piloting, the time of day is expressed in a 24-hour system that eliminates the designations of "A.M." and "P.M." Time is written in four-digit figures; the first two are the hour and the last two are the minutes. The day starts at 0000 or midnight; the next minute is 0001,

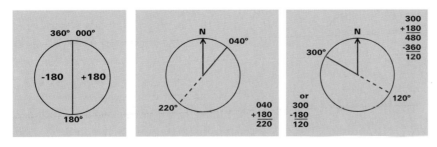

Figure 16-04 *The reciprocal of a given direction can be found by adding 180° to its value. If the total exceeds 360°, subtract 360°. Alternatively, subtract 180° from the original direction rather than doing this two-step addition and subtraction.*

12:01 A.M. in the "shore" system; 0100 would be 1 A.M., and so on to 1200 noon. The second half of the day continues in the same pattern with 1300 being 1 p.m., 1832 being 6:32 P.M., etc., to 2400 for midnight. (The time 2400 for one day is the same as 0000 for the next day.)

Time is spoken as "zero seven hundred" or "fifteen forty." *The word "hours" is not used.* The times of 1000 and 2000 are correctly spoken as "ten hundred" and "twenty hundred," *not* as "one thousand" or "two thousand."

When performing arithmetic computations with time, remember that when "borrowing" or "carrying" there are 60 minutes in an hour, and not 100. As obvious and simple a matter as this may be, miscalculations occur all too often.

Times Zones

A navigator in pilot waters must also be alert to TIME ZONES. Even in coastal or inland waters, you can cruise from one zone to another, necessitating the resetting of clocks and watches.

Daylight Time

A further complication in time is the prevalence of DAYLIGHT TIME during the summer months. Government publications are in standard time; local sources of information such as newspapers

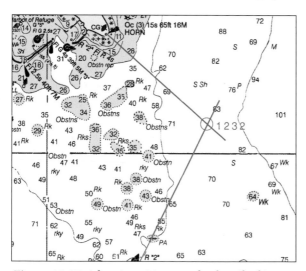

Figure 16-05 *A boat's position may be described in "relative" terms, such as distance and direction from an identifiable object such as a landmark or aid to navigation. In this example, it might be stated as "1.8 miles, 120° true, from Point Judith Light."*

and radio broadcasts use daylight time if it is in effect. Daylight time is one hour *later* than standard time. When converting from standard time to daylight, *add* one hour; from daylight to standard, *subtract* one hour.

Speed

No matter what type of boat you have, SPEED is an essential dimension of piloting. Speed is defined as the number of units of distance traveled in a specified unit of time. The basic unit of speed is MILES PER HOUR, whether these are nautical or statute miles, as determined by location. A nautical mile per hour is termed a KNOT. Since this term includes "per hour," it is incorrect to say "knots per hour." The unit "knot" may be abbreviated either as "kn" or "kt"; the former has a somewhat greater usage.

Conversion of Knots & mph

The conversion factors between statute miles per hour (mph) and knots are the same as for the corresponding units of distance—1 knot = 1.15 mph, or 7 knots roughly equals 8 mph. (1 knot = 1.852 km/h).

Position

The ability to describe the position of his vessel accurately is an essential requirement for a boater, and one that marks him or her as well qualified. To realize the importance and the difficulties of this seemingly simple task, listen to your radio on VHF Channel 16 or 22 on a weekend afternoon during the boating season. The hesitant, and inaccurate, attempts by skippers to simply say where they are surely must irritate the Coast Guard and embarrass competent boaters, and almost always delays the arrival of assistance.

Relative & Geographic Coordinates

POSITION may be described in two ways: in relative terms or by geographic coordinates. To state your boat's RELATIVE POSITION, describe it as being a certain distance and direction from an identifiable point such as a landmark or aid to navigation. Precision depends on the accuracy of the data on which you base the position: You

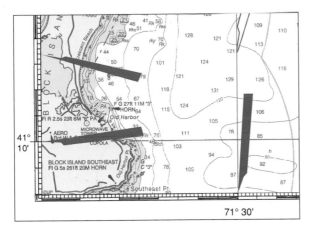

Figure 16-06 A boat's position may also be described in geographic coordinates. Using the subdivisions on the chart's borders, latitude and longitude are measured as shown here, and are recorded with time.

might say that you were "about two miles southeast of Point Judith Light"; or if you had the capability of being precise, you could say, "I'm 1.8 miles, 130° true from Point Judith Light." Be careful not to confuse the direction you measure *toward* the identifiable point with your report of position *from* the object. In relative positioning, the distance can, of course, be essentially zero, as would be the case with a position report such as "I am at Lighted Whistle Buoy 2"; see **Figure 16-05**.

These examples of position description have all used visible identifiable objects. You can also state your GEOGRAPHIC POSITION in terms of latitude and longitude using those straight, uniformly spaced lines on most charts. Using this procedure, measure the position from the markings on either side and on the top or bottom of your chart.

The units of measurement for geographic coordinates are degrees and minutes, but this degree is not the same unit as used in the measurement of direction, nor is this minute the same as the unit of time. Be careful not to confuse these units of position with other units with similar names. For more precise position definition, you can use either SECONDS or DECIMAL FRACTIONS OF MINUTES (usually tenths), as determined by your chart. The smallest unit on the marginal scales of NOS coast charts is tenths of minutes, but for harbor charts it is seconds; refer to Chapter 15, **Figures 15-12** and **15-13**.

To state your boat's geographic position, give the latitude first, before longitude, and follow the figures by "north" or "south" as appropriate. Similarly, longitude must be designated "east" or "west" to be complete. All U.S. waters are in north latitude and west longitude, but the position labels should be stated nevertheless; see **Figure 16-06**.

Skippers of boats with GPS normally describe their position in terms of latitude and longitude. Boaters with Loran-C receivers will normally use geographic coordinates, but sometimes describe their position in terms of "time difference" readings; this is acceptable to the Coast Guard in search and rescue operations.

Depths

The DEPTH of the water is important both for safety of a boat in preventing grounding, and for navigational purposes. Thus, this vertical measurement from the surface of the water to the bottom is an essential dimension of piloting. Measurements may be made continuously or only occasionally as appropriate.

In pilot waters, depths are normally measured in FEET; refer to **Figure 16-05**. In open ocean waters the small boat operator may use charts indicating depths in FATHOMS of six feet each. Some charts of other nations may use METERS and DECIMETERS (tenths of a meter). Check each chart when you buy it, and again when you use it, to note its unit of depth measurement. Check also the datum—the horizontal plane of reference, such as MEAN LOWER LOW WATER—from which depths on the chart are measured; refer to Chapter 15, **Figure 15-09**. Note that "mean lower low water" is the average of the lower low water of each tidal day, and there will be many days that will have a low water level *below* the mean; at those times, actual depths will be *less* that the figures printed on the chart. Charts of inland waters will have a datum at a specified level.

In many areas, depths often fluctuate from the chart's printed figures because of tidal changes; in other areas, depths change in seasonal patterns.

Heights

The HEIGHT or ELEVATION of objects is also of concern to a boater. The height of some landmarks and lighted aids to navigation may determine their range of visibility. Of more critical importance, however, are such vertical measurements as the clearance under a bridge; refer to Chapter 17, **Figure 17-02.** Heights, or vertical dimensions upward from the surface of the water, are measured in feet (or meters).

You will find that in tidal areas the plane of reference for heights is *not* the same as for depths.

The usual datum for height measurement is MEAN HIGH WATER. This will be an imaginary plane surface above the mean low-water datum for depths by an amount equal to the MEAN TIDE RANGE; charts usually show the height at mean high water; refer to Chapter 15, **Figure 15-17.**

Note that "mean high water" is the *average of all highs,* and there will be many instances of normal highs being *above* the datum, with correspondingly *lesser* vertical clearances.

THE INSTRUMENTS OF PILOTING

For piloting in coastal and inland waters, you will need a few simple tools or instruments. They are not particularly expensive items, but they should be of good quality, well cared for, and used with respect.

Direction

Many instruments are used for measuring direction—some directly and others on a chart. Still other instruments measure direction both from a chart and from observation.

Determining Direction

The basic instrument for determining direction is a COMPASS. With rare exceptions it will be a MAGNETIC compass as described in Chapter 13. Its directions are properly called "compass" directions—not "magnetic," not "true." Usually, before a direction such as 057°C can be used or plotted, it must be corrected for both deviation and variation (see Chapter 13, pages 447-450).

The compass is used primarily to determine the direction in which the boat is headed. Depending upon its mounting and its location in the boat, you can also use the steering compass to determine the direction of other objects from your boat. Readings may be taken by sighting across the compass itself and estimating the reading of the compass card. Steering compass sights are generally accurate enough, but physical obstructions usually limit them to objects forward of the beam.

Hand-bearing Compass You can take compass sights more flexibly with a HAND-BEARING COMPASS, which is held in the hand and not in a stationary mounting. These come in many styles, but each is basically a small liquid-filled compass with a suitable grip for holding in front of your eye, plus a set of sights and/or a prismatic optical system for simultaneously observing a distant object through the sights and reading the compass card. A typical hand-bearing compass is shown in **Figure 16-07**; this model uses a prism in lieu of sights. A small steering compass can sometimes be removed from its mounting (only if the construction is such that the compensating magnets are part of the mounting and do not come with the compass when it is removed) and taken to where there is an unobstructed line of

Figure 16-07 A hand-bearing compass can be used from almost any location on a boat, but be careful to keep away from large masses of magnetic material that could cause deviation errors.

sight to a distant object; refer to **Figure 16-01.** Some binoculars have a built-in compass that allows the user to simultaneously see the distant object more clearly and read its direction.

A hand-bearing compass is normally used on deck away from the usual causes of magnetic deviation, as discussed in Chapter 13, page 466. Take care, however, not to get too close to objects of iron or similar material, such as anchors or stays and shrouds. To find a sighting position on deck that you can be sure is free of magnetic influences, take bearings on a distant charted landmark with your boat in a known position. Compare your hand-bearing readings taken from various locations on deck with the magnetic bearing from the chart. Put the boat on several different headings as you do this, in case the orientation of its magnetic influences has an important effect on the hand-bearing compass. When taking the bearing make sure that your eyeglasses or other item, such as a spare battery in your shirt pocket, are not causing deviation.

Typically, you would find a clear space to stand and brace yourself (note that you will be concentrating on the sighting and not keeping a weather eye for the next large wave), then raise the hand-bearing compass to your eye and take the reading. In most situations, the compass is well clear of the various magnetic influences that cause deviation, but you should be alert to the possibility that you are standing too close to a mass of magnetic material.

Hand-bearing compasses are also very useful in determining whether a nearby vessel is changing position with respect to your boat. Are you on a collision course? Are you winning or losing ground in a race? A hand-bearing compass can help you answer these important questions—though not always definitively—while there is still time to do something about it.

Plotting Directions

Once you have determined a direction by compass, pelorus, or other device, you must plot it on the chart. There are several instruments for doing this, and they are the same tools used for determining direction from the chart itself.

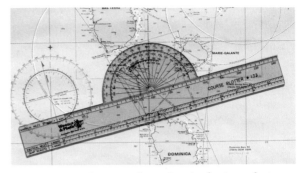

Figure 16-08 *A course plotter is a single piece of transparent plastic ruled with a set of lines parallel to the longer edges, and semicircular main and auxiliary scales in degrees. There may be distance scales on the two longer sides.*

Course Plotters   These are pieces of clear plastic, usually rectangular, which have one or more semicircular angular scales marked on them; see **Figure 16-08.** The center of the scales is at or near the center of one of the longer sides of the plotter and is usually emphasized with a small circle or bull's-eye. Plotters normally have two main scales, one from 000° to 180° and the other from 180° to 360°; each calibrated in degrees. (Some models may not follow the three-digit rule.) There may also be smaller AUXILIARY SCALES, which are offset 90° from the main scales. Lines are marked on the plotter parallel to the longer sides.

Course plotters are used in the following manner:

To determine the direction of a course or bearing from a given point: Place the plotter on

Figure 16-09 *The course plotter is lined up with the charted line along one of the longer sides, and is then moved until a meridian cuts through the bull's-eye. Direction can then be read from the appropriate main scale. If more convenient, the plotted line can be lined up with one of the parallel lines on the course plotter.*

the chart so that one of its longer sides is along your course or bearing line, and slide the plotter until the bull's-eye is over a MERIDIAN (longitude lines running North-South). Read the true direction on the scale where it is intersected by the meridian. Easterly courses are read on the scale that reads from 000° to 180° and westerly courses on the other main scale; see **Figure 16-09.** If it is more convenient, find your plotted course or bearing with one of the plotter's marked parallel lines rather than its edge. It is not essential that you actually draw in the line connecting the two points (the plotter can be aligned using only the two points concerned), but you will usually find it easier and safer to get in the habit of drawing in the connecting line.

When the direction to be measured is within 20° or so of due North or South, it may be difficult to reach a meridian by sliding the course plotter across the chart. The small inner auxiliary scales have been included on the plotter for just such cases. Slide the plotter until the bull's-eye intersects a PARALLEL OF LATITUDE (east-west line). The intersection of this line with the appropriate *auxiliary* scale indicates the direction of the course or bearings; see **Figure 16-10.**

To plot a specified direction (course or bearing) from a given point: Put a pencil point on the origin location, keep one of the longer edges of the course plotter snug against the pencil, and slide the plotter around until the center bull's-eye and the desired mark on the appropriate main scale both lie along the same meridian. With the plotter thus positioned, draw in the specified direction from the given point.

Alternatively, you can first position the plotter using the bull's-eye and scale markings without regard to the specified origin point, slide the plotter up or down the meridian until one of the longer edges is over the origin point and then draw in the direction line.

For directions nearly north or south, use one of the small auxiliary scales on a parallel of latitude.

To extend a line that must be longer than the length of the course plotter: Place a pair of dividers (see page 567), opened to three or four inches (7-10 cm), tightly against the edge of the plotter and then slide the plotter along using the divider points as guides. Draw in the extension of the course or bearing line after the plotter has been advanced.

To draw a new line parallel to an existing course or bearing line: Use the parallel lines marked on the course plotter as guides.

Some course plotter models do more than just measure directions. One, called a "Nautical Ruler," has distance scales along its longer sides for both nautical and statute miles at common chart scales. Loran-C interpolator scales are along the shorter edges and considerable other information is also printed on this device.

There are other plotting instruments, such as the Quik-Course; see **Figure 16-11.** This can be

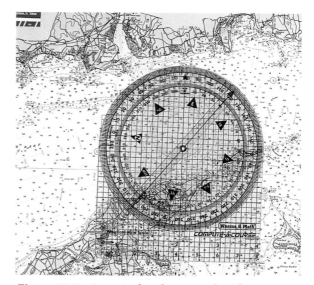

Figure 16-11 A particular plotting tool, such as a Quik-Course plotter, is handy to use in plotting course lines and bearing. It is particularly useful in smaller, open boats.

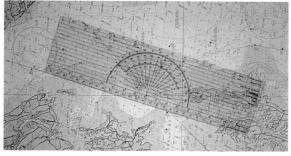

Figure 16-10 In the case of plotted lines within 10° to 20° of North or South, the inner auxiliary scale and a parallel of latitude can be used.

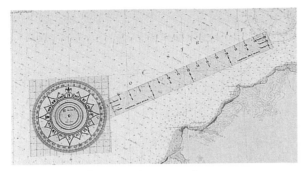

Figure 16-12 Some navigators prefer to use a course protractor for plotting. The long arm is moveable with respect to the square grid.

used to determine the direction of a course line by placing its center at any point along the line, orienting the horizontal and vertical lines with similar lines on the chart, and reading the true direction from the printed scales. After correction from compass to true, bearings can be plotted by placing the center of the Quik-Course on the object sighted upon, aligning the plotter, and placing a pencil mark on the chart for the reciprocal of the bearing as read on the scale around the outer edge of the plotter. After you remove the Quik-Course from the chart, you can draw a line from this pencil mark back to the location of the sighted object.

Course Protractors Many skippers use one of these as their primary plotting tool; see **Figure 16-12.** This instrument, with its moving parts, is slightly more complex and takes a little more practice to use comfortably and accurately than course plotters. Course protractors typically consist of a small clear plastic square marked with a 360° compass scale and a grid of fine lines. Riveted on the center of the circular scale is a clear plastic arm that revolves like the hands of a clock—but it is a very long arm as it extends about a foot (30.5 cm) beyond the circle of the compass scale The principle is to duplicate the orientation of the compass rose of the chart (particularly the magnetic circle) and transfer it to the point of interest on the chart.

Course protractors are used in the following manner:

To measure the direction of a course or bearing: Place the center of the course protractor on the chart exactly over the specified origin point, such as your boat's position or an aid to navigation. Then swing the protractor's arm around to the nearest compass rose on the chart, making the upper edge of the arm (which is in line with the center of the compass part of the course protractor) pass directly over the center of the compass rose.

Holding the course protractor arm firmly in this position, turn the compass part of the protractor around until the arm's upper edge cuts across the same degree marking of the protractor compass as it does at the compass rose (true or magnetic). The compass of the protractor and the rose on the chart are now parallel.

Holding the protractor compass firmly against the chart, move the protractor arm around until its edge cuts across the second point involved in the course or bearing. You can now read the direction in degrees (true or magnetic) directly from the protractor compass scale.

To lay off a line in a specified direction from the given point: Line up the protractor rose with the chart's compass rose as in the preceding instructions. Then rotate the arm until the desired direction is indicated on the compass scale, and draw in the line; extend the line back to the origin point after you have labeled the course and the protractor has been lifted off the chart.

Parallel Rulers These are traditional instruments for measurement and plotting directions on charts. Parallel rulers may be made of black or

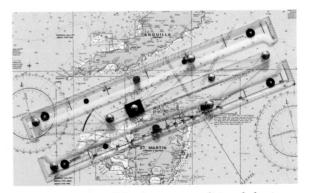

Figure 16-13 Parallel rulers are a traditional plotting instrument. Two straightedges are kept in parallel alignment by the connecting links. Transfer directions from one location to another by "walking" the rulers from plotted line to a compass rose, or vice versa.

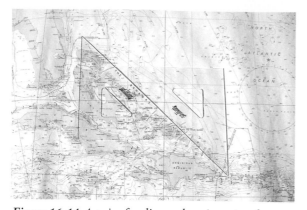

Figure 16-14 A pair of ordinary drawing triangles can be used for easily transferring a direction from one part of a chart to another, but not for long distances.

clear transparent plastic; see **Figure 16–13.** The two rulers are connected by linkages that keep their edges parallel and, like ordinary drawing rulers, have beveled edges that are convenient for drawing lines. To measure the direction of a line, line up one ruler with the desired objects on the chart and then "walk" the pair across the chart to the nearest compass rose by alternately holding one ruler and moving the other toward the compass rose or other objective using the two small knobs that are on each ruler. One ruler is held firmly in place on the chart while the other is advanced. Then this second ruler is held in place while the first is closed up on it; this process can be repeated as necessary. To plot a line of stated direction, reverse the process; start at the compass rose and walk to the desired origin point and draw a line to the length desired. In both procedures, take care that the rulers do not slip.

Normally the outer circle of a compass rose will be used, giving true directions. With experience, however, the inner circle can be used for measurement of magnetic directions; remember that deviation must be applied to get compass directions.

Closely related to parallel rulers is the recently developed "GPS PLOTTER," specifically designed for plotting latitude and longitude values taken from a GPS receiver—it works equally well with geographic coordinates from any source.

Drawing Triangles An ordinary plastic pair of these can also be used for transferring a direction

from one part of a chart to another, although not for very great distances. The two triangles need not be similar in size or shape; it is helpful if each triangle has a handle. Place the two hypotenuses (longest sides) together, and line up one of the other sides of one triangle with the course or bearing line, or with the desired direction at the compass rose; see **Figure 16-14.** Hold the other triangle firmly in place as a base, and slide the first one along its edge carrying the specified line to a new position while maintaining its direction. If necessary, alternately slide and hold the triangles for moving greater distances. Although it takes some practice to use this method, it does work.

Other Instruments There are a number of other instruments available for use in plotting directions, including patented variations on those mentioned above. You may use any that you feel comfortable with.

There are also several more comprehensive plotting systems available. These typically offer a means of mounting and protecting a chart, and also provide a set of several specialized plotting devices that can make chartwork much easier to execute and much more accurate in practice. While the principles are the same (and still must be thoroughly understood), such chartwork systems are especially desirable for small boat skippers who may often have to do their plotting in cramped, uncomfortable and/or wet circumstances. Each of these systems has its own operating method, so no

Figure 16-15 Various electronic plotting systems are available that can simplify and speed up many procedures. Some compute positions electronically once matched to the chart, and can accept input from other instruments.

attempt will be made to describe them here; one is illustrated in **Figure 16-15.**

Distance

Distance to an object can be measured directly by RADAR (see Chapter 21), and distance traveled can be measured directly by a SUMMING LOG, but many recreational craft have neither of these items of equipment.

A handheld OPTICAL RANGEFINDER can be used to measure distance to an object up to a thousand yards or so. Most often in piloting, however, distances are measured by taking them from a chart.

Chart Measurements for Distance

Dividers Distance is measured on a chart with a pair of these; see **Figure 16-16,** right. Open the two arms of the dividers and the friction at the pivot is sufficient to hold the separation between the points. Most dividers have some means for adjusting this friction; it should be enough to hold the arms in place, but not so much as to make opening or closing difficult. A special type of dividers has a center crosspiece (like the horizontal part of the capital letter "A") which can be rotated by a knurled knob to set and maintain the opening between the arms, thus the distance between the points cannot accidentally change; see **Figure 16-16,** left. This type of dividers is

particularly useful if kept set to some standard distance, such as one mile to the scale of the chart being used.

To measure distance with dividers: First open them to the distance between the two points on the chart, then transfer them without change to the chart's graphic scale. Although your first thought might be to place one divider pin on the zero position of the scale and then see where the other pin falls to read a distance, there is a more accurate procedure. For one pin of the dividers, choose a mark on the scale for a whole number of units so that the other pin falls on the subdivided unit to the left of zero; refer to Chapter 15, **Figure 15-07.** The distance measured is the sum of the whole units to the right of the zero mark and the fraction of a unit measured to the left of zero. Be sure to note the type of fraction used, such as seconds of latitude/longitude, tenths of a mile, or hundreds of yards/meters.

If the distance on the chart cannot be spanned with the dividers opened widely (about 60 degrees is the maximum practical opening), follow this procedure: Set the points for a convenient opening for a whole number of units on the graphic scale or latitude subdivisions; then step this off the necessary number of times by swinging one leg past the other as you set the points alternately along the line. Although you

Figure 16-16 Three styles of dividers are shown here. When using the more-common kind (left), the friction at the pivot holds the arms for the desired opening between the points. Another type (center) uses an adjustable center cross arm to maintain the seperation between the points. When using traditional "one-hand" dividers (right), squeeze the lower part of the arms to close the gap, the upper part to open it.

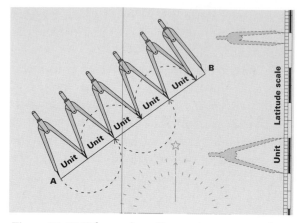

Figure 16-17 When a chart distance is too great to be measured with a single setting of the dividers, open the points to a whole number of units. Step these along the charted line for the required number of times, and then measure any smaller distance left over in the usual manner.

have probably drawn in a line on the chart, it is possible to step the dividers along the edge of a ruler; remember to count the number of steps. Then adjust the dividers to measure the odd remainder. The total distance is then the simple sum of the parts stepped off and measured separately; see **Figure 16-17**.

To mark off a desired distance on the chart: Set the right pin of the dividers on the nearest lower whole number of units, and the left pin on the remaining fractional part of a unit measured leftward from zero on the scale. The dividers are now properly set for the specified distance at the scale of the chart being used and can be applied to the chart. If the distance is too great for one setting of dividers, step it off in increments.

Charts at a scale smaller than 1:50,000 do not have a graphic scale; distances are measured on the *latitude* scales at either side of the chart. Take care to measure on these scales near the same latitude as the portion of the chart being used; in other words, move directly horizontally across the chart to either of its sides to use the scales; refer to **Figure 16-17.**

With a little experience you can set and use conventional dividers with one hand. Making sure that the friction at the pivot is properly adjusted, practice this technique until it is easy for you; it will add convenience and speed to your

piloting work. Traditional "one-hand" dividers have a pair of curved arms; squeezing them above or below the crossover opens or closes the gap between the points; refer to **Figure 16-16,** right.

An instrument that looks much like a pair of dividers, except that a pencil lead or pen is substituted for one point, is called a COMPASS (or DRAWING COMPASS to distinguish it from a magnetic compass). This is used primarily for drawing circles or arcs of circles.

Chart Measurer This device can also be used to measure distance across a chart, althought with reduced, but generally acceptable, accuracy. A chart measurer has a small wheel that rolls along the chart and is internally geared to an indicating dial. Chart measurers read distances directly in miles at various typical chart scales; there are separate models for charts using statute and nautical miles. They are particularly useful in measuring distances up and down rivers with many bends and changes of direction.

Time

Every skipper, no matter how small his or her boat, should have a dependable and reasonably accurate timepiece, whether a clock, wristwatch, or pocket watch. Long-term accuracy is of secondary importance in piloting, but short-term errors, those accumulated over the length of a day or half-day, should be small. A knowledge of the time of day within a few minutes is usually all you will need. If you use a clock, mount it where it is

Figure 16-18 A stopwatch, as shown here, or a wristwatch that includes a timing function, is useful for measuring elapsed times. It eliminates the possibility of mistakes that might be made in subtracting clock times.

clearly visible from the helm-seat or plotting table.

ELAPSED TIME is often of greater interest than ABSOLUTE TIME; a stopwatch is handy for this see **Figure 16-18.** Most stop watches have a second hand that makes one revolution per minute, and this is the simplest kind to use, but there are some that sweep completely around in 30 seconds, and even a few that have a 10-second period; some have a digital readout. Know for sure the type of stopwatch that you are using.

Also quite useful is a COUNTDOWN TIMER with alarm. This can be either a simple kitchen timer from the galley, or a wristwatch with the countdown feature. Countdown timers save you the trouble of keeping an eye on the clock to be ready for a course change or an expected sighting of an aid to navigation.

Digital wristwatches are excellent for use in piloting. Some models have many features in addition to ordinary timekeeping, such as settable alarm, stopwatch, and countdown timer with alarm.

Speed

Speed is a dimension that can either be measured directly or calculated from knowledge of distance and time. Direct reading instruments are convenient, but they give only the relative speed through the water, and not the SPEED MADE GOOD over the bottom.

In "olden days," the speed of a vessel through the water was measured by a "chip log." A weighted wooden float was attached to the end of a line that was allowed to run out off a reel. Knots were tied in this line at regular, specific intervals (47 feet, 3 inches) and counted as the line ran out for a specified time, measured by turning an hourglass (actually a 28-second glass). The number of knots that had passed gave the vessel's speed in nautical miles per hour, hence the speed was measured in, what else, "knots," and it still is today!

More modern marine speedometers use the pressure built up in a small tube by motion of the boat, or the rotation of an impeller. There are many different models with varying speed ranges, from those for sailboats to models reading high enough for fast powerboats; see **Figure 16-19.**

Figure 16-19 Many small craft are fitted with a marine speedometer. Some use a pressure tube in the flow of water past the hull, and others, such as seen here, use a small impeller mounted through the bottom of the craft. Displays are digital and can include distance as well as speed.

Speed made good (SMG), also termed SPEED OVER GROUND (SOG), can be manually calculated from distance covered and elapsed time, as discussed later in this chapter, or with special calculating devices. These calculators are adaptations of general mathematical slide rulers; they may be either linear or circular in form; see **Figure 16-20.**

Small electronic calculators are also very useful for speed-time-distance computations. Today's GPS receivers provide quite accurate SOG data. This is especially true when differential corrections are being used.

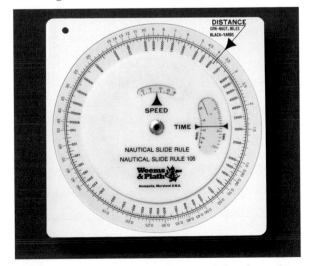

Figure 16-20 A circular calculator or slide rule, such as the one seen here, enables a navigator to solve time-distance-speed problems as well as other conversions or measurements. It provides easily read, accurate results.

Depth Measuring Tools

Depth of the water can be measured manually or electronically. A hand LEAD LINE is simple, accurate, and not subject to breakdowns, but it is awkward to use, inconvenient in bad weather, and can give only one or two readings per minute. A lead line can be used only at quite slow speeds, or to check depths around an anchored boat.

Many small boats today have an ELECTRONIC DEPTH SOUNDER—a convenient device that gives clear and accurate measurements of the depth of water beneath the boat. A depth sounder gives readings many times each second, so frequently that they appear to be a smooth, continuous depth measurement. For more information on these relatively inexpensive, but most useful, piloting aids, refer to Chapter 21.

Miscellaneous Piloting Tools

Among the most important of all piloting tools are ordinary PENCILS and ERASERS; see **Figure 16-21.** Pencils should be neither too hard nor too soft. If too hard they tend to score into the chart paper and if too soft they smudge. A medium (HB or No. 2) pencil works well; experiment to see what hardness is best for you. Keep several pencils available, well sharpened, and handy to the plotting table. Fine lead (0.5mm) mechanical pencils are excellent.

A soft eraser of the "Pink Pearl" type is good for most erasures; an art gum eraser works well for general chart cleaning.

Binocular A good binocular is essential for most piloting situations. In choosing a binocular remember that higher powers give greater magnification, bringing distant objects closer, but only at the cost of a more limited field of view. An adequate field of view makes it easier to find an object on small boats with their rapid and sometimes violent motion—just the time when you are most anxious to find that object.

A binocular is designated by two numbers, such as "6 x 30" or "10 x 50." The first figure indicates the power of magnification, the second is the diameter of the front lens in millimeters—a 6 x 30 binocular enlarges images six times and has a 30

Figure 16-21 Seen here are some of the basic tools for piloting: a high-quality, waterproof binocular, hand bearing compass, powerful searchlight, flashlight with magnifying lens, and, most important, pencil and eraser.

mm front lens. The size of the front lens is an important consideration as a larger lens gathers more light and is the main factor in determining how well the optics will assist your night vision in night use. Most authorities recommend a 7 x 50 binocular as best for marine use. A binocular may be individually focused (IF) for each eye, or centrally focused (CF) for both eyes, with a minor adjustment on one eyepiece to balance any difference between a person's two eyes. Both types are fine for marine use; choice is based on personal preference. There are also fixed-focus, nonadjusting binoculars.

More expensive, but highly advantageous, is a STABILIZED BINOCULAR. The human hand just cannot hold a binocular steady enough for boating use under many conditions; the greater the magnification, the greater the problem. Image Stabilization (IS) technology was developed for handheld video cameras, and has now been applied to the binocular. Clearer vision is achieved by one of two techniques: an internal gyroscopic mechanism or electronic sensors coupled to microprocessors; the results are the same. Small batteries are required for most stabilized binoculars, but they will be usable in the nonstabilized mode if batteries are lacking or go dead.

They are somewhat larger and heavier than a regular binocular, but for most boaters, their advantages will outweigh these negative factors.

Keep your binocular in its case when you are not using it, and make sure that the strap is around your neck when you are using it. Be careful when you put it down so that it cannot slide off and be damaged, even a rubber housing may not protect it from harm.

Flashlights Keep several FLASHLIGHTS or ELECTRIC LANTERNS on your boat for emergency use, and extra batteries for them. At least one flashlight should have a red lens or filter so you can use it for reading charts at night (white lights cause a temporary loss of night vision, red light helps preserve it). Handheld magnifiers with built-in red illumination are excellent for reading chart details underway at night.

Your Own Piloting Tools

Every navigator eventually has his own favorite set of piloting tools. Don't be concerned with choosing the "right" or the "best" instrument—choose tools with which you feel confident and learn to use them intuitively.

MEASUREMENTS

If you are considering the measurement of various quantities for use in piloting, and the calculations in which they are used, you must first consider the appropriate standards of accuracy and precision.

Although often used interchangeably in everyday language "accuracy" and "precision" are *not* synonymous. PRECISION relates to the degree of fineness of measurement of the value under consideration. ACCURACY relates to how closely the stated value is to the true or correct value.

Statements of distance as 32 miles or 32.0 miles are not quite the same things. The first merely says that to the best of observation and measurement the distance is not 31 nor 33 miles; the second says that it is not 31.9 nor 32.1 miles. Note the difference is the degree *preciseness* of these two statements of the same distance. Never write 32.0 for 32 unless your measurements are sufficiency precise to warrant it.

The accuracy of the value recorded, regardless of how precisely it may or may not be stated, is determined by the tools and/or techniques used to measure it. Accuracy is sometimes stated as a value, such as "accurate to a half-mile." It can be stated as a probability, such as "100 meters CPE (circular probable error)." Meaning that 50 percent of measurements will be within the stated distance.

Accuracy and precision are independent of each other. A measurement or calculation may be stated in very precise terms, but at the same time it may be inaccurate.

Standard Limits of Precision

The navigation of vessels of various sizes naturally involves different standards of precision and accuracy, as befitting the conditions encountered. The piloting of small boats does not permit so high a degree of accuracy as on large ships that offer a more stable platform.

Direction

Direction is measured in small-craft navigation to the nearest whole degree. It is not reasonable to measure or calculate directions to a finer degree of precision when a boat is seldom steered closer than 2 degrees or 3 degrees to the desired course.

Distance

Distances are normally expressed to the nearest tenth of a mile. This degree of precision, which works out to roughly 200 yards for a nautical mile, is reasonable in consideration of the size of the vessel and other measurement standards. On a chart at a typical scale of 1:40,000 this is less than 3/16 of an inch.

Time

Time is measured and calculated to the nearest minute. Fractions of a minute are rarely of any significance in routine piloting. In contests, however, time is calculated to decimal fractions and used in terms of seconds.

Speed

Measured electronically, speed through the water is usually indicated to the nearest tenth of a knot (miles per hour), especially at speeds less than 10

ROUNDING OF NUMBERS

In this chapter, the phrase "to the nearest…" is used frequently. ROUNDING is often employed to reduce various quantities to such limitations. For example, if you were to make a distance calculation for a speed of 13 knots for a time of 5 minutes, you would get 1.08333 on most electronic calculators (perhaps even more trailing "3s"). However, since distance is normally expressed to the nearest tenth of a mile, you would use it as 1.1 miles, the value arrived at by "rounding off," as described below.

Any mathematical expression of a quantity has a certain number of "significant figures." The quantity 4 has one significant figure, for instance; 4.2 or 14 each have two significant figures; 5.12, 43.8, and 609 each have three significant figures.

The process of reducing the number of significant figures is called "rounding." To have uniform results, rules have been established for the rounding of numbers.

1. If the digit to be rounded off is 4 or less, it is dropped or changed to a zero.

> 8.23 is rounded to 8.2
> 432 is rounded to 430

2. If the digit to be rounded off is 6 or larger, the preceding digit is raised to the next higher value and the rounded digit is dropped or changed to a zero.

> 8.27 is rounded to 8.3
> 439 is rounded to 440

3. If the digit to be rounded off is a 5, it is desirable to round to the nearest even value, up or down.

> 8.25 is rounded to 8.2
> 435 is rounded to 440

This rule may seem arbitrary, but it is followed for consistency in results; it has an advantage that when two such rounded figures are added together and divided by two for an average, the result will not present a new need for rounding.

Note, however, that slightly different figures will result from using an electronic calculator. When a calculator is set to display a fixed number of decimal places, a 5 to be rounded off nearly always results in the preceding digit being changed to the next higher—even or odd—number. (Internal calculations use the full range of numbers without rounding.) Computers, with their greater capabilities, can be programmed to round up only half of the time, when the preceding digit is odd; they round down for other numbers—this ensures less distortion of the final results.

4. Rounding can be applied to more than one final digit; but all such rounding must be done in one step. For example: 6148 is rounded to 6100 in a single action; do *not* round 6148 to 6150, and then round 6150 to 6200.

knots (mph). The accuracy of such readings does not support this level of precision unless the device has been carefully calibrated. Speed over the bottom (speed made good) may be accurately shown by a GPS receiver, and will be shown accurately when using Differential GPS. Speed is calculated to the nearest tenth of a knot or mile per hour. It is seldom accurately measurable to such fine units, but a calculation to the nearest tenth is not inconsistent with the expressed standards of precision of distance and time. This same degree of precision is used in calculations of current velocity.

Position

Geographic coordinates are expressed to the nearest tenth of a minute, or whole minute, of latitude and longitude, or to the nearest second, as determined by the scale of the chart. As explained in Chapter 15, latitude and longitude markings are subdivided into minutes and seconds on the larger-scale charts (1:49,000 and larger) and in fractions of minutes on smaller-scale charts (1:50,000 and smaller). The smallest scale charts may show whole minutes without fractions.

Don't be misled by the displays of GPS and Loran receivers. Most models show position in latitude and longitude to a finer degree of precision than is warranted by the radionavigation system being used—one more decimal place than is justified.

Depths & Heights of Tide

Tidal variations in the depth of water are normally tabulated to the nearest tenth of a foot (or meter); calculations are carried out to the same degree of precision. Remember, however, that the effects of tidal action by winds and atmospheric pressure make this degree of precision hardly warranted.

DEAD RECKONING

When operating your boat in large bodies of water, you should always have at least a rough knowledge of your position on the chart. Basic to such knowledge is a technique of navigation known as DEAD RECKONING (DR). This is the advancement of the boat's position on the chart from its last accurately determined location, using the courses steered and speeds though the water. Note that no allowance is made for the effects of wind, waves, current, or steering errors. This may seem strange, but the reasoning will become clear in Chapter 18, the chapter covering position determination.

Much piloting is now done with electronics, but equipment can fail—often at the worst possible time. It is dead reckoning that will get you safely to your destination. It is not some relic left over from the days of sailing ships; it is an essential part of the navigation of any vessel.

Terms Used in Dead Reckoning

Dead reckoning follows some important conventions for recording information on the chart. The DR TRACK (or DR TRACK LINE) is the path that a boat would be expected to follow, or is believed to be following, without any allowance for the offsetting influences mentioned above. It is represented on the chart by a line drawn from the last known position using courses and distances through the water. The path the boat actually travels may be different due to one or more offsetting influences, to be considered in Chapter 18.

COURSE, abbreviated "C," is the direction in which a boat is to be steered, or is being steered—in other words, the direction of travel through the water. Courses are normally plotted as true directions labeled with three-digit figures with leading zeros added as necessary: 8° becomes 008; 42° becomes 042. The degree symbol is not used. Some skippers may plot and label courses as magnetic or compass directions. There is no need to add a "T" following the numbers if the course is a true direction, but do add a space following with "M" or "C" to indicate a magnetic or compass direction, if applicable.

HEADING is different from course; it is the direction in which a boat is pointed at any given moment. For example, a sailboat proceeding upwind will typically have a heading that varies from its course by several degrees. Heading is often given in terms of magnetic or compass directions; these values are not part of a plot.

SPEED, abbreviated "S," is the rate of travel through the water. This is the DR track speed; it is used, with elapsed time, to determine DR POSITIONS along the track line. (Speed is shown on a plot only for a vessel underway.)

DISTANCE, abbreviated "D," may be used with a DR plot of a future intended track.

The Basic Principles of Dead Reckoning

You should follow these basic principles of dead reckoning:

1. *A DR track is always started from a known position.*

2. *For a DR track, use either true or magnetic courses consistently and label appropriately.*

3. *Only the speed through the water is used for determining distance traveled and a DR position* *along the track.* (The reason why speed over the bottom is not used is discussed in Chapter 18.)

Rules for when to plot a DR position are given on page 580.

The Importance of Dead Reckoning

You should always plot a DR track when navigating in large, open bodies of water, especially when aids to navigation or landmarks are not available, or when visibility is poor. You should also plot a DR track whenever there is the possibility of an emergency arising. In such a situation it might suddenly be necessary to report your position to the Coast Guard or other source of assistance. In other words, keeping a DR track is a part of safe boating and is almost always important.

A DR track is the primary representation of your boat's path, the base to which other factors, such as the effect of current, are applied. Dead reckoning is the basic method of navigation to which you will apply corrections and adjustments from other sources of information.

At the same time, remember that this DR track rarely represents your boat's actual progress. If there were no steering errors, speed errors, or external influences, the DR track could be used as a means of determining your boat's position at any time, as well as the ETA (ESTIMATED TIME OF ARRIVAL) at a destination. But even with errors and external influences a DR plot is always an important safety measure in the event of unexpected variations in current, and if you encounter fog or other loss of visibility.

Plotting

Fundamental to the use of dead reckoning is the use of charts and plots of a boat's intended and actual positions. You should always use standard SYMBOLS and LABELS so your chart work will be clear to you and understandable to another person (and to yourself at a later date!).

Basic Requirements

The basic requirements of plotting are *accuracy, neatness,* and *completeness.* All measurements taken from the chart must be made carefully, all direct observations must be made as accurately as conditions on a small boat permit, and all calculations should be made in full and in writing. If time permits, each of these actions should be repeated as a check; errors can be costly!

Neatness in plotting is essential to avoid confusion of information on the chart. Drawing extra or overly long lines on charts or scribbling extraneous notes on them may obscure vital information.

Information on a chart must also be complete. You will often need to refer back to information that you placed on the chart hours or days ago, and it can be dangerous to rely on memory to supply details.

Labeling

Draw lines on your charts lightly and no longer then necessary. Keep your straightedge slightly off the desired position of the line you are drawing, to allow for the thickness of the pencil point, no matter how fine it may be. Failure to do this may result in small errors that can accumulate and make your DR positions inaccurate

The requirements of neatness and completeness combine to establish a need for *labeling.* Immediately after drawing any line on a chart, or plotting any point, label it. The basic rules for labeling are:

1. *The label for any line is placed along that line.*

2. *The label for any point should not be along any line*—it should make an angle with any line so that its nature as the label of a point will be unmistakably clear.

The above basic rules are applied in the labeling of DR plots in the following manner:

• Use plain, block upper-case letters and numbers. Labels should be placed so that they can be read with the top or left side of the chart up. If space does not allow a label to be placed as described below, it is acceptable to place it in an adjacent clear area with an S-shaped arrow pointing to where it would normally appear.

• The direction label is placed *above* the track line as a three-digit number, preceded by "C" for course and followed, if applicable, by "M" or "C" to indicate magnetic or compass. Use a space between the figures and any letters. Note that "T" (for true direction), periods, and the degree symbol "°" are omitted.

• The speed along the track is indicated by numerals placed *under* the track line, usually directly beneath the direction and preceded by a space and the letter "S"; see **Figure 16-22.** Units, such as knots or mph, are omitted.

• A known position at the start of a DR track, a FIX (see Chapter 18), is shown as a circle across the line; a small dot may be placed on the line for emphasis. It is labeled with time *written horizontally;* the word "fix" is understood and is not shown; see **Figure 16-23.**

• A DR position, calculated as a distance along the track at the set speed through the water, is shown as a half-circle (with a dot) along the track line; it is labeled with the time *placed at an angle to the course line but not horizontally.* "DR" is understood and is not written in; see **Figure 16-24.**

• When planning and preplotting a run, speed, which is often affected by sea conditions, may not be known in advance. In this case, distance, "D," may be labeled *below* the course line in lieu of speed; units (nautical or statute miles) are not shown.

Further applications of the basic rules of labeling will be given as additional piloting procedures and situations are introduced in Chapters 17 and 18.

All lines on a chart should be erased when no longer needed, to keep the chart clear. Erasures should be made as lightly as possible to avoid damaging the chart and obscuring its printed information.

D, T & S Calculations

As mentioned earlier, calculations involving distance (D), time (T), and speed (S) are often made with a small mechanical (slide-rule or circular) calculator. Use of a calculator is acceptable, but you should also be able to make your calculations accurately and quickly without one, using only a simple set of equations and ordinary arithmetic. The three basic equations are:

$$D = ST \qquad S = \frac{D}{T} \qquad T = \frac{D}{S}$$

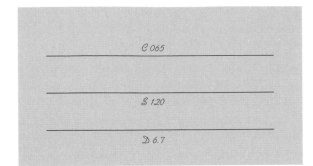

Figure 16-22 Course is labeled above the line with C followed by a space and the direction as a three-digit number (add leading zeros as necessary) followed by a space and then M or C if the direction is magnetic or compass; no letter is used if it is true. Speed is labeled beneath the line with the letter S in front of it. Or distance can be shown below the course line with the designator D. Note the space between the letters and the numbers here also.

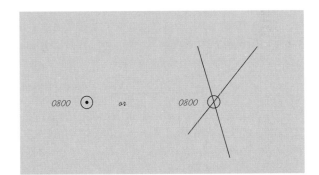

Figure 16-23 A known position of the boat is plotted as a dot with a small circle around it. If it is at the intersection of two lines, the dot need not be used. Label the position with the time as a four-digit number in the 24-hour system, written horizontally.

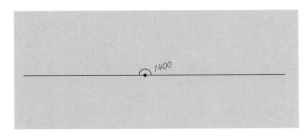

Figure 16-24 A DR position along a track, without a change in course or speed, is plotted as a half-circle around a dot on the line. Add the time as for a known position, but not written horizontally.

Where D is distance in miles, T is time in hours, and S is speed in knots or miles per hour as determined by the type of mile being used. Note carefully that T is in *hours* in these basic equations. To use time in *minutes,* as is more normally the case, the equations are modified to read:

$$D = \frac{ST}{60} \qquad S = \frac{60D}{T} \qquad T = \frac{60D}{S}$$

Examples of the use of these practical equations may serve to make them clearer:

1. You are cruising at 14 knots; how far will you travel in 40 minutes?

$$D = \frac{ST}{60} \qquad D = \frac{14 \times 40}{60} = 9.3 \text{ miles}$$

Note that the calculated answer of 9.33 is rounded to the nearest tenth according to the rule for the degree of precision to be used in stating distance.

2. On one of the Great Lakes, it took you 40 minutes to travel 11 miles; what is your speed?

$$S = \frac{60D}{T} \qquad S = \frac{60 \times 11}{40} = 16.5 \text{ mph}$$

3. You have 9.5 miles to go to reach your destination; on a broad reach you are sailing at 6.5 knots; how long will it take you to get there?

$$T = \frac{60D}{S} \qquad T = \frac{60 \times 9.5}{6.5} = 88 \text{ minutes}$$

Note again the rounding of results; the calculated answer of 87.6 minutes is used as 88 minutes. In powerboat piloting contests, however, it would probably be used as 87.6 minutes, or as 87 minutes 36 seconds.

The equations are also usable with kilometers and km/h. Memorize the three equations for distance, speed, and time. Practice using them until you are thoroughly familiar with them, and can get correct answers quickly.

The Three-Minute Rule

For short distances, the "Three-Minute Rule" is very handy. Add two zeros to the speed you are making in knots, and you will have the distance, in yards, that you will travel in three minutes, to an approximation close enough for practical navigation.

Use of Logarithmic Scale on Charts

Charts of the National Ocean Service (NOS) at scales of 1:40,000 and larger have printed on them a logarithmic speed scale.

To find speed: Place one point of your dividers on the mark on the scale indicating the distance in nautical miles, and the other point on the number corresponding to the time in minutes; see **Figure 16-25.** Without changing the spread between the divider arms, place the right point on the "60" at the right end of the scale; the left point will then indicate on the scale the speed in knots.

To determine time: Use the same logarithmic scale to determine the time required *to cover a given distance at a specified speed* (for situations not exceeding one hour). Set the two divider points on the scale marks representing speed in knots and distance in miles. Move the dividers, without changing the spread, until the right point is at "60" on the scale; the other point will indicate the time in minutes.

To determine distance: Using knowledge of time and speed, distance likewise can be determined from this logarithmic scale. Set the right point of the dividers on "60" and the left point at the mark on the scale corresponding to the speed in

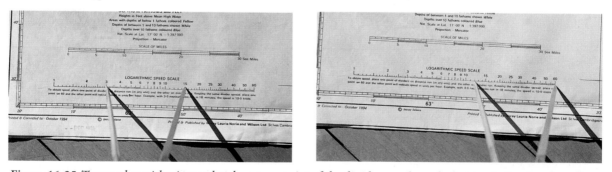

Figure 16-25 To use a logarithmic speed scale, set one point of the dividers on the scale division indicating the miles traveled, and the other point on the number corresponding to the time, in minutes. With the dividers maintaining the same spread, transfer them so that the right point is on the "60" of the scale; the left point then indicates the speed in knots or mph.

knots. Then, without changing the spread, move the right point to the mark on the scale representing the time in minutes; the left point indicates the distance in nautical miles.

The logarithmic scale is used in the same manner with distances in statute miles and speeds in mph.

NOS charts have instructions for determining speed printed beneath the logarithmic scale, but not the procedures for determining distance or time. In all cases, you must know two of the three quantities in order to determine the other.

Use of S-D-T Calculators

It is not practicable here to give detailed instructions for operating all models of speed-distance-time slide rule or circular calculators. In general, they will have two or more scales, each logarithmically subdivided. The calculator will be set using two of the factors and the answer, the third factor, will be read off at an index mark; refer to **Figure 16-20.**

If you have a calculator for S-D-T problems, read the instructions carefully and practice with it sufficiently, using simple, self-evident problems, to be sure you can get reliable results later even in emergency.

Speed Curves

Although many boats may have marine speedometers, the traditional method for determining speed of powerboats is through the use of engine speed as measured by a TACHOMETER in revolutions per minute (rpm). A SPEED CURVE is prepared as a plot on cross-section (graph) paper of the boat's speed in knots or mph for various engine speeds in rpm.

Factors Affecting Speed Curves

The boat's speed at a specified engine setting may be affected by several factors. The extent of each effect will vary with the size of the boat, type of hull, and other characteristics.

LOAD is a primary factor influencing a boat's speed. The number of people aboard, the amount of fuel and water in the tanks, and the amount and location of other weights on board will affect the depth to which the hull sinks into the water (the

displacement) and the angular trim. Both displacement and trim may be expected to have an effect on speed.

Another major factor affecting speed is the UNDERWATER HULL CONDITION. Fouling growth like barnacles or moss increases the drag (the resistance to movement through the water), and slows the boat at any speed. Fouling on the propeller itself will drastically affect performance.

Whenever preparing speed data on a boat, note the loading and underwater hull conditions as well as the figures for rpm and speed. If you make a speed curve at the start of the season, when the bottom is clean, check it later in the season if your boat is used in waters where fouling is a problem. You may need a new speed curve, or you may be able to determine a small correction that can give you a more accurate determination of speed. You should also know what speed differences to expect from full tanks to half or nearly empty; the differences can be surprising.

Obtaining Speed Curves

Speed curves are obtained by making repeated runs over a known distance using different throttle settings and timing each run accurately. You can use any reasonable distance, but it should not be less than a half-mile so small timing errors will not excessively influence the results; yet, it need not be more than a mile, to avoid excessive time and fuel requirements for the trials.

The run need not be an even half-mile or mile if the distance is accurately known. Do not depend upon floating aids to navigation—they

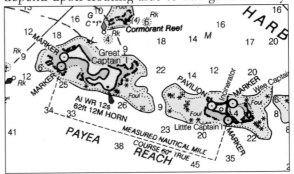

Figure 16-26 Measured miles are often established and indicated on charts for measuring vessel speed. Even if your boat has a speedometer, make timed runs over this distance to check its accuracy.

may be slightly off station, and, in any event, they have some scope on their anchor chains and will swing about under the effects of wind and current. Some areas will have a MEASURED MILE (or half-mile); see **Figure 16-26.** These are accurately surveyed distances with each end marked by a range. Use these courses whenever possible; they are accurate, and calculations are easier with the even-mile distance. But do not let the absence of a measured mile keep you from making a speed curve. Wharves, fixed aids to navigation, or points of land will also give you the accurate distance you need.

In most speed trials you will need to run the known distance twice, one in each direction, in order to allow for the effects of current. Even in waters not affected by currents, you should make round-trip runs for each throttle setting to allow for wind effects.

For each *one-way* run, measure the time and steer your boat carefully to make the most direct run. Compute the speed for each run by the equations on page 576. Tables are available that give speeds for various elapsed times over a measured mile. If the measured distance is an exact half-mile, just divide the tabulated speeds by two. Then average the *speeds* of each pair of runs at a given rpm, for the true speed of the boat through the water. The strength of the current is one-half the difference between the speeds in the two directions of any pair of runs. *Caution:* do *not* average the *times* of a pair of runs to get a single time for use in the calculations; this will *not* give you the correct value for speed through the water.

If time is measured with a regular clock or watch, be careful in making the subtractions to get "elapsed time." Remember that there are 60 seconds in each minute, not 100, and likewise 60

RPM	NORTH-SOUTH		SOUTH-NORTH		AVERAGE SPEED	CURRENT
	TIME	SPEED	TIME	SPEED		
900	7M 54S	7.59	11M 25S	5.25	6.42	1.14
1100	6M 53S	8.72	9M 14.2S	6.50	7.61	1.11
1300	6M 08.8S	9.76	7M 38.6S	7.85	8.92	0.95
1500	5M 35.8S	10.71	6M 40.4S	9.00	9.86	0.86
1700	5M 10.8S	11.58	5M 54.2S	10.17	10.88	0.71
1900	4M 38S	12.96	5M 06.4S	11.71	12.36	0.61
2150	3M 48.6S	15.75	4M 05.6S	14.67	15.21	0.54

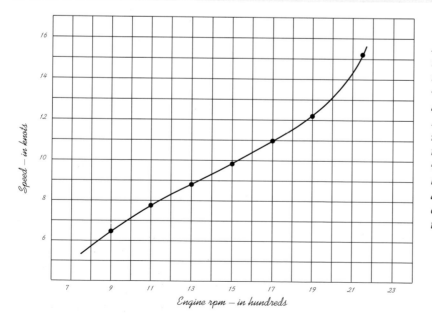

Figure 16-27 During the speed trials for Trident, the results were tabulated as shown at top. Runs were made in each direction to account for the effect of current. Entries in the craft's log were made for the hull bottom condition and the state of fuel and water tanks. The speed curve at bottom, plotted from this data, is accurate only for the load and hull conditions similar to those during the speed trials.

minutes in one hour. Most people are so used to decimal calculations that they make errors when "borrowing" in the subtraction of clock times.

If one is willing to use a slightly more complex equation, the boat's speed through the water (or the strength of the current) can be found from a single calculation using the times of the two runs of each pair.

$$S = \frac{60D(Tu + Td)}{2TuTd} \qquad Cur = \frac{60D(Tu - Td)}{2TuTd}$$

Where S is speed through the water in knots or mph

Cur is current in knots or mph

Tu is time upstream, in minutes

Td is time downstream, in minutes

D is distance, in nautical or statute miles

In preparing a speed curve for a boat, make enough pairs of runs to provide points for a plot of speed versus rpm; six or eight points will usually be enough for a satisfactory curve. With some types of hulls, there will be a break in the curve at a critical speed when the hull changes from displacement action to semi-planing action. At this portion of the curve you may need additional, more closely spaced measurements, so it is a good idea to calculate speed during runs and make a rough plot as you go along—obvious errors in timing will be readily seen.

You may also want to calculate the current's strength for each pair of runs. The current values will probably vary during the speed trials, but the variations should be small and in a consistent direction, either steadily increasing or decreasing, or going through a slack period. You will get the best results by running your trials at a time of minimum current.

Example of a Speed Curve

A set of speed trials was run for the motor yacht *Trident* over the measured mile off Kent Island in Chesapeake Bay. This is an excellent course because it is marked both by buoys offshore as well as by ranges on land. The presence of the buoys aids in steering a straight run from one end of the course to the other; the ranges are used for accuracy in timing.

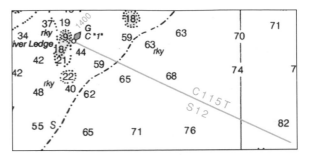

Figure 16-28 A dead reckoning (DR) plot is started when leaving a known position. This is plotted as a fix, with the time labeled; course and speed are labeled along the course line.

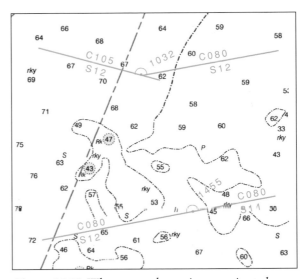

Figure 16-29 Whenever a change in course is made a DR position is plotted for that time; the new course and speed are labeled along the new DR track. If a variation in speed is made without a change in direction, B, a DR position is plotted for that time, and new course and speed labels are entered following it.

On this particular day, it was not convenient to wait for slack water, but a time was selected that would result in something less than maximum ebbing current. A table was set up in the log, and runs were made in each direction at speeds of normal interest from 900 rpm to 2150 rpm, which was maximum for the Detroit 6-71 diesels.

The results of the runs are shown in **Figure 16-27**, upper. An entry was also made in the log that these trials were made with fuel tanks 0.4 full, the water tanks approximately one-third full, and with a clean bottom. The column of the table marked "Current" is not necessary, but it serves as

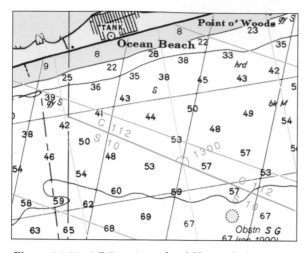

Figure 16-30 A DR position should basically be plotted every hour on the hour. In conditions of reduced visibility, the interval between DR positions should be shortened.

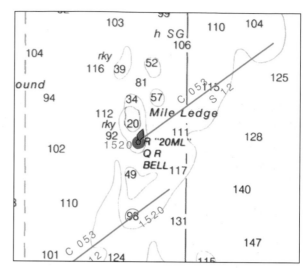

Figure 16-31 Start a new DR track whenever the boat's position is fixed. In this example, a fix is obtained when the craft passes alongside an identified aid to navigation. Label the old DR with the same time as the fix.

a flag to quickly expose any inconsistent data. Note that on these trials the current is decreasing at a reasonably consistent rate.

After the runs had been completed, a plot was made on cross-section paper of the boat's speed as a function of engine rpm. This resulted in the speed curve shown as **Figure 16-27,** lower.

Dead Reckoning Plots

With knowledge of dead reckoning terms and principles, the rules for labeling points and lines, and the procedures for making calculations involving distance, time, and speed, you can now consider the use of DR plots.

There are several specific rules for making and using DR plots.

• *A DR plot should be started when leaving a known position;* see **Figure 16-28.**

• *A DR position should be shown whenever a change is made in course;* see **Figure 16-30,** plot A; *or in speed;* see **Figure 16-29,** plot B.

• *A DR position should be plotted each hour on the hour (more frequently under conditions of reduced visibility);* see **Figure 16-30.**

• *A new DR track should be started each time the boat's position is fixed. The old DR position for the same time as the fix should also be shown at the end of the old DR track;* see **Figure 16-31.**

Tides & Currents

The Nature of Tides & Their Causes • Tidal Predictions & Calculations
Currents & Their Prediction • The Effects of Currents on Piloting

An understanding of tides and currents is important to a skipper in coastal waters, as these can to some extent affect where he or she can travel or anchor safely, how long it will take to get there—or the speed that will be needed to arrive at a given time—and the heading that must be maintained to make good a given course over the bottom.

Here we should reemphasize the proper meaning and use of some terms that often are used incorrectly. TIDE is the rise and fall of the ocean level as a result of changes in the gravitational attraction between earth, moon, and sun. It is a *vertical* motion only. CURRENT is the *horizontal* motion of water from any cause. TIDAL CURRENT is the flow of water from one point to another that results from a difference in tidal heights at those points. To say "The tide certainly is running strongly today!" is not correct, for tides may be high or low, but they do not "run." The correct expression would be "The tidal current certainly is strong today." Remember—tide is vertical change; current is horizontal flow.

TIDES

Tides originate in the open oceans and seas, but are only noticeable and significant close to shore. The effect of tides will be observed along coastal beaches, in bays and sounds, and up rivers generally as far as the first rapids, waterfall, or dam. Curiously, the effect of tides may be more noticeable a hundred miles up a river than it is at the

Previous Page: Figure 17-01 The rise and fall of ocean tidal levels cause a flow first into and then out of inland bodies of water such as bays, sounds, and the lower reaches of rivers. Because they can set a boat off its course, these tidal currents have important effects in piloting.

river's mouth, because water piles up higher in the river's narrower stretches; see **Figure 17-01**. Coastal regions in which the water levels are subject to tidal action are commonly referred to as "tidewater" areas.

Definition of Terms

In addition to the basic definition of tide as given above, certain other terms used in connection with tidal action must be defined. The height of tide at any specified time is the vertical measurement between the surface of the water and the tidal datum, or reference plane, typically at what is called mean lower low water; see page 585. Do not confuse "height of tide" with "depth of water." The latter is the total distance from the surface to the bottom. The tidal datum for an area is selected so that the heights of tide are normally positive values, but the height can at times be a small negative number when the water level falls below the datum.

HIGH WATER, or HIGH TIDE, is the highest level reached by an ascending tide; see **Figure 17-02**. Correspondingly, LOW WATER, or LOW TIDE, is the lowest level reached by a descending tide. The difference between high and low waters is the RANGE of the tide.

The change in tidal level does not occur at a uniform rate; starting from low water, the level builds up slowly, then at an increasing rate which in turn tapers off as high water is reached. The decrease in tidal stage from high water to low follows a corresponding pattern of a slow buildup to a maximum rate roughly midway between stages, followed by a decreasing rate. At both high and low tides, there will be periods of relatively no change in level; these are termed STAND. MEAN SEA LEVEL is the average level of the open ocean, and corresponds closely to mid-tide levels offshore; it is not used in navigation.

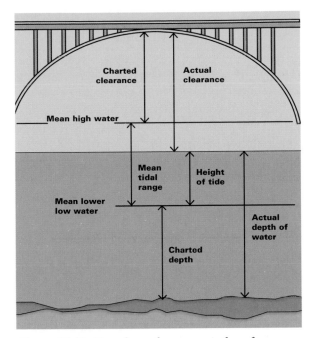

Figure 17-02 Mean lower low water is the reference level for all NOS tide levels. Bridge clearances are measured from mean high water. Tidal range is the difference between a given high water and the adjacent low water. Mean tidal range is the difference between mean lower water and mean high water.

Tidal Theory

Tidal theory involves the interaction of gravitational and centrifugal forces—the inward attractions of the earth on one hand and the sun and the moon on the other, balanced by the outward forces resulting from the revolution of the earth in its orbit; see **Figure 17-03.** The gravitational and centrifugal forces are in balance as a whole—otherwise the bodies would fly apart from each other or else crash together—but they are not quite in balance at most points on the earth's surface, and this is what causes the tides. The effects of the sun and moon will be described separately, even though, of course, they act simultaneously.

Earth-Sun Effects

Although not precisely the case, the earth can be thought of as revolving around the sun, and just as a stone tied to the end of a string tends to sail off when a young boy whirls it about his head, so the earth tends to fly off into space. This effect is known as centrifugal force; it is shown at the left

in **Figure 17-03.** (Remember that we are talking about the centrifugal force related to the sun-earth system, and not that of the spinning of the earth on its own axis.)

The earth is kept from flying off into space by the gravitational attraction of the sun, shown at the right in **Figure 17-03.** These forces are in overall balance.

This balance is not exact at all points. The centrifugal force is everywhere the same, and parallel to a line from the center of the earth to the center of the sun. Gravitational forces are *not* everywhere equal and parallel; from each point on the earth's surface, they extend toward the center of the sun, greater on the nearer side as a result of the lesser distance. **Figure 17-03** shows these forces at representative points, and the resultant force from their combination.

In theory, we can think of the earth as being a smooth sphere uniformly covered with water (no land areas). **Figure 17-04** shows how the resultant forces cause the water to flow toward the areas of the earth's surface that are *both nearest and farthest* from the sun; here there will be "high tides." As this water flows, the areas from which it comes will have less water, and hence "low tides." (The tides on the side of the earth nearer the sun are slightly greater than those on the far side, but the difference is not great, only about 5 percent.)

As the earth rotates on its axis, once every 24 hours, the line of direction to the sun constantly changes. Thus each point of the earth's surface

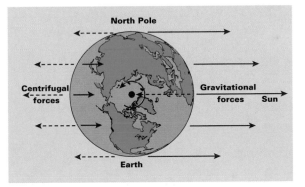

Figure 17-03 Tides result from the differences between centrifugal and gravitational forces. The forces illustrated here represent the interaction of the earth and sun; corresponding forces result from the relationship of the moon and the earth.

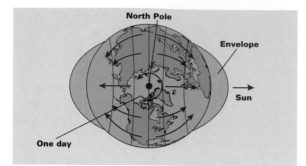

Figure 17-04 In a theoretical simplification, high tides are created on opposite sides of the earth at the same time. The gravitational attraction of the sun (or moon) pulls one way and the centrifugal force of the earth's orbit pulls the other way.

will have two high and two low tides each day. As a result of the tilt of the earth's axis, the pairs of highs, and those of the lows, will not normally be of exactly the same level.

Earth-Moon Effects

The moon is commonly thought of as revolving about the earth; actually, the two bodies revolve around a common point on a monthly cycle. This point is located about 2,900 miles (4,667 km) from the center of the earth toward the moon (about 1,100 miles or 1,770 km deep *inside* the earth).

Both tend to fly away from this common point (centrifugal force), but the mutual gravitational attraction acts as a counterbalance, and they remain the same distance apart. However, the gravitational pull of the moon effects the waters of the earth in the same manner as the pull of the sun.

Spring & Neap Tides

Now combine the earth-sun and the earth-moon systems. Although the mass of the moon is only a tiny fraction of that of the sun, it is much closer to the earth (about 238,860 miles or 384,400 km away). Thus its tidal forces are roughly 2¼ times greater than those of the sun (about 92,900,000 miles or 149,500,000 km away). The result is that the observed tide usually "follows the moon," but the action is somewhat modified by the sun's relative position. The two high and two low waters each day occur about 50 minutes later than the corresponding tides of the previous day.

In the course of any one lunar month, the three bodies line up in sun-moon-earth and sun-earth-moon relationships; see **Figure 17-05.** These are the times of the new and full moon, respectively. In both cases, the sun's effect lines up with and reinforces the moon's effect, tending to result in greater-than-average tidal ranges (usually about 20

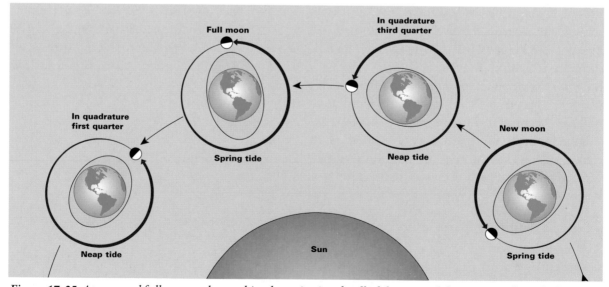

Figure 17-05 At new and full moons, the combined gravitational pull of the sun and the moon produce the largest tidal variations. These tides, which occur twice a month, are called "spring" tides. At the first and third quarters of the moon, the two gravitational forces partially offset each other and the net tidal effect is less; these tides are called "neap" tides.

percent) called SPRING TIDES; note that this name has nothing to do with the season of the year.

At other positions in **Figure 17-05,** when the moon is at its first and third quarters, the tidal "bulge" caused by the sun is at right angles to that caused by the moon (they are said to be "in QUAD-RATURE"). The two tidal effects are in conflict and partially cancel each other, resulting in smaller-than-average ranges (again about 20 percent); these are NEAP TIDES.

Note that the tidal range of any given point varies from month to month, and from year to year. The monthly variation results from the fact that the earth is not at the center of the moon's orbit. When the moon is closest to the earth (at PERIGEE), the lunar influence is maximum and tides will have the greatest ranges. Conversely, when the moon is farthest from the earth (at APOGEE), its effect and tidal ranges are least.

In a similar manner, the yearly variations in the daily ranges of the tides are caused by the changing gravitational effects of the sun as the body's distance from the earth becomes greater or less.

Actual Tides

The actual tide that we observe often seems to be at odds with the theoretical forces that govern it. Here are the main reasons for this:

• Great masses of land, the continents, irregularly shaped and irregularly placed, act to interrupt, restrict, and reflect tidal movements.

• Water, although generally appearing to flow freely, is actually a somewhat viscous substance that lags in its response to tidal forces.

• Friction is present as the ocean waters "rub" against the ocean bottom.

• The depth to the bottom of the sea, varying widely, influences the speed of the horizontal tidal motion.

• The depths of the ocean areas and the restrictions of the continents often result in "basins" that have their own way of responding to tidal forces.

Although these reasons account for great differences between theoretical tidal forces and actual observed tides, they nevertheless remain definite, constant relationships between the two at any particular location. By observing the tide, and relating these observations with the movements of the sun, moon, and earth, these constant relationships can be determined. With this information, tides can be predicted for any future date at a given place.

Types of Tides

A tide that each day has two high waters approximately equal in height, and two low waters also about equal, is known as a SEMIDIURNAL tide. This is the most common tide, and, in the United States, occurs along the East Coast; see **Figure 17-06,** left.

In a monthly cycle, the moon moves north and south of the equator; the importance of this action to tides is illustrated in **Figure 17-07.** Point *A* is under a bulge in the envelope. One half-day later, at point *B*, it is again under the bulge but the height is not as large as *A*. This situation, combined with coastal characteristics, tends to give rise to a "twice daily" tide with unequal high and/or low waters in some areas. This is known as the MIXED type of tide; refer to **Figure 17-06,** center. The term "low water" may be modified to indicate the more pronounced of the two lows. This tidal stage is termed LOWER LOW WATER and is averaged over a complete tidal

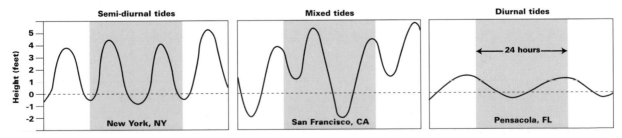

Figure 17-06 The daily cycle of tides (a 24-hour period is shown in blue) varies widely from place to place. There are three basic types—semidiurnal (left), mixed (center), and diurnal (right).

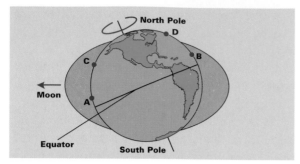

Figure 17-07 As the moon travels north and south of the earth's equatorial plane, it causes variations in the daily cycle at any given location on earth. Similar, but smaller, effects result from the sun's change in position with respect to the equator.

cycle of approximately 19 years to determine the "mean lower low water" (MLLW); this is used as the tidal datum in many areas subject to mixed tides; refer to **Figure 17-02**. Likewise, the more significant of the higher tides is termed HIGHER HIGH WATER.

Now consider point *C* in **Figure 17-07**. At this place, it is still under the bulge of the envelope. At point *D*, however, which is the same latitude as point *C*, it is above the low part. Point *C* will reach the orientation of point *D* after one half day of the earth's rotation. Hence the tidal forces tend to cause only one high and one low water each day (actually each 24 hours and 50 minutes approximately). This is the DIURNAL type, typified by Pensacola, Florida; refer to **Figure 17-06,** right.

Whenever the moon is farthest north (as in **Figure 17-07**) or south, there will be a tendency to have the diurnal or mixed type. When the moon lies over the equator, we tend to have the semidiurnal type. These are EQUATORIAL TIDES and the tendency toward producing inequality is then at a minimum.

These theoretical considerations are modified, however, by many practical factors such as the general configuration of the coastline.

Special Tide Situations

Peculiarities in the tide can be found almost everywhere, but none compare with those in the Bay of Fundy of eastern North America. Twice each day, the waters surge in and out of the Bay

producing, at Burntcoat Head, the highest tidal range in the world; a typical rise and fall of nearly 44 feet (13.4 meters). At normal spring tides, it rises 51.5 feet (15.7 m) and on perigee springs, as much as 53 feet or 16.2 meters.

The great range is often attributed to the funnel-like shape of the Bay, but this is not the main cause. Just as the water in a wash basin will slosh when you move your hand back and forth in just the right period of time, depending upon the depth of the water and the shape of the basin, so the tide will attempt to oscillate water in bays in cycles of 12 hours and 25 minutes. It would be a coincidence, indeed, if a bay were of such a shape and depth as to have a complete oscillation with a period of exactly 12 hours and 25 minutes. A bay can easily have a *part* of such an oscillation, however, such is the case in the Bay of Fundy.

A further factor in the large tidal ranges in the Bay of Fundy is that they are significantly affected by the Gulf of Maine tides, which, in turn, are affected by the open ocean tides. The relationships between these tides are such as to exaggerate their ranges.

Reference Planes

As mentioned, the heights of tides are reckoned from the specific reference plane, or datum. Although in the past, different datums were used on the Atlantic, Gulf, and Pacific Coasts of the United States, for all areas the predictions and charts of the National Ocean Service (NOS) are now based on a datum of mean lower low water.

The Importance of Tides

A good knowledge of tidal action is essential for safe navigation. The skipper of a boat of any size will be faced many times with the need to know the time of high water or low water, and their probable heights. He may want to cross some shoal area, passable at certain tidal stages but not at others. He may be about to anchor, and the scope to pay out will be affected by the tide's range. He may be going to tie up to a pier or wharf in a strange harbor, and needs to know about the tides to adjust his lines properly for overnight.

Sources of Tidal Information

The basic source of information on the time of high and low water, and their heights above (or below) the datum, are the TIDE TABLES prepared by the National Ocean Service. NOS no longer publishes these tables for sale to the public, but rather provides the data to several commercial contractors who do the actual printing in book format; refer to Chapter 15, **Figure 15-38.** This data is also used by companies that prepare programs of tidal information for personal computers and other electronic devices.

For information on predictions, contact NOAA/National Ocean Services, CO-OP, Products & Services Division, 1305 East-West Highway, Silver Spring, MD 20910-3281; voice 301-713-2815, Ext. 119; fax 301-713-4500 email to Tide.Predictions@noaa.gov; website www.co-ops.nos.noaa.gov. NOS can provide, for a fee, a complete compilation of predictions on a CD-ROM, or for a more limited area on 3.5-inch disks.

Any predictions appearing in newspapers or broadcast over radio and TV stations will have been extracted from these tables (and usually have been converted to daylight time, if in effect). Small-craft charts include tidal information in their margins or on the cover jacket, if one is used; see **Figure 17-08.**

Some reproduction of the tables in cruising guides may not use the table number, and may or may not be adjusted for daylight time.

Not to be overlooked is the possibility of "local knowledge." Never hesitate to ask experienced local boaters when you are in unfamiliar waters and need information of any kind. The best of the tables prepared by electronic computers sometimes cannot compare with a firsthand knowledge of what to expect that is based on years of local experience.

Tide Tables

Tide Tables are of great value in determining the height of water at any place at a given time. They are calculated in advance and published annually in four volumes, one of which covers the East Coast of North and South America, and another the West Coast of these continents.

The *Tide Tables* from various commercial publishers can usually be bought at any authorized sales agent for NOS charts or a nautical bookstore.

The *Tide Tables* give the predicted times and heights of high and low water for each day of the year at important points known as REFERENCE STATIONS. Portland, Boston, Sandy Hook, and Key West are examples of points for which detailed information is given in the East Coast *Tide Tables.* Reference stations in the West Coast *Tide Tables* include San Diego, the Golden Gate at San Francisco, and Aberdeen, Washington.

Crescent City, California, 2002
Times and Heights of High and Low Waters

		October							November							December				
		Time	Height			Time	Height			Time	Height			Time	Height			Time	Height	
		h m	ft	cm		h m	ft	cm		h m	ft	cm		h m	ft	cm		h m	ft	cm
1 Tu	0058 0804 1258 1842	0.6 5.3 3.7 6.3	18 162 113 192	**16** W	0215 0859 1448 2031	0.7 6.1 2.6 6.0	21 186 79 183	**1** F	0205 0839 1447 2042	0.5 6.8 1.6 6.4	15 207 49 195	**16** Sa	0250 0911 1546 2153	1.9 6.8 1.1 5.6	58 207 34 171	**1** Su	0214 0836 1525 2142	1.7 7.9 -0.1 6.0	52 241 -3 183	**16** M	0238 0851 1557 2229	3.1 7.2 0.4 5.4	94 219 12 165
2 W	0156 0847 1404 1951	0.2 5.7 3.1 6.6	6 174 94 201	**17** Th	0300 0932 1531 2122	0.8 6.3 2.1 6.1	24 192 64 186	**2** Sa	0253 0916 1537 2142	0.7 7.4 0.6 6.6	21 226 18 201	**17** Su	0326 0937 1621 2237	2.2 7.0 0.6 5.7	67 213 18 174	**2** M	0304 0917 1614 2241	2.1 8.3 -0.9 6.2	64 253 -27 189	**17** Tu	0319 0923 1633 2312	3.3 7.4 0.0 5.6	101 226 0 171
3 Th	0246 0923 1458 2052	-0.1 6.2 2.3 7.0	-3 189 70 213	**18** F	0338 1000 1608 2206	1.0 6.5 1.6 6.1	30 198 49 186	**3** Su	0338 0952 1625 2240	0.9 7.9 -0.3 6.7	27 241 -9 204	**18** M	0359 1003 1654 2319	2.5 7.2 0.2 5.8	76 219 6 177	**3** Tu	0352 0958 1701 ● 2337	2.5 8.6 -1.5 6.4	76 262 -46 195	**18** W	0358 0956 1708 2353	3.5 7.6 -0.4 5.8	107 232 -12 177

Figure 17-08 Small-craft charts provide annual tidal predictions for reference stations covered by the chart. Information tabulated for marinas and other boating facilities include data on the mean tidal range and the time difference from the applicable reference station.

San Diego, California

Times and Heights of High and Low Waters

January

Day	Time	ft	cm	Day	Time	ft	cm
1 W	0014	2.2	67	**16** Th	0553	6.4	195
	0639	6.3	192		1320	-0.9	-27
	1400	-0.7	-21		1950	3.9	119
	2027	3.9	119				
2 Th	0059	2.2	67	**17** F	0022	2.1	64
	0718	6.5	198		0644	7.0	213
	1435	-0.9	-27		1400	-1.5	-46
	2103	4.0	122		2029	4.2	128
3 F	0136	2.2	67	**18** Sa	0115	1.7	52
	0752	6.5	198		0733	7.4	226
	1504	-0.9	-27		1441	-1.9	-58
	2132	4.0	122		2104	4.6	140
4 Sa ●	0212	2.1	64	**19** Su ○	0206	1.4	43
	0824	6.5	198		0819	7.6	232
	1535	-0.9	-27		1521	-2.0	-61
	2202	4.1	125		2143	4.9	149
5 Su	0244	2.1	64	**20** M	0256	1.1	34
	0852	6.4	195		0907	7.5	229
	1603	-0.8	-24		1600	-1.9	-58
	2227	4.1	125		2222	5.2	158
6 M	0316	2.1	64	**21** Tu	0345	0.9	27
	0924	6.2	189		0953	7.0	213
	1629	-0.6	-18		1638	-1.5	-46
	2257	4.2	128		2302	5.4	165

February

Day	Time	ft	cm	Day	Time	ft	cm
1 Sa	0134	2.0	61	**16** Su	0113	1.3	40
	0743	6.2	189		0724	7.1	216
	1444	-0.8	-24		1419	-1.7	-52
	2108	4.2	128		2039	5.0	152
2 Su	0205	1.8	55	**17** M	0203	0.7	21
	0813	6.3	192		0813	7.2	219
	1511	-0.8	-24		1456	-1.7	-52
	2129	4.4	134		2111	5.5	168
3 M ●	0237	1.6	49	**18** Tu ○	0249	0.3	9
	0844	6.2	189		0859	6.9	210
	1533	-0.7	-21		1531	-1.4	-43
	2151	4.5	137		2146	5.8	177
4 Tu	0308	1.5	46	**19** W	0338	0.0	0
	0912	6.0	183		0944	6.4	195
	1556	-0.5	-15		1607	-0.9	-27
	2213	4.6	140		2221	6.0	183
5 W	0340	1.4	43	**20** Th	0425	0.0	0
	0941	5.7	174		1030	5.7	174
	†617	-0.2	-6		1639	-0.3	-9
	2235	4.7	143		2259	6.0	183
6 Th	0413	1.3	40	**21** F	0515	0.1	3
	1009	5.3	162		1118	4.9	149
	1639	0.1	3		1712	0.5	15
	2302	4.8	146		2338	5.8	177

March

Day	Time	ft	cm	Day	Time	ft	cm
1 Su	0123	1.7	52	**16** M	0111	0.7	21
	0724	5.7	174		0716	6.3	192
	1411	-0.5	-15		1349	-1.1	-34
	2029	4.5	137		2003	5.6	171
2 M	0155	1.3	40	**17** Tu	0157	0.0	0
	0756	5.8	177		0805	6.3	192
	1436	-0.4	-12		1425	-0.9	-27
	2050	4.8	146		2038	6.0	183
3 Tu	0224	1.0	30	**18** W ○	0243	-0.5	-15
	0828	5.7	174		0850	6.0	183
	1455	-0.3	-9		1457	-0.5	-15
	2109	5.0	152		2110	6.3	192
4 W ●	0256	0.7	21	**19** Th	0329	-0.8	-24
	0857	5.5	168		0936	5.6	171
	1516	-0.1	-3		1531	-0.1	-3
	2130	5.2	158		2142	6.4	195
5 Th	0326	0.6	18	**20** F	0411	-0.8	-24
	0929	5.2	158		1021	5.0	152
	1538	0.2	6		1603	0.5	15
	2151	5.3	162		2217	6.3	192
6 F	0401	0.4	12	**21** Sa	0457	-0.6	-18
	1001	4.8	146		1107	4.3	131
	1600	0.5	15		1632	1.1	34
	2214	5.4	165		2254	6.0	183

Figure 17-09 Each reference station is given four pages in Table 1, and each page covers three months. Tide levels are shown in feet and centimeters. The days of new and full moons are also indicated.

Additional data show the difference in times and heights between these reference stations and thousands of other points termed SUBORDINATE STATIONS. From these tables, the tide at virtually any point of significance along the coasts can easily be computed. The West Coast *Tide Tables,* for example, contain predictions for 40 reference stations, and differences for about 1,100 subordinate stations in North and South America.

Other nations have similar sets of tables for their waters.

Day	Time	ft	m	Day	Time	ft	m	Day	Time	ft	m
16 Tu	0435	6.7	2.0	1 M	0217	4.2	1.3	16 Tu	0306	6.1	1.9
	1023	10.1	3.1		0819	11.7	3.6		0835	9.7	3.0
	1749	1.9	0.6		1514	0.9	0.3		1543	1.6	0.5
					2153	9.6	2.9		2313	9.4	2.9
17 W	0128	9.3	2.8	2 Tu	0309	5.6	1.7	17 W	0412	6.9	2.1
	0559	7.4	2.3		0901	11.3	3.4		0919	9.2	2.8
	1111	9.7	3.0		1613	0.4	0.1		1643	1.6	0.5
	1849	1.4	0.4		2323	9.7	3.0				
18 Th	0237	10.0	3.0	3 W	0418	6.8	2.1	18 Th	0039	9.7	3.0
	0727	7.7	2.3		0951	10.9	3.3		0539	7.4	2.3
	1203	9.5	2.9		1719	0.0	0.0		1012	8.8	2.7

Figure 17-10 This Table 1 extract shows how a high or low tide may be omitted near midnight (see text); this might occur about once every two weeks.

Cautions

All factors that can be determined in advance are taken into account in tide predictions, but remember when using them that other factors can also influence the height of tides greatly. Such influences include barometric pressure and wind. In many areas the effect of a prolonged gale from a certain quarter can offset all other factors. Tidal rivers may be affected by the volume of water flowing down from the watershed. Normal seasonal variations of flow are allowed for in the predictions, but unexpected prolonged wet or dry spells may cause significant changes to tidal height predictions. Intense rainfall upriver may change both height and times of tides and such effects may not appear downstream for several days.

You should therefore be careful whenever using the *Tide Tables,* especially since low waters can go considerably lower than the level predicted.

Explanation of the Tide Tables

Table 1 of the *Tide Tables* gives the predicted times and heights of high and low water at the

Seattle, Washington
Times and Heights of High and Low Waters

October

Day	Time (h m)	ft	cm	Day	Time (h m)	ft	cm
11 M	0000	8.5	259	26 Tu	0219	8.8	268
	0635	1.6	49		0751	3.8	116
	1331	11.2	341		1353	10.8	329
	1948	4.0	122		2049	2.3	70
12 Tu	0119	9.1	277	27 W	0315	9.4	287
	0734	2.0	61		0840	4.3	131
	1407	11.4	347		1442	10.6	323
	2031	2.4	73		2121	1.4	43
13 W	0228	9.9	302	28 Th	0400	10.0	305
	0830	2.5	76		0923	4.8	146
	1439	11.7	357		1505	10.5	320
	2114	0.9	27		2146	0.7	21
14 Th	0329	10.8	329	29 F	0442	10.5	320
	0919	3.1	94		1001	5.3	162
	1515	11.9	363		1526	10.4	317
	2156	-0.5	-15		2218	0.1	3
15 F	0428	11.5	351	30 Sa	0517	10.9	332
	1011	3.7	113		1037	5.7	174
	1550	12.0	366		1551	10.4	317
●	2238	-1.6	-49	○	2248	-0.4	-12

November

Day	Time (h m)	ft	cm	Day	Time (h m)	ft	cm
11 Th	0239	10.1	308	26 F	0401	10.3	314
	0801	4.8	146		0854	6.7	204
	1348	12.0	366		1405	10.5	320
	2050	-0.9	-27		2120	-0.1	-3
12 F	0341	11.1	338	27 Sa	0443	10.9	332
	0900	5.4	165		0940	7.0	213
	1428	12.1	369		1436	10.5	320
	2134	-2.0	-61		2148	-0.7	-21
13 Sa	0437	11.9	363	28 Su	0518	11.4	347
	0953	5.9	180		1019	7.2	219
	1510	12.0	366		1505	10.5	320
●	2216	-2.8	-85	○	2223	-1.1	-34
14 Su	0532	12.4	378	29 M	0551	11.7	357
	1044	6.3	192		1100	7.3	223
	1552	11.8	360		1537	10.5	320
	2301	-3.1	-94		2256	-1.4	-43
15 M	0621	12.7	387	30 Tu	0625	12.0	366
	1137	6.6	201		1140	7.3	223
	1635	11.5	351		1613	10.4	317
	2346	-2.9	-88		2332	-1.6	-49

December

Day	Time (h m)	ft	cm	Day	Time (h m)	ft	cm
11 Sa	0353	11.4	347	26 Su	0435	11.1	338
	0845	7.2	219		0918	8.0	244
	1353	12.0	366		1354	10.5	320
	2118	-2.5	-76		2124	-0.8	-24
12 Su	0445	12.2	372	27 M	0507	11.6	354
	0944	7.4	226		1003	7.9	241
	1441	11.9	363		1433	10.5	320
	2203	-2.9	-88		2200	-1.3	-40
13 M	0532	12.7	387	28 Tu	0540	12.0	366
	1037	7.3	223		1043	7.7	235
	1530	11.6	354		1515	10.6	323
●	2246	-2.9	-88	○	2235	-1.6	-49
14 Tu	0616	13.0	396	29 W	0607	12.4	378
	1130	7.1	216		1122	7.4	226
	1616	11.2	341		1557	10.6	323
	2328	-2.5	-76		2313	-1.7	-52
15 W	0657	13.0	396	30 Th	0636	12.7	387
	1219	6.9	210		1204	6.9	210
	1704	10.6	323		1642	10.4	317
					2349	-1.4	-43

Figure 17-11 This is an extract from Table 1; it is used for working the examples of tide level calculations on pages 593-595.

main reference stations and is self-explanatory; note that heights are given in both feet and meters or centimeters; see **Figures 17-09, 17-10,** and **17-11.** Where no sign is given before the predicted height, the quantity is positive and is to be added to the depths as given on the chart. When the value is preceded by a minus (-) sign, the "heights" are to be *subtracted* from charted depths.

Time is given in the four-digit system from 0001 to 2400 (refer to Chapter 16). In many areas you must be careful regarding *daylight time* (DT); the *Tide Tables* are published in local *standard* time, and you must correct for a DT locality.

When there are normally two high and two low tides each date, they are roughly a little less than an hour later each succeeding day. Consequently, a high or low tide may skip a calendar day, as indicated by a blank space in the *Tide Tables;* see **Figure 17-10.** If it is a low tide that is skipped, for example, you will note that the previous corresponding low occurred late in the foregoing day, and the next one will occur early in the following day; see the sequence for late nighttime high tides on the 16th, 17th, and 18th in **Figure 17-10;** and refer to **Figure 17-06,** center.

Note also from a review of the *Tide Tables* that at some places there will be only one high and one low tide on some days, with the usual four tides on other days. This is not a diurnal tide situation, where a single high and low would occur every day. The condition considered here arises when the configuration of the land and the periods between successive tides are such that one tide is reflected back from the shore and alters the effect of the succeeding tide.

Sometimes the difference in the height of the two high or two low waters of a day is so increased as to cause only one low water each day. These tides are not unusual in the tropics and consequently are called TROPIC TIDES.

Table 2, Tidal Differences and Constants, gives the information necessary to find the time and height of tide for thousands of subordinate stations by applying simple corrections to the data given for the main reference stations; see **Figures 17-12** and **17-13.** The name of the applicable reference stations appears at the head of the particular section in which the subordinate station is listed. After the subordinate station number and name, the following information is given in the columns of Table 2:

TABLE 2-TIDAL DIFFERENCES AND OTHER CONSTANTS

No.	PLACE	POSITION		DIFFERENCES				RANGES		Mean Tide Level
		Latitude	Longitude	Time		Height				
				High Water	Low Water	High Water	Low Water	Mean	Diurnal	
		North	**West**	h m	h m	ft	ft			ft
				on Seattle, p.96				ft	ft	
	WASHINGTON–cont. Saratoga Passage and Skagit Bay Time meridian, 120° W									
1133	Sandy Point, Whidbey Island	48° 02.1'	122° 22.6'	+0 03	−0 01	*0.99	*1.00	7.56	11.25	6.60
1135	Holly Farms Harbor, Holmes Harbor, Whidbey I.	48° 01.6'	122° 32.1'	+0 01	−0 04	*1.01	*0.99	7.76	11.44	6.67
1137	Greenbank, Whidbey Island	48° 06.3'	122° 34.2'	−0 03	−0 06	*0.99	*0.99	7.6	11.3	6.6
1139	Crescent Harbor, N. Whidbey Island	48° 17'	122° 37'	+0 04	−0 04	*1.03	*0.99	8.0	11.6	6.8
1141	Coupeville, Penn Cove, Whidbey Island	48° 13.4'	122° 41.4'	+0 15	+0 09	*1.01	*0.99	7.8	11.5	6.7
1143	La Conner, Swinomish Channel	48° 23.5'	122° 29.8'	+0 21	+0 39	*0.90	*0.95	6.74	10.34	6.06
1145	Ala Spit, Whidbey Island	48° 23.8'	122° 35.2'	+0 12	+0 26	*0.92	*0.95	6.9	10.5	6.1
1147	Yokeko Point, Deception Pass	48° 24.8'	122° 36.9'	+0 26	+0 38	−1.0	−0.2	6.9	10.5	6.1
1149	Cornet Bay, Deception Pass	48° 24.1'	122° 37.4'	+0 15	+0 26	*0.89	*0.95	6.6	10.2	6.0

Figure 17-12 *This is an extract from Table 2 to be used in working the text examples. Note that the differences are to be applied to the Seattle reference station as indicated in the fourth column. Asterisk (*) indicates ratios. The height at the reference station is multiplied by this figure; see text.*

1. Latitude and longitude of the subordinate station.

2. Differences in time and height of high (and low) waters at the subordinate station and its designated reference station.

3. Mean and spring (or diurnal) tidal ranges.

4. Mean tide level.

As mentioned, note that the existence of a "minus tide" means that the actual depths of water will be *less* than the figures on the chart.

To determine the time of high or low water at any station in Table 2, use the column marked "Differences, Time." This gives the hours and minutes to be added to (+) or subtracted from (-) the time of the respective high or low water at the reference station shown in boldface type *above* the listing of the subordinate station. Be careful in making calculations near midnight. Applying the time difference may cause you to cross the line from one day to another. Simply add or subtract 24 hours as necessary.

The height of the tide at a station in Table 2 is determined by applying the HEIGHT DIFFERENCE, or in some cases the RATIO. A plus sign (+) indicates that the difference increases the height given for the designated reference station; a minus sign (-) indicates that it decreases the Table 1 value. Differences are not given in metric values; if needed, conversions from feet can be made using Table 7 in the *Tide Tables;* see also Appendix E, page 890.

Where height differences would give unsatisfactory predictions, ratios may be substituted for heights. Ratios are identified by an asterisk, and are given as a decimal fraction by which the height at the reference station is to be multiplied to determine the height at the subordinate station.

In the columns headed "Ranges," the MEAN RANGE is the difference in height between mean high water (MHW) and mean low water (MLW). This figure is useful in many areas where it may be added to mean low water to get mean high water, the datum commonly used for measuring vertical heights above water for bridge and other vertical

TABLE 2-TIDAL DIFFERENCES AND OTHER CONSTANTS

1093	Dupont Wharf, Nisqually Reach	47° 04.1'	122° 40.0'	+0 41	+0 49	*1.20	*1.04	9.63	13.51	7.77
1095	Longbranch, Filucy Bay	47° 12.6'	122° 45.2'	+0 38	+0 47	*1.20	*1.02	9.7	13.5	7.7
1097	Devils Head, Drayton Passage	47° 10.0'	122° 45.8'	+0 40	+0 50	*1.25	*1.10	9.98	14.18	8.09
1099	Henderson Inlet	47° 09.3'	122° 50.3'	+0 47	+0 58	*1.24	*1.06	10.0	14.0	8.0
1101	McMicken Island, Case Inlet	47° 14.8'	122° 51.7'	+0 40	+0 52	*1.24	*1.06	10.00	13.96	8.01
1103	Vaughn, Case Inlet	47° 20.5'	122° 46.5'	+0 51	+0 57	*1.26	*1.06	10.2	14.1	8.1
1105	Allyn, Case Inlet	47° 23.0'	122° 49.4'	+0 48	+0 59	*1.26	*1.07	10.20	14.16	8.13
1107	Walkers Landing, Pickering Passage	47° 16.9'	122° 55.4'	+0 44	+0 55	*1.26	*1.07	10.20	14.15	8.12
1109	Shelton, Oakland Bay	47° 12.9'	123° 05.0'	+1 26	+2 05	*1.26	*0.92	10.6	14.2	7.9
1111	Arcadia, Totten Inlet	47° 11.8'	122° 56.3'	+0 49	+1 05	*1.28	*1.06	10.4	14.4	8.2
1113	Burns Point, Totten Inlet	47° 07.3'	123° 03 4	+0 54	+1 07	**.33	*1.06	11.0	15.0	8.5

Figure 17-13 *Another extract from Table 2 used in working the tide level examples in the text. Seattle is again the reference station.*

clearances. The SPRING RANGE is the average semi-diurnal range occurring twice monthly when the moon is new or full. It is larger than the mean range where the type of tide is either semidiurnal or mixed, and is of no practical significance where the tide is of the diurnal type. Where this is the situation, the tables give the DIURNAL RANGE, which is the difference in height between mean higher high water and mean lower low water.

Special conditions at certain subordinate stations are covered by "endnotes" following Table 2. The format may vary slightly with different commercial publishers.

Table 3, Height of Tide at Any Time, is provided in order that detailed calculations can be made for the height of the tide at any desired moment between the times of high and low waters; see **Figure 17-14.** It is equally usable for either the reference stations in Table 1 or the subordinate stations of Table 2. Note that Table 3 is not a complete set of variation from one low to one high. Since the rise and fall are assumed to be symmetrical, only a half-table need be printed. Calculations are made from a high or low water, whichever is nearer to the specified time. In using Table 3, the nearest tabular values are used; interpolation is not necessary.

If the degree of precision of Table 3 is not required (it seldom is in practical piloting situations), a much simpler and quicker estimation can be made by using the following "one-two-three" rule of thumb. The tide may be assumed to rise or fall $1/12$ of the full range during the first and sixth hours after high and low water stands, $2/12$ during the second and fifth hours, and $3/12$ during the third and fourth hours. The results obtained by this rule will suffice for essentially all situations and locations, but should be compared with Table 3 calculations as a check when entering new areas.

The *Tide Tables* also include four other minor tables that, although not directly related to tidal calculations, are often useful. Table 4 provides sunrise and sunset data at five-day intervals for various latitudes. Table 5 lists corrections to convert the local mean times of Table 4 to standard zone time. Table 6 tabulates times of moonrise and moonset for certain selected locations.

Table 7, as noted above, allows direct conversion of feet to meters. The inside back cover of the publication lists other useful data, such as the phases of the moon, the times of solar equinoxes, and solstices.

Table 1 through Table 6 are each preceded by informative material that should be read carefully prior to use of the table concerned.

Tidal Effects on Vertical Clearances
The tide's rise and fall changes the vertical clearance under fixed structures such as bridges or overhead power cables. These clearances are stated on charts and in *Coast Pilots* as heights measured from a datum that is *not* the same plane as used for depths and tidal predictions. The datum for heights is normally mean high water, the average of all high water levels. The use of this datum ensures that clearances and heights are normally greater than charted or *Coast Pilot* values.

It will thus be necessary to determine the height of MHW above the tidal datum. Since the tidal datum is mean lower low water, the plane of mean high water is above MLLW by an amount equal to the sum of the "mean tide level" plus one-half of the "mean range"; both of these values are listed in Table 2 of the *Tide Tables* for all stations; also refer to **Figure 17-02.**

If the tide level at any given moment is below MHW, the vertical clearance under a bridge or other fixed structure is then greater than the figures shown on the chart; but if the tide height is *above* the level of MHW, the clearance is *less.* You should calculate the vertical clearance in advance if you anticipate a tight situation, but also observe the clearance gauges usually found at bridges. Clearances will normally be greater than the charted MHW values, but will occasionally be less.

Examples of Tidal Calculations
The instructions in the *Tide Tables* should be fully adequate for solving any problem. However, **Tide Level Examples 1 through 6** are worked here for various situations as guides to the use of various individual tables. Comments and cautions relating to the solution of practical problems involving the *Tide Tables* will also be given. The

TABLE 3-HEIGHT OF TIDE AT ANY TIME

Time from the nearest high water or low water

Duration of rise or fall, see footnote (h.m.)	h.m.	h.m.	h.m.	h.m.	h.m.	h.m.	h.m.	h.m.	h.m.	h.m.	h.m.	h.m.	h.m.	h.m.	h.m.
4 00	0 08	0 16	0 24	0 32	0 40	0 48	0 56	1 04	1 12	1 20	1 28	1 36	1 44	1 52	2 00
4 20	0 09	0 17	0 26	0 35	0 43	0 52	1 01	1 09	1 18	1 27	1 35	1 44	1 53	2 01	2 10
4 40	0 09	0 19	0 28	0 37	0 47	0 56	1 05	1 15	1 24	1 33	1 43	1 52	2 01	2 11	2 20
5 00	0 10	0 20	0 30	0 40	0 50	1 00	1 10	1 20	1 30	1 40	1 50	2 00	2 10	2 20	2 30
5 20	0 11	0 21	0 32	0 43	0 53	1 04	1 15	1 25	1 36	1 47	1 57	2 08	2 19	2 29	2 40
5 40	0 11	0 23	0 34	0 45	0 57	1 08	1 19	1 31	1 42	1 53	2 05	2 16	2 27	2 39	2 50
6 00	0 12	0 24	0 36	0 48	1 00	1 12	1 24	1 36	1 48	2 00	2 12	2 24	2 36	2 48	3 00
6 20	0 13	0 25	0 38	0 51	1 03	1 16	1 29	1 41	1 54	2 07	2 19	2 32	2 45	2 57	3 10
6 40	0 13	0 27	0 40	0 53	1 07	1 20	1 33	1 47	2 00	2 13	2 27	2 40	2 53	3 07	3 20
7 00	0 14	0 28	0 42	0 56	1 10	1 24	1 38	1 52	2 06	2 20	2 34	2 48	3 02	3 16	3 30
7 20	0 15	0 29	0 44	0 59	1 13	1 28	1 43	1 57	2 12	2 27	2 41	2 56	3 11	3 25	3 40
7 40	0 15	0 31	0 46	1 01	1 17	1 32	1 47	2 03	2 18	2 33	2 49	3 04	3 19	3 35	3 50
8 00	0 16	0 32	0 48	1 04	1 20	1 36	1 52	2 08	2 24	2 40	2 56	3 12	3 28	3 44	4 00
8 20	0 17	0 33	0 50	1 07	1 23	1 40	1 57	2 13	2 30	2 47	3 03	3 20	3 37	3 53	4 10
8 40	0 17	0 35	0 52	1 09	1 27	1 44	2 01	2 19	2 36	2 53	3 11	3 28	3 45	4 03	4 20
9 00	0 18	0 36	0 54	1 12	1 30	1 48	2 06	2 24	2 42	3 00	3 18	3 36	3 54	4 12	4 30
9 20	0 19	0 37	0 56	1 15	1 33	1 52	2 11	2 29	2 48	3 07	3 25	3 44	4 03	4 21	4 40
9 40	0 19	0 39	0 58	1 17	1 37	1 56	2 15	2 35	2 54	3 13	3 33	3 52	4 11	4 31	4 50
10 00	0 20	0 40	1 00	1 20	1 40	2 00	2 20	2 40	3 00	3 20	3 40	4 00	4 20	4 40	5 00
10 20	0 21	0 41	1 02	1 23	1 43	2 04	2 25	2 45	3 06	3 27	3 47	4 08	4 29	4 49	5 10
10 40	0 21	0 43	1 04	1 25	1 47	2 08	2 29	2 51	3 12	3 33	3 55	4 16	4 37	4 59	5 20

Correction to height

Range of tide, see footnote (Ft.)	Ft.	Ft.	Ft.	Ft.	Ft.	Ft.	Ft.	Ft.	Ft.	Ft.	Ft.	Ft.	Ft.	Ft.	Ft.
0.5	0.0	0.0	0.0	0.0	0.0	0.0	0.1	0.1	0.1	0.1	0.1	0.2	0.2	0.2	0.2
1.0	0.0	0.0	0.0	0.0	0.1	0.1	0.1	0.2	0.2	0.2	0.3	0.3	0.4	0.4	0.5
1.5	0.0	0.0	0.0	0.1	0.1	0.1	0.2	0.2	0.3	0.4	0.4	0.5	0.6	0.7	0.8
2.0	0.0	0.0	0.0	0.1	0.1	0.2	0.3	0.3	0.4	0.5	0.6	0.7	0.8	0.9	1.0
2.5	0.0	0.0	0.1	0.1	0.2	0.2	0.3	0.4	0.5	0.6	0.7	0.9	1.0	1.1	1.2
3.0	0.0	0.0	0.1	0.1	0.2	0.3	0.4	0.5	0.6	0.8	0.9	1.0	1.2	1.3	1.5
3.5	0.0	0.0	0.1	0.2	0.2	0.3	0.4	0.6	0.7	0.9	1.0	1.2	1.4	1.6	1.8
4.0	0.0	0.0	0.1	0.2	0.3	0.4	0.5	0.7	0.8	1.0	1.2	1.4	1.6	1.8	2.0
4.5	0.0	0.0	0.1	0.2	0.3	0.4	0.6	0.7	0.9	1.1	1.3	1.6	1.8	2.0	2.2
5.0	0.0	0.1	0.1	0.2	0.3	0.5	0.6	0.8	1.0	1.2	1.5	1.7	2.0	2.2	2.5
5.5	0.0	0.1	0.1	0.2	0.4	0.5	0.7	0.9	1.1	1.4	1.6	1.9	2.2	2.5	2.8
6.0	0.0	0.1	0.1	0.3	0.4	0.6	0.8	1.0	1.2	1.5	1.8	2.1	2.4	2.7	3.0
6.5	0.0	0.1	0.2	0.3	0.4	0.6	0.8	1.1	1.3	1.6	1.9	2.2	2.6	2.9	3.2
7.0	0.0	0.1	0.2	0.3	0.5	0.7	0.9	1.2	1.4	1.8	2.1	2.4	2.8	3.1	3.5
7.5	0.0	0.1	0.2	0.3	0.5	0.7	1.0	1.2	1.5	1.9	2.2	2.6	3.0	3.4	3.8
8.0	0.0	0.1	0.2	0.3	0.5	0.8	1.0	1.3	1.6	2.0	2.4	2.8	3.2	3.6	4.0
8.5	0.0	0.1	0.2	0.4	0.6	0.8	1.1	1.4	1.8	2.1	2.5	2.9	3.4	3.8	4.2
9.0	0.0	0.1	0.2	0.4	0.6	0.9	1.2	1.5	1.9	2.2	2.7	3.1	3.6	4.0	4.5
9.5	0.0	0.1	0.2	0.4	0.6	0.9	1.2	1.6	2.0	2.4	2.8	3.3	3.8	4.3	4.8
10.0	0.0	0.1	0.2	0.4	0.7	1.0	1.3	1.7	2.1	2.5	3.0	3.5	4.0	4.5	5.0
10.5	0.0	0.1	0.3	0.5	0.7	1.0	1.3	1.7	2.2	2.6	3.1	3.6	4.2	4.7	5.2
11.0	0.0	0.1	0.3	0.5	0.7	1.1	1.4	1.8	2.3	2.8	3.3	3.8	4.4	4.9	5.5
11.5	0.0	0.1	0.3	0.5	0.8	1.1	1.5	1.9	2.4	2.9	3.4	4.0	4.6	5.1	5.8
12.0	0.0	0.1	0.3	0.5	0.8	1.1	1.5	2.0	2.5	3.0	3.6	4.1	4.8	5.4	6.0
12.5	0.0	0.1	0.3	0.5	0.8	1.2	1.6	2.1	2.6	3.1	3.7	4.3	5.0	5.6	6.2
13.0	0.0	0.1	0.3	0.6	0.9	1.2	1.7	2.2	2.7	3.2	3.9	4.5	5.1	5.8	6.5
13.5	0.0	0.1	0.3	0.6	0.9	1.3	1.7	2.2	2.8	3.4	4.0	4.7	5.3	6.0	6.8
14.0	0.0	0.2	0.3	0.6	0.9	1.3	1.8	2.3	2.9	3.5	4.2	4.8	5.5	6.3	7.0
14.5	0.0	0.2	0.4	0.6	1.0	1.4	1.9	2.4	3.0	3.6	4.3	5.0	5.7	6.5	7.2
15.0	0.0	0.2	0.4	0.6	1.0	1.4	1.9	2.5	3.1	3.8	4.4	5.2	5.9	6.7	7.5
15.5	0.0	0.2	0.4	0.7	1.0	1.5	2.0	2.6	3.2	3.9	4.6	5.4	6.1	6.9	7.8
16.0	0.0	0.2	0.4	0.7	1.1	1.5	2.1	2.6	3.3	4.0	4.7	5.5	6.3	7.2	8.0
16.5	0.0	0.2	0.4	0.7	1.1	1.6	2.1	2.7	3.4	4.1	4.9	5.7	6.5	7.4	8.2
17.0	0.0	0.2	0.4	0.7	1.1	1.6	2.2	2.8	3.5	4.2	5.0	5.9	6.7	7.6	8.5
17.5	0.0	0.2	0.4	0.8	1.2	1.7	2.2	2.9	3.6	4.4	5.2	6.0	6.9	7.8	8.8
18.0	0.0	0.2	0.4	0.8	1.2	1.7	2.3	3.0	3.7	4.5	5.3	6.2	7.1	8.1	9.0
18.5	0.1	0.2	0.5	0.8	1.2	1.8	2.4	3.1	3.8	4.6	5.5	6.4	7.3	8.3	9.2
19.0	0.1	0.2	0.5	0.8	1.3	1.8	2.4	3.1	3.9	4.8	5.6	6.6	7.5	8.5	9.5
19.5	0.1	0.2	0.5	0.8	1.3	1.9	2.5	3.2	4.0	4.9	5.8	6.7	7.7	8.7	9.8

Figure 17-14 *Table 3 is used to determine the height of the tide at intermediate times between high and low water. To use this table, you must know three things—how long in hours and minutes between the high and low on either side of the time in which you are interested; the time in hours and minutes from that time to the nearer of the adjacent high and low; and the size of the rise or fall to the nearest half-foot. The answer produced from that data and Table 3 will give you a correction value to be applied to that high or low prediction.*

extracts from the *Tide Tables* that are necessary to work the **Tide Level Examples** are given in **Figures 17-11 through 17-14.**

CURRENTS

CURRENT is the horizontal motion of water. It may result from any one of several factors, or from a combination of two or more. Although certain of these causes are more important to a boater than others are, he or she should have a general understanding of all.

Types of Currents

The major causes of current flow are gravitational action, the flow of air (wind) across the surface of bodies of water, and geophysical differences such as variations in heat and salt. Water naturally flows "downhill" as in rivers or from higher tidal levels to lower ones. Persistent winds across large bodies of water cause a surface flow. Currents over large areas in oceans may be either seasonal or semipermanent.

Tidal Currents

Boaters in coastal areas will be affected most by TIDAL CURRENTS. The rise and fall of tidal levels is a result of the flow of water to and from a given locality. Such flow of water results in tidal current effects.

The normal type of tidal current, in bays and rivers, is called the REVERSING current that flows alternately in one direction and then in the opposite. Off shore, tidal currents may be of the ROTARY type, flowing with little change in strength, but while slowly and steadily changing direction.

A special form of a tidal current is known as the HYDRAULIC type, such as flows in a waterway connecting two bodies of water. Differences in the time and height of the high and low waters of the two bays, sounds, or other tidal waters cause a flow from one to the other and back again. A typical example of hydraulic current is the flow through the Cape Cod Canal between Massachusetts Bay and Buzzards Bay.

Remember to use the terms correctly—tide is the *vertical* rise and fall of water levels; current is the *horizontal* flow of water.

TIDE LEVEL EXAMPLE 3

Determining the level of the tide at a Reference Station at a given time between high and low waters.

Problem: What is the predicted height of the tide at Seattle at 1700 on Sunday 28 November?

Solution: From Table 1, note that the given time of 1700 falls between a high tide at 1505 and a low tide at 2223. We compute the duration of fall and range as follows:

Time	Height
15 05	10.5
22 23	-1.1
7:18 duration of fall	11.6 feet range

The desired time is nearer to the time of high water, so calculations will be made using this starting point.

1700	desired time
1505	time of nearest high water
1:55	difference

The given time is 1 h 55m after the nearest high water. Turn to Table 3, which is used to the nearest tabulated value; do not interpolate. Enter the upper part of the Table on the line for Duration of rise or fall of 7 h 20m (nearest value to 7h 18m) and read across to the entry nearest 1h 55m—in this case 1h 57m in the 8th column from the left. Follow down this column into the lower part of Table 3 to the line for Range of tide of 11.5 feet (nearest value to 11.6). At the intersection of this line and column is found the correction to the height of the tide: 1.9 feet.

Since, as we have noted, the tide is falling, and we are calculating from high water, the correction is subtracted from the height of high water:

10.5 – 1.9 = 8.6 feet.

Thus, the predicted height of the tide at Seattle at 1700 PST on Sunday 28 November is 8.6 feet above the tidal datum.

Make sure that calculations are made for the right pair of high and low tides—and that the calculations are made to the nearest high or low water. Also, be careful to apply the final correction to the nearest high or low water as used in the computation. Do not apply it to the range. Apply it in the right direction: down from a high or up from a low.

TIDE LEVEL EXAMPLE 4

Determining the predicted height of tide at a Subordinate Station at a given time.

Problem: What is the predicted height of the tide at Shelton, Oakland Bay, Puget Sound, at 2000 on Saturday 30 October?

Solution: First, use the steps from Tide Level Example 2—find Shelton in the index, locate its number on Table 2 and note the time and height differences. Now, the times of the high and low waters on either side of the stated time must be calculated for the Subordinate Station using Tables 1 and 2. This is done as follows:

High-water time	Height
15 51 at Seattle	10.4 feet
+1:26 difference	1.26 ratio
17 17 at Shelton	13.1 feet

Low-water time	Height
22 48 at Seattle	-0.4
+2:05 difference	0.92 ratio
00 53 at Shelton	0.37 (0.4)

Next we calculate the time difference and range:

Time	Range
00 53 low water	-0.4
17 17 high water	13.1
7:36 time difference	13.5 feet range

The time from the nearest high or low is calculated:

17 17	high water at Shelton
20 00	desired time
2:43	time from nearest high

With the data from the above calculations, enter Table 3 for a duration of rise or fall of 7h 40m (nearest to 7h 36m), a time from nearest high or low of 2 h 49m (nearest to 2h 43m), and a range of 13.5 feet.

From these data, we find a correction to height of tide of 4.0 feet. We know that the tide is falling and therefore the height at 2000 will be less than the height at the closest high water at 1717. Therefore, the correction is to be subtracted from the Shelton high water height: 13.1 – 4.0 = 9.1 feet. The height of the tide at Shelton, Oakland Bay, Puget Sound, at 2000 PST on Saturday 30 October is predicted to be 9.1 feet above datum.

Note: You must be sure to use the high and low tides occurring at the Subordinate Station on either side of the given time. In some instances, you may find that when you have corrected the times for the Subordinate Station, the desired time no longer falls between the corrected times of high and low tides. In this case, select another high or low tide so that the pair used at the Subordinate Station will bracket the given time.

TIDE LEVEL EXAMPLE 5

Determining the time of the tide reaching a given height at a Reference Station.

Problem: At what time on the morning of Tuesday 30 November will the height of the rising tide at Seattle reach 3 feet?

Solution: This is essentially Tide Level Example 3 in reverse. First determine the range and duration of the rise (or fall) as follows:

Time	Height
22 56 (29th low water	-1.4 feet
06 25　high water	12.0 feet
7:29　duration/range	13.4 feet range

It is noted that the desired difference in height of tide is from the low water –1.4 –3 = -4.4 or 4.4 feet.

Enter the lower part of Table 3 on the line for a range of 13.5 feet (nearest to actual 13.4 feet) and find the column in which the correction nearest 4.4 is tabulated: in this case, the nearest value (4.7) is found on the 12th column to the right.

Proceed up this column to the line in the upper part of the table for a duration of 7h 20m (nearest to the actual 7h 29m). The time from the nearest high or low found on this line is 2h 56m. Since our desired level is nearest to low water than high, this time difference is added to the time of low water: 2256 + 2:56 = 0152.

Thus the desired tidal height of 3 feet above datum is predicted to occur at 0152 PST on 30 November.

Note that a similar calculation can be made for a Subordinate Station by first determining the applicable high and low water times and heights at that station.

TIDE LEVEL EXAMPLE 6

Determination of predicted vertical clearance.

Problem: What will be the predicted vertical clearance under the fixed bridge across the canal near Ala Spit, Whidbey Island, at the time of morning high tide on 13 December?

Solution: Chart 18445 states the clearance to be 35 feet. The datum for heights is MHW.

From Tables 1 and 2, we determine the predicted height of the tide at the specified time as follows:

At Seattle	12.7 feet
Ratio	0.92
At Ala Spit	11.68 (11.7)

From Table 2 we calculate the height of mean high water for Ala Spit.

Mean tide level	6.1 feet
½ mean range	3.5
Mean high water	9.6 feet above tidal datum

The difference between predicted high water at the specified time and mean high water is 11.7 –9.6 = 2.1 This is above MHW and the bridge clearance is reduced; 35 – 2.1 = 33 feet, to the nearest whole foot.

On the morning of 13 December, the clearance at high tide under the fixed bridge across the canal near Ala Spit, Whidbey Island, is predicted to be 33 feet. This is less than the clearance printed on the chart.

River Currents

Boaters on rivers above the head of tidal action must take into account RIVER CURRENTS. (Where tidal influences are felt, river currents are merged into tidal currents and are not considered separately.) River currents vary considerably, with the width and depth of the stream, the season, and recent rainfall; refer to Chapter 22 for details. When rivers reach tidal areas, the currents there will be a combination of river flow and tidal level changes.

Ocean Currents

Offshore piloting will frequently require knowledge and consideration of OCEAN CURRENTS. These currents result from relatively constant winds such as the "trade winds" and "prevailing westerlies." The rotation of the earth and variations in water density and salinity are also factors in the patterns of ocean currents.

The ocean currents of greatest interest to American boaters are the Gulf Stream and the California Current; see **Figure 17-15.** The Gulf Stream is a northerly and easterly flow of warm water along the Atlantic Coast of the United States. It is quite close to shore along the southern part of Florida, but moves progressively further to sea as it flows northward, where it both broadens and slows.

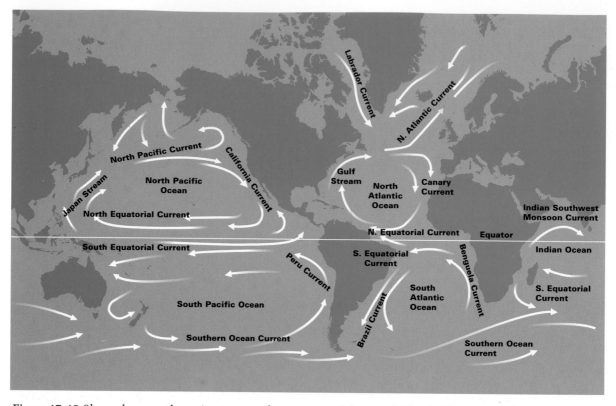

Figure 17-15 Shown here are the major ocean surface currents of the world. The Gulf Stream off the East Coast of the United States and Canada, and the California Current off the West Coast are those of most interest to North American boaters. Other currents exist at lower depths, as well as downwelling and upwelling.

The California Current flows generally southward and a bit eastward along the Pacific Coast of Canada and the United States, turning sharply westward of Baja California (Mexico). It is a flow of colder water and, in general, is slower and less sharply defined than the Gulf Stream, and exhibits some variation with season.

Wind-Driven Currents

In addition to the consistent ocean currents caused by sustained wind patterns, temporary conditions may create local WIND-DRIVEN CURRENTS. Wind blowing across the sea causes the surface water to move. The extent of this effect varies, but generally a steady wind for 12 hours or longer will result in a discernible current.

For a rough rule of thumb, the strength of a wind-driven current can be taken as 2 percent of the wind's velocity. The direction of the current will *not* be the same as that of the wind, a result of the earth's rotation. In the Northern Hemisphere, the current will be deflected to the right to a degree determined by the latitude and the depth of the water. The deflection may be as small as 15 degrees in shallow coastal areas, or as great as 45 degree on the high seas; it is greater in the higher latitudes.

Definition of Current Terms

Currents have both strength and direction. The proper terms should be used in describing each of these characteristics.

The SET of a current is the direction *toward* which it is flowing. A current that flows from north to south is termed a southerly current and has a set of 180 degrees. (Note the difference here from the manner in which wind direction is described—it is exactly the opposite: a wind from north to south is called a northerly wind with a direction described as 000 degrees.)

The DRIFT of a current is its speed, normally in knots, except for river currents, which are in mph (1 knot = 1.15 mph = 1.85 km/hr). Current drift is stated to the nearest tenth of a knot.

The term velocity is rarely used in connection with current, but if it is, it requires a statement of *both* strength and direction.

A tidal current is said to FLOOD when it flows in from the sea and results in higher tidal stages. Conversely, a tidal current EBBS when the flow is seaward and water levels fall.

Slack vs. Stand

As these currents reverse, there are brief periods of no discernible flow, called SLACK, or SLACK WATER. The time of occurrence of slack is *not* the same as the time of STAND, when vertical rise or fall of the tide has stopped. Tidal currents do *not* automatically slack and reverse direction when tide levels stand at high or low water. High water at a given point simply means that the level there will not get any higher. Further up the bay or river, the tide will not have reached its maximum height and water must therefore continue to flow in so that it can continue to rise. The current can still be flooding after stand has been passed at a given point and the level has started to fall.

For example, consider the tides and currents on Chesapeake Bay. High tide occurs at Baltimore some seven hours after it does at Smith Point, roughly half way up the 140 miles from Cape Henry at the Bay's entrance to Baltimore. On a certain day, high water occurs at 1126 at Smith Point, but slack water does not occur until 1304. The flooding current has thus continued for 1h 38m after high water was reached.

Corresponding time intervals occur in the case of low water stand and the slack between ebb and flood currents.

In many places, the time lag between a low or high water stand and slack water is not a matter of minutes but of hours. At the Narrows in New York Harbor, floor current continues for about two hours after high water is reached and the tide begins to fall, and continues to ebb for roughly two and a half hours after low water stand. After slack, the current increases until mid-flood or mid-ebb, and then gradually decreases. Where

ebb and flood last for about six hours—as along the Atlantic seaboard—current will be strongest about three hours after slack. Thus, the skipper who figures his passage out through the Narrows from the time of high water, rather than slack, will start about two and a half hours too soon and will run into an opposing current at nearly its maximum strength.

Current Effects

A current of any type can have a significant effect on the travel of a boat with respect to the bottom. Speed can be increased or decreased; the course made good can be markedly different from that steered. For safe and efficient navigation, a boater must know how to determine and apply current effects.

Effect on Course & Speed Made Good

A current directly in line with a boat's motion through the water will have a maximum effect on the speed made good, but no off-course influence. The effect can be of significance when figuring your ETA at your destination. It can even affect the safety of your boat and its crew if you have figured your fuel too closely and have run into a bow-on current.

A current that is nearly at a right angle to your course through the water will have a maximum effect on the course made good and a minor effect on the distance that you must travel to reach your destination.

Knowledge of current set and drift can assist your cruising. Select departure times to take advantage of favorable currents, or at least to minimize adverse effects. A 12-knot boat speed and a 2-knot current, reasonably typical situations, can combine to result in either a 10-knot or a 14-knot speed made good—the 40 percent gain of a favorable current over an opposing one is significant in terms of both time and fuel. For slower craft the gains are even greater: 50 percent for a 10-knot boat, 67 percent for an 8-knot craft, and 100 percent for one making only 6 knots.

Even lesser currents have some significance. A half-knot current would hinder a swimmer and make rowing a boat noticeably more difficult. A one-knot current can significantly affect a sailboat in light breezes.

Difficult Locations

In many boating areas, there are locations where current conditions can be critical. Numerous ocean inlets are difficult or dangerous in certain combinations of current and onshore surf. In general, difficult surf conditions will be made more hazardous by an outward-flowing (ebbing) current. The topic of inlet seamanship is covered in more detail in Chapter 10, on page 356. In many narrow bodies of water, the maximum current velocity is so high that passage is impossible for boats of limited power, and substantially slowed for boats of greater engine power; see **Figure 17-16.** Such narrow passages are particularly characteristic of Pacific Northwest boating areas, but do occur elsewhere. Currents in New York City's East River reach 4.6 knots, and they are more than 5 knots at the Golden Gate of San Francisco. Velocities of 3.5 to 4 knots are common in much-traveled passages like Woods Hole, Massachusetts, and Plum Gut, at the eastern end of Long Island, New York.

Tidal Current Predictions

Without experience or official information, local current prediction is always risky. For example, east of Badgers Island in Portsmouth (NH) Harbor the maximum ebb current is predicted at less than a half knot. Yet just southwest of the same island, the tabular maximum is 3.7 knots.

One rule is fairly safe for most locations—the ebb is stronger and lasts longer than the flood. Eighty percent of all reference stations on the Atlantic, Gulf, and Pacific coasts of the U.S. report currents stronger at the ebb. This is normal because river flow adds to the ebb, but hinders the flood.

On the Atlantic Coast, expect to find two approximately equal flood currents and two similar ebb currents in a cycle of 24 hours and 50 minutes approximately. On the Pacific Coast, however, two floods and ebbs differ markedly. On the Gulf Coast, there may be just one flood and one ebb in 25 hours. In each case these patterns are, of course, generally similar to tidal action in their respective areas.

Don't try to predict current velocity from the time that it takes a high tide to reach a given point from the sea's entrance. Dividing the distance from Cape Henry to Baltimore by the time that it takes high water to work its way up Chesapeake Bay gives a speed of 13 knots. True maximum flood current strength is only about one knot.

Another important fact about tidal currents is that tidal currents at different places *cannot* be forecast from their tidal ranges. You would expect strong currents at Eastport, Maine, where the difference between successive high and low

Figure 17-16 In some passages, tidal currents are so strong that all but the fastest boats must avoid running against the strongest flood and ebb. Skippers of less powerful craft must plan for passage at slack water or with a favorable current—in the right direction, a strong current can double the over-the-bottom speed of a displacement boat. And all skippers can gain to some degree from transiting when the current aids their passage.

waters reaches as much as 20 feet. And you would be right; there are 3-knot currents there. But Galveston, Texas, with only a 2-foot range of tides, has currents up to more than 2 knots. So has Miami with a 3-foot range, and Charleston, South Carolina, with a 6-foot range—these are stronger currents than Boston, where the range is often more than 10 feet and as strong as at Anchorage, Alaska, where it's as much as 35 feet from some highs to the next low.

A good forecasting rule for all oceans: expect strong tidal currents where two bays meet. The reason: tidal ranges and high water times in the two bodies of water are likely to be different.

For the coasting skipper, here is another tidal current fact that may be useful near the beach: flood and ebb don't usually set to and from shore, but rather parallel with it. This is as true off New Jersey and Florida as it is off California and Oregon. A few miles offshore, however, and in some very large bays, the current behaves quite differently—for example, the rotary current mentioned previously in this chapter.

Tidal Current Tables

At any given place, current strength varies with the phases of the moon and its distance from the earth. It will be strongest when tidal ranges are greatest—near new and full moon—and weakest when tidal ranges are least—near first and last quarters. Current speed may vary as much as 40 percent above and below its average value.

The relationship between currents and tides makes possible the prediction of tidal currents. NOS provides data for two volumes of predictions annually; one covers the Atlantic Coast of North America and the other the Pacific Coast of North America and Asia. These books are printed and sold commercially in the same manner as the *Tide Tables*.

Each volume includes predictions of tidal currents in bays, sounds, and rivers, plus ocean currents such as the Gulf Stream. General information on wind-driven currents is also included, although these, of course, result from temporary, local conditions and so cannot be predicted a year or more ahead. Your own past experience and local knowledge are the best source of information about how storm winds affect local waters.

TIDAL CURRENT TABLES are available at most sales agents for charts and nautical publications.

Description of Tables

The format and layout of the *Tidal Current Tables* is much the same as for the *Tide Tables* discussed earlier in this chapter. A system of reference stations, plus constants and differences for subordinate stations, is used to calculate the predictions for many points.

Table 1. There are 22 reference stations in the Atlantic Coast volume and 36 for the Pacific Coast; the Gulf of Mexico is included in the Atlantic Coast volume. For each station, there are tabulated and predicted times and strengths of maximum flood and ebb currents, plus the times of slack water. The direction of the flood and ebb currents is also listed; see **Figure 17-17**.

Table 2. Time differences and velocity ratios are listed for hundreds of subordinate stations; see **Figure 17-18**. Following the station number and descriptive location, there is depth at which the reading was taken and then the latitude and longitude to the nearest minute. Time differences are given for maximum flood and ebb, and for minimum current (usually slack) before flood and before ebb. Speed ratios are tabulated for maximum current in both directions (given in degrees, true, for direction *toward* which current flows). Also listed are average speeds and directions, including speed at "slack" as currents do not always decrease fully to zero velocity. A few stations will have only the entry "Current weak and variable"; this information, even though negative in nature, is useful in planning a cruise. A number of "endnotes" are used to explain special conditions at various stations; these are found at the end of Table 2.

Table 3. This ratio table is in two separate parts; one is for normal reversing currents (as in **Figure 17-19**) and the other (not shown) is for hydraulic currents at specified locations, and provides a convenient means for determining the current's strength at times intermediate between slack and maximum velocity.

Chesapeake Bay Entrance, Virginia

F-Flood, Dir. 300° True   E-Ebb, Dir. 129° True

October

Day	Slack h m	Max h m	knots	Day	Slack h m	Max h m	knots
1 F		0220	1.2E	16 Sa		0215	1.8E
	0529	0810	0.8F		0510	0757	1.6F
	1123	1456	1.2E		1126	1454	1.9E
	1811	2037	0.7F		1802	2028	1.2F
	2322				2330		
2 Sa		0249	1.2E	17 Su		0304	1.8E
	0603	0846	0.9F		0601	0848	1.5F
	1201	1527	1.2E		1218	1544	1.8E
	1851	2114	0.7F		1858	2120	1.1F
	2357						
3 Su		0320	1.2E	18 M	0023	0353	1.7E
	0640	0921	0.8F		0656	0939	1.4F
	1239	1600	1.1E		1311	1638	1.7E
	1932	2151	0.6F		1952	2212	1.0F
4 M	0032	0356	1.2E	19 Tu	0117	0448	1.5E
	0719	0956	0.8F		0753	1033	1.2F
	1317	1640	1.0E		1405	1739	1.5E
	2015	2230	0.5F		2050	2310	0.9F
5 Tu	0107	0437	1.1E	20 W	0212	0552	1.3E
	0800	1034	0.7F		0854	1132	1.0F
	1356	1729	0.9E		1502	1842	1.3E
	2059	2314	0.5F		2151		
6 W	0141	0527	1.0E	21 Th		0011	0.7F
	0843	1119	0.7F		0311	0657	1.2E
	1438	1824	0.9E		1000	1235	0.8F
	2149				1606	1943	1.2E
					2258		
7 Th		0001	0.4F	22 F ◐		0112	0.6F
	0218	0622	1.0E		0421	0801	1.1E
	0933	1209	0.6F		1111	1339	0.7F
	1531	1915	0.8E		1713	2047	1.1E
	2244						
8 F ○		0050	0.4F	23 Sa	0001	0220	0.5F
	0307	0715	1.0E		0532	0911	1.0E
	1030	1301	0.6F		1222	1458	0.6F
	1638	2008	0.9E		1813	2151	1.0E
	2339						
9 Sa		0143	0.4F	24 Su	0101	0345	0.5F
	0421	0813	1.0E		0636	1019	1.0E
	1132	1400	0.6F		1330	1617	0.6F
	1739	2108	0.9E		1904	2246	1.0E
10 Su	0030	0246	0.5F	25 M	0154	0443	0.6F
	0537	0918	1.1E		0733	1115	1.1E
	1233	1508	0.7F		1430	1703	0.6F
	1832	2206	1.1E		1947	2329	1.0E
11 M	0118	0350	0.7F	26 Tu	0239	0520	0.7F
	0644	1022	1.3E		0825	1203	1.1E
	1335	1611	0.8F		1519	1736	0.6F
	1922	2257	1.3E		2025		
12 Tu	0204	0442	0.9F	27 W		0006	1.0E
	0747	1120	1.4E		0316	0552	0.8F
	1432	1703	1.0F		0909	1246	1.1E
	2012	2346	1.4E		1559	1811	0.6F
					2100		
13 W	0250	0528	1.2F	28 Th		0038	1.1E
	0846	1216	1.6E		0349	0625	0.8F
	1527	1751	1.1F		0949	1326	1.2E
	2101				1637	1848	0.6F
					2135		
14 Th		0035	1.6E	29 F		0109	1.1E
	0336	0614	1.4F		0420	0700	0.9F
	0941	1311	1.8E		1026	1401	1.2E
	1619	1841	1.1F		1711	1928	0.6F
	2150				2209		
15 F ●		0125	1.7E	30 Sa ○		0142	1.2E
	0421	0705	1.5F		0452	0738	0.9F
	1034	1405	1.9E		1102	1434	1.2E
	1709	1934	1.2F		1749	2009	0.6F
	2240				2246		
				31 Su		0217	1.2E
					0528	0815	0.9F
					1139	1506	1.2E
					1828	2048	0.6F
					2323		

November

Day	Slack h m	Max h m	knots	Day	Slack h m	Max h m	knots
1 M		0253	1.2E	16 Tu	0002	0334	1.6E
	0604	0851	0.9F		0636	0919	1.4F
	1217	1539	1.2E		1251	1618	1.6E
	1909	2125	0.6F		1933	2152	0.9F
2 Tu	0001	0330	1.2E	17 W	0056	0426	1.5E
	0644	0926	0.9F		0731	1011	1.2F
	1255	1617	1.1E		1341	1714	1.5E
	1951	2203	0.5F		2028	2246	0.8F
3 W	0039	0411	1.2E	18 Th	0149	0525	1.3E
	0728	1004	0.8F		0830	1107	1.0F
	1334	1704	1.0E		1431	1814	1.3E
	2035	2244	0.5F		2124	2344	0.7F
4 Th	0118	0501	1.1E	19 F	0244	0629	1.2E
	0811	1047	0.8F		0931	1205	0.8F
	1414	1757	1.0E		1524	1909	1.2E
	2121	2333	0.5F		2223		
5 F	0201	0557	1.0E	20 Sa ◐		0043	0.6F
	0902	1137	0.7F		0348	0731	1.0E
	1458	1850	1.0E		1040	1304	0.7F
	2212				1619	2003	1.0E
					2322		
6 Sa		0025	0.5F	21 Su		0142	0.6F
	0257	0655	1.0E		0500	0836	0.9E
	1001	1230	0.7F		1150	1406	0.5F
	1552	1941	1.0E		1714	2059	1.0E
	2304						
7 Su ○		0119	0.5F	22 M	0019	0253	0.5F
	0416	0754	1.0E		0607	0946	0.9E
	1108	1330	0.7F		1300	1520	0.4F
	1653	2035	1.1E		1802	2155	0.9E
	2355						
8 M		0218	0.6F	23 Tu	0110	0406	0.6F
	0533	0900	1.1E		0705	1047	0.9E
	1214	1444	0.7F		1403	1623	0.4F
	1750	2133	1.2E		1845	2240	0.9E
9 Tu	0044	0323	0.8F	24 W	0156	0450	0.7F
	0639	1008	1.2E		0757	1136	1.0E
	1319	1545	0.7F		1457	1704	0.4F
	1844	2229	1.3E		1927	2317	1.0E
10 W	0132	0420	1.0F	25 Th	0236	0524	0.8F
	0740	1108	1.4E		0844	1218	1.0E
	1420	1643	0.8F		1539	1741	0.5F
	1937	2320	1.4E		2009	2351	1.0E
11 Th	0222	0508	1.3F	26 F	0311	0556	0.8F
	0837	1204	1.6E		0925	1258	1.1E
	1517	1733	0.9F		1614	1818	0.5F
	2032				2052		
12 F		0011	1.6E	27 Sa		0026	1.1E
	0311	0555	1.4F		0348	0630	0.9F
	0930	1258	1.7E		1003	1335	1.1E
	1608	1823	1.0F		1649	1857	0.6F
	2126				2134		
13 Sa ●		0104	1.6E	28 Su		0107	1.2E
	0400	0644	1.5F		0421	0707	0.9F
	1021	1351	1.8E		1040	1409	1.2E
	1658	1916	1.0F		1724	1940	0.6F
	2218				2215		
14 Su		0156	1.7E	29 M ○		0148	1.3E
	0449	0736	1.5F		0457	0746	1.0F
	1110	1441	1.8E		1117	1443	1.2E
	1748	2010	1.1F		1802	2021	0.6F
	2310				2255		
15 M		0246	1.7E	30 Tu		0229	1.3E
	0541	0829	1.5F		0535	0825	1.0F
	1201	1529	1.8E		1156	1518	1.3E
	1840	2102	1.0F		1842	2100	0.6F
					2336		

December

Day	Slack h m	Max h m	knots	Day	Slack h m	Max h m	knots
1 W		0309	1.3E	16 Th	0035	0406	1.4E
	0617	0903	1.0F		0712	0950	1.2F
	1235	1556	1.2E		1317	1645	1.4E
	1924	2138	0.6F		2001	2221	0.8F
2 Th	0019	0351	1.3E	17 F	0125	0457	1.3E
	0700	0942	1.0F		0807	1039	1.0F
	1313	1639	1.2E		1358	1736	1.3E
	2007	2220	0.6F		2051	2312	0.8F
3 F	0105	0439	1.2E	18 Sa	0215	0556	1.1E
	0749	1025	0.9F		0902	1132	0.8F
	1351	1730	1.2E		1438	1825	1.1E
	2051	2308	0.6F		2141		
4 Sa	0155	0537	1.1E	19 Su		0006	0.7F
	0840	1114	0.8F		0310	0655	1.0E
	1430	1822	1.2E		1003	1226	0.6F
	2138				1517	1910	1.0E
					2232		
5 Su		0000	0.6F	20 M ◐		0059	0.6F
	0255	0638	1.1E		0416	0752	0.9E
	0940	1209	0.8F		1111	1318	0.5F
	1514	1913	1.2E		1600	1952	0.9E
	2229				2326		
6 M ○		0055	0.7F	21 Tu		0155	0.6F
	0409	0738	1.1E		0525	0858	0.8E
	1048	1305	0.7F		1221	1418	0.3F
	1609	2005	1.2E		1649	2038	0.9E
	2320						
7 Tu		0151	0.8F	22 W	0018	0302	0.6F
	0524	0844	1.1E		0626	1008	0.8E
	1159	1408	0.6F		1329	1530	0.3F
	1711	2103	1.2E		1739	2131	0.9E
8 W	0013	0254	0.9F	23 Th	0107	0409	0.6F
	0630	0955	1.2E		0721	1102	0.8E
	1308	1521	0.6F		1428	1629	0.3F
	1813	2204	1.3E		1830	2223	0.9E
9 Th	0108	0358	1.1F	24 F	0153	0453	0.7F
	0730	1058	1.4E		0811	1145	0.9E
	1410	1626	0.7F		1511	1711	0.4F
	1912	2301	1.4E		1921	2307	1.0E
10 F	0201	0452	1.2F	25 Sa	0237	0527	0.8F
	0828	1154	1.5E		0856	1225	1.0E
	1508	1719	0.8F		1549	1749	0.5F
	2012	2355	1.5E		2012	2350	1.1E
11 Sa	0255	0540	1.3F	26 Su	0317	0602	0.9F
	0921	1248	1.6E		0937	1304	1.1E
	1558	1809	0.9F		1622	1828	0.5F
	2110				2102		
12 Su		0049	1.5E	27 M		0035	1.2E
	0347	0629	1.4F		0353	0638	0.9F
	1003	1341	1.7E		1016	1342	1.2E
	1646	1901	1.0F		1657	1910	0.6F
	2204				2148		
13 M ●		0143	1.6E	28 Tu ○		0122	1.3E
	0437	0721	1.4F		0430	0719	1.0F
	1059	1429	1.7E		1054	1419	1.3E
	1733	1954	1.0F		1732	1953	0.7F
	2255				2233		
14 Tu		0232	1.6E	29 W		0207	1.4E
	0527	0813	1.4F		0510	0800	1.1F
	1147	1514	1.7E		1132	1455	1.4E
	1822	2045	1.0F		1811	2035	0.7F
	2345				2318		
15 W		0319	1.6E	30 Th		0250	1.4E
	0619	0902	1.3F		0553	0841	1.1F
	1232	1559	1.6E		1211	1533	1.4E
	1912	2132	0.9F		1852	2115	0.8F
				31 F		0334	1.4E
					0640	0922	1.1F
					1249	1614	1.4E
					1933	2157	0.8F

Figure 17-17 This is an extract from Table 1 of the Tidal Current Tables; it will be used in all the tidal current examples shown in the text.

TABLE 2-CURRENT DIFFERENCES AND OTHER CONSTANTS

No.	PLACE	Meter Depth	POSITION Latitude	POSITION Longitude	Min. before flood	flood	Min. before Ebb	Ebb	SPEED RATIOS Flood	Ebb	Min. before Flood Knots	Dir.	Max. Flood Knots	Dir.	Min. before Ebb Knots	Dir.	Max. Ebb Knot	Dir.
	CHESAPEAKE BAY Time meridian, 75° W	ft	North	West	on Chesapeake Bay Entrance, p.44						Knots	Dir.	Knots	Dir.	Knots	Dir.	Knot	Dir.
4441	Cape Henry Light, 1.1 n.mi. NNE of	15d	36°56.33'	75°59.98'	+0 26	+0 03	-0 04	+0 10	1.3	1.3	--	--	1.0	296°	--	--	1.7	113°
	... do.	38d	36°56 33'	75°59.98'	-1 42	-1 41	-1 36	-1 52	1.4	1.0	0.2	003°	1.1	275°	0.2	189°	1.2	108°
4446	Cape Henry Light, 2.0 n.mi. north of	15d	36°57.53'	76°00.63'	+0 12	+0 25	+1 00	+0 20	1.5	0.9	0.1	210°	1.2	289°	--	--	1.1	110°
	... do.	39d	36°57.53'	76°00.63'	-0 23	+0 10	+0 55	-0 17	1.5	0.5	0.1	012°	1.2	277°	0.1	190°	0.7	110°
	... do.	54d	36°57.53'	76°00.63'	-1 03	+0 07	+0 34	-1 05	1.1	0.4	0.1	002°	0.9	263°	0.2	177°	0.5	111°
4451	CHESAPEAKE BAY ENTRANCE	15d	36°58.80'	75°59.88'	Daily predictions						0.0	--	0.8	300°	0.0	--	1.2	129°
4456	Cape Henry Light, 4.6 miles north of		37°00.1'	75°59.3'	-0 27	+0 09	+0 19	+0 23	1.6	1.0	--	--	1.3	294°	--	--	1.3	104°
4461	Cape Henry Light, 5.9 n.mi. north of	14d	37°01.40'	75°59.55'	-0 59	-0 09	-0 26	-0 36	0.8	0.5	0.1	228°	0.6	307°	--	--	0.7	140°
4466	Lynnhaven Roads		36°55.1'	76°04.9'	-0 20	+0 18	+0 15	-0 10	1.0	0.7	--	--	0.8	280°	--	--	0.9	070°
4471	Lynnhaven Inlet bridge		36°54.4'	75°05.6'	-1 18	-1 10	-1 43	-2 30	0.7	1.1	--	--	0.6	180°	--	--	1.4	000°
	Chesapeake Bay Bridge Tunnel Chesapeake Beach, 1.5 miles north of																	
4476		15d	36°56.69'	76°07.33'	+0 29	+0 48	+0 06	+0 00	1.0	0.7	--	--	0.8	305°	--	--	0.9	100°
4481	Thimble Shoal Channel (Buoy "10")	46d	36°58.73'	76°07.57'	-0 04	+0 30	+0 45	+0 16	1.4	0.6	0.1	228°	1.1	302°	--	--	0.7	122°
	... do.		30°58.73'	76°07.57'	-0 55	+0 15	+1 25	-0 17	0.8	0.2	--	--	0.7	285°	--	--	0.3	105°
4486	Tail of the Horseshoe		36°59.57'	76°06.20'	+0 05	+0 30	+0 16	+0 28	1.1	0.8	--	--	0.9	300°	--	--	1.0	110°
4491	Cape Henry Light, 8.3 mi. NW of	12	37°02.20'	76°06.60'	+0 16	+0 43	+0 45	+0 26	1.2	0.9	--	--	1.0	329°	--	--	1.1	133°
4566	Cape Charles City, 3.3 n.mi. west of	15d	37°15.87'	76°05.62'	+0 38	+1 18	+1 03	+1 01	1.2	0.8	0.2	280°	1.0	355°	0.1	094°	1.0	187°
	... do.	40d	37°15.87'	76°05.62'	+0 16	+0 43	+1 10	+0 30	1.1	0.7	--	--	0.9	356°	0.1	284°	0.8	182°
	... do.	95d	37°15.87'	76°05.62'	+0 29	+1 00	+1 37	+1 24	1.2	0.7	0.1	223°	1.0	322°	--	--	0.8	138°
4571	New Point Comfort, 4.1 n.mi. ESE of	15d	37°17.40'	76°11.45'	+1 07	+1 22	+0 46	+0 46	1.0	0.8	0.3	296°	0.8	018°	0.3	098°	1.0	202°
4576	Wolf Trap Light, 0.5 mile west of		37°23.4'	76° 11.9'	+1 43	+2 00	+1 34	+1 36	1.2	1.0	--	--	1.0	015°	--	--	1.2	190°
4581	Wolf Trap Light, 5.8 miles east of		37°23.1'	76°04.3'	+2 23	+2 40	+2 14	+2 16	1.1	1.0	--	--	0.9	015°	--	--	1.3	175°
4586	Church Neck Point, 1.9 n.mi. W of	15d	37°24.20'	76° 09.40'	+0 46	+1 37	+1 36	+0 50	0.6	0.3	--	--	0.4	003°	--	--	0.4	177°
4591	Wolf Trap Light, 6.1 n.mi. ENE of	14d	37°24.50'	76°03.83'	+1 40	+1 58	+2 28	+2 11	1.6	0.9	0.2	275°	1.3	006°	0.2	098°	1.1	191°
	... do.	29d	37°24.50'	76°03.83'	+0 26	+0 55	+1 27	+1 07	0.8	0.5	0.2	099°	0.7	012°	0.2	279°	0.7	173°
4596	Wolf Trap Light, 5.2 n.mi. ENE of	15d	37°24.50'	76°05.00'	+1 43	+2 34	+2 41	+2 09	1.6	0.9	0.2	283°	1.3	010°	0.2	098°	1.1	187°
	... do.	40d	37°24.50'	76°05.00'	+0 24	+1 22	+2 43	+1 19	1.0	0.5	--	--	1.0	352°	0.2	266°	0.7	183°
	... do.	63d	37°24.50'	76°05.00'	+0 24	+1 22	+2 05	+1 11	1.0	0.5	--	--	0.8	343°	--	--	0.6	158°
4601	Wolf Trap Light, 1.4 n.mi. NNE of	15d	37°24.67'	76° 10.57'	+1 38	+2 16	+1 52	+1 19	1.4	0.9	--	--	1.1	005°	0.2	088°	1.2	175°
4606	Wolf Trap Light, 2.0 n.mi. NE of	14d	37°25.90'	76° 12.90'	+0 03	+0 33	+1 05	+0 08	0.7	0.4	--	--	0.6	345°	--	--	0.6	166°
4611	Nassawadox Point, 1.9 n.mi. NW of	13d	37°29.97'	75°59.37'	+1 16	+1 43	+1 56	+1 36	0.8	0.5	--	--	0.6	352°	0.1	270°	0.6	178°
4616	Gwynn Island, 8.0 n.mi. east of	14d	37°29.70'	76°06.50'	+2 03	+3 03	+2 48	+2 33	1.2	0.9	0.2	267°	0.6	357°	0.2	090°	1.1	175°
	... do.	28d	37°29.70'	76°06.50'	+0 33	+1 07	+1 46	+0 23	0.7	0.4	0.2	102°	0.6	013°	0.3	281°	0.5	209°
4621	Gwynn Island, 1.5 n.mi. east of	16d	37°30.03'	76° 14.70'	+0 59	+0 54	+0 54	+0 22	0.6	0.4	--	--	0.5	331°	0.1	227°	0.5	159°
4626	Stingray Point, 5.5 miles east of		37°35.0'	76°10.4'	+2 28	+3 36	+3 21	+2 32	1.2	0.7	--	--	1.0	343°	--	--	0.9	179°
4631	Stingray Point, 12.5 miles east of		37°33.8'	76°02.3'	+2 18	+3 00	+2 09	+2 36	1.2	0.6	--	--	1.0	030°	--	--	0.8	175°
4636	Powells Bluff, 2.2 n.mi. NW of	17d	37°35.45'	76°58.10'	+1 21	+1 29	+1 54	+1 23	0.8	0.5	0.1	101°	0.6	015°	0.1	284°	0.6	201°
4641	Windmill Point Light, 8.3 n.mi. ESE of	14d	37°34.60'	76°03.80'	+2 18	+2 57	+3 04	+2 46	1.1	0.7	0.1	270°	0.9	359°	0.1	095°	0.8	182°
	... do.	33d	37°34.60'	76°03.80'	+1 06	+1 22	+3 07	+2 14	0.6	0.3	0.2	099°	0.5	017°	0.2	255°	0.4	172°

Figure 17-18 The tidal current examples in the text use this extract from Table 2 for time and speed differences to be applied to the reference station.

TABLE 3-SPEED OF CURRENT AT ANY TIME

Interval between slack and desired time vs. Interval between slack and maximum current

h. m.	1 20	1 40	2 00	2 20	2 40	3 00	3 20	3 40	4 00	4 20	4 40	5 00	5 20	5 40
0 20	0.4	0.3	0.3	0.2	0.2	0.2	0.2	0.1	0.1	0.1	0.1	0.1	0.1	0.1
0 40	0.7	0.6	0.5	0.4	0.4	0.3	0.3	0.3	0.3	0.2	0.2	0.2	0.2	0.2
1 00	0.9	0.8	0.7	0.6	0.6	0.5	0.5	0.4	0.4	0.4	0.3	0.3	0.3	0.3
1 20	1.0	1.0	0.9	0.8	0.7	0.7	0.6	0.6	0.5	0.5	0.4	0.4	0.4	0.4
1 40	.....	1.0	1.0	1.0	0.9	0.8	0.8	0.7	0.7	0.6	0.6	0.5	0.5	0.4
2 00	.....	.....	1.0	1.0	0.9	0.9	0.8	0.8	0.7	0.7	0.6	0.6	0.6	0.5
2 20	.....	.....	.....	1.0	1.0	1.0	0.9	0.9	0.8	0.8	0.7	0.7	0.6	0.6
2 40	.....	.....	.....	.....	1.0	1.0	1.0	0.9	0.9	0.8	0.8	0.7	0.7	0.7
3 00	.....	.....	.....	.....	.....	1.0	1.0	1.0	0.9	0.9	0.8	0.8	0.8	0.7
3 20	.....	.....	.....	.....	.....	.....	1.0	1.0	1.0	0.9	0.9	0.9	0.8	0.8
3 40	.....	.....	.....	.....	.....	.....	.....	1.0	1.0	1.0	0.9	0.9	0.9	0.9
4 00	.....	.....	.....	.....	.....	.....	.....	.....	1.0	1.0	1.0	0.9	0.9	0.9
4 20	.....	.....	.....	.....	.....	.....	.....	.....	.....	1.0	1.0	1.0	0.9	0.9
4 40	.....	.....	.....	.....	.....	.....	.....	.....	.....	.....	1.0	1.0	1.0	1.0
5 00	.....	.....	.....	.....	.....	.....	.....	.....	.....	.....	.....	1.0	1.0	1.0
5 20	.....	.....	.....	.....	.....	.....	.....	.....	.....	.....	.....	.....	1.0	1.0
5 40	.....	.....	.....	.....	.....	.....	.....	.....	.....	.....	.....	.....	.....	1.0

Figure 17-19 Table 3 of the Tidal Current Tables is used to determine the speed of the current at intermediate times between slack and maximum flow. It is in two parts; Table A, shown here, is used for all locations except for a few unique places that are covered in Table B (not shown).

TABLE 4: DURATION OF SLACK

TABLE A-PERIOD WITH SPEED NOT MORE THAN

Maximum current Knots	0.1 Knots Minutes	0.2 Knots Minutes	0.3 Knots Minutes	0.4 Knots Minutes	0.5 Knots Minutes
1.0	23	46	70	94	120
1.5	15	31	46	62	78
2.0	11	23	35	46	58
3.0	8	15	23	31	38
4.0	6	11	17	23	29
5.0	5	9	14	18	23
6.0	4	8	11	15	19
7.0	3	7	10	13	16
8.0	3	6	9	11	14

Figure 17-20 Slack is a period during which the current slows down and reverses. The length of slack is a question of how slow is slow enough. Table 4A, Duration of Slack, is in two parts: Part A, shown here, is applicable in all locations except for a few that are covered in Part B (not shown). This table permits the calculation of the predicted duration of a flow that is less than, or equal to, a desired value.

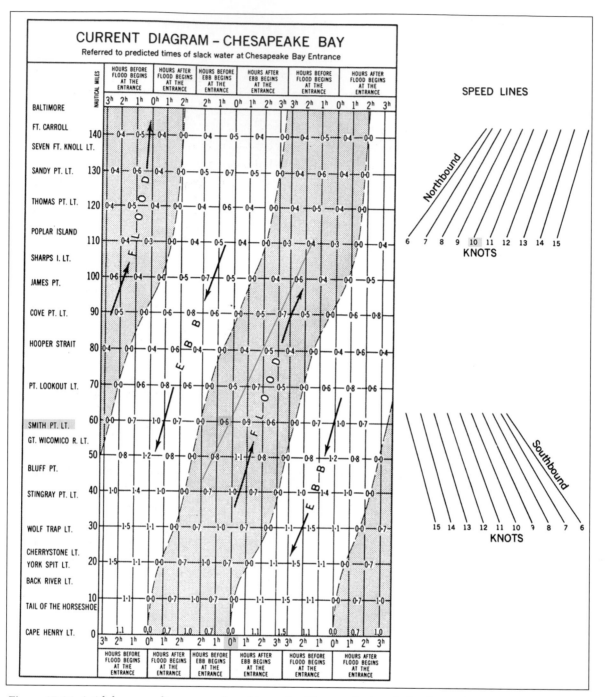

Figure 17-21 A tidal current diagram, such as this one for Chesapeake Bay, helps choose the time for a passage up or down the bay at a particular speed. See the text, Tidal Current Example 6 for how it is used.

Use the nearest tabulated values (as shown) without interpolation.

Table 4. Although slack water is only a momentary event, there is a period of time on either side of slack during which the current is so weak as to be negligible for practical piloting purposes. This period, naturally, varies with the maximum strength of the current, being longer for weak currents. Two sub-tables predict the duration of currents from 0.1 to 0.5 knots by tenths for normal reversing currents and for the hydraulic currents found at certain specified locations; see **Figure 17-20**.

Table 5. For the Atlantic Coast only, information is given on rotary tidal currents at various offshore points of navigational interest. These points are described in terms of general location and specific geographic coordinates. Predictions of velocity and direction are referred to times after maximum flood at designated reference stations.

The inside back cover of the *Tidal Current Tables* has the same astronomical data as is found in the *Tide Tables;* see page 587.

Tidal Current Diagrams

For a number of major tidal waterways of the United States, *Tidal Current Tables* give CURRENT DIAGRAM—graphic means for selecting a favorable time for traveling in either direction along these routes; see **Figure 17-21.**

Time

The *Tidal Current Tables* list all predications in *local standard time.* Be sure to make an appropriate conversion to daylight time if this is in effect. Subtract an hour from your watch time before using the tables, and add an hour to the results of your calculations. (Some commercial publishers make the conversion to daylight time; check carefully the tables that you use.)

Cautions: As with tidal predictions, the data in the *Tidal Current Tables* may often be upset by sustained abnormal local conditions such as wind or rainfall. Use the current predictions with caution during and immediately after such weather phenomena.

Note also that tidal current predictions are generally for a *spot location only;* the set and drift may be quite different only a mile or less away. This is at variance from predictions of high and low tides, which can usually be used over fairly wide areas around the reference station.

Examples of Tidal Current Calculations

The *Tidal Current Tables* contain all information needed for determining such predicted conditions as the time of maximum current and its strength, the time of slack water, and the duration of slack (actually, the duration of the very weak current conditions). Tidal current examples and solutions for typical problems follow with comments and cautions. The extracts from the *Tidal Current Tables* that are necessary to work **Tidal Current Examples 1 through 6** are given in **Figures 17-17 through 17-21.**

Supplementary Sources of Information

The ultimate source of current information is your own eyesight and past experience. These are most helpful even where there are predictions from the NOS tables. As noted before, the tabular data are to be expected under "normal" conditions, and may be easily upset by unusual circumstances. Strong winds will, for example, drive water into or out of bays and modify tidal levels and currents.

THE EFFECTS OF CURRENTS ON PILOTING

One of the more interesting problems in small-boat piloting is the matter of currents, their effect upon boat speed, the determination of courses, which must be steered to make good a desired track, and the time required to reach a destination. This is known as CURRENT SAILING (it applies to power vessels as well as sailing craft).

As a boat is propelled and steered through the water, it moves with respect to it. At the same time the water itself may be moving with respect to the bottom and the shore because of current. The resultant motion of the boat is the net effect of these two motions combined, with regard to both speed and direction. As a consequence, the actual course made good over the bottom will not be the same as the DR track, in terms of either course or speed.

Leeway, the leeward (away from the wind) motion of a vessel due to the wind, affects sailboats and, to a lesser extent, larger motorboats. However, the wind's effect need not be considered separately from current—the two may be lumped together along with such factors as wave action on the boat. The total offsetting influence of all of these factors collectively is termed "current."

TIDAL CURRENT EXAMPLE 1

Determining the predicted time and strength of maximum current, and the time of slack, at a Reference Station.

Problem: What is the predicted time and strength of the maximum ebb current at Chesapeake Bay Entrance during the afternoon of 16 October?

Solution: As Chesapeake Bay Entrance is a Reference Station, the answer is available by direct inspection of Table 1.

The table shown in **Figure 17-17** is a typical page from the Tidal Current Tables. We can see that the maximum ebb current on the specified afternoon is 1.9 knots and that it occurs at 1454 EST (1554 EDT). An entry at the top of the page tells us that ebbs at this station have a set of 129 degrees true.

Problem: What is the predicted time of the first slack before flood at this station on 21 October?

Solution: Table 1 does not directly identify the slacks as being "slack before ebb" or "slack before flood"; this must be determined by comparing the slack time with the nature of the next maximum current that occurs.

From the table, we can see that the earliest slack that will be followed by a flooding current at Chesapeake Bay Entrance on 21 October is predicted to occur at 1000 EST (1100 EDT).

Notes

1. The times obtained from the Tidal Current Tables are standard; add one hour for daylight saving time if it is in effect.

2. The direction of the current for a Reference Station is found at the top of the page in Table 1. It is also given in Table 2, which lists further information such as the geographic coordinates of the station.

3. The normal day at Chesapeake Bay Entrance, where the tide is of the semi-diurnal type, will have four slacks and four maximums. The tidal cycle of 24h and 50m will result in the occasional omission of a slack or maximum. You can see that a slack occurs very late on 20 October; the flood that follows it occurs on the following date.

TIDAL CURRENT EXAMPLE 2

Determining the time and strength of maximum current, and the time of slack, at a Subordinate Station.

Problem: What is the predicted time and strength of the morning maximum flood current at Lynnhaven Inlet bridge on 16 December?

Solution: Table 2 (refer to **Figure 17-18**) gives time differences and velocity ratios to be applied to the predictions at the appropriate Reference Station. There is an Index to Table 2 at the back of the Tidal Current Tables if it is needed to locate the given Subordinate Station.

For Lynnhaven Inlet bridge, the time difference and speed ratio are applied as follows:

Time		Velocity
09 50	Chesapeake Bay Entrance	1.2
-1:10	Lynnhaven factor	0.7
08 40	morning flood at Lynnhaven	0.8

The set (direction) of the current is also noted from the appropriate column of Table 2; in this case, it is 180° true. Thus the predictions are for a maximum current of 0.8 knot setting 180° true at Lynnhaven Inlet bridge at 0840 on 16 December.

Problem: What is the predicted time of the first afternoon slack water at Lynnhaven Inlet bridge on 17 October?

Solution: Table 1 shows the first afternoon slack for this date (1218) as a slack before ebb begins; but the time difference of –1.18 (from Table 2) makes it a morning slack at the Subordinate Station. So, the next slack, which is before flood at 1858, must be used.

18 58	Chesapeake Bay Entrance
-1:18	difference for Subordinate Station
17 40	at Lynnhaven Inlet bridge

Notes

1. Observe that Table 2 shows separate time differences for the four events of a tidal current cycle; always carefully check the column headings and select the proper time difference. Note also that the speed ratios for maximum flood and ebb currents are normally different.

2. The direction of the current at a Subordinate Station nearly always differs from that of a Reference Station; it must be taken from Table 2. No statement of current is complete without giving direction as well as strength.

3. Locations in Table 2 are often a point some distance and direction from a landmark or navigation aid. Many Subordinate Stations may be referred to the same Reference Stationbase.

TIDAL CURRENT EXAMPLE 3

Determining the strength and set of a current, at an intermediate time at a Reference Station.

Problem: What is the predicted strength and set of the current at Chesapeake Bay Entrance at 1720 EDT on 1 October?

Solution: Before entering the table, daylight saving time is first converted to standard time; 1720 EDT becomes 1620 EST. The times of slack and maximum current (ebb or flood) that bracket the desire time are found from Table 1. The interval between these times is determined, as is the interval between the desired time and slack.

18 11	time of slack
-14 56	time of maximum ebb current
3:15	interval, slack—maximum current

18 11	time of slack
-16 20	desired time
1:51	interval, slack—desired time

Once you have established these time intervals, Table 3A (see **Figure 17-19**) is used to determine the ratio of the strength of the current at the desired time to its maximum strength. The nearest tabulated values are used—with no interpolation. In this example, the ratio at the intersection of the line for 2h 00m (closed to 1h 51m) and the column for 3 h 20m (closest to 3h 15m) is found to be 0.8. Multiply the maximum current by this decimal fraction, 1.2 x 0.8 = 0.96 (which is used as 1.0).

From the times used, we note that the current is ebbing. From the top of Table 1, we determine that the direction is 129° true. So on 1 October, at 1720 EDT, the current at Chesapeake Bay Entrance will be 1.0 knots, setting 129° true.

Notes

1. Except as specially indicated, use Table 3A, the upper portion of Table 3; refer to Figure 17-19. The lower portion (B) is intended for use in designated waterways only.

2. Be sure that the interval is calculated between the desired time and the time of slack, whether or not this time is nearer to the given time than the time of maximum current.

3. Note that calculations of current strength are rounded to the nearest tenth of a knot.

TIDAL CURRENT EXAMPLE 4

Determining the current, at an intermediate time at a Subordinate Station.

Problem: What is the predicted strength and set of the current at a point 5.5 miles east of Stingray Point (the Subordinate Station) at 0935 EDT on 16 October?

Solution: First, the predictions for time of slack and maximum current must be found for the Subordinate Station. Before entering the tables, our desired time of 0935 EDT must be converted to 0835 EST.

Slack		Maximum	Max. Velocity
05 10	at Chesapeake Bay Entrance	07 57 flood	1.6 knots
+2:28	difference ratio	+3:36	1.2
07 38	at Subordinate Station	11 33	1.9 knots

With the information developed above, and the desired time, further calculations are made as follows:

11 33	time of maximum at Subordinate Station
-07 38	time of slack at Subordinate Station
3 55	interval between slack and maximum current

08 35	desired time when strength is needed
-07 38	time of slack at Subordinate Station
0 57	interval between slack and desired time

Using Table 3A, the intersection between the line of interval to desired time is 1h 00m (closed to 0h 57m) and the column for 4h 00m (closest to 3h 55m), the speed ratio is found to be 0.4. Next, multiply 0.4 x 1.9 (the maximum speed of current at the Subordinate Station) = 0.8.

Table 2 indicates that the direction of maximum flood current at Stingray Point is 343° true.

The current at 0935 EDT at a point 5.5 miles east of Stingray Point on 16 October is predicted to be 0.8 knot setting 343° true.

TIDAL CURRENT EXAMPLE 5

Determining the duration of slack (weak current) at a designated point.

Problem: For how long is it predicted that the current be not more than 0.4 knots around the time of first slack before ebb on 19 October at Chesapeake Bay Entrance?

Solution: Table 1 for this date shows the maximum currents on either side of this slack (0117) as 1.0 knots flood (2212 on the 18th) and 1.5 knots ebb (0448 on the 19th)

Use Table 4A (**Figure 17-20**) to find the duration of current less than 0.4 knot for each maximum. One-half of each such duration is used for the period from 0.4 to 0 knots and then 0 to 0.4 knots.

The value for the ending flood current is one-half of 94, or 47 minutes; for the beginning ebb current, it is one-half of 62, or 31 minutes. The duration will be 47 + 31 = 78m.

TIDAL CURRENT EXAMPLE 6

Use of a Current Diagram.

Problem: For an afternoon run up Chesapeake Bay from Smith Point to Sandy Point Light at 10 knots on 21 October, what time should you depart from Smith Point for the most favorable current conditions:

Solution: Use the Current Diagram for Chesapeake Bay; refer to **Figure 17-21**. Draw a line on the diagram parallel to the 10-knot northbound speed line so that it fits generally in the center of the shaded area marked "Flood." (You might use parallel rules to walk the line across.) Find the point where this 10-knot line intersects with the horizontal line marked 'Smith Point Light." Project downward from this point to the scale at the bottom of the diagram. The mark here is "0h after ebb begins at the entrance." Referring to Table 1, it will be seen that on the given date, the afternoon slack before ebb occurs at 1606.

For a run up Chesapeake Bay to Sandy Point Light at 10 knots on the afternoon of 21 October, it is predicted that the most favorable current will be available if you leave Smith Point Light at about 1606 EST (1706 EDT).

Notes

1. Similar solutions can be worked out for southbound trips, but on longer runs you will probably be faced with favorable and unfavorable current conditions. Choose a starting time to minimize adverse conditions.

2. Conditions shown on Current Diagrams are averages and for typical conditions—small variations should be expected in specific conditions.

A prediction of current effect can be added to a plot of a DR track to obtain an estimated position (EP), plotted as a small square with a dot in the center; see **Figure 17-22**.

Among all of these possible influences acting on a vessel, tidal current is by far the most important and it should never be underestimated. Unexpected current is always a threat to the skipper because it can quickly carry his boat off course, and possibly into dangerous water. Note that the overall risk is greater with slower boat speeds and under conditions of reduced visibility.

Piloting & Current Sailing Terms

The terms "course" and "speed" are used in DR plots for the motion of the boat through the water without regard to current. Before we consider the influence of currents on piloting, there are a few terms to become familiar with and to review; see **Figure 17-23**.

• The INTENDED TRACK is the expected path of the boat, as plotted on a chart, after consideration has been given to the effect of current.

• TRACK, abbreviated as TR, is the direction (true) of the intended track line.

• SPEED OF ADVANCE, SOA, is the intended rate of travel along the intended track line. Note that the intended tack will not always be the actual track, and so two more terms are needed:

• COURSE OVER THE GROUND, COG, is the direction of the actual path of the boat, the track made good; sometimes termed COURSE MADE GOOD (CMG).

• SPEED OVER THE GROUND, abbreviated as SOG, is the actual rate of travel along this track; it is sometimes termed SPEED MADE GOOD (SMG).

• SET is the direction *toward* which a current is

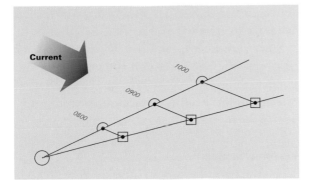

Figure 17-22 If the current is known, or can be estimated, a DR plot (the half-circles) can be modified to show a series of estimated positions (EPs, plotted as small squares).

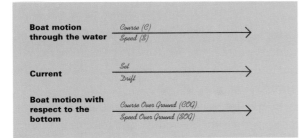

Figure 17-23 Just as lines are plotted on a chart, the DR current diagram must always be carefully labeled. Direction is shown above the line and speed below.

flowing—a current that is flowing from north to south is said to have a set of 180°. (Note that this is exactly the *opposite* from the manner in which wind direction is described.)

• DRIFT is the speed of a current. Its units may be knots or miles per hour as determined by the waters concerned.

Current Situations

A study of the effects of current resolves itself into two basic situations. The first situation occurs when the set of the current is in the same direction as the boat's motion, or is in exactly the opposite direction. In the second situation, the direction of the current is at an angle to the boat's course, either a right or an oblique angle.

The first situation is the simplest to solve. The speed of the current—the drift—is added to or subtracted from the speed through the water to obtain the speed over the ground. The course over

the ground (or intended track) is the same as the DR course—COG equals C, as does TR.

Vector Current Diagrams

When the boat's motion and the set of the current form an angle with each other, the solution for the resultant course and speed is more complex, but still not difficult. Several methods may be used, but a graphic solution using a vector current diagram is usually the easiest to understand.

The accuracy with which the resultant course and speed can be determined depends largely on the accuracy with which the current has been determined. Values of the current usually must be taken from tidal current tables or charts, or estimated by the skipper from visual observations.

Basically, a vector current diagram represents the two component motions separately, as if they occurred independently and sequentially—which, of course, they do not. These diagrams can be drawn in terms of velocities or distances. "Velocity" has a more detailed meaning than speed, since it is speed in a given linear direction, at a timed rate and within a frame of reference. The diagrams in this text will graph motions in terms of their velocities.

Such diagrams may also be called "vector triangles of velocity." The term "vector" in mathematics means quantity that has both magnitude and direction—directed quantities. In current sailing, the directed quantities are the motions of the boat and the water (the current).

Vectors

A vector may be represented graphically by an arrow, a segment of a straight line with an arrowhead indicating the direction, and the length of the line scaled to the speed; see **Figure 17-24.** If we specify that a certain unit of line length is equal to a certain unit of speed—that one inch equals one knot, for example—then two such vectors can graphically represent two different velocities. Any speed scale may be used, the larger the better for accuracy. However, the size of the available paper and working space will normally control the scale.

Vector current diagrams may be drawn on a chart either as part of the plot or separately. If

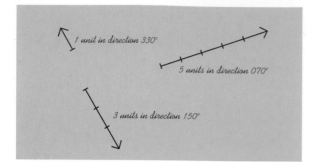

Figure 17-24 *A vector has direction as shown by the arrowhead. It has magnitude as shown by its length. Both are referenced to a convenient scale.*

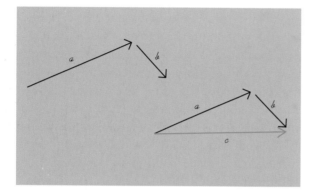

Figure 17-25 *Vectors may be combined—their quantities added—graphically. In this sketch, vectors a and b are added, and their sum is vector c. The sum vector can be measured for both magnitude (length) and direction in the same manner as you would measure a line on a chart.*

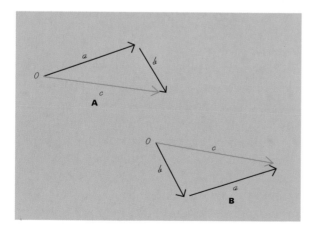

Figure 17-26 *Vector diagrams A and B appear to be different because vectors a and b have been drawn in reverse sequence. But the sum, c, is the same in both instances.*

drawn on plain paper it is wise to draw in a north line as the reference for measuring directions.

Since boats are subject to two distinct motions—the boat through the water, and the water with respect to the bottom—we will now consider how the resultant motion, or vector sum, is obtained by current diagrams.

Vector Triangles

When the two motions are not in line with each other, they form two sides of a triangle; see **Figure 17-25.** Completing the triangle gives the third side, which will be a vector representing the resultant motion or velocity. Consequently, when any two velocity vectors are drawn to the same scale and form the sides of a velocity triangle, the third side will be the resultant velocity vector (the vector sum of the other two), and its direction and magnitude may be measured from the diagram.

It may be easier to visualize the component motions if a time period of one hour is used and the points that are the corners of the triangle are considered as positions of the boat before and after certain motions, as follows:

- "O"—the origin
- "DR"—the DR position of the boat as a result solely of its motion through the water.
- "W"—the position of the boat solely as a result of the motion of the water.
- "P"—the position (intended or actual) of the boat as a result of the combined action of the component motions.

It should be noted that although in some cases two of the above letters are applicable to a position, it is customary to use only one.

"Tail-to-Head" Relationships

Note carefully how the vectors, one representing current and the other the boat's motion through the water are drawn "tail-to-head." (This rule applies only when one of the vectors is current, not when both represent the boat's motion.)

If boat motion through both the water and current are known, either may be drawn first from the origin. In **Figure 17-26,** drawing A and drawing B both yield the same result for vector *c*.

CASE 1: FINDING THE EFFECT OF CURRENT ON A BOAT'S COURSE & SPEED

If the set of the current is as shown in the diagrams in Figure 17-26, then the boat will be set off to the right of the direction in which it is being steered.

We will use a current diagram (shown at right) to determine the exact extent of this effect; we will also determine the path that the boat can be expected to follow, as well as its speed along that path (in other words, the intended track and speed of advance).

We first draw in a North line as a reference for measuring directions in the diagram, and then the vector for the boat's speed through the water, O-DR, a line drawn from the origin in the direction of 070° for a length of 10 units. Next, we add the vector for current, DR-W, three units in the direction of 130°. Note that we have observed the "tail-to-head" relationship rule. (Either of these two vectors could have been drawn first; the triangle would appear differently, but the result will be the same.)

Because these vectors form two sides of a triangle of velocities, the third side, O-W, is the resultant velocity at which the boat moves with respect to the bottom under the combined influences of its propulsion and the current. The point W can now be relabeled "P." The intended (or expected) track (TR) and the speed of advance (SOA) can be measured from the O-P line.

In this example, the results indicate that the boat can be expected to sail a course over the ground of 083° and to have a speed advance of 11.8 knots. Bear in mind that the directions of these vectors are plotted as true directions.

Summarizing briefly, we have drawn vectors to indicate independently the motion of the boat from two different influences—that of its own propulsion and that of the current. Actually, of course, the boat will not go first from O to DR and then on to P. All the time, it will travel directly along the intended track O-P. The boat is steered on course C, the direction of O-DR, but due to the effect of current, it is expected to travel along the intended track O-P. This is the intended route that must be considered for shoals and other hazards to navigation.

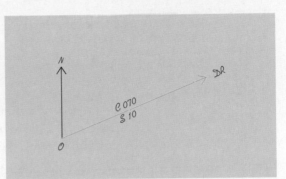

The north reference line is drawn first, but is not needed if the diagram is plotted directly on a chart. This shows the vector line for the course and speed.

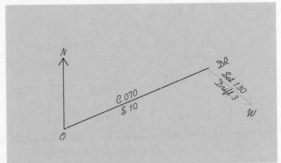

The vector for current set and drift is added; note the "tail-to-head" relationship of this second vector to the first one.

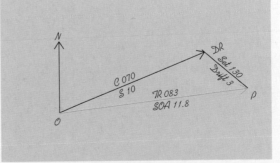

The connecting vector from O to P shows the resultant motion and speed of the boat over the bottom.

CASE 2: DETERMINING CURRENT SET & DRIFT

This is a situation in which you know the course you have steered and the speed through the water from either the speed curve of your boat or a marine speedometer. It is also obvious to you that you did not arrive at your DR position. From your chart plot, you have been able to determine the course and speed over the ground. Current has acted to set you off your course—you desire to know its set and drift.

After again drawing a north reference line, plot vectors for your motion through the water—C 255°, S 12 knots, and your motion with respect to the bottom—COG 245°, SOG 13.4 knots. These vectors are both drawn outward from the origin, O, to points DR and P respectively. The "tail-to-head" rule is not applicable as neither of these vectors represents current.

The action of the current has been to offset your boat from DR to P (which is also point W in this case), thus the set is the direction from DR toward P, and the drift is the length of this line in scale units.

In the diagram, the current is found to be setting 192° with a drift of 2.6 knots. This is the average current for the time period and the loca

tion of the run from O to P for which the calculations were made; it is not the current at P. For the next leg of your cruise, these current values can be used as is, or modified as required by the passage of time and/or the continuing change in position of the boat.

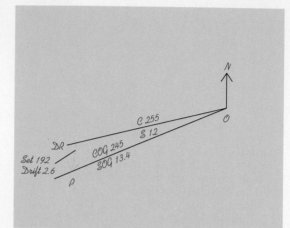

The prevailing current (actually the net effect of all offsetting influences) can be found graphically by plotting vectors for the DR track of the boat and its actual course and speed for a given time, then adding the vector from DR to P.

CASE 4: RENDEZVOUS

This is a variation of Case 3, in which you want to arrive at a specified point at a given time. It may be that you are competing in a predicted log contest, or merely that you have agreed to meet friends at that time and place. In addition to the data on current that you have, you have decided upon your track and your speed of advance. In the diagram at right, let us assume that the current sets 205° at 3 knots. You need to make good a track of 320°, and a quick distance-time speed calculation sets your required speed of advance at 11.5 knots.

From the north reference line, draw the current vector O-W and the intended track vector O-P. Complete the triangle with the vector W-P, which will give you the course to be steered (C 332 True) and the speed to run through the water (S 13.0) to arrive at the destination at the desired time. Line O-DR should be drawn in from the origin as a dead-reckoning track for the sake of safety.

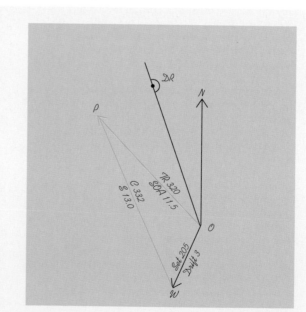

This problem concerns the course to be steered and the speed at which to run in order to arrive at a specified destination at a predetermined time. This could be used in establishing a rendezvous with another boat, or in predicted log or other navigation contests.

CASE 3: A TYPICAL CRUISING SITUATION

Here you know the track you desire to make good (TR 080°), you have decided to run at your normal cruising speed through the water (S 10 knots), and you have calculated (or estimated) the current's set (140°) and drift (4 knots). What you desire to know is the course to be steered (C) and the speed of advance (SOA), which can be used to figure your estimated time of arrival (ETA).

Draw in a North line and measure direction from it (see the diagram at right). Plot the current vector O-W, at the specified direction and length, and a line (not a vector yet) in the direction of the intended track—this line should be an indefinite length at this time. From point W, swing an arc, with dividers or drawing compass, equal in length to the speed through the water in scale units. The point at which this arc intersects the intended track line is point P and the vector triangle has been completed.

The direction of W-P is the course to be steered (C 060°); the length of the vector O-P is the speed over the ground (SOA 11.4) and from this the ETA can be calculated.

Let us look at the reasoning behind this graphic solution of Case 3. Again considering the component motions separately for the sake of simplicity, the boat is moved by current from O to W. It is to move from W at the specified speed through the water, but must get back on the intended track line—the problem is to find the point P on the track that is "S" units from point W. The solution is found by swinging an arc as described above. Remember that all vectors are plotted as true directions, including C, the course to be steered in the preceding solution. This must be changed to a compass direction (course) for actual use at the helm.

The DR Track

In accordance with the principles of dead reckoning, it is desirable to plot the DR track even though a current is known to exist. This line, drawn from point O in the direction C and with a length of S scale units, forms a basis for consideration of possible hazard if the current is not as calculated or estimated.

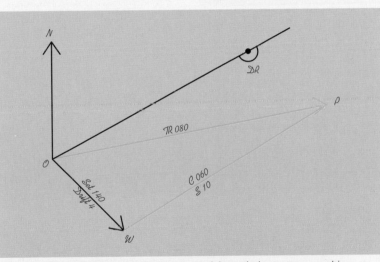

If you know your desired track, and your speed through the water, a graphic solution can be used to determine the course to be steered and the speed of advance. For safety, a DR plot is added.

The Four Cases of Current Problems

There are four typical current problems, designated for convenience as Cases 1, 2, 3, and 4; see pages 609-611.

• **Case 1:** What is the effect of a known current if no allowance is made for it while running the DR course?

• **Case 2:** What is the set and drift of an unknown current from observation on its effect?

• **Case 3:** What is the corrected course to be steered, without regard for the effect of speed or estimated time of arrival?

• **Case 4:** What is the course and speed to arrive at a specified time? This is the "rendezvous" or "contest" case; see **Figure 17-27.**

Figure 17-27 Proceeding toward a rendezvous point, this skipper compensates for the effect of current by adjusting his course and speed so that he arrives at his destination at the desired time.

Position Determination

Lines of Position • Visual Observations • Positioning Procedures • Radio & Radar Navigation • Using Depth Information • Specialized Techniques

It is your duty as skipper to make a careful judgment as to the precision and frequency with which your vessel's position should be fixed, and then to see that these fixes are carefully made and recorded. This is true whether you are doing the piloting or someone else is—you can delegate the function, but not the responsibility. Here we will cover procedures that you, as skipper, should be able to perform independent of any electronic positioning equipment you have at hand. Electronic positioning and navigation are covered in Chapter 21.

The actual procedures in position determination may vary widely in practice. When you are proceeding down a narrow channel, positioning is informal and a chart plot may not be maintained. In this case, position determination is not being omitted; rather it is being done continuously by visual reference to the aids to navigation. On the other hand, during an open ocean passage, a dead reckoning plot will be determined only three or four times each day, or even only once a day by noon sights.

Between these two extremes are the normal cruising situations in pilot waters. Cruising just offshore or in larger inland bodies of water, a skipper will usually maintain a DR plot of his track with periodic fixes, perhaps every 15 or 30 minutes, perhaps at hourly intervals.

Your ability to determine your position—to fix your position—with appropriate accuracy under any conditions of visibility or sea is essential. Your limitations in these skills must restrict the extent of your boating activities, setting the boundaries of the waters and weather conditions that you can accept without endangering your boat or its crew.

Remember that knowledge of where you are, extended from a recent position determination, is essential if you must call for help. If another boat is in trouble, you can set a direct course to render assistance *only* if you are both certain of each boat's location.

DEFINITION OF TERMS

A LINE OF POSITION (LOP) is a line along which an observer can be presumed to be located—actually two lines: one "real," one drawn on a chart; see **Figure 18-01.** In the absence of other information, the observer may be anywhere along the LOP. An LOP may result from an observation or measurement—from visual, electronic or celestial sources. It may be straight or curved. A circular LOP is sometimes called a circle of position; see **Figure 18-02.** An LOP, in a running fix (defined below), may be "advanced" to a later time according to the movement of the vessel; or, in a rare case, it may be "retired" to a previous time as needed.

A BEARING is the direction *toward* an object *from* the observer. Bearings are expressed in degrees as three-digit numbers: 005°, 056°, 157°,

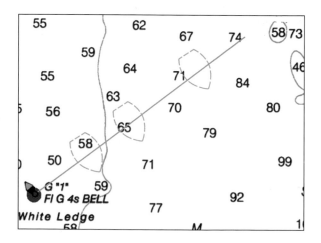

Figure 18-01 A line of position (LOP) is a line along which the observer is located. Although a single LOP does not determine position, it does tell you where the boat is not located, and such information can be useful in itself in many situations.

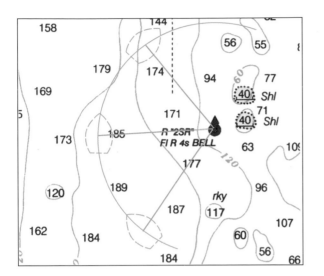

Figure 18-02 A line of position can be circular as well as straight. A circular LOP results from a measure of distance from an identified object. Usually it is plotted as an arc through the most likely area of position.

etc. A true bearing is one measured with reference to true North. A magnetic bearing is one measured with reference to local magnetic North, and a compass bearing is one taken over a compass and affected by the compass deviation at the time it was taken. (Refer to Chapter 13 for a discussion of true, magnetic, and compass direction.)

A RELATIVE BEARING is one measured with reference to the vessel's heading. It is measured *clockwise* from the fore-and-aft line, with 000° as dead ahead, 090° as broad on the starboard beam, and 180° as dead astern, etc.

A RANGE consists of two objects that can be observed in line with each other and the observer—all three are on the same straight line; see **Figure 18-03.**

A FIX is an accurately located position determined without reference to any assumption or estimation of prior position.

A RUNNING FIX (R FIX) may also be derived from two LOPs, one of which has been advanced (or retarded) from a different time—thus introducing an element of estimation.

An ESTIMATED POSITION (EP) is the best position obtainable short of a fix (or running fix). It is the most probable position, determined from incomplete or questionable data relating to course run, speed, and drift, etc.

Lines of Position

Lines of position are the basic element of position determination. An observer lies somewhere along the length of a line of position. If two LOPs intersect, the observer must be at the intersection—the only place where he or she can be on both lines at once. A fix is usually determined by crossing two, or more, LOPs.

When LOPs are drawn on charts they should be no longer than necessary and should be clearly and consistently labeled when they are drawn. Their labels should identify them completely; but extra information can be confusing on a much-used chart. The label must specify the time the LOP was observed or measured and its basic dimension such as direction toward or distance from the reference object.

A bearing is a line of position that has both time and direction. Time is always shown above the line of the bearing and direction below it; use plain, block letter styles. Remember to write time as a four-digit figure in the 24-hour system. Record the direction as a three-digit group with leading zeros as necessary; follow the figures with a space and the letter "M" if the direction is magnetic, the absence of a letter indicates a true direction (i.e., the noting of "T" for true is unnecessary and redundant). Note that the degree symbol (°) is omitted since all three-digit numbers in labels are obviously directions; see **Figure 18-04.**

A circle of position has dimensions of time and distance and may be plotted as a full circle or an arc.

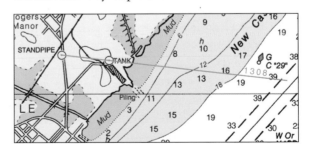

Figure 18-03 When two objects can be observed in line, this is a special LOP called a range. It is labeled only with the time of observation above the plotted line. Some range objects will have been set up specifically for that purpose, but any identifiable pair of charted objects or features can provide a range.

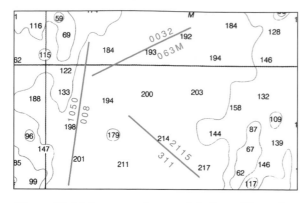

Figure 18-04 Prompt and correct labeling of lines of position is important; unlabeled or mislabeled lines cause confusion. Time is shown above the line in the 24-hour clock system. Direction is shown beneath the line as a three-digit number with "M" added if it is a magnetic direction.

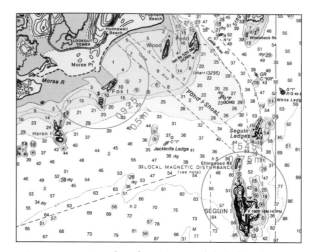

Figure 18-05 Circles of position are labeled in the same way as lines of position, with time written horizontally above the line and distance below (unit of distance may be shown). Time will be inside or outside the circle as determined by the curvature of the arc.

Time is written above the line, and distance (and units of distance) below (which may be "inside" or "outside" the circle or arc); see **Figure 18-05.**

A range is an LOP whose direction is self-evident from the two points that establish it. In this case, the label need show only time, which is written above the range line; refer to **Figure 18-03.** The line need not be plotted completely through both objects of the range—draw it only long enough to make clear which two objects define it. This will minimize the need to erase lines drawn over important chart symbols.

An LOP that has been advanced from an older line is labeled with both times above it—the original time first and the time to which it has been advanced, separated by a dash; see **Figure 18-06.**

Label your LOPs immediately to avoid mistakes. Unlabeled lines on a chart can be a dangerous source of confusion.

Fixes

A fix is an accurately located position. On many occasions in small-craft piloting, position will be determined by passing close by an identifiable object, often an aid to navigation. When such a fix is established, the skipper should note the time horizontally on the chart; see **Figure 18-07.**

A fix that is obtained from lines of position will be the intersection of two or more such lines; see **Figure 18-08.** Note that the angle of intersection

of two LOPs affects the accuracy of the position determination. When two lines cross at right angles (90°), an error of a couple of degrees in one or the other LOP will have the least effect. Where LOPs cross at small angles, however, an error in one or both observations or measurements will have far more serious implications; see **Figure 18-09.**

Two lines of position should intersect as nearly as possible at right angles and the angle should never be less than 60 degrees, if possible. A fix resulting from LOPs intersecting at angles smaller than 60 degrees may not be a fix at all and should be regarded with doubt.

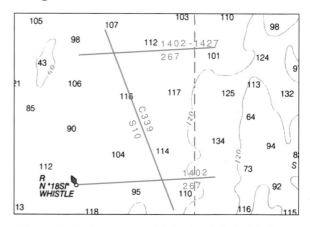

Figure 18-06 An advanced LOP is labeled with the original time and the time for which it was replotted. The direction remains the same and is repeated.

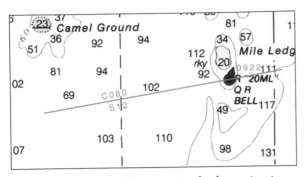

Figure 18-07 An excellent, yet simple, determination of position occurs when a boat passes close to an aid to navigation or other identifiable point. Note the time on the chart written horizontally, no circle needed.

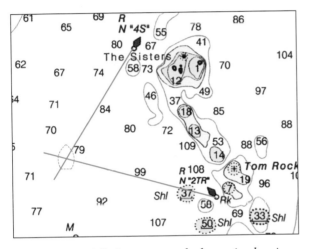

Figure 18-08 A fix is an accurately determined position for the observer and his or her vessel, determined from currently observed lines of position or other data.

Even lines that intersect at large angles will cover what are known as AREAS OF UNCERTAINTY. While we label our lines with specific directions, we know that there may be uncertainty in each line of 2 or 3 degrees. If the uncertainty is potentially dangerous, it should be represented graphically by adding two dashed lines on either side of the LOP that define the limits of the inaccuracy. LOPs from various sources will have different levels of inaccuracy—only an experienced navigator can judge these levels.

If both questionable LOPs are drawn with their dashed lines at the maximum and minimum possible values, the dashed lines will enclose an "area of uncertainty" at their intersection. The area of uncertainty is not the quadrilateral enclosed by the lines, but an elliptical area; it is

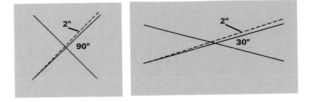

Figure 18-09 Note the difference in position of the intersection that a change of 2° in one LOP makes when the lines cross at 90° (left) or at 30° (right).

circular only if the two LOPs cross at exactly 90 degrees; see **Figure 18-10.**

Using More Than Two LOPs

Whenever possible, a third line of position should be drawn to reduce the uncertainty. Of course, a fourth and fifth LOP might also be available, but this is seldom the case and almost always unnecessary.

If the observer is on all three lines of position at the same time, then they should all intersect. The more common result is that they nearly intersect and instead of defining a point, they form a small triangle. (Theoretically the three bearings should be taken simultaneously, but in practice they can be taken in sequence, as the distance traveled by the boat in this short interval is too small to show up on the chart plot.)

The best result is obtained when all three LOPs form 60° (or 120°) angles. If this is the case, their inherent inaccuracy will have the least effect; see **Figure 18-11.**

In practice, two bearings should be taken promptly, one after the other, spaced as closely as possible to 90 degrees, and, if time permits, a third

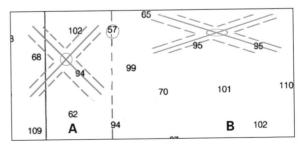

Figure 18-10 When both LOPs have a possible inaccuracy of several degrees, there is an area of uncertainty around the intersection point (A). This area grows as the intersection angle narrows (B). Be very cautious with intersection angles of 30° or less.

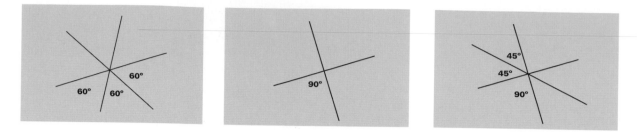

Figure 18-11 An optimum set of three LOPs cross at 60° or 120° (left), but this is seldom possible. Alternatively, you might choose objects whose LOPs would cross at 90° (or as near to 90° as possible) ensuring a good fix, and adding a third LOP at about 45° or 135° as insurance, if there is time and a suitable object available for the third observation.

chosen to split them as evenly as possible.

The triangle that almost always results when three LOPs are plotted is known as the triangle of position. A large triangle suggests a serious inaccuracy in at least one of the LOPs and a check should be made on the observation for error of reading, deviation, calculation, or plotting.

A small triangle (how small is a relative judgment depending on the proximity of danger) can be "eyeballed" to find its center, and this center used as the fix; see **Figure 18-12.**

Labeling the Fix

A fix is plotted on the chart as a small circle with a dot in its center; the dot, however, should be omitted from the symbol when it is placed at the intersection of two LOPs. The word "fix" is not needed, but the position must have a label, written horizontally, that records the time of the fix; see **Figure 18-13** and refer to Chapter 16, **Figure 16-24.** A running fix is shown with the same symbol, but the label should contain "R FIX" in addition to the time. When the fix is obtained by

passing close by an aid to navigation, the aid's symbol may take the place of the dot-and-circle. The usual distance off (50 to 100 yards or meters) is insignificant at most chart scales.

The Value of a Single LOP

While a fix is typically made with two or more LOPs, don't underestimate the value of a single LOP. Of course, a single LOP cannot tell the skipper where the boat is at the moment, but it can tell him (within its limits of accuracy) where the boat is not. This information, though lacking detail (and meaningful only in a negative sense), can nevertheless be reassuring where hazards may be close by.

Further, a single LOP can often be combined with a DR position to obtain a useful EP (estimated position). This EP is the position along the LOP that is closest to the DR position for the same time that the LOP was observed. To obtain such an EP, draw a line from the DR position, perpendicular to the LOP until the lines intersect. An EP is marked with a *square*. A square is used

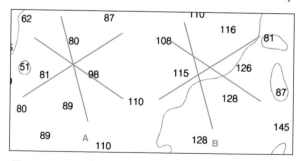

Figure 18-12 Plotting more than two LOPs increases the accuracy of the resulting fix. If they were perfectly accurate (A), all three would intersect at the same point. However, in actual navigation, they will almost always form a small triangle (B).

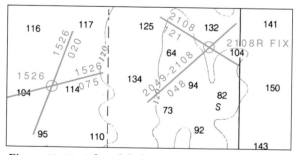

Figure 18-13 A fix is labeled with the time, written horizontally, but the word "fix" is not used. For a running fix, however, the label "R FIX" is added along with the time of the second observation, again written horizontally.

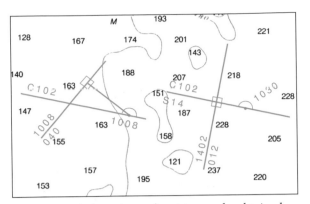

Figure 18-14 An estimated position can be obtained from a single LOP. It is the point on the LOP that is closest to the DR position for that time (left). If a beam bearing is used, the EP will be on the track line (right).

exclusively for EPs, so the label does not have to say "EP." Time may also be omitted because it is the same as the time that appears on the LOP or at the DR position; see **Figure 18-14.**

It is also possible to obtain an "EP with current." This requires an estimate of the set and drift of the current, either from predictions or from accurate measurements of the effects of the current on the boat's course and speed made good.

From the DR position for the specified time, an EP with current would be obtained as follows: A line is drawn representing the effect of the current during the time period since the DR track was started from the last fix. The line is drawn in the direction of the set of the current and to a length

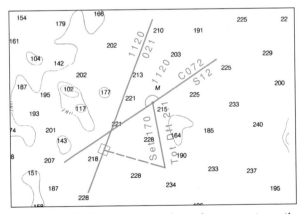

Figure 18-15 If information about the current is available, an improved "estimated position with current" can be plotted. The offsetting effect of the current (which includes wind effects) since the start of the DR track is calculated and plotted. The nearest point on the LOP from this current-influenced point is the EP.

equal to the total drift. (The length of the line would be drift multiplied by the elapsed time since the last fix.) This total drift line is labeled, and from its end another line is drawn to intersect the LOP at a right angle (just as in a regular EP plot). The intersection obtained is your EP with current; see **Figure 18-15.**

Running fixes, and the use of a single LOP with depth measurements, will be discussed later in this chapter.

VISUAL PILOTING

In typical small-craft navigation, the primary source of lines of position will be visual observation. Observations will include bearings, ranges and even horizontal and vertical angle measurements. Correct identification is essential. Although other methods and other equipment, such as GPS and Loran, radar bearings and distance measurements, and depth measurements, may also provide LOPs, these will normally be secondary to your visual observation. (The use of radios and radars in piloting is discussed later in this chapter; electronic navigation and positioning systems are covered in Chapter 21.)

The aids to navigation depicted on charts comprise a system consisting of fixed and floating objects with varying degrees of reliability. A prudent boater, therefore, will not rely on any *single* aid to navigation, especially a floating aid, to fix his or her position.

If a navigator has a choice of objects to sight for bearings, he or she should select the nearer ones provided they would make good intersection angles on the plot. The reason is that a measured angular inaccuracy, if one exits, will be the same whether the object is near or far. However, the linear inaccuracy will be amplified as the LOP is extended over a greater distance. For example, an angular error of one degree extending to one mile will result in an error of about 100 feet (30.5m). At two miles, the error will double. In a case where a light is being observed at night over a distance of a dozen miles, a one-degree error is potentially quite serious.

Simple Visual Bearings

Perhaps the simplest and most accurate visual observation is a bearing taken dead ahead and read from the vessel's steering compass; see **Figure 18-16.** The movement needed to swing the boat off course to line it up on an object is rarely important to the DR track since the boat is held on this heading just long enough for the boat to be lined up and for the compass to settle down and be read—perhaps only 20 or 30 seconds. Of course, this is somewhat more difficult on a sailboat because the dead-ahead alignment from the helm is more likely to be obscured by the mast.

The skipper must be sure of his general location and of surrounding traffic so that the off-course swing can be made safely. This is a quick, accurate, and simple way to get a bearing, and has the additional advantage that it can be accomplished by the helmsman alone; refer to **Figure 18-16.**

If the observed object on which the bearing is to be taken is on the beam, a swing off course to line it up with the bow may not be feasible. Perhaps the limited width of the channel, or other vessels, restricts such a deviation from the DR track. In this case, choose some part of the boat that will give you an accurate right angle from the centerline. This

Figure 18-16 *A simple, accurate way to take a bearing is to "aim" your boat directly at the sighted object and read the compass. Brief off-course swings for this purpose will not affect the DR plot materially, but be sure that there are no hazards alongside your course. Correct compass bearing to true directions before plotting them on your chart.*

might be a bulkhead, a seat back, etc. While the helmsman maintains course on the DR tract, the bearing taker waits until the object comes into view along this line. Such sights will determine when the object is dead abeam—either 090 or 270.

If waiting until the object comes abeam is not feasible or desirable, then the heading of the craft can sometimes be temporarily altered slightly to bring the sighted object on the beam more quickly. Should such a temporary change of heading be made, be sure that the 90 degrees is added to or subtracted from the compass reading at the moment the sighted object is abeam; do not use the normal base course.

It is extremely important to note that any of these bearings taken from the steering compass is a compass bearing and, as such, is subject to both deviation and variation. If you are to plot them as true bearings, you will have to correct for both (refer to Chapter 13).

In the case of the 90-degree adjustment for sightings abeam remember that 90 degrees must be added or subtracted *after,* not before, the compass reading has been corrected for deviation (and for variation) because, while variation will be the same on any heading, deviation will differ from one heading to another. The deviation is found on the deviation table opposite the boat's heading (because deviation varies with heading), not opposite the direction for the bearing.

A bearing in almost any direction can be taken by using one of several instruments: a hand-bearing compass, refer to **Figure 16-06;** a pelorus, refer to **Figure 16-08;** or a range finder, see **Figure 18-17.** Care must be taken to use the value of deviation of the boat's heading at the time of observation, *not the deviation value for the direction of the bearing.*

Plotting Bearings

The direction measured for a bearing is *from* the boat *toward* the object. When the plot is being done, the position of the boat is not yet known, but it is still possible to draw the bearing line of position so that it will have the correct direction and will lead to or through the point on the chart that locates the object.

It is also possible to plot a line outwards from the position of the sighted object toward the observer's position by using a reciprocal of the corrected bearing. If this method is being used, be sure to correct the bearing for deviation (as well as for variation, just to be consistent) *before* converting it to a reciprocal by adding or subtracting 180 degrees.

Avoid Magnetic Plotting

It is also possible to convert bearings to magnetic and to plot them as magnetic directions using the magnetic circle of the compass rose on the chart. However, this conversion is not recommended because it requires that all directions be plotted as magnetic—courses, ranges, and currents. A less confusing plot will result if you become accustomed to plotting in true directions.

Bearings Without Changing Heading

Getting a bearing, either dead ahead or abeam, may not always be safe or convenient, especially under sail. Of course, bearings can also be taken without changing the boat's heading. Such bearings may involve the boat's steering compass, a hand-bearing compass, or a pelorus.

On many boats, it may be possible to take a bearing in most directions by sighting over the steering compass. Sometimes the accuracy of such a bearing is increased by the use of sighting vanes placed over the compass, but usually the sighting can be taken across the card itself. Once again, be sure that you correct for deviation and variation, and that you use the deviation value appropriate to the *boat's heading*, not the direction of the bearing.

Using a Hand-bearing Compass

Very often, visual bearings are made with a hand-bearing compass; refer to Chapter 16, **Figure 16-06**. While such a compass is also vulnerable to deviation, the usual practice is to choose a location on board that is sufficiently distant from magnetic influences that a deviation correction is not needed. Some practice might be required to find a spot that is clear of obstruction, provides a secure platform and is free from magnet influence.

Figure 18-17 This navigation tool, a range finder, will provide a compass bearing, an estimation of distance, and the current time in a single observation.

(Remember, the metal frame of your glasses, the grommet in your cap, and the batteries in the flashlight you may be using to illuminate the card can affect the compass.) Once you have avoided magnetic influences you need only to correct the hand-bearing reading for variation to obtain a true bearing for plotting.

Using a Pelorus

A pelorus can also be used to obtain bearings, usually as relative bearings; refer to Chapter 16, **Figure 16-08.** A pelorus can be used anywhere that the object is clearly in view and where the pelorus card can be accurately aligned with the boat's fore-and-aft axis. In practice this might mean predetermining two or three convenient positions on deck.

Although the pelorus card can be adjusted (after fore-and-aft alignment) to the boat's compass heading, and sights made directly as compass bearings, this is less desirable than using the pelorus to read relative bearings, as described next. In all cases, the compass bearings must be converted to true bearings before plotting.

Relative Bearings

To take a relative bearing with a pelorus, the pelorus scale is set with 0° dead ahead. The helmsman is alerted and requested to steer a steady course, reading the compass continuously. Before the pelorus observation is made the reader calls "Stand by," and as it is made, the reader calls "Mark." At his call, the helmsman notes the reading on the steering compass and calls it out to the recorder. If the steering compass reading has not been accurate, the pelorus reading must be discarded. If it is very difficult to steer a steady course, the helmsman can instead call "Mark" each time he is confident of an accurate reading. The pelorus reader makes his observation at each "Mark."

The relative bearing that is obtained by either pelorus technique, or by simply sighting along a 90-degree line, must be corrected to true for plotting; see **Figure 18-18**. First the compass reading is corrected for deviation and variation, then the pelorus (or sighted) reading is added. (If the result exceeds 360, then 360 is subtracted.)

Once again, avoid a common error. Always be sure to use the deviation value appropriate to the boat's heading—not the bearing direction.

Let's look at the examples, shown in **Figure 18-18**. In the first case, an observer is on a boat that is heading 040 (true) and takes a relative bearing on a buoy at 055°. To determine the true bearing of this buoy, simply add the two numbers, 40 + 55 = 95, so the bearing is 095°.

Here's a more complicated example: A boat is heading 303° by compass when a relative bearing of 317° is measured. The variation for this location is 6°W and the deviation for this particular

compass at 30° is 2° E. Convert the boat's heading to true this way: 303 – 6 + 2 = 299°. The sum of the relative bearing and the true heading is 317 + 299 = 616. Subtract 360 and the true bearing is 256°.

Ranges

Lines of position from ranges are of exceptional value in position determination. They are free from all of the magnetic effects that might cause errors in bearings taken with reference to a compass (whether sighted on the bow or across the boat, or taken with a pelorus).

LOPs from ranges are also much more easily obtained than bearings. No matter how small the boat, or how rough the weather, if you can see both objects, you can line them up with absolute accuracy; refer to **Figure 18-03**. The accuracy of your LOP then depends only on the accuracy of the range locations on the chart. You now have half of a very accurate fix.

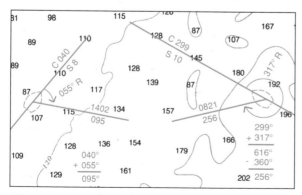

Figure 18-18 Relative bearings must be converted to true bearings before they are plotted. The relative bearing value is added to the boat's heading at the moment of observation; if the sum exceeds 360°, subtract 360°.

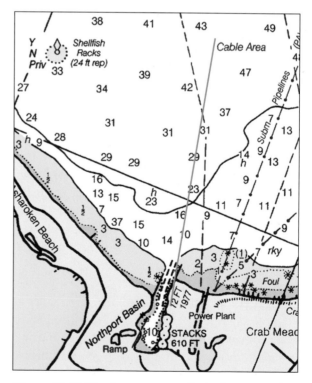

Figure 18-19 Navigators are not limited to ranges that have been established specifically as aids to navigation—many natural and man-made features make excellent incidental ranges. For example, these four stacks at Northport, Long Island, NY provide a range that is almost exactly magnetic south.

Ranges fall into two groups. First, there are those that consist of two aids to navigation constructed specifically to serve as a range and are charted with standard symbols. The direction of such a range can be measured from the chart, but is better determined from information in the *Light Lists*. However, any two objects that can be identified and located on the chart such as ordinary aids to navigation, spires, towers, radio towers, stacks, the center of bridges, and even clearly demarcated edges of natural features can be used for ranges; see **Figure 18-19**. Be careful using natural features because shoreline edges may change with changes in water level and exact points may be hard to determine. If possible,

avoid using buoys, as their location is not as exact as fixed aids to navigation.

Taking an LOP from a range requires no more than the observation of the time when your boat comes into alignment with the two objects. The LOP is plotted by lining up the symbols with a straight edge and drawing a light, solid line over the portion of the chart where your DR track or other LOP is likely to cross. The actual direction will not ordinarily be noted, but it should be labeled with the time as soon as it is drawn. The range LOP can be crossed with another range or an LOP from any other source. If none is available at the time of alignment, the range line of position can be advanced at a later time and used as part of a running fix. In this case, the direction should be noted so that the advanced line can be related to the original and easily labeled.

The U.S. Coast Guard, and other authorities, often establish ranges to indicate the center of a hazardous narrows, dredged channel, or simply an important waterway, especially if there are strong currents to contend with. Such a range line is printed on the chart, and it is often used for direct steering rather than as an LOP. Two cautions are needed: First, a vessel traveling in

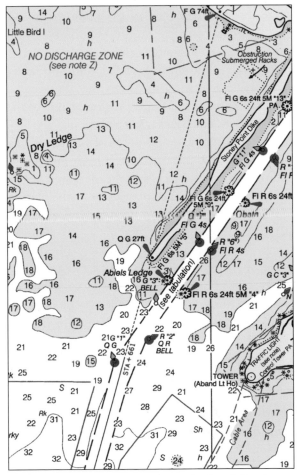

Figure 18-20 Caution must be used when following a range because there is always a limit to the extent of safe water. The range line on the chart will be solid for the length for which it is to be used, and dashed where it is not to be used. Often buoys or minor lights mark the beginning and end of a range-marked channel.

Figure 18-21 A sextant, such as the one seen above, is usually used for measuring vertical angles in celestial navigation, but it can also be used in piloting to measure horizontal or vertical angles to calculate distance off.

the opposite direction on the range will be on a collision course. Second, a range can be followed for too great a distance into dangerous waters. Buoys will often mark the limits of such a range, but study your chart carefully to determine when to turn off a range to avoid danger; see **Figure 18-20.**

Horizontal Angles

A way to obtain a fix without having to correct for compass error is to measure two horizontal angles having a common side. The two angles are taken using three objects identifiable on the chart. A sextant, normally used to measure vertical angles in celestial navigation, can be easily read sideways to a very high degree of accuracy; see **Figure 18-21.**

Horizontal angles can be plotted with a three-arm protractor; see **Figure 18-22.** The two measured angles are set on the outer arms in relation to the center arm. The protractor is moved on the chart, several positions being tried, until one allows all three arms to intersect the locations of the sighted objects, the edge of each arm representing a line of position. The center of the protractor (the apex of both angles) is the position of the observer. You plot it by placing a pencil point though a hole.

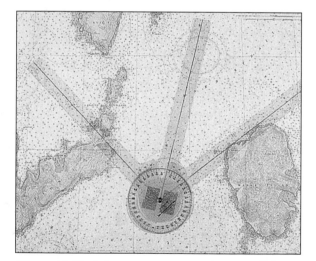

Figure 18-22 A three-arm protractor is a special plotting instrument for finding a position using two horizontal angles. The angles are carefully set on the protractor, then it is moved about on the chart until the arms lie over their respective objects.

The same plot can be accomplished with tracing paper. After drawing the angles on the tracing paper, they are moved around in the same way until all three are intersecting the locations of their respective objects; see **Figure 18-23.**

Be careful when selecting the three objects to be observed; if they and the boat all lie on the circumference of a circle, no fix can be obtained. When you study **Figure 18-24,** you will see three sighted objects—X, Y, and Z—and an observer at both A and at B. Both observations will give the same angle values, and will do the same almost anywhere between X and Z.

This situation, known as a "REVOLVER," can occur if the center object sighted is farther away from the observer than the other two. By selecting three objects so that they are essentially in line, or that the center one is closer to the observer, you can avoid an indeterminate situation.

A revolver should be avoided, but if one does develop it can be made usable by the addition of a single LOP, such as a single bearing on one of the three objects, or on any other point.

The geographic coordinates of a position can be calculated from the known latitude and longitude of the three objects and the measured angles between them, but the complexity of the mathematics makes the use of an electronic calculator or personal computer necessary.

Using a Horizontal Angle with a Radius

A fix can also be determined from LOPs derived from two horizontal angles that may or may not share a common point. Each angle can be used to establish a circle of position.

Consider one angle at a time. There is a circle, which contains both of the objects sighted upon (in measuring the horizontal angle) as well as the observer. The radius of this circle can be calculated using the distance between the sighted objects.

Here's how to proceed. First, measure the distance between the two sighted objects on the chart. Find the sine of the measured horizontal angle using your electronic or plastic circular calculator, or a trigonometric table from *Bowditch.* Next, multiply the sine by two and use that product to divide the distance between the

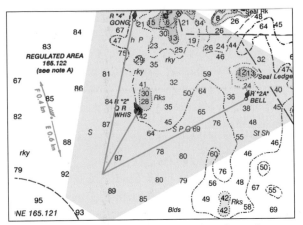

Figure 18-23 You can use horizontal angles to determine position by drawing them on tracing paper. Move the paper around on the chart until the lines intersect the objects that were sighted upon. The apex of the lines is the position at the time that the observations were taken.

objects. This is the radius of the circle on which your boat and all the sighted objects lie. (It's easy enough to find with a calculator.)

The next step is graphical. Set a pair of dividers (or a drafting compass) to that radius (on the chart scale), and scribe two intersecting arcs, one centered on one object and one on the other. That intersection is the center of the circle along which your boat and the two sighted objects lie, so put the compass point there and scribe as much of the circular LOP as you think you need.

Do the same procedure on your second set of objects. You now have two circular LOPs and you are at their intersection. (Actually, if you were to draw very long circular LOPs, there would be two intersections, but common sense or a third LOP will tell you which one is your position.)

While this procedure sounds complex, it is actually quite useful, especially aboard a boat in circumstances where the compass bearing is very hard to read because of rough weather. A simple plastic sextant and an appropriate calculator are quite inexpensive. You may also find this an interesting sampling of the sextant in more advanced navigating techniques.

Vertical Angles

All of the points (in a plane) that are a particular distance from an object lie in a circle—the distance is the radius of a circle. Such distances are often found by measuring the vertical angle from the bottom to the top of a known height, then using a simple trigonometric formula. For this reason, the heights of many man-made and natural features are carefully measured and recorded on your chart.

Such features include towers, lighthouses (usually measured to the light, not the top of the tower so as to be useful at night), radio towers, and bridges. Before you use such a recorded height, determine whether it has been measured from the base of the object or from some standard datum plane such as mean high water. Frequently, a correction will be required depending on the tidal level at the time of the observation (refer to Chapter 17).

Using a sextant, or some other device for measuring sighted angles, get an accurate measure of the angle from bottom (water level or base) to top. Call this angle "A" and the known height "h." This distance "d" can be calculated as: $d = h / \tan A$.

Again, use *Bowditch* or a calculator to find the tangent.

There are also specialized optical range finders, like the one shown earlier in **Figure 18-17,** that are adjusted to provide a reading from a scale.

Danger Bearings & Angles

Safety can often be ensured without a complete fix. As noted previously, a single LOP has value—it can tell you where you are not. In many situations, a line of position can be chosen that will keep a boat in safe waters without defining its position.

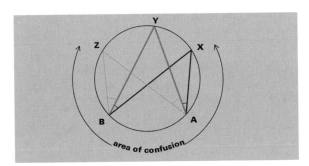

Figure 18-24 In a "revolver" situation, regardless of your position between X and Z, you will read the same angles if you happen to be on the circumference along with the sighted objects X, Y, and Z.

Danger Bearings

A bearing line can be chosen that will divide a safe area from an unsafe area. If you stay on the correct side of such a line, your vessel will be safe; crossing it will invite danger. Take the examples shown in **Figure 18-25:** Shoals are indicated on the chart, but not marked by any aid to navigation. A lighthouse on shore can be identified on the chart just beyond each shoal. The danger bearing is indicated, therefore, by a line that extends from the lighthouse toward your vessel tangent to the shoal. This line is drawn on the chart and its direction is measured. The line is labeled with the direction preceded by the letters "NMT" for "not more than," or "NLT" for "not less than." Time is not included in the label as this is not an observed line. Add hachures on the danger side or use a red pencil to emphasize the line's importance.

As the vessel approaches the area, a series of observations is made on the lighthouse (or whatever object was chosen). It should be beyond the danger area and on the same side of the boat. If the shoal lies to port, then any bearing on the lighthouse (or chosen object) greater than the danger bearing means that the boat has not yet crossed from unsafe to safe waters. Extra care should be taken until the bearing decreases below the NMT value.

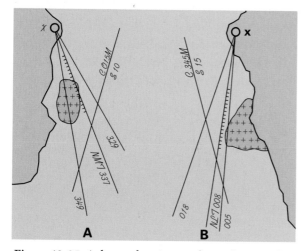

Figure 18-25 *A danger bearing can be used to avoid an unmarked hazardous area. In A above, any bearing on object X that is more than 337° indicates danger. In sketch B above, the opposite is true—a bearing less than 008° indicates danger.*

If the hazard were to starboard, the opposite would apply in relation to the NLT value.

Danger bearings are not always possible. They require a prominent object (which could be natural) that can be identified on the chart. It should be beyond the danger area and on the same side of the boat.

Horizontal Danger Angles

As we have seen, a horizontal angle measured between two objects (identifiable on the chart) defines a circle of position, or circular LOP. In **Figure 18-26,** left, an observer at either X or Y would measure the same angle between point A and point B. He would also measure the same angle at any point along that segment of the circular arc. If the observer were on the other side of the center of the circle, at X' or Y', or at other points along that segment, a constant (but different) angle would be observed. Note that the angle will be greater than 90 degrees in the first case (observer and objects on the same side of the circle), and less than 90 degrees in the second case; see **Figure 18-26,** right.

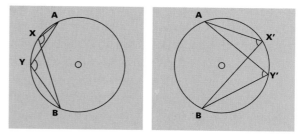

Figure 18-26 *The points at which there is a constant angle between the lines of sight to two objects form a circle as shown above. The angle between the lines to A and B is the same at X and Y, and all other points on the circle.*

Such a circle becomes very useful as a vessel approaches a hazard. It can establish a boundary between positions of safety and danger. When such a circular LOP is established, based on a horizontal angle, it is known as a HORIZONTAL DANGER ANGLE. A single horizontal danger angle is used to avoid a danger area, such as an unmarked shoal.

For passing a shoal between you and the shore, problem is how to stay far enough offshore to

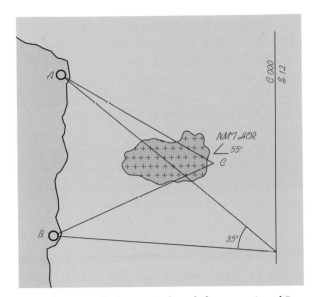

Figure 18-27 The horizontal angle between A and B is frequently measured as the boat proceeds along the track line toward the hazardous area. Any angle less than 55° means that the boat is in safe waters.

avoid the shoal. Find two prominent, identifiable objects that lie on the other side of the shoal from the area of safety. There's no need to actually draw the circle. Measure the angle on the chart from the most seaward point of the shoal to the chosen objects. This is the horizontal danger angle, shown in **Figure 18-27.** As you approach the shoal, frequent measurements of the horizontal

angle between the two objects will reveal whether or not you are standing outside the danger area. Angles less than the danger angle indicate that you are on a circular arc of a radius that is greater than the radius of the arc on which the danger lies. In other words, you're farther offshore than the tip of the shoal—and you are safe.

On the other hand, if the measured horizontal angle becomes greater than the danger angle, you are closer inshore than the tip of the shoal and may be in danger.

It is preferable to measure the angles with a sextant as you will have to take frequent and very accurate measurements, but they can also be determined by taking either relative or compass bearings on the objects.

The same technique can be used to pass inshore of a danger area—just make sure that your angles remain greater than the angle of the threatening extent of the shoal; see **Figure 18-28.**

Double Horizontal Danger Angles
The technique described above can be used to establish two horizontal danger angles where the problem is to pass safely between two offshore hazards. The principle is the same, as you will note from **Figure 18-29.** The safe angle lies between the upper and lower danger limits.

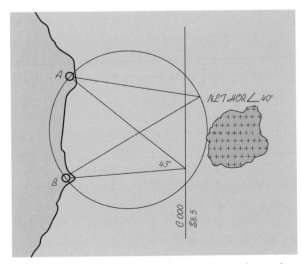

Figure 18-28 A horizontal danger angle can be used to pass between an offshore hazardous area and the shore itself. Here we see that the measured horizontal angle must be greater than the measured horizontal danger angle of 40°.

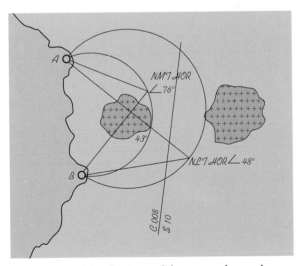

Figure 18-29 Two horizontal danger angles can be used to pass safely between two unmarked hazardous areas. The frequently measured angle must be between a minimum and maximum value; in the situation above, not less than 48° but not more than 76°.

Vertical Danger Angles

Where only a single object is available, it may be possible to use a vertical angle to establish a boundary between safe and hazardous waters. Using the vertical angle technique, a circle is drawn that has the identifiable object of known height at its center and encloses all of the hazards. The radius is measured from the chart and used in a formula $d = h / \tan A$ where "d" is distance, "h" is height, and $\tan A$ is the tangent of the angle. The angle itself can be found with a calculator or looked up in *Bowditch*, which also provides a table to substitute for the whole calculation (Table 15, 1995 or 2002 editions). The danger circle is labeled with the VERTICAL DANGER ANGLE.

On approach, a series of vertical angle measurements is taken and as these values approach the danger angle, course is altered to maintain or decrease the measured values. If the angle were maintained, the course would describe a circular arc around the sighted object (outside the area of hazard). A decreasing angle would mean that the boat was getting farther away from the sighted object and also from the hazardous area.

Vertical angles may also be used in pairs in a manner similar to that described for horizontal angles. Two vertical angles can be used to define a

safe passage between two hazards, one indicating the inshore limit and the other indicating the offshore limit. Range finders can also be used in this situation; refer to **Figure 18-17** and see below.

Using Range Finders

Range finders, generally designed to be used at distances less than a mile, are available in two types. One, called coincident, matches split images like a camera lens; the distance is read on a scale. Accuracy decreases with distance.

The other type of range finder uses a reticle graduation technique, like the periscope of a submarine. Its accuracy is relative to the height of the target in the viewer, distance and ability to match the target with the grid. For a 5 x 30 lens, the accuracy for a target 20 feet high will be, at 300 feet, ± 6 percent and at a quarter mile ± 25 percent (since the vertical height in the viewer is one-quarter of the first one).

POSITIONING PROCEDURES

Knowing where you are at all times is fundamental to boating safety. A fix is the best statement of position and should be obtained as often as possible. Of lesser significance, but not without value, are running fixes and estimates of position.

Basic Fixes

A basic fix is obtained by crossing two lines of position, and a third LOP is desirable. Such a fix assumes that the observations or measurements for these LOPs are made simultaneously, but the usual situation on a small boat is that there is only one bearing-taker. Observations are taken sequentially rather than simultaneously, but if they are taken quickly, the distance traveled between them is negligible and too small to be plotted on a chart. Adherence to the procedures that are described here will minimize the error from sequential observations.

As the boat moves along its course, a bearing angle will change. Those on the beam will change more rapidly than those on the bow or stern; bearings of closer objects will change more rapidly than those of distant objects. To obtain the most

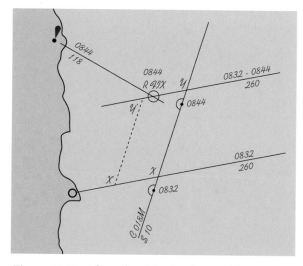

Figure 18-30 A line of position is advanced by moving forward any point on it an amount equal to the boat's motion during the time interval, and redrawing the LOP through the advanced point. The intersection of this line and the new LOP for the given time is a running fix.

accurate fix from two LOPs, deal first with the object whose bearing will change slowly—the one that is farthest forward or aft. Then take a sight on the second, faster-changing object and finally, do a check on the first. You now have three bearings on two objects. Plot them by using the average of the two bearings on the slowly changing object and the single bearing on the faster-changing object. If circumstances permit only two sightings, take the slowly changing one first.

Improving Your Fix

If you are able to sight three objects, take them in order of rate of change—the slower-changing ones first—and consider using the averaging technique if you are able. The time of the fix should be the approximate middle of the sequence. At typical cruising speeds and chart scales, a difference of a minute or two will not be significant. At 12 knots, for example, a boat will travel 0.2 miles in one minute; on a 1:80,000 scale chart, that's a distance of less than $\frac{3}{16}$ of an inch.

As described in Chapter 16, there are generally accepted standards of precision for the description of position. If geographic coordinates are used, latitude and longitude (in that sequence) are stated to the nearest tenth of a minute on charts with scales of 1:50,000 or smaller, and to the nearest second on charts of larger scale.

If the position is stated with respect to some aid to navigation or landmark, direction from that point is given to the nearest degree (true) and distance to the nearest tenth of a mile.

The Running Fix

In some cases it is possible to get a good sighting on one object, but no second object is available. In this situation a standard two-LOP fix is impossible, but a running fix (R fix) can be used instead. A running fix is usually not as reliable because it incorporates an element of dead reckoning rather than simple observation.

The technique is to observe and plot the single LOP that is available. Some time later, after the vessel has traveled a known distance, that plotted LOP will be advanced (or retired) to a new position on the chart. Think of the LOP sweeping

along across the water, without changing its angle, as your boat moves forward. To complete the running fix at a later time, a second LOP is plotted from a sighting on the same object or a new object and the "old" LOP is advanced to a new position—the position it would have reached in the period between the time it was sighted and the time the second LOP was sighted according to the speed and direction of the boat. You will note the dependence on an accurate measure of the speed and direction of the vessel in the intervening time.

Advancing an LOP

Here is how the technique is actually accomplished. The first LOP is observed and plotted, its time and direction carefully noted. A DR track is maintained. At a later time, a second sighting on the same object or some other object is made and plotted, time and direction recorded.

The "old" LOP must be "advanced" to a new position according to the DR track, so a point is selected somewhere on the older LOP and moved forward in the direction of the boat's travel for a distance representing the distance covered since the first sighting was observed. A new line is drawn through that advanced point—parallel to the old LOP. This new, advanced LOP is labeled as soon as it is drawn with the original time followed by a dash and the new time, and the original direction. The point where the advanced LOP crosses the LOP of the second observation is the position of the boat at the time of the second observation—the running fix; see **Figure 18-30.**

Sometimes, the LOP is an arc of a circle, such as when a vertical angle is used to establish distance away from an observed object. In that case, the point chosen to advance the old LOP to the new position is the center of the circular arc. The advanced LOP is scribed with the same radius as the old, but on an advanced center point; see **Figure 18-31.**

If the track of the boat in the interval between sightings is a straight line of constant speed, the DR is simple. However, the boat may vary both direction and speed between observations. This complicates the DR track, of course, but it does

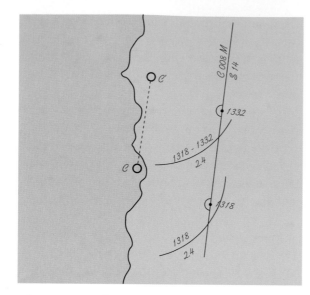

Figure 18-31 When a circular LOP has been used (as with a distance-off measurement), it can be advanced by moving its center by the same distance and in the same direction as the movement of the boat according to the DR track. The line C-C' is equal and parallel to the track line segment between the two DR positions.

not change the principle of advancing an LOP. Typically, the DR plot would be maintained through these variations of speed and direction. When it is time to advance the point on the LOP, it is advanced along a line parallel to and equal in length to a line drawn between the original DR position and the DR position at the time of the running fix; see **Figure 18-32**.

The Effect of Current

Current may also play a role in the advancement of the LOP. If current is predictable, the advanced point is moved according to the DR track, and then offset by the appropriate direction and distance according to the estimated drift and set of the current—both calculations using the elapsed time between observations; see **Figure 18-33**.

In all cases, a fix that is obtained from two simultaneous observations is preferable to a running fix because the accuracy of the original fix can only be decreased by errors and uncertainties in the DR data for the boat's speed and direction during the interval between first and second observation. When current is also a factor, this data becomes less and less certain.

Obviously, increasing the length of the time between observations decreases accuracy. Yet, enough time must be allowed to pass in order to pick up a second object, or to achieve a substantial angular change for the second observation of the same object.

In piloting, this interval is rarely more than 30 minutes, while in celestial navigation on the high seas, the interval might be as much as several hours since inaccuracy is less dangerous in those circumstances.

It is a matter of judgment whether a DR track should be interrupted and restarted on the basis of a running fix.

Observations on a Single Object

The running fix can be one form of observation on a single object (a running fix can also use two objects at different times), but there are other techniques for dealing with one available object. Successive observations of one object can use a method of bow-and-beam bearings, doubling the angle on the bow, two bearings and run between, or two relative bearings. Each of these different techniques is described in detail in this section.

Bow-and-Beam Bearings This technique uses two sightings that are easy to make with good

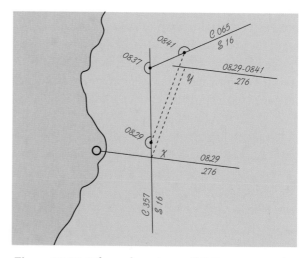

Figure 18-32 When advancing an LOP, you must take into account all changes of course and speed during the time interval. The net effect is determined by drawing a light dashed line (X-Y) between the two DR positions that define the time interval. You then advance the LOP for the length and direction of this line on a dashed line parallel to it.

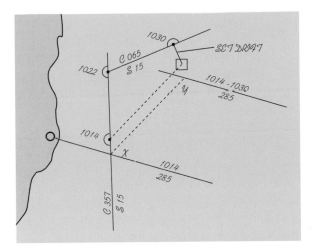

Figure 18-33 If the current is known or can be estimated, the advancement of an LOP can be made more accurately if that effect is included as shown above.

accuracy, even if no special tool is available—a 45-degree sighting off the bow and a 90-degree beam sighting off the same side. Both can be made with crude tools, even a 45-degree triangular drafting square, or no tools at all—just objects on deck that define a 45-degree and a 90-degree angle with the centerline. For this reason, bow-and-beam bearings can often be made by the helmsman single-handedly.

As the object comes into view, the observer waits for it to reach the 45-degree alignment. As usual, the time is recorded. Course and speed are

maintained. The same object is observed when it reaches the 90-degree alignment and the time is then recorded; see **Figure 18-34.**

Picture a 45-degree drafting triangle—the long edge corresponds to the LOP of the first (45-degree) observation. The other two edges are the same length. One of these edges is the LOP of the second observation and the other is the DR track of the boat between observations.

You have recorded the time of the first observation and of the second, so you can calculate how far the boat traveled in the interval. That traveled distance is equal to the distance from the object at the time of the second observation. You now have a distance and an LOP, so you can plot a fix.

Doubling the Angle on the Bow The technique of doubling the angle on the bow makes use of a similar principle as the bow-and-beam method, but it requires that relative angles be accurately measured, which means that two people are usually required.

As the boat approaches an observed object a relative bearing is taken. Let's assume that the bearing is 20 degrees to port. The boat continues along a DR track until the observed object bears 40 degrees to port. The time interval and the distance traveled are calculated. Again, as is the case with the bow-and-beam method, the

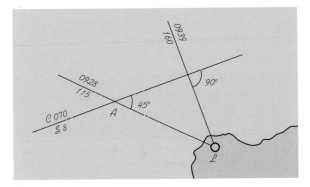

Figure 18-34 With only simple tools, and without an additional person to take bearings, a helmsman can determine his position. The time is noted when the sighted object bears 45° on either bow. The boat continues on with steady course and speed. The time is noted when the same object is broad on the beam. The distance traveled between the recorded times is calculated, and this is the distance that the boat was off the object at the time when it was abeam.

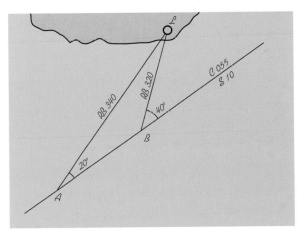

Figure 18-35 If two observations are made so that the second relative bearing is twice that of the first, as measured from the bow to either starboard or port, the distance to the object at the time of the second bearing is the same as the distance made good between the sightings—L to B equals A to B.

distance traveled between observations is equal to the distance from the object at the time of the second observation; see **Figure 18-35**.

There's an advantage with this method in that the boat's position can be fixed before the object is abeam. A hazard that may be present can more easily be avoided because the boat's course can be projected forward from the early known position. Typically, a headland can be sighted and given a wide berth well in advance.

Two Relative Bearings A more generalized solution from two relative bearings can be used. Table 18 of the 1995 or 2002 editions of *Bowditch* uses two items of information—the angle between the course and the first bearing (the first relative bearing), and the difference between the course and the second bearing (the second relative bearing). Columns of the table are in terms of the first item and lines of the table are in terms of the second item above; the interval between tabular entries is 2 degrees in both cases; see **Figure 18-36**.

For any combination of the two relative bearings within the limits of Table 18, two factors will be found. The first number is a factor by which the distance run between the bearings is multiplied to obtain the distance away from the sighted

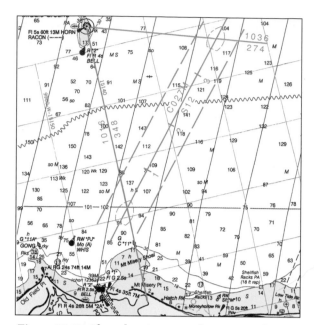

Figure 18-37 If two bearings are taken on a single object as a boat passes by, and these are plotted on the chart, only one point can be found on each bearing line where the boat's course and distance traveled will make a good fit. The second point is the boat's position at the time of the second observation. (The dashed lines on the chart extract above are shown only to illustrate how an improperly placed track line would be either too short or too long; they would not be used in actual piloting.)

object at the time of the second bearing. The second factor of the same entry in this table is the multiplier to be used to determine the distance off when the object is abeam, assuming, of course, that the same course and speed are maintained.

Two-Bearings-and-Run-Between Yet another method is available when only a single object can be observed. In this procedure, a bearing is taken on the object as before. The boat proceeds along its course. A second bearing is taken after the angle has changed by at least 30 degrees. The second bearing may be taken either before or after

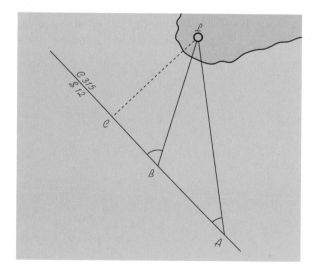

Figure 18-36 Distance off at the time of a second bearing, L-B, and distance off when abeam, L-C, can be found by using multiplying factors to the distance run, A-B, between the taking of the two bearings. These factors for various pairs of angles are given in Bowditch (1995 or 2002), Table 18. An extract of this table is shown at right.

TABLE 18													
Distance of an Object by Two Bearings													
Difference between the course and second bearing	Difference between the course and first bearing												
	34°		36°		38°		40°		42°		44°		46°
44	3.22	2.24											
46	2.69	1.93	3.39	2.43									
48	2.31	1.72	2.83	2.10	3.55	2.63							
50	2.03	1.55	2.43	1.86	2.96	2.27	3.70	2.84					
52	1.81	1.43	2.13	1.68	2.54	2.01	3.09	2.44	3.85	3.04			
54	1.63	1.32	1.90	1.54	2.23	1.81	2.66	2.15	3.22	2.60	4.00	3.24	
56	1.49	1.24	1.72	1.42	1.99	1.65	2.33	1.93	2.77	2.29	3.34	2.77	4.14	3.43
58	1.37	1.17	1.57	1.33	1.80	1.53	2.08	1.76	2.43	2.06	2.87	2.44	3.46	2.93

the object has passed abeam. A distance run between observations is calculated from the boat's DR track.

Both LOPs are plotted along with the course of the boat. A pair or dividers is opened to a span representing the distance run between observations. Then the dividers are placed in such a way as to have a point touching each LOP and have the line between them parallel to the boat's course. In other words, the boat's course is moved "sideways" until the distance traveled exactly spans the decreasing distance between the two LOPs. The divider points now indicate the boat's position at the time of each observation; see **Figure 18-37.**

Note that the distance run must be the distance over the bottom—suitable corrections having been made already for current. Accuracy depends on the usual factors, but it also depends on the accuracy of the course steered in the time interval between the observations. The net effect is to make this procedure somewhat less desirable than those described earlier.

RADIO & RADAR PILOTING

Several decades ago, radio direction finding (RDF) was a commonly used piloting technique for offshore cruising. The U.S. Coast Guard and comparable agencies in other countries operated hundreds of marine radiobeacon stations, and offshore cruising boats were equipped with RDF receivers. Large ships were also fitted with radio direction finders, often automatic (ADF) models. Bearings were taken of radiobeacons located onshore and on offshore aids to navigation; these were plotted on charts in a manner similar to visual bearings. Aeronautical radiobeacons were shown on charts if they were located so that they could aid in marine navigation. Bearings could also be taken on AM broadcast stations, and charts often had symbols marking the location of transmitting antennas. The fixes so obtained were less accurate than visual fixes, but had the advantage that they could be obtained at night and in conditions of reduced visibility, such as fog; they could also be obtained at distances far in excess of visual range. Bearings could also be taken on the radio signals of other vessels; this capability often aided rescue craft in "homing" in on a scene of distress.

With the switch to VHF and single sideband (SSB) for communications, and the use of Loran and satellite systems for navigation, radio direction finding as described above fell into disuse. It would be very rare indeed to find an RDF set on a modern recreational or commercial small craft. The U.S. Coast Guard has decommissioned many radiobeacons and converted the remainder into stations transmitting differential corrections for GPS. The call signs and frequency of many AM broadcast stations and the location of their transmitting antennas are still printed on charts, as are some aeronautical radiobeacons. However, these are not now used for direction finding for lack of onboard equipment—and the availability of better navigation systems.

VHF Radio Direction Finding

Radio direction finding has survived into the modern age in a specialized form. Automatic RDFs are available that indicate the direction of a received VHF signal to an accuracy of about 5°. Such sets are commonly found on Coast Guard utility boats and cutters and on some assistance-towing craft; see **Figure 18-38.** These are normally used in a "homing" mode to expedite the locating of a vessel requiring help; vessel operators are often asked to give a "long count from one to ten and back" while a bearing is taken. Coast Guard and other enforcement units can use a VHF ADF to locate a source of interfering

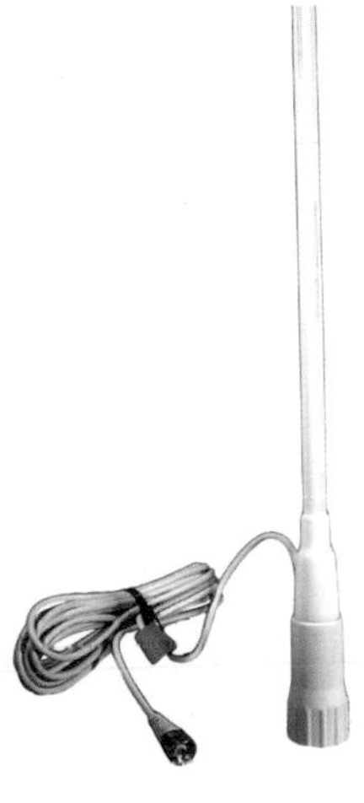

Figure 18-38
Automatic VHF radio direction finders (ADFs) will often be seen on assistance towboats that use them for locating craft in distress or needing assistance generally.

signals, such as a stuck microphone button. Bearings may also be taken on the 121.5 MHz signals of an EPIRB (if the ADF model being used covers this frequency); refer to Chapter 20.

VHF direction finders may also be seen on some sport fishermen that are seeking the most direct route to where the best fishing has been found! It must be remembered, however, that the Radio Act and FCC rules strictly forbid the use of intercepted radio communications for the benefit of anyone other than the addressee or his agent.

If a boat is so equipped, a VHF radio with the Digital Selective Calling (DSC) feature can be connected to an onboard GPS set and electronic chart plotter. When communicating with another craft having a VHF/DSC radio that is connected to its GPS receiver, the location of this other vessel will appear as an icon on the first boat's chart plotter.

Radar Piloting

While the subject of radar is covered in greater detail in Chapter 21, some mention of it in this section is appropriate. Radar has a unique advantage in navigation in that a single instrument can measure both direction and distance to both moving and still targets—and can do so under any

condition of visibility. Excellent detailed information on radar can be found in the NIMA Publication No. 1310, *Radar Navigation and Maneuvering Board Manual* (now available only in digital format as a CD-ROM or on the Internet at the NIMA Maritime Safety Information Division website, http://pollus.nss.nima.mil).

Radar measurements of direction are not as precise as those made visually, but radar can almost always make a measurement despite fog, light rain, or darkness. Heavy rain will often decrease radar's ability to detect targets.

On the other hand, measurements of distance are quite precise and accurate—much more so than vertical sextant measurements or optical range-finder readings.

Direction and distance fixes determined with radar are used in much the same manner as LOPs from visual sources. There are three different procedures for obtaining a position by radar; they are, in descending order of accuracy: radar measurement of distance to two objects, as in **Figure 18-39**; bearing on one object with a corresponding radar distance to that object, as in **Figure 18-40**; and two radar bearings. When the opportunity exists, an excellent combination is a visual direction LOP and a radar distance to the same object. Any fix involving radar is labeled with

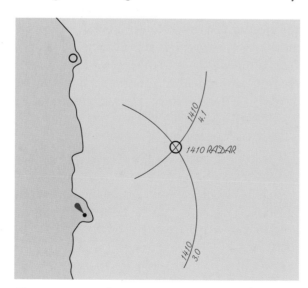

Figure 18-39 Radar ranges are more precise than radar bearings. When getting a position from radar alone, the best fix will be from the use of distances to two (or more) objects that can be identified on the radar display and on the chart.

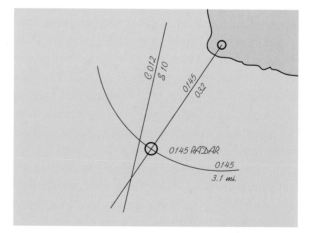

Figure 18-40 Radar is an excellent piloting tool as it can provide both direction and distance information on a single object. A fix from a radar observation is thus plotted as a line and an arc, with the fix labeled with the time and the block lettering "RADAR." If the direction information is from a visual bearing, the fix is more accurate.

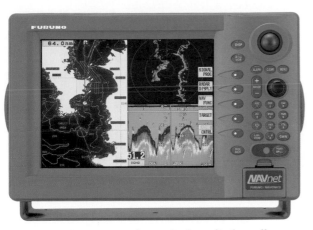

Figure 18-41 Many electronic chart displays allow simultaneous radar information. This provides an exceptionally good determination of the boat's position.

time and "RADAR." Radar distances can also be used in the manner described for vertical angles in order to avoid unmarked hazardous areas.

Radar observations of isolated objects such as buoys, offshore lighthouses, etc. are usually unambiguous. When the radar target is onshore, however, some identification problems may arise; there must be positive identification of the object on both the radar display and the chart.

Radar, even more than other piloting methods, requires considerable practice and accumulation of experience. Develop your radar procedures during fair weather and good conditions so that they are readily available in difficult circumstances and can use them with confidence; see **Figure 18-41.**

Racons

Racons, also referred to as radar beacons, radar transponders, and radar transponder beacons, are receiver/transmitter devices used as an aid to navigation to assist in identifying landmarks or buoys on a marine radar display. As also described in Chapter 14, a racon responds to a received radar pulse by transmitting back an active signal, not just a reflected echo, which becomes an identifiable mark on the radar display with a length of several miles, encoded for identification as a Morse code character beginning with a dash. The delay at the racon causes the displayed response to appear at a greater distance than the echo from the

structure on which the racon is mounted. Racons, and their identifying marks, are normally indicated on charts.

In the United States, racons are used:
• To identify aids to navigation, both on the water (buoys) and on the land (lighthouses);
• To identify landfall or positions on inconspicuous coastlines;
• To indicate navigable spans under bridges;
• To identify offshore oil platforms and similar structures.

Outside the United States, racons are also used:
• To mark new and uncharted hazards (using the letter "D");
• To identify center and turning points;

The U.S. Coast Guard operates approximately 80 racons on the Atlantic, Pacific, and the Gulf of Mexico coasts and on the North Slope of Alaska; most of these are dual-band units responding to both X-band and S-band radars. Their range should be 6 to 20 miles, depending on the heights of the racon and the radar. No additional equipment is required on a vessel, but some precautions are necessary in the operation of the radar. A rain clutter feature must be turned off (or, if necessary, set very low) to ensure that the racon signal is visible. U.S. Coast Guard racons are the "frequency-agile" type, responding on the exact frequency of the triggering radar; any interference rejection feature (clutter control) must be switched off.

USING DEPTH INFORMATION

The depth of water at a vessel's location is valuable piloting information. A single depth reading cannot tell a boater where he is, but it can tell him *where he is not*. If an accurate depth reading is 26 feet, you may be at any number of places that have a 26-foot depth, but you are not at a place that has significantly greater or less depth. When sufficient depth data have been obtained *and* have been also corrected for height of tide, they can be used for positive position determination in combination with an LOP from another source, or on their own.

Most depth sounders display the depth from the bottom of the water to the transducer, which is normally located a few feet below the water line. This distance must be added to get the depth of the water from the surface, the information needed for piloting. Some models, however, can have the display reading offset so the reading indicates the water depth below the keel or the depth from the surface, a preferable setup for use in piloting. Remember that depth figures on charts are for conditions at mean lower low water.

Depth Information and a Single LOP

Given a bottom with relatively uniform slope, it may be possible to get position information with depth and a single LOP. Typically this would be a beam bearing and a single depth reading. The LOP is plotted, then a point along the line is found that matches the depth indication on the chart, corrected for tidal stage; see **Figure 18-42.** Such a position should be regarded only as an estimated position and marked "EP." If there are several such points on the LOP, you will not be able to estimate your position.

In some instances a rough estimate of the boat's position can be obtained by matching a series of depth readings—one that corresponds to the density of depth figures on the chart in question. Mark your depth readings on tracing paper and move the paper around on the chart, keeping the line of soundings parallel to a line representing the direction of your course steered while the soundings were made. Look for the best match between your series, corrected for tidal stage, and a series

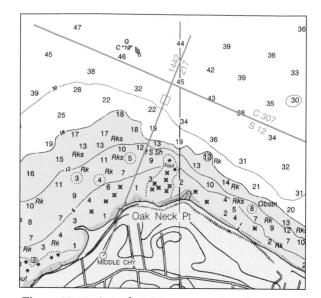

Figure 18-42 *A single LOP can sometimes be combined with depth information to provide an estimated position (EP). The LOP shown above is a beam bearing. A depth reading of 31 feet indicates that the estimated position is somewhat inshore of the DR track.*

on the chart. Don't expect to get an exact concurrence; see **Figure 18-43.**

This technique is not suited to shorelines foul with offshore rocks and areas of irregular or uniform depth. Confirmation of position cannot be positive but certain denial can be useful.

Fathom Curve Piloting

When cruising over a bottom of uniform slope, piloting can be simplified by choosing a depth curve that follows a safe path. The boat is steered so as to cross this depth, then along it with gentle course alteration to stay within a few feet of the

Figure 18-43 *A series of soundings can be plotted on a piece of tracing paper, each depth noted with time and spaced according to the boat's movement over the bottom. The tracing paper is then moved about on the chart until as good a match as possible is made between the measured depths and the depths shown on the chart. Remember to correct for the state of the tide.*

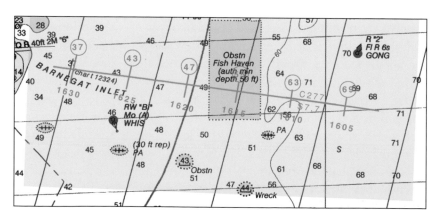

curve. Don't use this method when there is any chance of meeting hazards by covering more ground than anticipated or by distorting the curve at sudden, sharp changes in direction.

Currents & Piloting

Changes in depth resulting from tidal action cause a horizontal movement of water. A vessel thus travels in a body of water that in itself moving with respect to the bottom. This motion of the water—current—must be considered in determining a vessel's position. The effect of currents on the piloting of boats is covered in Chapter 17, pages 603-612.

SPECIALIZED TECHNIQUES

Beyond the basic techniques described in the preceding pages, as well as in Chapter 17 in the discussion of currents and piloting, there are many other specialized techniques that are useful in specific situations. These techniques should not be regarded as shortcuts. Their use requires a thorough understanding of principles, and they should not be approached until the basics have been learned.

Although the bow-and-beam technique has already been covered earlier in this chapter, you should know that there are other pairs of bearings that are not as easily obtained, but are easily used to plot a fix.

Special Pairs of Bearings

The following sets of bearings have a relationship to each other such that the run between the first bearing and the second will nearly equal the distance away from the sighted object when it is passed abeam:

20°-30°	21°-32°	22°-34°
23°-36°	24°-39°	25°-41°
27°-46°	29°-51°	30°-54°
31°-56°	32°-59°	34°-64°
35°-67°	36°-69°	37°-71°
38°-74°	39°-77°	40°-79°
41°-81°	43°-86°	44°-88°

Note that these are pairs of relative bearings to port as well as to starboard. In the table above,

"20°-30°" can be either relative bearings 020° and 030°, or 340° and 330°, "31°-56°" can be either RB 031° and 056°, or RB 329° and 304°, etc.

The Seven-Eighths Rule

If the observations are made when the relative bearings are 30° and 60° on either bow, simple calculations will give two useful items of information. The distance run between the observations is equal to the distance to the object at the time of the second bearing (remember doubling the angle on the bow). Also, this same distance multiplied by 7/8 (or more precisely, 0.866) is the distance that the boat will be off from the sighted object when it is broad on the beam, provided that the vessel's course has not changed; see Figure 18-44.

The Seven-Tenths Rule

A comparable situation to the seven-eighths rule above is one in which the relative bearings are 22.5°

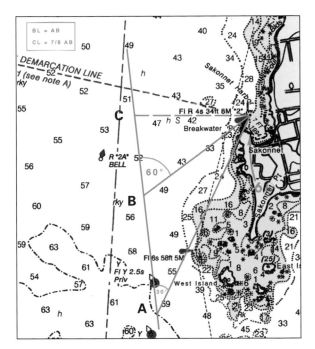

Figure 18-44 The "seven-eighths rule" is a special application of doubling the angle on the bow. If 30° and 60° are chosen as the first and second relative bearings, we know two things—the distance away at the second bearing is equal to the distance made good since the first bearing, and the distance off when abeam of the object will be seven-eighths of the distance between the first and second bearings.

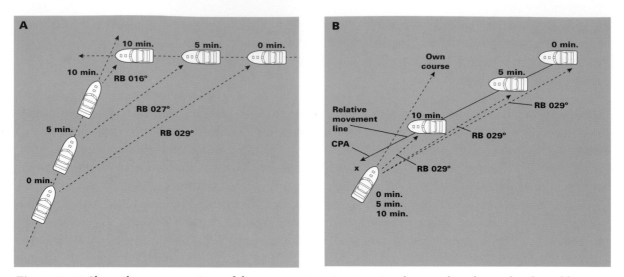

Figure 18-45 Shown here are two views of the same crossing situation. An observer directly overhead would see version A, while version B suggests the view from our own craft—the one that appears to be stationary. Crossing situations are much easier to predict if we imagine our own boat to be stationary and the other boat to be moving relative to our own.

and 45° to port or starboard. In this case, as before, the distance away from the sighted object is equal to the distance run between bearings, but the multiplier to determine distance off when the object is abeam is 0.7.

To Cross or Not to Cross

When determining the relative motion of another boat, it is necessary either to convert relative bearings to compass (or true) bearings, or to maintain a steady course. In practice, it is easier to maintain a steady course and observe

the change in relative bearings. The actual relative bearing is far less important than the direction and rate of change.

What we want to know in any crossing situation is: Will we cross ahead, or astern, or will we collide? Because we are interested in relative and not absolute motions, it is convenient to think of our own boat as being stationary.

We have three basic situations:

• The relative bearing of the other boat moves ahead (or toward our bow).

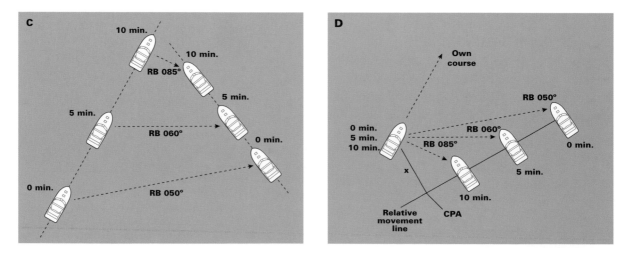

Figure 18-46 The other boat was goimg to cross ahead of our own in Figure 18-45. We could make this prediction because its relative bearing moved toward our bow. Here in versions C and D, the other craft's relative bearing moves aft. We know it will pass astern. In both cases, the separation at the closest point of approach is the distance x.

• The relative bearing of the other boat moves aft.

• The relative bearing of the other boat does not move at all.

The first situation, the other boat passing ahead, is shown in versions A and B in **Figure 18-45.** The successive positions of the two boats show a steadily decreasing bearing. Version A shows the boats are in absolute motion and version B shows how it looks from our own boat if we imagined it to be stationary.

The line connecting the two boats in versionB is the line of relative movement, the course and distance traveled by the other boat in relation to our own. Provided both boats maintain course and speed, it is a straight line. In this situation, when the line of relative motion is extended, it passes the bow of our "stationary" boat; therefore, the other boat following that line will cross ahead. The distance *x* is the minimum distance that will separate the two boats in this case. It occurs at the closest point of approach (CPA).

The second case, shown in **Figure 18-46,** versions C and D cover the situation when the relative bearing moves aft. The line of relative movement passes aft, and so will the other boat.

If the relative bearing does not change, the line of relative motion will pass through our boat's position. You might say that the CPA is zero, but you would be more likely to say "He's going to hit us!"

It is important to note that these illustrations are not actual chart plots of the boats. The position of the other boat cannot be plotted unless distance and bearing information were available, and this is unlikely unless you are using radar.

The significance here is that bearing information only, which is available to any skipper, will indicate how the two boats will converge and whether they will collide. The separation at CPA cannot actually be known unless a plot is made, but this is not significant.

Crossing Situations

The rules developed from the observations covered above are as follows:

• Maintain a reasonably steady course and speed.

• Observe the relative bearing of the other boat only when you are on your specified compass course. You must be on the same course each time you take a relative bearing.

• Watch the other boat for changes in course or speed that would obviously change the relative motion.

• If the relative bearing moves ahead, the other boat will pass ahead. If the relative bearing moves aft, the boat will pass astern. If the relative bearing is steady, there is a very real danger of collision; see versions E and F in **Figure 18-47.**

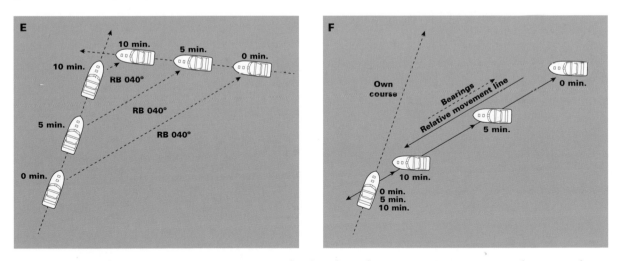

Figure 18-47 In this crossing situation, versions E and F, the relative bearing remains constant—unless one craft or the other alters course or speed, they will collide. The line of relative motion passes through our boat and there is "no separation" at the point of closest approach.

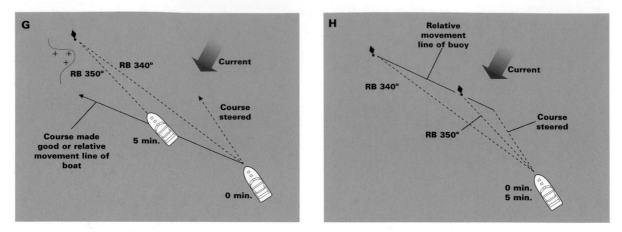

Figure 18-48 A plot of relative motion is also useful when the other object is stationary. In this situation, we can use the plot to determine whether we will leave the buoy to port or to starboard if we make no change in course or speed. In version G, our motion is relative to the buoy. In version H, its "motion" is relative to us.

Offsetting Effects of Current or Wind

Relative bearings can also be taken to help in compensating for the effects of offsetting currents or wind. In versions G and H of **Figure 18-48,** the skipper has put his boat on a course that he believes will put a buoy close aboard and avoid a shoal. At the time of the first bearing ("0 minutes") the buoy bears 340° relative. Five minutes later, the relative bearing is 350°. It is clear that the boat is being set down more than expected and that the line of relative movement of the buoy will pass ahead of the boat (the boat will pass on the shoal side). If the bearing on the buoy remained steady, the boat would pass close to it, and if the bearing shifted gradually away from the bow, the skipper would know that he would clear the shoal safely. In **Figure 18-48,** version G shows the problem in terms of the boat moving relative to the buoy, while in version H, the boat is considered to be stationary and the relative motion shown is that of the buoy. Note that the lines of relative movement in each case are parallel to each other, equal in length and opposite in direction.

Deliberate Course Offsets

A very useful technique in making a landfall confidently is to use a deliberate course offset—that is, by deliberately missing your target. When you lay your course you set it decidedly, to one side of your objective. The advantage of this procedure lies in the fact that when you do not arrive at your destination, you know which way to turn. If you had aimed directly and, through unpredicted current or steering errors, had not arrived at your destination, you would not be sure whether it lay on your port or starboard bow. With the deliberate offset, you can make a confident alteration of course, usually parallel to the shoreline.

For example: You've been fishing somewhere between Block Island and Martha's Vineyard. After several hours of trolling, drifting, and circling around your position is uncertain. Just as you decide that your fishing luck has run out and it's time to head back to Block Island, the fog

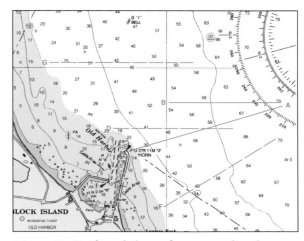

Figure 18-49 If you fail to make your predicted landfall, which way should you turn? To avoid this dilemma, make a large, deliberate "error" to one side or the other, then the choice is clear.

A SAILOR'S EYE

One of the easiest ways to acquire what is often referred to as a "sailor's eye" is to learn the simple but important principle of relative motion. For example, you find that your boat is converging on another boat that has the right of way. If you hold your course and speed, will you clear? What if your sailboat is on port tack and must yield right of way to a starboard tack boat? Do you hold and clear ahead, or pass under its stem? You have laid a course for a buoy, making allowances for current: Have you made the right allowance?

Relative motion is simply the motion of two boats in relation to each other. A boat approaching you on an opposite parallel course at 5 knots while you are making 4 knots has a relative motion of 9 knots. When meeting, if the skipper of the other boat turns to run alongside your boat to chat, your relative motion will be 1 knot, you will see his boat going slightly faster than yours.

The relative bearing of an object can be estimated within 5 or 10 degrees, with practice. When the direction of your own boat changes, the relative bearing also changes, though its true bearing remains the same.

For example, if you are on a course of 050° true and sight an object bearing 090° relative, the true bearing of the object will be 140° (50 + 90). If you change your course by coming left to a course of 020°, the relative bearing of the object will now be 120°. But the true bearing remains the same at 140° (20 + 120).

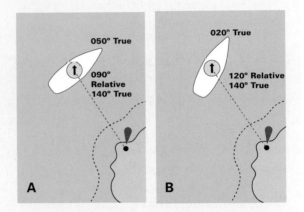

If a boat's heading changes, the relative bearing of an object is changed by the same amount. From the situation at A to that at B, the true heading of the boat has changed from 050° to 020°. The relative bearing has changed by the same amount, from 090° to 120°. Note: the sum of the heading and relative bearing remains constant (disregarding any forward boat movement).

closes in. Your best position estimate is that you are east of the bell buoy "1," marked as point *B* in **Figure 18-49.** You believe that you are somewhere near point *A* on the chart.

The solution to your problem is a deliberate offset. It's a good plan to lay your course for the off-lying bell buoy, but even if there were no buoy there is still merit in laying the course decidedly off to one side of the ultimate objective-Block Island Harbor.

Suppose you lay your course *A-B* to the bell buoy and miss it by ⅛ mile to the north. When you pick up the 3-fathom (18-foot) curve at *G*, you know you are north of the harbor—because you would have picked it up much sooner if you were south of the harbor entrance.

Had you missed it by ⅛ mile to the south and picked up the 3-fathom curve at *D*, you would still be able to follow the curve southeastward to buoy "3." Even if your position were ¼ mile south of *A* when you laid your course westward, you would still pick up the 3-fathom curve at the entrance to the harbor.

You find added assurance of your general position north of the harbor when you find depths holding generally at 3 fathoms on your course southeastward. If your calculations were completely wrong and you ran southeastward from any point below the harbor, depths would increase.

Let us consider, still in reference to **Figure 18-49,** what would have happened if you had laid a course directly for buoy "3" and had missed your objective, *E*, by ¼ mile to the south. Picking up the 3-fathom curve at *F*, you could not be sure whether you were north or south of the entrance.

Your first conclusion might be that, since you have run a few minutes overtime before reaching the 3-fathom curve, you are north of the harbor. But don't forget that you didn't accurately know your starting point. Suppose you had been several minutes eastward of where you thought you were when the fog set in. In this event, the additional few minutes' running time before reaching the 3-fathom curve is unreasonable.

On the assumption that you are indeed somewhat north of the harbor, you turn south, proceeding slowly and carefully. A few minutes pass, but still no buoy or harbor entrance. How far to continue? That buoy may be just ahead, obscured by the fog. On the other hand, doubt creeps in. You couldn't have been that far off in your reckoning—or could you? So you're in the fog—literally and figuratively.

In the first example, where you laid a deliberate offset, the intended track was about 3/8 mile to the north of the objective. How much deliberate offset should be made is a matter of judgment. On a long run in toward a long beach that runs for miles in either direction with few identifying marks, even if visibility is good, you may prefer to make allowances of a mile or more. But don't use this technique blindly. Study the chart carefully for possible dangers that may lie along the beach.

The same procedure may be used in other uncertain situations, such as crossing the Gulf Stream. Rather than attempting to make an exact allowance for the distance that the stream will set northward, make a somewhat over-generous allowance. If you don't pick up your target landfall after the allotted passage time, you can turn northward with confidence, rather than facing a 50-50 chance of being wrong.

Using a Predicted Timetable

If you are anticipating fog, you can take most of the worry out of the process by planning and plotting your run in advance. This same "timetable" technique can make a night run a pleasure instead of a trial.

Don't wait until you are underway to lay out your course, distances, running times, etc. Go over the entire trip in advance and acquaint yourself with each leg of the cruise, the aids to navigation that you will pass, the characteristics of lights, etc.

If you are piloting a powerboat and you can predict your speed with precision, set up a timetable. Set your time of departure as 0000 and note, in orderly fashion, the predicted time of arrival abeam of every light and buoy on both sides of your intended track. Alongside each entry show the characteristics of the navigational aid and the compass course at the time. You can also enter into your timetable the approximate times that major lights can be expected to become visible.

Use a watch or luminous clock with a luminous dial; set it at 0000 (12 o'clock) and start it when you leave your point of departure. The elapsed time of each event along the track will provide a quick aid to identification for each light or sound signal along the way.

By using elapsed time rather than actual time, you build some flexibility into your plan. A late or early departure will not upset your entire timetable. Any discrepancies that creep in can be compensated for by a reset of the clock.

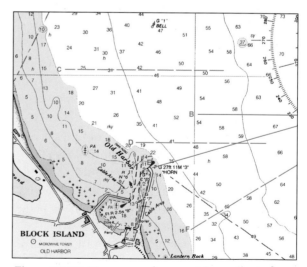

Figure 18-50 Many coastal areas with regular slopes toward deeper water offer depth information that can determine distance off. A rough, but useful, estimation of distance can also be made by using your height of eye at the helm and observing the buildings ashore.

Coastwise Piloting at Night

The lights of towns along shore can be used to estimate distance offshore. An experienced boater may be able to judge his distance by whether or not he can see the glow from the street and sign lights, or whether he sees the lighting directly. This might be a useful technique on a long, straight shoreline of consistent elevation. Of course the height at which the lights might be seen directly will vary with the observer's height of eye and should be tested by observing the shoreline at known distances.

You may also be able to follow a shoreline (without the help of a depth sounder) by noting the point at which the beach, or shoreline disappears from view. This requires straight shoreline of consistent elevation, as well as some experience, but it can be quite a useful check; see **Figure 18-50**.

Let's say you wish to parallel the New Jersey or Long Island beaches. From the deck of a typical small boat, at about 4.5 miles offshore, the beach will be under your horizon. If you can just see the beach, you are about 4 miles off. Fog and haze will make this observation unreliable and the height of your eye on your particular boat will also vary this distance.

You can also use your view of buildings on shore to estimate distance. For example, if you can make out individual windows on houses, you are probably about 2 miles offshore. With this rule of thumb, you could confidently stay from 2 to 4 miles off a long beach with no other reference.

Echo Piloting

An interesting variation on the technique for estimating distance off a beach is one used in Alaska and British Columbia, where the problem is often to maintain a distance off a rocky cliff face. It consists of sounding a short blast on the whistle or horn and timing the return of the echo.

The interval in seconds (preferably measured on a stopwatch) is divided by two because the sound wave goes to the cliff face and back. Multiply that figure by 1,100, which is a rough value for the speed of sound in air in feet per second. (Multiply by 340 for the distance in meters.)

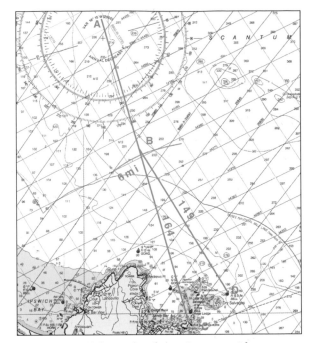

Figure 18-51 The "rule-of-sixty" can provide a shortcut for calculating the change in course required to clear an obstacle. It can be applied without making a chart plot.

For example, you sound a blast and the interval is 5 seconds. Multiply 2.5 seconds (the one-way trip) by 1,100 and you have 2,650 feet, or a distance off of slightly less than 0.5 nautical mile.

In some cases, a pilot might use an echo from both shores to stay in the middle of a passage simply by determining which one returns first, then altering course away from it.

The Rule-of-Sixty

This is another instance in which a convenient mental calculation can be made to reach a safe approximation. While it should never act as a substitute for position determination, this kind of calculation can be useful in making a decision while cruising shorthanded.

The rule-of-sixty provides a simple way of determining a new course to clear an off-lying danger area by the desired amount. You need to know your present course, your present distance off and the distance by which you would like to clear the danger area.

Let's assume that you are in the position shown on the chart. You have come out of Portsmouth

Harbor and are running a southerly course down the coast to Cape Ann. Somewhere off Newburyport you pick up the light on Straitsmouth Island, dead ahead; see **Figure 18-51,** at the bottom center, marked C. Your course made good along the line A-C has been 164° true. A bell buoy has been placed 1.5 miles eastward of the light, marking a number of rock ledges. You want to make a course change to clear the shoals. By how many degrees should you change course?

You could get out the chart and plot your position—which, if you are able to do so, is what you should do. However, you can also apply the rule-of-sixty and determine your new course in your head.

You know that the light you are seeing on the horizon is visible for 8 miles. (We'll assume that it is a clear night; if it isn't, you will have to establish distance by some other means.) The procedure is to divide 60 (the rule) by 8 (the distance) to get 7.5. Since you want to clear the light by 1.5 miles, multiply 7.5 by 1.5 and get 11.25. Round this to 11—the number of degrees by which you will have to change course. Thus your new course is 164° - 11° = 153° true. Long before you need to be concerned about the rock ledges, you will pick up the bell buoy north of Flat Ground.

The rule-of-sixty is never a substitute for proper plotting, but in rough weather or other difficult circumstances, it can be a reassuring guide.

Distance Along an Irregular Course

A pilot is often required to measure a total distance along a course that consists of several short, irregular legs. Of course, each leg can be measured and added, but there's a much easier, graphic method.

In **Figure 18-52,** the boat is at A. You need to know the total run to F, along the track B, C, D, E, F. The figure shows guidelines, which extend each leg outwards, but after you become familiar with the procedure you can use your eye to make the same extensions.

Place your divider points on A and B. Swing the A point to A1 (which lies along an extension of the next leg). Plant the divider point at A1 and stretch the other leg to C. Again, swing the A1 point to A2 (the extension of the next leg.) Plant the point at A2 and stretch the dividers to D. Repeat in this way until the dividers are planted at A4 and stretched to F.

Now you can lay that divider span along the graphic scale or the latitude scale at either side of the chart. You can make the measurement quickly and more accurately this way than by measuring and adding each leg.

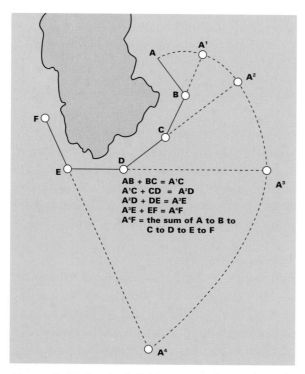

$$AB + BC = A^1C$$
$$A^1C + CD = A^2D$$
$$A^2D + DE = A^3E$$
$$A^3E + EF = A^4F$$
$$A^4F = \text{the sum of A to B to C to D to E to F}$$

Figure 18-52 A pair of dividers can make quick work of adding the lengths of several straight segments of a curved course. Span the first leg, A to B, then swing the point of the dividers from A to A1 in line with B and C and plant it. Next, move the point of the dividers that was at B to C; this adds the lengths A-B and B-C. Continue this procedure until you reach the final point, F in this example. Use the total span of the dividers on the chart's graphic scale to get the total distance.

Piloting Under Sail

The principles of piloting a small sailboat are no different from piloting a powerboat. However, much of successful piloting is not principle, but practice, and the practice aboard a sailboat may differ in several respects.

Most important is the fact that sailboat speeds are much more difficult to predict. While a

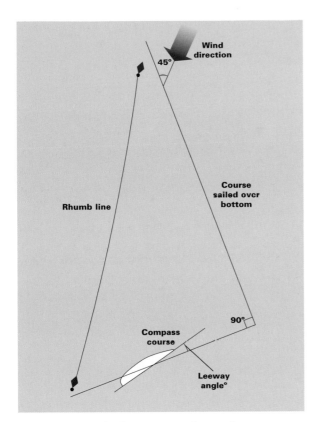

Figure 18-53 *The direct course (the one that a power-boat would take) is known as the rhumb line. The actual course that a sailboat might follow, both upwind and down, is considerably longer and more difficult to reckon. The values shown above are typical of a well-trimmed, deep keel craft.*

powerboat pilot might establish a timetable for a particular set of legs of his trip (refer to "Using a Predicted Timetable" above, page 642), a sailboat skipper would be much less likely to be able to predict the boat's speed several hours in advance along a particular leg of the trip.

In addition to dealing with the built-in complexity of a particular track, a sailboat navigator also makes extra calculations and plots to account for the fact that his boat will tack upwind and downwind too.

For the skipper of a powerboat, this leg may be a simple straight line with an easy-to-predict speed and direction. But for a sailor it becomes a series of doglegs, each with its own requirements (or estimates) and other variables to do with

steering the fastest possible course following a shifting wind, rather than a straight line; see **Figure 18-53.**

This makes it far more important for a sailboat navigator to keep track of his DR track at every tack and jibe, and to make an estimate of position just before the course is changed. It may be possible to sail equal times of each tack to simplify the calculation, but this is useful only when the destination is directly upwind, or down.

Since sailboats generally travel upwind with a "leeway angle" (refer to Chapter 8), allowances must be made for the difference between the compass orientation to the centerline of the hull and the hull's actual direction of travel through the water. It might vary by 2 or 3 degrees—much smaller than a typical steering error, but of potential significance as an additional factor over a very long leg.

All of these variations mean that a sailboat skipper must become adept at the calculations, described in this chapter, designed to resolve trigonometric problems.

A rule of thumb for sailing a tacking leg when the wind is not directly from or to your destination is to sail the longest leg first, except when the shorter leg may provide an opportunity for a fix that would be missing on the longer leg.

Finally, the actual chartwork aboard a sailboat can be more difficult due to a number of factors. The navigator may be working at an extreme angle of heel, for example, and is much more likely to be soaking wet.

Practice—And More Practice

Position determination cannot be learned totally "from the book." Study is essential, but you must put into practice the various procedures and techniques that you have studied. Remember, just as important as knowing the rules is knowing how to apply them. It's a good practice and good entertainment to "over-navigate" during daylight and in good weather so that you will be experienced, capable, and confidant when the sun sets and the weather closes in.

Electrical Systems

Fundamentals of Electricity & Electrical Circuits • Storage Batteries • Shorepower
Alternative Energy Sources • Electrical Equipment on Board

Electricity has become an essential ingredient in boating. Originally used for engine starting and lighting only, electrical power is now used for a multitude of tasks—for running communications and navigation equipment, for cooking and heating, and for such labor-intensive chores as raising the anchor and lifting the tender aboard.

Nowadays we take for granted the use of many electrical appliances that formerly would never have been afloat. More importantly, we place a greater reliance on electronic navigation and communication devices that must be reliably and constantly supplied with electrical power as a matter of safety rather than convenience.

Acquiring, storing, and delivering this power has become a complex matter, necessitating a knowledge of basic fundamentals, applicable standards, and an awareness that the boat's batteries are under constant demand; see **Figure 19-01.**

ELECTRICAL and ELECTRONIC are terms often used in an overlapping manner. In this book, "electrical equipment" includes such devices as motors, alternators, and lights. "Electronic equipment" refers to devices using transistors and integrated circuits, for example, radios, depth sounders, radar, and radionavigation systems. This chapter focuses on electrical systems whereas the following two chapters cover electronics; communications in Chapter 20, and navigation and other uses in Chapter 21.

GENERATING & STORING ELECTRICAL POWER

There is little need for a boater to delve deeply into the physics of electrical power—after all,

CAUTIONS FOR BOATERS

Just as on shore, 120V or 240V AC electrical circuits can produce a harmful, even deadly, electrical shock if improperly installed. This hazard exists not only to persons on board the boat, but also to persons swimming in the water in proximity to an improperly wired or improperly maintained vessel. If you do not possess a good degree of technical competence in this area, it is suggested that you always employ a fully qualified marine electrician to accomplish major repairs to your boat's electrical system, especially the 120V or 240V AC power.

most of us deal with electricity perfectly well at home without first undertaking a course in electromotive forces. Nevertheless, some fundamental background is helpful; with the convenience of electrical power aboard boats, come certain potential hazards and maintenance problems.

Basic Electrical Terminology

Electrical systems can be described in terms of the type of electricity used and the voltage level used.

Direct & Alternating Current

The terms "DC" and "AC" are used by just about everyone, but usually with little recognition of the differences between them. DIRECT CURRENT flows in one direction only and is substantially constant in value; DC is used on boats at a rela-

Opposite Page: Figure 19-01 The importance of electrical power on board boats has increased enormously in recent years. Every boater should as a minimum understand the fundamentals of electricity, and a skipper who cruises away from his home waters should be capable of diagnosing typical problems and making at least temporary repairs.

Figure 19-02 The basic source of electric power on boats is an alternator belt-driven from the propulsion engine. Most craft have 12-volt DC systems, although some larger vessels may have a 24-volt or 32-volt system. Higher voltages are likely to become available.

tively low voltage similar to how it is used on automobiles and trucks, typically described as "12 volts" although actually between 12 and 14; see **Figure 19-02.** Larger craft may use 32-volt DC systems. DC has the very advantageous ability to be stored in cells and batteries. (Technically, a single pair of positive and negative electrodes form a CELL; a group of cells connected together form a BATTERY—in common usage, however, individual cells are often referred to as "batteries.") Sizes vary widely, from tiny hearing aid and watch cells, to the ubiquitous AA, C, and D dry cells, to the large 8D storage batteries; see **Figure 19-03.**

ALTERNATING CURRENT reverses direction at regularly recurring intervals; AC electricity is widely used on shore and afloat, almost always at higher voltages than DC. Although AC cannot be stored in batteries, it has the advantageous property of being easily transformed from one voltage level to another, up or down. The most typical AC voltage is 120 volts, frequently referred to as "110." A higher voltage 240 volts ("220") is sometimes used for devices requiring a greater amount of power. AC power also has a characteristic of FREQUENCY. Alternating current in North America is 60 cycles per second (60 HERTZ); in Europe and most other parts of the world it is 50 Hertz (50 Hz). An electrical motor that is designed to run on 60-Hz AC will run slower when powered with 50-Hz AC. In some cases

that slowdown can cause operating problems, if not damage.

Shorepower (electrical power brought on board a boat from any source on land) is always alternating current, as is that produced by an AUXILIARY GENERATING PLANT (GENSET), or a DC to AC INVERTER. Power supplied by storage batteries is always direct current. However, it should not be assumed that, although a vessel's AC and DC systems are isolated from one another, there is never an interchange of power between them. Quite to the contrary, the AC power brought on board from a shorepower connection, and that produced by an onboard genset, can be changed by a battery charger into DC and used to recharge a vessel's storage batteries. Conversely, DC drawn from the ship's storage batteries can be changed into AC by an inverter and used to power the vessel's AC distribution system, but only for relatively low-power loads; see **Figure 19-04.**

Electrical Units & Calculations

Conceptually, the behavior of electricity flowing in wires can be likened to that of water flowing in pipes. The units of electrical measure are likewise analogous: VOLTAGE is analogous to pressure in a water pipe. An AMPERE (commonly called an

Figure 19-03 For times when the engine is not running, and the alternator is not producing electricity for the boat's needs, electrical power is stored in batteries. Groups of 2-volt cells are connected in series to form a battery providing the desired voltage. Shown here is a 12-volt battery consisting of six cells. For higher voltage systems batteries themselves may be connected in series, such as four 8-volt batteries in a 32-volt system.

Figure 19-04 Electrical power for 120-volt AC devices, such as those used at home, can be derived from the low-voltage DC system by using an inverter, but this is limited to relatively light loads that will not impose too great a drain on the boat's batteries. Some inverters also work in the reverse direction, supplying recharging power to batteries when AC power is available.

"amp") measures the amount of current that is flowing, which is comparable to the rate of flow of water moving through a pipe. And OHMS measure resistance, which can be visualized as corresponding to the friction that is generated when water flows through pipes.

There is a simple equation—Ohm's Law—that explains the relationship between current (I), voltage (E), and resistance (R),

$$I = \frac{E}{R}$$

Current flow is directly proportional to voltage and inversely proportional to the resistance in the circuit. In other words, the voltage *drop* in a circuit (E, in volts) equals the current flow in the circuit (I, in amperes, abbreviated "A") times the resistance of that circuit (R, in ohms).

$$E = I \times R$$

WATTS and KILOWATTS (1kW = 1,000 watts) are measures of power—the rate at which energy is consumed or generated. Using the water analogy, power compares to the volume of water moving through a pipe, and energy to the total volume of water that flows in a stated period of time.

Another simple equation expresses the relationship between watts, volts, and amps:

Watts = Volts x Amps.

This will be useful when we need to determine the electrical needs of a system we might want for a particular vessel; see page 651.

In DC systems, power requirements are commonly stated in amperes, and energy in AMPERE-HOURS (AH).

On-board Electrical Systems

The onboard source of electrical power can be divided into three broad categories:
- Power stored in batteries.
- Power brought aboard a vessel from land-lines via a shorepower connection.
- Power generated as needed and used.

Associated with each of these categories are one or more distinct, identifiable supply subsystems. For instance, electrical power that is created on board a boat as needed may be produced by alternators that are belt-driven by the vessel's main propulsion engine or engines. Often it may also be produced by a genset driven by its own separate engine.

Supply subsystems feed power to the vessel's electrical delivery systems, which consist of a network of distribution panels, bus bars, circuit breakers (or fuses), switches, wiring, outlets, and the like.

AC System Voltages

Not only does electrical current differ in terms of being direct or alternating; it differs in terms of voltage. Appliances designed for a specified voltage or voltage range must not be used on systems having other voltages. (Most modern electrical equipment is designed to cope with a modest range of voltage; but it is always important to check and comply with the manufacturer's specifications for that range. Otherwise irreversible damage to the equipment involved may occur.)

A system using a higher voltage has the advantage that, for a given wattage demand, it does not require as heavy wiring as at a lower voltage. Moreover, higher voltages are better at overcoming localized resistances, for example, minor buildups of corrosion at connecting terminals.

When high wattages are involved, the smaller wires that are practical with higher voltages are advantageous in terms of cost, weight, and the physical difficulties of installation. (Smaller

ELECTRICAL STANDARDS FOR BOATS

When it comes to understanding and following various standards of construction and recommended practices, there is no more important area for standards than that of the vessel's electrical systems. If improperly installed or poorly maintained, these systems can pose not only fire and explosion as well as corrosion hazards, but also the potential for electrocution.

The United States Coast Guard (USCG) has certain basic electrical standards, which are applicable to gasoline-powered vessels, and that speak primarily of ignition protection (reduction of explosion hazard) and overcurrent protection (to avoid overheating and fires). A review of these standards will show that they are very basic and provide little "practical" information on vessel wiring other than for these two purposes.

The National Fire Protection Association (NFPA) publishes *Standard No. 302 for Recreational and Commercial Motor Craft*. This covers a wide range of various topics with respect to fire protection, especially in the areas of electrical circuits and lightning protection.

However, by far the most comprehensive standards available today are those published by the American Boat and Yacht Council (refer to Appendix B). In covering almost every major system on a vessel, the ABYC Standards go into great detail on the subjects of DC and AC electrical systems, battery chargers and inverters, lightning protection, cathodic protection, and others. The ABYC Standards also have been used for the development of various international standards being adopted in Europe.

diameter wires are lighter and more flexible, making them easier to snake through the constricted passages available on boats.) This is why high-demand electric cooking ranges and household dryers are most often designed to operate on 240-volt AC, rather than the 120-volt electricity used for light bulbs, stereos, TVs, and the like.

At dockside in North America, you'll find 120-volt AC power and often also 240-volt AC power. Actually, these voltage designations are nominal—the designed voltages of shorepower will vary from 110 to 120 AC, and 220 to 240 AC, respectively. Moreover, in practice, shorepower voltage may drop well below these lower range limits. In Europe and many other parts of the world, nominal shorepower is 220-volt AC.

AC System Frequencies

Many items of equipment used on boats, such as battery chargers, microwaves, televisions, stereos, and fluorescent lights, contain transformers for the purpose of changing the voltage within the equipment. When operating on "foreign" power

(such as 50 Hz), it is imperative that this equipment be "compatible" with the 50-Hz shorepower source. This may be ascertained by looking at the nameplate on the equipment and verifying that it says "50/60 Hz." If this type of equipment is not installed on your boat, you have two choices: Either order special equipment to be compatible or, when in foreign ports, operate this equipment only from the vessel's genset in order to obtain the requisite 60-Hz power.

There are transformers that can step shorepower AC voltage up or down to match the voltage requirements of a vessel's AC equipment (see page 661). However, none of these change the frequency of the shorepower alternating current; so care must be taken when hooking up to foreign shorepower sources, even when you have managed to adapt to noncompatible outlet configurations. If a shoreline isolation transformer is installed on board the boat, it must be compatible with 50-Hz use if operation in foreign ports is anticipated where this frequency is to be encountered.

DC System Voltages

Today, direct current for shipboard use is generally either 12, 24, or 32 volts DC, with 12-volt systems being by far the most common. These voltage choices evolve from the fact that most batteries are made up of a number of individual nominal 2-volt cells, connected in a voltage-additive series, and the fact that manufactured batteries use certain common multiples of cells; 3 cells (6-volt battery), 4 cells (8-volt battery), and so forth. The fully charged nominal 2-volt cell will, in reality, produce a voltage of approximately 2.13 volts. Using this information, it is readily apparent that a 12-volt battery (6 cells) will have a fully charged voltage of approximately 12.8 volts, and a 32-volt battery (16 cells) will have a fully charged voltage of 34.1 volts. This becomes an important consideration when calculating voltage drop as discussed previously.

For 12-volt systems, a 12-volt battery is normally used. Alternatively, two 6-volt batteries (usually of the "golf cart" type) can be hooked together in series (positive post on one connected to the negative post on the other). Where the use of higher-voltage DC power is indicated, four 6-volt batteries can be wired in series for 24 volts, or four 8-volt batteries for 32 volts.

Determining Electrical Needs

Electrical power is the lifeblood of all electronic equipment. Although a few transistorized items may operate from self-contained batteries, most electronic equipment is powered from the boat's electrical system. With many of today's outboard motors having alternators, there is almost no lower limit to the size of boat that can have one or more electronic devices, but the total load must not exceed the electrical system's capacity.

For 12-volt DC systems, the load is usually stated in terms of amperes, and loads must be considered separately for instantaneous and longer-term situations. By adding the amperage "draw" of all the items likely to be operated simultaneously, you will have the maximum instantaneous value for selecting the size of wire and protective devices such as fuses or circuit breakers. If you will be running electrical and electronic equipment when your engines are shut down, such as overnight, you will have to multiply the amperage of each item by the number of hours of use. Added together for a cumulative load, this will give you the total number of ampere-hours of energy that your batteries will have to supply. If there were such as a "typical cruising boat," its daily consumption would be roughly 150 ampere-hours.

For 120-volt AC systems, the load is normally computed in watts. The wattage rating on an onboard item of equipment serves as a measure of the maximum amount of power that the electrical item will require when operated. By adding together the maximum wattage requirements of all equipment that will be operated simultaneously, a vessel's maximum requirements for AC electrical power can be determined. Wattage ratings also provide important information about the required sizes for wiring, and the required ratings for protective circuit breakers and/or fuses. Gensets are normally rated in terms of kilowatts; shorepower cords are rated in terms of ampere capacity.

Here is where we can apply the relationship between watts, volts, and amps: Watts = Volts x Amps. For example, using this equation, we can tell that a 120-volt appliance requiring 600 watts of power will draw 5 amps of current. Again using the sum of the amperes drawn simultaneously, you will know the required capacity of the shorepower connection or on-board AC auxiliary generating plant; see **Figure 19-05** and page 658.

It must be noted that in both DC and AC systems, the current draw labeled on equipment is the continuous running condition. For resistive loads such as incandescent lights and electric ranges, this value is all that is needed. However, loads such as fluorescent lights and induction-type motors have starting loads that are much higher, although for only brief moments, and this must be taken into consideration in system design.

Typical Boat Systems

Most small craft have a basic 12-volt DC system, consisting of storage batteries, an alternator on

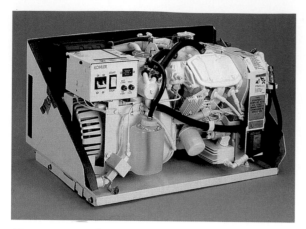

Figure 19-05 When the demands for 120-volt AC electrical power exceed what can be reasonably drawn from the boat's batteries, such as for electric stoves and air conditioners, an auxiliary generating plant (genset) must be installed. It should use the same fuel as the craft's main engines.

each propulsion engine, and perhaps a charger for use with shorepower. Typically, the boat will have both a STARTING BATTERY for each engine with its obvious use, plus one or more HOUSE BATTERIES that provide power for lights, pumps, radios, and other accessory equipment. The readily apparent advantage of such a system is that you can be assured of having adequate engine starting power no matter how much you use lights, fans, etc. These batteries have design differences. The primary characteristic of a starting battery is the ability to deliver large amounts of current for a limited time; a house battery should have the ability to deliver energy over many cycles of discharge and recharge. A battery undergoes a "deep cycle" when 20 percent or more of its stored energy is consumed before it is recharged; for maximum battery life, deep cycling should be limited to no more than 50 percent (voltage dropping to about 12.2 volts). A properly designed DEEP-CYCLE BATTERY can provide 200 to more than 3,000 discharge/recharge cycles. The cost for more cycles is greater, but the cost per cycle may be even less. Batteries designed for starting service may last only 50 or so deep cycles.

A separate 120-volt AC system will power "home-type" loads, such as cooking (if other fuels are not used), air conditioning, entertainment appliances, and additional lighting. Power from

this system can also be used to recharge the batteries of the DC system. While away from shore, power for the AC system must be generated as needed, since it cannot be stored. For lighter loads, an inverter can be run from the DC system; refer to **Figure 19-04;** but major loads will require the installation and use of an auxiliary generator powered by a separate small gasoline or diesel engine; refer to **Figure 19-05.** The fuel of this engine should always be the same as that for the main propulsion engine or engines; see below.

Storage Batteries

A boat's batteries store, and later release upon demand, electrical energy. They accomplish this by means of a natural galvanic (electrochemical) reaction between two molecularly dissimilar metals that are connected together and immersed in a current-carrying liquid.

The metals involved have differing natural electrical potentials (voltages). The one with the higher natural voltage is called the anode, while the one with the lower natural voltage is known as the cathode. The current-carrying liquid, meanwhile, is the electrolyte.

The battery most commonly found in marine (and automotive) applications is the wet-cell (sometimes called "flooded") lead-acid type. This form of battery utilizes lead-antimony and pure sponge-lead plates immersed in a water-diluted solution of sulfuric acid.

When a circuit is closed between a charged lead-acid battery and an electrical appliance (load), the lead dioxide and the sponge lead react chemically to form a lead sulfate. In the process, electrons flow from the sponge lead to the lead dioxide via the part of the circuit that is external to the battery, namely, the circuit leg running from the positive battery post through the electrical device involved to the negative battery post; and that flow of electrons powers the appliance. As the chemical reaction exhausts the available lead dioxide and sponge lead in the plates, the voltage of the battery drops, until it reaches a point where it is too low to be useful, at which point the battery must be recharged. (In actual practice, it should be recharged well before this point is

CARING FOR FLOODED WET-CELL BATTERIES

There are five essential components in the proper maintenance of wet-cell lead-acid batteries:

• Minimize or eliminate deep-discharge cycles.

Each time a storage battery is cycled (discharged, and then recharged), some of its useful life is lost. This is because the galvanic reaction that produces the discharge causes the plates to gradually deteriorate, and because most of the time some amount of lead-sulfate by-product remains unreconverted after recharging. Eventually, either the accumulation of unreconverted lead-sulfate or the degeneration of the cell plates, or both, is great enough to disrupt the battery's ability to function. At this point, replacement of the battery becomes necessary.

• Utilize properly controlled charging procedures.

Wet-cell lead-acid batteries are subject to other problems. If the recharging current is too high to be completely absorbed by the battery's chemical reaction, that current breaks down the water in the battery's electrolyte into components of hydrogen and oxygen gas. These gases then escape, causing the electrolyte level to drop, at times to the point of drying out and, consequently, irreversibly damaging some or all of the battery plates. More batteries are lost to improper charging procedures than are to the normal aging process.

• Maintain the correct electrolyte level.

You must check electrolyte levels regularly and replace any lost electrolyte by refilling with distilled water according to the manufacturer's specifications. (By using distilled water you will avoid the introduction of foreign chemicals and materials into the electrolyte.)

• Keep the battery clean and its terminal connections corrosion free and tight.

Regularly clean the tops of your batteries with a cloth dampened in a baking soda solution (the baking soda neutralizes any acid that has escaped via the cell vent caps). Be very careful not to let any baking soda solution get into the battery's interior, as that will degrade the electrolyte.

Using a wire brush, keep the terminals and cable connectors clean and shiny; make certain the connections are tight. After cleaning and reinstalling the cable connections, coat the terminals with an appropriate battery terminal compound to retard corrosion. Do not use petroleum jelly, which tends to liquefy and seep into the connection, causing more harm than good.

• Provide good ventilation.

The wet-cell type of lead-acid batteries produces explosive hydrogen gas during recharging. And although hydrogen gas is lighter than air and quickly dissipates, it does represent a danger that should not be ignored. Batteries can explode, so the prudent skipper is especially careful when working around them. When dealing with terminal connections, take care to vent the battery space well, make certain that the batteries are not being charged at the time, and take care not to create sparks. Moreover, it is always a good idea to wear splash-proof safety goggles when you are dealing with batteries. For further safety, remove all jewelry.

Caution: If you accidentally come in contact with battery acid, wash it off immediately to avoid severe burns to your skin. If battery acid contacts your eyes, flush them immediately with cool water, and seek medical attention. Also remember that battery acid will eat holes in most fabrics.

reached, as its life will be shortened if left in a discharged state for an extended time.)

Replacing the Energy

When energy has been taken from a battery to meet the boat's needs, it must be replaced in order to meet future needs—the battery must be recharged. On essentially all small craft, this energy will come from an ALTERNATOR, belt-driven from a main engine much the same as for cars and trucks; refer to **Figure 19-02.** Alternators have replaced the older "generators" as they have the advantage of a greater output at low engine rpm. The external result is the same for both devices: a DC voltage somewhat greater than that of the battery (about 14 volts for a 12-volt system), so that energy can be put into the battery against its natural tendency to discharge into a completed circuit.

The flow of energy from the alternator into the battery is through a VOLTAGE REGULATOR. This device prevents the alternator from over-charging the battery. For more on the operation of alternators and regulators, see books and pamphlets on engine electrical systems. Boats that are in port with people on board much of the time will need a BATTERY CHARGER, sometimes called a POWER CONVERTER; see **Figure 19-06.** This device takes 120-volt AC shorepower, TRANSFORMS it to a lower voltage, and then RECTIFIES it to DC. Thus as energy is taken from the battery it is replaced from shorepower, and the battery is completely or partially protected from becoming discharged. Battery charger

Figure 19-06 This advanced-design battery charger, or power converter, will charge batteries fast and full, but most importantly, it will protect the batteries from being overcharged by continuously sensing their state of charge.

MAINTAINING GEL-CELL BATTERIES

Maintenance-free gel-cell batteries are becoming more common. They offer some advantages. For example, their semi-solid electrolyte cannot spill out so they can be installed in any position.

Gel-cell batteries do, however, require somewhat different handling when it comes to charging, as they can be ruined quickly (gassed and dried out) by charging at too high a voltage. Of course, so can a wet-cell battery; but in the case of such an open-cell battery (with removable vent caps), you will be likely to notice the drop in liquid electrolyte. Then you can add water, and (hopefully) correct the problem before any permanent damage to the battery occurs. It is important to note that a gel-cell must *never* be opened once it leaves the factory; if this is done the outside air will "poison" the plates and ruin the recombinant chemistry.

In contrast, there is no easy visual way to measure deterioration of the semi-solid electrolyte in a gel-cell battery, so such batteries usually require re-regulation of the vessel's charging systems to a maximum 14.1 volts. After being fully charged, the "float" voltage should be 13.8 volts. For dockside charging, it is best to employ one of the newer type chargers on the market, those that have alternate programmed charging cycles available for gel-cells. Moreover, since the gel-cell suffers quickly when left in a partially (50 percent or more) discharged state for extended periods of time, it's critical to ensure that such batteries are "topped up" before leaving your boat for several days or more. Beyond that, what's good for the life of a common wet-cell lead-acid battery is good for a gel-cell.

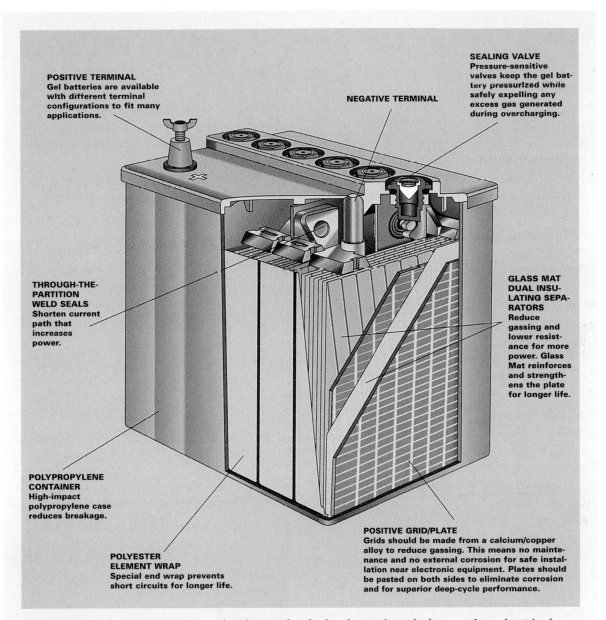

POSITIVE TERMINAL
Gel batteries are available with different terminal configurations to fit many applications.

NEGATIVE TERMINAL

SEALING VALVE
Pressure-sensitive valves keep the gel battery pressurized while safely expelling any excess gas generated during overcharging.

THROUGH-THE-PARTITION WELD SEALS
Shorten current path that increases power.

GLASS MAT DUAL INSULATING SEPARATORS
Reduce gassing and lower resistance for more power. Glass Mat reinforces and strengthens the plate for longer life.

POLYPROPYLENE CONTAINER
High-impact polypropylene case reduces breakage.

POLYESTER ELEMENT WRAP
Special end wrap prevents short circuits for longer life.

POSITIVE GRID/PLATE
Grids should be made from a calcium/copper alloy to reduce gassing. This means no maintenance and no external corrosion for safe installation near electronic equipment. Plates should be pasted on both sides to eliminate corrosion and for superior deep-cycle performance.

Gel-cell batteries offer the advantage that they can be tilted and turned upside down without the risk of spilling electrolyte. This is an advantage for any boat, but particularly for sailboats.

installation should be in accordance with ABYC Safety Standard A-20.

When a lead-acid battery is recharged, electrical energy from an external source—an engine-driven alternator, or AC-energized battery-charger—drives the above-described chemical reaction in reverse. In the process, lead sulfate is broken down, and the battery is restored to a "charged" condition.

Gel-cell & AGM Batteries

In increasing numbers, GEL-CELL storage batteries are being used on boats. These essentially maintenance-free batteries employ significantly different technology than the wet-cell lead-acid battery. In this newer type, the electrolyte is a gel composed either of sulfuric acid or a combination of sulfuric and phosphoric acids. A gel-cell operates on the "recombinant" principle by which the oxygen that is normally produced on the positive plate recombines with the hydrogen given off by the negative plate to form water, which replaces the moisture in the battery. The cells are sealed; there are no fill caps for adding water (there are, however, safety vents that are hopefully never needed). It is better fitted to deep-discharge service than a flooded cell, and has the advatageous property that the electrolyte is not sensitive to orientation. When recharging a gel-cell battery, procedures are slightly different; refer to page 654.

Another type of storage battery recently developed has ABSORBED GLASS MAT cells and is commonly referred to as an AGM battery. These do not use a gelled electrolyte, but rather the acid is absorbed and immobilized by a very fine fiber-glass mat between the plates. AGM batteries will accept very high rates of charge—75 percent or more of the ampere-hour capacity—that would destroy a wet-cell battery. Care must be taken that the charging device is not overloaded and damaged; an alternator regulator should have a high-temperature sensor. A discharge of 100 percent of capacity is said to not damage an AGM battery.

Gel-cell batteries are about 40 percent more expensive than flooded-cell batteries; with AGM batteries the cost differential is approximately 80 percent.

Choosing Battery Size & Type

It's extremely important to have appropriate type and size of battery for the job at hand. Each discharge-charge cycle in a storage battery results in a degree of irreversible chemical degradation of its plates. The "deeper" the cycle—that is, the more the battery is discharged before being recharged—the greater the resultant chemical degradation. For that reason, deep-cycling is one of the major factors in—if not the primary cause of—premature battery failure. Using a battery with a capacity two times (or more) greater than any anticipated total amp-hours draw is the best way to ensure maximum battery life.

However, capacity alone is not the sole consideration in determining what is the right size and

type of battery. Even though two batteries may have the same nominal capacity, a vessel's starting battery needs to be different from its service battery. Starting batteries are called upon to supply large amounts of current for very short periods of time, after which they are recharged quickly by an alternator driven by the vessel's propulsion engine. Starting batteries, therefore, are constructed with a large number of thin plates, which, for given external dimensions and a given overall weight, maximizes plate surface area, thereby facilitating the necessary chemical reactions.

Unfortunately, the numerous, thin plates of starting batteries do not provide the reserve capacity and resistance to sulfation required for the deeper cycling to which ship's service (used for all loads other than starting, such as lights, pumps, etc.) batteries are often subjected. Thus, ship's service batteries should be of the "deep-cycle" variety, constructed with relatively fewer and far thicker plates. Of course, a starting battery can be used for ship's service and vice versa, but maximum performance or longevity per unit size cannot then be expected.

Some so-called deep-cycle batteries are little more than relabeled starting batteries. So when buying batteries, check the specifications of similarly sized starting and deep-cycle batteries. For a

Figure 19-07 Storage batteries must be installed so that they are secure and firmly held in place. For most batteries, ventilation must be provided to prevent the build-up of explosive hydrogen gas (which tends to rise). Covers are essential to protect the terminals from accidentally being short-circuited should a conductive object, such as a wrench, fall on them.

given overall external size and weight, the deep-cycle battery will have fewer but thicker, plates.

ABYC Standard E-9 *Direct Current Electrical Systems* provides a great deal of additional information on the sizing of batteries for the anticipated load on board. ABYC Standard E-10 *Storage Batteries* contains information about the location, ventilation and mounting of batteries in order to be in compliance with both USCG regulations and voluntary industry standards; see **Figure 19-07.**

Battery Testing & Charging

After initial selection, the second most important factor in battery performance and longevity is proper control of discharge/recharge cycles. Draining a battery below about half its full charge before recharging greatly accelerates the deterioration of its plates. So does leaving a battery in a partial or fully discharged state for long periods of time.

It is wise to regularly check and pay close attention to the readings on your battery-condition gauges. At one time, the only battery-related gauges found aboard boats were ammeters, which measured either the current (amps) being drawn from the battery, or the current being pumped back in by the boat's charging system. On many boats, ammeters are supplemented with, and sometimes replaced by, voltmeters, which are often given special dial faces and called battery-condition meters; see **Figure 19-08.** More complete information on the state of each battery in the system can be shown by special electronic devices; see **Figure 19-09.**

For each battery, there is a maximum voltage point at which the battery is considered fully charged and a minimum voltage point at which it is effectively discharged.

There are slight differences between individual batteries, but most 12-volt units are considered fully charged at 12.8 volts and totally discharged at 10.5 volts. (But much electronic equipment may be nonoperational well before the voltage falls to 10.5.) In between those levels, the battery's state of charge can be measured as a percentage of fully charged voltage. That is what the voltmeters,

Figure 19-08 The state of charge of a storage battery can be determined from its voltage. Specially designed voltmeters are used for this purpose; the lower part of the voltage range is collapsed so that readings can be taken more precisely around the normal voltage range, usually 10 to 16 volts in a "12-volt" system.

with so-called "battery-condition" dial faces, actually do; refer to **Figure 19-08.**

Such battery-condition gauges are inexpensive compared with the cost of good quality batteries and they significantly aid in avoiding deep-cycling. They can also help ensure that your batteries are being fully recharged, a factor that is critical in a battery's longevity. There are also more expensive digital meters that indicate the countdown of stored ampere-hours as the battery is used, and the count back up of ampere-hours during recharging.

The specific gravity of the electrolyte in a lead-acid battery varies with the battery's state of charge. It is thus possible to measure state of charge with a hydrometer—in fact, for many years, this was the standard practice. (Using a hydrometer is still an easy way to identify a failing cell within a battery that is, otherwise, in good

Figure 19-09 A more precise and useful watch on battery condition can be accomplished with an electronic device designed for this purpose. It will show voltage, current presently being drawn from or charged into the battery, accumulated ampere-hours of discharge, and other data.

condition.) However, it is far more practical to use a voltmeter.

Your battery-condition meters may reveal that your batteries are not being fully charged when you run your engine. Or they may indicate that, while your starting battery comes to full charge, your ship's service battery, which has been drained overnight by your lights, refrigerator, radio, etc., does not. Such a situation is common and is one of the leading causes of accelerated battery deterioration.

Such deterioration occurs because the standard charging regulators fitted to most propulsion engine charging systems are designed only for recharging starting batteries. Starting batteries, on the other hand, are called upon to provide heavy current for a very, very brief period of time. Consequently, they can be recharged with a relatively large amount of current over a short period of time.

As a battery is recharged, its voltage rises. Standard regulators sense this voltage rise and taper off the charging current until it is too low to fully charge a ship's service battery within a reasonable time period. This causes problems when you are away from dockside hookups, and can also lead to accelerated deterioration due to failure to achieve a full recharge before you start the discharge period again.

Maintaining a proper charge in ship's service batteries sometimes requires a special charging regulator. These bypass or replace the preprogrammed cycle of a standard charging regulator and ensure that the ship's service battery receives the large amounts of current necessary for a full recharge. With such a device, it is also possible, from time to time, to intentionally "overcharge" the batteries slightly—a procedure called "equalization," which, in a lead-acid battery, drives excess unconverted lead sulfate back into solution.

This equalization reverses some otherwise permanent plate deterioration. However, it is critical to monitor very carefully battery temperature and peak voltage in accord with the manufacturer's recommendations as excess heat can build up and "gas out" electrolyte or damage the

battery's plates. In extreme cases, it can even melt down the battery case and cause a fire.

These special regulators for ship's service batteries are currently available in both manual and automatic types. The automatic units, though generally more expensive, guard against inadvertent damage to the batteries due to forgetting to cut back charging current as they reach full charge.

Multiple Charging Sources & Battery Isolators

On boats with multiple batteries and one or more sources of DC charging power (alternators and battery chargers), it is often desirable to be able to use one of the charging sources to serve at least two battery banks. An example of this is where one alternator would be used to charge both the cranking battery and the "house battery"; see **Figure 19-10.** (Other systems might have two alternators and more than two batteries.) In order to accomplish this, battery isolators are available from a number of sources. These are devices containing diodes which permit the flow of current in one direction only so that the output of the alternator or battery charger can be directed to both batteries simultaneously. The isolator prevents one battery from being charged or discharged by the other battery. It is important to note, however, that the use of isolators introduces a slight voltage drop in the charging circuit and, unless the charging device's output is adjusted higher, a little less than full charging will occur to the batteries.

Auxiliary Generating Plants (Gensets)

In addition to alternators that are belt driven by propulsion engine for the production of DC power, a vessel may have one or more auxiliary generating plants, known as gensets. These supply AC power in either nominal 120- or 240-volt systems for distribution to the vessel's wiring system.

Gensets are not connected to the vessel's drive train, but comprise a large alternator that is close-coupled to a dedicated engine, which may be cither a gasoline or diesel unit. Of course, the generator should use the same type of fuel as the propulsion engines. They also incorporate an engine-speed governing system, regulating circuitry, and sometimes special load-sensing circuitry that automatically starts (and stops) the unit according to demand. Gensets must be installed so that they will have easy access to check oil and water levels. Many are enclosed in a SOUND SHIELD to reduce the noise when they are operating; this must not be allowed to reduce the frequency of maintenance checks—"out of sight" must not mean "out of mind."

The advantage of a genset is that it can supply power for large, house-type electrical loads, while at the same time allowing a vessel to be independent of shorepower connections. The capacities of most manufacturers' lines of gensets typically start at about 2.5kW (2,500 watts) and extend up to 15kW and higher; refer to **Figure 19-05**.

Although the AC produced by a genset cannot be used directly to charge a vessel's storage batteries, it is possible to wire the genset so that it powers the same battery charger that would otherwise be driven by shorepower. In this way, any genset capacity in excess of the vessel's immediate needs can be used to recharge its batteries at times when its propulsion engines are not being run.

There are also DC gensets that can be run to directly charge the vessel's storage batteries.

Alternative Energy Sources

Using a source of energy that does not require the combustion of fossil fuels can both extend a skipper's cruising range and make him or her feel good for having relieved the environment of at least some hydrocarbon pollution. For boating applications, there may be some cost savings also from using the "free" energy of the sun and wind.

Solar Power

Sunlight can be converted into direct electricity by photovoltaic cells. The low voltage produced can be used to operate small electrical appliances—for instance, calculators and small ventilator fans. And a number of photovoltaic cells can be connected together in cased arrays called "solar panels" to charge, albeit in a limited way, a vessel's storage batteries; see **Figure 19-11**.

In order to charge storage batteries, the charging power must be at a higher voltage than the battery, whose voltage may be 12, 24, or 32 volts. In solar panels an appropriate number of individual photovoltaic cells are, therefore, first connected in voltage-additive series. Then a number of these cell groups may be arrayed in

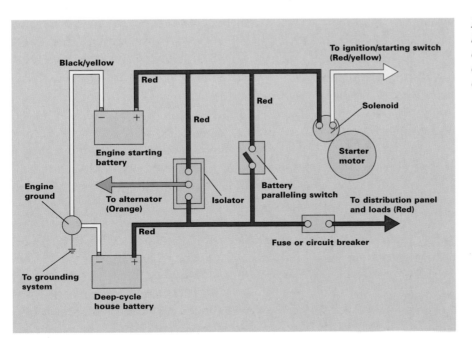

Figure 19-10 Shown here is a basic wiring diagram for two batteries charged from a single engine alternator.

current-additive parallel to provide greater amounts of energy; panels are normally rated in watts. The result is a quiet, nonpolluting onboard source of electrical power.

Unfortunately, it's often difficult to find enough deck space for enough panels to provide sufficient current for most shipboard devices. And most appliances whose current demands could be so satisfied directly, do not find their major use at times when there is sunlight to be converted. For example, a solar panel of practical size for, say, a 35-foot sailboat, could run an electric lamp. But the lamp would be needed most at times when there is no sunlight available to power the solar panel. For that reason, and because solar panels are still relatively expensive when measured against unit output, the practical onboard application of solar power is limited and usually relegated to supplementary charging of storage batteries.

The initial high cost of solar panels is partially offset by the fact that they require little maintenance other than occasional cleaning. They are available in several types at different efficiencies and costs. Solar panels are rated for the most favorable conditions: cloudless skies, perfect angle of incidence, sun well above horizon, proper ambient temperature, and clean panel surface. Significantly less energy will be developed in more typical conditions. The location of panels is usually fixed, but it may be possible to adjust their orientation so as to be more nearly perpendicular to the sun's rays. There will usually be some loss due to shadows on board that cannot be completely eliminated. Typically, solar panels will not produce enough energy to fully replace that used during a 24-hour period, but they will reduce the amount that must be obtained from other sources.

Wind Generators

In recent years, significant strides have been made in the manufacture of wind-driven generators for boats. Strong, ultralight composite materials have become available for rotor blades and other structural parts; and compact, efficient alternators have been developed. As a result, wind-driven genera-

Figure 19-11 Solar panels will provide small amounts of DC electrical power quietly and without the consumption of fuel. Flexible panels can be used in areas that are both convenient and out of the way.

tors are available in sizes and weights that make them practical for installation aboard yachts and other small craft; see **Figure 19-12.**

As an on-board source of electrical power, wind-driven generators offer some important advantages over solar panels: They produce appreciable amounts of energy, and they work at night and on cloudy or rainy days. They are also less expensive than a typical group of solar panels. Most wind generators start to produce a charging current with winds of about six knots, with output at significant levels with winds of 15 knots. However, they also have disadvantages: They're still relatively expensive for the amount of electrical power they develop; and they tend to be somewhat awkward looking, unless their installation is quite carefully designed and executed. The whirling blades of wind generators annoy some people, but the location on a sailboat—up on the backstay or pole-mounted at the transom—is out of the way. They're most useful at anchor, when a vessel is away from shorepower, lacks a genset, and is not running its propulsion engine(s). Consequently, they're usually found on sailing craft, for if properly installed, they can be used underway when under sail alone. After all, there would be little point in utilizing a wind-driven generator on a powerboat underway, as the propulsion engine(s)-driven alternator(s) would provide many more times the amount of current, at very little, if any, additional cost in fuel or engine wear.

Closely related, but seldom seen, are small hydro-generators towed in the water astern. A small rotor revolves in the water flow much the same as the larger propeller of a wind generator; the craft must be making way through the water for power to be generated.

Fuel Cells

Although well established as a source of electrical energy on shore and in space, FUEL CELLS are a promising source of power on boats as a replacement for gensets. Electrolysis is the familiar chemical process of using electrical energy to break down water into hydrogen and oxygen. Fuel cells work on the reverse process, combining hydrogen and oxygen to produce electricity with water as a by-product. They resemble batteries in that their DC electrical output is due to an electrochemical process, but they are producing energy, not storing it. Fuel cells get their oxygen input from a continuous stream of air. Hydrogen can be used directly, but is more easily and commonly obtained from fuels such as methane and methanol. Although hydrocarbons are used, there is no combustion and no polluting exhaust. Fuel cells are also unlike batteries in that their active elements are not consumed by the chemical reaction, and thus have a much longer service life. An individual fuel cell generates from 0.6 to 0.8 volts, and cells have to be stacked and connected in series to provide a useful power output. Fuel cell packages can be manufactured at a wide range of power output levels. Their potential for boats lies in their silent operation and lack of noxious exhaust fumes.

Transforming Power

Electrical appliances have fairly specific power requirements. For instance, a 24-volt DC electric motor will not run properly on 12-volt DC current, but instead will run too slowly, overheat, and possibly even burn up. Similarly, 24 or 40 volts fed into charge a 12-volt battery will overcharge and destroy it. Further, AC appliances will not operate on DC, and vice versa.

Some DC electronic equipment and other appliances are equipped with internal power circuitry that tolerates input voltages from, say, 10 to 40 volts; but this kind of tolerance does not generally extend to AC/DC appliances, except in today's onboard refrigeration systems and some other units that have the capacity to choose a higher voltage if both voltages are available (a refrigerator will choose 120 AC over 12 DC). And therefore, at times when the frequency and voltage characteristics of source currents do not match requirements of the equipment to be powered, it is necessary to employ a transformer (AC), an inverter (DC to AC), or a DC-DC converter.

Transformers

When a transformer is used simply to step up or step down the voltage of an AC system, without providing complete isolation from the shorepower system, it is known as a POLARIZATION TRANSFORMER. If the transformer is connected so as to provide complete galvanic isolation from the shorepower system, then it is known as an ISOLATION TRANSFORMER. ABYC Standard E-8 contains a great deal of additional information on the subject of both of these types of transformers.

Transformers are most frequently used to step the voltage of AC systems either up or down, but in some circumstances they are used without voltage change in order to isolate a vessel's onboard power system from a shorepower system. They can be so used because transformers magnetically couple their input and output circuits, creating current in the latter by induction, rather than by means of a direct conductive connection.

Figure 19-12
Though noisier than solar panels, a wind generator with its higher output in windy and less-than-perfect sunlight conditions, has become a symbol of electrical self-sufficiency among cruising sailors—they are even seen on some voyaging powerboats.

Inverters

If a vessel is wired for 120-volt AC or higher voltage, it will likely have onboard appliances that are designed specifically for these voltages, which the crew will undoubtedly want to continue to use when away from a shorepower hookup. If the vessel has an auxiliary generating plant of sufficient capacity, then the necessary supply of 120- or 240-volt AC power is no problem. However, there are cases in which the boat is too small to accommodate a genset comfortably; and there may be times when the crew wants 120-volt AC without the additional noise and vibration of a running genset—which is always present to some extent, however well-silenced and resiliently mounted the unit is. And in such instances, an inverter really shows its advantage.

Electric power inverters consist of a solid-state device that electronically steps-up and changes 12-volt (or 24- or 32-volt) DC power to 120-volt AC power. Such inverters are available in very small output capacities on up to capacities large enough to run small motor-operated equipment such as low-capacity air conditioners and under counter refrigerators, whose compressor motors require moderately high starting currents. (But keep in mind that the energy required by such appliances would be impractically large for most battery installations.) Size, weight, and cost are roughly proportional to output capacity; refer to **Figure 19-04.**

Beyond output capacity rating, some inverters are better than others at producing power whose wave pattern is closer, or identical with, the "sine wave" frequency characteristics of shorepower. The least expensive inverters produce what is known as "square wave" power. These are fine for running lights and other resistive appliances, as well as some appliances with small motors, such as coffee grinders, kitchen mixers, and blenders, and some (but only some) small electric tools. However, square-wave inverters may not be able to start some induction-type motors even if the nominal wattage rating of the motor is well within the inverter's capacity; and they may cause speed-sensitive equipment such as tape decks, CD players, and VCRs to run erratically.

The best all-around performance is secured with an inverter that produces either pure sine-wave power, or at least "modified sine-wave" power that is guaranteed by the manufacturer to operate all motors whose power draws are within the output capacities of the inverter. (In that respect, keep in mind that certain appliances, such as refrigerator and air conditioner compressor motors, may draw as much as three times their rated running current when they first start up.)

Today, there are some very advanced solid-state inverters on the market that incorporate highly sophisticated sensing circuitry, as well as sophisticated integral three-stage battery chargers (to replace the energy drawn out). These units are wired to the storage batteries and into the vessel's 120-volt distribution system. When there is 120-volt input from either a shorepower connection or a genset, the inverter automatically charges the storage batteries; when the input ceases, such units automatically switch to inverter mode to supply power in response to a sensed demand on their output circuit.

Provided that the inverter is of sufficient capacity, it is possible to run many types of "household style" devices on board, from fans to electric tools and kitchen appliances, without relying on either a shorepower connection or a shipboard genset. However, it's also necessary to have sufficient storage battery capacity, or you will run your batteries flat in a very short time. Keep in mind that a 100-watt lamp draws only 0.83 amps at 120 volts, but that, even neglecting inherent power losses (to heat) during current conversions, the inverter powering that lamp will be drawing 8.3 amps—10 times as much current. And if your ship's service battery is of average size for a small boat—say, 90 amp-hour capacity—and you allow for a 50 percent discharge, that single 100-watt lamp will use all the available stored power in less than 6 hours. So, if you want to use an inverter for more than, for example, running an electric drill for a few minutes at a time, you need to ensure that your ship's service storage batteries are of much greater capacity than normal.

The addition of a DC to AC inverter on board will be a complex installation at best to ensure the following: that batteries are properly sized, that DC wiring is of adequate capacity, that the device automatically switches itself off when shorepower is available, and that it is properly integrated into the vessel's electrical system so that it does not attempt to power up all AC loads simultaneously. When making such an installation, it is wise to employ a competent marine electrician; consult ABYC Standard E-8 *AC Electrical Systems* to ensure compliance with all necessary recommendations. A very handy small inverter, no larger than your fist, can plug directly into a cigarette-lighter socket and provide 120-volt AC power of 75 watts continuously (or 150 watts initial surge) to a single socket for a three-prong plug; this will run almost any AC accessory drawing not more than 0.6 Amp. If a bit more power is needed, there is a 150/300 watt unit that has a cigarette-lighter plug on a cord; both of these units provide modified sine-wave power and are moderately priced.

DC-DC Converters

Devices that take a higher DC voltage, such as 24 or 32 volts, and reduce it to a lower DC voltage, such as 12 volts, are called DC-DC converters. These are especially useful in powering certain items of electronic equipment that are generally available only in 12 volts when used on board vessels with 24- or 32-volt DC electrical systems. The DC-DC converter is preferable to a simple "dropping resistor" in that its output voltage is maintained at a constant level regardless of the connected load current.

Connecting to Shorepower

The shorepower connection is sometimes derided as the boat's "umbilical cord." This is because some boaters (basically, those without gensets or inverters) are loath to break the shorepower connection and give up the convenience of "house-type" AC devices. But the very nature of this disparagement indicates just how integrated the shore-to-ship power connection has become in boating today.

In North America, the voltage of shorepower current is usually nominal 120, but may in some cases be nominal 240, so diligent care needs to be taken at all times in hooking up and using such power. Shorepower connections should be made only to properly wired and protected outlets.

Further, the vessel should be equipped with proper shorepower cords (with lock-type fittings and water-shedding boots and collars), appropriate inlet fittings, and a correctly configured main distribution panel with circuit breakers. The design of proper cords and inlet fittings ensures that neither skipper nor crew will ever handle a "live" cord with exposed (male end) prongs—as that is a certain invitation to potentially fatal electric shock; see **Figure 19-13.**

As well, it is advantageous if the vessel's distribution panel incorporates both a voltmeter and an ammeter to measure the incoming power and avoid overloading of the shorepower cord and connections, and the shore circuit.

Properly wired AC outlets are found in a wide variety of configurations, each associated with particular combinations of voltage and current. For example, the size and pattern of 120-volt outlets with 15-, 30-, and 50-amp current capacity respectively differ from one another. And they all have configurations different from those of 240-volt outlets; refer to **Figure 19-13.**

Moreover, because wiring codes are not consistent across the Unites States, and certainly not across international borders, the outlets at a strange wharf or marina may not match the end on your shorepower cord. Therefore, if you travel far afield and wish to connect to shorepower, it may be necessary to have aboard a variety of ADAPTERS that will allow connection of your shorepower cord to different types of dock outlets; refer to **Figure 19-13.**

Regardless of what adapters you must use in order to accommodate the dock outlets, always ensure that the grounding conductor (green wire) is connected to an outlet or metallic device that truly provides an effective ground. Many, but not all, adapters will do this internally. All too often one sees adapters where a grounding (green wire) "pigtail" is connected via its clip to a piece of

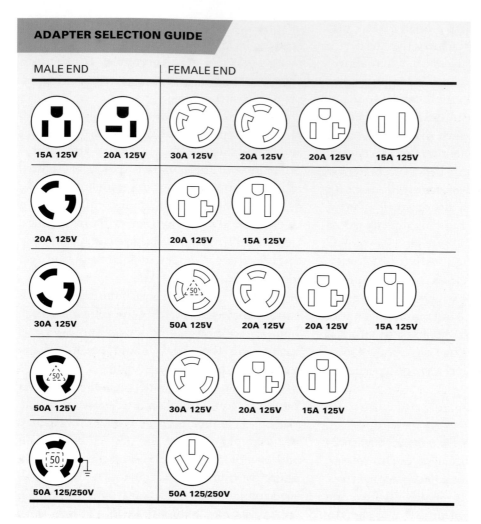

ADAPTER SELECTION GUIDE

MALE END	FEMALE END			
15A 125V 20A 125V	30A 125V	20A 125V	20A 125V	15A 125V
20A 125V	20A 125V	15A 125V		
30A 125V	50A 125V	20A 125V	20A 125V	15A 125V
50A 125V	30A 125V	20A 125V	15A 125V	
50A 125/250V	50A 125/250V			

Figure 19-13
Shorepower cords have a male connector at the landward end, shown here in the far-left column. The boat end is female and has the same wiring arrangement, which permits two cords to be connected end-to-end if necessary for a longer run. Sometimes, however, an adapter is required to fit between the power cord and a dissimilar shore outlet, such as the combination that appears at the bottom left.

plastic conduit or water pipe, or just left dangling. The grounding conductor is essential for the safety of persons on board and those in the water surrounding the vessel whenever it is connected to shorepower; *never sacrifice the grounding conductor's integrity.*

There are also adapters available (or which can be made up using proprietary, off-the-shelf parts) that can be used to split or merge current. For instance, if your boat has two 30-amp inlets, but the shore outlet is a single 50-amp unit, a properly wired adapter can likely be used to split the 50-amp outlet into connections for two 30-amp cords. Or if your boat has a single 50-amp inlet, and the shore two 30-amp outlets, the right adapter can be used to merge the two 30-amp outlets into a single 50-amp cord. There are adapters available that will match a 50-amp shore outlet to a 30-amp boat inlet without splitting. And conversely, there are adapters to match a 30-amp shore outlet to a 50-amp boat inlet, or a 15-amp shore outlet to a 30-amp boat inlet—though in these connections, it's important to remember that there may not be sufficient current available in such a hookup to run high-demand appliances that may be on board.

Another way of protecting yourself and your boat's electrical system is to verify the electrical connections on shore before hooking up. This is done with an outlet circuit tester; see Figure 19-14. Selling for just a few dollars, the instrument employs a combination of colored LEDs to indicate the following situations: correct wiring, open ground wire, open neutral wire, open hot wire, hot and ground reversed, and hot and neutral reversed. An outlet circuit tester is also a practical tool for testing extension cords, or for verifying any electrical work that has been done on the boat.

DISTRIBUTING ELECTRICAL POWER

It is quite obvious that electrical power generated, stored, or brought aboard via a shorepower connection is of little value unless it can be distributed properly to various onboard appliances. Yet, while much time, attention, and money is frequently spent on the source of onboard electricity, the distribution side of the system is almost as often given short shrift. And that's a shame, because relatively modest efforts and expenditures in this area can go a long way toward ensuring the reliable and safe utilization of onboard electrical power.

Caution: Whenever 120-volt or 240-volt AC systems are installed on board, there is the possibility that, due to the failure of equipment or insulation somewhere in the future, AC voltage can inadvertently be applied to the vessel's DC system. When and if this occurs, portions of the DC system, especially the engine and its propulsion system (which is connected via the battery negative), can now be energized at a potential of 120 volts AC above "ground." This poses an imminent danger, not only to persons on board who may inadvertently contact such equipment, but also to swimmers in the water, especially in freshwater areas, as they may be in the potential gradient or "field" created around the vessel.

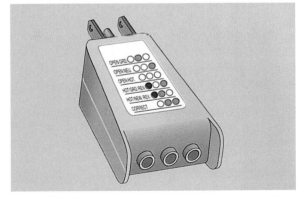

Figure 19-14 The circuit tester shown here is one of many available types that can quickly diagnose a faulty wiring situation.

Whenever using adapters, the following three actions must always be followed:

✓ Outlet and adapter must be of the same voltage rating.

✓ Total amperage drawn should never be allowed to exceed the amperage of the lowest-rated component of the connection.

✓ Polarity and grounding connection must be maintained.

In order to guard against this occurrence, the ABYC and NFPA Standards require the connection of the AC system grounding wire (green) to the DC system negative (ground) on board the vessel. This connection must be made on all vessels equipped with shorepower, other than those utilizing isolation transformers. The location of this connection should be ascertained, and its integrity checked on a regular basis. In years past, there have been articles written about disconnecting this circuit or "cutting" the green wire to shore to reduce the incidence of galvanic corrosion on board. *This is not only improper, but dangerous.* There are other ways to combat galvanic corrosion when using shorepower; these are covered later in this chapter.

Main Switches

The 12- (or 24- or 32-) volt DC and the 120-volt AC (or 240 volt AC, if applicable) subsystems should each be controlled by its own main switch that will cut power off entirely. This is an important protection, both for someone working on the system and in the event of an electrical or other fire, when it can be vitally important to be able to power down quickly and positively.

The one exception to this rule is the automatic bilge pump circuit. This circuit should be wired so as to remain active even if the main switches are turned off—especially if it's your practice, as it is with many boaters, to turn off the main switches whenever the boat is left unattended. That way, the protection of automatic bilge pumping will not be lost.

The main switch for the higher voltage subsystems (120 and 240 volts) will customarily be incorporated in the main distribution/circuit-breaker panel. However, since the lower DC voltage subsystems (12-, 24- and 32-volt varieties) supply current to the engine starter(s), the main switch for these circuits necessarily has to carry very high currents (often 300 amps or more); consequently, it is imperative that the switch be of robust construction. The low-voltage main switch is, therefore, often separated from the main distribution/circuit-breaker panel.

Low-voltage main switches are often constructed to control two separate battery banks. These switches can be identified by their labeling, which will show positions for bank 1, bank 2, all (or both), and off. The "all (or both)" position puts the two battery banks in parallel, thereby doubling the batteries' available capacity, while keeping voltage at the same level. This is handy at times for engine-starting under cold or otherwise difficult conditions. (Note that if this type of switch is to be used for battery paralleling, it must be rated by its manufacturer for that type of service, and selected according to the amount of cranking current that the starter on the engine will draw.)

Protecting the Alternator

The low-voltage main switches are often also wired to control the propulsion engine charging circuit, that is, starting current runs from the storage batteries to the starter(s) according to the setting of the switch, and charging current from the engine alternator(s) runs back to the battery or batteries according to the switch settings. Such an arrangement affords the advantage of being able to direct charging current to bank 1 or 2, or to both; see **Figure 19-15.**

However, when the main switch is used in this way in order to control the charging circuit, the boater must always take care that the main switch is of the "make-before-break" type, and also that it incorporates an alternator field disconnect circuit. (Note that with certain types of alternators, the field circuit is integral to the regulator built into the alternator and, therefore, it is impossible to utilize the field disconnect circuit provided on some battery switches. If this is the case, it is important always to ascertain that the alternator and its regulator are immune from damage that would otherwise result from disconnecting the alternator from the battery while it is operating.)

The reason for this precaution is that serious damage can occur to the alternator's rectifying and blocking diodes if ever the charging circuit is left without a battery connected to it while the engine is running—even momentarily. Thus, when you switch, say, from bank 1 to bank 2 with the engine running, the make-before-break type switch automatically connects bank 2 before disconnecting bank 1. Also, the alternator field disconnect circuit shuts down current to the alternator's field coil, thereby putting the alternator into "idle' or noncurrent-producing mode, if you should happen to turn the switch to the "OFF" position while the engine is running.

If the propulsion engine charging circuit is wired in such a way that it bypasses the main switch and goes directly to the storage batteries, the above precautions may not be necessary. But even if that is the case, it is usually necessary to

Figure 19-15 A battery selector switch provides positive battery disconnect, isolates all circuits, and also protects against the hazards of electrical fire and explosions. It can be separate or combined with the circuit breakers for individual circuits.

incorporate a battery isolator, as previously discussed, to prevent inadvertent crosscurrents between the vessel's starting and service battery banks, currents that can leave you with a flat starting battery.

The Distribution Panel

Of tutmost importance in the boat's electrical system are the various protective devices: switches, fuses, and circuit breakers. Every marine electrical system should have a main distribution panel where there are switches and overload protection devices. In addition to the switches on the individual pieces of electronic and electrical equipment that are used to turn them on and off, the various loads should be connected together into several branch circuits, each with a protective element and a means of shutting off power to that branch alone. Thus a short circuit or other failure on one branch will not require turning off all electrical power. Each branch circuit should be identified on the distribution panel.

Fuses provide overcurrent protection by means of the destruction of an internal metal strip that melts when a predetermined amount of current is drawn through it. Fuses are less expensive initially, but are a one-time-use device. Circuit breakers, although more expensive, perform the same function, but are resettable after the problem in the circuit has been corrected. Except in the smallest, least expensive boats, circuit breakers are today almost universally used in preference to fuses, at least when it comes to main distribution panels and when currents of 5 amps or greater are involved. (Occasionally an individual piece of sensitive electronic equipment will be additionally protected with an in-line fuse rated at 3 amps or less; and the manufacturer's installation manual should always be followed in this respect. Electronic components of some modern diesel engines are also protected in this manner.)

Fuses of the correct size offer safe onboard circuit protection. However, fuses have several disadvantages as compared to circuit breakers:

• When a fuse blows, it is more difficult to replace it than simply to reset a circuit breaker.

It is dangerously easy to replace a blown fuse with an improper one of excess current-carrying capacity.

• If a fuse blows and no replacement is handy, there is the temptation to shunt it with a length of wire, a practice which often leads to fire.

• In damp corrosive atmospheres, fuse clips tend to corrode, offering a high-resistance connection that results in voltage drop.

The main distribution panel is used to distribute current to various onboard circuits. There may be separate panels for DC and AC, or these can be combined; see **Figure 19-16**. For each of these, heavy conductors are brought to a heavy bus bar on the panel. Branch (or sub-) circuits are then wired on the panel from the bus bar through an appropriately rated circuit breaker, which is often also used as a switch for that branch circuit. In this way, circuit faults usually result in the

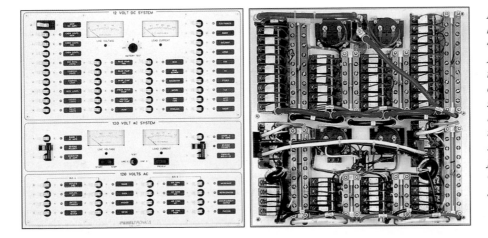

Figure 19-16 Shown here are front and back views of a combined AC and DC distribution panel. Note the careful labeling of each switch and circuit breaker. This panel also includes a transfer switch for changing from shorepower to the onboard auxiliary generating plant.

"tripping" of a breaker on the labeled main distribution panel, and are therefore easier to trace and correct. The use of a main distribution panel also facilitates checking the ON/OFF condition of various circuits. Trip-free circuit breakers are a recommended protective component for onboard application. These are designed so that the reset handle cannot be manually held to override the current interrupting mechanism—this makes "cheating" on the breaker impossible.

An Important Caution: When the low-voltage and higher-voltage distribution panels are combined into a single unit, or located in close proximity to each other, it is critical to make sure that no inadvertent cross-connections are made. Any such cross-connections would result in feeding 120- or 240-volt current into the vessel's 12-, 24- or 32-volt system. This in turn could cause at least the destruction of low-voltage equipment. In the worst-case scenario, it could cause fire or the electrocution of a crewmember or a swimmer.

The Wiring System

If the battery and alternator are the heart of a boat's electrical system, then the wires supplying power to the various electrical and electronic loads are the arteries and veins. The wires must be heavy enough—of sufficient cross-sectional area—to carry the current of the loads connected to the circuit.

Adequate wire size is determined by two factors: heating effect and voltage drop. Current passing through a wire increases its temperature; obviously, it must not become hot enough to become a fire hazard. As a general rule, a wire should not become warm to the touch when carrying its full load.

The voltage drop problem is the more common one. The heating losses mentioned above result in a lower voltage being delivered to the load than was put into the circuit at the battery. The voltage drop increases with an increase in the load, being directly proportional to the current in the circuit, and with an increase in the length of the wires.

The Right Size & Type of Wires

Many potential problems can be avoided by ensuring that all wiring is adequate in size for the amperage involved. Although it usually can be safely assumed that a boat will have proper size and type of wiring when it is delivered from the manufacturer, it is highly likely that additional equipment and accessories will be installed in the craft throughout its active life. Electrical problems encountered with new gear are often trace-

ELECTRICAL WIRE GAUGE SELECTION: NONCRITICAL 12-VOLT LOADS

Current (Amps.)	Wire length (feet): source to load, plus return to source					
	10 (or less)	15	20	30	40	50
5	18	18	18	18	16	16
10	18	18	16	14	14	12
15	18	16	14	12	12	10
20	16	14	14	12	10	10
25	16	14	12	10	10	8

Table 19-1 A 10 percent voltage drop can be tolerated by common electrical components. The American Boat & Yacht Council (ABYC) standards for noncritical loads, such as lights and pumps, are shown in the above table. All wires should be stranded to reduce the possibility of failure from mechanical fatigue.

ELECTRICAL WIRE GAUGE 12-VOLT WIRING FOR ELECTRONIC LOADS

Current (Amps.)	Wire length (feet): source to load, plus return to source					
	10 (or less)	15	20	30	40	50
5	18	16	14	12	10	10
10	14	12	10	10	8	6
15	12	10	10	8	6	6
20	10	10	8	6	6	4
25	10	8	6	6	4	4

Table 19-2 Electronic devices, such as radios and navigation equipment, are less tolerant of voltage drops in the wires supplying power to them than are common electrical loads—the ABYC standards call for a drop of not more than 3 percent. The necessary wire sizes are shown above for current drains and various lengths of wires.

able to the inadequacy of the original wiring. Thus a boat owner must know the correct wiring practices to support the added devices.

The higher the current (amperage) draw of a device, the heavier the wire that carries the current has to be. Insufficient wire size (diameter) means increased resistance. Excessively high resistance results in greater voltage drop (less voltage at the device) as well as greater heat. This results, at best, in a loss of efficiency (with power being lost in the conversion of electrical energy to heat), and at worst, in damage to electric motors and other appliances—even, in extreme cases, fire. Any wire, when subjected to excessive current, may overheat to the point of igniting adjacent combustible materials. It is for this reason that circuit breakers or fuses are utilized to limit the amount of current that can be loaded on a wire. Voltage drop also increases with the length of the circuit—the distance from the battery (or distribution panel) to the load device and back.

It's important to keep in mind that wire sizes in North America are generally specified according to American Wire Gauge (AWG) standards, under which a lower number designates a larger diameter (for example, No. 10 AWG wire is heavier than No. 16 AWG). The system is established so that a change of three numbers, either up or down, changes the cross-section area of the wire by a factor of two; this doubles, or halves, the resistance of the wire (but odd numbers are generally not used in small gauges). A change of six numbers changes the area, and resistance, by a factor of four; as resistance decreases, current-carrying capacity increases by the same factor.

When electrical wiring is in a marine environment, size is not the only consideration—wire type is also very important.

Wire with a solid conductor, or less than sixteen strands, should not be used on a boat because it is prone to fracture due to vibration, especially where the conductor may have been nicked when stripping the insulation for connection during installation. Instead, flexible, multistrand wire should be chosen for all systems.

It is recommended to use pretinned copper conductor in boat wiring, even though it is rela-

tively expensive. Conductor strands that are coated with tin resist corrosion are much better than bare copper ones. That's important not only at terminal fittings, where the copper is stripped for insertion into crimp-type or other terminal fittings, but all along the conductor. The type of corrosion to which copper is subject in a salt-damp environment tends to "creep" along bare copper wires, up under its protective insulation; and so plain copper conductor is potentially subject to severe and hidden corrosion when used in the marine environment.

Recommended Wire Gauges

In DC systems, typically 12- or 32-volt, the voltage drop that occurs due to the resistance of the wire becomes a critical consideration for certain types of equipment. ABYC recommends that "noncritical" applications (for example, where the voltage drop does not seriously compromise the function of the equipment, such as, motors, cabin lights, etc.) be limited to 10 percent. "Critical" devices, such as navigation lights, bilge blowers, and most electronics equipment, should have a voltage drop of not more than 3 percent. The ABYC Standards provide details and tables for these calculations; see **Tables 19-1** and **19-2**.

A simple check of equipment "as installed" can be made by using a DC voltmeter; first read the voltage at the fuse or breaker panel, then at the equipment itself. This must be done with all "normal" loads turned on and the DC charging source (engine or battery charger) operating. Additionally, the equipment under test must be running, in other words, pumping water with bilge pump or transmitting on the radio. If 13.2 volts were available at the distribution panel, then 12.8 volts (13.2 minus 3 percent of 13.2) should be the reading at the equipment for no more than a 3 percent drop.

Wiring Identification

In addition to having the right size and type of wires, the proper COLOR CODING of wiring should be observed without fail in order to facilitate the identification of circuits and the tracking of wires during troubleshooting procedures. See **Table 19-3.**

RECOMMENDED MARINE WIRING COLOR CODE

Color	Item	Use
DC Systems		
Green (G) or green w/yellow stripe(s) (GY)		DC grounding conductors
Black (Bl) or yellow (Y)*		DC negative conductors
Red (R)		DC positive conductors
Brown/yellow stripe (BY) or yellow (Y)**	Bilge blowers	Fuse or switch to blowers
Dark gray (Gy)	Navigation lights	Fuse or switch to lights
Brown (Br)	Pumps	Fuse or switch to pumps
Orange (O)	Accessory feeds	Distribution panel to accessory switch
Purple (Pu)	Instrument feed	Distribution panel to electric instruments
Dark blue (BL)	Cabin and instrument lights	Fuse or switch to lights
AC Systems		
Black (B)		Ungrounded conductor
White (W)		Grounded neutral conductor
Green (G)		Grounding conductor
Red, orange, blue		Additional ungrounded conductors
Black w/red stripe, black w/blue stripe or black w/orange stripe		Additional colors for ungrounded conductors (black).

* As of 1990, white for ground in the low voltage (DC) has been changed to yellow with the intention of recommending the use of black and white as high voltage (AC system) colors only.
** If yellow is used for DC negative, blower must be brown with a yellow stripe.
Note: These colors are associated with the boat, not the engine(s).

Table 19-3 ABYC Standard E-8 provides a system of color coding for the identification of wiring on small craft.

Identification should also be ensured with a complete wiring diagram that can be understood by a nonexpert. Enclose it in plastic and post it near the main switch panel. Keep it up to date as additions and changes are made. Proper terminal connections, bundling, and support of the wire runs should always be provided for, in order to minimize the potential for failures due to corrosion (connections lying loose in wet bilges) and failures due to mechanical problems (connections pulling loose under the substantial weight of wiring or due to vibration).

Wiring & the Compass

Wiring that supplies DC current to the compass's night-light and all other DC wiring in proximity to a vessel's autopilot heading sensor is a potential cause of serious magnetic deviation. When carrying current, such wiring can be the source of magnetic fields that will interfere with the proper functioning of the compass.

Even worse, because electrical circuits are sometimes on and sometimes off, and because the magnetic fields they generate change with variations in current, the magnetic interference they produce is sporadic and variable. Therefore, this form of magnetic deviation cannot generally be eliminated by compensating the compass, and so it is necessary to take a preventive, rather than a corrective, approach to the problem.

The primary preventive measure is to keep all DC wiring at least 3 feet—and preferably 6 feet—away from the vessel's magnetic compass (and the sensing unit of an autopilot). Obviously, that is not always possible, particularly in the case of wiring that runs to the compass's own night lighting. Wiring that cannot be routed well away from the compass should be run in twisted pairs, that is, each DC feed wire should be paired with a DC return wire and the two tightly (not loosely) twisted round and round together. This procedure will cause the magnetic field of one wire to be "canceled" by the field of the other.

The wiring installation should always be checked as a safety measure. You can do this by observing the compass while you switch the involved circuit first ON, then OFF. If the wires have been properly twisted, the compass card will not react. However, if the wires have not been properly paired and twisted, the card will shift quite rapidly to a new heading each time the circuit is switched.

ELECTRICAL APPLIANCES & EQUIPMENT

Clearly, electrical appliances are a boon for today's boater. Indeed, the convenience they afford is one of the two major reasons for having electrical power on board—the other being the use of modern sophisticated electronic navigation and communications equipment. Electrical appliances can, however, also be a bane; for, unless properly chosen and installed, they will deteriorate and break down quickly, as well as cause problems for critical electronics. The prudent skipper will, therefore, refer to the installation standards promulgated by such organizations as ABYC and NFPA and, in all cases, pay strict attention to the recommendations of the manufacturers of the equipment in question.

Just as for application ashore, choose electrical equipment that bears the listing mark of

Underwriters Laboratories (UL) whenever possible. Underwriters Laboratories "Marine" lists certain devices, especially electrical equipment, intended specifically for installation on board vessels. These listed devices should be used whenever there is a choice of equipment.

Microwave Ovens

For on-board use, microwave ovens offer some significant advantages over conventional electric ovens and ranges because they reduce cooking time, hence power consumption. They also reduce the amount of heat released into the surrounding cabin, which improves the comfort of the crew and, if the boat is simultaneously being air-conditioned, further reduces overall power consumption.

Microwave ovens are available in different sizes and wattage ratings. The larger ovens are usually more powerful (faster cooking) and require more current, but not in all cases; so it is important to check wattage ratings carefully when comparing units of the same physical size. Beyond that, choice of preferred size and wattage is determined basically by the same cooking considerations pertinent to shoreside applications; although final selection is limited by a number of other considerations relating specifically to on-board use.

First, on all but the largest yachts, galley space is relatively limited in comparison to on-shore applications—so it may not be possible to fit in a full- or apartment-size microwave; see **Figure 19-17.**

Second, unless the craft is fitted with a genset, supplying AC for the microwave can be a problem when shorepower is not available—for example, at anchor. Yet, such times are precisely when microwave cooking affords the greatest advantages. Consequently, it may be important to make sure that the unit can be powered by an existing inverter, and that there is sufficient storage battery capacity to supply current. For example, a 1,000 watt unit set on high power will draw about 8.33 amps at 120 volts. Assuming that the inverter has an efficiency of 85 percent (with 15 percent of the input energy lost to heat), the

MAKING THE CONNECTION—TERMINAL FITTINGS

In marine applications, winding a bared, twisted end of a conductor around the terminal screw on an appliance, circuit breaker, or bus bar just won't do. In fact, this practice is prohibited by industry standards. Such a connection is simply too prone to corrosion and to loosening due to vibration. Instead, some form of terminal fitting should be employed, one which provides a flanged fork (spade)— or even better, a ring— end that makes for a secure mechanical connection.

At one time, terminal fittings were soldered to the wire connector; but that procedure is both time-consuming and expensive; crimp fittings have gained almost universal acceptance. Crimp fittings are tinned copper fittings consisting of a tubular shank with a plastic sheathing at one end of which is a fork or a ring. The sheathing extends up over the wire insulation. The best-quality sheathing is nylon. Unlike the cheaper PVC, nylon will not crack or punch through when crimped, and resists the corrosive effects of ultraviolet (UV) light, oil, or diesel fuel.

The stripped end of the wire is inserted into the tubular shank of the crimp fitting, and a special tool is used to squeeze the shank tightly around the conductor. (The fitting must be of the proper size for the wire used.)

If properly done, the connection, although mechanical, is excellent and long-lasting. And if pretinned copper wire is used, and the terminals are tinned, the potential for corrosion between the wire and the crimped shank of the fitting is minimal.

It is possible to solder a crimped fitting after it has been crimped. But this is not preferred practice, as the heat will usually destroy the insulation that protects the shank on the crimp fitting. Additionally, the solder will "wick" part of the way up past the crimped fitting and, effectively, destroy the flexibility of the stranded wire, tending to make it stiff and prone to breakage from the vibration that exists on all boats. And where enhanced resistance to corrosion is desired, it is desirable to coat the terminal with one of the liquid vinyl compounds available for that purpose, or to

1 Strip the wire of its insulation, and slip it into the crimp fitting—a ring or a fork. Then squeeze the crimp with a special tool until exactly the right dimension is achieved.

2 Slide a length of heat-shrink tubing (available in several sizes) over the crimp.

employ modern vinyl heat-shrunk tubing.

Shrink tubing is applied by sliding a piece of appropriately sized material over the wire before crimping the terminal on. After crimping, the tubing is slipped into position so that it covers the shank of the crimp fitting and overlaps onto the wiring insulation. The assembly is then heated with a heat gun or a portable hair-dryer, whereupon the tubing shrinks tightly to the contours of the wire and fitting, at the same time exuding a sealant/

adhesive that seals the underlying connection from moisture intrusion. A more recent (and convenient) variation of this approach is a combination crimp and heat-shrink terminal fitting, which is first crimped in the normal manner, then heated.

Both standard crimp fittings and these combination crimp/heat-shrink fittings are also available in configurations for joining two or three wire ends; these are commonly called "butt connectors."

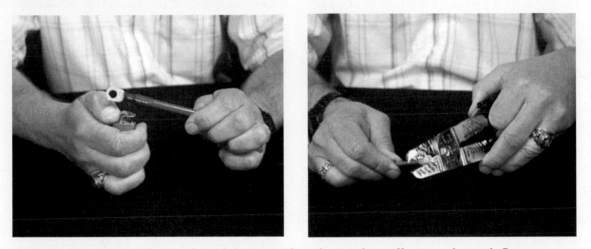

3 *Shrink the protective tubing with gentle heating. A hair-dryer is also as effective as the gentle flame of a lighter.*

current draw on a 12-volt battery will be about 93 amps—this is a pretty heavy load that would deeply discharge the average deep-cycle battery in less than half an hour.

In contrast, if the microwave were a 500-watt unit used for appropriately light duty, the battery draw would be about 47 amps; and since microwave cooking is, happily, fast, the 10 or so minutes needed would probably only discharge the vessel's batteries by about 7 to 8 amp-hours. And naturally, if the unit were in use on a power-boat underway, that amount of power would easily be supplied by the propulsion engine alternator(s), without a drain on the storage batteries.

Microwave ovens are relatively heavy and need to be securely mounted. It's also critical to make sure that they have sufficient ventilation, as lack of cooling ventilation is probably one of the most

frequent causes of failure in on-board use. Therefore, if the unit is being built in or enclosed in a locker, ventilation holes of adequate size should be cut in its enclosure.

Refrigeration & Air-Conditioning

Refrigerators and air-conditioning units that use sealed, electrically driven compressors are probably among the most, if not the most, reliable pieces of equipment to be found on board. One reason for this is that they incorporate shore-based technology that has reached a high level of refinement. In these units, the compressor motor is sealed inside the condenser casing with compressor itself, and so is protected from the ravages of the marine environment. If a fresh desiccant cartridge is soldered into the refrigerant circuit when it's first charged, and the system remains sealed, the basic unit will last for years without the need of attention, even if run continuously; see **Figure 19-18.**

This is not necessarily true of certain peripheral components, such as the evaporator fans and the electric pumps that supply cooling water to the condenser unit in water-cooled systems. But again, in the better systems, even these components are rated for years of operational life, even under frequent use over extended periods of time.

The important thing to remember about refrigeration and air-conditioning units is that their compressor motors draw starting current (amperage) that is at least twice, and can be as much as three times, their rated current draw when running. This means, for example, that a 6,000 BTU air-conditioning system that is rated at 7.5 amps at 120 volts can actually be drawing 15 or more amps each time the compressor starts up. It's critical to take this into account when matching gensets, inverters, wiring, and circuit breakers to such systems.

Ground Fault Circuit Interrupters

There are occasions when, due to faulty wiring, terminals, or other defects in a circuit, current will escape its normal (safe) path and head directly to ground via some other conductor. The condition is called a "ground fault" in an AC circuit. If the external conductor happens to be your body, you can be in big trouble, especially if

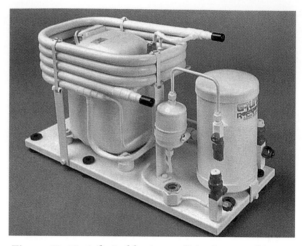

Figure 19-18 A desirable air-conditioning or refrigeration unit will have high-quality, long-lasting components. They will be well-mounted, secured against vibration and shocks, and protected against the harshness of the salt-water environment.

heavy current manages to pass through your heart. A GROUND FAULT CIRCUIT INTERRUPTER, or GFCI as it has come to be known, senses such a ground fault before any potentially injurious amount of current can be conducted, and in a fraction of a second breaks (interrupts) the power to the faulty circuit.

GFCIs are available in different sizes and capacities, some portable and some designed to be wired into the electrical distribution system; see **Figure 19-19.** No vessel with 120 or higher voltage on board should be without appropriate GFCIs in its distribution system. Standards call for GFCIs to be installed in all heads, galleys, machinery spaces, and on weather decks; any unit installed in the engine compartment of a gasoline-fueled boat must also be IGNITION PROTECTED (see below). Portable GFCIs should be employed as necessary on deck and on dock—indeed, anywhere near the water or where one might be showered upon—whenever electrical tools are employed. This caution simply cannot be overstated: Numerous fatalities have resulted from the failure to take these precautions, and when electrical tools have dropped in water or developed wiring faults while the operator was standing in a puddle or was otherwise well-grounded.

Caution: Most GFCIs are not listed as "ignition protected" devices and, in order to avoid an

Figure 19-17 A properly selected and installed microwave oven, as shown here above the stove, reduces cooking time, lessens heat generated, and generally enhances life afloat.

explosion hazard, should not be installed in the engine room or fuel tank areas of gasoline-powered vessels. Additional information about the use and installation of GFCI's is covered in ABYC Standard E-8, AC *Electrical Systems.*

PROTECTING YOUR BOAT & EQUIPMENT

Properly directed and controlled, electrical power can be a tremendous asset in the safe operation of a vessel. But stray or uncontrolled electrical currents can be destructive to both hull and gear, as well as potentially very dangerous to the crew and those who may be in proximity to the boat, whether in the water or out.

Ignition Protection

By their very nature, many electrical devices spark or "arc" in their normal operation; switches, relays, engine starters, and many DC motors and alternators are all examples of such devices. In the presence of gasoline or propane vapors, this "arc" can produce sufficient energy to ignite the vapors and produce a violent explosion.

In order to prevent this, the USCG, the ABYC, and the NFPA all require that electrical devices be "ignition protected" if they are to be installed in engine compartments or fuel tank compartments on gasoline-powered vessels. In addition, NFPA and ABYC have extended these ignition protection requirements to boats equipped with propane under certain conditions. There are various equipment test standards for ignition protection, including the Society of Automotive Engineers Standard SAE J1171 and Underwriters Laboratories Standard UL 1500. When installing or replacing any electrical component in compartments where vapors may be present, it is imperative that the component has been tested under one of these standards and the product itself is marked "ignition protected," or bears one of these two standard numbers.

Safe Battery Installation

Storage batteries must be installed in a ventilated area so that gases generated during charging will be

dissipated safely. They should also be protected from extreme heat and cold, and from spray. Starting batteries must be close to the engines in order to have short starter cables in order to reduce any voltage drop in the cables. Gasoline fumes are explosive and any spark from a battery connection is dangerous. Gasoline fumes should be kept away from the battery installation.

Batteries must be secured against shifting as well as against vertical motion that would allow them to pound. They should be chocked on all sides and supported by a nonabsorbent material that will not be affected by contact with electrolyte. Air should circulate all around the battery. A tray of fiberglass or other electrolyte-proof material must protect aluminum and steel surfaces of the boat.

Batteries should be accessible to inspection, cleaning, testing, and adding water to maintain the level of the electrolyte (wet-cell batteries only). They should also be covered with a nonconductive material so that a dropped wrench or other tool will not short-circuit the terminals. These covers must have sufficient small holes to allow the escape of any gases from charging.

Caution: Salt water reacts with battery acid to form chlorine gas, which can be deadly; refer to **Figure 19-09.**

Preventing Electrolytic Corrosion Damage

A boat owner must take precautions against electrical corrosion, also called "electrolysis." There

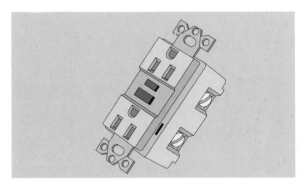

Figure 19-19 A ground fault circuit interrupter (GFCI) is designed to protect people from line-to-ground electrical shock hazards that may develop from faulty appliances, tools, or cords.

GALVANIC SERIES OF METALS IN SEAWATER

Metals & Alloys	Potential
More Active — Less Noble	
Magnesium and Magnesium Alloys	1.50 – 1.63
Zinc	0.98 – 1.03
Aluminum and Aluminum Alloys	0.76 – 1.00
Mild Steel; Wrought Iron; Cast Iron	0.60 – 0.71
Various Stainless Steels (active)	0.43 – 0.58
Aluminum Bronze	0.31 – 0.42
Tin	0.31 – 0.33
Various Brasses	0.30 – 0.40
Copper	0.30 – 0.57
Silicon Bronze	0.26 – 0.29
Stainless Steel Type 401 (passive)	0.26 – 0.35
Lead	0.19 – 0.25
Stainless Steel Type 304 (passive)	0.05 – 0.10
Stainless Steel Type 316 (passive)	0.00 – 0.10
Titanium	0.05 – +0.06
Platinum	+0.19 – +0.25
Graphite	+0.20 – +0.30
Less Active — More Noble	

Notes:
1. Variations are the result of varying degrees of purity.
2. All potentials are negative except where shown as "+".
3. There are many other metals not shown.

Table 19-4 In the galvanic series of metals in seawater the metals with the lower potential are variously termed the "less active" or "more noble" and act as the cathode in a galvanic circuit. On the other end of the scale (the top of this table) are metals that have higher potentials and are termed "more active" or "less noble"; these serve as the anode.

are three major forms of this—GALVANIC CORROSION, ON-BOARD STRAY CURRENT CORROSION, and EXTERNAL STRAY CURRENT CORROSION. Although the electro-chemical results are generally similar, these all have different causes and require different protective actions.

Galvanic Corrosion Principles

When two metals with widely differing electrical potential (voltage) are connected electrically and immersed in an ELECTROLYTE—that is, a current-carrying liquid such as salt water—a natural battery is formed. When that happens, direct current flows in the circuit comprised of the metal parts, the electrical connection, such as a bonding wire (see below) or a metal hull skin, and the electrolyte.

Different metals have different electric potentials as measured against a standard reference half-cell; the voltages for various metals in seawater are shown in **Table 19-4**. The difference in potential between any two metals determines the relative strength of the current flow and its direction. The metals with the lowest potential are variously termed the "most noble" or "most passive" and act as the CATHODE in a galvanic circuit. On the other end of the scale are metals that have higher potentials and are termed "least noble" or "most active"; these serve as the ANODE.

The direction of this current has important implications for the longevity of a vessel's underwater and bilge-mounted metal parts (including the hull if it is metal). In the segment of the circuit that is formed by the electrolyte (seawater), current flows from the anode to the cathode. This causes an anode to progressively disintegrate through the process of electrolysis; this is known as galvanic corrosion.

If the natural current in this circuit is supplemented by the introduction of current from an external source—for example, from an electrical wire that is shorting directly to ground—the rate of the anode's deterioration will be greatly accelerated. The natural galvanic corrosion is enhanced by the external current. The insulation on wiring should be protected from chafing and maintained in good general condition; wires should never be allowed to be in contact with bilge water. Each DC electrical device should have its own return wire of the same size as the "hot" wire returning directly to the negative bus at the distribution panel.

Protection Using Zincs

The terms "anode" and "cathode" are relative. In any galvanic circuit, the metal with the higher electrical potential behaves as the anode, while the metal with the lower potential acts as the cathode. Aluminum hull plating, for instance, will act as an anode relative to a copper radio grounding plate, which will be the cathode in this situation. However, a bar of pure zinc would be an anode relative to both the aluminum housing and the copper grounding plate. For this reason, the traditional method for protecting critical underwater parts is to bond them all together in a single circuit that includes one or more special SACRIFICIAL ZINC ANODES (commonly referred to simply as "zincs"); see **Figure 19-20.** When a piece of zinc of sufficient volume and exposed surface is introduced into a galvanic circuit, the higher voltage of the zinc overcomes the tendency of current to flow away from other metal parts in the circuit. Instead, current flows from the zinc to those parts that are in the process thus protected, although intentionally at the cost of the zinc. Magnesium sacrificial anodes also work well, even better than zinc, but are more expensive. *Caution: Never paint a zinc;* such would isolate it from the water and prevent its protective action.

A BONDING SYSTEM should be installed to connect all metal hull fittings exposed to bilge water or external water together, and to the external zinc electrode; see **Figure 19-21.** Connections to the bonding system must be checked regularly as they are particularly subject to corrosion in their wet or damp environment.

Since zincs are cheaper and easier to replace than critical metal parts, such as propellers, shafts, hull plating, and the like, this preventative for galvanic corrosion has, through the years, been almost universally used. Unfortunately, the use of static sacrificial zinc anodes doesn't always work as well as intended. The area of wetted surface of the zinc or zincs is critical: If too small, the desired effect of reversing destructive current flow will not be achieved.

Placement is also critical. If the zincs are too distant from the part or parts that require protection, the voltage of the zinc will not be able to overcome the resistance of the current path through the electrolyte; and therefore, the zinc(s) will fail to reverse potentially destructive galvanic currents in the region of the critical part or parts.

For both of these reasons, systems that provide more "active" corrosion protection have been developed in the last few years. These are IMPRESSED-CURRENT systems that sense and work actively to overcome potentially destructive voltage differentials. These systems divide into two types described below: anodic and cathodic.

Active Anodic Protection

Anodic impressed-current systems overcome the problems of size and anode-to-cathode distance, which frequently occur in a traditional arrangement of "static" sacrificial zincs. These anodic systems incorporate an electronic controller that senses voltage and/or current flow in a galvanic circuit. The controller then works to ensure that sufficiently high voltage is present on the system's sacrificial anode(s) by supplying current from an external source (such as the boat's battery) to the anode(s). And this in turn ensures that critical underwater metal parts are at all times in a cathodic (noncorroding) condition.

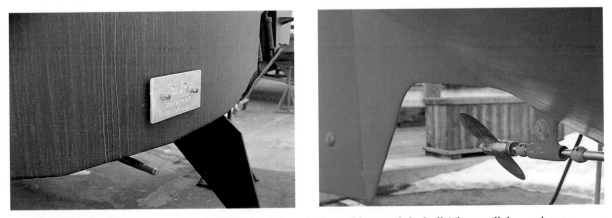

Figure 19-20 *Sacrificial zinc anodes should be placed on shafts, rudders, and the hull. These will do much to prevent galvanic corrosion. They should be expected to progressively deteriorate; periodic inspection and replacement is required for full effectiveness.*

Active Cathodic Protection

Cathodic impressed-current systems also incorporate an electronic controller, which senses the voltages and/or currents present in any galvanic couples. However, in cathodic systems, the controller uses external power to boost the voltage of a dedicated cathode to the point where that voltage is equal to the voltage of the anodes in the circuit. Then, since all metal parts in the galvanic circuit are at the same electrical potential, there is no current flow. Cathodic systems thus block the passage of destructive galvanic currents.

One system, such as, for example, Mercury Marine's Quicksilver MerCathode system, electronically measures the voltage of a boat's submerged critical metal parts, in particular, the aluminum stern-drive housing found on many smaller craft. Utilizing current from the boat's battery, it raises the voltage of a permanent, submerged titanium electrode (the cathode) so that it equals the voltage of the endangered part or parts (which become the anodes). With the titanium electrode and the otherwise endangered metal parts at the same electrical potential, there is no current flow, and thus no galvanic corrosion.

Avoid Dissimilar Metals

But whether a traditional system of sacrificial zincs is employed, or a more modern impressed-current system, the sensible boater still avoids, to the greatest extent practicable, mixing galvanically incompatible metals. Bronze through-hulls, for example, must not be used in direct contact with aluminum or steel hull plating. Instead, Type 316 stainless steel is often used, as it is much closer to aluminum and steel on the galvanic scale (thus there is less natural voltage differential between the two); refer to **Table 19-4.** Even better, nonconductive fiber-reinforced plastic fittings are sometimes used in smaller metal boats to completely eliminate the danger; such plastic fittings, however, are not generally available in sizes suitable for larger vessels.

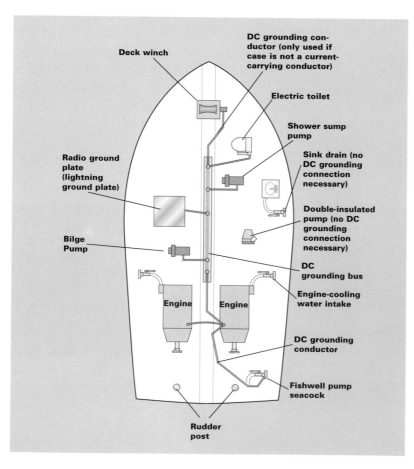

Figure 19-21 *A heavy copper strap should be run from one end of a boat to the other end to serve as a common bonding conductor. It is not to be used as a part of the return path of electrical power to DC equipment.*

Internal Stray Currents

Less common, but still possible, is corrosion caused by STRAY CURRENTS within a boat. If two pieces of metal in the bilge are at different potentials, possibly as a result of faulty wiring or poor connection to a bonding system (or lack of such a connection), current can flow from one to the other even if they are of the same metal. This action will result in metal being eaten away from the metal at the higher potential.

Zincs are of no use in such situations. The obvious prevention measures are careful initial wiring of all electrical equipment that might operate in or near bilge water (currents can flow across moist surfaces as well as in liquids), and the continued maintenance of both wire insulation and connections through regular checks.

External Stray Currents

If natural galvanic corrosion is an illness, electrolytic corrosion enhanced by an external current is a plague. The most common offenders are improperly wired shoreside electrical hookups and items of onboard equipment that are leaking current directly to the ground (the water) or to the boat's bonding system through shorted or defectively insulated internal components and/or bad wiring.

Correct Polarity Many shorepower-related electrolytic problems can be avoided by making certain that there is correct "polarity" when plugging in—that is, that the black wire is hot, the white is the neutral, and the green wire is connected to ground. Your boat's 120- or 240-volt main distribution panel may incorporate a reverse-polarity indicator, but such a unit provides less information and, ultimately, less protection than a simple and inexpensive hand-held indicator, of the type used by electricians; refer to **Figure 19-14.** What you really need to watch out for is a case in which improper shorepower wiring ends up with the current running to ground through the green wire, rather than through the white neutral wire.

Using an Isolation Transformer Additional protection can be had by incorporating, whenever possible, some form of "isolator" in any ship-to-shore electrical connection. In this respect, the best solution is an isolation transformer that will eliminate any direct conductive connection between the shorepower source and a vessel's electrical system. As previously mentioned on page 661, such transformers do not step the voltage up or down. Instead, they produce current for the boat's distribution system via a magnetic connection (induction) with the shorepower input. Unfortunately, isolation transformers are relatively large and heavy; they are also expensive. For these practical reasons, they are used for the most part only on larger yachts.

Using a Galvanic Isolator Where an isolation transformer is not practical for reasons of space or cost, one useful alternative is to install a "galvanic isolator" in the shorepower connection ground (green) line. These relatively inexpensive units work to isolate the boat's grounding system from the shorepower ground and, therefore, they help alleviate the potential for electrolytic corrosion. Since the galvanic isolator is connected in series with the AC system grounding conductor (green wire) to shore, it is imperative that the isolator meet certain minimum standards; otherwise the integrity of the grounding conductor will be compromised, if not lost completely. These requirements are reflected in ABYC Standard E-8 *AC Electrical Systems.* The only way you can be sure that you are complying with these standards is by using only galvanic isolators that bear the Underwriters Laboratories Marine listing mark.

Electronics
Communications

*Basic Radio Terminology • The Marine Radio System • VHF Radio Service • MF-HF
Single-Sideband Radio Service • The Global Maritime Distress & Safety System
(GMDSS) • Other Radio Communications • Other Means of Communications*

oday's electronic equipment has become so small and compact, and its drain on a boat's electrical system so reduced, that few craft are too small to carry one or more items of electronic equipment.

From a safety viewpoint, always essential in boating, the priority of purchase and installation in almost all cases will be a VHF radiotelephone for communications; see **Figure 20-01.** Other types of radios are also installed and used sometimes for specialized purposes. These include medium-frequency (MF) and high-frequency (HF) single-sideband (SSB) radios for longer range communications, amateur radio equipment which can serve many purposes for boaters, Citizens Band (CB) sets for communications that are not allowed on the marine service, and newer systems, such as satellite communications, the Family Radio Service (FRS), the General Mobile Radio Service (GMRS), and even cellular and satellite phones (which actually are radios).

BASIC RADIO TERMINOLOGY

Unless you are interested in obtaining an advanced (marine or general) radiotelephone operator's license, it's not necessary to delve deeply into the physics of radio transmission or, even more daunting, the esoterics of wave versus particle theory. For most boat owners, it's sufficient simply to understand a few very basic principles and distinctions, and to treat the rest in "black box" fashion—that is, to interface with marine radio as an intelligent user who is conversant with correct operating procedures, and without significant reference to what actually transpires inside the equipment. You will need to be familiar with certain characteristics of radio equipment to understand the proper selection, installation, licensing, and use of radiotelephones.

These characteristics include frequency bands, types of modulation, power, antenna requirements, and operating range. Almost all radios for small craft combine the transmitter and receiver into a single unit.

Frequency Bands

Radio energy is generated and transmitted as waves with specific physical characteristics. For our purposes, the two most important of these are amplitude (the height of the wave from trough to crest) and frequency (the rapidity with which the crests of the waves arrive at a given point). The unit of frequency equal to one cyle per second is a HERTZ (Hz). Frequency is today universally expressed in KILOHERTZ (kHz), where 1 kHz = 1,000 Hz, and MEGAHERTZ (MHz), where 1 MHz = 1,000 kHz; satellites, and sometimes radars, use frequencies measured in GIGAHERTZ (GHz), where 1 GHz = 1,000 MHz.

The total radio frequency spectrum is divided into various BANDS—from very-low frequency (VLF) to extremely high frequency (EHF); see **Figure 20-02.** Various communications and navigation systems work in one or more of these bands, as indicated in the spectrum bands of **Figure 20-02** and discussed below.

Radio communications for boats are in the medium frequency (MF), high frequency (HF), and very-high frequency (VHF) bands. The characteristics of each band are quite different, and the use of each is determined by its characteristics—primarily its operating range.

Opposite Page: Figure 20-01 A VHF marine radio should be the first item of electronic equipment for your boat—you will find many uses for it, but always use it in accordance with the FCC Rules. Smaller craft and dinghies can well use a handheld transceiver, less powerful but with many features of an installed set.

FREQUENCY SPECTRUM

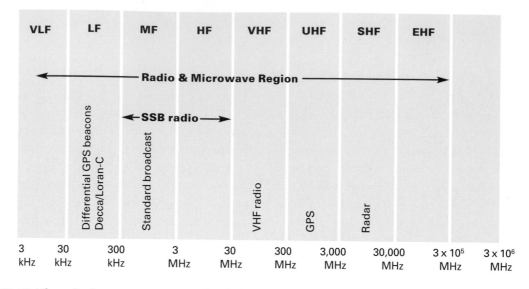

Figure 20-02 The radio frequency spectrum is divided into broad "bands" from very-low frequency (VLF) to extremely-high frequency (EHF). In boating, all bands from LF (differential GPS beacons) to SHF (radar) are used for various purposes. Marine radio communications are in the MF, HF, and VHF bands.

VHF The very-high frequency portion of the spectrum extends from 30 to 300 MHz, but the portion of interest to boaters lies between 156 and 163 MHz. VHF radio signals are often described as "line of sight," but actually the range is somewhat greater due to a slight degree of bending over the horizon. While the visual distance to the horizon is $1.17 \sqrt{H}$, where H is the height of eye above the surface in feet and distance is measured in nautical miles; an equation often used for VHF radio range calculations is $1.4 \sqrt{H}$, where H is height of the antenna. (The equation for range would be $2.5 \sqrt{H}$ if the height were in meters, with the distance still in nautical miles.)

These equations do not yield an exact or precise determination on range, and variations can be expected. It can be seen, however, that the height of an antenna is a primary factor in determining the communications range of any particular VHF installation. The amount of power used has some effect, but it is relatively slight, much less than you might expect. Normal maximum range is usually stated as about 20 miles assuming typical antenna heights for boats, but signals may sometimes be heard at distances of 200 miles or

more under so-called "freak" conditions. This usually occurs during temperature inversions where a "duct" is formed between the earth's surface and air layers at several thousand feet altitude that are warmer, rather than colder, than conditions at the surface.

MF and HF Medium frequencies (MF) lie between 300 and 3,000 kHz (3 MHz), and high frequencies (HF) between 3 and 30 MHz. Of interest to boatmen is a section of MF between 2 and 3 MHz and small slices of HF near 4, 6, 8, 12, 16, 22, and 25 MHz. The transmission characteristics of these frequency bands vary from one to another, from day to night, and, in some cases, from summer to winter. Propagation is both by GROUND WAVES, whereby the signal follows around the surface of the earth gradually diminishing in strength, and by SKY WAVES, where the signal is radiated straight outward at an angle to the horizon, encounters an IONIZED layer in the upper atmosphere, the IONOSPHERE, and is reflected back to earth; see **Figure 20-03**. These ionized layers (there are more than one) are at heights varying from 30 to 215 miles as determined by daylight/darkness conditions, season of

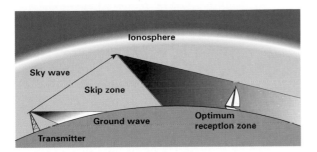

Figure 20-03 MF and HF radio signals are transmitted both by ground waves and sky waves. Ground waves spread out along the earth's surface for a few hundred miles. Sky waves start out at an angle above the earth's surface, are reflected by the ionosphere, and return to earth farther out as shown above. Between the reception area for ground waves and sky waves is the "skip zone," an area of no reception.

the year, and the status of the 11-year cycle of sunspots (radiation from the sun causes the ionization). Communications may be established over distances up to a few hundred miles by use of the ground waves, or out to thousands of miles using sky waves. There will normally be a SKIP ZONE between where reception of the ground wave fades out and the nearest range of reception of sky waves.

Selecting a frequency band for communications with a distant ship or shore station is a complex matter affected by the distance, time of day, and season of the year. Specific instructions will be found in the operation manuals of radios used for high-seas HF communications; experience gained by use of such equipment is of great assistance in selecting the optimum frequencies. In general terms, the following guidance can be offered:

• The 2 MHz band is usable for shorter distances of 20 to 100 miles day or night, with somewhat greater distances being reached at night. The FCC Rules, however, require that VHF must be used for shorter distances where its range is adequate.

• The 4 MHz band is a short-to-medium-distance band for 20 to 250 miles during the day, but can open out to longer distances at night—150 to 1,500 miles.

• The 8 MHz band is a medium-distance, 250 to 1,500 miles, band during the day, and a long-distance, 400 to 3,000 miles, band at night.

• The 12, 16, 22, and 25 MHz bands are for use over thousands of miles.

• The highest frequency band that can be used is normally the best choice, as signals will be stronger and atmospheric noise least.

An excellent way to determine which frequency band to use is to listen—if you can hear the distant station you want to communicate with, it will probably be able to hear you, after the channel clears. If you don't hear it on a specific frequency, try channels on higher and lower frequency bands.

Other Bands Very-low frequency (VLF) and low frequency (LF) bands are used for electronic navigation systems. Frequencies in the ultrahigh frequency (UHF), super-high frequency (SHF), and extremely high frequency (EHF) bands are used for radars and satellite systems. These bands will be covered in more detail in Chapter 21.

Types of Modulation

In order to be useful for communications, radio waves generated at a given frequency must be modulated. It is this modulation of the signal that ultimately produces audible voice emulation at the receiving end. Some ratio sets modulate their transmitted signals by means of frequency modulation (FM) and some by amplitude modulation (AM).

AM Amplitude modulation, in double sideband (DSB) form, employs a carrier wave plus two sidebands, one either side of the carrier. AM is used by regular broadcast stations in the 550 to 1600 kHz band. For many years, DSB AM was also used in marine radiotelephone communications, but has been replaced by single sideband (SSB) AM, which employs a reduced or suppressed carrier wave and only one sideband, for long-range communications.

An advantage of SSB transmission is that its "narrower" signals take up less space in a crowded spectrum, and so allow more channels to be used within a given band. Another plus factor is that this type of modulation provides more "talk power"—a greater portion of the transmitted power carries useful intelligence (a carrier wave bears no intelligence and the second sideband merely duplicates the first one.) There is also less interference between two adjacent SSB signals that there would be with DSB transmissions.

The disadvantage of single-sideband is that it requires a more complex transmitter and receiver; these are more expensive to purchase, and a bit more difficult to operate.

FM Frequency modulation does not employ a "carrier" wave or sidebands, but rather modulates its signal by varying the frequency of a signal having a steady strength. The frequency is varied at an audio rate by the information (voice, music, etc.) being transmitted. The extent to which it is varied is a measure of the "loudness" of the audio input.

FM radio signals have the advantage that they are not significantly affected by atmospheric noise (static) or noise from shipboard electrical equipment. They also exhibit what is known as "capture effect": When AM signals from two different stations are transmitted simultaneously on the same frequency, they interfere with one another and often render both unreadable. However, when FM signals from two transmitting stations are competing for the same channel, the stronger signal "captures" the receiver and is clearly read, to the exclusion of the other, weaker signal. This, by the way, is why signal output wattage is important; higher wattage may not significantly increase range, but it will help to get your signal through when a frequency is crowded with traffic.

Another advantage of FM is the relative immunity of the signals to atmospheric noise (static) and man-made electrical noise such as ignition interference. FM signals are normally of excellent intelligibility and clarity with properly functioning transmitters and receivers.

FM radio waves, however, have the disadvantage that, in virtue of their spread either side of their nominal frequency, they take up more "space" on the radio wave spectrum. Consequently, FM transmission is used only in the VHF and higher frequencies, where adequate radio spectrum space is still available.

Power

The power of a radio transmitter can be described and measured in a number of ways. VHF/FM transmitters are rated in OUTPUT POWER, the power delivered to the point where the antenna cable is connected; this is roughly 35 percent to 40 percent of the DC input power from the boat's electrical system. (The DC power consumed while receiving only is very slight.) VHF sets on boats are limited by regulations to 25 watts and must have a front-panel control to reduce this to 1 watt or less. (FCC rules require that the lower power be used for short-range contacts where such is sufficient; the use of low power for communications with nearby craft may result in more readable signals.)

Single-sideband radiotelephones are rated in terms of PEAK ENVELOPE POWER (PEP), a complex technical standard. SSB transmitters on vessels are subject to power limits between 150 and 1,150 watts, as determined by the geographic area concerned, the frequency used, and the type of communications involved. For practical purposes, however, few small craft will need more than 150 watts, and many can operate effectively with sets rated at 50 to 100 watts.

Antennas

The best transmitter-receiver combination is severely handicapped, or is even worthless, if it is not connected to an efficient antenna by an efficient feedline. The outgoing signal must be effectively radiated, and the incoming signal adequately picked up—the transmitting requirement is normally much more severe.

VHF A VHF/FM radiotelephone is virtually useless without an appropriate antenna. It can sometimes receive signals, but only relatively strong ones; and it cannot transmit. (Indeed, a radiotelephone's circuitry can be damaged if the transmitter is triggered without an antenna being attached.)

Virtually all VHF/FM radiotelephone antennas today are of the "whip" variety—that is, they're supported at their bottom end only. In shorter lengths (30 to about 42 inches), the whips are sometimes made of a self-supporting stainless steel rod; but in longer lengths, they are almost always constructed of a thin wire surrounded and supported by a flexible, wrapped fiberglass-reinforced plastic casing, the casing being "transparent" to radio waves.

At 156 to 163 MHz, a simple 36-inch piece of wire suffices as a basic "half-wavelength" antenna. Lengthening and other modifications of such a basic antenna can result in significant increases in effective radiating power. These increases are known as GAIN.

Gain is designated in decibels (dB), with every 3 dB representing a doubling of effective radiated power. For example, the effective radiated power of a given radiotelephone with a 3 dB gain antenna is double that of the same unit with a basic 0 dB gain antenna. With a 6 dB gain antenna the effective radiated power of the same unit is double that with the 3 dB gain antenna, or four times that with the 0 dB gain antenna. And with a 9 dB gain antenna, the radiated power is eight times what it would be if the unit were attached to a 0 dB gain antenna. It is clear that the use of a gain antenna significantly enhances transmission signal strength.

However, the proper course of action is *not* to install the highest-gain antenna possible, for two reasons. First, increased gain usually requires increased length; and physical limitations may prevent installation of a very high-gain antenna. In addition, as previously noted, radiated power does not have a major effect on range; only antenna height does. Therefore, it is sometimes more effective to use a lower gain antenna mounted high up, for instance, at the top of a sailboat mast, or on a powerboat antenna extension mast.

Secondly, gain antennas work by concentrating the radiated signal: They "squeeze" the normally more vertical limits of the wave pattern into a more horizontal configuration and, in doing so, lose less energy to useless skyward radiation. (Remember VHS signals are not, to any useful extent, reflected back to earth by the ionosphere.) See **Figure 20-04**. That horizontally concentrated pattern is an advantage only as long as the transmitting vessel remains relatively level. However, if the transmitting vessel heels or rolls to any great extent (for example, a sailboat under a press of sail, or a powerboat running in a heavy beam sea), this horizontally concentrated pattern results in the transmitted waves being, on one moment, directed into the sea (leeward heeled side) and, at the next moment, beamed uselessly skyward (windward heeled side). For that reason, it is usual practice *not* to choose an antenna gain greater than 3 dB for sailing vessels, and to limit gain to 6 to 9 dB on powerboats, depending on their size and stability.

Effective radiated power can often be improved significantly *without* resorting to an antenna with higher gain. Too many and/or poor coaxial connections in the cable run between the transceiver and its antenna can result in significant loss in signal strength (due to increased resistance). The same is true, more or less, of antenna cable that is too small or insufficiently shielded for the length of run involved. Consequently, in most cases, it's advantageous to minimize the number of coaxial connectors in the line, and to employ heavier cable of type RG8 or a high-performance equivalent cable in

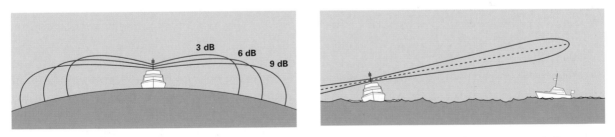

Figure 20-04 *Higher-gain antennas achieve greater range by "squeezing down" the radiation pattern (left), increasing signals at lower, desirable angles and decreasing the power that is wasted in upward, unproductive angles. An antenna with too much gain—too flat a radiation pattern—may be disadvantageous in rough water. As the boat rolls and pitches (right), the radiated signal may go above the receiving boat or down into the water. Either will cause fading and intermittent reception.*

preference to the lighter, more commonly supplied type RG58.

If a vessel operates in open waters in rough conditions (when distress calling is most likely needed), there is always the risk of losing or seriously damaging a vessel's whip antenna. The prudent skipper carries either a spare or an emergency antenna. The best is one that can be readily mounted on deck and is fitted with a cable of sufficient length and the correct coaxial connector for attachment to the vessel's VHF radiotelephone. (This is true for sailboats, as well as powerboats, since a sailboat is most likely to have lost its mast-mounted antenna during a partial or complete dismasting.)

MF and HF The antenna requirement for SSB transmitters in the MF and HF bands is a difficult one to effectively meet on small craft, especially powerboats. Except for sailboats, the antenna is normally a self-supporting pole of fiberglass with a wire conductor inside. This is electrically one-quarter of a wavelength—"electrically" because an actual physical quarter wavelength would be a structural impossibility—at 2 MHz, about 117 feet (35.6 m) high! In actual practice, a LOADING COIL may be built into the antenna near its midpoint so that it will appear electrically longer than its physical length. It is also the usual practice to use an ANTENNA TUNER near the antenna base to "match" the impedance of the antenna to the output circuit of the transmitter; this may be either manually or automatically tuned for the frequency used.

On sailboats, it is common to install an insulator near the upper and lower ends of a backstay and use the intervening length of metal wire as the antenna. On larger sailing craft, this makes quite an efficient antenna after loading and tuning adjustments have been made.

In addition to the problems of the antenna itself, most MF and HF radio installations on small craft present difficulties in grounding. A proper ground is a vital part of a SSB antenna system. There should be at least 100 square feet (9.3 m≈) of RF ground, preferably copper mesh built into the hull when the fiberglass was laid up. (A metal hull works wonder-

fully.) The problem is not the type of modulation, but the fact that an SSB set normally covers a very wide range of frequencies, from 2 MHz to as high as 25 MHz. (A few installations may use two or more different antennas for more efficient operation.) An SSB installation will normally require the services of an experienced technician.

Modes of Operation

Two different modes of operation are used in marine radio communications. Most marine communications are SIMPLEX—both stations transmit and receive on the same frequency. Thus the person on the receiving end cannot interrupt and communicate to the person currently transmitting, until the latter stops transmitting and provides the opportunity. This technique is sometimes difficult for a beginner to grasp in practice—but this is the reason why you must pause after transmitting and release the microphone button. In fact, this is the only way that you will be able to hear the reply from the party at the other end.

In SEMIDUPLEX (or HALF-DUPLEX) operation, two frequencies are used, each station transmitting on one and receiving on the other. FULL-DUPLEX allows a station to transmit and receive simultaneously, as you would with a conventional telephone on land—this is not possible on boats, except for some satellite circuits.

Radiotelephones

The radio communication equipment authorized for use on boats, and by persons holding no personal license or the rudimentary, easy-to-obtain Restricted Radiotelephone Operators Permit, is specially constructed to ensure that only certain designated frequencies are used, and that it is impossible to transmit inadvertently on unauthorized frequencies. This is accomplished by eliminating the need for operator tuning, and instead incorporating "switch-selectable" channels. And because the simplified operation of such units, and their primary devotion to voice communication, are reminiscent of shoreside telecommunications, the units have come to be known as radiotelephones. Such equipment is "Type Accepted" by the FCC, and by regulation are the only sets that can be used.

THE MARINE RADIO SYSTEM

In the very early days of electronic ship-to-shore and ship-to-ship communications, the use of Morse code predominated. This continued to be the case in military and commercial marine contexts for quite some time, but no longer. Today, however, the vast majority of marine electronic communications, especially for recreational boats, are effected through voice transmissions.

Marine voice transmissions are, for the most part, much like conversations between two persons over shoreside telephones. However, there are at least two important differences between ordinary onshore telephone conversations and marine communications.

Except for some VHF use, there are very specific federal licensing requirements and more stringent procedural regulations for marine communications. It should be noted that communications regulations and certain procedures vary from one country to another. Unless otherwise stated, the material in this chapter should be understood as pertaining exclusively to the United States. The rules and regulations of the Federal Communications Commission (FCC) uniformly refer to "ship stations"—boaters must understand that this applies to vessels of all sizes, even the smallest of boats.

Safety Communications

Perhaps the most important point for skippers of recreational craft to understand is that, by law, the primary function of regulated electronic communications at sea is *safety*, and that marine radio communications related to safety have absolute priority over all other types of communications. Certain other specified uses of marine radios are allowed; but the overriding rule is that if you're talking to another vessel or to a shore station about matters other than immediate safety—for example, the weather, or whether a destination

marina has a slip available for your arrival—you *must* without exception cease transmitting if there is a safety-related communication competing for the airwaves. In fact, even among safety-related communications there is a specific hierarchy of priority that must, again under law, be observed. These points will be discussed in more detail later in this chapter.

Operational Communications

In addition to safety, electronic voice communications is also allowed for "operational" purposes which, strictly speaking, are those having to do with the navigation, movement, and management of vessels at sea. In the recreational sector, these categories of operational uses are, for the most part, interpreted liberally. For example, ship-to-ship communications between two boats about where to stay for the night would be considered as having to do with "movement." And ship-to-shore communications between a yacht skipper and the attendant at a fuel dock would be considered as having to do with "management." However, a call to a marina to make dinner reservations at that facility's restaurant would *not* fall within this category and so would not be permissible.

Personal & Social Communications

It's important to keep in mind that, however liberally the concepts of "safety" and "operational" are interpreted, the laws governing marine communications strictly prohibit superfluous personal or social chitchat between boats on most channels (frequencies).

Communications of a strictly personal or social nature are allowed, but only in certain contexts and on certain channels specifically designed for that purpose. These circumstances and channels have primarily to do with ship-to-shore communications, in which a radio connection is made with a land-based telephone system via a "Marine Operator." In such cases, the boat's radiotelephone becomes part of the land-based telephone system; calls may be placed to, or received from, shoreside telephones for any purpose allowed under the laws governing land-

"RESCUE 21"

In the 1990s it became increasingly apparent that the communications network supporting search and rescue (SAR) operations of the U.S. Coast Guard was not up to the task – much of the technology dated back to the 1970s. Formally named the National Distress and Response System (NDRS), this VHF-based system supposedly had a range of 20 nautical miles offshore, but numerous coverage gaps. Direction finding capabilities were limited, and there was a lack of interoperability with the Coast Guard's various partners and customers. It used simplex radio operation, which prohibited a station in the system from receiving radio calls when engaged in transmitting.

In October 2002, the Coast Guard began the NDRS Modernization Project – the name was soon officially shortened to "Rescue 21." Implementation began in 2003 to be accomplished incrementally; some delays are being encountered, but all regions should be operational by late 2007.

Rescue 21 is an advance search and rescue communications system for the 21st century that will make it possible for the Coast Guard to more effectively locate and assist boaters in distress. It is designed to take the "search" out of search and rescue – it will provide automatic identification of incoming calls from DSC radios; it will provide automatic location of vessels in distress using DSC and GPS. The new system will eliminate gaps in coverage, enable immediate direction finding, and make possible the recording and instant playback of radio calls. Where Rescue 21 is operational, all boaters will benefit from improved communications with Coast Guard shore activities and vessels, but those craft equipped with radios using DSC, and especially those using Class D features (see page 694), will gain the most from the new system. Regardless of the type of radio on the craft in distress, direction finding will be possible to an accuracy of 2 degrees — SAR vessels will have a markedly smaller area to search.

An increase in the number of voice and data channels from one to six will allow multiple operations to be conducted simultaneously — no longer will a single caller in distress (or even worse, a hoax caller) prevent another caller from getting through. Encryption will provide security for sensitive Coast Guard communications. Enhanced digital playback of recorded incoming calls will improve the chances for unclear messages to be understood. The system will provide for the tracking of Coast Guard boats and cutters, improving the speed of response to emergency situations. Improved interoperability with federal, state, and local resources will increase the assets for SAR efforts.

The improved communications capabilities of Rescue 21 will also assist the Coast Guard in carrying out its homeland security and law enforcement missions as well as other critical operations.

---

based telecommunications. You should keep in mind, however, that calls placed through a Marine Operator are subject to "linkage" and possibly other charges.

The VHF radio rules do not apply to cellular telephone communications from vessels, or to such services as Citizen Band (CB) and the Family Radio Service (FRS).

Licensing

The regulations of the Federal Communications Commission (FCC) do not require individual station licenses for VHF/FM radios on "voluntarily equipped" boats that do not travel to foreign ports or engage in international communications; included in this exemption are radars and all types of EPIRBs (Emergency Position

Indicating Radiobeacons, see page 705). Cruising or fishing in international waters—beyond the 12-mile U.S. territorial limit—does not invoke the requirement for a station license provided that you do not enter waters under the jurisdiction of another county. This action benefits a large majority of U.S. boaters in that a fee no longer must be paid. Even though an individual license is not required, such a station must still be used in full compliance with all applicable operating regulations as before; the only exception is that now call signs will not be used as they no longer will be assigned.

Note carefully that this change in FCC rules does not exempt any craft *required* by law or regulation to be equipped with a radio. Also *not exempted* are HF-MF single-sideband (SSB) installations, and radio-equipped boats that do travel to foreign waters or communicate across national boundaries; these must have licenses as before. The exception here is for U.S. recreational vessels cruising in Canadian waters; no station license is required.

Before applying for *any* FCC license or permit, a person *must* obtain a "FCC Registration Number (FRN)." This can be done electronically at http://www.fcc.gov (click on button for "Commission Registration System—CORES") or by submitting a paper Form 160 to FCC Attn: CORES Administrator, Room CY-C140, 445 12th Street, Washington, DC 20554-0001. There is no fee.

Applying for a Station License

A station license may be issued to a U.S. citizen, corporation, or an alien individual, but not to the government of a foreign nation or its representative. This license can be applied for by mail using FCC Form 605—provided you have your state registration numbers or a U.S. Coast Guard documentation number. (Note: The FCC will accept only the current form; forms packed with radios by the manufacturer may be obsolete. Forms may be requested by calling 800-418-3676 or they may be downloaded from the Internet at www.fcc.gov/formpage.html.) Form 605 is a multipart form; detailed instructions for comple-

tion of the application appear on the first two pages. Read and heed these carefully to avoid having your application returned for correction or additional information. The next two pages are the actual application that will be mailed to the FCC. Be sure that you ask for all frequency bands that you know you will need, or which you can anticipate needing in the future.

Fees totaling $200 (as of October 2003; probably increasing slightly in future years) must accompany the application together with FCC Form 159 marked with payment code "PASR." Payment may be made by check or money order, payable to "FCC," or by credit card (Visa, MasterCard, American Express, or Discover Card). Send all required papers to Federal Communications Commission, Wireless Bureau Applications, P.O. Box 358130, Pittsburgh, PA 15251-5130. Fees are reviewed annually and may be changed. Application can be made electronically with payment by credit card. If the application is returned as defective, the returned papers may require a second application fee payment. Questions regarding fees can be made to 888-225-5322.

If you need immediate use of the radio, Schedule F at the end of Form 605 becomes a temporary license valid for 90 days, within which time you should receive the formal papers. It gives information on generating a temporary call sign (based on your registration or documentation numbers) that can be used for interim operation. Use of such a temporary call sign must cease on receipt of the regular license and call sign, even if the 90-day period has not expired.

Radio station licenses in the U.S. are issued in the name of the owner and the vessel. A station license is not automatically transferred to another person upon sale of the boat, nor may a license be moved with the radio set to a new boat owned by the same person; a new license must be applied for using Forms 605 and 159 marked with fee payment code "PASR," plus payment in the same amount as for a new license. A change in the licensee's legal name, mailing address, vessel name, official documentation number, or state registration number (but not a change in ownership) does not require license modification. Just send Form 605 for an "Administrative Update," no fee required to the FCC at 1270 Fairfield Rd., Gettysburg, PA 17325-7245, advising of the change; a copy of this form must be posted on board along with the license. A simple change in equipment requires no action at all. The only instance of a modification of a license during its term would be to add an FCC-issued Maritime Mobile Service Identity (MMSI) number; see page 694. The fee is $50; send Forms 605 and 159 using fee payment code "PASM." (An MMSI may be obtained without charge from BoatU.S. and several other authorized sources.) The license expiration date is not changed. A license may be modified at the time of renewal without additional cost beyond the normal renewal fee. If a station license is lost, a duplicate must be obtained; send Forms 605 and 159 and the fee of $50 using fee payment code "PADM."

FCC regulations require that a station license be conspicuously posted on board the vessel at the principal control point of the station. The license term is 10 years. Approximately 120 days before the expiration date, the FCC will send a renewal reminder. If this is not received by 30 days before expiration, renewal should be Form 605 and Form 159 marked with the fee payment code "PASR," together with the same fee as for a new license, to the FCC Wireless Bureau Applications, P.O. Box 358345, Pittsburgh, PA 15251-5245. Licenses can also be renewed on the Internet with payment by credit card. If you did make timely application for renewal, operation may continue even if you have not received the renewed license before the expiration date. If the boat is sold or use of the radio station is ever permanently discontinued, you should send Form 605 requesting cancellation of the license to the FCC at the Gettysburg address; this will preclude your being held responsible for any future misuse of the call sign concerned.

For changes in FCC rules, fees, and procedures go to www.fcc.gov/wtb.

Applying for an Operator Permit

A personal license, a radio operator permit, is not required for the operation of a VHF set on a boat exempted from having to have a station license as described above. An exception applies if a boat goes into Canadian waters: an operator permit is required (Canada has a station license exemption similar to the United States, but requires an operator permit for its boaters). If such license is required, a Restricted Radiotelephone Operator Permit or higher grade of license is also required.

For vessels carrying more than six passengers for hire, and for vessels over 65 feet in length on the Great Lakes, whether commercial or noncommercial, the operator must have a Marine Radio Operator Permit. At least a Restricted Permit is required on board vessels that must comply with the Bridge-to-Bridge Radiotelephone Act (see Chapter 5)—vessels over 65 feet in length, tugs over 26 feet and dredges in channels. A higher class license is available for trained individuals making tuning adjustments and repairs. In situations where a licensed operator is required, an unlicensed person may talk into the microphone, but a licensed operator must be present and responsible for the proper use of the station.

An applicant for any grade of U.S. operator's license must be a U.S. citizen or a foreign national eligible for work in the U.S. (there are some exceptions for special cases). For a Restricted Radiotelephone Operator Permit, you do not have to appear in person at any FCC office. It is obtained by filling out FCC Form 605 and mailing it to the Federal Communications Commission, Wireless Bureau Applications, P.O. Box 358130, Pittsburgh, PA 15251-5130. A fee of $50 must accompany the application and Form 159 marked with payment type code "PARR." The permit is issued, without test or examination, by declaration. The applicant must "certify" that he can speak and hear, keep at least a rough written log, and is familiar with the treaties, laws, and regulations governing the station that he will operate. He must also certify that he had need for a permit because he intends to engage in international voyages and is eligible for employment in the United States. The Restricted Permit is valid for the lifetime of the person to whom it is issued, unless it is suspended or revoked. Follow the instructions carefully to avoid having the application returned to you for correction. A portion of Form 605 may be retained as a temporary operator permit, valid for 60 days; this allows you to get on the air immediately if your operations require a permit.

For the Marine Radio Operator Permit, an examination is required, necessitating a visit to an FCC office. This test is nontechnical, in a multiple-choice format, covering only operating rules and procedures. You will find the examination not at all difficult if you prepare for it properly. A free *Study Guide* is available from FCC offices. Application is on Form 605; there is no fee. The permit is valid for five years and must be renewed using the same form and paying a fee of $50, accompanied by Form 159 with payment type code "PACS" marked. For skippers of recreational boats the privileges of this higher class license are no greater than those of a Restricted Permit, but for many it is a matter of pride to qualify and post it on board their craft.

If your radio operator permit is lost or becomes illegible, apply immediately for a duplicate. Use the same form as for an original and a fee of $50 with Form 159 marked PADM. State the circumstances fully and, if the license has been lost, you must certify that a reasonable search has been made. Continued operation is authorized if a signed copy of the application for a duplicate is posted. If a lost license is found later, send either that license or the duplicate to the FCC for cancellation.

• **Canadian licensing** Canadian yachts are subject to parallel installation and operator licensing requirements, the only significant difference being that the Canadian Restricted Operator Certificate (Maritime) requires the passing of a brief exam on the correct operating procedures; this exam is only given by units of the Canadian Power & Sail Squadrons, see Chapter 26, page 872. The Certificate is available without charge, but must be obtained before applying for a Noncompulsory Station License. (Starting with C$46 up to April, the cost is based on the remaining number of months in the year; renewal is C$35.) Such a station license is required only for those vessels sailing to waters other than those of Canada and the United States.

Information on the current licensing procedures and the appropriate forms can be obtained from Industry Canada, 473 Albert Street (4th Floor), Ottawa, Ontario K1R 5B4. Telephone: 613-998-3693; fax: 613-998-5919.

VHF/FM RADIO SERVICE

For small craft, the maritime communications system is divided into two parts—short range and long range. Each of these portions involves different equipment—VHF/FM for short range, and MF-HF/SSB for long range.

Most marine electronic voice communications, especially in the recreational sector, use a VHF/FM radiotelephone. In fact, by law, a VHF/FM radio must be installed on board as a precondition to the licensing and installation of any other form of marine radiotelephone. The reason for this is that VHF/FM is, by domestic law and international treaty, the prescribed vehicle for local communications, both ship-to-ship and ship-to-shore.

Channels

The marine VHF communications band stretches from 156 to 162.5 MHz. Within this band, there are numbered CHANNELS spaced 25 kHz apart. Actual frequencies are rarely used in marine communications; the general procedure is to speak of channel numbers. Channels, or groups of channels, are assigned specific uses, and may not be used for other purposes; see Table 20-1. Most are simplex channels, others are semiduplex. In the United States, some channels internationally assigned for duplex use are employed for simplex communications on the lower frequency of the pair; these have the letter "A" as a suffix, such as 22A. VHF transceivers have a USA/International or button to selct the appropriate channels. Remember "A" in "USA" when communicating with the U.S. Coast Guard.

VHF/FM transmissions are basically line-of-sight—that is, the signals are *not* reflected by the ionosphere under normal conditions, nor do they significantly bend around the curvature of the earth. Consequently, VHF/FM transmission is

SELECTED VHF MARINE CHANNELS & THEIR USES

Channel Number	Frequency (MHz) Transmit	Frequency (MHz) Receive	Communications Purpose
06	156.300	156.300	Intership safety communications only.
07A	156.350	156.350	Commercial intership and ship-to-coast; also channels 08*, 10, 18A, 19A, 79A, 90A and others for specific geographic areas (* = intership only).
09	156.450	156.450	Commercial and noncommercial intership and ship-to-coast commercial docks, marinas and some clubs); also used by recreational boaters as alternate calling channel. Also used at some locks and bridges.
12	156.600	156.600	Port Operations—traffic advisory—also USCG secondary working channel with non-USCG vessels.
13	156.650	156.650	Navigational—ship's bridge to ship's bridge (1 watt only). Available to all vessels and is required on passenger and commercial vessels (including many tugs), as well as all power-driven vessels more than 20 meters (65.6 ft.) in length. Used at some bridges.
14	156.700	156.700	Port Operations (intership and ship-to-coast)
16	156.800	156.800	Distress Safety and Calling (mandatory). All distress calls should be made on Channel 16.
22A	157.100	157.100	Coast Guard Liaison and Maritime Safety Information Broadcasts; used for communications with USCG ship, coast, and aircraft stations after first establishing communications on Channel 16.
24	157.250	161.850	Public telephone (Marine Operator); also Channels 25, 27, 84, 85, 86, 88.
26	157.300	161.900	Public telephone (Marine Operator).
28	157.400	162.000	Public telephone (Marine Operator).
65A	156.275	156.275	Port Operations (intership and ship-to-coast); also Channels 20A*, 66A, 73, 74, 77† (* = intership only; †= communications with pilots only).
67	156.375	156.375	Commercial intership all areas, plus noncommercial intership (Puget Sound and Strait of Juan de Fuca). In the Lower Mississippi River, use limited to navigational bridge-to-bridge navigational purposes (1watt).
68	156.425	156.425	Noncommercial intership and ship-to-coast (marinas, yacht clubs, etc.).
69	156.475	156.475	Noncommercial intership and ship-to-coast.
70	156.525	156.525	Distress and safety calling, and general purpose calling; may only be used by vessels equipped with Digital Selective Calling (DSC).
71	156.575	156.575	Noncommercial intership and ship-to-coast.
72	156.625	156.625	Noncommercial intership only.
78A	156.925	156.925	Noncommercial intership and ship-to-coast.
79A	156.975	156.975	Commercial intership and ship-to-coast. Noncommercial intership on Great Lakes only.
80A	157.025	157.025	Commercial intership and ship-to-coast. Noncommercial intership on Great Lakes only.
WX1		162.550	Weather broadcasts (receive only).
WX2		162.400	Weather broadcasts (receive only).
WX3		162.475	Weather broadcasts (receive only).

Table 20-1 This table lists selected VHF channels, their operating frequencies, and their general purposes, focusing primarily on the interests of recreational (noncommercial) boaters. Some additional commercial and noncommercial channels are available in specific limited areas. The FCC has numerous additional conditions and limitations on certain channels too complex to be shown here. The "A" suffix indicates a channel used only in U.S. waters and is different from its frequencies and purpose in International usage. Wx1, Wx2, and Wx3 are widely used as the primary channels for continuous weather reports and forecasts. Additional Channels Wx4 – Wx7 are used in specific areas, as necessary, to avoid possible interference with a primary channel.

fairly well restricted to a limited geographical area, on average 10 to 15 nautical miles in ship-to-ship situations, and 25 to 30 miles ship-to-shore, depending on the heights of both the transmitting and receiving antennas. That means a boat transmitting in, say, Jacksonville, Florida, on 156.3 MHz will not interfere with one transmitting on the same frequency at the exact same time in St. Augustine, Florida, 45 miles away. And the potential for interference is further decreased in VHF/FM radiotelephones by the legal limitation of their maximum output power to 25 watts, the requirement for a switch-selectable, one-watt output for close-in communications, and by the capture effect previously mentioned.

Equipment Selection

There are many manufacturers of VHF radio equipment for boats and ships—and each manufacturer has many models. The selection of a VHF set for your boat should be undertaken with study and care. As with most electronic devices, greater price brings better quality construction and more features, but you may not need the very "top-of-the-line" transceiver. Compare different models, and ask other boaters what has been their experience with different manufacturers and models; see **Figure 20-05**.

Power & Channels

VHF/FM radiotelephones are limited by law to 25 watts output power and required to have a 1-watt switchable low-power setting. Output power does not bear directly on operating range, which can be considered as line-of-sight between the transmitting and receiving antennas, regardless of transmitting or radiating power. However, output power does have a bearing on capture effect, namely, the ability of the signal to be received clearly in spite of potential interference from simultaneous signals from other transmitters. As a practical matter, every VHF/FM set now manufactured, except handheld models, is built with the maximum allowable 25 watts output power. Handheld units will usually have an output power of 5 watts, sometimes less.

Figure 20-05 A VHF transceiver must be "Type Accepted" by the FCC. Power is switch-selectable between 25 watts and 1 watt. Low power should be used for short distances to reduce interference to other stations and is mandatory (automatic) for Channel 13.

VHF radios—full-size and handheld—have the legally required channels and many more.

Sensitivity & Selectivity

Technical factors in equipment selection are sensitivity and selectivity (adjacent channel rejection). Sensitivity is usually expressed as the number of microvolts needed to produce 20 decibel (db) "quieting." (When comparing nominal specifications, it's important to confirm that the 20 dB standard is being used.) This rating effectively measures the minimum signal strength that will trigger a set's receiver capability. And in this case, the lower the microvolt number, the higher the radiotelephone's sensitivity, and thus the better its ability to receive weak or distant transmissions.

Selectivity is usually expressed as a negative dB number (for example, "-65 db") and measures a set's ability to screen out interfering signals on channels or frequencies close to the one being used. The higher the absolute dB number, the better the set's selectivity (-70 dB is better than -60 db) and the better the set will be at rejecting potential interference from simultaneous transmissions on other frequencies.

Other Considerations & Features

Beyond channel capability, sensitivity, and selectivity, there are other features of potential interest, the inclusion of which directly affects a unit's price. One factor is water-resistance. Some units are more "splash-proof" than others, thus more suitable for exposed locations; some are even rated as waterproof—submersible to a limited depth for a limited time.

Nearly all sets are capable of scanning in various modes: all channels or only selected channels. Also common is a button that allows instant, direct access to Channel 16, or 16 and 9.

Most units incorporate an automatic "dual watch" and/or scanning feature that allows you to monitor (as you must under law when the radio is on) Channel 16 plus one or more other channels on which you might be expecting to receive a call. Some sets also have "tri-watch" so that Channels 16 and 9 plus a selected channel can be concurrently monitored.

LCD displays show the selected channel and other operating information. These are backlit for night use, frequently with adjustable light levels. A few more expensive models can display information from a GPS receiver, such as latitude and longitude, speed and course, and date and time. Some microphones have buttons that allow a change of channel up or down, or a switch to 16, without reference to the radio itself. There are even wireless speaker/mike combinations.

Most installed VHF receivers have the capability of feeding a remotely located auxiliary speaker so that a watch can be kept below decks; some can be used as a loud hailer and automatic foghorn.

Some incorporate a weather alert system that sounds a warning tone to advise of a special hazardous weather broadcast on the local VHF weather channel. Many sets have digital selective calling (DSC), see below, built-in; others have the capability of adding it as an option.

Digital Selective Calling

Digital Selective Calling (DSC) is a semiautomated method of making a radio contact. It has been internationally established for MF, HF, and VHF communications and is a part of the Global Maritime Distress and Safety System (GMDSS); see page 704. DSC will eventually replace aural watches on distress frequencies and be used for routine and urgent maritime safety information broadcasts. (VHF Channel 16 audio watches on large ships and by the U.S. Coast Guard was scheduled to end in 2005 but this date has been extended indefinitely.)

DSC uses a digital transmission to send a specific set of information. This includes the caller's MMSI (Maritime Mobile Service Identity), a nine-digit number that uniquely identifies the vessel; the requested working frequency and mode; priority of the call; and other data. DSC calls can be made to an individual ship or shore station, a group of stations, a specific set of stations, such as all USCG units, all receivers in a prescribed geographic area, or all receivers within range, such as for distress calls or if the called station's MMSI is not known. The called station uses DSC to respond, then the contact is carried out normally on Channel 16 if it is a distress situation or on a normal working channel if it is not distress communications. A DSC-equipped vessel or shore station can call using a "data stream" on Channel 70; a connection can be made and the set switched to a working channel without first transmitting the call on Channel 16. A ringer alerts an operator to an incoming call—bringing radiotelephone communication ever closer to the ease and convenience of shoreside telephone use.

DSC distress calls can include the vessel's location, either directly inputted from GPS or Loran receivers, or keyed in manually. Calls can even indicate the nature of the distress, such as "sinking," "on fire," etc.

DSC Types DSC transceivers are divided into various classes. In the U.S., most small craft will use a VHF radio with SC-101, or the even better Class D, capabilities. Such sets are capable of sending and receiving distress, safety, and routine calls. A Class D transceiver has a second receiver built-in that continuously monitors Channel 70 for DSC calls even when the basic receiver and transmitter are being used on another channel. An SC-101 radio has only one receiver that is inoperable when transmitting. A Class "A" DSC radio includes a second receiver plus additional features. It has extensive calling number memory and caller ID capabilities, and a keypad similar to that found on conventional telephones that simplifies the entry of the MMSI number; see

Figure 20-06. The operation of a Class A DSC radio closely resembles that of using a cellular telephone.

Many currently used marine radios have DSC capability or can be upgraded to DSC, and all equipment type-approved by the FCC after June 1999 must include at least a basic DSC function. Sets that were type-approved before that date can continue to be manufactured and sold. Older radios can still be used; there is no requirement that a recreational boat have a DSC radio, but the new system does have advantages.

In any event, a wise skipper will compare the latest specifications and features of a number of units in a given price range before making a final selection of VHF/FM radiotelephone equipment.

Handheld Units

Over the last few years, small portable (as opposed to full-size installed) VHF/FM radiotelephones have gained significantly in popularity. Generally referred to as handheld units, this type is fitted with an integral microphone, speaker, and antenna, as well as a rechargeable battery; see **Figure 20-07.** (Some more expensive models now use a lithium-ion battery rather than the more-common nickle-cadmiums; these have more power for longer life and are free of the "memory-effect" that plagues "Ni-Cads.") A dual capability of also using ordinary alkaline AA dry cells is desirable. Most hand-helds have a

Figure 20-07 Small handheld VHF transceivers now have essentially all the features of a full-size installed set, except for output power. These include coverage of all channels, dual-watch, scanning in one or more modes, one-button switching to Channel 16 (on some sets 16 and 9), and other features such as Weather Alert.

5-watt output rating, some have a 6-watt output. But there are a few of lesser power for smaller size and lighter weight. As with all marine VHF radios, hand-helds must have a low power (1-watt or less) switch; operating at the lower power will considerably extend battery life.

Many hand-helds incorporate additional features: jacks for a separate speaker and/or microphone and the capability of replacing the normal attached "rubber-ducky" antenna with an adapter (Radio Shack No. 278-120) for attaching a cable leading to an external antenna, usually larger and mounted higher. Various degrees of weather and water resistance are available, including full submersibility; transparent plastic cases are available for the protection of sets that are not water-resistant, some are large enough that the antenna can be left on and the set operated while safely protected in the case.

As a result of advancing technology, hand-helds may have all the features of installed sets—dual- and tri-watch, scanning of all or selected channels, weather channels and alerting capability, battery status indicator, backlit display of channel in use and other information, locking of the key pad so as to avoid accidental channel change, and others, even voice scrambling for privacy! Some are so small that they can fit into a shirt pocket. Few features are sacrificed for smaller size—power may be less (not too important) and battery life may be less (can be critical).

A handheld unit can be valuable as follows:

• For communication between a dinghy or tender and the vessel that it accompanies.

• As a back-up for the regular radiotelephone.

Figure 20-06 VHF transceivers must now have at least a minimal capability of Digital Selective Calling (DSC). Sets with a numeric keypad are advantageous for entering the nine-digit MMSI (Maritime Mobile Service Identity) number for the station or stations you wish to call. Many sets will have memory storage for frequently used MMSIs.

• On larger vessels where it is sometimes useful to have a radio capability when away from the regular installation.

• For two-way emergency communication in the event of having to abandon ship.

Keep in mind, however, that it is *not* legal to use a handheld radio to communicate with the vessel's main radio from a position *on board that vessel*. In other words, you cannot legally use a marine handheld set for intercom purposes.

Hand-helds also have other significant limitations. First, they have limited output power. Second, their integral antennas are much shorter and less efficient, and are, naturally, situated no higher than the hand that holds the unit. These factors combine to make hand-helds unsuitable for anything more than relatively close-in communications. And so, while they definitely have their place, they are rarely, if ever, an adequate substitute for full-power, fully featured installed sets.

There is an additional point regarding hand-helds, which is often overlooked in practice, and worth considering: Contrary to uninformed belief and all-too-common practice, handheld VHF/FM marine radiotelephones are *not authorized* as walkaround, portable units. Except for licensed stationary shore stations, mobile marine radio is authorized only for shipboard use (which includes yachts and tenders). Using a hand-held from an onshore location—for example, to call your vessel from a shoreside shop—is a violation of the marine radiotelephone regulations.

Installation & Maintenance

Most of today's VHF/FM radiotelephones come from the factory fully tested and ready to operate, requiring only connection to a power source and an appropriate antenna. Installation does not necessarily require the services of a trained technician.

If you choose to install one of these units yourself, it's important to keep a few points in mind. When hooking the radio up to the vessel's DC electrical system, be certain that correct polarity is observed, and that an appropriate in-line fuse is used. (Refer to Chapter 19 and the radiotelephone manufacturer's installation instructions.) Mount the unit in as protected a location as possible, consistent with convenient use for both receiving and transmitting; because the speaker contains a powerful magnet, it should not be placed close to a compass. As some heat is generated from the operation of the set, allow for adequate ventilation around the case. When mounting the unit, remember that it's necessary to run not only power to it, but the antenna cable as well. Never attempt to splice coaxial cable, but instead employ, when necessary, appropriate cable couplers (PL-259) available at any marine electronics dealer or electronics store (such as, Radio Shack No. 278-1369). And avoid sharp bends in the antenna cable by employing, if necessary, a right-angle cable connector (UG-646; Radio Shack No. 278-199). Make sure that all coaxial cable connections are correctly made; use properly soldered connectors, which are much more reliable in a marine environment than so-called solderless connectors. Finally, be sure to ground the radio case according to manufacturer's recommendations. Although grounding is not necessary for the operation of a VHF/FM radiotelephone, it will help eliminate interference from adjacent electronic equipment.

Once a VHF/FM radiotelephone is installed, there is actually very little maintenance that can be performed by the operator who is not also a trained radio technician; actually very little is needed. It's wise to inspect the antenna and power line connections periodically for signs of resistance-inducing corrosion. And the same is true for the ferrules of in-line fuses. Any corrosion should be removed, and any soldered connections redone if broken or deteriorated.

It's good practice to operate the radiotelephone frequently, at the very least in receiving mode. When turned on, a unit's internal circuitry produces dehumidifying heat that helps forestall internal condensation and consequent corrosion. It's also good practice to work all of the unit's switches and buttons periodically, as many of these have self-cleaning contacts that, when operated, remove any buildup of corrosion—something they do better if the corrosion is not allowed to build up from nonuse over a period of time.

Beyond that, dust, dirt, and salt spray residue should be removed regularly from the unit's case with a soft rag dampened (not flooded) with fresh water and a mild detergent used to remove greasy fingerprints.

A newly purchased handheld transceiver may require a period of battery charging before it is ready for full use. Many hand-helds have removable antennas with BNC connectors; these can be connected to an installed antenna by use of an adapter (such as, Radio Shack No. 278-120).

Operating Rules & Procedures

The FCC Rules regarding the keeping of a watch on Channel 16 were changed in October 2003. A "voluntarily equipped" vessel (a recreational boat) not equipped with DSC is now required *at all times when underway* to have its radio on and monitoring Channel 16 when it is not being used to communicate on another channel. A voluntary vessel equipped with DSC must, *when underway*, maintain a watch on either Channel 70 or Channel 16 when the radio is not in use on another channel.

Establishing Contact

Calls not related to distress of safety may be initiated on Channel 16, but such transmissions must be limited to establishing contact and determining a working channel (see below) to be used. Any single calling transmission must not exceed 30 seconds duration, and if no reply is received, a 2-minute pause must be observed before repeating the call. A maximum of three call attempts, separated by 2-minute silences, may be made before a 15-minute silence must be observed (this silence may be reduced to 3 minutes if the call transmissions will not interfere with traffic from other stations). No transmissions on Channel 16 may exceed 1 minute. These limitations do not apply to emergency situations. Nonemergency transmissions on Channel 16 are absolutely limited to reaching agreement on the working channel to be used; not even the briefest messages are to be transmitted.

In order to lessen the congestion on Channel 16, which has been steadily increasing, the FCC

has authorized the voluntary use of Channel 9 by noncommercial vessels for calling. You are cautioned, however, maintaining a watch for calls on Channel 9 may result in not hearing warnings and announcements from Coast Guard stations, calls from Marine Operators, and other important transmissions, as well as calls for your boat from others who are not aware of your Channel 9 watch. Remember, Channel 16 is the only channel to be used for distress calls and messages. If you have a set with the dual-watch or tri-watch feature, it would be an excellent practice to monitor both Channel 16 and 9.

The use of digital selective calling on Channel 70 is highly recommended if you know that the vessel with which you wish to communicate is so equipped.

After Contact Has Been Made

Once contact is made on an appropriate working channel (see below), the ensuing exchange of transmission must be:

- Of a legally permissible nature.
- Of the minimum possible duration.

The phonetic alphabet should be used to spell call signs, names, places, etc., *only* when absolutely necessary to ensure clarity. In most circumstances, when reception is clear, use of phonetics, while it sounds "professional" to some, only prolongs exchanges unnecessarily.

Further, superfluous words and phrases, such as "Do you read me?" and "Come in, Bluejay" should be avoided as much as possible in order to shorten transmission times. And to avoid unnecessary interference with other transmissions on the same frequency, the minimum practical transmitting power setting must by law be used—1 watt will suffice more often than you think.

Station Identification

Licensed stations with call signs must identify themselves at the start and end of an exchange of transmissions; it is not necessary to again state the call sign upon shifting to a working channel. Boats now without call signs must also identify themselves, but do so routinely by stating the vessel's name.

The Privacy of Communications

The Communications Act of 1934 as subsequently amended and the radio operating rules set down by the FCC forbid any person from divulging, except to the intended addressee or his authorized agent, any information gained from receiving or intercepting any radio transmissions not addressed to him, *and from using to his own benefit any such information.* This does not apply to distress communications or to public broadcasts, but it does apply to all other conversations.

Priority Channels

The most important frequency on the VHF radiotelephone band is Channel 16 (156.8 MHz), the international distress, safety, and calling frequency. It is on Channel 16 that all "Mayday," "Pan-Pan" (pronounced "pahn-pahn") and "Securite" (pronounced "saycuritay") calls are made (refer to Chapter 12).

Mayday calls are absolute first-priority distress calls involving imminent danger of loss of life or vessel. Pan-Pan calls are second-priority urgent communications concerning the safety of a ship, aircraft, other vessel or person in sight or on board. Securite calls are third-priority safety messages concerning navigation or weather. When a transmission is preceded by one of these priority call identifiers, other operators must stay clear of the channel (even if that means cutting short a communication in progress) until it is clear that the priority call has been concluded.

It's important to understand and use these priority signal identifiers correctly, as misuse, especially of the Mayday signal, can cause dangerous confusion and expensive false alarms. For example, while running aground on a falling tide in a calm sea a couple of hundred yards from shore may be inconvenient, it does *not* generally warrant a Mayday call. If, in such a case, your stranded vessel would be a hazard to navigation say, in a heavy fog, such a situation might warrant a Securite call, but probably just a normal call to advise the Coast Guard of your situation and location, and to ask them to switch to their working channel would be more in order. The same is true if you have simply run out of fuel, or if your engine has died or won't start.

Channel 16 is also the international channel on which initial brief contact with another ship or shore station may be made for the purpose of switching to an appropriate working channel. This type of traffic is allowed on Channel 16 to ensure that a great many stations will be listening on the channel at any one time, thereby improving chances that an urgent or distress signal, even a weak one, will be heard. Hailing calls in the U.S., however, have undermined the distress purpose of the channel to such an extent that in addition to Channel 16, recreational craft can use Channel 9 for initial contacts, but this lessens the possibility of a distress call being heard.

Mayday Calls

If you are in distress, transmit a Mayday call (refer to Chapter 12, page 410), repeating at intervals until an answer is received. If an answer is not received on Channel 16 after a number of attempts, repeat the message on another available channel, such as a working channel used in that area, where it is most likely to draw attention.

If your Mayday is received by the Coast Guard, you may be asked to perform a "long count" (typically saying "One, Two, Three . . . up to Ten and then back down) or other suitable extended signal transmission to permit radio direction finding stations to determine your position. Always end your transmissions with the name of your vessel and your ship station call sign.

If you must abandon ship, consider taping down your VHF radiotelephone microphone button; this will provide a continuing signal on which rescue vessels may home. (This is best done by arrangement with any rescue vessel, with your set tuned to a channel other than 16, as locking onto Channel 16 will interfere with ongoing rescue-related communications; this applies to handheld sets only if connected to the vessel's power supply and an external antenna.) Recent models of installed VHF sets, however, are required to have circuitry that shuts the signal off after five minutes of continuous transmitting.

When VHF radios first became available for recreational boats, frequency control was by use of a pair of crystals—one for receiving and one for transmitting—and associated circuit components. Space was limited, so most sets had provisions for only 12 channels, and some were limited to just six. Crystals were relatively expensive, and to keep the cost of the sets down, not all channels were activated (even so, the costs were several times what they are today). For boat-to-boat communications there were all the present channels, plus Channel 70—few if any craft were set up to talk on all 12 channels. To make contacts between skippers more practical, manufacturers decided that all sets would have at least one common channel for intership contacts, and that this would be channel 68.

The habit of saying "Switch to 68" persists today—even among many boaters, recreational and commercial, who don't know how it started. There's nothing magic about "68"; there is much to be gained by using 69, 71, 76, or 78—clearer, less busy channels. So the next time you need to shift off of "16," try using one of the "other channels."

Working Channels

VHF/FM radio operations are much facilitated by having enough channels to assign separate ones for the different types of communications, and even for various types of vessels. *The success of the VHF marine radio service depends upon the use of the correct channel for the specific type of communications and vessels involved.*

Features of the VHF service are the assignment of *different channels* to commercial and noncommercial vessels for operational communication, and the limited range of VHF which excludes interference from stations 30 to 50 miles or more away. Noncommercial craft are assigned five exclusive channels for intership traffic (plus additional ones in specific limited geographic areas); commercial vessels have 12 other channels of their own. The most used intership noncommercial channel is 68; it is greatly overused in preference to other available channels; see the sidebar, "In the Beginning . . ." and refer to **Table 20-1.** Channel 9 (also called 09) can be used by both noncommercial and commercial vessels; it is the only channel properly available for any necessary intercommunication between these two types of vessels.

Ship-shore communications to a marine operator (in FCC terms, a PUBLIC COAST STATION) are possible on a number of channels. Certain ones, such as 26 and 28, are assigned in preference to others so as to limit the number of different frequencies on which a boat must be capable of operating (important in the early days of VHF, but of no significance now). Ship-shore radio contacts are also possible on VHF with yacht clubs, marinas, and similar PRIVATE COAST STATIONS as they are designated in the FCC Rules; these use other channels such as 9, 68, 69, 71, or 78.

Channel 22 (sometimes called 22A) is basically a U.S. government frequency, but nongovernment vessels, including recreational boats, are allowed to use it for nondistress communications with the Coast Guard. It should not be used for any other communications.

Channel 13 (67 in some areas) is restricted to "bridge-to-bridge" communications. The term "bridge" originally meant only the control station of a vessel and the channel was used for directing the safe passage of vessels past one another. More recently, this channel has been authorized for use for communications with the operating personnel of drawbridges to request and acknowledge openings (see Chapter 5, page 168). Large vessels, tugs, and dredges in channels must GUARD (maintain a listening watch on) this in addition to Channel 16. It is used with abbreviated operating procedures to ensure navigational safety while maneuvering in close quarters. It must not be used for any other purpose, and power is limited to 1 watt. It is not required for recreational craft, but may often be of use, especially where drawbridges are radio equipped.

OPERATING PROCEDURES

Ship-to-ship communications are usually initiated on Channel 16; recreational craft may also use Channel 9. Immediately after contact is established, the communicating stations are required to shift to an appropriate "working" channel. A typical contact and shift would proceed roughly as follows:

"Bluejay . . . Bluejay, this is Desolate, over." (Boat names can be repeated up to three times each, but this is not normally necessary, and is undesirable as it lengthens transmissions.)

"Desolate" (repeated only if necessary because of poor conditions) "this is Bluejay."

"Bluejay, this is Desolate. Switch six-nine."

"This is Bluejay. Roger, six-nine."

(It is desirable to acknowledge the number of the working channel to avoid possible loss of contact when switching due to misunderstanding.)

(Both stations retune to Channel 69.)

"Bluejay, this is Desolate, over."

"Desolate, this is Bluejay . . ."

(And at the end of the call):

"Desolate, out."

"Bluejay, out."

The procedure words "Over" and "Out" should *never* be used together as they have contrary meanings. The procedure word "Roger" (meaning received and understood) should never be said more than once. When each station is hearing the other clearly, the use of "Over" and "Out" can be omitted—this is desirable to shorten each transmission.

Noncommercial craft are required to keep to their specifically designated working channels, except when communicating with a commercial vessel, in which case Channel 9 (or 09) is to be used.

Ship-to-shore communications are sometimes initiated on Channel 16, but where possible should be made directly on an appropriate working channel when it is known that the shore station being called—for example, a marina dockmaster's office or a bridgetender—monitors that channel.

Calls to the Marine Operator are normally initiated directly on the working channel. And even if a call is initiated by the Marine Operator on Channel 16, a ship station should respond only on the appropriate working channel, as the Marine Operator will be expecting the reply on that frequency.

Under limited conditions, aircraft are authorized to use Channels 6, and 16; 9, 68, and 72; and 8, 18, and 67 for communications with ships and boats.

Channel 70 is designated for "digital selective calling" (DSC). This is a new high-technology procedure whereby transmissions can be addressed to a specific vessel, a group or class of vessels, or to all vessels. Once this new technique is fully implemented, a few years in the future, a boat equipped with a DSC set will not hear the normal radio traffic such as is now heard on Channel 16. The receiver will remain silent until it is specifically addressed, or is included in a group call, or there is a Mayday. Similarly, transmissions from your boat will be digitally addressed to other stations, ashore or afloat. Even though the DSC system is not yet in full use, Channel 70 may be used now *only* for distress and safety calling, or general purpose calling, *using digital selective calling techniques.* (There are also DSC channels for single-sideband use on the medium- and high-frequency bands.)

Channel assignments in Canada are generally the same as in the United States as both nations follow the international agreements. There are, however, slight differences and a U.S. boater planning to cruise into Canadian waters should get specific information for the area to be visited; also, weather channels there are on different frequencies than in the U.S.

Commercial vs. Noncommercial Channels

As noted above, there are separate radio channels allocated for use by commercial craft and by noncommercial (recreational) boats. Unfortunately, in many areas, commercial craft, such as charter sport fishing and drift fishing boats make use of the noncommercial channels on which they are not authorized by the FCC. This crowds the frequencies that are being used properly by recreational craft. The commercial boats gain nothing by doing this as their own channels actually are much less congested.

Modern VHF sets are capable of transmitting on many more channels than are authorized for any particular type of craft. All boat skippers—commercial and noncommercial—should learn just which channels they are authorized to communicate on, and use only them, to avoid receiving violation citations from the FCC.

Radio Information Services

In the U.S., marine weather information and forecasts are broadcast continuously from many locations by the National Weather Service. In Canada and many other countries, similar continuous weather broadcasts are made by equivalent government agencies.

Virtually every VHF marine radiotelephone today has switch-selectable capability for receiving such broadcasts. There are seven U.S. continuous weather broadcast channels in current use, but nearly all stations use one of the first three. The location, channel number, and coverage area of NWS continuous VHF broadcast stations is indicated on a series of Marine Weather Service Charts published by NOAA (see page 547, in Chapter 15). The Canadian weather service uses two other frequencies. An additional frequency is assigned to continuous weather broadcasting, but unused in North America, for a total of nine channels, usually designated by WX-1 through WX-9. Commercial broadcast stations and various Marine Operators also transmit weather information, but of varying timeliness and accuracy.

At any time, the U.S. Coast Guard may broadcast special safety information, including weather summaries and forecasts, on Channel 22A, the Coast Guard's assigned working channel. Such special broadcasts are preceded by an alerting announcement (and possible warning tone) transmitted on Channel 16. (Alpha "A" symbols are assigned to those channels used within the U.S., where the frequencies are different from those same channels used in the International Service—remember "A" for U.S.A.)

MF-HF SINGLE-SIDEBAND (SSB) RADIO SERVICE

VHF radio is intended mainly for short-range communications. Reliable direct voice communication over distances greater than about 25 miles (depending on antenna heights) requires the use either of medium-frequency (MF) and/or high-frequency (HF) radiotelephones, or equipment that sends signals to relaying communications satellites. Satellite communications are discussed in a later section.

Marine radiotelephone equipment that operates in the MF and HF bands is today universally, and by international treaty, of the single-sideband (SSB) variety; see **Figure 20-08**. SSB is amplitude modulated, though it utilizes only a single sideband adjacent to, rather than double sidebands on either side of, a carrier wave. MF and HF marine radio is sometimes referred to as AM radio, but this is a holdover from the days when marine MF

Figure 20-08 MF-HF single-sideband (SSB) transceivers are sold and installed with pretuned channels for many frequencies. A general knowledge of the propagation characteristics of the different frequency bands, and a bit of experience, is needed for the selection of the best band to use at a particular time of day to communicate over a given distance.

and HF sets were of the double sideband (DSB) type—it's currently more accurate and usual to use the term "SSB" when referring to them.

Licensing MF-HF Radios

A vessel cannot be licensed for SSB radiotelephone unless it is already equipped with a VHF/FM set. Moreover, in order to help ease the crowding on the MF and HF bands, an SSB operator is required by law to attempt communication on VHF *before* using the 2-3 MHz band or higher frequencies—unless the transmitting station is clearly beyond normal VHF range. (MF and HF transmissions carry for very great distances because of signal "bounce," and SSB signals tend to interfere with one another.)

In most cases, a Restricted Radiotelephone Operator permit is sufficient licensing for SSB operation. That permit is good for equipment up to and including 100-watts carrier wave power or 400-watts peak envelope power (PEP). Higher-level licenses, such as the Marine Radio Operator permit and various commercial radio operator licenses, are valid for SSB operation.

Selection of SSB Sets

SSB transceivers are commonly available with output power from 50 to 150 watts. Unlike the range of VHF transmissions, which is essentially line-of-sight and remains relatively unaffected by output power, the range of SSB transmissions is affected by, among other things, the strength of the radiated signal.

By regulation, all marine SSB radiotelephone stations in the 2-3 MHz band must be able to operate on 2182 kHz, the international distress and calling frequency (the DSC equivalent is 2187.5 kHz). They must also be able to operate on at least two other frequencies. However, in order to achieve maximum utility from an SSB installation, the savvy skipper will usually pick a set with a much wider frequency capability, as frequency selection affects range. Most sets will have the desirable feature of one-button selection of 2182 kHz distress frequency, and some systems will also automatically generate the radiotelephone alarm signal on this channel. The frequencies 4125

and 6215 kHz may also be used for distress calling. There are calling frequencies in each HF band for various Coast Guard shore communications stations for distress or safety traffic.

The maximum reliable range of SSB transmission in the 2-3 MHz (MF) band during the day is 50 to 150 miles. Transmission in the HF bands can reach for thousands of miles, depending on a number of factors such as the frequency used, atmospheric noise and other interference, the time of day, even the level of sunspot activity. The likely range of signals in the HF bands is discussed on page 682.

There are working frequencies in the MF band and each of the HF bands, two, three, or more, some simplex and some half-duplex (often listed as simply "duplex") in each band. Operating frequencies are usually referred to by a "channel number" rather than a value in megahertz. These designations consist of three- or four-digits in which the first one or two are derived from the frequency band in megahertz and the final two digits are assigned sequentially.

Not all HF/SSB radiotelephones are capable of operating on all eight available bands. Less expensive equipment will typically operate on the lower bands—these are fully adequate for skippers who do not need to communicate over the vast distances requiring the higher-frequency bands. Current models use a frequency synthesizer and can operate on any frequency within their overall range, but are factory-set to transmit and receive only on authorized channels that can be accessed by simple push-button keypad operation.

Digital Selective Calling (DSC) is also now available on SSB sets. DSC-equipped SSB radiotelephones can automatically alert an operator to a call incoming on any of a number of bands without the need to maintain an audio watch. Information on the incoming call will be shown on the radio's display screen, and all of the information in a distress call will be recorded; in the case of a distress call being received, the set will be automatically switched to 2.182 MHz or an appropriate higher distress frequency.

Skippers who plan to cruise to areas where VHF and MF radio does not afford adequate communications capability should consider MF-HF sets that can transmit and receive on the frequencies assigned to the Coast Guard's CALL (Contact And Long-range Liaison) system, which is also used for high seas emergency, voice-weather, navigation information, and medical communications.

Some models of marine MF-HF equipment are capable of operating on amateur radio bands (see page 713) if properly licensed for such use. However, the reverse is not true—sets sold for amateur radio use may be capable of operating on marine frequencies, but should *not* be used for this purpose as they are not "Type Accepted" by the FCC for marine communications.

Figure 20-09 Single-sideband (SSB) radios are desirable, even necessary, for boats that are going to cruise beyond reliable VHF range. They are larger than VHF sets, but not so large as to present mounting problems for medium-size or larger craft. Installation will normally require the services of a properly trained and licensed technician.

Other MF & HF Channels

There are many simplex frequencies and half-duplex frequency pairs in the 2-3 MHz band and in each HF band—too many to list here. Normally, when a marine SSB set is purchased, a list of frequencies or channels is included in or with the operator's manual. The transceiver will have been factory-tuned to these channels, and all the operator has to do is to know which ones can be used to meet his or her particular communications needs. SSB sets normally have extensive memory capabilities for storing the settings for frequencies and channels commonly used; many of these will have been preprogrammed by the manufacturer.

Information on MF and HF channels and their specific uses can be obtained from the U.S. Coast Guard Navigation Information Center at www.navcen.uscg.gov/marcomms.

Installation of MF-HF Radios

Installation of MF-HF equipment usually requires the services of a trained and licensed technician; see **Figure 20-09**. Most SSB sets today come pretested and adjusted. Unlike VHF/FM radio, a SSB set requires a large GROUND PLANE in order to radiate its signals—which, except on metal hulls, needs to be installed in the form of a large copper mesh panel (sometimes built into the fiberglass hull). As

well, SSB is much more subject to interference from shipboard electrical equipment, and so often requires the installation of special isolators and noise-suppression filters in the vessel's electrical system. Sets equipped for DSC must be connected to a GPS (or Loran) receiver so that geographic position information will be transmitted in distress calls and can optionally be sent in routine communications. SSB radios are larger than VHF sets, and often come in two units, a "control head" and a "black box" with the remainder of the circuitry.

With MF-HF sets, antenna selection and installation is also more complicated, since SSB generally requires a physically much longer antenna than VHF, and different antenna "tuning" for different bands. Antennas are employed in both "long wire" and whip form; and most SSB systems currently incorporate automatic antenna-tuning couplers. The final choice of one or more antennas should be made in consultation with a qualified technician and in view of the physical limitations imposed by one's vessel and rigging. Sets equipped with Class D DSC have a second receiver for continuously monitoring DSC frequencies, and this will require a second antenna, which can be a simple whip or short length of wire; no tuner is required.

THE GLOBAL MARITIME DISTRESS & SAFETY SYSTEM (GMDSS)

Since the invention of radio at the end of the 19th century, ships at sea have relied on Morse code, invented by Samuel Morse and first used in 1844, for distress and safety telecommunications; refer to **Figure 20-16.** The need for ship and coast radio stations to have and use radiotelegraph equipment, and to listen to a common radio frequency for Morse-encoded distress calls, was recognized after the sinking of the liner Titanic in the North Atlantic in 1912. The U.S. Congress enacted legislation soon after, requiring U.S. ships to use Morse code radiotelegraph equipment for distress calls. The International Telecommunications Union (ITU), now a United Nations agency, followed suit for ships of all nations. Morse-encoded distress calling has saved thousands of lives since its inception almost a century ago, but its use requires skilled radio operators spending many hours listening to the radio distress frequency. Its range on the medium-frequency (MF) distress band (500 kHz) is limited, and the amount of traffic Morse signals can carry is also limited.

The Development of GMDSS

Over fifteen years ago the International Maritime Organization (IMO), a United Nations agency specializing in safety of shipping and preventing ships from polluting the seas, began looking at ways of improving maritime distress and safety communications. In 1979, a group of experts drafted the *International Convention on Maritime Search and Rescue*, which called for development of a global search and rescue plan. This group also passed a resolution calling for development by IMO of a Global Maritime Distress and Safety System (GMDSS) to provide the communication support needed to implement the search and rescue plan. This new system, which the world's maritime nations, including the United States, are implementing, is based upon a combination of satellite and terrestrial radio services, and has changed international distress communications from being primarily ship-to-ship based to ship-to-shore (Rescue

Coordination Center) based. It spelled the end of Morse code communications for all but a few users, such as amateur radio. The GMDSS provides for automatic distress alerting and locating in cases where a radio operator doesn't have time to send an SOS or Mayday call, and, for the first time, requires ships to receive broadcasts of maritime safety information which could prevent a distress from happening in the first place. In 1988, IMO amended the *Safety of Life at Sea Convention* (SOLAS), requiring ships subject to it fit GMDSS equipment. Such ships were required to carry NAVTEX and satellite EPIRBs (see below) by 1 August 1993, and had to fit all other GMDSS equipment by 1 February 1999. U.S. ships were allowed to fit GMDSS in lieu of Morse telegraphy equipment by the Telecommunications Act of 1996.

The GMDSS consists of several systems, some of which are new, but many of which have been in operation for many years. The system will be able to reliably perform the following functions: alerting (including position determination of the unit in distress), search and rescue coordination, locating (homing), maritime safety information broadcasts, general communications, and bridge-to-bridge communications. Specific radio carriage requirements depend upon the ship's area of operation (see below) rather than its tonnage. The system also provides redundant means of distress alerting, and emergency sources of power.

Features of GMDSS

The Global Maritime Distress and Safety System (GMDSS) is now the internationally recognized distress and radio communication safety system for ships replacing the previous ship-to-ship safety system, described above. The GMDSS is an automated ship-to-shore system using satellites and digital selective calling (DSC) technology. The GMDSS is mandated for all ships by the International Maritime Organization (IMO).

Significant advantages are provided over the former system: GMDSS

• Provides worldwide ship-to-shore alerting, it is not dependent upon passing ships.

- Simplifies radio operations, alerts may be sent by two simple actions.
- Ensures redundancy of communications, it requires two separate systems for alerting.
- Enhances search and rescue, operations are coordinated from shore centers.
- Minimizes unanticipated emergencies at sea, maritime safety broadcasts are included.
- Eliminates reliance on a single person for communications; it requires at least two licensed GMDSS radio operators and typically two maintenance methods to ensure distress communications capability at all times.

Sea Areas

GMDSS uses four coverage areas: A1, A2, A3, and A4 to cover the sea areas of the world for distress watchkeeping.

- Sea Area A1 is an area within VHF range of a coast station fitted with DSC (about 30 - 40 miles).
- Sea Area A2 is an area within MF range of a coast station fitted with DSC (about 150 miles).
- Sea Area A3 is an area covered by the Inmarsat Satellite System (excluding A1 and A2 areas).
- Sea Area A4 is basically the polar regions which are not covered by the above.

GMDSS Component Systems

The GMDSS consists of many separate systems that are being implemented in a coordinated and agreed-upon manner. Some of these systems are discussed below:

The COSPAS-SARSAT System

COSPAS-SARSAT is an international satellite-based search and rescue system, established by Canada, France, the U.S.A., and Russia. These four countries jointly helped develop a 406-MHz satellite emergency position-indicating radiobeacon (EPIRB), an element of the GMDSS designed to operate with the COSPAS-SARSAT system: see **Figure 20-10.** These automatic-activating EPIRBs, now required on SOLAS ships, commercial fishing vessels, and other ships, are designed to transmit to a rescue coordination center a vessel identification

and an accurate location of the vessel from anywhere in the world.

Emergency Position Indicating Radiobeacon (EPIRB)

Every boat that goes offshore beyond reliable VHF radio range—roughly 20 miles (37 km)—should carry an EPIRB (Emergency Position Indicating RadioBeacon). The original models, many of which are still in use, operate on two frequencies: 121.5 MHz, the emergency channel for civilian planes, and 243.0 MHz, the "guard" channel (for maintaining a listening watch on) for military aircraft. When one or more of these detect the distinctive tone signal of an EPIRB, a report is

Figure 20-10 A Position Indicating Radiobeacon (EPIRB) of the newer type operating on 406 MHz is an essential safety item for a boat cruising farther from shore than reliable VHF radio range. When activated, a distress signal is picked up by an orbiting satellite and relayed to rescue authorities ashore. All EPIRBs transmit an identification number that has been registered with government authorities after purchase. Advanced models can be interfaced with a GPS or Loran receiver to include the position of the vessel; some units even have an internal GPS receiver that can continue to send location data even after being put overboard from an abandoned vessel.

made to airway control authorities, who pass the information to search-and-rescue activities. Equipment on orbiting satellites of the COSPAS/SARSAT system can relay EPIRB 121.5 / 243.0 MHz signals if the satellite can "see" both the EPIRB and a ground terminal simultaneously.

The beacon's position is determined by multiple reports from aircraft and/or orbiting satellites. To determine a position and initiate rescue efforts may take 4 to 6 hours; in some cases, up to 12 hours. Location is usually within 12 to 15 miles (22 to 28 km).

These EPIRBs are divided into Class A (float-free, automatic activation) and Class B (manually activated). Class B units, acceptable for voluntarily equipped craft, may cost only a few hundred dollars.

First-generation EPIRBs suffered from voice-communications interference on their working frequencies and the units have a very high incidence of false alarms—as many as 95 plus percent of such EPIRB alerts were determined to be nonemergency situations. Because of this the processing of signals from Class A and B units by the COPAS/SARSAT system will be discontinued on February 1, 2009.

The Second Generation

Advances in technology have led to the development of a new type, referred to as a "406" EPIRB—the name derived from its operating frequency of 406.0 MHz. This is a dedicated frequency free of interference from other communications. Beacon signals are picked up by orbiting satellites of COSPAS/SARSAT. The distress signals are transmitted to a ground station and passed on to rescue authorities. If a ground station is not in view when the distress signals are received, they are stored by the satellite for retransmission when one comes within range. The distress signals can also be received and relayed by GEOS weather satellites and other geostationary satellites of the GEOSAR system.

When COSPAS/SARSAT satellites are used, position is determined by the Doppler effect of the signals and may take 1 to 2 hours. Location is determined within 1 to 3 miles (2 to 5 km). If the

PERSONAL LOCATOR BEACON (PLB)

Although not a part of the GMDSS, a PERSONAL LOCATOR BEACON (PLB) can serve much the same needs of a boater as an EPIRB. A PLB is intended to be associated with an individual—a hiker, hunter, mountain climber, and of course, a boater—rather than with a vessel. It is smaller and lighter, and transmits the same 406 and 121.5 MHz signals. It transmits a distress message with identification that is specific to that unit. Some models may have an input for GPS position data. It does not have a strobe light, and although it will float, it will not function in that situation. Its battery is smaller and it is intended to operate for a shorter period than an EPIRB.

For several years PLBs have been in wide use in Europe and other parts of the world. As of July 1, 2003, the FCC authorized the sale and use of PLBs in the United States. These units must be registered. If used on a boat, it is recommended that item 9 on the registration form include basic information on the type, size, color, etc., of the craft.

signals are detected by a GEOSTAR satellite, the distress alert is immediate, but no position information is provided.

A major advantage of second-generation equipment is that each 406 EPIRB transmits a unique registration number for identification. Each unit is entered into a database that provides vital information on the vessel's name and characteristics, its owner, a point of contact, etc. The purchaser of a 406 EPIRB is legally required to register it immediately; there are penalties for failing to comply. For information, call 888-212-7283 within the U.S. or 1-301-457-5430 from elsewhere; registration forms may be obtained online at www.sarsat.noaa.gov/epirb-form.pdf. A confirmation letter will be sent, plus a proof-of-registration decal that must be affixed to the

EPIRB. In order to keep the database current, registration is for two years only, and re-registration is required. Any change in EPIRB registration data must be reported in writing without delay—it is essential for your safety that the information on file is correct and current. There are no fees and registration may save *your* life.

The 406 EPIRBs are available in Category I (float-free, automatic activation) and Category II (manual activation). Both models also have a 121.5 MHz low-power beacon for final search and a strobe light for final location. Second-generation EPIRBs are considerably more expensive, in the vicinity of a thousand-plus dollars, but their far greater effectiveness makes them worthwhile. For occasional needs, 406 EPIRBs can be rented from the BoatU.S. Foundation for Boating Safety; call 888-663-7472, or check at any BoatU.S. Marine Center.

And Now We Have . . .

A further development is a model of a 406 EPIRB with a connection for position data from an onboard GPS receiver being used for navigation. The vessel's position is continually updated and stored in the EPIRB every 20 minutes. Such a beacon not only alerts for a distress situation and identifies itself, it also transmits its location. Reports from GEOSAR satellites, as well as COSPAS/SARSAT, will carry position information.

And yet another development is the GPIRB—a 406 EPIRB with an integral GPS receiver. Upon being activated, the GPS will determine its position within about 2 minutes and add that data to the transmitted signal. The GPS then shuts down to conserve battery power, but every 20 minutes it reactivates and provides a new position. Rescue authorities can use successive positions to determine drift should the GPIRB cease functioning.

The cost of an EPIRB with GPS interconnect capability is greater than that of a standard 406 EPIRB; the cost of a GPIRB is even greater, in the vicinity of two thousand dollars. But with both such units the distress location is clearly established to less than a half mile (1 km).

There are also Inmarsat Class E EPIRBs that transmit a distress message, including GPS position, on 1646.0 MHz via Inmarsat communications satellites. These are not sold in the U.S.

Use & Maintenance

Once any EPIRB is activated, *it must be left on*. To turn it off "to save the battery" severely disrupts rescue operations. Testing must be strictly limited to conditions stated in the unit's manual.

The only maintenance required is the replacement of the battery at the intervals specified by the unit's manual.

NAVTEX

NAVTEX is an international, automated system for instantly distributing maritime navigational warnings, weather forecasts and warnings, search and rescue notices, and similar safety information to ships; see **Figure 20-11.**

A small, low-cost and self-contained "smart" printing radio receiver installed in the pilot house of a ship or boat checks each incoming message to see if it has been received during an earlier transmission, or if it is of a category of no interest to the ship's master. If it is a new and wanted message, it is printed on a roll of adding-machine-size paper;

Figure 20-11 A NAVTEX receiver is a small "black box" that receives navigation information, weather warning, search and rescue information, and related safety data from a series of shore stations all transmitting on the same frequency at scheduled times. Some models print out the information on paper tape; other units display the information on an LCD screen. All received data is stored for later review.

if not, the message is ignored. Some models show the information on a LCD screen, with printing possible through a connection to a personal computer's printer.

A new ship coming into the area will receive many previously broadcast messages for the first time; ships already in the area that had already received the message won't receive it again. No person needs to be present during a broadcast to receive vital information.

There is a large number of transmitting stations, all operating at scheduled times on 518 kHz. NAVTEX reception extends out to a range of 200 to 400 nautical miles.

Inmarsat

Satellite systems operated by the International Mobile Satellite Organization (Inmarsat), are also important elements of the GMDSS. Three types of Inmarsat ship earth station terminals are recognized by the GMDSS:

Inmarsat A, B, and C The Inmarsat A and B, an updated version of the A, provide ship-shore, ship-ship and shore-ship telephone, telex and high-speed data services, including a distress priority telephone and telex service to and from rescue coordination centers. The Inmarsat C provides ship-shore, shore-ship and ship-ship store-and-forward data and telex messaging, the capability for sending preformatted distress messages to a rescue coordination center, and the SafetyNET service. The Inmarsat C SafetyNET service is a satellite-based worldwide maritime safety information broadcast service of high seas weather warnings, NAVAREA navigational warnings, radionavigation warnings, ice reports and warnings generated by the USCG-conducted International Ice Patrol, and other similar information not provided by NAVTEX. SafetyNET works similarly to NAVTEX in areas outside NAVTEX coverage.

Inmarsat C equipment is relatively small and lightweight, and costs much less than an Inmarsat A or B.

Inmarsat A and B ship earth stations require relatively large gyro-stabilized antennas; the antenna size of the Inmarsat C is much smaller.

Inmarsat also operates an EPIRB system, the Inmarsat L, which is similar to that operated by COSPAS-SARSAT.

Under a cooperative agreement with the National Oceanic and Atmospheric Administration (NOAA), combined meteorological observations and AMVER reports can now be sent to both the USCG AMVER Center, and NOAA, using an Inmarsat C ship-earth station, at no charge. There is also no charge to register for this service and to receive the necessary Inmarsat C software. For more information, see the NOAA SEAS (Shipboard Environmental data Acquisition System). It is strongly urged that Inmarsat C equipment have an integral satellite navigation receiver, or be externally connected to a satellite navigation receiver. That connection will ensure accurate location information to be sent to a rescue coordination center if a distress alert is ever transmitted.

High-Frequency Communications

The GMDSS includes HF radiotelephone and radiotelex (narrow-band direct-printing) equipment, with calls initiated by digital selective calling. Worldwide broadcasts of maritime safety information are also made on HF narrow-band direct printing channels.

To meet these GMDSS requirements, the Coast Guard has improved high-frequency (HF) ship-shore radio safety services from its Communication Stations to the maritime community, as well as narrow-band direct-printing broadcasts.

SART (Search-And-Rescue radar Transponder)

The GMDSS installation on ships include one or more search and rescue radar transponders, devices that are used to locate survival craft or distressed vessels by creating a series of dots on a rescuing ship's X-band (3 cm) radar display. The detection range between these devices and ships, dependent upon the height of the ship's radar mast and the height of the SART, is normally about eight nautical miles. Note that a marine radar may not detect a SART even within this

Automatic Identification System (AIS)

A small-craft boater will not be directly involved in the AUTOMATIC IDENTIFICATION SYSTEM (AIS) for ships, but he or she should have general knowledge of what it is and how it works.

Visualize a shipboard radar display, with overlaid electronic chart data, that shows a mark for every significant vessel within radio range, each shown with a velocity vector showing course and speed. Each ship "mark" could also indicate the size of the vessel and its position to GPS or DGPS accuracy. With a "click" on the mark, you could learn the vessel's name, course and speed, classification, call sign, registration number, MMSI, and other information. Maneuvering information, closest point of approach (CPA), time to CPA, and other navigational information, more accurate and timely than information from an automatic radar plotting aid (ARPA) could also be available. Every ship would have a display of information previously available only to modern Vessel Traffic Service centers.

This complex, high-technology system uses data links on VHF marine band frequencies to exchange information. AIS transponders would continuously transmit whether near shore or on the high seas. The system provides for automatic sharing of the channels used so that a vessel does not interfere with others, several thousands of vessels could be in the same area without a problem. Basic information is transmitted every 2 to 10 seconds while underway and every 3 minutes while at anchor. Additional information, such as the dimensions of the ship and its draft, its destination and ETA there, is transmitted every 6 minutes. There are two classes of AIS installations: Class A includes all features; Class B has more limited capabilities, but sufficient to adequately participate in the system.

The Homeland Defense initiative has accelerated and emphasized the use of AIS in U.S. waters. More information can be found at www.navcen.uscg.gov/marcomms.

distance, if the radar settings are not optimized for SART detection.

Digital Selective Calling

The IMO also introduced digital selective calling (DSC) on VHF, MF, and HF maritime radios as part of the GMDSS system. DSC distress alerts, which consist of a preformatted distress message, are used to initiate emergency communications with ships and rescue coordination centers. When fully implemented, DSC will eliminate the need for persons on a ship's bridge or on shore to continuously guard radio receivers on voice radio channels, including VHF Channel 16 and 2182 kHz now used for distress, safety and calling. A listening watch aboard GMDSS-equipped ships on 2182 kHz ended on 1 February 1999; watches on VHF Channel 16 will continue indefinitely, but eventually will be discontinued.

It is urged that the DSC-equipped VHF and MF/HF radios be externally connected to a satellite navigation receiver. That connection will ensure accurate location information is sent to a rescue coordination center if a distress alert is ever transmitted. FCC regulations actually require that ship's position be manually entered into the radio every four hours on ships required to carry GMDSS equipment, while that ship is underway.

Once SOLAS ships are allowed to disband watchkeeping on VHF and MF radiotelephone channels, other ships (and boats) are going to need DSC-equipped radios to contact these ships, particularly in a passing situation, especially when outside U.S. waters. It is considered that VHF, MF, and HF radiotelephone equipment carried on ships should include a DSC capability as a matter of safety. To achieve this, the FCC has required that all VHF and MF/HF maritime radiotelephones type-accepted after June 1999 have at least a basic DSC capability.

VHF digital selective calling also has other capabilities beyond those required for the GMDSS. The Coast Guard uses this system to track vessels in Prince William Sound, Alaska, Vessel Traffic Service. IMO and the USCG also plan to require ships carry a Universal Automatic Identification System (AIS), which will be DSC-compatible. Countries having a GMDSS A1 Area will be able to identify and track AIS-equipped vessels in its waters without any additional radio equipment.

A DSC-equipped radio cannot be interrogated and tracked unless that option was included by the manufacturer, and unless the user configures it to allow tracking.

U.S. shore-based radio stations currently exist to support every element of the GMDSS, except for digital selective calling. As of September 2003, the United States had not declared the boundaries of A1 Sea Areas or A2 Sea Areas, but plans to eventually have both areas in place.

Use of GMDSS for Routine Communications
GMDSS telecommunications equipment should not be reserved for emergency use only. The International Maritime Organization in COMSAR Circular 17 encourages mariners to use that equipment for routine as well as safety telecommunications.

Boaters & the GMDSS
Small craft are not directly concerned with the mandatory equipment requirements of GMDSS, but boaters who will be operating in waters used by compulsorily equipped vessels may benefit generally with the several forms of communications services provided by GMDSS.

VHF DSC radios can automatically keep watch on VHF channel 70 and will activate when there is an incoming call for your vessel, an "all ships" call, urgency, or safety, a distress call or distress relay. The radio will indicate which channel to use for the subsequent communications such as Channel 16 for distress working, or 72 for ship-to-ship. If the set has only a single receiver, a watch on Channel 70 can be substituted for the normally required watch on Channel 16 *only* if your boat is within the service area of a USCG station that has DSC capability.

If your boat is fitted with a dual-receiver (Class D) VHF DSC set, you should keep an automatic watch (silent) on Channel 70 and, if practicable, an audible dual watch on channels 16 and 13 to ensure that you monitor distress, safety, and shipping traffic. If you sail within an area that has a port operation or vessel traffic service (the management of ships' movements) then you should keep watch on that channel rather than channel 13. If you are unsure what channel that will be, or whether you are in an area that monitors ships' movements, check the appropriate publication or contact the relevant harbor authority or your local Coast Guard unit.

OTHER RADIO COMMUNICATIONS
Other forms of "two-way" radio found on board recreational vessels include Citizens Band (CB) radio, amateur ("ham") radio, Family Radio System (FRS), General Mobile Radio System GMRS), cellular and satellite telephones, and other forms of satellite systems. With the exception of satellite systems, these "alternate" forms of radio communication can sometimes be less expensive to buy and install than marine radio with equivalent range capability. However, none can be considered a substitute for true marine radio, since only the designated marine frequencies are monitored continuously for distress calls by the USCG and the search and rescue bodies of other countries.

Citizens Band Radio Service
As its name implies, the Citizens Band Radio Service is intended to give the general public economical access to two-way radio communications. CB sets are relatively inexpensive, easy to install, and simple to operate; see **Figure 20-12**. The CB service has its own particular functions, and these do not overlap or conflict with other established services. It is *not* a substitute for the

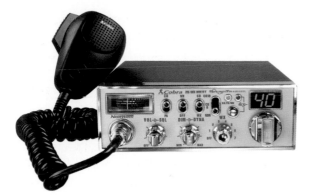

Figure 20-12 Citizen Band (CB) radios can serve a useful purpose on recreational boats as they do not have the restriction of marine radios against personal and social conversations. Models for both fixed installation and handheld use are available at relatively inexpensive prices.

safety features of the regular VHF marine radio service, nor for ship-to-shore connections into the public telephone service, nor is it a type of hobby or amateur service for casual contacts at great distances. While CB use is not now as widespread as it was two decades ago, it still is available and can meet particular communications needs of some boaters.

CB Channels & Equipment

CB is allocated 40 specific frequencies between 29.965 and 27.405 MHz, commonly referred to as channels 1 through 40. Any channel may be used with single or double sideband amplitude modulation (although older 23-channel sets are compatible with newer 40-channel sets only on channels 1 to 23). Except for Channel 9, reserved for "emergency communications involving the immediate safety of life or the immediate protection of property, or for traveler assistance," no channel is assigned to a particular use or user group.

Sets are available as full-size units or handhelds. More expensive models have features such as dual watch, one-touch access for Channels 9 and 19, weather radio access and continuous monitoring, and others. All CB sets must be unmodified FCC-certified units. If not manufactured for marine use, a CB set must be well protected from the relatively harsh environmental conditions found on boats.

CB stations are limited to 4 watts carrier wave output power on DSB AM, and 12 watts PEP on SSB AM. The usual reliable range of CB is 5 miles, but may, in favorable conditions, extend to 15 or more. These are ranges for ground waves; sky waves can sometimes reach and be received thousands of miles away. For this reason, external power amplifiers are strictly prohibited by regulation—although some CB "outlaws" illegally boost the output power of their sets many times over. Such illegal power amplification crowds the airwaves and interferes with the intended purpose as a medium for local communications. FCC rules strictly prohibit CB communication between stations more than 155.3 miles (250 km) apart.

CB Operation

CB radio operation does not require a license, and there are no specific operating procedures. But the FCC does require:

• That all communications be restricted to the minimum practical transmission time.

• That exchanges between stations be limited to a maximum 5-minute duration.

• That when exchanges have reached the 5-minute limit, both stations remain off the air for a minimum of 1 minute.

• These rules do not apply in any case involving emergency communications.

CB communications may be in any language, but use of any code other than the "ten code" is prohibited. Station identification is encouraged, though not required; and its form is only "suggested." Common practice is to use a CB "handle" or nickname, though the FCC encourages this only in conjunction with a call sign composed of the letter K followed by the operator's initials and residence ZIP code or an organization name and unit number. "Handles" alone are preferred by many operators because they are untraceable.

A CB station may *not* be used for any illegal activity, to transmit music or sound effects, to advertise the sale or solicit the sale of goods and services, to intentionally interfere with another CB station, or any of several other actions set forth in the FCC Rules. Profane, obscene, or indecent language is specifically prohibited.

CB radios can be used wherever the FCC has jurisdiction on land and on vessels and aircraft (with permission of the captain); they may be used in international waters. They are not authorized for use on land or waters under the jurisdiction of a foreign nation (except Canada), but that country might have its own equivalent service.

If you want to install a CB set on your boat, be sure the unit chosen is designed or adapted for conditions at sea. You should use an antenna specifically intended for marine applications; the standard automotive-type will not function satisfactorily.

Family Radio Service

The Family Radio Service (FRS) is a direct outgrowth of the Citizens Band Radio Service. It is the result of advances in technology and the availability of additional frequencies. It carries the same general types of communications, but at lesser ranges—no more than two miles, and often much less.

FRS units are small, not much larger than cellular phones, and quite inexpensive; see **Figure 20-13.** They must be FCC-certified units, but no license is required; there are no age or citizenship restrictions. Power is limited to not more than 0.5 watt. No external amplifier may be attached to increase the range; any external antenna must be part of the FCC certification. Some units are water-resistant; some include a receiver for VHF continuous weather broadcasts. Although usually hand-held, models are available that can be worn as a headset. FRS radios are often bought in pairs. There are some models that integrate a GPS receiver into an FRS radio, and even a few that include basic charts for use with the GPS location information.

Using the FRS

The FRS operates on 14 channels in the 462 MHz portion of the spectrum; the least expensive models may operate on only one or several of these channels. There are 38 "quiet codes" (tones), one of which can be transmitted to activate a specific

station with whom you wish to communicate—this lessens the annoyance of others using the same channel. You may use the FRS unit to transmit one-way communications only to establish communications with another person, send an emergency message, provide traveler assistance, make a voice page, or to conduct a brief test. There is no specific assigned use for any channel. You must share any channel with other users; no channel is available for the exclusive use for any person or group. Emergency communications take precedence over other traffic. FRS radios may not be connected to the public landline telephone service.

FRS radios have the same geographic authorizations and restrictions as CB stations as noted above. On larger boats some skippers use FRS radios to communicate with crew in the boat while anchoring. Others use it instead of UHF hand-helds to maintain contact on shore or from dock to dinghy or primary vessel.

General Mobile Radio Service

The General Mobile Radio Service (GMRS) is a personal radio service available to an individual person. It is a two-way voice communication

Figure 20-13 Inexpensive handheld radios of the Family Radio Service (FRS) can be very useful in boating. Although their range is quite limited, they can be used for on-board communications, to a dinghy, or to a person on shore. Multiple channels with subgroup codes are available; no license is required. They can interconnect with radios of the higher-powered licensed General Mobile Radio Service (GMRS).

service to facilitate the activities of that individual's immediate family members. Before any station transmits on any channel authorized in the GMRS from any point within or over the territorial limits of any area where radio services are regulated by the FCC, the responsible party must obtain a license for a GMRS system. An individual 18 years of age or older, who is not a representative of a foreign government, is eligible to apply for a GMRS system license. Application for a GMRS system license is made on FCC Form 605. There is a filing fee—in mid-2003, it was $75.

GMRS Systems

Each GMRS system consists of station operators, a mobile station (often comprised of several mobile units) and sometimes one or more land stations. A small base station is one that has an antenna no more than 20 feet above the ground or above the tree on which it is mounted.

Normally, you and your family members would communicate between yourselves over the general area of your residence, such as an urban or rural area. This area must be within the territorial limits of the fifty United States, the District of Columbia, and the Caribbean and Pacific Insular areas. In transient use, mobile station units from one GMRS system may communicate with mobile station units from other GMRS systems with certain restrictions.

There are twenty-three GMRS channels in the 462 and 467 MHz portions of the spectrum. The GMRS is a higher-powered, licensed extension of the Family Radio Service—seven of the GMRS channels match channels of the FRS, and inter-communication is allowed. In addition there are eight other GMRS channels for simplex use. None of the GMRS channels are assigned for the exclusive use of any system. License applicants and licensees must cooperate in the selection and use of the channels in order to make the most effective use of them and to reduce the possibility of interference. Other channels are for duplex systems and for relay stations.

Every GMRS system station operator must cooperate in sharing the assigned channel with station operators in other GMRS systems by monitoring the channel before initiating transmissions, waiting until communications in progress are completed before initiating transmissions, engaging in only permissible communications and limiting transmissions to the minimum practical transmission time.

GMRS stations may use up to 5 watts effective radiated power. Expect a communications range of five to twenty-five miles. You cannot make a telephone call with a GMRS unit.

Amateur Radio

Amateur ("ham") radio is used worldwide, with capabilities for both short- and long-range communications. It is authorized for personal, but not business, communications; it is useful to boaters who cruise to faraway ports, and who want to communicate economically over very long distances.

Ham radio is assigned a multiplicity of frequency bands from 1.8 to 450 MHz, with additional specialized bands up to 250,000 MHz, in fact more frequencies than marine VHF/FM or SSB. Within this spread, there is a suitable frequency for communication at about any distance around the world at some time of the day. One of the major workhorse ham frequencies is 14.313 MHz, where members of relay "nets" meet to handle permissible traffic and arrange landline telephone patches for mobile marine stations. Because of this network, ham radio can be useful to communicate across great distances with people who may or may not have access to marine radiotelephone equipment.

Radiotelegraph (Morse code), radiotelephone (AM or FM), radioteletype, and television signals are also transmitted by properly licensed ham operators on specified subbands. Indeed, some hams even "moon-bounce" signals.

Regulations & Licensing

The rules governing ham operations do not provide for a specific emergency channel, but several frequencies—such as 7.268 MHz and 14.313 MHz—have historically been used as emergency channels and are regularly monitored by hams worldwide.

Amateur radio operation requires both a station and an operator license. Ham operator's licenses are issued in different grades—in ascending order, Technician, General, and Amateur Extra. (The former grades of Novice, Technician Plus, and Advanced are "grandfathered" into the new system, but new licenses of these grades are no longer being issued.) Each grade up grants the operator wider access to assigned bands and different modes. Even though only the ability to engage in voice communication may be desired, a demonstrated ability to send and receive Morse code at the speed of only five words per minute is now required for all grades, except Technician. A "no-code" Technician license restricts operation to frequencies above 50 MHz, generally suitable only for shorter-range communications. Holders of a Technician license can take the Morse code test, and if passed, operation is allowed on four long-distance HF bands. The holder of a General class license can operate on all 27 amateur bands; the Amateur Extra license grants access to otherwise restricted subbands with the regular band limits.

An amateur radio operator license is not overly easy to obtain, but neither is it impossible for anyone who seriously desires it and will devote some time to study and code practice. The drop in required Morse code speed from the former 13 words per minute to the current 5 words per minute has opened up ham radio to a wider field of boaters and other persons.

Additional information can be obtained from stores that sell ham radio equipment, by mail from the American Radio Relay League, Newington, CT 06111, or on the Internet at www.arrl.org.

Cellular Telephones

Cellular telephone systems use a large number of transceiving antennas/stations. Each one serves a limited geographic area, called a "cell," and is linked together through relay and controlling stations into a network. That network is further patched into the landline telephone system. Although the range of both a cellular telephone and a cell antenna/station is relatively short, the ultimate calling range of the system is very great because of the relays and the landline patches accomplished by the cellular telephone network.

Each cellular telephone (actually a radiotelephone) has its own identifier code. When a call is placed to a cellular phone, the network tries to contact it by broadcasting its code. If successful, the called cellular phone "rings" and is answered much like a conventional telephone. A call is placed from a cellular phone in the same way as from a regular phone.

Advantages & Disadvantages of Cellular Phones for Boaters

The major advantages of the system are:

• Its user interface is much the same as with the standard telephone network, so operator licensing is not required.

• It affords mobile users full access to land-based telephone systems, and vice versa.

• It employs relatively short-range radio technology (that avoids over-congestion of the airwaves), while overall affording users the capabilities for long-range communications.

The maximum range of a cellular phone to and from a cell antenna/station varies, but is basically line-of-sight. In some circumstances, coverage range can be only a few miles; in others, it can be a near equivalent of VHF radio. Range for boaters is further complicated by the fact that most cell antenna/stations are placed with land-based use in mind, so the distance offshore that a vessel can stay in contact with a cell antenna/station is often short. The limited range of a cell phone can be significantly increased if its small on-unit antenna is replaced by a fixed marine-type antenna mounted as high as practical on the boat. The range can be increased if its fraction-of-a-watt output signal is increased to two or three watts by an external amplifier before being sent to this antenna.

A cellular phone can be useful and extremely convenient, but *it is no substitute for proper marine radiotelephony when it comes to safety.* The call for help will not be heard by other vessels that may be nearby, and Coast Guard and other assistance towing vessels do not have the capability of radio direction finding on cell phone transmissions. If within range though, in some, but not all, areas, simply dialing "*CG" will reach the local USCG unit. In some assistance cases, Coast Guard units have been known to ask if the vessel concerned has a cellular phone, with the objective of shifting communications to that mode with more positive contact and no interference from other stations.

Cellular telephone service is continually improving because of expanding service areas and advancing technology. Portable phones of Personal Communication Service (PCS) networks look much like cellular phones and are used in the same way, but operate in separate systems on higher frequencies.

Boaters should seek the latest available information from both equipment manufacturers and network service providers before making decisions regarding equipment selection or the purchase of cellular telephone service.

Satellite Telephones

While cellular systems depend on terrestrial antennas, satellite telephone systems (satphones) reach much higher, sending and receiving their voice and data messages using numerous satellites

Figure 20-14 Craft of roughly 40 feet length or more can be fitted for satellite service—voice, data, television, or a combination of these. Antennas within a "dome" are stabilized to keep them pointed in the correct direction regardless of motions of the vessel. Domes will vary in size depending upon the service used.

orbiting about 500 miles in space. Though there are a number of systems on the drawing boards of Europe and Asia, two most talked about in the U.S. are Iridium and Globalstar. Except for Africa and parts of Malaysia, Globalstar covers much of the world, including North America and the Caribbean out to about 200 miles offshore. Iridium, with its 66 satellites, has worldwide coverage.

The advantages of these systems are instantaneous voice and data connections on land and sea; large coverage areas (especially Iridium), and handy, handheld hardware.

The disadvantages are high hardware costs—in the vicinity of a thousand dollars or more—and service costs, which include quite expensive only per-minute charges in some cases, per-minute plus monthly fees in others.

As more and more users sign up for satphone services, the cost, of course, will drop.

Other Satellite Communications

Satellite communications systems (SATCOM) beam signals via earth-based and orbiting space relay stations. SATCOM affords users full access to voice, telex, facsimile, and data networks. It is now practical for vessels down to 40 feet in length; see **Figure 20-14.**

Ship-to-shore, ship-to-ship and shore-to-ship communications are made via Coast Earth Stations (CESes), the links into the network's space segment for onshore subscribers. In the U.S., the CESes are operated by Telenor Satellite Services (formerly COMSAT), which provides access to the worldwide satellite communications space segments supplied by the International Maritime Satellite Organization (Inmarsat).

Procedures for placing and receiving calls via Inmarsat are highly automated. CES Maritime Services operators give directory, calling and related assistance on a 24-hour, 7-day-per-week basis. The operators also provide distress assistance in concert with governmental Rescue Coordination Centers.

The shipboard unit used for linking into the Inmarsat system is designated a Ship Earth Station (SES). There are a number of distinct types of SES, each providing a different array of access capabilities to the Inmarsat satellites and thereby to worldwide public telex and telephone networks.

Inmarsat-A supports telex and high-quality voice communications, as well as high-speed data and facsimile transmissions on its voice-quality channels. Its shipboard terminal, however, employs a relatively large stabilized tracking dish antenna that is suitable for installation on only large vessels.

Inmarsat-C uses a compact omnidirectional antenna convenient for smaller vessels. It supports data transmissions at up to 600 bps, but does not support voice communications.

Inmarsat-B is a digital version of Inmarsat-A.

Inmarsat-M and Mini-M is a small digital voice terminal with a simplified tracking dish antenna. A receive-only version of Inmarsat-C SES is available for automatic reception of maritime safety broadcasts in offshore and other areas not reached by NAVTEX. Now higher-speed data and e-mail services are available in Inmarsat's new FLEET products.

There are now several systems that provide cellular-telephone-like service in specific service areas or globally, using multiple satellites in low-earth orbits (LEO) or somewhat higher medium-earth orbit (MEO); see above "Satellite Telephones."

Violations & Penalties

You should never be in violation of the FCC Rules and you should have no need for the knowledge of the procedures and penalties involved. Yet things do not always work out that way, so it is just as well to be informed.

If you receive a CITATION OF VIOLATION from the FCC, you must reply in duplicate within ten days, to the office that issued the citation. If a complete reply cannot be given in that time, send an interim reply and supplement it as soon as possible. If for reasons beyond your control you cannot reply at all within ten days, do so at the earliest date practicable, and fully support your reasons for the delay. Each letter to the FCC must be complete and contain all the facts without cross-reference to other correspondence.

The answer must contain a full explanation of the incident and describe the actions taken to prevent a recurrence of it. If personnel errors are involved, your reply must state the name and license number of the operator concerned.

You may be lucky, however, and receive a WARNING NOTICE rather than a citation. Generally in this instance, no reply is required. The FCC form that you receive will indicate whether or not an answer is necessary. If one is required, don't get yourself into further trouble by failing to answer *within ten days.*

Revocation & Suspension of License

A station license may be revoked for any one of a number of specified violations of the Communications Act or the FCC Rules. Operator licenses and permits normally are not revoked but are suspended for varying periods of time, up to the balance of the license term. Notice of suspension must be given in writing and is not effective until 15 days after receipt. Within this period, you can apply for a hearing, and this automatically defers the suspension until after the hearing has been held and the FCC has ruled.

Fines Imposed

In addition to the revocation or suspension of licenses, the FCC can prosecute violators in the Federal District Courts. Any violation of the Communications Act may be punished by a fine of not more than $10,000, or imprisonment for not more than one year, or both. A second offense, not necessarily a repeat of the first, increases the minimum limit on the prison term to two years. For a violation of any FCC rule, regulation, restriction, or condition, or of any treaty provision, a court may additionally impose a fine of not more than $500 for each and every day during which the violation occurred.

Administrative Forfeitures

To avoid the delays, costs, and cumbersome procedures of formal court prosecutions, the FCC has the authority to levy its own ADMINIS-TRATIVE FORFEITURES—actually small fines—for

12 specific violations. These are in addition to any other penalties that may be imposed by law.

Among these twelve, the violations of principal concern to the operators of radio stations on boats are:

• Transmission of any authorized communications on a distress or calling frequency.

• Failure to identify the station at the times and in the manner prescribed by the FCC rules.

• Interference with a distress call or distress communications.

• Operation of a station without a valid permit or license of the proper grade.

• Transmission of any false call contrary to the FCC rules.

• Failure to respond to official communications from the FCC.

The maximum forfeiture for a single violation, or a series of violations all falling within a single category as listed above, is $100. If more than one category is involved, however, the maximum liability is raised to $500 for a station licensee, or $400 for an individual operator. Note that the term "operator" may be applied to any person using the equipment, whether or not licensed by the FCC. In some cases, if two different persons are involved in an incident involving one station, forfeitures may be assessed against both station licensee and the person who was operating the station.

The procedures for the imposition of these administrative fines have been kept simple, yet ample protection is afforded to the rights of individuals. Upon receipt of a NOTICE OF APPARENT LIABILITY FOR FORFEITURE, the addressed person has three possible courses of action. He can pay the fine and so close the incident; or he may, within 30 days, submit a written statement to the FCC giving the reasons why he should be allowed to pay a lesser fine, or none at all; or he may request an interview with an FCC official. These last two courses of action can be combined, submitting both an explanation and a request for an interview. If either or both of these actions are taken, the FCC will review all information relating to the case, and make a final determination.

There is no judicial appeal from the FCC's ruling, and you had best pay up as there are established procedures for turning over cases of nonpayment to a U.S. District Attorney for prosecution.

OTHER MEANS OF COMMUNICATIONS

There is often a need for communications at very short distances, a few yards to perhaps a quarter- or half-mile from the boat—or on board the boat itself.

Hailers

For voice communications boat-to-boat or boat-to-shore over distances up to a hundred yards or so, a LOUD HAILER is very useful. This may be either an installed item of equipment or a portable POWER MEGAPHONE; an installed unit will have the most power and greatest range, but a handheld model will be more convenient on smaller motorboats and on sailboats.

Various models of installed hailers offer additional useful features such as auxiliary use as a foghorn, perhaps sounding automatically at selected intervals. A valuable feature is a listening capability whereby the speaker can also act as a microphone to pick up distant sounds, aiding in *two-way* voice communications, or the early detection of sound-producing aids to navigation.

In selecting equipment, be sure to get a unit with adequate power, 25 to as much as 80 watts is desirable. The "P.A." output from CB sets is only 2 to 4 watts, and the "hailer" function on some VHF radios is only 5 to 10 watts.

Proper installation is essential. A hailer requires adequate primary power wiring (a powerful hailer will draw 10 amps or more; check the voltage at the unit while using it). Adequate wiring from the unit to the speaker is also important. And perhaps most important is the proper location and mounting of the speaker (to disperse the sound in the desired direction and prevent feedback into the microphone). Note that despite what is seen on many craft, the proper mounting is with the longer axis of a rectangular speaker opening vertical, not horizontal; see **Figure 20-15.** An excellent feature of some installations is the mounting of the speaker either on the searchlight or on a similar mount that can be both trained in direction and elevated in a vertical plane. This permits the efficient use of the hailer to persons off to one side or a bridgetender high above the boat. The combination of a hailer that can pick up and amplify distant sounds with a trainable mount will permit "audio direction-finding" on fog signals to a surprising degree of precision—a real help in zero-visibility piloting situations.

Intercom Systems

While most people think of a boat being too small and too compact to have internal communications problems, there are numerous applications for simple intercom systems. The interior of many larger cruisers, particularly those of the double-cabin type, are so divided that voices do not carry well from one compartment to another. A simple three-station intercom system connecting the bridge, after cabin, and forward cabin or galley can facilitate conversation between these locations and save many steps. On a boat with a small crew, such as a couple living on board by themselves, a quick and reliable communications system is truly a safety item, and the helmsman need not leave his position to or divert his attention to carry on a conversation or summon assistance.

On a larger craft, the intercom system can be expanded to include a unit in a weatherproof box on the foredeck. Then the person at the helm can have positive contact with a crewmember raising or lowering an anchor, picking up a mooring pennant, or handling dock lines. Just try to get up a badly fouled anchor without good communications with the helmsman, and you will quickly appreciate this small electronic device.

Morse Code Communications

Contrary to what many contemporary skippers believe, Morse code and other forms of signaling have not been totally replaced by electronic voice and data communications. Although radiotelephony and radiotext transmissions predominate, especially in the recreational sector, there remains

Figure 20-15 An installed loud hailer is excellent for direct-voice communications over distances from tens of yards to a half-mile or more. Some models will pick up incoming sounds to make two-way communications possible. When installed on a boat, the longer axis of the speakers horn, shown here horizontally, should be vertical.

a place for radio communications (other than in ham radio) that employ Morse code, and for visual forms of signaling, such as the use of hoisted flags.

The International Morse Code

The use of Morse code offers a number of significant advantages in radio communications. Because a keyed continuous wave (CW) signal does not require microphone or modulation circuits, the equipment necessary for successfully sending Morse code messages is simple, low-cost, and easy to build and maintain. Moreover, exceptionally low output power—as little as 2 or 3 watts—is often sufficient to transmit CW signals across open ocean to a range in the thousands of miles. And because an experienced radio operator can usually distinguish even a weak Morse code CW signal amid static and interfering transmissions, these signals can often get through in circumstances where both VHF/FM and SSB would likely fail.

Memorizing Morse code characters, shown in **Figure 20-16,** takes time, but it can be done by anyone. Once learned, and occasionally used, they will not be forgotten.

Flag Signaling

There is an established International Code of flag signals. One or more flags are hoisted aloft on a halyard where they can be seen by another vessel The set of code flags—shown on page 720—consists of one each of 26 alphabet flags, 10 numeral pennants, 3 substitutes (or repeaters) and an answering pennant (the Navy and Coast Guard use a fourth repeater). The substitutes are used when a given flag or pennant has already been used once in a hoist; and flags and pennants are mixed in a hoist as required.

NIMA Publication No 102, *International Code of Signals* provides sets of one- and two character signals for commonly used messages, plus signals of more characters for more complex communications (a revised edition in digital format is available on a CD-ROM and on-line.). These are used with flag hoists and other methods of visual and sound signaling. For example, hoisting the alphabet flag 'H' means "I have a pilot on board." The alphabet flags 'N' plus 'C' means, "I am in distress and require immediate assistance."

Today, few yachts carry a full set of international code flags, but many carry one or more that have special uses, for instance, the yellow 'Q' flag that must be hoisted when entering, and requesting permission to use, a foreign port. Racing sailboats (and judging committee boats), however, regularly have recourse to flag signaling; and the sailing skipper who engages in racing needs to be fully familiar with the specialized signals involved; refer to page 720, for "International Flags & Pennants," and to page 721, for "Signaling Using Flags."

Flashing Light Signaling

Signaling by short and long flashes of light is much faster than flag signaling and more information can be communicated. Moreover, because light signals can be narrowly aimed, they are less likely to be intercepted by other than the communicating vessels. Consequently, light signals are still widely used by naval vessels.

On board ships, light signaling is often accomplished by means of an Aldis light, a very bright, highly aimable light with a convenient trigger switch. However, light signaling can be accomplished with any form of light that is readily turned on and off, even a flashlight. If it is not feasible to turn the light off and on fast

The International Morse Code Alphabet

A •—	M ——	Y —•——
B —•••	N —•	Z ——••
C —•—•	O ———	1 •————
D —••	P •——•	2 ••———
E •	Q ——•—	3 •••——
F ••—•	R •—•	4 ••••—
G ——•	S •••	5 •••••
H ••••	T —	6 —••••
I ••	U ••—	7 ——•••
J •———	V •••—	8 ———••
K —•—	W •——	9 ————•
L •—••	X —••—	0 —————

Punctuation & Procedural Signals
Period •—•—•—
Comma ——••——
Interrogative ••——•• (IMI)
Distress call •••———••• (SOS)
From —••• (DE)
Invitation to transmit (go ahead) —•— (K)
Wait •—••• (AS)
Error •••••••• (EEEE, etc.)
Received •—• (R)
End of each message •—•—• (AR)

Equivalents
A dash is equal to three dots.
The space between parts of the same letter is equal to one dot.
The space between two letters is equal to three dots.
The space between two words is equal to five dots.

Figure 20-16 Morse code signaling is not frequently used, but it can be of great help in some situations. It can be used by sound and flashing light. Learning is not difficult if studied and practiced occasionally.

enough for signaling, a shutter can be operated close in front of the light to form short and long flashes. Therefore, there are circumstances in which light signaling can be advantageous to a small craft skipper.

Unfortunately, light signaling requires the ability to send and read Morse code—a rarity among recreational boaters. So it is unlikely to have application for most boat operators—unless perhaps one night he or she is aground, with a general failure of electrical power for radio communication and an urgent need to communicate with a Coast Guard rescue vessel or helicopter, in which case the ability to send light signals with a battery-powered flashlight could prove critical.

INTERNATIONAL FLAGS & PENNANTS

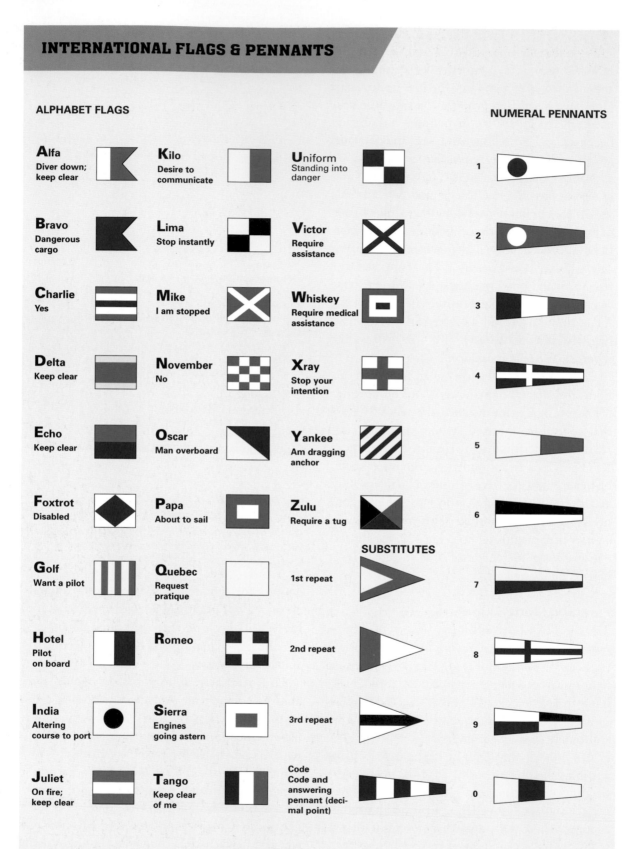

ALPHABET FLAGS

Alfa
Diver down;
keep clear

Bravo
Dangerous
cargo

Charlie
Yes

Delta
Keep clear

Echo
Keep clear

Foxtrot
Disabled

Golf
Want a pilot

Hotel
Pilot
on board

India
Altering
course to port

Juliet
On fire;
keep clear

Kilo
Desire to
communicate

Lima
Stop instantly

Mike
I am stopped

November
No

Oscar
Man overboard

Papa
About to sail

Quebec
Request
pratique

Romeo

Sierra
Engines
going astern

Tango
Keep clear
of me

Uniform
Standing into
danger

Victor
Require
assistance

Whiskey
Require medical
assistance

Xray
Stop your
intention

Yankee
Am dragging
anchor

Zulu
Require a tug

SUBSTITUTES

1st repeat

2nd repeat

3rd repeat

Code
Code and
answering
pennant (deci-
mal point)

NUMERAL PENNANTS

1

2

3

4

5

6

7

8

9

0

SIGNALING USING FLAGS

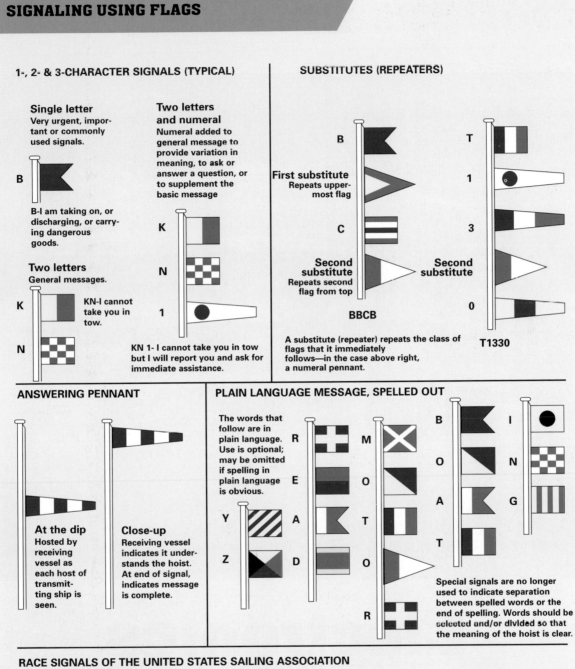

1-, 2- & 3-CHARACTER SIGNALS (TYPICAL)

Single letter
Very urgent, important or commonly used signals.

B

B-I am taking on, or discharging, or carrying dangerous goods.

Two letters
General messages.

K

N

KN-I cannot take you in tow.

Two letters and numeral
Numeral added to general message to provide variation in meaning, to ask or answer a question, or to supplement the basic message

K

N

1

KN 1- I cannot take you in tow but I will report you and ask for immediate assistance.

SUBSTITUTES (REPEATERS)

B

First substitute
Repeats uppermost flag

C

Second substitute
Repeats second flag from top

BBCB

T

1

3

Second substitute

0

T1330

A substitute (repeater) repeats the class of flags that it immediately follows—in the case above right, a numeral pennant.

ANSWERING PENNANT

At the dip
Hosted by receiving vessel as each host of transmitting ship is seen.

Close-up
Receiving vessel indicates it understands the hoist. At end of signal, indicates message is complete.

PLAIN LANGUAGE MESSAGE, SPELLED OUT

The words that follow are in plain language. Use is optional; may be omitted if spelling in plain language is obvious.

R

E

Y

Z

M

O

A

D

B

O

A

T

R

I

N

G

Special signals are no longer used to indicate separation between spelled words or the end of spelling. Words should be selected and/or divided so that the meaning of the hoist is clear.

RACE SIGNALS OF THE UNITED STATES SAILING ASSOCIATION

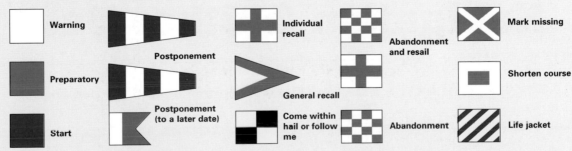

Warning

Postponement

Individual recall

Abandonment and resail

Mark missing

Preparatory

Postponement (to a later date)

General recall

Shorten course

Start

Come within hail or follow me

Abandonment

Life jacket

Electronics
Navigation & Other Uses

*Depth Sounders & Fish Finders • Global Positioning System (GPS) • Loran
Chart Plotters • Radar • Onboard Data Networks • Radio Direction Finding*

While most of the attention to electronic equipment for boats is normally focused on radiotelephones, there are many other devices ranging from those that are highly desirable, even necessary, to those that may be classed as merely useful for convenience or comfort. Equipment in all these categories will be considered in this chapter.

DEPTH SOUNDERS & FISH FINDERS

Today's replacement for the handheld lead lines used for centuries to determine the depth of water beneath a vessel is an electronic device called a DEPTH SOUNDER. Modern electronic devices furnish a vastly greater amount of information, and do it with far greater ease, especially in nasty weather. A depth sounder provides both safety and convenience, so it is doubly advantageous to have on board. They have a wide range of use—lakes, rivers, bays, and offshore.

Now depth sounders have been carried one step further—they have evolved into FISH FINDERS. These units do indicate the depth of the water, but go beyond that capability to show a video display of the water between the boat and the bottom, with an emphasis on indicating any fish occupying that area.

How Depth Is Measured & Displayed

Depth sounders determine depth by measuring the roundtrip time required for pulses of ultrasonic energy to travel from the boat to the bottom of the water and then to be reflected back to the vessel—the velocity of sound in water is about 4,800 feet/second. These are sound waves, but of a frequency above that which the human ear can hear. Ultrasonic frequencies used ranges from 25 kHz to 400 kHz, with 50 kHz and 200 kHz being typical. Lower frequencies will penetrate to greater depths, but higher frequencies will allow narrower beam widths and better definition of echoes in shallower water. The beam width can be as wide as 45° or as sharp as 15°; some depth sounders and fish finders provide for a selection of a lower or a higher operating frequency. The pulses are sent out from a TRANSDUCER, and the same device picks up the returning echoes, and sends them to a RECEIVER, where they are processed to eliminate undesired "noise" and are then sent to some type of DISPLAY (the transmitter and receiver are combined into a single unit that also includes the display); see **Figure 21-01**.

Transducers are normally mounted as a through-hull fitting, but transom mounts are available for smaller craft. Careful placement of the transducer is necessary to avoid turbulence that would prevent proper operation. Occasionally, a depth sounder transducer is bonded to the

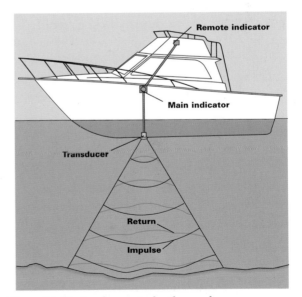

Figure 21-01 An electronic depth sounder measures the distance to the bottom by the time that it takes for pulses of ultrasonic sound to travel to the bottom and back.

Figure 21-02 Modern depth sounders display the depth digitally on an LCD screen. The units of depth are normally selectable between feet, fathoms, and meters. Values less than 10 usually are shown to one decimal place.

inside of a hull or mounted in an oil-filled box within the hull. The angle of the beam should not be greater than 15° from the vertical, and the hull must be solid fiberglass, not with a core of other material. The cable from the transducer to the main unit to the transducer is part of a "tuned circuit" of the system. Do not cut off any excess; coil it up at either end or somewhere along its length.

Liquid crystal displays (LCD) are commonly used—a digital display that is easily read in daylight and does not require a light shield in bright-light conditions, such as in an open boat on a flying bridge; these can also be backlighted for night use (red backlighting is preferable); see **Figure 21-02**. Depth information generally is available in feet, fathoms, or meters. There is at least one model of "black box" depth sounder that has no display of its own and connects by a cable to a personal computer for a video display.

A video display sounder presents a visual "elevation" picture of the bottom, using an LCD panel, plus underwater objects such as large fish or schools of smaller fish, thus becoming a "fish finder"; see **Figure 21-03.** The display changes constantly as the boat moves along its course showing the current depth and depths just passed; on many sounders you can "freeze" it for a more detailed study.

Correction to "Zero" Depth Indication

A depth sounder's transducer generally is mounted on the hull several feet below the water surface, but for its own protection, at some distance up from the lowest point of the keel. As depths are measured from the transducer, its readings will be *neither* the actual depth of the water nor the clearance between the keel and the bottom. On many models, the zero reading can be offset plus or minus a few feet so that the depth indications will be either the true water depth or the clearance under the boat, without having to mentally add or subtract a fixed amount.

Although actual water depth readings are advantageous for navigation, some skippers prefer a direct reading of clearance under the keel.

Interpreting Displays

A depth sounder shows the depth over a small area as defined by the beam width of the transducer; it does not identify the bottom by type. Digital displays will commonly show depths to a tenth of a foot below 10 feet and whole numbers of feet for greater depths. A unit should be selected that has large enough figures that it can be comfortable read from a reasonable distance. Some models also incorporate a seawater temperature sensor and this value can be displayed alternately with depth. Other models incorporate speed data from a separate sensor. Many depth sounders have a digital output that can be sent over a data

Figure 21-03 Fish finders show the bottom and schools of fish, or larger individual fish, beneath the boat. Most models will show the depth digitally, and some can also show other data such as water temperature and speed. Various controls allow adjustment for the best picture of the water column.

network (see page 745) to other navigation instruments such as a GPS receiver, radar, or a chart plotter.

Portable depth sounders and even fish finders are available that can be hand-held over the side of a small boat, but their capabilities are less than that of installed units.

Depth Alarms

Most depth sounders have at least a shallow-water alarm, and some have multiple depth alarms. The latter are useful when the boat is anchored. With one alarm set just below the present depth and the other set just above it, with allowance made for tidal changes, the unit sounds if the boat drags anchor toward either shallower or deeper water. Dual alarms are also useful for depth contour piloting (see Chapter 18, page 635); set the alarms for one or two feet (or meters) less, and the same distance greater than, the depth curve that you desire to follow.

Handheld Lead Lines

You should still carry a handheld lead line! It can be very useful for taking depth measurements around your boat if you run aground—its readings can tell you the best direction to go to get off; it's not always dead astern. The line need not be long, 10 feet or so with marking every foot, plus a special mark at your boat's draft. A handheld lead line can also be useful for taking measurements from a dinghy ahead of your boat if you are outside a channel or pass, about whose depths you are uncertain.

Fish Finders

As mentioned above, the electronic depth sounder principles can be extended to create a newer device, the fish finder; refer to **Figure 21-03.** Here the depth of the water is indicated, but the primary focus of attention is on the water column between the boat and the bottom—are there any fish there? This is much like an underwater radar, either looking only downward or scanning around.

LCD video displays for fish finders may be either monochrome or color, with the latter being

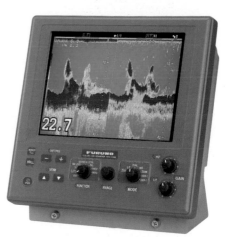

Figure 21-04 Fish finders are available with color LCD displays that provide greater and more easily interpreted information, but these are more expensive than monochrome models. Some models can have a GPS module added so as to also show position.

more expensive; see **Figure 21-04.** A digital display of depth, and sometimes water temperature, is shown in addition to the "picture" of the water column beneath the boat. Monochrome displays can have multiple shades of gray or green to show various features, and a white line for the bottom. Color displays use various colors for this purpose. Care must be taken when selecting a fish finder that the screen is readable in all types of ambient light that will be encountered.

The ability to zoom in at different ratios on a specific portion of the water column provides greater information than a simple depth finder with only a single "elevation" display of the entire column of water beneath the boat. Some fish finders feature multiple selectable beams to view the area around the boat and at least one of those with multiple selectable beams will project a beam ahead or behind the craft. Split screens are available on many models. There are other special features on the more expensive units, varying with the manufacturer and model.

A distinct advantage of fish finders over simple depth finders is their ability to give a general indication of the nature of the bottom, such as hard rock, firm sand, soft mud, etc.

HOW A GPS RECEIVER DETERMINES POSITION

In essence, what a marine GPS receiver does is measure the distance between itself and three satellites in space, use those distances as the radii of three spheres, each having one of the satellites as its center, then, using spherical geometry, it determines its position as the intersection of those three spheres.

Here's how it does that: The signal transmitted by each GPS satellite has two parts. One is a digital code, unique to that particular satellite, which identifies it. Superimposed over that code is a navigation message that contains updated information about that satellite's orbit (technically referred to as "ephemeris data"); what time it is as far as the satellite is concerned (GPS time); almanac data for all the satellites in the constellation; and coefficients the receiver can then plug into a computer model stored in its memory to calculate how the atmosphere is affecting the signal's transmission through the ionosphere. (This is known as its PROPAGATION.)

The satellite tells the receiver the instant in GPS time that it transmitted its signal, and the receiver synchronizes itself (approximately) to GPS time. Since time, speed, and distance are interrelated—by multiplying the difference between the time that the satellite transmitted the signal and the time that it reached the receiver by the signal's speed (186,000 statute miles per second)—the receiver calculates its approximate distance (called a PSEUDORANGE) from the satellite. The receiver's computation of this distance could be absolutely accurate if it contained an atomic clock, but that would make the receiver prohibitively expensive. Instead, a GPS receiver uses for a time reference an affordable crystal oscillator that synchronizes it and the satellite with near but not total accuracy.

If the receiver could determine distance with absolute accuracy, signals from two satellites would be sufficient to fix latitude and longitude. Since it cannot determine distance with absolute accuracy, it acquires the pseudorange from a third satellite and adjusts the three pseudoranges in equal amounts until the three LOPs converge to

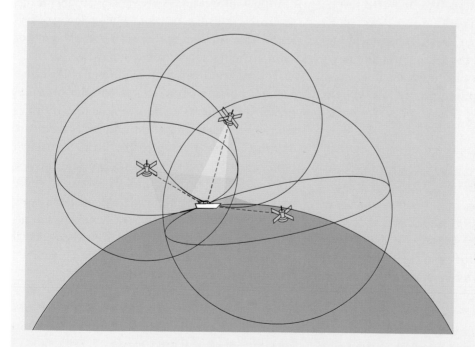

As shown in this illustration, A GPS receiver determines vessel position by taking virtually instantaneous readings from at least three satellites, each of whose distance becomes the radius of a sphere. The receiver calculates the vessel's position as the point at which the three spheres intersect.

determine the clock error in all three signals and then eliminate it.

The receiver uses the pseudoranges it has computed from the satellites it is observing to solve three simultaneous equations (one for each satellite), with three unknowns (latitude, longitude and clock error), and produces an estimate of its position.

It next must account for its own velocity during the process of acquiring and processing the satellite signals. It does this by comparing the frequencies of the satellite signals against that of a reference signal that the receiver generates internally. From the Doppler effect (this is the effect you note in the sound-wave frequency of a train's whistle as it approaches you, passes you, then recedes into the distance) the receiver computes its velocity relative to each of the satellites that it is observing. The receiver then recalculates the earlier three equations using velocity rather than pseudoranges. After using the solution to those three equations to allow for its own velocity in the earlier estimated position, the receiver produces a fix. This is shown in drawing on the opposite page.

Fish finders are available in a range of sizes, and one can be fitted on almost any length fishing boat. Of greater importance than overall size is the "resolution" of the display, usually stated in the number of "pixels" shown, either a total number or the number horizontally and vertically—more is better.

If both a fish finder and a depth sounder are mounted on a boat, care should be taken that they operate on different frequencies to avoid interference problems.

Scanning Fish Finders

"Scanning sonar" units are available for larger vessels—commercial fishing craft and yacht-size sportfishing boats. These can direct a beam of ultrasonic sound pulses 360° around a vessel or to any desired sector 6° or wider; the center of the sector can be set on dead ahead or astern, or any direction to the side. The beam can be directed from 5° upward to 90° downward to greatly expand the volume of water that is being checked. Angles of 0° to 5° down from the horizontal will show fish swimming near the surface, but nothing of the bottom. Down angles of 30° to 40° will show the bottom; intermediate angles will show some of the bottom and the water area above the bottom. These are large and expensive units; the transducer dome retracts within the hull of the vessel when not in use, and speed is limited to about 15 knots when it is lowered. For smaller craft, units with a phased array of transducers (no moving parts) can scan either vertical from the surface to the bottom looking forward, or horizontally through a 90° or 180° arc centered on dead ahead, depending on the model installed; beam width is 12°.

Though these sound like the ideal device to warn of underwater obstructions, they must be used with caution as in shallow water where they could be most useful, sonar echoes become so chaotic that they cannot be correctly interpreted by an inexperienced operator.

GLOBAL POSITIONING SYSTEM (GPS)

The Global Positioning System (GPS) is an advanced worldwide radionavigation system designed and operated by the U.S. Department of Defense (DOD) as the principal electronic navigation system for the U.S. military forces and allies. GPS is also available to civilian users at a level of accuracy somewhat less than that available to the military. The DOD began designing the system in 1973, and started launching initial test satellites in 1978. By 1991, enough satellites were in place for mariners to reliably determine latitude and longitude virtually anywhere in the world. Launch of the 24th satellite in 1994 completed the system. After testing and verification, "Full Operation Capability" was declared on July 17, 1995.

GPS Satellites

GPS is based on a constellation of 21 active and three fully functional but "spare" satellites that operate in six orbital planes at an altitude of 10,900 nautical miles (20,200 km) and at an inclination angle to the equator of 55°. Each satellite takes about 12 hours to complete a single orbit and follows the same ground pattern on each orbit, but is observable from a fixed position on earth approximately 4 minutes earlier each 24 hours due to the difference between its orbital speed and the speed of the earth's rotation.

The satellites' orbits are subject to small, gradual changes. Since the entire system is based on the satellites being able to transmit their precise location in space to GPS receivers, their orbit information must be periodically updated. Satellite orbits are tracked by five monitoring stations that feed data on changes to the system's Master Control Station at Colorado Springs, Colorado. The Master Control Station recomputes that information and feeds updated navigation messages back to the satellites through a network of five ground antennas. Each satellite now transmits on two frequencies: L1 at 1575.42 MHz and L2 at 1227.6 MHz. Nonmilitary users can receive and process only L1, which carries a Coarse/Acquisition (C/A) code. Military receivers use signals on both frequencies. Future plans call for a second civilian frequency for improved system operation, and updates to the military precision service

Because of the satellites' altitude and orbital patterns, at least six satellites are observable by a ground-based GPS receiver at all times; at times as many as 8, or even 10, can be simultaneously received. This means fixes can be obtained from the system continuously. Signals from any three satellites are sufficient to fix latitude and longitude. However, reception of signals from a fourth satellite is needed to determine altitude, which is not a requirement for recreational marine applications. Additional satellite signals increase the accuracy of the position data. All satellites transmit on the same frequencies, but the "message" from each of these has identifying information.

Figure 21-05 Handheld GPS receivers can be very small and convenient with their built-in antenna and internal batteries for power. Many models can be placed in a bracket near a boat's helm and connected to the craft's electrical power. They thus become essentially an installed unit, but with the capability of being taken into a dinghy or life raft.

GPS Is Everywhere!

GPS has become truly universally used—not only for maritime and air navigation. GPS receiving capabilities will be found in nearly every mode of transportation from wilderness hikers to rail and bus systems. Some applications will tell the user where he or she is. In other instances, the location information will be automatically transmitted by radio to a central plotting location where movements of vehicles are tracked; the movements of wild animals, especially endangered species, can be similarly monitored.

Advanced applications of GPS using computer processing of data provide centimeter accuracy of positions and have become the accepted means of land surveying.

Some cellular telephones are already equipped for GPS, and soon all new phones will have this capability—when you call 911, the emergency service operator may know where you are even better than you do!

GPS Accuracy

GPS produces two levels of fix accuracy (defined in terms of meters). One, the Standard Positioning Service (SPS), is available to all users and normally produces positions that will have, with Selective Availability (see below) turned off, a horizontal accuracy of 13 meters (14 yds) or less for 95 percent of all fixes. The vertical accuracy is not as good, being 22 meters (24 yds) or less, but this is of little interest to boaters.

The Precision Positioning Service (PPS), available only to U.S. military forces and its allies as well as a very limited number of nonmilitary users, has higher accuracy and encrypted data.

GPS & Nautical Charts

GPS should be used *only* with up-to-date nautical charts labeled as being on the NAD-83 (North American Datum, 1983) or WGS-84 (World Geodetic System, 1984) datum systems—for practical purposes, these are the same. If used with older charts based on the NAD-27 datum, position errors of up to 160 meters (525 ft) may result. However, many GPS receivers have stored in their memories correction factors for numerous older and foreign chart datums.

An often overlooked factor in GPS positioning is that the location information may be more accurate than the nautical chart that is being used! GPS-level accuracy was not possible when many charts were first surveyed, and if your GPS receiver shows you on a pier, for example, instead of alongside it, the GPS is more likely to be accurate than the chart! You might even be aground, with the GPS showing that you are in the charted channel. There are even cases where islands or other geographical features are incorrectly charted to the extent of several miles. *It is not the GPS that is in error, but rather the charts!*

Another factor is that GPS positions will be shown to a degree of precision, such as hundredths or even thousands of a minute of latitude and longitude. Lines, symbols, and the like on even the largest scale charts are wider and larger than such very small dimensions. The third decimal place (approximately 6 feet or 2 meters), and often even the second decimal place (60 feet or 20 meters), generally has little practical meaning in navigation.

Selective Availability

When GPS was first made available to civilian users, DOD downgraded its accuracy "for national security reasons" by the application of "Selective Availability (SA)." It was still a fine

system for marine navigation, just not as accurate as it could be. SA was "set to zero"—effectively removed—in May 2000, but all it takes to restore it is a presidential decision, and the throwing of a switch. It has been reported that DOD has the capability to activate SA in specific geographic areas only, such as regions subject to ongoing military operations. With SA turned on, the stated system accuracy is 100 meters (109 yds), but users have reported consistent accuracies on the order of 30 meters (33 ft).

GPS Integrity

GPS has no inherent way to alert users if one of more satellites have malfunctioned and are transmitting incorrect data; it is possible that if a satellite failed, it could transmit incorrect information for up to an hour or more before the problem was detected by a control station and that satellite was set to nonusable. This normally is not a problem for mariners because with six satellites in view at all times, their receivers can calculate a fix from three healthy satellites; it is a much greater problem for aviation users. This lack of integrity information in GPS, however, again points up the maxim that the prudent navigator will never rely on a single source for determining position but will always verify his position by at least one other navigational means.

Differential GPS signals (see below) incorporate information that alerts users if a GPS satellite is malfunctioning.

GPS Receivers

Many models of both portable and installed GPS receivers are available from many manufacturers. Some portable units are designed only to be handheld and operate off an integral antenna; see **Figure 21-05.** Others can be handheld and operated off an integral antenna, or mounted in a holder at a vessel's navigation station or helm, using an externally mounted antenna and drawing power from the boat's electrical system. For offshore cruisers, a handheld GPS receiver is a valuable component of the "abandon-ship bag."

Some installed GPS receivers include their signal acquisition and navigation computing equipment along with their display in a single unit mounted at a vessel's navigation station or helm; see **Figure 21-06.** Other installed receivers have their signal acquisition and computing equipment in an antenna, called a GPS sensor, mounted in an out-of-the-way location and a separate display mounted at the navigation station or helm. The two components must be connected by cables. For vessels with more than one helm, these units can operate multiple displays from a single antenna; position information can also be transmitted over a data network for display on a fish finder, radar, or chart plotter.

GPS Receiver Features

A full-function GPS receiver can do much more than simply tell of a vessel's geographical position with a usable degree of accuracy. Also commonly shown in a GPS display is the vessel's course and speed made good, information continuously computed internally from successive positions with the data being "smoothed" over a user-selected interval (typically 5 to 20 seconds) for greater accuracy. Courses and bearings can be shown as true, magnetic with stored values for variation, or magnetic based on user-entered variation. Since course and heading information is derived from successive positions, heading information is not available when the craft is stationary. There are, however, GPS COMPASSES that use either two or three antennas spaced apart from each other and a special receiver to derive heading information to a high degree of accuracy.

Internal memory can be used to store the coordinates of WAYPOINTS for future use; ROUTES can be preplanned using a series of waypoints. Most sets can store multiple routes and can, with a single key press, reverse the direction of a route. Along a route, transfers from one leg to the next can be automatic or manual, with an alarm being sounded as each waypoint is approached; some models can be programmed to switch from one route to another.

Internal computing capabilities can determine the distance and direction (true or magnetic) between pairs of waypoints. Using computed track and present position data, a GPS receiver can show cross-track error, and how to steer to get back on track. This information can be fed into an autopilot for continuous course correction without action by the helmsman. (But always remember to keep a sharp lookout for other vessels and navigational hazards.) Combining its knowledge of speed, distance, and time, a GPS receiver can display how long it will take to reach a certain point and give an ETA.

Most GPS receivers allow an operator to save vessel position at any time with a simple push of a button. This feature is normally used to establish new waypoints, but could be extremely valuable in a man-overboard situation; when so used the GPS receiver will compute the heading and distance back to the MOB position.

GPS signals also include very precise time information, which can be dipslayed either as local zone time or mean solar time at the prime meridian (0° longitude), formerly known as GMT (Greenwich Mean Time), but now referred to as Coordinated Universal Time (abbreviated UTC, after the French name); but you must be aware that "GPS Time" is *not* the same as actual, correct UTC. UTC is adjusted every year or so to compensate for the very gradual slowing of the earth's rotation, a "leap second" is added to UTC. The clocks of GPS

Figure 21-06 GPS receivers that are fixed-mounted at a boat's helm position usually have larger screens and can simultaneously display more information. All GPS receivers display much more data than just latitude and longitude. Many can also show geographic information from internal memory and become simple chart plotters.

satellites, out in space, are not adjusted. Thus GPS time has gradually diverged 13 or more seconds from correct UTC, and the difference will increase in the coming years. Some GPS receivers have a correction built-in as of the date of their manufacture, others do not. If very accurate time is needed, compare the reading of your GPS receiver with a time signal from WWV (the radio station of the National Institute of Standards and Technology at Fort Collins, Colorado, that broadcasts highly accurate time information on highly accurate frequencies) or other radio source, and determine what the difference is for your specific GPS receiver; this will remain constant only until the next leap second is added to UTC. Some units will also give sunrise and sunset times for the current position of the vessel.

Some GPS receivers incorporate internal memory or use read-only-memory (ROM) cards for storing and displaying monochrome or multicolored chart representations on their own screens. These can also superimpose on the chart an icon indicating the vessel's position, together with course and speed.

Many GPS receivers can also be programmed to stand an anchor watch by describing a small circle around a vessel's anchored position and having the receiver sound an alarm if the vessel drifts outside that circle. Other alarms and alerts can be established for off-track error greater than a preset amount, approaching a place to be avoided, and functions as an alarm clock or count-down timer; a valuable function is a "watch alert" that can be set to sound at preset intervals and must be manually turned off by the helmsman, who might have dozed off.

GPS Antennas

External GPS antennas are small. Some are 1 to 2 inches in diameter and 12 to 15 inches high; others are 3 inches in diameter, but only 2 inches high; refer to Chapter 4, **Figure 4-04.** All must be mounted on a vessel's exterior with a 360-degree view of the horizon. Mounting should only be high enough to provide a clear view all around the horizon—too great a height results in excessive motion of the antenna due to the pitch and roll of the vessel that can degrade the accuracy of the position.

A GPS antenna should not be mounted where it will be in the beam of radar pulses, but a separation of only a few feet is adequate from communications antennas.

Differential GPS

Even in the absence of Selective Availability, the accuracy of fixes obtained from GPS by civilian users of the system is degraded by the fact that the C/A code contains only a predicted model of how the atmosphere is delaying GPS signals' propagation, not how it is affecting the signals in real time. This source of error, however, can be offset by a refinement of GPS called Differential GPS (DGPS).

The Maritime DGPS network is operated by the U.S. Coast Guard to provide the high degree of accuracy required for Harbor and Harbor Approach navigation that cannot be provided by the civilian mode of GPS alone (whether or not SA is activated).

The system employs a series of fixed reference stations with known precise geographical coordinates. As these stations receive signals from GPS satellites, they compare their position as indicated by the signals with their known position and compute the difference, generating a compensating correction for each satellite that is in sight. These stations then transmit data corrections within their broadcast range, 75 to several hundred miles, varying with the particular station; see **Figure 21-07.**

The broadcasts are made over frequencies—285-325 kHz— already approved by international treaties for maritime radionavigation beacons. Although DGPS was initially planned as a Harbor and Harbor Approach system, the overlapping coverage of its transmitters now provides DGPS for all the coastal waters of the contiguous U.S., including the Great Lakes, Alaska, Hawaii, and Puerto Rico out to as much as 200 nautical miles or more offshore. Because of the value of highly accurate position information, the network is being extended as the

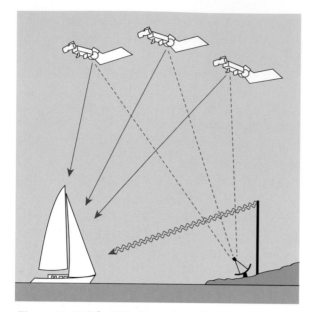

Figure 21-07 The U.S. Coast Guard operates a number of Differential GPS radiobeacons. The difference between the accurately known location and the observed position is determined and corrections are transmitted that can be received by boats and ships to improve the accuracy of their position. Numerous foreign countries operate similar systems.

National DGPS (NDGPS) to provide full coverage of the continental United Sates, thus all inland waters. Canada and many other foreign nations provide a compatible differential correction service.

In DGPS, a separate, independent integrity monitor is associated with each reference station; this can alert users if a satellite is transmitting an unreliable signal.

On-board DGPS Equipment

To use DGPS-transmitted corrections, a GPS receiver must be "DGPS-capable"—able to use the SC-104, version 2.0 data broadcast format. The DGPS receiver may be integral to the GPS set, or it may be a separate unit linked by cable; a separate antenna is usually required. Some differential receivers are manually tuned by the user, but most now search for, and automatically select, the strongest available signal and can switch to the next strongest if the first signal is lost.

The stated system accuracy of DGPS is 10 meters (11 yds), but in actual use accuracies are generally better—on the order of 1 meter (1.1 yds) out to a distance of 100 nautical miles from the station transmitting the corrections, and increasing 1 meter for each additional 100 nautical miles from the station.

The more accurate positions of DGPS also result in better and more stable readings of course and speed made good.

WAAS Differential Corrections

The U.S. Department of Transportation is developing the WIDE AREA AUGMENTATION SYSTEM (WAAS) to provide differential corrections for aeronautical services. It will have its own nationwide network of ground stations and will transmit error-correction information to aircraft in flight via geostationary satellites that are in orbit for multiple other purposes. The WAAS data is transmitted on the same frequency as the basic GPS signals and no separate receiver (and antenna) is needed—internal software decodes and applies the corrections. The end result is similar to that achieved by using the low-frequency (LF) Coast Guard signals. Some marine GPS receivers are available that use WAAS corrections in lieu of the marine broadcasts.

WAAS corrections are not available for distant waters, but differential GPS broadcasts similar to the USCG service may be received from the local foreign government.

LORAN

Though the term Loran is an acronym for Long Range Navigation, it is actually a medium-range navigation system for both marine vessels and aircraft. Unlike the Global Positioning System, Loran covers only the United States and Canadian coasts and the Great Lakes, plus a limited number of other areas of the world, as discussed opposite.

Despite the system's limited coverage, within the areas where its signals can be received, a good Loran receiver is a versatile and valuable navigation instrument. Although GPS is now the system of choice and few new Loran installations are being made on boats, there are many craft fitted with Loran receivers and the system will continue in operation for a number of years to come. New receivers with advanced technology are still being produced by at least one manufacturer.

A primary reason for the continued operation of the Loran service is that no navigator should depend on a single means of position determination. GPS is very highly reliable, but it could have failures, and it has some vulnerabilities to hostile action.

The Loran-C System

Today's Loran system (technically called Loran-C) was deployed during the late 1950s and is based on the earlier Loran-A system, which was developed during World War II for use by the United States military. This association with the military helps explain Loran's somewhat spotty coverage pattern, since its areas of coverage were initially designed to strategically benefit the military forces of the United States and its allies.

With the advent of GPS, many feared that support of the Loran system by the United States government would be withdrawn. While the United States has terminated its support for overseas Loran stations, it is committed to maintaining and improving the Loran system covering the contiguous 48 states plus southern and southeastern Alaska. U.S.-operated Loran stations will remain on the air well into this century. Extensive funding has resulted in improved transmitters and associated equipment, including uninterruptable power sources to ensure continued operation in times of emergencies. Receiver and receiving antenna designs have benefited from advances in technology. Research is being conducted to improve the overall system, such as redesigning receivers to use all received signals regardless of which chain they are part of. Although there are major technical problems, consideration is being given to transmitting GPS differential corrections as part of Loran signals.

Loran-C Chains

Loran utilizes a network of shore-based radio transmitters that are grouped in "chains." Loran chains are designed to provide accurate navigational fixes within 50 nautical miles from shore or out to the 100-fathom curve, whichever is greater. (In practice, usable Loran signals can be received at much greater distances; sometimes more than 1,000 miles.)

A Loran chain consists of one master transmitter (designated M) and two, three, or four secondary transmitters (designated W, X, Y and Z), each of which sends out pulsed radio signals, on 100 kHz, which travel through the atmosphere at 186,000 miles per second. In order to enable Loran receivers to identify the source of these signals, the transmitters send out their pulses in sequence at precise intervals of an assigned number of microseconds (millionths of a second). The interval between transmissions from the master transmitter is referred to as the Group Repetition Interval (GRI), and each chain is assigned a distinctive GRI. There are presently 24 Loran USCG stations (some operating in more than one chain); the coverage area includes all of the continental United States plus much of Alaska.

Assuming all transmitters in a chain are transmitting properly, fixes can be obtained from the system continuously. A typical Loran receiver updates its position approximately once every second.

Foreign Loran Systems

The operation and maintenance of overseas Loran systems originally installed and operated by the United States have been taken over by the governments in the areas that they serve. Canada, for instance, now has full responsibility for the Loran systems covering its own coastal waters. The United States and Russia jointly operate a chain that covers the area between western Alaska and eastern Russia, and Russia has both eastern and western systems. Japan and South Korea have a chain of stations for their waters. Several northern European governments operate chains covering waters adjacent to their nations. Saudi Arabia and India each operate two chains, and China maintains four chains.

Loran Accuracy

Loran ground wave transmissions generally have a maximum range of 1,000 to 1,200 miles from

HOW LORAN WORKS

Once a Loran receiver captures the radio signals from the master transmitter and one secondary transmitter in a chain whose geographical positions have been programmed into its memory, it measures the difference in time it took the two signals to reach it. Since speed, time, and distance are interrelated, that TIME DIFFERENCE (TD) locates the receiver on a hyperbolic line-of-position (LOP); see left sketch below. (A hyperbola is a curve generated by a point so moving that the difference in the distance between two points is a constant.) The receiver then almost instantaneously repeats the process with signals from the master and a different secondary to establish a second LOP; see middle sketch below. Using the two LOPs, a position is established; see right sketch below. A modern Loran receiver converts the TD information to a display of latitude and longitude that can be plotted on any chart. It is also possible to display the TD readings and plot a position using that information on a chart that is overprinted with Loran lines.

It is important to remember that, unlike GPS, a Loran-C receiver is not concerned with its absolute distance from any transmitter, only with its relative distances from the master transmitter and the secondary transmitters in a given Loran chain.

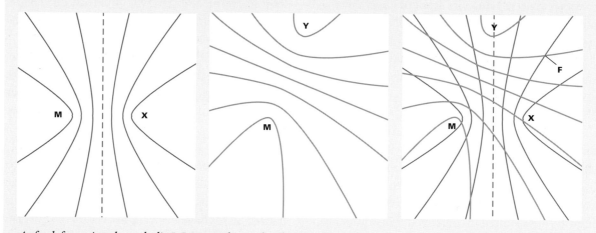

At far left, various hyperbolic LOPs are shown for the two stations, M and X. At middle, another set of Loran LOPs is shown for stations M and Y. At right, these LOPs are combined and a fix occurs at the intersection of any pair of lines, such as at F.

their transmitters. Within the ground wave coverage area, the absolute accuracy of initial fixes normally is within 0.25 nautical mile.

Repeatability

The accuracy of Loran's repeatability—its ability to reestablish a position that it has fixed earlier—is even greater than the absolute accuracy of initial fixes. In ideal situations, it can be on the order of 50 meters (55 yds), or even better. For the greatest repeatability accuracy, the same pairs of TDs should be used consistently; this may not always occur in receivers that automatically select the TD pair to be used.

As with GPS, discussed earlier, Loran should be used only with up-to-date nautical charts labeled as being based on the NAD-83 (North American Datum, 1983) or WGS-84 (World Geodetic System, 1984) datum systems. If used with older charts based on the NAD-27 datum, position errors of up to 160 meters (175 yds) can result.

If a Loran transmitter malfunctions, an element is incorporated into its signal that causes the display on receivers within its coverage area to blink, thereby alerting users that its signal should not be used for navigation.

Onboard Loran Equipment

Most Loran receivers include their signal acquisition and navigation computing equipment, along with their displays, in a single unit that is mounted at a vessel's navigation station or helm; see **Figure 21-08.** Other installed receivers have their signal acquisition and computing equipment in one "black box" that can be mounted in an out-of-the-way location, and a separate display that is mounted at the navigation station or helm. These two components must be connected by cables. For vessels that have more than one helm, these units can power multiple displays from a single "black box."

A typical external Loran antenna is an 8-foot metal whip encased in fiberglass and connected to a coupler that adds about 1 to 1½ feet to its height. The antenna should be mounted as far as possible from metal objects such as masts and rigging. The receiver should be well grounded.

Loran Receiver Capabilities

While Loran receivers find position by time differences (TDs) and can display position in that format, all Loran receivers also are able to convert TDs to latitude and longitude and express posi-

Figure 21-08 A Loran-C receiver can show position in terms of Loran time differences (TDs) or in terms of latitude and longitude—there are advantages and disadvantages of both methods. Cross-track error and distance to go to a designated destination or waypoint can also be shown on the model shown here.

tion in that format as well. (The same TD data in different Loran receivers may yield slightly different values of latitude and longitude because of different conversion processes.)

Like GPS receivers (pages 729 to 730), a full-function Loran receiver can tell a mariner a great deal more than his or her vessel's geographical position with a usable degree of accuracy. It can display elapsed time and distance from given points astern, and provide the vessel's cross-track error, with optional audible alarm. It can also calculate and display vessel course-over-ground and speed-of-advance, display the course required to reach points ahead (waypoints) and how far away they are, and indicate which way the helmsman should steer to stay on course. It can display how long it will take to reach a certain point and the vessel's ETA. It can also be interfaced with an autopilot to steer the vessel to waypoints in a route, and can sound an alarm as the vessel draws close to a particular location. Most Loran receivers can be programmed with a hundred or more waypoints in 10 or more routes.

More sophisticated Loran receivers have ASF correction built into their circuitry. In boundary areas where the coverage of two Loran overlap, most advanced Loran receivers will automatically select signals from the secondary transmitters providing the strongest signals, and if the vessel on which they are carried cruises from the coverage area of one Loran chain into the coverage area of another chain, will automatically switch to the new chain's GRI (Group Repetition Interval).

Some Loran receivers also can be interfaced with a radar or video depth sounder to superimpose a digital display of vessel position, course, and speed on the radar or video depth sounder screen. Some Loran receivers can be interfaced with electronic chart plotters (see below) to superimpose a graphic/digital display of position, course and speed on a monochrome or multicolored representation of a chart or a full-color digitized chart on the plotter's screen. Fully integrated Loran receivers incorporate read-only-memory (ROM) cards for storing and displaying monochrome representations of navigation charts on their own screens, on which position, course, and speed can be graphically/digitally superimposed.

Although in nearly all present piloting situations GPS is the primary electronic navigation system, a backup capability of Loran is desirable. Unfortunately, as of early 2003, there were no receivers available that combined GPS and Loran navigation systems.

CHART PLOTTERS

Electronic charts were covered in Chapter 15—here we will consider how they are used. Electronic charts are most commonly stored on compact disks that appear the same as those so widely used to store music; they are, however, CD-ROMs, compact disks for read-only memory. Also used are data cards or "cartridges."

A "Chart Plotter" is also referred to by some as a "Chartplotter" or an "Electronic Charting System"; see **Figure 21-09**. These are the small-craft parallels to the Electronic Chart and Information Display Systems (ECDISs) used on large ships. It must be remembered, however, that the chart plotter on a boat is *not* a substitute for having the proper paper charts on board.

An electronic chart reader can be a stand-alone device merely displaying the information that is stored internally or inputted from a CD-ROM or data card, but more often they are combined with a GPS or DGPS receiver so that the vessel's position is shown on the chart display. (Disks and cards are available from several commercial sources.) In this manner, the tedious step of transferring the location in latitude and longitude from the GPS display to a paper chart is avoided, and the possibility of plotting error is eliminated. (Some GPS receivers have rudimentary chart information internally stored in memory, but without the capability of receiving external chart information, these are not true "chart plotters.") Chart plotter displays are LCD panels, either monochrome or color; the number of pixels (resolution) will vary with the size and cost of the unit. Screens are normally backlit at variable intensity for nighttime use; some models will have a transflective display for usable visibility in conditions of bright light, such as on a flybridge; these displays get brighter as the light falling on them gets stronger. Chart plotters with a range of screen size are available in a comparable range of price. Displays can be selected as "north up" or "heading up" similarly to radar displays.

The full range of internally calculated information from a GPS receiver (see page 729) is usually available for display at the margins of a chart

Figure 21-09 A chart plotter is used to display the contents of an electronic chart, often at the helm of a boat. It is usually combined with a GPS or DGPS receiver so that the position of the craft is shown directly on the chart being used. Additionally, information on speed, heading, and other navigational data will be shown in the margins of the chart area.

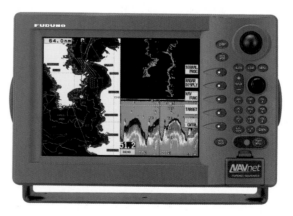

Figure 21-10 A chart plotter capable of split-screen operation can show the usual chart on one half and another presentation on the other half. This additional capability greatly enhances the use of this device.

plotter screen. A split screen may allow the simultaneous display of data and a chart, or a chart and a fish finder view of the water beneath the boat; some can show a chart and an aerial photograph of the same area, usually a harbor or harbor entrance; see **Figure 21-10.** Radar displays can be superimposed on a chart at the same scale, or shown on a split screen. On some models, the overlaid radar display can be made semitransparent so that chart details can be read through it.

Data from other electronic devices that can be shown on some models include depth information, speed through the water, water temperature, wind speed and direction, etc. Chart plotters interconnected with a VHF-DSC radio can show the position of a vessel in distress if the Mayday message contains that information; if set up to do so, the location of any boat calling can be shown on the plotter, and the DSC radio can request another boat to transmit its position, which will be shown. Some models, on craft fitted with appropriate sensors, can even display fuel usage and remaining availability—the possibilities are almost endless!

A recently developed chart plotter, when used with an appropriate electronic chart, can sound an alarm when a preset depth, or less, appears in the path ahead of the boat; this is based on the charted depth and must be adjusted for actual tidal conditions; no measurements are taken. It can also warn of land, man-made objects, and other charted features as selected. The unit takes an input of position from its internal GPS receiver and scans the chart in an arc 15° either side of dead ahead out to a distance selectable from 1/4 to 1 mile; the distance should be chosen with reference to the speed of the craft. Caution: This system relies upon the information included on the chart; it cannot warn against an uncharted depth or obstruction.

Caution It must always be remembered that on small craft a chart plotter is not a full replacement for paper charts. Even a 10-inch color display will not show nearly all the information that you can quickly scan from a conventional chart. Knowing how to zoom, pan, and scroll the display on your chart plotter will help, but you must still have a full-size chart at hand for when you need the full picture.

Software on a Personal Computer

As an alternate to a specialized chart plotter, an onboard personal computer, usually laptop or notebook style, can be used with navigation software and electronic charts; see **Figure 21-11.** A major disadvantage of this procedure is the fact that the displays on most portable computers simply cannot be read in bright light, thus preventing their use on flybridges and at other exposed helm stations. They work well belowdecks, but this requires a second person and a reliable means of communication between him or her and the helmsman. Portable computers with "sunlight-readable" displays, or separate displays, are available, but they are considerably more expensive; it is important that a very bright screen have the capability to be sufficiently reduced in brightness for satisfactory use at night.

Many navigation programs for use on a PC while underway can also be used while in port or at home for cruise planning.

Figure 21-11 A portable computer can be used on a boat in many ways. With navigation software, it can be the equivalent of a chart plotter. With specialized software, it can calculate tidal heights and times, and other marine data. With regular software, it can run word processing, database, and spreadsheet programs. It can run games and entertainment programs, and often can be used to connect to the Internet.

Almost every electronic device that is mentioned in this chapter operates on internal "firmware"—computer programming that is not normally changed by the operator but which can be upgraded by the installation of new data from the manufacturer. Upgrading can often significantly improve the operation of your equipment. Information on available upgrades may or may not be available from local dealers; the best source of information is directly from the manufacturer, usually from its website—check your owner's manual or do a search on the Internet.

The electronic charts used with a chart plotter, and the navigational software used with a personal computer, may also include a database with additional information such as available marine facilities, tide predictions, and other information useful to a cruising boater. Computer software programs are available from several sources and in various levels of sophistication and capabilities. Most programs are for the Windows operating system, but there are some are available for Macintosh computers.

Because of the possibility of equipment failure or loss of electrical power, the availability of such supplemental information should be considered as a convenience only—a full backup of texts and tables should always be on board.

Specialized CD-ROMs are available showing "fishing hot spots"; shoreside street maps and points of interest; highways and topographic features; and other nonmarine information.

RADAR

Radar is an acronym for Radio Detection And Ranging. The basic technology that radar employs has been available since before WW II, but the advent in recent years of digital signal processing and integrated circuitry has allowed a number of improvements in its ability to define (clearly outline) targets, as well as in how its information is displayed. A good radar set is an extremely valuable piece of equipment because of its ability to detect the presence, range, and bearing of distant objects in any weather, and to track some forms of weather, such as rainstorms.

Radar serves two purposes on board ships and boats. Although often primarily thought of as a collision-avoidance device, radar can be an essential tool in navigation (see Chapter 18, pages 633 to 635).

Radar Equipment

A radar's components consist of a transmitter that generates radio waves and includes a modulator that causes the radio waves to be generated in brief pulses; an antenna that radiates the radio waves and collects the returning echoes (see **Figure 21-12**); a receiver that detects the returned reflections and amplifies them to usable strength; and a display that presents the pattern of received echoes on a cathode-ray tube (CRT) or liquid crystal display (LCD) and includes rotary knobs

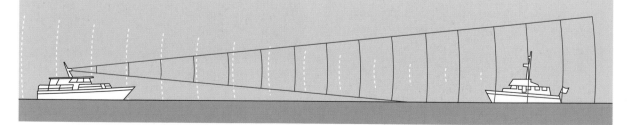

Figure 21-12 A marine radar operates by transmitting very brief pulses of super high frequency radio waves. These are reflected back by other vessels, aids to navigation, landmasses, and other "targets." The speed of the pulses is so great that an echo is received before the next pulse is sent out.

HOW RADAR DETECTS OBJECTS

Radar works by transmitting a tightly focused beam of super high frequency radio waves from a rotating antenna mounted as high as practical on a vessel, then measuring the time it takes those radio wave pulses to be reflected off distant objects and return to the antenna; refer to **Figure 21-12.** By multiplying that time interval by the speed of radio waves—161,875 nautical miles per second (299,793 km/s)—the system can determine the distance between the antenna and the objects that reflected radio waves back to it.

The bearing to an object is determined by the direction in which the antenna is pointing when it transmits its radio wave beam and receives a reflection (often called an echo). The antenna's rotation during the time interval between the pulse being sent out and its return is not a factor in determining the bearing of an object because it makes only one revolution every 2 to 4 seconds but transmits pulses of radio waves at the rate of 400 to 6,000 per second. Since it takes the radio waves only a fraction over 12 microseconds (millionths of a second) per nautical mile of range to make their round trip, the antenna can send and receive up to 30 pulses in the time it takes to rotate just one degree, which means that, electronically speaking, it is standing still.

Because the radio waves that a radar trans-mits bend slightly to follow the earth's curvature, its horizon at any particular mounting height is about 7 percent farther away than the horizon of the human eye at that same height. The maximum range at which a particular radar can detect an object and the clarity with which it can define targets depend on four factors—the strength of the radio wave signal it transmits, the sensitivity with which it can detect and interpret reflected radio waves, the length of its antenna and the height at which the antenna is mounted on the vessel, and the height of the object itself (see illustration below).

As the reflected radio waves are received, they are displayed on a screen normally mounted adjacent to a vessel's helm. The pattern of all the reflected radio waves that are received on a single sweep of the antenna clearly reveals the existence of the objects they detect.

This does not necessary mean that the image displayed on the radar screen will match exactly what is seen with the human eye or on a navigation chart. Low-lying targets such as a beach along a coast will not show up as well as tall buildings several hundred yards inland. Radar cannot "see" through a mountain to reveal a harbor entrance on the other side, and the reflection from a large object such as a commercial ship can mask the reflection of a smaller vessel behind it or nearby.

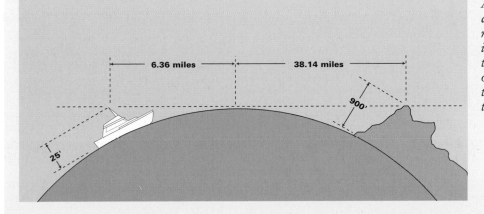

6.36 miles   38.14 miles

900'

25'

A radar's range depends on the mounting height of its antenna and on the height of the objects that reflect the radio waves it transmits.

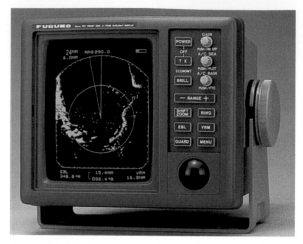

Figure 21-13 A standard radar display presents the vessel's position at the center of the screen and the vessel's heading at the 12 o'clock position. With each rotation of the antenna, reflected radar pulses reveal the objects that they detect.

and buttons, and sometimes a joystick or trackball for certain operator-controlled functions; see **Figure 21-13.**

The radars used on small craft normally group these components in two units. The antenna, the transmitter, and a portion of the receiver are housed in one unit, mounted as high on the vessel as practical. The remainder of the receiver and the display are housed in a second unit, normally installed near the vessel's helm. Some manufacturers also offer a remote display that allows a second presentation of the picture on the master display at a second steering station such as on a powerboat's flybridge or a navigator's station below.

Transmitters for use on recreational vessels are rated by their peak pulse power output and range from 1 kW to about 10 kW—the power taken from the boat's electrical system is much less, from 100 watts to about 300 watts.

Radar Antennas

Small-craft radar antennas range in length from about 17 inches to 6.5 feet (45 cm to 2.0 m). Antennas under about 2 feet (61 cm) in length in some cases are enclosed in a RADOME, a fiberglass housing most often used to prevent a sailboat's sails from becoming entangled in the rotating antenna. A radome does not affect the quality of

an antenna's radio wave transmission but does limit the size of an antenna.

The longer an antenna, the narrower the horizontal width of the beam of radio waves it transmits. A 17-inch (43-cm) radome antenna, for example, would typically transmit a 5.7° horizontal beam; a 3.5-foot (1.1-m) open array antenna might transmit a 2.4° beam; and a 6.5-foot (2.0 m) antenna might transmit a 1.23° beam. The narrower a radar's beam width is, the greater will be its ability to define targets; this is called BEARING DISCRIMINATION; see **Figure 21-14.**

Beam width is greater in the vertical plane than for the horizontal. It is much the same for all antennas regardless of size. Greater vertical beam width allows for vessel motion and has no discrimination penalty.

Radar sets are designed with a number of different range scales—longer ranges for coverage of a larger area and the earlier detection of "targets"; shorter ranges for better detail of nearby waters. The maximum range scales for radars found on board recreational boats generally vary from about 16 to 72 nautical miles, but these figures can be misleading. The maximum range at which an object can be detected is most limited by the height of the antenna—output power levels and size of the antenna are lesser factors in the performance of the set. Although a longer range may be used for tracking weather, such as thunderstorms or large rainsqualls, a boat radar is usually operated on a range scale of 4 to 8 miles. When navigating a channel, or in close quarters with other craft, the range scale will usually be reduced to a mile or less. Some models have a wider display and can be operated with a split screen, one part using a long-range setting and the other providing a shorter-range close-in view.

Radar Displays

Radar displays using CRTs "paint" a presentation of reflected radio waves on phosphor screens with each sweep of the antenna. Because the signal display of conventional radars has to be relatively weak to keep from burning an image into the phosphor, it fades rapidly. Newer "raster scan"

Figure 21-14 *The larger a radar antenna is, the better will be its bearing discrimination, the ability to separate two targets close together. In some instances, however, such as on a sailboat, it may be necessary to use a smaller antenna enclosed in a radome.*

radars with LCD displays can keep signals from fading before the next antenna sweep.

Digitally processed signals can be "frozen" to allow a more precise range or bearing to be taken on a detected object.

Most radars found on recreational vessels have a monochrome display in either green or amber. Some models offer varying levels of "quantization," which means they present the strongest echoes they receive in the darkest green or amber, and the weakest echoes received in the lighter shades of green or amber. More expensive radars provide a display that presents echoes of different strengths in different colors: Red for the strongest, yellow for those of medium strength, and blue or green for the weakest. Some models have an extra wide screen and can simultaneously display radar information at two different ranges, such as near-maximum range and close in.

Radar for All Sizes of Boats

Modern electronic technology has reduced the size of radar sets, and their demands for electrical power from the boat's electrical system, to the point that they can be installed in craft as small as 25 feet (7.6 m) or so. If your boat is this size or larger, you can, and should, consider the installation of this very useful item of electronic equipment.

Radar Capabilities

Radar displays allow an operator to select from a variety of scales ranging from ⅛ mile up to the unit's maximum range. Most use concentric circles ("rings") of light to divide the selected range into a number of equal units to allow rapid estimates of the distance to any object that is reflecting the antenna's transmitted radio waves. Most also offer at least one VARIABLE RANGE MARKER (VRM), a movable concentric circle that the operator can place directly over the image of a detected object with a knob, push-button, joystick, or trackball. The display will then read out digitally the range to the object. Another common feature is an ELECTRONIC BEARING LINE (EBL), a movable straight line that pivots around the center point of the screen, which the operator can place over the image of a detected object. The display will then digitally read out the relative bearing from the vessel to the object. More expensive radars offer multiple VRMs and EBLs.

Some radars allow the operator to zoom in on a portion of the display to present that segment in greater detail. While most radars display the vessel's position at the center of the screen, some radars allow the operator to "off-center" the display to provide greater coverage to one particular portion of the display.

The standard orientation of a radar display is "heads up"—the vessel's heading is always toward the 12 o'clock position on the radar screen. The display of radars that are interfaced with an electronic compass can present a "north-up" display in which compass north is at the 12 o'clock position on the screen. Some electronic compasses can be programmed to automatically compute variation and present true North at the 12 o'clock position on the screen of an interfaced radar.

More sophisticated radars also offer such features as echo tracking, which graphically presents the track of other vessels on the display screen. Some radar manufacturers also offer optional target plotter adapters, which allow selected models of their radars to track up to 10 targets simultaneously; display their range, bearing, and CLOSET POINT OF APPROACH (CPA); and sound an alarm if a target violates preset CPA limits. If these radars are also interfaced with an appropriate navigation sensor such as a GPS or Loran receiver, they can also display target courses in relative or true degrees and present the TIME TO CLOSEST POINT OF APPROACH (TCPA).

More sophisticated radars can be interfaced with navigation sensors such as GPS or Loran receivers to digitally display own vessel course and speed over the ground on the radar screens. Some can utilize read-only-memory (ROM) cards to display computerized chart representations on their screens and, if they are interfaced to appropriate navigation sensors, can graphically plot the vessel's track on either their radar picture or the chart representation.

Most radars allow a guard zone, all-round or sector only, to be drawn around the vessel on which they are installed, and sound an alarm if that zone is violated. This feature can be valuable as an anticollision device when underway, and also as an anchor watch. Many radars also can indicate if they detect radar operating on another vessel in their vicinity.

The Use of Radar

Radar offers an excellent means of extending the coverage provided by a visual lookout, especially at night and in reduced visibility. This greater range of detection affords more time for a vessel to maneuver in order to avoid another craft or a detected obstacle. With radar plot, an early determination can be made of another vessel's course and speed. Radar also helps when making a landfall from offshore; running a coast and picking up landmarks for fixes; or traveling in confined waters, entering an inlet, and the like. Radar has real advantages, even in the daytime, and of course becomes particularly helpful at night or in conditions of reduced visibility.

It is very important that every skipper fully understand that while the Navigation Rules require that a radar, if one is on board, be used in

COMPUTERS ON BOARD

Computers—in the form of microchips—are now at the heart of virtually every piece of marine electronic equipment, and increasingly, boaters are using on-board computer systems to assist them in the operation of their vessels.

With the advance of solid-state technology, which packages more and more power and versatility in smaller and smaller components, using a sophisticated personal computer with a rechargeable power supply on board a recreational vessel is not difficult or complicated.

Typical desktop personal computers require 120-volt AC power input, but that's because they are designed primarily for use on land where that is the power normally available. In fact, the computer circuits themselves run on less than 6 volts of DC electrical current, which is provided by the computer's "power supply" (a step-down transformer plus a rectifier that converts 120-volt AC power to multiple DC voltages such as 12, 5, or 3.3). The easiest way to use a personal computer on board a boat with 12-volt battery power is with an inverter that changes the battery's 12-volt DC power to 120-volt AC power, which the computer's power supply will then step down and rectify to the required voltages. The computer's power supply should be from a dedicated circuit with its own breaker on the main distribution panel to protect it from sudden voltage drops as other equipment comes on and off line. The computer should then be connected to the inverter through a surge protector to guard against sudden voltage spikes.

At 120-volt input, the current draw of a personal computer is about 2 amps (200 watts). If the AC power is being produced by an inverter, that equates to approximately a 23-amp DC draw on a 12-volt

A notebook computer can serve many purposes on a boat including navigation, log keeping, and administration of supplies and spare parts. It can also serve the same uses as a computer at home or in an office—word processing, data recording, and entertainment. In some instances, connections can be made to the Internet.

system, after allowing for the inverter's 15 percent efficiency loss. While this is an easily manageable power level on board a boat equipped with an AC generator, it could be too great for a vessel that relies strictly on an engine alternator to recharge its batteries.

A more practical approach on medium-size and smaller craft, especially those without an AC generator, is a portable "laptop" or "notebook" computer that can be operated for several hours on an internal battery; see the photo. With some portable computers, the battery can be recharged externally by using a small solid-state DC-DC voltage converter to change the boat's electrical power—actually about 13.2 volts—to an appropriate voltage for the computer's battery; great care should be taken to avoid damaging the battery by charging too rapidly or for too long a period of time. This should not be attempted with the battery installed in the computer unless specifically approved by the manufacturer. The drain from the boat's power system is so small—less than one amp—that it should present no problem. Some portable computers have connections for an external full-sized keyboard, mouse, printer, and even a monitor, making them, in effect, compact and lightweight equivalents of a desktop PC. More and more computers specifically designed for marine use are entering the market.

Available software includes programs for tide and current predictions, current sailing, Mercator and great circle sailing, celestial navigation, and other boating activities. And, of course, the computer can be used for the same word processing, database, and spreadsheet work as at home or the office; and the younger members of the crew can play their games. A primary application is with navigation software to serve as a chart plotter. Internet connections are frequently possible while in port, and may even be feasible while underway.

Precautions

• Computer equipment must be carefully protected from rain and spray. This equipment should be run periodically to ensure that internal parts are dry.

• Disk and CD-ROM drives and printers have moving parts that can be damaged by vibration and shock. They must be mounted securely and cushioned as much as possible. Laptop and notebook computers, being designed to travel, are more resistant to shock and vibration, but even they should be cushioned when underway.

• Computer circuits often generate radio interference and should be mounted well away from sensitive navigation and communications electronics.

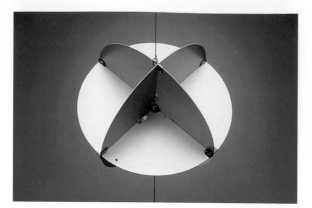

Figure 21-15 Whether or not your boat is equipped with a radar, it is highly advisable to use a passive radar reflector to make sure that your craft shows up on the screen of vessels that are using their radar. Without such a reflector, there is a good chance that your craft will not be detected by a ship's radar.

conditions of reduced visibility, *radar is not a substitute for a human lookout required by Rule 5*; refer to Chapter 5, and **Figure 5-06.**

Radar Piloting

Radar's ability to measure distance is also helpful in establishing fixes. A single bearing on an object whose position is known will provide only an LOP along which your vessel lies. Combining such a bearing, visual or radar, with the radar's ability to determine your distance from that same object allows you to determine a fix. Using radar to establish your distance from two or more objects whose location is known can also produce a fix. As range discrimination is usually better than bearing discrimination, a fix from two measurements of distance is to be preferred over one using two bearings. More on the use of radar in piloting will be found in Chapter 18.

Developing Radar Skills

It is not possible to simply install a radar on your boat and immediately use it effectively. For both navigation and collision avoidance, the scene shown on the display will require interpretation, and this will require both study and experience. The full value of having a radar on your boat will not be realized until you can use it skillfully and with confidence.

Most manuals that come with radar sets provide rudimentary information regarding the use of the many controls on the equipment. There are a number of books devoted to the user of radar, some focused particularly on small craft. There are also videotapes and programs for personal computers that can be run interactively to simulate radar operation. Some larger electronic stores offer instructional courses that are well worthwhile for a skipper not experienced in radar use.

Radar Detectors

In all but a few areas where they are illegal, RADAR DETECTORS will be found on many cars and trucks—they also have an application for boats (although not the same models). A radar detector is a small receiver with a small nonrotating antenna and a simple display. When this device detects incoming radar pulses, it will show a visual indication of the general direction from which they are coming; an audible alarm is also available. While very useful, particularly when operating short-handed, it must be remembered that no signal is returned to the vessel whose radar has "illuminated" your craft, and that skipper may be entirely unaware of your presence and location.

Passive Radar Reflectors

The strength of radar echoes is based on the reflectivity of objects that return a minute portion of the outgoing radio energy from the radar set. Such common boat-building materials as fiberglass have less reflectivity than metal, and thus are relatively poor radio wave reflectors.

A boat owner who does not have radar equipment on board can still use radar to increase safety by installing a PASSIVE RADAR REFLECTOR as a desirable "defensive" device to alert radar-equipped vessels in his vicinity as to his presence and position. Even radar-equipped craft should have a passive reflector as high as reasonably practical. Having an operating radar on board a boat does not increase the likelihood of its being detected by other vessels unless those vessels themselves carry operative equipment that detects the presence and source of radar emissions.

Most passive radar reflectors consist of thin metal sheets arranged in mutually perpendicular planes. These may fold for storage, but must be flat and rigid with respect to each other when open for use. A reflector with each surface only about 2 feet (60 cm) square can provide a strong return signal if properly used. For maximum effectiveness, a reflector should be hoisted from three corners so that one of the eight "pockets" is straight up; this is sometimes termed the "rain-catching" position; see **Figure 21-15.** In certain cases, the reflector planes are held in their optimum configuration within a fiberglass shell.

Radar Transponders

An active electronic device that detects the arrival of a radar pulse and returns its own pulse or pulses after an extremely short delay is termed a RADAR TRANSPONDER. They are placed on some major aids to navigation and other navigation-sensitive locations such as bridges—these are commonly called radar beacons, refered to as "racons." Racons are relatively low-powered and have a range of 6 to 8 miles if located on a buoy, farther if installed at a greater height. To conserve power, those on buoys are not operated continuously, but typically with a duty-cycle of 20 seconds on, 20 seconds off.

The transmitted pulses appear on a radar display as radial lines just beyond the echo of the detected object. The pulses can be read as dashes of the Morse code and racons are assigned various identifications consisting of single letters that are all dashes—T, M, and O. (Racons in some foreign waters may signal "D" [- · ·] on new and uncharted hazards.)

ONBOARD DATA NETWORKS

One of the more interesting developments in marine electronics has been the ability to interconnect various devices for the exchange of data—and continuing advances in data and video networking can be expected in the years ahead; see **Figure 21-16.**

A GPS receiver inputs information from a differential beacon receiver and outputs data to an autopilot. A VHF radio receives position information from a GPS or Loran receiver and adds that data to an outgoing distress message. A chart plotter receives depth information from an electronic sounder and includes that information in its display. A radar receives information on the vessel's course and speed from a GPS receiver and adds that to its screen. And many instruments can be used with a second display so that the same information is available in two locations. There are also LCD display-only units that can receive inputs from various navigation devices, switching from one to another as desired; The concentration of all displays in a single unit is a great space-saver on crowded helm consoles. Such devices can even be used to display the output from a TV set, VCR, or DVD player!

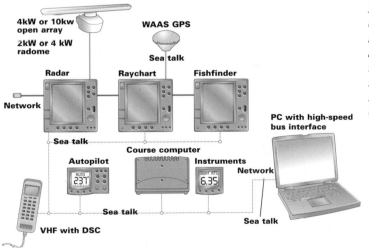

Figure 21-16 Many items of electronic equipment can be connected by a network so that information can be shared. It is advantageous, for example, for a fish finder to also display position data and course and speed information. A radar display may share space on a chart plotter, and many other combinations are possible.

In order that devices sending data, called "talkers," and devices receiving data, called "listeners," can understand each other, the National Marine Electronics Association (NMEA) has developed standards to be used by the makers of on-board electronic equipment. The standard NMEA 0180 was followed by NMEA 0183 in several versions; more recently NMEA 2000 has been published. In some instances, the standards were not followed exactly by a manufacturer and difficulties were encountered in connecting a pair of devices from different sources, but in general, the standards worked well. The best results and least problems were encountered if the two items of electronic equipment were from the same manufacturer. If purchasing items from different makers, be sure that you can return one or both if interoperability problems arise and cannot be overcome. NMEA 2000 is a more detailed specification and will be more rigidly enforced; interoperability problems should be less.

While manufacturers have used NMEA standards to send data to and from electronic units, it's more recently that they have developed their own video networks based on Ethernet protocols as used for computers in offices and homes; improved connectors are used to meet marine environmental conditions. The various devices are connected to a "hub" as in small businesses and homes with several computers. A different technique uses proprietary cables and software to link devices together in a string using T-connectors at all units except those at the ends of the string.

These networks usually have a trademarked name. They are quite satisfactory in use, but do have the limitation of requiring all devices from one manufacturer. Others use Arcnet, which does require a hub.

RADIO DIRECTION FINDING

Although radio direction finding in the low and medium frequency bands was the first electronic navigation system, equipment for this (known as RDF) has entirely disappeared from small craft. Such equipment was used in taking radio bearings on marine and aviation radiobeacons, AM-band broadcast stations and other ships using double-sideband (AM) radios in the MF band. These bearings were plotted on a chart in a manner similar to visual bearings. Often more than two bearings were taken, if possible, as radio bearings are less precise than visual observations. Now, however, much better means of positioning are available.

Marine Radiobeacons

The U.S. Coast Guard formerly operated more than 100 marine radiobeacons along and just offshore the coasts and the Great Lakes. Most of these have now been disestablished, and the remaining ones have been converted to transmit correctional information for GPS; the resulting Differential GPS (DGPS) positions are much more accurate than those from uncorrected GPS data; see above, page 729.

VHF Radio Direction Finding

Direction finders for the VHF band are of the automatic (ADF) type. Many USCG utility boats and cutters, and assistance towing vessels, have these devices on board for search and rescue efforts. The Coast Guard does not operate any radiobeacons on the VHF band, but the continuous transmission of the NOAA weather stations provide a good signal for determining an LOP; the range would be the same as in regular reception of weather information with an accuracy of 5 to 10 degrees. You

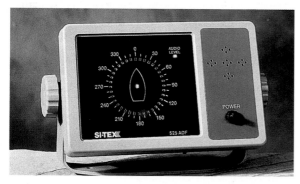

Figure 21-17 This add-on unit for VHF radio direction finding covers 130 to 180 MHz and is internally computer controlled. It can be attached to a conventional VHF radio to take bearings on other vessels, or to steer directly toward them. Bearings are shown by a bright red LED that appears on the azimuth scale within a half-second of signal reception. The VHF radio can still be used for all its normal functions.

must know the location of the transmitting antenna and have that plotted on the chart you are using; locations are shown on Marine Weather Services Charts published by NOS (see Chapter 24, page TK, and Appendix A). This will normally provide only one LOP, but in limited areas it may be possible to receive two weather stations and, therefore, to obtain a rough fix. Coast Guard stations and Marine Operators normally have multiple antenna sites, and it is not possible to use their signals for taking bearings for lack of knowledge of which antenna was currently being used.

Equipment for VHF direction finding may be either a self-contained unit or an add-on for a conventional communications transceiver; see **Figure 21-17.** In the latter case, no modification is required of the basic radio and it can continue to be used for its normal functions. But in both cases, a special antenna is required to sense the direction from which the VHF signals are coming; an automatic switch protects the RDF unit when the set transmits; see **Figure 21-18.** The display can be either the relative bearing of the source of the signals, accurate to about 10 degrees, or the cross-track error for heading directly to the other vessel.

The primary application of VHF direction finding is "homing," the determination of the direction in which the source of the signal lies, and the direct course to that source. This is extremely helpful in most expeditiously reaching a vessel in need of assistance.

Another common use of a VHF ADF set is taking bearings, or homing on radio transmissions of vessels reporting successful fishing activities. It must be noted, though, that such actions are illegal. The use of intercepted radio messages not addressed to you for your own benefit is prohibited by federal law (47 USC 605 and 18 USC 2511) and FCC regulation (47 CFR 80.88).

MISCELLANEOUS EQUIPMENT

Many small items of electronic equipment can be installed on a boat for greater safety and convenience of those on board. Remember that each extra item will add to the load on the battery and elec-

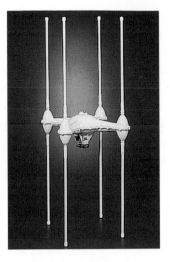

Figure 21-18 Radio direction finding on the VHF band requires an antenna of special design in addition to the actual ADF unit. It must be mounted in the clear and properly oriented.

trical wiring. Although they are all not directly related to navigation purposes, they are nonetheless considered important by many boaters.

Autopilots

Autopilots are becoming more and more common on smaller and smaller craft, because they offer two considerable operational advantages and at least one safety aspect.

But first, what is an autopilot? It is an electronic device using mechanical or hydraulic power to steer a boat (or ship). The name is somewhat unfortunate as the equipment does not perform any true "piloting" functions, such as determining position or deciding what course to steer to a destination. A better name might be an "automatic helmsman." An autopilot is basically a device that will ensure that a boat is maintained on a preset heading. More advanced models can receive positional information and adjust that heading to make good a desired track.

The operational advantages are: (1) the person at the helm is relieved of the job of constantly steering the boat, which can be tiresome and tedious (and cold, wet, and uncomfortable at times on some craft); and (2), the autopilot will in many, if not most, cases do a better job than a human for maintaining a desired heading! The safety aspect comes into play because the person at the helm will have much more time to act as a lookout for other vessels and hazards to navigation.

The heading sensor is usually an electronic compass of the flux-gate type, which should be installed in a stable location (usually low in the hull) and well away from varying magnetic influences (steady influences can be compensated out by the autopilots computer). Data from this unit is sent to the central processor, which can be located anywhere that is convenient. From this electronic "brain," signals are then sent to a mechanical or hydraulic drive unit to turn the rudder(s) in a direction that will correct a heading error. To make control more effective and smoother, a rudder angle sensor will provide "feedback" to the control unit. Sailboats may use a masthead wind vane to maintain a steady heading with respect to the apparent wind, and may be able to automatically take up a heading 100° (or other value set in) greater or lesser following a tacking maneuver.

The power requirements from a boat's electrical system are moderate and usually cause no problems. The convenience achieved by having an autopilot will be much appreciated by all on board who stand a watch at the helm. Although there may be some instances where it will be necessary for a human to steer—a significant following or quartering sea—you will be amazed and satisfied as to the large percentage of the time that an autopilot can take over the job of steering your craft.

Auxiliary Functions & Features

As noted above, many autopilots will accept positional information in the form of CROSS-TRACK ERROR from a GPS or Loran receiver. This will alter the desired heading to compensate for offsetting influences such as currents or crosswinds.

A DODGE feature will allow the set heading to be overridden temporarily to avoid an obstruction in the waters ahead; the prior heading will be resumed when the dodging action has ended.

A handheld remote unit will make it possible to control the autopilot from a position away from the helm. Various alarms are included in many autopilots. An OFF-COURSE ALARM will be sounded if the vessel gets more than a preselected distance from the established track. A WATCH ALARM can be set to sound an audible signal at regular intervals until manually turned off—no more sleeping undisturbed at the helm! Some

---

OTHER ELECTRICAL & ELECTRONIC EQUIPMENT

- Battery chargers (*Chapter 19*)
- Carbon-monoxide detectors (*Chapter 11*)
- Electronic compasses (*Chapter 13*)
- EPIRBs (*Chapter 20*)
- Fuel-vapor detectors (*Chapter 11*)
- Inverters (*Chapter 19*)
- NAVTEX receivers (*Chapter 20*)
- Weather instruments (*Chapter 24*)

---

autopilots can be used in a POWER-STEERING MODE without the heading sensor being active.

Rudder Position Indicators

A RUDDER POSITION INDICATOR is a very simple instrument much like the rudder angle sensor of an autopilot (some autopilots include a display of this information). On a stand-alone device, the display is often an "upside-down" electrical meter whose pointer will simulate the position of the rudder, straight down showing that the rudder is centered; a marked scale will show the extent to which the rudder(s) had been turned to either side.

A quick glance at this instrument just before getting underway will often prevent your having an unpleasant surprise!

Speed Measuring Instruments

A GPS or Loran receiver will usually give you information on the speed that you are making good over the bottom and toward your objective. But it may also be desirable to know the speed of your craft through the water. Some nonelectronic devices do this by measuring water pressure of a sensor facing forward, but more accurate readings are obtained by using an electronic device. Most speed logs have a very small paddle-wheel extending down from the bottom of the boat, connected by a small cable to a control head that translates the revolutions of the wheel into a digital readout of speed, which can be stated in user-selected units such as statute miles per hour, knots, or kilometers per hour; see **Figure 21-19**.

Some units can add in a time factor and also provide distances traveled through the water.

Engine Synchronization

On twin-engine craft, a lack of synchronization between the two power trains can produce an annoying "beat note," and can even be damaging. There are available electronic devices to indicate a lack of synchronization so that the helmsman can take corrective action. There are also electro-mechanical units that will automatically adjust the throttle of a "slave" engine to bring it into step with a "master" engine.

Alarm Systems

There are many situations on a boat where an alarm system may prevent an unsafe situation or an expensive failure. Engine alarms will indicate low oil pressure or excessively high cooling water temperature; a separate alarm may alert the skipper to a loss of water flow in the exhaust system. A high-water alarm in the bilge will give a warning of water inflow greater than the bilge pumps can handle. An anchor watch alarm associated with an electronic navigation system will quickly bring attention to the fact that the anchor is not holding firmly.

Security alarm systems will help protect against burglary and vandalism; these may also be connected to the high bilge water alarm mentioned above and fire sensors. Security alarms may be connected to sound the boat's horn, monitored in marina offices, or by professional security services; some will even initiate a phone call to the home of the owner of the craft.

Entertainment Systems

Just because you are out in your boat, doesn't mean that you have to be without your "news, weather, and sports." Or even without your music. Even the smallest of craft have room for a portable tape, CD, or MP3 player. Just be sure that your gear is reasonably water-resistant, or protect it well from spray and rain.

Boats with a cabin can have more sophisticated entertainment systems, with built-in radios, music players, and even TVs and DVDs.

Equipment requiring 120V AC power can be used when alongside a pier or underway if you have an auxiliary generating plant, commonly called a "genset"; see Chapter 19, page 658. Smaller items can be operated for reasonable periods of a few hours from an inverter running on the boat's electrical system—just don't overdo it and fail to leave enough power in your battery for starting the engine when you want to head for home.

VCR tapes and DVDs will provide you with movies, if that is what you wish for entertainment. A good choice is a set combining a small TV set, often 13-inch size, with a VCR or DVD player. Sometimes your home berth will be within the normal service area of one or more TV stations; if not, an external omnidirectional amplified antenna can be mounted on a short mast on a powerboat or part way up the mast of a sailboat. This can also provide good reception of FM radio stations.

There are two new radio services with signals from satellites that provide coverage over all the lower 48 states and to about 300 miles off shore. Intended primarily for automobile reception, they are well adaptable for use on boats. The two systems—Sirius and XM Radio—are generally similar, offering 100 or more channels with a wide selection of digital-quality programs of music, news, weather, sports, and other entertainment, some without commercials. Receivers are available from several manufacturers and are reasonably priced; some are complete, others play through an existing FM radio; all require their own special antenna to receive the satellite signals.

Figure 21-19 Small panel instruments can digitally show speed through the water and distance traveled. This information is sometimes shown on a larger instrument that also shows other data such as elapsed time, water temperature, depth, etc.

Inland Boating

Piloting & Seamanship on Inland Waters—Rivers, Canals & Lakes
The Proper Procedures for Using Locks

Boating on inland rivers, canals, and lakes is different in some respects from that on coastal rivers, bays, and sounds, and along saltwater shores. The differences are not total; many aspects of safe recreational boating are the same on all waters. But where differences do exist, they should be carefully considered.

The Pleasures of Inland Boating

Some of the finest cruising is found on the network of rivers and lakes giving access to areas far removed from tidal waters. Throughout the United States there are more than 30,000 miles (48,000 km) of waterways navigable by small boats. Using the Mississippi, the Great Lakes, the N.Y. State Canal System, and other waterways linking these with the Atlantic and Gulf Intracoastal Waterways, a boater can circumnavigate the entire eastern portion of the United States, a cruise of more than 5,000 miles (8,000 km). Only a small-portion of this would be in the open sea, although the Great Lakes are, of course, sizeable bodies of water, comparable to the ocean insofar as small craft cruising is concerned; see **Figure 22-01.**

To these vast networks of interconnected waterways must be added the many navigable, but isolated, stretches of rivers and the thousands of lakes large enough for recreational boating. Many of these lakes have been formed behind dams in regions far removed from what is normally thought of as "boating areas." Today, there are few places where one would be surprised to see a sign reading "Marina" or "Boating Supplies."

Limitations

All cruising areas have their disadvantages and limitations; see **Figure 22-02.** Some rivers and lakes may have shoals and rocks. Other rivers may have problems with overhead clearance; a fixed bridge might arbitrarily determine your "head of navigation."

On some of the principal inland waterways, the overhead clearance is severely limited—on some sections of the N.Y. State Canal System it is only 15.5 feet (4.7 m). Boaters must unstep masts or fold down signal masts, radio antennas, and outriggers. Fixed overhead power cables are usually high enough to cause no problems to masted vessels, however, and their clearance is noted on charts. Unusually high water stages on rivers reduce overhead clearance by the amount of the rise over the "normal levels"; use extra caution at such times. Look for notes that explain what the clearances are based on; for instance, charts for the Ohio River give vertical clearance for high water, based on 1936-67 levels; refer to **Figure 22-10.**

RIVER BOATING

While rivers seldom offer vast open expanses where you will need the usual techniques of coastline piloting, they do require special piloting skills. Local lore often outweighs certain piloting principles that are the coastal skipper's law, because a river's ever-changing conditions put a premium on local knowledge; see **Figure 22-03.** River navigation is thus often more an art than a science.

River Piloting

The fundamental difference is, of course, the closeness of the shore, usually with easily identifiable landmarks or aids to navigation. Knowing where you are, therefore, is *not* a problem. The skill of piloting here lies in directing your boat to avoid hazards—on many rivers, this is not a simple matter; see **Figure 22-04.**

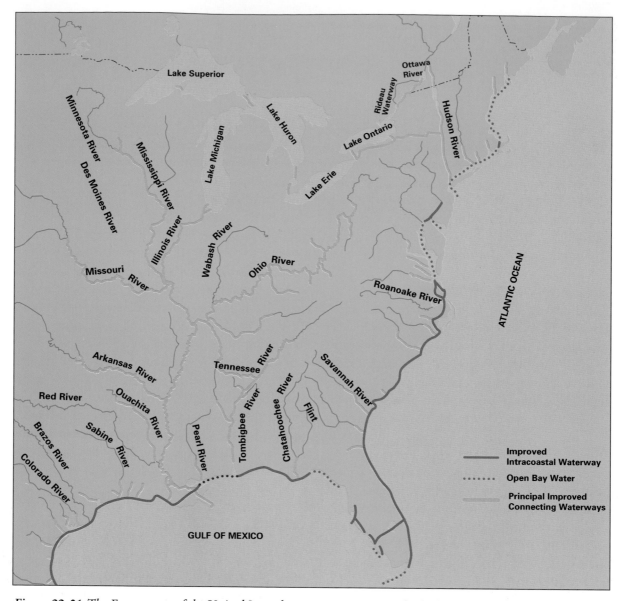

Figure 22-01 *The Eastern part of the United States has an extensive network of inland waterways, including those that are natural, improved, or entirely man-made. On the Pacific Coast, there are the Sacramento and Colorado rivers, and throughout the nation there are many lakes and reservoirs that provide boating opportunities.*

Water-Level Changes

Inland waters are termed "nontidal," but that doesn't mean they have no fluctuations in water level; see **Figure 22-05**. The variations are apt to be of a seasonal nature, such as spring freshets, loaded with debris, flood down from the headwaters, overflow banks, and course rapidly on down to the sea. The annual changes in level can be astounding; at St. Louis the seasonal fluctuation in river level from winter-spring flood conditions to

low level in late summer and fall may be as much as 50 feet (15 m). In smaller navigable streams, sudden heavy rains may raise water level several feet (about a meter) or more in a matter of hours.

River Currents

Broadly speaking, river currents, although they fluctuate in velocity, will always trend in one direction—from the headwaters to the mouth. Tidal rivers may nevertheless have strong tidal

Figure 22-02 Each waterway system has at least a few of its own variations on the basic U.S. system. Careful reading of chart notes, Light Lists, and Local Notices to Mariners is just as important for inland skippers as for coastal navigators. Visiting boaters should make a practice of seeking out local knowledge.

Figure 22-04 River piloting differs from that in coastal waters in that the skipper usually can tell at all times exactly where he is. The navigational problem consists mainly of avoiding underwater hazards such as shoals, sand bars, and snags. On many rivers, aids to navigation are not numbered in the usual sense, but rather carry a dayboard marked with the number of statute miles upriver from a designated starting point.

Figure 22-03 The most often encountered hazards in river boating are shoals, sand bars, and submerged rocks. In man-made lakes, decaying trees and stumps may be present.

conditions at the mouth, which back the water up so that you can take advantage of a favorable current going *upstream*. On the Hudson, for example, an economy-minded skipper electing to run at 9 to 10 knots can time his trip to carry a favorable current all the way from New York City to Albany, 150 miles (241 km) inland. Tides at this latter city, even so far from the sea, may range in excess of 6 feet (1.8 m), although at other points far downstream the range will be only half that amount.

Current Strengths The strength of river currents varies widely from river to river, and from season to season for any particular river. Speeds on some sections of the Mississippi range from 1 to 6 mph (1.6 and 9.7 km/hr) under average conditions. At extreme high-water stages, current strengths may be much greater—9 mph (14.5 km/hr) or more in narrow and constricted areas.

River currents sometimes attain such speeds that navigation upstream is not feasible, although capably handled boats can be taken down safely. In the St. Lawrence River Galop Rapids, for

Figure 22-05 The Guntersville Yacht Club in Alabama uses floating piers to accommodate the seasonal fluctuation in water level.

instance, the current may run as fast as 13 mph (20.9 km/h). Some river boats have power enough to ascend certain rapids, but as a general rule rapids are best avoided in favor of the canals and locks that bypass them, unless the skipper has local knowledge or engages the service of a local pilot; see also "Locks & Dams," page 765.

"Selecting" Your Current River current characteristics are of the utmost importance to the masters of deep-draft commercial vessels. The surface current acting on a small boat may actually be contrary to that which grips a large ship's keel near the river bottom. Even surface currents vary from bank to midstream. Friction of the bank and bottom slows the water. The commercial skipper—to whom fuel costs and time of run are especially important—knows this difference. He uses the strength of the midstream current for his run downstream, and on the way back upstream he runs as close to the bank as he safely can, even turning into small coves, to take advantage of the countercurrents.

You may be less concerned with the economic factors that the professional pilot weighs so carefully, but you can profitably heed the same principles. You can cut running time and fuel costs by running courses that make the river's current work for you, or minimize its adverse effect. A 12-mph boat in a 4-mph current is making good either 8 or 16 mph, depending on direction of travel—a significant effect! Even for a 20-mph craft the difference between 16- and 24-mph speeds is 50 percent.

Channels at River Bends

As a river flows around a bend, it tends to carve out the outside of the curve and slow down around the inside, depositing silt, forming shoals and ultimately a sand bar out from the point around which it is turning. Man-made structures and unusual bottom contours may alter this tendency, but it generally means that river channels going around bends will shoal on one side and deepen on the other over time; see **Figure 22-06.**

Study a river chart that gives depth (NOS charts, for example) and note this river flow characteristic. Then when you are on a river whose charts do not give depths (charts of the Mississippi and Ohio rivers do not), you will have a better feeling for where to find deeper water. With this understanding of natural channels at bends you will be less likely to run straight courses from marker to marker, cutting corners and risking getting hung up on a bar.

Figure 22-06 By staying in mid-channel, this small boat avoids the shoals that tend to build up along the inside of river bends. A deep-draft vessel may need to follow the outside curve of the bend in order to make sure that there is sufficient depth.

Figure 22-07 Generally, the outside edge of a river bend provides the deepest water, The contour of the riverbank is also an indication of the underwater contour, but experience and judgment are required for correct interpretation. Local knowledge is a valuable commodity for a visitor.

The proper course at each end is, of course, a curved line roughly following the trend of the river as a whole. If there are no aids to navigation to guide you, keep about a quarter of the river's width off the *outside* bank at a bend in the river.

On some river charts, even the markings showing the topography ashore give clues to the river itself. Contour lines crowded close together near shore indicate a cliff rising steeply from the bank, with a good chance of deep water close under the bluff. The cliff may also be a landmark to steer by; see **Figure 22-07.**

Channel Crossing Where a river bends in an "S" curve—a curve in one direction followed by a curve in the opposite direction—the straight section between the curves is termed a CROSSING. On major rivers, these are usually marked by ranges or directional lights. In some instances, such as at low-water stages, seasonal buoys may be added to mark the route of best water; these buoys may be found in pairs or singly; see below.

Aids to Navigation

The basic U.S. system of buoyage (see Chapter 14) is used on the Great Lakes. The larger inland rivers, those that are navigable from the sea, have aids to navigation maintained by the U.S. Coast Guard. Many of their lights, buoys, and daybeacons are like those discussed in Chapter 14, but a few are of special design for their "inland" purpose. Some rivers under state jurisdiction may still have aids to navigation conforming to the now-obsolete Uniform State Waterway Marking System, but most waterways have been converted to the system used in waters marked by the U.S. Coast Guard.

The "Right" and "Left" Banks of a River Designation of a river's banks may at first be confusing. Left and right banks—called "port" and "starboard" banks—are named relative to a vessel's course *downstream*, not to the vessel herself; the left (port) bank is the one on your left as you face in the direction that the river flows; see **Figure 22-08.**

On the New York State Canal System, however, when regulations refer to the "starboard" side of the Canal, they mean the right side when entering from Waterford (near Albany). Thus the starboard side of the Champlain Canal is the east side; but on the Erie Canal westward, the starboard side is the north side. Check your charts. There are also numerous marinas that provide dockage, fuel, and other services.

Mileage Markers A "mile" on an inland waterway is a statute (land) mile, not a nautical mile. Aids to navigation along many major rivers

Figure 22-08 Particular attention must be paid to the notion of the "right" and "left" banks of a river. The choice is not always intuitive, but is fundamental to the coloring of buoys.

are conspicuously marked with mileages showing the distance from a designated reference point; refer to **Figure 22-04**. It is always easy to get a "fix"; just relate the mileage on a daybeacon or light structure with the mileage figures on your chart. These mileage figures often take the place of arbitrary odd and even numbers used on coastal waters, and they are helpful in computing distance and speed.

Daymarks   The Western Rivers Buoyage System uses PASSING DAYMARKS—square green with green reflective borders on the right side (descending the river) or triangular red with red reflective borders on the left side. There are also CROSSING DAYMARKS that are diamond-shaped, red or green as appropriate, with small reflective squares of the same color in each corner. These indicate that the channel is crossing from one bank to the other.

Daymarks on some rivers consist of two white boards on posts or trees on shore, in the form of a large "X"; refer to **Figure 22-04.**

Lights   Most lights on major rivers, such as the Mississippi, show through 360°—they are visible all around the horizon. Sometimes a beam projects in one direction only, however, or the intensity of an all-round light is increased in a certain direction by a special lens. The beam's width varies with the locations; a narrower beam marks a more critical channel. Flashing lights on the right (proceeding downstream) side of the river show a single green or white flash; those on the left side show double red or white flashes.

Generally speaking, lights on the "Western Rivers" (see Chapter 4) are placed strategically at upper and lower ends of "crossings" as marks to steer by, with additional lights between as needed. Where there are no crossings, lights along the banks serve as passing lights—lights that mark specific points along the banks. Your chart will show how a specific light should be used.

Buoys   The skipper who is familiar with the basic U.S. system of buoyage will have no difficulty with buoyage on rivers. Buoys generally follow the same basic principles: green can-type buoys on the left and red nun-type buoys on the right when proceeding upstream from seaward.

On the Mississippi and its tributaries, many buoys are unnumbered.

Buoys on the Mississippi River carry reflectors similar to those used on shore aids—red on the channel's right (when ascending—returning from the sea, as in "red, right, returning"—see Chapter 14, page 485) and green on those on the left side. Lighted buoys show a red light (double flash) if on the right side of a channel (ascending) and a green light (single flash) if on the left side; a few buoys on either side show a white flashing light in the same single or double flash pattern. Buoys marking wrecks at the side of a channel show a quick flashing light of the appropriate color.

Buoys marking channel junctions or obstructions that can be passed on either side are horizontally banded either green-over-red or red-over-green as in the IALA system. If lighted, they show a group (2 + 1) flashing light of the same color as the top band.

Caution Required   In all cases, check buoys ahead of time by referring to your charts; some rivers deviate from conventional systems.

Ranges   On some of our major rivers, like the Hudson and the Connecticut, where channels through flats are stabilized and maintained by dredging, ranges with conspicuous markers on shore will help you stay within narrow channel limits. If you align the front and rear markers properly, you can hold your course safely in mid-channel despite any offsetting forces of current or wind.

Buoys and daymarks used on the Western Rivers are illustrated along with those used on other waters in Chapter 14; see page 501.

River Charts

River charts are commonly issued in the form of books, the pages covering successive short stretches of the river in strip form. A typical example is the bound volume published annually by the Mississippi River Commission, Vicksburg, Miss., to cover that river from Cairo, Illinois, to the Gulf of Mexico. The scale is 1:62,500 (roughly 1 inch = 1 mile, or 1.6 cm = 1 km). All depth information (with a few exceptions) and detailed positions of rocks, reefs,

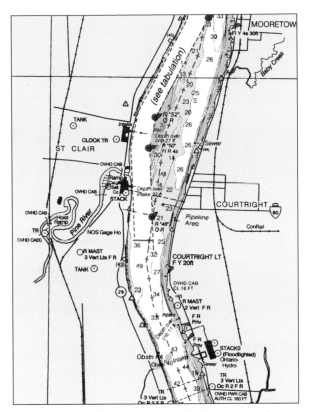

Figure 22-09 This section of NOS Chart 14852 shows the boundary between Canada (on the right) and the United States. Depths are reference to the Great Lakes datum and will vary with changing lake levels.

River charts are usually on a "polyconic" projection (see Chapter 15), and elevations normally refer to a specified mean water level.

Variations in River Charts River charts from different sources, such as the Army Corps of Engineers or NOS do not all use the same symbol and coloring scheme; see **Figure 22-09.** Before you use one, study it very carefully—particularly its LEGEND. This gives aids to navigation symbols, abbreviations, topographic and hydrographic information, and often illustrations of characteristics peculiar to that chart. The symbols for buoys on charts of the Ohio River, for example, are unique to that waterway and may cause initial confusion to strangers unless carefully studied; see **Figure 22-10.**

Upper and Lower Mississippi River charts show water in blue and man-made features in black; red is used for the sailing line, aids to navigation, and submerged features.

The book of Illinois Waterway charts shows the main channel in white with shoal areas tinted blue; land areas are colored yellow.

A booklet of charts for Navigation Pools 25 and 26 of the Mississippi River shows hazard areas—depths under 6 feet (1.8 m)—in bright red shading, harbors or anchorage areas with an anchor symbol, and the availability of fuel, water, marine railways, launching ramps, and repair and docking facilities.

Charts in the New York State Canals book, NOS Chart 14786, resemble the coastal charts described in Chapter 15. Land areas are screened gold tint, channels 12 feet (3.7 m) deep or more are white, with lesser depths light blue and depth contour lines for 6 and 12 feet (1.8 and 3.7 m), and black lines delineating the banks. Buoy symbols have magenta discs if they are lighted. Aids to navigation are numbered, and scattered depth figures give the skipper a good idea as to whether he dare venture out of the channel to seek an anchorage or for any other reason. Rocks and wrecks are indicated with standard symbols from Chart No. 1; see Chapter 15. Arrows indicating current flow direction, used on many other inland charts, do not appear on those of New York inland waterways.

shoals, and ledges that are shown on coastal charts are omitted. In their place, the course of the river is traced in blue tint between heavy black lines delineating the banks. A broken red line indicates the channel. Navigation lights are shown by a star and dot symbol with a number showing its distance upstream from a reference point—in this case, AHP, "Above the Head of Passes." The Head of Passes is the point not far above the mouth of the river where the river splits into separate channels ("passes") leading through the delta into the Gulf. Mileages are given every five miles (statute), with small red circles at one-mile intervals. Mileages above and below the Head of Pass appear in red. A detailed alphabetical table lists all towns, cities, bridges, mouths of tributary rivers, and other important features adjacent to the main channel, with distances (AHP) in miles and number of the chart on which the feature appears.

Figure 22-10 On this Army Corps of Engineers chart of the Cumberland River, of Tennessee and Kentucky, locations of bulletin boards that show river stages are shown, as well as the reference point for gauge readings. Symbols for nun and can buoys differ from those used on NOS charts. These and other river chart symbols are shown in the legend at right, excerpted from the chart.

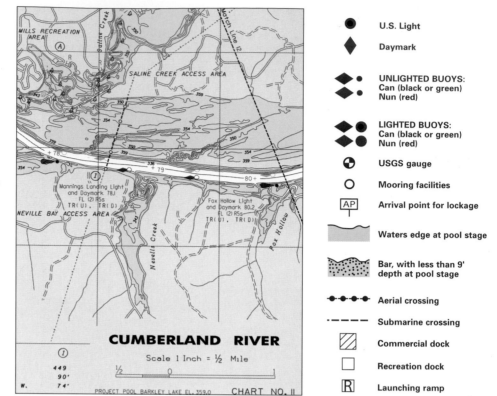

Missing from the typical river chart is the compass rose of coastal and offshore charts which enables the navigator to lay a compass course. Instead river charts generally carry an arrow indicating true North. To make the best use of space on the printed sheet, North is rarely toward the top of the chart; refer to **Figure 22-10.**

Publications

Charts can convey a great amount of information, and you should always use the most detailed and latest editions you can get. Yet for space reasons, these charts cannot show all you need to know. Valuable additional data is published in the form of books and pamphlets; see also Appendix A.

U.S. Army Corps of Engineers Publications The Army Engineers at Vicksburg, Mississippi, publishes a pamphlet called *Mississippi River Navigation,* which contains not only interesting background information on Mississippi River navigation, but also a few pages of explicit instructions "For Part-Time Pilots."

Since channels, water levels, and other conditions on the Mississippi, Ohio, and other major rivers are constantly changing, the river boater must keep posted on the latest information at all times. Army Engineer District and Division offices issue several regular publications about current conditions. There are variously termed *Divisional Bulletins, Navigational Bulletins, Navigational Notices, Notices to Navigational Interests* (weekly), and *Special Notices to Navigation Interests* (as required). These small publications show up-to-date river conditions, such as channel depths and widths, estimated current velocities, controlling bridge clearances for specified sketches of rivers, construction projects and other hazards, and facilities like marine railways and lifts.

U.S. Coast Guard Notices The 8th Coast Guard District, with Headquarters in New Orleans, issues a *Western Rivers Edition* of *Local Notices to Mariners* covering changes in aids to navigation, hazards, etc., for the Mississippi River System. The USCG also issues *Channel Reports* noting the least depth found by Coast Guard cutters and buoy tenders on their river patrols.

Light List One of the most helpful documents to the river skipper is the U.S. Coast Guard's *Light List, Volume V*, covering all of the Mississippi River System. It tabulates lights, buoys, and other aids to navigation and gives mileages (in statute miles) from a specified point. Aids are described in greater detail than chart symbols and abbreviations can provide; see **Figure 22-11.**

Navigation "Tools"

On most rivers—unlike other waters—there is usually no need to plot a course or bearing, so there is little use of a compass. Generally, a binocular will be used to sight from one navigational aid to the next. In fog, most recreational boat traffic comes to a near-standstill, although commercial vessels normally carry on with radar. This does not mean you can dispense with compasses on all inland rivers; some are wide enough that you can continue in fog using a compass, speed curve, watch or clock, *and due caution*. Also, some rivers feed into large lakes.

Shoals & Dredging

Shoaling is a serious problem in most rivers, and dredging in many rivers is nearly continuous. Spring floods build up current velocities, stir up silt in river bottoms, wash away parts of riverbanks, and carry all this dirt downriver in suspension, to be deposited as mud flats and sand bars where the strength of the current lessens; these flats and bars become hazards to navigation.

The Connecticut River is a good example of the shoaling problem; its channels must be dredged to authorized depths each year, at great expense. In the Mississippi River, a jellied mass of muck, called "flocculation," is deposited as sediment on the river bottom to a depth of 10 to 15 feet (3.0-4.6 m) each year. Deep-draft vessels will plow through it, and high-water stages of the river flushes it out into the Gulf, so the Army Engineers do not bother to dredge it at low-water stages. Over the centuries, this is how the river's delta has been built up.

Shoals or bars that build up at the mouth of a river, or at the confluence of two rivers, can cause a serious problem. Rough seas and difficult wave patterns can build up here when strong out-flowing currents are opposed by a crosswind.

"Eyeball" Piloting

Much of a river pilot's success depends on his acquired skill of interpreting what he sees. For example, no flat statement can be made about what certain surface conditions reveal about relative depths of water, although they do present clues within the context. On one hand, where there is a chop in the channel there may be areas of smoother water over the bars, especially if there is any weed growth present. On the other hand there may be wind-current conditions where the channel will be comparatively smoother with ripples revealing the bars. The experienced pilot will know which condition prevails.

(1) No.	(2) Name and Location	(3) Position	(4) Characteristic	(5) Height	(6) Range	(7) Structure	(8) Remarks
		MISSISSIPPI RIVER (Louisiana) - Eighth District					
13475	ENGLISH TURN LIGHT 80A LDB mile 78.3.	29 52 42 N 89 57 36 W	Fl R 2.5s	22	5	TR on dolphin.	
13482	Lower 12 Mile Point Anchorage Lower Daybeacon 78.6	29 53 00 N 89 57 24 W				NY on pile.	Ra ref.
13482.5	STOLT-NIELSON DOCK LIGHT LDB mile 79.6	29 52 17 N 89 56 44 W	Fl R 2.5	10		On dock.	Private aid.
13483	Lower 12 Mile Point Anchorage Upper Daybeacon 80.8	29 52 06 N 89 55 24 W				NY on pile.	Ra ref.

Figure 22-11 Information on the charts for the Mississippi River system including the Illinois Waterway is supplemented by the USCG Light List, Volume V, which provides more details than can be shown on the charts.

In some narrower river channels, with wind against current, a small sea builds up in which the larger waves disclose the deeper water and grow smaller until there are no seas at the channel's edge. Under any conditions, the experienced boater will quickly learn to take advantage of nature's signs.

Watch Your Wake In unfamiliar waters, even your wake can give a clue to the safety of your course. As it rolls off into shallow water, its smooth undulations give way to a sharper formation, even cresting on the flats in miniature "breakers." When the waves reach a shoal or a flooded area where submerged stumps are close to the surface, the difference will show. If your wake closes up toward your stern and appears short and peaked, sheer off, and fast, away from the side of the channel where this telltale signal appears.

Practice Makes Perfect As you develop a sense of river piloting, you'll become more conscious of the actual track you should make good over the bottom relative to shoals and the sides of channels. Where currents do occasionally flow diagonally across your course, you will allow for them instinctively and look astern frequently to help maintain that sense of position. *Always know to which side you should turn if the water shoals.*

Local Knowledge

Not even the best of charts and publications can "tell all" about a particular stretch of a river. Rivers are particularly prone to seasonal or irregular changes, and if you are new to a specific portion of a river, you should take every chance to ask experienced local people about hazards or recent changes.

River Seamanship

Boaters on inland rivers are subject to many of the general requirements for safety and good seamanship covered in other chapters. They must also be prepared for the special conditions that relate to specific bodies of waters. For example, boat handling at piers, and on entering or leaving slips, may be complicated by swift river currents. Grounding hard on river shoals may be more troublesome than it is on tide-

water, where the next rising tide will often free a boat without any other assistance.

River Cruising

Cruising can be exceptionally enjoyable on rivers, but requires careful planning and execution. Problems of where to make fast or anchor for the night are a part of cruising in any waters. On rivers you can often find shelter from blows close at hand, yet you will encounter areas big enough to work up a sizeable chop or even seas, especially when wind opposes current. You'll also need protection from wakes and wash of passing river traffic, and you need to decide whether to seek the seclusion of quiet anchorages off the beaten track, or the activity associated with towns and cities.

New marinas on many inland waters—the Tennessee-Tombigbee Waterway, for example—have been a boon to river cruising. They offer a place to make fast for the night, and easy access to fuel and supplies.

Safety Harbors and Landings Many rivers now provide safety harbors and landings for use in bad weather, mechanical difficulty, or other emergencies; their locations are shown on charts. Safety harbors are usually coves off the navigable channel. Direction boards on shore indicate the entrance, and cross boards mark the upper and lower limits.

Safety landings are areas where the banks have been cleared of stumps, boulders, snags, or other underwater hazards so that boats can safely come to shore, with upper and lower limits marked by direction boards. These signs are typically color-coded; for instance, on the Tennessee, white if a 9-foot (2.7 m) depth is available at all water stages, orange if this depth is not available at lower levels.

The Erie Canal provides terminals at intervals along its route; these are only occasionally in use by commercial vessels, and are available to recreational craft at other times. The terminals are concrete with rather rough faces, so you will need fenders and fender boards.

To allow for the seasonal range in water levels (or stages) most Western River marinas and yacht clubs are afloat on strings of barges. At low-water stages, you may have a long climb up the riverbank to get to town.

Anchoring

Your chart will often reveal a likely place to anchor for the night. A widening of the river may offer you the chance to get out of the reach of traffic, or a small tributary or slough may invite exploration (enter with caution and check depths as you go), or the natural configuration of riverbanks and bars may provide a natural "harbor" with complete protection. Islands in midriver often leave a secondary channel for small boats on the side opposite that used by deeper draft commercial vessels. When a river cuts a channel behind a section of bank, a "towhead" is formed. Sometimes these are filled in or dammed across at the upper end by river deposits, forming a natural protected harbor that can be entered from the lower end.

You may also be able to get your boat behind a pile dike—a structure designed to keep river-banks from washing away. The dike juts into the river and, by tying up to one of the piles just inside the outer end on the downstream side, you will be protected from passing traffic as well as from floating debris.

Use Caution Outside Channels When entering sloughs between islands or between an island and the bank, beware of submerged wing dams at the upstream end. To be safe, enter and leave from the downstream end.

When anchoring on the larger rivers near a sandbar or island—or when beaching a small boat there to go ashore—it's wise to pick the down-stream rather than the upper end. If your anchor drags, or if you somehow get aground on the upstream end, the current will be pushing you harder ashore. Water at the downstream end is likely to be quieter and the eddies that normally exist there may help to free you.

Sandy bars that are exposed at low water may be quite unstable. Be careful when using them for camping or swimming.

Check Characteristics of the Bottom The character of the bottom varies widely on inland waterways. Particularly in their lower reaches, river bottoms are often soft mud, so you should carry at least one broad-fluked anchor of a design that will dig down until it reaches a good holding. A grapnel anchor, with its spidery arms and flukes, would pull through mud and provide no holding power at all; but on a hard or rocky bottom it is likely to be a better choice than the other type.

When anchoring over rocky bottoms, or in areas full of snags and roots, it is best to rig a TRIP LINE, a light line from the anchor's crown to a small buoy—an empty plastic bottle will do—at the surface. If the anchor snags and will not come free in a normal fashion, pick up the buoy and raise the anchor with the trip line, crown first; see Chapter 9, page 312.

Leave an anchor light burning all night if there is any chance of other vessels being underway nearby; if you are not sure whether you need an anchor light, be on the safe side and have one showing.

Making Fast to the Bank

In many areas, cruising boaters make fast to the river's bank for a lunchtime break in the day's journey, or even overnight. Be cautious when doing this. First, check that the depth is adequate and the area is free of underwater obstacles; approach the shore slowly. Avoid vertical banks

Figure 22-12 This typical Mississippi River bank is riprapped with concrete to protect against erosion. Use care near such banks to avoid damage to your boat's bottom.

that may be in a stage of active caving; exposed tree roots in the bank may be evidence of recent erosion. Avoid rock riprap along the banks; it can damage a boat's bottom; see **Figure 22-12.**

Allowance for Water-Level Changes On inland rivers your docking lines generally need not allow for the tidal changes common on the coasts, except, of course, on tidal rivers. On nontidal waterways, however, there is always the chance of a change in level with hard thunderstorms or other heavy rainfalls. Dams may have sudden discharges, both scheduled and unscheduled, of large amounts of water—use extra caution when on the downstream side of a dam and obey all "Keep Out" signs. Observe the practices of local boats, and be guided accordingly.

Tying up to a barge or float that will itself rise or fall with a change in levels is advantageous. Here, you need simply to leave enough slack in lines to accommodate the wake of a passing vessel.

River Cruising Problems

Boaters who have cruised a given river may have conflicting reports of its hazards, or the absence of them. One may have made the cruise in the early spring, encountering high-water, flood conditions, racing currents, and floating debris, while another made his trip in September or October with low-stage water levels and slower currents so that he encountered few, if any, obstacles, except perhaps more numerous shoals. At extreme flood conditions, as a rule, river navigation is not recommended without the services of an experienced pilot.

Eddies and "Whirlpools" On the Mississippi, "sand boils" may be caused by sand piling up on the riverbed. During flood stages these whirlpool-like disturbances can be so violent that they can throw a boat out of control. In more favorable months, they may be no worse than surface eddies—felt, but certainly of no danger to a boat.

Debris Floating and partially submerged debris, such as tree trunks and branches, are a hazard for small boats. Keep a sharp lookout in waters where they have been reported. Floating debris is usually at its worst in the spring months, when flood water levels have swept away downed

trees and other materials from above the normal high-water line.

Misplaced Buoys Another hazard of river piloting at springtime high-water levels is that buoys can be moved from their charted position, dragged by strong currents or floating debris.

Submerged Buoys River currents sometimes flow so fast that buoys are towed under and completely submerged, leaving only a V-shaped eddy on the surface to reveal their location. Sometimes the buoy's top will be visible to a boat bound upstream, or the wake of a passing vessel will expose it momentarily. The surface eddy of a towed-under buoy always points upstream as its "wake" divides downstream around it. Avoid *any* surface disturbance like this; a submerged obstacle is likely lurking beneath.

Do not confuse the towed-under eddy with the condition of two currents converging at the downstream end of a middle bar. That condition may also show a V-shaped eddy, but pointing downstream.

Problems from Silt Some river boaters have reported underwater bearings ruined, engine jackets or heat exchangers filled with silt, and water pump impellers worn out at the end of a single river run. In all waters heavily laden with silt, you are wise to carry protection against it: raw water strainers, freshwater-cooling systems, cutless-type underwater bearings, and pump impellers that can handle mud and sand.

Special Hazards Some rivers present special hazards. The Army Engineers caution against regarding the Mississippi with insufficient respect; as in the example above of eddies and "whirlpools." The lower river is very large, with low-water widths of 2,500 feet (0.8 km) and high-water (bank-full) widths up to 9,000 feet (2.7 km). The bank-full stages generally occur between December and July, most frequently in March or April. Low-water stages occur in the fall months.

The Mississippi River's Lake Pepin typifies the kind of exposed area that you may encounter. This "lake," actually a broadening of the river proper, is 21 miles (33.8 km) long and up to 2.5 miles (4 km) wide; sizeable seas can build up in such a body of water.

You can find many kinds of equipment at work

along rivers, especially the larger ones. Hydraulic pipeline dredges may have lengths of floating pipeline you must avoid. Barges carrying bank-protection equipment may extend hundreds of feet out from shore, often in the swiftest part of the current. When passing any form of construction or maintenance equipment, keep *well clear* because of hazard of being swept under it, and slow down to avoid damage from your wake. Regulations exist governing lights and day shapes for dredges and other "floating plant" working on river projects, and for the passing of such equipment by other vessels. Use your VHF radio to contact the working vessel and get permission to pass, and advice on how to do so safely.

Confusing Lights Special caution is required when running rivers at night, even those with numerous lighted aids to navigation. Shore lights may cause confusion; searchlights used by commercial traffic may blind you. Floating debris often cannot be seen at all.

Signals

Whistle signals for passing other vessels, or for use in conditions of restricted visibility and other special situations, are prescribed in the Inland Navigational Rules. Details are in Chapter 5.

With few exceptions, the signal for requesting a drawbridge opening is one prolonged blast followed by one short blast. Where there are more than one bridge in close proximity, signals must be given for each bridge separately; see Chapter 5, page 167. VHF radio communications are much preferable to whistle signals.

Passing Commercial Traffic

Most U.S. inland waterways handle considerable commercial traffic. Whether you are cruising or just out for the day, you must know how to handle your boat in a situation with a large commercial vessel. At night, be especially watchful for the navigation lights of other vessels—if you see both the red and green sidelights, you are dead ahead, and in danger. In a narrow channel, a big tug or tanker requires much of the available water. As she approaches, you'll see a sizeable bow wave built up ahead of her, and

the water drawn away by suction to lower the level at her sides amidships. Give her as wide a berth as you possibly can, and be alert for violent motions of your boat as she passes.

Tugs with tows astern in narrow waterways present a real problem to approaching small boats. Fortunately, most of the river "towing" today is done by pushing scows and barges ahead of the tug; see **Figure 22-13**. This keeps the whole tow under better control as a single unit. Passing at a bend is more dangerous than on a straightaway, and sometimes must be avoided entirely; the tug and its barges cannot help but make a wide swing; and where there is ample room to pass at the beginning of the turn, there may be none at all later. If small boats *must* pass at a bend, it is usually wiser for them to take the *inside* of the curve.

Jumbo Tows on the Mississippi Big rafts of Mississippi River barges bunched together in one vast tow may cover acres of water. You

Figure 22-13 Under no circumstances should you compromise the maneuvering room available to river tows (a series of linked barges pushed by a powerful, deep-draft tug). Avoid passing them in river bends.

WATERWAYS INFORMATION

The overall source for U.S. waterway information is the U.S. Army Corps of Engineers, whose map *Major Waterways and Ports of the United States* presents the whole picture. Color maps of smaller river regions show details of interest to boaters—marinas, ramps, sanitary facilities, camping and picnic sites, as well as dams and locks. Their series of *Lakeside Recreation* maps for each region of the U.S. is particularly useful. These are available from every Corps office and from the U.S. Army Corps of Engineers, Publications Department (see Appendix A).

In addition, each local office of the Corps publishes its own series of maps. An example is the Mississippi River. The Chicago District covers the middle and upper region, and the Vicksburg, Mississippi District covers the lower Mississippi. Refer to Appendix A.

The U. S. Geological Survey (USGS) publishes a series of brochures, *River Basins of the United States.* These include general maps of major rivers, along with information of historical, hydrographic and geological interest.

Another service, the Tennessee Valley Authority's Mapping Services Branch publishes navigational charts of the waters under its jurisdiction.

A further source of information on U.S. lakes and rivers, particularly the "Wild and Scenic River System," is the National Park Service of the United State Department of the Interior in Washington, DC.

In Canada, all but the smallest lakes and rivers are charted by the Canadian Hydrographic Service; the exceptions are covered by other agencies. The Canada Map Office publishes topographic maps showing water areas, but without depth information.

The Ontario Ministry of Natural Resources publishes provincial *Fishing Maps*, which show water depths as well as other fishing-related detail. Canada's major subarctic lakes and rivers are charted by the Saskatchewan Property Management Corporation at a scale of 1:50,000 as well as by the Canadian Hydrographic Service. Maps Alberta supplies charts of that province's lakes and rivers.

should never jeopardize their activities, regardless of right-of-way. Integrated tows may consist of a bowpiece, a group of square-ended barges, and a towboat (at the stern)—all lashed together in one streamlined unit 1,000 feet (305 m) or more in length. At night, the lights of the towboat may be more conspicuous than the sidelights on the tow far out ahead. To make barges more visible, the Inland Rules require that those pushed ahead must show a quick-flashing yellow light all the way forward on the centerline; watch carefully for such a light; see Chapter 4.

Give All Tows a Wide Berth On all rivers, you should give tows a wide berth. In particular, *stay away from in front of tows*; if you should lose power, the tow could probably never stop or steer clear in time. A commercial

tow must maintain speed to be able to steer, and may at times need a half-mile to come to a full stop.

When approaching a tow from astern, intending to pass, watch out for sunken logs and other debris that may be stirred up from the bottom by the wash from the tug's powerful propeller; these will be low in the water and difficult to see. Use caution in passing through the turbulence resulting from this wash. Pass by at as large a distance as possible to avoid being sucked toward the tug when you come abreast of its stern.

Small-boat whistle signals are usually inaudible at the noisy control station of large vessels some distance away. If you need to communicate, use VHF radio, Channel 13 or 16. (On the Mississippi below Baton Rouge, Channel 67 is used rather than 13.) A passing is often verbally described over the radio, saying "one-whistle" or "two-whistle," as if actual blasts were being sounded.

Watch Your Wake

Much inland boating is done on waterways that are quite narrow. Regulate your speed so that no *destructive* wake results; excessive wake can cause damage to other boats and to shore installations. Some wake is almost inevitable from motorboats, but it must not be "destructive"; keep your speed, and your wake, down when passing boats and shoreline facilities.

CANAL BOATING

Before construction of DAMS and LOCKS, many of our rivers were unnavigable. Water coursed down valleys at the land's natural gradient, dropping hundreds of feet in not many miles, running too fast and encountering too many natural obstacles for safe navigation. To overcome such obstacles, engineers dam natural waterways at strategic spots to create a series of POOLS or levels that may be likened to a stairway. Good examples of how closely these can resemble an actual flight of stairs are at places like Waterford, N.Y., and Rideau Waterway at Ottawa, where vessels descend or ascend a series of locks in immediate succession. This section covers boating on both completely man-made waterways, which might be termed "pure canals," and on "canalized" natural rivers.

Water Levels

To a river pilot, the term POOL STAGE indicates the height of water in a pool at any given time with reference to the datum for that pool. On many rivers, pool stages are posted on conspicuous bulletin boards along riverbanks so as to be easily read from passing vessels. Charts show the locations of these bulletin boards; refer to **Figure 22-10**.

On the Ohio River, gauges at the locks of each dam show the depth of the pool impounded by the next dam downstream. For example, if the chart indicates a 12-foot gauge reading for a normal pool, a reading of 11.7 feet indicates that the next pool is 0.3 feet below normal elevation.

Figure 22-14 Locks have made water travel possible on many waterways with dams and otherwise unnavigable sections such as rapids. More than one boat at a time may be passed through a lock, sometimes in company with a larger vessel.

Locks & Dams

Without locks, the dams on our inland waterways would restrict river cruising to the individual pools and would prevent through navigation except for boats light enough to be PORTAGED— carried on land by hand or on vehicles—around the dams. Locks, in conjunction with the dams, permit boats to move from level to level. Locks vary in size, but since they almost invariably handle commercial traffic, their dimensions offer no restrictions to the movement of recreational boats. Most locks can accommodate several vessels at the same time; see **Figure 22-14**.

Principles of Locks & Locking

Locks are virtually watertight chambers with gates at each end, and with valves admitting

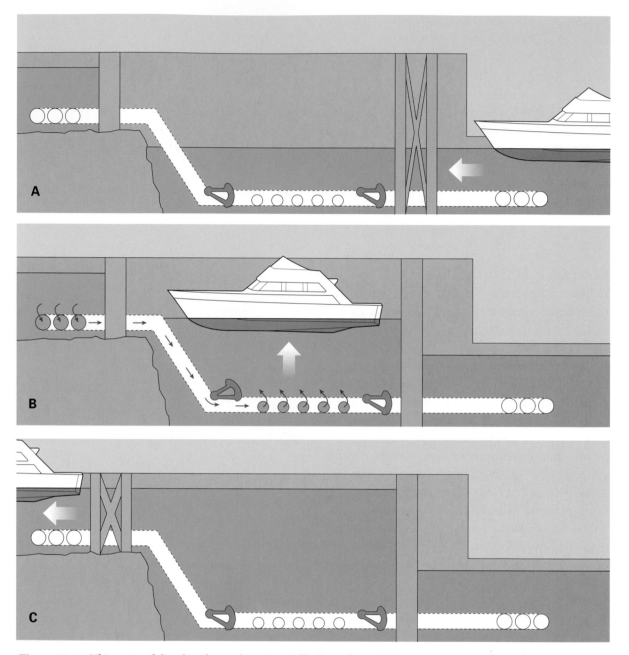

Figure 22-15 *This series of sketches shows the process of locking through for an upbound craft. With the water in the lock at the downriver level, A, the boat enters the lock. The downriver gates are closed and water enters the lock chamber, B. (Water is shown here entering from valves in sides of the lock; in many locks, there are no such valves and the upriver gates are opened just a bit to let water in.) At C, the water in the lock chamber has risen to the upriver level, the gates are opened, and the boat proceeds on its way.*

water to them as required. When a vessel is to be locked upstream to a higher level, first all gates are closed and valves on the lock's downstream side are opened to let the water run out to the lower level. Then the downstream gates are opened so that the vessel can enter the lock. The downstream gates are then closed and water flows into the lock from above through another set of valves until the chamber is full to the level of the upper pool, with the boat rising along with the water. The upstream gates are now opened, and the vessel resumes her course upstream.

Locking a vessel down is the reverse of this process; see **Figure 22-15.**

Water is not pumped at river locks; the natural flow is utilized, which is why some canals limit the number of lockings each day during droughts or annual dry seasons.

Variations in Lock Design

There are various kinds of locks, all of which accomplish the same result. Gates may swing to the side or roll back; sometimes they lift vertically and boats go under them.

Smaller locks and those with a minimal water-level change may not have underwater valves; water is let in or out of the chamber by opening the gates just a crack at first, then gradually widening the opening as the levels begin to equalize.

On one section of the Trent-Severn Waterway in Canada, the remarkable lock at Peterborough, Ontario is actually a hydraulic elevator in which two large water-filled chambers, containing vessels, counterbalance as they rise and fall to the upper and lower levels. At another location on the same waterway, an ingenious marine railway with a unique cradling device is used to carry boats up and down a steep grade and deposit them at the other end. Through passage on a waterway like the Trent-Severn is obviously limited to boats within the capacity of the railway, both as to length and weight.

Whistle Signals

Signals are prescribed for vessels approaching a lock, to be answered by the lockmaster. The signals vary in different areas, so familiarize yourself with the signals that apply to the waterway you are using. At many locks, VHF/FM radios are used for direct communications between vessels and the lockmaster.

On the Ohio River, vessels sound a long and a short blast on the whistle from a distance of not more than one mile from the lock. Approaching boats must wait for the lockmaster's signal before entering.

Where locks are in pairs (designated as LAND-WARD and RIVERWARD), the lockmaster on the Ohio may also use an air horn to give directions as follows: one long, enter landward lock; two longs, enter riverward lock; one short, leave landward lock; two shorts, leave riverward lock.

On the Mississippi, signs on the river face of the guide-wall warn small boats not to pass a certain point until signaled by the lock tender. Boaters use a signal cord near this sign, if their own horns are not loud enough, to attract the attention of the lock attendant. Similar arrangements are found on the Okeechobee Waterway crossing Florida, and elsewhere.

Signal Lights

Traffic signal lights at the Ohio locks resemble those you find on city streets—red, amber (or yellow), and green vertically arranged. Flashing red warns: "do not enter, stand clear." Flashing amber (or yellow) cautions: "approach, but under full control." Flashing green is the "go-ahead: all clear to enter."

On the N.Y. State Canal System, a fixed green is the signal to enter; a fixed red requires the vessel to wait. Six flashes of a red or green light means "stay where you are and await further instructions." If there are no signal lights showing, you must wait or make fast to the approach wall.

As with sound signals, VHF radio communications are often used to supplement light signals.

Precedence at Locks

The Secretary of the Army has established an order of priority for the users of locks controlled by the Corps of Engineers, as follows: (1) U.S. military vessels; (2) mail boats; (3) commercial passenger boats; (4) commercial tows; (5) commercial fishermen; (6) noncommercial boats.

In the descending order of precedence, the lockmaster also takes into account whether vessels of the same priority are arriving at landward or riverward locks (if locks are paired), and whether they are bound upstream or downstream.

Recreational boats *may*, at the direction of the lockmaster, be locked through with commercial vessels if a safe distance can be maintained between them, and if the commercial vessels are *not* carrying petroleum products or other hazardous substances.

Locking Procedures

The concrete walls of locks are usually rough and dirty. Some older locks have metal-sheathed inside surfaces, but most are hard on small boats, so keep your fenders ready; see **Figure 22-16**. Ordinary cylindrical fenders pick up dirt and roll on the wall to smear your topsides. Instead, you should use fender boards consisting of a plank (generally 2 by 6 inches, several feet long) suspended horizontally outside the usual fenders hung vertically. They will normally work well amidships or where a boat's sides are reasonably straight.

Bags of hay have the same objection as cylindrical fenders, except on heavily flared bows and at the edge of the deck where they flatten down and work fairly well. Auto tires wrapped in burlap would be ideal except that their use is illegal in most canals (if they came adrift they would sink and probably foul the lock's valves or gates).

As you can't be sure which side of the next lock you will be using, it's wise to have duplicate fender systems for each side.

Entering & Leaving

Since moving quickly around the deck while watching upward is an easy way to slip and fall, make sure that all persons outside on deck are wearing PFDs before entering a lock.

It is very important to enter locks with enough speed to maintain good steerage since there may be some turbulence from the valves or the propellers of large vessels, but not so much speed that you cannot stop quickly. Small boats may be rafted alongside larger vessels, or as groups of two or more. This is entirely practicable if all skippers are cooperative and cautious; it is usually good strategy for smaller boats to enter the lock last.

Occasionally you will hear about boats being tossed about as water boils into the lock from open valves. Be alert for this possibility, but lock tenders on our inland waterways are almost always careful to control the rate of inflow to minimize any turbulence in the lock chamber, and you need not fear the locking process for this reason. With a light boat, however, use extra caution when locking through in company with large commercial vessels. A boat directly astern of

a tug, for example, can be tossed around when the tug leaves and its big propeller starts to kick out its wash astern.

Approaching a Lock From Upstream

Be cautious when approaching a lock from the upstream side; follow the marked channel closely. There are stories on every waterway of boats missing the upstream lock entrance and going *over* the adjacent dam. Looking down a river from above a dam, it is sometimes virtually impossible to see any break in the water's surface, especially at night. Yet there is virtually no chance for such an accident if a skipper pays close attention to the buoys as on his chart, or to the general configuration of the dam and locks if there are no buoys.

Actually there are some circumstances where it *is* proper to go over a dam. The Ohio River has a special type of dam that has a lock chamber on one side and BEAR TRAPS on the other. Between them, there are movable wickets that can be held in an upright position during low-water stages, and lowered at times of high water. When the wickets are up, vessels use the lock. With the

Figure 22-16 Adequate fendering is a must in using locks; the side walls are always fouled by growth since they are submerged much of the time. Fenders will become dirty, possibly to the extent that they can no longer be cleaned for regular use—use your oldest, or some substitute (see text).

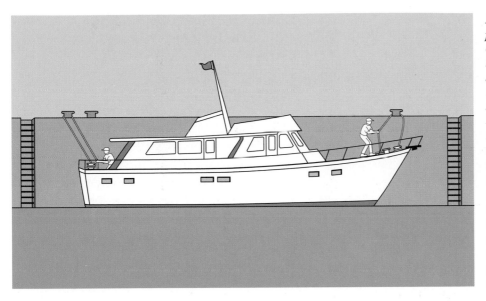

Figure 22-17 One procedure makes use of two long lines, leading from the bow and stern to bollards at the top of the lock wall and back to the boat. While they can be snubbed to a cleat to reduce the strain on the person tending them, they should never be fully cleated when locking down. Some skippers lead their lines to the side of their craft away from the wall if the lock is very deep.

wickets down, at high water, vessels run through the NAVIGABLE PASS, right over the submerged dam without locking. By day, it is important to watch the bulletin boards at the locks to know whether the lock or pass is to be used. At night, control lights are shown at the guide walls. When the navigable pass is being used, a gauge reading on the powerhouse board shows the depth of water over the pass sill at the dam; the figures are in red on a white background, preceded by the word "Pass."

Have Enough Line

Another essential in locking is adequate line. Its diameter depends on the size of your boat; and its length on the depth of the locks. Lines for locking through can be slightly smaller in diameter than your normal mooring lines; ½-inch line is often used for boats in the 35-to-50-foot (10.7-15.2 m) range, ⅜-inch for smaller boats. (If it can be found, manila is preferable to synthetic material because of its lower cost; locking lines will soon get too dirty for further use and must be discarded.) Some locks may provide lines, but be prepared; don't count on their availability.

In general, bow and stern lines should be at least twice the depth of the deepest lock that you plan to go through. This length permits running the line around a bollard on the top of the lock wall and back to your boat where it is constantly tended by hand. Then at the final level when you are ready to cast off, you can turn loose one end and haul in on the other without assistance from above (which you are not likely to get); see **Figure 22-17.** When locking down, it's *extremely* dangerous to make fast to a bollard above and then secure the line to a bitt or cleat on the boat. If the water level drops unexpectedly, the boat can be "hung up" and seriously damaged, with possible injuries to those on board. When locking up, line must be taken in steadily to keep the lines taut and the boat under control. Many experienced river boaters snub their lines on the side of their craft away from the lock wall so that the lines angle upward and inward to the top of the lock tending to pull the boat closer to the wall.

Use of Ladders & Other Methods

Lock walls often have ladders recessed into them, should someone be unlucky enough to fall in. On some canals, small boats may follow a ladder up or down, rung by rung, holding on with boathooks or short lengths of line. On other canals, rules do not permit this and the ladders must be kept clear for emergency use.

In addition to bollards at the top, some locks have posts recessed in the walls at intervals in a vertical line. Locking up, you can transfer your

Figure 22-18 Safety should always be your principal concern. You will need one crew member forward and one aft to tend lines. Handling lines alone is not recommended. Special caution is needed when the boat's gunwale is above the wall.

lines successively from lower posts to higher ones as you rise in this chamber.

In some new locks, floating mooring posts built into the walls move up and down with the water level. This makes for the easiest locking through of all, because you can use relatively short lines and they need no adjustment as your boat moves up or down.

Tend Your Lines Carefully

The watchword in locks is "Safety." Whether the water level is rising or falling, tend your lock lines carefully at all times; see **Figure 22-18.** You will need one crewmember forward and another aft; with only two people aboard, the helmsman can usually tend whichever line is nearest to him or her, generally the stern line. Single-handing in locks is definitely not recommended and may be prohibited by regulations. In some locks, coming up, special caution is required at the top of the lift. The boat may have been adequately fendered against the lock wall, but when the lock chamber is nearly full the boat's gunwale may be above the wall and the topsides are then unprotected, particularly at a bow with flare.

The Army Corps of Engineers publishes an informative illustrated leaflet entitled *Locking Through.* Write to the U.S. Army Engineer District, P.O. Box 59, Louisville, KY 40101 for a copy; see also Appendix A. It sets forth, concisely, the essentials as they apply to the Ohio River.

Spillways

Recreational boaters *must* keep clear of the spillway area below dams. The fishing there may be particularly good because fish tend to congregate below dams, but the hazards, too, are great. Spillway areas are subject to sudden changes as the dam's gates and valves open and close; placid waters become turbulent with no warning at all as a heavy stream of water boils up unexpectedly from beneath the surface. Heed the warning signs and stay out of spillway areas.

Artificial Land Cuts

Not all waterways are merely improved versions of natural rivers and lakes. Artificial land cuts are often needed to interconnect navigable waterways and provide continuous passage between major bodies of water. Lake Champlain, for example, is accessible from the upper reaches of the Hudson River only because of a 24-mile (38.6 km) completely artificial waterway cut into the land. A dredged land cut many miles long is also found at the western end of the Eire Canal, to connect Lake Erie with rivers in the middle of the state

Narrow land cuts pose problems of their own. A typical cross section of a dredged canal might have a surface width of, for example, 125 feet (38 m), but a bottom width of only 75 feet (23 m) with a depth of 12 feet (3.7 m). If normal cruising speeds were maintained through such portions of a canal, the bank would be quickly washed down into the channel. In artificial waterways, therefore, speed limits are rigidly enforced; see **Figure 22-19.** In N.Y. State Canals, the speed limit is 10 mph (16 km/h) unless otherwise posted. A telephone network between the various locks enables lock tenders to know when a boat running the proper speed is due; violators are quite easily caught! Some sets of locks also operate on time schedules and it serves no purpose to go too fast, only to wait at the next lock.

Some land sections are cut through solid rock, perhaps only 100 feet (30.5 m) or less in width.

This makes a virtual trough with ragged walls of blasted rock. In a confined channel such as this, the wakes of a group of boats may combine and reinforce each other in a synchronized pattern, building up out of all proportion to the wakes of each boat individually. Unless speed is held down as required by circumstances, regardless of the legal limit, small boats can get out of control, with the possibility of being thrown into the rock walls and suffering serious damage.

Speed limits are established for good reasons, and must be obeyed.

Regulations

On the Western Rivers, no special permission or clearance is necessary for passage through the locks; there are, however, regulations to be observed. You can get copies of these from the Engineer District Offices at Chicago or St. Louis; see Appendix A.

The N.Y. Canal Corporation publishes a pamphlet describing the routes, vertical clearances, regulations, permits and tolls, and general safety information for its inland waterways. For copies and a free map of the Erie Canal and Connecting Waterways, see Appendix A.

LAKE BOATING

The term "lake boating" has extreme limits. The water area involved can range from the smallest of natural or man-made lakes and reservoirs to the Great Lakes, really a group of inland seas; see **Figure 22-20**.

Some lakes are "protected waters" at all times; others, particularly the Great Lakes, can produce waves hazardous even to ships of considerable size. While waves on these lakes are seldom of remarkable height, they are usually very steep and often require more caution than ocean waves in similar wind conditions.

An inland boater can cruise hundreds of miles and never be far from shelter in case of bad weather, but he must still treat the larger lakes with respect. Lake Superior, for example, is the one of the largest bodies of fresh water in the world. Deep, with rock-lined coasts and subject

Figure 22-19 Much of our inland waterway system is man-made and requires on-going maintenance. Speeds on both artificial and natural sections may be strictly regulated. Sailboats with masts up must be alert for overhead power lines.

to storms and fog as well, it can present a challenge to even the saltiest skipper. On Lake Erie, smaller and comparatively shallow, seas in a gale cannot shape up in the normal pattern of open ocean waves. Instead they are short and steep, frequently breaking in heavy squalls. Even Lake Oneida in midstate New York on the Barge Canal route can build up seas that would be challenging to an offshore boater.

Figure 22-20 Many lakes provide a surprisingly large cruising area and sufficient depths for larger yachts. However, trailerable boats are the best choice for the boater who wants to explore more inaccessible locations.

Water Levels

Lake levels vary from year to year and show a seasonal rise and fall as well—low in the winter and high in the summer. Monthly bulletins published during the navigation season show present and projected levels of the Great Lakes as well as average and record levels. More current information is contained in weekly reports released to newspapers and radio and television stations, and availavble on the Internet at www.glerl.noaa.gov/data/now.

In larger lakes, a steady, strong wind will lower levels to windward and pile up water on the leeward side. Barometric pressure can also influence lake levels, sometimes causing a sudden and temporary, but drastic, change in water level on any portion of a lake; this phenomenon is called a SEICHE.

Lake Piloting

Many smaller lakes do not require "navigation" by the skipper and thus do not have charts, as such. On the larger lakes, however, shore lines may be many miles long; you should have a chart, sometimes called a map, and keep track of where you are at all times—piloting may be required, especially in changeable weather conditions or fog. On the largest lakes, you need to plot your course using a compass, make time-speed-distance calculations, and even take bearings and fixes—essentially all the actions of piloting except tidal calculations; see **Figure 22-21.**

Great Lakes Charts

Charts of the Great Lakes, published by the National Ocean Service (NOS), are excellent, covering features of the navigable water in great detail. They show depths of water (the lesser depths in blue tint), safe channels, submerged reefs and shoals, aids to navigation, adjacent shorelines with topographic features and landmarks, types of bottom, and much related information. Scales vary from as large as 1:2,500 to 1:20,000 for harbor charts to 1:400,000 or 1:500,000 for general charts of individual lakes. The smallest scale used is for the general chart (14500) of all the Great Lakes at 1:1,500,000. The projection used for Great Lakes charts is usually polyconic. Several use the Mercator projection, and a few are published in a metric edition.

Great Lakes Charts have a compass rose showing both true and magnetic directions with the variation stated. Magnetic variation in the Great Lakes varies from 13° W in the eastern end to 1°E in the extreme western waters; there is a small area in which the variation is 0°. In isolated areas, great deposits of iron ore in the earth produce strong local effects; this is most pronounced along the north shore of Lake Superior, where variation has been observed to change from 7° to 27° within a distance of only 650 feet (200 meters)!

Many lake charts show the principal routes between major ports, giving the course in degrees (true) and distance in statute miles. Comparative elevations are referred to mean tide as calculated at New York City. Local heights and depths are measured from an established datum for each lake.

The Great Lakes are partly Canadian waters, and excellent charts for these areas are available from the Canadian Hydrographic Survey, Ottawa. These all use the Mercator projection.

Coast Pilot 6 (Great Lakes Pilot)

To supplement the information on Great Lakes charts, get a copy of the current edition of the *Coast Pilot 6,* published by the NOS. This most useful volume provides full descriptions of the waters charted, laws and regulations governing navigation, bridge clearance, signals for locks and bridges, dimensions and capacities of marine railways, and weather information. Keep your copy corrected from *Local Notices to Mariners* issued by the 9th Coast Guard District, Cleveland, Ohio. Similar texts are published by the Canadian Hydrographic Service.

Great Lakes Light List

The U.S. Coast Guard publishes the *Light List, Volume VII,* covering the Great Lakes; see Chapter 15, page 549-550.

This *Light List* includes some Canadian buoys and lights, identified by the letter "C"

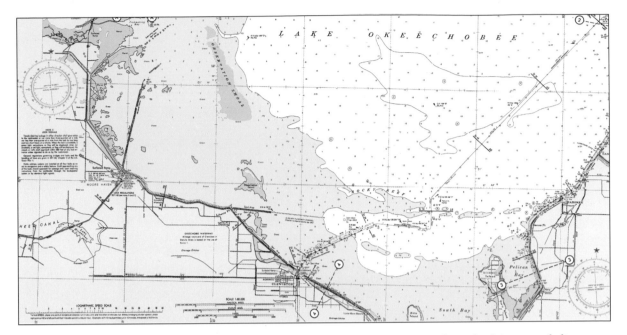

Figure 22-21 *On larger lakes, you will need to plot your course using a compass and standard time-speed-distance calculations. Lake charts, such as those for the Great Lakes (not shown here), often show principal routes between major ports, giving the course in degrees (true) and the distance in statute miles.*

following the name of the aid. Except for minor differences in design, the buoyage systems used for Canada and the United States are the same. The Canadian buoyage system also makes greater use of cardinal buoys (see Chapter 14) than the U.S. Coast Guard.

Caution Along Some Shores

In some lakes, such as Lake Champlain, depth becomes a factor. Certain shores may be particularly inviting because of their scenic attractions, but they may have depths of several hundred feet running right up to sheer cliff shores. If your engine fails, your anchor will be of little use in such deep water, and if the breeze is toward those cliffs you can be blown against them.

Rules & Regulations

Many smaller inland lakes do not fall under federal jurisdiction and are regulated by the appropriate states or other agencies. Other lakes are considered "navigable waters of the United States" where federal rules and regulations apply. Check on the status of unfamiliar waters, if you have any doubts.

Navigation Rules

The U.S. Inland Navigational Rules apply to all vessels on waters subject to federal regulations; refer to Chapters 4 and 5. The Canadian side of the Great Lakes and other border waterways are, of course, subject to Canada's rules.

Pollution-Control Regulations

Water pollution is a very serious concern on all lakes, especially those that are a source of domestic drinking water. Many complex regulations may be in effect. Overboard discharge of sewage regulations are very strictly enforced and are particularly important for boaters crossing state or international boundaries. Some states are known for their zealous application of environmental laws, especially regarding recreational boating. When visiting a new area, be sure to check with the local authorities; also see Appendix A.

Marlinespike Seamanship

Ropes & Lines • How They Are Made & Used • Knots & Splices
Care & Maintenance of Lines • Blocks & Tackle

From anchor rodes to sheets, vangs, and whippings, anyone concerned with the work of a boat becomes involved with lines, knots, and splices—and their proper use. This knowledge and the related hand skills are as important to a powerboat skipper as they are to the owner of a sailboat. They comprise a subject recognized for its fascinating lore, for the beautiful artifacts that are a part of it, and for its sheer practicality. Working with CORDAGE—the collective name for ropes, lines, and "small stuff"—is an ancient skill that now takes in new technologies.

The information that follows is intended to give you a picture of:

• The construction, materials, and characteristics of various kinds of modern cordage

• The tools, techniques, and special words used in working with cordage

• The procedures for making and using knots, bends, hitches, and splices

• The coiling and storage of lines, as well as their care and inspection

The nautical name for this special information and skill is marlinespike seamanship. Once used extensively with rigging, marline is a two-strand twine; a marlinespike is a useful tool, often one blade of a sailor's rigging knife.

ROPES & LINES

Rope is bought as "rope." But once it is in use on board a boat it is called LINE, or by name of the rigging part it has become. Sailors will tell you that there aren't many ropes aboard a ship or boat. There is the bolt rope at the foot or luff of a sail, or a tiller rope, or a foot rope, or a bell rope, or a few other rare ones. Everything else is a line.

Rope Materials

Like a sailor's knife, rope goes back thousands of years. For centuries rope was made from natural fibers, especially flax and hemp, including jute, sisal, and manila (from the wild banana plant). Most rope was LAID, usually three STRANDS twisted together. Each strand is composed of three YARNS, each of which is composed of multiple FIBERS; see **Figure 23-01**. Boaters work with knots and splices that have been in use for centuries, based on the standard way rope was made by twisting fibers.

Since the mid-20th century, there have been more technological changes in rope than in the preceding thousand years. New synthetic fibers have altered the form of rope and even the way particular splices or knots are made and used. The new kinds of cordage are so superior that a boater has little reason to pay any attention to most of the old materials, although he may have difficulty in making the right choice among the new forms.

The most obvious change is in the form of rope itself—probably more than half the rope used in recreational boating in the U.S. is PLAITED, BRAIDED, or DOUBLE-BRAIDED (a core inside a cover), compared to the traditional, three-strand laid rope. Small stuff, used for whippings and seizings is also greatly changed.

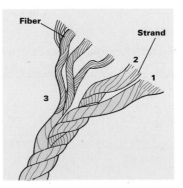

Figure 23-01
"Three-strand rope" is made up of three strands twisted clockwise in a right-hand lay. The individual strands have a left-hand lay, and the fibers will normally have a right-hand twist.

Shock cord and even monofilament line have special uses, all made possible by new materials.

Synthetic Materials

The first important synthetic fiber to appear was polyamide (nylon). Nylon rope is strong (more than twice as strong as the best yacht manila for the same size), has useful qualities of elasticity or controlled stretch, and has gone through successive improvements. This rope can be given various degrees of softness or hardness, some variation in surface textures, and can be obtained in various colors to fit its intended uses. With its shock-absorbing elasticity it is particularly well suited for dock lines and anchor lines.

High-intensity polyester fiber (Dacron, Terylene, Duron, Fortrel, A.C.E., and Kodel are trademarks) is made into rope that is virtually as strong as nylon but has one important difference: the rope can be made to have very little stretch. This property makes polyester fiber superior for special purposes like the running rigging on sailboats, where elasticity is undesirable. In manufacturing, polyester rope can be given varied finishes: woolly, smooth, or textured to make it easy to grip, as required; it also can be colored.

Aramid fiber (Kevlar), a newer material used for marine rope, combines strength and strong dimensional stability (near zero stretch). It is comparatively expensive and is used chiefly on competitive sailboats.

Polypropylene rope is least expensive among the synthetics; it is as strong as nylon or Dacron but tends to deteriorate rapidly from exposure to the ultraviolet component of sunlight. Its main advantage is that it floats, which the others do not do, so it is suited to some commercial fishing applications as well as to waterski tow ropes and dinghy painters. Any other use aboard a boat is an economy measure and may be unwise. For appropriate special purposes, it should be a larger size (compared to nylon) and renewed frequently.

Rope Construction

The construction of three-strand laid rope has changed little in thousands of years except for varying surface textures. New materials and new types of rope-making machines have caused one particularly significant development in rope construction, however: braided and double-braided ropes.

The various kinds of rope "geometry" are worth looking at in some detail, starting with the oldest.

Three-Strand Rope

Some knowledge of the anatomy of three-strand rope makes it easier to work with, especially in splicing and in finishing off the ends (a subject discussed at the end of this chapter).

If you hold the rope so that the end is away from your body, the strands will seem to have a twist that is clockwise. This is called "right-hand lay." Most rope is right-land lay, and has been since the pyramids were built. If you look at the twist in just one of the three strands, it is a left-hand twist. Finally, with all but the smallest ropes the fibers have an opposite twist within the strand; refer to **Figure 23-01.**

Because some tension is put on the rope in manufacturing, these opposite twists, of strand and rope, tend to keep the rope from UNLAYING, or untwisting.

The reason for being aware of the lay of the rope is this: when you splice you will be working with these twists, sometimes retwisting a short length of strand with your fingers, and SPLICING (interweaving) the strands back into the normal lay of the rope. Since virtually all laid rope is right-handed, your fingers should learn to work with the twist, whether you are tying knots, splicing, or coiling.

Laid rope comes in several degrees of hardness or stiffness. The technical terms are SOFT LAY, MEDIUM LAY, and HARD LAY. For boating purposes you will probably use only medium lay. (SAILMAKER'S LAY is another variation, but unless you're making sails you won't need it.) Very soft lay is sometimes on sale, and is superficially attractive—silky soft, like milkweed seedpods. It's of little use on a boat because it kinks easily. Hard-laid rope, used commercially, may be too difficult to work with to be of any value on small craft.

You may read about, but seldom see, FOUR-STRAND ROPE and LEFT-HAND LAY ROPE; both are

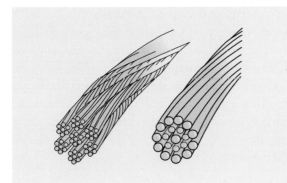

Figure 23-02 Wire rope is stranded in 7 x 7 format, left, which is often used for running rigging, or in 1 x 19 format, right, the type used for sailboat standing rigging.

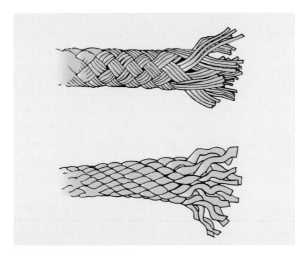

Figure 23-03 Braided line may be either single-braid, lower, or eight-part plaited braid, upper. Single-braid in small diameters (1/4-inch and smaller) is used for flag halyards, sail bag ties, and similar purposes.

for special purposes. And there is one more "twist" about rope—to make very large cables, such as those that tugs or large ships use, three right-hand lay ropes can be twisted together, left-hand lay; this is called CABLE LAY.

Most wire rope is made the same way: by twisting strands; the more intricate strandings, with 7 x 7 and 1 x 19 strands, are seen most often. In 7 x 7, seven strands, each in turn consisting of seven wires, are twisted together; in 1 x 19, 19 single strands make up the rope. This 1 x 19 wire rope is stronger but less flexible than the 7 x 7 type, and is used primarily for standing rigging; see **Figure 23-02.**

*Figure 23-04 Braided line may be either single-braid (refer to **Figure** 23-03) or double -braid, above. Double-braid, sometimes called braid-on-braid, is used for many purposes on boats of all types and sizes. It has some stretch, but less than three-strand twisted line.*

Braided Line

Small diameter (¼-inch and smaller) single-braided is used for flag halyards, to tie the ends of sailbags, and for special purposes such as awnings; see **Figure 23-03.** Most single-braid line can't be spliced unless it's a hollow braid.

Double-Braided Double-braided line is a widely used type. It has a braided core inside a braided cover; see **Figure 23-04.** For low-stretch applications the cover is polyester; the core is often a mixture of fibers with greater stretch. This construction has advantages for many purposes, but it requires special techniques for splicing.

Double-braid is very flexible because both the cover and the core are composed of small strands. Its stretch depends on the materials used. Its resistance to abrasion is excellent because the wear is distributed over many strands. Braided line tends to coil evenly and, unlike laid line, is virtually kink free (does not hockle).

On both sail and power boats you will often see double-braid nylon used for dock lines because of its smooth running and easy-on-the-hands characteristics; occasionally it will be used for anchor lines. You'll see double-braid poly-ester used for sheets and halyards on racing sail-boats.

Other Types of Rope

In addition to stranded and braided rope, several other forms of flexible materials have special uses aboard boats. These materials are not traditional cordage, but they do some of the same things rope or small lines will do.

Figure 23-05
Shock cord is made of rubber strands with a braided cover. It is generally used in short lengths with loops and toggles, or hooks, at the ends.

Shock cord, which is multistrand rubber with a synthetic cover, see **Figure 23-05.** It can stretch twice its length. The uses of shock cord are endless: to hold topping lifts out of the way, to make quick lash-ups for furling sails, to hold halyards away from the mast, and to hold a pair of oars on a cabin top or books in a book rack. Shock cord is not as strong as rope; its extreme elasticity makes it unsuitable for many purposes, and it cannot be spliced. Its ends are usually made up with plastic or metal clips to prevent fraying; eyes (actually looped ends in the shape of eye splices) are made the same way. A loop at one end of a short piece of shock cord and a toggle inset at the other end makes a good tie to keep a coil of line in place.

Webbing is made of woven nylon or polyester, see **Figure 23-06.** It is used for sail stops (replacing the traditional sewn strips of doubled sailcloth) and for dinghy tie-downs as well as hold-downs for boats on trailers. Webbing is very strong, and when used for sail ties it holds well with a square knot or a slippery reef knot. Webbing is either single or hollow flat (double).

Monofilament is another kind of line found on boats. Its main use is for fishing lines and a heavier piece makes a good lanyard for a pocket stopwatch or small calculator. Monofilament fish line must be knotted only in certain specific ways or it will invariably come untied.

Small stuff is a term used by the typical old salt, sitting on a hatch cover making up whippings, servings, and seizings. Waxed nylon line and flat braid (also called parachute cord) is used for whippings and to prevent chafe. Marline, a tan-colored two-strand string used for servings, in now scarce. Cod-line, a similar three-strand material, is useful if you can get it.

Selecting the Correct Rope

In the course of boat ownership, you will need to make decisions about what size and type of rope to buy for new dock and anchor lines, or how to improve the rigging when replacing a sheet, vang, or halyard. In addition to the factors already reviewed concerning elasticity and the form of rope, you need to consider other points, including size.

Sizes

The size of rope, in the United States, is customarily given as its diameter in inches, particularly in the recreational-boat sizes. But since most of the rest of the world measures rope by its circumference and in millimeters, you will see more and more line described by "nominal" size with metric comparison tables. In addition, manufacturers and sellers of rope know very well that a piece of braided rope, held loosely, is thicker than one stretched out. Because of this, they market such rope by its weight, which is a more accurate measure of the amount of material. At some marine stores, however, you will find all types of rope sold by length, often in prepackaged kits.

Strength Ratings

Experts, concerned with safety and dependability, say that the working load for laid line should not exceed 11 percent of its TENSILE STRENGTH—the load, in pounds of "pull," at which the rope would break (part). Braided rope is normally specified for use at, or under, 20 percent of its tensile strength. As rope ages it inevitably suffers from

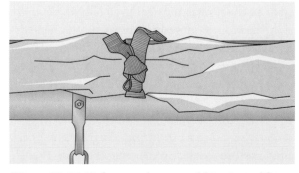

Figure 23-06 Nylon or polyester webbing is used for sail stops, for lashing a dinghy on deck, or as tie-downs to secure a boat on its trailer.

FIBER CORDAGE—TYPICAL WEIGHTS & MINIMUM BREAKING STRENGTHS (POUNDS)*

Nominal Size (inches) Diameter	Nylon (High Tenacity—N.Y.)			Du Pont Dacron or H.T. Polyester			Polyolefins (H.T.) (Polypropylene and/or Polyethylene)			Double Nylon Braid			Polyester/ Polyolefin Double Braid		
	Net Wt. 100'	Ft. per lg.	Breaking strength	Net Wt. 100'	Ft. per lg.	Breaking strength	Net Wt. 100'	Ft. per lg.	Breaking strength	Net Wt. 100'	Ft. per lg.	Breaking strength	Net Wt. 100'	Ft. per lg.	Breaking strength
3/8	100	100.0	1 000	1.3	77.0	1 000	0.7	137.0	750	NA	NA	NA	0.8	133.0	900
1/4	1.5	66.6	1 700	2.1	47.5	1 700	1.2	80.0	1 250	1.7	60.3	2 100	1.7	60.2	1 700
5/16	2.5	40.0	2 650	3.3	30.0	2 550	1.9	53.0	1 850	2.8	36.0	3 500	2.6	38.4	2 600
3/8	3.6	28.0	3 650	4.7	21.3	3 500	2.9	34.5	2 600	3.3	30.0	4 200	3.5	28.5	3 500
7/16	5.0	20.0	5 100	6.3	15.9	4 800	3.9	25.5	3 400	5.0	20.0	6 000	5.1	20.0	5 100
1/2	6.6	15.0	6 650	8.2	12.2	6 100	4.9	20.4	4 150	6.7	14.9	7 500	6.8	15.0	6800
9/16	8.4	11.9	8 500	10.2	9.8	7 700	6.2	16.0	4 900	8.3	12.0	9 500	NA	NA	NA
5/8	10.5	9.5	10 300	13.2	7.6	9 500	7.8	12.8	5 900	11.1	9.0	12 000	11.0	9.0	11 000
3/4	14.5	6.9	14 600	17.9	5.6	13 200	11.1	9.0	7 900	15.0	6.7	17 000	15.0	6.7	15 000
7/8	20.0	5.0	19 600	24.9	4.0	17 500	15.4	6.5	11 000	20.8	4.8	23 700	20.0	5.0	20 000
1 000	26.0	3.8	25 000	30.4	3.3	2 200	18.6	5.4	13 000	25.0	4.0	28 500	28.0	3.6	28

*These figures on synthetics are an average of those available from four large cordage manufacturers. Those for the rope you buy should be available from your dealer. Check them carefully.

Table 23-1 When buying rope, keep these points in mind: A soft, sleazy rope may be stronger and easier to splice, but it will not wear as well and is more apt to hockle or unlay than a well "locked-up" rope. Blended ropes, part polyolefins and part other fibers, may be found. Multifilament (fine filament) polypropylene looks like nylon, but don't expect it to be as strong—it floats, nylon doesn't. Spun, or stapled, nylon and high-intensity polyester (such as Dacron) are not as strong as ropes made of continuous filaments, but are easier to grasp; these are sometimes used for sheets on sailboats.

abrasion and sunlight. Braided rope has the advantage that the core, providing a major part of the strength, is protected. All parts of laid rope suffer from wear. See **Table 23-1** for data on the weight and breaking strength of various types of rope in a range of typical sizes.

In practice, a common-sense approach is often the determining factor. A small size of rope might be strong enough for a jib sheet, but a larger size will be easier to grasp with the hands.

Varieties Available

There are dozens of brands, configurations, and combinations of materials, particularly in braided rope. Sometimes one characteristic, reduced stretch, for example, changes another, such as ease of splicing.

The surface textures of braided polyester ropes vary. Those made with continuous filaments are shiny, smooth, and strong. Those made with spun yard (short filaments) are softer, fuzzier, and not quite as strong. Select the shiny ones for halyards, and the fuzzier ones for sheets, where being easier on the hands and better gripping of the drums of winches are important qualities.

Some skippers who do a lot of night sailing use lines of different surface texture, with different feel for different purposes, such as sheets and guys.

Color Coding

The use of color coding for racing and cruising sailboats is common. The lines may have a solid color, or be white with a colored "tracer." A recommended standard is:

• Mainsail, sheet and halyard—white
• Jib/genoa, sheets and halyards—blue
• Spinnaker, sheets and halyard—red
• Topping lifts—green
• Vangs and travelers—orange

Matching Size with Use

For most uses, the appropriate size of rope is one that is large enough to be comfortable in the hands under normal working situations. A flag halyard, which has very little strain on it, can be thin to reduce wind resistance.

Sail halyards must be strong enough to take the tremendous strain of the sail filled with wind, with minimum stretch, be resistant to abrasion at the sheaves, and still offer the least possible wind resistance.

The proper size of a line may be determined by still another factor: chafing. A dock line or anchor line, for instance, is used many times, sometimes chafes seriously and sometimes not at all, and yet should always be strong enough to hold under extreme storm conditions. A mooring pennant needs to be many times stronger than is required for the worst possible storm conditions, partly because the big fall storm may come at the end of the season, when the line has already been weakened by various small chafings. (See Chapter 9 for more details on anchor and mooring lines.)

Matching Rope Size and Blocks If a line is a bit too large for a block or other type of fairlead, or a chock, you run the risk of binding, jamming, or chafing; see **Figure 23-07.** Sometimes the solution is not a smaller line but a larger fitting.

If a line is too small for a particular block, it can get caught between the sheave and the shell—another kind of jam. (Refer to **Figure 23-20** for the parts of a block.) If a wire sheave is adapted for rope, the sheave must be dressed down for a proper groove. (Be aware that for comparable sizes, rope will have only a fraction of the strength of wire.)

The diameter of the sheave in a block can also be important. If a line makes a 180° change of direction over a very small sheave, the stress on the line is obvious. Sometimes naval architects use two small blocks at the top of the mast to solve

Figure 23-07 Blocks should be matched to the lines used. Otherwise, you run the risk of lines binding, jamming, or chafing.

this problem—each block gives the halyard a 90° turn. Similarly, a fairlead that makes a change in direction in a line results in a certain amount of friction; if the line goes through the fairlead at an extreme angle, the friction is greater. In such a situation a block might well be better than a simpler fairlead, to make the line handling easier as well as to minimize abrasion.

Use Quality Rope

The problems of cheap rope may be hidden, but they are real. Some polypropelene rope, at the bottom of the cost scale, is made from large-diameter filaments. Rope with finer filaments costs more, but lasts longer and is much stronger. Hard-lay nylon, which may be old, is so difficult to work with that it may not be worth its low price.

As you work with the variety of lines aboard a boat, you will form the habit of constantly checking for chafe and other problems: a splice that is beginning to fray, a chock with a rough corner that will weaken a dock line by chafing, a block whose sheave tends to be stiff and needs cleaning and lubricating. Frequent inspection of gear and rigging, and replacement, lubrication, or other suitable repair is an important part of good seamanship.

Information on inspection details and procedures is given near the end of this chapter under "Care & Maintenance of Lines"; see page 793.

Availability

The retail availability of special kinds of rope can be a problem for some boaters. An inland hardware store may stock several kinds and sizes of rope—suitable mainly for farmers and homeowners. Preferences and needs also vary among commercial fishermen, recreational powerboat owners, and sailors.

Sometimes there are special solutions. If you can't find waxed flat braid for whippings at a marine dealer, talk to a sailmaker. If all you need at the moment is a small size, waxed nylon dental tape is roughly similar. If you plan on making up a polypropylene dinghy painter that will float, and thus stay out of the way of propeller blades, try a source that supplies commercial fishing boats; and get the black rope—it's the most resistant to sunlight.

MARLINESPIKE TOOLS

For most everyday work with rope you need only your fingers and a good knife. But many marlinespike jobs need special tools, a few professional techniques, and some standard materials.

Here is what you would find in an experienced sailor's "ditty bag," and some of the extras that might be in the tool locker or perhaps on a home workbench—for most kinds of marlinespike seamanship:

A good knife, preferably the type called a rigging knife, with a built-in marlinespike and probably a hasp that is used for opening and closing shackles; see **Figure 23-08.** The blade should be sharp; often a keen but slightly jagged edge works well on synthetic rope. If you don't have a sharpening stone a file from the engine toolbox will keep the blade sharp.

A large fid or **marlinespike,** for separating the strands of laid rope when splicing. You can usually splice small sizes of laid line, if it's fairly soft, using only your fingers. But a fid (usually of wood or plastic) or metal spike, used to separate the strands and to get the strand you are working with through quickly and easily, makes any splicing easier, and is usually a necessity for larger sizes of rope.

Figure 23-08 The combination knife and marlinespike is the tool most often used in marlinespike work. Some sailors carry separate knives and fids.

Special fids will be needed for splicing double-braided rope, different sizes matched to the diameter of the rope. Several types of hollow fids and other special tools are on the market.

Sailmaker's needles (keep them in a small plastic bottle) for making whippings and repairing sail slide attachments and jib hank fastenings. Keep several sizes of needles on hand.

A sailmaker's palm to push the needles through the rope; see **Figure 23-09.** Even if you don't expect to repair sails, a palm is a good hand-tool. Keep the leather soft by applying neat's-foot oil twice a year.

A pair of scissors.

A pair of pliers. Simple sharp-nosed are best.

Waxed sail twine (tape and/or cord) and perhaps some old-fashioned brown marline for a traditional-looking project. As you'll see at the end of this chapter, waxed nylon twine or lacing tape is used to make whippings on the ends of

Figure 23-09 A traditional sailmaker's palm is needed to push needles through heavy sailcloth when making repairs. Strong waxed thread is used in this work.

lines. Lacing tape, which is flat and plaited, is also used for sail fittings; even if you never sew a sail you'll need twine or tape for lashings. Many people also keep a piece of beeswax in their ditty bags, for waxing twine.

A source of heat is needed to melt and seal the ends of synthetic rope. A candle and matches or the flame in a galley stove will do, if you follow a careful safety procedure of heating an old knife blade and then applying it ot the rope to melt it. On shore (or if your boat has 120-volt AC power) an electric hot knife is best; see below.

An electric rope cutter. Not everyone needs this professional tool, which plugs into an electrical outlet and uses a hot wire or blade to *melt* the rope (quickly, smoothly, and sealing the ends). However, many amateur sailors who like to work with rope own one. Perhaps the handiest tool for the boat owner is an electric soldering gun, with a special cutting head obtainable from hardware stores. This knife-like head is also useful for melting and smoothing the fine strands of rope that are left after a splice is made. Electric rope cutters or hot knives require 120-volt AC power.

Plastic tape for temporary whippings. White tape with some stretch to it, black electrical tape,

waterproof sail repair tape, or first-aid tape will do. These are all adhesive tapes unlike the nylon lacing tapes referred to earlier.

Liquid, **quick-drying plastic** for dipping rope ends into as a substitute for a twine whipping or other end finish for a line. They are called Whip-It, Whip End Dip, or similar names.

Keep all the tools and materials well enclosed against moisture, which can make scissors and knives useless. A canvas ditty bag with plastic wraps for the metal tools will do, as will a tight-closed plastic box; see **Figure 23-10.**

USE OF ROPES & LINES

So far we have been looking at rope and line primarily as the raw materials of marlinespike seamanship. Now we turn our attention to their use, and you will notice the additional special language that is used aboard boats.

Use of Lines on Boats

Various lines find common use on powerboats and sailboats—dock lines, anchor rodes, lines for towing, and others. Sailing craft, of course, have many other lines specifically for their mode of propulsion. These numerous applications are covered in other chapters in this book.

KNOTS, BENDS & HITCHES

The first principle in dealing with laid rope is that it has a twist, and you must work with it, not against it. This applies to splicing and knotting as well as to coiling.

You will also feel how a little friction of one part of the rope against another holds it fast. That's the second principle for any kind of rope: in knots, splices, bends, or hitches, the pressure of the rope against itself, as it tightens, is what does the holding.

The third principle is a rule, a definition: a good knot is one that can be made almost automatically (your fingers learn to do it, just as they learn to write your name), that holds securely in the usage it is meant for, and that can be unfastened or untied readily. With practice, you will be able to tie knots in the dark or in more than one position.

Figure 23-10 A typical ditty bag includes a number of marlinespike tools, from a sailmaker's palm to an electric hot knife. Keep all tools and materials protected from moisture, which can render scissors and other tools useless. A canvas ditty bag with plastic wraps for the metal tools will do, as will a tight-closing plastic box.

DEFINING MARLINESPIKE TERMS

Many of the special terms used in marlinespike seamanship are best understood by handling line or by looking at illustrations. The STANDING PART is the long end of a piece of line. If you loop the working part back on itself, you form a BIGHT. If the bight is around an object or the rope itself, it's a TURN; if it's a complete circle, it's a ROUND TURN. The extreme other end of the line is the BITTER END; see the illustration. All BENDS, HITCHES, KNOTS, and even SPLICES are technically KNOTS, but to the purist there are differences. A splice was only a form of interweaving of the strands—until braided rope came along with a new form.

A WHIPPING is small twine or tape wrapped tightly around and through the end of a rope to keep it from unraveling. A SEIZING is a similar wrap-around, but for another purpose, such as binding two parts of a line together in a piece of rigging, or binding a sail hank to the sail. PARCELING is a more complex wrap-around, combining twine and tape, to take wear or prevent chafe. The illustrations allow you to compare these somewhat similar methods . Another term is LOCKING, which means sewing through the throat of a braided line eye splice to hold it in place.

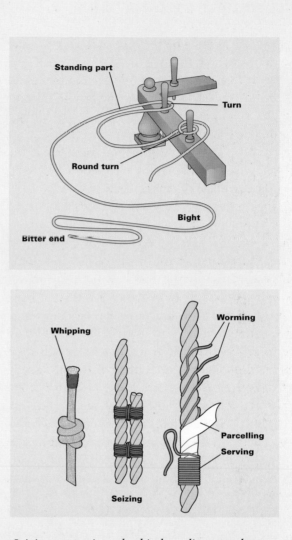

Whipping, left, prevents the end of the line from unlaying. Seizing, center, is used to bind two lines together. Worming, serving, and parcelling, right, are used to protect a line against severe chafing.

Some knots are adjustable; others are not. At times, the choice of which knot to use depends on the size or character of the line involved—there are variations in the way line works, as will be mentioned in this chapter.

Most of the following information about specific knots concerns their efficient use. The illustrations on pages 786–788, in the sidebar, "Most-Used Knots on Board Recreational Boats," are for identification; the paragraphs below give additional information about tying or using each one.

Cleat Hitches

One of the simplest knots, certainly the most used aboard a boat, involves nothing more than turns around a cleat. You may not have even thought of this as a knot—but it is. When fastening a line to a cleat, as with many things at sea, a small error at the start can cause problems later.

Look closely at the illustrations, page 788, and see how the dock line at the right comes in at an angle to the base of the cleat. It then goes around the base of the cleat so that it passes under each horn once. This keeps the strain low on the cleat.

COILING & STOWING LINES

When you handle lines on board any boat, you soon learn some basic techniques; one of these is how to coil a line, and another is how to stow it.

Coiling a Line

Laid line, having its natural twist built in, should always be coiled clockwise so it won't hockle (kink) or tangle. If it's an unused dock line, either end can be used to start a coil. Otherwise, always start at the secured end—where the halyard or sheet is cleated, for example, and work toward the free end. Never start at the free end—you'll end up with a twisted, awkward coil that's anything but docile. If the line to be coiled is loose and untangled, it's easy. If it looks the least bit tangled, "overhaul" it by running it through your hands from one end to the other, so it's ready to be coiled.

Now, start by holding the line in your left hand. With an easy sweeping motion, using your right hand, bring each coil to your left hand and take it in with your fingers. Remember that the coils are always clockwise.

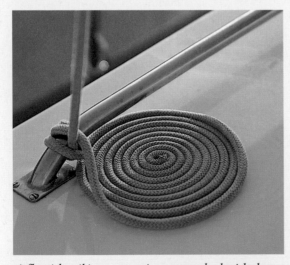

A flemish coil is an attractive way to deal with the free end of a line in use, but don't leave it in place too long.

An even sweep of your arm, the same distance each time, will result in coils of the same size. Sometimes your thumb is used to add or control a twist—it takes practice.

Don't try to wind up the line over your elbow, unless you're a landlubber in the backyard doing clothesline. (If you are naturally left-handed, you may want to reverse the "left" and "right" instructions above.)

When working with braided line, which has no lay or twist to it, it's not necessary to coil it. Simply hand a length from your right hand to your left hand and you will see a figure eight develop. From this eight, the line will always pay out without kinking or fouling. But since coiling line is a frequent task aboard boats, sometimes with one kind of line and sometimes with another, get into the habit of making clockwise coils no matter what type of line you are handling.

Stowing a Coiled Line

What you do next with the coil or figure eight depends on circumstances. If the line is the end of a jib sheet that will be used again in a few minutes, or the unused part of a dock line that you need to keep ready, just turn the coil so the free end is down and lay it on the deck, in the corner of the cockpit, or wherever is convenient.

If the coil is to be hung up, which it will be in most cases, there are several ways to do it. A completely free coil of line, such as a fairly heavy spare anchor line that is to be stowed for a while, can be tied up—using using shock cord or rope straps made up for the purpose, or small pieces of spare line. A newer, convenient method is to use cinch straps of Velcro self-adhering tape. If it is a very heavy and long line you would do best to lay it onto the deck in figure eights when coiling—you couldn't hold the coil in your hand anyway. On a ship this is called FAKING (sometimes FLAKING) DOWN.

A free coil, such as an unused dock line that you may use again soon, is often handled as follows: take a short arm's length of the end of the line and wrap the coil with three, four, or five turns and then, using the last length of line, pass a loop through the entire end of the coil. Hang the coil up, on a cleat or hook, using this loop. When you want to use the line, the loop comes out quickly and the whole coil is readily available.

A halyard is handled somewhat similarly, except that:

1. Don't wrap the coil. Leave it free, for quickest availability when the sail is to be dropped.

2. Use the standing part of the line, not the free end, to make the pass-through loop, and to keep it from slipping loose give it a turn or two as you hang it on the cleat.

There is another way to deal with the free end of a line that is somewhat more decorative, a FLEMISH COIL; see opposite. This is easy to do on deck or pier, and look "yachtlike," but if you leave it there for an extended period of time, it will pickup up dirt and moisture, and leave a soiled mark behind when it is picked up.

Of course, an eye splice is very useful in one end of a dock line; it makes a good loop with which to hang up the line.

When wrapping a coil, make a loop with the free end, pass it over the top and pull on the free end.

To hang a halyard coil, use the standing line to make a pass through the loop that goes on the cleat.

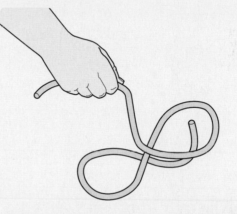

The term "faking a coil," or "flaking," means, simply, to lay the rope in the form of a figure eight.

The cleat should be mounted so that it is at an angle to the expected direction of strain.

Even half a turn, plus a firm hold on the line, usually creates enough friction to hold a boat at a dock until the whole turn can be completed. In fact, you should always take a half turn around a cleat when a load is coming on the line; this is an essential part of good line handling called SNUBBING. Never try to hold a load-bearing line in your bare hands—it can slip and seriously burn your fingers and palm. Note that in the illustration on page 788 the snubbing is nearly a whole turn; and note also that the crossover that will make the figure eight should

be made after the line goes around *both* horns of the cleat.

One and a half or two figure eights are enough; more would add no security and just take time to undo later.

There are two ways to complete the hitches on a cleat: you can leave the last turn free, perhaps keeping it under your eye if it is a jib sheet, for example. In this way the line can be instantly thrown off if necessary.

For more security you can turn the last hitch over, so it is tightened to bind against itself. This might be best for a dock line or halyard, but is not safe if instant release may be necessary. In a small

MOST-USED KNOTS ON BOARD RECREATIONAL BOATS

OVERHAND KNOT

Shown here chiefly because it's simple, and helps explain the figure-eight knot shown at left. Use it sparingly; it's almost impossible to untie after it is tightened. (It is useful to hold the end of a winch line on a trailer hitch.)

FIGURE-EIGHT KNOT

With one more turn into the overhand knot you have a stopper knot, to keep the end of a line from running through a block or small grommet. Easy to untie.

BOWLINE

This is the most useful of all knots aboard a boat. Once learned (and practice is necessary) it is easy to make, never slips or jams, and can always be untied. Two bowlines, one on each line, are an excellent combination when you need to tie two lines together.

TWO HALF HITCHES

For fastening a line to something else, such as a grommet in the corner of an awning. Quick and easy, but for many special purposes there are better knots you will prefer. A single half hitch also has some special uses.

REEF KNOT OR SQUARE KNOT

If you are tying a bundle, this knot works; note that the two bitter ends are on the same side of the standing parts. If the line is under constant pressure, and if both ends are the same size, it can still be untied. If it is made with a strip of canvas or webbing, as when securing a furled sail, it is a useful knot and easily untied even when wet. If it is used to tie two lines together, to make a longer line, it is a mistake. Use the reef knot sparingly.

GRANNY KNOT

This is a knot that too many people tie automatically when they are trying to tie a square knot. They should teach their fingers to go the other way, because the granny is a useless knot. Sometimes it slips, sometimes it jams. It has no value at all on a boat.

COW HITCH OR LARK'S HEAD

A small existing loop (usually an eye splice, not shown here) turned inside itself when you want to fasten a line to a large piling. It is also useful to fasten such a loop to a ring, provided the other end of the line is free. Many people use this hitch to fasten a jib sheet to the clew of a jib on a small sailboat.

SLIPPERY REEF KNOT

Half a square bow-knot. Good for furling a sail. This is always easier to untie than a square knot.

SHEET BEND

This is an excellent way to tie two lines together, especially if they are of different sizes or textures. As you will realize when you practice tying knots, some are just variations on a theme. You can use part of a sheet bend to fasten onto a loop

BECKET HITCH

This is really a sheet bend, in which one line has a loop, such as an eye splice (shown here) or bowline. If an extra round turn is taken (near left), this is called a double becket hitch. This version is especially useful when the added-on line is smaller than the one with the loop.

BUNTLINE HITCH

This is excellent for fastening a halyard to a shackle. It is its own stopper knot and won't jam in a block as an eye splice might. Sometimes called the "inside clove hitch," or the "studding sail tack bend," this is easy to tie and untie. Another use is on a trailer winch snap shackle—a modern use for a hitch from square-rigger days.

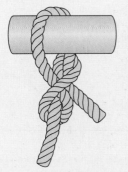

CARRICK BEND

This is one of the traditional ways to fasten two lines of the same size together. It looks beautiful in a drawing, but under strain it changes appearance. The carrick bend is probably best for fairly heavy, stiff lines of the same size.

ROLLING HITCH

To tie a small line to the standing part of a larger one, so it won't slip, use the rolling hitch. You can use this hitch to hold a jib sheet while riding turns are removed from a winch, to haul on any line, or to make an adjustable loop for an awning tie-down. The rolling hitch is also used to attach a line to a round wooden or metal object with the least possibility of slipping sideways. It will hold best when a second rolling hitch is made with the free end. It is also very useful for making a fender line fast to a lifeline or rail.

ANCHOR BEND

Also called fisherman's bend. This is a standard way to fasten an anchor line to the ring of an anchor. It is excellent for making up a spare anchor, and it may be used in many other situations.

The double loop reduces possible chafe and makes the half hitches more secure. Of course there are other ways to make an anchor line fast, including a bowline or an eye splice over a thimble, plus a shackle. Seizing the free end of the standing end gives extra security.

MOST-USED KNOTS (CONTINUED)

SURGEON'S KNOT

Tying the ordinary square or reef knot, even around a parcel, often requires a helper—someone to hold a finger on the half-formed knot until it is completed. If you take the extra turn of a surgeon's knot, the friction/tension holds it while you complete the knot. Surgeons, of course, call it a suture knot.

MARLINESPIKE HITCH

This is used to take up on a whipping or serving while it's being made—a good way to get it very tight. Withdraw the spike, and the hitch vanishes.

ASHLEY'S STOPPER KNOT

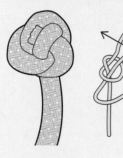

This makes a hefty stopper for the end of a line, looks seamanlike, and is easily undone. It takes a little longer to tie than the figure eight, and should be drawn up with some care.

CLOVE HITCH

Commonly used to tie a line to a piling. This is often a mistake. Although very adjustable, it tends to slip, especially with slippery nylon line. It is best to take an extra half hitch (or two

half hitches) to make it secure. If you use the same line from the bow to a piling, and then to the stern, the clove hitch is ideal. Both ends are taut and you have the adjustable feature.

REVERSE SURGEON'S KNOT

Aboard a sailboat there is one special purpose for a version of the surgeon's knot; tying the strings at the end of the older type of batten pocket. While the square knot will usually shake loose, perhaps leading to the loss of the batten, there is a cure. If you tie a reverse surgeon's knot—the extra twist in the second half of the knot is what's important –it will hold tightly no matter how the wind shakes it.

MONKEY FIST

Used to make a ball at the end of a heaving line. Make three loops around your hand, some 4 feet from the end of the line. Take the working end to make three more loops around, at right angles to the first three. The final set of loops is made around the inner group. Insert a pebble, if needed, and work turns to take up the slack.

CLEAT HITCH—CLEATING A LINE

Start with a turn around the cleat, then go around the cleat so that the line passes under each horn once. Finish with a half hitch over one horn. More wrappings and hitches are not needed, and they only slow the process of casting-off.

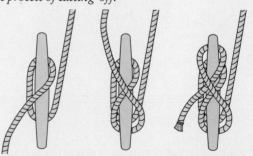

sailboat, in puffy winds, you probably wouldn't cleat the main sheet all the way—you'd take one turn and hold it tight in your hand.

Similar figure-eight turns are sometimes used on mooring bitts.

Using the Right Knot

The knots described, and shown in detail on pages 786–788, in the sidebar, "Most-Used Knots on Board Recreational Boats," can be divided into two groups: basic knots used generally on boats, and a few specialized knots that come in handy at certain times.

You have seen that some knots are echoes of others, and that more than one knot is sometimes used for the same purpose. Here are some reasons: A knot may work well with rough-textured rope, but tend to slip when tied with slippery synthetic line. One knot may work well with small line, while another works out better with heavier and stiffer line. The sheet bend can be tied in a hurry; it takes more time to make two bowlines when tying two long lines together, as for a tow. One bowline, with half the sheet bend tied into it (the becket bend), has the advantage that it can be unfastened quickly.

Some of the potential problems are most easily solved by alternate methods. An anchor bend, for example, is customarily given some extra security with a short seizing or a constrictor knot made with sail twine; see **Figure 23-11,** left. On other occasions, where the knot won't be in use for as

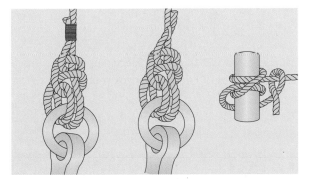

Figure 23-11 *Twine seizing, left, can be used to give extra security to an anchor bend. A variation, center, is to pass the free end through a strand of the standing part. A clove hitch, right, is better secured if it is finished with a half-hitch (or two) around the standing part of the line.*

KNOTS & STRENGTH OF LINE	
Type of knot, bend, or hitch	Percentage of retained strength
Anchor bend	
Over ⅝" dia. ring	55-65%
Over 4" dia. post	80-90%
Two half hitches	
Over ⅝" dia. ring	60-70%*
Over 4" dia. post	65-75%*
Square Knot	43-47%**
Sheet bend	48-58%*
Carrick bend	55-60%
Bowline	67-75%

* Smaller sizes of nylon are likely to slip without breaking
** Both nylon and combination ropes in smaller sizes are liable to slip.

Table 23-2 The use of knots and splices reduces the overall strength of lines in which they are used.

long a time as an anchor line might be, the free end can be passed through a strand of laid line (see **Figure 23-11,** center), or an extra half hitch can be used; see **Figure 23-11,** right—a clove hitch with an extra half hitch or two half hitches.

Effect on Strength

The use of knots (and splices) reduces the overall strength of any line—be aware of this, and select a size of line that provides adequate strength for the use to which it is put. Factors that are to be applied to the basic working load of a line to account for the use of knots and splices are listed in **Table 23-2.**

SPLICES & SPLICING

Most stock sailboats are delivered with all the rigging supplied; it is not until something new is added or something old is replaced that a splice is even thought about. Power and sailing craft may have a made-up anchor line (usually not as long as it should be), but probably will not have enough dock lines. Marine dealers often sell dock lines of various lengths already made up, or you may want to make your own. A sailmaker will often be a good source for new jib sheets, other lines, or small stuff. But in spite of the fact that many boat owners do not need to do much splicing, it is a good idea to know the basics. You can be a wise customer, and you can make the occasional emergency repair if you know the rudiments of splicing.

Splicing, like knotting, is a finger art. In small to moderate sizes of laid ropes you can make splices without tools, although a knife and fid are extremely helpful. If you are splicing heavier line or braided line, simple tools are necessary—a fid or marlinespike for laid line, and a special fid for braided line.

Splicing Principles

As you can easily see in the illustrations of **Figure 23-12,** or by looking at a splice that is already made in laid line, the principle is simple: three strands are tucked over and under so that they interweave with three other strands. If you are splicing the ends of two lines together in a SHORT SPLICE, the result is obviously thicker. A short splice, therefore, won't go through a block of the correct size for the diameter of the line. A LONG SPLICE is the solution—part of each strand is taken out and the tapered result makes a thin splice (with less strength). Most boat owners, however, would replace a broken line rather than splice it.

Short Splice

The best way to learn how to make a short splice is to start to make one! The sequence of actions is shown and described in **Figure 23-12,** A through E. A slightly modified beginning is shown in **Figure 23-12,** F.

Eye Splice

Although the short splice is the easiest to learn, an EYE SPLICE is much more often needed. An eye splice is most useful in one end, sometimes both ends, of a dock line. A good practice is to make the eye about three times larger than the size of any piling or bollard that is likely to be used. The reason: a too-small eye splice, under strain, tends to pull apart at its throat.

The same principle as in a short splice—interweaving—applies; see **Figure 23-13.** But there is

one point where an error is easily made; note **Figure 23-13,** B, very carefully.

Start the eye splice by unlaying the strands of the free end six to ten turns of lay. Now tape or heat-seal the end of each strand to prevent its unlaying while being handled; whipping can be applied to the strand ends, but this action is rarely done as this is only a temporary intermediate action if the ends are to be tapered. It is sometimes helpful to place tape around the unlaid strands every 4 to 6 inches to maintain the "turn" in the strand.

Next form a loop in the line by laying the end back along the standing part. Hold the standing part away from you in the left hand, loop toward you. The unlaid end can be worked with the right hand.

The size of loop is determined by the point X (**Figure 23-13,** A) where the opened strands are first tucked under the standing part of the line. If the splice is being made around a thimble, the line is laid snugly in the thimble groove and point X will be at the tapered end of the thimble. The line may be temporarily taped or tied into the thimble until the job is finished.

Now lay the three opened strands across the standing part as shown in **Figure 23-13,** A, so that the center strand *b* lies over and directly along the standing part. Left-hand strand *a* leads off to the left, right-hand strand *c* to the right of the standing part.

Tucking of strand ends, *a*, *b*, and *c* under the three strands of the standing part is the next step. Get this right and the rest is easy.

Always start with the center strand *b*. Select the topmost strand *2* of the standing part near point X and tuck *b* under it. Pull it up snug, but not so tight as to distort the natural lay of all strands. Note that the tuck is made from right to left, *against* the lay of the standing part.

Now take left-hand strand *a* and pass it over strand *2* and then tuck it under strand *1*. Similarly, take strand *c* and tuck under strand *3*, which lies to the right of strand *2*—*be sure to tuck from right to left in every case.*

The greatest risk of starting wrong is in the first tuck of strand *c*. It should go under *3*, from right

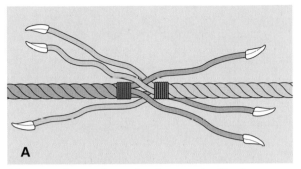

A

To start a short splice, *unlay the strands of both rope ends for a short distance, about ten turns of the lay. Tape or fuse the six strands, or whip them, to prevent unlaying. A seizing is often made around each of the ropes, or each is wrapped with a piece of tape, to prevent strands from unlaying too far. These seizings or tape will be cut as the splice is completed.*

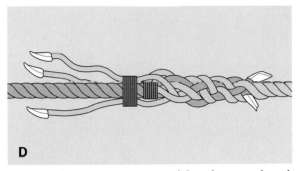

D

Next cut the temporary seizing of the other strands and the rope and repeat, splicing these three remaining strands into the opposite rope.

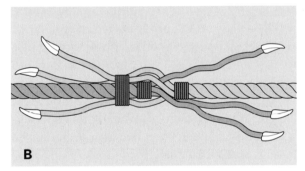

B

Next, "marry" the ends so that the strands of each rope lie alternately between strands of the other as show. Now tie all three strands of one rope temporarily to the other—this is desirable, but not essential.

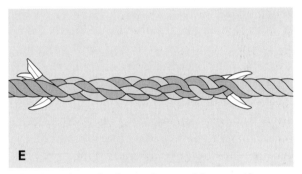

E

This shows how the short splice would appear if not tapered, after trimming off the ends of strands. Never cut the ends too close; otherwise when a heavy strain is put on the rope, the last tuck tends to work out.

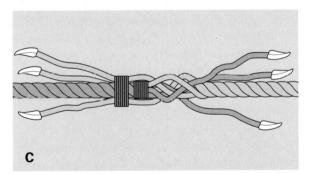

C

Working with the three free strands, remove temporary seizing from around the other rope and splice the strands into it by tucking the loose strands over and under successive strands from right to left against the lay of the rope. When first tucks have been made, snug down all three strands. Then tuck two or three more times on that side

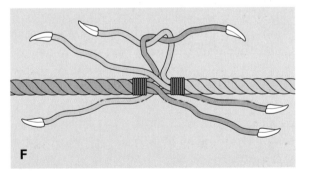

F

An alternative to the short splice technique shown in Steps A through E, which some find easier, is to start as in Step A and tie pairs of strands from opposite ends in an overhand knot. This, in effect, makes the first tuck.

Figure 23-12 *The five steps of a short splice are shown above, A through E. An alternative beginning is shown at F.*

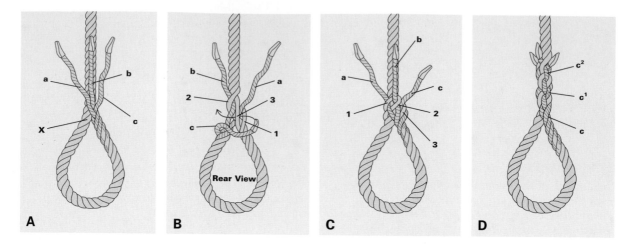

Figure 23-13 An eye splice forms a permanent loop in the end of a line. It may be made around a thimble to guard against chafe (as occurs on an anchor line), or as a larger eye without a thimble for use as a dock line.

to left and look like the drawing in **Figure 23-13, B.** The way you do it is to flop the whole thing over in your hands before making the tuck of strand c. You'll notice only one free strand (that's c) untucked, and only one of the original strands in the standing part that doesn't have a strand under it. Be sure you make the third tuck in the right direction; see **Figure 23-13,** B.

If the first tuck of each of strands, a, b, and c is correctly made, the splice at this point will look as shown in **Figure 23-13,** C.

The splice is completed by making at least three additional tucks with each of strands a, b, and c. As each added tuck is made be sure it passes over one strand of the standing part, then under the strand next above it, and so on, the tucked strand running against the lay of the strands of the standing part. This is clearly shown in **Figure 23-13,** D, after the first three tucks have been made. Note that c, c1, and c2, are the *same* strand as it appears after each of the three successive tucks.

Suggestions The splice can be made neater by tapering. This is done by cutting out part of the yarns from the tucking strands before the finishing tucks. In any case, the first four tucks in synthetic line are made with full strands. (Four tucks are necessary as synthetics are often slippery.) After that, some experienced skippers prefer to cut out about a third of each strand and

make one last tuck. This produces an even taper. After the splice is finished, roll it on deck under foot to smooth it up. Then put a strain on it and finally cut off the projecting ends of the strands. Do not cut off the "tails" too short. If desired, locking can be applied at the throat of the splice.

The loose fibers at the end of each strand can be fused with a rope-cutting tool such as a soldering gun, or with a flame, but be careful not to melt or set fire to the rope.

• The eye splice is often made on a metal or plastic thimble. When used this way it is necessary to work the splice very tightly and it is almost always desirable to add a locking, using a needle and waxed nylon twine or tape (see instructions for whipping on page 797).

• Another way to make a synthetic rope splice tight is to place it in boiling water so that the rope shrinks.

• In all splicing, careful re-laying of the rope—so that every strand is under the same even tension—is important.

• It is important to insert the thimble or other captive fitting into your splice *before* finalizing it. This is often forgotten when making an eye splice, even by experts.

Back Splice

One other splice is seen occasionally on boats: the BACK SPLICE at the end of a line. This makes a

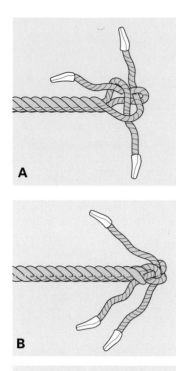

Figure 23-14 A back splice is started by bringing each strand over the one to its left, and under the next one, as in A. The strands are then tucked as shown in B for at least three tucks each. Longer strands can be used, and trimmed in thirds (after the basic tucks) to provide a tapered finish.

good, neat finish to a line, but it has a major disadvantage: if you want to unreeve the line at the end of the season, or to replace it, the back splice probably won't go through the blocks; see **Figure 23-14.** A well-made whipping makes an equally neat finish (refer to **Figures 23-20** and **23-21**). You can tie a figure eight or Ashley stopper knot to keep the end from going through a block when you don't want it to.

Splicing Double-Braided Line

An eye splice in double-braid looks difficult—but is relatively simple to learn. The technique has almost nothing to do with other kinds of splicing—it is just a logical way to use the cover and core of the braided line since both are hollow. A thimble can be inserted during the splicing process. The eight steps of the procedure are described, with explanatory illustrations that

show how special tools are used, in **Figure 23-15a through 23-15h**, on pages 794-795.

Splicing Line to Wire Rope & Chain

Splices in wire rope, best left to professionals, and wire-to-rope, surely left to professionals, use techniques somewhat similar to laid rope splices, but differing in details.

Anchor lines (rodes) that use a combination of three-strand nylon line and chain are common (see Chapter 9). These can join an eye splice in the line to a link of the chain by use of a shackle, but only if a windlass is *not* used. If a windlass is used, the line must be spliced to the chain in order that the junction will pass smoothly over the drum. This is frequently left to a professional, but should be within the capability of a boater who has some splicing experience. The technique used is much like a combination of an eye splice and a back splice. Two strands of the line are passed through the end link of the chain in one direction, and the other strand is passed through the same link in the opposite direction. Strands are then interwoven in a manner common to all splices, taking care that they are pulled up snuggly and are tapered off at the finish of the splice.

CARE & MAINTENANCE OF LINES

The many lines on your craft not only represent a significant financial investment, they are also important safety equipment. Taking the proper care of them will lengthen their lives and postpone the day when they have to be replaced. Proper care will also ensure that they have their full rated strength when they are used; see **Figure 23-16.**

Routine Care for Lines

The various lines on your boat will serve you better and last longer if they are used properly and are given continuing attention.

Keep Lines Clean. Dirt, sand, oil, and acids are destructive to synthetic rope. To wash rope, put it in a mesh bag or dirt pillowcase—that way it won't foul up your washing machine. Mild

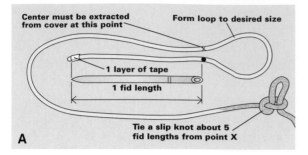

Figure 23-15a *Tightly tape end with one layer of tape. Mark a big dot one fid length from end of line, and from this dot form a loop the size of the eye you want. Mark an X where the loop meets the dot.*

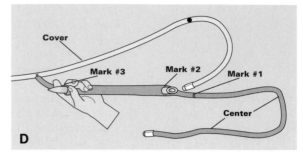

Figure 23-15d *Insert fid into center at Mark #2, and slide it lengthwise through "tunnel" until point comes out at Mark #3.*

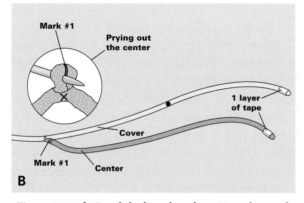

Figure 23-15b *Bend the line sharply at X, and spread the strands apart firmly to make an opening so the center can be pried out. Mark one big line on the center where it comes out (this is Mark #1), and use your fingers to pull all the center out of the cover from X to the end. Pull on the paper tape inside the cover until it breaks back at the slip knot, and pull it out. Put a layer of tape on center end.*

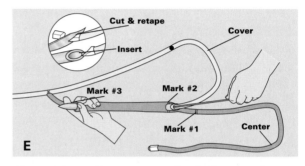

Figure 23-15e *Cut across taped end of cover to form a point, and retape tightly with one layer of tape. Jam this point into open end of the fid; jam pusher into fid behind the tape. Hold center gently at Mark #3 and push both fid and cover through center until dot almost disappears at Mark #2.*

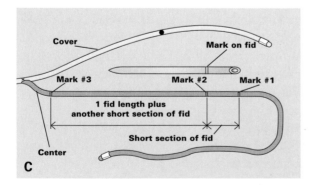

Figure 23-15c *Pull out more of the center. From Mark #1 measure a distance equal to the short section of the fid, and mark two heavy lines (this is Mark #2). Mark #3 is three heavy lines at a distance of one fid length plus one short section of the fid from Mark #2.*

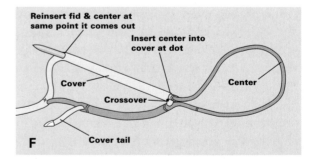

Figure 23-15f *Note how center tail must travel through the cover. It must go in close to dot, and come out through the opening at X. On large eyes several passes may be needed for fid to reach X. When this occurs, simply reinsert fid at the point it came out and continue to X. To start, insert fid in cover at dot and slide it through tunnel to X. Form a tapered point on center tail, jam it into the open end of fid, and push fid and center through the cover. After fid comes out at X, pull all center tail through cover until tight, then pull cover tail tight.*

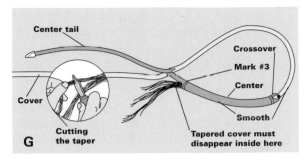

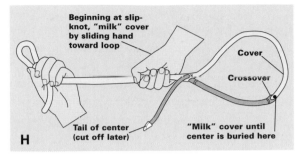

Figure 23-15g *Unravel cover tail braid all the way to Mark #3, and cut off groups of strands at staggered intervals to form a tapered end. Hold loop at crossover in one hand, and firmly smooth both sides of loop away from crossover. Do this until the tapered tail disappears inside Mark #3.*

Figure 23-15h *Hold rope at slipknot, and gently begin to "milk," or slide, the cover slack toward the loop. You'll see the center begin to disappear into the cover. Go back to the knot, and continue sliding more cover firmly until all center and the crossover are buried.*

washing power should be used, and a bit of fabric softener may be added.

Don't Let It Kink . Kinking (hocking) of a line is not only annoying, but it can also result in problems that lead to breakage. Sometimes coiling new three-strand rope first against the lay (counterclockwise), and then with the lay (clockwise), helps to get it so it will coil and run smoothly. Rope, including braided rope, should be taken off its original spool in a direct unwinding pull—not looped off over the top of the spool. As mentioned earlier, larger, stiffer ropes may need different handling from small, flexible lines. Double-braid can

develop a twist when used off and on winches. This can lead to kinking. Overhaul the line and take out the twist, as needed.

Guard Against Chafing & Abrasion. You can use a leather or plastic chafe guard, which is better, or, if your line is small enough, one of the kind made from split garden hose. You can whip or serve (by wrapping line of a smaller size around the line to take the wear) a place in a dock line that goes over a gunwale or through a chock. Using small braided tape or cord is good for such a whipping because if it wears through it breaks and you can see it. Special chafing tape is also available.

Figure 23-16 *The way that lines are handled and stowed is an indication of the way that a boat is generally cared for.*

Some skippers prewhip dock lines and anchor lines at a number of convenient places and then adjust the lines so the whippings will be in the chocks.

You should "change the nip" on an anchor line periodically, letting out or taking in a short length; don't let the wear come on the same place over an extended time.

Avoid Friction Damage. Slipping, on a power winch or windlass, can result in friction heat that will damage a line.

Use the Right Size Line in a Proper Manner. A line that jams in a block can tear itself apart. Heavy strains that do not break a rope can nevertheless weaken it. Both continual stretching and sudden shocks are damaging.

Maintenance for Lines

Maintenance of the lines on board a boat should be an ongoing procedure, but such action should be supplemented by a complete annual or semiannual inspection of all lines, those in use and those merely waiting to be used

Make Small Repairs Promptly. If an eye splice is coming undone, or a whipping breaks, fix it with care before relying on that line again. An incomplete eye splice can be dangerous, and an unwhipped line end will keep right on coming apart until it is fixed.

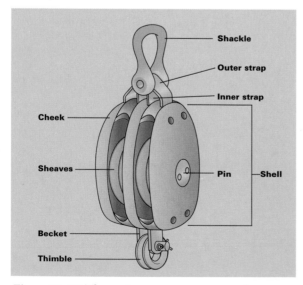

Figure 23-17 The various component parts of a double-sheave block are identified in the above sketch.

Inspect Your Lines & Rigging. Inspection of rope means unlaying a number of strands, looking for broken fibers. Frayed strands, powdered fibers inside the rope, and stiffness are the signs of serious deterioration. In addition, you should go over the entire length of line, looking for cuts and nicks, exterior signs of abrasion, and burns.

A slight abrasion fuzz on synthetic line, laid or braided, acts as a protective cushion. Pulled or cut strands in braided line are more serious; they can affect 2 percent or more of the line strength for each strand involved.

Eye splices should be inspected, inside and out, for distortion of the thimbles as well as a tendency for the splice to come undone. Whipping and servings, of course, should be inspected regularly for excessive wear, so they can be renewed. Several times a season halyards should get a special inspection where they run through the block at the masthead when in use, because here the small motion always in the same place around the block, plus sharp bends in the line, lead to breakdowns. Because of this, anyone who has had a sail drop suddenly in a strong wind knows the wisdom of checking halyards.

Any three-strand lines that have had severe kinks, or hockles, can be assumed to have lost 30 percent of their strength. Never use force to straighten a kink. Instead, turn the line in your hands or trail it astern.

An old-fashioned cure for wear on a line is still useful with synthetic rope: reversing the line end for end. In other cases a small repair, a whipping to take the chafing, or a slight shortening of the line to make a new eye splice may be the cure.

BLOCKS & TACKLE

The use of a BLOCK AND TACKLE (sometimes pronounced "tay-kle"), or to use a higher sounding name, mechanical appliance, on board small craft is most often found on sailboats. On powerboats, such gear is generally limited to the lowering and hoisting aboard of dinghies and tenders. Nonetheless, any boater should have a basic knowledge of it, as its use enables one man to do the work of many.

ROPE & BLOCK SIZES

Size of Block (Length of Shell) (Inches)	Diameter of Rope (Inches)
3	$\frac{3}{8}$
4	$\frac{1}{2}$
5	$\frac{9}{16}$ - $\frac{5}{8}$
6	$\frac{3}{4}$
7	$\frac{13}{16}$
8	$\frac{7}{8}$ - 1

Table 23-3 Matching rope and block sizes.

Blocks and tackle are used where hoisting sails, as well as setting them, requires some means for one or two people to provide the strength of many. No matter how small the sailboat, the sheets usually run through one or more blocks, meaning there is a mechanical appliance providing a mechanical advantage. To see how beneficial this is, go sailing in a 20-foot boat, in a moderate breeze, and bend a line to the boom. While underway, attempt to trim in the sail with your improvised sheet. It will come in, but it will be a struggle; so try the exercise with the regular system of blocks and tackle and you will see with what ease the sail comes in.

Terminology

A BLOCK consists of a frame of wood or metal inside of which is fitted one or more SHEAVES (pulleys)—the word is pronounced "shiv"—and is designated according to the number of sheaves it contains, such as single, double, or triple; see **Figure 23-17**. The size of the block to be used is, of course, determined by the size of the rope that will run through it. If a fiber rope is being used, the size of the block should be about three times the *circumference* of the rope and the sheave diameter about twice the circumference. Therefore, for 5/8-inch rope (about 2 inches in circumference), the block could be 6 inches (three times the circumference) and the sheave diameter 4 inches (twice the circumference). This is an approximation; see **Table 23-3** for recommended block sizes and rope diameters. Today, blocks are designed

for a narrow range of line sizes. Choosing the maximum possible diameter of sheave will help to reduce friction, thereby extending the life of lines and equipment.

Wire rope is also used for running rigging, but usually only as halyard leads on sailboats. This should be stainless steel and sheaves should be as large as possible for long rope life. Make sure the rope cannot be squeezed between the sheave and the sideplate (also called the cheek or shell) of the block or your line may become jammed.

The term TACKLE is used for an assemblage of FALLS (lines) and BLOCKS. When you pass rope through the blocks, you REEVE them and the part of the fall made fast to one of the blocks, or to the load, as the case may be, is known as the STANDING PART, while the end upon which the force is to be applied is called the HAULING PART. To OVERHAUL the falls is to separate the blocks; to ROUND IN is to bring them together; and CHOCK-A-BLOCK or TWO-BLOCKED means they are positioned tight together.

Types of Tackle

Tackles are named in several ways; see **Figure 23-18**; according to the number of sheaves in the blocks that are used (single, two-fold, three-fold PURCHASES), or according to the purpose for which the tackle is used, or from names handed down from the past (luff-tackles, watch-tackles, gun-tackles, Spanish-burtons, etc.). The tackles that may be found aboard cruising boats are now generally classified by ratio, as below:

Ratio 1 to 1. Traditionally called a single whip, this is a single fixed block and fall. There is no gain in power—the gain is only in height of lift or change in direction of pull.

Ratio 2 to 1 or 3 to 1. Traditionally called a gun tackle, this consists of two single blocks. If lower block is movable, double force is gained. If upper block is movable, triple force is gained.

Ratio 3 to 1 or 4 to 1. Traditionally called a luff tackle, this consists of a double block and a single block. The force gained is three if the single block is movable, four if the double block is movable.

Ratio 4 to 1 or 5 to 1. Traditionally called a two-fold or double tackle, this consists of two

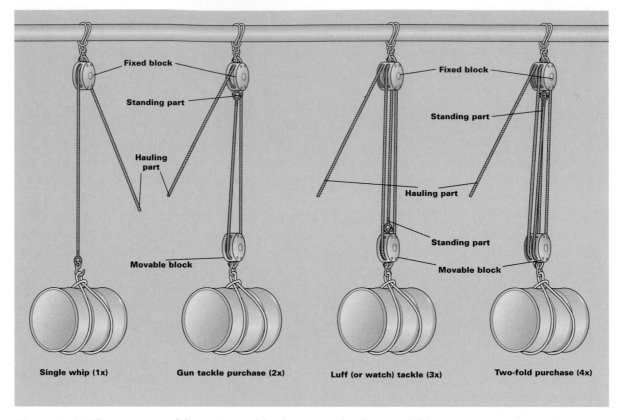

Figure 23-18 These are some of the various tackles that are used on boats and ships.

double sheave blocks. Force gained is four or five, depending upon block movement.

Calculating the Power of a Tackle

The force gained in all these tackle combinations is theoretical only, as the friction of the blocks is ignored. The usual method of compensating for this friction, and calculating the actual force required, is to add 5 percent to the weight of the object (W) for each sheave in the tackle before dividing by the number of falls (with modern gear, this may be a bit on the conservative side). For example: in the two-fold purchase of **Figure 23-18,** if the weight of the drum is 500 pounds, 5 percent is 25 pounds; 4 sheaves x 25 pounds = 100 pounds. Thus the total W to be considered is 500 + 100 = 600 pounds. With four falls, the force needed to lift the drum would be 600 ÷ 4 or 150 pounds, rather than the theoretical 125 pounds if friction was disregarded—a significant difference. The actual friction will, of course, vary with the type of bearings and pins, state of lubrication, and sheave diameter.

There are, of course a number of other purchases, the heaviest commonly used aboard ship being a three-fold purchase, which consists of two triple blocks.

It must be remembered that the hauling part on a three-part block should be reeved around the *center* sheave. If this is not done, the block will cant, causing it to bind, and in extreme cases to break.

AT THE BITTER END

If a piece of rope is cut, it will start to fray and unravel at the end—sometimes in seconds; see **Figure 23-19,** A and B. If it is taped before cutting, or if the cutting is done with an electric cutter that melts the fibers, the end won't fray, at least not immediately.

Taping or Dipping

But the end of a line still needs protection for almost any use. There are a variety of ways that a

BLOCK MAINTENANCE

Maintenance for a block relates closely to its construction. Older blocks needed grease to ease friction. Today's use of synthetics and precision machining provides a product that is almost maintenance-free. Maintenance is now reduced to the following: Inspect periodically for fatigue, in particular for cracked or elongated shackles. Rinse often with fresh water to keep clean, and if lubrication is needed, a dry lubricant will usually suffice.

Avoid leaving heavy tools on blocks when not in use. This may slightly deform the bearings.

Sheaves are now designed to accommodate the following: wire only, wire-rope combination (halyards), Kevlar and Spectra line with a special configuration that allows the line to flatten to avoid stress concentration, and ratchet sheaves with their many-sided design that grips sheets tenaciously but allows line to be eased smoothly.

Large boats' sheaves and blocks generally come in three types of bearing systems:

• Ball bearing for the freest running system; they have the lowest load carrying ability.

• Roller bearings can carry more load, but they have more friction at low loads. Combinations of ball and roller bearing give a free rolling system for loads that are moderate to high.

• Bushings, impregnated with Teflon, combined with side-load balls are used for loads too high even for roller bearings. These produce more friction than balls or rollers at low loads. Good examples are: masthead sheaves, runner block sheaves, wire sheaves, and steering cable sheaves. Most blocks previously had a friction load of approximately 5 percent per sheave. Today's technology has brought it down to as low as 2 percent per sheave.

line can be protected; some are good if you're in a hurry, some fit one situation relating to line handling, others are right for different purposes.

A careful taping of the end of a line is useful but hardly looks seamanlike; one might say it's a good way to handle a coil of spare rope that you're storing in a locker before putting it to use; see **Figure 23-19, C.** A rope end with adhesive tape is at least ready for a more sophisticated finish later.

The air-drying liquid plastics mentioned earlier can also be used for rope ends and may make color coding possible; see **Figure 23-19, D.**

Whipping

Braided and double-braided line is more difficult to finish with a traditional yet functional end. An eye splice on a braided dock line is an obviously correct solution for one end—this end is protected and the eye splice is ready to use. On the other end, a whipping, **Figure 23-19,** E, preferably one made very tight with a sailmaker's needle, results in a usable finish.

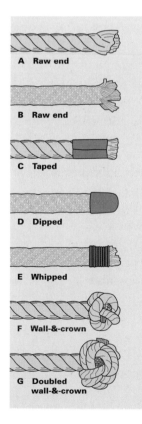

A Raw end

B Raw end

C Taped

D Dipped

E Whipped

F Wall-&-crown

G Doubled wall-&-crown

Figure 23-19 The ends of three-strand or braided line can be taped, dipped, or whipped to prevent unlaying. Also shown is the wall-and-crown, a good-looking finish that combines two separate knots, and the manrope knot, a doubled wall-and-crown.

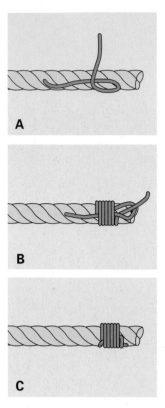

Figure 23-20 *To make a plain whipping, begin at least 1 inch from the bitter end. Lay a loop of cord across the line, leaving a tail of 5 or 6 inches on the bitter end, A. Then with the working piece of cord, wrap around the line from the trail end toward the apex of the loop, B. To finish off the whipping, insert the working end of the cord through the loop. Pull on the bitter end of the cord until the loop slides completely out of sight, then clip the ends closely, C.*

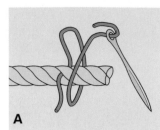
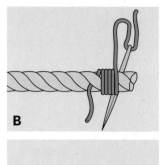

Figure 23-21 *A sailmaker's whipping is started by stitching the cord through the line, A. Wind six or more turns around the line, B, and stitch back through it. Then bring the cord back over the turns along a groove between the strands. Stitch through a strand to the next groove, and bring the cord back along this. Stitch through the next strand to the final groove, C, and finish with a square knot in the cord.*

With laid line, however, the marlinespike arts of the sailor provide more opportunity. A variety of whippings, knots, or a back splice are among the choices.

To make a plain whipping, you need the right size of waxed nylon twine or lacing and your hands; see **Figure 23-20.**

A far better whipping, called a sailmaker's whipping, requires a palm and sailmaker's needle, as well as the cord or lacing twine; see **Figure 23-21** for instructions. This whipping will last longer as well as look better.

Ending with a Splice or Knot

A standard way to make a good-looking end for a line—provided it doesn't have to go through a block—is a back splice. Properly tapered, perhaps polished off with a little extra whipping, it will last a long time; refer to **Figure 23-14.**

Two fancier rope ends, from many that are available, are illustrated here without instructions. You can learn to make them—as you can learn other ornamental and useful knots and rope work—in any of several advanced books on marlinespike seamanship.

• The wall-and-crown (see **Figure 23-19,** F) is a good-looking finish that combines two simple knots.

• The manrope knot is really a doubled wall-and-crown (see **Figure 23-19,** G). Finished with a back splice it looks good on the end of a bucket rope—and helps you hold the bucket.

Weather

The Basic Forces That Make Weather • Clouds • Fog • Highs & Lows Air Masses & Fronts • Storms & Severe Weather • Forecasts & How To Get Information • Weather Observing & Weather Proverbs

eather is an important element of your boating; it can add to or detract from your environment, and it can have a vital bearing on your safety.

As the skipper of a small craft you really need two different kinds of weather information: the current or "nowcast" conditions, how these conditions may change in the next few hours, what conditions should be like over the next two or three days, and, for longer term planning, a forecast of what conditions will be like through the remainder of the week. You need not be qualified as a weather forecaster, but you must be able to obtain up-to-date information and utilize this information as it relates to your individual plans. And you must be able to correctly interpret local weather signs—wind shifts, changes in cloud patterns or ocean swells.

What Makes the Weather

Weather doesn't just happen; there are basic causes and effects. An appreciation of these influences will lead to a better understanding of weather systems and their movement. This is the basis for weather forecasting.

The Earth's Atmosphere

The earth is enveloped in its ATMOSPHERE—a constantly changing, fluid-like mixture of gasses, mostly nitrogen and oxygen—that extends upward with decreasing density for many miles. Half of all this air is in the lower 3.5 miles (5.6 km), but from a weather standpoint, we are usually concerned only with that portion which lies below about 20 miles (32 km).

The atmosphere consists of several layers. Of these, only the lower two (the TROPOSPHERE and the STRATOSPHERE) and the boundary area between them (the TROPOPAUSE) will be of interest to us.

The height of the troposphere varies with latitude, averaging 11 miles (18 km) at the equator but only 5 miles (8 km) above the poles. This is the area that contains our weather systems, and most of our clouds.

Heat from the Sun

Although the sun is some 93 million miles (150 million km) away, and only an infinitesimal fraction of its energy falls on the earth, this is enough to make the earth habitable and to establish our climate and weather patterns. About 29 percent of the sun's energy is reflected back into space or

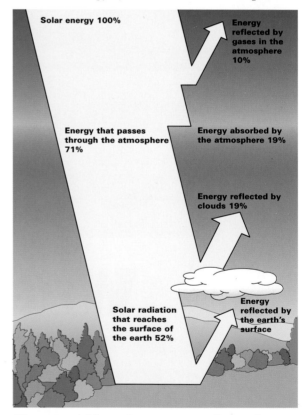

Figure 24-01 The sun's rays encounter layers of gasses in the atmosphere that either stop the rays, reflect them, or let them through. Only about half of the sun's radiated energy reaches the earth's surface, where it is reflected or absorbed and partially reradiated.

absorbed by the atmosphere. Clouds reflect another 19 percent, and 52 percent reaches the earth. Much of the solar energy that does reach the earth's surface is reradiated as heat rays of longer wavelength. These are trapped in the lower atmosphere in much the way air in a greenhouse is warmed to grow plants—hence the much-talked-about "greenhouse effect" and the general warming of the planet. Various types of surfaces absorb and reflect different percentages of the incoming solar rays; these differences result in both climatic differences between geographic regions and local differences between land and sea areas; see **Figure 24-01.**

The atmosphere moderates the sun's effect, filtering out excess (and harmful) rays by day, and holding in heat at night. Without our atmosphere, we would have to cope with extremes like those on the moon, +200° Fahrenheit (F) or more in sunlight, -200° F or less in darkness (+93 to -129° Celsius (C). Clouds directly affect the cooling of the air at night as they reflect back a portion of the heat rising from the earth's surface; on clear nights, more heat is lost.

CLOUDS

The most visible manifestation of weather is clouds; winds and temperature can be felt, but not seen. Many cloud patterns are not only beautiful and interesting to watch, but they can also be meaningful in interpreting weather conditions and trends.

Moisture in the Air

There is more water in the air than you might think; it evaporates from the oceans, lakes, and rivers and can exist in the air in any of three physical states—vapor, liquid, and solid. A term you will often hear is RELATIVE HUMIDITY—the amount of water vapor present in the air as a *percentage* of the maximum possible amount for air at that temperature. This maximum amount decreases with a decrease in temperature. The relative humidity of a mass of air *increases* as its temperature *falls* even though the actual amount of moisture is unchanged. When air is cooled after

---

DESCRIBING WATER VAPOR CONTENT

- **Condensation** A process in which a gas changes to a liquid, as from steam to water.
- **Dew point** The temperature at which air would become saturated if cooled at constant pressure.
- **Evaporation** A process in which a liquid turns to a vapor without its temperature reaching the boiling point.
- **Relative humidity** The actual amount of water vapor in the air divided by the amount of water vapor that would be present if the air were saturated at the same temperature and pressure. It is expressed as a percentage.

Dew point indicates indirectly the amount of water vapor present, while relative humidity expresses the degree of saturation. Therefore, air that has a temperature and dew point of 75°F and 50°F respectively contains more water vapor than air with a temperature and dew point of 45°F and 45°F respectively. However, the relative humidity is higher in the latter case.

- **Saturation** The point at which air will not absorb more moisture. The higher the temperature, the more water vapor the air can hold before it becomes saturated.
- **Sublimation** Conversion directly from a solid to a vapor or vice versa without going through the liquid state.

---

the relative humidity reaches 100 percent, some moisture condenses into a visible form. The temperature at which this occurs is the DEW POINT.

Formation of Clouds

When air moves upward (e.g., moving over mountains, moving over domes of colder air, or moving upward in cumuloform clouds), it expands and cools. As it cools, the relative humidity increases until the air becomes saturated and clouds are formed. There may also be precipitation in the form of RAIN (liquid) or SNOW, SLEET, or HAIL (solid). (When this saturation occurs at or very near the surface, this is FOG. The various types of fog and the circumstances of their formation are discussed in detail on pages 807–811.)

Cooling can also come with horizontal air movement. For example, air cools when moving from warmer water surfaces to cooler land surfaces. Again, when air cools to the dew point, clouds form and precipitation can fall.

Types of Clouds

There is an international system of cloud classification. The different cloud types have descriptive names that depend mainly upon appearance. However, they may also sometimes be classified upon the processes of formation as seen by an observer. Despite an almost infinite variety of shapes and forms, it is still possible to define ten basic types; see **Figure 24-02a** through **Figure 24-02u** on this and following pages.

High Clouds

HIGH CLOUDS are found above about 18,000 to 20,000 feet (5500 to 6000 m) and are composed of ice crystals. Their various types are described below; see **Figures 24-02a-f.**

Cirrus (Ci) Detached clouds in the form of white, delicate filaments, or white or mostly white patches or narrow bands. These clouds have a fibrous (hair-like) appearance, or a silky sheen, or both. Experienced boaters will often use wispy cirrus clouds as the first sign that an approaching cold front will arrive in about 24 hours.

Figure 24-02a Cirrostratus covers the entire sky, with some thicker patches of altostratus below it. As cirrus clouds thicken, the lower portions become water droplets.

Figure 24-02b Cirrocumulus cloud puffs are smaller in apparent size than the sun or moon, which they would not obscure. This is sometimes called a "mackerel sky."

Figure 24-02c Cirrostratus is a high veil of ice crystal cloud through which the sun can be seen, along with a well-defined halo; it may herald an approaching storm system.

Figure 24-02d Ground haze, mixed with industrial smog, dissipates in morning sunlight which is not blocked by a think layer of cirrostratus cloud.

Figure 24-02e Cirrocumulus clouds are heavier and thicker than cirrus, but still without shading. Small elements may be more or less arranged in repeating patterns.

Figure 24-02f Cirrus are high, thin clouds, either in white filaments or patches and narrow bands. They may have a fibrous (hairlike) appearance or a silky sheen, or both.

Figure 24-02g *Altocumulus—white or gray, or both—often appears in regular patterns across large areas of the sky. The pattern above is called a "mackerel sky."*

Figure 24-02h *Altostratus represents warm air riding over cold air ahead of a warm front. The layer will grown thicker and lower, with continuous rain or snow.*

Figure 24-02i *More altostratus that covers the entire sky, with widely scattered stratocumulus beneath it. This followed a day of warm, hazy sunshine in late May.*

Figure 24-02j *Nimbostratus, just prior to the onset of a steady rainfall. If the sun were in the picture, its image would be blurred, and there would be no halo.*

Figure 24-02k *Stratus has a thick, almost uniform look. This indicates stable air, and as there is little turbulence in this, any precipitation will be fine drizzle.*

Figure 24-02l *Stratocumulus is white with dark patches in thick portions of the clouds. This type may appear as rounded masses or rolls that may or may not be merged.*

Cirrocumulus (Cc) Thin, white patch, sheet, or layer of cloud, without shading, composed of very small elements. These elements are in the form of grains or ripples, merged or separate, and more or less regularly arranged. Most of the elements have an apparent width of less than one degree of arc.

Cirrostratus (Cs) Transparent, whitish cloud veil of fibrous (hair-like) or smooth appearance, totally or partly covering the sky, and generally producing halos around the sun or the moon.

Middle Clouds

MIDDLE CLOUDS are found from about 7,000 feet up to 18-20,000 feet (2000 up to 5500-6,000 m). These are water droplet clouds and are described below; see **Figures 24-02g-i.**

Altocumulus (Ac) White or gray (or both

white and gray), patch, sheet, or layer of cloud, generally with shading, composed of layers, rounded masses, rolls, etc., which are sometimes partly fibrous or diffuse, and which may or may not be merged. Most of the regularly arranged small elements usually have an apparent width of between one and five degrees of arc.

Altostratus (As) Grayish or bluish cloud sheet or layer of striated, fibrous, or uniform appearance, totally or partly covering the sky, and having parts thin enough to reveal the sun at least vaguely, as through ground glass. Altostratus does not show halo phenomena.

Low Clouds

LOW CLOUDS, described below, are found from near ground up to about 7,000 feet (2000 m); see **Figures 24-02j-l.**

Figure 24-02m Cumulus of little development indicate continued fair weather; following the passage of a cold front, they may be accompanied by brisk winds.

Figure 24-02n More fair-weather cumulus. If they form in warm air ahead of a cold front, however, they can be accompanied by squalls and thunderstorms.

Figure 24-02o Cumulonimbus base as a line of heavy thunderstorms approaches. Squall winds reached 50 knots in gusts, and the accompanying rain was torrential.

Figure 24-02p Cumulus clouds normally are associated with fair weather, but local hot spots and extreme development can change them into storm cumulonimbus.

Figure 24-02q Cumulus may build in the afternoon, but later in the day will flatten as the surface cools and the supply of rising warm, most air diminishes.

Figure 24-02r Stratocumulus is a thick, solid layer with a lumpy base. It is often formed by the spreading out of cumulus, and may be followed by clearing at night.

Nimbostratus (Ns) Gray cloud layer, often dark, the appearance of which is rendered diffuse by more or less continuously falling rain or snow, which in most cases reaches the ground. These clouds are thick enough throughout to blot out the sun. Low, ragged clouds frequently occur below the layer, with which they may or may not merge.

Stratocumulus (Sc) Gray or whitish (or both gray and whitish), patch, sheet, or layer cloud. These almost always have dark parts, composed of tessellations (covering without gaps), rounded masses, or rolls, which are non-fibrous (except for "virga"—precipitation trails) and which may or may not be merged. Most of the regularly arranged elements have an apparent width of more than five degrees of arc.

Stratus (St) Generally gray cloud layer with a fairly uniform base, which may yield drizzle, ice prisms, or snow grains. When the sun is visible through the cloud, its outline is clearly discernible. Stratus does not produce halo phenomena (which is an ice crystal cloud effect) except, possibly, at very low temperatures. Sometimes stratus appears in the form of ragged patches.

Clouds of Vertical Development (Cumuloform)

As opposed to the clouds described above, which normally form in sheets or layers, there are clouds that have significant vertical extent. These develop with a significant rising action; see **Figures 24-02m-u.**

Cumulus (Cu) Detached clouds, generally dense and with definite outlines, developing vertically in the form of rising mounds, domes, or towers, of which the bulging upper part often

Figure 24-02s *Cumulus development culminates in an anvil-topped
cumulonimbus thunderhead that
may tower 20,000 to 50,000 feet
above the surface of the earth.*

Figure 24-02t *Cumulonimbus
associated with summer showers
results from local developments of
cumulus clouds. Rainfall is likely to
be brief, but moderately heavy.*

Figure 24-02u *Altostratus here is a
thick, almost uniform cloud layer
about 10,000 feet high. If this
thickens and lowers, precipitation is
on the way.*

resembles a cauliflower. The upper sunlit parts
are mostly brilliant white; their bases are relatively dark and horizontal. Sometimes cumulus
is ragged.

Cumulonimbus (Cb) Heavy and dense cloud,
with a considerable vertical extent in the form of a
mountain or huge towers. This is a thunderstorm;
see **Figure 24-02s** and pages 819–823. Depending
where on the earth they form, the tops of these
clouds may extend to over 100,000 ft (30km). At
least part of the upper portion is usually smooth,
or fibrous or striated, and nearly always flattened.
This part of a cumulonimbus cloud often spreads
out in the shape of an anvil or vast plume. Under
the base of this cloud, which is often very dark,

there are frequently low ragged clouds, either
merged with it or not, and precipitation.

Variations

It should be noted that cloud groupings as above
are not absolute or exclusive. For example, cumulonimbus often become mid-level altocumulus or
altostratus while the tops of these are high level
cirrus clouds

FOG

Fog is merely a cloud whose base rests upon the
earth, either land or water. It consists of water
droplets that are suspended in the air. Each
droplet is so small that it cannot be distinguished
individually, yet present in such tremendous
numbers that objects close at hand are obscured;
see **Figure 24-03.**

If we are to have innumerable water droplets
suspended in the air, there must be much water
vapor already in that air. If droplets are to form
from this vapor, the air must somehow be cooled
so the vapor will condense. If the droplets are to
condense in the air next to the earth, the cooling
must take place at the surface of the earth. If the
fog is to have any depth, successively higher layers
of air must be cooled sufficiently to allow condensation in them also. Fog usually forms from the
surface up. Thus, the land or water must be colder
than the air next to it; and this must be colder than
air above.

Figure 24-03 *Fog forms when warm, moist air is
cooled to the point where the water vapor in it
condenses out. Fog forms from the surface up;
as successive layers of air are cooled enough to cause
condensation, the depth of the fog increases.*

Air is said to be SATURATED with water vapor when its water vapor content would remain unchanged if it were placed above a level surface of pure water at its own temperature—it could absorb no more moisture. The amount of water vapor required to saturate a given volume of air depends on the temperature of the air, and increases as the temperature increases. (Remember, the higher the temperature, the more water vapor the air can hold before it becomes saturated.)

If a mass of air is originally in an unsaturated state, it can be saturated by cooling it down to a temperature at which its content of water vapor is the maximum containable amount, that is, to the DEW-POINT TEMPERATURE. Or it can become saturated by more water being caused to evaporate into it until it can hold no more. In this latter process, unsaturated air, as it passes over rivers and lakes, over the oceans or over wet ground, picks up water vapor and has its relative humidity raised. Also, rain falling from higher clouds will increase the amount of water vapor in unsaturated air near the earth.

Types of Fog

As a boater, you can be affected by four types of fog: (1) RADIATION FOG, formed in near-calm conditions by the cooling of nearby land on a clear night as a result of radiation of heat from the ground to the clear sky; (2) ADVECTION FOG, formed by the flow of warm air over cold sea or lake; (3) STEAM FOG, or SEA SMOKE, formed when cold air blows over much warmer water; and (4) PRECIPITATION FOG, formed when rain coming out of warm air aloft falls through a shallow layer of cold air at the earth's surface.

Note that both steam fog and rain fog are basically the result of evaporation from relatively warm water, a process that increases the dew point. These fogs can be described as WARM-SURFACE FOGS. On the other hand, radiation fog and advection fog can be considered COLD-SURFACE FOGS.

There are also two other types of fog, but they are ones less likely to be a problem in boating: these are commonly referred to as UPSLOPE FOG and ICE FOG.

Radiation Fog

There are four requirements for the formation of radiation fog (sometimes called GROUND FOG). First, the air must be stable, and the air next to the earth must be colder than the air a short distance aloft. Second, the air must be relatively moist. Third, it must be night and the sky must be clear so that the earth readily can lose heat by radiation to outer space. The fourth requirement is that the wind must be light to calm.

The third requirement of the clear night sky enables the ground to become colder than the overlying air, which subsequently is cooled below its dew point both by contact with the ground (conduction of heat) and by radiative loss of heat to the ground. The characteristics of the fog developed vary with the degree of the fourth requirement of calmness. If there is a dead calm, the lowest strata of air will not mix with the ones above, and fog will likely form only to a height of two to four feet (0.6 to 1.2 m). If there is a slight motion of the air (a wind of three to five knots) and, hence, some turbulent mixing, the cooling is spread through a layer which may extend to a height of several hundred feet (perhaps 125 m) above the ground. With stronger winds, the cooling effect is distributed through so deep a layer that temperature does not fall to the dew point and fog does not form.

Radiation fog is most prevalent in middle and high latitudes; it can be predicted with considerable accuracy; see page 843. It is local in character and occurs most frequently in valleys and lowlands, especially near lakes and rivers where you might be cruising. The cooled air drains into these terrain depressions; the lake or river aids the process of fog formation by contributing water vapor, which raises the dew point. Often there is dense radiation fog in narrow rivers and channels leading to a large body of water that is absent of fog away from shore.

This type of fog may be patchy or uniformly dense. It affects boaters mainly in the late summer or early autumn. Having formed at night, it will usually start to evaporate ("burn off") over land shortly after sunrise. The lower layers are the first to go. It is slower to clear over water, however, since the temperature of the water warms less from night to day than does the land.

Advection Fog

Whereas radiation fog bothers boaters chiefly in the late summer and early autumn, advection fog can be a problem at any season. Advection means "transport by horizontal motion," which relates to the production of this type of fog by winds carrying warm, moist air over a colder surface. The dew point of the air must be higher than the temperature of the surface over which the air is moving. The air can be cooled below its dew point by conduction and by radiation of heat to the colder surface. Other requirements for the formation of advection fog are: (a) the air at a height of 100 feet (30 m) or so must be warmer than the air just above the surface; and (b) the temperature of the surface—be it land or water—must become progressively colder in the direction toward which the air is moving. Advection fog may form day or night, in any season of the year, especially over the sea.

Coastal Fog For boaters, the most bothersome variety of advection fog is COASTAL FOG. When steady winds blow landward and carry warm oceanic air across cold coastal water, the resulting fog may blanket a great length of coastline and, especially at night, may extend many miles inland up bays and rivers. It can be seen on land as it blows past streetlights. For example, consider the Pacific Coast, where the water close to the land is often colder than the water well offshore. The prevailing winds in summer are onshore and the air (which frequently has come from mid-Pacific) is usually nearly saturated with water vapor. The same thing happens when southerly winds carry air across the Gulf Stream and thence northward across the colder Atlantic coastal waters.

For inland boaters, advection fog may be a problem as it forms over large lakes whenever relatively warm and moist air is carried over their colder surfaces.

Advection fog is generally dissipated less easily than is radiation fog. Unlike radiation fog, sunshine usually has no effect on advection fog over water. Usually, a wind shift or a marked increase in wind velocity is required.

Precipitation Fog

When rain, after descending through a layer of warm air aloft, falls into a shallow layer of colder air at the earth's surface, there will be some evaporation from the warm raindrops into the colder air. Under certain conditions, this will raise water vapor content of the cold air above the saturation point and precipitation fog, also called RAIN FOG, will form. Because this type of fog is often found near frontal activity, it is sometimes known as FRONTAL FOG.

Steam Fog

On large rivers, such as the Mississippi or the Ohio, steam fog can be a particular hazard to late evening or early morning boating in the autumn. When cold air passes over much warmer water, the lowest layer of air is rapidly supplied with heat and water vapor. Mixing of this lowest layer with unmodified cold air above, can, under certain conditions, produce a SUPERSATURATED (foggy) mixture. Because the water is much warmer than the air, vertical air currents are created, and we observe the phenomenon of steaming, in much the same way as steam forms over a hot bath; see **Figure 24-04.**

Sea Smoke In winter when cold air below about 10°F (-12°C) blows off the land and across

Figure 24-04 Cold air passing over warm water picks up enough heat and moisture to form steam fog. It is most prevalent, morning and evening, during autumn months. It is found most often on inland rivers as well as small lakes and ponds.

Figure 24-05 Sea smoke at Great Harbor, Woods Hole, Massachusetts. Water temperature at the time of this photograph was +31.6°F (-0.2°C), and the air temperature, 30 feet (9.1m) was +5°F (-15°C). The wind was from the northwest at about 20 knots.

the adjacent coastal waters, steam fog may be widespread and very dense, and is then termed sea smoke; see **Figure 24-05.** Along North American coastal waters, steam fog occurs most frequently off the coasts of Maine and Nova Scotia, and in the Gulf of St. Lawrence, where it can be a serious navigational hazard. However, its occurrence is not restricted to the higher latitudes. Off the east coast of the U. S. it has been observed as far south as Florida, and it also occurs occasionally over the coastal waters of the Gulf of Mexico.

Other Types of Fog

When a low, moving blanket of air is gradually elevated toward a cooler altitude by the slope of the land, "upslope fog" forms. Occurring frequently on the sides of mountains, this type of fog is common, for example, at New Hampshire's Mount Washington and in the Great Plains where a southeast wind blows moist air from the Gulf of Mexico toward the Rocky Mountains. If winds are too strong, however, stratus or stratocumulus clouds will form instead of fog.

At very low temperatures, usually below -25°F (-32°C), the air may become full of ice crystals. This "ice fog" can seriously restrict visibility. In this case, the water vapor in the air has turned directly into ice through the sublimation process.

Distribution of Fog (Contiguous 48 States)

In the United States, the coastal sections most frequently beset by fog range from the Strait of Juan de Fuca to Point Arguello, California, on the Pacific Coast, and from the Bay of Fundy to Montauk Point, New York, on the Atlantic Coast. On these waters, the average annual number of hours of fog occurrence exceeds 900—more than 10 percent of the year. In the foggiest parts of these areas, off the coast of Northern California and the coast of Maine, fog is present about 20 percent of the year.

Going southward along both the Atlantic and Pacific coasts, the frequency of fog decreases, more rapidly on the Atlantic Coast than on the Pacific. The average annual fog frequency over the waters near Los Angeles and San Diego, for example, is about three times that in the same latitude along the Atlantic Coast.

Seasonal Frequencies

The time of maximum occurrence of fog off the Pacific Coast varies somewhat with the various localities and, of course, with the individual year. In general, however, over the stretch from Cape Flattery, Washington, to Point Arguello, the season of most frequent fog runs from July through October, with more than 50 percent of the annual number of foggy days occurring during these months. However, along the lower coast of California, from Los Angeles southward, the foggiest months are those from September through February, and the least foggy are from May through July.

On the Atlantic side, off the coast of New England, the foggiest months are usually June, July, and August, with a maximum of fog generally occurring during July. In this month, fog is normally encountered about 50 percent of the time. Off the Middle Atlantic Coast, however, fog occurs mostly in the winter and spring months, with a tendency toward minimum frequency in summer and autumn. Along the South Atlantic Coast (from Cape Hatteras to the tip of Florida) and in the Gulf of Mexico fog rarely creates a problem for boaters. It is virtually nonexistent during the summer, and even in the winter and early spring season (December through March), when it has maximum frequency, the number of days with fog rarely exceeds 20 during this four-month period.

The Great Lakes as a whole tend to have fog in the warmer season. The explanation for this is to be found in the comparison of the lake temperatures with the air temperatures over the surrounding land. From March or April to the beginning of September, the lakes tend to be colder than the air. Hence, whenever the dew-point temperature is sufficiently high, conditions favor the formation of advection fog over the water.

The greatest fogginess occurs when and where the lakes are coldest in relation to the air blowing off the surrounding land. On Lake Superior, north-central Lake Michigan, and northwestern Lake Huron, the time of maximum frequency is late May and June; elsewhere it is late April and May. Since the lake temperatures become colder from south to north and from the shores outward, the occurrence of fog increases northward and toward the lakes' centers.

WINDS

One of the major weather elements is WIND—the horizontal movement of air. Winds have a major impact on people and their activities, not the least of which is boating.

Circulation Patterns

Wind is explained by a fundamental law of physics. As a gas (in this case, air) is heated, it expands, becoming less dense (lighter), and thus tends to rise. Conversely, cooling air contracts, becoming more dense (heavier) and tends to sink. Air is primarily heated by contact with the earth's surface; this air rises and surrounding surface air rushes in to fill the relative void, which is, in turn, replaced by cooler air sinking from aloft. This process of CIRCULATION is essentially continuous, resulting in horizontal and vertical air movements over wide areas.

The nearer the equator, the more nearly vertical the angle of the sun's rays are all year, resulting in greater heating at the surface. Thus, the equatorial air rises and flows toward the poles. Rising air is then replaced by a stream of colder air from the poles toward the tropical regions. This simple pattern is modified by the earth's rotation (known, for the person who described it, as the Coriolis effect) and by the distribution of landmasses.

In the northern hemisphere, the northward flowing air at high altitudes is bent eastward and, by the time that it reaches about 30° latitude, it has started to build up an area of higher pressure forcing some of the flow downward and back toward the equator. This portion becomes a steady flow near the surface back toward the equator that is bent westward by the earth's rotation—the reliable "northeast trade winds" of the northern subtropical zone. The portion that continues northward toward the pole eventually descends as the "prevailing westerlies" of the higher midlatitudes. Between these regions there are the "horse latitudes," near 30°, where winds are weaker and less constant. Near the equator, where the warmed air rises and turns north or south, the region of weaker winds is called the "doldrums"; see **Figure 24-06.**

Local Wind Patterns

Temperature differences—heating and cooling air—cause localized breezes as well as global winds. Land areas usually heat up more quickly than water areas during hours of sunlight; air rising over the land is replaced by air coming in from seaward—these are the refreshing "sea breezes"; see **Figure 24-07,** upper.

Subsequently, at night, the land loses its heat more quickly, the water's surface becomes the relatively warmer areas, and "land breezes" flow towards the sea. In both cases, these breezes are felt quite close to the surface; there is a counter-flow of air at higher elevations to complete the local circulation pattern; see **Figure 24-07,** lower.

Both of these breezes, interacting with general wind patterns, can generate showers and thunderstorms.

Winds Afloat

Wind direction and strength are a matter of constant interest, and sometimes concern, to every boater. The measurement of these values, and their use in forecasting immediate and future weather conditions will be covered later in this chapter.

HIGHS & LOWS

Familiarity with atmospheric pressure is essential in understanding weather because the pressure distribution in the atmosphere controls the winds and, to a considerable extent, the occurrence of clouds and precipitation. For a boater watching the weather, it is important to comprehend how the winds and other elements relate to the pressure distribution on a weather map.

The global circulation of the atmosphere resulting from unequal heating results in the building up of areas where the weight of air (atmospheric pressure) is greater than or less than that surrounding it. These are the HIGHS and LOWS that are seen on weather maps, usually designated by large letters "H" and "L."

General Characteristics

Highs, also called "anticyclones," generally bring dry weather. Lows, also called "cyclones" (this term is used to generically describe weather events having a strong cyclonic circulation and is also used specifically to describe hurricanes in the Indian Ocean) generally bring unsettled weather and precipitation. Highs and Lows are rather large areas of "weather" measured in many hundreds of miles or kilometers across. In the northern hemisphere, circulation around an area of high pressure is clockwise; around lows, it is counter-clockwise. (Circulation is the opposite in the southern hemisphere.) Winds are generally weaker in highs than in low-pressure systems.

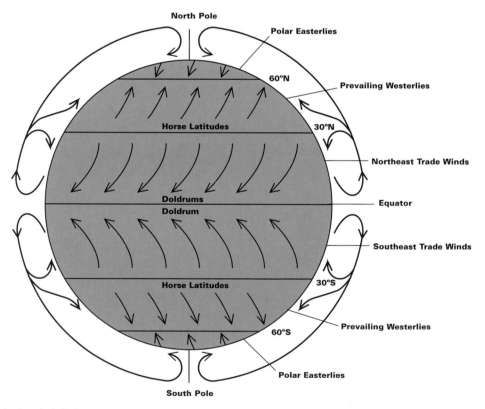

Figure 24-06 These idealized global air circulation patterns are based to a large extent on the heated air that rises along the equator and descends as cold air at the poles, and at latitudes approximately 30° from the equator, the "horse latitudes."

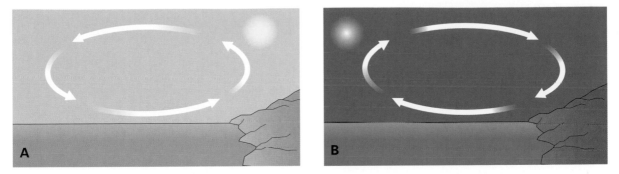

Figure 24-07 In the daytime, A, when the land is warmer, air rises over the land and is replaced by cooler air coming in from seaward. This activity creates a "sea breeze." At night, B, the opposite occurs when the temperature of the land is lower than that of the sea. There is then a "land breeze."

The Formation of Highs

In the earth's general circulation system, areas of high pressure are formed by the descent of cold, dense air toward the surface in polar regions and in the horse latitudes (near 30° latitude); refer to **Figure 24-06.** As air flows outward toward areas of lower pressure, the rotation of the earth changes its direction so that a clockwise circulation is established. Highs form sequentially in the north polar region and move southward; as they reach the latitudes of the prevailing westerlies, they are carried first southeastward, than eastward, and often finally northeastward.

The existence of continents and oceans distorts the theoretical picture of the formation of highs and lows; the actual process is quite complex. High-pressure "breeding zones" form in relatively specific areas rather than in broad zones; these areas change between summer and winter.

The Formation of Lows

The formation of low-pressure cells (see page 819) usually is quite different from that of highs, although large scale lows, for example, annually develop over deserts and other relatively warm spots. However, the following describes what is usually considered when a Low is discussed. The boundary between two masses of air of different temperatures is termed a FRONT. This is a major weather phenomenon that will be considered in detail in the following section. On such a boundary, a horizontal wavelike situation develops; refer to **Figure 24-14.** This grows and becomes more and more distinct and may even "break" as an ocean wave does on the beach.

AIR MASSES & FRONTS

A general knowledge of air masses and fronts will make weather forecasts more understandable, and more useful.

Air Masses

An air mass is any large body of air (covering as much as several hundred thousand square miles (a million or more square kilometers) in which the conditions of temperature and moisture are essentially homogeneous.

Basic Characteristics

Air masses derive their basic characteristics from the surface beneath them. The homogeneous properties are acquired as the mass remains over the SOURCE AREA for an extended period of time until the uniformity is achieved. This source area can be continental or maritime and polar or tropical. Once developed, the mass tends to retain those characteristics even while moving over different surfaces; see **Table 24-1.** Those characteristics and their comparison with those of the surface over which the air mass is moving—warmer or colder—define the air mass. **Figure 24-08** shows the principal air masses that affect North America and their general normal movement.

Maritime and continental air masses differ significantly in their characteristics of temperature and humidity and generate different kinds of weather. Oceans experience less extreme variations of heat and cold than do continents, and maritime air masses change less with seasons. As a result a maritime air mass moving over land tends to moderate any conditions of excess heat or cold.

Most active weather is generated around Lows or at the boundaries between air masses. However, showers or thunderstorms frequently occur within moist air masses, especially warm moist air masses.

Weather Fronts

A general knowledge of air masses is important as it leads directly to our consideration of weather fronts. A front is the boundary between two different air masses; the bodies of air do *not* tend to mix, but rather each moves with respect to the other. The passage of a front results in a change of weather conditions at that location. The bigger the difference in characteristics between two adjacent air masses, the stronger the front is said to be. And, the stronger the front, the greater is the potential for active, sometimes violent, weather.

Cold Fronts

With a COLD FRONT, the oncoming cold air mass, being denser, pushes under the warm air mass and forces it upward; see **Figure 24-09**. In the northern hemisphere, cold fronts generally lie along a NE-SW line and move eastward or southeastward. The rate of movement is roughly 400-500 statute miles (650-800 km) per day. The stronger the cold front, the faster it tends to move. Since air masses tend to be most diverse in the transition seasons, fronts generally will move the fastest in late winter and spring.

A strong, rapidly moving cold front will bring weather changes that may be quite intense but relatively brief in duration. These active cold fronts are often characterized by a line of strong thunderstorms. In late summer, when air mass differences are smaller, slower

AIR-MASS CHARACTERISTICS		
Observed Weather	Stable Air Mass	Unstable Air Mass
Visibility	Poor	Good
Winds	Steady	Gusty
Clouds	Stratoform	Cumuloform
Precipitation	Steady	Showery

Table 24-1 An air mass is a body of air in which temperature and moisture conditions are essentially the same in all directions horizontally. It may be described as stable or unstable, as shown in the table above.

moving cold fronts may be accompanied by scattered clouds along the frontal boundary, but no precipitation.

A SQUALL LINE is a line of thunderstorms ahead of an approaching cold front. In fact, there may be more than one squall line in very unstable air masses. Squall lines may be very turbulent with strong winds endangering small craft. A strong increase in wind (called a SQUALL) often accompanies a squall line. Boaters need to understand the difference between GUSTS and SQUALLS. A gust is a rapid fluctuation of wind with a variation of at least 10 knots between peaks and lulls. Gusty conditions may last for several days. A squall, on the other hand, is a sudden increase in which the average wind speed raises at least 15 knots and remains at 20 knots or more for over one minute. Although both are potentially dangerous, the squall, because of the suddenness and intensity of change, is usually worse. A squall line appears as a wall of very dark, threatening clouds. A squall line may produce weather more severe than that of the front itself.

The approach of a cold front is indicated by a shift of the wind toward the south, then to the southwest. Barometric pressure readings fall. As the front approaches, tall cumuloform clouds are usually present with the bottoms (bases) of these dropping closer to the earth's surface. Rain starts slowly but may increase rapidly.

As the front passes the wind continues to veer (change in a clockwise direction), westward, northwestward, and then sometimes northerly. After passage the sky clears quickly, temperatures drop, pressure builds up quickly, and the wind

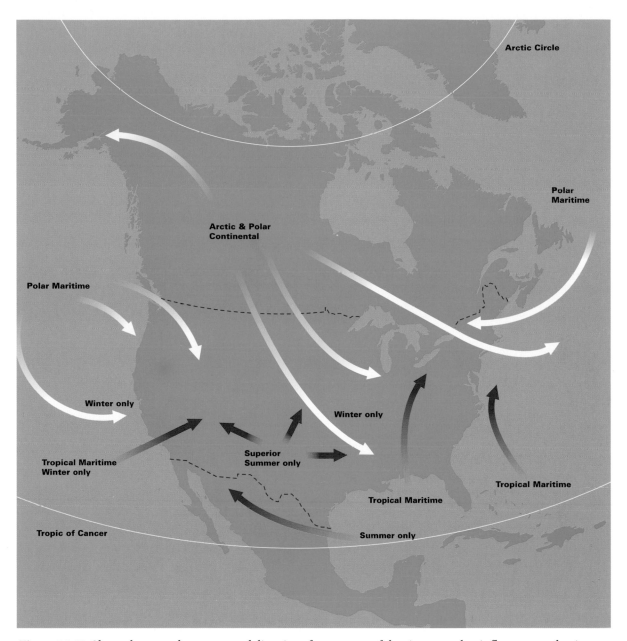

Figure 24-08 Shown here are the sources and direction of movement of the air masses that influence weather in North America. The properties of an air mass, and its conflicts with adjacent air masses, are the causes of weather changes. Note that some are seasonal only, such as those above the south-central U.S. (near Texas) called "superior," meaning it is an exceptionally dry air mass.

may continue to veer to the northeast. For a few days at least, the weather will have the characteristics of a cold air mass although gusty winds may continue, especially if the front was strong.

Warm Fronts

A WARM FRONT occurs when an advancing warm air mass reaches colder air. The warmer air, being less dense, cannot push under the cold air such as in a cold front. It rides up over it; see **Figure 24-10.** Warm fronts are generally oriented in directions NS, NW-SE or EW and change their direction more often than cold fronts do. The rate of movement is slower, 150-200 miles (240-320 km) per day, and thus warm fronts are eventually overtaken by the next following cold front.

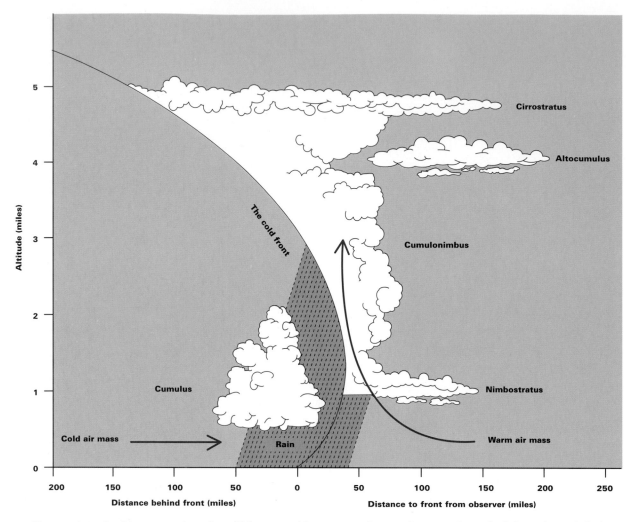

Figure 24-09 In this cross section of a cold front, a cold air mass is shown advancing from the left, pushing aloft the warm air mass it displaces. Thunderstorms usually occur when the temperature differences are great, and rapidly rising warm air ahead of the cold front forms towering cumulus clouds.

Warm-front weather is usually milder than that of a cold front and may extend several hundreds of miles (500-600 km) in advance of the actual front. Clouds are found at lowering levels as the front approaches and rainfall is generally more moderate but extended in time. The approach of a warm front is signaled by a falling barometer (but falling more slowly than for an approaching cold front), a buildup of clouds, and the onset of rain or drizzle. The winds are generally from an easterly direction north of the front and gradually veer to the south as the front passes. After the front passes there will be cumulus clouds and temperatures will rise; the barometer will also slowly rise.

Stationary Fronts

Occasionally fronts will slow down to the point of little or no forward movement. A STATIONARY FRONT hanging over you will bring conditions of clouds and rain much like those of a warm front.

Occluded Fronts

An occluded front is a more complex situation where we have warm air, cold air, and colder air. It occurs after a cold front, because of its faster movement, overtakes a warm front and lifts the warm air mass off the ground. Either the warm front or the cold front is pushed upward from the earth's surface; see **Figure 24-11** and **Figure 24-12**. The appearance on a weather map is that of a

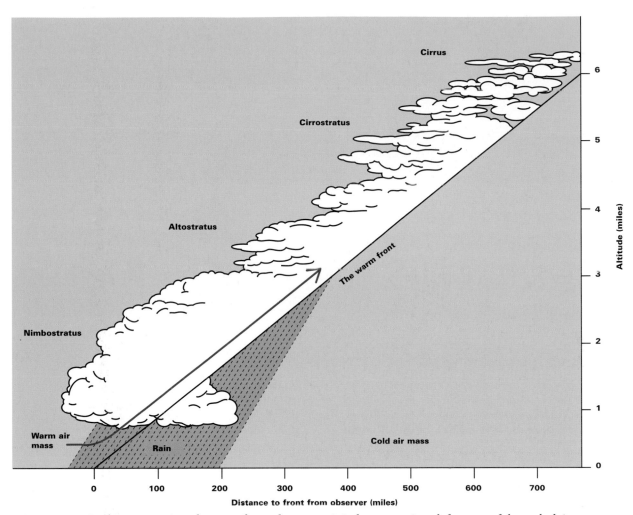

Figure 24-10 *In this cross section of a warm front, the warm air is shown moving aloft on top of the underlying wedge of cold air, which retreats as the warm air advances. The cloud sequence at the front is first cirrus, then cirrostratus, then altostratus, and finally nimbostratus in the rain area.*

curled "tail" extending back toward the Low from the junction of the cold and warm fronts. In a satellite photo, this looks like a comma. Both warm and cold front type precipitation can occur surrounding an occlusion.

STORMS & SEVERE WEATHER

Although a boater is interested in whatever the weather is and what is forecast, real attention is focused on the possibility of STORMS. While sunny skies and fair winds are eagerly awaited, it is the approach of a storm that causes concern for the safety of the crew, passengers, and for the boat itself.

Extra-Tropical Cyclones

The principal source of rain, winds, and generally foul weather in the U.S. is the EXTRA-TROPICAL CYCLONE. Although some other types of storms may be more destructive, the extra-tropical cyclone is the ultimate cause of most active weather. Such a storm (in the northern hemisphere) is defined as a traveling system of winds rotating counterclockwise around a center of low barometric pressure and containing at least a warm front and a cold front. The warm air mass is typically moist tropical air, and the cold air mass is polar continental.

Development of an Extra-Tropical Cyclone

The development of an extra-tropical cyclone is

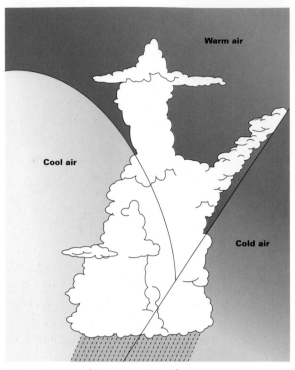

Figure 24-11 *This cross section of a warm-type occlusion illustrates how the advancing cool air rides up on the cold air ahead—acting somewhat like a warm front—and the warm air then is pushed aloft.*

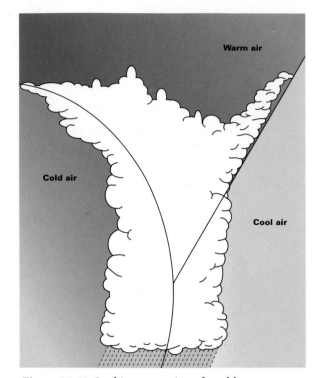

Figure 24-12 *In this cross section of a cold-type occlusion, the advancing cold air moves under the cool air forcing the cool air aloft—acting like a cold front. Once again, the warm air is moved above the surface.*

shown in **Figure 24-13.** At *A*, there is a warm air mass, typically moist tropical air, flowing northeastward bordering a cold air mass, typically polar continental, flowing southwestward. They are separated by a heavy line representing the front between them. At *B*, a small wave has formed on the front. The cold air from behind pushes under the warm air; the warm air rushes up over the cold air ahead of it. A cold front is born on the left, a warm front on the right. Where they are connected, the barometric pressure is lowered and the air starts circulating counterclockwise. A Low is developed. This also causes a High to be seen behind the cold front.

Pushed by the earth's general circulation patterns, the whole system keeps moving in a general easterly direction. When warm, moist air is lifted, as it is when a cold air mass pushes under it or when it rushes up over cold air ahead, it cools by expansion. After its temperature has fallen to the dew point, excess water vapor condenses to first form clouds and then precipitation; the dotted area represents this.

At *C*, in **Figure 24-13**, the storm is steadily developing with the low-pressure area intensifying more and more. The clouds and rain are increasing, and the winds are becoming stronger. At *D*, the storm is approaching maturity. Note how the gap has narrowed between the fronts.

By the time *E* is reached, the cold front has begun to catch up with the warm front and an occluded front is formed; the storm is now at its height. When the situation at *F* is reached, the storm has begun to weaken and the weather will soon clear as a high behind the cold front reaches the area. (Exception—cold air over warm water may actually enhance the development of showers and thunderstorms.)

Extra-tropical cyclones are constantly forming, moving, and dying around the globe. It takes about one day (24 hours) for any one disturbance to reach maturity. However, although most usually dissipate within three or possibly four days, some can last for a week or more. In winter, these storms occur on the average of twice a week in the U.S.; in summer they occur somewhat less frequently and are less intense. Their movement is generally eastward to north of east at a speed in winter of about 700 miles (1,100 km) per day and in summer perhaps 500 miles (800 km). Such storms usually cover a large area; they can affect a given locality for two days or more.

Thunderstorms

While extra-tropical cyclones are the principal source of wind, rain, and generally foul weather for large areas, there are also local, small-scale but intense THUNDERSTORMS, which you must be prepared to handle. These are embedded in extra-tropical cyclones usually linked to the cold and occluded fronts. If the air comprising the warm sector is sufficiently unstable, however, which is often the case in spring or summer, thunderstorms may also be associated with the warm front or be found with the warm sector itself.

A thunderstorm is a storm of short duration, arising only from a cumulonimbus cloud, attended by thunder and lightning, and marked by abrupt fluctuations of temperature, pressure, and wind. A LINE SQUALL, now usually referred to in meteorological terms as a squall line, is a lengthy row of thunderstorms that may stretch for 100 miles (160 km) or more.

Incidentally, a SHOWER (as opposed to gentle, steady rain) is a smaller brother to the thunderstorm, though the rainfall and wind in it may be of considerable intensity. A shower is the product of relatively large cumulus (TOWERING CUMULUS) clouds separated from one another by blue sky. A shower is over quickly and is not accompanied by thunder and lightning. However, they may be strong enough to generate waterspouts.

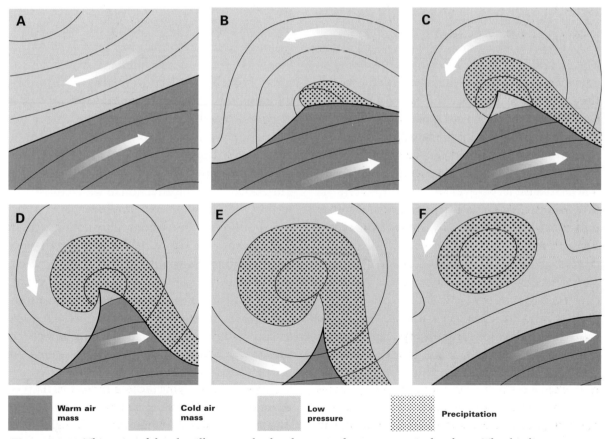

| Warm air mass | Cold air mass | Low pressure | Precipitation |

Figure 24-13 *This series of sketches illustrates the development of an extra-tropical cyclone,. The thin lines are isobars that pass through points of equal barometric pressure. Arrows indicate wind directions.*

Figure 24-14 *This sequence of photographs shows the growth of an anvil top. The left photo was taken at noon, the middle at 1220, and the right photo at 1230.*

Requirements for Thunderstorm Formation

There are three requirements for the development of a thunderstorm.

• **Lifting Mechanism** There must be strong upward air currents, such as those caused by a cold front burrowing under warm air or by the heating of air in contact with the surface of the earth on a summer day, to lift surface air.

• **Instability** The air parcels forming the storm must be buoyant (warmer) relative to the air outside the storm and be able to keep on ascending higher and higher until they pass the freezing level.

• **Moisture** The air must have a large concentration of water vapor. The most promising thunderstorm air is of tropical maritime origin; whenever it appears in your cruising area, especially when a cold front is approaching, you need to be watchful.

The life cycle of a thunderstorm usually lasts about an hour. However, subsequent thunderstorms will often develop near where the former one dissipated, feeding off the moisture left by the earlier storm, making it seem as if the storm were longer-lived than it actually was. Also, the cooler, denser air brought to the earth's surface by the downdrafts induced in the previous thunderstorm can act as the lifting mechanism for generating the next one.

As the thunderstorm cycle begins, a cumulous cloud forms and grows vertically. Boaters should watch such growing clouds and developing storms very closely and be prepared to take evasive or protective actions; see **Figure 24-14.** Vacuuming air from miles around its base, and feeding on moisture that may have been carried aloft by earlier clouds, the cumulus cloud continues growing. It becomes a towering cumulus and, eventually, it develops into a cumulonimbus (thunderstorm) cloud. Rain drops or ice particles form and, as they become too heavy for the updraft to support, fall, inducing downdrafts. Over time, these downdrafts cut off the air inflow, and the growth process ceases. The cloud essentially precipitates itself away leaving residual middle- and high-level clouds.

Characteristics of a Thunderstorm

In all cases, the prime danger signal for a thunderstorm is a cumulus cloud growing larger. Every thunderstorm cloud has four distinctive features, although you may not always be able to see all four as other clouds may intervene in your line of sight. **Figure 24-15** is a drawing of a cumulonimbus cloud showing these four features diagrammatically. Starting at the top, notice the layer of cirrus clouds, shaped like an anvil (consequently called an ANVIL TOP), leaning in the direction toward which the upper wind is blowing; this generally tells us the direction in which the storm is moving. The anvil-top development is illustrated in **Figure 24-14;** these three photographs were taken from the same position over a time interval of only one-half hour!

The next feature is the main body of the cloud—a large cumulus of great height with cauliflower sides. It must be of great height, as it must extend far above the freezing level if the cirrus anvil top is to form. (Cirrus clouds are composed of ice crystals, not water droplets.)

The third feature is the ROLL CLOUD. This is formed by violent air currents along the leading edge of the base of the cumulus cloud.

The fourth and final feature is the dark area within the storm and extending from the base of

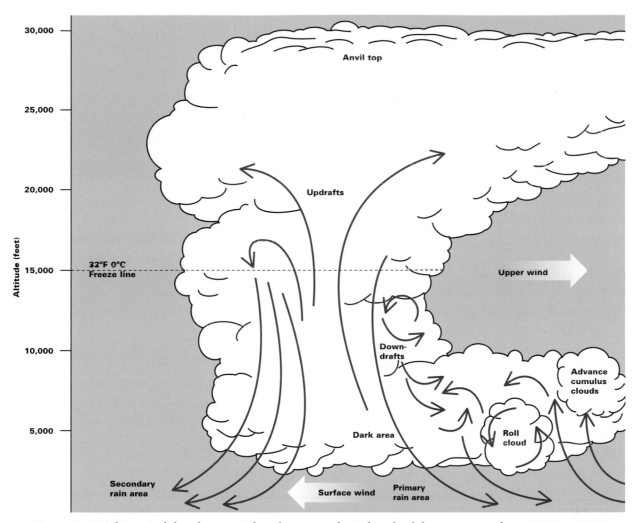

Figure 24-15 *This typical thunderstorm is based on a cumulonimbus cloud that may tower from 25,000 to 50,000 feet high. The anvil top indicates the direction that the wind is blowing.*

the cloud to the earth; at the center of this is precipitation. This core is generally beneath the strongest part of the thunderstorm. Hail and heavy precipitation are most likely to be found in this core area.

Ahead of a thunderstorm the wind may be steady or variable, but as the roll cloud draws near, the wind may weaken or become unsteady; see **Figure 24-15.** As the roll cloud passes overhead, violent shifting winds accompanied by strong downdrafts may be expected. The wind velocity may reach 60 knots or more. Heavy precipitation, and sometimes hail, begins to fall just behind the roll cloud. The weather usually clears quickly after the passage of the storm. The precipitation usually has brought cooler air to the surface so, for at least a time, temperatures and humidity are lower.

Individually, thunderstorms can produce TORNADOES, WATERSPOUTS, or MICROBURSTS with winds measuring over 120 knots. They can spawn hailstones as large as grapefruits and can generate lightning bolts of unbelievable power. The thunderstorm is the single most powerful weather element there is. All severe weather comes from or, like the hurricane, is made up of thunderstorms. Never take these for granted. When you hear thunderstorms in the forecast, or see them in your area, heighten your alert.

Frequency of Thunderstorms

Thunderstorms occur most frequently, and with the greatest intensity, in the spring and summer over all parts of the U.S. While they may strike at

LIGHTNING & THUNDER

A buildup of dissimilar positive and negative electrical charges occurs within a vertically developing cumulonimbus cloud, between the cloud and the earth below (the earth normally has a negative charge), or between neighboring clouds. When the buildup of opposite charges becomes great enough, a LIGHTNING FLASH occurs. These can occur within a cloud, from one cloud to another, or between the cloud and ground. Actually what we think of as a flash is really a series of strikes *back and forth* over a period of roughly two-tenths of a second. A flash to the surface usually starts with a faint "leader" from the cloud followed instantly by a massive strike upward from the surface. About two-thirds of all lightning flashes are within clouds and never reach the surface. A lightning flash is almost unbelievably powerful—up to 30,000,000 volts at 100,000 amperes; it happens so quickly that it is essentially explosive in nature.

The sudden, vast amount of heat energy released by a lightning flash causes the sound waves termed THUNDER. This release of energy comes from the collapse of the atmosphere around the lightning strike.

Lightning protection for boats is discussed on page 390.

any hour, they are most common in the late afternoon and early evening over inland and coastal waters. The surrounding land has been a good "stove" for many hours, heating the air to produce strong upward currents. Over the ocean, well away from shore, thunderstorms more commonly occur between midnight and sunrise. Finally, thunderstorms are most frequent and most violent in subtropical latitudes. The southeastern part of the U.S. may have four or more thunderstorms per week in summer.

If the cumulonimbus cloud is fully developed and towers to normal thunderstorm altitudes, 35,000 feet (10.7 km) or more in spring and summer, the storm will likely be violent. If the anvil top is low, only 20,000 feet (6.1 km) or so, as is usual in winter and autumn, the storm will likely be less severe. If the cumulonimbus cloud is not fully developed, particularly if it lacks the anvil top, and the roll cloud is missing, only a shower is most likely.

Anticipating Thunderstorms

The possibility of a thunderstorm may be first noticed from static crashes on an AM radio receiver. You can plot the approach, once the cumulonimbus cloud is visible, with a series of bearings; you can also estimate its distance from you. The thunder and lightning occur simultaneously at the point of lightning discharge, but we see the lightning discharge much sooner than we hear the thunder. Time this interval in seconds. Multiply the number of seconds by 0.2 (or divide by 5); the result will be approximate distance off in statute miles (multiply by 0.34, or divide by 3, to get distance off in kilometers). Take care, however, that you are properly associating a particular flash with its thunder; this may be difficult if there is nearly continuous lightning.

A good safety guide is the "30/30" rule. The first "30" represents 30 seconds or about 6 miles. If the time between lightning and thunder is less than 30 seconds, you or your vessel can be struck. The second "30" is to remind the boater to wait 30 minutes after the last lightning flash to move from shelter. More than half of the lightning deaths each year occur after a thunderstorm has passed. Also remember, lightning may impact an area out to 60 feet or more from where it has hit the surface.

Take precautions well before lightning begins. Don't wait. Lower radio antennas, outriggers, sails, and drop anchors, if necessary. Go into the cabin if possible, or at least keep a low profile below the freeboard. Avoid contact with the hull or with metal fittings, especially those associated with the lightning conduction system. Don't touch radio equipment or wiring. Depending on your situation, you might want to disconnect power cables from expensive equipment separating these wires as far apart as possible. And, keep your life jacket on in case you are rendered unconscious.

Tornadoes

Tornadoes are whirlpools of small horizontal extent that extend downward from a thunderstorm and have a funnel-like appearance; see **Figure 24-16.** (The only exception, weak tornadoes can be generated when spiraling surface winds are caught in the updraft of a rapidly developing towering cumulus cloud.) The average diameter of the visible funnel cloud is about 250 yards (230 m), but the destructive effects of this system of whirling winds may extend outward from the tornado center as much as one-half mile (0.8 km) on each side. The wind speed near the core can only be estimated, but it is at least as high as 300 knots. Any thunderstorm can produce a tornado. However, the bigger the cumulonimbus cloud, the more likely it is that a tornado will form. Although tornadoes can occur at any time and in any location that a thunderstorm is found, they usually are seen, in boating areas, adjacent to

Figure 24-16 A tornado funnel is a cloud of water droplets mixed with dust and debris that are drawn up because of the greatly reduced atmospheric pressure with the funnel. This pressure drop causes the wind to whirl inward and upward.

the Atlantic and Gulf of Mexico coasts of North America and in all inland boating areas east of the Rocky Mountains.

Thunderstorms producing tornadoes move with or to the right of the upper level winds pushing the storm. This wind is usually from the southwest. The air mass in which the storm develops typically consists of two layers, a very moist one (source: Gulf of Mexico) near the ground and a relatively dry layer above. The temperature decreases with altitude rather rapidly in each layer. When this combination of air layers is lifted along a squall line or cold front, excessive instability develops and violent updrafts are created.

Waterspouts

Tornadoes do occur over water. When this occurs, they are called WATERSPOUTS. Although there are other less intense features over the water that are also called waterspouts (similar to dust devils over the desert), boaters should treat any such feature with respect and allow a lot of distance between it and their vessel. They are a threat to small craft. The conditions favoring the formation of waterspouts at sea are similar to those conducive to the formation of tornadoes over land. However, they are much more frequent in the tropics than in middle latitudes.

A waterspout, like a tornado, forms under a towering cumulus or cumulonimbus cloud. A funnel-shaped protuberance (FUNNEL CLOUD) first appears at the base of the parent cloud and grows downward toward the sea. Beneath it the water becomes agitated and a cloud of spray forms. The funnel cloud descends until it merges with the spray; it then assumes the shape of a tube that stretches from the sea surface to the base of the cloud; see **Figure 24-17.**

The diameter of a waterspout may vary from 20 to 200 feet (6-60 m) or more. Its length from the sea to the base of the cloud is usually between 1,000 and 2,000 feet (300-600 m). It may last from ten minutes to half an hour. Its upper part often travels at a different speed and in a different direction from its base, so that it becomes bent and stretched-out. Finally, the tube breaks at a point about one-third

MICROBURST: A DISASTROUS FORCE

Tornadoes are not the only strong winds that can come from a thunderstorm. There is a potential danger lurking in the form of a MICROBURST. This is a concentrated column of sinking air that spreads out in all directions when it reaches the surface. These straight-line winds may reach 30 to 40 knots, but, in some instances, have been estimated at over 120 knots. Microbursts often occur in a series of varying powers and dimensions. Although they last only a few minutes, they are known to have capsized and destroyed boats. The greatest threat is to sailboats underway with normal sails set—the almost instantaneous onset of winds from an unpredicted direction (squall) is a major threat. Unlike a dry squall, which can usually be seen approaching across the water, a microburst's winds will strike your boat before anyone takes notice. They frequently appear in groups; don't relax after one passes!

Although microbursts are usually associated with seasonal thunderstorms, they can also occur during rainstorms that are not accompanied by thunder and lightning, such as along squall lines. The strongest winds are in or near the center of the storm where heavy rain, and frequently hail, is falling. Often the gust front precedes the microburst; this is a frontal zone of advancing cold air, characterized by a sudden increase in wind speed, and followed by gusty winds. The combination of these two strong wind systems can easily be fatal.

The best protection against microbursts is avoidance. Prepare for every boating trip by obtaining the latest marine weather forecasts. Listen to the NOAA Weather Radio channels or the U.S. Coast Guard. Continuous broadcasts of the latest marine weather information are provided on various frequencies; see page 692. And keep aware of what is happening around you. Remember that thunderstorms are dangerous weather systems that can have strong, gusty winds that vary in direction and speed. Be sure that your boat has adequate stability to help you cope with strong winds in the event of their unexpected occurrence.

Another phenomenon associated with thunderstorms is the MACROBURST. This is, essentially, a microburst that covers a wider area, more than 2.5 miles in diameter, with generally similar conditions.

of the way up to the cloud base, and the "spout" at the sea surface quickly subsides.

The considerably reduced air pressure at the center of a waterspout is clearly indicated by the visible variations of the water level. A mound of water, a foot (0.3 m) or so high, sometimes appears at the core, because the atmospheric pressure inside the funnel is perhaps 30 to 40 millibars less than that on the surface of the water surrounding the spout. This difference causes the rise of water at the center.

Remember, tornadoes and waterspouts are winds. You cannot see the wind. What you see in each is cloud material that has been sucked down by the whirling action or surface material (water, dirt, or other debris) picked up by the strong winds. Such material may be carried for long distances. For example, considerable quantities of salt spray, picked up by the strong winds at the base of the spout, are sometimes carried far aloft. This has been verified by observations of a fall of salty rain following the passage of a waterspout.

Boaters need to understand that tornadoes that form over land and then move out over water are called something different. Special Marine Warnings are issued to alert boaters of such an occurrence. These are broadcast over VHF NOAA Weather Radio and by the U.S. Coast Guard.

Figure 24-17 A waterspout over St. Louis Bay, off Henderson Point, Mississippi. Note the cloud of spray just above the sea surface. This is the marine equivalent of a tornado, although usually smaller.

Hurricanes: The Tropical Cyclones

HURRICANE is the popular term for a TROPICAL CYCLONE in North America. Unlike the extra-tropical cyclone, it is not related to warm and cold fronts. A hurricane is defined as a storm of tropical origin with a counterclockwise circulation reaching a strength of 64 knots (74 mph) or more at the center.

In its earlier stages, with winds less than 33 knots (38 mph) but with a closed circulatory pattern, the term is a TROPICAL DEPRESSION. When the winds increase beyond 33 knots, it is a TROPICAL STORM until it reaches hurricane strength. In the Western Pacific Ocean, the term used for tropical cyclones is TYPHOON, and because of the greater expanse of ocean there, these storms often become even larger and more intense than hurricanes. In the Indian Ocean, these are called CYCLONES.

Frequency of Tropical Cyclones

The frequency of hurricanes and typhoons varies around the world. In the Far East, typhoons may occur in any month, although they are most common in late summer and early autumn. In North American waters, the period from early December through May is usually, but not always, hurricane-free. August, September, and October are the months of greatest frequency; in these months hurricanes typically, but again not always, form over the tropical Atlantic, mostly between latitudes of 8°N and 20°N. The infrequent hurricanes of June and November almost always originate in the southwestern part of the Caribbean Sea. Interestingly, hurricanes do *not* occur in the South Atlantic.

Hurricanes also occur in the Eastern Pacific off the coast of Mexico, and, infrequently, the direct effect of these storms reaches well into the southwestern U.S. More frequently, the swells generated by these storms can cause much damage to coastal regions of southern California. Some of these storms may affect the Hawaiian Islands.

Development of a Hurricane

The birthplace of a hurricane typically lies within a diffuse and fairly large area of relatively low pressure situated somewhere in the 8°N-20°N latitude belt. In the Atlantic, they often develop from weak storms moving off the Sahara Desert. The winds around the low-pressure area are not particularly strong, and, although cumulonimbus clouds and showers are more numerous than is usual in these latitudes, there is no clearly organized "weather system." This poorly defined condition may persist for several days before hurricane development commences. The development of highly sophisticated WEATHER SATELLITES has greatly improved the ability of forecasters to watch vast ocean areas where these storms originate for any signs of conditions favorable for hurricane development.

When development starts, however, it takes place relatively quickly. Within an interval of 12 hours or less the barometric pressure drops 15 millibars or more over a small, almost circular area. (See page 839 for explanation of units of pressure.) Winds increase and form a ring around the area; the width of this ring is at first only 20 to 40 miles (37 to 74 km). Clouds and thunderstorms become well organized and show a spiral structure. At this stage the growing tropical cyclone acquires an EYE. This is the inner area enclosed by the ring of stronger winds, which has expanded to a width of 100 miles (160 km) or more by the time the cyclone reaches maturity. Within the eye we find the lowest barometric reading. As the tropical cyclone intensifies as the central pressure

Figure 24-18 Heading west from the Bahamas, Hurricane Andrew hit the coast of southeast Florida, as shown in this satellite image. The storm cut a swath of destruction across the state before spinning out over the Gulf of Mexico, and then turning northwest into Louisiana and Mississippi.

continues to fall, the features become more defined and the winds speeds increase.

Hurricane eyes average about 15 miles (28 km) in diameter but may be as large as 25 miles (46 km). The wind velocities in the eye of a hurricane are seldom greater than 15 knots and often are less. Cloud conditions vary over a wide range. At times there are only scattered clouds, but usually there is more than 50 percent cloud cover. Through the openings, the sky is visible overhead, and, at a distance, the dense towering clouds of the hurricane ring can extend to great heights. This feature is the EYE WALL. Seas within the eye are heavy and confused; the "calm" is only with respect to winds.

Hurricane Tracks

Hurricanes have such an impact that they may seem to move in any direction they choose. However, the usual track of an Atlantic hurricane is a parabola around the semipermanent Azores-Bermuda high-pressure area. Thus, after forming, a hurricane will move westward on the southern side of the Azores-Bermuda High, at the same time tending to work away from the equator. When the hurricane reaches the western side of this High, it begins to follow a more northerly track and its

direction of advance changes progressively toward the right. The position where the westward movement changes to an eastward movement is known as the POINT OF CURVATURE.

Occasionally when a hurricane is in a position near the southeast Atlantic coast, the Azores-Bermuda High happens to have an abnormal northward extension. In this situation the hurricane may fail to execute a complete recurvature in the vicinity of Cape Hatteras. It will skirt the western side of the High and come ashore along the southeast U.S. Coast, as occurred with Hurricane Andrew, a major storm of 1992; see **Figure 24-18.**

The rate of movement of tropical cyclones while they are still in low latitudes and heading westward is about 15 knots, which is considerably slower than the usual rate of travel of extra-tropical cyclones. After recurving, they begin to move faster and usually attain a forward speed of at least 25 knots. They may reach 50 to 60 knots in the latter stages before dissipating.

Other storms, particularly early in the season, form in the Caribbean Sea and move westward and north into the Gulf of Mexico. And still other hurricanes follow quite erratic paths, even looping back on their prior track.

Hurricanes gradually decrease in intensity after they reach middle and high latitudes and move over colder water. They quickly lose strength after moving on shore. All tropical cyclones lose their identity, eventually becoming large extra-tropical cyclones.

Effects of El Niño

The phenomenon called "El Niño," a disruption of the ocean-atmosphere system in the tropical Pacific Ocean, has important consequences for weather and climate around the globe. Basically, every few years the water across a huge area in the eastern Pacific warms. This, of course, warms the air above it. The result is that the earth's entire circulation pattern changes. Of most significance is that this changes the position of the JET STREAM winds (high-speed winds near the tropopause, generally westerly). Since storm systems tend to follow the jet stream, for about a year or so, the usual time period of an El Niño, unusual weather patterns result. For example, rainfall may be increased in the southern part of the U.S. and Peru while drought conditions develop in Australia and neighboring countries.

Of principal interest here are the effect on hurricanes. It has been generally accepted that during the existence of El Niño conditions the frequency and intensity of Atlantic hurricanes is lessened.

WEATHER FORECASTS

Some years ago, to be considered a fully qualified skipper, you had to be able to take a series of complex daily weather maps and forecast your own weather; see **Figure 24-19**. Now this is no longer necessary, although the ability to read and understand a simplified weather map will always be useful. The ready availability of weather forecasts by radio, TV, marine facsimile, and the Internet does much of the work for you—but

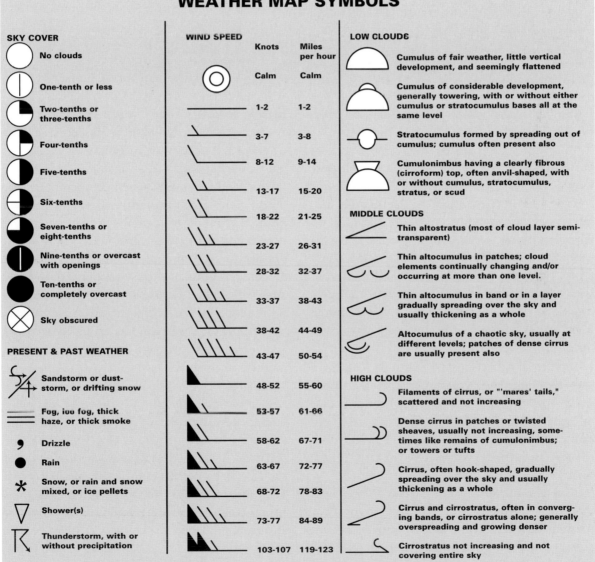

Figure 24-19 *The symbols shown above are those found on weather maps used professionally by the National Weather Service. The sample Station Model,* **Figure 24-20,** *shows how these are used. The average boater need know only a few of them.*

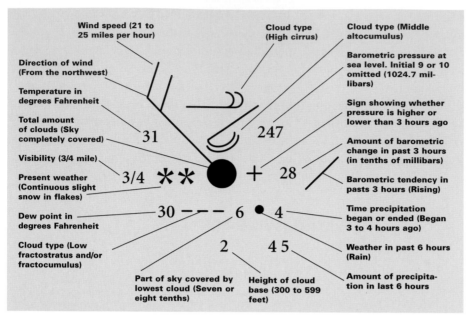

Wind speed (21 to 25 miles per hour)

Direction of wind (From the northwest)

Temperature in degrees Fahrenheit

Total amount of clouds (Sky completely covered)

Visibility (3/4 mile)

Present weather (Continuous slight snow in flakes)

Dew point in degrees Fahrenheit

Cloud type (Low fractostratus and/or fractocumulus)

Part of sky covered by lowest cloud (Seven or eight tenths)

Height of cloud base (300 to 599 feet)

Cloud type (High cirrus)

Cloud type (Middle altocumulus)

Barometric pressure at sea level. Initial 9 or 10 omitted (1024.7 millibars)

Sign showing whether pressure is higher or lower than 3 hours ago

Amount of barometric change in past 3 hours (in tenths of millibars)

Barometric tendency in pasts 3 hours (Rising)

Time precipitation began or ended (Began 3 to 4 hours ago)

Weather in past 6 hours (Rain)

Amount of precipitation in last 6 hours

31   247   3/4 ✳✳   + 28   30 – – – 6 ● 4   2   4 5

Figure 24-20 The sample station model shown here illustrates how the many different symbols depicted in **Figure 24-19** *are combined to give a complete indication of the existing conditions at a specific location.*

you still have the responsibility to get, and heed, the information.

Although weather forecasting is a science that has improved in recent years, every boater knows that it is far from infallible. Get your forecasts by any and every means possible, but keep an eye on present conditions, especially on changes in them. A forecast of good, safe conditions for your general area does not preclude temporary local differences that could be hazardous. Keep alert for special warnings broadcast by the Coast Guard on VHF Channe 22A (or 22) following a preliminary announcement on Channel 16.

Incidentally, if you see conditions that differ from that forecasted, especially if they are potentially life threatening, try to forward that information to the NWS so they can let others know. There are lots of places where the NWS has no observations; you may be the only "eyes" they have.

Weather Maps

As with your navigation charts, information on weather maps is presented by use of symbols. Some of the more frequently encountered symbols will be described below; the many others now used only by professionals are omitted; refer to **Figure 24-19.**

Station Models

A complete STATION MODEL for a reporting location will tell you much more than you need to know; see **Figure 24-20.** It includes information on wind direction and speed; temperature; visibility; cloud type, amount, and height; current pressure and past change plus current tendency; precipitation in past three hours; dew point temperatures; and current weather. Simplified models omit much of this and often show only current weather, temperature, and wind direction and speed.

Current weather is indicated by the appearance of the circle in the center of the station model—open for clear, partially or totally solid for degrees of cloudiness. Current weather—rain, snow, drizzle, etc.—is shown by a symbol immediately to the left of the station circle. Wind direction is indicated by a WEATHER VANE line and wind speed by the number, size, and shape of the FEATHERS on the end of the weather vane. Temperature will normally be given in degrees Fahrenheit (degrees Celsius in Canada and other areas using the metric system).

Air Masses & Fronts

Air masses may or may not be shown in detail. If their characteristics are shown, large block letters will be used: P for polar and T for tropical. Either of these may be further described as maritime (m) or continental (c). Thus we have cP, mP, and mT—the most common of air masses—as well as cT. Since k indicates colder than the land mass over which it is moving and w indicates warmer that the land mass over which it is moving, more precise labels would include cPk and mPw, for example.

Usually, weather maps show simply Highs and Lows, with a large block letter, H or L; occasionally the word High or Low will be spelled out, or a circle drawn around the letter.

Fronts are shown as a heavy line. Cold fronts have a series of solid triangles on the line that point in the direction of movement; see **Figure 24-21.** Warm fronts have solid half-circles on the line; again the side that they are on indicating the direction of movement of the front. An occluded front has alternating triangles and half-circles on the *same side* of the line. A stationary front has the same alternating symbols but with the triangles on one side of the line and the half-circles on the other, indicating no movement.

In some simplified sketches, a cold front is shown by a solid heavy line whereas a warm front is two parallel fine lines; an occluded front is thus a broken line with alternating solid and open segments. On less detailed maps, a front may be shown as merely a heavy line labeled "Cold" or "Warm," or "Stationary" Front. On weather maps in color, a warm front is normally shown in red, with a cold front in blue.

Isobars

A line connecting points of equal barometric pressure is termed an ISOBAR. (See page 839-841 for explanation of units of pressure.) Such lines are usually drawn on weather maps at intervals of four millibars of pressure—996, 1000, 1004, etc.—and are labeled along the line or at each end (96, 00, 04, etc.). On some weather maps, isobars will be labeled for pressure in terms of inches of mercury: 29.97, 30.00, 30.03, etc.

Precipitation

Any precipitation—rain, snow, or hail—is shown by one of a series of symbols; refer to **Figure**

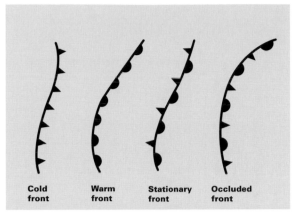

Figure 24-21 Fronts are shown on weather maps by solid lines, usually heavier than other lines, with triangles or half-circles used singly or in combination to indicate the type of front. These symbols face the direction in which the pressure system and its front are moving.

24-19. On less detailed maps, areas of precipitation are often shown by shading or crosshatching, with a descriptive word nearby or different forms of shading used to distinguish rain, snow, and other forms of precipitation.

Using Weather Maps

Unless your boat has a weather facsimile (fax) machine or access to the Internet, it is unlikely that you would be able to receive a weather map while out cruising. But if you are so equipped, or can get them on shore, you might like to try your hand at making predictions from one or more weather maps.

Predictions from a single map are, of course, less accurate and reliable than those based on a series of weather maps over regular intervals of time. A forecast from a single map can only be made for 6 to 12 hours ahead—there are too many factors that can upset an orderly flow of events. (Make sure that you are using a map of *actual* conditions, as of a specified recent time; many weather maps now printed in newspapers are for *predicted* conditions for the day of publication.) Assume that a front is advancing at roughly 20 miles an hour in the normal direction of movement. Sketch in the position of the front 12 hours after the date and time of the map—assuming that your map of actual conditions is

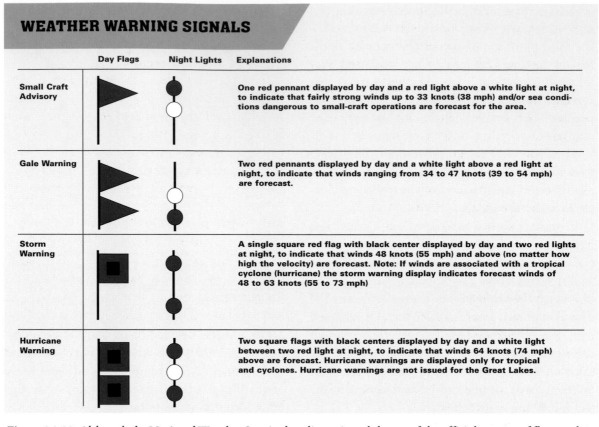

WEATHER WARNING SIGNALS

	Day Flags	Night Lights	Explanations
Small Craft Advisory			One red pennant displayed by day and a red light above a white light at night, to indicate that fairly strong winds up to 33 knots (38 mph) and/or sea conditions dangerous to small-craft operations are forecast for the area.
Gale Warning			Two red pennants displayed by day and a white light above a red light at night, to indicate that winds ranging from 34 to 47 knots (39 to 54 mph) are forecast.
Storm Warning			A single square red flag with black center displayed by day and two red lights at night, to indicate that winds 48 knots (55 mph) and above (no matter how high the velocity) are forecast. Note: If winds are associated with a tropical cyclone (hurricane) the storm warning display indicates forecast winds of 48 to 63 knots (55 to 73 mph)
Hurricane Warning			Two square flags with black centers displayed by day and a white light between two red light at night, to indicate that winds 64 knots (74 mph) above are forecast. Hurricane warnings are displayed only for tropical and cyclones. Hurricane warnings are not issued for the Great Lakes.

Figure 24-22 Although the National Weather Service has discontinued the use of the official systems of flags and lights shown here, these may still be seen from some shore installations such as yacht clubs and marinas.

recent enough that you still have time in which to make a usable 12-hour forecast. Then with the advanced front, and knowledge of the conditions accompanying this front, you can make your own forecast.

If you have a series of maps of existing conditions at daily or half-daily intervals, you can make a much better forecast. Predict your frontal movement based on trends as well as actual events. If weather trends tend to repeat themselves in your areas, file sets of weather maps for typical frontal passages as additional guidance. Keep a record of your forecasts, and compare them later with the conditions that actually occurred. Do this over a period of time and the accuracy of your predictions is sure to improve. You can also compare your forecasts with those received by radio or TV from professionals—but don't peek, make your forecasts first, then compare.

Newspaper Weather Maps

The weather maps printed in daily newspapers vary widely in how much information is presented and how details are shown; invariably these maps are less detailed than are official NWS weather maps. Basic information will be shown sufficiently to get a very generalized picture of nationwide weather, but little more than that. As noted above, maps are usually for predicted conditions rather than a report of actual events.

Television Weather Maps

Weather maps shown as part of local or network news programs also vary widely in level of detail. They do have advantages over newspaper maps in that they frequently show current conditions, and color is used for a more vivid presentation. Most TV weather reporters use animation to show predicted movement of fronts and weather patterns. Often satellite photographs, either still photos or time-lapse loops, are shown to explain conditions or trends. Current and recent weather radar scans are also interesting and helpful in visualizing rain patterns out to about 125 miles (230 km).

Many local cable TV systems carry "The Weather Channel"—a continuous live broadcast of current weather conditions and forecasts. Information is quite comprehensive and several specialized services are included. Weather maps in a number of formats are shown, as well as satellite pictures and radar plots from areas of significant weather activity. Periodically, the national broadcast is interrupted for local reports and predictions.

Other Weather Maps

There are many other weather maps besides the ones usually seen by the public—the "surface analysis" maps. These include upper-air maps for constant pressure levels, such as the 500-millibar map for an altitude of roughly 18,000 feet (5,500 m). Winds at these levels do much to "steer" surface weather patterns, but use of upper-air maps requires specialized training and experience.

Weather Forecasts

Professional meteorologists take great care in the preparation of their forecasts. Your responsibility is to read or listen carefully—don't see or hear something that isn't there, something that you were hoping for. Most times on a boat you will get your forecast by listening to a radio transmission. If it is a scheduled broadcast, get a pencil and paper ready and take notes; if you have to use an abbreviated format to keep up with the flow of information, expand your fragments into complete form as soon as possible while the data are still fresh in your mind. Using a small tape recorder can help. If it is a continuous broadcast, still take notes, but listen a second time to expand your initial notes. Listen as many times as necessary to get the details fully and accurately. Special warnings on NWS stations are preceded by a ten-second high-pitched tone. If you hear this, grab paper and a pencil and stand by to record the

information. Newer VHF radios have a weather alert feature. If this feature is activated and a warning is broadcast, the radio will automatically tune in the appropriate channel.

If you are watching a TV weather report and forecast, it is just as important to take notes, dividing your attention between the picture on the screen and your notepad.

In most instances, you will be able to get a forecast for your local waters. If you can't, try to get a forecast for the region upwind (usually westward) of you, and apply your knowledge of weather movement to make a forecast for your own area.

Keep your notes on weather forecasts received, and compare them with actual conditions later. You may be able to detect a pattern of error in the forecasts, such as weather frequently arriving 12 hours or so later than is forecast—apparently some forecasters would rather have you prepared a bit early for the arrival of a storm than to be caught short.

Weather Forecast Terms

The National Weather Service has an ascending series of alerting messages—advisories, watches, and warnings—for boaters, keyed to increasingly hazardous weather and sea conditions.

The former system of flag and light signals was discontinued by NWS some years ago, but the various levels of alerts remain in effect, and displays may still be seen from various shore activities such as marinas and yacht clubs; see **Figure 24-22.** Boaters should check locally to learn where the signals continue to be flown. Some locations may display only the day signals, others both the day and night signals. In some areas, the Small Craft Advisory pennant is flown on law-enforcement patrol craft when that condition is established.

The Weather Service emphasizes that visual storm warnings are only *supplementary* to the written advisories and warnings given prompt and wide distribution by radio, television, and other media. Important details of the forecasts and warnings with regard to the time, intensity, duration, and direction of storms cannot be given satisfactorily through visual signals alone.

Use of Small-Craft Advisories

The term SMALL-CRAFT ADVISORY needs some explanation. Although there is now no Weather Service definition of Small Craft, you can usually infer that this refers to "small boats, yachts, tugs, barges with little freeboard, or any other low-powered craft." However, much depends on the skill of the mariner. It is the responsibility of each person to decide if his or her seamanship skills and the seaworthiness of his or her vessel are capable of coping with expected wind and sea conditions. Each person has to make the decision to go or stay.

A small-craft advisory does not distinguish between the expectation of a general, widespread, all-day blow of 25 knots or so and, for example, a forecast of isolated, late-afternoon thunderstorms in which winds dangerous to small craft (but not expected to reach warning levels) will be localized and of short duration. It is up to you to deduce from your own observations, supplemented by information you can obtain from any source, which type of situation the advisory applies to and to plan your day's cruise accordingly.

Hurricane Watches & Warnings

Official information is issued by hurricane centers describing all tropical cyclone advisories, watches, and warnings in effect. These bulletins include tropical cyclone locations, intensity, movement, and special precautions that should be taken. ADVISORIES describe tropical cyclones and subtropical cyclones prior to the issuance of watches and warnings. When a hurricane threatens, an NWS watch or warning may result. A HURRICANE WATCH is an announcement for specific areas that a hurricane or incipient hurricane condition poses a threat to coastal areas—generally within 36 hours. A HURRICANE WARNING informs the public that sustained winds of 64 knots (74 mph) or higher associated with a hurricane are expected in a specific coastal area within 24 hours. This warning can remain in effect when dangerously high water or a combination of

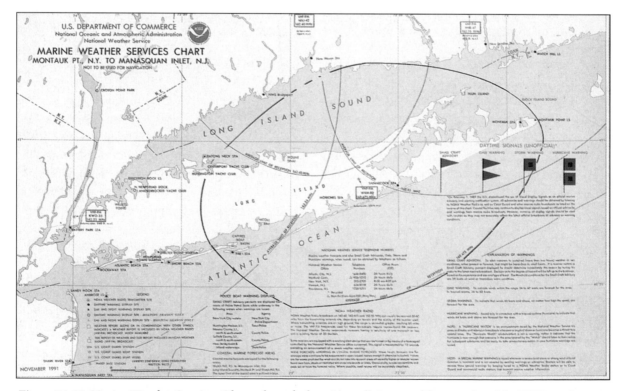

Figure 24-23 Marine Weather Services Charts show the location, call signs, and frequencies of the VHF continuous weather broadcast stations in the charted area. Some of these charts will show the nominal coverage area of each station. Other information of general interest is also shown.

dangerously high water and exceptionally high waves continues, even though winds may be less than hurricane force.

Marine Weather Services Charts

The National Weather Service publishes a series of 15 MARINE WEATHER SERVICES CHARTS covering the coastal waters of all 50 United States, Puerto Rico and the U.S. Virgin Islands, Guam and the northern Mariana Islands, and the Great Lakes. These charts, of which **Figure 24-23** is an example, contain detailed information regarding the times of weather broadcasts from commercial stations, the locations of NWS continuous FM broadcasts and their frequencies, and much other information useful to boaters. The day and night visual signals—no longer official, but continued from some locations—are illustrated and explained. These charts can be viewed and information on how to procure these found over the Internet (see below).

Boaters will find much interesting weather information on the various *Pilot Charts* of the North Atlantic and North Pacific oceans issued by the National Imagery and Mapping Agency (NIMA). The *Pilot Charts* show average monthly wind and weather conditions over the oceans and in addition contain a vast amount of supplemental data on subjects closely allied to weather. They are a valuable source of information for skippers of all sizes of vessels on ocean passages; see page 551.

Each volume of the *Coast Pilot* also contains information on climate conditions and weather broadcasts within its coverage area.

Weather Maps at Sea

Just because you are offshore and not receiving your daily newspaper or able to see your local weather show, you need not be without a reliable and up-to-date weather map. Facsimile radio (RADIOFAX) transmissions can be received by a high-frequency receiver and processed in a unit that prints a weather map line by line; see **Figure 24-24.** An onboard personal computer and printer can be used with special hardware and software making a number of different charts available, such as surface analysis, prognosis

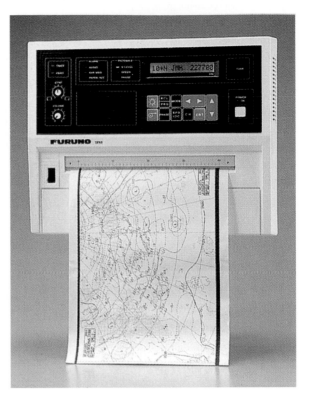

Figure 24-24 A weather fax machine prints out weather maps that can enable you to track the approach of a major disturbance long before it enters your area. Such equipment, which requires a single-sideband (SSB) radio receiver (unless one is integral with the fax equipment) is found on some larger seagoing craft and on most ships.

(forecasts for various periods), upper-air winds, wave analysis, seawater temperature, satellite photographs, and others. Although there is some cost involved, these charts have significant advantages over voice announcements, as you have a specific "hard-copy" picture of current or forecast conditions to study in detail.

Using special peripheral equipment, facsimile weather charts can also be received on board with a high-frequency radio receiver and a personal computer and printer.

Weather Information from the Internet

As with almost any topic, the Internet can be an excellent source for weather information—current and recent conditions, forecasts, and special situations such as hurricanes. The obvious place to start looking is the homepage of the National Weather Service at www.weather.gov. From here you can click your way to just about any weather information you need: current conditions; local and marine forecasts, including offshore areas; weather maps; radar scans; satellite images; past weather and climate data; Marine Weather Service Charts (see above), and many more interesting items.

Some of the same information, presented differently, plus other items, can be obtained from the website of the Weather Channel, www.weather.com.

USING LOCAL WEATHER SIGNS

While weather forecasts are helpful, and you should always take care to get them, they are not completely dependable and they are normally made for a relatively large area. To supplement the official forecast, look around your boat frequently. Notice both the current weather and changes over the last hour or so. And finally, you should know how to interpret the weather signs that you see in clouds, winds, and pressure and temperature changes. If you are not in home waters, local advice may assist you with weather just as it does with navigation.

Cloud Observations

First, identify the cloud form (or forms) observed in the sky, and note whether they are *increasing* or *decreasing* in amount and whether they are *lowering* or *lifting*. In general, thickening and lowering of a cloud layer, be it a layer of cirrostratus, altocumulus, or altostratus, are signs of approaching *wet* weather. And when a layer of clouds shows signs of evaporation, that is, when holes or openings begin to appear in a layer of altostratus, or the elements of an altocumulus layer are frayed and indistinct at the edges, we have an indication of *improving* weather or, at least, delay of any development of foul weather.

Finally, note the *sequence of cloud forms* during the past few hours. Cirrus clouds are frequently the advance agents of an approaching extra-tropical

Weather Proverbs

With all of modern weather forecasting's scientific instruments, high-speed computers, and highly trained professionals, don't overlook the guidance inherent in traditional weather proverbs. Their origins have been lost in the passage of time, and their originators did not know why they were true, but their survival over centuries attests to their general validity. Use them, with caution, and adapt them to local waters.

cyclone, especially if they are followed by a layer of cirrostratus. In this case, the problem is to forecast the track the low-pressure center will take to one side or the other of your location, the nearness of approach of the center, and the intensity of the low.

As the clouds thicken steadily from cirrus to cirrostratus and then to altostratus, you should expect further development to nimbostratus with its rain or snow. There are usually contrary indications if such is not be the case or if the precipitation will arrive late, amount to little, end soon, or will come in two brief periods separated by several hours of mild, more or less sunny weather.

If the northern horizon remains clear until a layer of altostratus clouds overspreads most of the sky, the low-pressure center will probably be passing to the south without bringing precipitation. If the northern horizon is slow in clouding up but becomes covered by the time the cloud sheet is principally altostratus, there will probably be some precipitation but not much. If the cloud sheet, after increasing to altostratus, breaks up into altocumulus and the sky above is seen to have lost most of its covering of cirrostratus, the low-pressure area is either weakening or passing on to the north.

You can often detect the approach of a line of thunderstorms an hour or more in advance by observing the thin white arch of the cirrus border to the anvil top of the approaching cumulonimbus cloud. The atmosphere ahead of a squall line is often so hazy that only this whitish arch

> **Mackerel skies and mares' tails
> Make tall ships carry low sails.**
>
> **I**f high-flying cirrus clouds are few in the sky
> and resemble wisps in a mare's tail in the
> wind, this is a sign of fair weather. Only when
> the sky becomes heavy with cirrus, or with
> mackerel, clouds—cirrocumulus that resemble
> wave-rippled sand on a beach—can you expect
> a storm. There is an exception to the mare's tail
> proverb, however. If cirrus clouds form as
> mare's tails with the hairs pointing upward or
> downward, the probability is for rain, even
> though the clouds may be scattered.

will reveal the presence of a moderately distant cumulonimbus, as the shadowed air under the dense anvil will be invisible behind the sunlit hazy blue air near the observer. Thus, this part of the sky will appear to be clear and will resemble the blue sky above the cirrus arch.

Wind Observations

Sailboat skippers are familiar with the wind direction indicators that can be mounted at the masthead, and these are now often seen on medium-size and larger powerboats. Because a boat anchored or underway can head in any direction all around the compass, a few mental calculations are necessary before we can use this indicator, a yarn, an owner's flag, or club burgee to determine the true direction of the wind. At anchor, the fly will give us the bearing of the wind relative to the boat's bow; this must be converted to the true bearing of the wind itself. We can use our compass to obtain these values, provided we know its deviation on our heading and know the variation for our anchorage. In addition, we need to remember that wind direction is always stated as the true direction *from* which, not *toward* which, the wind is blowing.

For measuring wind strength we need something else. This is an ANEMOMETER; the principal parts of the instrument are illustrated in **Figure 24-25,** upper. The anemometer is essentially a

speedometer. It consists of a rotor with hemispherical or conical cups attached to the ends of the spokes. It is designed for mounting at the masthead, where the wind is caught by the cups and causes them to turn at a speed proportional to wind speed. Indications of the rotor's speed are electrically transmitted to an indicator mounted at the helm or in the cabin on your boat. In the type of instrument illustrated in **Figure 24-25,** lower, the indicator is direct-reading with its scale marked both in knots (0 to 50) and Beaufort force numbers (0 to 12); see below. Battery drain (0.09A) is insignificant. A 60-foot (18 m) cable is supplied to connect the rotor aloft with the illuminated indicator below. At anchor, the reading is the actual or true wind velocity at masthead height.

Models are available that have a digital display and can "remember" the maximum wind velocity since the last time that it was reset. Such instruments can also measure temperature and combine

Figure 24-25 An anemometer rotor is shown above on this sailboat's masthead fixture. It is connected by a cable to an indicator, usually mounted in the cockpit or at the navigator's position. The display unit shown here, lower, shows wind speeds to 50 knots and gives the Beaufort scale force numbers.

> **Red sky at morning**
> **Sailors take warning;**
> **Red sky at night**
> **Sailor's delight.**
>
> **T**here is a simple explanation for this old and quite reliable proverb. A red sunset results from viewing the sun through dusty particles in the air, the nuclei necessary for the formation of rain. This air probably would reach an observer the following day. Since weather tends to flow west to east in most places, if tomorrow's weather appears to the west as a line of wetness, the sun shining through the mass appears as a yellow or grayish orb. On the other hand if the weather lying to the west is dry, the sun will show at its reddish.
>
> Red sky in the morning is caused by the rising, eastern sun lighting up the advance guard of high cirrus and cirrostratus, which will be followed later on by the lowering, frontal clouds. Red sky at night—a red-tinted sunset—often derives from the sky clearing at the western horizon, with the clouds overhead likely to pass before the night is done.

> **Rainbow in morning**
> **Sailors take warning;**
> **Rainbow toward night**
> **Sailor's delight.**
>
> **T**his is also quite an old weather jingle, and a little reasoning, particularly in view of the explanation about the "red sky at morning" saying, would tell you it is true.
>
> As noted, storm centers usually move from the west. Thus, a morning rainbow would have to be viewed from its position already in the west with the sun shining on it from the east. (A rainbow is always seen in a direction opposite to the sun.) The storm would move in your direction, and you could confidently expect rain. A late-afternoon rainbow, however, viewed toward the east, would tell you that the storm has already passed.

that data with wind speed to display a value for wind chill.

True & Apparent Wind

So far we have been considering the determination of the direction and speed of the wind while at anchor. Underway, the determination is more difficult. But the Oceanographic Office of the Navy has worked out the problem, so we may as well use their results. **Table 24-2** is based on wind tables published in *Bowditch*. Using our true course and speed, we can determine from this table the approximate TRUE WIND DIRECTION and SPEED, provided we know the apparent direction and speed. Our wind indicator or owner's flag will give the apparent direction and our anemometer will give us the apparent strength.

The Beaufort Scale

Another method is to estimate the strength of the wind in terms of the BEAUFORT SCALE of wind force. Visually we can observe the sea condition and note the Beaufort number to which it corresponds; see **Table 24-3.** The range of wind speed represented by each force number on the Beaufort scale is shown in knots, statute miles per hour, and kilometers per hour in the table. Wind direction can also be judged by observing the direction from which the smallest ripples are coming since these ripples always run with the wind, responding instantly to changes in wind direction; see **Figure 24-26.**

You don't need to determine wind direction and strength with great precision, but reasonable estimates are helpful in preparing your own local forecasts. Estimating direction within 15 degrees is sufficient and within one Beaufort number is enough for strength. By observing wind direction and speed regularly and making a record of them you can obtain clues concerning potential weather developments as the wind shifts direction and changes its strength.

TRUE FORCE & DIRECTION OF THE WIND FROM ITS APPARENT FORCE & DIRECTION ON A BOAT UNDER WAY

SPEED OF BOAT

Apparent Wind Velocity (Knots)	5 Knots		10 Knots		15 Knots		20 knots	
	True Wind		True Wind		True Wind		True Wind	
	Points off Bow	Velocity Knots	Points off Bow	Velocity Knots	Points off Bow	Velocity Knots	Points off Bow	Velocity Knots
I. Apparent Wind Direction is Dead ahead								
Calm	D. As.	5 K.	D. As.	10 K.	D. As.	15 K.	D. As.	20 K.
4 K.	D. As.	1 K.	D. As.	6 K.	D. As.	11 K.	D. As.	16 K.
8 K.	D. Ah.	3 K.	D. As.	2 K.	D. As.	7 K.	D. As.	12 K.
12 K.	D. Ah.	7 K.	D. Ah.	2 K..	D. As.	3 K.	D. As.	8 K.
16 K.	D. Ah.	11 K.	D. Ah.	6 K.	D. Ah.	1 K.	D. As.	4 K.
22 K.	D. Ah.	17 K.	D. Ah.	12 K.	D. Ah.	7 K.	D. Ah.	2 K.
30 K.	D. Ah.	25 K.	D. Ah.	20 K.	D. Ah.	15 K.	D. Ah.	10 K.
42 K.	D. Ah.	37 K.	D. Ah.	32 K.	D. Ah.	27 K.	D. Ah.	22 K.
60 K.	D. Ah.	55 K.	D. Ah.	50 K.	D. Ah.	45 K.	D. Ah.	40 K.
II. Apparent Wind Direction Is 4 Points (Broad) Off the Bow								
4 K.	11 pts.	4 K.	14 pts.	8 K.	15 pts.	12 K.	15 pts.	17 K.
8 K.	7 pts.	6 K.	11 pts.	7 K.	13 pts.	11 K.	14 pts.	15 K.
12 K.	6 pts.	9 K.	9 pts.	9 K.	11 pts.	11 K.	13 pts.	14 K.
16 K.	5 pts.	13 K.	7 pts.	11 K.	10 pts.	12 K.	11 pts.	14 K.
22 K.	5 pts.	19 K.	6 pts.	16 K.	8 pts.	15 K.	9 pts.	16 K.
30 K	5 pts.	27 K.	6 pts.	24 K.	7 pts.	22 K.	8 pts.	21 K.
42 K.	4 pts.	39 K.	5 pts.	36 K.	6 pts.	33 K.	6 pts.	31 K.
60 K	4 pts.	57 K.	5 pts.	53 K.	5 pts.	51 K.	6 pts.	48 K.
III. Apparent Wind Direction Is 8 Points Off the Bow (Abeam)								
4 K.	13 pts.	6 K.	14 pts.	11 K.	15 pts.	16 K.	15 pts.	20 K.
8 K.	11 pts.	9 K.	13 pts.	13 K.	14 pts.	17 K.	14 pts.	22 K.
12 K.	10 pts.	13 K.	12 pts.	16 K.	13 pts.	19 K.	13 pts.	23 K.
16 K.	10 pts.	17 K.	11 pts.	19 K.	12 pts.	22 K.	13 pts.	26 K.
22 K.	9 pts.	23 K.	10 pts.	24 K.	11 pts.	27 K.	12 pts.	30 K.
30 K.	9 pts.	30 K.	10 pts.	32 K.	10 pts.	34 K.	11 pts.	36 K.
42 K.	9 pts.	42 K.	9 pts.	43 K.	10 pts.	45 K.	10 pts.	47 K.
60 K.	8 pts.	60 K.	9 pts.	61 K.	9 pts.	62 K.	10 pts.	63 K.
IV. Apparent Wind Direction Is 12 Points Off the Bow (Broad on the Quarter)								
4 K.	14 pts.	8 K.	15 pts.	13 K.	15 pts.	18 K.	15 pts.	23 K.
8 K.	14 pts.	12 K.	14 pts.	17 K.	15 pts.	21 K.	15 pts.	26 K.
12 K.	13 pts.	16 K.	14 pts.	20 K.	14 pts.	25 K.	15 pts.	30 K.
16 K.	13 pts.	20 K.	14 pts.	24 K.	14 pts.	29 K.	14 pts.	33 K.
22 K.	13 pts.	26 K.	13 pts.	30 K.	14 pts.	34 K.	14 pts.	39 K.
30 K.	13 pts.	34 K.	13 pts.	38 K.	13 pts.	42 K.	14 pts.	46 K.
42 K.	12 pts.	46 K.	13 pts.	50 K.	13 pts.	54 K.	13 pts.	58 K.
60 K.	12 pts.	64 K.	13 pts.	67 K.	13 pts.	71 K.	13 pts.	75 K.

CONVERSION OF POINTS OFF BOW TO TRUE DIRECTION OF WIND
BOAT'S HEADING – TRUE

Points Off Bow	000°	045°	090°	135°	180°	225°	270°	315°
I. When Wind Direction Obtained from Table Above Is off Port Bow								
Dead Ahead	N	NE	E	SE	S	SW	W	NW
4 points	NE	E	SE	S	SW	W	NW	N
8 points	E	SE	S	SW	W	NW	N	NE
12 points	SE	S	SW	W	NW	N	NE	E
Dead Astern	S	SW	W	NW	N	NE	E	SE
II. When Wind Direction Obtained from Table Above Is Off Port Bow								
Dead Ahead	N	NE	E	SE	S	SW	W	NW
4 points	NW	N	NE	E	SE	S	SW	W
8 points	W	NW	N	NE	E	SE	S	SW
12 points	SW	W	NW	N	NE	E	SE	S
Dead Astern	S	SW	W	NW	N	NE	E	SE

To Use This Table
Abbreviations: D. As = Dead Astern. D. AH = Dead Ahead. K. = Knots. Pts. = Points off bow.
1. With Wind Direction Indicator: Determine Apparent Wind Direction off the Bow.
2. With Anemometer: Determine Apparent Wind Velocity, in Knots.
3. Enter Upper Part of Table: Use portion for nearest Apparent Wind Direction Opposite Apparent Wind Velocity and under nearest Speed of Boat, read Wind Direction in Points off Bow and True Wind Velocity in Knots. Note whether True Wind Direction is off Starboard or Port Bow.
4. Enter Lower Part of the Table: Use portion for proper Bow: Starboard or Port. Opposite Points off Bow and under Nearest Boat's True Heading, read True Wind Direction.
5. Log: Record True Wind Direction as obtained from Lower Part of Table and True Wind Velocity as obtained from Upper Part of Table in Boat's Weather Log.

Table 24-2 *This table will allow you to find the true force and direction of the wind from its apparent force and direction on a boat underway.*

THE BEAUFORT WIND SALE

BEAUFORT NUMBER	MPH	KM/HR	KNOTS	INTERNATIONAL DESCRIPTION	EFFECTS OBSERVED ON WATER
0	under 1	under 1	under 1	Calm	Sea like a mirror.
1	1-3	1-5	1-3	Light air	Ripples with appearance of scales; no foam crests.
2	4-7	6-11	4-6	Light breeze	Small wavelets; crests of glassy appearance, not breaking.
3	8-12	12-19	7-10	Gentle breeze	Large wavelets; crests begin to break, scattered whitecaps.
4	13-18	20-28	11-16	Moderate	Small waves 0.5-1.25 meters high, becoming longer; numerous whitecaps.
5	19-24	29-38	17-21	Fresh	Moderate waves of 1.25-2.5 meters taking longer form; many whitecaps; some spray.
6	25-31	39-49	22-27	Strong	Larger waves 2.5-4 meters forming; whitecaps everywhere; more spray.
7	32-38	50-61	28-33	Near gale	Sea heaps up, waves 4-6 meters; white foam from breaking waves begins to blow in streaks.
8	39-46	62-74	34-40	Gale	Gale Moderately high (4-6 meters) waves of greater length; edge of crests begin to break into spindrift; foam is blown in well-marked streaks.
9	47-54	75-88	41-47	Strong gale	High waves (6 meters); sea begins to roll; dense streaks of foam; spray may reduce visibility.
10	55-63	89-102	48-55	Storm	Very high waves (6-9 meters) with overhanging crests; sea takes a white appearance as foam is blown in very dense streaks; rolling is heavy and visibility is reduced.
11	64-73	103-117	56-63	Violent storm	Exceptionally high (9-14 meters) waves; sea covered with white foam patches; visibility still more reduced.
12	74-82	118-131	64-71	Hurricane	Air filled with foam; waves over 14 meters; sea completely white with driving spray; visibilty greatly reduced.

Table 24-3 This table is based roughly on a scale for estimating wind speeds developed in 1805 by Admiral Sir Francis Beaufort of the British Royal Navy. The original Beaufort Scale was based on the effect of various wind speeds on the amount of sail that a full-rigged ship could carry. It has since been modified and modernized.

Wind Force & Its Effect on the Sea

Boaters frequently use the Beaufort scale to log wind speed and the condition of the sea, but too often the description of sea conditions relies on verbal statements like "moderate waves," "large waves," "moderately high waves" (see **Table 24-3,**

THE BUYS-BALLOT'S LAW

Christophorus Buys-Ballot, a Dutch meteorologist, used the direction of the swirl of the wind in a low-pressure cell to find the center of a storm. In 1858, he formulated a law stating that winds are perpendicular to the lines of barometric slope. Two years later, he put his observations into a paper entitled *Some Rules for Predicting Weather Changes in the Netherlands.* In that

Low pressure

paper was his well-known rule, "with your back to the wind, low pressure is to the left, higher pressure to the right." (In the southern hemisphere, you would face the wind to find the low-pressure center with your left hand.) The application of this law has enabled many sailors to head for calmer waters

column for "Effects Observed on Water") which leaves the boaters pretty much "at sea" in trying to visualize exactly what these terms imply.

The British Meteorological Office has solved this problem by issuing a State of Sea card (M.O. 688A) with photographs to accompany each of the descriptions of 13 wind forces of the Beaufort scale. Thus an observer has a guide in estimating

Rainbow to windward, foul fall the day; Rainbow to leeward, rains run away.

This is another old seafarer's saying about rainbows, but it is certainly worth remembering because it is almost infallibly true. If a rainbow is behind or with the direction of the prevailing wind, then you can expect its curtain of moisture to reach you. But if the rainbow appears to the lee of the wind, then you know rain has already passed and the gray line of showers is receding, moving away from you.

wind strength (in knots) when making weather reports or in logging sea conditions. Fetch, depth of water, swell, heavy rain, current, and the lag effect between the wind picking up and the sea increasing may also affect the appearance of the sea. Range of wind speed and the mean wind speed are given for each force. By special permission, we reproduce six of these photographs (Forces 1, 3, 5, 8, 10, 12); refer to **Figure 24-26.** Forces 0, 2, 4, 6, 7, 9, and 11, though not illustrated, may be estimated in relation to those above and below them in the scale.

Pressure Observations

Another weather instrument you should be familiar with is the ANEROID BAROMETER; see **Figure 24-27.** The one illustrated has several interesting features.

First, there is the pressure scale. You probably are accustomed to thinking of barometric pressure in terms of INCHES OF MERCURY, so the scale is graduated in these units. Weather reports and forecasts now use pressures shown in MILLIBARS. So, another scale graduated in millibars helps. You thus would not have to worry about conversions between units.

Figure 24-26 *Photographs taken from a National Weather Service NOAA publication show wind forces and their effect on open waters. Beaufort Force 1 (calm air) is shown at upper-left. Force 3 (gentle breeze) is at upper-right. Force 5 (fresh breeze) appears at center-left. Force 8 (gale) is at center-right. Force 10 (storm) is shown at lower-left. Finally, at lower-right is Force 12 (hurricane); note how in hurricane-force winds the surface of the sea may be completely obscured by driving foam.*

The "standard atmospheric pressure" of 29.92 inches of mercury is equal to 1013.2 millibars; 1 inch equals 33.86 millibars, or 1 millibar equals 0.03 inches of mercury.

Second, it is a rugged instrument and it has a high order of accuracy. Third, it has a reference hand, for keeping track of changes in pressure. The words "Fair-Change-Rain," in themselves, when they appear on the face of an aneroid barometer, are decorative. It is not the actual barometric pressure that is important in forecasting; it is the direction and rate of change in pressure.

Figure 24-27 The barometer shown here has scales both in inches of mercury and in millibars. Markings such as "Rain," "Change," or "Fair" are traditional, but are of little practical value.

How a Barometer Is Used

A good barometer is a helpful instrument provided you read it at regular intervals and keep a record of the readings and provided you remember that there is much more to weather than just barometric pressure.

An individual reading of the barometer tells you only the pressure being exerted by the atmosphere on the earth's surface at a particular point of observation at that time. But suppose you have logged the pressure readings at regular intervals, as follows:

Time	Pressure	Change
0700	30.02	—
0800	30.00	-0.02
0900	29.97	-0.03
1000	29.93	-0.04
1100	29.88	-0.05
1200	29.82	-0.06

The pressure is falling, and it is falling at an increasing rate. Trouble is brewing. A fall of 0.02 inch per hour is a low rate of fall; consequently, this figure would not be particularly disturbing. But a fall of 0.05 inch per hour is a rather high rate.

Next, there is a normal daily change in pressure. The pressure is usually at its maximum

value about 1000 and 2200 each day and at its minimum value about 0400 and 1600. The variation between minimum and maximum may be as much as 0.05 inch change in these six-hour intervals (about 0.01 inch change per hour). Thus, when the pressure normally would increase about 0.03 inch (0700 to 1000) our pressure actually must have fallen 0.09 inch.

Suppose, now, that at about 1200 you also observed that the wind was blowing from the NE with increasing force and that the barometer continued to fall at a high rate. A severe northeast gale is probably on its way. On the other hand, given the same barometer reading of about 29.80, rising rapidly with the wind going to west, you could expect improving weather. Quite a difference!

Barometric Changes & Wind Velocity

Let us now relate barometric changes to wind velocity. First, it is generally true that a rapidly falling barometer forecasts the development of strong winds. This is so because a falling barometer indicates the approach or development of a Low, and the pressure gradient is usually steep in the neighborhood of a low-pressure center. On the other hand, a rising barometer is associated with the prospect of lighter winds to come. This is true because a rising barometer indicates the approach or development of a High, and the pres-

**Winds that swing against the sun
And winds that bring the rain are one.
Winds that swing around the sun
Keep the rainstorm on the run.**

This old saying is based on the direction a weathervane is pointing, but observing a flag will do as well. It means that a wind that changes against the sun's movement, blowing first from the west, then the east, brings dirty weather with it. But, a wind that changes its direction so it moves from east to west, as the sun moves, almost always results in clear skies.

**A backing wind says
storms are nigh;
But a veering wind will clear the sky.**

This folklore observation generally refers to
storms running in a southerly direction.

sure gradient is characteristically smaller in the neighborhood of a high-pressure center.

The barometer does not necessarily fall before or during a strong breeze. The wind often blows hard without any appreciable accompanying change in the barometer. This means that a steep pressure gradient exists (isobars close together, as seen on the weather map), but that the well-developed High or Low associated with the steep pressure gradient is practically stationary. In this case the wind may be expected to blow hard for some time; any slackening or change will take place gradually.

It not infrequently happens that the barometer falls quite rapidly, yet the wind remains comparatively light. If you remember the relation between wind velocity and pressure gradient, you can conclude that the gradient must be comparatively

Appearance of the Moon Proverbs

The shape and color of the moon as indicators of coming weather changes have long been a subject of controversy mostly among those meteorological experts who declare that the moon has no appreciable control over the weather beyond a very small tidal effect on the atmosphere. But for now, let's be content with the observation that as far as weather portents are concerned, the moon is one of the most visible and absolutely reliable signs of weather change. It is not the moon's influence that makes the following sayings ring with truth, it is other atmospheric conditions that influence the moon's appearance.

small (isobars relatively far apart). The rapid fall of the barometer must be accounted for, then, in either one or two ways. Either a Low with a weak pressure gradient on its forward side is approaching rapidly, or there is a rapid decrease of pressure taking place over the surrounding area, or both. In such a situation, the pressure gradient at the rear of the Low is often steep, and in that case, strong winds will set in as soon as the barometer commences to rise. (It will rise rapidly under these circumstances.) The fact that the barometer is now rising, however, indicates that decreasing winds may be expected soon.

The Barometer & Wind Shifts

Nearly all extra-tropical cyclones display an unsymmetrical distribution of pressure. The pressure gradients are seldom the same in the front and rear of an extra-tropical cyclone. During the approach of a Low, the barometer alone gives no clue as to how much the wind will shift and what velocity it will have after the passage of the low-pressure system. This is particularly applicable to situations in which the wind blows from a southerly direction while the barometer is falling. The cessation of the fall of the barometer will coincide with a veering (gradual or sudden) shift of the wind to a more westerly direction. Unfortunately, if you have no information other than the variations in atmospheric pressure indicated by your barometer, you cannot foretell the exact features of the change.

In using barometric indications for local forecasting, remember that weather changes are influenced by the characteristics of the earth's surface in your locality. Check all rules against experience in your own cruising waters before you place full confidence in them.

Temperature Observations

Thermometer readings will not give as much information for weather predicting as data from other instruments, but they are not without some value.

Cold air carried down from a thunderstorm cloud with the rain may be felt as much as three

Sharp horns on the moon threaten high winds.

When you can clearly see the sharp horns or ends of a crescent moon with your naked eye, it means there are high-speed winds aloft which are sweeping away cloud forms. Inasmuch as these high winds always descend to earth, you can predict a windy day following.

Figure 24-28. By recording these temperatures and plotting their spread over a period of several hours, as is indicated by that part of the curve drawn as a solid line, you will have a basis for forecasting the time at which you are likely to be fogbound. The broken-line portion of the curve represents actual data, but it could just as easily have been drawn by extending the solid portion. If an error were made in this extrapolation, it would probably indicate that the fog would form

miles in advance of the storm itself. Thus, a warning is given and the approach of the storm is confirmed.

Judging the Likelihood of Fog

In order to judge the likelihood of fog formation, you can periodically measure the air temperature and dew-point temperature and see if the SPREAD (difference) between them is getting smaller.

A graph derived from a series of air and dew-point temperatures (see below) is shown in

When a halo rings the moon or sun The rain will come upon the run.

Halos are excellent atmospheric signs of rain. Halos around the moon after a pale sun confirm the advent of rain, for you are viewing the moon through the ice crystals of high cirriform clouds. When the whole sky is covered with these cloud forms, a warm front is approaching, bringing a long, soft rain.

GENERAL BAROMETER RULES

• Foul weather is usually forecast by a falling barometer with winds from the east quadrant.

• Except after a wintertime cold frontal passage in a relatively warm marine area, clearing and fair weather is usually forecast by winds shifting to west quadrants from a rising barometer.

• When the wind sets in from points between south and southeast and the barometer falls steadily, a storm is approaching from the west or northwest, and its center will pass near or north of the observer within 12 or 24 hours, with the wind veering to northwest by way of south and southwest.

• When the wind sets in from points between east and northeast and the barometer

starts to fall steadily, a storm is approaching from the south or southwest, and its center will pass near or to the south of the observer within 12 or 24 hours, with the wind backing to northwest by way of north.

• The rapidity of a storm's approach and the storm's likely intensity will be indicated by the rate and by the the amount of fall in the barometer.

• A falling barometer and a rising thermometer often forecast precipitation.

• Barometer and thermometer rising together often forecast fine weather.

• A slowly rising barometer forecasts settled weather.

• A steady, slow fall of pressure indicates forthcoming unsettled or wet weather.

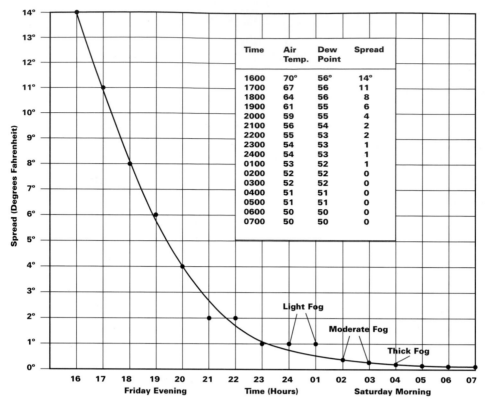

Time	Air Temp.	Dew Point	Spread
1600	70°	56°	14°
1700	67	56	11
1800	64	56	8
1900	61	55	6
2000	59	55	4
2100	56	54	2
2200	55	53	2
2300	54	53	1
2400	54	53	1
0100	53	52	1
0200	52	52	0
0300	52	52	0
0400	51	51	0
0500	51	51	0
0600	50	50	0
0700	50	50	0

Figure 24-28 Shown here is a plot of a series of air and dewpoint temperatures at hourly intervals based on the values in the table, inset. Indications of the density of fog at various times is also shown.

at an earlier hour. This is on the safe side; you would be secure in your anchorage sometime before the 59th minute of the 11th hour.

Note that while the average decrease in spread is about 1.5° F per hour, the decrease is at a much greater rate in the earlier hours of the day. So long as you do not make unreasonable allowances for a slowing up in the rate of change of the spread, this also will help keep you on the safe side.

Determining the Dew Point

You can determine the dew point by means of a simple-to-operate, inexpensive device known as a SLING PSYCHROMETER; see **Figure 24-29.** A sling psychrometer consists of two thermometers mounted in a single holder with a handle that permits it to be whirled overhead. One thermometer, known as the DRY BULB, has its bulb of mercury exposed directly to the air and thus shows the actual temperature of the air. The other thermometer, the WET BULB, has its bulb covered with a piece of gauze; soak this gauze in fresh water so that the bulb is moistened. If the air is not saturated with water vapor, evaporation then

takes place from the wet-bulb thermometer as it is whirled and, since the process of evaporation requires the expenditure of heat, the wet bulb is

When boat horns sound hollow, Rain will surely follow.

Anyone who has spent any time around boats knows the truth of this time-honored prophecy. Nor do you have to be sitting on a piling in a marina to notice the unusual sharpness of sounds on certain days—the more penetrating sound of a bell ringing or voices that carry longer distances are signs of the acoustical clarity when bad weather lowers the cloud ceiling toward the earth. The tonal quality of sound is improved because the cloud layer bounces the sounds back, the way the walls of a canyon echo a cry. When the cloud barrier lifts, the same clouds dissipate in space.

A halo around the sun indicates the approach of a storm within three days, from the side which is the most brilliant.

Halos predict a storm at not great distance, and the open side of the halo tells the quarter from which it may be expected.

hese two sayings at first reading may seem contradictory, but they are more explicit in their forecasting than the simple "halo rings the moon" saying. As cirrus and cirrostratus fronts push across the sky in the region of the moon or sun, the halo first appears and subsequently becomes brightest in that part of the arc from which a low-pressure system is approaching. Later, the halo becomes complete and the light is uniform throughout. As the storm advances, altostratus clouds arrive and obliterate the original, and for a time, the brightest part of the halo—that is, the side nearest the oncoming storm. Both sayings are useful, but they refer to different times in the life of the halo.

It is also true that when halos are double or triple, they signify that cirrostratus clouds are relatively thick, such as would be the case in a deep and well-developed storm. Broken halos indicate a much disturbed state in the upper atmosphere, with rain close at hand.

Now, to put any confusion to rest about the forecast persistence of rain by the appearance of sun and moon halos, the U.S. Weather Service has verified through repeated observations that sun halos will be followed by rain about 75 percent of the time. Halos around the moon have a rain forecasting accuracy of about 65 percent.

cooled. Continue whirling until there is no more lowering of this. The reduced temperature shown by the wet-bulb thermometer, the WET-BULB TEMPERATURE, thus represents the lowest temperature to which the air can be cooled by evaporating water into it.

When you whirl the psychrometer you create a draft around it, thereby increasing the efficiency of the evaporation process and making the wet bulb more reliable than it would be with little or no air movement past it—hence the psychrometer's design for whirling.

From the wet-bulb and dry-bulb temperatures, you can determine the dew point by referring to a suitable table. As you are far more interested in knowing the spread between air temperature and dew point, however, use **Table 24-4,** explained below.

If the air is already saturated with water vapor, no water can evaporate from the gauze and both thermometers will show the same value. The spread between air temperature and dew point is

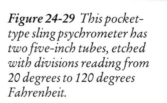

Figure 24-29 This pocket-type sling psychrometer has two five-inch tubes, etched with divisions reading from 20 degrees to 120 degrees Fahrenheit.

zero. But if the air is not already saturated with water vapor, subtract the wet-bulb temperature from the dry-bulb temperature. With this difference and the dry-bulb (the air) temperature, consult **Table 24-4** and find the corresponding spread between the air temperature and the dew-point temperature. This is the figure you want.

Difference Dry-bulb minus wet-bulb	AIR TEMPERATURE SHOWN BY DRY-BULB THERMOMETER												
	35	40	45	50	55	60	65	70	75	80	85	90	95
1	2	2	2	2	2	2	2	1	1	1	1	1	1
2	5	5	4	4	4	3	3	3	3	3	3	3	2
3	7	7	7	6	5	5	5	4	4	4	4	4	4
4	10	10	9	8	7	7	6	6	6	6	5	5	5
5	14	12	11	10	10	9	8	8	7	7	7	7	6
6	18	15	14	13	12	11	10	9	9	8	8	8	8
7	22	19	17	16	14	13	12	11	11	10	10	9	9
8	28	22	20	18	17	15	14	13	12	12	11	11	10
9	35	27	23	21	19	17	16	15	14	13	13	12	12
10	—	33	27	24	22	29	18	17	16	15	14	14	13
11	—	40	32	28	25	22	20	19	18	17	16	15	15
12	—	—	38	32	28	25	23	21	20	18	17	17	16
13	—	—	45	37	31	28	25	23	21	20	19	18	17
14	—	—	—	42	35	31	28	26	24	22	21	20	19
15	—	—	—	50	40	35	31	28	26	24	23	21	21

Table 24-4 *This table will allow you to use the air temperature as shown by the dry-bulb thermometer of a sling psychrometer and the difference between that reading and the wet-bulb reading to determine dew-point spread. All figures are in degrees Fahrenheit at 30 inches barometric pressure.*

If, in the late afternoon or early evening, the spread between the air temperature and dew point is *less* than approximately 6° F, and the air temperature is falling, you will probably encounter fog or greatly restricted visibility in a few hours. These critical values are emphasized by the heavy line below them in **Table 24-4**.

Incidentally, should you ever want to know the dew-point temperature itself, all you need do is to subtract the spread figure given in the table from the temperature shown by the dry-bulb thermometer. The formula used for converting Fahrenheit temperature to Celsius temperature is: (°F-32) x 0.56 = °C.

The Weather Log

Although the latest Weather Service forecasts are readily available via various media, it is often

---

Lightning from the west or northwest will reach you, Lightning from the south or southeast will pass you by.

This is a true saying, if you live in the North Temperate Zone. Lightning comes hand in hand with storm clouds, and thunderheads always loom over the horizon from the west or northwest, and usually move east. So lightning anywhere from the south or southeast will pass you by.

Sound traveling far and wide A stormy day does like betide.

This is another (English) version of the saying about "sound" and bad weather; this one suggests that you actually can hear bad weather approaching, say, when a faraway train whistle is audible when normally it would be faint. The reason the sound carries farther is that the whistle was blown under a lowering cloud ceiling whose extending barrier may not have reached your position yet.

BOAT WEATHER LOG

Yacht________ At/ Passage________ to ________

Day_____ Date_____ Time Zone_____ Skipper_____

1. Latest Weather Map: Date_____ Time_____ Summary of forecast and of principal regional weather features: ________

2. Radio Weather Reports Received (state source and time): ________

3. Local Weather Observations

4. Remarks and Local Forecast for Next_____ Hours (state time forecast effective): ________

LOCAL WEATHER OBSERVATIONS

Time

Latitude—degrees, minutes

Longitude—degrees, minutes

Course—degrees mag.

—degrees true

Speed—Knots

Barometer—in. or mb.

—tendency

Clouds—form

—moving from

—amount

—changing to

Sea—condition

—swells

—moving from

Temperatures—air, dry bulb

—dewpoint

—water

Visibility

Wind—direction, true

—shifting to

—velocity, true

—force (Beaufort)

Weather—present

Figure 24-30 *A weather log of this general format, left, can be used to record information developed from weather maps, or received by radio, and the forecast developed from this data. The reverse side, right, is used for local weather observations. By recording this information and keeping the record, it is possible to develop considerable skill in making forecasts.*

helpful to record your own cloud and weather observations. You can then check the reliability of the latest prediction. Occasionally the professional forecaster misjudges the future rate of travel of the weather pattern, which may move faster or slower than anticipated. Or a new, unforeseen development in the pattern may occur.

A form of WEATHER LOG that is suitable for use on recreational boats is shown in **Figure 24-30,** left. This is the front sheet; **Figure 24-30,** right, shows the reverse side. The first weather items recorded are based on a reading of the latest weather map (if available) and a summary of any radio reports received. Then use the reverse side to jot down your local observations. Sufficient columns are available to permit the entry of these data six times during one 24-hour day, at four-hour intervals. Entries may be made using standard weather code symbols or any other method you choose, provided you use the same system consistently.

From these records you can estimate how and to what extent the actual weather during the next few hours might differ from those predicted in the official forecast.

Boating Customs

Courtesy Afloat • The Etiquette of Flags, Afloat & Ashore

Boating is an informal kind of recreation, no longer bound to the ceremonies of "yachting etiquette." However, there are many occasions when proper observances are expected, even if as only common courtesy to your boating neighbors.

You need not belong to a yacht club, but it helps to understand club practices that you might encounter. You should be able to recognize a race in progress, for example, and take steps to avoid it. Likewise, you should be able to drop your hook in an anchorage, or make fast at a marina, or raft up with other boats without causing friction. You should know the proper procedures for displaying flags.

This chapter covers boating customs, as they exist today. In the main, they simply represent good sense and good manners afloat.

COURTESY AFLOAT

Except when cruising the high seas, or on some remote inland waters, you will generally be boating within sight of other boats. Often you will be close enough that any maneuvers you make, even activities on board your boat, will have an impact on others. Some actions are beyond those required by the Navigation Rules. The situations suggested below are a matter of good manners, of causing the least interference to the vessel with the most limited maneuverability.

When Underway

A faster boat overtaking a slower one in restricted waters, such as a channel or narrow river, should slow down sufficiently to cause no damage or discomfort. Often overlooked is that it may be necessary for the slower boat itself to reduce speed. For example, if the slower boat is making 8 knots, the faster boat can slow only to about 10 knots in order to have enough speed differential left to get past. But at that speed the passing boat may make a wake that is uncomfortable to the other craft. The overtaken boat should slow to about 4 knots, or even less, to allow the other boat to pass at 5 or 6 knots with little wake; see **Figure 25-01**.

If an adequate depth of water extends outward on one or both sides of the course, it is courteous for the passing boat to swing well out to a safe side in order to minimize the discomfort to the overtaken boat. A powerboat should pass a sailboat well to leeward, or astern if it is in a crossing situation, so as to not disturb the flow of air on its sails; refer to Chapter 8, page 273.

Near Regattas & Other Events

A fleet of sailboats all headed in the same general direction is a sure indication of a race in progress. While it might be possible to pass through such a fleet "legally," observing the proper Navigation Rules, this action might interfere with the courses and tactics of the racing skippers. Stay well clear so that neither your wake nor your "wind shadow" will have any effect on the race boats.

Although cruising-type sailboats engaged in a long-distance race may not be easy to identify as competitors in an event, whether such a boat is racing or just cruising, it is best to take no action which would interfere with its progress.

Marine parades, powerboat races, and other such types of event may be held—with a regatta permit from the U.S. Coast Guard—in waters that are otherwise subject to normal marine

Opposite Page: Figure 25-01 It is courteous for a faster boat to slow down when passing a slower craft, such as a sailboat. However, such passing will be accomplished most comfortably for the slower boat if that craft also slows down in order that the faster craft can pass at a true "no wake" speed.

Figure 25-02 Boating waters are patrolled by many different law-enforcement craft. These may be boats of the Coast Guard, USCG Auxiliary, or state or local police agencies. Whatever the source of the patrolling craft, instructions and orders from them must be promptly obeyed.

Figure 25-04 When two or more boats are rafted, the boat at the anchor (according to plan, the last one to depart) must have adequate ground tackle. All rafted boats should be well protected by fenders.

traffic. The Coast Guard, USCG Auxiliary, or the organization sponsoring the event may provide patrol boats to keep nonparticipating craft clear of the event; see **Figure 25-02.** You must obey instructions given from any such patrol boat. In addition to the danger in blundering out into the path of speeding race boats, it is discourteous to interfere with the performance of any regatta.

Anchorages, Moorings & Marinas

Be a good boating neighbor when you drop the hook in an anchorage, lie at a mooring, or make fast at a yacht club or marina pier. Enter an

Figure 25-03 At an anchorage or marina, turn down radios or similar equipment and keep other noise levels low. Many boaters turn in early after a day's cruise

anchorage dead slow; a wake that upsets someone's dinner or drink will not win friends among other boaters. In addition, refrain from the unnecessary use of your searchlight. Avoid anchoring too close to other boats: Keep in mind that when a wind shift changes the boats' positions, anchor rodes can foul in a matter of minutes, and hulls can be damaged if they bang together. Remember the first boat to anchor has a right to an appropriate swinging radius. Also consider the state of the tide and the effect of its range on your swinging radius. If a guest mooring is free, use it only after you have obtained permission; it may be reserved for another boat, or it may be unsuitable for your craft. As for fuel piers, make fast to them only briefly. When others are waiting, never use fueling time as an opportunity to make a trip to the store. Likewise, when boating in some salt-water areas, avoid using a marina's limited fresh-water reserves to wash your boat without first asking for permission.

In the evening hours, take care not to disturb people on other boats in the area. Sound travels exceptionally well across water, and many cruising boat crews turn in early for dawn departures; see **Figure 25-03.** You should resist the temptation to visit among the other boats with a dinghy and outboard motor. The quiet of using oars will be appreciated by others. Make sure that those aboard your boat keep their voices down and play music only at low levels. Remember that any comments you make about other boats will carry as well. If you are one of the early departees, leave the mooring with an absolute minimum of noise, and again, at dead slow speed.

When rafting, the boat that will be last to leave is the one to take the mooring, lie alongside the pier or wharf, or drop the anchor (provided that its ground tackle is adequate). The others should lash up in order of departure, so that the first to leave will be farthest outboard. This is only common sense—but it must be remembered; see **Figure 25-04.**

Don't throw trash and garbage overboard; even if it is biodegradable, it is unsightly and illegal. Secure any flapping halyards; they can be a most annoying source of noise (and can chafe the surface of the mast). Dogs should be well trained to avoid barking in an anchorage. Exercise them ashore in authorized areas, or well away from normal traffic areas; make sure you pick up after your pet; see **Figure 25-05.** When you go ashore, for whatever reason, leave the area as you found it—or even cleaner. Observe all signs and regulations, extinguish fires, and dispose of refuse if permitted.

Cruising in Company

When on a group cruise, maintain speed and keep a constant distance from the other boats, according to a prearranged plan. Agree in advance about places to stop for fuel, supplies, sightseeing, or other reasons. Do not use your VHF marine radio for social communication between boats: This equipment is for safety and operational traffic only. CB and FRS radios, however, if available, are suitable for social use.

If you are rafted, avoid crossing from one boat to another unnecessarily and, unless you are on informal terms with your neighbors, ask permission before you do so. Be sure to supply your share of fenders, fenderboards, and lines—as well as ingredients for parties and meals that are planned.

Clubs & Organizations

If you are a member of a recognized yacht club, often other yacht clubs will extend you courte-

Figure 25-05 *Whether on the water for a day, or departing for an extended cruise, taking the family pet along presents extra responsibilities. Fair weather or foul, you must be prepared to take a dog ashore periodically—and to clean up after it.*

sies—the use of guest slips, moorings, and clubhouse facilities, for example. Remember, though, that proper procedure requires asking permission to use such facilities, even if you wish to make fast briefly at the club dock to pick up a member who is planning to join you.

When visiting a yacht club of which you are not a member, take the time to inform yourself about the actions and routines of the local owner-members and club officers. This can be especially important in respect to evening "colors," the lowering of flags: Remember that not all clubs strictly calculate the daily time of sunset, and some sunset signals for colors may be earlier than you would normally expect; see **Figure 25-06.**

Yacht clubs and organizations such as the United States Power Squadrons generally have by-laws or handbooks that spell our requirements for ceremonial procedures, such as the exchange of salutes, daily color ceremonies, salutes between vessels, precedence in boarding or leaving launches, and flag courtesies.

In many cases a 0800 gun is sounded as a signal to raise colors and a sunset gun for lowering colors. If you expect to be away from your boat at the time of sunset, take in the applicable flags before you leave the boat.

If hired personnel are not on hand when a boat is coming in to make fast near your position, it is good manners to offer to help with the docking lines; see **Figure 25-07.** Always ask permission before boarding another boat. As for approaching

Figure 25-06 The national ensign should always be raised briskly in the morning, but lowered slowly and ceremoniously at sunset. Other flags are raised after the U.S. flag, and lowered before it.

an anchored or moored boat in your dinghy or tender, traditional naval practice suggests pulling alongside that boat's starboard side.

THE ETIQUETTE OF FLAGS

There is no legislation governing the flying of any flag on noncommercial vessels. However, through the years, customs have been established for the types of flags that may be flown and when and where they are to be displayed. In recent years, new procedures have evolved, such as flying the national ensign from the stern staff of a sailboat underway.

The term "colors" strictly applies only to the flag at the stern of a vessel to denote the boat's nationality. In practice, however, it has come to be used for all flags flown and will be used in that context in this chapter.

In general, it is not considered proper practice to fly more than one flag on a single hoist. There

are a few exceptions, however. Many vessels, because of their size or construction, cannot accommodate single hoisting; these may have a multiple hoist where necessary, with proper order of precedence observed—the more "senior" flags are flown above the others. If there is more than one hoist on a starboard spreader, they can be used, with the more "senior" flag on the outboard hoist.

U.S. Power Squadrons guidelines for flag display are given in **Table 25-1.** See "Flag Display Afloat," on pages 860–861, which shows the flags, pennants, and burgees that may be flown from American-owned recreational boats, and the proper methods for their display.

Flying Various Flags
• **The United States ensign** is proper for all U.S. craft without reservation. This is "Old Glory," with 50 stars and 13 stripes. It is flown from the stern staff of powerboats underway on inland waters. On the high seas it need be flown only when meeting or passing other vessels. If the powerboat has a mast and gaff, the proper display is at the gaff. On a sportfisherman, where a stern staff would be in the way of the action, the practice is to fly the ensign from a halyard rigged just behind the tuna tower, often on a short gaff.

On Marconi-rigged sailboats under sail alone, the practice for many years has been to fly the ensign from the leech of the aftermost sail, approximately two-thirds the length of the leech above

Figure 25-07 If there are no club or marina employees around, it is always a friendly and helpful action to take a line from an arriving craft—many fine friendships have started from this simple act of courtesy.

USPS GUIDE TO ONBOARD FLAG DISPLAY

Flag	When Flown	Power Yacht without Mast	Power Yacht with Signal Mast	Sailing Yacht with One Mast	Power or Sail with Two Masts Yachet
U.S. Ensign, U.S. Yacht Ensign, USPS Ensign (when flown in lieu of U.S. Ensign)	0800 to sunset	Flag staff	Flag staff	Flag staff. Optional when underway; peak of gaff if so rigged or 2/3 up leech of mainsail or equivalent position along backstay	Flag staff. Optional when underway; peak of aftermast gaff if so rigged or 2/3 up leech of aftertaste sail or equivalent position along backstay
Foreign Ensign or commercial ensign when flown as courtesy flag	In foreign ports and waters (after customs clearance)	Bow staff	Starboard spreader (outboard halyard)	Starboard spreader (outboard halyard)	Starboard spreader (outboard halyard) of foremost mast
Foreign Ensign—in respect to foreign dignitary	When foreign dignitary is on board	Bow staff	Bow staff	Forestay	Bow staff or forestay
USPS Ensign (when not flown in lieu of U.S. Ensign)	Day and night except 0800 to sunset when flown in lieu of U.S. ensign.* Only when in commission and under command of USPS member	Antenna or staff amidships (preferably to starboard)*	Starboard spreader. If foreign ensign flown; inboard starboard spreader halyard, if equipped, or port spreader*	Starboard spreader. If foreign ensign flown, then on inboard halyard or port spreader*	Foremost starboard spreader. If foreign ensign flown, on inboard halyard or port spreader*
Officer (either present or past)	Day and night when in commission	Antenna or staff amidships (alternative: bow staff)	Masthead	Masthead	Aftermost masthead
Private Signal (House Flag)	Day and night when in commission	Bow staff	Masthead	Masthead	Aftermost masthead
Squadron Burgee, Yacht Club Burgee	Day and night when in commission	Bow staff	Bow staff	Masthead	Foremost masthead
Officer-in-Charge	Day and night during activity of which in charge	Above or in lieu of officer flag	Above or in lieu of officer flag	Above or in lieu of officer flag	Above or in lieu of officer flag

* In U.S. waters the USPS ensign may be flown in lieu of (and at the same times and locations as) the U.S. ensign.

Table 25-1 The United States Power Squadrons fulfills its mandate to provide information to the boating community at large by designing education aids, including the table above. This quick-reference guide identifies flags, pennants, and burgees that may be flown from U.S.-owned recreational boats and the proper methods for their display.

the clew. This puts it in about the same position it would occupy if the boat were gaff-rigged, and on gaff-rigged sailboats it is still proper to fly the ensign from the peak of the aftermost gaff.

The advent of the modern high-aspect-ratio rig, with the boom end well inboard of the stern, has made it possible to fly the ensign from the stern staff of a sailboat underway, and this is now accepted practice. However, the ensign should never be displayed while the boat is racing. Under power alone, or at anchor or made fast, the ensign should be flown from the stern staff of all sailboats. If an overhanging boom requires that the staff be off-center, it should be on the starboard side.

• **The United States yacht ensign** is the 13-star flag, with a fouled anchor in the union of a circle of stars. Originally restricted to documented vessels of a specific classification, it is now flown on recreational boats of all types and sizes instead of the national ensign. Some yacht clubs now have bylaws requiring that the U.S. yacht ensign be flown regardless of boat size or documentation status. However, when a boat is taken into international or foreign waters, the 50-star U.S. ensign is the proper flag to display, not the yacht ensign, which is not a "national" flag.

• **The United States Power Squadrons ensign,** blue and white vertical stripes with a red union, is flown as a signal that the boat is commanded by a USPS member in good standing. The USPS, described in Chapter 26, is a national organization of boaters dedicated to better and safer boating through education and civic service.

The preferred location for flying the USPS ensign is the starboard yardarm or spreader, underway, at anchor, or made fast to shore, on both motor and sailing craft. It may be flown from the stern staff in place of the U.S. or yacht ensign, but this is only for U.S. waters, and is usually done only on smaller boats that lack a mast. On sailboats underway, it may be flown from the aftermost peak or leech in place of other ensigns.

The USPS ensign may be flown at its proper location on boats displaying the USCG Auxiliary ensign to indicate that the owner is a member of both organizations; however, it cannot be flown if the craft is under U.S. Coast Guard orders.

• **The U.S. Coast Guard Auxiliary ensign,** known as the "blue ensign," is flown on a boat that has been approved as a "Facility" by the organization for the current year, as described in Chapter 26. This flag is flown both day and night.

On a vessel without a mast, the blue ensign is flown at the bow staff; if there is one mast, it is flown at the masthead. On a vessel with two or more masts, the USCG Auxiliary ensign is displayed at the main masthead. It is never flown in place of the national ensign.

When this ensign is displayed, it is improper to hoist a guest, owner absent, meal, cocktail, or other novelty flag.

• **The United States Coast Guard Auxiliary operational ensign** is only flown by the boat of a member of the USCG Auxiliary that meets a particularly high standard of equipment and availability, called an "Operational Facility," and that is called on for use under Coast Guard orders in assistance and patrol missions. The U.S. Coast Guard Auxiliary operational ensign is white with the Coast Guard's "racing stripes" of red and blue—in place of the "blue ensign."

• **The yacht club burgee** is generally triangular in shape, although sometimes swallow-tailed; a yacht club burgee may be flown by day only, or by day and night, as specified by the individual club. It is flown from the bow staff of mastless and single-masted powerboats, at the foremost masthead of vessels with two or more masts, and the main masthead of ketches or yawls. The burgee may be flown while underway (but not racing) and at anchor. You may substitute the owner's private signal (see below) for the burgee on single-masted yachts without bow staff, when the boat is underway.

• **The U.S. Power Squadron pennant,** which has been authorized by the U.S. Power Squadrons Governing Board, may be flown in lieu of a club burgee and from the same positions. This pennant may be flown by day only, or both day and night.

• **Owner's private signal** is generally swallow-tailed in shape, but it may be rectangular or pennant-shaped. It is flown from the masthead of a single-masted motorboat or sailboat, or from the aftermost mast of a power or sailing vessel with two or more masts. It may be flown by day only, or day and night.

A mastless motorboat may fly this signal from the bow staff in place of a club burgee.

• **Officer flags** designating yacht club or USPS officers are rectangular in shape, blue (with white design) for senior officers; red for next lower in rank; and white (with blue design) for lower ranks. Other officers' flags (except fleet captain and fleet surgeon) may be swallow-tailed or triangular in shape, as provided in the regulations of those organizations making provisions for such flags.

An officer's flag is flown in place of the owner's private signal on all rigs of motor and sailing vessels except single-masted sailboats, when it is flown in place of the club burgee at the masthead. On smaller motorboats without a signal mast, a USPS officer flag may be flown from a radio antenna either singly or beneath the USPS ensign.

• **USCG Auxiliary officer flag** flies day and night when the officer is on board. On a vessel without a mast, it is flown at the bow staff in place of the Auxiliary ensign; on a vessel with a mast, it is flown at the starboard spreader. Past officers' burgees are displayed in the same manner.

Only one officer's flag may be flown at a time, and an incumbent officer's flag invariably takes precedence.

Size of Flags

Although flags come in a fixed, standardized series of sizes, there are guidelines that will help in selecting the proper size for your boat.

Keeping in mind that flags are more often too small than too large, use the rules given below and round upward to the nearest larger standard size:

The flag at the stern of your boat—U.S. ensign, yacht ensign, or USPS ensign—should be one inch on the fly for each foot of overall length. The hoist will normally be two-thirds of the fly, but some flags such as the USCG Auxiliary ensign have different proportions; refer to Chapter 1, **Figure 1-32.**

Other flags such as club burgees, officers' flags, and private signals for use on sailboats should be approximately ½-inch on the fly for each foot of the highest mast above the water. For flying on powerboats, these flags should be roughly ⅝ inch on the fly for each foot of overall length. The shape and proportions of pennants and burgees will be prescribed by the appropriate organization to which they relate. A Union Jack should be the same size as the corresponding portion of the national ensign.

Not all flags available for purchase in the U.S. have the correct proportions—this is particularly true of the flags of some foreign nations; a ratio of 1:2 for hoist to fly is quite common. Information on the proper dimensions can usually be obtained from encyclopedias, from consulates or embassies, or on the Internet. If you intend to purchase a foreign flag to be used as a courtesy flag on arrival in that country's waters, try to get one that is of the correct shape; also remember that some nations, such as the Bahamas, use a different flag for vessels than the one flown on land. Federal law prescribes the dimensions of U.S. flags to be used by governmental agencies in terms of 11 numbered sizes. The basic proportions of the U.S. national flag are 10:19 (not 3:5 as you will find in most stores), but there are some numbered sizes with quite different ratios.

Raising & Lowering Flags

"Colors are made" each morning at 0800; as mentioned, at yacht club and similar organization docks or anchorages, this may be signaled by a morning gun. The national ensign or yacht ensign is first hoisted at the stern (or set in place on its staff). This is followed by the USPS ensign at the starboard spreader (if not already flying on a day-and-night basis), provided the skipper is a USPS member. Then comes the club burgee or Squadron pennant at the bow, and the private signal at the masthead. (An officer's flag, if flown in place of a private signal, would be flown continuously.)

If the boat bears a valid USCG Auxiliary Facility decal, it would be flying the Auxiliary ensign at the masthead, day and night. The USCG Auxiliary officer's pennant or burgee may be flown, day and night, at the starboard spreader. On smaller craft, the same sequence should be followed, with the flags on their staffs being set in the appropriate locations as illustrated in the sidebar, "Flag Display Afloat," on pages 860–861.

At sunset, colors not properly flown on a day-and-night basis should be lowered in reverse sequence, the ensign at the stern always being the last to be secured. A cannon report also may be used as a sunset signal.

Dressing Ship

On national holidays, at regattas, and on other special occasions, yachts often "dress ship" with signal flags. Officers' flags, club burgees, and national flags are not used. A vessel is dressed at 0800, and remains so dressed until evening colors (while at anchor only, except for a vessel's maiden and final voyages, and participation in a marine parade or other unique situation).

Figure 25-08 "Dressing ship" can add a fine touch of ceremony to the proper yachting event. International Code flags and pennants are strung from the water's edge at the bow across the boat to the water's edge aft. The proper sequence of flags and pennants is given in the text.

In dressing ship, the yacht ensign is hoisted at the stern staff, and the Union Jack may be displayed at the jack (bow) staff. A rainbow of flags of the International Code is arranged, reaching from the waterline forward to the waterline aft, by way of the bowsprit end (or stem if no bowsprit exists) and the masthead(s); see **Figure 25-08.** Flags and pennants are bent on alternately, rather than in an indiscriminate manner. Since there are twice as many letter flags as numeral pennants, it is good practice, as in the Navy, to follow a sequence of two flags, one pennant, two flags, one pennant, throughout. The sequence recommended here provides a harmonious color pattern throughout. Staring from the bow: AB2, UJ1, KE3, GH6, IV5, FL4, DM7, PO Third Repeater, RN First Repeater, ST Zero, CX9, WQ8, ZY Second Repeater.

Honoring Other National Flags

As a matter of courtesy, it is proper to fly the flag of a foreign nation on your boat when you enter and operate on its waters. There are only a limited number of positions from which flags may be displayed; consequently, when a COURTESY FLAG of another nation is flown, it usually must displace one of the flags commonly displayed in home waters. It is not hoisted until clearance has been completed and the yellow "Q" flag has been removed.

The following are general guidelines to follow regarding courtesy flags:

• On a mastless powerboat, the courtesy flag of another nation is now most commonly flown from a radio antenna on the starboard side (the most forward antenna if there is more than one on that side). This approximates the location of a starboard spreader of a mast.

• When a motorboat has a mast with spreaders, the courtesy flag is flown at the starboard spreader.

• On a two-masted motorboat, the courtesy flag displaces any flag normally flown at the forward starboard spreader.

• On a sailboat, the courtesy flag is flown at the boat's starboard spreader, whether the United States ensign is at the stern staff or is flown from

FLYING NATIONAL & YACHTING FLAGS

Flags are flown aboard boats and on shore to convey a variety of information to the boating community. An ensign—the national flag—identifies the country of registration. A burgee indicates a yacht club or boating organization of which the boat owner is a member. Other flags give information about the owner—office held in a club or organization, for example. A pennant, such as some of those shown in "Flag Display Afloat," on pages 860 and 861, is generally a signal flag. The flags shown below include flags commonly seen on boats in North America.

U.S NATIONAL ENSIGN & MERCHANT FLAG
is flown from the stern staff of all boats at anchor and underway according to the circumstances (see page TK).

U.S. YACHT ENSIGN
May be flown on noncommercial craft, except in international or foreign waters.

U.S. CUSTOMS FLAG
Flown at every U.S. Customs Service office.

U.S. COAST GUARD ENSIGN
Flown day and night on active USCG units afloat or ashore.

MEXICAN NATIONAL ENSIGN
Identifies Mexican vessels.

CANADIAN NATIONAL ENSIGN
Identifies Canadian vessels—naval, merchant, or recreational—and Canadian Customs offices.

BAHAMIAN CIVIL ENSIGN
Flown by ships and boats of all sizes; different from flag flown ashore.

YACHT CLUB BURGEE (TYPICAL)
Usually triangular in shape; design varies widely.

YACHT CLUB COMMODORE'S FLAG
Identifies Commodore's boat or presence ashore.

YACHT PRIVATE SIGNAL
Inidividual yacht owners may have their own flags; the one above is typical.

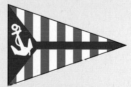

POWER SQUADRONS BURGEE (TYPICAL)
Design varies widely.

TRANSPORTATION OR TENDER FLAG
Is used to request launch service boats and an International Code flag "T."

DIVER'S FLAG
Generally flown on a boat hosting divers or on a small float near a diver, warns other crafts to "stay clear."

RIGID REPLICA OF INTERNATIONAL CODE FLAG "A"
Signals underwater operations as specified in the Navigation Rule 27(e).

YACHT PROTEST
Also International Code flag "B," is seen at sailing races and other events.

the leech. If there is more than one mast, the courtesy flag is flown from the starboard spreader of the forward mast.

• No other flag should ever be flown on the same halyard as a courtesy flag, nor on a halyard outboard of one.

Although these points serve as protocol in most waters, keep in mind that customs observed in various foreign waters differ from one another; in case of doubt, inquire locally or observe other craft from your country.

As noted previously, it is proper for U.S. vessels while in international or foreign waters to fly the U.S. ensign (50-star flag) at the stern, gaff, or leech, rather than the yacht ensign or the USPS ensign. When the starboard spreader is used for the courtesy ensign of the foreign country, the USPS ensign or similar flag may be flown from the port spreader; if the vessel has multiple flag halyards on the starboard spreader, the USPS ensign is flown there, inboard from the courtesy ensign.

The U.S. ensign, club burgee, officer's flag, and private signal are flown as in home waters.

Do not fly a foreign courtesy ensign after you have returned to U.S. waters. Although this may show that you've "been there," it is not proper flag etiquette.

Display of State Flags

Any citizen of any state may fly the flag of that state, unless doing so is specifically prohibited by

FLAG DISPLAY ASHORE

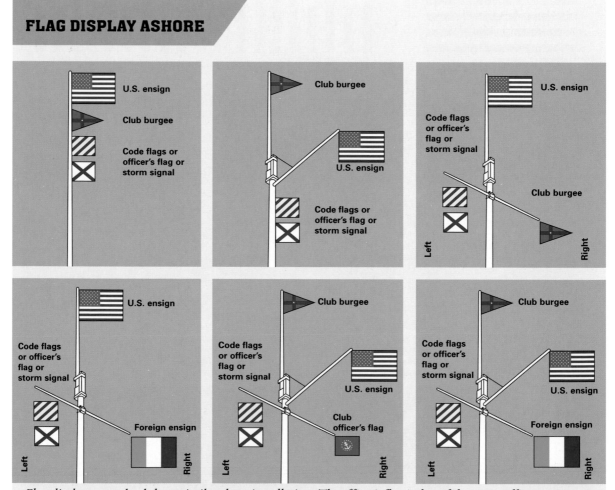

Flag displays at yacht clubs or similar shore installations. The officer's flag is that of the senior officer present on the grounds or on board his boat in the club anchorage. Storm signals may be substituted for the International Code flags, which are displayed on national holidays or other days of special significance.

state law. On a vessel with one or more masts, the state flag is flown at the main masthead in place of the private signal, officer's flag, or USCG Auxiliary ensign (and in this case an Auxiliary officer cannot fly the officer's pennant from the starboard spreader). When the state flag displaces a yacht club or USPS officer's flag, the officer's flag cannot be flown from any other hoist. On a mastless boat, the state flag can be flown at the bow staff in lieu of a club burgee, or it may replace any flag flown from a suitable radio antenna.

The flying of a state flag at the stern of a boat is not proper; nor is it proper to fly from this place of honor any Confederate, "pirate," or other "gag" flag, and certainly not the flag of a foreign country of one's heritage.

Flag Display Ashore

The flagpole or mast of a yacht club is considered to represent the mast of a vessel, and the peak of the gaff, if one is used, is the place of honor from which the U.S. ensign is flown, just as it would be on a gaff-rigged boat. The location of the gaff on the pole is opposite to the direction to the water—as if it were on a ship standing out to sea. The flag should be hoisted briskly but lowered slowly and ceremoniously.

There has been some confusion because proper flag etiquette requires no other flag to be flown above the U.S. ensign, and obviously another flag, such as a yacht club burgee at the masthead, will be higher than the U.S. flag when the latter is at the gaff. This is entirely proper because "above," in flag etiquette, means "directly on top of." The illustrations in "Flag Display Ashore," opposite, show the standard mast and pole displays as if you were ashore, facing seaward.

Note that signal flags should be flown from a conspicuous hoist; and that on national holidays and days of special yachting significance you may fly the flags of the International Code. Flags flown ashore at private homes may follow the code used for yacht clubs and similar organizations.

Half-masting Flags

A flag is flown at HALF-MAST (or HALF-STAFF) in respect for a deceased person. Although there

are no laws governing the half-masting of flags on private vessels, or at private homes and clubs, most citizens follow the flag display customs used on U.S. government buildings and ships. Only the President or the governor of a state, territory, or possession can direct that the U.S. ensign be flown at half-mast. The duration varies from a few days (usually until sunset on the day of burial) to 30 days, according to the deceased person's position. It is not correct for a yacht club commodore or similar organization official to order the U.S. ensign half-masted—only the burgee or organization flag. On Memorial Day, the U.S. flag is flown at half-mast until 1220, the time of the final gun of the traditional 21-gun salute commencing at noon.

On a simple flagstaff—as at a vessel's stern or flagpole ashore—"half-mast" position is about three-fourths the way up to the top. If the flagpole has a yardarm, or yardarm and gaff, half-mast position is level with the yardarm. When the U.S. flag is displayed at half-mast on a vessel, other flags remain at their normal position. When it is half-masted ashore, fly only a private signal or club burgee at the masthead of a gaff-rigged mast with it.

When the U.S. ensign is flown at half-mast, it should be hoisted fully and smartly, then lowered ceremoniously to half-mast position. Before lowering, it is again raised to full height and lowered from there. Some yacht clubs fly their burgee at half-mast for a period of mourning on the death of a club member. A private signal may be flown at half-mast on the death of the vessel's owner.

Flag Display at Meetings

The flag of the United States should be displayed either from a staff or flat against the wall above and behind the speaker's table or lectern.

The flag of the United States should never be draped or laid over anything except a casket, at which time special rules apply.

When displayed flat against a wall, it should be fastened by the upper edge only, with union to the flag's right (to a viewer's left). This is applicable whether the flag is hung with the stripes hori-

FLAG DISPLAY AFLOAT

Where the illustrations below specify "at the starboard spreader" it means the spreader that is on the most forward mast if there is more than one, and by the most outboard hoist on that spreader.

When referring to the illustration captions, note that conventions for a vessel "at anchor" also apply to other non-underway statuses—at a mooring or made fast to the shore.

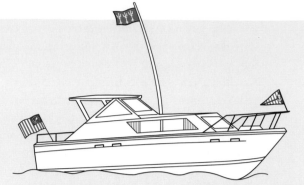

On a typical small powerboat with radio antenna, a USPS officer's or past officer's flago, or a USCG Auxiliary ensign may be flown from the antenna a the same height as if on a signal mast. Flags at the bow and stern are the same on a craft with signal mast with spreader.

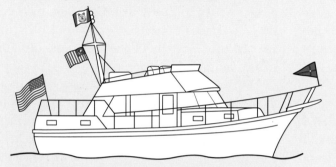

On a powerboat with signal mast with spreaders, the U.S. or yacht ensign is flown from the stern staff, and the squadron pennant or club burgee is at the bow staff. The officer's flag, private signal, or USCG Auxiliary ensign is at the masthead. An owner-absent or guest flag, or the USPS ensign (if not flown at the stern), is displayed at the starboard spreader.

On a small powerboat with a s mast, flags are displayed in the manner as for the craft with sig mast with spreaders (top left).

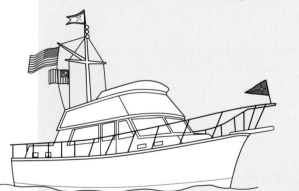

When a gaff is added to the signal mast, it is the place for the U.S. or yacht ensign, while underway. At anchor, these are flown at the stern.

On a sportfishermen, the U.S., USPS, or yacht ensign is flown abaft the tuna tower to keep the cockpit coaming clear at the stern for fishing lines.

On a mastless motorboat the U.S. ensign (or if not in foreign waters, the USPS or yacht ensign) is flown from a stern staff and the club burgee, USPS Squadron pennant, USCG Auxiliary ensign, or private signal is flown from the bow staff.

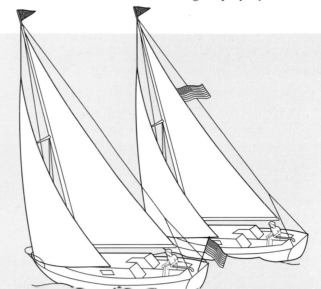

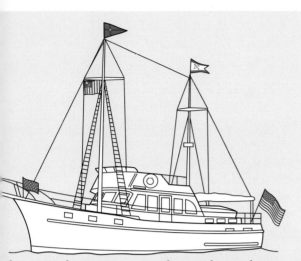

documented two-master motorboat with spreaders on
ach mast (above) at anchor. The U.S. or yacht ensign is at
e stern staff; USPS or USCG Auxiliary ensign at the
rward starboard spreader; club burgee or Squadron burgee
the forward masthead; and private signal or officer's flag
the after masthead. The Union Jack is at the bow (jack)
aff; this is displayed only when the vessel is not underway.

A single-masted sailboat underway may fly the U.S., USPS,
or yacht ensign at a stern staff (above, left) or at the leech of
the mainsail approximately two-thirds the length of the leech
above the clew (above, right). The club burgee, Squadron
burgee, private signal, or officer's flag is at the masthead. If
not flown from the stern or leech, the USPS ensign may be
flown from the starboard spreader.

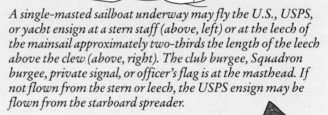

On a yawl or ketch, the club burgee or
Squadron burgee is at the main masthead and
the private signal or officer's flag is at the
mizzen masthead. At anchor or in port, the U.S.
or yacht ensign is flown from the stern staff; and
the USPS ensign at the starboard main
spreader, if the boat is operated by a member.
Underway, the ensign can be flown at the stern
or from the leech of the aftermost sail or from
the backstay at the height shown above.

On a schooner underway (right), flag arrangement is the same as
for a yawl or ketch, even though the relative height of the masts
is reversed. The U.S. or yacht ensign may be flown from a stern
staff while underway (not racing) if the length of the aftermost
boom permits.

GUIDE TO MISCELLANEOUS FLAGS

• **Diver Down** There are two flags flown in connection with diving operations: a red flag with a single diagonal stripe of white and a rigid replica of the International Code flag "A." It is not proper for them to be flown on shore or by any boat not engaged in diving operations.

• **Race Committee or Regatta Committee Flag** is a blue rectangular flag with a single vertical fouled anchor in white with the letters "R" and "C" beside the anchor in white or red. It is often large, and may be flown at any position for greatest visibility. Often other flags are taken down to avoid confusion.

• **Transportation or Tender Flag** is used in many harbors where boats lie at moorings, and where yacht clubs or commercial operators provide launch (water taxi) service to and from the shore. This is the International Code flag "T"; it is used to request service and may be used with a sound signal; it may be flown by craft providing such service.

• **Quarantine Flag,** the International Code letter "Q" (plain yellow, rectangular), is flown when entering a foreign port (except Canada and a few others), or returning to a U.S. port from a foreign cruise. It signals that the vessel is "healthy" and requests clearance into the port; it is taken down after customs and immigration formalities have been completed.

• **Protest Flag,** the International Code flag "B" (plain red, swallow-tailed), is seen at sailing or other contests. It signals that the vessel flying it will file a protest on another vessel (or vessels) at the event's conclusion.

• **Man Overboard** is generally recognized as the International code flag for the letter "O" (red-and-yellow divided diagonally; rectangular); this flag is often fixed to a staff, which in turn is attached to a life ring.

• **Union Jack** is a rectangular blue flag with 50 stars (the equivalent of the upper-left quadrant of the national ensign). It may be flown only at the jack staff on sailing yachts or the jack staff of motor yachts with more than one mast, only during the day, and only while not underway on Sundays and national holidays, or when "dressing ship." On modern craft, the normal bow staff is used as the "jack staff." It should be the same size as the corresponding portion of the national flag being flown.

• **Owner Absent & Guest Flags** Some larger yachts will fly a rectangular plain blue flag when the owner is not on board. This is flown at the starboard main spreader; a blue light is shown at night.

When an owner is not present, but guests are on board and in charge of the yacht, the flag flown is blue with a diagonal white stripe and is flown from the port main spreader.

zontal or vertical; a horizontal position of the stripes is preferable.

When displayed on a staff indoors, the U.S. national ensign is stood at the right of the speaker-regardless of whether or not there is a platform or stage at the front of the room. A state or organizational flag, if displayed, is placed at the speaker's left. (If the flag of another nation is displayed, it should be at the speaker's right, just inboard of the U.S. flag.) If the flag of the United States and another flag are displayed with crossed staffs, as at the head of a room, the U.S. flag should be at its right and with its staff in front of the staff of the other flag.

If the flag of the United States is flown with other flags in a group, it should be in the center and slightly higher, or it should be in front of the other flags.

Chapter
26

Boating
Organizations

United States Power Squadrons • Canadian Power & Sail Squadrons
The United States Coast Guard • The United States Coast Guard Auxiliary

In addition to private and commercial yacht clubs and boating schools, boaters in the U.S. and Canada have access to educational and other boating-related activities from both non-commercial and governmental organizations. In the private sector, the United States Power Squadrons and the Canadian Power and Sail Squadrons fill an important role. The never-ending work of the United States Coast Guard, with assistance from the civilian-supported USCG Auxiliary, touches the vast majority of all U.S. boaters. In Canada, the Canadian Coast Guard and its Auxiliary operate in a somewhat different, but no less important, manner.

UNITED STATES POWER SQUADRONS

In 1912, the motorboat was beginning to challenge the sailboat for a position in the field of recreational boating. A group in the Boston Yacht Club felt that there was a serious lack of knowledge on the part of some who were adopting this new form of boating. They decided to improve the situation by conducting classes on recreational boating. The program that was established led to the formation of the "Power Squadron of the Boston Yacht Club," and set the educational basis for the United States Power Squadrons (USPS).

On 2 February 1914, with Charles F. Chapman in attendance, a meeting held at the New York Yacht Club resulted in the formation of the "United States Power Squadrons." Following World War I, the programs of the USPS were reor

Previous Page: A primary mission of the United States Power Squadrons is teaching basic boating safety to the public and advanced courses, such as piloting, navigation, and course planning, to its members.

ganized into a new format that emphasized instruction as a service to boaters and boating in general. Growth was rapid and steady, with local Squadrons being organized in numerous coastal and inland boating areas.

With the end of World War II, recreational boating boomed, and with it new U.S. Power Squadrons were formed in areas around the world, including Japan and Okinawa (now part of Japan), as well as Hawaii, Alaska, Puerto Rico, U.S. Virgin Islands, and the Panama Canal Zone, although not all are still active.

The USPS Today

The United States Power Squadrons today is a nongovernmental membership organization, self-supporting in its efforts to enhance boating safety through education. In 2003, the U.S. Power Squadrons comprised more than 60,000 members, both men and women, in more than 450 Squadrons assigned to 33 Districts across the United States.

The purposes of the USPS may be described by quoting the "Objects" of the organization as stated in its bylaws:

"To selectively associate congenial persons of good character having a common love and appreciation of yachting as a nationwide fraternity of boatmen;

"To encourage and promote yachting, power and sail, and to provide through local squadrons and otherwise a practical means to foster fraternal and social relationships among persons interested in yachting;

"To encourage and promote a high amateur standard of skill in the handling and navigation of yachts, power and sail; to encourage and promote the study of the science and art of navigation, seamanship, and small boat handling; to develop and promote instructional programs for the benefit of members; and to stimulate members to increase their knowledge of and skill

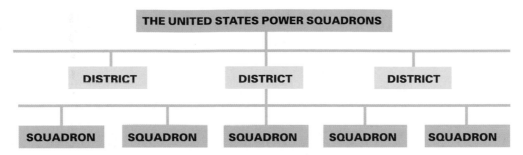

Figure 26-01 Simplified USPS organizational chart. There are 33 Districts and more than 450 local Squadrons. The number of Squadrons in a District varies from five to more than 30. Each echelon of the organization is led by elected officers.

in yachting, through instruction, self-education, and participation in marine sports events and competitions;

"To encourage its members to abide by recognized yachting traditions, customs, and etiquette; and "To render and encourage its members to render such altruistic, patriotic, or other civic service as it may from time to time determine or elect."

The USPS Ensign

The USPS ensign, pictured on page 866, consists of seven blue and six white vertical stripes with a union of red, on which is the same white fouled anchor and circle of stars as on the yacht ensign.

The ensign of the United States Power Squadrons may be flown on boats only when they are skippered by members of the organization. Rules for where and when it can be flown are given in Chapter 25.

In the form of decals and stickers, automobile emblems, boating cap insignia, etc., the USPS design can be worn or displayed only by Power Squadron members in good standing. Those members also receive *The Ensign*, the USPS monthly publication.

Membership

Members of the USPS may be male or female over 16 years of age who have applied for membership, have met entrance qualifications set by the national organization and who have been selected by the local unit. Members are classified as either active or family.

Active members have all the privileges of membership in USPS. Family members must be related by blood, marriage, or adoption to an active member and either reside in the household with or are dependents of the active member. Family members may not vote or hold office but may take courses and serve on committees.

As a volunteer organization, USPS depends on its members for support. Therefore, it is important that members be willing to "give" of their time and talents, as well as "take" advantage of the knowledge and opportunity to improve skills that USPS offers.

Organization

The basic unit of USPS is the local Squadron. These have names of geographic significance, and may have as few as 20 members or as many as 500 or more.

Squadrons are grouped into Districts, which are numbered; this is the intermediate level between the local unit and the National organization; see **Figure 26-01**.

All levels of organization are led by elected officers. Squadrons and Districts have a Commander plus several Lieutenant Commanders and Lieutenants. The USPS as a whole is directed by a Chief Commander and five department heads with the rank of Vice Commander. National Committee Chairmen and other national staff officers hold the rank of Rear Commander or Staff Commander. All officers are unpaid volunteers; there is a paid office staff at the National Headquarters at Raleigh, NC.

Although the United States Power Squadrons is not a military organization, it has winter and summer, formal and informal yachting-type uniforms for men and women. Members are not

United States Power Squadrons Flags & Insignia

USPS ENSIGN

The Ensign of United States Power Squadrons may be displayed only by enrolled members of USPS. It is an outward and visible sign that the vessel displaying it is under the charge of a person who has made a study of piloting and small boat handling, and will recognize the rights of others and the traditions of the sea. The Squadrons' Ensign also marks a craft as being under the command of a man who has met certain minimum requirements and is so honored for meeting them.

NATIONAL OFFICERS

OFFICE	INSIGNIA	FLAG	SLEEVE
CHIEF COMMANDER			
VICE COMMANDERS			
REAR COMMANDERS			
STAFF COMMANDERS			
NATIONAL FLAG LIEUTENANT			
AIDES TO C/C CHAPLAIN			

DISTRICT OFFICERS

OFFICE	INSIGNIA	FLAG	SLEEVE
DISTRICT COMMANDER			
DISTRICT LIEUTENANT COMMANDERS			
DISTRICT 1st LIEUTENANTS			
DISTRICT LIEUTENANTS			
DISTRICT FLAG LIEUTENANT			
DISTRICT AIDES CHAPLAIN			

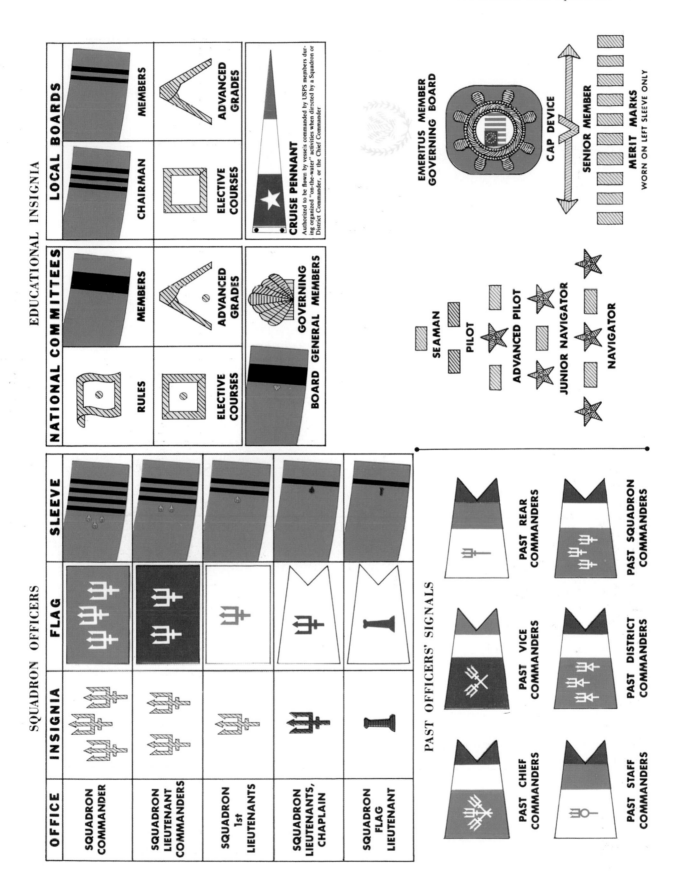

EDUCATIONAL INSIGNIA

NATIONAL COMMITTEES

LOCAL BOARDS

MEMBERS

ADVANCED GRADES

CHAIRMAN

ADVANCED GRADES

MEMBERS

RULES

ELECTIVE COURSES

ELECTIVE COURSES

GOVERNING BOARD GENERAL MEMBERS

CRUISE PENNANT

Authorized to be flown by vessels commanded by USPS members during organized "on-the-water" activities when directed by a Squadron or District Commander, or the Chief Commander

EMERITUS MEMBER GOVERNING BOARD

CAP DEVICE

SENIOR MEMBER

MERIT MARKS

WORN ON LEFT SLEEVE ONLY

SEAMAN

PILOT

ADVANCED PILOT

JUNIOR NAVIGATOR

NAVIGATOR

SQUADRON OFFICERS

OFFICE	INSIGNIA	FLAG	SLEEVE
SQUADRON COMMANDER			
SQUADRON LIEUTENANT COMMANDERS			
SQUADRON 1st LIEUTENANTS			
SQUADRON LIEUTENANTS, CHAPLAIN			
SQUADRON FLAG LIEUTENANT			

PAST OFFICERS' SIGNALS

PAST REAR COMMANDERS

PAST SQUADRON COMMANDERS

PAST VICE COMMANDERS

PAST DISTRICT COMMANDERS

PAST CHIEF COMMANDERS

PAST STAFF COMMANDERS

Figure 26-02 *As a public service function, each Squadron presents one or more of the public education courses each year. USPS members can wear any one of a series of blue or white uniforms as determined by the nature of the Squadron activity and season of the year. Many members elect to wear an informal blazer to most occasions. While officers are expected to have them, other members are not required to purchase uniforms.*

required to purchase these uniforms, and many do not. Most officers, however, do wear uniforms for meetings, rendezvous, ceremonies, and other special occasions. Uniforms may or may not be worn to various USPS educational classes.

An officer's rank in the United States Power Squadron is indicated on the uniform coat by sleeve braid and embroidered insignia; see pages 866–867 and page 873. A varying number of dark blue stripes is used with three different widths of braid that are used in combination. White shirts have shoulder board insignia but not the braid.

The uniform cap may be worn with all the various USPS uniforms. The rank of various Squadron, District and National officers is also indicated on the cap. A USPS cap ornament may be worn on non-uniform boating caps, and may show insignia of rank.

An illustrated table of information on USPS officers' sleeve braid and insignia, cap insignia and flags is found on pages 866–867.

Educational Programs

Educational programs constitute a major part of USPS activities. They are divided into three segments. Basic public education courses are open to everyone; there is no formal lower age limit,

but it is suggested that children should be at least 12 years old and accompanied by a parent. see **Figure 26-02.** Advanced grades courses and elective courses are currently available only to USPS members and to military and reserve personnel in times of national emergency. A general description of these courses is given below.

Basic Public Education Courses

USPS offers a choice of basic boating courses for the public. Four of these meet the National Association of State Boating Law Administrators (NASBLA) standards for minimum safety education recommended for all recreational boaters. All four of these courses cover:

- Boat types, terminology, hull features, and propulsion systems
- Fueling, pre-departure checklists, boat handling, docking, and anchoring
- Personal watercraft (PWC) and other water sports
- Boating safety, courtesy afloat, and environmental concerns
- Registration, required equipment, and other recommended equipment
- Federal and state-specific regulations
- Navigation rules and aids to navigation
- Adverse conditions, emergencies, and marine radiotelephone use

USPS course materials are developed and distributed nationwide, as is the applicable end-of-course examination. Instruction is by local USPS members, all of whom are unpaid volunteers. They are aided at times by outside experts and local marine law enforcement deputies. Course costs are nominal and vary by locale. Many students also find it desirable to purchase supplementary materials such as the recommended text (*Chapman Piloting & Seamanship*) and plotting instruments. Family groups are urged to take a basic course together.

Boat Smart is the most popular USPS course nationwide and is designed to be classroom-taught in eight hours.

America's Boating Course is the newest USPS public course, available to boaters anywhere in the world. It was developed in partnership with the

U.S. Coast Guard Auxiliary. This course features interactive electronic courseware that is available on-line via the Internet; www.americasboating-course.com. The electronic courseware also comes on a CD-ROM that accompanies the course manual. *America's Boating Course* is also offered in a classroom venue, lasting about eight hours.

The Squadron Boating Course is a 12-hour classroom course that covers, in addition to the above,

- Marine compass installation and use
- Bearings and other lines of position
- Basic chartwork, plotting, and labeling
- Finding your position and plotting a course

The USPS Video Boating Course is a VHS video version of the *Squadron Boating Course* for those unable to attend a classroom course. It is closed-captioned for the hearing impaired.

Each Squadron is required to offer at least one series of basic public education classes each year. Many squadrons offer classes throughout the year, some on a virtually continuous basis. They usually vary the times and places of classes in order to reach the greatest numbers of boaters and their families. The nearest squadron can be located by calling toll-free to 1-888-FOR-USPS (1-888-367-8777) or by visiting the USPS web site at www.usps.org.

USPS also offers the public several shorter special-interest courses.

Chart Smart is nominally a four-hour program on marine compasses and basic chartwork, plotting, and labeling. *Jet Smart* is a four-hour course (including a VHS video) on personal watercraft (PWC) operation. *USPS Learning Guides* are short self-study programs available from Squadrons or marine stores. Currently available *Learning Guides* are listed at the end of this section.

Advanced Grades Courses

In keeping with its stated purpose of encouraging the study of the science of navigation, USPS offers its members a series of five advanced grades courses. These include: Seamanship; Piloting and Advanced Piloting (a two-part study of inland and coastal navigation); and Junior Navigation and Navigation (a two-part study of electronic and celestial offshore navigation).

All courses are, or soon will be, comprised of a series of two or three modules of approximately twelve hours class time each. This provides the student with maximum flexibility. The student can take whatever modules he or she wishes and does not lose credit for work done as often happens when one is forced to drop out part way through a longer course due to illness or travel.

Seamanship builds on the basics learned in *Boat Smart*, *America's Boating Course*, or the *Squadron Boating Course*. It is an important foundation for other advanced grades courses and is the recommended first course for new members. Seamanship covers practical marlinespike, hull design and construction, Navigation Rules operation under normal and adverse conditions, responsibilities of the skipper, fire prevention and control, basic first aid, common courtesies on the water, boat care, marina operations, and nautical customs and flag etiquette.

Piloting is the first of a two-part program studying inland and coastal navigation. Its focus is on the fundamentals of piloting—keeping track of a boat's movements, determining one's position at any time, and laying out courses to planned destinations. Included are instruction on charts and their uses, aids to navigation, the mariner's compass, variation and deviation of the compass, lines of position and steering courses, dead reckoning, plotting, and labeling charts.

Advanced Piloting is the second part of the inland and coastal navigation series. Its emphasis is on the use of modern electronic navigation systems and other advanced techniques for finding position. Topics covered include basic electronic navigation—radar, loran, GPS, and electronic charts, tides, tidal and river currents and their effects on piloting, finding one's position using bearings and angles, running fixes, simple use of the mariner's sextant, and how to construct one's own chart.

Junior Navigation is the first of a two-part program of study in offshore navigation. It is designed as a practical "how to" course, covering

Figure 26-03 The Advanced Grades program of USPS education culminates in the Junior Navigation and Navigation courses. These cover all aspects of offshore and celestial navigation, and the grade of "N" is highly esteemed by USPS members.

offshore electronic navigation, precise time determination, use of the nautical almanac, taking sextant sights of the sun, moon, planets and stars, reducing sights to establish lines of position, special charts and plotting sheets for offshore navigation, and navigational routines for offshore recreational craft; see **Figure 26-03**.

Navigation is the second part of the study of offshore navigation, further developing the student's understanding of celestial navigation theory. Focus is on honing skills in sight taking and positioning, advanced sight-reduction techniques, orderly methods for the navigator's daily work at sea, navigational coordinate systems and theory, and navigating with minimal resources, as under emergency conditions or in a lifeboat.

Elective Courses

USPS also offers its members six elective courses—five on high-interest aspects of recreational boating and one of a life-skills nature. These courses may be taken in any order. Elective courses are also comprised of two or three modules of approximately twelve hours class time each.

Cruise Planning is designed for both sail and power boaters who plan to cruise for a weekend, a week, or even a year. It covers such topics as planning and financing a voyage, managing commitments back home, how to equip a cruising boat, crew and guest selection, provisioning, voyage management, entering and clearing foreign ports, emergencies afloat, and security measures.

Engine Maintenance attempts to make students more self-reliant afloat, with trouble-diagnosis and temporary remedies given special emphasis. It covers both marine gasoline and diesel engines—inboard, outboard, and inboard-outboard (I/O). Focus is on concepts of operation, maintenance and repair of engine cooling, electrical, fuel, and lubricating systems, power train components, and ancillary propulsion components; see **Figure 26-04**.

Marine Electronics provides essential knowledge about a boat's electrical and electronic systems, including proper wiring, grounding, corrosion and electrolysis control, batteries and their maintenance, depth finders, marine radiotelephones, radar, loran, GPS, electronic charts, and other electronic navigation systems.

Sail provides a thorough study of the terminology and dynamics of sailing. The course covers types of hulls and rigs, types of running and standing rigging and their adjustments, hull and water forces caused by wind and waves, forces vs. balance, the theory of sailing, points of sail, sail handling, sailing under various wind conditions, and navigation rules unique to sailing vessels

Weather is designed to teach a student how to make weather observations and predictions for

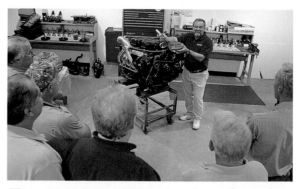

Figure 26-04 Engine Maintenance is one of several elective courses available to members. Others cover weather, sailing, marine electronics, and cruise planning. A special course is provided to help members to be better instructors.

ADDITIONAL USPS FLAG & INSIGNIA

During the last several years, the USPS has made additions to the official insignia and flags. The insignia, Port Captain's flag, and "life member" crest are shown below. Also shown at bottom right is the insignia for Senior Navigator, awarded for having taken all courses (Full Certificate).

The Port Captain's Flag, a white tapered swallow-tail flag with a red lighthouse, is to be flown in home waters only.

After receiving 25 Merit Marks, Life Membership is awarded and this insignia can be worn in lieu of the Senior Member device.

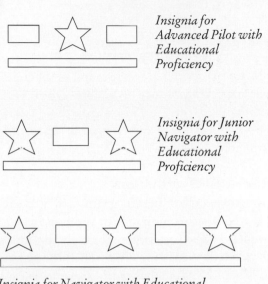

Insignia for Advanced Pilot with Educational Proficiency

Insignia for Junior Navigator with Educational Proficiency

Insignia for Navigator with Educational Proficiency

Insignia for recipient of Educational Achievement Award (completion of all Advanced Grades and Elective Courses); this carries the grade of Senior Navigator, abbreviated SN.

more enjoyable boating. The principal text is USA Today's *The Weather Book*. Topics include awareness of weather phenomena, how to read a weather map and the sky, how to understand and anticipate weather development, structure and characteristics of the atmosphere, factors considered in weather forecasting, sources and use of weather reports and forecasts, instrument and visual observations the skipper can make.

Instructor Development, unlike other USPS courses, is not designed to enhance boating skills. Rather, it deals with effective communications for the speaker and teacher, a quality that benefits the individual in all walks of life. Emphasis is on the special demands of teaching

adults. It offers practical instruction in preparing for teaching assignments, preparing for meeting presentations, effective teaching techniques, conducting efficient meetings, and selection and use of audiovisual aids.

Learning Guides, as mentioned above under "Basic Public Education," are available to anyone, whether or not a member of USPS. They are designed as short, self-study programs. Many also lend themselves well to team study or seminar presentation. *Learning Guide* titles currently available include: *Amateur Radio; Boat Design & Construction; Boat Insurance; Calculators for Navigation; Compass Adjusting; Global Positioning System; How to Fly Flags; Introduction to*

Sailing; Knots, Bends, and Hitches; Navigational Astronomy; Oceanography; Plotting and Labeling Standards; Predicted Log Contest; Radar; Sight Reduction Methods; Skipper Saver; USPS Nautical Glossary; and *Water Sports.*

More are under development at all times. *Learning Guides* are available from local Squadrons, from USPS headquarters (1-888-367-8777), or from many marine stores and suppliers.

Other USPS activities

Cooperative Charting Program USPS coordinates the boating activities of thousands of its members in an effort to report changes to nautical and geodetic charts for NOS. The limited field facilities of NOS are thus much strengthened and expanded, resulting in more accurate charts.

Vessel Safety Checks Members and units of the USPS participate extensively with the Vessel Safety Check program that is operated jointly with the Coast Guard Auxiliary; see page 396.

Port Captain Program Port Captains are knowledgeable local USPS members who are willing to share their expertise with other members on request. They can provide information and guidance on subjects such as water hazards, anchorages, marinas, repair facilities, and other shoreside services.

Social activities. At the USPS, it's not "all work and no play." Squadrons hold a wide variety of social activities both afloat and ashore. Each District has a fall and spring conference. Although these are working sessions, they are usually preceded or followed by evening social gatherings. The national level Annual Meeting in January, and the Spring and Fall Governing Board Meetings, combine both intense official events with those of a much lighter nature.

Figure 26-05 Members of the Canadian Power and Sail Squadrons (CPS)—fly this flag.

CANADIAN POWER & SAIL SQUADRONS

The success of the United States Power Squadrons in the fields of boating education and public service has led to the formation of roughly parallel organizations in several other countries. The leading one of these is in our "Neighbor to the North."

Mission Statement

To increase awareness and knowledge of safe boating by educating and training members and the general public, by fostering fellowship among members, and by establishing partnerships and alliances with both organizations and agencies interested in boating.

Organization

Founded in 1938, Canadian Power Squadrons became Canadian Power and Sail Squadrons (CPS) in 1985, and is Canada's largest nationwide organization of boating enthusiasts. The French equivalent of the name is *les Escadrilles canadiennes de plaisance*, and forms part of the corporate title. Like its U.S. counterpart, CPS is dedicated to improving boating safety through education. A variety of courses are offered to the general public; some Advanced Courses are available only to CPS members. CPS is a charitable, individual-membership organization, incorporated under the Companies Act of Canada, and all instructional work is done by members on a volunteer basis. Members fly the flag shown in **Figure 26-05.**

The basic unit of CPS is the Squadron. It is at the Squadron level that courses, in both English and French, are offered to the boating community, and the camaraderie of membership begins. A number of Squadrons in a geographic region are generally grouped together to form a District. The Districts assist in the administration and communication of information throughout their Squadron network.

In addition to training recreational boaters on the principles of safe boating, many local lawenforcement agencies and municipal authorities request courses from CPS; see **Figure 26-06.** Effective representation on various government

Figure 26-06 *The Canadian Power and Sail Squadrons are recognized as the foremost educational boating authority in Canada. They offers a wide variety of courses coast to coast.*

councils and Canadian Coast Guard (CCG) working groups, a good working relationship and active dialogue with several levels of government, and excellent partnerships with various corporations and organizations involved in the marine sector are other ways that CPS represents the recreational boater.

The organization's head office, staffed by paid employees, is located at 26 Golden Gate Court, Toronto, Ontario M1P 3A5. Contact can be made by phone, fax, or e-mail: (416) 293-2445, toll-free in Canada 888-277-2628 (CPS-BOAT), e-mail hqg@cps-ecp.ca, and a web site at www.cps-ecp.ca.

Public Courses

The Boating Course is open to the boating public and may be taken in the classroom or by correspondence. Subjects covered include boat handling under normal and adverse conditions, seamanship and common emergencies, aids to navigation, government regulations and equip-

ment requirements, rules of the road, compass and chart familiarization, and introduction to piloting. *The Boating Course* provides all of the information needed to meet the Canadian Coast Guard (CCG) Boating Safety Course Standard. The successful completion of the supervised CCG accredited test will enable the student to obtain the CCG Pleasure Craft Operator Card. The card is required for any operator of a power-driven boat born after April 1, 1983, any operator of a power-driven boat under 4 meters and by all operators of power-driven boats, regardless of age or size of boat, by September 15, 2009. The successful completion of the CCG Test offers the opportunity for CPS Associate membership. Passing the Boating Course Test entitles the student to become a Regular CPS member.

The Boat Pro Manual has also been CCG accredited, and successful completion of the supervised exam will lead to the CCG Pleasure Craft Operator Card. Completion also offers the opportunity for CPS associate membership. A unique feature of *The Boat Pro Manual* is that it is also approved by the National Association of State Boating Law Administrators (NASBLA), making it truly a North American boater's safety manual.

Boatwise is designed for children 8 to 12 years of age. Among other things, youngsters learn to identify various boats and parts of a boat, use of safety equipment, the rules of the road, the importance of life jackets, an understanding of aids to navigation, and the importance of watching the weather.

The Maritime Radiotelephone Course (VHF) teaches the phonetic alphabet and correct marine radiotelephone operating procedure. Also, the Restricted Radiotelephone Operator's Certificate exam is normally given at the end of each session.

The Enviro Boater Guide is another informational publication, and stresses environmentally friendly boating. It contains tips on cleaning a boat, how to avoid polluting the water, usage of approved products, recycling methods, a no-dumping attitude and how to work together to keep waterways clean and safe.

Figure 26-07 CPS Squadrons across Canada offer advanced and elective boating courses in English and/or French.

Elective Courses

Once exclusive to the membership of CPS, Elective Courses are now open to the public. However, membership does have its benefits, as non-members can expect higher enrollment fees.

Powerboating provides knowledge needed to be a safe and proficient operator of a power-driven vessel. The course discusses engine and trouble diagnosis, and much more.

Seamanship Sail teaches some of the basic techniques for safe operation of a sailboat under various conditions. The topics explore all aspects of sailing, from the vessel to handling, encouraging the participant to become a more competent sailor.

Extended Cruising focuses on the unique aspects and challenges of long-rang cruising, in order to maximize enjoyment and minimize risks for those on board. The *Seamanship Sail* course is recommended in preparation for this course.

Weather courses are offered by CPS in the following manner. *Fundamentals of Weather* covers the basic understanding of weather, including: the causes of weather, winds, the atmosphere, clouds; weather fronts, and forecasting. *Global Weather* details worldwide weather topics.

Marine Maintenance covers seasonal maintenance and repairs to hulls. Sections are also devoted to maintenance of marine engines and other information needed to keep a well found boat.

Marine Electronics is for the boater who wants to take advantage of modern electronic devices for navigation and safety afloat. The course covers electricity, DC and AC systems, wiring, galvanic and stray current corrosion, and electrical interference. Auxiliary equipment and some of the electronic navigation equipment are introduced.

Advanced Courses

Successful completion of the exam for *The Boating Course* qualifies a boater for CPS membership, and offers the opportunity to expand your boating enjoyment through advanced courses; see **Figure 26-07.**

Piloting builds on knowledge acquired in *The Boating Course*, adding relative bearings and running fixes, effects of current and leeway, and new skills in coastal navigation.

Advanced Piloting offers the *Piloting* course graduate advanced coastal navigation principles to be able to determine the vessel's position at all times, using landmarks and aids to navigation and allowing for current, leeway, tides and currents.

Celestial Navigation incorporates skills learned in *Advanced Piloting* and provides a thorough understanding of celestial navigational coordinates. This course shows how to establish lines of position, from celestial observations, by sextant—using corrections to provide a reliable fix by various sight reduction methods. *Great Circle Sailing*, with the study of *Pilot Charts*, gives the navigational skills needed for open sea passage.

Electronic Navigation is a series of seminars discussing the use and installation of various electronic navigation systems. *Navigating with GPS* covers the details of GPS including chart datum, the use of waypoints, creating and using routes, and methods of using GPS efficiently. Seminars on radar, depth sounders, and electronic charting are being developed.

Other Activities

Port captains assist the boating traveler by providing a contact and a source of information about local conditions and facilities such as location of marinas, yacht clubs, repair facilities, marine supplied, fuel, pump-outs, charts and publications, restaurants, grocery stores, and places of interest.

Marep (Marine Report) Hydrographic Program lets CPS aid the Hydrographic Service in updating nautical charts and publications by reporting changes observed by members, such as obstructions in or out of the water, new or altered marine facilities, and new landmarks that could be useful for navigation.

Marep Weather Program by CPS assists Environment Canada in giving updated, accurate weather information to mariners. Data are relayed to Environment Canada via the CCG on VHF radio.

Social Activities

Many Squadrons arrange one or more events during the summer months—a cruise, predicted log race, sail past, picnic, or some other rendezvous; see **Figure 26-08.** In winter, it is common practice for Squadrons to organize monthly social evenings, which may include special guest speakers, wine and cheese nights, student nights, various parties and, most importantly, graduation night for the many students completing *The Boating Course.*

What Makes CPS Successful?

The dedication of CPS members provides an unequaled community service to boaters and would-be boaters. The CPS organization thrives on the knowledge and experience of its members,

Figure 26-08 Along with administrative and educational work, CPS members schedule social events each year, such as this cruise to Desolation Sound, about 100 miles north of Vancouver, British Columbia.

who without formal recognition, donate their time, energy and personal resources to safe, proficient, and fun-filled boating in Canada.

For details on courses, call toll-free in Canada 888-CPS-BOAT (277-2628). Web site: www.cps-ecp.ca.

THE UNITED STATES COAST GUARD

The United States Coast Guard (USCG) is a military service and a branch of the Armed Forces. It is not, as many people think, normally a part of the Department of Defense. In 1967, the Coast Guard, which had been a part of the Treasury Department for many decades, was transferred to the then-new Department of Transportation. In March 2003, it was again transferred, this time to the newly created Department of Homeland Security. This transfer was complete, including not only the obvious security missions but also all other functions such as boating safety, aids to navigation, search and rescue, fisheries enforcement, environmental protection, and icebreaking. These are peacetime activities—in time of war or national emergencies, however, vessels and units of the Coast Guard may be placed under the control of the Department of the Navy.

The flag of the U.S. Coast Guard, its distinctive ensign, is closely connected with the organization's history. The ensign bears 16 red-and-white vertical stripes, which represent the number of states in the Union when the flag was first authorized in 1799.

The Coast Guard ensign (page 857) has the unusual feature in that it is flown day and night on active USCG units afloat as well as ashore—a constant reminder that the Coast Guard is always on duty to render assistance.

Coast Guard cutters, ships, boat, aircraft, and vehicles are easily identified by the distinctive red-and-blue slanted stripes, with the USCG emblem on the red; see **Figures 26-09, 26-10,** and **26-11.**

Functions Relating to Boating

Boaters generally come into contact with the U.S. Coast Guard for two reasons: law enforcement

Figure 26-09 Medium-size Coast Guard cutters such as this one fill the gaps between the smaller craft that operate near shore and on inland waters and the ocean-going cutters of several hundred feet in length.

Figure 26-10 United States Coast Guard operations such as search and rescue and law enforcement use both helicopters and fixed-wing aircraft.

Figure 26-11 Small Coast Guard craft, such as the "utility boat" shown here, are equipped to handle many types of emergencies as well as search and rescue operations.

and safety. The following aspects of Coast Guard operations directly affect recreational boating.

• **Boating Regulations** Many of the federal laws relating to boating are implemented by regulations issued by the Commandant of the Coast Guard. The Federal Boat Safety Act of 1971 is an important law, and serves as the basis for the registration and numbering of motorboats. The Coast Guard performs this task itself only in Alaska; the boat-registration systems of the other states carry out this function for boaters in their respective states, and must be approved by the Commandant. Coast Guard patrol vessels, however, have the authority to check the registration papers of boats on all U.S. waters.

As discussed in Chapter 2, boats of more than a specified minimum size may be "documented" rather than registered and numbered. For all states and U.S. territories, this function is performed in a centralized location by officials of the Coast Guard.

As discussed in Chapter 3, Coast Guard regulations also spell out the details of the safety equipment required by the various federal laws. USCG personnel are authorized to make inspections of boats to determine the adequacy of such equipment. Boardings may be made at any time without a search warrant to check for illegal activities.

• **Safety Activities** Coast Guard vessels make frequent patrols to keep a watchful eye for any reckless operation of boats and all hazards to navigation. Many races, regattas, and other marine events are patrolled to ensure the safety of both participants and spectators.

In addition, the Coast Guard often has booths and exhibits at boat shows and other marine events. These provide boaters with information, advice, and assistance on problems relating to safety on the water. According to Coast Guard philosophy, the organization would much rather prevent an accident than rescue victims.

• **Aids to Navigation** From unlighted buoys and daybeacons to lighthouses, the Coast Guard is responsible for operating thousands of aids to navigation. It also operates transmitting stations of the Loran-C electronic navigation system and radiobeacons that broadcast corrections for Differential GPS.

This is a quiet and unspectacular, but most necessary, service to all who travel on the water. The installation and maintenance of lighted and unlighted aids to navigation are major functions of the Coast Guard, and affect boaters every time they leave their moorings.

• **Search & Rescue** Many boaters venture out on the waters, offshore or inland, with a greater sense of security knowing that the Coast Guard is standing by to help, living up to its motto "Semper Paratus"—"Always Ready." The rescue of mariners in distress is probably the most dramatic activity of the Coast Guard, the one that makes the headlines—when a ship goes down in a storm, for example. Less publicized, but equally important, are the many instances when the USCG comes to the aid of the skipper who has lost his way at sea, gone aground, suffered dismasting or engine failure, or merely run out of fuel. However, requests for assistance in non-life-threatening situations, such as mechanical or fuel problems in stable weather conditions, are referred by the Coast Guard to commercial towing assistance companies.

Coast Guard search and rescue surface units include ships known as "cutters" and small craft of many sizes. Fixed-wing aircraft and helicopters extend the search capabilities of surface vessels and in many cases are used to perform rescue missions when wind and sea conditions permit.

Organization & Personnel

The Commandant of the Coast Guard, an Admiral, and his staff are located at USCG Headquarters in Washington, D.C. Operational activities are grouped geographically into Districts; see **Figure 26-12**. Each District has a Commander, who is a Rear Admiral. For operational matters, the Districts of the Atlantic/Gulf of Mexico and Pacific coasts have been placed under the Atlantic Area and the Pacific Area commands respectively.

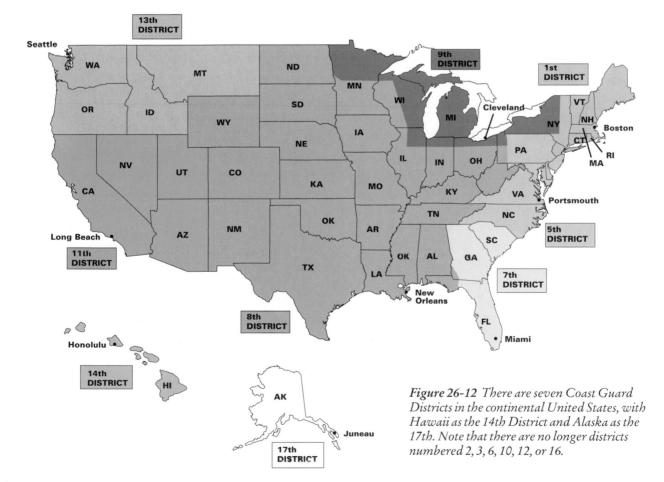

Figure 26-12 There are seven Coast Guard Districts in the continental United States, with Hawaii as the 14th District and Alaska as the 17th. Note that there are no longer districts numbered 2, 3, 6, 10, 12, or 16.

Operating units of the Coast Guard—individual bases, stations, cutters, boats, aircraft units, etc.—may be under the direct control of a District, or these may be under an intermediate level, called a "Group." Groups are being changed to "Sectors" additionally including local shore activities such as Marine Inspection Offices and Captains of the Port; aviation activities are sometimes included.

Personnel of the Coast Guard include commissioned officers, warrant officers, and enlisted men and women, and their ranks are the same as in the U.S. Navy. The distinguishing United States Coast Guard device is a small shield that is worn above an officer's stripes on both uniform jacket sleeves and on the lower right sleeve of an enlisted man or woman's uniform jacket. There is a United States Coast Guard Reserve to support the regular establishment. There are also civilian employees in many shore-based activities. (The Coast Guard Auxiliary is entirely distinct from the USCG Reserve).

Functions of the United States Coast Guard not directly related to boating include the Merchant Marine Inspection Program that sets and enforces safety standards for vessels and crews and pollution control for spills of oil and toxic chemicals. Icebreakers and cutters of reinforced construction keep harbors open for commercial navigation in winter; each spring, cutters and aircraft work with the International Ice Patrol tracking icebergs in the North Atlantic.

The Coast Guard is responsible for enforcement of offshore fishery laws out to 200 miles (370 km). In recent years, the interdiction of drug smugglers and illegal aliens has become a primary task in certain coastal areas.

Responsibility for port and waterway security has long been a task of the Coast Guard, but since September 2001, this function has become a larger part of everyday activity of Coast Guard vessels and personnel.

The final major function of the Coast Guard is to maintain at all times a high state of readiness to function as a specialized service in the Navy in time of war.

THE U.S. COAST GUARD AUXILIARY

In 1939, Congress established "a United States Coast Guard Reserve" administered by the Commandant and composed of unpaid, volunteer U.S. citizens who owned motorboats and yachts. In 1941, Congress created a military Coast Guard Reserve and renamed the original volunteer reserve as the "Coast Guard Auxiliary."

Membership

The Coast Guard Auxiliary (USCGAux, not USCGA, which is the abbreviation for the Coast Guard Academy) is a volunteer civilian organization functioning under the direction of the Commandant of the U.S. Coast Guard. It is composed of people interested in the Coast Guard and its principles—people who are dedicated to the interest of their country, and concerned about the safety and welfare of their fellow men and women. Despite its uniforms and insignia, the Auxiliary is a nonmilitary body.

Membership is open to any citizen of the U.S. and its territories and possessions who is 17 years of age or older. Ownership of a boat, aircraft, or radio station, or a special needed skill, is desirable but not mandatory. Membership is also open to all currently active or honorably discharged members of the regular and reserve uniformed services, including the Coast Guard. Auxiliarists donate their time and abilities to the cause of safety on the water. The only compensation for services rendered is personal satisfaction and only minor reimbursement of expenses for some official activities.

To become a member, an applicant must meet the general eligibility requirements and complete the New Member Initial Orientation and Entry Training Program. Members are encouraged to take advanced training toward the higher status of AUXOP member and/or "Auxiliary Coxswain." A boat, aircraft, or radio station is termed a "Facility."

Flags

A boat that has qualified as a Facility may fly the Coast Guard Auxiliary Ensign. This rectangular

U.S COAST GUARD AUXILIARY FLAGS & INSIGNIA

COAST GUARD AUXILIARY
ENSIGN

NATIONAL COMMODORE

AUXILIARY PATROL BOAT ENSIGN

NATIONAL VICE COMMODORE

NATIONAL REAR COMMODORE

DISTRICT COMMODORE

DIVISION CAPTAIN

FLOTILLA COMMANDER

DISTRICT VICE COMMODORE
(White field, blue markings,
Dist. Rear Commodore)

DIVISION VICE CAPTAIN

FLOTILLA VICE COMMANDER

CHIEF OF DEPARTMENT
3 Bars—Division Chief
2 Bars—Branch Chief and
Aide to National Commodore
1 Bar—Branch Assistant

DISTRICT STAFF OFFICER
1½ Bars—Assistant DSO

DIVISION STAFF OFFICER

FLOTILLA STAFF OFFICER
(Also Aide to District Commodore)

AUXILIARY COXSWAIN

CAP DEVICE   SHIELD   SHIELD   DEVICE   AUXOP DEVICE   AUXILIARY AVIATOR

METAL COLLAR INSIGNIA[1]	SHOULDER BOARDS[2]		METAL COLLAR INSIGNIA[1]	SHOULDER BOARDS[2]
National Commodore		Division Vice Captain With Red "A": Branch Chief; Dist. Staff Officer; Aide to NACO DCO Admin. Officer		
National Vice Commodore		Aide to DCO Admin. Asst. to DCO Flotilla Commander With Red "A": Branch Asst.; Asst. Dist. Staff Officer		
National Rear Commodore		Flotilla Vice Commander With Red "A": Division Staff Officer		
District Vice Commodore District Rear Commodore With Red "A": Department Chief		Flotilla Staff Officer; Aide to DCO		
Division Captain With Red "A": Division Chief NACO Admin. Officer		Member		

[1]Large metal shoulder insignia are worn on blue raincoats and windbreakers; the same insignia in smaller size are worn on the collars of light blue and blue flannel shirts for certain uniforms, and on garrison caps.
[2]Shoulder Boards are worn on blue coats, and white dinner jackets, and on light blue shirts for certain uniforms.

THE CANADIAN COAST GUARD

The Canadian Coast Guard (CCG) is part of the federal Department of Fisheries and Oceans. Its mandate is to ensure a safe and efficient marine transportation system and to protect the marine environment in waters under the jurisdiction of the Government of Cananda. The organization operates under the CCG flag—the Canadian national ensign, shown in Chapter 25, page 857.

Among other services, CCG vessels place and remove buoys, deliver supplies to lightstations, service radio and radar beacons and provide icebreaking and pollution clean-up support.

blue flag with a white diagonal slash on which the USCG Auxiliary emblem appears; see page 879. Like the USCG Ensign, the Auxiliary Ensign may be flown from boats day and night.

The Coast Guard Auxiliary Operational Ensign is white with the Coast Guard red-and-blue slanted stripes; the Auxiliary emblem is on the red stripe. This is flown in place of the blue-and-white flag when a Facility is operating under USCG orders; see page 879.

Purposes

The U.S. Coast Guard Auxiliary has several fundamental purposes that are stated as follows in the Act of Congress that established the organization:

• To promote safety and effect rescues on and over the high seas and on the navigable waters

• To promote efficiency in the operation of both motorboats and yachts

• To foster a wider knowledge of, and better compliance with, the laws, rules, and regulations governing the operation of motorboats and yachts

• To facilitate other operations of the Coast Guard

In 1966 the purpose of the Auxiliary was expanded by Act of Congress to read "to assist the Coast Guard as authorized by the Commandant in performing any USCG function, power, duty, role, mission, or operation authorized by law." (There is an exception for combat and direct law enforcement.) The same Act authorized the Commandant to use the Auxiliary to assist other federal agencies, state authorities, and local governments in areas other than recreational boating safety. With the Coast Guard's added responsibilities under the Department of Homeland Security, considerable use is being made of the resources of the Auxiliary.

Activities

In support of its commitment to recreational boating safety, the Auxiliary has active programs of Public Education, Vessel Examination, and Operations, as described below.

• **Public Education** The Auxiliary offers several courses to the boating public. These courses are tailored to meet the needs of various types of boating—power or sail, large or small. Courses consist of from one to eight lessons, with classes held in the evenings or on weekends. Constant attention is given to the improvement of these courses and the development of new lessons or courses as required.

• **Member Training** Auxiliary members are actively encouraged to take "specialty" courses to improve their knowledge and increase their value to the organization. Various subjects of study would include communications, search and rescue, patrol procedures, and weather.

• **Vessel Examinations** Many members of the Auxiliary are active in the Courtesy Marine Examination (CME) program, now called the "Vessel Safety Check" (VSC). Boat owners are urged each year to request a VSC. This purely voluntary action ensures that a thorough check is made of all safety-related equipment. Boats that pass the examination are awarded the VSC sticker for the current calendar year. Boats that do not pass are not reported to any authority; the owner is simply advised of the deficiencies and is encouraged to resubmit the boat for another check when they have been corrected; see **Figure 26-13.**

Auxiliarists are also busy each year inspecting the boats of other members to determine their

Figure 26-13 *In addition to regular Coast Guard boarding, thousands of voluntary Vessel Safety Checks are made each year by members of the Auxiliary and USPS on boats of all types and sizes. Deficiencies are brought to the attention of the owner, but are not reported to any law-enforcement authority.*

fitness for continued designation as Facilities. Such boats have higher safety standards and equipment requirements, as they will be allowed to fly the Auxiliary flag. The highest standards are required for a craft that is designated an "Operational Facility," as it will be used in operational programs under Coast Guard orders.

• **Operational Programs** Personnel and vessels of the Auxiliary are used to perform various missions in fields where the resources of the regular Coast Guard are not sufficient to meet the demands placed upon them—regatta patrols and search and rescue missions, for example. This often occurs on weekends and during holiday periods. For such duties, orders are issued by a designated Coast Guard officer.

To improve operational efficiency, the Auxiliary conducts an extensive *Boat Crew Qualification Program* for its members engaged in such work. This leads progressively to designation as "Crewman" and "Auxiliary Coxswain."

Auxiliary members have no law-enforcement powers. When a Coast Guard officer or petty officer is embarked in the Auxiliary vessel, however, it may fly the regular Coast Guard Ensign.

Auxiliary vessels conduct safety patrols as well as patrols to check on aids to navigation and to report errors and needed changes on charts—a part of the Chart Updating Program of the National Ocean Service.

Auxiliary aircraft may be used to supplement regular Coast Guard units in search and rescue operations and administrative support missions. In some areas Auxiliary aircraft even make "Twilight patrols" at the end of days of heavy boating activity to spot any boat that may need aid in reaching port safely.

• **Fellowship Activities** Units of the Auxiliary work hard at their basic responsibilities but not to the complete exclusion of social activities. Rendezvous, parties, dances and other Auxiliary events promote goodwill and fellowship.

Organization

The basic unit of the Auxiliary is the FLOTILLA. This is a local group of members and their facilities who work together in the various programs. Depending on the group, membership may include dozens, even hundreds, of members. Flotillas are grouped geographically into DIVISIONS—the normal intermediate level between local Flotilla and DISTRICT. In some cases, though, a District (which corresponds to USCG Districts, as shown in **Figure 26-12**) is divided into two or more REGIONS for better control. Districts are assigned to one of three AREAS—Atlantic (East), Atlantic (West), and Pacific.

Auxiliary units are headed by their own elected officers—Flotilla Commander, Division Captain, or District Commodore. These are assisted by other elected and appointed officers. The Auxiliary as a whole is headed by a National Commodore, four National Vice Commodores, and three National Directorate Commodores. At all levels, there are appointed staff officers for the various operational and administrative functions.

At Coast Guard Headquarters in Washington, D.C., a USCG officer with the rank of Captain is designated as the Chief Director of Auxiliary. At each Coast Guard District Headquarters, there is an officer, usually at the rank of Commander, who is the Director of Auxiliary for that district. At both of these levels, these officers are assisted by a small military and civilian staff .

Uniforms & Insignia

Auxiliary uniforms have evolved through several distinct phases and are now more "military" than "yachting," although the organization remains basically civilian in nature.

The Auxiliary has "dinner dress," "service dress," and "undress," plus "tropical" and "working" uniforms. A member need not own all of these, only those appropriate to his or her area and normal activities. Uniform jackets and raincoats are also available. Uniforms are required for certain activities, such as official patrols and participation in Vessel Safety Checks; instructors normally wear uniforms. The purchase and upkeep of uniforms is at the individual Auxiliarist's expense.

The office held by members is indicated by sleeve stripes, shoulder boards, and pin-on insignia, all patterned after those worn by regular Coast Guard officers but with differences that distinguish the Auxiliarist. Stripes on the sleeves and shoulder boards is of silver rather than gold and worn in stripes, half-stripes, and broad stripes in a series comparable to those by Ensigns to Vice Admirals in the Coast Guard and Navy. The Auxiliary, however, does not use rank titles like those of the regular and reserve services; insignia are prescribed for offices held rather than rank titles.

Shoulder boards, worn on many uniforms, carry a varying number of stripes. Shoulder boards of the most senior Auxiliary officers are of solid silver braid with one, two or three stars as appropriate to the office held. The Auxiliary shield is above the stripes or stars of shoulder boards and sleeve stripes.

Collar insignia consist of the same series of designs used for officers of the U.S. Armed Forces, but with a letter "A" superimposed in blue or red. Similar insignia, in larger sizes, are worn on uniform jackets (windbreakers) and raincoats.

Officers and members of the Auxiliary wear frame caps similar to those used by regular officers. Chin straps of member's frame caps are black; those of officers are silver. Visor ornamentation in silver is worn on the caps of senior officers. A "working cap" of boating style is authorized in Coast Guard Blue. The fore-and-aft "garrison cap" may be worn with service dress or working uniforms when more convenient than the frame cap.

How to Join the USCG Auxiliary

If you are an eligible boater, why not join the Auxiliary? The rewards include learning a great deal about boating safety and enjoyment. In addition, there is nothing finer than the sense of satisfaction that comes from helping others. Ask any local Coast Guard unit or Auxiliarist where you can "sign up."

APPENDIX A

CHART, CRUISING & SAFETY INFORMATION SOURCES

Note: The details of addresses, especially Internet Websites, may change or become inoperable.

Charts of Various Waterways
U.S. Coastal Waters and Great Lakes Atlantic, Pacific, and Gulf Coasts; Atlantic and Gulf Intracoastal Waterways; Hudson River north to Troy, New York; Great Lakes and connecting rivers; Lake Champlain; New York State Canals; and Minnesota-Ontario Border Lakes: Published by National Ocean Service; available from FAA/National Aeronautical Charting Office, AVN-530, 6303 Ivy Lane, Suite 400, Greenbelt MD 20770-1479; 800-638-8972; fax 301-436-6829; 9-AMC-CHARTSALES/FAA@faa.gov; http://naco.faa.gov. Also available from many local sales agents.

Mississippi River, full length and some tributaries Published by U.S. Army Corps of Engineers; available from U.S. Army Engineers, Mississippi Valley Division, 1400 Walnut Street, Vicksburg, MS 39180-3262; 601-634-7110; www.mvd.usace.army.mil.

Ohio River and tributaries U.S. Army Engineers, Great Lakes and Ohio River Division, P.O. Box 1159, Cincinnati, OH 39180-1159; 513-684-3010; www.lrd.usace.army.mil.

Missouri River and tributaries U.S. Army Engineers, Kansas City District, 601 E. 12th Street, Kansas City, MO 64106-2808; 816-983-3201; www.nwk.usace.army.mil *or* U.S. Army Engineers, Omaha District, 106 S. 15th Street, Omaha NE 68102-1618; 402-221-3900 or toll-free 888-835-5971; www.nwo.usace.army.mil.

Tennessee River and tributaries Tennessee Valley Authority, Map Store, 1101 Market Street, Chattanooga, TN 37402-2801; 423-751-6277 or 800-627-7882; fax 423-751-6216; mapstore@tva.gov; www.tva.gov.

Canadian Waters Chart Distribution Office, Canadian Hydrographic Service, Department of Fisheries and Oceans, P.O. Box 8080, 830 Industrial Avenue, Unit 19, Ottawa, ON K1G 3H6; 613-998-4931; fax 613-998-1217; chs_sales@dfo.gc.ca (info only; retail sales only via authorized dealers); www.charts.gc.ca/chs. Digital chart products: Nautical Data International, Inc., P.O. Box 127, St. John's, Newfoundland A1C 5H5; 800-563-0634 or 709-576-0634; fax 709-576-0636; support@digital-ocean.ca; www.digitalocean.ca.

Waters of Other Nations Published by National Imagery and Mapping Agency (NIMA). Nine regional catalogs are available (free). NIMA nautical publications are available for purchase from the U.S. Government Printing Office and its regional bookstores and authorized sales agents; 202-521-1800; fax 202-512-2250; http://bookstore.gpo.gov. Send mail orders to Superintendent of Documents, P.O. Box 371954, Pittsburgh, PA 15250-1954.

Coast Pilots
U.S. Waters Atlantic, Gulf, and Pacific Coasts; Atlantic and Gulf Intracoastal Waterways; the Great Lakes. Published by National Ocean Service; available from FAA/National Aeronautical Charting Office, AVN-530, 6303 Ivy Lane, Suite 400, Greenbelt MD 20770-1479; 800-638-8972; fax 301-436-6829; 9-AMC-CHARTSALES/FAA@faa.gov; http://naco.faa.gov. Also available from many local sales agents as listed in each NOS chart catalog.

Canadian Waters Published by Canadian Hydrographic Service. Information from Chart Distribution Office, CHS, Department of Fisheries and Oceans, P.O. Box 8080, 830 Industrial Avenue, Unit 19, Ottawa, ON K1G 3H6; 613-998-4931; fax 613-998-1217; chs_sales@dfo.gc.ca. (Info only; retail sales only via authorized dealers) 613-998-4931; fax 613-998-1217; chs_sales@chshq.dfo.ca; www.charts.gc.ca/chs. Titles are listed in chart catalogs.

Cruising Guides
Cruising Guide to the New York State Canal System N.Y. State Canal Corporation, P.O. Box 189. Albany, NY 12201-0189; 800-422-6254; www.canals.state.ny.us. Published by Northern Cartographic, 4040 Williston Road, South Burlington, VT 05403-6062; ncarto@together.net.

Waterway Guide Regional editions provide annually updated information on the Intracoastal Waterway and adjacent waters. Northern: Maine to Chesapeake Bay and Delaware Canal; Champlain Waterway. Mid-Atlantic: Chesapeake Bay and Delaware Canal to Georgia/Florida border. Southern: Georgia/Florida border to Brownsville, Texas; and the Bahamas; 443-482-9377 or 800-233-3359; www.waterwayguide.com.

Cruising Charts, Guides and Booklets for State of Texas Local Convention & Visitors Bureaus; 800-452-9292.

Quimby's Cruising Guide This guide covers all navigable inland waterways with details of harbors, locks, dams, hazards, as well as onshore services, transportation, and attractions; the guide provides sources of navigation charts and books. Waterway Journal, 319 N. 4th Street, Suite 650, St. Louis, MO 63102-1994; 314-241-7354.

Guide for Cruising Maryland Waters Twenty full-color charts, with over 200 courses and distances plotted; includes marina and facility information: Department of Natural Resources, Tawes State Office Building. Annapolis, MD 21401; 410-974-3211. Also available: a Maryland boating course.

Ports Cruising Guides Lake Ontario/Thousand Islands; Georgian Bay/North Channel/Lake Huron; Trent-Severn Waterway/Lake Simcoe: Ports Cruising Guides, 94 Wheeler Ave., Toronto, Ontario M4L 3V2; 416-691-5347; fax 416-691-0488.

Yachtsman's Guide to the Bahamas Annual guide to the Bahamas: Tropic Island Publishers, Inc., P.O. Box 8010, Red Bank, NJ 07701-8010; 877-922-9653; fax 732-389-9139, www.yachtsmansguide.com. Mailing & Shipping Office: P.O. Box 610938, North Miami, FL 33261-0938; 305-893-4277.

Guide to the Virgin Islands Guide to waters of U.S. and British Virgin Islands and eastern Puerto Rico: Tropic Island Publishers, Inc. (see above).

Light Lists
U.S. Light Lists Published by USCG: Available from Superintendent of Documents, U.S. Government Printing Office, Washington, DC 20402; 202-512-1800; fax 202-512-2250. Mail-order Superintendent of Documents, P.O. Box 371954, Pittsburgh, PA 15250-1954. Available at GPO Regional Bookstores and some chart sales agents. Text of each *Light List* volume may be accessed at ww.navcen.uscg.gov/pubs/LightLists/LightLists.htm. Pdf files (all or portions) may be printed for use.

Navigation Rules
Navigation Rules, International—Inland The 1996 edition contains the International Regulations for Preventing Collisions at Sea (the 72 COLREGS) and the Inland Navigational Rules, which supersede the old Inland Rules, Western Rivers Rules, Great Lakes Rules and other Pilot Rules. It includes sections on COLREGS demarcation lines. Penalty provisions, alternative compliance, and the Vessel Bridge-to-Bridge Radiotelephone Regulations. Published by USCG. Available from Superintendent of Documents, U.S. Government Printing Office, Washington, DC 20402; 202-512-1800; fax 202-512-2250. Send mail orders to Superintendent of Documents, P.O. Box 371954, Pittsburgh, PA 15250-1954. Also available at GPO regional bookstores and authorized sales agents for charts and publications.

Notices to Mariners
U.S. Notice to Mariners Weekly publication of the National Imagery and Mapping Agency, prepared jointly with the National Ocean Service and the USCG; NavNotices@nima.mil; http://pollux.nss.nima.mil.

Canadian Notices to Mariners Available from authorized Canadian Hydrographic Service Chart Dealers; information on ordering can be obtained from CHS Chart Distribution Office 830 Industrial Avenue, Unit 19, P.O. Box 8080, Ottawa, ON K1G 3H6; 613-998-4931; fax 613-998-1217; chsinfo@dfo-mpo.gc.ca; www.charts.gc.ca.

Local Notices to Mariners Issued weekly by Coast Guard District Commanders; now distributed only electronically.

Publications of NIMA/NGA
National Imagery and Mapping Agency (now **National Geospatial-Intelligence Agency**) publications are available from the FAA/National Aeronautical Charting Office, AVN-530, 6303 Ivy Lane, Suite 400, Greenbelt MD 20770-1479; 800-638-8972; fax 301-436-6829; 9-AMC-CHART-SALES/FAA@faa.gov; http://naco.faa.gov. Also available from many local sales agents.

Each regional NOAA/NOS catalog of NIMA products lists popular index charts, world charts, general nautical charts, magnetic charts, oceano-graphic charts, aeronautical charts, and Loran charts published by the agency.

Sailing Directions Books supplementing NIMA charts containing descriptions of coastlines, harbors, dangers, aids, port facilities, and other data that cannot be shown conveniently on charts.

Pilot Charts Monthly information on ocean currents and weather probabilities for various waters.

List of Lights, Radio Aids, and Fog Signals For foreign waters, similar to USCG Light Lists.

Miscellaneous NIMA Publications
Pub. 9. American Practical Navigator, originally by Nathaniel Bowditch, 2002.†
Pub. 102. International Code of Signals.†
Pub. 117. Radio Navigation Aids, Marine Direction-Finding Stations, Radio Beacons, Time Signals, Navigational Warnings, Distress Signals, Medical Advice and Quarantine Stations, and Loran, and Regulations on Use of Radio in Territorial Waters.†
Pub. 150. World Port Index.†
Pub. 151. Distances Between Ports †
Pub. 1310. Radar Navigation and Maneuvering Board Manual.‡
† Available in printed version with CD-ROM.
‡ Available only as a CD-ROM.

Safety Publications
Standards and Recommended Practices for Small Craft Available from ABYC, 3069 Solomon's Island Road, Edgewater, MD 21037-1416; 410-956-1050; fax 410-956-2737; info@abycinc.org; www.abycinc.org.

Fire Protection Standard #302-94 for Motor Craft (Pleasure and Commercial) Available from NFPA, 1 Batterymarch Park, P.O. Box 9101, Quincy, MA 02269-9101; 617-770-3000; fax 617-770-0700; www.nfpa.org.

Tide & Current Tables

U.S. Tide Tables and Tidal Current Tables NOS data are available in book format through private publishers and distributors: International Marine, P.O. Box 182607, Columbus, OH 43218-2607; 800-722-4726. Thomas Reed Publications, 293 S. Main Street, Providence, RI 02903-2910 401-454-8300 or 800-995-4995 (orders only); fax 401-454-8455; info@reedsalmanac.com; www.reedsalmanac.com.

Canadian Waters Tide and current tables and complementary publications: Rules of the Road. Information from Chart Distribution Office, CHS, Department of Fisheries and Oceans, P.O. Box 8080, 830 Industrial Avenue, Unit 19, Ottawa, Ontario K1G 3H6; 613-998-4931; fax 613-998-1217; chs_sales@dfo.gc.ca. (Info only; retail sales only via authorized dealers) chs_sales@chshq.dfo.ca; www.charts.gc.ca/chs.

U.S. Coast Guard Publications

A variety of materials on recreational boating safety are available free of charge by calling the USCG Customer Infoline: 800-368-5647; www.uscgboating.org.

Federal Requirements and Safety Tips for Recreational Boats An operator booklet on U.S. laws, equipment requirements and safety recommendations for recreational vessels. Available at all Coast Guard offices.

Coast Guard Safety on the Internet The USCG provides a Website that contains a wealth of information of interest to recreational boaters: www.navcen.uscg.mil. In addition to Recreational Boating Safety, there are other pages of interest.

Weather Publications

Worldwide Marine Weather Broadcasts Broadcast schedules of marine weather information from all areas of the world where service is available. Purchase from the U.S. Government Printing Office and its bookstores and sales agents; 202-521-1800; fax 202-512-2250; http://bookstore.gpo.gov. Send mail orders to Superintendent of Documents, P.O. Box 371954, Pittsburgh, PA 15250-1954.

Miscellaneous Publications

The American Nautical Almanac Compact publication from the United States Naval Observatory contains all ephemeris material essential to the solution of problems of navigational position; star chart is included. Available from Superintendent of Documents, U.S. Government Printing Office, Washington, DC 20402; 202-512-1800; fax 202-512-2250. Send mail orders to Superintendent of Documents, P.O. Box 371954, Pittsburgh, PA 15250-1954. Available at GPO Regional Bookstores and some sales agents for charts.

Dutton's Navigation and Piloting by Elbert S. Maloney; 14th Edition, 1985. Customer Service, USNI Operations Center, 2062 Generals Hwy., Annapolis, MD 21401-6780; 410-224-3378 or 800-233-8764; fax 410-571-1703; customer@usni.org; www.usni.org/webstore. The Naval Institute Press publishes many other books of interest to boaters.

Reed's Nautical Almanac Comprehensive nautical reference available in East Coast, West Coast and Caribbean Editions. Thomas Reed Publications, Inc. 293 S. Main Street, Providence, RI 02903-2910; 401 454-8300 or 800-995-4995 (orders only); fax 401-454-8455; info@reedsalmanac.com; www.reedsalmanac.com.

Canadian Addresses

Canadian Coast Guard Office of Boating Safety, 200 Kent Street, 5th Floor, Ottawa, Ontario K1A 0E6; 613 - 993-0999 or 800-267-6687; fax 613-990-1866; obs-bsn@dfo-mpo.gc.ca; www.dfo-mpo.gc.ca

Hydrographic Chart Distribution Office Department of Fisheries and Oceans, P.O. Box 8080, 830 Industrial Avenue, Unit 19, Ottawa, ON K1G 3H6; 613-998-4931; fax 613-998-1217; chs_sales@dfo.gc.ca (info only; retail sales only via authorized dealers); www.charts.gc.ca/chs

Environmental Canada Main Floor, 351 St., Joseph Blvd., Hull, Quebec K1A 0H3; 819-997-2800 or 1-800-668-6767; fax 819-953-2225; enviroinfo@ec.gc.ca

APPENDIX B

ASSOCIATIONS & ORGANIZATIONS

The American Boat & Yacht Council Inc. (ABYC) 3069 Solomon's Island Road; Edgewater, MD 21037-1416; 410-956-1050; fax 410-956-2737; info@abycinc.org; www.abycinc.org.

American Boat Builders & Repairers Association 817 Main Street; Warren, RI 02885-4325; 401-247-0318; fax 401-247-0074; info@abbra.org; www.abbra.org.

American Bureau of Shipping (ABS) 1535 Richmond Terrace; Staten Island, NY 10310-1114; 718-981-2535; www.eagle.org.

American Power Boat Assocation (APBA)
17640 E. Nine Mile Road; P.O. Box 377; Eastpointe, MI 48021-0377; 586-773-9700; fax 586-773-6490; apbahq@apba-racing.com; www.apba.org.

Boat Owners Association of the United States (BoatU.S.) 880 South Pickett Street; Alexandria, VA 22304-4606; 703-823-9550; fax 703-461-2847; mail@boatus.com; www.boatus.com.

British Meteorological Office London Road; Bracknell, Berkshire RG12 2SZ; England; 44-(0)1-344-855680; fax 44-(0)1344-855681; enquiries@metoffice.com; www.met-office.gov.uk.

BUC Information Services 1314 N.E. 17th Court; Fort Lauderdale, FL 33305; 800-327-6929; in Florida 954-565-6715; fax 954-561-3095; info@buc.com; www.buc.com.

Canadian Yachting Association (CYA) 1600 James Naismith Drive, Suite 504; Gloucester, Ontario K1B 5N4; Canada; 613-748-5687; fax 613-748-5688; sailcanada@sailing.ca; www.sailing.ca.

Cruising Club of America P.O. Box 4024; Boston, MA 02101-4024; www.cruisingclub.org.

Lloyds of London 1 Lime Street; London, EC3M 7HA; England; www.lloyds.com.

Marine Department of Underwriters Laboratories (UL) 12 Laboratory Drive; P.O. Box 13995; Research Triangle Park, NC 27709-3995; 919-549-1400; fax 919-547-6000; rtp@ul.com; www.ul.com/marine.

National Association of State Boating Law Administrators (NASBLA) 1500 Leestown Road, Suite 330; Lexington, KY 40511-2047; 859-225-9487; fax 859-231-6403; info@nasbla.org; www.nasbla.org.

National Boating Federation P.O. Box 4111; Annapolis, MD 21403-4111; 410-626-8566; www.n-b-f.org.

National Fire Protection Association (NFPA) 1 Batterymarch Park; P.O. Box 9101; Quincy, MA 02269-9101; 617-770-3000; fax 617-770-0700; www.nfpa.org.

National Marine Electronics Association 7 Riggs Avenue; Severna Park, MD 21146-3819; 410-975-9425; fax 410-975-9450; info@nmea.org; www.nmea.org.

National Marine Manufacturers Association (NMMA) 200 E. Randolph Drive, Suite 5100; Chicago, IL 60601-6528; 312-946-6200; fax 312-946-0388; www.nmma.org.

United Safe Boating Institute
P.O. Box 30428; Raleigh, NC 27622-0428; 919-755-0092; fax 919-836-1813. For information on boating courses, call 1-800-336-BOAT; president@usbi.org; www.usbi.org.

United States Sailing Association (US SAILING)
P.O. Box 1260; Portsmouth, RI 02871-0907; 401-683-0800; fax 401-683-0840; info@ussailing.org; www.ussailing.org.

Yacht Architects & Brokers Association
105 Eastern Avenue, Suite 104; Annapolis, MD 21403-3366; 410-263-1014; fax 410-263-1659; www.yachtbrokersusa.org.

APPENDIX C

STATE BOAT REGISTRATION OFFICES

All undocumented vessels equipped with propulsion machinery must be registered in the "state of principal use" as required by the Federal Boat Safety Act of 1971 (FBSA/71). Some states require all vessels to be numbered. A certificate number will be issued upon registering the vessel. These numbers must be displayed on your vessel. The owner/operator of a vessel must carry a valid certificate of number whenever the vessel is in use. When moved to a new state of principal use, the certificate is valid for 60 days. Check with your state numbering authority for numbering requirements. Following is a list of vessel registration authorities for states (in alphabetical order by postal code abbreviations) and U.S. territories:

Titling and Registration
Division of Motor Vehicles
3300B Fairbanks Street
Anchorage, **AK** 99503-4153
907-269-5559; fax 907-269-6084;
www.state.ak.us/dmv/reg/boat.htm

Boat Titling and Registration
Marine Police Division
Dept. of Conservation and Natural Resources
64 North Union Street, Room 438
Montgomery, **AL** 36130-1451
334-353-2628; fax 334-242-0336;
www.dcnr.state.al.us/MP/registration.htm

Licensing Division
Dept. of Finance & Administration
P.O. Box 1272, Revenue Division
Little, Rock, **AR** 72203-1272
501-682-4703; www.state.ar.us

Boat Titling and Registration
Law Enforcement Branch
Arizona Game & Fish Dept.
2221 West Greenway Road
Phoenix, **AZ** 85023-4312
602-789-2403; fax 602-789-3729;
www.azgfd.com

Vessels Section, Mail Stop E-272
Dept. of Motor Vehicles
P.O. Box 825341
Sacramento, **CA** 94269-5341
800-777-0103;
www.dmv.ca.gov/boatsinfo/boat.htm

Boat Registration Office
Division of Parks & Outdoor Recreation
Department of Natural Resources
13787 South Highway 85
Littleton, **CO** 80125-9721
303-791-1920; fax 303-297-1657;
www.parks.state.co.us/boating

Marine Vessel Section
Dept. of Motor Vehicles
60 State Street
Wethersfield, **CT** 06161-3032
860-263-5116; fax 860-263-5555;
www.ct.gov/dmv

Harbor Section
Metropolitan Police Dept.
550 Water Street, S.W.
Washington, **DC** 20024-2399
202-727-4584; fax 202-727-3663; www.dc.gov

Boat Registrations
Division of Fish & Wildlife
Dept. of Natural Resources & Environmental
Control
P.O. Box 1401
Dover, **DE** 19903
302-739-3498; fax 302-739-6157;
www.dnrec.state.de.us/fw

Bureau of Titling & Registration
Department of Highway Safety and Motor Vehicles
2900 Apalachee Parkway
Tallahassee, **FL** 32399-6552
850-922-2472; fax 850-4124-9379;
www.hsmv.state.fl.us/dmv/faqboat.html

Boating Registration Unit
Wildlife Resources Division
Department of Natural Resources
2189 Northlake Parkway
Building 10. Suite 108
Tucker, **GA** 30084-4111
770-414-3337; fax 770-414-3344;
http://georgiawildlife.dnr.state.ga.us

Division of Boating & Ocean Recreation
Department of Land & Natural Resources
333 Queen Street, Suite 300
Honolulu, **HI** 96813-5341; 808-587-1966;
fax 8089-587-1977; www.state.hi.us/dlnr/dbor

Licensing Bureau
Fish & Wildlife Division
Dept. of Natural Resources
Wallace State Office Building
E. Ninth and Grand Avenue
Des Moines, **IA** 50319-0034
515-281-8688; fax 616-281-6794; www.iowadnr.com

Licensing Section
Dept. of Parks & Recreation, Boating Program
P.O. Box 83720
Boise, **ID** 83720-0065; 208-334-4197; fax 208-334-3741; www.idahoparks.org/rec/permits_boating.html

Boat Registration & Titling
Office of Law Enforcement
Dept. of Natural Resources
524 South Second Street
Springfield, **IL** 62701-1787
217-782-2138; fax 217-782-9599; www.dnr.state.il.us

Bureau of Motor Vehicles
100 North Senate Avenue, Room N440
Indianapolis, **IN** 46204-2214; 317-233-6000; fax
317-233-0053; www.state.in.us/bmv/watercraft

Administrative Services Division
Division of Law Enforcement
Dept. of Wildlife & Parks
512 S.E. 25th Avenue
Pratt, **KS** 67124-8174
620-672-5911 Ext. 127; fax 620-672-3013;
www.kdwp.state.ks.us/boating/boating.html

Title Branch
Department of Transportation
P.O. Box 2014
Frankfort, **KY** 40622-0001
502-564-2737; fax 502-564-1686;
www.kdfwr.state.ky.us/boating.htm

Motorboat Registration Division
Dept. of Wildlife & Fisheries
P.O. Box 14796
Baton Rouge, **LA** 70898-4796
225-765-2881; fax 225-763-5421; www.wlf.state.la.us

Registration Bureau
Division of Law Enforcement
Dept. of Fisheries, Wildlife & Environmental Law
Enforcement
251 Causeway Sreet
Boston, **MA** 02114-2194; 617-626-1611;
fax 617-626-1630; www.sport.state.ma.us

Licensing & Watercraft Registration Services
580 Taylor Avenue
Building E3
Annapolis, **MD** 21401-2397
410-260-8233; fax 410-260-8239;
www.dnr.state.md.us/service

Licensing & Registration
Dept. of Inland Fisheries & Wildlife
284 State Street
August, **ME** 04333-0001
207-287-3128; fax 207-287-6395;
www.state.me.us/ifw/licreg/licandreg.htm

Dept. of State Vessel Registration
430 W. Allegan Street
Lansing, **MI** 48918-0001
517-322-1460; www.michigan.gov/sos

Registration & Titling
Dept. of Natural Resources
500 Lafayette Road
St. Paul, **MN** 55155-4046
651-297-3227; fax 651-297-8851;
www.dnr.state.mn.us/licenses/watercraft

Motor Vehicle Bureau
P.O. Box 100
Jefferson City, **MO** 65105-0100
573-751-8383; fax 573-751-3551;
www.dor.state.mo.us/mvdl/motorv/h2o

Boating Division
Dept. of Wildlife, Fisheries & Parks
1505 Eastover Drive
Jackson, **MS** 39211-6322
601-432-2186; fax 601-432-2071;
www.ms.gov/gf/boating

Registrar's Bureau
Dept. of Justice
925 Main Street
Deer Lodge, **MT** 59722
406-846-2436; fax 406-846-6039;
www.fwp.state.mt.us/fishing/boatrestrictions.asp

Boat Licensing
Game & Fish Department
100 North Bismarck Expressway
Bismarck, **ND** 58501-5095
701-328-6334; fax 701-328-6374;
www.state.nd.us/gnf/licenses/boat-and-water.html

Boat Registration
Nebraska Game & Parks Commission
2200 N. 33rd Street
Lincoln, **NE** 68503-0370
402-471-5462; fax 402-471-5528;
www.ngpc.state.ne.us/boating/BGregister.html

New Hampshire Dept. of Safety
Division of Motor Vehicles
10 Hazen Drive
Concord, **NH** 03305-0002; 603-271-2333;
www.gencourt.state.nh.us/rules/saf-c2300.html

Marine Law Enforcement Bureau
New Jersey State Police
Division of Motor Vehicles
P.O. Box 7068
West Trenton, **NJ** 08628-0068
609-292-6500 or 888-486-3339 (NJ only);
www.state.nj.us/mvs/boats.htm

Vehicles Services Bureau
Motor Vehicles Dept.
P.O. Box 1028
Santa Fe, **NM** 87504-1028
505-827-2294; fax 505-827-0395;
www.state.nm.us/tax/trd_form.htm

License Office
Law Enforcement Division
Division of Wildlife
1100 Valley Road
Reno, **NV** 89512-2817
775-688-1512; fax 775-688-1509;
www.nevadadivisionofwildlife.org/
license/licburo.htm

Bureau of Registration
Dept. of Motor Vehicles
Swan Street Building
Empire State Plaza
Albany, **NY** 12228-0001
518-474-0921; fax 514-486-6581;
www.nydmv.state.ny.us/dmvfaqs.htm#BOATS

Registration & Titling
Division of Watercraft
Dept. of Natural Resources
4435 Fountain Square Drive
Columbus, **OH** 43224-1300
614-265-6490; fax 614-267-8883;
www.dnr.state.oh.us/watercraft/reg

Boats & Outboard Motors Division
Motor Vehicle Division
Oklahoma Tax Commission
2501 Lincoln Blvd.
Oklahoma City, **OK** 73194-0013
405-521-3221; fax 405-522-0991;
www.oktax.state.ok.us/mvreg.html

Boat Registration
State Marine Board
435 Commercial Street, N.E., #400
Salem, **OR** 97301-3453
503-373-1405 Ext. 254; fax 503-378-4597;
www.marinebd.osmb.state.or.us/Laws

Boat Registration Division
Bureau of Boating & Education
Fish & Boat Commission
P.O. Box 67000
Harrisburg, **PA** 17106-7000
717-705-7932; fax 717-705-7931;
www.fish.state.pa.us

Licensing Unit
Division of Business Affairs
Dept. of Environmental Management
235 Promenade Street, 4th Floor
Providence, **RI** 02908-5734
401-222-6647; fax 401-222-1181;
www.state.ri.us/dem/programs/
bpoladm/manserv/hfb/index.htm

Titling & Registration
P.O. Box 167
Columbia, **SC** 29202-0167
803-734-3852; fax 803-734-4086;
http://pop.scdnr.state.sc.us/boating/wcma.htm

Titling & Registration
Division of Motor Vehicles
445 E. Capital Avenue
Pierre, **SD** 57501-3185
605-773-3541; fax 605-773-4117;
www.state.sd.us/revenue/forms/mv/dmvforms.htm

Boat Registration
Boating Division
Wildlife Resource Agency
P.O. Box 40747
Nashville, **TN** 37204-0747
615-781-6618; fax 615-781-5268;
www.state.tn.us/twra/boat002.html

Titling & Registration
Law Enforcement Division
Texas Parks & Wildlife Dept.
4200 Smith School Road
Austin, **TX** 78744-3218
512-389-4675; fax: 512-389-4330;
www.tpwd.state.tx.us/boat/boat.htm

Motor Vehicle Division
State Tax Commission
210 North 1950 West
Salt Lake City, **UT** 84134-0001
801-297-7500; fax 801-297-7697;
www.stateparks.utah.gov/parks/boating/high-
light_1.htm

Boat Registration & Titling
Dept. of Game & Inland Fisheries
P.O. Box 11104
Richmond, **VA** 23230-1104
804-367-1189; fax 804-367-1064;
www.dgif.state.va.us/boating/boat_registration.html

Marine Division
Dept. of Motor Vehicles
120 State Street
Montpelier, **VT** 05603-0001
808-828-2000; fax 808-828-2170;
www.aot.state.vt.us/dmv/Vehicles/Motorboat/
MotorboatRegistration.htm

Titling & Registration Services
Dept. of Licensing
1125 Washington Street
Olympia, **WA** 98504-0001
360-902-3754; fax 360-902-4098; www.dol.wa.gov

Bureau of Customer Service
Licensing & Registration Division
Dept. of Natural Resources
125 S. Webster Street
Madison, **WI** 53703-3420
608-266-2107; fax 608-264-6130;
www.dnr.state.wi.us/org/es/enforcement/
safety/boatreg.htm

Division of Motor Vehicles
Division of Transportation
Capital Complex
Building 3
Charleston, **WV** 25305-0001
304-558-5351; www.wvdot.com/6_motorists/
dmv/6g4_applications.htm

License Sales Accounting
Fiscal Division
Wyoming Game & Fish Dept.
5400 Bishop Blvd.
Cheyenne, **WY** 82006-0001
307-777-4683;
http://gf.state.wy.us/fish/boating/index.asp

U.S. Territories
Boat Registration (Guam)
Police Dept.
Building 233, Central Avenue
Tiyan, **GM** 96913

Numbering & Registration (Puerto Rico)
Office of the Commissioner of Navigation
Dept. of Environment & Natural Resources
P.O. Box 9066600
San Juan, **PR** 00906-6600
787-725-2340; fax 787-725-7335

Boating Registration (U.S. Virgin Islands
Dept. of Planning & National Resources
Cyril E. King Airport, 2nd Floor
St. Thomas, **USVI** 00802
340-775-3320 Ext. 5138; fax 340-775-5706

Note: The details of addresses, especially Internet
Websites, may change or become inoperable.

APPENDIX D

USCG DISTRICT OFFICES

Contact the Recreational Boating Safety Specialist at the District Office with jurisdiction for your state or territory.

Note: Some "mil" Websites may not be available for security reasons.

First Coast Guard District
Connecticut, Maine, Massachusetts, New Hampshire, New Jersey (northern portion), New York, Rhode Island, Vermont.
Capt. John Foster Williams Building
408 Atlantic Avenue
Boston, MA 02110-3350
617-223-8480; www.uscg.mil/d1

Fifth Coast Guard District
Delaware, District of Columbia, Maryland, New Jersey (southern portion), North Carolina, Pennsylvania, Virginia.
Federal Building
431 Crawford Street
Portsmouth, VA 23704-5004
757-398-6287; www.uscg.mil/d5

Seventh Coast Guard District
Florida, Georgia, Puerto Rico, South Carolina, U.S. Virgin Islands.
Brickell Plaza Federal Building
909 SE First Avenue
Miami, FL 33131-3050
305-536-5654; www.uscg.mil/d7

Eighth Coast Guard District
Alabama, Arkansas, Colorado, Illinois, Iowa, Kansas, Kentucky, Louisiana, Mississippi, Missouri, Nebraska, New Mexico, North Dakota, Oklahoma, South Dakota, Tennessee, Texas, West Virginia, Wyoming.
Hale Boggs Federal Building
500 Camp Street
New Orleans, LA 70130-3396
504-589-6298; www.uscg.mil/d8

Ninth Coast Guard District
Michigan, Minnesota, Ohio, Wisconsin.
1240 East 9th Street
Cleveland, OH 44199-2060
216-902-6001; www.uscg.mil/d9

Eleventh Coast Guard District
Arizona, California, Nevada, Utah.
Coast Guard Island
Alameda, CA 94501-5100
510-437-3701; www.uscg.mil/d11

Thirteenth Coast Guard District
Idaho, Montana, Oregon, Washington.
Jackson Federal Building
915 Second Avenue
Seattle, WA 98174-1067
206-220-7237; www.uscg.mil/d13

Fourteenth Coast Guard District
Hawaii, Guam, American Samoa, Northern Mariana Islands.
Prince Kalanianaole Federal Building
300 Ala Moana Boulevard, 9th Floor
Honolulu, HI 96850-4982
808-541-2051; www.uscg.mil/d14

Seventeenth Coast Guard District
Alaska.
P.O. Box 25517
Juneau, AK 99802-5517
907-463-2025; www.uscg.mil/d17

APPENDIX E

THE METRIC SYSTEM

The Metric Conversion Act of 1975 (amended by the Omnibus Trade and Competitiveness Act of 1988) declares, as the policy of the United States, that the metric system of measurement is the preferred system of weights and measures for U.S. trade and commerce. To date, little progress has been made in converting the everyday thinking of the general U.S. population, including boaters; most persons continue to use a system that is variously called "Customary," "English," or "Inch-Pound." An understanding of the metric system, however, is becoming increasingly necessary as its use continues to expand—Navigation Rules, internal-combustion engines, liquor and wine, the nautical charts of other nations (and now some U.S. charts), etc.

The terms "metric system," "SI," "SI metric," and "SI units" refer to units belonging to the International System of Units (abbreviated SI from the French *Le Système International d'Unités*). They include the SI units (together with their multiples and submultiples); three other metric units—the liter, hectare, and metric ton—that are accepted for use with the SI units because of their practical importance; and a small number of other metric units that are accepted because of their use in specialized fields. SI provides a logical and interrelated framework for measurements in science, industry, commerce, and other forms of human endeavor.

The modern metric system is based on a foundation of base units, with multiples and submultiples expressed in a decimal system using various prefixes.

The SI Units
The base units of most interest to boaters are length, weight, and time. These units and their symbols are:

Length	meter (m)*
Mass (weight)	kilogram (kg)**
Time	second (s)***

Other base units of wide interest are temperature and electrical current:

| Temperature | Kelvin (K)**** |
| Electrical current | Ampere (A) |

* The international spelling is "metre," but for United States usage "meter" has been adopted (the pronunciation is the same).
** The kilogram is the only base unit that integrally includes a multiplier (see below).
*** Although the base SI unit for time is the second, units of minute, hour, and day are accepted for use with SI.
**** For nonscientific use, the degree Celsius (C) is more commonly used. The size of the units is the same; the difference is in the zero degree temperature. Degree "Celsius" was formerly known as "centigrade (also symbol "C").

The symbols, shown in parentheses, are *not* abbreviations. Most are written in lowercase letters except for those units (such as Ampere and degrees Celsius and Kelvin) that are named after a person. Unit symbols are not changed for the plural form. In the statement of a quantity, a space is inserted between the numerical value and the symbol; a hyphen is normally used in the adjectival form (exception: no space is used between values of degrees, minutes, and seconds and the symbols). Periods are not used with any symbols (except at the end of a sentence).

Derived Units
Other units in the metric system are derived from the base units. Typical of those expressed in combinations of base units and of interest to boaters are:

Area	square meter (m²)
Volume	cubic meter (m³)
Speed, velocity	meter per second (m/s) kilometer per hour (km/h)
Frequency	Hertz (Hz) [cycles per second]
Energy, work	Joules (J)
Power	Watt (W) [Joules/s]

Multiples & Submultiples
Units larger and smaller than the base units are formed by adding prefixes to make multiples and submultiples. The prefix symbol is added to the symbol for the base unit. Prefixes that are multiples or submultiples of 1,000 (kilo, centi, milli) are generally preferred as follows (there are others for larger and smaller multipliers, but such are of lesser interest):

1,000,000,000	10^9	giga	G*
1,000,000	10^6	mega	M*
1000	10^3	kilo	k
100	10^2	hecto	h
10	10	deka	da*
0.1	10^{-1}	deci	d
0.01	10^{-2}	centi	c
0.001	10^{-3}	milli	m
0.000,001	10^{-6}	micro	μ (Greek letter "mu")

* Note the exception to the capitalization and single-letter rules for "G," M," and "da" to prevent confusion with "g," "m," and "d."

Retained Non-SI Units
Certain units that are not metric units are so widely used that they are accepted for use with the metric system.

Non-SI Units of Interest to Boaters
Of interest to boaters are degrees (°), minutes ('), and seconds (") as measurements of arc. (The radian is the metric measurement of plane angles, but its use has been limited to scientific applications.)

Other Non-SI Units
There are other non-SI units, which are continued for a limited time subject to future review, include the nautical mile and knots as measurements of distance and speed. Also retained are the "bar" and "millibar" for atmospheric pressure.

The "liter" as a unit of volume is widely used—it is equal to 0.001 m² or 1,000 cm². The international symbol for liter is the lowercase letter "l"; but because of the similarity of this character with the numeral "1," the uppercase letter, "L" is commonly used in the United States.

The "metric ton"(t) of 1,000 kilograms is not strictly a part of SI, but is widely used.

Conversion
Conversion factors are given on the following page (page 892). These factors are rounded for general use; however, in most cases these will yield quite acceptable practical results.

Metric System Conversion Factors

Customary Units to Metric

Known value		Multiply by	To find	
in	inches	25.4	millimeters	mm
ft	feet	0.3048	meters	m
yd	yards	0.9144	meters	mst
mi	statute miles	1.609	kilometers	km
n mi	nautical miles	1.852	kilometers	km
oz	ounces (weight)	28.35	grams	g
lb	pound	0.4536	kilograms	kg
oz	ounce (liquid)	30.28	milliliters	mL
qt	quarts	0.9464	liters	L
gal	gallons	3.785	liters	L
hp	horsepower	0.746	kilowatts	kW
°F	degrees Fahrenheit (temperature)	⁵/₉ after subtracting 32	degrees Celsius (temperature)	°C

Metric Units to Customary

Known value		Multiply by	To find	
cm	centimeters	0.3937	inches	in
m	meters	3.281	feet	ft
m	meters	1.094	yards	yd
km	kilometers	0.6214	statute miles	st mi
km	kilometers	0.5400	nautical miles	n mi
g	grams	0.03527	ounces (weight)	oz
kg	kilograms	2.205	pounds	lb
mL	milliliters	0.03381	ounces (liquid)	oz
L	liters	1.057	quarts	qt
L	liters	0.2642	gallons	gal
KW	kilowatts	1.34	horsepower	hp
°C	degrees Celsius (temperature)	9.5 then add 32	degrees Fahrenheit (temperature)	°F

When converting in either direction, care must be taken that multiplication does not result in a value implying a higher degree of precision (see Chapter 16, pages 571-572) than the value in the original system. Rounding should be applied to the converted value to yield the same number of ignificant digits (do not round either the original value or the conversion factor).

Using the Internet

Conversions in either direction for any unit or value are quickly, easily, and accurately made by using one of the several available Websites on the Internet, such as: www.digitaldutch.com/unitconverter.

APPENDIX F

ABBREVIATIONS & ACRONYMS

ABYC American Boat and Yacht Council. (*See also Glossary.*)
AC Alternating Current.
ADF Automatic Direction Finder, an advanced variation of a radio direction finder.
AM Amplitude Modulation, one form of radio transmission, modulating the carrier wave in accordance with the strength of the audio signal.
AP Advanced Piloting, a course and a grade in the U.S. Power Squadrons.
ATON Coast Guard acronym for Aids to Navigation.

c metric prefix for 1/100.
C (1) Course, used in marking charts while plotting. (2) Celsius, the metric temperature scale (formerly "centigrade").
CE Center of Effort.
CB Citizens Band, a short-wave radio frequency service; compass bearing.
CLR Center of Lateral Resistance.
CMG Course Made Good.
CNG Compressed Natural Gas, a fuel sometimes used for cooking and heating.
CO Carbon monoxide, a poisonous gas.
CO_2 Carbon dioxide; a type of fire extinguishing agent.
COLREGS USCG acronym for International Regulations for the Prevention of Collisions at Sea.
CPS Canadian Power and Sail Squadrons.
CQR A brand of plow anchor.

D (1) Direction, used in labeling data on a chart plot. (2) Distance, also used in labeling data on a chart plot.
DC Direct Current.
DF (1) Direction Finder. (2) Direction Finding.
DGPS Differential GPS (USCG corrections).
DR Dead Reckoning, a form of navigation.

E East, cardinal compass point.
EHF Extremely High Frequency (radar).
EP Estimated Position.
EPIRB Emergency Position Indicating Radiobeacon. (*See also Glossary.*)
ETA Estimated Time of Arrival.
ETD Estimated Time of Departure.

F Fahrenheit, usually shown as °F, a temperature scale.
FAA Federal Aviation Administration.
FBSA Federal Boat Safety Act (U.S.).
FCC Federal Communications Commission, the U.S. regulator and licenser of radio transmission facilities.

FM Frequency Modulation, a communications technology that changes the frequency of the transmitting radio wave in accordance with the information being transmitted.
FRP Fiberglass reinforced plastic, usually referred to as simply as "fiberglass."

G metric prefix for 1,000,000,000.
GMT Greenwich Mean Time; essentially the same as Universal Time Coordinated (UTC).
GPO Government Printing Office, a sources of U.S. publications and documents.
GPS Global Positioning System, a radio navigation system using signals from satellites.

HF High Frequency (radio).
HIN Hull Identification Number.
hp Horsepower, a unit of power, equal to 746 watts.
Hz Hertz, a unit of frequency measurement, equivalent to cycles per second.
ICW Intracoastal Waterway.

JN Junior Navigator, a course and a grade in the U.S. Power Squadrons.

k metric prefix for 1,000.
kHz Kilohertz, unit of radio frequency, one thousand Hertz.
km Kilometer, one thousand meters, 0.62 of a statute mile, 0.54 of a nautical mile.
kn Knot, speed measurement, one nautical mile per hour (sometimes "kt").

lat Latitude.
LF Low Frequency (Loran-C).
LNM Local Notice to Mariners.
LOA Length overall. (*See also Glossary.*)
long Longitude.
LOP Line of Position.
LORAN-C Long Range Navigation system using several timed radio pulses from different locations.
LPG Liquefied Petroleum Gas, a fuel.
LWL Length of a vessel on the waterline or load waterline. (*See also Glossary.*)

m (1) meter, unit of linear measurement. (2) metric prefix for 1/1,000.
M metric prefix for 1,000,000.
MF Medium Frequency (radio).
MHW Mean High Water, a tidal datum for heights.
MHz Megahertz, unit of radio frequency, one thousand kHz, or one million Hertz.
MLLW Mean lower low water, a tidal datum.
MLW Mean low water.
MSD Marine Sanitation Device.

N (1) North, cardinal compass point. (2) Navigator, a course and highest educational grade in the U.S. Power Squadrons.

NFPA National Fire Protection Association.
NGA National Geospatial-Intelligence Agency.
NIMA National Imagery and Mapping Agency.
NM Notice to Mariners.
NMMA National Marine Manufacturers Association.
NOAA National Oceanic and Atmospheric Administration.
NOS National Ocean Service, a unit of NOAA.
NWS National Weather Service, a unit of NOAA.

P Piloting, a course and a grade in the U.S. Power Squadrons.
PFD Personal Floatation Device.
PPI Plan Position Indicator, a type of radar display.

Q flag (1) Yellow quarantine flag, so-called. (2) The International Signal Code is "My vessel is healthy and I request free practique."

RACON A radar beacon which, when triggered by pulses from a vessel's radar, transmits a reply.
RDF Radio Direction Finder. (*See also Glossary.*)
rpm Revolutions per minute.

S (1) South, cardinal compass point. (2) Seamanship, a course and grade in the U.S. Power Squadrons.
SAR Search and Rescue, Coast Guard and CG Auxiliary term.
SDGPS Satellite Differential GPS (FAA system).
SE Southeast, intercardinal compass point.
SHF Super High Frequency (radar).
SN A U.S. Power Squadrons designation for a member who has completed all courses.
SOLAS Safety of Life at Sea Convention.
SOS Morse code signal of distress.
SSB Single Side Band, radio term for a shortwave communications technique.

T flag Transportation flag, signal flag hoisted as a signal requesting a tender or launch service.

UHF Ultra High Frequency (radio)
UL Underwriters Laboratories, a safety organization that conducts product tests.
USCG United States Coast Guard.
USCG Aux United States Coast Guard Auxiliary.
USN United States Navy.
USPS United States Power Squadrons.
UTC Universal Time Coordinated.

VHF Very High Frequency (radio).
VLF Very Low Frequency.

W West, cardinal compass direction.
WAAS Wide Area Augmentation System (FAA).
WWV Continuous broadcast time signal station, transmitting from Colorado.
WWVH 24-hour radio time signal station, Hawaii.

APPENDIX G

GLOSSARY OF SELECTED TERMS

The definitions that follow are for the nautical use of these terms; many will have additional definitions in other fields of interest. More specialized terms are defined in appropriate chapters throughout *Chapman Piloting & Seamanship*. Refer to the Index (page 907) for further information.

abaft (1) Behind. (2) Toward the stern.

abeam (1) To one side of a vessel. (2) At a right angle to the fore-and-aft line.

abovedeck On deck as opposed to within the boat; actually being above deck level is described as being aloft.

abreast (1) Even with. (2) By the side of. (3) Side by side.

ABYC American Boat and Yacht Council, Inc., the organization that sets voluntary safety and construction standards for small craft in the U.S.A.

admeasure To measure a vessel for the purpose of documentation.

adrift Floating free without propulsion; not moored, aground, nor fastened to the shore.

admiralty law Law of the sea; a term for maritime law derived from the British.

aft, after Near or at the stern.

aground With the keel or bottom fast on the sea bottom.

aids to navigation Markers on land or sea that are established to enable navigators to avoid danger and fix their position; typically buoys, lights, daybeacons, and radiobeacons.

aloft Above the deck, usually in the rigging.

AMVER (Automated Mutual-Assistance Vessel Rescue) The USCG's unique, computer-based, and voluntary global ship reporting system used worldwide by search and rescue authorities to arrange for assistance to persons in distress at sea.

amidship (1) In the center. (2) The center portion of the vessel.

anchor A metal device, fastened to chain or line, to hold a vessel in position, partly because of its weight, but chiefly because the designed shape digs into the bottom.

anchorage A customary, suitable, and (usually) designated harbor area in which vessels may anchor.

anchor bend A specific knot, generally used to fasten an anchor line to an anchor.

anchor light An all-round white light required by the Navigation Rules when a vessel is at anchor or moored; also called a riding light.

anchor rode A line or chain, used to hold a vessel fast to the anchor.

anchor watch Person or persons kept alert on deck while the vessel is at anchor or moored in order to cope with unexpected situations.

anemometer An instrument that measures wind velocity.

aneroid barometer A device to measure and indicate air pressure for meteorology, using a mechanical means, rather than a liquid such as mercury. The pressure is generally indicated as the equivalent of so many millibars, or as inches of mercury.

antifouling A type of paint, used on the bottoms of boats, that repels barnacles, marine grass and many other undesirable adhesions.

apparent wind The direction and force of the wind relative to a moving vessel, differing from true wind. The motion of a sailboat or powerboat underway makes the effective wind, acting on sails or hull, vary from the actual wind. Apparent wind can be indicated by a telltale or instruments.

astern (1) The direction toward the stern of a vessel. (2) Beyond the stern.

athwart At right angles to the centerline.

auxiliary A sailboat that has an engine.

aweigh Off the bottom, said of an anchor.

backdrafting A potentially dangerous condition caused by air movement over or around a boat, creating a low-pressure area at the stern that can increase CO levels on board.

backing (wind) Wind changing its direction, counterclockwise in the northern hemisphere, clockwise in the southern hemisphere; opposite of veering.

backsplice A splice in which the strands are reversed and interwoven, to make a rope end.

backstay A stay supporting the mast, running from the masthead to the stern.

ballast Additional weight placed low in the hull to improve stability; ballast may be either internal or external.

bar A sand, mud, or debris shoal, as across the mouth of a river or harbor.

batten down To close all openings, such as hatches, and fasten all loose gear, in heavy weather; wooden hatches used to be covered with a tarpaulin, and then fastened with battens and wedges.

battens Thin flexible strips of wood or plastic, used in batten pockets of a sail to support (stiffen to keep flat) the roach; battens are also used in awnings.

beam One of the principal dimensions of a boat, the width; also, the direction at right angles to the centerline of a vessel, as "the lighthouse is broad on the beam."

beam reach A point of sailing with the apparent wind blowing at right angles to the boat's fore-and-aft line.

bearing The direction of an object (vessel, buoy, etc.) from an observer; bearings can be visual, or by radio or radar.

bear off (1) To turn away from the wind. (2) To turn leeward; also "to bear away."

beating Sailing against the wind, in alternate tacks.

Beaufort wind scale A scale indicating the force of the wind, invented by Admiral Beaufort in 1808; the original scale indicated the effect on a full-rigged frigate under sail; it has been extended to cover effects on shore as well as at sea, plus criteria that can now be measured, such as speed of the wind; the scale usually shows wind forces 0 through 12, but it has been expanded to 17. Each increase of force (number) means a doubling of the pressure (not velocity) of the wind.

becket (1) A loop or eye made in the end of rope or wire. (2) A rope handle.

bedding compound Caulking material used for mating two surfaces, rendering them watertight.

bend One of several types of knots, a combination of turns and tucks, used to fasten a line to a spar or another line; to fasten by means of a bend or knot.

berth (1) A position, as a place to sleep. (2) A place in which a vessel may be made fast.

bight (1) The middle part of a slack rope. (2) A loop. (3) An indentation in a shoreline.

bilge (1) The lowest point of a vessel's interior hull. (2) The part of the exterior between the bottom and the topsides, the "turn of the bilge."

binnacle A compass box or case, or a stand, usually illuminated at night.

binocular A telescopic instrument for the use of both eyes at once, having two tubes, each furnished with lenses and prisms to minimize the size.

bitt A strong post of wood or iron, similar to a samson post, on deck in the bow or the stern, to which anchor, mooring, and towing lines may be fastened.

bitter end (1) Inboard end of an anchor rode. (2) The extreme end of any line.

block-and-tackle Arrangement of blocks (pulleys) and line to gain a mechanical advantage.

boarding ladder A temporary set of steps placed over a vessel's side.

boat (1) A small vessel, propelled by oars, sail, or power. Many consider a boat as being not over 65 feet in length. Another dividing point might be 20 meters (65.6 ft), as used in the Navigation Rules. (2) A vessel that can be carried on board a ship.

boathook A pole with a hook on one end, used for retrieving or picking up objects and for fending off.

bollard A strong vertical fitting, usually iron, on deck or on a pier or wharf, to which mooring lines may be fastened.

boom A spar used to extend the foot of a sail.

boom vang A system of and line to hold the boom down under some sailing conditions.

bosun A boatswain, a petty officer in charge of hull, rigging, and sail maintenance as well as deck operations; other spellings are bos'n, bo's'n, bo'sun.

bosun's chair A seat, sometimes a rigid plank or made of canvas, used to hoist a person aloft to repair rigging; pockets for tools are often included.

bow The forward part of a vessel.

bow & beam bearings A set of bearings on an object ashore or an aid to navigation whose position is known, used to determine distance off.

Bowditch A standard reference work on navigation, containing useful tables and instructional text; it is named after Nathaniel Bowditch, the nineteenth-century author of the first "Bowditch" (Publication No. 9 from NIMA).

bowline The "king of knots," used to make a loop in a line; this knot is simple, strong, virtually slip proof and is very easily untied.

bowsprit A fixed spar, projecting from the bow, to which forestays and/or the headstay are fastened; also useful for anchor handling.

braided line A modern configuration of rope (usually called "line" on board a boat or ship); it may be a single braid or double braid, one braid (core) inside another.

breakwater A structure, usually stone or concrete, built to create waves coming on shore in order to create a harbor or improve an existing one.

breast line Mooring or dock line, extending laterally from the vessel to a pier or float, as distinguished from a spring line, which controls fore and aft movement of the vessel.

bridge (1) The control station of a vessel; the persons in charge of a vessel, or (by extension) of an organization, such as the U.S. Power Squadrons. (2) A structure over water to carry pedestrian, vehicular or railroad traffic.

brightwork (1) Polished brass, bronze or stainless steel aboard a vessel. (2) Varnished wood as trim.

Bristol fashion Shipshape; clean, neat, orderly, and conforming to high standards of seamanship.

broach to, broaching The sudden, unplanned, and uncontrolled turning of a vessel so that the hull is broadside to the seas or to the wind.

broad on the beam At a right angle to a vessel's fore-and-aft axis.

broad reach A point of sailing with the apparent wind broad just aft of the beam.

bulkhead A transverse wall in the hull; the interior compartmentalization of a vessel is created by bulkheads; in some cases bulkheads are watertight, adding to the safety in case of damage to the hull.

buntline hitch A simple, useful hitch for attaching a halyard to a shackle; strong, secure, easily undone.

buoy (1) A floating aid to navigation showing channels or otherwise indicating location, rocks and other obstructions, and prohibited areas on the water; turning points in races. (2) To buoy an anchor is to temporarily fasten the anchor line to a float, so that the anchor need not be raised when a vessel is leaving its anchorage.

burdened vessel Under the Navigation Rules, the vessel that must "give way" to another vessel in a crossing or overtaking situation.

burgee A special flag flown on a vessel or on a flagstaff of a shore installation, indicating either the ownership of the vessel or the identity of a yacht club or similar organization.

camber Curvature of either sail or keel; the curve of the deck usually being higher in the center so that the water can run off.

can A cylindrical buoy, generally green.

canvas (1) Firm, closely woven cloth (originally hemp, linen or cotton) used for sails and awnings. (2) A set of sails; today the word "sailcloth" is generally used for modern sailmaking fabrics such as polyester (Dacron) and nylon.

capsize (1) For a vessel: to turn over. (2) To turn bottom side up.

capstan A vertical winch on deck, used for hauling, such as the anchor line.

cardinal points The four principal compass points: North, East, South, and West.

carlins Fore and aft members of the deck frame; they support the coamings of the cockpit, the cabin trunk sides and the hatch coamings.

carry away To break loose, said of gear that is stressed beyond the strength of its fastenings.

cast off (1) To loose or unfasten. (2) To undo all mooring lines in preparation for departure.

catamaran A twin-hulled vessel, sail or power.

catboat A simple rig for a sailboat, with one mast and one sail, which may be either Marconi rig or with a gaff.

catenary In a rope or chain run between two points, the sag from a straight line due to the effect of gravity.

cavitate, cavitation Turbulence in the water caused by the overfast rotation of a propeller; causes wear on the propeller and a reduction in propeller efficiency.

ceiling (1) The inside lining of the hull. (2) The height of cloud cover.

celestial navigation Position determination (and the total process of navigation based on it) by reference to sun, stars and moon. Usually a sextant measures the altitude of the observed heavenly body, a highly accurate source of time information is used to determine the time of the sight, and tables and/or a navigational electronic calculator are used to determine a position line; the place where two position lines cross is a fix.

centerboard A board or metal plate, moving vertically or pivoting up and down in a slot in the keel, which adds lateral resistance to the hull form of a sailboat; in effect the boat's sideways motion through the water is thus controlled by increasing the area of the keel.

chafe (1) Abrasion. (2) Wear.

chafing gear Cloth, tape, or other material fastened around a line or other rigging to prevent wear.

chain locker Stowage space for anchor chain.

chainplates Fittings on the sides of the hull or the outer edges of the deck of a sailboat, to which the port and starboard rigging, shrouds, are fastened.

chandlery (1) Items of nautical gear. (2) A store where nautical gear is sold.

channel (1) The navigable portion of a waterway. (2) The marked and designated area where there is a known depth of water; boats may not normally anchor in a channel.

Charlie Noble A stovepipe fitting in a cabin top or deck, through which the metal "chimney" of a boat's cooking or heating stove passes; usually equipped with a cooling rim of water and a partial cap, to exclude rain and spray, and to control smoke.

chart Seagoing map; most charts are issued by governmental sources, and their data is based on surveys of the land and underwater areas, showing depths as well as buoys and other aids to navigation; they are updated periodically.

chine The intersection between the topsides and bottom of the hull of a vessel.

chock A rigging fitting, essentially shaped like a U or an O, normally mounted on deck or in the toe rail, to control a rigging or mooring line.

classes Organized groups of boats (essentially for racing), with either identical measurements and specifications, or variable measurements to fit a formula, designed to equalize boat performance to some degree and thus put a premium on skill and tactics.

cleat A rigging fitting to which mooring lines, sail control line such as sheets and halyards, and miscellaneous lines are temporarily attached.

cleat hitch The distinctive crisscross or figure-eight hitch used to fasten (belay) a line to a cleat.

clevis pin A large pin that secures one fitting to another.

clew The lower, after corner of a sail, to which the sheet is attached.

close-hauled Hard on the wind, a point of sailing in which the sheets are hauled tight, enabling the boat to sail "against the wind."

clove hitch A double-lock hitch, generally used around a piling or bollard; easily adjusted, but it can work loose.

club-footed Foot of sail, such as a jib or foresail, supported by a small boom.

coaming A raised edge, as around part or all of a cockpit, that prevents the seawater from entering the boat.

cockpit A space for the crew, lower than the deck and often watertight or self-draining.

cockpit sole The actual floor of a cockpit.

code In signaling, any of several systems used to transmit messages visually, by sound or electronically; alphabet code flags and dot-dash (Morse) system are most often used; in addition to spelling out words, code flags are used in combinations to transmit brief phrases or to describe marine situations such as emergency conditions.

cold molding Process of bending multiple thin layers of wood in sequence with glue to achieve a total desired thickness as opposed to forming by steam bending or sawing.

colors (1) The national ensign. (2) Sometimes applied to all flags flown from a vessel. (3) The act or ceremony of raising the colors, including other flags.

COLREGS USCG term for the International Regulations for Preventing Collisions at Sea, also known as the International Navigation Rules.

come about (1) To tack. (2) To change direction relative to the wind.

companionway A hatch or entrance, from deck to cabin.

compass (1) Navigation instrument, either magnetic needles or bars attached, which floats or pivots in a bowl; older compasses used a system of graduated points while most modern ones use the 0 to 360 degree system. (2) A plotting tool used to draw circles or circular arcs.

cordage A term that includes all rope and small line.

cored construction The use of a core material sandwiched between an outer layer and inner layer, e.g. deck made of fiberglass inner and outer layers and balsa core.

Corinthian An amateur yachtsman or boater.

counter The portion of the hull, at the stern, above the waterline and extending aft.

course (1) The direction in which a vessel is to be steered (2) In racing, the present course or series of courses, often triangular, to be followed.

cowls (scoops) Direct the flow of air and vapors in or out of ducts.

cradle A frame used to support a vessel on land.

cringle A rope loop or circular eye, made on a metal or plastic thimble, used for fastening the corner of a sail, awning, or other canvas item.

critical value table A table prepared for each whole degree of deviation; opposite this is listed on one side the range of compass headings for which that value of deviation is applicable; on the other side is the range of magnetic headings which have that value of deviation.

crossing situation When two vessels meet, not head on or nearly head on but with each having the other forward of a direction 22.5 degrees aft the beam; the vessel having the other on its starboard side is the give-way vessel and must keep clear.

cunningham A line controlling tension along a sail's luff, invented by Briggs Cunningham.

current Horizontal movement of water, as from the normal flow of a river or when caused by the rise and fall of tides.

Dacron Trademark name for a type of polyester fiber, may be cloth or line.

daggerboard A centerboard that is retracted vertically rather than hinged.

danger angle A measured angle between the bearings of two points—such as buoys, landmarks, or rocks—indicates to the mariner an unsafe area for his/her vessel.

davit A swing-out device, a crane, used to hoist; a pair of davits, at the stern or at the side of the vessel, handles a dinghy or other small boat; a single davit at the bow is often used to handle a heavy anchor.

dayboard A sign with a specified geometric shape and color atop a pile or dolphin as part of an aid to navigation; the combination of the dayboard and pile or dolphin if unlighted is a "daybeacon," if lighted it is termed a "light."

daysailer A boat without a cabin that is used for short sails or racing.

dayshape A special geometric marker, such as a black ball, cone, or cylinder hung aloft to indicate a vessel's type, occupation or state; one black ball means "at anchor," three means "aground."

dead ahead, dead astern Direction exactly ahead of or behind a vessel.

deadlight A fixed skylight, comparatively small, in a deck or cabin top, admitting light to the space below; a non-opening port.

dead reckoning The navigation means used to determine position, calculated from the course steered and the speed through the water, without obtaining a fix; a dead reckoning position is indicated on a chart by marking a half circle with a dot on the track line; the time is placed at an angle to the horizontal and to the track line.

deadrise Height between the bottom of a vessel and its widest beam, also expressed as an angle.

departure, point of The last fix obtained by an outward bound vessel; it is marked on the chart as the beginning of the track until the next fix or estimated position. A vessel "takes departure" from such a position.

depth sounder An electronic depth-finding instrument, measuring the time an ultrasonic pulse takes to go from the vessel to the bottom and return, then displaying the result in feet, fathoms or meters.

deviation The amount by which a ship's magnetic compass needle points to one side or the other of magnetic north; iron, steel, magnets, and DC current in wires cause the compass to vary by different amounts on differing headings.

dinghy A small boat used as a tender; the term is also used for a small racing sailboat.

displacement The weight of the water displaced by a floating hull; the volume of water will vary depending on whether it is fresh water or seawater.

displacement hull A vessel supported by its own buoyancy while in motion; see planing hull.

distress signals Standardized or improvised signals, which may be visual, audible or electronic, that are used on board a boat to indicate distress and seek assistance; listed in the Navigation Rules.

ditty bag A small bag for tools and personal items.

dock An enclosed or nearly enclosed water area; a place where vessels can make fast, as at a pier, wharf, or floating structure; frequently used incorrectly to refer to the pier or wharf itself.

dolphin (1) A small group of piles, in the water, tied together into a single structure, generally used for mooring or as part of an aid to navigation. (2) A species of marine mammal. (3) A species of fish.

dorade vent Specially designed deck box ventilation to keep water out with a baffle while letting air in below decks.

douse (1) To drop or lower a sail quickly. (2) To put out a lamp or a fire.

downhaul (1) A rigging line used to haul down. (2) To hold down a spar or sail.

draft (1) The vertical distance from the waterline to the lowest point of the hull or attachments such as propellers and rudders, thus the minimum depth of water in which a vessel will float; a vessel is said to "draw" a certain amount of water. (2) The curvature built into a sail.

dressing ship On national holidays, at regattas, and on other special occasions, yachts often "dress ship" with International Code signal flags; A vessel is dressed at 0800, and remains so dressed until the time of evening colors (while at anchor only, except for a vessel's maiden and final voyages, and participation in a marine parade or other situation).

drift (1) Movement of a vessel through the water without propulsion. (2) Speed of a current.

drydock An enclosed dock from which the water can be pumped out, so a ship can have its lower hull cleaned or repaired.

dry rot Decay of wood timbers, as in a boat, actually occurring in most conditions.

ease To let out a line under full control, gradually as with a sheet or a docking line.

ebb A tidal current flowing toward the sea.

ensign (1) The national flag. (2) The flag of an organization such as the Coast Guard Auxiliary or the U.S. Power Squadrons.

entry Forward-designed section of hull in the water; qualifies the type of hull in terms of efficiency and behavior in relation to wave action (for example, a sharper entry means faster hull speed for a racing hull).

estimated position (EP) A navigational point (less precise than a fix) based on course run, speed, and estimates of such factors as drift caused by wind or currents.

eye splice A fixed loop in the end of a line, made by intertwining strands of rope or by tucking an outer core of double-braid rope back into itself.

fairlead A rigging fitting designed to change the direction of a line, control the line and minimize friction.

fastening (1) Any of several methods of holding planks in a wooden boat to the frames. (2) Screws, nails, rivets. (3) A screw or bolt used to fasten rigging and plumbing fixtures.

fathom A nautical linear measurement, 6 feet, used primarily to measure depth and anchor rodes.

fathometer The formerly trademarked name for one brand (Raytheon) of electronic instrument for measuring depth of water; now used generically for electronic depth sounders.

fender A cushioning device hung between the boat and a float, pier or another craft.

fetch (1) The distance across water over which the wind is or has been blowing. (2) To sail a course that will clear a buoy or shoal, also "lay."

fid A tapered, pointed tool used to separate strands of rope, as in splicing.

figure-eight A knot, usually in the end of a line as a stopper, to prevent the end of the line from passing through a block or fairlead.

fin keel Keel shaped like the fin of a fish, shorter and deeper than a full-length keel.

fix The position of a vessel, determined by bearings, either visual or electronic, or by any other means believed to be acceptably accurate.

flame arresters A safety device, such as a metal mesh protector, to prevent an exhaust backfire from causing an explosion; operates by absorbing heat.

flare (1) A pyrotechnic signal that can indicate distress. (2) The outward curvature of the topsides.

flashing A lighted aid to navigation that is on less than it is off in a regular sequence of single flashes occurring less than 30 times in each minute.

flemish To coil a line spirally, laid flat on deck, either for appearance or to make a mat.

float plan A plan given to a responsible person on shore that tells where you intend to cruise and when you expect to make port again including a description of the boat; a form, not required, is available from many sources (do not attempt to file a plan with the USCG; they do not have the manpower to keep track of boats).

flood An incoming tidal current.

flotsam Wreckage debris floating on the water.

fluke The flat palm-shaped or shovel-shaped part of an anchor (on the end of each arm) that digs in to the bottom to prevent dragging.

flying bridge A high steering position, usually above the normal wheelhouse of a power cruiser, also called a "fly bridge."

following sea Waves from astern.

foot (1) The bottom edge of a sail; also. (2) To steer slightly lower than close-hauled in order to increase boat speed.

fore Located at the front, as of a vessel.

fore-and-aft From stem to stern, from front to back, oriented parallel to the keel.

forecast Formalized weather prediction.

forecastle The forward portion, below decks, of a vessel; the place where the crew is quartered. Pronounced and often spelled fo'c'sle.

foredeck The forward part of the main deck of a vessel.

forestay A stay, from high on the mast to the foredeck; the headstay runs from the top of the mast, or near there. to the bow and is the outermost stay.

forestaysail A sail attached to the forestay, similar to a jib, which is on the headstay.

foretriangle The area bounded by the mast, foredeck, and headstay.

forward On board a vessel, the direction to the front, toward the bow.

fractional rig A rig in which the jib of a sloop does not reach to the top of the mast, a three-quarter rig is an example of this rig.

frames Transverse structural members of a vessel, also called "ribs."

freeboard The vertical distance between the waterline and the top of the deck.

fronts Boundaries between air masses that have different temperatures.

fully battened Sail with battens running full width of the sail horizontally.

furling Folding, rolling, or gathering a sail on its boom when it is not in use.

gaff (1) A spar holding the upper side (head) of a four-sided sail. (2) A device used to bring on board a large fish.

galley The kitchen on a boat or ship.

garboard strake The strake (plank) next to the keel.

gel coat Standard finish of a fiberglass boat.

genoa An overlapping jib.

geographic position Charted position.

give-way vessel The vessel that does not have the right of way in a crossing or overtaking situation; the vessel that is burdened.

grab rail A convenient grip, on a cabin top or along a companion ladder.

great circle A circle formed on a sphere, such as the earth, by the intersection of a plane passing through the center of the sphere. An arc of a great circle is the shortest distance between two points, hence a great circle route is the shortest route between the points.

grommet A ring or eyelet, as in a sail; a rope grommet is a circle made by unlaying the rope, then using one strand spirally, twisted onto itself, replacing the original strands.

gross tonnage The total interior space of a ship, including non-cargo space, computed at 40 cubic feet equals one ton; **net tonnage** is found by subtracting engine rooms, crew's quarters, stores, and navigation space; **displacement tonnage** is the weight of the vessel, which is the same as the weight of the water displaced.

ground swells Swells that become shorter and steeper as they near the shore, because of the shoaling water.

ground tackle Anchor, anchor rode (line or chain), and the shackles and other gear used for attachment.

gunwale The upper edge of the side of a boat, usually a small projection above the deck; toe rail.

guy A rigging line for control, attached to the end of a movable spar.

hail A call to a ship or boat.

half-hitch The simplest knot, usually part of another knot, such as two half-hitches or a fisherman's bend.

halyard A line used to hoist a spar or sail aloft.

hand lead A weight, attached to a line, lowered into the water to find out the depth.

handsomely Slowly and carefully, as to "ease a line handsomely," in a proper manner.

handy-billy Block and tackle (movable).

hank Small snap hook securing the jib luff to the headstay.

harbor (1) A safe anchorage, protected from most storms; may be natural or man-made, with breakwaters and jetties. (2) A place for docking and loading or unloading.

hard over All the way in one direction, as a tiller or wheel can be "hard over" to make an abrupt turn.

hauling (1) Hauling out is removing a boat from the water. (2) Pulling on an anchor line, halyard, or a rope or line is simply called hauling.

hauling part The part of a fall or tackle to which power is applied.

hawse hole An opening in the hull, through which mooring lines are run.

hawsepipes Fittings in the hawse holes through which dock or anchor lines may be run, and, in larger vessels, in which the upper part of the anchor may be stowed.

head (1) The bow or forward part of a vessel. (2) The upper end of a vertical part, such as the rudder head. (3) The upper corner of a triangular sail; the upper edge of a four-sided sail. (4) The toilet on board ship (fixture only or entire compartment).

heading The direction in which a vessel is pointed at any given moment.

headsail Any of several sails set forward of the mast (in the foretriangle).

head seas Waves coming from the direction in which a vessel is heading.

headstay (1) A stay from the bow to a point high on the mast. (2) The foremost stay.

headway Forward motion of a vessel through the water.

heave (1) To pull strongly on a line. (2) To throw a line.

heaving line A light line, coiled and thrown from vessel to vessel or between vessel and shore, to be used for pulling in a larger line, such as a dock line.

heaving to (1) Setting the sails so that a boat makes little headway, usually in a storm or a waiting situation. (2) In power-driven vessels, heading into the seas, or nearly so, and reducing speed to the minimum necessary to maintain control.

heel, heeling To tip, to lean to one side; heeling may result from uneven distribution of weight or the force of the wind; a list is a continuous; a roll is a repeated inclination, from side to side.

heeling error The additional or changing deviation in a compass caused by heeling, when the relative position of heavy iron (keel, engine) is changed so that the magnetic force varies.

helm The tiller, wheel, and other steering gear; a boat is said to have a weather helm if it tends to turn its bow to windward; lee helm if it tends to fall away to leeward.

high tide, high water The highest level reached as a result of tidal action.

hitch (1) A knot attaching a line to an object, such as a cleat, ring, spar. (2) The device used to connect a trailer to a towing vehicle.

horizontal angle An angle, usually measured with a sextant, between two landmarks, providing a line of position (the arc of a circle).

horseshoe buoy Personal Flotation Device (PFD), used in rescues, shaped like a U and mounted in a bracket at the rail; for man-overboard situations.

hydrofoil A type of boat with underwater foils that lifts the hull clear of the water when high speeds are reached.

hydrography The science of surveying the waters of the earth.

in irons Up in the wind and unable to pay off on either tack. A sailboat that loses headway (and therefore steerageway) when attempting to come about is said to be "in irons" or "in stays."

inboard (1) More toward the center of a vessel. (2) inside; a motor fitted inside the boat.

Inflatable boat A craft that has an inflatable structure; an inflatable boat with a rigid bottom is often referred to as a RIB.

Inland Rules Navigation Rules for vessel operations in certain harbors, rivers, lakes, and inland waterways of the United States.

Intracoastal Waterways (ICW) Bays, rivers, and canals along coasts (such as Atlantic and Gulf of Mexico coasts), connected so vessels may travel without entering the open sea.

isobars On a weather map, lines drawn connecting places of equal atmospheric pressure; isobars close together indicate a steeper gradient of pressure and stronger winds.

isogonic lines Lines, on a chart, connecting points of equal magnetic variation.

jetty A structure, usually masonry, projecting out from the shore; a jetty may protect a harbor entrance.

jib A triangular sail, set on the headstay.

jibe To change direction, when sailing with the wind aft, so that the wind comes on a different quarter and the boom swings over to the opposite side; an accidental jibe can be dangerous.

keel The main structural member of a vessel, the backbone; the lateral area beneath the hull to provide steering stability and reduce leeway.

ketch A two-masted sailing rig; the after (mizzen) mast is shorter than the forward (main) mast and stepped forward of the rudder post, so the mizzen sail on a ketch is relatively larger than it might be on a yawl.

king spoke The topmost spoke of a steering wheel when the rudder is in a centered position.

knot (1) Unit of speed, one nautical mile per hour. (2) A general term for a hitch or bend.

laid up Not in commission and ready for use.

latitude Geographic distance north or south of the equator, measured in degrees, minutes, and seconds or fractions of a minute.

launch (1) To move a boat into the water from land. (2) A powerboat used as a ferry between land and a moored boat; also "shore boat."

laying-to Underway with little or no way on; an alternative to anchoring under certain circumstances.

lazarette A small storage compartment at the stern.

lead A shaped weight on a marked line, used to measure water depth and to pick up bottom samples (mud, clay, sand).

lead line, hand lead A weight, attached to a line, lowered into the water to find out the depth.

lee The direction toward which the wind blows, an object sheltered from the wind is "in the lee." A lee shore is the coast lying in the direction toward which the wind is blowing.

leeboards Boards attached to the gunwale (in lieu of an external keel) to reduce leeway.

leech Trailing edge of a sail.

lee helm The tendency of a sailboat to turn the bow to leeward, as distinguished from weather helm, unless corrective rudder action is taken.

leeway Sideways drift of a boat, primarily caused by the wind or a current.

length on the waterline (LWL) The length of a vessel when measured at the line of flotation.

length overall (LOA) The distance between the tip of the bow and the end of the stern, excluding projecting spars or rudder.

lifelines Lines, usually of wire rope, often covered with plastic, at the sides of the boat's deck to keep persons from falling overboard.

life preserver A flotation coat, vest, ring, or cushion; called Personal Flotation Device (PFD) by the USCG.

Light Lists A series of seven volumes published by the USCG for the coastal and inland waters that provide more complete information concerning aids to navigation than can be shown on charts; but they should not be used for navigation in lieu of charts and *Coast Pilots*.

lights Lighthouses or beacons; fixed aids to navigation that are equipped with light sources having certain prescribed characteristics.

line A rope in use aboard a vessel; laid line is formed by twisting three (sometimes four) strands; braided line may be single or braid over a core.

line of position (LOP) A line, straight or curved, along which an observer can be presumed to be located derived from observation or measurement by visual, electronic, or celestial sources; there are two lines: one "real," one drawn on a chart.

linestoppers Also called **jamcleats**; they will keep the tension on a line while stopped or jammed.

list (1) A continuous leaning to one side, often caused by an imbalance in stowage or a leak into one compartment. (2) A *Light List* is a printed listing of aids to navigation, in geographical order.

locker A storage place, a closet.

log (1) A device for measuring distance run through the water. (2) A written record, usually in a book, of a vessel's course, speed, weather encountered, radio transmissions and receptions, as well as other details of navigation and maintenance.

long splice A splice joining two rope ends, made by untwisting strands, thinning and removing the ends, so that the final splice is no thicker than the original line; a long splice will thus go through a block without jamming.

lubber's line The index mark, usually inside the compass, by which the course is read and the vessel is steered.

luff The forward part or leading edge of a sail.

magnetic bearing, course, heading A bearing, course, or heading named in relation to magnetic north; usually this is an intermediate step in converting a "compass" reading related to the direction of the north point of the compass to get a "true" reading related to the direction of true north.

magnetic meridian A line of horizontal magnetic force of the earth to which a compass, without local disturbances (deviation), aligns itself.

magnetic north The direction a compass needle points when there are no local disturbing influences (deviation).

mainsail The sail hoisted on the after side of the mainmast, pronounced "mains'l."

make fast Action of attaching a line, such as making a boat fast to a pier or the shore.

marline Light two-stranded line (formerly of hemp), tarred or untarred, used for lacings, whippings, seizings, and servings.

marlinespike (1) A pointed steel tool for splicing line. (2) That portion of seamanship devoted to the use of lines, knots, and related matters.

masthead light A white light, at or near the masthead, used underway by a vessel under power at night; the range of visibility required varies with the size of the vessel; the arc of visibility is from dead ahead to 22.5 degrees abaft the beam, on both sides.

MAYDAY A radio-telephone distress call, from the French *m'aidez* (help me).

meridian A line passing through both poles and intersecting the equator at right angles, known as longitude. The prime meridian is that of Greenwich (0 degrees).

messenger A light line used to carry another line such as a halyard or a larger hawser from a ship to the shore or to another vessel; see heaving line.

midships Location near the center of a vessel measured either from side to side or fore-and-aft.

mile The statute mile is 5280 feet; the nautical mile is 6076.12 feet (1852 meters exactly).

mizzen The aftermost mast in a ketch, yawl, or schooner with three or more; the mizzen sail is set on this mast.

moored Anchored, made fast to a pier, wharf, etc.

mooring (1) Permanent ground tackle. (2) A place where vessels are kept at anchor.

Morse code A communication code developed by Samuel Morse, originally for the land telegraph; the code, modified for radio use, uses dots and dashes for letters, numerals, and a few special signs.

motorboat A boat propelled by an internal-combustion engine; the U.S. Motor Boat Act divides motorboats into four classes based on length.

motorsailer An auxiliary sailboat with a larger than usual engine.

mouse, mousing Turns of twine, taken across a hook, to prevent accidental unhooking.

nautical mile 6076.12 feet (1852 m), an international standard; for practical purposes, equals one minute of latitude, but not one minute of longitude.

naval architect Architect specializing in marine design.

navigation The art and science of determining a vessel's position and guiding it safely and efficiently to another position; coastal navigation, using visual (surface) reference points, is more usually called piloting; celestial navigation uses observations of heavenly bodies (usually with instruments) and tables or calculators; electronic navigation (radionavigation) is the technical term when electronic devices and systems are used.

navigation lights Lights shown by a vessel that indicate course, position, and status such as fishing or towing.

Navigation Rules The Rules of the Road in the U.S., governing navigation lights, rules for vessels meeting or passing, sound signals, and distress signals; the Rules for International and U.S. waters differ in only a few small details.

neap tide One occurring when the sun and moon are farthest from being in line (quarter and three-quarter moons); neap tides have the least range (rise and fall). *See* spring tide.

net tonnage A vessel's capacity, determined by measuring its hull interior and subtracting the volume of non-cargo spaces (engine room, crew quarters, etc.) *See* gross tonnage.

nylon A polyamide synthetic material with a long-chain molecule; nylon fibers are used for rope and some sailcloth, when elasticity is desirable; hard nylon is used for some rigging parts, such as sheaves.

oarlock A U-shaped, or sometimes O-shaped, pivoting device in which oars are set when rowing.

offshore (1) Out of sight of land. (2) From the land; toward the water.

off-soundings Waters deeper than where depths can normally be measured; usually assumed to 100 fathoms or 200 meters.

outboard (1) Outside or away from a vessel's hull; opposite of inboard. (2 A propulsion unit for boats, attached at the transom; includes motor, driveshaft and propeller; fuel tank and battery may be integral or could be installed separately in the boat.

outdrive A propulsion system for boats, with an inboard motor operating an exterior drive, with driveshaft, gears, and propeller; also called stern drive and inboard/outboard (I/O).

overall length (LOA) The extreme length of a vessel, excluding spars or rigging fittings.

painter A towline or tie-up line for a small boat.

parallax error The error in reading an instrument such as a compass or gauge from off to one side, resulting from the distance between the needle or pointer and the numerical scale.

parcel To wrap tape or other small stuff around a wire or fiber rope, to prevent chafe; usually used with "worming" that fills in the spaces between the twisted strands of rope.

passage (1) One leg of a voyage. (2) A journey.

patent log A device, including rotor on a towline and counter, for measuring distance run and speed.

pay out To release line in a controlled manner, as with an anchor rode.

pelorus A sighting device, without a compass, used to determine relative bearings.

pennant (1) A small flag, typically a signal flag. (2) A short length of line or cable between a mooring chain and the boat, sometimes called a pendant.

PFD U.S. official terminology for life preserver; personal flotation device.

pier A structure, usually wood or masonry, extending into the water, used as a landing place for boats and ships.

pile, piling A vertical wooden, concrete, or metal pole, driven into the bottom; may be a support for a pier or floats or an aid to navigation; also used for mooring.

piloting Navigation using visual reference points (aids to navigation, landmarks, etc.) and water depths.

pitch (1) The alternating rise and fall of the bow of a vessel proceeding through waves. (2) The theoretical distance advanced by a propeller in one revolution. (3) tar and resin used for caulking between the planks of a wooden vessel.

planing hull A hull designed so that forward speed creates water lift, reducing friction and increasing speed.

planking Lengths of wood used for the external skin or the deck of a vessel.

Pleasure Vessel License A form of USCG documentation that does not allow commercial use.

plumb bow Hull with vertical bow shape.

Polyester Synthetic material (typical trade name, Dacron) used for fibers for rope and sailcloth; polyester is stronger and has less elasticity than nylon.

port (1) Left, as the port side of a boat, or a direction, as "to turn to port." (2) An opening, for light and/or ventilation, in the side of a vessel. (3) General area of a shore establishment having facilities for landing and maintaining vessels.

port tack A sailing vessel with the wind coming from the left, or port, side is said to be on the port tack; such a vessel normally does not have the right of way when meeting a vessel on the starboard tack.

position finding The process of determining the position of a vessel on a chart or in the water.

pram A small boat used as a tender; a dinghy in the U.S., usually with a squared-off bow.

prime meridian The meridian of longitude through Greenwich, England (0°).

privileged vessel One having right-of-way, both course and speed, when meeting another vessel.

psychrometer A weather instrument, usually two hygrometers, one dry and one with a wet bulb, to measure the moisture in the air.

pulpit The forward railing structure at the bow of a boat.

purchase (1) A mechanical device for lifting or pulling. (2) On board ship, the term is used specifically for a block and tackle.

Q flag A plain yellow flag—the letter "Q" of the International Code Flag set—must be hoisted by any vessel arriving in the port of a country from the waters of another country; it must be kept flying until the vessel is "cleared" by customs and immigration officials of the arrival port.

quarter The side of a vessel, from amidships to the stern; the term is used to identify dock lines as in "fasten the quarter spring."

quartering sea Seas coming from the quarter.

quay A structure, usually of masonry or stonework, parallel to the water's edge, where vessels can make fast, and load and unload cargo; a wharf.

radar An electronic system using super high-frequency radio waves; when reflected they show on a screen the position, size and distance of an object; radar is used at night and in bad visibility for both collision avoidance and navigation.

radio bearing A direction determined by radio.

radio direction finder (RDF) A radio receiver with special antenna and circuitry used to determine the direction to a source of radio waves.

radionavigation (1) Electronic piloting. (2) The determination of a vessel's position, course, and speed by various electronic devices and systems.

rafting, rafted The mooring procedure for two or

more vessels, made fast side-by-side at a dock or on an anchor or mooring buoy.

rail (1) A protective edge on deck. (2) A solid bar on supports, similar to a lifeline.

raised deck Deck level arranged to be higher than the actual gunwale.

rake (1) The slant, fore and aft, of a mast. (2) The slant of a ship's funnels, bow, or stern.

reach, reaching (1) To sail across the wind. (2) A channel between the mainland and an island.

reciprocal A direction precisely opposite another; differing by 180°.

reef (1) An underwater barrier, such as rock or coral. (2) To shorten sail by reducing the area exposed, by rolling the sail on a boom or tying in reef points.

reeving Leading a line through a block or fairlead as in setting up a purchase, or rigging a halyard.

registration The numbering or licensing of a boat.

relative bearing A direction in relation to the bow of a vessel, expressed in degrees.

reverse sheer The reverse of normal sheer. The sheerline rises above the straight line from stem to stern instead of curving below.

rhumb line A straight line on a Mercator chart; it intersects all meridians at the same angle; for short distances it provides and adequate course, but a great circle is actually the shorter distance.

RIB *See* rigid inflatable.

ribs Another term for frames, the transverse members of a wooden hull to which the planks are fastened.

riding light The anchor light.

rig (rigs) (1) The spars, standing rigging, and sails; (2) To make a boat ready for sailing or to prepare a sail or piece of gear for use.

rigging The wire rope, rods, lines, hardware, and other equipment that support and control the spars and sails; standing rigging is semi-permanent once set up; running rigging is continually adjusted as the sails are hoisted, doused, trimmed, or reefed.

right-hand lay The twist of stranded rope commonly used, with the strands twisting to the right; Z-twist.

right-of-way In both normal boat operation and racing, certain boats (privileged or stand-on vessels) have priority in crossing or overtaking situations, or at turns in races; the other craft (burdened or give-way vessel) must yield to the boat that has the right-of-way in particular situation; the boat on starboard tack, or the vessel coming from the right in the case of power boats, will have the right-of-way under most conditions.

rigid inflatable Inflatable boat with a rigid bottom (also called a RIB).

rode The anchor line, which may be line (fiber rope), chain, or a combination of line and chain.

roll The alternating motion of a boat, leaning alternately to port and starboard; the motion of a boat about its fore-and-aft axis.

roller furling The method of furling a sail by winding it on a stay, most used for jibs but used for mainsails on some cruising boats.

roller reefing Reduction of sail area by winding the sail on a rotating boom.

rolling hitch A knot useful for attaching a line to another line or to a spar.

rope Cordage, lines made of fiber or steel; rope may be braided or formed with twisted strands; when in use aboard ships it is generally called line.

round turn A turn, of line, around an object or a line; part of a knot.

rub rail, strake, or guard An outer member on the side of a vessel's hull, designed to absorb friction and pounding from contact with pilings, docks, etc.

rules of the road A general term for the regulations governing vessels, used to prevent collisions; in the U.S. the technical name is Navigation Rules; the rules vary slightly for inland and international waters, but are generally similar.

running fix A navigation fix obtained by using a line of position (LOP) taken at or near the current time together with another earlier LOP that has been advanced for the movement of the vessel between these two times.

running lights The required lights, called navigation lights, that a vessel shows at night or in poor visibility, to indicate position, course, and status.

running rigging The adjustable lines (and certain hardware items) for the control of spars and sails.

safety harness Harness with webbing used with a safety line to lessen chances of persons on deck falling overboard.

sailboard More or less a large surfboard with a mast and small sail partially supported by the person standing who steers by shifting both the positions of the sail and his or her weight on the board.

samson post In a small vessel, a single bitt forward used to fasten the anchor and dock lines.

satellite navigation Position finding using radio transmissions from satellites orbiting in space with sophisticated on-board automatic equipment.

schooner A fore-and-aft rigged sailing vessel with two or more masts, with the foremast shorter than the mainmast.

scope The ratio of length of anchor rode in use to the vertical distance from the bow of the vessel to the bottom of the water.

screw A propeller; sometimes called a wheel.

scudding Running before the wind in a gale.

scuppers Drain holes on deck, in the toe rail, or in bulwarks, or (with drain pipes) in the deck itself.

scuttlebutt Gossip, rumors, so called because sailors used to gather around the scuttlebutt, a cask for drinking water.

sea anchor Canvas shaped like a parachute or a cone with an opening at the tip to keep a boat's bow to the seas in open water and reduce drift to a minimum; not a means of anchoring to the bottom.

sea cock A valve placed on the inside of a through-hull fitting to regulate the flow of water from the outside into the hull.

seakindly Comfortable in rough seas, moving through the water without undue motion or strain; said of a vessel's hull design.

seamanship All the arts and skills of boat handling, ranging from maintenance and repairs to steering, anchoring, docking, sail handling, marlinespike work, and rigging.

seiche An oscillation of the surface of a lake or landlocked sea that varies in period from a few minutes to several hours.

seizing Binding two lines together, or a rope to a spar, and so on, using light line.

sentinel Weight suspended from an anchor rode to help keep the pull on the anchor as horizontal as possible to prevent dragging in rough weather; also called a "kellet."

serving Covering and protecting a portion of a line, to prevent wear; a serving may be as simple as a whipping (small stuff wrapped around) or more elaborate, with worming, parceling, and the addition of waterproofing.

set (1) To raise a sail. (2) The direction of a current.

sextant A precision navigating instrument, used for measuring angles, as in celestial navigation when the altitudes of heavenly bodies are taken, or in piloting, when the known heights of objects ashore or the known distance of two objects from each other can be used to find distance.

shackle A metal link fitting with a pin across the throat, used to connect lines to an anchor, fasten blocks to a spar in rigging, or a line to a sail.

sheave A grooved wheel or pulley over which rope or rigging wire runs, used to change the direction of force; often sheaves are parts of blocks.

sheer (1) The curvature of the deck, fore and aft, as seen from the side. (2) A turn off course, from poor helmsmanship or difficult steering. (3) A swing, as on a moored boat.

sheet A line used to control a sail's lateral movement, either directly or by limiting the movement of a boom or other spar.

sheet bend A knot useful for bending a line to an eye or to join two lines of different sizes.

ship (1) A large seagoing vessel. (2) A three-mastered sailing vessel with square sails, called "full-rigged," on each mast. (3) To take something aboard, as water in rough seas. (4) To place gear in place, as to ship a rudder or to ship oars, bringing them inboard when not in use.

shipshape In good order, in good condition, properly rigged and ready.

shrouds Fixed rigging on either side of the mast.

sidelights Red and green navigation lights, visible from forward or on the beam. *See* running lights.

signal halyard Halyard for hoisting the signal flags and pennants.

slack (1) Not moving. (2) Loose. (3) To ease.

slack water The period of little or no water movement between flood and ebb tidal currents.

sliding hatch Hatch using slides for opening.

slip (1) A berth for a boat between two piers or floats or piles. (2) The percentage difference between the theoretical and the actual distance that a propeller advances when turning in water under load.

small stuff Cordage in small sizes, such as marline, spun yarn, sail twine; primarily used for whippings and servings.

snub a line To check a running rope quickly, usually by tension around a bitt or cleat.

sole The cabin or cockpit deck.

soundings Measurements of water depth as shown on a chart; a vessel is "off soundings" if in water too deep to use a long (deep sea) lead line; inside the 100 fathom line is usually "on soundings."

spars Masts, booms, gaffs, and poles used in sailboat rigging; today spars are made of wood, aluminum extrusions, and composites of synthetics.

spinnaker A three-cornered sail of light cloth, usually nylon, used in downwind sailing.

splice To join two lines, or make an eye, by tucking strands or otherwise interweaving parts of rope; braided rope that has a core and a cover is usually spliced by tucking one inside the other.

spring line One of the standard dock lines, used to control fore and aft motion of a boat made fast in to a pier or float.

spring tide One that occurs when there is a new moon, with the sun and moon conjunction, or when there is a full moon, the moon and sun being in opposition; at such times, high tides are higher than normal, and low tides are lower; the tidal range is greater. *See* neap tide.

squall A sudden and violent windstorm often accompanied by rain; a line squall or line of squalls quite often accompanies an advancing cold front.

square knot Another name for the reef knot, useful for tying two ends of a line together, as around an object; not a suitable knot to use when fastening two lines where the strain will be intermittent.

square rigged Vessel rigged with sails that are hung laterally and of square shape.

stanchion A metal post, used to hold lifelines along a deck.

stand Period of time when vertical rise or fall of the tide has stopped.

standing part (1) The portion of a line not used in making a knot, or the part of the line around which the knot may be tied. (2) In a block and tackle, the part of the purchase that does not move when power is applied to the hauling part.

standing rigging The permanent stays and shrouds, as well as some other rigging parts, used mainly to hold up the mast and take the strain of the sails; although necessarily somewhat adjustable the standing rigging is not continually changed as is the running rigging.

stand-on vessel The boat that has the right of way in a crossing or overtaking situation; the privileged vessel. *See* give-way vessel.

starboard (1) The right side of a vessel as related to facing the bow; the starboard side remains starboard no matter what the orientation of a person on board. (2) The right bank of a river as you face in the direction that the river flows is called its "starboard" bank, thus related to the river's flow *downstream*, not to the vessel herself.

starboard tack A vessel sailing with the wind coming over the starboard side is on the starboard tack and generally has the right-of-way over a boat on the port tack.

stateroom Sleeping quarters for guests or captain.

statute mile Unit of measurement on land and most U.S. inland waters, 5,280 feet. *See* nautical mile.

stays Rigging, generally wire or roods, used to support the masts in a fore- and-aft direction and to carry certain sails.

staysail An additional sail that is set between the mast and the jib, or between masts.

steadying sail Sail hoisted more for steadying effect of the wind on it than for propulsion.

steerageway Sufficient motion through the water to enable a vessel to respond to its rudder.

stem The forward member of the hull, or the corresponding portion of the hull in composite construction.

step (1) At the base of the mast, the special part of the boat in which the heel of the mast is set. (2) To raise the mast and put it in place.

stepped Referring to the mast, keel-stepped or deck-stepped.

stern The after portion of the boat.

stern drive An inboard/outboard engine system, with the motor inside the hull; steering is done by turning the outboard (propeller) unit.

stern line The dock or mooring line that runs from the stern of a vessel to the pier, float, or pile.

sternway Opposite of headway; having a reverse motion through the water.

stow To put in the proper place.

strakes Lines of planking, as from stem to stern. *See* sheer strake *and* garboard strake.

stuffing box A through-hull fitting for the drive shaft or rudder post, also called a gland.

suit of sails The full complement of a boat's sails.

superstructure Cabins and other structures above deck.

surf Waves breaking on a shore, reef, or bar.

survey Inspection of a vessel for any reason by a qualified professional (marine surveyor).

swamp To fill with water, not from a leak but from water coming over the deck and gunwales.

swell A long, large wave that does not crest; swells come from such a distance that the wind causing them is not apparent locally.

swim platform Low platform installed at the transom for ease of boarding.

tack (1) The forward bottom corner of a sail, or either bottom corner of a square sail. (2) Each leg of a zigzag course sailed to windward or downwind.

tackle A purchase, a block and tackle, a combination rig of one or more blocks with lines to obtain mechanical advantage.

tack rag A slightly sticky cloth used to pick up dust and dirt from brightwork before varnishing.

telltale A wind-direction indicator, mounted on the rigging, sail, or mast.

tender (1) A small boat accompanying a yacht or other recreational vessel, used to transport persons, gear, and supplies; a dinghy. (2) A vessel is said to be tender if it is relatively unstable.

tensile strength The load, in pounds of "pull," at which a rope, chain, or other item would break.

thimble Metal fitting used in rigging, forming a reinforced place of attachment.

throat The forward upper corner of a four-sided fore-and-aft sail; the point where the throat halyard attaches.

thwart A crossways seat, usually contributing to structural strength in a rowboat or other small open boat.

tides The vertical rise and fall of ocean water, and waters affected by the ocean, caused by the gravitational forces of the moon and the sun.

tiller An arm or lever attached to the top of a rudder post for the purpose of controlling the position of the rudder and so steering the craft.

toe rail The low bulwark on a small decked boat.

tonnage A measure of the capacity or displacement of a vessel. *See* gross tonnage, net tonnage.

topping lift A running rigging line to control a spar; typically an adjustable topping lift would run over a sheave or through a block at the top of the mast down to the end of a boom or spinnaker pole.

topsides (1) The sides of a vessel above the waterline. (2) On deck as opposed to below deck.

track (1) Metal or plastic rigging fitting, used to control spars, blocks and other rigging parts. (2) The path, normally shown on a chart, between one position and another, as a dead reckoning track.

Traffic Separation Scheme (TSS) A plan, generally internationally agreed on, by which vessels in congested areas use one-way lanes to lessen the danger of collisions.

transom The transverse part of the stern.

trim, trimmed (1) The way in which a vessel floats, on an even keel, or trimmed by the head (bow) or stern, for example; adjustable by shifting ballast. (2) To set sails, to adjust by means of sheets and certain other rigging lines.

trip line A line fast to the crown of an anchor by means of which the anchor can be hauled out when dug in too deeply or fouled; a similar line used on a sea anchor to bring it aboard.

true course A course corrected for variation and deviation; one that is referenced to geographic north.

true north Geographic north.

true wind The actual direction and force of the wind, as distinct from apparent wind as felt by a person on board or indicated by a telltale, which varies with the speed and direction of the vessel.

tumblehome The inward curving of the topsides, above the waterline.

tune (1) To adjust the rigging and sails for maximum efficiency. (2) To adjust an engine for optimum efficiency.

tunnel hull Hull with tunnels shaped for the propeller to reduce draft.

turnbuckle A threaded, adjustable rigging fitting, used for stays, lifelines, and sometimes other rigging.

turning circle The course followed by a boat when it is turning; the smallest possible circle when the rudder is hard over.

twine Small stuff, light line used for whippings or servings; sail twine is also used for sewing.

two-blocked Fully closed up, raised as far as the gear permits, as when both blocks in a purchase are drawn completely together.

two half-hitches A useful knot, in which the hitches are made upon the standing part of the line and then drawn up (tightened).

underway A vessel not at anchor or aground or made fast to the shore.

Underwriters Laboratories One of the principal testing organizations involved in setting safety standards in the United States.

upwind To the windward of.

USPS United States Power Squadrons, a private membership organization that specializes in boating education and good boating practices.

V-drive Mechanism used with an engine installation that has the normally aft-facing end of the engine facing forward.

V-hull Hull shaped in a V.

variation A compass "error" resulting from the fact that at most points on the earth's surface the direction of the magnetic lines of force is not toward the geographic north pole or south pole; at any location, the difference between a true direction and a magnetic direction.

vector A line drawn to represent magnitude and direction, such as leeway a boat makes in a given time period as a result of wind or water current.

veer (1) To change direction, to swerve. (2) To veer out is to let out rope, as an anchor line. (3) When the wind veers it changes direction clockwise, as opposed to backing (counterclockwise).

vessel A boat, ship, or other moving, floating craft; a barge is a vessel, a float at a pier is not a vessel.

VHF radio A Very High Frequency electronic communications system.

voyage A complete trip, as distinguished from a passage.

wake The track in the water of a moving vessel; commonly used for the disturbance of the water (waves) resulting from the passage of the vessel's hull.

wash The loose or broken water left behind a vessel as it moves along; the surging action of waves.

weather helm The tendency of a vessel to turn to windward, requiring a slight amount of helm to keep it on course; normally this is considered a sailboat safety element.

weather shore The coast lying in the direction from which the wind is blowing, as opposed to a lee shore. *See* lee.

weather side Side of a boat upon which the wind is blowing.

well-found With adequate equipment and stores, well supplied and fitted out.

wetted surface The area of the wetted part of a hull (including rudder) in the water, affecting speed.

wharf A structure, parallel to the shore, for docking vessels.

wheel (1) The steering wheel. (2) A propeller.

whipping Twine wound around a line, as on the end or at an eye splice, to add strength and prevent fraying or abrasion.

whistle signal A standard communication signal between boats, to indicate change of course, danger, or other situations.

Wide Area Augmentation System (WAAS) An FAA radionavigation system that transmits corrections to basic GPS signals to improve position accuracy.

wide berth To pass well clear of another vessel or an object.

winch A device, on deck, on a spar, or otherwise mounted, which is used to haul on a line; if geared or used with a handle (lever) it provides a mechanical advantage.

windage Wind resistance.

windlass A special form of winch, a rotating drum device for hauling a line or chain.

windward The direction from which the wind is blowing.

working sails The sails used in normal winds, as distinguished from light weather sails or storm sails.

worm To fill in the spaces in laid rope, as part of the procedure known as worm-and-parcel.

yacht A pleasure vessel, a pleasure boat; in American usage, the idea of size and luxury is conveyed, either sail or power.

yard (1) A spar, crossing the mast, on which square sails are fitted. (2) A place where boats are stored, constructed, or repaired.

yaw To swing or steer off course, as when running with a quartering sea.

yawl A rig for two-masted sailboats, in which there is a mainmast and a smaller mizzen mast, stepped aft of the rudder post.

Index

PHOTO CREDITS

6 Katie Dietz/Camera Graphics; 7 Courtesy Motor Boating & Sailing; 8 Courtesy Motor Boating & Sailing; 10 Courtey New York Yacht Club; 11 Rosenfeld Collection/Mystic Seaport Museum; 12 Courtesy Carver Boat Corp.; 14 (top left) Courtesy Benford Design Group; 14 (lower left) Courtesy Hinckley Co.; 15 (top left) Ed Homonylo; 15 (bottom right) Courtesy Catamaran Co.; 16 (top right) Courtesy Vaudrey Miller Yachts NZ Ltd.; 17 Courtesy Sea-Doo/Bombardier; 19 Ed Homonylo; 20 (top right) Courtesy C. Raymond Hunt Associates; 22 (top left) Courtesy C&C International Yachts; 22 (bottom right) Courtesy Grady-White Boats Inc.; 25 Courtesy C&C International Yachts; 26 Ed Homonylo; 27 Courtesy Boston Whaler; 28 (top left) Courtesy Sea Ray Boats; 28 (lower right) Ed Homonylo; 29 Courtesy Four Winns, a member of the Genmar family; 33 (top left) Eric Schweikardt; 33 (lower right) Ed Homonylo; 34 Ed Homonylo; 35 Courtesy Sea Ray Boats; 37 (top left) Elbert S. Maloney; 37 (top right) Elbert S. Maloney; 37 (lower right) Courtesy Freedom Fenders; 39 Eric Schweikardt; 40 Courtesy Chesapeake Yachting Center; 41 Courtesy Sea Ray Boats; 43 Courtesy Volvo Penta of North America; 44 (top left) Courtesy Yamaha Motors; 44 (lower right) Courtesy Mercury Marine; 46 Courtesy Johnson Marine Products; 48 Courtesy U.S. Coast Guard; 49 (top) Courtesy U.S. Coast Guard; 50 Courtesy Marine Electronics; 52 Courtesy U.S. Coast Guard; 53 Eric Schweikardt; 54 Courtesy Reliance Foundry Ltd.; 55 Courtesy Deck to Dock Inc.; 56 Courtesy N.Y. Canal Corp.; 59 Courtesy U.S. Department of Transportation; 60 Courtesy U.S. Coast Guard; 61 Courtesy Sea Doo/Bombardier; 62 Courtesy Vanguard Sailboats; 63 (top left) Eric Schweikardt; 63 (bottom right) Eric Schweikardt; 64 (bottom right) Eric Schweikardt); 66 Courtesy U.S. Coast Guard; 67 Courtesy U.S. Coast Guard; 70 Courtesy N.Y. City Police Department; 72 Courtesy Dan Fales; 75 (top left) Eric Schweikardt; 75 (bottom right) Jerry L. Routt; 78 Courtesy Dan Fales; 83 Eric Schweikardt; 88 Courtesy Mercury Marine; 94 Courtesy Mustang Survival Corp.; 95 Courtesy Stearns Inc.; 97 Courtesy Amerex Corp.; 101 Eric Schweikardt; 106 (top left) Philip C. Jackson; 106 (lower right) Courtesy Raritan Engineering Co., Inc.; 110 (top left) Ed Homonylo; 110 (lower right) Courtesy Forespar Products Corp.; 111 (top left) Courtesy Zodiac of North America; 111 (lower right) Courtesy Johnson Marine Products; 112 Robert Steimle; 113 Eric Schweikardt; 114 (bottom left) Courtesy ITT Industries Jabsco, Rule & Flojet; 114 (bottom right) Courtesy ITT Industries Jabsco, Rule & Flojet; 115 (top left) Courtesy Fireboy-Xintex Marine Safety Equipment; 115 (bottom right) Courtesy Fireboy-Xintex Marine Safety Equipment; 116 Courtesyof ACR Electronics, Inc.; 117 Ed Homonylo; 118 Courtesy Volvo Penta of North America; 119 Courtesy Kohler Power Systems; 122 Courtesy U.S. Department of Transportation; 123 Eric Schweikardt; 131 (top left) Elbert S. Maloney; 131 (lower left) Elbert S. Maloney; 131 (lower right) Courtesy Sea-Dog; 132 Courtesy Sea Dog; 144 Courtesy Sea-Dog; 146 Courtesy U.S. Coast Guard; 149 Eric Schweikardt; 153 Eric Schweikardt; 174 Courtesy Sea Ray Boats; 178 (top right) Courtesy Egg Harbor Yacht Co.; 179 Eric Schweikardt; 181 Courtesy Twin Disc; 185 Courtesy Correct Craft Inc.; 189 (all) Ed Homonylo; 196 Eric Schweikardt; 197 Eric Schweikardt; 199 Eric Schweikardt; 202 Courtesy Freedom Fenders; 205 Ed Homonylo; 211 Eric Schweikardt; 213 (all) Ed Homonylo; 217 (all) Ed Homonylo; 220 Courtesy Yamaha Motor Corp., USA; 222 Eric Schweikardt; 223 (lower left) Courtesy Grady White Boats; 227 Courtesy Ranger Boats, a member of the Genmar family; 228 (top right) Courtesy Talon Boats; 228 (lower left) Courtesy Yamaha Motor Corp., USA; 229 (top left) Courtesy Yamaha Motor Corp., USA; 232 Courtesy SeaSense Marine Accessories; 233 (top right) Courtesy Tie Down Engineering, Inc.; 233 (lower left) Courtesy Zodiac of North America; 235 Courtesy Yamaha Motor Corp., USA; 237 Courtesy Four Winns, a member of the Genmar family; 239 Eric Schweikardt; 241 Ed Homonylo; 244 (top left) Courtesy Boat Master; 244 (bottom left) Courtesy Boat Master; 247 Ed Homonylo; 249 Courtesy Trailex, Inc.; 250 (top left) Courtesy Boat Master; 250 (bottom left) Courtesy PowerWinch; 251 Eric Schweikardt; 252 Courtesy Boat Master; 254 Courtesy Mercury Marine; 255 (top left) Eric Schweikardt; 255 (Bottom Right) Eric Schweikardt; 258 Courtesy Canvas Craft; 262 (all) Ed Homonylo; 263 (all) Ed Homonylo; 264 (all) Ed Homonylo; 265 (top left) Ed Homonylo; 265 (bottom right) Eric Schweikardt; 268 Courtesy Zodiac of North America; 269 Courtesy Bayliner Yachts; 274 Eric Schweikardt; 285 Courtesy Vanguard Sailboats; 289 Ed Homonylo; 291 Eric Schweikardt; 305 Courtesy Harken Fittings; 306 (all) Eric Schweikardt; 308 Eric Schweikardt; 309 Eric Schweikardt; 311 Ed Homonylo; 313 Courtesy Jeanneau Trimarans; 316 Eric Schweikardt; 318 Courtesy Tie Down Engineering, Inc.; 320 (top left) Courtesy Fortress Anchors; 320 (bottom right) Courtesy Simpson Lawrence USA; 321 Courtesy Simpson Lawrence USA; 322 (top left) Courtesy Bruce Anchor Group; 322 (bottom right) Courtesy Creative Marine Products; 323 (top left) Courtesy Best Marine Imports; 323 (bottom right) Courtesy Best Marine Imports; 326 (all) Eric Schweikardt; 327 (all) Eric Schweikardt; 329 (all) Eric Schweikardt; 331 Eric Schweikardt; 327 Courtesy Taylor Made Products; 329 Courtesy Tie Down Engineering, Inc.; 342 Eric Schweikardt; 344 (top left) Courtesy Davis Instrument Corp.; 344 (bottom right) Eric Schweikardt; 347 Eric Schweikardt; 350 Ed Homonylo; 353 Courtesy U.S. Coast Guard; 360 Story Litchfield; 363 Eric Schweikardt; 369 Courtesy Sea Ray Boats; 372 Eric Schweikardt; 374 (all) Eric Schweikardt; 375 (bottom right) Eric Schweikardt; 378 Courtesy U.S. Power Squadrons; 378 Courtesy U.S. Coast Guard Auxiliary; 379 (top left) Courtesy American Red Cross; 379 (bottom right) Courtesy American Boat & Yacht Council; 381 (bottom right) Courtesy National Fire

Prevention Association; **382** Eric Schweikardt; **383** Eric Schweikardt; **383** Eric Schweikardt; **386** Courtesy Fireboy-Xintex Marine Safety Equipment; **387** Courtesy SeaSense Marine Accessories; **394** Courtesy Datrex Inc.; **395** Robert Chartier; **398** Courtesy Broadwater Marine Stoves; **400** Eric Schweikardt; **408** Courtesy U.S. Coast Guard; **414** Courtesy U.S. Coast Guard; **419** Courtesy U.S. Coast Guard; **423** Ed Homonylo; **425** Courtesy Port Supply, Watsonville, CA; **426** Courtesy Nick Souza/Maersk; **428** (top right) Courtesy U.S. Coast Guard; **428** (bottom left) Eric Schweikardt; **429** Courtesy U.S. Coast Guard; **432** Robert Steimle; **436** Courtesy Ritchie Navigation; **437** Courtesat of Weems & Plath; **440** Eric Schweikardt; **443** Eric Schweikardt; **445** Courtesy KVH Industries, Inc.; **471** Courtesy Ritchie Navigation; **473** Eric Schweikardt; **476** Courtesy U.S. Coast Guard; **477** (top left) Courtesy U.S. Coast Guard; **477** (bottom left) Courtesy U.S. Coast Guard; **477** (bottom right) Courtesy U.S. Coast Guard; **478** (top left) Courtesy U.S. Coast Guard; **478** (lower right) Courtesy U.S. Coast Guard; **479** Courtesy U.S. Coast Guard; **481** Eric Schweikardt; **482** Eric Schweikardt; **489** Eric Schweikardt; **491** Courtesy N.O.A.A.; **492** (top left) Courtesy N.O.A.A.; **492** (bottom left) Courtesy N.O.A.A.; **492** (bottom middle) Courtesy N.O.A.A.; **492** (bottom right) Courtesy N.O.A.A.; **503** Eric Schweikardt; **535** Eric Schweikardt; **545** Courtesy Furuno Marine Electronics; **556** Courtesy Davis Instrument Corp.; **562** Courtesy Weems & Plath; **563** (top right) Courtesy Weems & Plath; **563** (bottom right) Courtesy Weems & Plath; **564** (bottom left) Courtesy Weems & Plath; **564** (bottom right) Courtesy Weems & Plath; **565** (top left) Courtesy Weems & Plath; **565** (bottom right) Courtesy Weems & Plath; **566** (top left) Eric Schweikardt; **566** (bottom right) Courtesy KVH Industries, Inc.; **567** (all) Courtesy Weems & Plath; **568** Courtesy Yamaha Motors; **569** (top right) Courtesy Yamaha Motors; **569** (bottom right) Courtesy Weems & Plath; **570** Robert Chartier; **576** (all) Eric Schweikardt; **581** Eric Schweikardt; **598** Eric Schweikardt; **612** Ed Homonylo; **613** Eric Schweikardt; **620** Eric Schweikardt; **621** Courtesy KVH Industries, Inc.; **623** Ed Homonylo; **624** Courtesy Weems & Plath; **633** Courtesy Midland Radio Corp.; **635** Courtesy Furuno Marine Electronics; **647** Ed Homonylo; **648** (top left) Eric Schweikardt; **648** (bottom right) Courtesy West Marine; **649** Courtesy Trace Engineering Co.; **652** Courtesy Kohler Power Systems; **654** Courtesy Newmar; **656** Elbert S. Maloney; **657** (top right) Courtesy Blue Sea Systems; **657** (bottom right) Courtesy Xantrex Technology Inc.; **660** Courtesy United Solar Systems; **661** Ed Homonylo; **666** Courtesy Blue Sea Systems; **667** Courtesy Paneltronics; **672** (all) Ed Homonylo; **673** (all) Ed Homonylo; **674** (top right) Courtesy Marine Air Sysytems; **674** (bottom left) Courtesy Bayliner Yachts; **677** (all) Eric Schweikardt; **680** Courtesy Vaudrey Miller Yachts NZ Ltd.; **693** Courtesy ICOM America Inc.; **695** (top right)

Courtesy Raytheon Marine; **695** (bottom left) Courtesy Courtesy SEA, A Division of Datamarine International, Inc.; **701** Courtesy ICOM America, Inc.; **703** Courtesy Furuno Marine Electronics; **705** Courtesy ACR Electronics, Inc.; **707** Courtesy Furuno Marine Electronics; **711** Courtesy Cobra Electronics, Inc.; **712** Courtesy Cobra Electronics, Inc.; **715** Courtesy Sea Tel, Inc.; **718** Courtesy Raymarine; **722** Courtesy Sea Ray Boats; **724** (top left) Courtesy Silva; **724** (bottom right) Courtesy Humminbird; **725** Courtesy Furuno Marine Electronics; **728** Courtesy Silva; **730** Courtesy Vaudrey Miller Yachts NZ, Ltd.; **735** Courtesy Furuno Marine Electronics; **736** (bottom left) Courtesy Silva; **736** (bottom right) Courtesy Furuno Marine Electronics; **737** Courtesy Marine Computer Systems; **740** Courtesy Furuno Marine Electronics; **741** Courtesy Furuno Marine Electronics; **743** Courtesy Marine Computer Systems; **744** Courtesy Davis Instrument Corp.; **746** Courtesy SiTex; **747** Ed Homonylo; **749** Coutesy of Silva; **750** Courtesy New York Canal Corp.; **753** (all) Eric Schweikardt; **754** (top left) Courtesy Guntersville Yacht Club; **754** (bottom right) Ed Homonylo; **755** (top left) Courtesy Arizona Office of Tourism; **755** (bottom right) Ed Homonylo; **761** Courtesy Army Corp of Engineers; **763** Eric Schweikardt, Courtesy Bayliner Yachts; **765** Eric Schweikardt, Courtesy Bayliner Yachts; **768** Ed Homonylo; **770** Courtesy NY Canal Corp.; **771** (top right) Courtesy NY Canal Corp.; **771** (bottom right) Courtesy National Park Service; **774** Robert Steimle; **777** Courtesy New England Ropes; **780** Ed Homonylo; **781** (top right) Courtesy Davis Instrument Corp.; **781** (bottom right) Courtesy Southern Crown Boatworks; **782** Ed Homonylo; **784** Eric Schweikardt; **795** Courtesy Harken Fittings; **801** Courtesy U.S. Coast Guard; **804** (all) Courtesy N.O.A.A.; **805** (all) Courtesy N.O.A.A.; **806** (top right) Peg Bottomley; **806** (bottom right) Tom Bottomley; **806** (top left, top center, bottom center, bottom left) Courtesy N.O.A.A.; **807** (top left, top center) Courtesy N.O.A.A.; **807** (top right) Tom Bottomley; **807** (bottom left) Courtesy U.S. Coast Guard; **809** Courtesy U.S. Coast Guard; **810** Courtesy U.S. Coast Guard; **820** (all) Courtesy British Meteorological Society; **823** Courtesy N.O.A.A.; **825** Courtesy N.O.A.A.; **833** Courtesy Furuno Marine Electronics; **835** (top right) Courtesy Davis Instrument Corp.; **835** (bottom right) Courtesy Silva; **840** (all) Courtesy N.O.A.A.; **841** Courtesy Weems & Plath; **845** Courtesy NovaLynx; **848** Eric Schweikardt; **850** (all) Eric Schweikardt; **851** Ed Homonylo; **853** (all) Eric Schweikardt; **856** Eric Schweikardt; **863** Courtesy U.S. Power Squadrons; **868** Courtesy U.S. Power Squadrons; **870** (top left) Courtesy Weems & Plath; **870** (bottom right) Eric Schweikardt; **873** Courtesy Canadian Power & Sail Squadrons; **874** Courtesy Canadian Power & Sail Squadrons; **876** Courtesy Canadian Power & Sail Squadrons; **876** (all) Courtesy U.S. Coast Guard; **881** Courtesy U.S. Coast Guard

ACKNOWLEDGMENTS

The marine charts presented in this edition of Chapman are courtesy of Maptech, Inc., a digital mapping technology company. Because they have access to government databases including those updated and maintained by the National Oceanic and Atmospheric Administration, Maptech offers superior mapping, charting, and reference products to serve consumers, industry, and government needs in marine, topographic, and aeronautical fields. At www.maptech.com they maintain a free-of-charge server for reference access to all their charting products. For more information, contact Maptech toll-free at 888-849-5551.

ACIF Inc., Montreal, QC, Canada
Brian Aitken, Toronto, ON, Canada
American Red Cross, Washington, DC
Applied Biochemists, Mequon, WI
Arizona Office of Tourism, Phoenix, AZ
Astro Pure Water Purifiers, Margate, FL
Curtis Baer, Baltimore, MD
Robert Berger, U.S. Coast Guard (Boston)
Kelley Birtz, Rouses Point, NY
Jon Blair, Port Sandfield, ON, Canada
John Bleasby, Toronto, ON, Canada
Boathouse, Dorval, QC, Canada
Bombardier Corp., Sea-Doo Division, Palm Bay, FL
Huguette Brazeau, Dollard-des-Ormeaux, QC, Canada
Bristol Flare Corporation, Bristol, PA
Frances Brochu, Montreal, QC, Canada
Canadian Coast Guard, Ottawa, ON, Canada
Canadian Department of Transportation, Ottawa, ON, Canada
Canadian Hydrographic Service, Dept. of Fisheries & Oceans, Ottawa, ON, Canada
Canadian Power & Sail Squadrons/Escadrilles canadiennes de plaisance, Scarborough, ON, Canada
Canadian Red Cross, Ottawa, ON, Canada
Eric Cassini-Brochu, Montreal, QC, Canada
Center for Marine Conservation, Washington, DC
Chesapeake Bay Foundation, MD
Clayton Antique Boat Museum, Clayton, NY
Alston Colihan, U.S. Coast Guard
Cordage Institute, Hingham, MA
D.B.H. Cordage Products Inc., Dorval, QC, Canada
Pierce Crosbie, Toronto, ON, Canada
Robert David, National Boating Federation
Steve Davis, Port Townsend, WA
Dale Dawson, Vermont Ware, VT
Lorraine Doré, Montreal, QC, Canada
East Penn Manufacturing Co., Inc., Lyon Station, PA
Andrea Elvidge, Toronto, ON, Canada
Federal Communications Commission, Washington, DC
Mike Fitzsimmons, Alexandria Bay, NY
Foster & Associates, Hingham, MA
Friends of the Earth, Ottawa, ON, Canada
Melanie Gagnon, Montreal, QC, Canada
E. Charles Game, P.E., Consulting Engineer, Asheboro, NC

General Ecology of New England, Trumbull, CT
André Giasson, Montreal, QC, Canada
Rory Gilsenan, Washington, DC
Glendinning Marine Products, Inc., Conway, SC
Grand Banks Yacht, Greenwich, CT
Eric Gravel, Outremont, QC, Canada
Derek Griffiths, Toronto, ON, Canada
The Guest Company, Inc., Meriden, CT
Haft/SL Marine Products, Bradenton, FL
Harken, Pewaukee, WI
Dave Harris, Toronto, ON, Canada
Hathaway, Reiser & Raymond, Inc., Stamford, CT
Frederick Hayes (Lifesling), Bellevue, WA
Joseph Hershey, U.S. Coast Guard
Kristin Hianassen, NY Canal Corporation
High Seas Technology, Inc., Fort Lauderdale, FL
Henry R. Hinckley & Co., Southwest Harbor, ME
Ariel Home-Douglas, Montreal, QC, Canada
Marty Hornstein, St. Jerôme, QC, Canada
Marsh Howard, Dorval, QC, Canada
Paul Howard, Toronto, ON, Canada
Robert Hudson, Toronto, ON, Canada
Sonya Hudson, Toronto, ON, Canada
Jeff Isom, Mercury Marine
Jeff Kauzlaric, Furuno Marine Electronics
Steve Killing, Port McNicholl, ON, Canada
Brenda Kokiv, Montreal, QC, Canada
Solange Laberge, Blainville, QC, Canada
Jacques Lacasse, St. Bruno, QC, Canada
Land and Sea, Grand Rapids, MI
Les Expertises Marine Nord-Sud Inc., Ile Perrot, QC, Canada
Aben MacKenzie, Ste Anne de Bellevue, QC, Canada
Freya MacKenzie, Ste Anne de Bellevue, QC, Canada
Jan MacNeill, Ottawa, ON, Canada
The Mailing Co. Hubbell, West Haven, CT
David Manley, San Juan Bautista, CA
Nicholas Manley, San Juan Bautista, CA
Marina Bo-Bi-No, Laval, QC, Canada
Marina Jean Beaudoin Inc., Montreal, QC, Canada
Marine Patrol, Clinton County Sheriff's Department, Plattsburgh, NY
Albert Marm, U.S. Coast Guard
McGarr Marine, Longueuil, QC, Canada
McGill Maritime Services, Montreal, QC, Canada
John McMurray, Flint, MI
Mercury Marine, Fond du Lac, WI
Midwest Industries, Idagrove, IA
Alex Milne Associates, Toronto, ON, Canada
Alf Mortimer, Port Sandfield, ON, Canada
Motor Boating & Sailing, New York, NY
Mystic Seaport Museum Library, Mystic, CT
National Safe Boating Council, Inc., Washington, DC
National Oceanic & Atmospheric Administration (NOAA), Rockville, MD
National Ocean Service (NOAA)
National Weather Service (NOAA)

National Wildlife Federation, Washington, DC
Martin Nelson, National Weather Service (Miami)
Ian Nener, Montreal, QC, Canada
The New England Lighthouse Foundation, Wells, ME
Paul Oler, Baltimore, MD
Steve Olver, Toronto, ON, Canada
PMI Technologies, Newport News, VA
Paneltronics, Hialeah Gardens, FL
Para-Tech Engineering, Santee, CA
Charles-Guy Paré, Pompano Beach, FL
Brian Parsons, Montreal, QC, Canada
Petrokem, Patterson, NJ
Jean Poliquin, Montreal, QC, Canada
Deborah Pollard, Rouses Point, NY
Denis Poupart, Lachine, QC, Canada
Ian Quarrier, Maptech
RGM Industries Inc., Titusville, FL
Ronald Ramsay, Dollard des Ormeaux, QC, Canada
Revenue Canada, Public Relations, Montreal, QC, Canada
Donald Richardson, Ottawa, ON, Canada
Ritchie Navigation Instruments, Pembroke, MA
Mathew Ruddick, U.S. Coast Guard (Boston)
St. John Ambulance, Montreal, QC, Canada
Odette Sévigny, Montreal, QC, Canada
Shewmon, Inc., Safety Harbor, FL
Kathy Simo, Toronto, ON, Canada
Si-Tex Marine Electronic Inc., Clearwater, FL
State of Vermont, Agency of Natural Resources, Waterbury, VT
Dr. Charles J. Stine, Ellicott City, MD
Jodie Stine, Baltimore, MD
Story Litchfield, Bangor, ME
Catherine Szabo, Rouses Point, NY
Laleah Tanguay, Montreal, QC, Canada
Debbie Thomas, Toronto, ON, Canada
Kirk Thompson, Ottawa, ON, Canada
Cathie Trogdon, Weems & Plath
Margie Troy, Baltimore, MD
Elissa Turnbull, Toronto, ON, Canada
Joyce H. Turnbull, Toronto, ON, Canada
Simon Turnbull, Toronto, ON, Canada
Twin Disc Inc., Racine, WI
U.S. Marine Corporation, Arlington, WA
U.S. Coast Guard Auxiliary, Washington DC
U.S. Army Corps of Engineers, Washington DC
U.S. Coast Guard Headquarters, Washington, DC
U.S. Power Squadrons, Raleigh, NC
U.S. Sailing Association, Newport, RI
VA Sea Grant, University of North Carolina, Charlottesville, VA
Jan VanderKap, Toronto, ON, Canada
Voiles Windyne Sails, Dorval, QC, Canada
Jocelyn Wakefield, Montreal, QC, Canada
Kevin Wallace, LTJG, U.S. Coast Guard
George Webber, U.S. Coast Guard
West Products, Watsonville, CA
John Whiting, Block Island, RI
Sara Wood, Toronto, ON, Canada
Zodiac of North America, Inc., Stevensville, MD